D0225220

Full-Circle Learning

MyLab™: Learning Full Circle for Marketing, Management, Business Communication, and Intro to Business

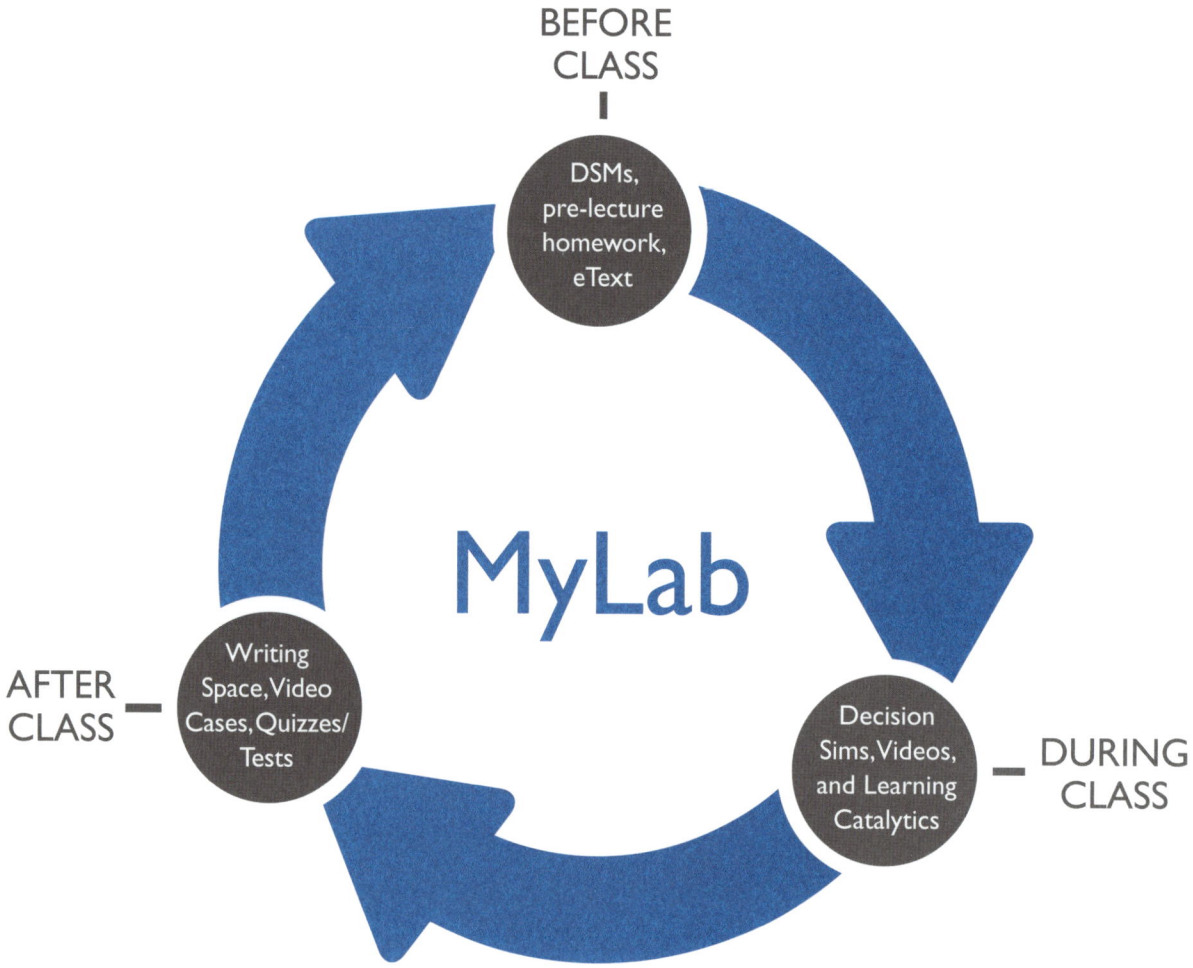

MyManagementLab®: Improves Student Engagement Before, During, and After Class

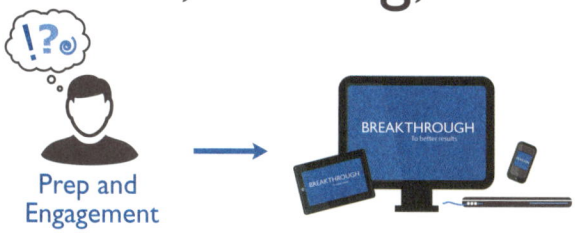

- **Personal Inventory Assessments (PIA) – NEW!** Online questionnaires designed to promote self-reflection and engagement in students, because students learn better when they can connect what they are learning to their personal experience. Student results include a written explanation along with a graphic display that shows how their results compared to the class as a whole. Instructors will also have access to this graphic representation of results to promote classroom discussion.

- **NEW! VIDEO LIBRARY –** Robust video library with over 100 new book-specific videos that include easy-to-assign assessments, the ability for instructors to add YouTube or other sources, the ability for students to upload video submissions, and the ability for polling and teamwork.

- **Decision-making simulations – NEW and improved feedback for students.** Place your students in the role of a key decision-maker! Simulations branch based on the decisions students make, providing a variation of scenario paths. Upon completion students receive a grade, as well as a detailed report of the choices and the associated consequences of those decisions.

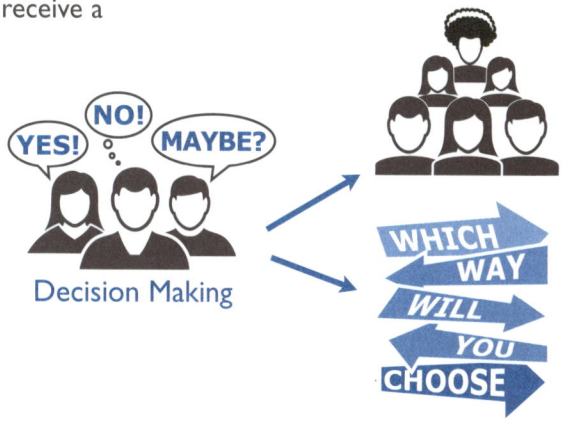

- **Video exercises – UPDATED with new exercises.** Engaging videos that bring business concepts to life and explore business topics related to the theory students are learning in class. Quizzes then assess students' comprehension of the concepts covered in each video.

- **Learning Catalytics –** A "bring your own device" student engagement, assessment, and classroom intelligence system helps instructors analyze students' critical-thinking skills during lecture.

- **Dynamic Study Modules (DSMs) – UPDATED with additional questions.** Through adaptive learning, students get personalized guidance where and when they need it most, creating greater engagement, improving knowledge retention, and supporting subject-matter mastery. Also available on mobile devices.

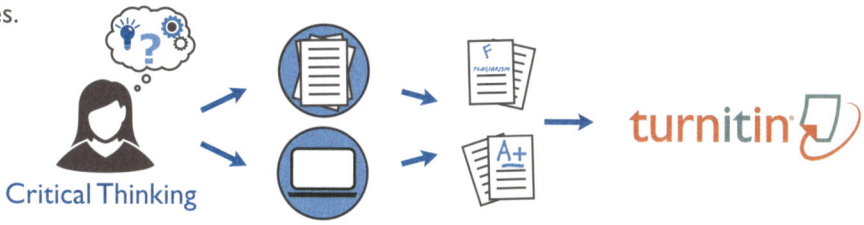

- **Writing Space – UPDATED with new commenting tabs, new prompts, and a new tool for students called Pearson Writer.** A single location to develop and assess concept mastery and critical thinking, the Writing Space offers automatic graded, assisted graded, and create your own writing assignments, allowing you to exchange personalized feedback with students quickly and easily.

  Writing Space can also check students' work for improper citation or plagiarism by comparing it against the world's most accurate text comparison database available from **Turnitin**.

http://www.pearsonmylabandmastering.com

WHERE WE ARE NOW

The framework above introduces each chapter and makes the following point: That the firm's HR policies and practices should produce the employee skills and behaviors the company needs to achieve its strategic aims.

Human Resource Management

Human Resource Management

Fifteenth Edition

GARY DESSLER
Florida International University

PEARSON

Boston Columbus Indianapolis New York San Francisco Amsterdam Cape Town
Dubai London Madrid Milan Munich Paris Montréal Toronto Delhi
Mexico City São Paulo Sydney Hong Kong Seoul Singapore Taipei Tokyo

Vice President, Business Publishing: Donna Battista
Editor-in-Chief: Stephanie Wall
Senior Acquisitions Editor: Kris Ellis-Levy
Development Editor: Kerri Tomasso
Editorial Assistant: Lauren Russell
Vice President, Product Marketing: Maggie Moylan
Director of Marketing, Digital Services and Products: Jeanette Koskinas
Executive Field Marketing Manager: Adam Goldstein
Field Marketing Manager: Lenny Ann Kucenski
Product Marketing Assistant: Jessica Quazza
Team Lead, Program Management: Ashley Santora
Program Manager: Sarah Holle
Team Lead, Project Management: Jeff Holcomb
Project Manager: Kelly Warsak
Senior Operations Specialist: Carol Melville
Creative Director: Blair Brown
Art Director: Janet Slowik
Vice President, Director of Digital Strategy and Assessment: Paul Gentile
Manager of Learning Applications: Paul DeLuca
Digital Editor: Brian Surette
Director, Digital Studio: Sacha Laustsen
Digital Studio Manager: Diane Lombardo
Digital Studio Project Manager: Monique Lawrence
Digital Studio Project Manager: Alana Coles
Digital Studio Project Manager: Robin Lazrus
Full-Service Project Management and Composition: Margaret McConnell/Integra Software Services
Interior Designer: Integra Software Services, Inc.
Cover Designer: Integra Software Services, Inc.
Cover Art: Corbis Images
Printer/Binder: Manufactured in the United States by RR Donnelley
Cover Printer: Phoenix Color/Hagerstown

Microsoft and/or its respective suppliers make no representations about the suitability of the information contained in the documents and related graphics published as part of the services for any purpose. All such documents and related graphics are provided "as is" without warranty of any kind. Microsoft and/or its respective suppliers hereby disclaim all warranties and conditions with regard to this information, including all warranties and conditions of merchantability, whether express, implied or statutory, fitness for a particular purpose, title and non-infringement. In no event shall Microsoft and/or its respective suppliers be liable for any special, indirect or consequential damages or any damages whatsoever resulting from loss of use, data or profits, whether in an action of contract, negligence or other tortious action, arising out of or in connection with the use or performance of information available from the services.

The documents and related graphics contained herein could include technical inaccuracies or typographical errors. Changes are periodically added to the information herein. Microsoft and/or its respective suppliers may make improvements and/or changes in the product(s) and/or the program(s) described herein at any time. Partial screen shots may be viewed in full within the software version specified.

Microsoft® and Windows® are registered trademarks of the Microsoft Corporation in the U.S.A. and other countries. This book is not sponsored or endorsed by or affiliated with the Microsoft Corporation.

Copyright © 2017, 2015, 2013 by Pearson Education, Inc. or its affiliates. All Rights Reserved. Manufactured in the United States of America. This publication is protected by copyright, and permission should be obtained from the publisher prior to any prohibited reproduction, storage in a retrieval system, or transmission in any form or by any means, electronic, mechanical, photocopying, recording, or otherwise. For information regarding permissions, request forms, and the appropriate contacts within the Pearson Education Global Rights and Permissions department, please visit www.pearsoned.com/permissions/.

Acknowledgments of third-party content appear on the appropriate page within the text.

PEARSON, ALWAYS LEARNING, and MyManagementLab® are exclusive trademarks owned by Pearson Education, Inc. or its affiliates in the U.S. and/or other countries.

Unless otherwise indicated herein, any third-party trademarks, logos, or icons that may appear in this work are the property of their respective owners, and any references to third-party trademarks, logos, icons, or other trade dress are for demonstrative or descriptive purposes only. Such references are not intended to imply any sponsorship, endorsement, authorization, or promotion of Pearson's products by the owners of such marks, or any relationship between the owner and Pearson Education, Inc. or its affiliates, authors, licensees, or distributors.

Library of Congress Cataloging-in-Publication Data

Dessler, Gary
Human resource management/Gary Dessler.—15 Edition.
pages cm
Revised edition of the author's Human resource management, 2013.
ISBN 978-0-13-423545-5—ISBN 0-13-423545-2
1. Personnel management. I. Title.
HF5549.D4379 2015
658.3—dc23

2015030092

10 9 8 7 6 5 4 3 2 1

PEARSON

ISBN 10: 0-13-423545-2
ISBN 13: 978-0-13-423545-5

FOR CLAUDIA

BRIEF CONTENTS

Preface xxix
Acknowledgments xxxv

PART ONE **INTRODUCTION** **1**

1 **Introduction to Human Resource Management** 1
2 **Equal Opportunity and the Law** 30
3 **Human Resource Management Strategy and Analysis** 66

PART TWO **RECRUITMENT, PLACEMENT, AND TALENT MANAGEMENT** **94**

4 **Job Analysis and the Talent Management Process** 94
5 **Personnel Planning and Recruiting** 126
6 **Employee Testing and Selection** 165
7 **Interviewing Candidates** 201

PART THREE **TRAINING AND DEVELOPMENT** **231**

8 **Training and Developing Employees** 231
9 **Performance Management and Appraisal** 272
10 **Managing Careers and Retention** 307

PART FOUR **COMPENSATION** **344**

11 **Establishing Strategic Pay Plans** 344
12 **Pay for Performance and Financial Incentives** 385
13 **Benefits and Services** 416

PART FIVE **ENRICHMENT TOPICS IN HUMAN RESOURCE MANAGEMENT** **449**

14 **Building Positive Employee Relations** 449
15 **Labor Relations and Collective Bargaining** 479
16 **Safety, Health, and Risk Management** 513
17 **Managing Global Human Resources** 559
18 **Managing Human Resources in Small and Entrepreneurial Firms** 588

APPENDICES

APPENDIX A **HRCI PHR® and SPHR® Certification Body of Knowledge** 612

APPENDIX B **About the Society for Human Resource Management (SHRM) Body of Competency and Knowledge™ Model and Certification Exams** 618

APPENDIX C **Comprehensive Cases** 630

Glossary 646

Name/Organization Index 655

Subject Index 667

CONTENTS

Preface xxix

Acknowledgments xxxv

PART ONE **INTRODUCTION** 1

1 **Introduction to Human Resource Management** 1

WHAT IS HUMAN RESOURCE MANAGEMENT? 3
- Why Is Human Resource Management Important to All Managers? 3
- Line and Staff Aspects of Human Resource Management 5
- Line Managers' Human Resource Management Responsibilities 5
- The Human Resource Department 6

THE TRENDS SHAPING HUMAN RESOURCE MANAGEMENT 7
- Workforce Demographics and Diversity Trends 7
- Trends in How People Work 8

■ **IMPROVING PERFORMANCE: HR AS A PROFIT CENTER:** Boosting Customer Service 9
- Globalization Trends 10
- Economic Trends 10
- Technology Trends 12

TODAY'S NEW HUMAN RESOURCE MANAGEMENT 13
- A Brief History of Personnel/Human Resource Management 13
- Distributed HR and the New Human Resource Management 13

■ **TRENDS SHAPING HR:** Digital and Social Media 14
- A Quick Summary 14
- HR and Strategy 15

■ **IMPROVING PERFORMANCE: THE STRATEGIC CONTEXT:** Building L.L.Bean 15
- HR and Performance 16
- HR and Performance and Sustainability 17
- HR and Employee Engagement 17

THE NEW HUMAN RESOURCE MANAGER 18
- HR and the Manager's Skills 19
- HR and Ethics 19
- HR Manager Certification 19
- HR and the Manager's Human Resource Philosophy 20

THE PLAN OF THIS BOOK 21
- The Basic Themes and Features 21
- Practical Tools For Every Manager 21

CHAPTER CONTENTS OVERVIEW 22
- Part 1: Introduction 22
- Part 2: Recruitment, Placement, and Talent Management 22
- Part 3: Training and Development 22
- Part 4: Compensation 22
- Part 5: Enrichment Topics in Human Resource Management 22

THE TOPICS ARE INTERRELATED 23

CHAPTER SECTION SUMMARIES 23

DISCUSSION QUESTIONS 24

INDIVIDUAL AND GROUP ACTIVITIES 24

EXPERIENTIAL EXERCISE 25

APPLICATION CASE: JACK NELSON'S PROBLEM 25

CONTINUING CASE: CARTER CLEANING COMPANY 25

KEY TERMS 27

ENDNOTES 27

2 Equal Opportunity and the Law 30

EQUAL OPPORTUNITY LAWS ENACTED FROM 1964 TO 1991 32
- Title VII of the 1964 Civil Rights Act 32
- Executive Orders 32
- Equal Pay Act of 1963 33
- Age Discrimination in Employment Act of 1967 33
- Vocational Rehabilitation Act of 1973 33
- Pregnancy Discrimination Act of 1978 33
- Federal Agency Guidelines 33
- Early Court Decisions Regarding Equal Employment Opportunity 34

THE LAWS ENACTED FROM 1991 TO THE PRESENT 35
- The Civil Rights Act of 1991 35
- The Americans with Disabilities Act 35
- Uniformed Services Employment and Reemployment Rights Act 37
- Genetic Information Nondiscrimination Act of 2008 (GINA) 37
- State and Local Equal Employment Opportunity Laws 37
- In Summary: Religious and Other Types of Discrimination 37
- Recent Trends in Discrimination Law 38
- Sexual Harassment 38

■ **TRENDS SHAPING HR:** Digital and Social Media 42

DEFENSES AGAINST DISCRIMINATION ALLEGATIONS 42
- The Central Role of Adverse Impact 42
- Bona Fide Occupational Qualification 45
- Business Necessity 46

■ **KNOW YOUR EMPLOYMENT LAW:** Examples of What You Can and Cannot Do 47

THE EEOC ENFORCEMENT PROCESS 49
- Voluntary Mediation 51
- Mandatory Arbitration of Discrimination Claims 52

■ **IMPROVING PERFORMANCE: HR TOOLS FOR LINE MANAGERS AND SMALL BUSINESSES** 52

DIVERSITY MANAGEMENT 53
- Potential Threats to Diversity 53

■ **IMPROVING PERFORMANCE: HR AS A PROFIT CENTER** 54
- Managing Diversity 54

■ **IMPROVING PERFORMANCE: HR AS A PROFIT CENTER** 55
- Implementing the Affirmative Action Program 55
- Reverse Discrimination 57

CHAPTER SECTION SUMMARIES 57
DISCUSSION QUESTIONS 58
INDIVIDUAL AND GROUP ACTIVITIES 59
EXPERIENTIAL EXERCISE 59
APPLICATION CASE: AN ACCUSATION OF SEXUAL HARASSMENT IN PRO SPORTS 60
CONTINUING CASE: CARTER CLEANING COMPANY 60
KEY TERMS 61
ENDNOTES 61

3 Human Resource Management Strategy and Analysis 66

THE STRATEGIC MANAGEMENT PROCESS 68
- The Management Planning Process 68
- What Is Strategic Planning? 69
- The Strategic Management Process 69

TYPES OF STRATEGIES 71
- Corporate Strategy 71
- Competitive Strategy 72
- Functional Strategy 73
- Managers' Roles in Strategic Planning 73

STRATEGIC HUMAN RESOURCE MANAGEMENT 73
What Is Strategic Human Resource Management? 74
■ IMPROVING PERFORMANCE: THE STRATEGIC CONTEXT: The Shanghai Ritz-Carlton Portman Hotel 74
■ IMPROVING PERFORMANCE: HR AS A PROFIT CENTER: The Zappos "WOW" Way 75
Sustainability and Strategic Human Resource Management 75
Strategic Human Resource Management Tools 76
HR METRICS, BENCHMARKING, AND DATA ANALYTICS 78
Improving Performance Through HRIS: Tracking Applicant Metrics for Improved Talent Management 78
Benchmarking 78
Strategy and Strategy-Based Metrics 79
What Are HR Audits? 80
■ TRENDS SHAPING HR: Digital and Social Media 81
■ TRENDS SHAPING HR: Science in Talent Management 82
HIGH-PERFORMANCE WORK SYSTEMS 83
EMPLOYEE ENGAGEMENT GUIDE FOR MANAGERS: EMPLOYEE ENGAGEMENT AND PERFORMANCE 84
The Employee Engagement Problem 85
What Can Managers Do to Improve Employee Engagement? 85
How to Measure Employee Engagement 85
How Kia Motors (UK) Improved Performance with an HR Strategy Aimed at Boosting Employee Engagement 85
CHAPTER SECTION SUMMARIES 87
DISCUSSION QUESTIONS 88
INDIVIDUAL AND GROUP ACTIVITIES 88
EXPERIENTIAL EXERCISE 89
APPLICATION CASE: SIEMENS BUILDS A STRATEGY-ORIENTED HR SYSTEM 89
CONTINUING CASE: CARTER CLEANING COMPANY 89
TRANSLATING STRATEGY INTO HR POLICIES AND PRACTICES CASE: IMPROVING PERFORMANCE AT THE HOTEL PARIS 90
KEY TERMS 92
ENDNOTES 92

PART TWO RECRUITMENT, PLACEMENT, AND TALENT MANAGEMENT 94

4 Job Analysis and the Talent Management Process 94
THE TALENT MANAGEMENT PROCESS 96
Improving Performance Through HRIS: Talent Management Software 96
THE BASICS OF JOB ANALYSIS 97
What Is Job Analysis? 97
Uses of Job Analysis Information 98
Conducting a Job Analysis 98
■ IMPROVING PEFORMANCE: HR AS A PROFIT CENTER: Boosting Productivity Through Work Redesign 99
METHODS FOR COLLECTING JOB ANALYSIS INFORMATION 100
The Interview 101
Questionnaires 102
Observation 105
Participant Diary/Logs 105
Quantitative Job Analysis Techniques 105
Electronic Job Analysis Methods 106
WRITING JOB DESCRIPTIONS 108
Diversity Counts 108
Job Identification 109
Job Summary 109
Relationships 109
Responsibilities and Duties 109

■ **TRENDS SHAPING HR:** Digital and Social Media 112
■ **KNOW YOUR EMPLOYMENT LAW:** Writing Job Descriptions That Comply with the ADA 112
Standards of Performance and Working Conditions 113
■ **IMPROVING PERFORMANCE: HR TOOLS FOR LINE MANAGERS AND SMALL BUSINESSES:** Using O*NET 113
O*NET 114
WRITING JOB SPECIFICATIONS 116
Specifications for Trained versus Untrained Personnel 116
Specifications Based on Judgment 117
Job Specifications Based on Statistical Analysis 117
The Job-Requirements Matrix 117
EMPLOYEE ENGAGEMENT GUIDE FOR MANAGERS 118
USING COMPETENCIES MODELS 118
■ **IMPROVING PERFORMANCE: THE STRATEGIC CONTEXT:** Daimler Alabama Example 119
How to Write Competencies Statements 119
CHAPTER SECTION SUMMARIES 120
DISCUSSION QUESTIONS 121
INDIVIDUAL AND GROUP ACTIVITIES 121
EXPERIENTIAL EXERCISE 122
APPLICATION CASE: THE FLOOD 122
CONTINUING CASE: CARTER CLEANING COMPANY 123
TRANSLATING STRATEGY INTO HR POLICIES AND PRACTICES CASE: IMPROVING PERFORMANCE AT THE HOTEL PARIS 123
KEY TERMS 124
ENDNOTES 124

5 **Personnel Planning and Recruiting** 126

INTRODUCTION 128
WORKFORCE PLANNING AND FORECASTING 128
Strategy and Workforce Planning 129
■ **IMPROVING PERFORMANCE: THE STRATEGIC CONTEXT:** Four Seasons 129
Forecasting Personnel Needs (Labor Demand) 130
Forecasting the Supply of Inside Candidates 132
Forecasting the Supply of Outside Candidates 133
Predictive Workforce Monitoring 134
■ **IMPROVING PERFORMANCE: HR AS A PROFIT CENTER:** Predicting Labor Needs 134
Matching Projected Labor Supply and Labor Demand 134
Succession Planning 134
WHY EFFECTIVE RECRUITING IS IMPORTANT 135
The Recruiting Yield Pyramid 136
■ **KNOW YOUR EMPLOYMENT LAW:** Recruiting Employees 136
INTERNAL SOURCES OF CANDIDATES 137
Finding Internal Candidates 137
EMPLOYEE ENGAGEMENT GUIDE FOR MANAGERS 138
Promotion from Within 138
OUTSIDE SOURCES OF CANDIDATES 138
Informal Recruiting and the Hidden Job Market 138
Recruiting via the Internet 139
Improving Performance Through HRIS: Using Applicant Tracking 139
■ **TRENDS SHAPING HR:** Science in Talent Management 140
■ **TRENDS SHAPING HR:** Digital and Social Media 141
Advertising 142
Employment Agencies 142
Recruitment Process Outsourcers 144

Temporary Workers and Alternative Staffing 144
■ **KNOW YOUR EMPLOYMENT LAW:** Contract Employees 145
■ **TRENDS SHAPING HR:** The New Extended Workforce 146
Offshoring and Outsourcing Jobs 146
Executive Recruiters 147
■ **IMPROVING PERFORMANCE: HR TOOLS FOR LINE MANAGERS AND SMALL BUSINESSES:** Recruiting 101 148
Referrals and Walk-Ins 149
On-Demand Recruiting Services 149
College Recruiting 149
Telecommuters 150
Military Personnel 150
■ **IMPROVING PERFORMANCE: HR AS A PROFIT CENTER:** Cutting Recruitment Costs 151
RECRUITING A MORE DIVERSE WORKFORCE 151
Recruiting Women 151
Recruiting Single Parents 152
Older Workers 152
Diversity Counts 153
Recruiting Minorities 153
The Disabled 153
DEVELOPING AND USING APPLICATION FORMS 154
Purpose of Application Forms 154
Application Guidelines 154
■ **KNOW YOUR EMPLOYMENT LAW:** Application Forms and EEO Law 155
Using Application Forms to Predict Job Performance 156
Mandatory Arbitration 156
CHAPTER SECTION SUMMARIES 157
DISCUSSION QUESTIONS 157
INDIVIDUAL AND GROUP ACTIVITIES 158
EXPERIENTIAL EXERCISE 158
APPLICATION CASE: FINDING PEOPLE WHO ARE PASSIONATE ABOUT WHAT THEY DO 159
CONTINUING CASE: CARTER CLEANING COMPANY 159
TRANSLATING STRATEGY INTO HR POLICIES AND PRACTICES CASE: IMPROVING PERFORMANCE AT THE HOTEL PARIS 160
KEY TERMS 161
ENDNOTES 161

6 **Employee Testing and Selection** 165
WHY EMPLOYEE SELECTION IS IMPORTANT 167
THE BASICS OF TESTING AND SELECTING EMPLOYEES 167
Reliability 167
Validity 168
■ **TRENDS SHAPING HR:** Digital and Social Media 169
Evidence-Based HR: How to Validate a Test 170
Bias 172
Utility Analysis 172
■ **IMPROVING PERFORMANCE: HR AS A PROFIT CENTER:** Using Tests to Cut Costs and Boost Profits 172
Validity Generalization 173
■ **KNOW YOUR EMPLOYMENT LAW:** Testing and Equal Employment Opportunity 173
Test Takers' Individual Rights and Test Security 173
Diversity Counts: Gender Issues in Testing 174
How Do Employers Use Tests at Work? 174
TYPES OF TESTS 175
Tests of Cognitive Abilities 175

Tests of Motor and Physical Abilities 175
Measuring Personality and Interests 176
■ **IMPROVING PERFORMANCE: HR PRACTICES AROUND THE GLOBE:** Testing for Assignments Abroad 176
Achievement Tests 177
Improving Performance Through HRIS: Computerization and Online Testing 177
■ **IMPROVING PERFORMANCE: THE STRATEGIC CONTEXT:** Crowdsourcing at Google 178
WORK SAMPLES AND SIMULATIONS 178
Using Work Sampling for Employee Selection 178
Situational Judgment Tests 179
Management Assessment Centers 179
Situational Testing and Video-Based Situational Testing 180
The Miniature Job Training and Evaluation Approach 181
Realistic Job Previews 181
Choosing a Selection Method 181
■ **IMPROVING PERFORMANCE: HR TOOLS FOR LINE MANAGERS AND SMALL BUSINESSES:** Employee Testing and Selection 182
BACKGROUND INVESTIGATIONS AND OTHER SELECTION METHODS 183
Why Perform Background Investigations and Reference Checks? 183
■ **KNOW YOUR EMPLOYMENT LAW:** Giving References 184
How to Check a Candidate's Background 184
■ **TRENDS SHAPING HR:** Digital and Social Media 186
Using Preemployment Information Services 186
Making the Background Check More Valuable 187
The Polygraph and Honesty Testing 188
Testing for Honesty: Practical Guidelines 189
Graphology 189
"Human Lie Detectors" 190
Physical Exams 190
Substance Abuse Screening 190
Drug Testing Legal Issues 191
Complying with Immigration Law 191
CHAPTER SECTION SUMMARIES 192
DISCUSSION QUESTIONS 193
INDIVIDUAL AND GROUP ACTIVITIES 193
EXPERIENTIAL EXERCISE 193
APPLICATION CASE: THE INSIDER 194
CONTINUING CASE: CARTER CLEANING COMPANY 194
TRANSLATING STRATEGY INTO HR POLICIES AND PRACTICES CASE: IMPROVING PERFORMANCE AT THE HOTEL PARIS 195
KEY TERMS 196
ENDNOTES 196

7 **Interviewing Candidates** 201

BASIC TYPES OF INTERVIEWS 203
Structured Versus Unstructured Interviews 203
Interview Content (What Types of Questions to Ask) 204
How Should We Conduct the Interview? 206
■ **TRENDS SHAPING HR:** Digital and Social Media 207
■ **IMPROVING PERFORMANCE: THE STRATEGIC CONTEXT:** Urban Outfitters 208
Avoiding Errors That Can Undermine an Interview's Usefulness 208
First Impressions (Snap Judgments) 209
Not Clarifying What the Job Requires 209
Candidate-Order (Contrast) Error and Pressure to Hire 209
Nonverbal Behavior and Impression Management 210
Effect of Personal Characteristics: Attractiveness, Gender, Race 210

Diversity Counts: Applicant Disability and the Employment Interview 211
■ **IMPROVING PERFORMANCE: HR PRACTICES AROUND THE GLOBE:** Selection Practices Abroad 211
Interviewer Behavior 212
HOW TO DESIGN AND CONDUCT AN EFFECTIVE INTERVIEW 212
Designing a Structured Situational Interview 212
■ **IMPROVING PERFORMANCE: HR TOOLS FOR LINE MANAGERS AND SMALL BUSINESSES:** How to Conduct an Effective Interview 213
Profiles and Employee Interviews 216
EMPLOYEE ENGAGEMENT GUIDE FOR MANAGERS 217
Building Engagement: A Total Selection Program 217
The Toyota Way 217
■ **TRENDS SHAPING HR:** Science in Talent Management 218
DEVELOPING AND EXTENDING THE JOB OFFER 219
CHAPTER SECTION SUMMARIES 220
DISCUSSION QUESTIONS 220
INDIVIDUAL AND GROUP ACTIVITIES 221
EXPERIENTIAL EXERCISE 221
APPLICATION CASE: THE OUT-OF-CONTROL INTERVIEW 222
CONTINUING CASE: CARTER CLEANING COMPANY 223
TRANSLATING STRATEGY INTO HR POLICIES AND PRACTICES CASE: IMPROVING PERFORMANCE AT THE HOTEL PARIS 223
KEY TERMS 224
ENDNOTES 224
APPENDIX 1 FOR CHAPTER 7 STRUCTURED INTERVIEW GUIDE 227
APPENDIX 2 FOR CHAPTER 7 INTERVIEW GUIDE FOR INTERVIEWEES 230

PART THREE **TRAINING AND DEVELOPMENT** **231**

8 **Training and Developing Employees** 231
ORIENTING AND ONBOARDING NEW EMPLOYEES 233
The Purposes of Employee Orientation/Onboarding 233
The Orientation Process 233
EMPLOYEE ENGAGEMENT GUIDE FOR MANAGERS: ONBOARDING AT TOYOTA 234
OVERVIEW OF THE TRAINING PROCESS 235
■ **KNOW YOUR EMPLOYMENT LAW:** Training and the Law 235
Aligning Strategy and Training 235
■ **IMPROVING PERFORMANCE: THE STRATEGIC CONTEXT:** The Training Program That Turned Macy's Around 236
The ADDIE Five-Step Training Process 236
Conducting the Training Needs Analysis 236
Designing the Training Program 239
Developing the Program 242
■ **TRENDS SHAPING HR:** Digital and Social Media 242
IMPLEMENTING THE TRAINING PROGRAM 243
On-the-Job Training 243
Apprenticeship Training 243
Informal Learning 245
Job Instruction Training 245
Lectures 245
Programmed Learning 246
Behavior Modeling 246
Audiovisual-Based Training 246
Vestibule Training 247
Electronic Performance Support Systems (EPSS) 247
Videoconferencing 247

Computer-Based Training (CBT) 247
Simulated Learning and Gaming 247
Lifelong and Literacy Training Techniques 248
■ **IMPROVING PERFORMANCE: HR PRACTICES AROUND THE GLOBE:** Diversity Training at ABC Virtual Communications, Inc. 248
Team Training 249
Internet-Based Training 249
The Virtual Classroom 250
■ **TRENDS SHAPING HR:** Digital and Social Media 250
■ **IMPROVING PERFORMANCE: HR TOOLS FOR LINE MANAGERS AND SMALL BUSINESSES:** Creating Your Own Training Program 251
IMPLEMENTING MANAGEMENT DEVELOPMENT PROGRAMS 252
Strategy's Role in Management Development 252
Succession Planning 252
Improving Performance Through HRIS: Succession Systems 253
Candidate Assessment and the 9-Box Grid 253
Managerial On-the-Job Training and Rotation 254
■ **IMPROVING PERFORMANCE: HR PRACTICES AROUND THE GLOBE:** Global Job Rotation 254
Off-the-Job Management Training and Development Techniques 255
Leadership Development at GE 257
■ **TRENDS SHAPING HR:** Customized Talent Management Through Differential Development Assignments 257
MANAGING ORGANIZATIONAL CHANGE PROGRAMS 258
Lewin's Change Process 258
Using Organizational Development 259
EVALUATING THE TRAINING EFFORT 260
Designing the Study 260
Training Effects to Measure 261
CHAPTER SECTION SUMMARIES 263
DISCUSSION QUESTIONS 264
INDIVIDUAL AND GROUP ACTIVITIES 264
EXPERIENTIAL EXERCISE 265
APPLICATION CASE: REINVENTING THE WHEEL AT APEX DOOR COMPANY 265
CONTINUING CASE: CARTER CLEANING COMPANY 265
TRANSLATING STRATEGY INTO HR POLICIES AND PRACTICES CASE: IMPROVING PERFORMANCE AT THE HOTEL PARIS 266
KEY TERMS 267
ENDNOTES 268

9 **Performance Management and Appraisal** 272

BASICS OF PERFORMANCE APPRAISAL 274
The Performance Appraisal Process 274
Why Appraise Performance? 274
Defining the Employee's Goals and Performance Standards 275
■ **IMPROVING PERFORMANCE: HR AS A PROFIT CENTER:** Setting Performance Goals at Ball Corporation 275
■ **IMPROVING PERFORMANCE: HR TOOLS FOR LINE MANAGERS AND SMALL BUSINESSES:** How to Set Effective Goals 275
Who Should Do the Appraising? 276
TECHNIQUES FOR APPRAISING PERFORMANCE 278
Graphic Rating Scale Method 278
Alternation Ranking Method 278
Paired Comparison Method 278
Forced Distribution Method 280
Critical Incident Method 280
Narrative Forms 282

Behaviorally Anchored Rating Scales 283
Mixed Standard Scales 285
Management by Objectives 285
Computerized and Web-Based Performance Appraisal 286
Electronic Performance Monitoring 286
Conversation Days 287
Appraisal in Practice: Using Multiple Methods 287
■ **TRENDS SHAPING HR:** Customized Talent Management 287
■ **IMPROVING PERFORMANCE: THE STRATEGIC CONTEXT:** TRW's New Global Performance Appraisal/Management System 288
DEALING WITH RATER ERROR APPRAISAL PROBLEMS 288
Potential Rating Problems 288
Diversity Counts: The Problem of Bias 290
The Need for Fairness 290
■ **KNOW YOUR EMPLOYMENT LAW:** Appraising Performance 291
MANAGING THE APPRAISAL INTERVIEW 292
How to Conduct the Appraisal Interview 292
How to Handle a Defensive Subordinate 293
How to Criticize a Subordinate 293
How to Handle a Formal Written Warning 294
EMPLOYEE ENGAGEMENT GUIDE FOR MANAGERS 295
Use the Appraisal Interview to Build Engagement 295
PERFORMANCE MANAGEMENT 296
Total Quality Management and Performance Appraisal 296
What Is Performance Management? 296
■ **TRENDS SHAPING HR:** Digital and Social Media 297
■ **IMPROVING PERFORMANCE: HR PRACTICES AROUND THE GLOBE:** Performance Management at General Dynamics Armament Systems (GDAS) 298
The Manager's Role in Performance Management 299
CHAPTER SECTION SUMMARIES 299
DISCUSSION QUESTIONS 300
INDIVIDUAL AND GROUP ACTIVITIES 300
EXPERIENTIAL EXERCISE 300
APPLICATION CASE: APPRAISING THE SECRETARIES AT SWEETWATER U 301
CONTINUING CASE: CARTER CLEANING COMPANY 302
TRANSLATING STRATEGY INTO HR POLICIES AND PRACTICES CASE: IMPROVING PERFORMANCE AT THE HOTEL PARIS 302
KEY TERMS 303
ENDNOTES 303

10 **Managing Careers and Retention** 307

CAREER MANAGEMENT 309
Careers Today 309
The Psychological Contract 309
The Employee's Role in Career Management 310
The Employer's Role in Career Management 311
Employer Career Management Methods 311
Improving Performance Through HRIS: Integrating Talent Management and Career and Succession Planning 312
Diversity Counts: Toward Career Success 313
The Manager as Mentor and Coach 313
■ **IMPROVING PERFORMANCE: THE STRATEGIC CONTEXT** 314
EMPLOYEE ENGAGEMENT GUIDE FOR MANAGERS 314
Career Management 314
Commitment-Oriented Career Development Efforts 315
■ **IMPROVING PERFORMANCE: HR PRACTICES AROUND THE GLOBE:** Career Development at Medtronic 315

MANAGING EMPLOYEE TURNOVER AND RETENTION 316
■ IMPROVING PERFORMANCE: HR AS A PROFIT CENTER: Turnover and Performance 316
Managing Voluntary Turnover 317
A Comprehensive Approach to Retaining Employees 317
■ TRENDS SHAPING HR: Digital and Social Media 318
Job Withdrawal 319
EMPLOYEE LIFE-CYCLE CAREER MANAGEMENT 319
Making Promotion Decisions 320
■ KNOW YOUR EMPLOYMENT LAW: Establish Clear Guidelines for Managing Promotions 320
Diversity Counts: The Gender Gap 321
Managing Transfers 322
Managing Retirements 322
MANAGING DISMISSALS 324
Grounds for Dismissal 324
■ KNOW YOUR EMPLOYMENT LAW: Termination at Will 325
Avoiding Wrongful Discharge Suits 326
Security Measures 326
Supervisor Liability 327
The Exit Process and Termination Interview 327
Layoffs and the Plant Closing Law 328
Adjusting to Downsizings and Mergers 329
CHAPTER SECTION SUMMARIES 330
DISCUSSION QUESTIONS 330
INDIVIDUAL AND GROUP ACTIVITIES 331
EXPERIENTIAL EXERCISE 332
APPLICATION CASE: GOOGLE REACTS 332
CONTINUING CASE: CARTER CLEANING COMPANY 332
TRANSLATING STRATEGY INTO HR POLICIES AND PRACTICES CASE: IMPROVING PERFORMANCE AT THE HOTEL PARIS 333
KEY TERMS 334
ENDNOTES 334
APPENDIX FOR CHAPTER 10 MANAGING YOUR CAREER AND FINDING A JOB 337

PART FOUR COMPENSATION 344

11 Establishing Strategic Pay Plans 344
BASIC FACTORS IN DETERMINING PAY RATES 346
Aligning Total Rewards with Strategy 346
Equity and Its Impact on Pay Rates 346
Legal Considerations in Compensation 347
■ KNOW YOUR EMPLOYMENT LAW: The Workday 348
■ KNOW YOUR EMPLOYMENT LAW: The Independent Contractor 350
Union Influences on Compensation Decisions 352
Pay Policies 352
■ IMPROVING PERFORMANCE: THE STRATEGIC CONTEXT: Wegmans Food Markets 353
■ IMPROVING PERFORMANCE: HR PRACTICES AROUND THE GLOBE: Compensating Expatriate Employees 354
JOB EVALUATION METHODS 354
Compensable Factors 354
Preparing for the Job Evaluation 355
Job Evaluation Methods: Ranking 356
Job Evaluation Methods: Job Classification 357
Job Evaluation Methods: Point Method 358

Computerized Job Evaluations 358
HOW TO CREATE A MARKET-COMPETITIVE PAY PLAN 359
1. Choose Benchmark Jobs 359
2. Select Compensable Factors 359
3. Assign Weights to Compensable Factors 360
4. Convert Percentages to Points for Each Factor 360
5. Define Each Factor's Degrees 361
6. Determine for Each Factor Its Factor Degrees' Points 361
7. Review Job Descriptions and Job Specifications 361
8. Evaluate the Jobs 362
9. Draw the Current (Internal) Wage Curve 363
10. Conduct a Market Analysis: Salary Surveys 363
11. Draw the Market (External) Wage Curve 364
12. Compare and Adjust Current and Market Wage Rates for Jobs 365
13. Develop Pay Grades 366
14. Establish Rate Ranges 367
15. Address Remaining Jobs 368
16. Correct Out-of-Line Rates 368
■ IMPROVING PERFORMANCE: HR TOOLS FOR LINE MANAGERS AND SMALL BUSINESSES: Developing a Workable Pay Plan 368
PRICING MANAGERIAL AND PROFESSIONAL JOBS 369
What Determines Executive Pay? 369
Compensating Executives 370
Compensating Professional Employees 370
Improving Performance Through HRIS: Payroll Administration 371
CONTEMPORARY TOPICS IN COMPENSATION 371
Competency-Based Pay 372
■ IMPROVING PERFORMANCE: HR PRACTICES AROUND THE GLOBE: JLG's Skill-Based Pay Program 372
Broadbanding 373
Comparable Worth 374
Diversity Counts: The Pay Gap 375
Board Oversight of Executive Pay 375
EMPLOYEE ENGAGEMENT GUIDE FOR MANAGERS 376
Total Rewards Programs 376
■ TRENDS SHAPING HR: Digital and Social Media 376
Total Rewards and Employee Engagement 376
CHAPTER SECTION SUMMARIES 377
DISCUSSION QUESTIONS 378
INDIVIDUAL AND GROUP ACTIVITIES 378
EXPERIENTIAL EXERCISE 379
APPLICATION CASE: SALARY INEQUITIES AT ASTRAZENECA 379
CONTINUING CASE: CARTER CLEANING COMPANY 379
TRANSLATING STRATEGY INTO HR POLICIES AND PRACTICES CASE: IMPROVING PERFORMANCE AT THE HOTEL PARIS 380
KEY TERMS 381
ENDNOTES 381

12 **Pay for Performance and Financial Incentives** 385

MONEY'S ROLE IN MOTIVATION 387
Incentive Pay Terminology 387
Linking Strategy, Performance, and Incentive Pay 387
Motivation and Incentives 387
■ KNOW YOUR EMPLOYMENT LAW: Employee Incentives and the Law 389
INDIVIDUAL EMPLOYEE INCENTIVE AND RECOGNITION PROGRAMS 389
Piecework 389
Merit Pay as an Incentive 390

Incentives for Professional Employees 391
Nonfinancial and Recognition-Based Awards 392
■ **TRENDS SHAPING HR:** Digital and Social Media 392
■ **IMPROVING PERFORMANCE: HR TOOLS FOR LINE MANAGERS AND SMALL BUSINESSES** 393
Job Design 394
■ **IMPROVING PERFORMANCE: THE STRATEGIC CONTEXT:** The Fast-Food Chain 394
INCENTIVES FOR SALESPEOPLE 395
Salary Plan 395
Commission Plan 395
Combination Plan 396
Maximizing Sales Results 396
Sales Incentives in Action 397
■ **TRENDS SHAPING HR:** Digital and Social Media 397
INCENTIVES FOR MANAGERS AND EXECUTIVES 397
Strategy and the Executive's Long-Term and Total Rewards Package 398
Short-Term Incentives and the Annual Bonus 398
■ **IMPROVING PERFORMANCE: HR PRACTICES AROUND THE GLOBE** 401
Some Other Executive Incentives 402
TEAM AND ORGANIZATION-WIDE INCENTIVE PLANS 402
How to Design Team Incentives 403
Evidence-Based HR: Inequities That Undercut Team Incentives 404
Profit-Sharing Plans 404
Scanlon Plans 404
Other Gainsharing Plans 405
At-Risk Pay Plans 405
Employee Stock Ownership Plans 406
Incentive Plans in Practice: Nucor 406
EMPLOYEE ENGAGEMENT GUIDE FOR MANAGERS 407
Incentives and Engagement 407
CHAPTER SECTION SUMMARIES 407
DISCUSSION QUESTIONS 408
INDIVIDUAL AND GROUP ACTIVITIES 408
EXPERIENTIAL EXERCISE 409
APPLICATION CASE: INSERTING THE TEAM CONCEPT INTO COMPENSATION—OR NOT 409
CONTINUING CASE: CARTER CLEANING COMPANY 410
TRANSLATING STRATEGY INTO HR POLICIES AND PRACTICES CASE: IMPROVING PERFORMANCE AT THE HOTEL PARIS 411
KEY TERMS 412
ENDNOTES 412

13 **Benefits and Services** 416

INTRODUCTION: THE BENEFITS PICTURE TODAY 418
Policy Issues 418
PAY FOR TIME NOT WORKED 419
Unemployment Insurance 419
Vacations and Holidays 419
■ **KNOW YOUR EMPLOYMENT LAW:** Some Legal Aspects of Vacations and Holidays 421
Sick Leave 421
■ **IMPROVING PERFORMANCE: HR AS A PROFIT CENTER:** Controlling Sick Leave 421
Leaves and the Family and Medical Leave Act 422
■ **KNOW YOUR EMPLOYMENT LAW:** FMLA Guidelines 422
Severance Pay 423
Supplemental Unemployment Benefits 424
INSURANCE BENEFITS 424
Workers' Compensation 424

Hospitalization, Health, and Disability Insurance 425
■ **KNOW YOUR EMPLOYMENT LAW:** Patient Protection and Affordable Care Act of 2010 426
Trends in Employer Health-Care Cost Control 428
■ **IMPROVING PERFORMANCE: HR AS A PROFIT CENTER:** The Doctor Is on the Phone 430
Long-Term Care 430
Life Insurance 430
Benefits for Part-Time and Contingent Workers 431
RETIREMENT BENEFITS 431
Social Security 431
Pension Plans 431
■ **KNOW YOUR EMPLOYMENT LAW:** Pension Planning and the Law 433
Pensions and Early Retirement 433
Improving Performance Through HRIS: Online Benefits Management Systems 434
■ **TRENDS SHAPING HR:** Digital and Social Media 434
PERSONAL SERVICES AND FAMILY-FRIENDLY BENEFITS 435
Personal Services 435
Family-Friendly (Work–Life) Benefits 436
Other Personal Services Benefits 437
Diversity Counts 437
■ **IMPROVING PERFORMANCE: THE STRATEGIC CONTEXT** 437
Executive Perquisites 438
FLEXIBLE BENEFITS PROGRAMS 438
The Cafeteria Approach 438
■ **IMPROVING PERFORMANCE: HR TOOLS FOR LINE MANAGERS AND SMALL BUSINESSES:** Benefits and Employee Leasing 439
Flexible Work Schedules 440
EMPLOYEE ENGAGEMENT GUIDE FOR MANAGERS 441
Costco's Compensation Plan 441
CHAPTER SECTION SUMMARIES 441
DISCUSSION QUESTIONS 442
INDIVIDUAL AND GROUP ACTIVITIES 442
EXPERIENTIAL EXERCISE 443
APPLICATION CASE: STRIKING FOR BENEFITS 443
CONTINUING CASE: CARTER CLEANING COMPANY 443
TRANSLATING STRATEGY INTO HR POLICIES AND PRACTICES CASE: IMPROVING PERFORMANCE AT THE HOTEL PARIS 444
KEY TERMS 445
ENDNOTES 445

PART FIVE **ENRICHMENT TOPICS IN HUMAN RESOURCE MANAGEMENT** 449

14 **Building Positive Employee Relations** 449
WHAT IS EMPLOYEE RELATIONS? 451
EMPLOYEE RELATIONS PROGRAMS FOR BUILDING AND MAINTAINING POSITIVE EMPLOYEE RELATIONS 451
Ensuring Fair Treatment 451
■ **IMPROVING PERFORMANCE: THE STRATEGIC CONTEXT:** A New HR Strategy at the Foxconn Plant in Shenzhen, China 453
Bullying and Victimization 453
Improving Employee Relations Through Communications Programs 454
Develop Employee Recognition/Relations Programs 454
Use Employee Involvement Programs 455
■ **TRENDS SHAPING HR:** Digital and Social Media 455

■ **IMPROVING PERFORMANCE: HR AS A PROFIT CENTER:** The Cost-Effective Suggestion System 456

THE ETHICAL ORGANIZATION 456

Ethics and Employee Rights 457
What Shapes Ethical Behavior at Work? 458
The Person (What Makes Bad Apples?) 458
Which Ethical Situations Make for Ethically Dangerous Situations (Bad Cases)? 458
What Are the "Bad Barrels"?—The Outside Factors That Mold Ethical Choices 458
How Managers Can Create More Ethical Environments 459
How Human Resource Managers Can Create More Ethical Environments 459

■ **IMPROVING PERFORMANCE: HR TOOLS FOR LINE MANAGERS AND SMALL BUSINESSES:** Small Business Ethics 460

■ **KNOW YOUR EMPLOYMENT LAW:** Electronic Monitoring 462

■ **TRENDS SHAPING HR:** Digital and Social Media 463

MANAGING EMPLOYEE DISCIPLINE 464

The Three Pillars of Fair Discipline 464
Diversity Counts 465
How to Discipline an Employee 465
Discipline Without Punishment 466

EMPLOYEE ENGAGEMENT GUIDE FOR MANAGERS 467

How Companies Become "Best Companies to Work For" 467
The "Best Companies to Work For" 467
SAS: Great Benefits, Trust, and Work-Life Balance 467
Google: Happiness and People Analytics 468
FedEx: Guaranteed Fair Treatment 468
A "Best Company" Human Resource Philosophy? 469

CHAPTER SECTION SUMMARIES 470
DISCUSSION QUESTIONS 471
INDIVIDUAL AND GROUP ACTIVITIES 471
EXPERIENTIAL EXERCISE 472
APPLICATION CASE: ENRON, ETHICS, AND ORGANIZATIONAL CULTURE 472
CONTINUING CASE: CARTER CLEANING COMPANY 473
TRANSLATING STRATEGY INTO HR POLICIES AND PRACTICES CASE: IMPROVING PERFORMANCE AT THE HOTEL PARIS 473
KEY TERMS 475
ETHICS QUIZ ANSWERS 475
ENDNOTES 475

15 **Labor Relations and Collective Bargaining** 479

THE LABOR MOVEMENT 481

■ **IMPROVING PERFORMANCE: THE STRATEGIC CONTEXT:** The "Anti-Walmart's" Revenues 481

Why Do Workers Organize? 481
Employee Engagement and Unionization 482
What Do Unions Want? 482
The AFL-CIO and the SEIU 483

UNIONS AND THE LAW 484

Period of Strong Encouragement: The Norris-LaGuardia (1932) and National Labor Relations (or Wagner) Acts (1935) 484
Period of Modified Encouragement Coupled with Regulation: The Taft-Hartley Act (1947) 485
Unfair Union Labor Practices 486

THE UNION DRIVE AND ELECTION 487

Step 1. Initial Contact 487
Step 2. Obtaining Authorization Cards 488
Step 3. Hold a Hearing 489
Step 4. The Campaign 490

Step 5. The Election 490
How to Lose an NLRB Election 491
Evidence-Based HR: What to Expect the Union to Do to Win the Election 492
The Supervisor's Role 492
■ **KNOW YOUR EMPLOYMENT LAW:** Rules Regarding Literature and Solicitation 493
Decertification Elections: Ousting the Union 493
■ **IMPROVING PERFORMANCE: HR PRACTICES AROUND THE GLOBE:** France Comes to the Workers' Aid 493
THE COLLECTIVE BARGAINING PROCESS 494
What Is Collective Bargaining? 494
What Is Good Faith? 494
The Negotiating Team 495
Costing the Contract 495
Bargaining Items 495
Building Negotiating Skills 496
Bargaining Hints 496
Impasses, Mediation, and Strikes 497
■ **TRENDS SHAPING HR:** Digital and Social Media 500
The Contract Agreement 500
DEALING WITH DISPUTES AND GRIEVANCES 501
Sources of Grievances 501
The Grievance Procedure 501
Guidelines for Handling Grievances 502
■ **IMPROVING PERFORMANCE: HR TOOLS FOR LINE MANAGERS AND SMALL BUSINESSES:** How to Handle a Grievance Situation 503
THE UNION MOVEMENT TODAY AND TOMORROW 503
What Are Unions Doing About It? 504
Cooperative Clauses 505
■ **IMPROVING PERFORMANCE: HR AROUND THE GLOBE:** Labor-Management Cooperation and Works Councils in America 506
CHAPTER SECTION SUMMARIES 506
DISCUSSION QUESTIONS 507
INDIVIDUAL AND GROUP ACTIVITIES 507
EXPERIENTIAL EXERCISE 508
APPLICATION CASE: NEGOTIATING WITH THE WRITERS GUILD OF AMERICA 508
CONTINUING CASE: CARTER CLEANING COMPANY 509
TRANSLATING STRATEGY INTO HR POLICIES AND PRACTICES CASE: IMPROVING PERFORMANCE AT THE HOTEL PARIS 509
KEY TERMS 510
ENDNOTES 510

16 **Safety, Health, and Risk Management** 513

INTRODUCTION: SAFETY AND THE MANAGER 515
Why Safety Is Important 515
■ **IMPROVING PERFORMANCE: HR AS A PROFIT CENTER:** Improving Safety Boosts Profits 515
Management's Role in Safety 515
■ **IMPROVING PERFORMACE: THE STRATEGIC CONTEXT:** Deepwater Horizon 516
The Supervisor's Role in Accident Prevention 516
MANAGER'S BRIEFING ON OCCUPATIONAL SAFETY LAW 516
OSHA Standards and Record Keeping 517
Inspections and Citations 518
Responsibilities and Rights of Employers and Employees 520
■ **IMPROVING PERFORMANCE: HR TOOLS FOR LINE MANAGERS AND SMALL BUSINESSES:** Free On-Site Safety and Health Services 521

■ **TRENDS SHAPING HR:** Digital and Social Media 522
WHAT CAUSES ACCIDENTS? 523
What Causes Unsafe Conditions? 523
What Causes Unsafe Acts? 524
HOW TO PREVENT ACCIDENTS 524
Reducing Unsafe Conditions 524
Diversity Counts: Protecting Vulnerable Workers 528
Reducing Unsafe Acts 529
Reducing Unsafe Acts Through Screening 529
Reducing Unsafe Acts Through Training 529
Improving Performance Through HRIS: Online Safety Training 530
Reducing Unsafe Acts Through Posters, Incentives, and Positive Reinforcement 530
■ **IMPROVING PERFORMANCE: HR AS A PROFIT CENTER:** Using Positive Reinforcement 530
Reducing Unsafe Acts by Fostering a Culture of Safety 532
Reducing Unsafe Acts by Creating a Supportive Environment 532
Reducing Unsafe Acts by Establishing a Safety Policy 532
Reducing Unsafe Acts by Setting Specific Loss Control Goals 532
Reducing Unsafe Acts Through Behavior-Based and Safety Awareness Programs 532
Reducing Unsafe Acts Through Employee Participation 532
■ **TRENDS SHAPING HR:** Digital and Social Media 533
Conducting Safety and Health Audits and Inspections 533
EMPLOYEE ENGAGEMENT GUIDE FOR MANAGERS 534
Milliken & Company—World-Class Safety Through Employee Engagement 534
Involvement-Based Employee Engagement 534
WORKPLACE HEALTH HAZARDS: PROBLEMS AND REMEDIES 535
Chemicals and Industrial Hygiene 535
■ **IMPROVING PERFORMANCE: HR PRACTICES AROUND THE GLOBE:** Safety at Saudi Petrol Chemical 535
■ **KNOW YOUR EMPLOYMENT LAW:** Hazard Communication 537
Asbestos Exposure at Work and Air Quality 537
Alcoholism and Substance Abuse 537
Stress, Burnout, and Depression 539
Solving Computer-Related Ergonomic Problems 540
Repetitive Motion Disorders 541
Infectious Diseases 541
Workplace Smoking 541
OCCUPATIONAL SECURITY AND RISK MANAGEMENT 542
Enterprise Risk Management 542
Preventing and Dealing with Violence at Work 542
Securing the Facility 544
Company Security and Employee Privacy 545
Business Continuity and Emergency Plans 546
■ **TRENDS SHAPING HR:** Digital and Social Media 546
Twitter Notifications 546
Terrorism 546
CHAPTER SECTION SUMMARIES 547
DISCUSSION QUESTIONS 547
INDIVIDUAL AND GROUP ACTIVITIES 548
EXPERIENTIAL EXERCISE 548
APPLICATION CASE: THE NEW SAFETY AND HEALTH PROGRAM 552
CONTINUING CASE: CARTER CLEANING COMPANY 553
TRANSLATING STRATEGY INTO HR POLICIES AND PRACTICES CASE: IMPROVING PERFORMANCE AT THE HOTEL PARIS 553
KEY TERMS 554
ENDNOTES 554

17 **Managing Global Human Resources** 559

THE MANAGER'S GLOBAL CHALLENGE 561
What Is International Human Resource Management? 561
ADAPTING HUMAN RESOURCE ACTIVITIES TO INTERCOUNTRY DIFFERENCES 561
Cultural Factors 562
Economic Systems 563
HR Abroad Example: The European Union 563
HR Abroad Example: China 564
■ **IMPROVING PERFORMANCE: HR PRACTICES AROUND THE GLOBE:** Comparing Small Businesses, HR Practices in the United States and China 565
STAFFING THE GLOBAL ORGANIZATION 565
International Staffing: Home or Local? 566
■ **IMPROVING PERFORMANCE: HR AS A PROFIT CENTER:** Reducing Expatriate Costs 567
■ **TRENDS SHAPING HR:** Digital and Social Media 567
Management Values and International Staffing Policy 568
Ethics and Codes of Conduct 568
Selecting International Managers 569
Diversity Counts: Sending Women Managers Abroad 570
Avoiding Early Expatriate Returns 570
■ **IMPROVING PERFORMANCE: HR TOOLS FOR LINE MANAGERS AND SMALL BUSINESSES:** Some Practical Solutions to the Expatriate Challenge 571
TRAINING AND MAINTAINING EMPLOYEES ABROAD 571
Orienting and Training Employees on International Assignment 571
Performance Appraisal of International Managers 572
Compensating Managers Abroad 573
Union Relations Abroad 575
Terrorism, Safety, and Global HR 575
■ **IMPROVING PERFORMANCE: HR PRACTICES AROUND THE GLOBE:** Business Travel 576
Repatriation: Problems and Solutions 576
EMPLOYEE ENGAGEMENT GUIDE FOR MANAGERS 577
Engagement Around the Globe 577
MANAGING HR LOCALLY: HOW TO PUT INTO PRACTICE A GLOBAL HR SYSTEM 577
■ **IMPROVING PERFORMANCE: THE STRATEGIC CONTEXT:** Hitachi 578
Developing a More Effective Global HR System 579
Making the Global HR System More Acceptable 579
Implementing the Global HR System 579
CHAPTER SECTION SUMMARIES 580
DISCUSSION QUESTIONS 581
INDIVIDUAL AND GROUP ACTIVITIES 581
EXPERIENTIAL EXERCISE 581
APPLICATION CASE: "BOSS, I THINK WE HAVE A PROBLEM" 582
CONTINUING CASE: CARTER CLEANING COMPANY 582
TRANSLATING STRATEGY INTO HR POLICIES AND PRACTICES CASE: IMPROVING PERFORMANCE AT THE HOTEL PARIS 583
KEY TERMS 584
ENDNOTES 584

18 **Managing Human Resources in Small and Entrepreneurial Firms** 588

THE SMALL BUSINESS CHALLENGE 590
How Small Business Human Resource Management Is Different 590

Diversity Counts: Necessity and the Entrepreneur 591
Why HRM Is Important to Small Businesses 591
USING INTERNET AND GOVERNMENT TOOLS TO SUPPORT THE HR EFFORT 591
Complying with Employment Laws 592
Employment Planning and Recruiting 593
■ **TRENDS SHAPING HR:** Digital and Social Media 593
Employment Selection 594
Employment Training 596
Employment Appraisal and Compensation 596
Employment Safety and Health 596
LEVERAGING SMALL SIZE WITH FAMILIARITY, FLEXIBILITY, FAIRNESS, AND INFORMALITY 597
Simple, Informal Employee Selection Procedures 597
■ **IMPROVING PERFORMANCE: HR TOOLS FOR LINE MANAGERS AND SMALL BUSINESSES:** A Streamlined Interviewing Process 597
Flexibility in Training 598
Flexibility in Benefits and Rewards 598
Fairness and the Family Business 600
USING PROFESSIONAL EMPLOYER ORGANIZATIONS 600
How Do PEOs Work? 600
Why Use a PEO? 601
Caveats 601
MANAGING HR SYSTEMS, PROCEDURES, AND PAPERWORK 602
Introduction 602
■ **IMPROVING PERFORMANCE: THE STRATEGIC CONTEXT:** City Garage 602
Basic Components of Manual HR Systems 603
Automating Individual HR Tasks 604
Human Resource Information Systems (HRIS) 604
Improved Transaction Processing 604
Online Self-Processing 605
Improved Reporting Capability 605
HR System Integration 605
HRIS Vendors 605
■ **TRENDS SHAPING HR:** Digital and Social Media 605
CHAPTER SECTION SUMMARIES 606
DISCUSSION QUESTIONS 606
INDIVIDUAL AND GROUP ACTIVITIES 606
EXPERIENTIAL EXERCISE 607
APPLICATION CASE: NETFLIX BREAKS THE RULES 607
CONTINUING CASE: CARTER CLEANING COMPANY 608
TRANSLATING STRATEGY INTO HR POLICIES AND PRACTICES CASE: IMPROVING PERFORMANCE AT THE HOTEL PARIS 608
ENDNOTES 609

APPENDICES

APPENDIX A **HRCI PHR® and SPHR® Certification Body of Knowledge** 612
APPENDIX B **About the Society for Human Resource Management (SHRM) Body of Competency and Knowledge™ Model and Certification Exams** 618
APPENDIX C **Comprehensive Cases** 630

Glossary 646
Name/Organization Index 655
Subject Index 667

PREFACE

Human Resource Management, 15th edition, provides students in human resource management courses and practicing managers with a full and practical introduction to modern human resource management concepts and techniques in a highly readable form. With employers increasingly shifting HR tasks to managers and employees, I feel even more strongly than I did when I wrote the first edition that all managers—not just HR managers—need a strong foundation in human resource management concepts and techniques to do their jobs. You will therefore find an emphasis here on practical material you need to perform your day-to-day management responsibilities, even if you never spend one day as a human resource manager.

Things are changing fast in human resource management, and as this book makes clear we are today on the cusp of what is really the New Human Resource Management. For example, Accenture estimates that social media tools like LinkedIn will soon produce up to 80% of new recruits.[1] Cloud computing and intuitive user interfaces let managers monitor goal attainment and give real-time performance feedback continuously and interactively, rather than once or twice per year.[2] Mobile applications enable HR capabilities ranging from employee location monitoring to checking digital identities at time clocks. Websites like Knack and True Office help employers add gaming features to training, performance appraisal, and recruiting. Data mining and talent analytics revolutionized how employers such as Google and Xerox identify competencies and recruit and select job candidates.[3]

As we'll see with real examples throughout this book, tools like these are doing more than changing how employers recruit, select, appraise, train, and pay employees—they're also changing who "does" HR. In the New Human Resource Management, digital devices and social media are shifting more HR tasks from central human resource departments to employees and line managers: For instance, easily finding and vetting capable candidates through social media already let many line managers bypass HR to find their own recruits.[4] Changes like these give the line managers more human resource management responsibilities. And they mean that many human resource managers can refocus their efforts *from* day-to-day activities like interviewing candidates *to* broader, strategic efforts, such as formulating plans for boosting employee performance and engagement.

CHANGES AND NEW FEATURES

You'll therefore find six important changes for this edition:

- **New *Trends Shaping HR* Features**

Many employers are living the future of HR management today. To bring this New Human Resource Management to life, just about every chapter has one or more **Trends Shaping HR** features, each focusing on Digital and Social

[1] Accenture, "Top Trends That Will Reshape the Future of HR: The Future of HR," www.accenture.com/us-en/insight-future-of-hr.aspx, accessed March 6, 2015.

[2] https://go.oracle.com/LP=3174?elqCampaignId=6310&src1=ad:pas:go:dg:tal&src2=wwmk14054343mpp012&SC=sckw=WWMK14054343MPP012, accessed April 4, 2015.

[3] Josh Bersin, "Big Data in Human Resources: Talent Analytics (People Analytics) Comes of Age," www.forbes.com/sites/joshbersin/2013/02/17/bigdata-in-human-resources-talent-analytics-comes-of-age/, accessed March 29, 2015.

[4] Accenture, "Top Trends That Will Reshape the Future of HR."

Media, Customized Talent Management, Science in Talent Management, or The Extended Workforce. Here are some examples from the book:

TRENDS SHAPING HR: *Digital and Social Media*

Digital and social media tools and the new human resource management.
Digital and social media tools are changing how people look for jobs, and how companies recruit, retain, pay, and train employees. In doing so, they've transformed the practice of human resource management, and created, in a sense, a new human resource management. Here are some examples.

TRENDS SHAPING HR: *Customized Talent Management*

There has always been some customizing of appraisals. For example, rating a salesperson based on whether she attained her sales goals assumes she had her own customized goals to meet.

Today, some employers are customizing their appraisal in other ways. For example, it is increasingly common for companies to adapt their appraisals to how critical the employees are to the company's strategic success—their "mission-critical" employees. For example, GE prioritizes jobs and focuses on what it calls its employee "game changers."[53] Unilever includes 15% of employees per management level in its high-potential list each year.[54] Shell China appoints "career stewards" to meet regularly with "emerging leaders."[55] McKinsey & Co. recommends limiting the "high

TRENDS SHAPING HR: *Science in Talent Management*

Most employers use tools like job boards to produce large numbers of recruits, and then use ATS and screening systems to cut those numbers down. Google's "People Operations" (HR) group is more scientific. When their research showed that tools like job boards weren't cost-effective for them, they created their own in-house recruiting firm. This in-house team uses a proprietary candidate database called gHire. Google's recruiters continually expand and winnow this candidate list, by searching social networking and other sites, by searching who's working where, and by reaching out to prospective hires and maintaining dialogues with them, sometimes for years. These in-house recruiters produce hand-picked candidates and account for about half of Google's yearly hires.[73]

TRENDS SHAPING HR: *The New Extended Workforce*

Many employers today build their staff wholly or in part around an extended workforce consisting, for instance, of freelance programmers, designers, or marketers. Freelancer community websites enable such employers to recruit the right freelance team based on the freelancer's reputation and work product. For example, Elance.com (see www.elance.com/) reports its members' skills assessments, and lists detailed project work experience, making it easier for prospective employers to decide who to hire. Similarly, the TopCoder.com (see www.topcoder.com/how-it-works/) programming community site enables employers to identify top programmers based on the reputations they earned within the community. New hiring sites like these may have a big impact on HR. Some employers may well use them to democratize HR, by letting their line managers recruit and hire new employees directly. ■

- **New *The Strategic Context* Features**

As employers devolve more HR tasks to supervisors and employees and use performance management systems to link employees' actions to the company's goals, supervisors and employees need a "line of sight" that shows them how their HR actions impact the company's goals. I've therefore added to this edition **The Strategic Context** features. Integrated with chapter-opening scenarios, these features show how actual managers adjusted their HR actions to produce the employee competencies and skills that were needed to achieve the company's strategic aims.

In addition, a **Fully Integrated Strategy Case and Strategy Maps** again provide the most comprehensive treatment of strategic human resource management in any HR survey text:

✓ Chapter 1 introduces and Chapter 3 presents the concepts and techniques of human resource strategy.

✓ Each chapter starting with Chapter 3 contains a continuing "Hotel Paris" case, written to help make strategic human resource management come alive for readers. The continuing case shows how this hotel company's HR director uses that chapter's human resource management concepts and techniques to create HR policies and practices that produce the employee skills and behaviors the Hotel Paris needs to improve its service and thereby achieve its strategic goals.

✓ An overall strategy map for the Hotel Paris on the book's inside back cover, and chapter-specific Hotel Paris strategy maps in the accompanying MyManagementLab®, help readers understand and follow the strategic implications of the hotel's HR decisions.

✓ "Eiffel Tower" callouts in each chapter draw students' attention to the Hotel Paris case.

- **New *Employee Engagement Guide for Managers* Features**

Employee engagement refers to being psychologically involved in, connected to, and committed to getting one's jobs done. Trends including intensifying global competition and more millennials in the workforce make employee engagement crucial today (a fact recognized by the new Employee Engagement section in the Society for Human Resource Management's certification exams). Recent surveys show that about 70% of employees are disengaged at work. I use new *Employee Engagement Guide for Managers* sections in Chapters 3–17 to show

how managers use human resource activities to improve employee engagement. For example, Chapter 3's guide shows how Kia Motors (UK) improved employee engagement, Chapter 6's guide shows how Toyota uses a total selection program to improve engagement, and Chapter 14's guide shows how "Great Companies to Work For" like Google and SAS develop the positive employee relations that help foster employee engagement.

- **New *SHRM* Coverage**

Starting in 2015,the Society for Human Resource Management (SHRM) began offering its own competency and knowledge-based testing and certifications for SHRM Certified Professionals and SHRM Senior Certified Professionals, based on its own certification exams.[5] The new SHRM exams put new emphases on Employee Engagement and on Employee Relations, two topics that this new 15th edition covers more comprehensively than does any other survey book with which I'm familiar (with the exception of my *Fundamentals of Human Resource Management, 4th edition*, Pearson 2015).

I've also summarized separately the SHRM and the HR Certification Institute's (HRCI's) knowledge bases in Appendices A and B of this book, (pages 612–629). One covers SHRM's functional knowledge areas (such as employee relations). The other covers HRCI's seven main knowledge areas (such as Strategic Business Management and Workforce Planning and Employment). The latter also lists about 91 specific HRCI "Knowledge of" subject areas within these seven main topic areas with which those taking the test should be familiar. You'll also find throughout this book special Knowledge Base icons starting in Chapter 2 to denote coverage of SHRM and/or HRCI knowledge topics.

- **Revised Chapter 10 (Managing Careers) and Chapter 14 (Building Positive Employee Relations)**

With the new Employee Engagement Guide for Managers features in most chapters, I revised Chapter 10 (Managing Careers and Retention, formerly Managing Employee Retention, Engagement, and Careers) to focus more on career management practices and employee retention techniques. With SHRM's new emphasis on employee relations, I also revised Chapter 14 (formerly Ethics, Employee Relations, and Fair Treatment at Work) to more comprehensively address (unique to this book) how real companies build employee relations.

- **New: Sustainability and HRM**

In a world where sea levels are rising, glaciers are crumbling, and increasing numbers of people view financial inequity as outrageous, more and more people say that businesses can't just measure "performance" in terms of maximizing profits. This 15th edition contains all-new material on sustainability and on the roles of HR management in implementing companies' sustainability efforts.

MYMANAGEMENTLAB SUGGESTED ACTIVITIES

For the 15th edition, I am excited that Pearson's MyManagementLab has been integrated fully into the text. The new features are outlined below. Making these assessment activities available online for students to complete before coming to class should give you, the professor, more discussion time during class to review areas that students may be having difficulty with.

Learn It

Students can be assigned the Chapter Warm-Up before coming to class. Assigning these questions ahead of time will hopefully help ensure that students come to class prepared.

[5] www.shrm.org/certification/pages/default.aspx#sthash.JRZQeAWR.dpuf, accessed September 8, 2015.

Watch It

Recommends a video clip that can be assigned to students for outside classroom viewing or for in-classroom use. The video I chose for each chapter corresponds to the chapter material and is accompanied by multiple-choice questions that reinforce students' comprehension of the chapter content.

Try It

Recommends a mini-simulation that can be assigned to students as an outside classroom activity or that can be done in the classroom. As students watch the simulation, they will be asked to make choices based on the simulation scenario. At the end of the simulation, students receive immediate feedback based on their answers. These simulations reinforce the chapter's concepts, as well as students' comprehension of those concepts.

Talk About It

These are discussion-type questions that can be assigned as an activity within the classroom.

Assisted-Graded Writing Questions

These are short essay questions that the students can complete as an assignment and submit to you, the professor, for grading.

FEATURES CONTINUED FROM 14TH EDITION

Given the very positive response to the 14th edition and to the continuing challenges that world economies still face, I continued the 14th edition's emphasis on improving performance, productivity, and profitability in this 15th edition, and kept several features:

Improving Performance: features again demonstrate real-world human resource management tools and practices that managers actually use to improve performance. The discussion questions within each of the three boxed Improving Performance features are also in the accompanying MyManagementLab®. These features include:

IMPROVING PERFORMANCE: *HR as a Profit Center*

Turnover and Performance

What is the link between turnover and organizational performance? Perhaps surprisingly, the issue isn't clear (although it would seem obvious that firing an incompetent employee would be a positive).[33] The problem is that what might be a positive in individual cases becomes a negative when the employer repeatedly loses employees. One study concludes that *all* turnover, voluntary or involuntary,

Improving Performance: HR as a Profit Center: contains actual examples of how human resource management practices add value by reducing costs or boosting revenues.

Improving Performance: HR Tools for Line Managers and Small Businesses: explains that many line managers and entrepreneurs are "on their own" when it comes to human resource management, and describes work sampling tests and other straightforward HR tools that line managers and entrepreneurs can create and safely use to improve performance.

IMPROVING PERFORMANCE: *HR Tools for Line Managers and Small Businesses*

How to Conduct an Effective Interview

You may not have the time or inclination to create a structured situational interview. However, there is still much you can do to make your interviews systematic and productive.

Step 1: **First, know the job.** Do not start the interview unless you understand the job's duties and what human skills you're looking for. Study the job description.

Step 2: **structure the interview.** Any structuring is better than none. If pressed for time, you can still do several things to ask more consistent and job-relevant questions, without developing a full-blown structured interview.[77] For example:[78]

- Base questions on *actual job duties*. This will minimize irrelevant questions.
- Use *job knowledge, situational, or behavioral questions*. Questions that simply ask for opinions and attitudes, goals and aspirations, and self-descriptions and self-evaluations allow candidates to present themselves in an overly favorable manner or avoid revealing

Improving Performance: HR Practices Around the Globe: shows how actual companies around the globe use HR practices to improve their teams' and companies' performance, while illustrating the challenges managers face in managing internationally.

IMPROVING PERFORMANCE: *HR Practices around the Globe*

Career Development at Medtronic[30]

Medtronic is a global medical technology company with more than 85,000 employees around the world. The company offers a wide range of career planning and development support tools aimed at helping employees understand their occupational strengths and weaknesses and reach their potential. These tools include customized development plans, self-assessment and feedback tools, mentoring programs,

Improving Performance Through HRIS: are embedded features that demonstrate how managers use human resource technology to improve performance.

And as in the 14th edition:

Know Your Employment Law sections within each chapter discuss the practical implications of the employment laws that apply to that chapter's topics, such as the laws relating to recruitment (Chapter 5), selection (Chapter 6), training (Chapter 8), and safety (Chapter 16).

Diversity Counts features provide practical insights for managing a diverse workforce, for instance, regarding gender bias in selection decisions, bias in performance appraisal, and "hidden" gender bias in some bonus plans (Chapter 12).

Treatment of Global HR and Small Business HR Management

While this 15th edition again has two chapters devoted to Global HR and to Small Business HR, you will also find in this new 15th edition *Managing HR Around the Globe* boxed features throughout the book, and, similarly, *HR Tools for Line Managers and Small Businesses* boxed features throughout the book.

INSTRUCTOR RESOURCES

At the Instructor Resource Center (www.pearsonhighered.com/irc), instructors can easily register to gain access to a variety of instructor resources available with this text in downloadable format. If assistance is needed, our dedicated technical support team is ready to help with the media supplements that accompany this text. Visit http://247.pearsoned.com for answers to frequently asked questions and toll-free user support phone numbers.

The following supplements are available with this text:

- Instructor's Resource Manual
- Test Bank
- TestGen® Computerized Test Bank
- PowerPoint Presentation
- Additional videos illustrating the most important subject topics are available in MyManagementLab under the Instructor Resources: Business Today.

ACKNOWLEDGMENTS

Everyone involved in creating this book is proud of what we've achieved. *Human Resource Management* is one of the top-selling books in this market, and, as you read this, students and managers around the world are using versions translated into about a dozen languages, including Thai, French, Spanish, Indonesian, Russian, and Chinese.

Although I am responsible for *Human Resource Management*, I want to thank several people for their assistance. They include, first, the faculty who carefully reviewed the 14th edition, and who made many useful and insightful suggestions:

John Durboraw, *Columbia College*
Lisa Nieman, *Wesleyan University*
Brooke Sorrells, *Virginia College*
Craig Tunwell, *Troy University*

I am very grateful to Gordon Schmidt (Indiana University/Purdue University Fort Wayne) and Angela Boston (University of Texas) for their hard work on updating and improving the supplements for the 15th edition, and to the MyLabs team of Project Manager Toni Ackley, Gordon Schmidt (Indiana University/Purdue University Fort Wayne), Susan C. Schanne (Eastern Michigan University), and Leslie Carnes, SPHR (Ivy Tech Community College).

At Pearson, thank you for the support and dedicated assistance of all involved. I particularly appreciate the insights, suggestions, and personal involvement of Editor-in-Chief Stephanie Wall and Senior Acquisitions Editor Kris Ellis-Levy. Thank you again to my outstanding production team, with whom I've worked for many years: Jeff Holcomb, Project Management Team Lead, and Kelly Warsak, my irreplaceable Project Manager. Thanks to Lenny Ann Kucenski, Field Marketing Manager, and the Pearson sales staff, without whose efforts this book would languish on the shelf, and to Sarah Holle, Program Manager, and Lauren Russell, Editorial Assistant. I want to thank everyone at Pearson International for successfully managing *Human Resource Management's* internationalization. Development editor Kerri Tomasso was extraordinarily helpful, and thank you to Margaret McConnell at Integra.

At home, I want to thank my wife, Claudia, for her support during the many hours I spent working on this edition. My son, Derek, always a source of enormous pride, was very helpful. Lisa, Samantha, and Taylor are always in my thoughts. My parents were always a great source of support and encouragement and would have been very proud to see this book.

1

Introduction to Human Resource Management

Kwanbenz/Shutterstock

LEARNING OBJECTIVES

1-1 Explain what human resource management is and how it relates to the management process.

1-2 Briefly discuss and illustrate each of the important trends influencing human resource management.

1-3 Briefly describe "distributed HR" and other important aspects of human management today.

1-4 List at least four important human resource manager competencies.

1-5 Outline the plan of this book.

For many people today Elance (www.elance.com) symbolizes much of what's new in human resource management. Millions of freelancers from graphic designers to translators, accountants, and lawyers register on the site. Employers then use Elance to find, screen, hire, and pay the talent they need, in more than 180 countries.[1]

WHERE ARE WE NOW ...

The purpose of this chapter is to explain what human resource management is, and why it's important to all managers. We'll see that human resource management activities such as hiring, training, appraising, compensating, and developing employees are part of every manager's job. And we'll see that human resource management is also a separate function, usually with its own human resource or "HR" manager. The main topics we'll cover here include what is human resource management, the trends shaping human resource management, human resource management today, the new human resource manager, and the plan of this book. The framework above (which introduces each chapter) makes this point: That the firm's HR policies and practices should produce the employee skills and behaviors the company needs to achieve its strategic aims.

What is Human Resource Management?

LEARNING OBJECTIVE 1-1

Explain what human resource management is and how it relates to the management process.

To understand what human resource management is, it's useful to start with what managers do. Elance is an *organization.* An **organization** consists of people (in this case, people like Elance's own in-house sales managers and Web designers) with formally assigned roles who work together to achieve the organization's goals. A **manager** is someone who is responsible for accomplishing the organization's goals, and who does so by managing the efforts of the organization's people.

organization
A group consisting of people with formally assigned roles who work together to achieve the organization's goals.

manager
Someone who is responsible for accomplishing the organization's goals, and who does so by managing the efforts of the organization's people.

Most writers agree that **managing** involves performing five basic functions: planning, organizing, staffing, leading, and controlling. In total, these functions represent the **management process**. Some of the specific activities involved in each function include:

managing
To perform five basic functions: planning, organizing, staffing, leading, and controlling.

management process
The five basic functions of planning, organizing, staffing, leading, and controlling.

- ***Planning.*** Establishing goals and standards; developing rules and procedures; developing plans and forecasts
- ***Organizing.*** Giving each subordinate a specific task; establishing departments; delegating authority to subordinates; establishing channels of authority and communication; coordinating the work of subordinates
- ***Staffing.*** Determining what type of people should be hired; recruiting prospective employees; selecting employees; setting performance standards; compensating employees; evaluating performance; counseling employees; training and developing employees
- ***Leading.*** Getting others to get the job done; maintaining morale; motivating subordinates
- ***Controlling.*** Setting standards such as sales quotas, quality standards, or production levels; checking to see how actual performance compares with these standards; taking corrective action as needed

In this book, we will focus on one of these functions—the staffing, personnel management, or *human resource management* function. **Human resource management (HRM)** is the process of acquiring, training, appraising, and compensating employees, and of attending to their labor relations, health and safety, and fairness concerns. The topics we'll discuss should therefore provide you with the concepts and techniques every manager needs to perform the "people" or personnel aspects of management. These include:

human resource management (HRM)
The process of acquiring, training, appraising, and compensating employees, and of attending to their labor relations, health and safety, and fairness concerns.

- *Conducting job analyses* (determining the nature of each employee's job).
- *Planning labor needs* and *recruiting* job candidates.
- *Selecting* job candidates.
- *Orienting and training* new employees.
- *Managing wages and salaries* (compensating employees).
- *Providing incentives and benefits.*
- *Appraising performance.*
- *Communicating* (interviewing, counseling, disciplining).
- *Training employees*, and *developing managers.*
- *Building employee relations and engagement.*

And what a manager should know about:

- Equal opportunity and affirmative action.
- Employee health and safety.
- Handling grievances and labor relations.

Why Is Human Resource Management Important to All Managers?

The concepts and techniques in this book are important to all managers for several reasons.

AVOID PERSONNEL MISTAKES First, having a command of this knowledge will help you avoid the *personnel mistakes you don't want to make* while managing. For example, you don't want

- To have your employees not doing their best.
- To hire the wrong person for the job.
- To experience high turnover.
- To have your company in court due to your discriminatory actions.
- To have your company cited for unsafe practices.
- To let a lack of training undermine your department's effectiveness.
- To commit any unfair labor practices.

Carefully studying this book can help you avoid mistakes like these.

IMPROVING PROFITS AND PERFORMANCE More important, it can *help ensure that you get results—through people.*[2] Remember that you could do everything else right as a manager—lay brilliant plans, draw clear organization charts, set up modern assembly lines, and use sophisticated accounting controls—but still fail, for instance, by hiring the wrong people or by not motivating subordinates. On the other hand, many managers—from generals to presidents to supervisors—have been successful even without adequate plans, organizations, or controls. They were successful because they had the knack for hiring the right people for the right jobs and then motivating, appraising, and developing them. Remember as you read this book that *getting results* is the bottom line of managing and that, as a manager, you will have to get these results through people. This fact hasn't changed from the dawn of management. As one company president summed it up:

> For many years it has been said that capital is the bottleneck for a developing industry. I don't think this any longer holds true. I think it's the workforce and the company's inability to recruit and maintain a good workforce that does constitute the bottleneck for production. I don't know of any major project backed by good ideas, vigor, and enthusiasm that has been stopped by a shortage of cash. I do know of industries whose growth has been partly stopped or hampered because they can't maintain an efficient and enthusiastic labor force, and I think this will hold true even more in the future.[3]

Because of global competition, technological advances, and economic turmoil, that statement has never been truer than it is today. Human resource management methods like those in this book can help any line manager/supervisor (or HR manager) boost his or her team's and company's levels of engagement, profits and performance. Here are two examples we'll meet in this book:

> *At one Ball Corp.* packaging plant, managers trained supervisors to set and communicate daily performance goals. Management tracked daily goal attainment with team scorecards. Employees received special training to improve their skills. Within 12 months production was up 84 million cans, customer complaints dropped by 50%, and the plant's return on investment rose by $3,090,000.
>
> *A call center* averaged 18.6 vacancies per year (about a 60% turnover rate). The researchers estimated the cost of a call-center operator leaving at about $21,500. They estimated total annual cost of agent turnover for the call center at $400,853. Cutting that rate in half would save this firm about $200,000 per year.

YOU MAY SPEND SOME TIME AS AN HR MANAGER Here is another reason to study this book: *you might spend time as a human resource manager*. For example, about a third of large U.S. businesses surveyed appointed non-HR managers to be their top human resource executives. Thus, Pearson Corporation (which publishes this book) promoted the head of one of its publishing divisions to chief human resource executive at its corporate headquarters. Why? Some think these people may be better equipped to integrate the firm's human resource activities (such as pay policies) with the company's strategic needs (such as by tying executives' incentives to corporate goals).[4] Appointing non-HR people can also be good for the manager. For example, one CEO served a three-year stint as chief human resource officer on the way to becoming CEO. He said the experience he got was invaluable in learning how to develop leaders and in understanding the human side of transforming a company.[5]

However most top human resource executives do have prior human resource experience. About 80% of those in one survey worked their way up within HR. About 17% had the HR Certification Institute's Senior Professional in Human Resources (SPHR) designation, and 13% were certified Professional in Human Resources (PHR). The Society for Human Resource Management (SHRM) offers a brochure describing alternative career paths within human resource management.[6] Find it at www.shrm.org.

HR FOR SMALL BUSINESSES And here is one other reason to study this book: you *may well end up as your own human resource manager*. More than half the people working in the United States work for small firms. Small businesses as a group also account for most of the 600,000 or so new businesses created every year. Statistically speaking, therefore, most people graduating from college in the next few years either will work for small businesses or will create new small businesses of their own.[7] Small firms generally don't have the critical mass required for a full-time human resource manager (let alone an HR department).[8] The owner and his or her other managers (and perhaps assistant) handle tasks such as signing employees on. Gaining a command of the techniques in this book should help you to manage a small firm's human resources more effectively. We'll address human resource management for small businesses in later chapters.

Line and Staff Aspects of Human Resource Management

All managers have always been, in a sense, human resource managers, because they all get involved in recruiting, interviewing, selecting, and training their employees. Yet most firms also have a human resource department with its own top manager. How do the duties of this human resource manager and department relate to the human resource duties of sales and production and other managers? Answering this requires a short definition of line versus staff authority. **Authority** is the right to make decisions, to direct the work of others, and to give orders. Managers usually distinguish between line authority and staff authority.

authority
The right to make decisions, direct others' work, and give orders.

In organizations, **line authority** traditionally gives managers the right to *issue orders* to other managers or employees. Line authority therefore creates a superior (order giver)–subordinate (order receiver) relationship. When the vice president of sales tells her sales director to "get the sales presentation ready by Tuesday," she is exercising her line authority. **Staff authority** gives a manager the right to *advise* other managers or employees. It creates an advisory relationship. When the human resource manager suggests that the plant manager use a particular selection test, he or she is exercising staff authority.

line authority
Traditionally gives managers the right to issue orders to other managers or employees.

staff authority
Gives a manager the right to advise other managers or employees

On the organization chart, managers with line authority are **line managers**. Those with staff (advisory) authority are **staff managers**. In popular usage, people tend to associate line managers with managing departments (like sales or production) that are crucial for the company's survival. Staff managers generally run departments that are advisory or supportive, like purchasing and human resource management. Human resource managers are usually staff managers. They assist and advise line managers in areas like recruiting, hiring, and compensation.

line manager
A manager who is authorized to direct the work of subordinates and is responsible for accomplishing the organization's tasks.

staff manager
A manager who assists and advises line managers.

Line Managers' Human Resource Management Responsibilities

However, line managers do have many human resource duties. This is because the direct handling of people has always been part of every line manager's duties, from president down to first-line supervisors. One major company outlines its line supervisors' responsibilities for effective human resource management under these general headings:

1. Placing the right person in the right job
2. Starting new employees in the organization (orientation)
3. Training employees for jobs that are new to them
4. Improving the job performance of each person
5. Gaining creative cooperation and developing smooth working relationships
6. Interpreting the company's policies and procedures
7. Controlling labor costs
8. Developing the abilities of each person
9. Creating and maintaining departmental morale
10. Protecting employees' health and physical conditions

And we'll see in this chapter that, if anything, digital tools like *LinkedIn hiring* and cloud computing are actually expanding many line managers' HR responsibilities.

The Human Resource Department

In small organizations, line managers may carry out all these personnel duties unassisted. But as the organization grows, line managers usually need the assistance, specialized knowledge, and advice of a separate human resource staff. In larger firms, the *human resource department* provides such specialized assistance. Figure 1-1 shows human resource management jobs in one organization. Typical positions

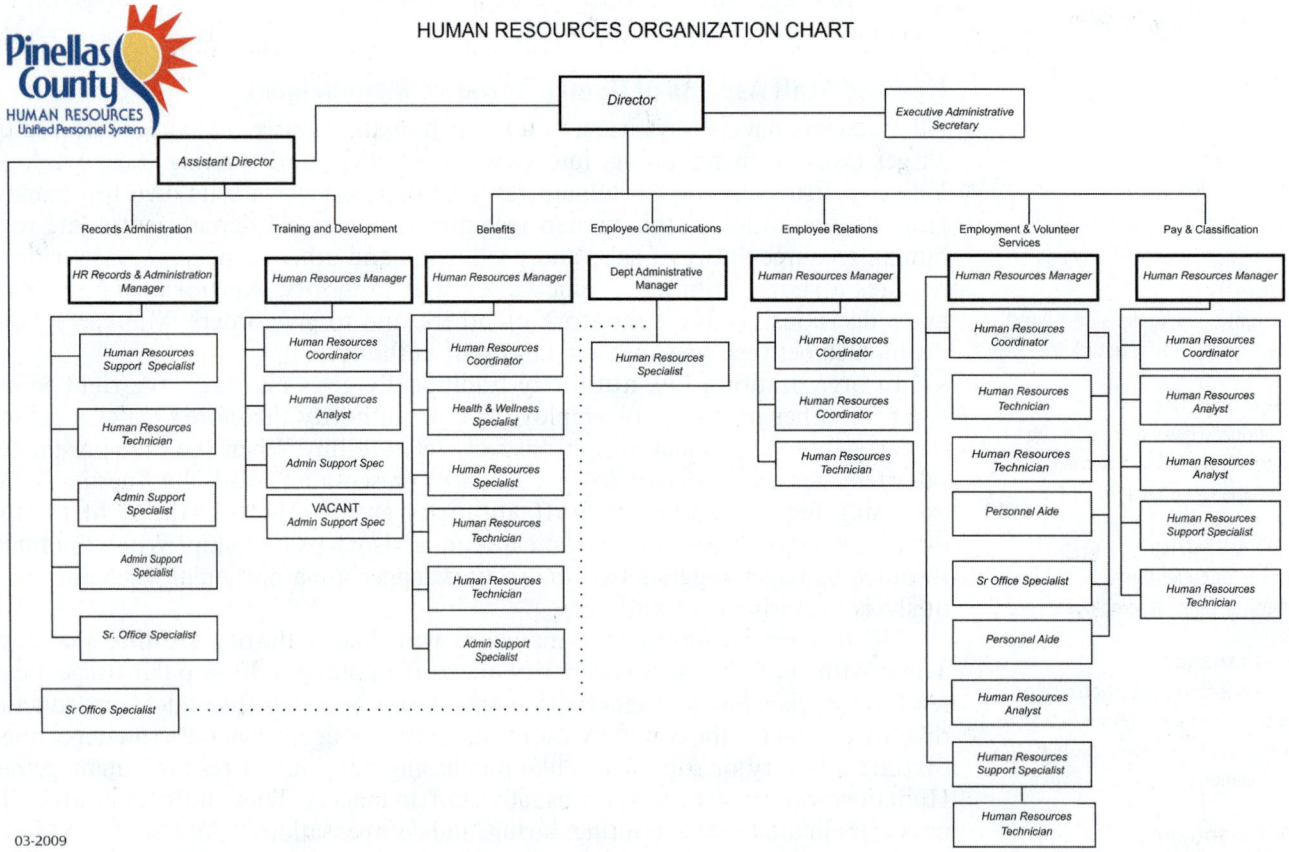

FIGURE 1-1 Human Resource Department Organization Chart Showing Typical HR Job Titles

Source: "Human Resource Development Organization Chart Showing Typical HR Job Titles," www.co.pinellas.fl.us/persnl/pdf/orgchart.pdf. Courtesy of Pinellas County Human Resources. Reprinted with permission.

include compensation and benefits manager, employment and recruiting supervisor, training specialist, and employee relations executive. Examples of job duties include:

- ***Recruiters:*** Maintain contacts within the community and perhaps travel extensively to search for qualified job applicants.
- ***Equal employment opportunity (EEO) representatives or affirmative action coordinators:*** Investigate and resolve EEO grievances, examine organizational practices for potential violations, and compile and submit EEO reports.
- ***Job analysts:*** Collect and examine detailed information about job duties to prepare job descriptions.
- ***Compensation managers:*** Develop compensation plans and handle the employee benefits program.
- ***Training specialists:*** Plan, organize, and direct training activities.
- ***Labor relations specialists:*** Advise management on all aspects of union–management relations.

NEW APPROACHES TO ORGANIZING HR However, what HR departments do and how they do it are changing. Because of this, many employers are taking a new look at how they organize their human resource functions.[9] For example, one survey found that 44% of the large firms surveyed planned to change how they organize and deliver HR services.[10] Most plan to use technology to institute more "*shared services*" (or "transactional") arrangements.[11] These establish centralized HR units whose employees are shared by all the companies' departments to assist the departments' line managers in human resource matters. These shared services HR teams generally offer their services through intranets or centralized call centers; they aim to provide managers and employees with specialized support in day-to-day HR activities (such as discipline problems). You may also find specialized *corporate HR teams* within a company. These assist top management in top-level issues such as developing the personnel aspects of the company's long-term strategic plan. *Embedded HR teams* have HR generalists (also known as "relationship managers" or "HR business partners") assigned to functional departments like sales and production. They provide the selection and other assistance the departments need. *Centers of expertise* are basically specialized HR consulting firms within the company. For example, one center might provide specialized advice in areas such as organizational change to all the company's various units.

The Trends Shaping Human Resource Management

LEARNING OBJECTIVE 1-2

Briefly discuss and illustrate each of the important trends influencing human resource management.

Working cooperatively with line managers, human resource managers have long helped employers hire and fire employees, administer benefits, and conduct appraisals. However, trends are occurring in the environment of human resource management that are changing how employers get their human resource management tasks done. These trends include workforce trends, trends in how people work, technological trends, and globalization and economic trends.

Workforce Demographics and Diversity Trends

The composition of the workforce will continue to change over the next few years; specifically, it will continue to become more diverse with more women, minority group members, and older workers in the workforce.[12] Table 1-1 offers a bird's-eye view. Between 1992 and 2022, the percent of the workforce that the U.S. Department of Labor classifies as "white" will drop from 85% to 77.7%. At the same time, the percent of the workforce that it classifies as "Asian" will rise from 4% to 6.2%, and those of Hispanic origin will rise from 8.9% to 19.1%. The percentages of younger workers will fall, while those over 55 years of age will leap from 11.8% of the workforce in 1992 to 25.6% in 2022.[13] Many employers call "the aging workforce" a big problem. The problem is that there aren't enough younger workers to replace the projected

TABLE 1-1 Demographic Groups as a Percent of the Workforce, 1992–2022

Age, Race, and Ethnicity	1992	2002	2012	2022
Age: 16–24	16.9%	15.4%	13.7%	11.3%
25–54	71.4	70.2	65.3	63.1
55+	11.8	14.3	20.9	25.6
White	85.0	82.8	79.8	77.7
Black	11.1	11.4	11.9	12.4
Asian	4.0	4.6	5.3	6.2
Hispanic origin	8.9	12.4	15.7	19.1

Source: Based on U.S. Bureau of Labor Statistics Economic News Release December 19, 2013. www.bls.gov/news.release/ecopro.t01.htm, accessed May 12, 2015.

number of baby boom–era older workers (born roughly 1946–1964) retiring.[14] Many employers are bringing retirees back (or just trying to keep them from leaving).

With overall projected workforce shortfalls (not enough younger workers to replace retirees), many employers are hiring foreign workers for U.S. jobs. The H-1B visa program lets U.S. employers recruit skilled foreign professionals to work in the United States when they can't find qualified American workers. U.S. employers bring in about 181,000 foreign workers per year under these programs, although such programs face opposition.[15]

Other firms are shifting to nontraditional workers. Nontraditional workers are those who hold multiple jobs, or who are "temporary" or part-time workers, or those working in alternative arrangements (such as a mother–daughter team sharing one clerical job). Others serve as "independent contractors" for specific projects. Almost 10% of American workers—13 million people—fit this nontraditional workforce category.

Some employers find millennials or "generation Y" employees (those born roughly between 1982 and 2004) a challenge to deal with, and this isn't just an American phenomenon. For example, the *New York Times* recently reported that because China's one-child rule led many parents to pamper their children, China's senior army officers are having problems getting millennial-aged volunteers and conscripts to shape up.[16]

On the other hand, millennials also bring a vast array of skills. They've grown up with social media and are expert at collaborating online. And, having grown up with Apple and Google, they're comfortable with innovation.

Trends in How People Work

At the same time, work has shifted from manufacturing jobs to service jobs in North America and Western Europe. Today over two-thirds of the U.S. workforce is employed in producing and delivering services, not products. By 2020, service-providing industries are expected to account for 131 million out of 150 million (87%) of wage and salary jobs overall. So in the next few years, almost all the new jobs added in the United States will be in services, not in goods-producing industries.[17]

ON-DEMAND WORKERS Anyone who has registered on Uber already knows something about on-demand workers.[18] At last count, Uber was signing up almost 40,000 new independent contractor drivers per month, a rate that was doubling every few months.

Today, in more and more companies like Uber, Elance, and Airbnb, employees aren't employees at all, but are freelancers and independent contractors who work when they can on what they want to work on, when the company needs them.[19] So, for example, Airbnb can run in essence a vast lodging company with only a fraction of the "regular" employees one like Hilton Worldwide would need (because the lodgings are owned and managed by the homeowners themselves). Other sites tapping on-demand workers include Amazon's Mechanical Turk, Elance-oDesk, TaskRabbit, and Handybook (which lets users tap Handy's thousands of freelance cleaners and furniture assemblers when they need jobs done).[20] The head of Elance-oDesk, which places millions of short-term professionals via its site, says those on its site are viewed as "mobile, independent bundles of skills."[21]

The fact that employers increasingly rely on such Uber-like "extended workforces" has implications for HR. For example, companies that rely on freelancers, consultants, and other such nontraditional employees will need to create personnel policies on matters like compensation for these "nonemployees," and become more expert as talent brokers in matching specific workers with specific tasks that need to be done.

On-demand models like Elance's and Uber's have detractors. Some people who work for on-demand services say the sometimes menial jobs can make them feel somewhat disrespected. One critic says such work is unpredictable and insecure. An article in the *New York Times* said this: "The larger worry about on-demand jobs is not about benefits, but about a lack of agency—a future in which computers, rather than humans, determine what you do, when and for how much."[22] Some Uber drivers recently sued to become regular (rather than freelance independent contractor) employees.

HUMAN CAPITAL One big consequence of such demographic and workforce trends is employers' growing emphasis on their workers' knowledge, education, training, skills, and expertise—in other words on their "human capital."

Service jobs like consultant and lawyer always emphasized education and knowledge. And today's proliferation of IT-related businesses like Google and Facebook of course demands high levels of human capital. The big change is that even "traditional" manufacturing jobs like assembler are increasingly high-tech. Similarly bank tellers, retail clerks, bill collectors, mortgage processors, and package deliverers today need a level of technological sophistication they wouldn't have needed a few years ago. So in our increasingly knowledge-based economy, "... the acquisition and development of superior human capital appears essential to firms' profitability and success."[23]

For managers, the challenge here is that they have to manage such workers differently. For example, empowering workers to make more decisions presumes you've selected, trained, and rewarded them to make more decisions themselves. Employers therefore need new human resource management practices to select, train, and engage these employees.[24] The accompanying HR as a Profit Center illustrates how one employer took advantage of its human capital.

IMPROVING PERFORMANCE: *HR as a Profit Center*

Boosting Customer Service

A bank installed special software that made it easier for its customer service representatives to handle customers' inquiries. However, the bank did not otherwise change the service reps' jobs in any way. Here, the new software system did help the service reps handle more calls. But otherwise, this bank saw no big performance gains.[25]

A second bank installed the same software. But, seeking to capitalize on how the new software freed up customer reps' time, this bank also had its human resource team upgrade the customer service representatives' jobs. This bank taught them how to sell more of the bank's services, gave them more authority to make decisions, and raised their wages. Here, the new computer system dramatically improved product sales and profitability, thanks to the newly trained and empowered customer service reps. Value-added human resource practices like these improve employee performance and company profitability.[26] ■

Based on "Human Resources Wharton," www.knowledge.wharton.upe.edu; Anthea Zacharatos et al., "High-Performance Work Systems and Occupational Safety," *Journal of Applied Psychology*, 90, no. 1, 2005, pp. 77–93. See also Jennifer Schramm, "Effective HR Practices Drive Profit," *HR Magazine*, November 2012, p. 88.

If your professor has assigned this, go to the Assignments section of **mymanagementlab.com** to complete this discussion.

Talk About It 1: Discuss three more specific examples of what you believe this second bank's HR department could have done to improve the reps' performance.

Globalization Trends

Globalization refers to companies extending their sales, ownership, and/or manufacturing to new markets abroad. Thus Toyota builds Camrys in Kentucky, while Apple assembles iPhones in China. Free trade areas—agreements that reduce tariffs and barriers among trading partners—further encourage international trade. The North American Free Trade Agreement (NAFTA) and the European Union (EU) are examples.

Globalization has boomed for the past 50 or so years. For example, the total sum of U.S. imports and exports rose from $47 billion in 1960, to $562 billion in 1980, to about $5.1 *trillion* recently.[27] Evolving economic and political philosophies drove this boom. Governments dropped cross-border taxes or tariffs, formed economic free trade areas, and took other steps to encourage the free flow of trade among countries. The fundamental economic rationale was that by doing so, all countries would gain, and indeed, economies around the world did grow quickly until recently.

At the same time, globalization vastly increased international competition. More globalization meant more competition, and more competition meant more pressure to be "world class"—to lower costs, to make employees more productive, and to do things better and less expensively.

As multinational companies jockey for position, many transfer operations abroad, not just to seek cheaper labor but to tap into new markets. For example, Toyota has thousands of sales employees based in America, while GE has over 10,000 employees in France. The search for greater efficiencies prompts some employers to *offshore* (export jobs to lower-cost locations abroad, as when Dell offshored some call-center jobs to India). Some employers offshore even highly skilled jobs such as lawyer.[28] Managing the "people" aspects of globalization is a big task for any company that expands abroad—and for its HR managers.[29]

Economic Trends

Although globalization supported a growing global economy, the past 10 or so years were difficult economically. As you can see in Figure 1-2, gross national product (GNP)—a measure of the United States of America's total output—boomed between 2001 and 2007. During this period, home prices (see Figure 1-3) leaped as much as 20% per year. Unemployment remained docile at about 4.7%.[30] Then, around 2007–2008, all these measures fell off a cliff. GNP fell. Home prices dropped by 10% or more (depending on city). Unemployment nationwide soon rose to more than 10%.

Why did all this happen? It's complicated. Many governments stripped away rules and regulations. For example, in America and Europe, the rules that prevented commercial banks from expanding into new businesses such as investment

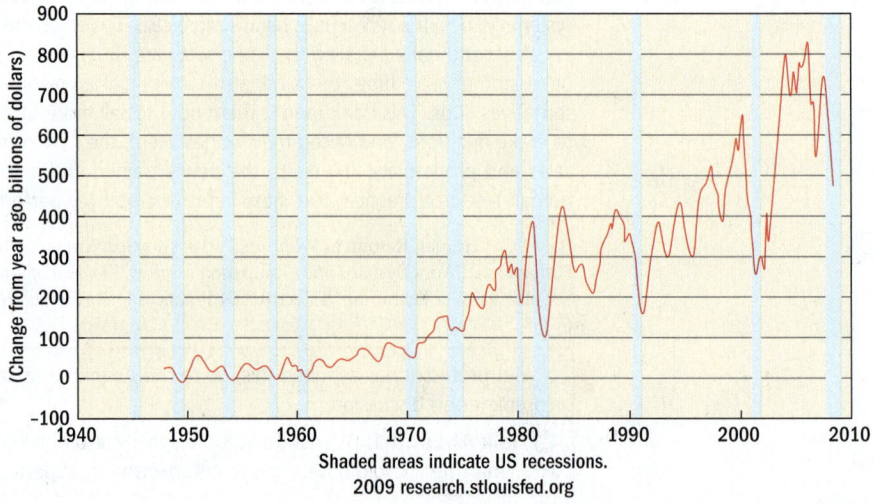

FIGURE 1-2 Gross National Product, 1940–2010

Source: Based on "Gross National Product (GNP)" by FRED Economic Data/St. Louis Fed., from Federal Reserve Bank of St. Louis.

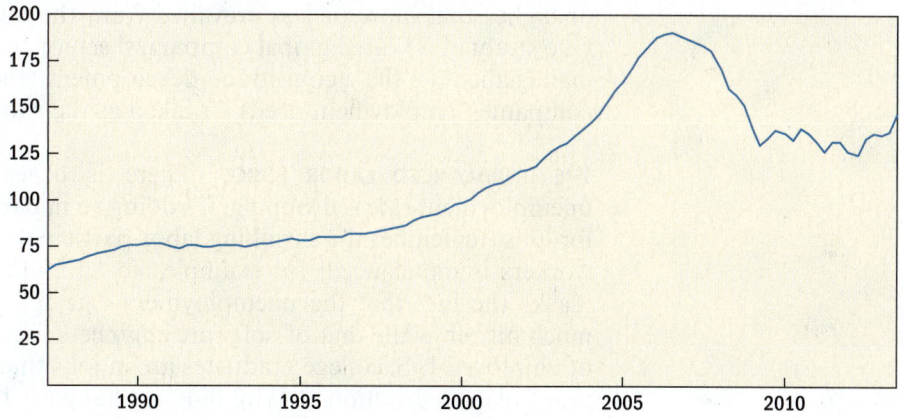

FIGURE 1-3 Case-Shiller Home Price Indexes June 1988–June 2013

Source: Based on Case-Shiller Home Price Indexes June 1988–June 2013, S&P Dow Jones Indices LLC. Accessed September 30, 2013.

banking were relaxed. Giant, multinational "financial supermarkets" such as Citibank emerged. With fewer regulations, more businesses and consumers were soon deeply in debt. Homebuyers bought homes with little money down. Banks freely lent money to developers to build more homes. For almost 20 years, U.S. consumers spent more than they earned. The United States became a debtor nation. Its balance of payments (exports minus imports) went from a healthy *positive* $3.5 billion in 1960, to a huge *minus* (imports exceeded exports) $497 billion deficit more recently.[31] The only way the country could keep buying more from abroad than it sold was by borrowing money. So, much of the boom was built on debt.

Around 2007, all those years of accumulating debt ran their course. Banks and other financial institutions found themselves owning trillions of dollars of worthless loans. Governments stepped in to try to prevent their collapse. Lending dried up. Many businesses and consumers stopped buying. The economy tanked.

Economic trends are pointing up today, and hopefully they will continue to do so. For example, the unemployment rate had fallen from a high of more than 10% a few years ago to around 5% in 2015, and economic activity was also picking up.

However, that doesn't necessarily mean clear sailing for the economy. For one thing, the "Great Recession" of 2007–2009 certainly grabbed everyone's attention. After seeing the economy tank the way it did, many companies became hesitant to spend a lot expanding factories and equipment. The financial meltdown and writing off excessive debt left banks reluctant to make new loans, so prospective small business owners find it hard to start new businesses. With their mortgages (often still) underwater, their credit card and tuition loan debts still hanging over them, and many still without good jobs, consumers are understandably wary about pulling out all the stops when it comes to spending.[32] The Federal Reserve Board, which supported economic expansion after the Great Recession, began reducing support in 2014 (because the economy was looking better, and because of the huge debts it had run up supporting the recovery). At the same time, productivity increases are slowing, which may further retard economic growth.[33] And after what the world went through in 2007–2009, it's doubtful that the deregulation, leveraging, and globalization that drove economic growth for the previous 50 years will continue unabated.

LABOR FORCE TRENDS Complicating all this is the fact that the labor force in America is growing more slowly than expected (which is not good, because if employers can't get enough workers, they can't expand). To be precise, the Bureau of Labor Statistics projects the labor force to grow at 0.5% per year 2012 to 2022, compared with an annual growth rate of 0.7% during the 2002–2012 decade.[34] Why the slower labor force growth? Mostly because with baby boomers aging, the "labor force participation rate" is declining—in other words, the *percent* of the population that wants to work is declining. Add it all up, and the bottom line looks to be slower economic growth ahead. The Bureau of Labor Statistics projects that gross domestic product (GDP) will increase by 2.6% annually from 2012 to 2022, slower than the 3%

or higher that more or less prevailed from the mid-1990s through the mid-2000s.[35] One study of 35 large global companies' senior human resource officers said "talent management"—the acquisition, development and retention of talent to fill the companies' employment needs—ranked as their top concern.[36]

THE UNBALANCED LABOR FORCE There is other economic news. Although the unemployment rate is dropping, it's doing so in part because fewer people are looking for jobs (remember the shrinking labor participation rate). Furthermore, demand for workers is unbalanced; for example, an "average" unemployment rate of, say, 5% masks the fact that the unemployment rate for, say, recent college graduates was much higher, while that of software engineers was much lower.[37] In fact, almost half of employed U.S. college graduates are in jobs that generally require less than a four-year college education.[38] Why did this happen? In brief, because most of the jobs that the economy added in the past few years don't require college educations, and the Bureau of Labor Statistics says that will probably continue. Occupations that *do not* typically require postsecondary education employed nearly two-thirds of workers a few years ago.[39] And, "two-thirds of the 30 occupations with the largest projected employment increases from 2012 to 2022 typically do not require postsecondary education for entry."[40]

The result is an unbalanced labor force: in some occupations (such as high-tech) unemployment rates are low, while in others unemployment rates are still very high; recruiters in many companies can't find candidates, while in others there's a wealth of candidates[41]; and many people working today are in jobs "below" their expertise (which may or may not help to explain why about 70% of employees report being psychologically disengaged at work). In any case, slow growth and labor unbalances mean more pressure on employers (and their human resource managers and line managers) to get the best efforts from their employees.

Technology Trends

However, it may be technology that most characterizes the trends shaping human resource management today.[42] For example, the consulting firm Accenture estimates that social media connections via tools like LinkedIn will soon produce as many as 80% of new recruits—often letting line managers bypass the human resource management unit.[43]

Five main types of digital technologies are driving this transfer of functionality from HR professionals to automation. Employers increasingly use *social media* tools such as Twitter, Facebook, and LinkedIn (rather than, say, as many employment agencies) to recruit new employees. Employers use new *mobile applications*, for instance, to monitor employee location and to provide digital photos at the facility clock-in location to identify workers. The feedback, fun, and objectives inherent in *gaming* support many new training applications, and websites such as Knack, Gild, and True Office enable employers to inject gaming features into training, performance appraisal, and recruiting. *Cloud computing* and more intuitive user interfaces enable employers to monitor and report on things like a team's goal attainment and to provide real-time evaluative feedback. Finally, *data analytics* basically means using statistical techniques, algorithms, and problem-solving to identify relationships among data for the purpose of solving particular problems (such as what are the ideal candidate's traits, or how can I tell in advance which of my best employees is likely to quit?). When applied to human resource management, data analytics is called *talent analytics*.

As one example, talent analytics is revolutionizing how employers look for job candidates. For example, one employer reportedly operated for many years on the assumption that what mattered was the school the candidate attended, the grades they had, and their references. A retrospective talent analytics study showed that these traits didn't matter at all. What mattered were things like: their résumés were grammatically correct, they didn't quit school until obtaining some degree, they were successful in prior jobs, and they were able to succeed with vague instructions.[44]

Technological change is also affecting the nature of jobs.[45] When someone thinks of "tech jobs," jobs at Apple and Google come to mind, but technology affects all sorts of jobs. At Alcoa's Davenport Works plant in Iowa, a computer at each work station helps each employee control his or her machines or communicate data. One former college student became a team leader in a plant with automated machines. He and his team type commands into computerized machines that create precision parts.[46] As another example, about 17 million people now use information technology to work from remote locations at least once per month. "Co-working sites" offer freelance workers office space and access to Wi-Fi and office equipment.[47]

Today's New Human Resource Management

LEARNING OBJECTIVE **1-3**

Briefly describe "distributed HR" and other important aspects of human management today.

A Brief History of Personnel/Human Resource Management

"Personnel management" is not new.[48] Ancient armies and organized efforts always required attracting, selecting, training, and motivating workers. But personnel tasks like these were mostly just part of every manager's job, something that lasted in most countries until the late 1800s. At that time, labor problems began arising in many of the post–industrial revolution's new factories. Soon employers were setting up "welfare offices" and "welfare secretaries" to manage activities like factory washrooms, and "safety bureaus" to oversee plant safety. By 1900, employers set up the first "hiring offices," training programs, and factory schools. Personnel management had begun.

In these early firms, personnel managers took over hiring and firing from supervisors, ran the payroll departments, and administered benefits plans. As expertise in testing emerged, personnel departments played a greater role in employee selection and training.[49] New union laws in the 1930s added "Helping the employer deal with unions" to personnel's tasks. New equal employment laws in the 1960s made employers more reliant on personnel management to avoid discrimination claims.[50] By the 1970s globalization made gaining a competitive edge through engaged employees—and therefore personnel management—increasingly important. Today economic and demographic trends (recall the diminishing workforce participation rate and aging population, for instance) make finding, hiring, and motivating employees more challenging, while more high tech and service jobs means employers must excel at managing employees' knowledge, skills, and expertise (human capital) through aptly renamed human resource management departments. Furthermore, as we've seen, technological trends including mobile and social media are changing how employers recruit, select, train, appraise, and motivate employees.[51] In a sense, a new human resource management is emerging. We'll look at this next.

Distributed HR and the New Human Resource Management

Perhaps most importantly, more and more human resource management tasks are now being redistributed *from* a central HR department *to* the company's employees and line managers, thanks to digital technologies like mobile phones and social media.[52] For example, employees at Washington-based LivingSocial use a digital tool called Rypple to comment on each other's work. LivingSocial then uses these comments as an input to its formal employee appraisals. Similarly, hiring managers in some companies bypass human resource management to find candidates directly via LinkedIn. At Google, when someone applies for a job, his or her information goes into a system that matches the recruit with current Google employees based on interests and experiences. In a process Google calls "crowdsourcing," Google employees then get a big say in who Google hires.

Some experts say that if current trends continue, many aspects of HR and talent management will become "fully embedded in how work gets done throughout an organization [distributed], thereby becoming an everyday part of doing business."[53] So, somewhat ironically, we seem to be shifting in some respects back toward the time before the first personnel departments when line managers did more of the personnel tasks. As an example, Hilton Worldwide is placing more HR activities in the hands of employees, while redirecting the savings thus attained to building up the more strategic aspects of what its human resource managers do.[54] In the following chapters, we'll use Trends Shaping HR features like the accompanying one to present more examples.

TRENDS SHAPING HR: *DIGITAL AND SOCIAL MEDIA*

Digital and social media tools and the new human resource management.
Digital and social media tools are changing how people look for jobs, and how companies recruit, retain, pay, and train employees. In doing so, they've transformed the practice of human resource management, and created, in a sense, a new human resource management. Here are some examples.

Career sites now make the inner workings of employers more transparent than they've ever been.[55] Sites such as Glassdoor, CareerBliss, CareerLeak, and JobBite let their members share insights into hundreds of thousands of employers, including specific company-by-company commentaries, salary reports, and CEO approval ratings. According to one report, 48% of job seekers surveyed said they've used Glassdoor during their job search, including checking before applying for employment at a company.[56] Among other things, such transparency prompted sensible human resource (and other) managers to redouble their efforts to ensure that their internal processes (such as promotion decisions, pay allocations, and performance appraisals) are fair, and that their recruitment processes are civil—for instance, by responding to rejected job candidates and providing them with some closure.

PhotosIndia.com/Getty Images

Like many employers, Hilton Worldwide is "distributing HR"—placing more HR activities in the hands of employees.

Recruitment is one of the most familiar ways that digital and social media revolutionized human resource management. For example, as we'll see in Chapter 5, managers use LinkedIn to find passive employment candidates (those not actively looking for jobs), and to check out active candidates. Another site, Gild, lets managers find skilled software engineers by searching the Web for open source code, and then evaluating the code's programmers in part by scanning technology forums to assess the programmers' reputations.

Talent analytics algorithms help managers improve employee retention. They do this, for example by identifying the factors (such as experience, career advancement, performance reviews, compensation, and even a surge in activity on social media sites) that flag high-potential employees who are more likely to leave.

To improve training, talent analytics tools synthesize information from learning management systems (such as training courses taken) and customer management systems (such as each salesperson's sales performance) to identify which training courses have the biggest impact, and why.

Rather than just matching mentors and protégés informally, new, eHarmony-type tools let managers match them also based on personality.

And with about 70% of all openings now available online, new analytical tools scrutinize online job ads and identify hiring trends by industry and occupation, and real-time competitive pay and benefits information. ■

A Quick Summary

We can summarize important trends to this point as follows:

- One big consequence of globalized competition, economic and demographic trends, and the shift to high-tech and service jobs is the growing emphasis by employers on getting the best from their "human capital," in other words, from their workers' knowledge, education, training, skills, and expertise.

FIGURE 1-4 What Trends Mean for Human Resource Management

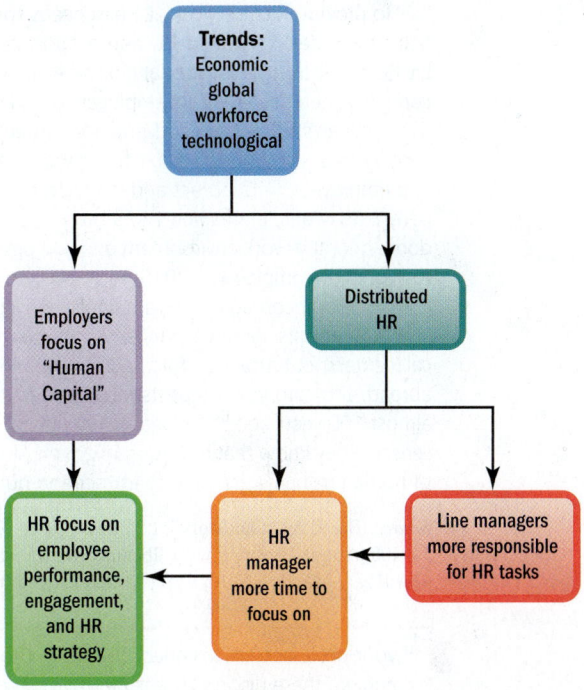

- This requires, among other things, using human resource methods to improve employee performance and engagement.
- Thanks to digital devices and social media, employers are shifting (distributing) more HR tasks from central human resource departments to employees and line managers.
- This gives many line managers more human resource management responsibilities.
- And this means that many human resource managers can refocus their efforts *from* day-to-day activities like interviewing candidates *to* broader efforts, such as formulating strategies for boosting employee performance and engagement. Figure 1-4 illustrates this.

We'll look next at human resource management's roles in strategy, performance, and employee engagement next.

HR and Strategy

strategic human resource management
Formulating and executing human resource policies and practices that produce the employee competencies and behaviors the company needs to achieve its strategic aims.

First, today's human resource managers are focusing more on longer term, strategic "big picture" issues. We'll see in Chapter 3 (Strategy) that **strategic human resource management** means formulating and executing human resource policies and practices that produce the employee competencies and behaviors the company needs to achieve its strategic aims. We illustrate this throughout this book with Strategic Context features such as the accompanying one.

IMPROVING PERFORMANCE: *The Strategic Context*

Building L.L.Bean

Strategic human resource management means formulating and executing human resource policies and practices that produce the employee competencies and behaviors the company needs to achieve its strategic aims.

L.L.Bean illustrates how companies do this. The heart of L.L.Bean's strategy has always been offering great outdoor equipment with outstanding service and expert advice. As its company history said, "L.L.Bean, Inc., quickly established itself as a trusted source for reliable outdoor equipment and expert advice. The small company grew. Customers spread the word of L.L.Bean's quality and service."[57]

To provide such service, L.L.Bean needs special people as employees, ones whose love of the outdoors helps them deal knowledgably and supportively with the company's customers. To paraphrase its Website, L.L.Bean is looking for a special type of employee, one (like its customers) who loves the outdoors, and the company therefore treats its employees just as well as it famously treat its customers.[58]

L.L.Bean's HR policies and practices attract and develop just such employees. For one thing, the company knows just who to recruit for. It wants sociable, friendly, experienced, outdoors-oriented applicants and employees.[59] To attract and cultivate these sorts of employee competencies and behaviors, the company uses multiple interviews to screen out applicants who might not fit in. And L.L.Bean offers an outdoors-oriented work environment and competitive pay and benefits. It was a *Fortune* "100 Best Companies to Work For" employer in 2015.

To help encourage great employee service, L.L.Bean also provides a supportive environment. For example, when its Web sales recently for the first time exceeded phone sales, L.L.Bean closed four local call centers, but arranged for the 220 employees to work from their homes. And instead of sending jobs abroad, the company keeps its jobs close to the town where Leon Leonwood Bean started his company almost 100 years ago.[60] L.L.Bean's managers built the firm's strategy and success around courteous, expert service. They know that having the right employees is the key to its success, and that it takes the right blend of human resource practices to attract and nurture such employees. ■

Source: Based on "Our Story", L.L.Bean, pp. 1-19, from www.llbean.com/customerService/aboutLLBean/images/110408_About-LLB.pdf; www.llbean.com/; Michael Arndt, "L.L.Bean Follows Its Shoppers to the Web," *Business Week*, March 1, 2010. http://www.llbean.com/llb/shop/515428.

If your professor has assigned this, go to the Assignments section of **mymanagementlab.com** to complete these discussion questions.

Talk About It 2: What would you say are (1) L.L.Bean's strategic aims, (2) its required employee behaviors and skills to achieve these aims, and (3) HR policies and practices it needs to produce these necessary employee behaviors and skills?

As in the Strategic Context feature, today's employers want their HR managers to put in place practices that will produce the employee behaviors that help the company achieve its strategic aims. We use a model opening each chapter to illustrate this idea, but in brief the model follows this three-step sequence: Set the firm's strategic aims → Pinpoint the employee behaviors and skills we need to achieve these strategic aims → Decide what HR policies and practices will enable us to produce these necessary employee behaviors and skills.

HR and Performance

Employers also expect their human resource manager/"people experts" to spearhead employee performance-improvement efforts. Here they can apply three levers. The first is the *HR department lever*. The HR manager ensures that the human resource management function is delivering services efficiently. For example, this might include outsourcing certain activities such as benefits management, and using technology to deliver its services more cost-effectively.

The second is the *employee costs lever*. For example, the human resource manager takes a prominent role in advising top management about the company's staffing levels, and in setting and controlling the firm's compensation, incentives, and benefits policies.

The third is the *strategic results lever*. Here the HR manager puts in place the policies and practices that produce the employee competencies and skills the company needs to achieve its strategic goals. That's what was done at L.L.Bean, for instance.

HR AND PERFORMANCE MEASUREMENT Improving performance requires measuring what you are doing. For example, when IBM's former chief HR officer needed $100 million to reorganize its HR operations several years ago, he told top management, "I'm going to deliver talent to you that's skilled and on time and ready to be deployed. I will be able to measure the skills, tell you what skills we have, what [skills] we don't have [and] then show you how to fill the gaps or enhance our training."[61]

Human resource managers use performance measures (or "metrics") to validate claims like these. For example, median HR expenses as a percentage of companies' total operating costs average just under 1%.[62] We'll address this in Chapter 3.

HR AND EVIDENCE-BASED MANAGEMENT Basing decisions on such evidence is the heart of *evidence-based human resource management*. This is the use of data, facts, analytics, scientific rigor, critical evaluation, and critically evaluated research/case studies to support human resource management proposals, decisions, practices, and conclusions.[63] Put simply, evidence-based human resource management means using the best-available evidence in making decisions about the human resource management practices you are focusing on.[64] The evidence may come from *actual measurements* (such as, how did the trainees like this program?). It may come from *existing data* (such as, what happened to company profits after we installed this training program?). Or, it may come from published *research studies* (such as, what does the research literature conclude about the best way to ensure that trainees remember what they learn?).

Sometimes, companies translate their findings into what management gurus call *high-performance work systems,* "sets of human resource management practices that together produce superior employee performance."[65] For example, at GE's assembly plant in Durham, North Carolina, highly trained self-directed teams produce high-precision aircraft parts. We'll also discuss how they do this in Chapter 3.

HR AND ADDING VALUE The bottom line is that today's employers want their human resource managers to *add value* by boosting profits and performance. Professors Dave Ulrich and Wayne Brockbank describe this as the "HR Value Proposition."[66] They say human resource programs (such as benefits plans) are just a means to an end. The HR manager's ultimate aim must be to add value. *Adding value* means helping the firm and its employees improve in a measurable way as a result of the human resource manager's actions. We'll see in this book how human resource practices do this. For example, we'll use, in each chapter, HR as a Profit Center features like the one on page 9 to illustrate this.

HR and Performance and Sustainability

In a world where sea levels are rising, glaciers are crumbling, and people increasingly view financial inequity as offensive, more and more people say that businesses can't just measure "performance" in terms of maximizing profits. They argue that companies' efforts should be "sustainable," by which they mean judged not just on profits, but on their environmental and social performance as well.[67] As one example, PepsiCo has a goal to deliver "Performance with Purpose"—in other words, to deliver financial performance while also achieving human sustainability, environmental sustainability, and talent sustainability. PepsiCo wants to achieve business and financial success while leaving a positive imprint on society (click www.pepsico.com, then click *What We Believe*, and then *Performance with Purpose*). In one survey, about 80% of large surveyed companies report their sustainability performance.[68] We'll see that sustainability trends have important consequences for human resource management.

HR and Employee Engagement

employment engagement
The extent to which an organization's employees are psychologically involved in, connected to, and committed to getting their jobs done.

Employee engagement refers to being psychologically involved in, connected to, and committed to getting one's jobs done. Engaged employees "experience a high level of connectivity with their work tasks," and therefore work hard to accomplish their task-related goals.[69]

Employee engagement is important because it drives performance. For example (as we will discuss in Chapter 3), based on one Gallup survey, business units with the highest levels of employee engagement have an 83% chance of performing above the company median; those with the lowest employee engagement have only a 17% chance.[70] A survey by consultants Watson Wyatt Worldwide concluded that companies with highly engaged employees have 26% higher revenue per employee.[71]

The problem for employers is that, depending on the study, only about 21–30% of today's employees nationally are engaged.[72] In one survey, about 30% were engaged, 50% were not engaged, and 20% were actively disengaged (anti-management).[73]

We will see in this book that managers improve employee engagement by taking concrete steps to do so. For example, a few years ago, Kia Motors (UK) turned its performance around, in part by boosting employee engagement.[74] As we will discuss more fully in Chapter 3, it did this with new HR programs. These included new *leadership development* programs, new *employee recognition* programs, improved *internal communications* programs, a new *employee development* program, and by modifying its *compensation and other policies.* We use special Employee Engagement Guide for Managers sections in most chapters to show how managers use human resource activities such as recruiting and selection to improve employee engagement.

The New Human Resource Manager

LEARNING OBJECTIVE 1-4
List at least four important human resource manager competencies.

It's more complicated being a human resource manager today.[75] Tasks like formulating strategic plans and making data-based decisions require new competencies and skills. HR managers can't just be good at traditional personnel tasks like hiring and training. Instead, they must "speak the CFO's language" by defending human resource plans in measurable terms (such as return on investment).[76] To create strategic plans, the human resource manager must understand strategic planning, marketing, production, and finance.[77] As companies merge and expand abroad, they must be able to formulate and implement large-scale organizational changes, drive employee engagement, and redesign organizational structures and work processes. None of this is easy.

When asked, "Why do you want to be an HR manager?" many people basically say, "Because I'm a people person." Being sociable is certainly important, but it takes much more. What does it take to be a human resource manager today? Recently, the Society for Human Resource Management (SHRM) introduced a new "competency model" (called the SHRM Body of Competency and Knowledge™); it itemizes the competencies, skills, and knowledge and expertise human resource managers need. Here are the behaviors or competencies (with definitions) SHRM says today's HR manager should be able to exhibit:

- ***Leadership & Navigation*** The ability to direct and contribute to initiatives and processes within the organization.
- ***Ethical Practice*** The ability to integrate core values, integrity, and accountability throughout all organizational and business practices.
- ***Business Acumen*** The ability to understand and apply information with which to contribute to the Organization's strategic plan.
- ***Relationship Management*** The ability to manage interactions to provide service and to support the organization.
- ***Consultation*** The ability to provide guidance to organizational stakeholders.
- ***Critical Evaluation*** The ability to interpret information with which to make business decisions and recommendations.
- ***Global & Cultural Effectiveness*** The ability to value and consider the perspectives and backgrounds of all parties.
- ***Communication*** The ability to effectively exchange information with stakeholders.

SHRM also says human resource managers must have command of the basic knowledge in the functional areas of HR, such as employee relations. The basic knowledge of principles, practices, and functions they need here should cover:

- Functional Area #1: Talent Acquisition & Retention
- Functional Area #2: Employee Engagement
- Functional Area #3: Learning & Development
- Functional Area #4: Total Rewards
- Functional Area #5: Structure of the HR Function
- Functional Area #6: Organizational Effectiveness & Development
- Functional Area #7: Workforce Management

HR managers can't just be good at traditional personnel tasks like hiring and training, but must "speak the CFO's language" by defending human resource plans in measurable terms.

Dmitriy Shironosov/Alamy

- Functional Area #8: Employee Relations
- Functional Area #9: Technology & Data
- Functional Area #10: HR in the Global Context
- Functional Area #11: Diversity & Inclusion
- Functional Area #12: Risk Management
- Functional Area #13: Corporate Social Responsibility
- Functional Area #14: U.S. Employment Law & Regulations
- Functional Area #15: Business & HR Strategy

HR and the Manager's Skills

The aim of this book is to help every manager develop the skills he or she needs to carry out the human resource management–related aspects of his or her job, such as recruiting, selecting, training, appraising, and incentivizing employees, and providing them with a safe and fulfilling work environment.[78] Special HR Tools for Line Managers and Small Businesses features provide small business owners/managers in particular with techniques to better manage their small businesses. Know Your Employment Law features highlight the practical information all managers need to make better HR-related decisions that work. Employee Engagement Guide for Managers features show how managers improve employee engagement.

HR and Ethics

Regrettably, news reports today are filled with stories of otherwise competent managers who have run amok. For example, prosecutors filed criminal charges against several Iowa meatpacking plant human resource managers who allegedly violated employment law by hiring children younger than 16.[79] Behaviors like these risk torpedoing even otherwise competent managers and employers. **Ethics** means *the standards someone uses to decide what his or her conduct should be*. We will see that many serious workplace ethical issues—workplace safety and employee privacy, for instance—are human resource management related.[80]

ethics
The principles of conduct governing an individual or a group; specifically, the standards you use to decide what your conduct should be.

HR Manager Certification

Many human resource managers use certification to demonstrate their mastery of contemporary human resource management knowledge and competencies. Managers have, at this writing, at least two testing processes to achieve certification.

The oldest is administered by the HR Certification Institute (HRCI), an independent certifying organization for human resource professionals (see www.hrci.org). Through testing, HRCI awards several credentials, including Professional in Human Resources (PHR), and Senior Professional in Human Resources (SPHR). Managers can review HRCI's Knowledge Base and take an online HRCI practice quiz by going to www.hrci.org and clicking on Exam Preparation and then on Sample Questions.[81]

Starting in 2015, SHRM began offering its own competency and knowledge-based testing and certifications, for SHRM Certified Professionals, and SHRM Senior Certified Professionals, based on its own certification exams.[82] The exam is built around the SHRM Body of Competency and Knowledge™ model which includes functional knowledge and skills as well as competencies.

We've summarized separately the SHRM and the HRCI knowledge bases in Appendices A and B of this book, pp. 612–629). One covers SHRM's functional knowledge areas (such as employee relations). The other covers HRCI's seven main knowledge areas (such as Strategic Business Management, and Workforce Planning and Employment. It includes about 91 specific HRCI "Knowledge of" subject areas within these seven main topic areas with which those taking the test should be familiar.

You'll find throughout this book special Knowledge Base icons starting in Chapter 2 to denote coverage of SHRM and/or HRCI knowledge topics.

HR and the Manager's Human Resource Philosophy

Technical expertise is important, but at the end of the day, people's actions are always based in part on the basic assumptions they make, and this is especially true in regard to human resource management. The basic assumptions you make about people—Can they be trusted? Do they dislike work? Why do they act as they do? How should they be treated?—together comprise your philosophy of human resource management. And every personnel decision you make—the people you hire, the training you provide, your leadership style, and the like—reflects (for better or worse) this basic philosophy.

How do you go about developing such a philosophy? To some extent, it's preordained. There's no doubt that you will bring to your job an initial philosophy based on your experiences, education, values, assumptions, and background. But your philosophy doesn't have to be set in stone. It should evolve as you accumulate knowledge and experiences. For example, after a worker uprising in China at the Hon Hai-owned Foxconn plant that assembles Apple iPhones, the personnel philosophy at the plant softened in response to the workers' (and Apple's) discontent.[83] In any case, no manager should manage others without first understanding the personnel philosophy that is driving his or her actions.

One of the things molding your own philosophy is that of your organization's top management. While it may or may not be stated, it is usually communicated by the managers' actions and permeates every level and department in the organization. For example, here is part of the personnel philosophy of the founder of the Polaroid Corp., stated many years ago:

> To give everyone working for the company a personal opportunity within the company for full exercise of his talents—to express his opinions, to share in the progress of the company as far as his capacity permits, and to earn enough money so that the need for earning more will not always be the first thing on his mind. The opportunity, in short, to make his work here a fully rewarding and important part of his or her life.[84]

Current "best companies to work for" lists include many organizations with similar philosophies. For example, the CEO of software giant SAS has said,

> We've worked hard to create a corporate culture that is based on trust between our employees and the company . . . a culture that rewards innovation, encourages employees to try new things and yet doesn't penalize them for taking chances, and a culture that cares about employees' personal and professional growth.[85]

Similarly, when Google founders Larry Page and Sergey Brin began building Google, they set out to make it a great place to work. Google doesn't just offer abundant benefits and stock options.[86] Google's team of social scientists run experiments, for instance, to determine successful middle managers' skills.[87] The aim is to keep "Googlers" happy (and Google successful and growing). We'll look closer at how managers maintain positive employee relations in Chapters 3 and 13.

Watch It!
How does a company actually go about putting its human resource philosophy into action? If your professor has assigned this, go to to the Assignments section of mymanagementlab.com to complete the video exercise titled *Human Resource Management (Patagonia)*.

The Plan of This Book

LEARNING OBJECTIVE **1-5**
Outline the plan of this book.

The Basic Themes and Features

In this book, we'll use four themes and features to highlight particularly important issues, and to provide continuity from chapter to chapter.

Practical Tools For Every Manager

First, human resource management is the *responsibility of every manager*—not just those in human resources. Throughout every page in this book, you'll therefore find an emphasis on practical material that you as a manager will need to perform your day-to-day management responsibilities, even if you never spend one day as an HR manager.

Second, managers use human resource management techniques to *improve performance, productivity, and profitability*. To highlight this, you will find special boxed features titled:

Improving Performance: HR Tools for Line Managers and Small Businesses. These features highlight actual tools and practices any manager can use to improve performance at work.

Improving Performance: HR as a Profit Center. We've seen that employers need human resource management practices that add value. To illustrate this throughout the book, most chapters contains an illustrative Improving Performance: HR as a Profit Center feature. These show actual examples of how human resource management practices add measurable value—by reducing costs or boosting revenues.

Improving Performance: HR Practices Around the Globe. These features highlight how actual companies around the globe use effective HR practices to improve their teams' and companies' performance.

Improving Performance Through HRIS. These features highlight how managers use human resource technology to improve performance.

Diversity Counts. These features provide insights and guidelines for managing a diverse workforce.

Third, the book emphasizes how digital and high-tech trends are shaping human resource management. You'll therefore find *Trends* features such as ***Trends Shaping HR: Digital and Social Media*** in most chapters.

Fourth, particularly with today's "distributed HR", every line and staff manager should understand how the employer's human resource management policies and practices produce the employee skills and performance the company needs *to achieve its strategic aims*. Special chapter-opener scenarios and ***Improving Performance: The Strategic Context*** features illustrate this in most chapters. And use the Hotel Paris continuing case starting in Chapter 3 to apply that idea.

Chapter Contents Overview

Following is a brief overview of the chapters and their content.

Part 1: Introduction

Chapter 1: Introduction to Human Resource Management. The manager's human resource management jobs; crucial global and competitive trends; how managers use technology and modern HR measurement systems to create high-performance work systems.

Chapter 2: Equal Opportunity and the Law. What you should know about equal opportunity laws; how these laws affect activities such as interviewing, selecting employees, and evaluating performance; *Know Your Employment Law* features highlight important laws in each chapter.

Chapter 3: Human Resource Management Strategy and Analysis. What is strategic planning; strategic human resource management; building high-performance HR practices; tools for evidence-based HR; employee engagement at Kia Motors.

Part 2: Recruitment, Placement, and Talent Management

Chapter 4: Job Analysis and the Talent Management Process. How to analyze a job; how to determine the human resource requirements of the job, as well as its specific duties; and what is talent management.

Chapter 5: Personnel Planning and Recruiting. Human resource planning; determining what sorts of people need to be hired; recruiting them.

Chapter 6: Employee Testing and Selection. Techniques you can use to ensure that you're hiring the right people.

Chapter 7: Interviewing Candidates. How to interview candidates effectively.

Part 3: Training and Development

Chapter 8: Training and Developing Employees. Providing the training and development to ensure that your employees have the knowledge and skills needed to accomplish their tasks.

Chapter 9: Performance Management and Appraisal. Techniques you can use for appraising employee performance.

Chapter 10: Managing Careers and Retention. Causes of and solutions for employee turnover, and how to help employees manage their careers.

Part 4: Compensation

Chapter 11: Establishing Strategic Pay Plans. How to develop equitable pay plans for your employees.

Chapter 12: Pay for Performance and Financial Incentives. Pay-for-performance plans such as financial incentives, merit pay, and incentives that help tie performance to pay.

Chapter 13: Benefits and Services. Providing benefits that make it clear the firm views its employees as long-term investments and is concerned with their welfare.

Part 5: Enrichment Topics in Human Resource Management

Chapter 14: Building Positive Employee Relations. Developing employee relations programs and employee involvement strategies; ensuring ethical and fair treatment through discipline and grievance processes

Chapter 15: Labor Relations and Collective Bargaining. How to deal with unions, including the union organizing campaign; negotiating and agreeing upon a collective bargaining agreement between unions and management; and managing the agreement via the grievance process.

Chapter 16: Safety, Health, and Risk Management. How to make the workplace safe, including the causes of accidents; laws governing your responsibilities for employee safety and health; risk management methods.

Chapter 17: Managing Global Human Resources. Special topics in managing the HR side of multinational operations.

Chapter 18: Managing Human Resources in Small and Entrepreneurial Firms. Special topics for managing human resources in smaller firms.

The Topics Are Interrelated

In practice, do not think of each of this book's topics as being unrelated to the others. Each topic interacts with and affects the others, and all should align with the employer's strategic plan. For example, hiring people who don't have the potential to learn the job will doom their performance, regardless of how much training they get. Similarly, we will see throughout this book that each human resource management function, from job analysis to recruiting, selecting, training, and rewarding employees, should aim to produce the employee behaviors and competencies that the company needs to achieve its strategic goals.

Chapter Review

MyManagementLab® Go to **mymanagementlab.com** to complete the problems marked with this icon. ✪

Chapter Section Summaries

1-1. All managers should be able to answer, **What is human resource management, and why is it important?** Doing so helps managers avoid problems like hiring the wrong person for the job. And more important, it can help ensure that managers get results through people. Line managers' human resource duties include placing the right person on the job, and orienting and training new employees.

1-2. **The trends shaping human resource management** are influencing what human resource managers do and how they do it. Globalization means more competition, and more competition means more pressure to lower costs and to make employees more productive and quality conscious. Technology is requiring more employees to be technologically well informed and pressuring employers to improve their human resource processes by applying new distributive technological tools. There is more emphasis on "knowledge work" and therefore on building "human capital," the knowledge, education, training, skills, and expertise of a firm's employees. Workforce and demographic changes mean that the workforce is becoming older and more diverse.

1-3. New digital technologies such as mobile and social media will make **human resource management today** more distributed. Traditionally, personnel/HR managers focused on administrative issues such as running the payroll department. Today, employers expect their human resource management teams to focus more on big-picture issues, including instituting human resource policies and practices that support the companies' strategic objectives, and to foster high performance through engaged employees.

1-4. To do so, **the human resource managers** need **new competencies.** They should be able to apply evidence-based human resource management, which means the use of data, facts, analytics, scientific rigor, critical evaluation, and critically evaluated research/case studies to support human resource management proposals, decisions, practices, and conclusions.

1-5. In understanding the overall **plan of this book,** keep several important themes in mind: that human resource management is the responsibility of every manager, that the workforce is increasingly diverse, that employers and their human resource managers face the need to manage in challenging economic times, and that human resource managers must be able to defend their plans and contributions in measurable terms—to use evidence-based management—to show they've added value.

Discussion Questions

✪ **1-1.** Explain what HR management is and how it relates to the management process.

1-2. Give examples of how HR management concepts and techniques can be of use to all managers.

1-3. Illustrate the HR management responsibilities of line and staff managers.

✪ **1-4.** Compare the authority of line and staff managers. Give examples of each.

Individual and Group Activities

1-5. Working individually or in groups, develop outlines showing how trends like workforce diversity, technological innovation, globalization, and changes in the nature of work have affected the college or university you are attending now. Present in class.

1-6. Working individually or in groups, contact the HR manager of a local bank. Ask the HR manager how he or she is working as a strategic partner to manage human resources, given the bank's strategic goals and objectives. Back in class, discuss the responses of the different HR managers.

1-7. Working individually or in groups, interview an HR manager. Based on that interview, write a short presentation regarding HR's role today in building competitive organizations.

1-8. Working individually or in groups, bring several business publications such as *Bloomberg Businessweek* and the *Wall Street Journal* to class, or access them in class via the Web. Based on their contents, compile a list titled "What HR Managers and Departments Do Today."

1-9. Based on your personal experiences, list 10 examples showing how you used (or could have used) human resource management techniques at work or school.

1-10. Laurie Siegel, former senior vice president of human resources for Tyco International, took over her job just after numerous charges forced the company's previous board of directors and top executives to leave the firm. Hired by new CEO Edward Breen, Siegel had to tackle numerous difficult problems starting the moment she assumed office. For example, she had to help hire a new management team. She had to do something about what the outside world viewed as a culture of questionable ethics at her company. And she had to do something about the company's top-management compensation plan, which many felt contributed to the allegations by some that some former company officers had used the company as a sort of private ATM.

Siegel came to Tyco after a very impressive career. For example, she had been head of executive compensation at Allied Signal, and was a graduate of the Harvard Business School. But, as strong as her background was, she obviously had her work cut out for her when she took the senior vice president of HR position at Tyco.

Working individually or in groups, conduct an Internet search and/or library research to answer the following questions: What human resource management–related steps did Siegel take to help get Tyco back on the right track? Do you think she took the appropriate steps? Why or why not? What, if anything, do you suggest she do now?

1-11. Appendices A and B at the end of this book (pages 612–629) list the knowledge someone studying for the HRCI (Appendix A) or SHRM (Appendix B) certification exam needs to have in each area of human resource management (such as in Strategic Management, and Workforce Planning). In groups of several students, do four things: (1) review Appendix A and/or B; (2) identify the material in this chapter that relates to the Appendix A and/or B required knowledge lists; (3) write four multiple-choice exam questions on this material that you believe would be suitable for inclusion in the HRCI exam and/or the SHRM exam; and, (4) if time permits, have someone from your team post your team's questions in front of the class, so that students in all teams can answer the exam questions created by the other teams.

Experiential Exercise

HR and "The Profit"

Purpose: The purpose of this exercise is to provide practice in identifying and applying the basic concepts of human resource management by illustrating how managers use these techniques in their day-to-day jobs.

Required Understanding: Be thoroughly familiar with the material in this chapter, and with at least one or two episodes of CNBC's *The Profit* with Marcus Lemonis www.tv.com/shows/the-profit/watch/. (Access a library of past episodes at URLs such as www.cnbc.com/live-tv/the-profit)

How to Set Up the Exercise/Instructions:

- Divide the class into teams of several students.
- Read this: As you may know by watching billionaire Marcus Lemonis as he works with actual small businesses in which he's taken an ownership share, human resource management often plays an important role in what he and the business owners and managers need to do to be successful. For example, at Grafton Furniture, a lack of clarity about who does what (a lack of up-to-date job descriptions) leads to inadequate supervision of some ongoing orders and to lower profit margins. Questions also arise at Grafton about, for instance, the effectiveness of the training that some managers (including the owner's son) have received.
- Watch several of these shows (or reruns of the shows), and then meet with your team and answer the following questions:

1-12. What specific HR functions (recruiting, interviewing, training, and so on) can you identify Mr. Lemonis addressing on this show? Make sure to give specific examples based on the show.

1-13. What specific HR functions can you identify as being problematical in this company? Again, please give specific answers.

1-14. In terms of HR functions (such as recruiting, selection, interviewing, compensating, appraising, and so on) what exactly would you recommend doing to improve this company's performance?

1-15. Present your team's conclusions to the class.

Application Case

Jack Nelson's Problem

As a new member of the board of directors for a local bank, Jack Nelson was being introduced to all the employees in the home office. When he was introduced to Ruth Johnson, he was curious about her work and asked her what the machine she was using did. Johnson replied that she really did not know what the machine was called or what it did. She explained that she had only been working there for 2 months. However, she did know precisely how to operate the machine. According to her supervisor, she was an excellent employee.

At one of the branch offices, the supervisor in charge spoke to Nelson confidentially, telling him that "something was wrong," but she didn't know what. For one thing, she explained, employee turnover was too high, and no sooner had one employee been put on the job than another one resigned. With customers to see and loans to be made, she continued, she had little time to work with the new employees as they came and went.

All branch supervisors hired their own employees without communication with the home office or other branches. When an opening developed, the supervisor tried to find a suitable employee to replace the worker who had quit.

After touring the 22 branches and finding similar problems in many of them, Nelson wondered what the home office should do or what action he should take. The banking firm generally was regarded as being a well-run institution that had grown from 27 to 191 employees during the past 8 years. The more he thought about the matter, the more puzzled Nelson became. He couldn't quite put his finger on the problem, and he didn't know whether to report his findings to the president.

Questions

1-16. What do you think is causing some of the problems in the bank's home office and branches?

1-17. Do you think setting up an HR unit in the main office would help?

1-18. What specific functions should an HR unit carry out? What HR functions would then be carried out by supervisors and other line managers? What role should the Internet play in the new HR organization?

Source: From Supervision in Action: The Art of Managing Others, 4th edition, Pearson Education, Inc., Upper Saddle River, New Jersey.

Continuing Case

Carter Cleaning Company

Introduction

A main theme of this book is that human resource management activities like recruiting, selecting, training, and rewarding employees are not just the job of a central HR group but rather a job in which every manager must engage. Perhaps nowhere is this more apparent than in the typical small service business. Here the owner/manager usually has no HR staff to rely on. However, the success of his or her enterprise (not to mention his or her family's peace of mind) often depends largely on the effectiveness through which workers are recruited, hired, trained, evaluated, and rewarded. Therefore, to help illustrate and emphasize the front-line manager's HR role, throughout this book we will use a continuing case based on an actual small business in the southeastern United States. Each chapter's segment of the case will illustrate how the case's main player—owner/manager Jennifer Carter—confronts and solves personnel problems each day at work by applying the concepts and techniques of that particular chapter. Here is background information that you will need to answer questions that arise in subsequent chapters. (We also present a second, unrelated "application case" case incident in each chapter.)

Carter Cleaning Centers

Jennifer Carter graduated from State University in June 2008 and, after considering several job offers, decided to do what she always planned to do—go into business with her father, Jack Carter.

Jack Carter opened his first laundromat in 1998 and his second in 2001. The main attraction of these coin laundry businesses for him was that they were capital- rather than labor-intensive. Thus, once the investment in machinery was made, the stores could be run with just one unskilled attendant and none of the labor problems one normally expects from being in the retail service business.

The attractiveness of operating with virtually no skilled labor notwithstanding, Jack had decided by 2004 to expand the services in each of his stores to include the dry cleaning and pressing of clothes. He embarked, in other words, on a strategy of "related diversification" by adding new services that were related to and consistent with his existing coin laundry activities. He added these for several reasons. He wanted to better utilize the unused space in the rather large stores he currently had under lease. Furthermore, he was, as he put it, "tired of sending out the dry cleaning and pressing work that came in from our coin laundry clients to a dry cleaner 5 miles away, who then took most of what should have been our profits." To reflect the new, expanded line of services, he renamed each of his two stores Carter Cleaning Centers and was sufficiently satisfied with their performance to open four more of the same type of stores over the next 5 years. Each store had its own on-site manager and, on average, about seven employees and annual revenues of about $500,000. It was this six-store chain that Jennifer joined after graduating.

Her understanding with her father was that she would serve as a troubleshooter/consultant to the elder Carter with the aim of both learning the business and bringing to it modern management concepts and techniques for solving the business's problems and facilitating its growth.

Questions

1-19. Make a list of five specific HR problems you think Carter Cleaning will have to grapple with.

1-20. What would you do first if you were Jennifer?

MyManagementLab

Go to **mymanagementlab.com** for Auto-graded writing questions as well as the following Assisted-graded writing questions:

1-21. From a practical point of view, why is it important for all managers and future managers to have a good command of human resource management concepts and techniques?

1-22. Think of some companies that you are familiar with or that you've read about where you think the human resource managers have been successful in "adding value." What do the HR managers do to lead you to your conclusion?

1-23. MyManagementLab Only—comprehensive writing assignment for this chapter.

✪ Try It!

How would you apply the concepts and skills you learned in this chapter? If your professor has assigned this, go to the Assignments section of mymanagementlab.com to complete the simulation: *Human Resources Management*.

✪ PERSONAL INVENTORY ASSESSMENTS

Personal Assessment of Management Skills

Complete this assessment to learn more about your management skills.

Key Terms

organization, 3
manager, 3
managing, 3
management process, 3
human resource management (HRM), 3
authority, 5
line authority, 5
staff authority, 5
line manager, 5
staff manager, 5
strategic human resource management, 15
employment engagement, 17
ethics, 19

Endnotes

1. www.elance.com/p/lpg/freelancing/?rid=1TN5N&utm_source=bing&utm_medium=cpc&utm_campaign=c-bBrand-Exact&utm_term=elance%20odesk&ad={creative}&bmt=e&adpos={adposition}, accessed May 12, 2015. Note that the owner of Elance and its related company oDesk recently rebranded itself as Upwork, www.upwork.com, accessed May 12, 2015.
2. See, for example, Seongmin Ryu and Sunghoon Kim, "First-Line Managers' Involvement and HR Effectiveness: The Case of South Korea," *Human Resource Management* 52, no. 6 (November–December 2013), pp. 947–966.
3. Fred K. Foulkes, "The Expanding Role of the Personnel Function," *Harvard Business Review,* March–April 1975. See also www.bls.gov/oco/ocos021.htm, accessed October 3, 2011.
4. Steve Bates, "No Experience Necessary? Many Companies Are Putting Non-HR Executives in Charge of HR with Mixed Results," *HR Magazine* 46, no. 11 (November 2001), pp. 34–41. See also Adrienne Fox, "Do Assignments Outside HR Pay Off?" *HR Magazine,* November 2011, p. 32.
5. "Why Chief Human Resources Officers Make Great CEOs," *Harvard Business Review*, December 2014, p. 31.
6. "A Profile of Human Resource Executives," *BNA Bulletin to Management,* June 21, 2001, p. S5; "Today's HR Executives: How Career Paths Have Changed—and Stayed the Same," http://knowledge.wharton.upenn.edu/article/todays-hr-executives-how-career-paths-have-changed-and-stayed-the-same, accessed July 25, 2014.
7. See "Small Business: A Report of the President" (1998), www.SBA.gov/ADV/stats, accessed March 9, 2006; and www.census.gov/econ/smallbus.html, accessed May 13, 2015.
8. Susan Mayson and Rowena Barrett, "The 'Science' and 'Practice' of HR in Small Firms," *Human Resource Management Review* 16 (2006), pp. 447–455.
9. Some firms have recently worked on eliminating their traditional human resource departments, with generally mixed results. See, for example, Todd Henneman, "Is HR at Its Breaking Point?" *Workforce Management,* March 22, 2013, pp. 29–33.
10. See Dave Ulrich, "The New HR Organization," *Workforce Management,* December 10, 2007, pp. 40–44, and Dave Ulrich, "The 21st-Century HR Organization," *Human Resource Management* 47, no. 4 (Winter 2008), pp. 829–850.
11. "Technology to Play Role in Updating HR Delivery Services, Report Finds," *Bloomberg BNA Bulletin to Management,* September 4, 2012, p. 281. See also Meg McSherry Breslin, "Strategic Move? Report Examines Future of HR," *Workforce Management,* November 2012, p. 14.
12. www.bls.gov/news.release/ecopro.t01.htm, accessed July 29, 2012.
13. "Percent Growth in Labor Force, Projected 1990–2020," www.bls.gov/news.release/ecopro.t01.htm, accessed July 29, 2012.
14. "Talent Management Leads in Top HR Concerns," *Compensation & Benefits Review,* May/June 2007, p. 12; www.bls.gov/news.release/ecopro.t01.htm, accessed May 12, 2015.
15. Rita Zeidner, "Does the United States Need Foreign Workers?" *HR Magazine,* June 2009, pp. 42–44.
16. Jane Perlez, "Coddled Recruits Are Hindering China's Army," *New York Times,* February 18, 2015, p. 85.
17. See "Charting the Projections: 2010–2020," *Occupational Outlook Quarterly,* Winter 2011; www.bls.gov/ooq/2011/winter/winter2011ooq.pdf, www.bls.gov/emp/optd/optd003.pdf, accessed July 29, 2012.
18. Farhad Manjoo, "Uber's Business Model Could Change Your Work," *New York Times,* January 29, 2015, pp. B1, B8.
19. Accenture, "Top Trends That Will Reshape the Future of HR: The Future of HR," www.accenture.com/us-en/Pages/insight-future-of-HR.aspx, accessed March 6, 2015.
20. Lauren Weber and Rachel Silverman, "On-Demand Workers: 'We Are Not Robots,'" *Wall Street Journal,* January 28, 2015, pp. B1, B7.
21. Erica Fry, "Start Up: You," *Fortune* 171, no. 1 (January 1, 2015), pp. 84–87.
22. Manjoo, "Uber's Business Model Could Change Your Work," p. B8.
23. Russell Crook et al., "Does Human Capital Matter? A Meta-Analysis of the Relationship Between Human Capital and Firm Performance," *Journal of Applied Psychology* 96, no. 3 (2011), pp. 443–456.
24. Peter Drucker, "The Coming of the New Organization," *Harvard Business Review,* January–February 1988, p. 47. See also James Guthrie et al., "Correlates and Consequences of High Involvement Work Practices: The Role of Competitive Strategy," *International Journal of Human Resource Management,* February 2002, pp. 183–197.
25. "Human Resources Wharton," www.knowledge.wharton.upe.edu, accessed January 8, 2006.
26. See, for example, Anthea Zacharatos et al., "High-Performance Work Systems and Occupational Safety," *Journal of Applied Psychology* 90, no. 1 (2005), pp. 77–93. See also Jennifer Schramm, "Effective HR Practices Drive Profit," *HR Magazine,* November 2012, p. 88.
27. www.census.gov/foreign-trade/statistics/historical/gands.pdf, accessed June 30, 2015.
28. "Study Predicts 4.1 Million Service Jobs Offshored by 2008," *BNA Bulletin to Management,* August 2, 2005, p. 247; and Patrick Thibodeau, "Offshoring Shrinks Number of IT Jobs, Study Says," *Computerworld,* March 21, 2012, www.computerworld.com/s/article/9225376/Offshoring_shrinks_number_of_IT_jobs_study_says_, accessed October 5, 2012.
29. Due to rising costs abroad and customer pushback, many firms today are bringing jobs back. See, for example, "Here, There and Everywhere," *The Economist,* January 19, 2013, pp. 1–20.
30. www.bls.gov/opub/ted/2006/may/wk2/art01.htm, accessed April 18, 2009.
31. Ibid.
32. Rich Miller, "Yellen Fed Resigns Itself to Diminished Growth Expectations," *Bloomberg,* May 2, 2014, www.bloomberg.com/news/2014-05-02/yellen-s-fed-resigned-to-diminished-growth-expectations.html, accessed May 2, 2014.
33. Peter Coy, "This Economist Foresees 15 Years of Labor Shortages," *Bloomberg BusinessWeek,* March 21, 2014, www.businessweek.com/printer/articles/191219-this-economist-foresees-15-years-of-labor-shortages, accessed April 30, 2014.
34. Bureau of Labor Statistics, "Employment Projections: 2012–2022 Summary," December 19, 2013, www.bls.gov/news.release/ecopro.nr0.htm, accessed April 30, 2014.
35. Ibid.
36. "Talent Management Leads in Top HR Concerns," *Compensation & Benefits Review,* May/June 2007, p. 12; "Talent Management, ACA Among Top Issues Facing HR in 2013," *Bloomberg BNA Bulletin to Management,* January 15, 2013, p. 22. See also Douglas Ready, Linda Hill, and Robert Thomas, "Building a Game-Changing Talent Strategy," *Harvard Business Review,* January–February 2014, pp. 63–68.
37. Darrell West, "The Paradox of Worker Shortages at a Time of High National Unemployment," *Brookings,* April 10, 2013, www.brookings.edu/research/

papers/2013/04/11-worker-shortage-immigration-west, accessed April 30, 2014.
38. Richard Vedder, Christopher Denhart, and Jonathan Robe, "Why Are Recent College Graduates Underemployed?" *The Center for College Affordability,* http://centerforcollegeaffordability.org/uploads/Underemployed%20 Report%202.pdf, accessed April 30, 2014.
39. Bureau of Labor Statistics, "Economic Projections: 2012–2022 Summary."
40. Ibid.
41. See, for example, David Ferris, "X-factor for Factories Is Factoring-In Recruiting," *Workforce Management,* December 2012, p. 8.
42. Anthony Abbatiello, "The Digital Override," *Workforce*, May 2014, pp. 36–39.
43. Accenture, "Top Trends That Will Reshape the Future of HR."
44. Josh Bersin, "Big Data in Human Resources: Talent Analytics (People Analytics) Comes of Age," www.forbes.com/sites/joshbersin/2013/02/17/bigdata-in human-resources-talent-analytics-comes-of-age, accessed March 29, 2015.
45. See "A Third Industrial Revolution," *The Economist,* April 21, 2012, pp. 1–20; and Jeffrey Immelt, "The CEO of General Electric on Sparking an American Manufacturing Renewal," *Harvard Business Review,* March 2012, pp. 43–46.
46. Timothy Appel, "Better Off a Blue-Collar," *Wall Street Journal,* July 1, 2003, p. B1.
47. Adrienne Fox, "At Work in 2020," *HR Magazine,* January 2010, pp. 18–23.
48. This is based on Bruce Kaufman, "The Historical Development of American HRM Broadly Viewed," *Human Resource Management Review* 24 (2014), pp. 196–218. See also D. Ulrich and J. H. Dulebohn, "Are We There Yet? What's Next for HR?" *Human Resource Management Review* 25, no. 2 (June 2015), pp. 188–204; and D. J. Cohen, "HR Past, Present and Future: A Call for Consistent Practices and a Focus on Competencies," *Human Resource Management Review* 25, no. 2 (June 2015), pp. 205–215.
49. For a book describing the history of human resource management, see, for example, SHRM, *A History of Human Resources,* www.shrmstore.shrm.org/a-history-of-human-resources.html, accessed October 4, 2012.
50. "Human Capital Critical to Success," *Management Review,* November 1998, p. 9. See also "HR 2018: Top Predictions," *Workforce Management* 87, no. 20 (December 15, 2008), pp. 20–21; and Edward Lawler III, "Celebrating 50 Years: HR: Time for a Reset?" *Human Resource Management* 50, no. 2 (March–April 2011), pp. 171–173.
51. See, for example, D. L. Stone, D. I. Deadrick, J. M. Lukaszewski, and R. Johnson, "The Influence of Technology on the Future of Human Resource Management," *Human Resource Management Review* 25, no. 2 (June 2015), pp. 216–231.
52. Abbatiello, "The Digital Override."
53. Tim Good, Catherine Farley, Himanshu Tambe, and Susan Cantrell, "Trends Reshaping the Future of HR: Digital Radically Disrupts HR," Accenture 2015.
54. Ibid. Some companies today think they're better off without an HR department, but the results are decidedly mixed. Lauren Weber and Rachel Feintzeig, "Is It a Dream or a Drag? Companies Without HR," *Wall Street Journal*, April 9, 2014, pp. 81, B7.
55. This is based on "The Future of Business: Human Resources, How HR Leaders Are Reinventing Their Roles in Transforming Business," *The Economist Intelligence Unit,* 2014.
56. Ibid.
57. www.llbean.com/customerService/aboutLLBean/images/110408_About-LLB.pdf, accessed June 1, 2011; www.llbean.com/llb/shop/515428, accessed May 14, 2015.
58. http://llbeancareers.com/culture.htm, accessed February 28, 2010; www.llbean.com/llb/shop/515428, accessed May 14, 2015.
59. http://llbeancareers.com/culture.htm, accessed February 28, 2010; www.llbean.com/llb/shop/515428, accessed May 14, 2015.
60. Michael Arndt, "L.L.Bean Follows Its Shoppers to the Web," *Business Week*, March 1, 2010.
61. Robert Grossman, "IBM's HR Takes a Risk," *HR Magazine,* April 1, 2007.
62. Chris Brewster et al., "What Determines the Size of the HR Function? A Cross National Analysis," *Human Resource Management* 45, no. 1 (Spring 2006), pp. 3–21.
63. See, for example, www.personneltoday.com/blogs/hcglobal-human-capital-management/2009/02/theres-no-such-thing-as-eviden.html, accessed April 18, 2009.
64. The evidence-based movement began in medicine. In 1996, in an editorial published by the *British Medical Journal,* David Sackett, MD, defined *evidence-based medicine* as "use of the best-available evidence in making decisions about patient care" and urged his colleagues to adopt its tenets. "Evidence-Based Training™: Turning Research into Results for Pharmaceutical Sales Training," an AXIOM White Paper © 2006 AXIOM Professional Health Learning LLC. All rights reserved.
65. "Super-Human Resources Practices Result in Better Overall Performance, Report Says," *BNA Bulletin to Management,* August 26, 2004, pp. 273–274. See also Wendy Boswell, "Aligning Employees with the Organization's Strategic Objectives: Out of Line of Sight, Out of Mind," *International Journal of Human Resource Management* 17, no. 9 (September 2006), pp. 1014–1041. A study found that some employers took a lower-cost approach to human resource practices, with mixed results. See Soo Min Toh et al., "Human Resource Configurations: Investigating Fit with the Organizational Context," *Journal of Applied Psychology* 93, no. 4 (2008), pp. 864–882.
66. Susan Wells, "From HR to the Top," *HR Magazine,* June 2003, p. 49. See also "HR Will Have More Opportunities to Demonstrate Value in 2012," *Bloomberg BNA Bulletin to Management,* January 17, 2012, p. 22.
67. Sully Taylor, Joyce Osland, and Caroline Egri, "Guest Editors' Introduction: Introduction to HRM's Role in Sustainability: Systems, Strategies, and Practices," *Human Resource Management* 51, no. 6 (November–December 2012), p. 789.
68. Cathy Dubois and David Dubois, "Strategic HRM as Social Design for Environmental Sustainability Organization," *Human Resource Management* 51, no. 6 (November–December 2012), p. 799.
69. Michael Christian, Adela Garza, and Jerel Slaughter, "Work Engagement: A Quantitative Review and Test of Its Relations with Task and Contextual Performance," *Personnel Psychology* 60, no. 4 (2011), pp. 89–136.
70. Adrienne Fox, "Raising Engagement," *HR Magazine,* May 2010, pp. 35–40.
71. Except as noted, this is based on Kathryn Tyler, "Prepare for Impact," *HR Magazine* 56, no. 3, (March 2011), pp. 53–56.
72. www.gallup.com/strategicconsulting/163007/state-american-workplace.aspx; Bruce Louis Rich et al., "Job Engagement: Antecedents and Effects on Job Performance," *Academy of Management Journal* 53, no. 3 (2010), pp. 617–635; "Special Report: Employee Engagement—Losing Lifeblood," *Workforce Management,* July 2011, pp. 24–27.
73. "Five Ways to Improve Employee Engagement Now," *Gallup Business Journal.* Gallup.com, accessed April 7, 2014.
74. Ibid.
75. Richard Vosburgh, "The Evolution of HR: Developing HR as an Internal Consulting Organization," *Human Resource Planning* 30, no. 3 (September 2007), pp. 11–24; and the RBL Group, "2012 Human Resource Competency Study," www.rbl.net/index.php/hrcs/index/overview, accessed October 4, 2012.
76. Dave Ulrich and Wayne Brockbank, *The HR Value Proposition.* Boston: Harvard Business School Publishing, 2005.
77. See, for example, "Employers Seek HR Executives with Global Experience, SOX Knowledge,

Business Sense," *BNA Bulletin to Management,* September 19, 2006, pp. 297–298; and Robert Rodriguez, "HR's New Breed," *HR Magazine,* January 2006, pp. 67–71.

78. HR-related questions that line managers have to address include: What are our talent needs? How should we meet our talent needs? How can we do a better job of hiring? How can we develop internal talent? And, How can we manage our employees' career paths? (These are quoted from Peter Cappelli, "HR for Neophytes," *Harvard Business Review,* October 2013, pp. 25–27.)
79. "Meatpacking Case Highlights HR's Liability," *Workforce Management,* September 20, 2008, p. 6.
80. Kevin Wooten, "Ethical Dilemmas in Human Resource Management," *Human Resource Management Review* 11 (2001), p. 161. See also Ann Pomeroy, "The Ethics Squeeze," *HR Magazine* 51, no. 3 (March 2006), pp. 48–55.
81. SHRM and HRCI generally do not make it possible for college graduates without HR experience to sit for one of the certification exams. However, they do provide sample practice questions. See, for example, www2.shrm.org/assuranceoflearning/StudentMaterials.html, accessed July 25, 2014.
82. www.shrm.org/certification/pages/default.aspx#sthash.JRZQeAWR.dpuf, accessed September 8, 2014.
83. See, for example, "When the Jobs Inspector Calls," *The Economist,* March 31, 2012, p. 73; and Paul Mozur, "Foxconn Workers: Keep Our Overtime," *Wall Street Journal,* December 18, 2012, pp. B1–B2.
84. Fred Foulkes and Henry Morgan, "Organizing and Staffing the Personnel Function," *Harvard Business Review,* May–June 1977.
85. "Working at SAS: An Ideal Environment for New Ideas," SAS website, April 20, 2012. Copyright © 2011 by SAS Institute, Inc. Reprinted with permission. All rights reserved.
86. Manjoo, "Uber's Business Model Could Change Your Work."
87. Ibid.

2

Equal Opportunity and the Law

Photographee.eu/Shutterstock

LEARNING OBJECTIVES

2-1 Explain the importance of and list the basic features of Title VII of the 1964 Civil Rights Act and at least five other equal employment laws.

2-2 Describe post-1990 employment laws including the Americans with Disabilities Act and how to avoid accusations of sexual harassment at work.

2-3 Illustrate two defenses you can use in the event of discriminatory practice allegations, and cite specific discriminatory personnel management practices in recruitment, selection, promotion, transfer, layoffs, and benefits.

2-4 List the steps in the EEOC enforcement process.

2-5 Discuss why diversity management is important and how to install a diversity management program.

A university recently fired its career services director after years of good evaluations. This happened about a year after his new boss gave him his first poor evaluation while peppering him with questions like "when are you going to retire?" The dismissed employee soon sued for age discrimination.[1] We will see how to avoid such problems.

WHERE ARE WE NOW . . .

Every HR action you take as a manager, from interviewing applicants to training, appraising, and rewarding them, has equal employment implications. Therefore, the purpose of this chapter is to provide you with the knowledge to deal more effectively with equal employment questions on the job. The main topics we cover are equal opportunity laws enacted from 1964 to 1991, the laws enacted from 1991 to the present, defenses against discrimination allegations, illustrative discriminatory employment practices, the EEOC enforcement process, and diversity management.

Equal Opportunity Laws Enacted from 1964 to 1991

Hardly a day goes by without equal opportunity lawsuits at work.[2] One survey of corporate counsels found that such lawsuits were their biggest litigation fears.[3] Performing day-to-day supervisory tasks like hiring employees without understanding these laws is fraught with peril.

LEARNING OBJECTIVE 2-1

Explain the importance of and list the basic features of Title VII of the 1964 Civil Rights Act and at least five other equal employment laws.

Actually, laws barring discrimination against minorities in the United States are nothing new. The Fifth Amendment to the U.S. Constitution (ratified in 1791) states that "no person shall be deprived of life, liberty, or property, without due process of the law." The Thirteenth Amendment (1865) outlawed slavery, and courts have held that it bars racial discrimination. The Civil Rights Act of 1866 gives all persons the same right to make and enforce contracts and to benefit from U.S. laws.[4] But as a practical matter, Congress and presidents avoided dramatic action on implementing equal employment until the early 1960s. At that point, civil unrest among minorities and women and changing traditions prompted them to act. Congress passed a multitude of new civil rights laws.

Title VII of the 1964 Civil Rights Act

Title VII of the 1964 Civil Rights Act

The section of the act that says an employer cannot discriminate on the basis of race, color, religion, sex, or national origin with respect to employment.

Title VII of the 1964 Civil Rights Act was one of the first of these laws. As amended by the 1972 Equal Employment Opportunity Act, Title VII states that an employer cannot discriminate based on race, color, religion, sex, or national origin. Specifically, it states that it shall be an unlawful employment practice for an employer:

1. To fail or refuse to hire or to discharge an individual or otherwise to discriminate against any individual with respect to his or her compensation, terms, conditions, or privileges of employment, because of such individual's race, color, religion, sex, or national origin.
2. To limit, segregate, or classify employees or applicants for employment in any way that would deprive or tend to deprive any individual of employment opportunities or otherwise adversely affect his or her status as an employee, because of such individual's race, color, religion, sex, or national origin.

Title VII bars discrimination on the part of most employers, including all public or private employers of 15 or more persons and most labor unions. It also covers all private and public educational institutions, the federal government, and state and local governments. It bars public and private employment agencies from failing or refusing to refer for employment any individual because of race, color, religion, sex, or national origin.

Equal Employment Opportunity Commission (EEOC)

The commission, created by Title VII, empowered to investigate job discrimination complaints and sue on behalf of complainants.

Title VII established the **Equal Employment Opportunity Commission (EEOC)** to administer and enforce the Civil Rights Act at work. It consists of five members appointed by the president with the advice and consent of the Senate. Each member serves a 5-year term. In popular usage, the EEOC also includes the thousands of staff the EEOC has around the United States. They receive and investigate job discrimination complaints from aggrieved individuals. When the EEOC finds reasonable cause that the charges are justified, it attempts (through conciliation) to reach an agreement.[5] If this fails, it can go to court. The EEOC may file discrimination charges on behalf of aggrieved individuals, or the individuals may file on behalf of themselves.[6] We'll discuss the EEOC procedure later in this chapter.

Executive Orders

affirmative action

Steps that are taken for the purpose of eliminating the present effects of past discrimination.

Office of Federal Contract Compliance Programs (OFCCP)

This office is responsible for implementing the executive orders and ensuring compliance of federal contractors.

Various U.S. presidents signed executive orders expanding equal employment in federal agencies. For example, the Johnson administration (1963–1969) issued Executive Orders 11246 and 11375. These required that government contractors with contracts of more than $50,000 and 50 or more employees take **affirmative action** to ensure employment opportunities for those who may have suffered past discrimination. They also established the **Office of Federal Contract Compliance Programs (OFCCP)**. It implements the orders and ensures compliance.[7]

Equal Pay Act of 1963

Equal Pay Act of 1963
The act requiring equal pay for equal work, regardless of sex.

Under the **Equal Pay Act of 1963** (amended in 1972), it is unlawful to discriminate in pay on the basis of sex when jobs involve equal work; require equivalent skills, effort, and responsibility; and are performed under similar working conditions. Pay differences derived from seniority systems, merit systems, and systems that measure earnings by production quantity or quality or from any factor other than sex do not violate the act. Unfortunately, this act notwithstanding, women still earn only about 70% as much as men in similar jobs; we'll address this inequity and how to deal with it in our chapter on establishing strategic pay plans.

Age Discrimination in Employment Act of 1967

Age Discrimination in Employment Act of 1967 (ADEA)
The act prohibiting arbitrary age discrimination and specifically protecting individuals over 40 years old.

The **Age Discrimination in Employment Act of 1967 (ADEA)** made it unlawful to discriminate against employees or applicants who are between 40 and 65 years of age. Subsequent amendments effectively ended most mandatory retirement at age 65. Most states and local agencies, when acting as employers, must also adhere to the ADEA.[8]

You can't get around the ADEA by replacing employees who are, say, 60 with someone over 40. In one case the U.S. Supreme Court held that an employee who is over 40 years of age might sue for discrimination if a "significantly younger" employee replaces him or her, even if the replacement is also over 40. The Court didn't specify what "significantly younger" meant. Here the plaintiff was replaced by someone 16 years younger.[9]

Younger managers especially may have to guard against ageist prejudices. For example, a 54-year-old former manager alleged that Google fired him because his supervisor said he wasn't a "cultural fit." Such comments prompted the California Court of Appeals to let the manager's case proceed.[10]

Lawyers like the ADEA. It allows jury trials and double damages to those proving "willful" discrimination.[11]

Vocational Rehabilitation Act of 1973

Vocational Rehabilitation Act of 1973
The act requiring certain federal contractors to take affirmative action for disabled persons.

The **Vocational Rehabilitation Act of 1973** requires employers with federal contracts of more than $2,500 to take affirmative action in employing handicapped persons. It does not require hiring unqualified people. It does require an employer to take steps to accommodate a handicapped worker unless doing so imposes an undue hardship on the employer.

Pregnancy Discrimination Act of 1978

Pregnancy Discrimination Act
An amendment to Title VII of the Civil Rights Act that prohibits sex discrimination based on "pregnancy, childbirth, or related medical conditions."

The **Pregnancy Discrimination Act** of 1978 prohibits using pregnancy, childbirth, or related medical conditions to discriminate in hiring, promotion, suspension, or discharge, or in any term or condition of employment. Furthermore, under the act, if an employer offers its employees disability coverage, then it must treat pregnancy and childbirth like any other disability, and include it in the plan as a covered condition.[12]

More women are suing under this act, and progressive human resources notwithstanding, it's easy to see why.[13] As one example, an auto dealership fired an employee after she said she was pregnant. The reason? Allegedly, "In case I ended up throwing up or cramping in one of their vehicles. They said pregnant women do that sometimes, and I could cause an accident. . . ."[14] Managers therefore should base such decisions on "medical documentation, not on a manager's interpretation."[15]

Federal Agency Guidelines

Uniform Guidelines
Guidelines issued by federal agencies charged with ensuring compliance with equal employment federal legislation explaining recommended employer procedures in detail.

The federal agencies charged with ensuring compliance with these laws and executive orders have their own implementing guidelines. These spell out recommended procedures for complying with the law.[16]

The EEOC, Civil Service Commission, Department of Labor, and Department of Justice together issued **Uniform Guidelines**.[17] These set forth "highly recommended" procedures for things like employee selection and record keeping. As an example, they specify that employers must *validate* any employment selection devices (like tests) that screen out disproportionate numbers of women or minorities, and they explain how to do so. (We explain this procedure in Chapter 6.) The EEOC and other agencies also periodically issue updated guidelines clarifying and revising their positions on matters such as sexual harassment. The American Psychological Association has its own (non–legally binding) Standards for Educational and Psychological Testing.

Early Court Decisions Regarding Equal Employment Opportunity

Several court decisions between 1964 and 1991 helped clarify courts' interpretations of equal employment opportunity (EEO) laws such as Title VII.

GRIGGS V. DUKE POWER COMPANY *Griggs* was a landmark case because the Supreme Court used it to define unfair discrimination. Lawyers sued the Duke Power Company on behalf of Willie Griggs, an applicant for a job as a coal handler. The company required its coal handlers to be high school graduates. Griggs claimed this requirement was illegally discriminatory. He said it wasn't related to success on the job, and it resulted in more blacks than whites being rejected for these jobs. Griggs won the case. The Court's decision was unanimous. In his written opinion, Chief Justice Burger laid out three crucial guidelines affecting equal employment legislation.

(Adj.) overt: done or shown openly; plainly or readily apparent, not secret or hidden

- First, the Court ruled that the *discrimination does not have to be overt to be illegal.* The plaintiff does not have to show that the employer intentionally discriminated against the employee or applicant. Instead, the plaintiff just has to show that discrimination took place.
- Second, the Court held that an employment practice (in this case, requiring the high school degree) *must be job related* if it has an unequal impact on members of a **protected class**. (For example, if arithmetic is not required to perform the job, don't test for arithmetic.)
- Third, Chief Justice Burger's opinion placed the *burden of proof on the employer* to show that the hiring practice is job related. Thus, the employer must show that the employment practice (in this case, requiring a high school degree) is necessary for satisfactory job performance if the practice discriminates against members of a protected class. Said Justice Burger,

protected class
Persons such as minorities and women protected by equal opportunity laws, including Title VII.

> The act proscribes not only overt discrimination, but also practices that are fair in form, but discriminatory in operation. The touchstone is business necessity. If an employment practice which operates to exclude Negroes cannot be shown to be related to job performance, the practice is prohibited.[18]

For employers, *Griggs* established these five principles:

1. A test or other selection practice must be job related, and the burden of proof is on the employer.
2. An employer's intent not to discriminate is irrelevant.[19]
3. If a practice is "fair in form but discriminatory in operation," the courts will not uphold it.
4. *Business necessity* is the defense for any existing program that has adverse impact. The court did not define business necessity.
5. Title VII does not forbid testing. However, the test must be job related (valid), in that performance on the test must relate to performance on the job.

ALBEMARLE PAPER COMPANY V. MOODY In the *Albemarle* case, the Court provided more details on how employers could prove that tests or other screening tools relate to job performance.[20] For example, the Court said that if an employer wants to test candidates for a job, then the employer should first clearly document and understand the job's duties and responsibilities. Furthermore, the job's performance standards should be clear and unambiguous. That way, the employer can identify which employees are performing better than others. The Court's ruling also established the EEOC (now Federal) Guidelines on validation as the procedures for validating employment practices.

LEARNING OBJECTIVE 2-2

Describe post-1990 employment laws including the Americans with Disabilities Act and how to avoid accusations of sexual harassment at work.

The Laws Enacted from 1991 to the Present

The Civil Rights Act of 1991

Civil Rights Act of 1991 (CRA 1991)
The act that places the burden of proof back on employers and permits compensatory and punitive damages.

Several subsequent Supreme Court rulings in the 1980s limited the protection of women and minority groups under equal employment laws. For example, they raised the plaintiff's burden of proving that the employer's acts were in fact discriminatory. This prompted Congress to pass a new Civil Rights Act. President George H. W. Bush signed the **Civil Rights Act of 1991 (CRA 1991)** into law in November 1991. The effect of CRA 1991 was to roll back equal employment law to where it stood before the 1980s decisions, and to place more responsibility on employers.

BURDEN OF PROOF First, CRA 1991 addressed the issue of *burden of proof.* Burden of proof—what the plaintiff must show to establish possible illegal discrimination, and what the employer must show to defend its actions—plays a central role in equal employment cases.[21] Today, in brief, once an aggrieved applicant or employee demonstrates that an employment practice (such as "must lift 100 pounds") has an adverse impact on a particular group, then the burden of proof shifts to the employer, who must show that the challenged practice is job related.[22] For example, the employer has to show that lifting 100 pounds is required for performing the job in question, and that the business could not run efficiently without the requirement—that it is a business necessity.[23]

MONEY DAMAGES Before CRA 1991, victims of *intentional* discrimination (which lawyers call *disparate treatment*) who had not suffered financial loss and who sued under Title VII could not then sue for compensatory or punitive damages. All they could expect was to have their jobs reinstated (or to get a particular job). They were also eligible for back pay, attorneys' fees, and court costs.

CRA 1991 makes it easier to sue for *money damages* in such cases. It provides that an employee who is claiming intentional discrimination can ask for (1) compensatory damages and (2) punitive damages, if he or she can show the employer engaged in discrimination "with malice or reckless indifference to the federally protected rights of an aggrieved individual."[24]

"mixed-motive" case
A discrimination allegation case in which the employer argues that the employment action taken was motivated not by discrimination, but by some nondiscriminatory reason such as ineffective performance.

MIXED MOTIVES Some employers in **"mixed-motive" cases** had taken the position that even though their actions were discriminatory, other factors like the employee's dubious behavior made the job action acceptable. Under CRA 1991, an employer cannot avoid liability by proving it would have taken the same action—such as terminating someone—even without the discriminatory motive.[25] *If there is any such motive, the practice may be unlawful.*[26]

The Americans with Disabilities Act

Americans with Disabilities Act (ADA)
The act requiring employers to make reasonable accommodations for disabled employees; it prohibits discrimination against disabled persons.

The **Americans with Disabilities Act (ADA)** of 1990 prohibits employment discrimination against qualified disabled individuals.[27] It prohibits employers with 15 or more workers from discriminating against qualified individuals with disabilities, with regard to applications, hiring, discharge, compensation, advancement, training, or other terms, conditions, or privileges of employment.[28] It also says employers must make "reasonable accommodations" for physical or mental limitations unless doing so imposes an "undue hardship" on the business.

The ADA does not list specific disabilities. Instead, EEOC guidelines say someone is disabled when he or she has a physical or mental impairment that "substantially limits" one or more major life activity. Initially, impairments included any physiological disorder or condition, cosmetic disfigurement, or anatomical loss affecting one or more of several body systems, or any mental or psychological disorder, but the list is growing.[29] The act specifies conditions that it does *not* regard as disabilities, including homosexuality, compulsive gambling, pyromania, and certain disorders resulting from the current illegal use of drugs.[30]

Mental disabilities account for the greatest number of ADA claims.[31] Under EEOC ADA guidelines, "mental impairment" includes "any mental or psychological disorder, such as…emotional or mental illness." Examples include major depression, anxiety disorders, and personality disorders. The ADA also protects employees with intellectual disabilities, including those with IQs below 70–75.[32] The guidelines say employers should be alert to the possibility that traits normally regarded as undesirable (such as chronic lateness, hostility, or poor judgment) may reflect mental impairments. Reasonable accommodation might then include providing barriers between work spaces.

qualified individuals
Under ADA, those who can carry out the essential functions of the job.

QUALIFIED INDIVIDUAL Just being disabled doesn't qualify someone for a job, of course. Instead, the act prohibits discrimination against **qualified individuals**—those who, with (or without) a reasonable accommodation, can carry out the *essential functions* of the job. The individual must have the requisite skills, educational background, and experience. A job function is essential when, for instance, it is the reason the position exists, or it is so highly specialized that the employer hires the person for his or her expertise or ability to perform that particular function. For example, when an Iowa County highway worker had an on-the-job seizure, his driver's license was suspended and the court ruled he had no ADA claim because he couldn't perform the essential functions of the job.[33]

REASONABLE ACCOMMODATION If the individual can't perform the job as currently structured, the employer must make a "reasonable accommodation" unless doing so would present an "undue hardship."[34] Reasonable accommodation might include redesigning the job, modifying work schedules, or modifying or acquiring equipment or other devices; widening door openings or permitting telecommuting are examples.[35] For example, about 70% of working-age blind adults are unemployed or underemployed. Existing technologies such as screen-reading programs might enable most to work successfully.[36]

Attorneys, employers, and the courts continue to work through what "reasonable accommodation" means.[37] In one classic case, a Walmart door greeter with a bad back asked if she could sit on a stool while on duty. The store said no. The federal district court agreed door greeters must act in an "aggressively hospitable manner," which can't be done from a stool.[38] Standing was an essential job function. You can use technology and common sense to make reasonable accommodation (see Figure 2-1).

THE ADA AMENDMENTS ACT OF 2008 (ADAAA) Employers traditionally prevailed in almost all—96%—federal circuit court ADA decisions.[39] One case typifies what plaintiffs faced. An assembly worker sued Toyota, arguing that carpal tunnel syndrome prevented her from doing her job.[40] The U.S. Supreme Court ruled that the ADA covers carpal tunnel syndrome only if her impairments affect not just her job performance, but also her daily living activities. The employee admitted that she could perform personal chores such as washing her face and fixing breakfast. The Court said the disability must be central to the employee's daily living (not just to his or her job).[41]

However, the ADA Amendments Act of 2008 (ADAAA) has made it easier for employees to show that their disabilities are influencing one of their "major life activities," such as reading and thinking.[42] For example, sensitivity to perfume might be considered a disability.[43] Employers must therefore redouble their efforts to ensure they're complying with the ADA.[44]

Many employers simply take a progressive approach. Common employer concerns about people with disabilities (for instance, that they are less productive and

FIGURE 2-1 Examples of How to Provide Reasonable Accommodation

- Employees with *mobility or vision impairments* may benefit from voice-recognition software.
- Word-prediction software suggests words based on context with just one or two letters typed.
- Real-time translation captioning enables employees to participate in meetings.
- Vibrating text pagers notify employees when messages arrive.
- Arizona created a disability-friendly website to help link prospective employees and others to various agencies.

FIGURE 2-2 ADA Guidelines for Managers and Employers

- *Do not* deny a job to a disabled individual if the person is qualified and able to perform the essential job functions.
- *Make* a reasonable accommodation unless doing so would result in undue hardship.
- *Know* what you can ask applicants. In general, you may *not* make preemployment inquiries about a person's disability before making an offer. However, you *may* ask questions about the person's ability to perform essential job functions.
- *Itemize* essential job functions on the job descriptions. In virtually any ADA legal action, a central question will be, what are the essential functions of the job?
- *Do not* allow misconduct or erratic performance (including absences and tardiness), even if that behavior is linked to the disability.

John Lee/First Light/AGE Fotostock

Technology enables employers to accommodate disabled employees.

have more accidents) are generally baseless.[45] For example, Walgreens tries to fill at least one-third of the jobs at its large distribution centers with people with disabilities.[46]

Figure 2-2 summarizes some important ADA guidelines for managers and employers.

Uniformed Services Employment and Reemployment Rights Act

Under the Uniformed Services Employment and Reemployment Rights Act (1994), employers are generally required, among other things, to reinstate employees returning from military leave to positions comparable to those they had before leaving.[47]

Genetic Information Nondiscrimination Act of 2008 (GINA)

The Genetic Information Nondiscrimination Act of 2008 (GINA) prohibits discrimination by health insurers and employers based on people's genetic information. Specifically, it prohibits the use of genetic information in employment, prohibits the intentional acquisition of genetic information about applicants and employees, and imposes strict confidentiality requirements.[48]

State and Local Equal Employment Opportunity Laws

In addition to federal laws, all states and many local governments prohibit employment discrimination. The state or local laws usually cover employers (like those with less than 15 employees) not covered by federal legislation.[49]

Employers ignore city and state EEO laws at their peril. In New York City, for instance, city law applies to employers with as few as 4 employees (not 15, as under Title VII).[50] Connecticut recently became the first state to require that employers provide paid sick leave to employees. Hawaii and Massachusetts prohibit employers from asking about criminal convictions on applications.[51] Managers use manuals such as *HR Compliance Basics: Your State and Federal Employment Law Manual* (available from the SHRM) to understand local EEO requirements.

KNOWLEDGE BASE

State and local equal employment opportunity agencies (often called *Human Resources Commissions* or *Fair Employment Commissions*) also play a role in equal employment compliance. When the EEOC receives a discrimination charge, it usually defers it for a limited time to the state and local agencies that have comparable jurisdiction. If that doesn't achieve satisfactory remedies, the charges go back to the EEOC for resolution.

In Summary: Religious and Other Types of Discrimination[52]

The EEOC enforces laws prohibiting discrimination based on age, disability, equal pay/compensation, genetic information, national origin, pregnancy, race/color, religion, retaliation, sex, and sexual harassment. The EEOC has also held that discrimination against an individual because that person is transgender is discrimination because of sex and therefore covered under Title VII. The Commission has also found that sexual orientation claims by lesbian, gay, and bisexual individuals alleging sex stereotyping have a sex discrimination claim under Title VII.

Religious discrimination involves treating someone unfavorably because of his or her religious beliefs. The law protects not only people who belong to traditional, organized religions, such as Buddhism, Christianity, Hinduism, Islam, and Judaism, but also others who have sincerely held religious, ethical, or moral beliefs. Unless it would be an undue hardship on the employer, an employer must reasonably accommodate an employee's religious beliefs or practices. This applies to schedule changes or leave for religious observances, as well as to such things as religious dress or grooming practices. These might include, for example, wearing particular head coverings or other religious dress (such as a Jewish yarmulke or a Muslim headscarf), or wearing certain hairstyles or facial hair (such as Rastafarian dreadlocks or Sikh uncut hair and beard). Religious discrimination claims are increasing. In one case truck drivers claimed that requiring them to deliver alcoholic drinks violated their religious faith.[53]

Recent Trends in Discrimination Law

Some trends are broadening the impact of equal employment laws, while others are forming new headwinds.

In terms of the former, the U.S. Supreme Court held that the federal Defense of Marriage Act's exclusion of state-sanctioned, same-sex marriages was unconstitutional.[54] In a guidance from the Department of Labor (DOL), the DOL said that under the Employee Retirement Income Security Act (ERISA), "The term 'spouse' will be read to refer to any individuals who are lawfully married under any state law, including those married to someone of the same sex who were legally married in a state that recognizes such marriages, but who are domiciled in a state that doesn't recognize such marriages."[55] In 2014, President Obama signed an executive order barring federal contractors from discriminating against lesbian, gay, bisexual, and transgender employees, for instance in terms of benefits.[56] The DOL recently passed final regulations requiring that federal contractors adopt quantifiable hiring goals for individuals with disabilities.[57] Employers who don't employ a minimum of 7% disabled workers may face penalties, possibly including loss of their contracts unless they take immediate remedial actions.[58] The 2013–2016 Equal Employment Opportunity Commission enforcement priorities focus on (among other things) eliminating hiring barriers, such as credit history checks, that might unfairly discriminate.[59]

But other recent decisions may produce headwinds. For example, the U.S. Supreme Court upheld a Michigan constitutional amendment that bans affirmative action in admissions to the state's public universities. One effect would seem to be to permit voters in individual states to eliminate affirmative action–based admissions to their public universities.[60] And in two other recent decisions, the U.S. Supreme Court made it more difficult for someone to bring a retaliation claim against an employer; it also more strictly defined "supervisor," reducing the likelihood someone could show that an employer was responsible for a "supervisor's" harassing behavior.[61] Table 2-1 summarizes selected equal employment opportunity laws, actions, executive orders, and agency guidelines.

Sexual Harassment

sexual harassment
Harassment on the basis of sex that has the purpose or effect of substantially interfering with a person's work performance or creating an intimidating, hostile, or offensive work environment.

Under Title VII, **sexual harassment** generally refers to harassment on the basis of sex when such conduct has the purpose or effect of substantially interfering with a person's work performance or creating an intimidating, hostile, or offensive work environment. In one recent year, the EEOC received 11,717 sexual harassment charges, about 15% of which were filed by men.[62] (The U.S. Supreme Court held, in *Oncale v. Sundowner Offshore Services Inc.*, that same-sex sexual harassment is also actionable under Title VII.[63]) One study found "women experienced more sexual harassment than men, minorities experienced more ethnic harassment than whites, and minority women experience more harassment overall than majority men, minority men, and majority women."[64]

TABLE 2-1 Summary of Important Equal Employment Opportunity Actions

Action	What It Does
Title VII of 1964 Civil Rights Act, as amended	Bars discrimination because of race, color, religion, sex, or national origin; instituted the EEOC.
Executive orders	Prohibit employment discrimination by employers with federal contracts of more than $10,000 (and their subcontractors); establish office of federal compliance; require affirmative action programs.
Federal agency guidelines	Indicate guidelines covering discrimination based on sex, national origin, and religion, as well as employee selection procedures; for example, require validation of tests.
Supreme Court decisions: *Griggs v. Duke Power Co., Albemarle v. Moody*	Rule that job requirements must be related to job success; that discrimination need not be overt to be proved; that the burden of proof is on the employer to prove the qualification is valid.
Equal Pay Act of 1963	Requires equal pay for men and women for performing similar work.
Age Discrimination in Employment Act of 1967	Prohibits discriminating against a person age 40 or over in any area of employment because of age.
State and local laws	Often cover organizations too small to be covered by federal laws.
Vocational Rehabilitation Act of 1973	Requires affirmative action to employ and promote qualified handicapped persons and prohibits discrimination against handicapped persons.
Pregnancy Discrimination Act of 1978	Prohibits discrimination in employment against pregnant women, or those with related conditions.
Vietnam Era Veterans' Readjustment Assistance Act of 1974	Requires affirmative action in employment for veterans of the Vietnam War era.
Ward Cove v. Atonio	Made it more difficult to prove a case of unlawful discrimination against an employer.
Americans with Disabilities Act of 1990	Strengthens the need for most employers to make reasonable accommodations for disabled employees at work; prohibits discrimination.
Civil Rights Act of 1991	Reverses various U.S. Supreme Court decisions; places burden of proof back on employer and permits compensatory and punitive money damages for discrimination.
ADA Amendments Act of 2008	Makes it easier for employee to show that his or her disability "substantially limits" a major life function.
Genetic Information Nondiscrimination Act	Signed into law in May 2008, prohibits discriminating against employees and applicants based on their genetic information.

Source: Based on The actual laws. From www.usa.gov/Topics/Reference Shelf/Laws.shtml, accessed September 21, 2013.

Under EEOC guidelines, employers have an affirmative duty to maintain workplaces free of sexual harassment and intimidation. CRA 1991 permits victims of intentional discrimination, including sexual harassment, to have jury trials and to collect compensatory damages for pain and suffering and punitive damages, where the employer acted with "malice or reckless indifference" to the person's rights.[65] The **Federal Violence Against Women Act of 1994** further provides that a person "who commits a crime of violence motivated by gender and thus deprives another" of her rights shall be liable to the party injured.

Federal Violence Against Women Act of 1994
The act that provides that a person who commits a crime of violence motivated by gender shall be liable to the party injured.

WHAT IS SEXUAL HARASSMENT? EEOC guidelines define *sexual harassment* as unwelcome sexual advances, requests for sexual favors, and other verbal or physical conduct of a sexual nature that takes place under any of the following conditions:

1. Submission to such conduct is made either explicitly or implicitly a term or condition of an individual's employment.
2. Submission to or rejection of such conduct by an individual is used as the basis for employment decisions affecting such individual.
3. Such conduct has the purpose or effect of unreasonably interfering with an individual's work performance or creating an intimidating, hostile, or offensive work environment.

PROVING SEXUAL HARASSMENT There are three main ways someone can prove sexual harassment:

1. ***Quid Pro Quo.*** The most direct is to prove that rejecting a supervisor's advances adversely affected what the EEOC calls a "tangible employment action," such as hiring, firing, promotion, demotion, and/or work assignment. In one case, the employee showed that continued job success and advancement were dependent on her agreeing to the sexual demands of her supervisors. "Sexual harassment" generally requires that the behavior be pervasive or severe. Thus, in one case, the court ruled that although the supervisor had touched the employee's shoulder twice as he drove her back from work and also mentioned that she "owed him" for hiring her, she did not have a trial-able sexual harassment claim.[66]
2. ***Hostile Environment Created by Supervisors.*** The harassment need not have tangible consequences such as demotion. For example, one court found that a male supervisor's behavior had substantially affected a female employee's emotional and psychological ability to the point that she felt she had to quit her job. Therefore, even though the supervisor made no direct threats or promises in exchange for sexual advances, his advances interfered with the woman's performance and created an offensive work environment. That was sufficient to prove sexual harassment. Courts generally do not interpret as sexual harassment sexual relationships that arise during the course of employment but that do not have a substantial effect on that employment.[67] The U.S. Supreme Court also held that sexual harassment law doesn't cover ordinary "intersexual flirtation." In his ruling, Justice Antonin Scalia said courts must carefully distinguish between "simple teasing" and truly abusive behavior.[68]
3. ***Hostile Environment Created by Coworkers or Nonemployees.*** Coworkers or nonemployees can trigger such suits. One court held that a mandatory sexually provocative uniform led to lewd comments by customers. When the employee refused to wear the uniform, she was fired. The employer couldn't show there was a job-related necessity for the uniform, and only female employees wore it. The court ruled that the employer, in effect, was responsible for the sexually harassing behavior. Such abhorrent client behavior is more likely when the clients are in positions of power, and when they think no one will penalize them.[69] Employers are also liable for the sexually harassing acts of nonsupervisory employees if the employer knew or should have known of the conduct.

WHEN IS THE ENVIRONMENT "HOSTILE"? Hostile environment sexual harassment generally means the intimidation, insults, and ridicule were sufficiently severe to alter the employee's working conditions. Courts look at several things. These include whether the discriminatory conduct is *frequent or severe*; whether it is *physically threatening* or humiliating, or a mere offensive utterance; and whether it unreasonably *interferes* with an employee's work performance.[70] Courts also consider whether the employee subjectively *perceives* the work environment as being abusive. For example, did he or she welcome the conduct or immediately complain?[71]

SUPREME COURT DECISIONS The U.S. Supreme Court used a case called *Meritor Savings Bank, FSB v. Vinson* to endorse broadly the EEOC's guidelines on sexual harassment. Two other Supreme Court decisions further clarified sexual harassment law.

In the first, *Burlington Industries v. Ellerth*, the employee accused her supervisor of *quid pro quo* harassment. She said her boss propositioned and threatened her with demotion if she did not respond. He did not carry out the threats, and she was promoted. In the second case, *Faragher v. City of Boca Raton*, the employee accused the employer of condoning a hostile work environment. She said she quit her lifeguard job after repeated taunts from other lifeguards. The Court ruled in favor of the employees in both cases.

The Court's written decisions have two implications for employers and managers. First, in *quid pro quo* cases it is *not* necessary for the employee to suffer a tangible job action (such as a demotion) to win the case. Second, the Court laid out an important defense against harassment suits. It said the employer must show that it took "reasonable care" to prevent and promptly correct any sexually harassing behavior *and* that the employee unreasonably failed to take advantage of the employer's policy.

Implications for Employers and Managers These decisions suggest an employer can defend itself against sexual harassment liability by showing two things:

- First, it must show "that the employer exercised reasonable care to *prevent* and *correct promptly* any sexually harassing behavior."[72]
- Second, it must demonstrate that the plaintiff "unreasonably *failed to take advantage* of any preventive or corrective opportunities provided by the employer." The employee's failure to use formal reporting systems would satisfy the second component.[73]

Prudent employer steps therefore include:[74]

- Take all complaints about harassment seriously.
- Issue a strong policy statement condemning such behavior. Describe the prohibited conduct, assure protection against retaliation, describe a confidential complaint process, and provide impartial investigation and corrective action.
- Take steps to prevent sexual harassment from occurring. For example, communicate to employees that the employer will not tolerate sexual harassment, and take immediate action when someone complains.
- Establish a management response system that includes an immediate reaction and investigation.
- Train supervisors and managers to increase their awareness of the issues, and discipline managers and employees involved in sexual harassment.

WHEN THE LAW ISN'T ENOUGH Unfortunately, two practical considerations often outdo the legal requirements. First, "Women perceive a broader range of sociosexual behaviors (touching, for instance) as harassing."[75] In one study, about 58% of employees reported experiencing potentially harassment-type behaviors at work. Overall, about 25% found it flattering and about half viewed it as benign. But on closer examination, about four times as many men as women found the behavior flattering or benign.[76] Sexual harassment training and policies can reduce this problem.[77]

A second problem is that employees often won't complain. For example, two Air Force generals recently appeared before the U.S. Congress' House Armed Services Committee to explain (among other things) how 23 instructors at an Air Force base could engage in unprofessional relationships or sexual assaults against 48 female trainees. The Air Force blamed both a climate of fear among female personnel (who believed that reporting the offenses to superior officers would be futile or counterproductive) and "a weak command structure."[78]

WHAT THE EMPLOYEE CAN DO First, complain. Remember that courts generally look to whether *the harassed employee used the employer's reporting procedures to file a complaint promptly.* If the employer has an effectively communicated complaint procedure, use it and then cooperate in the investigation.[79] In that context, steps an employee can take include:

1. File a verbal contemporaneous complaint with the harasser and the harasser's boss, stating that the unwanted overtures should cease because the conduct is unwelcome.
2. If the unwelcome conduct does not cease, file verbal and written reports regarding the unwelcome conduct and unsuccessful efforts to get it to stop with the harasser's manager and/or the human resource director.
3. If the letters and appeals to the employer do not suffice, contact the local office of the EEOC to file the necessary claim. In very serious cases, the employee can also consult an attorney about suing the harasser for assault and battery, intentional infliction of emotional distress, and injunctive relief, and to recover compensatory and punitive damages.

Watch It!
How does an employer actually deal with problems such as sexual harassment? If your professor has assigned this, go to the Assignments section of www.mymangementlab.com to complete the video exercise titled *Equal Employment (UPS)*.

TRENDS SHAPING HR: *DIGITAL AND SOCIAL MEDIA*

For employers, social media brings both benefits and reasons for caution. For one thing, some employees will use Facebook and other accounts to harass and bully co-workers (as with disparaging comments). Here, employers must distinguish between illegal online harassment (that applying to race, religion, national origin, age, sex/gender, genetic information, and disability discrimination) and common personality conflicts. However, at a minimum, employers should have a zero-tolerance policy on bullying.[80]

On the positive side, we'll see that social media has been a boon for staffing, for instance for finding candidates on LinkedIn or for checking out current applicants on Facebook. However, viewing an applicant's social media profile can be problematic, as it may reveal information on things like religion, race, and sexual orientation.[81] Some states forbid employers from requiring or even requesting employees' or applicants' passwords. It's therefore sensible to put in place policies restricting who can check out candidates online and how they can do it. And supervisors should think twice about doing such checking themselves. ■

LEARNING OBJECTIVE 2-3
Illustrate two defenses you can use in the event of discriminatory practice allegations, and cite specific discriminatory personnel management practices in recruitment, selection, promotion, transfer, layoffs, and benefits.

Defenses Against Discrimination Allegations

To understand how employers defend themselves against employment discrimination claims, we should first briefly review some basic legal terminology.

Discrimination law distinguishes between disparate *treatment* and disparate *impact*. *Disparate treatment* means intentional discrimination. Disparate treatment "exists where an employer treats an individual differently because that individual is a member of a particular race, religion, gender, or ethnic group."[82] A rule that says "we don't hire drivers over 60 years of age" exemplifies this.

Disparate impact means that "an employer engages in an employment practice or policy that has a greater adverse impact (effect) on the members of a protected group under Title VII than on other employees, regardless of intent."[83] A rule that says "employees must have college degrees to do this particular job" exemplifies this (because more white males than some minorities earn college degrees).

Disparate impact claims do not require proof of discriminatory intent. Instead, the plaintiff must show that the apparently neutral employment practice (such as requiring a college degree) creates an adverse impact—a significant disparity—between the proportion of (say) minorities in the available labor pool and the proportion you hire. Thus, disparate impact allegations require showing that the act produced an adverse impact. If it has, then the employer will probably have to defend itself (for instance, by arguing that there is a business necessity for the practice). Adverse impact "refers to the total employment process that results in a significantly higher percentage of a protected group in the candidate population being rejected for employment, placement, or promotion."[84] Then the burden of proof shifts to the employer.

adverse impact
The overall impact of employer practices that result in significantly higher percentages of members of minorities and other protected groups being rejected for employment, placement, or promotion.

The Central Role of Adverse Impact

Showing that one of the employer's employment practices or policies has an **adverse impact** therefore plays a central role in discriminatory practice allegations.[85] Under Title VII and CRA 1991, a person who believes that (1) he or she was a victim of unintentional discrimination because of an employer's practices need only (2) establish

Employees who believe they are victims of harassment should have a mechanism for filing a complaint.

Maurice van der Velden/Getty Images

a *prima facie* case of discrimination. This means showing, for instance, that the employer's selection procedures (like requiring a college degree for the job) did have an adverse impact on the protected minority group.

So, for example, if a minority applicant feels he or she was a victim of discrimination, the person need only show that the employer's selection process resulted in an adverse impact on his or her group. (For example, if 80% of the white applicants passed the test, but only 20% of the black applicants passed, a black applicant has a *prima facie* case proving adverse impact.) Then the burden of proof shifts to the employer. It becomes the employer's task to prove that its test (or application blank or the like) is a valid predictor of performance on the job (and that it applied its selection process fairly and equitably to both minorities and nonminorities).

In practice, an applicant or employee can use one of the following five methods to show that one of an employer's procedures (such as a selection test) has an adverse impact on a protected group.

disparate rejection rates
A test for adverse impact in which it can be demonstrated that there is a discrepancy between rates of rejection of members of a protected group and of others.

4/5ths rule
Federal agency rule that a minority selection rate less than 80% (4/5ths) of that for the group with the highest rate is evidence of adverse impact.

DISPARATE REJECTION RATES The **disparate rejection rate** method compares the rejection rates for a minority group and another group (usually the remaining nonminority applicants).[86]

Federal agencies use a **"4/5ths rule"** to assess disparate rejection rates: "A selection rate for any racial, ethnic, or sex group which is less than four-fifths or 80% of the rate for the group with the highest rate will generally be regarded as evidence of adverse impact, while a greater than four-fifths rate will generally not be regarded as evidence of adverse impact." For example, suppose the employer hires 60% of male applicants but only 30% of female applicants. Four-fifths of the 60% male hiring rate would be 48%. Because the female hiring rate of 30% is less than 48%, adverse impact exists as far as these federal agencies are concerned.[87]

THE STANDARD DEVIATION RULE Similarly, the courts have used the *standard deviation rule* to confirm adverse impact. (The standard deviation is a statistical measure of variability. It is a measure of the dispersion of a set of data from its mean. Suppose we calculate the average height of students in your management class. In simplest terms, the standard deviation helps to describe, among other things, how wide a range there is in height between the shortest and tallest students and the class's average student height.) In selection, the standard deviation rule holds that, as a rule of thumb, the difference between the numbers of minority candidates we *would have expected* to hire and whom *we actually hired* should be less than two standard deviations.

Consider this example. Suppose 300 applicants apply for 20 openings; 80 of the applicants are women, and the other 220 are men. We use our screening processes and hire 2 females and 18 males. Did our selection process have an adverse impact? To answer this, we can compute the standard deviation:

$$SD = \sqrt{\frac{(\textit{Number of minority applicants})}{(\textit{Number of total applicants})} \times \frac{(\textit{Number of non-minority applicants})}{(\textit{Number of total applicants})} \times (\textit{Number of applicants selected})}$$

In our case:

$$SD = \sqrt{\left(\frac{80}{300} \times \frac{220}{300} \times 20\right)} = \sqrt{(0.2667 \times 0.7333 \times 20)}$$

$$= \sqrt{3.911} = SD = 1.977$$

In our example, women are 26% (80/300) of the applicant pool. We should therefore *expect* to hire 26% of the 20 people hired, or about 5 women. We *actually* hired 2 women. The difference between the numbers of women we would expect to hire and whom we actually hired is 5 − 2 = 3. We can use the standard deviation rule to gauge if there is adverse (disparate) impact. In our example, the standard deviation is 1.977. Again, the standard deviation rule holds that as a rule of thumb, the difference between the numbers of minority candidates we would have expected to hire and whom we actually hired should be less than two standard deviations. Two times 1.9777 is about 4. Since the difference between the number of women we would have expected to hire (5) and actually hired (2) is 3, the results suggest that our screening did not have adverse impact on women. (Put another way, in this case, hiring just 2 rather than 5 is not a highly improbable result.)[88]

restricted policy
Another test for adverse impact, involving demonstration that an employer's hiring practices exclude a protected group, whether intentionally or not.

RESTRICTED POLICY The **restricted policy** approach means demonstrating that the employer's policy intentionally or unintentionally excluded members of a protected group. Here the problem is usually obvious—such as policies against hiring guards less than 6 feet tall. Evidence of restricted policies such as these is enough to prove adverse impact and to expose an employer to litigation.

POPULATION COMPARISONS This approach compares (1) the percentage of minority/protected group and white workers in the organization with (2) the percentage of the corresponding group in the labor market.

"Labor market," of course, varies with the job. For some jobs, such as secretary, it makes sense to compare the percentage of minority employees with the percentage of minorities in the surrounding community, since they will come from that community. But determining whether an employer has enough black engineers might involve determining the number available nationwide, not in the surrounding community.

Employers use *workforce analysis* to analyze the data regarding the firm's use of protected versus nonprotected employees in various job classifications. The process of comparing the percentage of minority employees in a job (or jobs) at the company with the number of similarly trained minority employees available in the relevant labor market is *utilization analysis*.

MCDONNELL-DOUGLAS TEST Lawyers in disparate impact cases use the previous approaches (such as population comparisons) to test whether an employer's policies or actions have the effect of unintentionally screening out disproportionate numbers of women or minorities. Lawyers use the McDonnell-Douglas test for showing (intentional) disparate treatment, rather than (unintentional) disparate impact.

This test grew out of a case at the former McDonnell-Douglas Corporation. The applicant was qualified, but the employer rejected the person and continued seeking applicants. Did this show that the hiring company intentionally discriminated against the female or minority candidate? The U.S. Supreme Court set four rules for applying the McDonnell-Douglas test:

1. that the person belongs to a protected class;
2. that he or she applied and was qualified for a job for which the employer was seeking applicants;
3. that, despite this qualification, he or she was rejected; and
4. that, after his or her rejection, the position remained open and the employer continued seeking applications from persons with the complainant's qualifications.

If the plaintiff meets all these conditions, then a *prima facie* case of disparate treatment is established. At that point, the employer must articulate a legitimate non-discriminatory reason for its action, and produce evidence but not prove that it acted based on such a reason. If it meets this relatively easy standard, the plaintiff then has the burden of proving that the employer's articulated reason is merely a pretext for engaging in unlawful discrimination.

ADVERSE IMPACT EXAMPLE Assume you turn down a member of a protected group for a job with your firm. You do this based on a test score (although it could have been interview questions or something else). Further, assume that this person feels he or she was discriminated against due to being in a protected class, and decides to sue your company.

Basically, all he or she must do is show that your procedure (such as the selection test) had an adverse impact on members of his or her minority group. The plaintiff can apply five approaches here. These are disparate rejection rates, the standard deviation rule, restricted policy, population comparisons, and, for disparate *treatment* cases, the McDonnell-Douglas test. Once the person proves adverse impact (to the court's satisfaction), the burden of proof shifts to the employer. The employer must defend against the discrimination charges.

There is nothing in the law that says that because your procedure has an adverse impact on a protected group, you can't use it. In fact, it may well happen that some tests screen out disproportionately higher numbers of, say, blacks than they do whites. What the law does say is that once your applicant has made his or her case (showing adverse impact), the burden of proof shifts to you. Now the employer must defend use of the procedure.

There are then two basic defenses employers use to justify an employment practice that has an adverse impact on members of a minority group: the bona fide occupational qualification (BFOQ) defense and the business necessity defense.

Bona Fide Occupational Qualification

bona fide occupational qualification (BFOQ)
Requirement that an employee be of a certain religion, sex, or national origin where that is reasonably necessary to the organization's normal operation. Specified by the 1964 Civil Rights Act.

An employer can claim that the employment practice is a **bona fide occupational qualification (BFOQ)** for performing the job. Title VII specifically permits this defense. Title VII provides that "it should not be an unlawful employment practice for an employer to hire an employee … on the basis of religion, sex, or national origin *in those certain instances where religion, sex, or national origin is a bona fide occupational qualification* reasonably necessary to the normal operation of that particular business or enterprise."

However, courts usually interpret the BFOQ exception narrowly. It is usually a defense to a disparate treatment case based upon direct evidence of *intentional* discrimination, rather than to disparate impact (unintentional) cases. As a practical matter, employers use it mostly as a defense against charges of intentional discrimination based on age.

AGE AS A BFOQ The Age Discrimination in Employment Act (ADEA) permits disparate treatment in those instances when age is a BFOQ.[89] For example, age is a

BFOQ when the Federal Aviation Agency sets a compulsory retirement age of 65 for commercial pilots.[90] Actors required for youthful or elderly roles suggest other instances when age may be a BFOQ. However, courts set the bar high: The reason for the age limit must go to the essence of the business. A court said a bus line's maximum-age hiring policy for bus drivers was a BFOQ. The court said the essence of the business was safe transportation of passengers, and, given that, the employer could strive to employ the most qualified persons available.[91]

RELIGION AS A BFOQ Religion may be a BFOQ in religious organizations or societies that require employees to share their particular religion. For example, religion may be a BFOQ when hiring persons to teach in a religious school. But again, courts construe this defense very narrowly.

GENDER AS A BFOQ Gender may be a BFOQ for positions like actor, model, and restroom attendant requiring physical characteristics possessed by one sex. However, for most jobs today, it's difficult to claim that gender is a BFOQ. For example, gender is not a BFOQ just because the position requires lifting heavy objects. A Texas man filed a complaint against Hooters of America alleging that one of its franchisees would not hire him as a waiter because it "merely wishes to exploit female sexuality as a marketing tool to attract customers and ensure profitability" and so was limiting hiring to females.[92] Hooters argued a BFOQ defense before reaching a confidential settlement.

NATIONAL ORIGIN AS A BFOQ A person's country of national origin may be a BFOQ. For example, an employer who is running the Chinese pavilion at a fair might claim that Chinese heritage is a BFOQ for persons to deal with the public.

Business Necessity

"Business necessity" is a defense created by the courts. It requires showing that there is an overriding business purpose for the discriminatory practice and that the practice is therefore acceptable.

It's not easy to prove business necessity.[93] The Supreme Court made it clear that business necessity does not encompass such matters as avoiding an employer inconvenience, annoyance, or expense. For example, an employer can't generally discharge employees whose wages have been garnished merely because garnishment (requiring the employer to divert part of the person's wages to pay his or her debts) creates an inconvenience. The Second Circuit Court of Appeals held that business necessity "must not only directly foster safety and efficiency" but also be essential to these goals.[94] Furthermore, "the business purpose must be sufficiently compelling to override any racial impact…."[95]

However, many employers use the business necessity defense successfully. In an early case, *Spurlock v. United Airlines*, a minority candidate sued United Airlines. He said that its requirements that pilot candidates have 500 flight hours and college degrees were unfairly discriminatory. The court agreed that the requirements did have an adverse impact on members of the person's minority group. But it held that in light of the cost of the training program and the huge human and economic risks in hiring unqualified candidates, the selection standards were a business necessity and were job related.[96]

In general, when a job requires a small amount of skill and training, the courts closely scrutinize any preemployment standards or criteria that discriminate against minorities. There is a correspondingly lighter burden when the job requires a high degree of skill, and when the economic and human risks of hiring an unqualified applicant are great.[97]

Attempts by employers to show that their selection tests or other employment practices are *valid* are examples of the business necessity defense. Here the employer must show that the test or other practice is job related—in other words, that it is a valid predictor of performance on the job. Where the employer can establish such validity, the courts have generally supported using the test or other employment practice as a business necessity. In this context, *validity* means the degree to which the test or other employment practice is related to or predicts performance on the job; Chapter 6 explains validation. The following Know Your Employment Law feature sums up how to apply all this.

KNOW YOUR EMPLOYMENT LAW

Examples of What You Can and Cannot Do

Before proceeding, we should review what federal fair employment laws allow (and do not allow) you to say and do.

Federal laws like Title VII usually don't expressly ban preemployment questions about an applicant's race, color, religion, sex, or national origin. In other words, "with the exception of personnel policies calling for outright discrimination against the members of some protected group," it's not the questions but their impact.[98] Thus, illustrative inquiries and practices like those on the next few pages are not illegal per se. For example, it isn't illegal to ask a job candidate about her marital status (although such a question might seem discriminatory). You can ask. However, be prepared to show either that you do not discriminate or that you can defend the practice as a BFOQ or business necessity.

But, in practice, there are two reasons to avoid such questions. First, although federal law may not bar such questions, many state and local laws do.

Second, the EEOC has said that it will disapprove of such practices, so just asking the questions may draw its attention. Such questions become illegal if a complainant can show you use them to screen out a greater proportion of his or her protected group's applicants, and you can't prove the practice is required as a business necessity or BFOQ.

Let's look now at some of the potentially discriminatory practices to avoid.[99]

Recruitment

Word of Mouth You cannot rely upon word-of-mouth dissemination of information about job opportunities when your workforce is all (or mostly all) white or all members of some other class such as all female, all Hispanic, and so on. Doing so reduces the likelihood that others will become aware of the jobs.

Misleading Information It is unlawful to give false or misleading information to members of any group, or to fail or refuse to advise them of work opportunities and the procedures for obtaining them.

Help-Wanted Ads "Help wanted—male" and "help wanted—female" ads are violations unless gender is a bona fide occupational qualification for the job. The same applies to ads that suggest age discrimination. For example, you cannot advertise for a "young" man or woman.

Selection Standards

Educational Requirements Courts have found educational qualifications to be illegal when (1) minority groups are less likely to possess the educational qualifications (such as a high school degree) and (2) such qualifications are also not job related. However, there may be jobs for which educational requirements (such as college degrees for pilot candidates) are a necessity.

Tests Courts deem tests unlawful if they disproportionately screen out minorities or women *and* they are not job related. According to a former U.S. Supreme Court Chief Justice,

> Nothing in the [Title VII] act precludes the use of testing or measuring procedures; obviously they are useful. What Congress has forbidden is giving these devices and mechanisms controlling force unless they are demonstrating a reasonable measure of job performance.

The employer must be prepared to show that the test results are job related—for instance, that test scores relate to on-the-job performance.

Preference to Relatives Do not give preference to relatives of current employees with respect to employment opportunities if your current employees are substantially nonminority.

Height, Weight, and Physical Characteristics Physical requirements such as minimum height are unlawful unless the employer can show they're job related. For example, a U.S. Appeals Court upheld a $3.4 million jury verdict against Dial Corp. Dial rejected 52 women for entry-level jobs at a meat-processing plant because they failed strength tests, although strength was not a job requirement.[100] *Maximum* weight rules generally don't trigger adverse legal rulings. To qualify for reasonable accommodation, obese applicants must be at least 100 pounds above their ideal weight or there must be a physiological cause for their disability. However, legalities aside, managers should be vigilant.[101] Studies show that obese individuals are less likely to be hired, less likely to receive promotions, more likely to get undesirable sales assignments, and more likely to receive poor customer service.[102]

Arrest Records Unless the job requires security clearance, do not ask an applicant whether he or she has been arrested or spent time in jail, or use an arrest record to disqualify a person automatically. Due to racial and ethnic disparities in arrest and prison rates, both the EEOC and the Office of Federal Contract Compliance Programs (OFCCP) recently set forth new guidance discouraging employers from using blanket exclusions against individuals with criminal records.[103]

Application Forms Employment applications generally shouldn't contain questions about applicants' disabilities, workers' compensation history, age, arrest record, or U.S. citizenship. It's generally best to collect personal information required for legitimate reasons (such as emergency contact) after you hire the person.[104]

Discharge Due to Garnishment Disproportionate numbers of minorities suffer garnishment procedures (in which creditors make a claim to some of the person's wages). Therefore, firing a minority member whose salary is garnished is illegal, unless you can show some overriding business necessity.

Sample Discriminatory Promotion, Transfer, and Layoff Practices

Fair employment laws protect not just job applicants but also current employees. For example, the Equal Pay Act requires that equal wages be paid for substantially similar work performed by men and women. Therefore, courts may hold that any employment practices regarding pay, promotion, termination, discipline, or benefits that

1. are applied differently to different classes of persons,
2. adversely impact members of a protected group, and
3. cannot be shown to be required as a BFOQ or business necessity are illegally discriminatory.

Personal Appearance Regulations and Title VII Employees sometimes file suits against employers' dress and appearance codes under Title VII. They usually claim sex discrimination, but sometimes claim racial or even religious discrimination. A sampling of court rulings follows:[105]

- Dress. In general, employers do not violate the Title VII ban on sex bias by requiring all employees to dress conservatively. For example, a supervisor's suggestion that a female attorney tone down her attire was permissible when the firm consistently sought to maintain a conservative dress style and counseled men to dress conservatively. However, Alamo Rent-A-Car lost a case when it tried to prevent a Muslim woman employee from wearing a headscarf.

- Hair. Courts usually favor employers here. For example, employer rules against facial hair do not constitute sex discrimination because they discriminate only between clean-shaven and bearded men, discrimination not qualified as sex bias under Title VII. Courts have also rejected arguments that prohibiting cornrow hairstyles infringed on black employees' expression of cultural identification.
- Uniforms. When it comes to discriminatory uniforms and/or suggestive attire, however, courts frequently side with employees. For example, requiring female employees (such as waitresses) to wear sexually suggestive attire as a condition of employment has been ruled as violating Title VII in many cases.[106]
- Tattoos and body piercings. About 38% of Millennials in one survey had tattoos as compared with 15% of baby boomers. About 23% of Millennials had body piercings as compared with 1% of baby boomers. One case involved a waiter with religious tattoos on his wrists at Red Robin Gourmet Burgers. The company insisted he cover his tattoos at work; he refused. Red Robin settled the suit after the waiter claimed that covering the tattoos would be a sin based on his religion.[107] ■

If your professor has assigned this, go to the Assignments section of **mymanagementlab.com** to complete these discussion questions.

Talk About It 1: Have you ever had an experience in which an employer apparently violated one or more of the guidelines above—for example, told you to change your hairstyle—or have you ever simply noticed a violation (such as a store posting a sign that said "delivery boy wanted")? What was your reaction? What did you do? Are there situations in which the employer may have been within the law to do what he or she did?

Finally, keep three other things in mind:

1. *Good intentions are no excuse.* As the Supreme Court held in the *Griggs* case, Good intent or absence of discriminatory intent does not redeem procedures that operate as built-in headwinds for minority groups and are unrelated to measuring job capability.
2. One cannot claim that a *union agreement necessitates some discriminatory practice*. Equal employment opportunity laws prevail.[108]
3. A strong defense *is not your only recourse.* The employer can agree to eliminate the illegal practice and (when required) to compensate the people discriminated against.

The EEOC Enforcement Process

LEARNING OBJECTIVE **2-4**

List the steps in the EEOC enforcement process.

Even careful employers eventually face employment discrimination claims and have to deal with the EEOC.[109] All managers (not just human resource managers) play roles in this process. Figure 2-3 provides an overview of this EEOC enforcement process.[110]

- ***File Charge.*** The process begins when someone files a claim with the EEOC. Either the aggrieved person or a member of the EEOC who has reasonable cause to believe that a violation occurred must file the claim in writing and under oath.[111] Under CRA 1991, the discrimination claim must be filed within 300 days (when there is a similar state law) or 180 days (where there is no similar state law) after the alleged incident took place (2 years for the Equal Pay Act).[112] The U.S. Supreme Court, in *Ledbetter v. Goodyear Tire & Rubber Company,* held that employees claiming Title VII pay discrimination must file their claims within 180 days of when they first receive the allegedly discriminatory pay. Congress then passed, and President Obama signed, the Lilly Ledbetter Fair Pay Act into law. Employees can now file such claims anytime, as long as they're still receiving an "infected" paycheck. (In fiscal year 2012, individuals filed 99,412 charges with the EEOC; the two largest categories were for retaliation [37,836 charges] and racial discrimination [33,512].[113]) One may obtain employment practices liability insurance against discrimination claims.[114]

FIGURE 2-3 The EEOC Charge-Filing Process

Note: Parties may settle at any time.
Source: Based on www.eeoc.gov.

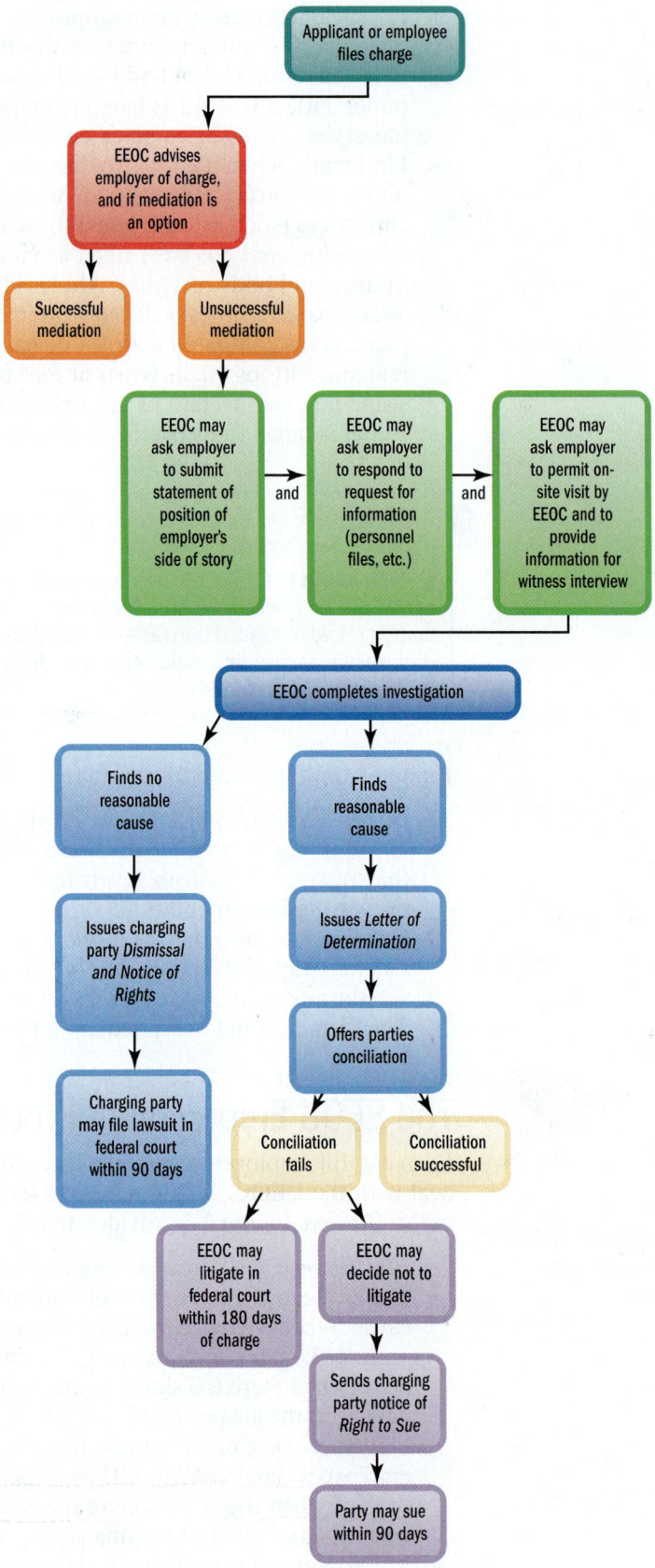

FIGURE 2-4 Questions to Ask When an Employer Receives Notice That the EEOC Has Filed a Bias Claim

Source: Based on Bureau of National Affairs, Inc., "Fair Employment Practices: Summary of Latest Developments," January 7, 1983, p. 3; Kenneth Sovereign, *Personnel Law* (Upper Saddle River, NJ: Prentice Hall, 1999), pp. 36–37; Equal Employment Opportunity Commission, "The Charge Handling Process," http://www.eeoc.gov/employers/process.cfm, accessed August 30, 2013.

1. Exactly what is the charge, and is your company covered by the relevant statutes? (For example, Title VII and the Americans with Disabilities Act generally apply only to employees with 15 or more employees.) Did the employee file his or her charge on time, and was it processed in a timely manner by the EEOC?
2. What protected group does the employee belong to?
3. Is the EEOC claiming disparate impact or disparate treatment?
4. Are there any obvious bases upon which you can challenge and/or rebut the claim? For example, would the employer have taken the action if the person did not belong to a protected group?
5. If it is a sexual harassment claim, are there offensive comments, calendars, posters, screensavers, and so on, on display in the company?
6. In terms of the practicality of defending your company against this claim, who are the supervisors who actually took the allegedly discriminatory actions, and how effective will they be as potential witnesses? Have you received an opinion from legal counsel regarding the chances of prevailing?

- ***Charge Acceptance.*** The EEOC's common practice is to accept a charge and orally refer it to the state or local agency on behalf of the charging party. If the agency waives jurisdiction or cannot obtain a satisfactory solution, the EEOC processes it upon the expiration of the deferral period.[115]
- ***Serve Notice.*** After a charge is filed (or the state or local deferral period has ended), the EEOC has 10 days to serve notice on the employer. Attorneys advise against submitting lengthy statements in response to a charge. Instead, provide a concise explanation describing why the actions were lawful.[116] Figure 2-4 lists some questions to ask after receiving a bias complaint from the EEOC.
- ***Investigation/Fact-Finding Conference.*** The EEOC then investigates the charge to determine whether there is reasonable cause to believe it is true; it has 120 days to decide.[117] Early in the investigation, the EEOC holds an initial *fact-finding conference.* The EEOC's focus here is often to find weak spots in each party's position. It uses these to push for a settlement.
- ***Cause/No Cause.*** If it finds no reasonable cause, the EEOC must dismiss the charge, and must issue the charging party a Notice of Right to Sue. The person then has 90 days to file a suit on his or her own behalf.
- ***Conciliation.*** If the EEOC does find cause, it has 30 days to work out a conciliation agreement. The EEOC conciliator meets with the employee to determine what remedy would be satisfactory. It then tries to negotiate a settlement with the employer.
- ***Notice to Sue.*** If this conciliation is not satisfactory, the EEOC may bring a civil suit in a federal district court, or issue a Notice of Right to Sue to the person who filed the charge.

Voluntary Mediation

The EEOC refers about 10% of its charges to a voluntary mediation mechanism, "an informal process in which a neutral third party assists the opposing parties to reach a voluntary, negotiated resolution of a charge of discrimination."[118] If the parties don't reach agreement (or one of the parties rejects participation), the EEOC processes the charge through its usual mechanisms.[119]

Faced with an offer to mediate, the employer has three options: Agree to mediate the charge; make a settlement offer without mediation; or prepare a "position statement" for the EEOC. If the employer does not mediate or make an offer, the position statement is required. It should include a robust defense, including information relating to the company's business and the charging party's position; a description of any rules or policies and procedures that are applicable; and the chronology of the offense that led to the adverse action.[120]

Mandatory Arbitration of Discrimination Claims

Many employers, to avoid EEOC litigation, require applicants and employees to agree to arbitrate such claims. The EEOC does not favor mandatory arbitration. However, the U.S. Supreme Court's decisions (in *Gilmer v. Interstate/Johnson Lane Corp.* and similar cases) make it clear that "employment discrimination plaintiffs [employees] may be compelled to arbitrate their claims under some circumstances."[121] Given this, employers "may wish to consider inserting a mandatory arbitration clause in their employment applications or employee handbooks."[122] To protect such a process against appeal, the employer should institute steps to protect against arbitrator bias, allow the arbitrator to offer a claimant broad relief (including reinstatement), and allow for a reasonable amount of prehearing fact finding.

alternative dispute resolution or ADR program
Grievance procedure that provides for binding arbitration as the last step.

Rockwell International has a grievance procedure that provides for binding arbitration as the last step. Called (as is traditional) an **alternative dispute resolution or ADR program**, Rockwell gradually extended the program to all nonunion employees at some locations. New hires at Rockwell must sign the agreement. Current employees must sign it prior to promotion or transfer. U.S. federal agencies must have ADR programs.[123] ADR plans are popular, although the EEOC generally prefers mediation for handling bias claims.[124]

The accompanying HR Tools feature provides some guidelines to follow in addressing EEOC claims.

IMPROVING PERFORMANCE: *HR Tools for Line Managers and Small Businesses*

Chances are the EEOC won't file a suit, but getting a notice saying it's investigating is still scary. Whether you are managing one team or your own small business, every manager should know in advance what the EEOC will be looking for and what to do. A checklist follows.[125]

During the EEOC Investigation:

- ✓ *Conduct your own investigation* to get the facts.
- ✓ Ensure that there is information in the EEOC's file *demonstrating lack of merit* of the charge.
- ✓ *Limit the information supplied* to only those issues raised in the charge itself.
- ✓ *Get as much information* as possible about the *charging party's claim*.
- ✓ *Meet with the employee* who made the complaint to clarify all the relevant issues. For example, what happened? Who was involved?
- ✓ Remember that *the EEOC can only ask (not compel) employers* to submit documents and ask for the testimony of witnesses under oath.
- ✓ Give the EEOC a *position statement*. It should contain words to the effect that "the company has a policy against discrimination and would not discriminate in the manner charged in the complaint."
- ✓ Support the statement with documentation.

During the Fact-Finding Conference:

- ✓ Because the only official record is the notes the EEOC investigator takes, *keep your own records*.
- ✓ Bring an *attorney*.
- ✓ Make sure you are *fully informed* of the charges and facts of the case.
- ✓ Before appearing, *witnesses (especially supervisors) need to be aware* of the legal significance of the facts they will present.

During the EEOC Determination and Attempted Conciliation:

- ✓ If there is a finding of cause, *review it carefully*, and point out inaccuracies in writing to the EEOC.
- ✓ Use this letter to try again to convince the parties that the charge is *without merit*.
- ✓ *Conciliate prudently*. If you have properly investigated the case, there may be no real advantage in settling at this stage.
- ✓ Remember: Odds are that *no suit will be filed* by the EEOC.

Finally, prudent supervisors should keep two other things in mind. First, know that courts may hold you personally liable for your actions. *Management malpractice* is aberrant managerial conduct that has serious consequences for the employee's personal or physical well-being, or that "exceeds all bounds usually tolerated by society."[126] In one outrageous example, the employer demoted a manager to janitor and took other steps to humiliate him. The jury awarded the man millions. Supervisors who commit management malpractice may be personally liable for paying some of the judgment.

Second, *retaliation* is illegal. The EEOC says, "All of the laws we enforce make it illegal to fire, demote, harass, or otherwise 'retaliate' against people because they filed a charge, complained to their employer... or because they participated in a discrimination investigation or lawsuit."[127] Retaliation is the most common charge filed with the EEOC.[128] In one case, the employee complained to the employer that she was paid less than male counterparts. The employer soon fired her fiancé. Finding for the employee, the U.S. Supreme Court decision said, "A reasonable worker might be dissuaded from engaging in protected activity" if she knew that her fiancé would be fired.[129] ■

If your professor has assigned this, go to the Assignments section of **mymanagementlab.com** to complete these discussion questions.

Talk About It 2: Check with the EEOC's website and compile a list of the biggest financial settlements this past year for retaliation claims. About how much was the average claim? What you would do to *avoid* doing something that prompted the EEOC to become interested in your company?

Diversity Management

LEARNING OBJECTIVE **2-5**

Discuss why diversity management is important and how to install a diversity management program.

White males no longer dominate the labor force. Women and minorities will account for most labor force growth in the near future.[130] Employers today therefore often strive for diversity not just because the law says they must but due to self-interest.[131] **Diversity** means being diverse or varied and at work means having a workforce composed of two or more groups of employees with various racial, ethnic, gender, cultural, national origin, handicap, age, and religious backgrounds.[132] We introduce diversity and diversity management here, and then address them in features throughout the book.

diversity
The variety or multiplicity of demographic features that characterize a company's workforce, particularly in terms of race, sex, culture, national origin, handicap, age, and religion.

stereotyping
Ascribing specific behavioral traits to individuals based on their apparent membership in a group.

discrimination
Taking specific actions toward or against a person based on the person's group.

tokenism
When a company appoints a small group of women or minorities to high-profile positions, rather than more aggressively seeking full representation for that group.

ethnocentrism
The tendency to view members of other social groups less favorably than members of one's own group.

gender-role stereotypes
The tendency to associate women with certain (frequently nonmanagerial) jobs.

Potential Threats to Diversity

Workforce diversity produces both benefits and problems for employers. Unmanaged, it can produce behavioral barriers that reduce cooperation. Potential problems include:

- **Stereotyping**. Here someone ascribes specific behavioral traits to individuals based on their apparent membership in a group.[133] For example, "older people can't work hard." *Prejudice* is a bias toward prejudging someone based on that person's traits, as in "we won't hire him because he's old." Some people's biases are subconscious. To check, try asking questions like, "Do I typically hire the same type of person?" and "To whom do I generally assign the best projects?"[134]
- **Discrimination** is prejudice in action. It means taking specific actions toward or against the person based on the person's group.[135] Of course, it's generally illegal to discriminate at work based on someone's age, race, gender, disability, or national origin. But in practice, discrimination may be subtle. For example, many argue that a "glass ceiling," enforced by an "old boys' network" (friendships built in places like exclusive clubs), hinders women from reaching top management. Discrimination against Muslim employees is prohibited under Title VII. The number of such charges in rising quickly.[136]
- **Tokenism** means a company appoints a small group of women or minorities to high-profile positions, rather than more aggressively seeking full representation for that group.[137]
- **Ethnocentrism** is the tendency to view members of other social groups less favorably than one's own. Thus, in one study, managers attributed the performance of some minorities less to their abilities and more to help they received from others. The same managers attributed the performance of *non*minorities to their own abilities.[138]
- Discrimination against women goes beyond glass ceilings. Working women also confront **gender-role stereotypes**, the tendency to associate women with certain (frequently nonmanagerial) jobs.

On the other hand, diversity can be an engine of performance, as the following feature shows.

IMPROVING PERFORMANCE: *HR as a Profit Center*

Diversity can actually drive higher profits. In one study, researchers examined the diversity climate in 654 stores of a large U.S. retail chain. They defined *diversity climate* as the extent to which employees in the stores said the firm promotes equal opportunity and inclusion. They found the highest sales growth in stores with the highest pro-diversity climate, and the lowest in stores where subordinates and managers reported less hospitable diversity climates.[139] Another study found racial discrimination to be related negatively to employee commitment, although organizational efforts to support diversity reduced such negative effects.[140]

More than 50 of the largest U.S. companies, including GE, Microsoft, and Walmart, recently filed briefs with the U.S. Supreme Court arguing that affirmative action produces increased sales and profits. Thus, when Merck needed halal certification for one of its medicines, it turned to its Muslim employees. They helped Merck bring the product to market faster and helped ensure its acceptance among Muslims.[141] ■

If your professor has assigned this, go to the Assignments section of **mymanagementlab.com** to complete these discussion questions.

Talk About It 3: What do you think accounts for the fact that diversity apparently seems to produce higher profits? Do you think that would always be the case? Why or why not?

Managing Diversity

managing diversity
Maximizing diversity's potential benefits while minimizing its potential barriers.

The key to deriving such benefits is properly managing diversity's potential problems. **Managing diversity** means maximizing diversity's potential benefits while minimizing the potential problems—such as prejudice—that can undermine cooperation. In practice, diversity management involves both compulsory and voluntary actions. However, compulsory actions (particularly EEO law compliance) can't guarantee cooperation. Managing diversity therefore usually relies on taking voluntary steps to encourage employees to work together productively.[142]

Typically, this starts at the top. The employer institutes a *diversity management program*. A main aim is to make employees more sensitive to and better able to adapt to individual cultural differences.

Here one writer advocates a four-step "AGEM" diversity training process: Approach, Goals, Executive commitment, and Mandatory attendance. First, determine if diversity training is the solution or if some other approach is more advisable. If training is the solution, then set measurable program goals, for instance, having training participants evaluate their units' diversity efforts. Next, make sure a high-visibility executive commits to the program. Finally, make training mandatory.[143]

To expand on this, five sets of voluntary organizational activities often constitute such company-wide diversity management programs:[144]

Provide strong leadership. Companies with exemplary reputations in managing diversity typically have CEOs who champion the cause of diversity. Leadership here means, for instance, becoming a role model for the behaviors required for the change. One study concluded that top managers who excelled at creating inclusive organizations were also those who were personally passionate about encouraging inclusion and diversity.[145]

Assess the situation. One study found that the most common tools for assessing a company's diversity include equal employment hiring and retention metrics, employee attitude surveys, management and employee evaluations, and focus groups.

Provide diversity training and education. The most common starting point for a diversity management effort is usually some type of employee education program.

Change culture and management systems. Combine education programs with other concrete steps aimed at changing the organization's culture and management systems. For example, change the performance appraisal procedure to appraise supervisors based partly on their success in reducing intergroup conflicts.

Evaluate the diversity management program. For example, do employee attitude surveys now indicate any improvement in employees' attitudes toward diversity?

McDonald's Corp. doesn't call its diversity program a "program" at all—because it says diversity management should be an ongoing effort. At McDonald's, employee attendance at the company's Intercultural Learning Lab facilitates dialogue and communication among employees.[146]

One expert helps turn high-potential minority employees into senior leaders; he says employers tend to make four mistakes when cultivating minorities for higher positions. Rather than centralizing diversity management, *they distribute diversity tasks* among various recruiting teams, while limiting their diversity departments primarily to retention and inclusiveness; the solution here is more central direction. They *focus on "inputs"* such as mentoring programs, rather than on outcomes such as the number of diversity candidates who gained promotions; goal setting is one solution. They focus on "*fixing the culture,*" which is typically a multiyear process; cultural change should be just one element of the process. Finally, they often *staff* their diversity departments with new minority employees; the solution is to rotate high-performance minority or nonminority line executives into diversity roles.[147]

The following HR as a Profit Center feature provides another example of diversity management's benefits.

IMPROVING PERFORMANCE: *HR as a Profit Center*

Workforce diversity makes strategic sense. With strong top-management support, IBM created several minority task forces focusing on groups such as women and Native Americans. One effect of these teams has been internal: In the 10 or so years since forming them, IBM has boosted the number of U.S.-born ethnic minority executives by almost 2 ½ times.[148]

However, the firm's diversity program also aided IBM's strategy of expanding its markets and business results. For example, one task force decided to focus on expanding IBM's market among multicultural and women-owned businesses. It did this in part by providing "much-needed sales and service support to small and midsize businesses, a niche well populated with minority and female buyers."[149] As a direct result, this IBM market grew from $10 million to more than $300 million in revenue in just 3 years. ■

If your professor has assigned this, go to the Assignments section of **mymanagementlab.com** to complete this discussion question.

Talk About It 4: In terms of reducing costs and/or boosting sales, what other benefits do you think diversity management could bring to an employer?

Implementing the Affirmative Action Program

Equal employment opportunity aims to ensure that anyone, regardless of race, color, disability, sex, religion, national origin, or age, has an equal opportunity based on his or her qualifications. *Affirmative action* means taking actions (in recruitment, hiring, promotions, and compensation) to eliminate the current effects of past discrimination.

Affirmative action is still a significant workplace issue today. The incidences of major court-mandated affirmative action programs are down, but courts still use them. Furthermore, many employers must still engage in voluntary programs. For example, Executive Order (EO) 11246 (issued in 1965) requires federal contractors to take affirmative action to improve employment opportunities for groups such as women and racial minorities. It covers about 22% of the U.S. workforce.[150]

good-faith effort strategy
An affirmative action strategy that emphasizes identifying and eliminating the obstacles to hiring and promoting women and minorities, and increasing the minority or female applicant flow.

Under guidelines such as EO 11246, the key aims of affirmative action programs are (1) to use numerical analysis to determine which (if any) target groups the firm is underutilizing relative to the relevant labor market, and (2) to eliminate the barriers to equal employment. Many employers pursue these aims with a **good-faith effort strategy**; this emphasizes identifying and eliminating the obstacles to hiring and promoting women and minorities, and increasing the minority or female applicant flow. Reasonable steps to take include those shown in Figure 2-5.

It's useful to place recruiting ads on online minority-oriented job sites. For example, Recruiting-Online.com lists dozens of online diversity candidate resources (www.recruiting-online.com/course55.html). Diversity candidate

Diversity management can blend a diverse workforce into a close-knit and productive community.

Jetta Productions/Getty Images

websites with job banks include the National Urban League, Hispanic Online, Latino Web, Society of Hispanic Engineers, Gay.com, Association for Women in Science, and Minorities Job Bank.

EMPLOYEE RESISTANCE Avoiding employee resistance to affirmative action programs is important. Here, studies suggest that current employees need to believe the program is fair. *Transparent selection procedures* (making it clear what selection tools and standards the company uses) help in this regard. *Communication* is also crucial. Show that the program doesn't involve preferential selection standards. Provide details on the qualifications of all new hires (both minority and nonminority). *Justifications* for the program should emphasize redressing past discrimination and the practical value of diversity, not underrepresentation.[151]

PROGRAM EVALUATION How can one tell if the diversity initiatives are effective? Some commonsense questions can be asked:

- Are there women and minorities reporting directly to senior managers?
- Do women and minorities have a fair share of the jobs that are the traditional stepping-stones to successful careers in the company?

FIGURE 2-5 Steps in an Affirmative Action Program

1. Issue a written equal employment policy indicating that the firm is an equal employment opportunity employer and the employer's commitment to affirmative action.
2. Demonstrate top-management support for the equal employment policy—for instance, appoint a high-ranking EEO administrator.
3. Publicize internally and externally the equal employment policy and affirmative action commitment.
4. Survey current minority and female employment by department and job classification to determine where affirmative action programs are especially desirable.
5. Carefully analyze employer human resources practices to identify and eliminate hidden barriers.
6. Review, develop, and implement specific HR programs to improve female and minority utilization.
7. Use focused recruitment to find qualified applicants from the target group(s).
8. Establish an internal audit and reporting system to monitor and evaluate progress.
9. Develop support for the affirmative action program, inside the company and in the community.

- Do women and minorities have equal access to international assignments?
- Is the employer taking steps that ensure that female and minority candidates will be in the company's career development pipeline?
- Are turnover rates for female and minority managers the same or lower than those for white males?
- Do employees report that they perceive positive behavior changes as a result of the diversity efforts?[152]

Reverse Discrimination

reverse discrimination
Claim that due to affirmative action quota systems, white males are discriminated against.

Reverse discrimination means discriminating against *non*minority applicants and employees. Many court cases addressed these issues, but until recently, few consistent answers emerged.

In one of the first such cases, *Bakke v. Regents of the University of California* (1978), the University of California at Davis Medical School denied admission to white student Allen Bakke, allegedly because of the school's affirmative action quota system, which required that a specific number of openings go to minority applicants. In a 5-to-4 vote, the U.S. Supreme Court struck down the policy that made race the only factor in considering applications for a certain number of class openings and thus allowed Bakke's admission.

Bakke was followed by many other cases. In June 2009, the U.S. Supreme Court ruled in an important reverse discrimination suit brought by Connecticut firefighters. In *Ricci v. DeStefano*, 19 white firefighters and one Hispanic firefighter said the city of New Haven should have promoted them based on their successful test scores. The city argued that certifying the tests would have left them vulnerable to lawsuits from minorities for violating Title VII.[153] The Court ruled in favor of the (predominantly white) plaintiffs. In New Haven's desire to avoid making promotions that might appear to adversely impact minorities, Justice Kennedy wrote that "the city rejected the test results solely because the higher scoring candidates were white." The consensus of observers was that the decision would make it harder for employers to ignore the results obtained by valid tests, even if the results disproportionately impact minorities.[154]

The bottom line seems to be that employers should emphasize the external recruitment and internal development of better-qualified minority and female employees, "while basing employment decisions on legitimate criteria."[155]

Chapter Review

MyManagementLab® Go to **mymanagementlab.com** to complete the problems marked with this icon.

Chapter Section Summaries

2-1. Several of the most important equal employment opportunity laws became law in the period from 1964 to 1991.

- Of these, Title VII of the 1964 Civil Rights Act was pivotal, and states that an employer cannot discriminate based on race, color, religion, sex, or national origin. This act established the Equal Employment Opportunity Commission, and covers most employees.
- Under the Equal Pay Act of 1963 (amended in 1972), it is unlawful to discriminate in pay on the basis of sex when jobs involve equal work, skills, effort, and responsibility and are performed under similar working conditions.
- The Age Discrimination in Employment Act of 1967 made it unlawful to discriminate against employees or applicants who are between 40 and 65 years of age.
- The Vocational Rehabilitation Act of 1973 requires most employers with federal contracts to take affirmative action when employing handicapped persons.
- The Pregnancy Discrimination Act of 1978 prohibits using pregnancy, childbirth, or

related medical conditions to discriminate in hiring, promotion, suspension, or discharge or in any term or condition of employment.

- The EEOC, Civil Service Commission, Department of Labor, and Department of Justice together issued Uniform Guidelines that set forth "highly recommended" procedures regarding HR activities like employee selection, record keeping, and preemployment inquiries.
- One of the most important cases during this early period was *Griggs v. Duke Power Company.* Here, Chief Justice Burger held that in employment, discrimination does not have to be overt to be illegal, and an employment practice that discriminates must be job related.

2-2. Equal employment law continues to evolve, with important **new legislation being enacted since 1990–1991**.

- The Civil Rights Act of 1991 reversed the effects of several Supreme Court rulings—for instance, underscoring that the burden of proof is the employer's once a plaintiff establishes possible illegal discrimination.
- The Americans with Disabilities Act prohibits employment discrimination against qualified disabled individuals. It also says employers must make "reasonable accommodations" for physical or mental limitations unless doing so imposes an "undue hardship" on the business.
- Although Title VII made sexual harassment at work illegal, the Federal Violence Against Women Act of 1994 provided women with another way to seek relief for (violent) sexual harassment. Basically, sexual harassment refers to unwelcome sexual advances, requests for sexual favors, and other verbal or physical conduct of a sexual nature that takes place, for instance, when such conduct is made either explicitly or implicitly a term or condition of an individual's employment. Three main ways to prove sexual harassment include *quid pro quo*, hostile environment created by supervisors, and hostile environment created by coworkers who are not employees.

2-3. Employers use various **defenses against discrimination allegations**. In defending themselves against discrimination allegations, employers need to distinguish between disparate treatment (intentional discrimination) and disparate impact (a policy that has an adverse impact regardless of intent). Plaintiffs show adverse impact by the standard deviation rule or by showing disparate rejection rates, restricted policy, or population comparisons, or by applying the McDonnell-Douglas test. Employers defend themselves by showing that the employment practice is a bona fide occupational qualification (for instance, gender is a BFOQ for a position such as model). Or they may defend themselves by using the business necessity defense, which requires showing that there is an overriding business purpose.

Given this, it is useful to have a working knowledge of *discriminatory employment practices*. For example, in recruitment, employers no longer use "help wanted—male" ads and endeavor to ensure that educational requirements are necessary to do the job. Similarly, in promotion and transfer, the Equal Pay Act requires that equal wages be paid for substantially similar work performed by men and women.

2-4. All managers play an important role in **the EEOC enforcement process.** The basic steps in this process include filing the charge, charge acceptance by the EEOC, serving notice on the employer, the investigation/fact-finding conference, a finding of cause/no cause, conciliation efforts, and (if necessary) a notice to sue. The EEOC refers about 10% of its charges to voluntary mediation mechanisms.

2-5. With an increasingly diverse workforce, **diversity management** is a key managerial skill. Managing diversity means maximizing diversity's potential benefits while minimizing the potential barriers. In one typical approach, the steps include providing strong leadership, assessing the situation, providing diversity training and education, changing the culture and management systems, and evaluating the diversity management program's results. Affirmative action generally means taking actions to eliminate the present effects of past discrimination. Many employers still pursue voluntary, good-faith effort strategies in identifying and eliminating the obstacles to hiring and promoting women and minorities, while some employers are under court-mandated requirement to do so.

Discussion Questions

✪ **2-1.** What important precedents were set by the *Griggs v. Duke Power Company* case? The *Albemarle v. Moody* case?

✪ **2-2.** Explain each of the four examples of a bona fide occupational qualification.

2-3. What is sexual harassment? How can an employee prove sexual harassment?

2-4. What is the difference between disparate treatment and disparate impact?

Individual and Group Activities

2-5. Working individually or in groups, respond to these three scenarios based on what you learned in this chapter. Under what conditions (if any) do you think the following constitute sexual harassment? (a) A female manager fires a male employee because he refuses her requests for sexual favors. (b) A male manager refers to female employees as "sweetie" or "baby." (c) A female employee overhears two male employees exchanging sexually oriented jokes.

2-6. Working individually or in groups, discuss how you would set up an affirmative action program.

2-7. Compare and contrast the issues presented in *Bakke* with more recent court rulings on affirmative action. Working individually or in groups, discuss the current direction of affirmative action.

2-8. Working individually or in groups, write a one-page paper titled "What the Manager Should Know About How the EEOC Handles a Person's Discrimination Charge."

2-9. Explain the difference between affirmative action and equal employment opportunity.

2-10. Assume you are the manager in a small restaurant; you are responsible for hiring employees, supervising them, and recommending them for promotion. Working individually or in groups, compile a list of potentially discriminatory management practices you should avoid.

2-11. Appendices A and B at the end of this book (pages 612–629) list the knowledge someone studying for the HRCI (Appendix A) or SHRM (Appendix B) certification exam needs to have in each area of human resource management (such as in Strategic Management, and Workforce Planning). In groups of several students, do four things: (1) review Appendix A and/or B; (2) identify the material in this chapter that relates to the Appendix A and/or B required knowledge lists; (3) write four multiple-choice exam questions on this material that you believe would be suitable for inclusion in the HRCI exam and/or the SHRM exam; and, (4) if time permits, have someone from your team post your team's questions in front of the class, so that students in all teams can answer the exam questions created by the other teams.

Experiential Exercise

"Space Cadet" or Victim?

Discrimination lawsuits are rarely simple, because the employer will often argue that the person was fired due to poor performance rather than discrimination. So, there's often a "mixed-motive" element to such situations. The facts of a case illustrate this (*Burk v. California Association of Realtors*, California Court of Appeals, number 161513, unpublished, 12/12/03). The facts were as follows. The California Association of Realtors maintained a hotline service to provide legal advice to real estate agents. One of the 12 lawyers who answered this hotline was a 61-year-old California attorney who worked there from 1989 to 2000. Until 1996 he received mostly good reviews. At that time, association members began filing complaints about his advice. His supervisor told him to be more courteous.

Two years later, association members were still complaining about this individual. Among other things, association members who called in filed complaints referring to him as "a space cadet" and "incompetent." Subsequently, his supervisor contacted six association members whom the 61-year-old lawyer had recently counseled; five of the six said they had had bad experiences. The association fired him for mistreating association members and providing inadequate legal advice.

The 61-year-old lawyer sued the association, claiming that the firing was age related. To support his claim, he noted that one colleague had told him that he was "probably getting close to retirement" and that another colleague had told him he was "getting older." The appeals court had to decide whether the association fired the 61-year-old lawyer because of his age or because of his performance.

Purpose: The purpose of this exercise is to provide practice in analyzing and applying knowledge of equal opportunity legislation to a real problem.

Required Understanding: Be thoroughly familiar with the material presented in this chapter. In addition, read the preceding "space cadet" case on which this experiential exercise is based.

How to Set Up the Exercise/Instructions:

- Divide the class into groups.
- Each group should develop answers to the following questions:

  2-12. Based on what you read in this chapter, on what legal basis could the 61-year-old California attorney claim he was a victim of discrimination?

2-13. On what laws and legal concepts did the employer apparently base its termination of this 61-year-old attorney?

2-14. Based on what laws or legal concepts could you take the position that it is legal to fire someone for poor performance even though there may be a discriminatory aspect to the termination? (This is not to say that there necessarily was such a discriminatory aspect with this case.)

2-15. If you were the judge called on to make a decision on this case, what would your decision be, and why?

- The court's decision follows, so please do not read this until you've completed the exercise.

In this case, the California State Appeals court held that "the only reasonable inference that can be drawn from the evidence is that [plaintiff] was terminated because he failed to competently perform his job of providing thorough, accurate, and courteous legal advice to hotline callers."

Based on "On Appeal, Hotheaded Hotline Lawyer Loses Age, Disability Discrimination Claims," *BNA Human Resources Report*, January 12, 2004, p. 17.

Application Case

An Accusation of Sexual Harassment in Pro Sports

The jury in a sexual harassment suit brought by a former high-ranking New York Knicks basketball team executive awarded her more than $11 million in punitive damages. Officials of Madison Square Garden (which owns the Knicks) said they would appeal the verdict. However, even if they were to win on appeal (which one University of Richmond Law School professor said was unlikely), the case still exposed the organization and its managers to a great deal of unfavorable publicity.

The federal suit pitted Anucha Browne Sanders, the Knicks' senior vice president of marketing and business operations (and former Northwestern University basketball star), against the team's owner, Madison Square Garden, and its president, Isiah Thomas. The suit charged them with sex discrimination and retaliation. Ms. Browne Sanders accused Mr. Thomas of verbally abusing and sexually harassing her over a 2-year period. She said the Garden fired her about a month after she complained to top management about the harassment. At the trial, the Garden cited numerous explanations for the dismissal, saying she had "failed to fulfill professional responsibilities." At a news conference, Browne Sanders said that Thomas "refused to stop his demeaning and repulsive behavior and the Garden refused to intercede." Mr. Thomas vigorously insisted he was innocent. According to one report of the trial, her claims of harassment and verbal abuse had little corroboration from witnesses, but neither did the Garden's claims that her performance had been subpar. After the jury decision came in, Browne Sanders's lawyers said, "This [decision] confirms what we've been saying all along, that [Browne Sanders] was sexually abused and fired for complaining about it." The Garden's statement said, in part, "We look forward to presenting our arguments to an appeals court and believe they will agree that no sexual harassment took place."

Questions

2-16. Do you think Ms. Browne Sanders had the basis for a sexual harassment suit? Why?

2-17. From what you know of this case, do you think the jury arrived at the correct decision? If not, why not? If so, why?

2-18. Based on the few facts that you have, what steps could Garden management have taken to protect itself from liability in this matter?

2-19. Aside from the appeal, what would you do now if you were the Garden's top management?

2-20. "The allegations against Madison Square Garden in this case raise ethical questions with regard to the employer's actions." Explain whether you agree or disagree with this statement, and why.

Sources: "Jury Awards $11.6 Million to Former Executive of Pro Based on "Jury Awards $11.6 Million to Former Executive of Pro Basketball Team in Harassment Case," BNA Bulletin to Management, October 9, 2007, p. 323; Richard Sandomir, "Jury Finds Knicks and Coach Harassed a Former Executive," *New York Times*, www.nytimes.com/2007/10/03/sports/basketball/03garden.html?em&ex 1191556800&en 41d47437f805290d&ei5087%0A accessed November 30, 2007. and "Thomas Defiant in Face of Harassment Claims," espn.com accessed November 30, 2007.

Continuing Case

Carter Cleaning Company

A Question of Discrimination

One of the first problems Jennifer faced at her father's Carter Cleaning Centers concerned the inadequacies of the firm's current HR management practices and procedures.

One problem that particularly concerned her was the lack of attention to equal employment matters. Each store manager independently handled virtually all hiring; the managers had received no training regarding such fundamental matters as the types of questions they should not ask of job applicants. It was therefore not unusual for female applicants to be asked questions such as "Who's going to take care of your children while you are at work?" and for minority applicants to be asked questions about arrest records and credit histories. Nonminority applicants—three store managers were white males and three were white females—were not asked these questions, as Jennifer discerned from her interviews with the managers. Based on discussions with her father, Jennifer deduced two reasons for the laid-back attitude toward equal employment: (1) her father's lack of insight about the legal requirements and (2) the fact that, as Jack Carter put it, "Virtually all our workers are women or minority members anyway, so no one can come in here and accuse us of being discriminatory, can they?"

Jennifer decided to mull that question over, but before she could, she was faced with two serious equal rights problems. Two women in one store privately confided to her that their manager was making unwelcome sexual advances toward them. One claimed he had threatened to fire her unless she "socialized" with him after hours. And during a fact-finding trip to another store, an older gentleman—he was 73 years old—complained of the fact that although he had almost 50 years of experience, he was paid less than people half his age in the same job. Jennifer's review of the stores resulted in the following questions.

Questions

2-21. Is it true, as Jack Carter claims, that "virtually all our workers are women or minority members anyway, so no one can come in here and accuse us of being discriminatory"?

2-22. How should Jennifer and her company address the sexual harassment charges and problems?

2-23. How should she and her company address the possible problems of age discrimination?

2-24. Given the fact that each of its stores has only a handful of employees, is her company covered by equal rights legislation?

2-25. And finally, aside from the specific problems, what other personnel management matters (application forms, training, and so on) have to be reviewed given the need to bring them into compliance with equal rights laws?

MyManagementLab

Go to **mymanagementlab.com** for Auto-graded writing questions as well as the following Assisted-graded writing questions:

2-26. Explain the main features of Title VII, the Equal Pay Act, the Pregnancy Discrimination Act, the Americans with Disabilities Act, and the Civil Rights Act of 1991.

2-27. What are the two main defenses you can use in the event of a discriminatory practice allegation, and what exactly do they involve?

2-28. MyManagementLab Only—comprehensive writing assignment for this chapter.

✪ Try It!

How would you apply the concepts and skills you learned in this chapter? If your professor has assigned this, go to the Assignments section of mymanagementlab.com to complete the simulation: *HR and Diversity*.

✪ PERSONAL INVENTORY ASSESSMENTS

Intercultural Sensitivity Scale

How sensitive to different cultures are you? Complete this assessment to learn more about your personality.

Key Terms

Title VII of the 1964 Civil Rights Act, 32
Equal Employment Opportunity Commission (EEOC), 32
affirmative action, 32
Office of Federal Contract Compliance Programs (OFCCP), 32
Equal Pay Act of 1963, 33
Age Discrimination in Employment Act of 1967 (ADEA), 33
Vocational Rehabilitation Act of 1973, 33
Pregnancy Discrimination Act, 33
Uniform Guidelines, 33
protected class, 34
Civil Rights Act of 1991 (CRA 1991), 35
"mixed-motive" case, 35
Americans with Disabilities Act (ADA), 35
qualified individuals, 36
sexual harassment, 38
Federal Violence Against Women Act of 1994, 39
adverse impact, 42
disparate rejection rates, 43
4/5ths rule, 43
restricted policy, 44
bona fide occupational qualification (BFOQ), 45
alternative dispute resolution or ADR program, 52
diversity, 53
stereotyping, 53
discrimination, 53
tokenism, 53
ethnocentrism, 53
gender-role stereotypes, 53
managing diversity, 54
good-faith effort strategy, 55
reverse discrimination, 57

Endnotes

1. Michael Winerip, "Pushed Out of a Job Early," *New York Times,* December 7, 2013, pp. B1, B2.
2. For example, see http://eeoc.gov/eeoc/newsroom/index.cfm. As another example, in a recent conciliation agreement between FedEx Corp. and the Department of Labor's Office of Federal Contract Compliance Programs, FedEx agreed to pay $3 million and amend its practices to settle charges that it discriminated against thousands of applicants. "FedEx to Pay $3 Million, Amend Practices to Settle OFCCP Charges of Bias in Hiring," *Bloomberg BNA Bulletin to Management*, March 27, 2012, p. 97.
3. Betsy Morris, "How Corporate America Is Betraying Women," *Fortune,* January 10, 2005, pp. 64–70.
4. Based on or quoted from International Association of Official Human Rights Agencies, *Principles of Employment Discrimination Law* (Washington, DC.). See also Bruce Feldacker, *Labor Guide to Labor Law* (Upper Saddle River, NJ: Prentice Hall, 2000); "EEOC Attorneys Highlight How Employers Can Better Their

Nondiscrimination Practices," *BNA Bulletin to Management*, July 20, 2008, p. 233; and www.eeoc.gov, accessed August 4, 2013. Plaintiffs still bring equal employment claims under the Civil Rights Act of 1866. For example, in 2008 the U.S. Supreme Court held that the act prohibits retaliation against someone who complains of discrimination against others when contract rights (in this case, an employment agreement) are at stake. Charles Louderback, "U.S. Supreme Court Decisions Expand Employees' Ability to Bring Retaliation Claims," *Compensation & Benefits Review*, September/October 2008, p. 52. Employment discrimination law is a changing field, and the appropriateness of the rules, guidelines, and conclusions in this chapter may also be affected by factors unique to the employer's operation. They should be reviewed by the employer's attorney before implementation.

5. For a recent conciliation agreement, see "FedEx to Pay $3 Million, Amend Practices to Settle OFCCP Charges of Bias in Hiring," *Bloomberg BNA Bulletin to Management*, March 27, 2012, p. 97.
6. Individuals may file under the Equal Employment Act of 1972.
7. "The Employer Should Validate Hiring Tests to Withstand EEOC Scrutiny, Officials Advise," *BNA Bulletin to Management*, April 1, 2008, p. 107. President Obama's administration recently directed more funds and staffing to the OFCCP. "Restructured, Beefed Up OFCCP May Shift Policy Emphasis, Attorney Says," *BNA Bulletin to Management*, August 18, 2009, p. 257.
8. See, for example, "Divided EEOC Approves Draft of Rule Amending Age Discrimination Regulations," *BNA Bulletin to Management*, November 22, 2011, p. 369.
9. "High Court: ADEA Does Not Protect Younger Workers Treated Worse Than Their Elders," *BNA Bulletin to Management* 55, no. 10 (March 4, 2004), pp. 73–80. See also D. Aaron Lacy, "You Are Not Quite as Old as You Think: Making the Case for Reverse Age Discrimination Under the ADEA," *Berkeley Journal of Employment and Labor Law* 26, no. 2 (2005), pp. 363–403; Nancy Ursel and Marjorie Armstrong-Stassen, "How Age Discrimination in Employment Affects Stockholders," *Journal of Labor Research* 17, no. 1 (Winter 2006), pp. 89–99; and www.eeoc.gov/laws/statutes/adea.cfm, accessed October 3, 2011.
10. "Google Exec Can Pursue Claim," *BNA Bulletin to Management*, October 20, 2007, p. 342; and "Fired Google Manager May Proceed with Age Bias Suit, California Justices Rule," *BNA Bulletin to Management*, August 10, 2010, p. 249.
11. www.eeoc.gov/laws/statutes/adea.cfm, accessed October 3, 2011.
12. The U.S. Supreme Court ruled in *California Federal Savings and Loan Association v. Guerra* that if an employer offers no disability leave to any of its employees, it can (but need not) grant pregnancy leave to a woman disabled for pregnancy, childbirth, or a related medical condition.
13. John Kohl, Milton Mayfield, and Jacqueline Mayfield, "Recent Trends in Pregnancy Discrimination Law," *Business Horizons* 48, no. 5 (September 2005), pp. 421–429; and www.eeoc.gov/eeoc/statistics/enforcement/pregnancy.cfm, accessed October 3, 2011.
14. Nancy Woodward, "Pregnancy Discrimination Grows," *HR Magazine*, July 2005, p. 79.
15. "Pregnancy Claims Rising; Consistent Procedures Paramount," *BNA Bulletin to Management*, November 23, 2010, p. 375.
16. www.uniformguidelines.com/uniformguidelines.html, accessed November 23, 2007.
17. The EEOC and the OFCCP agreed to coordinate their efforts more closely and to share information on employers with federal contracts or subcontracts. "EEOC, OFCCP Issue Updated Agreement on Coordinated Enforcement, Data Sharing," *BNA Bulletin to Management*, November 22, 2011, p. 371.
18. *Griggs v. Duke Power Company*, 3FEP cases 175.
19. This is applicable only to Title VII and CRA 91; other statutes require intent.
20. James Ledvinka, *Federal Regulation of Personnel and Human Resources Management* (Boston: Kent, 1982), p. 41.
21. Bruce Feldacker, *Labor Guide to Labor Law* (Upper Saddle River, NJ: Prentice Hall, 2000), p. 513.
22. "The Eleventh Circuit Explains Disparate Impact, Disparate Treatment," *BNA Fair Employment Practices*, August 17, 2000, p. 102. See also Kenneth York, "Disparate Results in Adverse Impact Tests: The 4/5ths Rule and the Chi Square Test," *Public Personnel Management* 31, no. 2 (Summer 2002), pp. 253–262; and "Burden of Proof Under the Employment Non-Discrimination Act," www.civilrights.org/lgbt/enda/burden-of-proof.html, accessed August 8, 2011.
23. We'll see that the process of filing a discrimination charge goes something like this: The plaintiff (say, a rejected applicant) demonstrates that an employment practice (such as a test) has a disparate (or "adverse") impact on a particular group. *Disparate impact* means that an employer engages in an employment practice or policy that has a greater adverse impact (effect) on the members of a protected group under Title VII than on other employees, regardless of intent. (Requiring a college degree for a job would have an adverse impact on some minority groups, for instance.) Disparate impact claims do *not* require proof of discriminatory intent. Instead, the plaintiff's burden is to show two things. First, he or she must show that a significant disparity exists between the proportion of (say) women in the available labor pool and the proportion hired. Second, he or she must show that an apparently neutral employment practice, such as word-of-mouth advertising or a requirement that the jobholder "be able to lift 100 pounds," is causing the disparity. Then, once the plaintiff fulfills his or her burden of showing such disparate impact, the *employer* has the heavier burden of proving that the challenged practice is job related. For example, the employer has to show that lifting 100 pounds is actually required for effectively performing the position in question, and that the business could not run efficiently without the requirement—that it is a business necessity.
24. Commerce Clearing House, "House and Senate Pass Civil Rights Compromise by Wide Margin," *Ideas and Trends in Personnel*, November 13, 1991, p. 179.
25. Mark Kobata, "The Civil Rights Act of 1991," *Personnel Journal*, March 1992, p. 48.
26. Again, though, if the "employer shows that it would have taken the same action even absent the discriminatory motive, the complaining employee will not be entitled to reinstatement, back pay, or damages"; www.eeoc.gov/policy/docs/caregiving.html#mixed, accessed September 24, 2011.
27. Elliot H. Shaller and Dean Rosen, "A Guide to the EEOC's Final Regulations on the Americans with Disabilities Act," *Employee Relations Law Journal* 17, no. 3 (Winter 1991–1992), pp. 405–430; and www.eeoc.gov/ada, accessed November 20, 2007.
28. "ADA: Simple Common Sense Principles," *BNA Fair Employment Practices*, June 4, 1992, p. 63; and www.eeoc.gov/facts/ada17.html, accessed September 24, 2011.
29. Shaller and Rosen, "A Guide to the EEOC's Final Regulations," p. 408. Other specific examples include "epilepsy, diabetes, cancer, HIV infection, and bipolar disorder"; www1.eeoc.gov//laws/regulations/adaaa_fact_sheet, accessed October 3, 2011.
30. Shaller and Rosen, "A Guide to the EEOC's Final Regulations," p. 409. Thus, one court recently held that a worker currently engaging in illegal use of drugs was "not a qualified individual with a disability" under the ADA. "Drug Addict Lacks ADA Protection, Quarter Firms," *BNA Bulletin to Management*, April 26, 2011, p. 133.
31. James McDonald Jr., "The Americans with Difficult Personalities Act," *Employee Relations Law Journal* 25, no. 4 (Spring 2000), pp. 93–107; and Betsy Bates, "Mental Health Problems Predominate in ADA Claims," *Clinical Psychiatry News*, May 2003, http://findarticles.com/p/articles/mi_hb4345/is_5_31/ai_n29006702, accessed September 24, 2011. For a detailed discussion of dealing with this issue, see www.eeoc.gov/facts/intellectual_disabilities.html, accessed September 2, 2011.
32. "EEOC Guidance on Dealing with Intellectual Disabilities," *Workforce Management*, March 2005, p. 16.
33. "Driver Fired After Seizure on Job Lacks ADA Claim," *BNA Bulletin to Management*, January 4, 2011, p. 6.
34. www.ada.gov/reg3a.html#Anchor-Appendix-52467, accessed January 23, 2009.
35. See "EEOC Guidance on Telecommuting as ADA Accommodation Discussed," *Bloomberg BNA Bulletin to Management*, October 16, 2012, p. 335.
36. Martha Frase, "An Underestimated Talent Pool," *HR Magazine*, April 2009, pp. 55–58; and Nicole LaPorte, "Hiring the Blind, While Making a Green Statement," *New York Times*, March 25, 2012, p. b3.
37. M. P. McQueen, "Workplace Disabilities Are on the Rise," *Wall Street Journal*, May 1, 2007, p. A1.
38. "No Sitting for Store Greeter," *BNA Fair Employment Practices*, December 14, 1995, p. 150. For more recent illustrative cases, see Tillinghast Licht, "Reasonable Accommodation and the ADA-Courts Draw the Line," at http://library.findlaw.com/2004/Sep/19/133574.html, accessed September 6, 2011.
39. For example, a U.S. circuit court recently found that a depressed former kidney dialysis technician could not claim ADA discrimination after the employer fired him for attendance

problems. The court said he could not meet the essential job function of predictably coming to work. "Depressed Worker Lacks ADA Claim, Court Decides," *BNA Bulletin to Management*, December 18, 2007, p. 406. See also www.eeoc.gov/press/5-10-01-b.html, accessed January 8, 2008.

40. *Toyota Motor Manufacturing of Kentucky, Inc. v. Williams.* 534 U.S. 184 (2002).
41. "Supreme Court Says Manual Task Limitation Needs Both Daily Living, Workplace Impact," *BNA Fair Employment Practices*, January 17, 2002, p. 8.
42. "EEOC Issued Its Final Regulations for ADA Amendments Act," *Workforce Management*, June 2011, p. 12.
43. "Rise in ADA Cases Calls for Focus on Accommodations, Job Descriptions," *Bloomberg BNA Bulletin to Management*, September 25, 2012, p. 310.
44. Lawrence Postol, "ADAAA Will Result in Renewed Emphasis on Reasonable Accommodations," *Society for Human Resource Management Legal Report*, January 2009, pp. 1–3.
45. Mark Lengnick-Hall et al., "Overlooked and Underutilized: People with Disabilities Are an Untapped Human Resource," *Human Resource Management* 47, no. 2 (Summer 2008), pp. 255–273.
46. Susan Wells, "Counting on Workers with Disabilities," *HR Magazine*, April 2008, p. 45.
47. "Wachovia Violated USERRA by Failing to Reinstate Reservist to Comparable Job," *BNA Bulletin to Management*, September 20, 2011, p. 297.
48. www.eeoc.gov/press/2-25-09.html, accessed April 3, 2009; and Susan Hauser, "Sincerely Yours, Gina," *Workforce Management*, July 2011, pp. 16–18.
49. James Ledvinka and Robert Gatewood, "EEO Issues with Preemployment Inquiries," *Personnel Administrator* 22, no. 2 (February 1997), pp. 22–26.
50. "Employers More Vulnerable Under New York City Statute," *BNA Bulletin to Management*, July 31, 2012, p. 245.
51. Joanne Deshenaux and Dori Meinert, "States, Cities Go Beyond Federal Government," *HR Magazine*, February 2013, pp. 28–32.
52. Quoted or paraphrased from www.eeoc.gov/laws/types/index.cfm; www.eeoc.gov/laws/types/religion.cfm; www.eeoc.gov/eeoc/internal_eeo/index.cfm; and www.eeoc.gov/federal/otherprotections.cfm, all accessed May 9, 2013.
53. Melanie Trottman, "Religious Discrimination Claims on the Rise," *Wall Street Journal*, October 28, 2013, p. B1.
54. "Employer Should Respond to DOMA with Steps That Offset Risks, Attorneys Say," *Bloomberg BNA Bulletin to Management*, July 2, 2013, pp. 209–210.
55. "DOL Says 'Spouse' and 'Marriage' in ERISA Include Same-Sex Legally Married Couples," *Bloomberg BNA Bulletin to Management*, September 24, 2013, p. 305.
56. "OFCCP Announces Final Rule Protecting LGBT Federal Contractor Workers from Bias," *Bloomberg BNA Bulletin to Management*, December 9, 2014.
57. "OFCCP Announces 'Higher Historic' Final Rules on Contractor Hiring of Veterans, Disabled," *Bloomberg BNA Bulletin to Management*, September 3, 2013, p. 281.
58. Lauren Weber, "Are You Disabled? Now Your Boss Wants to Know," *Wall Street Journal*, March 19, 2014, p. B1.
59. "Lipnic Says EEOC Intends to Combat Hiring Barriers, Explore Accommodation," *Bloomberg BNA Bulletin to Management*, May 7, 2013, p. 145.
60. Adam Liptak, "Justices Back Ban on Race as Factor in College Entry," *New York Times*, April 23, 2014, pp. A1, A12.
61. Melanie Trottman and Lauren Weber, "Bar Is Raised in Worker Bias Cases," *Wall Street Journal*, June 25, 2013, p. B1, B8.
62. www.eeoc.gov/types/sexual_harassment.html, accessed April 24, 2009; and www.eeoc.gov/eeoc/statistics/enforcement/sexual_harassment.cfm, accessed October 3, 2011.
63. Richard Wiener et al., "The Fit and Implementation of Sexual Harassment Law to Workplace Evaluations," *Journal of Applied Psychology* 87, no. 4 (2002), pp. 747–764. Recently, for instance, a U.S. Court of Appeals told a male Walmart employee that he could proceed with his claim that a female supervisor had sexually harassed him. "Man's Harassment Claims Advanced," *BNA Bulletin to Management*, September 6, 2011, p. 285.
64. Jennifer Berdahl and Celia Moore, "Workplace Harassment: Double Jeopardy for Minority Women," *Journal of Applied Psychology* 91, no. 2 (2006), pp. 426–436.
65. Larry Drake and Rachel Moskowitz, "Your Rights in the Workplace," *Occupational Outlook Quarterly* (Summer 1997), pp. 19–29.
66. "EEOC: "Boss's Shoulder Touching Not Sexual Harassment," *Bloomberg BNA Bulletin to Management*, February 11, 2014, p. 45.
67. Patricia Linenberger and Timothy Keaveny, "Sexual Harassment: The Employer's Legal Obligations," *Personnel* 58 (November/December 1981), p. 64; and "Court Examines Workplace Flirtation," http://hr.blr.com/HR-news/Discrimination/Sexual-Harassment/Court-Examines-Workplace-Flirtation, accessed October 2, 2011.
68. Edward Felsenthal, "Justice's Ruling Further Defines Sexual Harassment," *Wall Street Journal*, March 5, 1998, p. B5.
69. Hilary Gettman and Michele Gelfand, "When the Customer Shouldn't Be King: Antecedents and Consequences of Sexual Harassment by Clients and Customers," *Journal of Applied Psychology* 92, no. 3 (2007), pp. 757–770.
70. See the discussion in "Examining Unwelcome Conduct in a Sexual Harassment Claim," *BNA Fair Employment Practices*, October 19, 1995, p. 124. See also Michael Zugelder et al., "An Affirmative Defense to Sexual Harassment by Managers and Supervisors: Analyzing Employer Liability and Protecting Employee Rights in the U.S.," *Employee Responsibilities and Rights* 18, no. 2 (2006), pp. 111–122.
71. Ibid.; "Examining Unwelcome Conduct in a Sexual Harassment Claim," p. 124.
72. For example, a server/bartender filed a sexual harassment claim against Chili's Bar & Grill. She claimed that her former boyfriend, also a restaurant employee, had harassed her. The court ruled that the restaurant's prompt response warranted ruling in favor of it. "Ex-Boyfriend Harassed, but Employer Acted Promptly," *BNA Bulletin to Management*, January 8, 2008, p. 14.
73. See Mindy D. Bergman et al., "The (Un)reasonableness of Reporting: Antecedents and Consequences of Reporting Sexual Harassment," *Journal of Applied Psychology* 87, no. 2 (2002), pp. 230–242. See also www.eeoc.gov/policy/docs/harassment-facts.html, accessed October 2, 2011.
74. Adapted from *Sexual Harassment Manual for Managers and Supervisors* (Riverwood, IL: CCH Incorporated, a Wolters-Kluwer Company, 1991); www.eeoc.gov/types/sexual_harassment.html, accessed May 6, 2007; and www.eeoc.gov/policy/docs/harassment-facts.html, accessed October 2, 2011.
75. Maria Rotundo et al., "A Meta-Analytic Review of Gender Differences in Perceptions of Sexual Harassment," *Journal of Applied Psychology* 86, no. 5 (2001), pp. 914–922. See also Nathan Bowling and Terry Beehr, "Workplace Harassment from the Victim's Perspective: A Theoretical Model and Meta Analysis," *Journal of Applied Psychology* 91, no. 5 (2006), pp. 998–1012.
76. Jennifer Berdahl and Karl Aquino, "Sexual Behavior at Work: Fun or Folly?" *Journal of Applied Psychology* 94, no. 1 (2009), pp. 34–47.
77. Jathan Janov, "Sexual Harassment and the Three Big Surprises," *HR Magazine* 46, no. 11 (November 2001), p. 123ff. California mandates sexual harassment prevention training for supervisors: See "California Clarifies Training Law; Employers Take Note," *BNA Bulletin to Management*, November 20, 2007, p. 375.
78. Ana Campoy and Julian Barnes, "Air Force Combats Sex Misconduct," *Wall Street Journal*, November 15, 2012, p. A-8; and James Risen, "Air Force Leaders Testify on Culture That Led to Sexual Assaults of Recruits," *New York Times*, January 24, 2013, p. A-15.
79. Mary Rowe, "Dealing with Sexual Harassment," *Harvard Business Review*, May–June 1981, p. 43; the quoted material goes on to say that "the employer still bears the burden of proving that the employee's failure was unreasonable. If the employee had a justifiable fear of retaliation, his or her failure to utilize the complaint process may not be unreasonable" and is quoted from www.uiowa.edu/~eod/policies/sexual-harassment-guide/employer-liablity.htm, accessed October 3, 2011.
80. "Employers Should Address Inappropriate Behavior on Social Sites," *Bloomberg BNA*, February 19, 2013, p. 62.
81. "Be Careful with Social Media When Vetting Potential Workers," *Bloomberg BNA Bulletin to Management*, June 25, 2013, p. 206.
82. John Moran, *Employment Law* (Upper Saddle River, NJ: Prentice Hall, 1997), p. 166.
83. "The Eleventh Circuit Explains Disparate Impact, Disparate Treatment," p. 102.
84. John Klinefelter and James Thompkins, "Adverse Impact in Employment Selection," *Public Personnel Management*, May/June 1976, pp. 199–204; and www.eeoc.gov/policy/docs/factemployment_procedures.html, accessed October 2, 2011.
85. Moran, *Employment Law*, p. 168.
86. Employers use several types of statistics in addressing adverse impact. (For a discussion, see Robert Gatewood and Hubert Feild, *Human Resource Selection* [Fort Worth, TX: The Dryden Press, 1994], pp. 40–42, and Jean Phillips and Stanley Gulley, *Strategic Staffing* [Upper

Saddle River, NJ: Pearson, 2012], pp. 68–69.) For example, *stock statistics* might compare *at a single point in time* (1) the percentage of female engineers the company has, as a percentage of its total number of engineers, with (2) the number of trained female engineers in the labor force as a percentage of the total number of trained engineers in the labor force. Here, the question of relevant labor market is important. For example, the relevant labor market if you're hiring unskilled assemblers might be the local labor market within, say, 20 miles from your plant, whereas the relevant labor market for highly skilled engineers might well be national and possibly international. *Flow statistics* measure proportions of employees, in particular, groups at two points in time: before selection and after selection takes place. For example, when comparing the percentage of minority applicants who applied with the percentage hired, the employer is using flow statistics. An employer's company-wide minority hiring statistics may be defensible company-wide but not departmentally. The employer therefore may employ *concentration statistics* to drill down and determine the concentration of minorities versus nonminorities in particular job categories.

87. One study found that using the 4/5ths rule often resulted in false-positive ratings of adverse impact, and that incorporating tests of statistical significance could improve the accuracy of applying the 4/5ths rule. See Philip Roth, Philip Bobko, and Fred Switzer, "Modeling the Behavior of the 4/5ths Rule for Determining Adverse Impact: Reasons for Caution," *Journal of Applied Psychology* 91, no. 3 (2006), pp. 507–522.
88. The results must be realistic. In this example, hiring 2 out of 5 women suggests there is no adverse impact. But suppose we had hired only 1 woman. Then the difference between those we would be expected to hire (5) and whom we actually hired (1) would rise to 4. Hiring just one less woman might then trigger adverse impact issues, because twice the standard deviation is also about 4. However, realistically, it probably would not trigger such concerns, because with such small numbers, one person makes such a difference. The point is that tools like the 4/5ths rule and the standard deviation rule are only rules of thumb. They do not themselves determine if the employer's screening process is discriminatory. This fact may work both for and against the employer. As the Uniform Guidelines (www.uniformguidelines.com/qandaprint.html) put it, "Regardless of the amount of difference in selection rates, unlawful discrimination may be present, and may be demonstrated through appropriate evidence…."
89. The ADEA does not just protect against intentional discrimination (disparate treatment). Under a Supreme Court decision (*Smith v. Jackson,* Miss., 2005), it also covers employer practices that seem neutral but that actually bear more heavily on older workers (disparate impact). "Employees Need Not Show Intentional Bias to Bring Claims Under ADEA, High Court Says," *BNA Bulletin to Management* 56, no. 14 (April 5, 2005), p. 105.
90. The Fair Treatment for Experienced Pilots Act raised commercial pilots' mandatory retirement age from 60 to 65 in 2008. Allen Smith, "Congress Gives Older Pilots a Reprieve," *HR Magazine*, February 2008, p. 24.
91. *Usery v. Tamiami Trail Tours*, 12FEP cases 1233. Alternatively, an employer faced with an age discrimination claim may raise the factors other than age (FOA) defense. Here, it argues that its actions were "reasonable" based on some factor other than age, such as the terminated person's poor performance.
92. www.foxnews.com/story/0,2933,517334,00.html, accessed January 7, 2010.
93. Howard Anderson and Michael Levin-Epstein, *Primer of Equal Employment Opportunity* (Washington, DC: The Bureau of National Affairs, 1982), pp. 13–14.
94. *U.S. v. Bethlehem Steel Company*, 3FEP cases 589.
95. *Robinson v. Lorillard Corporation*, 3FEP cases 653.
96. *Spurlock v. United Airlines*, 5FEP cases 17.
97. Anderson and Levin-Epstein, *Primer of Equal Employment Opportunity*, p. 14.
98. Ledvinka and Gatewood, "EEO Issues with Preemployment Inquiries," pp. 22–26.
99. Ibid.; www.eeoc.gov/laws/practices/index.cfm, accessed August 2, 2013.
100. "Eighth Circuit OKs $3.4 Million EEOC Verdict Relating to Pre-Hire Strength Testing Rules," *BNA Bulletin to Management*, November 28, 2006, p. 377.
101. Svetlana Shkolnikova, "Weight Discrimination Could Be as Common as Racial Bias," www.usatoday.com/news/health/weightloss/2008-05-20-overweight-bias_N.htm, accessed January 21, 2009.
102. Jenessa Shapiro et al., "Expectations of Obese Trainees: How Stigmatized Trainee Characteristics Influence Training Effectiveness," *Journal of Applied Psychology* 92, no. 1 (2007), pp. 239–249. See also Lisa Finkelstein et al., "Bias Against Overweight Job Applicants: Further Explanations of When and Why," *Human Resource Management* 46, no. 2 (Summer 2007), pp. 203–222. For an interesting study, see T. A. Judge and D. M. Cable, "When It Comes to Pay, Do the Thin Win? The Effect of Weight on Pay for Men and Women," *Journal of Applied Psychology,* January 2011.
103. "OFCCP Issues Criminal Records Directive, Cautions Contractors on Blanket Exclusions," *Bloomberg BNA Bulletin to Management*, February 12, 2013, p. 49; and "EEOC to Focus on Hiring, Pay and Harassment," *HR Magazine*, February 2013, p. 11.
104. See, for example, www.eeoc.gov/policy/docs/guidance-inquiries.html, accessed June 28, 2009.
105. This is based on *BNA Fair Employment Practices*, April 13, 1989, pp. 45–47; and "Crossed: When Religion and Dress Code Policies Intersect," www.mcguire_woods.com/news-resources/item.asp?item=3108, accessed October 2, 2011.
106. Eric Matusewitch, "Tailor Your Dress Codes," *Personnel Journal* 68, no. 2 (February 1989), pp. 86–91; Matthew Miklave, "Sorting Out a Claim of Bias," *Workforce* 80, no. 6 (June 2001), pp. 102–103, and "Laws and Cases Affecting Appearance," www.boardmanlawfirm.com/perspectives_articles/appearance.php, accessed September 8, 2011.
107. Rita Pyrillis, "Body of Work," *Workforce Management*, November 7, 2010, pp. 20–26.
108. This isn't ironclad, however. For example, the U.S. Supreme Court, in *Stotts*, held that a court cannot require retention of black employees hired under a court's consent decree in preference to higher-seniority white employees who were protected by a bona fide seniority system. It's unclear whether this decision also extends to personnel decisions not governed by seniority systems. *Firefighters Local 1784 v. Stotts* (*BNA*, April 14, 1985).
109. In its most recent plan, the EEOC said it would focus on hiring, and particularly enforcing its guidance on indiscriminate use of criminal conduct in background screening; on gender-based pay discrepancies; and on enforcing its requirements against harassment based on race, ethnicity, religion, age, and disability. "EEOC to Focus on Hiring, Pay and Assessment," p. 11.
110. Prudent employers often purchase employment practices liability insurance to insure against some or all of the expenses involved with defending against discrimination, sexual harassment, and wrongful termination–type claims. Antone Melton-Meaux, "Maximizing Employment Practices Liability Insurance Coverage," *Compensation & Benefits Review*, May/June 2008, pp. 55–59.
111. Litigants must watch the clock. In an equal pay decision, the U.S. Supreme Court held (in *Ledbetter v. Goodyear Tire & Rubber Company*) that the employee must file a complaint within 180 (or 300) days of the employer's decision to pay the allegedly unfair wage. The clock starts with that first pay decision, not with the subsequent paychecks that the employee receives. "Justices Rule 5–4 Claim-Filing Period Applies to Pay Decision, Not Subsequent Paycheck," *BNA Bulletin to Management* 58, no. 23 (June 5, 2007), pp. 177–184; and www.eeoc.gov/eeoc/statistics/enforcement/charges.cfm, accessed May 1, 2012. A recent U.S. Supreme Court case will make it more difficult for plaintiffs to file class-action claims for discrimination. See "Supreme Court Hands Wal-Mart Big Victory: Reverses Approval of Class-Action Claim," *BNA Bulletin to Management*, June 21, 2011, p. 193.
112. In 2007, the U.S. Supreme Court, in *Ledbetter v. Goodyear Tire & Rubber Company,* held that employees claiming Title VII pay discrimination must file their claims within 180 days of when they first receive the allegedly discriminatory pay. As of 2009, Congress was working to formulate new legislation enabling an employee to file a claim at any time, as long as the person is still receiving an "infected" paycheck.
113. www.eeoc.gov/eeoc/statistics/enforcement/charges.cfm, accessed March 20, 2013.
114. "EPLI Now Established Employer Litigation Strategy," *BNA Bulletin to Management*, November 29, 2011, p. 382.
115. If the charge was filed initially with a state or local agency within 180 days after the alleged unlawful practice occurred, the charge may then be filed with the EEOC within 30 days after the practice occurred or within 30 days after the person received notice that the state or local agency has ended its proceedings.
116. "Attorneys: Employer Should Handle EEOC Discharges Strategically," *Bloomberg BNA Bulletin to Management,* October 15, 2013, p. 334.
117. "EEOC Attorneys Stress the Importance of Cooperation

During Investigations," *BNA Bulletin to Management*, March 8, 2011, p. 73.

118. www.eeoc.gov/mediate/facts.html, accessed June 29, 2009.
119. "EEOC's New Nationwide Mediation Plan Offers Option of Informal Settlements," *BNA Fair Employment Practices*, February 18, 1999, p. 21; and www.eeoc.gov/employees/mediation.cf, accessed October 2, 2011.
120. Timothy Bland, "Sealed Without a Kiss," *HR Magazine*, October 2000, pp. 85–92.
121. Stuart Bompey and Michael Pappas, "Is There a Better Way? Compulsory Arbitration of Employment Discrimination Claims After *Gilmer*," *Employee Relations Law Journal* 19, no. 3 (Winter 1993–1994), pp. 197–216, and www.eeoc.gov/policy/docs/mandarb.html, accessed September 5, 2011. The EEOC says here, for instance, that "the employer imposing mandatory arbitration is free to manipulate the arbitral mechanism to its benefit."
122. See Bompey and Pappas, pp. 210–211.
123. David Nye, "When the Fired Fight Back," *Across-the-Board*, June 1995, pp. 31–34; and www.eeoc.gov/federal/fed_employees/adr.cfm, accessed October 3, 2011.
124. "EEOC Opposes Mandatory Arbitration," *BNA Fair Employment Practices*, July 24, 1997, p. 85; and www.eeoc.gov/employees/mediation.cfm, accessed October 2, 2011.
125. *Sources:* "Tips for Employers on Dealing with EEOC Investigations," *BNA Fair Employment Practices*, October 31, 1996, p. 130; "Conducting Effective Investigations of Employee Bias Complaints," *BNA Fair Employment Practices*, July 13, 1995, p. 81; Commerce Clearing House, *Ideas and Trends*, January 23, 1987, pp. 14–15; http://eeoc.gov/employers/investigations.html, accessed October 4, 2009; and www.eeoc.gov/employers/process.cfm, accessed August 1, 2012.
126. Kenneth Sovereign, *Personnel Law*, 4th edition (Upper Saddle River, NJ: Prentice Hall, 1999), p. 220. Perhaps surprisingly, more senior managers than nonmanagers report suffering retaliation when reporting workplace misconduct. *Bloomberg BNA Bulletin to Management*, September 11, 2012, p. 294. This includes what one report calls "traceable retaliation," such as demotions, physical harm, and online harassment.
127. www.eeoc.gov/laws/types/retaliation.cfm, accessed August 19, 2011; and Adam Liptak, "Fiancé's Firing Is Ruled an Illegal Reaction to a Discrimination Claim," *New York Times*, January 25, 2011, p. A16.
128. See "Retaliation Becomes Most Common Charge," *HR Magazine*, March 2011, p. 16. For instance, there were recently 37,836 private-sector retaliation charges filed, 33,512 race discrimination charges, and 33,566 discrimination charges. "Retaliation Most Frequent EEOC Charge in Fiscal Year 2012," *Bloomberg BNA Bulletin to Management*, February 5, 2013, p. 45.
129. Liptak, "Fiancé's Firing," p. A16.
130. See, for example, "Diversity Is Used as Business Advantage by Three Fourths of Companies, Survey Says," *BNA Bulletin to Management*, November 7, 2006, p. 355; and Claire Armstrong et al., "The Impact of Diversity and Equality Management on Firm Performance: Beyond High Performance Work Systems," *Human Resource Management* 49, no. 6 (November–December 2010), pp. 977–998.
131. Brian O'Leary and Bart Weathington, "Beyond the Business Case for Diversity in Organizations," *Employee Responsibilities and Rights* 18, no. 4 (December 2006), pp. 283–292.
132. See, for example, Michael Carrell and Everett Mann, "Defining Work-Force Diversity in Public Sector Organizations," *Public Personnel Management* 24, no. 1 (Spring 1995), pp. 99–111; Richard Koonce, "Redefining Diversity," *Training and Development Journal*, December 2001, pp. 22–33; and Kathryn Canas and Harris Sondak, *Opportunities and Challenges of Workplace Diversity* (Upper Saddle River, NJ: Pearson, 2008), pp. 3–27. Others list race and ethnicity diversity, gender diversity, age diversity, disability diversity, sexual diversity, and cultural and national origin diversity as examples. Lynn Shore et al., "Diversity in Organizations: Where Are We Now and Where Are We Going?" *Human Resource Management Review* 19 (2009), pp. 117–133.
133. Taylor Cox Jr., *Cultural Diversity in Organizations* (San Francisco, CA: Berrett Kohler Publishers, Inc., 1993), p. 88; also see Stefanie Johnson et al., "The Strong, Sensitive Type: Effects of Gender Stereotypes and Leadership Prototypes on the Evaluation of Male and Female Leaders," *Organizational Behavior and Human Decision Processes* 106, no. 1 (May 2008), pp. 39–60.
134. "Outsmarting Our Brains: Overcoming Hidden Biases to Harness Diversity's True Potential," Ernst & Young LLP, 2013; and Dana Wilkie, "Bringing Bias into the Light," *HR magazine*, December 2014, pp. 32–27.
135. Cox, *Cultural Diversity in Organizations*, p. 64.
136. "Workplace Bias Against Muslims Increasingly a Concern for Employers," *BNA Bulletin to Management*, October 26, 2010, p. 337. See also Robert Grossman, "Valuable but Vulnerable," *HR Magazine*, March 2011, pp. 22–27.
137. Cox, *Cultural Diversity in Organizations*, pp. 179–80.
138. J. H. Greenhaus and S. Parasuraman, "Job Performance Attributions and Career Advancement Prospects: An Examination of Gender and Race Affects," *Organizational Behavior and Human Decision Processes* 55 (July 1993), pp. 273–298. Much research here focuses on how ethnocentrism prompts consumers to avoid certain products based on their country of origin. See, for example, T. S. Chan et al., "How Consumer Ethnocentrism and Animosity Impair the Economic Recovery of Emerging Markets," *Journal of Global Marketing* 23, no. 3 (July/August 2010), pp. 208–225.
139. Patrick McKay et al., "A Tale of Two Climates: Diversity Climate from Subordinates' and Managers' Perspectives and Their Role in Store Unit Sales Performance," *Personnel Psychology* 62 (2009), pp. 767–791.
140. Maria del Carmen Triana, Maria Fernandez Garcia, and Adrian Colella, "Managing Diversity: How Organizational Efforts to Support Diversity Moderate the Effects of Perceived Racial Discrimination on Affective Commitment," *Personnel Psychology* 63 (2010), pp. 817–843.
141. "Selling the Supremes on Diversity," *Bloomberg Businessweek*, October 20–October 28, 2012, p. 38.
142. As another example, leaders who facilitated high levels of power sharing within their groups helped to reduce the frequently observed positive relationship between increased diversity and increased turnover. But leaders who were inclusive of only a select few followers "may actually exacerbate the relationship between diversity and turnover" (p. 1422). Lisa Nishii and David Mayer, "Do Inclusive Leaders Help to Reduce Turnover in Diverse Groups? The Moderating Role of Leader—Member Exchange in the Diversity to Turnover Relationship," *Journal of Applied Psychology* 94, no. 6 (2009), pp. 1412–1426.
143. Faye Cocchiara et al., "A Gem for Increasing the Effectiveness of Diversity Training," *Human Resource Management* 49, no. 6 (November–December 2010), pp. 1089–1106.
144. For diversity management steps, see Cox, *Cultural Diversity in Organizations*, p. 236. See also Patricia Digh, "Creating a New Balance Sheet: The Need for Better Diversity Metrics," *Mosaics*, Society for Human Resource Management, September/October 1999, p. 1; and Richard Bucher, *Diversity Consciousness* (Upper Saddle River, NJ: Pearson Prentice Hall, 2004), pp. 109–137.
145. Boris Groysberg and Katherine Connolly, "Great Leaders Who Make the Mix Work," *Harvard Business Review*, September 2013, pp. 68–76.
146. Susan Hauser, "The Clone Danger," *Workforce Management*, April 2013, p. 40.
147. John Rice, "Why Make Diversity So Hard to Achieve?" *Harvard Business Review*, June 2012, p. 40.
148. David Thomas, "Diversity as Strategy," *Harvard Business Review*, September 2004, pp. 98–104; see also J. T. Childs Jr., "Managing Global Diversity at IBM: A Global HR Topic That Has Arrived," *Human Resource Management* 44, no. 1 (Spring 2005), pp. 73–77.
149. Ibid., p. 99.
150. David Harrison et al., "Understanding Attitudes Toward Affirmative Action Programs in Employment: Summary and Meta-Analysis of 35 Years of Research," *Journal of Applied Psychology* 91, no. 5 (2006), pp. 1013–1036; and Margaret Fiester et al., "Affirmative Action, Stock Options, I-9 Documents," *HR Magazine*, November 2007, p. 31.
151. David Harrison et al., "Understanding Attitudes Toward Affirmative Action Programs in Employment: Summary and Meta-Analysis of 35 Years of Research," *Journal of Applied Psychology* 91, no. 5 (2006), pp. 1013–1036.
152. Bill Leonard, "Ways to Tell If a Diversity Program Is Measuring Up," *HR Magazine*, July 2002, p. 21; and Ye Yang Zheng and Brenda White, "The Evaluation of a Diversity Program at an Academic Library," *Library Philosophy and Practice*, 2007, http://unllib.unl.edu/LPP/yang.pdf, accessed October 2, 2011.
153. http://newsfeedresearcher.com/data/articles_n17/tests-city-court.html, accessed April 24, 2009.
154. Adam Liptak, "Supreme Court Finds Bias Against White Firefighters," *New York Times*, June 30, 2009, pp. A1, A13.
155. Ibid., p. 560.

3

Human Resource Management Strategy and Analysis

Tang dewei/imaginechina/AP Images

LEARNING OBJECTIVES

4-1 Define talent management and explain why it is important.

4-2 Discuss the process of job analysis, including why it is important.

4-3 Explain how to use at least three methods of collecting job analysis information, including interviews, questionnaires, and observation.

4-4 Explain how you would write a job description.

4-5 Explain how to write a job specification.

4-6 List some human traits and behaviors you would want an employee to bring to a job if employee engagement is important to doing the job well.

4-7 Explain competency-based job analysis, including what it means and how it's done in practice.

When Daimler opened its Mercedes-Benz assembly plant in Alabama, its managers had a dilemma. Their strategy was to create a high-performance plant, one Daimler could then extend to its other plants in America, South Africa, Brazil, and Germany. The dilemma was that plant managers could not hire, train, or pay their employees unless they knew what each employee was expected to do. But in this plant, self-managing teams would assemble the vehicles, so team-members' jobs might change every day. How do you hire people when their job duties are always changing?[1] We'll see what they did.

WHERE ARE WE NOW ...

Because managers should know what a job entails before deciding who to recruit and hire for it, human resource management really starts with deciding what the job entails. The main purpose of this chapter is to show you how to analyze jobs and write job descriptions. We discuss several techniques for analyzing jobs, and explain how to write job descriptions and job specifications. The main topics we address include the talent management process, the basics of job analysis, methods for collecting job analysis information, writing job descriptions, writing job specifications, employee engagement and job analysis, and using models and profiles in talent management. Then, in Chapter 5 (Personnel Planning and Recruiting), we'll turn to the methods managers use to actually find the employees they need.

The Talent Management Process

LEARNING OBJECTIVE 4-1
Define talent management and explain why it is important.

For many people, Chapters 4–13 represent the heart of the book, specifically recruitment, selection, training, appraisal, career planning, and compensation. Managers traditionally view these activities as a series of steps:

1. Decide what positions to fill, through job analysis, personnel planning, and forecasting.
2. Build a pool of job applicants, by recruiting internal or external candidates.
3. Obtain application forms and perhaps have initial screening interviews.
4. Use selection tools like tests, interviews, background checks, and physical exams to identify viable candidates.
5. Decide to whom to make an offer.
6. Orient, train, and develop employees so they have the competencies to do their jobs.
7. Appraise employees to assess how they're doing.
8. Compensate employees to maintain their motivation.

This stepwise view makes sense. For example, the employer needs job candidates before selecting whom to hire.

The problem with the stepwise view is twofold. First, the process usually isn't really stepwise. For example, managers do not just train employees (step 6 above) and then appraise how they're doing (step 7). Instead (to use our example), the appraisal may well also loop back to shape the employee's subsequent training. So, first, rather than view these eight HR activities as stepwise, it is best to view them holistically—because the steps interactively affect each other and work together. The second problem is that focusing just on each step may cause the manager to miss, as it were, the forest for the trees. It's not just each step but the *results you obtain* by applying them together that's important. So, second, it's important to remember that each and every step should be focused on achieving, in unison, some specific result (such as, say, improving customer service).

talent management
The goal-oriented and integrated process of planning, recruiting, developing, managing, and compensating employees.

Recognizing all this, the trend today is to view these eight activities not stepwise but as part of a coordinated *talent management* effort.[2] We will define **talent management** as *the holistic, integrated and results and goal-oriented process of planning, recruiting, selecting, developing, managing, and compensating employees*.[3] What does this mean in practice? As an example, the manager who takes a talent management approach tends to take actions such as the following:

1. He or she starts with the results and asks, "What recruiting, testing, training, or pay action should I take to produce the employee competencies we need *to achieve our company's goals*?"
2. He or she treats activities such as recruiting and training as interrelated. For example, the manager knows that having employees with the right skills depends as much on recruiting and training as on applicant testing.
3. Because talent management is holistic and integrated, he or she will probably use the same "profile" of required human skills, knowledge, and behaviors ("competencies") for formulating a job's recruitment plans as for making selection, training, appraisal, and compensation decisions for it.
4. He or she takes steps to actively coordinate/integrate talent management functions such as recruiting and training. For example, HR managers meet to make sure they are using the same skills profile to recruit as to select, train, and appraise for a particular job, or use talent management software like the following to do so.

Improving Performance Through HRIS: Talent Management Software

Because talent management is holistic and interdependent, many employers use talent management software systems to coordinate their talent-related activities. For example, Talent Management Solutions' (www.talentmanagement101.com) *Talent Management Suite* includes recruiting, employee performance management, a learning management system, and compensation management support. It "ensures that all levels of the organization are aligned—all working for the same goals."[4] SilkRoad Technology's Talent Management Solution includes applicant tracking, onboarding, performance management, and compensation support. It helps you "... recruit, manage, and retain your best employees."[5] ■

The Basics of Job Analysis

Talent management starts with understanding what jobs need to be filled, and the human traits and competencies employees need to do those jobs effectively.

LEARNING OBJECTIVE 4-2

Discuss the process of job analysis, including why it is important.

What Is Job Analysis?

Organizations consist of positions that have to be staffed. The organization chart (see Figure 4-1) shows the title of each supervisor's position and, by means of connecting lines, who is accountable to whom, who has authority for each area, and who is expected to communicate with whom. **Job analysis** is the procedure through which you determine the duties of the company's positions and the characteristics of the people to hire for them.[6] Job analysis produces information for writing **job descriptions** (a list of what the job entails) and **job** (or "person") **specifications** (what kind of people to hire for the job). Virtually every personnel-related action—interviewing applicants, and training and appraising employees, for instance—requires knowing what the job entails and what human traits one needs to do the job well.[7]

job analysis
The procedure for determining the duties and skill requirements of a job and the kind of person who should be hired for it.

job descriptions
A list of a job's duties, responsibilities, reporting relationships, working conditions, and supervisory responsibilities—one product of a job analysis.

job specifications
A list of a job's "human requirements," that is, the requisite education, skills, personality, and so on—another product of a job analysis.

The supervisor or human resources specialist normally collects one or more of the following types of information via the job analysis:

- ***Work activities.*** Information about the job's actual work activities, such as cleaning, selling, teaching, or painting. This list may also include how, why, and when the worker performs each activity.
- ***Human behaviors.*** Information about human behaviors the job requires, like sensing, communicating, lifting weights, or walking long distances.
- ***Machines, tools, equipment, and work aids.*** Information regarding tools used, materials processed, knowledge dealt with or applied (such as finance or law), and services rendered (such as counseling or repairing).
- ***Performance standards.*** Information about the job's performance standards (in terms of quantity or quality levels for each job duty, for instance).

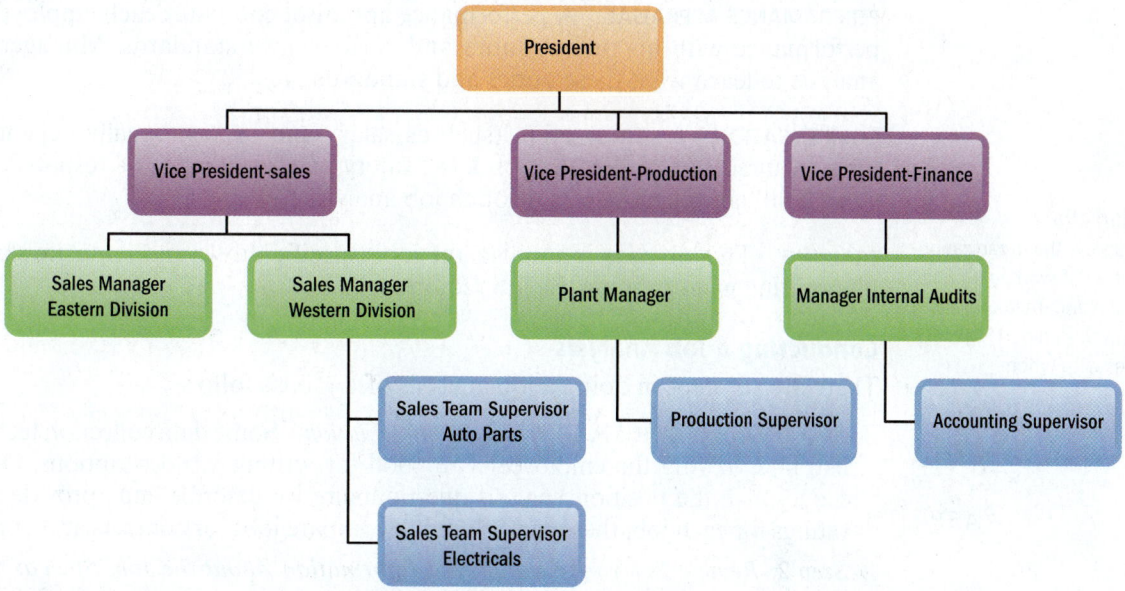

FIGURE 4-1 Organization Chart

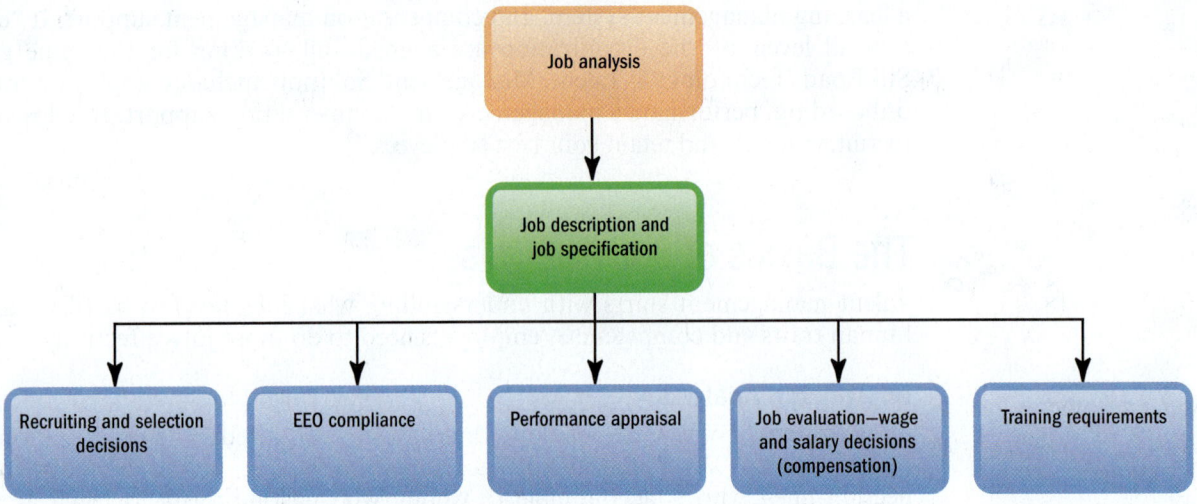

FIGURE 4-2 Uses of Job Analysis Information

- ***Job context.*** Information about such matters as physical working conditions, work schedule, incentives, and, for instance, the number of people with whom the employee would normally interact.
- ***Human requirements.*** Information such as knowledge or skills (education, training, work experience) and required personal attributes (aptitudes, personality, interests).

Uses of Job Analysis Information

As Figure 4-2 summarizes, job analysis is important because it supports just about all human resource management activities.

RECRUITMENT AND SELECTION Information about what duties the job entails and what human characteristics are required to perform these duties helps managers decide what sort of people to recruit and hire.

EEO COMPLIANCE Job analysis is crucial for validating all major human resources practices. For example, to comply with the Americans with Disabilities Act, employers should know each job's essential job functions—which in turn requires a job analysis.

PERFORMANCE APPRAISAL A performance appraisal compares each employee's actual performance with his or her duties and performance standards. Managers use job analysis to learn what these duties and standards are.

COMPENSATION Compensation (such as salary and bonus) usually depends on the job's required skill and education level, safety hazards, degree of responsibility, and so on—all factors you assess through job analysis.

organization chart
A chart that shows the organization-wide distribution of work, with titles of each position and interconnecting lines that show who reports to and communicates with whom.

TRAINING The job description lists the job's specific duties and requisite skills—thus pinpointing what training the job requires.

Conducting a Job Analysis

There are six steps in doing a job analysis of a job, as follows.

Step 1: Decide How You Will Use the Information Some data collection techniques—like interviewing the employee—are good for writing job descriptions. Other techniques, like the position analysis questionnaire we describe later, provide numerical ratings for each job; these can be used to compare jobs for compensation purposes.

Step 2: Review Relevant Background Information About the Job, Such as Organization Charts and Process Charts[8] It is important to understand the job's context. For example, **organization charts** show the organizationwide division of work,

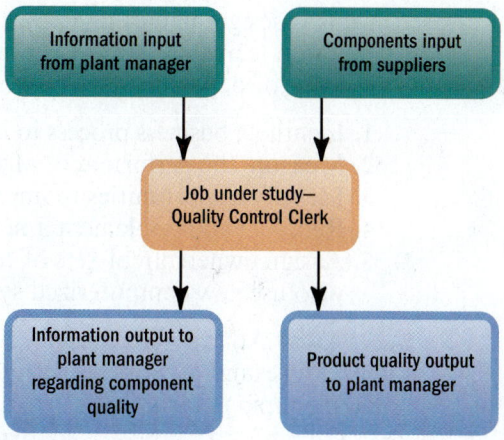

FIGURE 4-3 Process Chart for Analyzing a Job's Workflow

Source: Henderson, Richard I., Compensation Management in a Knowledge -Based World, 9th Ed., © 2003, p.137. Reprinted and Electronically reproduced by permission of Pearson Education, Inc., Upper Saddle River, New Jersey.

process chart
A workflow chart that shows the flow of inputs to and outputs from a particular job.

and where the job fits in the overall organization. A **process chart** provides a detailed picture of the workflow. Thus, in the process chart in Figure 4-3, the quality control clerk should review components from suppliers, check components going to the plant managers, and give information regarding the components' quality to these managers. Finally, an existing job description may provide a starting point for revising the job description.

Workflow Analysis Reviewing the organization chart, process chart, and job description helps the manager identify what a job's duties and demands are now. However, it does *not* answer questions like "Does how this job relates to other jobs make sense?" or "Should this job even exist?" To answer such questions, the manager may conduct a *workflow analysis*. **Workflow analysis** is a detailed study of the flow of work from job to job in one identifiable work process (such as processing a mortgage application). In turn, this analysis may lead to changing or "reengineering" the job. The accompanying HR as a Profit Center feature illustrates workflow analysis.

workflow analysis
A detailed study of the flow of work from job to job in a work process.

IMPROVING PEFORMANCE: *HR as a Profit Center*

BOOSTING PRODUCTIVITY THROUGH WORK REDESIGN

The Atlantic American insurance company in Atlanta conducted a workflow analysis to identify inefficiencies in how it processes its insurance claims. As the firm's HR director said, "We followed the life of a claim to where it arrived in the mail and where it eventually ended up" in order to find ways to improve the process.[9]

The workflow analysis prompted several performance-boosting redesigns of the insurance claim jobs. The firm reduced from four to one the number of people opening mail, replacing three people with a machine that does it automatically. A new date stamping machine lets staff stamp 20 pages at a time rather than 1. A new software program adds bar codes to each claim automatically, rather than manually. The new system lowered costs. ■

Source: Based on Ron Miller, "Streamlining Claims Processing," eWeek 23, no. 25 (June 19, 2006), pp. 33, 35.

If your professor has assigned this, go to the Assignments section of **mymanagementlab.com** to complete these discussion questions.

Talk About It 1: Based on your experience, what would the workflow look like for the process a dry-cleaning store uses to accept and chronicle a new order of clothes from a customer? How might this process be improved?

In conducting a workflow analysis, the manager may use a *flow process chart*; this lists in order each step of the process. The manager may convert this step-by-step flow process chart into a diagrammatic process chart. This shows, with arrows and circles, each step in the process.

business process reengineering
Redesigning business processes, usually by combining steps, so that small multifunction process teams using information technology do the jobs formerly done by a sequence of departments.

Business Process Reengineering The workflow analysis at American Atlantic led to a *reengineering* of its claims processing operation. **Business process reengineering**

means redesigning business processes, usually by combining steps, so that small multifunction teams, often using information technology, do the jobs formerly done by a sequence of departments. The basic reengineering approach is to

1. Identify a business process to be redesigned (such as processing an insurance claim)
2. Measure the performance of the existing processes
3. Identify opportunities to improve these processes
4. Redesign and implement a new way of doing the work
5. Assign ownership of sets of formerly separate tasks to an individual or a team who use new computerized systems to support the new arrangement

As at Atlantic American, reengineering usually requires redesigning individual jobs. For example, workers doing date stamping must now know how to use the new date-stamping machine.

Job Redesign Early economists enthusiastically described why specialized jobs were more efficient (as in, "practice makes perfect"). Today, most agree that specialized jobs can backfire, for instance by sapping morale. Experts typically suggest three ways to redesign specialized jobs to make them more challenging. **Job enlargement** means assigning workers additional same-level activities. Thus, the worker who previously only bolted the seat to the legs might attach the back too. **Job rotation** means systematically moving workers from one job to another.

job enlargement
Assigning workers additional same-level activities.

job rotation
Systematically moving workers from one job to another.

Psychologist Frederick Herzberg argued that the best way to motivate workers is through what he called job enrichment. **Job enrichment** means redesigning jobs in a way that increases the opportunities for the worker to experience feelings of responsibility, achievement, growth, and recognition—and therefore more motivation. It does this by *empowering* the worker—for instance, by giving the worker the skills and authority to inspect the work, instead of having supervisors do that. Herzberg said empowered employees would do their jobs well because they wanted to, and quality and productivity would rise. That philosophy, in one form or another, is the theoretical basis for the team-based self-managing jobs in many companies around the world today.

job enrichment
Redesigning jobs in a way that increases the opportunities for the worker to experience feelings of responsibility, achievement, growth, and recognition.

Step 3: Select Representative Positions With a job to analyze, the manager then generally selects a sample of positions to focus on. For example, to analyze an assembler's job, it is usually unnecessary to analyze the jobs of all the firm's 200 assembly workers; instead a sample of 10 jobs will do.

Step 4: Actually Analyze the Job In brief, the actual job analysis involves greeting each job holder; briefly explaining the job analysis process and the participants' roles in this process; spending about 15 minutes interviewing the employee to get agreement on a basic summary of the job; identifying the job's broad areas of responsibility, such as "calling on potential clients"; and then interactively identifying specific duties/tasks within each area using one of the methods we describe just below.[10]

Step 5: Verify the Job Analysis Information with the Worker Performing the Job and with His or Her Immediate Supervisor This will help confirm that the information (for instance, on the job's duties) is factually correct and complete and help to gain their acceptance.

Step 6: Develop a Job Description and Job Specification The *job description* lists the duties, activities, and responsibilities of the job, as well as its important features, such as working conditions. The *job specification* summarizes the personal qualities, traits, skills, and background required for getting the job done.

Methods for Collecting Job Analysis Information

LEARNING OBJECTIVE 4-3
Explain how to use at least three methods of collecting job analysis information, including interviews, questionnaires, and observation.

There are many ways (interviews, or questionnaires, for instance) to collect job information. The basic rule is to use those that best fit your purpose. Thus an interview might be best for creating a list of job duties. The more quantitative "position analysis questionnaire" method may be best for quantifying each job's worth for pay purposes. Before actually analyzing the job, keep several things in mind.

LEARNING OBJECTIVES

3-1 Explain with examples each of the seven steps in the strategic management process.

3-2 List with examples the main types of strategies.

3-3 Define *strategic human resource management* and give an example of strategic human resource management in practice.

3-4 Give at least five examples of HR metrics.

3-5 Give five examples of what employers can do to have high-performance systems.

3-6 Describe how you would execute a program to improve employee engagement.

When the Ritz-Carlton Company took over managing the Portman Hotel in Shanghai, China, the hotel already had a good reputation among business travelers. However, many luxury hotels were opening there. To stay competitive, the Portman's new managers decided to reposition the hotel with a new strategy, one that emphasized outstanding customer service. But they knew that improving the service would require new employee behaviors, and therefore new selection, training, and pay policies and practices. We will see what they did.

WHERE ARE WE NOW ...

The next part of this book, Part 2, turns to the nuts and bolts of human resource management, including activities like analyzing jobs and recruiting and selecting employees. Ideally, activities like these should produce the employee behaviors and competencies the firm needs to achieve its strategic goals. Therefore, the main purpose of the present chapter is to explain how managers formulate human resource strategies for their companies. We'll address the strategic management process, types of strategies, strategic human resource management, HR metrics and benchmarking, high-performance work systems, and employee engagement. We'll turn in the following chapter to how to analyze jobs and recruit employees.

The Strategic Management Process

LEARNING OBJECTIVE 3-1
Explain with examples each of the seven steps in the strategic management process.

Employers can't intelligently design their human resource policies and practices without understanding the role these policies and practices are to play in achieving their companies' strategic goals. In this chapter, we look at how managers design strategic and human resource plans, and how they evaluate the results of their plans. We start with an overview of the basic management planning process.

The Management Planning Process

The basic management planning process consists of five steps: setting objectives, making basic planning forecasts, reviewing alternative courses of action, evaluating which options are best, and then choosing and implementing your plan. A *plan* shows the course of action for getting from where you are to the goal. *Planning* is always "goal-directed" (such as, "double sales revenue to $16 million in fiscal year 2017").

In companies, it is traditional to view the goals from the top of the firm down to front-line employees as a chain or *hierarchy of goals*. Figure 3-1 illustrates this. At the top, the president sets long-term or "strategic" goals (such as "double sales revenue to $16 million in fiscal year 2017"). His or her vice presidents then set goals for their units that flow from, and make sense in terms of accomplishing, the president's goal (see Figure 3-1). Then their own subordinates set goals, and so on down the chain.[1]

KNOWLEDGE BASE

Policies and procedures provide day-to-day guidance employees need to do their jobs in a manner that is consistent with the company's plans and goals. Policies set broad guidelines delineating how employees should act. For example, "It is the policy of this company to comply with all laws, regulations, and principles of ethical conduct." *Procedures* spell out what to do if a specific situation arises. For example,

> Any employee who believes this policy has been violated must report this belief to the employee's immediate supervisor. If that is not practical, the employee should file a written report with the Director of Human Resources. There is to be no retaliation in any form.[2]

Employers write their own policies and procedures, or adapt ones from existing sources (or both). For example, most employers have employee manuals listing the company's human resource policies and procedures. A Google search would produce many vendors of such policies and procedures.[3] They offer prepackaged HR policies manuals covering appraisal, compensation, equal employment compliance, and other policies and procedures.

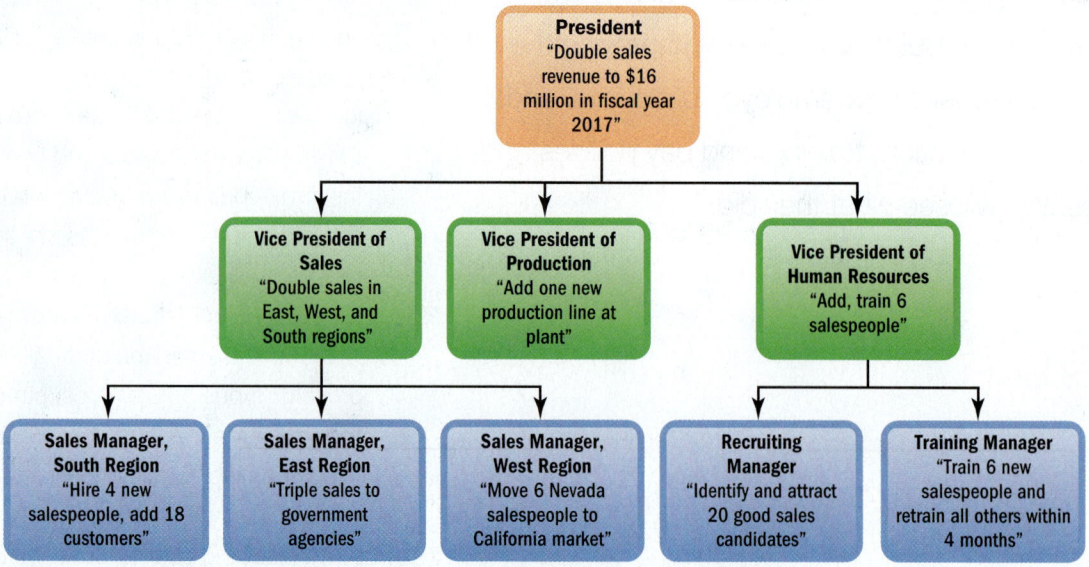

FIGURE 3-1 Sample Hierarchy of Goals Diagram for a Company

What Is Strategic Planning?

strategic plan
The company's plan for how it will match its internal strengths and weaknesses with external opportunities and threats in order to maintain a competitive advantage.

As noted, the company's hierarchy or chain of goals flows from top management's overall strategic plan for the company. A **strategic plan** is the company's overall plan for how it will match its internal strengths and weaknesses with its external opportunities and threats in order to maintain a competitive position. The strategic planner asks, "Where are we now as a business, and where do we want to be?" He or she then formulates a strategic plan to help guide the company to the desired destination.[4] When Yahoo! tries to figure out whether to sell its search business to concentrate on offering more content, or when Apple branches out into selling watches, they are engaged in strategic planning.

Strategic plans are similar to but not the same as *business models*. Those investing in a business will ask top management, "What's your business model?" A business model "is a company's method for making money in the current business environment." It pinpoints whom the company serves, what products or services it provides, what differentiates it, its competitive advantage, how it provides its product or service, and, most importantly, how it makes money.[5] For example, Google doesn't make money by requiring people to pay for searches; it makes money by offering targeted paid advertisements based on what you're searching for.

strategy
A course of action the company can pursue to achieve its strategic aims.

A **strategy** is a course of action. Both PepsiCo and Coca-Cola face the same basic problem—people are drinking fewer sugared drinks. However, they each chose different strategies to deal with this. PepsiCo *diversified* by selling more food items like chips. Coca-Cola *concentrated* on sweet beverages, and on boosting advertising to (hopefully) boost Coke sales.

strategic management
The process of identifying and executing the organization's strategic plan by matching the company's capabilities with the demands of its environment.

Finally, **strategic management** is the process of identifying and executing the organization's strategic plan by matching the company's capabilities (strengths and weaknesses) with the demands of its environment (its competitors, customers, and suppliers, for instance).

The Strategic Management Process

Figure 3-2 summarizes the strategic management process. Its seven steps include (1) ask, "What business are we in now?" (2) evaluate the firm's internal and external strengths, weaknesses, opportunities, and threats, (3) formulate a new business direction, (4) decide on strategic goals, and (5) choose specific strategies or courses of action. Steps (6) and (7) are to implement and then evaluate the strategic plan.

The strategic management process begins (step 1) by asking, "What business are we in?" Here the manager defines the company's current business. Specifically, "What products do we sell, where do we sell them, and how do our products or services differ from our competitors'?" For example, the Coca-Cola Company sells mostly sweetened beverages such as Coke and Sprite, while PepsiCo sells drinks but also foods such as Quaker Oats and Frito chips.

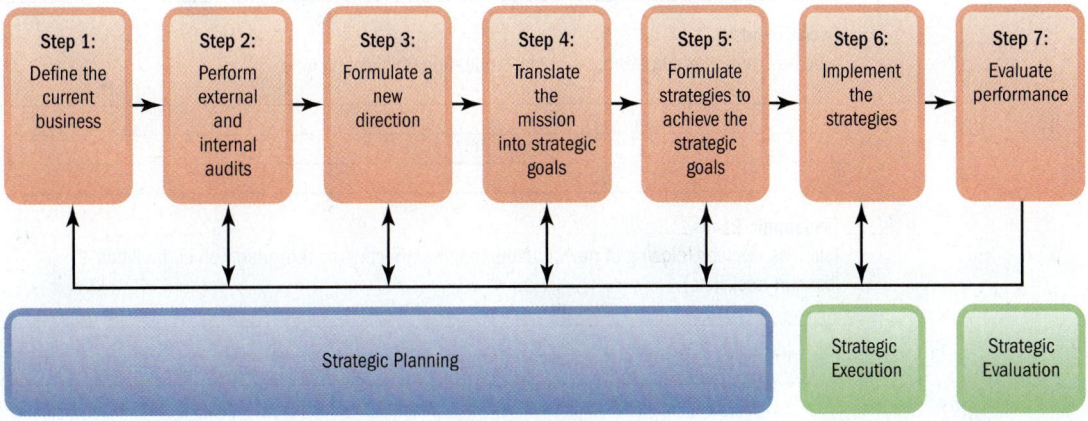

FIGURE 3-2 **The Strategic Management Process**

The second step is to ask, "*Are we in the right business* given our strengths and weaknesses and the challenges that we face?" To answer this, managers "audit" or study both the firm's environment and the firm's internal strengths and weaknesses. The *environmental scan worksheet* in Figure 3-3 is a guide for compiling information about the company's environment. As you can see, this includes the economic, competitive, and political trends that may affect the company. The *SWOT chart* in Figure 3-4 is widely used. Managers use it to compile and organize the company strengths, weaknesses, opportunities, and threats. This audit may also include analyzing the so-called PEST factors. These include Political factors such as government regulations and employment laws; Economic factors including unemployment and economic growth; Social factors such as changing demographics and health consciousness trends; and Technological factors such as use of social media and digitalization and of self-driving vehicles. In any case, the manager's aim is to create a strategic plan that makes sense in terms of the company's strengths, weaknesses, opportunities, and threats.

FIGURE 3-3 Worksheet for Environmental Scanning

Economic Trends
(such as recession, inflation, employment, monetary policies)

_____
_____
_____
_____

Competitive and Market Trends
(such as market/customer trends, entry/exit of competitors, new products from competitors)

_____
_____
_____
_____

Political Trends
(such as legislation and regulation/deregulation)

_____
_____
_____
_____

Technological Trends
(such as introduction of new production/distribution technologies, rate of product obsolescence, trends in availability of supplies and raw materials)

_____
_____
_____
_____

Social Trends
(such as demographic trends, mobility, education, evolving values)

_____
_____
_____
_____

Geographic Trends
(such as opening/closing of new markets, factors affecting current plant/office facilities location decisions)

_____
_____
_____
_____

FIGURE 3-4 SWOT Matrix, with Generic Examples

Potential Strengths

- Market leadership
- Strong research and development
- High-quality products
- Cost advantages
- Patents

Potential Weaknesses

- Large inventories
- Excess capacity for market
- Management turnover
- Weak market image
- Lack of management depth

Potential Opportunities

- New overseas markets
- Failing trade barriers
- Competitors failing
- Diversification
- Economy rebounding

Potential Threats

- Market saturation
- Threat of takeover
- Low-cost foreign competition
- Slower market growth
- Growing government regulation

Next, based on this analysis (in other words, on the environmental scan, SWOT, and PEST analyses), the task in step 3 will be to decide *what should our new business be*, in terms of what we sell, where we will sell it, and how our products or services differ from competitors' products and services? Some managers express the essence of their new business with a *vision statement*. A **vision statement** is a general statement of the firm's intended direction; it shows, in broad terms, "what we want to become."[6] PepsiCo's vision is "Performance with Purpose." CEO Indra Nooyi says her company's executives choose which businesses to be in based on Performance with Purpose's focus on human sustainability, environmental sustainability, and talent sustainability.[7] For example, that vision prompted PepsiCo to add the healthy Quaker Oats and Gatorade to its lineup of products.

vision statement
A general statement of the firm's intended direction; it shows, in broad terms, "what we want to become."

Whereas the vision statement describes in broad terms what the business should be, the company's **mission statement** summarizes what the company's main tasks are today. Several years ago, Ford adopted what was for several years a powerful Ford mission statement—making "Quality Job One."

mission statement
Summarizes the answer to the question, "What business are we in?"

In any case, the manager's next step (step 4) is to translate the desired new direction into *strategic goals*. At Ford, for example, what exactly did making "Quality Job One" mean for each department in terms of how they would boost quality? The answer was laid out in goals such as "no more than 1 initial defect per 10,000 cars."

Next, (step 5) the manager *chooses strategies*—courses of action—that will enable the company to achieve its strategic goals. For example, how should Ford pursue its goal of no more than 1 initial defect per 10,000 cars? Perhaps open two new high-tech plants, and put in place new, rigorous employee selection, training, and performance-appraisal procedures.

Step 6, *strategy execution,* means translating the strategies into action. This means actually hiring (or firing) people, building (or closing) plants, and adding (or eliminating) products and product lines.

Finally, in step 7, the manager *evaluates* the results of his or her planning and execution. Things don't always turn out as planned. All managers should periodically assess the progress of their strategic decisions.

Types of Strategies

LEARNING OBJECTIVE 3-2
List with examples the main types of strategies.

In practice, managers engage in three types or levels of strategic planning, *corporate-level* strategic planning, *business unit* (or *competitive*) strategic planning, and *functional* (or *departmental*) strategic planning (see Figure 3-5, page 72).

Corporate Strategy

corporate-level strategy
Type of strategy that identifies the portfolio of businesses that, in total, comprise the company and the ways in which these businesses relate to each other.

For any business, the corporate strategy answers the question, "What businesses will we be in?" Specifically, the **corporate-level strategy** identifies the portfolio of

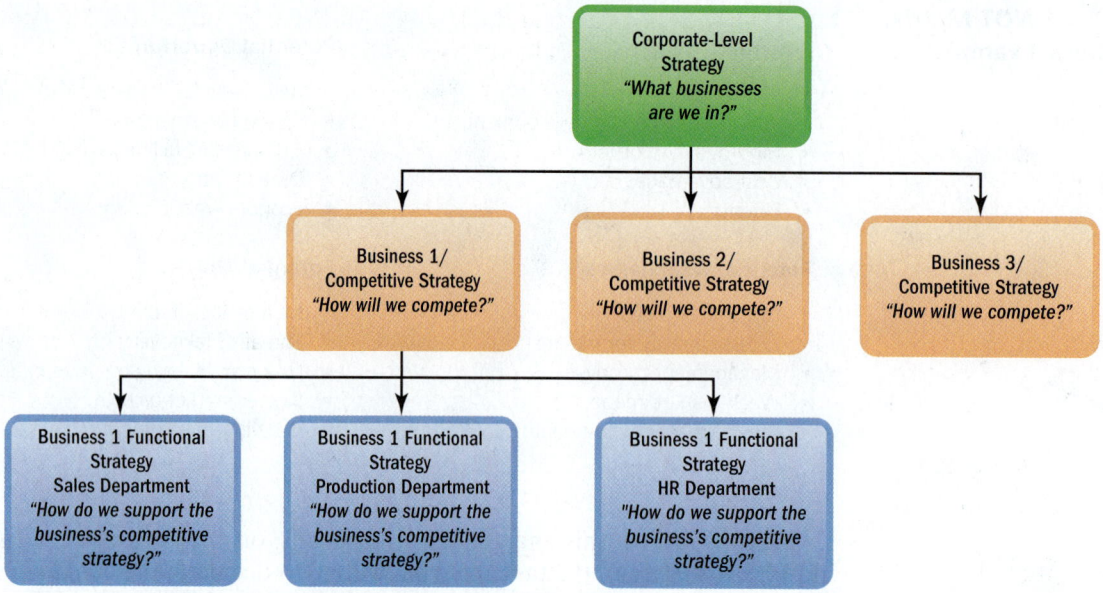

FIGURE 3-5 Type of Strategy at Each Company Level

businesses that, in total, comprise the company and how these businesses relate to each other. For example, with a *concentration* (single-business) corporate strategy, the company offers one product or product line, usually in one market. WD-40 Company is one example. With one spray lubricant its product scope is narrow. A *diversification* corporate strategy means the firm will expand by adding new product lines. PepsiCo is diversified. Thus, PepsiCo added Frito-Lay chips and Quaker Oats to its drinks businesses. Here product scope is wider. A *vertical integration* strategy means the firm expands by, perhaps, producing its own raw materials, or selling its products directly. Thus, Apple opened its own Apple stores. With a *consolidation* strategy, the company reduces its size. With *geographic expansion*, the company grows by entering new territorial markets, for instance, by taking the business abroad.

Competitive Strategy

On what basis will each of our businesses compete? Within a company like PepsiCo, each business unit (such as Pepsi and Frito-Lay) needs a *business-level competitive strategy.* A **competitive strategy** identifies how to build and strengthen the business unit's long-term competitive position in the marketplace.[8] It shows, for instance, how Pizza Hut will compete with Papa John's, or how Walmart will compete with Target.

competitive strategy
A strategy that identifies how to build and strengthen the business's long-term competitive position in the marketplace.

Managers build their competitive strategies around their businesses' competitive advantages. **Competitive advantage** means any factors that allow a company to differentiate its product or service from those of its competitors to increase market share. Coca-Cola has a "secret formula" that shows how to create its famous beverage. However, competitive advantages needn't be tangible. For example, here is how a former vice president of human resources at the Toyota Motor Manufacturing facility in Georgetown, Kentucky, described the importance of human capital as a competitive advantage:

competitive advantage
Any factors that allow an organization to differentiate its product or service from those of its competitors to increase market share.

> People are behind our success. Machines don't have new ideas, solve problems, or grasp opportunities. Only people who are involved in thinking can make a difference . . . Every auto plant in the United States has basically the same machinery. But how people are utilized and involved varies widely from one company to another. The workforce gives any company its true competitive edge.[9]

Managers typically adopt one or more of three standard competitive strategies—cost leadership, differentiation, or focus—to achieve competitive advantage. *Cost leadership* means becoming the low-cost leader in an industry. Walmart is an example. With *differentiation,* the firm seeks to be unique in its industry along dimensions that are widely valued by buyers.[10] Thus, Volvo stresses the safety of its cars, and Papa John's stresses fresh ingredients. *Focusers* carve out a market niche (like Bugatti cars). They offer a product or service that their customers cannot get from generalist competitors (such as Toyota).

Functional Strategy

functional strategy
A strategy that identifies the broad activities that each department will pursue in order to help the business accomplish its competitive goals.

Each department should operate within the framework of its business's competitive strategy. **Functional strategies** identify what each department must do to help the business accomplish its strategic goals. Thus, for, say, P&G to make its Oil of Olay products a top-tier brand, its product development, production, marketing, sales, and human resource departments must engage in activities that are consistent with this unit's high-quality mission. Inferior products, cheap packaging, or sloppy salespeople would not do.

Managers' Roles in Strategic Planning

Devising the company's overall strategic plan is top management's responsibility. However, few top executives formulate strategic plans without lower-level managers' input. No one knows more about the firm's competitive pressures, product and industry trends, and employee capabilities than do the company's department managers.

For example, the human resource manager is in a good position to supply "competitive intelligence"—information on competitors. Details regarding competitors' incentive plans, employee opinion surveys about customer complaints, and information about pending legislation such as labor laws are examples. Human resource managers should also be the masters of information about their own firms' employees' strengths and weaknesses.

In practice, devising the firm's overall strategic plan involves frequent discussions among and between top and lower-level managers. The top managers then use this information to hammer out their strategic plan.

EXAMPLE: IMPROVING MERGERS AND ACQUISITIONS Mergers and acquisitions (M&A) are among the most important strategic decisions companies make. When mergers and acquisitions fail, it's often not due to financial issues but to personnel-related ones, such as employee resistance.[11] Prudent top managers therefore tap their human resource managers' input early in the merger process.

Critical human resource M&A tasks include choosing top management, communicating changes to employees, merging the firms' cultures, and retaining key talent.[12] Human resource consulting companies such as Towers Watson assist firms with merger-related human resource management services. For example, they identify potential pension shortfalls, identify key talent and suitable retention strategies, help clients combine payroll systems, and help determine which employee is best for which role in the new organization.[13]

Strategic Human Resource Management

LEARNING OBJECTIVE 3-3
Define *strategic human resource management* and give an example of strategic human resource management in practice.

The company's top managers choose overall corporate strategies, and then choose competitive strategies for each of the company's businesses. Then departmental managers within each of these businesses formulate functional strategies for their departments. Their aim should be to have functional strategies that will support the competitive strategy and the company-wide strategic aims. The marketing department would have marketing strategies. The production department would have production strategies. The human resource management ("HR") department would have *human resource management strategies*.

HR in Practice at the Hotel Paris Starting as a single hotel in a Paris suburb in 1990, the Hotel Paris is now a chain of nine hotels, with two in France, one each in London and Rome, and others in New York, Miami, Washington, Chicago, and Los Angeles. To see how managers use strategic human resource management to improve performance, see the Hotel Paris Case on pages 90–91 and answer the questions.

What Is Strategic Human Resource Management?

Every company's human resource management policies and activities should make sense in terms of the firm's strategic aims. For example, a high-end retailer like Neiman-Marcus will have different employee selection, training, and pay policies than will Walmart. **Strategic human resource management** means formulating and executing human resource policies and practices that produce the employee competencies and behaviors the company needs to achieve its strategic aims. The following Strategic Context feature illustrates.

strategic human resource management
Formulating and executing human resource policies and practices that produce the employee competencies and behaviors the company needs to achieve its strategic aims.

IMPROVING PERFORMANCE: *The Strategic Context*

The Shanghai Ritz-Carlton Portman Hotel

When the Ritz-Carlton Company took over managing the Portman Hotel in Shanghai, China, the new management reviewed the Portman's strengths and weaknesses, and its fast-improving local competitors. They decided that to compete, they had to improve the hotel's level of service. Achieving that in turn meant formulating new human resource management plans for hiring, training, and rewarding hotel employees. It meant putting in place a new human resource strategy for the Portman Hotel, one aimed at improving customer service. Their HR strategy involved taking these steps:

- *Strategically*, they set the goal of making the Shanghai Portman outstanding by offering superior customer service.
- To achieve this, Shanghai Portman employees would have to exhibit new *skills and behaviors*, for instance, in terms of how they treated and responded to guests.
- To produce these employee skills and behaviors, management formulated new human resource management *plans, policies, and procedures*. For example, they introduced the Ritz-Carlton Company's *human resource system* to the Portman: "Our selection [now] focuses on talent and personal values because these are things that can't be taught … it's about caring for and respecting others."[14]

Management's efforts paid off. Their new human resource plans and practices helped to produce the employee behaviors required to improve the Portman's level of service, thus attracting new guests. Travel publications were soon calling it the "best employer in Asia," "overall best business hotel in Asia," and "best business hotel in China." Profits soared, in no small part due to effective strategic human resource management. ■

If your professor has assigned this, go to the Assignments section of **mymanagementlab.com** to complete this discussion question.

✪ **Talk About It 1:** Asian culture is different from that in the United States. For example, team incentives tend to be more attractive to people in Asia than are individual incentives. How do you think these cultural differences would have affected how the hotel's new management selected, trained, appraised, and compensated the Shanghai Portman's employees?

The basic idea of strategic human resource management is this: In formulating human resource management policies and activities, the manager should aim to formulate policies that produce the employee skills and behaviors that the company needs to achieve its strategic goals.

Figure 3-6 outlines this idea. First, the manager formulates *strategic plans* and goals. Next, he or she asks, "What *employee skills and behaviors* will we need to achieve these plans and goals?" And finally, he or she asks, "Specifically what recruitment, selection, training, and other *HR policies and practices* should we put in place so as to produce the required employee skills and behaviors?" Managers often refer to their specific HR policies and practices as *human resource strategies*.[15] The accompanying HR as a Profit Center feature presents another strategic human resource management example.

IMPROVING PERFORMANCE: *HR As a Profit Center*

The Zappos "WOW" Way

When your strategy involves selling shoes and clothes online to people who can't try them on, you need employees who are energized and enjoy what they're doing—Zappos wants employees to deliver "WOW" through service.[16] That's why Zappos' founders knew they needed special methods for hiring, developing, and retaining employees, and that's just what they created. As their website says, "This ain't your mama's HR! Recruiting, benefits, and employee relations keep this cruise ship afloat with fun, inventive ways of getting employees motivated and educated about the Zappos Family of companies, their benefits, and the other fun stuff going on around here!"[17]

While they may not appeal to everyone, these "fun, inventive techniques" include interviewing job applicants in what looks like the set of a talk show, asking employees to submit their own designs for Steve Madden shoes, and (during Zappos' annual "Bald & Blue Day") having some employees volunteer to shave their heads or dye their hair blue.[18] And, by the way, if you're not happy working at Zappos, the company will pay you to leave—it wants no one there who doesn't truly want to be there.

Again, that may not be for everyone, but it works for Zappos. It knows that selling online successfully requires energized employees who really enjoy what they're doing. Management uses these special HR practices to cultivate the energized and fun environment that Zappos needs to execute its strategy, and judging from Zappos' success they seem to be working. ■

If your professor has assigned this, go to the Assignments section of **mymanagementlab.com** to complete this discussion question.

✪ **Talk About It 2:** Why do you think Zappos' top managers believe it is so important for employees to provide a "WOW" factor in their business?

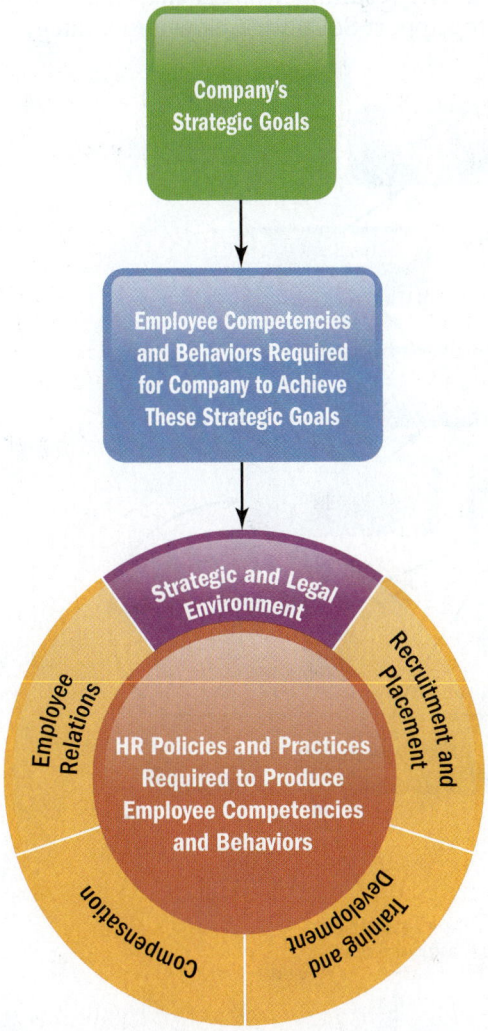

FIGURE 3-6 The HR Strategy Model

Note: This figure opens each chapter of this book and says this: The company's HR policies and practices should produce the employee competencies and behaviors that the company needs to achieve its strategic goals.

✪ **Watch It!**

How does a company actually go about developing a human resource strategy? If your professor has assigned this, go to the Assignments section of **mymanagmentlab.com** to complete the video exercise titled *Strategic Management (Joie de Vivre Hospitality)*.

Sustainability and Strategic Human Resource Management

Today's emphasis on *sustainability* has important consequences for human resource management. *Strategic human resource management* means having human resource policies and practices that produce the employee skills and behaviors that are necessary to achieve the company's strategic goals, and these include sustainability goals.

For example, PepsiCo wants to deliver "Performance with Purpose." This means achieving financial performance while also achieving human sustainability, environmental sustainability, and talent sustainability.[19] PepsiCo's human resource managers can help the company achieve these goals.[20] For example, they can use its *workforce planning* processes to help determine how many and what sorts of environmental sustainability ("green") jobs the company will need to recruit for. They can work with top management to institute *flexible work arrangements* that help sustain the environment by reducing commuting. They can change its employee *orientation* process to include more emphasis on socializing new employees into PepsiCo's sustainability goals. They can modify its *performance appraisal* systems to measure which managers and employees are successful in reaching their individual sustainability goals. They can use *incentive systems* that motivate employees to achieve PepsiCo's sustainability goals.[21] The bottom line is that HR policies and practices can support a firm's sustainability strategy and goals.

Strategic Human Resource Management Tools

Managers use several tools to translate the company's strategic goals into human resource management policies and practices. These tools include the strategy map, the HR scorecard, and the digital dashboard.

strategy map
A strategic planning tool that shows the "big picture" of how each department's performance contributes to achieving the company's overall strategic goals.

STRATEGY MAP The **strategy map** summarizes how each department's performance contributes to achieving the company's overall strategic goals. It helps the manager and each employee visualize and understand the role his or her department plays in achieving the company's strategic plan. Management gurus sometimes say that the map clarifies employees' "line of sight." It does this by visually linking their efforts with the company's ultimate goals.[22]

Figure 3-7 presents a strategy-map example for Southwest Airlines. The top-level target is to achieve its profitability, costs, and revenue goals. Then the strategy map shows the chain of activities that help Southwest Airlines achieve these goals. Like Walmart, Southwest has a low-cost-leader strategy. So, for example, to boost revenues and profitability Southwest must fly fewer planes (to keep costs down), maintain low prices, and maintain on-time flights. In turn (further down the strategy map), on-time flights and low prices require fast turnaround. This, in turn, requires motivated ground and flight crews. The resulting strategy map helps each department understand what it needs to do to support Southwest's low-cost strategy.[23]

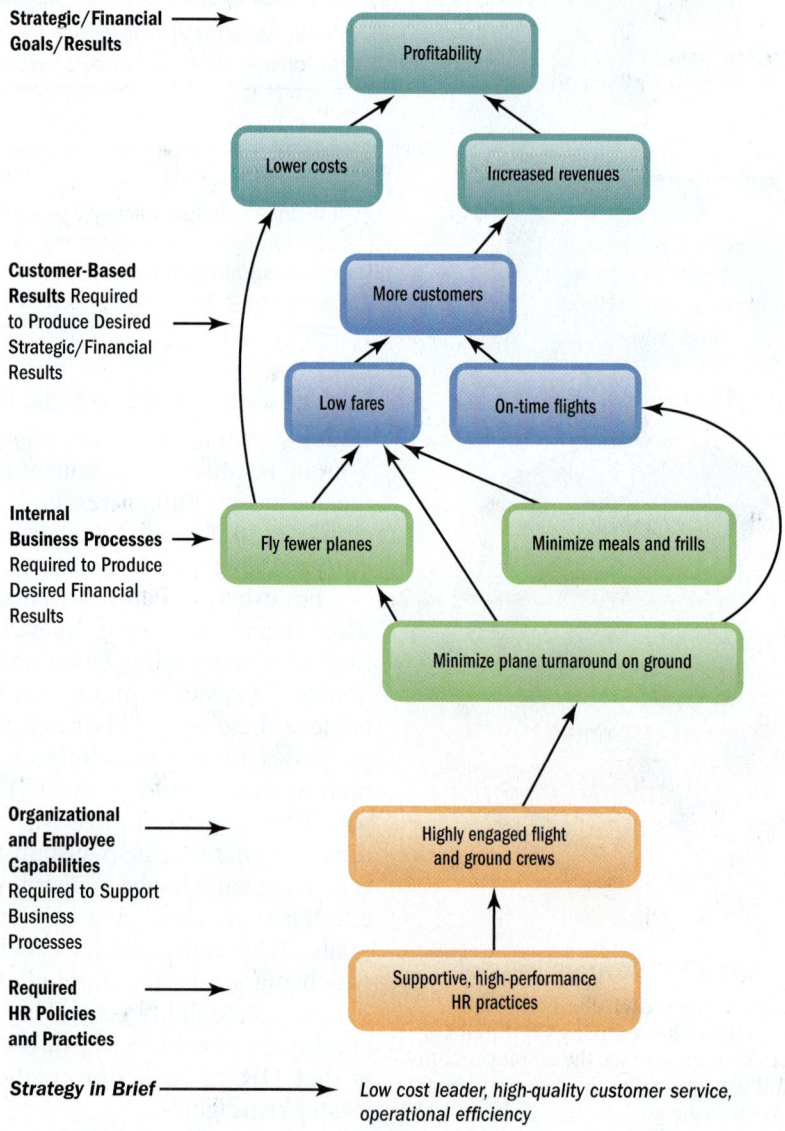

FIGURE 3-7 Strategy Map for Southwest Airlines

Source: Based on TeamCHRYSALIS.com, accessed July 2006; http://mcknightkaney.com/Strategy_Maps_Primer.html; www.strategymap.com.au/home/StrategyMapOverview.html.

For example, what steps must Southwest's human resource team take to boost the motivation and dedication of its ground crews?

HR scorecard
A process for assigning financial and nonfinancial goals or metrics to the human resource management–related chain of activities required for achieving the company's strategic aims and for monitoring results.

THE HR SCORECARD Many employers quantify and computerize the strategy map's activities. The HR scorecard helps them to do so. The **HR scorecard** is not a scorecard. It refers to a process for assigning financial and nonfinancial goals or metrics to the human resource management–related strategy-map chain of activities required for achieving the company's strategic aims.[24] (Metrics for Southwest might include airplane turnaround time, percent of on-time flights, and ground crew productivity.) The idea is to take the strategy map and to quantify it.

Managers use special scorecard software to facilitate this. The computerized scorecard process helps the manager quantify the relationships between (1) the HR activities (amount of testing, training, and so forth), (2) the resulting employee behaviors (customer service, for instance), and (3) the resulting firm-wide strategic outcomes and performance (such as customer satisfaction and profitability).[25] The HR scorecard derives from the "balanced scorecard" planning approach, which aims to balance hard data such as financial measures with soft data such as customer satisfaction in assessing a company's performance.

digital dashboard
Presents the manager with desktop graphs and charts, and so a computerized picture of where the company stands on all those metrics from the HR scorecard process.

DIGITAL DASHBOARDS The saying "a picture is worth a thousand words" explains the purpose of the digital dashboard. A **digital dashboard** presents the manager with desktop graphs and charts, showing a computerized picture of how the company is doing on all the metrics from the HR scorecard process. As in the accompanying illustration, a top Southwest Airlines manager's dashboard might display real-time trends for various strategy-map activities, such as fast turnarounds and on-time flights. This enables the manager to take corrective action. For example, if ground crews are turning planes around slower today, financial results tomorrow may decline unless the manager takes action.

Figure 3-8 summarizes the three strategic planning tools.

A digital dashboard presents the manager with desktop graphs and charts, showing a computerized picture of how the company is doing on all the metrics from the HR scorecard process.

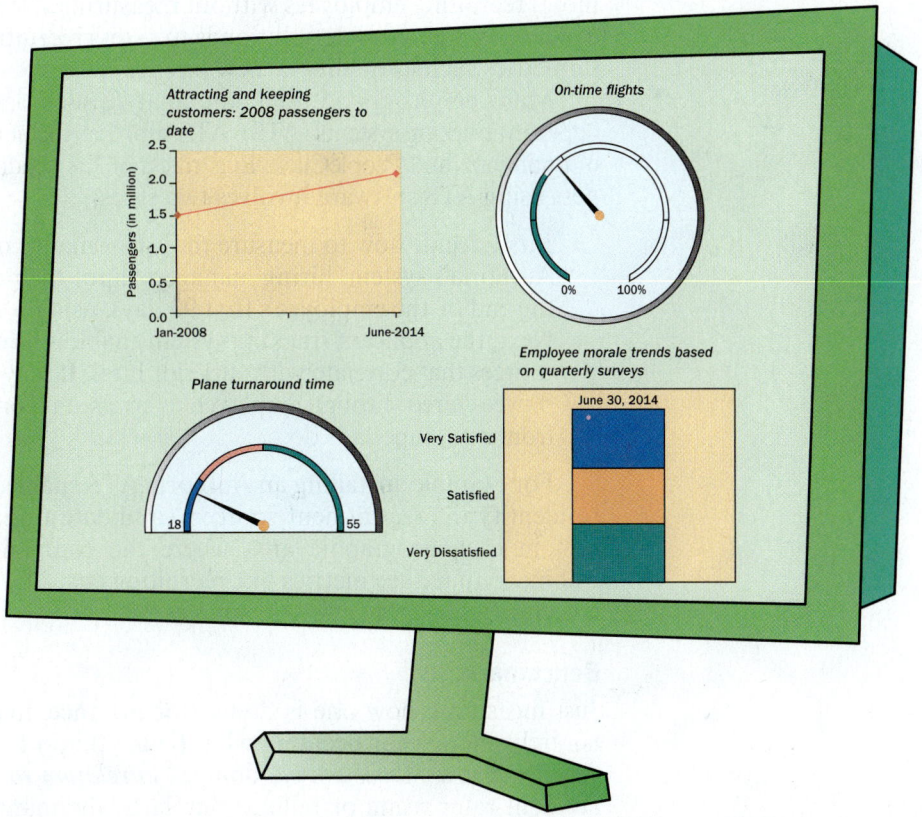

Strategy Map
Graphical tool that summarizes the chain of activities that contribute to a company's success, and so shows employees the "big picture" of how their performance contributes to achieving the company's overall strategic goals.

HR Scorecard
A process for assigning financial and nonfinancial goals or metrics to the human resource management–related chain of activities required for achieving the company's strategic aims and for monitoring results.

Digital Dashboard
Presents the manager with desktop graphs and charts, so he or she gets a picture of where the company has been and where it's going, in terms of each activity in the strategy map.

FIGURE 3-8 Three Important Strategic HR Tools

HR Metrics, Benchmarking, and Data Analytics

LEARNING OBJECTIVE 3-4
Give at least five examples of HR metrics.

We've seen that strategic human resource management means formulating HR policies and practices that produce the employee competencies and behaviors the company needs to achieve its strategic goals. Being able to measure results is essential to this process. For example, it would have been futile for the Ritz-Carlton Portman Shanghai's managers to set "better customer service" as a goal if they couldn't measure customer service.[26] Relevant measures might include, for instance, hours of training per employee, productivity per employee, and (via customer surveys) customer satisfaction.

human resource metrics
The quantitative gauge of a human resource management activity, such as employee turnover, hours of training per employee, or qualified applicants per position.

Human resource managers use many such measures (or "**human resource metrics**"). For example, there is (on average) one human resource employee per 100 company employees for firms with 100–249 employees. The HR employee-to-employee ratio drops to about 0.79 for firms with 1,000–2,499 employees and to 0.72 for firms with more than 7,500 employees.[27] Figure 3-9 illustrates other human resource management metrics. They include employee tenure, cost per hire, and annual overall turnover rate.[28]

Improving Performance Through HRIS: Tracking Applicant Metrics for Improved Talent Management

As an example of using metrics, many employers spend thousands of dollars (or more) recruiting employees without measuring which hiring source produces the best candidates. The sensible solution is to assess recruitment effectiveness using measures or metrics such as quality of new hires.[29]

Many employers do track and analyze such data with the help of computerized applicant tracking systems (ATS). ATS suppliers include Authoria, PeopleFilter, Wonderlic, eContinuum, and PeopleClick. Regardless of the vendor, analyzing recruitment effectiveness using ATS software involves two steps:

- First, decide how to measure the performance of new hires. For example, with Authoria's system, hiring managers input their evaluations of each new hire at the end of the employee's first 90 days, using a 1-to-5 scale.[30]
- Next, the applicant tracking system enables the employer to track the recruitment sources that correlate with superior hires. It may show, for instance, that new employees hired through employee referrals stay longer and work better than those from newspaper ads do.

For example, installing an Authoria ATS enabled the Thomson Reuters Company to identify the recruitment sources, candidate traits, and hiring practices that work best in each geographic area where the company does business.[31] This enabled Thomson to reduce metrics like recruiting costs, by shifting recruitment dollars from less effective to more effective sources. ■

Benchmarking

Just measuring how one is doing (for instance, in terms of employee productivity) is rarely enough for deciding what (if anything) to change. Instead, most managers want to know "How are we doing?" *in relation to something*. For example, are our accident rates rising or falling? Similarly, the manager may want to *benchmark* the

Organizational Data

- Revenue
- Revenue per FTE
- Net Income Before Taxes
- Net Income Before Taxes per FTE
- Positions Included Within the Organization's Succession Plan

HR Department Data

- Total HR Staff
- HR-to-Employee Ratio
- Percentage of HR Staff in Supervisory Roles
- Percentage of HR Staff in Professional/Technical Roles
- Percentage of HR Staff in Administrative Support Roles
- Reporting Structure for the Head of HR
- Types of HR Positions Organizations Expect to Hire in 2011

HR Expense Data

- HR Expenses
- HR Expense to Operating Expense Ratio
- HR Expense to FTE Ratio

Compensation Data

- Annual Salary Increase
- Salaries as a Percentage of Operating Expense
- Target Bonus for Non-Executives
- Target Bonus for Executives

Tuition/Education Data

- Maximum Reimbursement Allowed for Tuition/Education Expenses per Year
- Percentage of Employees Participating in Tuition/Education Reimbursement Programs

Employment Data

- Number of Positions Filled
- Time-to-Fill
- Cost-Per-Hire
- Employee Tenure
- Annual Overall Turnover Rate
- Annual Voluntary Turnover Rate
- Annual Involuntary Turnover Rate

Expectations for Revenue and Organizational Hiring

- Percentage of Organizations Expecting Changes in Revenue in 2011 Compared to 2010
- Percentage of Organizations Expecting Changes in Hiring in 2011 Compared to 2010

Metrics for More Profitable Organizations

- Total HR Staff
- HR-to-Employee Ratio
- HR Expenses
- HR Expense to Operating Expense Ratio
- HR Expense to FTE Ratio
- Annual Salary Increase
- Target Bonus for Non-Executives
- Target Bonus for Executives
- Maximum Reimbursement Allowed for Tuition/Education Expenses per year
- Percentage of Employees Participating in Tuition/Education Reimbursement Programs
- Time-to-Fill
- Cost-Per-Hire
- Annual Overall Turnover Rate

FIGURE 3-9 Metrics for the SHRM® 2011–2012 Customized Human Capital Benchmarking Report

Source: Reprinted with permission from the Society for Human Resource Management. All rights reserved.

results—compare high-performing companies' results to your own, to understand what makes them better.[32]

The Society for Human Resource Management's (SHRM's) benchmarking service enables employers to compare their own HR metrics with those of other companies. The employer can request comparable (benchmark) figures not just by industry, but by employer size, company revenue, and geographic region. (See http://shrm.org/research/benchmarks/.)

Figure 3-10 illustrates one of the SHRM's many sets of comparable benchmark measures. It shows how much employers are spending for tuition reimbursement programs.

Strategy and Strategy-Based Metrics

Benchmarking provides one perspective on how your company's human resource management system is performing.[33] It shows how your human resource management system's performance compares to the competition. However, it may *not* reveal the extent to which your firm's HR practices are supporting its strategic goals. For example, if the strategy calls for doubling profits by improving customer service, to what extent are our new training practices helping to improve customer service?

strategy-based metrics
Metrics that specifically focus on measuring the activities that contribute to achieving a company's strategic aims.

Managers use *strategy-based metrics* to answer such questions. **Strategy-based metrics** measure the activities that contribute to achieving a company's strategic aims.[34]

FIGURE 3-10 SHRM Customized Human Capital Benchmarking Report

Source: "HR Expense Data," from *SHRM Customized Human Capital Benchmarking Report*. Reprinted with permission from the Society for Human Resource Management. All rights reserved. www.shrm.org/Research/benchmarks/Documents/sample_humnba_capital_report.pdf.

Tuition/Education Data					
	n	25th Percentile	Median	75th Percentile	Average
Maximum reimbursement allowed for tuition/education expenses per year	32	$1,000	$5,000	$7,500	$6,000
Percentage of employees participating in tuition/education reimbursement programs	32	1.0%	3.0%	5.0%	4.0%

Thus, for the Portman Shanghai, the strategic HR metrics might include 100% employee testing, 80% guest returns, incentive pay as a percent of total salaries, and sales up 50%. If changes in HR practices such as increased training have their intended effects, then strategic metrics like guest returns should also rise.

What Are HR Audits?

Human resource managers often collect data on matters like employee turnover and safety via *human resource audits*. One practitioner calls an **HR audit** "an analysis by which an organization measures where it currently stands and determines what it has to accomplish to improve its HR function."[35] The HR audit generally involves using a checklist to review the company's human resource functions (recruiting, testing, training, and so on), as well as ensuring that the firm is adhering to regulations, laws, and company policies. The HR auditor may first review payroll data, focusing on what and when each employee was paid. He or she will then turn to whether the human resource records are in order (for instance, are medical records kept separate from résumés?). He or she will also review the employer's handbooks and policies, for instance, checking for disability accommodation policies, social media policies, and family and medical leave policies.[36] He or she may also want to benchmark the results to comparable companies'.

HR audit
An analysis by which an organization measures where it currently stands and determines what it has to accomplish to improve its HR functions.

HR audits vary in scope. Typical areas audited include:[37]

1. Roles and headcount (including job descriptions, and employees categorized by exempt/nonexempt and full- or part-time)
2. Compliance with federal, state, and local employment-related legislation
3. Recruitment and selection (including use of selection tools, background checks, and so on)
4. Compensation (policies, incentives, survey procedures, and so on)
5. Employee relations (union agreements, performance management, disciplinary procedures, employee recognition)
6. Mandated benefits (Social Security, unemployment insurance, workers' compensation, and so on)
7. Group benefits (insurance, time off, flexible benefits, and so on)
8. Payroll (such as legal compliance)
9. Documentation and record keeping. For example, do our files include résumés and applications, offer letters, job descriptions, performance evaluations, benefit enrollment forms, payroll change notices, and documentation related to personnel actions such as employee handbook acknowledgments?[38]
10. Training and development (new employee orientation, development, technical and safety, career planning, and so on)
11. Employee communications (employee handbook, newsletter, recognition programs)
12. Termination and transition policies and practices

TRENDS SHAPING HR: *DIGITAL AND SOCIAL MEDIA*

Data like monthly labor costs are interesting but relatively useless until converted to information. Information is data presented in a form that makes it useful for making decisions. For example knowing your cost per hire is interesting. However, presenting cost-per-hire data in a way that shows whether the cost is trending up or down provides information you can use to make decisions. Yet in one study, only 10% of respondents said they use such data to analyze their workplace practices' effectiveness.[39]

But this is changing. *Data analytics* means using statistical and mathematical analysis and algorithms to find relationships and make predictions. For example, when online bookstores use algorithms to predict which books you're most likely to buy based on things like what books you've already bought and similarities between you and other groups, they are using data analytics.[40] Data analytics relies on data mining. Data mining sifts through huge amounts of employee data to identify correlations that employers then use to improve their employee-selection and other practices. *Data mining* is "the set of activities used to find new, hidden, or unexpected patterns in data."[41]

Big data is basically data analytics on steroids. The basic idea (of scientifically analyzing data to find relationships and make predictions) is the same. However, with "big data" the volume, velocity, and variety of data that are analyzed are much greater. In terms of *volume*, for example, Walmart now collects about 2.5 petabytes of data—2.5 million gigabytes—*every hour* from its customer transactions.[42] Similarly, in terms of *velocity*, all these data are being created more or less instantaneously (as at Walmart); that means companies can use them to more quickly to adapt in real time (for instance, to who's buying what products, and therefore how to adjust online promotions). Finally, big data capitalizes on the huge *variety* of data now available. For instance, data come not just from Walmart's transactions but from customers' mobile phones, GPS, and social networks too.

TALENT ANALYTICS Data analytics tools like these enable employers (including Walmart) to analyze together employee data (like employee demographics, training, and performance ratings) from traditional sources such as employee records, as well as data from new sources (like company internal social media sites, GPS tracking, and e-mail activity).[43] Employers then use *talent analytics* (data analytics applied to HR issues) to answer questions that in the past they couldn't answer, or couldn't answer as well. For example, human resource consultant Aon Hewitt has an "analytics engine" that analyzes its client's employee and performance data. Computer dashboards then enable its clients to answer questions such as "Are there potential turnover trends we should further analyze to head off potential problems?" [44] "What factors drive our high-performing salespeople?" And, "what sorts of people are most likely to have accidents and submit claims?"

Talent analytics can produce striking profitability results. For example, Best Buy used talent analytics to discover that a 0.1% increase in employee engagement led to a more than $100,000 rise in a Best Buy store annual operating income.[45] Employers use talent analytics to answer several types of talent management questions.

Human Capital Facts For example, "What are the key indicators of my organization's overall health?" JetBlue found that employee engagement correlated with financial performance.

Analytical HR For example, "Which units, departments, or individuals need attention?" Lockheed Martin collects performance data in order to identify units needing improvement.

Human Capital Investment Analysis For example, "Which actions have the greatest impact on my business?" By monitoring employee satisfaction levels, Cisco was able to improve its employee retention rate from 65% to 85%, saving the company nearly $50 million in recruitment, selection, and training costs. A Google talent analytics team analyzed data on employee backgrounds, capabilities, and performance.[46] It identified factors (such as an employee feeling underutilized) likely to lead to the employee leaving—and thus helped it reduce turnover. Microsoft identified correlations among the schools and companies its employees arrived from and the employees' subsequent performance. This helped it improve its recruitment and selection practices.[47] By gathering thousands of observations across 100 variables about managers, Google identified what traits its best managers shared, including: good coach; empowers and does not micromanage; expresses interest in and concern for team members' success and personal well-being; productive and results-oriented; good communicator; helps with career development; has a clear vision and strategy for the team; and has key technical skills the team needs.[48] ConAgra Foods uses talent analytics to discover relationships among employee demographics, training, and performance and their relationships with various performance indicators.[49] ■

If your professor has assigned this, go to the Assignments section of **mymanagementlab.com** to complete this discussion question.

Talk About It 3: Could Best Buy or some of these other companies have made the same discoveries without using sophisticated computerized tools? How?

Digital tools like talent analytics disrupt how HR departments do things. They require HR managers to be more scientific and analytical. And, they often shift "who does HR" (for instance, Aon Hewitt's digital dashboard shows line managers when there's a turnover problem) *from* the human resource department *to* other departments (such as finance), and sometimes to line managers like the heads of departments.

Digital tools like these also show great promise. In one study, 82% of high-performing organizations gave human resource management leaders such analytical workforce data, compared with 33% of low-performing ones.[50]

TRENDS SHAPING HR: *SCIENCE IN TALENT MANAGEMENT*

Data analytics permits making decisions based on a measurable and objective review of the situation. Managers have a name for this. *Evidence-based human resource management* means using data, facts, analytics, scientific rigor, critical evaluation, and critically evaluated research/case studies to support human resource management proposals, decisions, practices, and conclusions.[51]

You may sense that being evidence based is similar to being scientific, and if so, you are correct. A recent *Harvard Business Review* article even argues that managers must become more scientific and "think like scientists" when making business decisions.[52]

But how can managers think like scientists? Objectivity, experimentation, and prediction are the heart of science. In gathering evidence, scientists (or managers) first need to be *objective*, or there's no way to trust their conclusions. Recently, a medical school disciplined several professors. They had failed to reveal that they were on the payroll of the drug company that supplied the drugs, the results of which the doctors were studying. Who could trust their objectivity or conclusions?

Being scientific also requires *experimentation.* An experiment is a test one sets up in such a way as to ensure that he or she understands the reasons for the results obtained. For example, in their *Harvard Business Review* article, "A Step-by-Step Guide to Smart Business Experiments," the authors argue that if you want to judge a new incentive plan's impact on corporate profits, don't start by implementing the plan with all employees. Instead, implement it with an "experimental" group (which gets the incentive plan) *and* with a "control" group (a group that does *not* get the incentive plan). Doing so will help you gauge if any performance improvement stemmed from the incentive or from some other cause (such as a new company-wide training program).[53] And, it will enable you to *predict* how changing the incentive plan will affect performance.

For managers, the point of being "scientific" is to make better decisions by forcing you to gather the facts. "Is this sales incentive plan really boosting sales?" "We've spent $40,000 in the past 5 years on our tuition-refund plan; what (if anything) did we get out of it?" What's the evidence?

Successful HR managers need to be scientific today. As an example, the chemical company BASF Corp. used talent analytics to analyze data on the relationship among stress, health, and productivity in its 15,000 U.S. headquarters staff. Based on that analysis, the company instituted health programs that it calculated would more than pay for themselves in increased productivity by reducing stress.[54]

Throughout this book we will show examples of how managers use evidence to make better human resource management decisions. For example: Which recruitment source produces our best candidates? Does it pay to use this testing program? And, does our safety program really lead to fewer accidents? ■

If your professor has assigned this, go to the Assignments section of **mymanagementlab.com** to complete this discussion question.

Talk About It 4: If it is apparently so easy to do what BASF did to size up the potential benefits of health programs, why do more employers not do so?

LEARNING OBJECTIVE 3-5

Give five examples of what employers can do to have high-performance systems.

High-Performance Work Systems

high-performance work system (HPWS)
A set of human resource management policies and practices that promote organizational effectiveness.

One reason to measure, benchmark, and scientifically analyze HR practices is to promote high-performance work practices. A **high-performance work system (HPWS)** is a set of human resource management policies and practices that together produce superior employee performance.

What exactly are these high-performance work practices? In one recent study, researchers collected data from 359 firms before, during, and after the 2007–2009 recession. They found that firms that used more effective staffing and training outperformed competitors before, during, and after the recession.[55]

Another study looked at 17 manufacturing plants, some of which adopted high-performance work system practices. The high-performance plants paid more (median wages of $16 per hour compared with $13 per hour for all plants), trained more, used more sophisticated recruitment and hiring practices (tests and validated interviews, for instance), and used more self-managing work teams.[56] Those with the high-performance HR practices performed significantly better than did those without such practices. Service companies (such as hotels) particularly gain from such high-performance work systems and practices.[57]

Studies like these show that high-performance work systems' policies and practices do differ from less productive ones (Table 3-1). For example, high-performing companies recruit more job candidates, use more selection tests, and spend many more hours training employees. Table 3-1 illustrates three things:

First, it shows examples of *human resource metrics* such as hours of training per employee, or qualified applicants per position. (In Table 3-1, the metric for "Number of qualified applicants per position" is 37 in the high-performing companies.) Managers use these to assess their companies' performance and to compare one firm with another.[58]

Second, it illustrates *what employers must do* to have high-performance systems. For example, high-performing companies have more than four times the number of qualified applicants per job than do low performers. They also hire based on validated selection tests, and extensively train employees.

Third, Table 3-1 shows that high-performance work practices usually *aspire to encourage employee involvement and self-management.* In other words, an aim of the high-performance recruiting, screening, training, and other human resources practices is to nurture an engaged, involved, informed, empowered, and self-motivated workforce.[59]

TABLE 3-1 Examples Selected from Several Studies of How Recruitment, Selection, Training, Appraisal, Pay, and Other Practices Differ in High-Performance and Low-Performance Companies

	Lower-Performance Companies' HR Practice Averages (e.g., company performance in terms of sales/employee, innovation, and employee retention)*	Higher-Performance Companies' HR Practice Averages (e.g., company performance in terms of sales/employee, innovation, and employee retention)*
Recruitment: Average number of qualified applicants per position	8	37
Selection: Average percentage of employees hired based on a validated *selection* test	4%	30%
Training: Average number of hours of *training* for new employees	35 hours	117 hours
Appraisal: Average percentage of employees receiving a regular *performance appraisal*	41%	95%
Pay Practices: Average percentage of the workforce eligible for *incentive pay*	28%	84%
Use of Teams: Average percentage of the workforce routinely working in all teams: semiautonomous, cross-functional, or project teams	11%	42%
Self-Directed Teams: Percent of companies with *semiautonomous or autonomous* work teams	9%	70%
Operational Information Sharing: Employees receive relevant operating performance information	62%	82%
Financial Information Sharing: Employees receive relevant financial performance information	43%	66%

*Findings rounded.

Based on "Comparison of HR Practices in High-Performance and Low-Performance Companies," by B. E. Becker, et al., from *The HR Scorecard: Linking People, Strategy and Performance* (Boston: Harvard Business School Press, 2001); Barry Macy, Gerard Farias, Jean-Francois Rosa, and Curt Moore, "Built to Change: High-Performance Work Systems and Self-Directed Work Teams—A longitudinal Field Study," *Research in Organizational Change and Development,* 16, pp. 339–418, 2007; James Gathrie, Wenchuan Liu, Patrick Flood, and Sarah MacCurtain, "High Performance Work Systems, Workforce Productivity, and Innovation: A Comparison of MNCs and Indigenous Firms," The Learning, Innovation and Knowledge (LINK) Research Centre Working Paper Series, WP 04-08, 2008.

Employee Engagement Guide for Managers: Employee Engagement and Performance

LEARNING OBJECTIVE 3-6

Describe how you would execute a program to improve employee engagement.

Employee engagement refers to being psychologically involved in, connected to, and committed to getting one's jobs done. Engaged employees "experience a high level of connectivity with their work tasks," and work hard to accomplish their task-related goals.[60]

Employee engagement is important because it drives performance and productivity. For example, based on a Gallup survey, business units with the highest levels of employee engagement have an 83% chance of performing above the company median; those with the lowest employee engagement have only a 17% chance.[61] According to one review of the evidence, employee engagement is correlated with employees' customer service productivity, and improvements in employee engagement were associated with significant increases in sales, product quality, productivity, safety incidents at work, retention and absenteeism, and revenue growth.[62] One consulting firm estimates that a 5% increase in employee engagement correlates to a 0.7% increase in operating margins.[63] Companies with highly engaged employees are also less likely to be unionized.[64] In one survey, highly engaged employees lost only about 7.5 days of productivity per year, compared to about 14 days for disengaged employees.[65] A survey by consultants Watson Wyatt Worldwide concluded that companies with highly engaged employees have 26% higher revenue per employee.[66]

The Employee Engagement Problem

The problem is that, depending on the study, only about 21–30% of employees nationally are engaged.[67] Gallup distinguishes among engaged employees "who work with passion and feel a profound connection to their company," not-engaged employees who are essentially "checked out," and actively disengaged employees. The latter "act out their unhappiness" by undermining what their engaged coworkers are accomplishing.[68] Gallup found that about 30% of employees were engaged, 50% were not engaged, and 20% were actively disengaged.

What Can Managers Do to Improve Employee Engagement?

Managers improve employee engagement by taking concrete steps to do so. We'll look more closely at how they do this in a moment, but one important activity is *providing supportive supervision.* For example, a Gallup survey found that managers who focus their support and coaching on their employees' strengths can "practically eliminate active disengagement"; conversely, "bosses from hell" kill employee engagement.[69] Other steps managers can take to foster engagement include making sure employees (1) *understand* how their departments contribute to the company's success; (2) *see how their efforts contribute* to achieving the company's goals; (3) get a *sense of accomplishment* from working at the firm;[70] and (4) are highly *involved*—as when working in self-managing teams.[71] Employers should also *hold managers responsible* for employee engagement. For example, WD-40 Company has its managers meet periodically with their employees to discuss how to improve employee engagement.[72]

How to Measure Employee Engagement

Firms like Gallup (www.gallup.com), and Towers Watson (go to www.towerswatson.com/en-US, then click Solutions, and then Surveys) offer comprehensive employee engagement survey services. However, monitoring employee engagement needn't be complicated. With about 180,000 employees worldwide, the consulting firm Accenture uses a three-part "shorthand" method it calls "say, stay, and strive." First, Accenture assesses how positively the employee speaks about the company and recommends it to others. Second, it looks at who stays with the company, and why. Third, it looks at "strive." For instance, "do employees take an active role in the overall success of the organization by moving beyond just doing tasks to going above and beyond?"[73]

The Employee Engagement Guide for Managers sections in this and the following chapters will show how managers use human resource activities to improve employee engagement.

How Kia Motors (UK) Improved Performance with an HR Strategy Aimed at Boosting Employee Engagement

Kia Motors today is a successful automobile manufacturer employing tens of thousands of employees around the world, and one famous for its 10-year warranty and for the quality and value of its products. However, Kia was not always so successful. In July 1997, Kia was under bankruptcy protection and having difficulty servicing its $10.6 billion of debt.[74] In 1998, Hyundai Motorcar Company of Korea purchased 51% of Kia. That triggered a multiyear program aimed at improving Kia's operating performance. Today, Hyundai owns about one-third of Kia Motors, although Kia is still a close-knit part of Hyundai Motor Group.

THE CHALLENGES After several years of improving operating conditions under Hyundai Motor Group, Kia (as well as most auto manufacturers around the world) ran into strong headwinds as credit tightened and consumers cut spending around 2006. Looking at the situation in 2006–2007, Kia's chairman, writing in the company's annual report said,

> In today's automobile industry, competition is so severe that even the bold at heart, if well-informed, would be hesitant to confidently predict future victors

> in the car market. Japanese automobile companies are unrelenting in their measures against us, while latecomers, such as China, are speeding up to catch up with us as far as they can. Stagnation and the world economic growth, coupled with exchange-rate risks and other major threats, present unfavorable economic conditions for any global player.[75]

In the face of these challenges, the chairman went on to lay out what Kia's strategy for dealing with this intense global competition would be. As he said:

> We intend to base future growth on raising our competencies as a global maker in all areas including production, sales, marketing, branding, as well as before and after servicing. We will also concentrate on our global quality management we have driven so far. We will first strengthen our basic competitiveness in terms of production costs and final products. Second, we will exclude all the unnecessary elements from the management through advanced systems to groundwork the base of stable profit making. Third, we will efficiently invest in new future businesses with our specialized R&D and global production bases.[76]

Also in 2006–2007, Kia Motor's UK subsidiary (Kia UK), which employed about 2,500 people, faced particularly dire circumstances; these included rapidly falling sales, increased financial losses, and low levels of employee engagement. Employee turnover was 31%. The direct cost to the company from the 31% turnover alone was estimated at about 600,000 British pounds (about $1 million) in 2006 (due to higher than necessary recruitment, legal, and employee dismissal costs).[77]

THE NEW HUMAN RESOURCE MANAGEMENT STRATEGY Gary Tomlinson, Kia UK's newly appointed head of HR, believed that Kia UK's low employee engagement was probably both a cause and an effect of the unit's poor performance. In fact, a survey of Kia UK employees had identified numerous personnel issues including possibly poor morale and communications. He knew Kia UK needed a new HR strategy to address this. He also knew that this strategy should support the parent company's strategy of basing "future growth on raising our competencies as a global maker in all areas including production, sales, marketing, branding, as well as before and after servicing."

Tomlinson (with the support of Kia UK's top management) wisely decided to develop, as he put it, "an employee engagement strategy to improve employee morale and address the high levels of employee turnover."[78] In brief, the idea was that, by (1) putting in place new HR policies and practices aimed at improving employee engagement, he could (2) change Kia UK employees' behavior (improve performance and reduce turnover, for instance) and thereby (3) support the parent company's stated strategy of "raising our competencies as a global maker in all areas." The following shows what he actually did to boost employee engagement.

HOW TO EXECUTE AN EMPLOYEE ENGAGEMENT STRATEGY Actually executing Kia UK's employee engagement HR strategy involved six steps (and these provide a roadmap for any such endeavor). First, Kia UK set *measurable objectives* for the program. These objectives included improving by at least 10% survey feedback scores for line managers' behaviors in terms of communication, the quality of appraisal feedback they gave their direct reports, the recognition of work done, and the respect between manager and employee.[79] Other objectives included reducing employee turnover employment costs (e.g., recruitment costs) by at least 10% per year.

Second, Kia UK held an extensive *leadership development* program. For example, it sent all managers for training to improve their management skills. Kia then tested the new skills with "360-degree" assessment tools (having managers' bosses, peers, and subordinates rate the managers' new leadership skills).

Third, Kia UK instituted new *employee recognition programs.* These included, for instance, giving "Outstanding Awards" to selected employees quarterly, and "Kia thank you" cards for jobs well done.[80]

Fourth, Kia UK *improved internal communications.* For example, it instituted quarterly employee briefings and more extensive use of performance appraisals, and launched a new corporate intranet called Kia Vision (this provided key business information and other useful communiqués to all employees). Based on employee feedback, Kia UK also decided, as part of the enhanced communications, to institute an *employee forum.* This consisted of one representative from each department; the forum in effect empowered and involved employees by enabling them to express opinions, suggestions, and concerns about their jobs.

Fifth, Kia instituted a new *employee development program.* This involved using the company's appraisal process to identify employees' training needs. Kia then created training plans for each employee. It based these plans on Kia's needs and on the employee's stated career aspirations.

Sixth, Kia UK made a number of changes to its *compensation and other policies.* For instance, it eliminated bonuses and substituted fixed-rate percentage-based salary increases. It also rewrote the entire employee handbook and all HR policies and procedures "to ensure they were aligned with [Kia UK's new] cultural values."[81]

THE RESULTS The results of the new employee engagement program were impressive. Employee surveys of employee engagement and of line managers' communications and other behaviors improved markedly; employee turnover fell from 31% in 2006 to 15% in 2007, to 5% in 2008, and to below 2% by the end of 2009. Recruitment and turnover costs fell by more than 400,000 British pounds within two years, a 71% reduction.[82]

Earlier we said that *strategic human resource management* means having the HR policies and practices that will produce the employee competencies and behaviors that the company needs to achieve its strategic goals. Kia UK's employee engagement program illustrates how one company actually did this.

Chapter Review

MyManagementLab® Go to **mymanagementlab.com** to complete the problems marked with this icon ✪.

Chapter Section Summaries

3-1. All managers' personnel and other decisions should be consistent with the goals that cascade down from the firm's overall strategic plan. Those goals form a hierarchy, starting with the president's overall strategic goals (such as double sales revenue to $16 million) and filtering down to what each individual manager needs to do in order to support that overall company goal.

The strategic planning process's seven steps include: (1) ask, "Where are we now as a business?" (2) evaluate the firm's internal and external strengths, weaknesses, opportunities, and threats, (3) formulate a new business direction, (4) decide on strategic goals, and (5) choose specific strategies or courses of action; steps (6) and (7) are to implement and then evaluate the strategic plan.

3-2. We distinguished among **three types of strategies:** corporate, business/competitive, and functional/department strategies.

3-3. Each function or department in the business needs its own functional strategy, and **strategic human resource management** means formulating and executing human resource policies and practices that produce the employee competencies and behaviors the company needs to achieve its strategic aims. Human resource strategies are the specific human resource management policies and practices managers use to support their strategic aims. Important and popular **strategic human resource management** tools include the strategy map, the HR scorecard, and digital dashboards.

3-4. The manager will want to gather and analyze data prior to making decisions. **Human resource metrics** (quantitative measures of some human resource management activities such as employee turnover) are critical in creating high-performance human resource policies and practices.

3-5. A **high-performance work system** is a set of human resource management policies and practices that together produce superior employee performance.

3-6. Employee engagement is important because it drives performance and productivity. For example, based on a Gallup survey, business units with the highest levels of employee engagement have an 83% chance of performing above the company median; those with the lowest employee engagement have only a 17% chance.

Actually **executing Kia UK's employee engagement HR strategy** involved six steps. These were: set *measurable objectives* for the program; provide *leadership development,* for example, send all managers for training to improve their management skills; institute new *employee recognition programs,* for instance, giving "Outstanding Awards" to selected employees quarterly; institute a new *employee development program,* for instance, using the company's appraisal process to identify employees' training needs and to create training plans for each employee; and change the *compensation* and *other policies* to ensure they are aligned with the new cultural values.

Discussion Questions

3-1. Give an example of hierarchical planning in an organization.

✪ **3-2.** What is the difference between a corporate strategy and a competitive strategy? Give one example of each.

3-3. Explain why strategic planning is important to all managers.

3-4. Explain with examples each of the eight steps in the strategic management process.

3-5. Explain with examples how human resources management can be instrumental in helping a company create a competitive advantage.

✪ **3-6.** Outline how you would implement an employee engagement program.

Individual and Group Activities

3-7. With three or four other students, form a strategic management group for your college or university. Your assignment is to develop the outline of a strategic plan for the college or university. This should include such things as strategic goals; and corporate, competitive, and functional strategies. In preparing your plan, make sure to show the main strengths, weaknesses, opportunities, and threats the college faces, and which prompted you to develop your particular strategic plans.

3-8. Using the Internet or library resources, review the annual reports of five companies. Bring to class examples of how those companies say they are using their HR processes to help the company achieve its strategic goals.

3-9. Interview an HR manager and write a short report on "The Strategic Roles of the HR Manager at XYZ Company."

3-10. Using the Internet or library resources, bring to class and discuss at least two examples of how companies are using an HR scorecard to help create HR systems that support the company's strategic aims. Do all managers seem to mean the same thing when they refer to HR scorecards? If not, how do they differ?

3-11. In teams of several students, choose a company for which you will develop an outline of a strategic HR plan. What seem to be this company's main strategic aims? What is the firm's competitive strategy? What would the strategic map for this company look like? How would you summarize your recommended strategic HR policies for this company?

3-12. Appendices A and B at the end of this book (pages 612–629) list the knowledge someone studying for the HRCI (Appendix A) or SHRM (Appendix B) certification exam needs to have in each area of human resource management (such as in Strategic Management, and Workforce Planning). In groups of several students, do four things: (1) review Appendix A and/or B; (2) identify the material in this chapter that relates to the Appendix A and/or B required knowledge lists; (3) write four multiple-choice exam questions on this material that you believe would be suitable for inclusion in the HRCI exam and/or the SHRM exam; and, (4) if time permits, have someone from your team post your team's questions in front of the class, so that students in all teams can answer the exam questions created by the other teams.

Experiential Exercise

Developing an HR Strategy for Starbucks

A few years ago, Starbucks was facing serious challenges. Sales per store were stagnant or declining, and its growth rate and profitability were down. Many believed that its introduction of breakfast foods had diverted its "baristas" from their traditional jobs as coffee-preparation experts. McDonald's and Dunkin' Donuts were introducing lower-priced but still high-grade coffees. Starbucks' former CEO stepped back into the company's top job. You need to help him formulate a new direction for his company.

Purpose: The purpose of this exercise is to give you experience in developing an HR strategy, in this case, by developing one for Starbucks.

Required Understanding: You should be thoroughly familiar with the material in this chapter.

How to Set Up the Exercise/Instructions: Set up groups of three or four students for this exercise. You are probably already quite familiar with what it's like to have a cup of coffee or tea in a Starbucks coffee shop, but if not, spend some time in one prior to this exercise. Meet in groups and develop an outline for an HR strategy for Starbucks Corp. Assume that for a corporate strategy Starbucks will remain primarily an international chain of coffee shops. Your outline should include four basic elements: a business/competitive strategy for Starbucks, the workforce requirements (in terms of employee competencies and behaviors) this strategy requires, specific HR policies and the activities necessary to produce these workforce requirements, and suggestions for metrics to measure the success of the HR strategy.

Application Case

Siemens Builds a Strategy-Oriented HR System

Siemens is a 150-year-old German company, but it's not the company it was even a few years ago. Until recently, Siemens focused on producing electrical products. Today the firm has diversified into software, engineering, and services. It is also global, with more than 400,000 employees working in 190 countries. In other words, Siemens became a world leader by pursuing a corporate strategy that emphasized diversifying into high-tech products and services, and doing so on a global basis.

With a corporate strategy like that, human resource management plays a big role at Siemens. Sophisticated engineering and services require more focus on employee selection, training, and compensation than in the average firm, and globalization requires delivering these services globally. Siemens sums up the basic themes of its HR strategy in several points. These include:

1. **A living company is a learning company.** The high-tech nature of Siemens' business means that employees must be able to learn on a continuing basis. Siemens uses its system of combined classroom and hands-on apprenticeship training around the world to help facilitate this. It also offers employees extensive continuing education and management development.
2. **Global teamwork is the key to developing and using all the potential of the firm's human resources.** Because it is so important for employees throughout Siemens to feel free to work together and interact, employees have to understand the whole Siemens process not just bits and pieces. To support this, Siemens provides extensive training and development. It also ensures that all employees feel they're part of a strong, unifying corporate identity. For example, HR uses cross-border, cross-cultural experiences as prerequisites for career advances.
3. **A climate of mutual respect is the basis of all relationships—within the company and with society.** Siemens contends that the wealth of nationalities, cultures, languages, and outlooks represented by its employees is one of its most valuable assets. It therefore engages in numerous HR activities aimed at building openness, transparency, and fairness, and supporting diversity.

Questions

3-13. Based on the information in this case, provide examples for Siemens of at least four strategically required organizational outcomes, and four required workforce competencies and behaviors.

3-14. Identify at least four strategically relevant HR policies and activities that Siemens has instituted in order to help human resource management contribute to achieving Siemens' strategic goals.

3-15. Provide a brief illustrative outline of a strategy map for Siemens.

Continuing Case

Carter Cleaning Company

The High-Performance Work System

As a person who keeps up with the business press, Jennifer Carter is familiar with the benefits of programs such as total quality management and high-performance work systems.

Jack, her father, actually installed a total quality program of sorts at Carter, and it has been in place for about 5 years. This program takes the form of employee meetings. Jack holds employee meetings periodically, but particularly when there is a serious problem in a store—such as poor-quality work or machine breakdowns. When problems like these arise, instead of trying to diagnose them himself or with Jennifer, he contacts all the employees in that store and meets with them when the store closes. Hourly employees get extra pay for these meetings. The meetings have been useful in helping Jack to identify and rectify several problems. For example, in one store all the fine white blouses were coming out looking dingy. It turned out that the cleaner/spotter had been ignoring the company rule that required cleaning ("boiling down") the perchloroethylene cleaning fluid before washing items like these. As a result, these fine white blouses were being washed in cleaning fluid that had residue from other, earlier washes.

Jennifer now wonders whether these employee meetings should be expanded to give the employees an even bigger role in managing the Carter stores' quality. "We can't be everywhere watching everything all the time," she said to her father. "Yes, but these people only earn about $8 to $15 per hour. Will they really want to act like mini-managers?" he replied.

Questions

3-16. Would you recommend that the Carters expand their quality program? If so, specifically what form should it take?

3-17. Assume the Carters want to institute a high-performance work system as a test program in one of their stores. Write a one-page outline summarizing important HR practices you think they should focus on.

Translating Strategy into HR Policies and Practices Case*,§

**The accompanying strategy map for this chapter is in the MyManagementLab, and the overall map on the inside back cover of this text outlines the relationships involved.*

CHAPTER 3

Improving Performance at the Hotel Paris

The Hotel Paris International

Starting as a single hotel in a Paris suburb in 1990, the Hotel Paris is now a chain of nine hotels, with two in France, one each in London and Rome, and others in New York, Miami, Washington, Chicago, and Los Angeles. As a corporate strategy, the Hotel Paris's management and owners want to continue to expand geographically. They believe doing so will let them capitalize on their reputation for good service, by providing multicity alternatives for their satisfied guests. The problem is, their reputation for good service has been deteriorating. If they cannot improve service, it would be unwise for them to expand, since their guests might prefer other hotels after trying the Hotel Paris.

Several things are complicating their problem. Elected in 2012, French president Francois Hollande has found it hard to halt or even slow the country's economic decline. His attempts to impose incremental tax rates of 75% on wealthy citizens prompted many to contemplate leaving France. Furthermore, many tourists—faced with similar economic challenges elsewhere—are increasingly staying at short-term rental apartments in Paris, found on the Web, (often through sites such as airbnb.com) for a fraction of what a fine hotel stay might cost.

The Strategy

Top management, with input from the HR and other managers, and with the board of directors' approval, chooses a new competitive strategy and formulates new strategic goals. It decides: "The Hotel Paris International will use superior guest services to differentiate the Hotel Paris properties, and to thereby increase the length of stays and the return rate of guests, and thus boost revenues and profitability." All Hotel Paris managers—including the director of HR services—must now formulate strategies that support this competitive strategy.

The Strategically Required Organizational Outcomes

The Hotel Paris's basic strategy is to use superior guest services to expand geographically. For HR director Lisa Cruz, reviewing the hotel's activities makes it clear that achieving the hotel's strategic aims means achieving a number of required organizational outcomes. For example, Lisa and her management colleagues must take steps that produce fewer customer complaints and more written compliments, more frequent guest returns and longer stays, and higher guest expenditures per visit.

The Strategically Relevant Workforce Competencies and Behaviors

The question facing Lisa, then, is this: What competencies and behaviors must our hotel's employees exhibit, if we are to produce required organizational outcomes such as fewer customer complaints, more compliments, and more frequent guest returns? Thinking through this question helps Lisa come up with an answer. For example, the hotel's required employee competencies and behaviors would include, "high-quality front-desk customer service," "taking calls for reservations in a friendly manner," "greeting guests at the front door," and "processing guests' room service meals efficiently." All require motivated, high-morale employees.

The Strategically Relevant HR Policies and Activities

The HR manager's task now is to identify and specify the HR policies and activities that will enable the hotel to produce these crucial workforce competencies and behaviors. For example, "high-quality front-desk customer service" is one such required behavior. From this, the HR director identifies HR activities to produce such front-desk customer service efforts. For example, she decides to *institute practices to improve the disciplinary fairness and justice in the company*, with the aim of *improving employee morale*. Her assumption is that enhanced fairness will produce higher morale and that higher morale will produce improved front-desk service.

The Strategy Map

Next, Lisa, working with the hotel's chief financial officer (CFO), outlines a strategy map for the hotel. This outlines the cause-and-effect links among the HR activities, the workforce behaviors, and the organizational outcomes (the figure on this book's inside back cover shows the overall map; you'll find detailed maps for each HR function in each chapter's related MyManagementLab page).

This map and its linkages reflect certain assumptions on Lisa's part. For example, based on experience and discussions with the firm's other managers, she formulates the following *hypothesis* about how HR affects hotel performance: Improved grievance procedures cause improved morale, which leads to improved front-desk service, which leads

§Written by and copyright Gary Dessler, PhD.

to increased guest returns, which leads to improved financial performance. The HR director then chooses metrics to measure each of these factors. For example, she decides to measure "improved disciplinary procedures" in terms of how many grievances employees submit each month. She measures "improved morale" in terms of "scores on our hotel's semiannual attitude survey," and measures "high-quality front-desk customer service" in terms of "customer complaints per month."

She moves on to quantifying the cause-and-effect links among these measures. For example: "Can we show top management that there is a measurable, sequential link between improved disciplinary procedures, high morale, improved front-desk service, number of guest return visits, and hotel financial performance (revenues and profits)?" If she can show such links, she has a persuasive case that shows HR's measurable contribution to the hotel's bottom-line financial performance.

In practice, the HR manager may well just rely on a largely subjective but logical argument to make the case for such cause-and-effect linkages. But ideally, she will use statistical methods such as correlation analysis to determine if measurable links exist, and (if so) what their magnitudes are. In this way, she might find, for instance, that a 10% improvement in grievance rates is associated with an almost 20% improvement in morale. Similarly, a 20% improvement in morale is associated with a 30% reduction in customer front-desk complaints. Furthermore, a 30% reduction in complaints is associated with a 20% increase in guest return visits, and a 20% increase in return rate is associated with a 6% rise in hotel revenues. It would appear that a relatively small HR effort in reducing grievances might have a big effect on this hotel's bottom-line performance!

Several things complicate this measurement process. For example, it's risky to draw cause–effect conclusions from correlation measures like these (do fewer grievances lead to higher morale, or vice versa?). Furthermore, it's rare that a single factor (such as grievance rates) will have such effects alone, so we may want to measure the effects of several HR policies and activities on morale simultaneously.

As explained in this chapter, computerization could enable Lisa to build a more comprehensive HR scorecard process, one that might handle links among dozens of cause-and-effect metrics. (Several vendors supply such scorecard software.) If not, then she will rely more on the logic and common sense underlying the strategy map to make her case.

How We Will Use the Hotel Paris Case

A Hotel Paris case in each chapter will show how Lisa, the Hotel Paris's HR director, uses that chapter's concepts and techniques to: (1) create HR policies and practices that help the Hotel Paris (2) produce the employee competencies and behaviors the company needs (3) to produce the customer service the Hotel Paris requires to achieve its strategic goals.

For example, she will endeavor to improve workforce competencies and behaviors by instituting improved recruitment processes (Chapter 5), and measure improved recruitment in terms of "number of qualified applicants per position." Similarly, she will recommend to management that they change the company's pay policies, so that the "target percentile for total compensation is in the top 25%." She could argue, based on competitors' experience, that doing so will translate into improved customer service behavior, more satisfied customers, and improved hotel performance. In practice, all the human resource management functions we discuss in this book influence employee competencies and behaviors, and thereby organizational performance.

You will find the strategy map for each Dessler *Human Resource Management* chapter's topic in the chapter's MyManagementLab; the summary map on the inside back cover of this book outlines the overall relationships involved for the Hotel Paris.

Questions

3-18. Draw a more simplified and abbreviated strategy map for the Hotel Paris. Specifically, summarize in your own words an example of the hierarchy of links among the hotel's *HR practices*, necessary *workforce competencies* and behaviors, and required *organizational outcomes*.

3-19. Using Table 3-1 and Figure 3-9, list at least 15 metrics the Hotel Paris could use to measure its HR practices.

MyManagementLab

Go to **mymanagementlab.com** for Auto-graded writing questions as well as the following Assisted-graded writing questions:

3-20. Define and give at least two examples of the cost-leadership competitive strategy and the differentiation competitive strategy.

3-21. You own a small business and your friend, over lunch, just mentioned that "it sounds like you have an employee engagement problem." What exactly would you do to improve employee engagement in your company now?

3-22. MyManagementLab only—comprehensive writing assignment for this chapter.

✪ Try It!

How would you apply the concepts and skills you learned in this chapter? If your professor has assigned this, go to the Assignments section of **mymanagementlab.com** to complete the simulation: *Strategic Management*.

✪ PERSONAL INVENTORY ASSESSMENTS

Effective Empowerment and Delegation

Personality plays a big role in empowering employees. Complete this assessment to learn more about your personality.

Key Terms

strategic plan, 69
strategy, 69
strategic management, 69
vision statement, 71
mission statement, 71
corporate-level strategy, 71
competitive strategy, 72
competitive advantage, 72
functional strategy, 73
strategic human resource management,74
strategy map, 76
HR scorecard, 77
digital dashboard, 77
human resource metric, 78
strategy-based metrics, 79
HR audit, 80
high-performance work system (HPWS), 83

Endnotes

1. For a good discussion of aligning goals, see, for example, Eric Krell, "Change Within," *HR Magazine,* August 2011, pp. 43–50.
2. James Jenks, *The Hiring, Firing (And Everything in Between) Personnel Forms Book* (Round Lake Publishing Co., 1994).
3. Such as http://store.bizmanualz.com/Human-Resources-Policies-and-Procedures-p/abr41m.htm.
4. For perspectives on strategic planning, see, for example, Donald Sull and Kathleen Eisenhardt, "Simple Rules for a Complex World," *Harvard Business Review*, September 2012, pp. 69–75; and Martin Reeves, Claire Love, and Philipp Tillmann, "Your Strategy Needs a Strategy," *Harvard Business Review*, September 2012, pp. 76–83.
5. Thomas Wheelen and J. David Hunger, *Strategic Management and Business Policy* (Upper Saddle River, NJ: Pearson Education, 2010), pp. 142–143.
6. See, for example, Fred David, *Strategic Management* (Upper Saddle River, NJ: Prentice Hall, 2007), p. 11.
7. Tony Bingham and Pat Galagan, "Doing Good While Doing Well," *Training & Development*, June 2008, p. 33. See also www.pepsico.com/Purpose/Our-Mission-and-Values, accessed July 31, 2014.
8. Paul Nutt, "Making Strategic Choices," *Journal of Management Studies*, January 2002, pp. 67–96.
9. Commerce Clearing House, "HR Role: Maximize the Competitive Advantage of People," *Ideas and Trends in Personnel*, August 5, 1992, p. 121.
10. Michael Porter, *Competitive Strategy* (New York: The Free Press, 1980), p. 14. See also Chris Zook and James Allen, "The Great Repeatable Business Model," *Harvard Business Review,* November 2011, pp. 107–112.
11. Andy Cook, "Make Sure You Get a Prenup," *European Venture Capital Journal*, December/January 2007, p. 76, www.accessmylibrary.com/coms2/summary_0286-29140938_ITM, accessed June 29, 2009.
12. www.towersPerrin.com, accessed December 4, 2007. See also Ingmar Bjorkman, "The HR Function in Large-Scale Mergers and Acquisitions: The Case of Nordea," *Personnel Review* 35, no. 6 (2006), pp. 654–671; Elina Antila and Anne Kakkonen, "Factors Affecting the Role of HR Managers in International Mergers and Acquisitions: A Multiple Case Study," *Personnel Review* 37, no. 3 (2008), pp. 280–299; Linda Tepedino and Muriel Watkins, "Be a Master of Mergers and Acquisitions," *HR Magazine*, June 2010, pp. 53–56; and Yaakov Weber and Yitzak Fried, "Guest Editor's Note: The Role of HR Practices in Managing Culture Clash During the Post Merger Integration Process," *Human Resource Management* 50, no. 5 (September–October 2011), p. 565.
13. This is paraphrased or quoted from "HR Services, Service Offerings: Mergers, Acquisitions and Restructuring," www.towers Perrin.com, accessed December 4, 2007.
14. See, for example, Evan Offstein, Devi Gnyawali, and Anthony Cobb, "A Strategic Human Resource Perspective of Firm Competitive Behavior," *Human Resource Management Review* 15 (2005), pp. 305–318.
15. Brian Hults, "Integrate HR with Operating Strategy," *HR Magazine,* October 2011, pp. 54–56. One review of strategic human resource management research in the United States concluded that "strategic human resource management researchers as a group deserve a D to F grade." Bruce Couchman, "Strategic Human Resource Management Research in the United States: A Failing Grade After 30 Years?" *Academy of Management Perspectives*, May 2012, pp. 12–34.
16. Michael Hargis and Don Bradley III, "Strategic Human Resource Management in Small and Growing Firms: Aligning Valuable Resources," *Academy of Strategic Management Journal* 10, no. 2, July 2011, pp. 105–126; http://about.zappos.com/our-unique-culture/zappos-core-values, accessed March 16, 2015.
17. "Meet the Zappos Family: Human Resources" from Zappos website. Copyright © 1999–2012 by Zappos.com, Inc. http://about.zappos.com/meet-zappos-family/zapposcom-inc/human-resources. Reprinted with permission.
18. www.weknownext.com/workplace/delivering-hr-at-zappos-hr-magazine-june-2011, accessed August 23, 2012.
19. www.pepsico.com/Purpose/Performance-with-Purpose/Goals, accessed May 5, 2014.
20. For an excellent discussion of how human resource management practices can support sustainability goals, see Dubois and Dubois, op. cit., pp. 816–818.
21. www.pepsico.com/Purpose/Performance-with-Purpose/Goals, accessed May 5, 2014.
22. Paul Buller and Glenn McEvoy, "Strategy, Human Resource Management and Performance: Sharpening Line of Sight," *Human Resource Management Review* 22 (2012), pp. 43–56.
23. Managers can use the Active-Strategy Company's *Active-Strategy Enterprise* to create and automate their strategy maps, and to access them through an iPhone or similar devices. See www.activestrategy.com/solutions/strategy_mapping.aspx, accessed March 24, 2009.
24. When focusing on HR activities, managers call this an *HR scorecard*. When applying the same process broadly to all of the company's activities, including, for example, sales, production, and finance, managers call it the "balanced scorecard process."
25. The "balanced" in *balanced scorecard* refers to a balance of goals—financial and nonfinancial.
26. See, for example, "Using HR Performance Metrics to Optimize Operations and Profits," *PR Newswire*, February 27, 2008; and "How to 'Make Over' Your HR Metrics," *HR Focus* 84, no. 9 (September 2007), p. 3.
27. SHRM Human Capital Benchmarking Study: 2007 Executive Summary.
28. For additional information on HR metrics, see, for example, Karen M. Kroll, "Repurposing Metrics for HR: HR Professionals Are Looking Through a People-Focused Lens at the CFO's Metrics on Revenue and Income per FTE," *HR Magazine* 51, no. 7 (July 2006), pp. 64–69; and http://shrm.org/metrics/library_publishedover/measurementsystemsTOC.asp, accessed February 2, 2008.
29. Connie Winkler, "Quality Check: Better Metrics Improve HR's Ability to Measure—and Manage—the Quality of Hires," *HR Magazine* 52, no. 5 (May 2007), pp. 93–94, 96, 98.
30. Ibid.
31. Ibid.
32. See, for example, "Benchmarking for Functional HR Metrics," *HR Focus* 83, no. 11 (November 2006), p. 1; and John Sullivan, "The Last Word," *Workforce Management,* November 19, 2007, p. 42. SHRM makes various metrics calculators available at www.shrm.org/TemplatesTools/Samples/Metrics/Pages/GeneralHumanResources.aspx, accessed October 6, 2012.
33. See Brian Becker and Mark Huselid, "Measuring HR? Benchmarking Is Not the Answer!" *HR Magazine* 8, no. 12 (December 2003), www.charmed.org, accessed February 2, 2008.
34. Ibid.
35. Lin Grensing-Pophal, "HR Audits: Know the Market, Land Assignments," SHRM Consultants Forum, December 2004, www.shrm.org/-hrdisciplines/consultants/Articles/Pages/CMS_010705.aspx, accessed July 7, 2010.
36. "Best Practices for a Human Resources Compliance Audit," *Bloomberg BNA Bulletin to Management,* January 21, 2014, pp. 22–24.
37. Grensing-Pophal, "HR Audits: Know the Market"; and Bill Coy, "Introduction to the Human Resources Audit," La Piana Associates, Inc., www.lapiana.org/consulting, accessed May 1, 2008.
38. Dana R. Scott, "Conducting a Human Resources Audit," *New Hampshire Business Review,* August 2007. See also Eric Krell, "Auditing Your HR

CHAPTER 3

Department," *HR Magazine,* September 2011, pp. 101–103.
39. "Executive Workplace Analytics," www.aon.com/human-capital-consulting/hrbpo, accessed March 19, 2013.
40. Andrew McAfee and Erik Brynjolfsson, "Big Data: The Management Revolution," *Harvard Business Review,* October 1, 2012, https://hbr.org/2012/10/big-data-the-management-revolution/ar, accessed April 4, 2015.
41. George Marakas, *Decision Support Systems* (Upper Saddle River, NJ: Prentice Hall, 2003), p. 326.
42. Ibid.
43. Josh Bersin, "Big Data in Human Resources: Talent Analytics (People Analytics) Comes of Age," February 17, 2013, http://www.forbes.com/sites/joshbersin/2013/02/17/bigdata-in-human-resources-talent-analytics-comes-of-age/ accessed June 20, 2015.
44. Ibid., p. 54. See also Cliff Stevenson, "Five Ways High Performance Organizations Use HR Analytics," www.i4cp.com/print/trendwatchers/2012/12/12/five-ways-high- performance-organizations-use-hr-analytics, accessed July 14, 2013.
45. Thomas Davenport, Jeanne Harris, and Jeremy Shapiro, "Competing on Talent Analytics," *Harvard Business Review*, October 2010, pp. 52–58.
46. Ed Frauenheim, "Keeping Score with Analytics Software," *Workforce Management* 86, no. 10 (May 21, 2007), pp. 25–33. See also Andrew McAfee and Eric Brynjolfsson, "Big Data: The Management Revolution," *Harvard Business Review*, October 2012, pp. 61–68.
47. Steven Baker, "Data Mining Moves to Human Resources," *Bloomberg Businessweek*, March 12, 2009, www.BusinessWeek.com/magazine/, accessed April 13, 2011.
48. Howard Risher, "Investing in Managers to Improve Performance," *Compensation & Benefits Review* 45, no. 6, 2013, pp. 324–328; D. Garvin, "How Google Sold Its Engineers on Management," *Harvard Business Review* 91, no. 2 (2013), pp. 74–82.
49. Dave Zielinski, "Get Analytical," *HR Magazine,* November 2014, pp. 61–62.
50. Cliff Stevenson, "Five Ways High Performance Organizations Use HR Analytics," www.i4cp.com/print/trendwatchers/2012/12/12/five-ways-high-performance-organizations-use-hr-analytics, accessed July 14, 2013.
51. See, for example, www.personneltoday.com/blogs/hcglobal-human-capital-management/2009/02/theres-no-such-thing-as-eviden.html, accessed October 2, 2012.
52. Eric Anderson and Duncan Simester, "A Step-by-Step Guide to Smart Business Experiments," *Harvard Business Review*, March 2011, pp. 98–105.
53. Ibid.
54. Bill Roberts, "How to Put Analytics on Your Side," *HR Magazine*, October 2009, pp. 43–46.
55. Youngsang Kim and Robert Ployhart, "The Effects of Staffing and Training on Firm Productivity and Profit Growth Before, During, and After the Great Recession," *Journal of Applied Psychology* 99, no. 3 (2014), p. 378.
56. www.bls.gov/opub/ted/2006/may/wk2/art01.htm, accessed April 18, 2009; and "Super Human Resources Practices Result in Better Overall Performance, Report Says," *BNA Bulletin to Management*, August 26, 2004, pp. 273–274. See also Wendy Boswell, "Aligning Employees with the Organization's Strategic Objectives: Out of Line of Sight, Out of Mind," *International Journal of Human Resource Management* 17, no. 9 (September 2006), pp. 1014–1041. A study found that some employers, which the researchers called *cost minimizers*, intentionally took a lower-cost approach to human resource practices, with mixed results. See Soo Min Toh et al., "Human Resource Configurations: Investigating Fit with the Organizational Context," *Journal of Applied Psychology* 93, no. 4 (2008), pp. 864–882.
57. Samuel Aryee et al., "Impact of High Performance Work Systems on Individual—and Branch—Level Performance: Test of a Multilevel Model of Intermediate Linkages," *Journal of Applied Psychology* 97, no. 2 (2012), pp. 287–300. See also Achim Krausert, "HRM Systems for Knowledge Workers: Differences Among Top Managers, Middle Managers, and Professional Employees," *Human Resource Management* 53, no. 1 (January–February 2014), pp. 67–87.
58. See, for example, www.halogensoftware.com/blog/are-you-using-hr-analytics-and-metrics-effectively, accessed August 27, 2014.
59. See, for example, J. G. Messersmith, "Unlocking the Black Box: Exploring the Link Between High-Performance Work Systems and Performance," *Human Resource Management International Digest* 20, no. 3 (2012), pp. 1118–1132.
60. Michael Christian, Adela Garza, and Jerel Slaughter, "Work Engagement: A Quantitative Review and Test of Its Relations with Task and Contextual Performance," *Personnel Psychology* 60, no. 4 (2011), pp. 89–136.
61. Adrienne Fox, "Raising Engagement," *HR Magazine*, May 2010, pp. 35–40. See also www.gallup.com/strategicconsulting/163007/state-american-work place.aspx.
62. Kevin Kruse, "Why Employee Engagement? (These 28 Research Studies Prove the Benefits)," September 4, 2012, www.forbes.com.
63. Ibid.
64. "Employee Engagement and Labor Relations," *Gallup Business Journal*, www.businessjournal.gallup.com, accessed April 10, 2014.
65. "Fatter Bottom Line Results from Sustained Engagement," *Bloomberg BNA Bulletin to Management*, July 30, 2013, p. 243.
66. Except as noted, this is based on Kathryn Tyler, "Prepare for Impact," *HR Magazine*, 56, no. 3 (March 2011), pp. 53–56.
67. www.gallup.com/strategicconsulting/163007/state-american-workplace.aspx; Bruce Louis Rich et al., "Job Engagement: Antecedents and Effects on Job Performance," *Academy of Management Journal*, 53, no. 3 (2010), pp. 617–635; "Special Report: Employee Engagement—Losing Lifeblood," *Workforce Management*, July 2011, pp. 24–27.
68. "Five Ways to Improve Employee Engagement Now," *Gallup Business Journal*: www.businessjournal.gallup.com, accessed April 7, 2014.
69. www.gallup.com/strategicconsulting/163007/state-american-workplace.aspx and http://www.gallup.com/services/178514/state-american-workplace.aspx accessed June 20, 2015.
70. Rich et al., "Job Engagement."
71. Alison Konrad, "Engaging Employees through High-Involvement Work Practices," *Ivey Business Journal*, March/April 2006, p. 1.
72. Michael Tucker, "Make Managers Responsible," *HR Magazine*, March 2012, pp. 75–78. See also J. Anitha, "Determinants of Employee Engagement and Their Impact on Employee Performance," *International Journal of Productivity and Performance Management* 63, no. 3 (2014), pp. 308–323.
73. Paula Ketter, "What's the Big Deal About Employee Engagement?" *Training & Development*, January 2008, pp. 47–48.
74. "Kia Motors in Big Trouble," *Business Career* 14, no. 8 (August 1997), pp. 12–13.
75. Kia Motors Corporation, 2006 annual report, page 6.
76. Ibid.
77. Gary Tomlinson, "Building a Culture of High Employee Engagement," *Strategic HR Review* 9, no. 3 (2010), pp. 25–31.
78. Ibid.
79. Ibid.
80. Ibid.
81. Ibid.
82. Ibid. Note that during these years economic activity in the UK was tumbling, which may account for at least some of the reduced turnover.

4

Job Analysis and the Talent Management Process

Michael Latz/vario Images/AGE Fotostock

It is helpful to spend several minutes prior to collecting job analysis information explaining the process that you will be following.

Walter Hodges/Flame/Corbis

- Make the job analysis a *joint effort by a human resources manager, the worker, and the worker's supervisor.* The human resource manager might observe the worker doing the job, and have both the supervisor and worker fill out job questionnaires. Then he or she lists the job's duties and required human traits. The supervisor and worker then verify the HR manager's list of job duties.
- *Make sure the questions and the process are both clear* to the employees. (For example, some might not know what you mean when you ask about the job's "mental demands.")
- *Use several job analysis methods.* For example, a questionnaire might miss a task the worker performs just occasionally. Therefore it's prudent to follow up the questionnaire with a short interview.

KNOWLEDGE BASE

The Interview

Job analysis interviews range from unstructured ("Tell me about your job") to highly structured ones containing hundreds of specific items to check off.

Managers may conduct individual interviews with each employee, group interviews with groups of employees who have the same job, and/or supervisor interviews with one or more supervisors who know the job. Use group interviews when a large number of employees are performing similar or identical work, since this can be a quick and inexpensive way to gather information. As a rule, the workers' immediate supervisor attends the group session; if not, you can interview the supervisor separately.

The interviewee should understand the reason for the interview. There's a tendency for workers to view such interviews, rightly or wrongly, as "efficiency evaluations." If so, interviewees may hesitate to describe their jobs accurately.

TYPICAL QUESTIONS Typical interview questions include the following:

What is the job being performed?

What exactly are the major duties of your position?

What physical locations do you work in?

What are the education, experience, skill, and [where applicable] certification and licensing requirements?

In what activities do you participate?

What are the job's responsibilities and duties?

What are the basic accountabilities or performance standards that typify your work?

What are your responsibilities? What are the environmental and working conditions involved?

What are the job's physical demands? The emotional and mental demands?

What are the health and safety conditions?

Are you exposed to any hazards or unusual working conditions?

STRUCTURED INTERVIEWS Many managers use questionnaires to guide the interview. Figure 4-4 presents one example. It includes questions regarding matters like the general purpose of the job; supervisory responsibilities; job duties; and education, experience, and skills required.

Such structured lists are not just for interviews. Job analysts who collect information by personally observing the work or by using questionnaires—two methods explained later—can also use structured lists.[11]

PROS AND CONS The interview's wide use reflects its advantages. It's a simple and quick way to collect information. Skilled interviewers can also unearth important activities that occur only occasionally, or informal contacts that aren't on the organization chart. The employee can also vent frustrations that might otherwise go unnoticed.

Distortion of information is the main problem.[12] Job analysis often precedes changing a job's pay rate. Employees therefore may legitimately view it as pay-related, and exaggerate some responsibilities while minimizing others. In one study, researchers listed possible job duties either as simple task statements ("record phone messages and other routine information") or as ability statements ("ability to record phone messages and other routine information"). Respondents were more likely to report the ability-based versions of the statements. There may be a tendency for people to inflate their job's importance when abilities are involved, to impress the perceptions of others.[13] Employees will even puff up their job titles to make their jobs seem more important.[14]

INTERVIEWING GUIDELINES To get the best information possible:

- Establish rapport with the interviewee. Know the person's name, speak understandably, briefly review the interview's purpose, and explain how the person was chosen for the interview.
- Use a structured guide that lists questions and provides space for answers. This ensures you'll identify crucial questions ahead of time and that all interviewers (if more than one) cover all the required questions. (However, also ask, "Was there anything we didn't cover with our questions?")
- Make sure you don't overlook crucial but infrequently performed activities—like a nurse's occasional emergency room duties. Ask the worker to list his or her duties in order of importance and frequency of occurrence.
- After completing the interview, review the information with the worker's immediate supervisor and with the interviewee.

Questionnaires

Having employees fill out questionnaires to describe their job duties and responsibilities is another good way to obtain job analysis information.

Some questionnaires are structured checklists. Here each employee gets an inventory of perhaps hundreds of specific duties or tasks (such as "change and splice wire"). He or she must indicate if he or she performs each task and, if so, how much time is normally spent on each. At the other extreme, the questionnaire may simply ask, "describe the major duties of your job."

In practice, the best questionnaire often falls between these two extremes. As illustrated in Figure 4-4, a typical job analysis questionnaire might include several open-ended questions (such as "Give a brief description of the main function/purpose of your job?") as well as structured questions (concerning, for instance, education required).

All questionnaires have pros and cons. A questionnaire is a quick and efficient way to obtain information from a large number of employees; it's less costly than

FIGURE 4-4 Job Analysis Questionnaire for Developing Job Descriptions

Source: Adapted from www.tsu.edu/PDFFiles/Human%20Resources/HR%20Forms/JAQ%20FORM_rev%20100809%20a.pdf; www.delawarepersonnel.com/class/forms/jaq/jaq.shtml; www.uh.edu/human-resources/forms/JAQ.doc; www.tnstate.edu/hr/documents/.../Job%20Analysis%20Questionnaire.doc (all accessed July 24, 2013).
*Copyright Gary Dessler, PhD

JOB ANALYSIS QUESTIONNAIRE*

PURPOSE AND INSTRUCTIONS

Because no one knows the job as well as the person doing it, we are asking you to complete this form. The purpose is to obtain current information on your job based on a review of job duties and responsibilities. We are not asking you about your job performance; only what your job requires you to do.

EMPLOYEE DATA (PLEASE PRINT):

Your Name: _____ Today's date _____

Employee ID: _____

Location/Department: _____

Your Job Title: _____ Job Code: _____

How long have you been in your current position: _____

Work Telephone Number: _____

Supervisor's Name: _____ Supervisor's Title: _____

SUMMARY OF DUTIES/RESPONSIBILITIES

Give a brief description of the main function/purpose of your job. This statement should be a brief summary of the responsibilities listed in the next section.

_____

_____

_____

Listing of Job Duties

What do you do on your job? Please list your job's specific duties/responsibilities in the space below. In doing so:

Please list the most important duties/responsibilities first. Write a separate statement for each duty/responsibility.

At the end of each statement please indicate the approximate percent of your workday (25%, 7%, etc.) you spend on that duty.

Please place an asterisk (*) next to the duties that you consider to be absolutely essential to this job.

_____

_____

_____

_____

_____

(Add additional duties as necessary)

Are there duties you are now performing that are not now in your job description? If so please list them on back of this page.

(Continued)

FIGURE 4-4 *Continued*

Minimum Level of Education (or Equivalent Experience) This Job Requires

What is the minimum level of education necessary to perform your job? Select only one please:

1. Elementary education.
2. Some high school.
3. A high school diploma or equivalent (G.E.D.).
4. A formal vocational training program (approximately one year), an apprenticeship, or some formal college education.
5. An Associate's degree (AA, AS) .
6. A bachelor's degree (BA, BS) .
7. A Master's degree (MA, MS, MBA, MPA) .
8. A doctorate degree (Ph.D., MD, JD, EED).
9. Are you required to be licensed or certified to perform your work?

[ ] Yes [ ] No List type _____

Required Training on Job

What is the level of on-the-job or classroom training someone requires to do your job? Please select one choice below:

1. No additional training required.
2. A day or two.
3. A week.
4. A month.
5. Several months.
6. One year.
7. Two years or more.

SUPERVISORY RESPONSIBILITIES

Do you supervise others as part of your job? If so please briefly describe the nature of your supervisory responsibilities.

PHYSICAL JOB DEMANDS

Please briefly describe this job's main physical demands. For example, does it involve Sitting? Walking? Standing? Lifting? Detailed repetitive motions? Climbing? Etc.

Working Conditions: Environmental and Safety Job Demands

Please list this job's working conditions, such as: air-conditioned office work; outdoor or indoor extreme heat or cold; wet; noise; job hazards; working in elevated conditions; etc.

EMPLOYEE COMMENTS

Is there any other information that would be important in understanding your job? If so, please give us your comments below.

SUPERVISOR'S REVIEW

Based on your understanding of the job as it currently exists, please review the employee's response and provide your own comments in the space below. **Please do not change the employee's responses.**

*Copyright Gary Dessler PhD

interviewing hundreds of workers, for instance. However, developing the questionnaire and testing it (perhaps by making sure the workers understand the questions) can be time-consuming. And as with interviews, employees may distort their answers.

Observation

Direct observation is especially useful when jobs consist mainly of observable physical activities—assembly-line worker and accounting clerk are examples. However, observation is usually not appropriate when the job entails a lot of mental activity (lawyer, design engineer). Nor is it useful if the employee only occasionally engages in important activities, such as a nurse who handles emergencies. *Reactivity*—the worker's changing what he or she normally does because you are watching—is another problem.

Managers often use direct observation and interviewing together. One approach is to observe the worker on the job during a complete work cycle. (The *cycle* is the time it takes to complete the job; it could be a minute for an assembly-line worker or an hour, a day, or longer for complex jobs.) Here you take notes of all the job activities. Then, ask the person to clarify open points and to explain what other activities he or she performs that you didn't observe.

Participant Diary/Logs

diary/log
Daily listings made by workers of every activity in which they engage along with the time each activity takes.

Another method is to ask workers to keep a **diary/log**; here for every activity engaged in, the employee records the activity (along with the time) in a log.

Some firms give employees pocket dictating machines and pagers. Then at random times during the day, they page the workers, who dictate what they are doing at that time.

Quantitative Job Analysis Techniques

Qualitative methods like interviews and questionnaires are not always suitable. For example, if your aim is to compare jobs for pay purposes, a mere listing of duties may not suffice. You may need to say that, in effect, "Job A is twice as challenging as Job B, and so is worth twice the pay." To do this, it helps to have quantitative ratings for each job. The position analysis questionnaire and the Department of Labor approach are quantitative methods for doing this.

position analysis questionnaire (PAQ)
A questionnaire used to collect quantifiable data concerning the duties and responsibilities of various jobs.

POSITION ANALYSIS QUESTIONNAIRE The **position analysis questionnaire (PAQ)** is a very popular quantitative job analysis tool, consisting of a questionnaire containing 194 items.[15] The 194 items (such as "written materials") each represent a basic element that may play a role in the job. The items each belong to one of five PAQ basic activities: (1) Having Decision-Making/Communication/Social Responsibilities, (2) Performing Skilled Activities, (3) Being Physically Active, (4) Operating Vehicles/Equipment, and (5) Processing Information. The final PAQ "score" reflects the job's rating on each of these five activities. To get those scores, the job analyst decides if each of the 194 items (such as one on using "written materials") applies to the job and, if so, to what extent. For example, within the "Processing Information" activity section an item on the extent to which the job requires using "written materials" such as books and reports might get a rating of 4. Since the PAQ scale ranges from 1 to 5, a 4 suggests that written materials do play a significant role in this job. The analyst can use an online version of the PAQ (see www.paq.com) for each job he or she is analyzing.

One of the PAQ's strengths is in assigning jobs to job classes for pay purposes. With ratings for each job's decision-making, skilled activity, physical activity, vehicle/equipment operation, and information-processing characteristics, you can quantitatively compare jobs relative to one another,[16] and then classify jobs for pay purposes.[17]

DEPARTMENT OF LABOR (DOL) PROCEDURE Experts at the U.S. Department of Labor did much of the early work developing job analysis.[18] They used their results to compile what was for many years the bible of job descriptions, the *Dictionary of Occupational*

Titles. This mammoth book contained detailed information on virtually every job in America. Internet-based tools have largely replaced the *Dictionary*. However, the U.S. Department of Labor job analysis procedure remains a good example of how to quantitatively rate, classify, and compare jobs. As Table 4-1 shows, the DOL method uses a set of standard activities called *worker functions* to describe what a worker must do with respect to *data, people*, and *things*. With respect to data, for instance, the functions include synthesizing and copying. For people, they include mentoring and supervising. For things, basic functions include manipulating and handling.

Each worker function has an importance rating. Thus, "coordinating" is 1, whereas "copying" is 5. If you were analyzing the job of a receptionist/clerk, for example, you might label the job 5, 6, 7 to represent copying data, speaking/signaling people, and handling things. You might code a psychiatric aide in a hospital 1, 7, 5 in relation to data, people, and things. In practice, you would score each task that the worker performed as part of his or her job in terms of data, people, and things. Then you would use the highest combination (say 4, 6, 5) to rate the overall job, since this is the highest level that you would expect a successful job incumbent to attain. If you were selecting a worker for that 4, 6, 5 job, you'd expect him or her to be able to at least compute (4), speak/signal (6), and tend (5). If you were comparing jobs for pay purposes, a 4, 6, 5 job should rank higher (see Table 4-1) than a 6, 8, 6 job. The manager can then present a summary of the job along with its 3-digit rating on a form such as in Figure 4-5.[19]

Electronic Job Analysis Methods[20]

Employers increasingly rely on electronic or Web-based job analysis methods. For example, the manager or job analyst may use the Web to review existing information about a job. Then, rather than collecting information about a job through direct interviews or questionnaires, the analyst uses online systems to send job questionnaires to job experts (often job incumbents) in remote locations. The Web also facilitates sharing and discussing responses, for instance, via Skype. The job analyst may thereby convene job experts to discuss and finalize the knowledge, skills, abilities, and other characteristics required for doing the job and its tasks.[21]

Conducting the job analysis via the Internet is often an obvious choice.[22] Most simply, the human resource department can distribute standardized job analysis questionnaires to geographically disbursed employees via their company intranets, with instructions to complete the forms and return them by a particular date.

Of course, the instructions should be clear, and test the process first. Without a job analyst actually sitting there with the employee or supervisor, there's a chance that the employees won't cover important points or that misunderstandings will cloud the results.

TABLE 4-1 Basic Department of Labor Worker Functions

	Data	People	Things
Basic Activities	0 Synthesizing	0 Mentoring	0 Setting up
	1 Coordinating	1 Negotiating	1 Precision working
	2 Analyzing	2 Instructing	2 Operating/controlling
	3 Compiling	3 Supervising	3 Driving/operating
	4 Computing	4 Diverting	4 Manipulating
	5 Copying	5 Persuading	5 Tending
	6 Comparing	6 Speaking/signaling	6 Feeding/offbearing
		7 Serving	7 Handling
		8 Taking instructions/helping	

Note: Determine employee's job "score" on data, people, and things by observing his or her job and determining, for each of the three categories, which of the basic functions illustrates the person's job. "0" is high; "6," "8," and "7" are lows in each column.

FIGURE 4-5 Sample Report Based on Department of Labor Job Analysis Technique

Job Analysis Schedule

1. Established Job Title DOUGH MIXER
2. Ind. Assign (bake prod.)
3. SIC Code(s) and Title(s) 2051 Bread and other bakery products

4. JOB SUMMARY:

Operates mixing machine to mix ingredients for straight and sponge (yeast) doughs according to established formulas, directs other workers in fermentation of dough, and curls dough into pieces with hand cutter.

5. WORK PERFORMED RATINGS:

	D	P	(T)
Worker Functions	Data	People	Things
	5	6	2

Work Field Cooking, Food Preparing

6. WORKER TRAITS RATING (to be filled in by analyst):

Training time required
Aptitudes
Temperaments
Interests
Physical demands
Environment conditions

The U.S. Navy used Internet-based job analysis.[23] To keep ambiguities to a minimum, it had the employees complete structured online job analysis forms step by step and duty by duty, as follows:

- First, the online form lists *a set of work activities* (such as "Getting Information" and "Monitor the Process") from the Department of Labor online O*NET work activities list (see Figure 4-6).[24]
- Next, the form directs employees to *select those work activities* that are important to their job.
- Then, the form asks them to *list actual duties* of their jobs that fit each of those selected work activities. For example, suppose an employee chose "Getting Information" as an important work activity. Now he or she would list next to "Getting Information" specific job duties, such as "watch for new orders from our vendors and bring them to the boss's attention."

Again, the main issue with online job analysis is to strip the process of ambiguities. The Navy's online method proved effective.[25]

Watch It!

If your professor has assigned this, go to the Assignments section of **mymanagementlab.com** to see how an actual company uses job analysis, and to complete the video exercise titled *Weather Channel: Talent Management*.

Figure 4-6 O*NET Generalized Work Activities Categories

Note: The U.S. Navy employees were asked to indicate if their jobs required them to engage in work activities such as: Getting Information; Monitoring Processes; Identifying Objects; Inspecting Equipment; and Estimating Quantifiable Characteristics.
Source: From O*NET website, www.onetonline.org.

Print-friendly Version
(Outline View | Description View)

- **Generalized Work Activities** — General types of job behaviors occurring on multiple jobs
  - Information Input — Where and how are the information and data gained that are needed to perform this job?
    - Looking for and Receiving Job-Related Information — How is information obtained to perform this job?
      - **Getting Information** — Observing, receiving, and otherwise obtaining information from all relevant sources.
      - **Monitor Processes, Materials, or Surroundings** — Monitoring and reviewing information from materials, events, or the environment, to detect or assess problems.
    - Identify and Evaluating Job-Relevant Information — How is information interpreted to perform this job?
      - **Identifying Objects, Actions, and Events** — Identifying information by categorizing, estimating, recognizing differences or similarities, and detecting changes in circumstances or events.
      - **Inspecting Equipment, Structures, or Material** — Inspecting equipment, structures, or materials to identify the cause of errors or other problems or defects.
      - **Estimating the Quantifiable Characteristics of Products, Events, or Information** — Estimating sizes, distances, and quantities; or determining time, costs, resources, or materials needed to perform a work activity.

Writing Job Descriptions

LEARNING OBJECTIVE 4-4
Explain how you would write a job description.

The most important product of job analysis is the job description. A job description is a written statement of what the worker actually does, how he or she does it, and what the job's working conditions are. You use this information to write a job specification; this lists the knowledge, abilities, and skills required to perform the job satisfactorily.[26]

HR in Practice at the Hotel Paris In reviewing the Hotel Paris's employment systems, the HR manager was concerned that virtually all the company's job descriptions were out of date, and that many jobs had no descriptions at all. She knew that without accurate job descriptions, all her improvement efforts would be in vain. To see how this was handled, see the case on pages 122–123 of this chapter.

Diversity Counts

Most people assume that job descriptions are only of use in business settings, but that's not the case. In fact, for parents who want the best care for their kids, writing up a job description before hiring a child-care worker could be quite useful. For example, because what children learn when they're very young predicts their future academic and career success, facilitating early-childhood learning is a crucial task for many caregivers.[27] And yet few parents write a job description before recruiting their child-care workers. Many, therefore, hire this important person not clearly understanding what they want this person to do.

A well-thought-out job description might benefit everyone involved. The parent—knowing that supporting early-childhood learning is so important—might put more effort into finding and training the child's caregiver (95% of whom are women). The child might benefit from a more nurturing learning environment. And the caregiver would gain if, after recognizing how many challenging tasks she is responsible for, the parent would raise her salary from the current national average of about $19,000 per year—just about the poverty level for a family of three. ■

There is no standard format for writing a job description. However, most descriptions contain sections that cover:

1. Job identification
2. Job summary

3. Responsibilities and duties
4. Authority of incumbent
5. Standards of performance
6. Working conditions
7. Job specification

Figures 4-7 and 4-8 present two sample forms of job descriptions.

Job Identification

As in Figure 4-7, the job identification section (on top) contains several types of information.[28] The *job title* specifies the name of the job, such as supervisor of data processing operations, or inventory control clerk. The Fair Labor Standards Act (FLSA) status section identifies the job as exempt or nonexempt. (Under the FLSA, certain positions, primarily administrative and professional, are exempt from the act's overtime and minimum wage provisions.) *Date* is the date the job description was actually approved.

There may also be a space to indicate who approved the description and perhaps a space showing the location of the job in terms of its facility/division and department. This section might also include the immediate supervisor's title and information regarding salary and/or pay scale. There might also be space for the grade/level of the job, if there is such a category. For example, a firm may classify programmers as programmer II, programmer III, and so on.

Job Summary

The job summary should summarize the essence of the job, and include only its major functions or activities. Thus (in Figure 4-7), the telesales rep "... is responsible for selling college textbooks...." For the job of mailroom supervisor, "the mailroom supervisor receives, sorts, and delivers all incoming mail properly, and he or she handles all outgoing mail including the accurate and timely posting of such mail."[29]

Some experts state unequivocally that "one item frequently found that should never be included in a job description is a 'cop-out clause' like 'other duties, as assigned,'"[30] since this leaves open the nature of the job. Finally, state in the summary that the employee is expected to carry out his or her duties efficiently, attentively, and conscientiously.

Relationships

There may be a "relationships" statement (not in Figure 4-7) that shows the jobholder's relationships with others inside and outside the organization. For a human resource manager, such a statement might say:[31]

Reports to: Vice president of employee relations.

Supervises: Human resource clerk, test administrator, labor relations director, and one secretary.

Works with: All department managers and executive management.

Outside the company: Employment agencies, executive recruiting firms, union representatives, state and federal employment offices, and various vendors.[32]

Responsibilities and Duties

This is the heart of the job description. It should present a list of the job's significant responsibilities and duties. As in Figure 4-7, list each of the job's major duties separately, and describe it in a few sentences. In the figure, for instance, the job's duties include "achieve quantitative sales goal ..." and "determine sales priorities...." Typical duties for other jobs might include making accurate postings to accounts payable, maintaining favorable purchase price variances, and repairing production-line tools and equipment. This section may also define the jobholder's authority limits. For example, the jobholder might have authority to approve purchase requests up to $5,000, grant time off or leaves of absence, discipline department personnel, recommend salary increases, and interview and hire new employees.

Usually, the manager's basic question here is, "How do I determine what the job's duties are and should be?" The answer first is, from the *job analysis*; this should reveal what the employees on each job are doing now.

Standard Occupational Classification (SOC)
Classifies all workers into one of 23 major groups of jobs that are subdivided into minor groups of jobs and detailed occupations.

Second, you can review various sources of standardized job description information. For example, the U.S. government's **Standard Occupational Classification (SOC)** (www.bls.gov/soc/socguide.htm) classifies all workers into one of 23 major groups of jobs, such as "Management Occupations" and "Healthcare Occupations." These in turn contain 96 minor groups of jobs, which in turn include 821 detailed occupations, such as the marketing manager description in Figure 4-8. The employer

JOB TITLE: Telesales Respresentative	**JOB CODE:** 100001
RECOMMENDED SALARY GRADE:	**EXEMPT/NONEXEMPT STATUS:** Nonexempt
JOB FAMILY: Sales	**EEOC:** Sales Workers
DIVISION: Higher Education	**REPORTS TO:** District Sales Manager
DEPARTMENT: In-House Sales	**LOCATION:** Boston
	DATE: April 2013

SUMMARY (Write a brief summary of job.)

The person in this position is responsible for selling college textbooks, software, and multimedia products to professors, via incoming and outgoing telephone calls, and to carry out selling strategies to meet sales goals in assigned territories of smaller colleges and universities. In addition, the individual in this position will be responsible for generating a designated amount of editorial leads and communicating to the publishing groups product feedback and market trends observed in the assigned territory.

SCOPE AND IMPACT OF JOB

Dollar responsibilities (budget and/or revenue)

The person in this position is responsible for generating approximately $2 million in revenue, for meeting operating expense budget of approximately $4000, and a sampling budget of approximately 10,000 units.

Supervisory responsibilities (direct and indirect)

None

Other

REQUIRED KNOWLEDGE AND EXPERIENCE (Knowledge and experience necessary to do job)

Related work experience

Prior sales or publishing experience preferred. One year of company experience in a customer service or marketing function with broad knowledge of company products and services is desirable.

Formal education or equivalent

Bachelor's degree with strong academic performance or work equivalent experience.

Skills

Must have strong organizational and persuasive skills. Must have excellent verbal and written communications skills and must be PC proficient.

Other

Limited travel required (approx 5%)

(Continued)

FIGURE 4-7 Sample Job Description, Pearson Education

Source: Reprinted and electronically reproduced by permission of Pearson Education, Inc., Upper Saddle River, New Jersey.

PRIMARY RESPONSIBILITIES (List in order of importance and list amount of time spent on task.)

Driving Sales (60%)

- Achieve quantitative sales goal for assigned territory of smaller colleges and universities.
- Determine sales priorities and strategies for territory and develop a plan for implementing those strategies.
- Conduct 15–20 professor interviews per day during the academic sales year that accomplishes those priorities.
- Conduct product presentations (including texts, software, and Web site); effectively articulate author's central vision of key titles; conduct sales interviews using the PSS model; conduct walk-through of books and technology.
- Employ telephone selling techniques and strategies.
- Sample products to appropriate faculty, making strategic use of assigned sampling budgets.
- Close class test adoptions for first edition products.
- Negotiate custom publishing and special packaging agreements within company guidelines.
- Initiate and conduct in-person faculty presentations and selling trips as appropriate to maximize sales with the strategic use of travel budget. Also use internal resources to support the territory sales goals.
- Plan and execute in-territory special selling events and book-fairs.
- Develop and implement in-territory promotional campaigns and targeted email campaigns.

Publishing (editorial/marketing) 25%

- Report, track, and sign editorial projects.
- Gather and communicate significant market feedback and information to publishing groups.

Territory Management 15%

- Track and report all pending and closed business in assigned database.
- Maintain records of customer sales interviews and adoption situations in assigned database.
- Manage operating budget strategically.
- Submit territory itineraries, sales plans, and sales forecasts as assigned.
- Provide superior customer service and maintain professional bookstore relations in assigned territory.

Decision-Making Responsibilities for This Position:

Determine the strategic use of assigned sampling budget to most effectively generate sales revenue to exceed sales goals.
Determine the priority of customer and account contacts to achieve maximum sales potential.
Determine where in-person presentations and special selling events would be most effective to generate the most sales.

Submitted By: Jim Smith, District Sales Manager	Date: April 10, 2013
Approval:	Date:
Human Resources:	Date:
Corporate Compensation:	Date:

FIGURE 4-7 ***Continued***

can use standard descriptions like these to identify a job's duties and responsibilities, such as "Determine the demand for products."

The employer may also use other popular sources of job description information, such as www.jobdescription.com. Another simple solution is just to *Google* the job description you want, by seeing online what others are doing. Thus, someone writing job descriptions for jobs such as marketing manager would readily find relevant online descriptions as follows:

Go to http://hiring.monster.com. Then click Resource Center, then Recruiting and Hiring Advice, then Job descriptions, then Sample job descriptions. Then scroll down to Marketing and Sales Manager Sample Job Description.[33]

FIGURE 4-8 Marketing Manager Description from Standard Occupational Classification

Source: U.S. Department of Labor, Bureau of Labor Statistics.

U.S. Department of Labor
Bureau of Labor Statistics
Standard Occupational Classification

www.bls.gov Advanced Search | A-Z Index

BLS Home | Programs & Surveys | Get Detailed Statistics | Glossary | What's New | Find It! In DOL

11-2021 Marketing Managers

Determine the demand for products and services offered by a firm and its competitors and identify potential customers. Develop pricing strategies with the goal of maximizing the firm's profits or share of the market while ensuring the firm's customers are satisfied. Oversee product development or monitor trends that indicate the need for new products and services.

Go to www.careerplanner.com. Then click Job Descriptions, then scroll down to Marketing Manager Job Description.[34]

O*NET online, as noted, is another option for finding job duties. We present an example in the hr Tools for Line Managers and Small Businesses feature at the end of this section.

TRENDS SHAPING HR: *DIGITAL AND SOCIAL MEDIA*

Social media is helping to democratize HR, by enabling line managers to do things for which they formerly required HR managers, thus bypassing HR. For example, the hiring manager can easily unearth job titles and duties using social media like LinkedIn. Thus (to paraphrase what someone posted on LinkedIn): *I hope some of you IT recruiters out there can help me to better understand what I need to put into the job descriptions that I'm writing for the O*NET developers and development managers I'm recruiting for*. The first of many replies listed 12 tasks including: (1) Do technical skills match the desired job? (2) What technical problems were solved by the job seeker? and (3) Did job seeker know about Cloud Deployment?[35]

But some of the job titles you'll find on social media may be more creative than usable. For example, Pinterest calls its designers Pixel Pushers![36] ■

Writing clear job duties is an art. For a teacher, for example, one duty might be:[37]

Incorrect: Ensures that students learn 5th grade English with the aim of passing the required common exam.

Comment: What the teacher does is ambiguous, and the expected process and results of the teacher's actions aren't clear.

Correct: Studies past common English exams to understand what they typically involve, prepares yearly, weekly, and daily lesson plans, presents each day's lesson clearly with follow up questions to ensure learning, administers weekly tests to confirm learning, and counsel students with one on one in class lessons as necessary.

KNOW YOUR EMPLOYMENT LAW

Writing Job Descriptions That Comply with the ADA

The list of job duties is crucial to employers' efforts to comply with the Americans with Disabilities Act (ADA). Under the ADA, the individual must have the requisite skills, educational background, and experience to perform the job's essential functions. The

EEOC says, "Essential functions are the basic job duties that an employee must be able to perform, with or without reasonable accommodation."[38] Factors to consider include:

- Whether the position exists to perform that function,
- The number of other employees available to perform the function,
- The degree of expertise or skill required to perform the function.
- Whether employees in the position are actually required to perform the function.[39]
- What the degree of expertise or skill required to perform the function is.[40]

As an example, answering calls and directing visitors to the proper offices might be essential functions for a receptionist's job. The EEOC says it will consider both the employer's judgment about which functions are essential, and a written job description prepared before advertising or interviewing for a job as evidence of essential functions. Other evidence includes the actual work experience of present or past employees in the job, the time spent performing a function, and the consequences of not requiring that an employee perform a function.

If the disabled individual can't perform the job as currently structured, the employer is required to make a "reasonable accommodation," unless doing so would present an "undue hardship." The EEOC says reasonable accommodation may include:

- acquiring or modifying equipment or devices,
- job redesign/restructuring,
- part-time or modified work schedules,
- reassignment to a vacant position,
- adjusting or modifying examinations, training materials, or policies,
- providing readers and interpreters, and
- making the workplace readily accessible to and usable by people with disabilities. ■

Standards of Performance and Working Conditions

A "standards of performance" section lists the standards the company expects the employee to achieve for each of the job description's main duties and responsibilities. One way to set standards is to finish the statement, "I will be completely satisfied with your work when…." This sentence, if completed for each listed duty, should result in a usable set of performance standards. For example:

***Duty:* Accurately Posting Accounts Payable**

1. Post all invoices received within the same working day.
2. Route all invoices to the proper department managers for approval no later than the day following receipt.
3. Commit an average of no more than three posting errors per month.

The job description may also list the job's working conditions, such as noise level, hazardous conditions, or heat.

IMPROVING PERFORMANCE: *HR Tools for Line Managers and Small Businesses*

Using O*NET

Without their own job analysts or even HR managers, many small business owners face two hurdles when doing job analyses. First, most need a more streamlined approach than those provided by questionnaires like that in Figure 4-4. Second is the concern that, in writing their job descriptions, they'll overlook duties that subordinates should be assigned. What they need is an encyclopedia listing all the possible positions they might encounter, including a list of the duties normally assigned to these positions.

The small business owner has at least three options. The *Standard Occupational Classification*, mentioned earlier, provides detailed descriptions of thousands of jobs and their human requirements. Web sites like www.jobdescription.com provide customizable descriptions by title and industry. And the Department of Labor's O*NET is a third alternative. We'll focus here on how to write a job description using O*NET (http://online.onetcenter.org).[41] It is free to use.

O*NET

The U.S. Department of Labor's online occupational information network, called O*NET, enables anyone to see the most important characteristics of various occupations, as well as the experience, education, and knowledge required to do each job well. Both the Standard Occupational Classification and O*NET list the specific duties associated with numerous occupations. O*NET also lists skills, including *basic skills* such as reading and writing, *process skills* such as critical thinking, and *transferable skills* such as persuasion and negotiation.[42] An O*NET job listing also includes information on worker requirements (required knowledge, for instance), occupation requirements (such as compiling, coding, and categorizing data, for instance), and experience requirements (including education and job training). Employers and career planers also use O*NET to check the job's labor market characteristics, such as employment projections and earnings data.[43]

The steps in using O*NET to facilitate writing a job description follow.

Step 1. *Review your Plan.* Ideally, the jobs you need should flow from your departmental or company plans. Do you plan to enter or exit businesses? What do you expect your sales to be in the next few years? What departments will have to be expanded or reduced? What kinds of new positions will you need?

Step 2. *Develop an Organization Chart.* Start with the organization as it is now. Then produce a chart showing how you want it to look in a year or two. Microsoft Word includes an organization charting function.[44]

Step 3. *Use a Job Analysis Questionnaire.* Next, gather information about each job's duties. (You can use job analysis questionnaires, such as those shown in Figures 4-4 and 4-9).

FIGURE 4-9 Simple Job Description Questionnaire

Source: Copyright Gary Dessler, PhD.

Background Data for Job Description

Job Title _____ Department _____

Job Number _____ Written by _____

Today's Date _____ Applicable DOT Codes _____

I. Applicable DOT Definition(s):

II. Job Summary:
(List the more important or regularly performed tasks)

III. Reports To:

IV. Supervises: _____

V. Job Duties: _____
(Briefly describe, for each duty, what employee does and, if possible, how employee does it. Show in parentheses at end of each duty the approximate percentage of time devoted to duty.)

A. Daily Duties:

B. Periodic Duties:
(Indicate whether weekly, monthly, quarterly, etc.)

C. Duties Performed at Irregular Intervals:

Source: Reprinted by permission of O*NET OnLine.

o·net OnLine

Occupational Information Network
O·NET OnLine

Related Links | OnLine Help

Find Occupations | Skills Search | Crosswalk

Welcome to O*NET™ OnLine!

Making occupational information interactive and accessible for all...

About New Data in OnLine

Find Occupations
Find occupations using keywords, O*NET-SOC codes, Job Families, or by viewing a complete list.

Skills Search
Use a list of your skills to find matching O*NET-SOC occupations.

Crosswalk
Use other classification systems (DOT, SOC, MOC, and RAIS) to find matching O*NET-SOC occupations.

If your search identifies occupations that require skills or abilities that may be difficult to use because of a health problem or disability, please consider job accommodations. Accommodations may involve a change in the work environment, the way a specific job is performed, or the use of special equipment.

For assistance in identifying accommodation options, contact the Job Accommodation Network (JAN), a service of the U.S. DOL Office of Disability Employment Policy, or go directly to SOAR (Searchable Online Accommodation Resource).

The Occupational Information Network (O*NET) and O*NET OnLine were developed for the US Department of Labor by the National O*NET Consortium. For more information about O*NET and the O*NET Consortium, please visit the O*NET Consortium Website.

o·net Resource Center | o·net Code Connector | CAREER onestop

Find Occupations | Skills Search | Crosswalk
Related Links | Content Model | Online Help

A

o·net OnLine

Occupational Information Network
O·NET OnLine

Related Links | OnLine Help

Find Occupations | Skills Search | Crosswalk

Job Family Search Results for:
Sales and Related (30 matches)

Sales and Related | Go

O*NET-SOC Code	O*NET-SOC Title	Reports (help)		
41-1011.00	First-Line Supervisors/Managers of Retail Sales Workers	Summary	Details	Custom
41-1012.00	First-Line Supervisors/Managers of Non-Retail Sales Workers	Summary	Details	Custom
41-2011.00	Cashiers	Summary	Details	Custom
41-2012.00	Gaming Change Persons and Booth Cashiers	Summary	Details	Custom
41-2021.00	Counter and Rental Clerks	Summary	Details	Custom
41-2022.00	Parts Salespersons	Summary	Details	Custom
41-2031.00	Retail Salespersons	Summary	Details	Custom
41-3011.00	Advertising Sales Agents	Summary	Details	Custom
41-3021.00	Insurance Sales Agents	Summary	Details	Custom
41-3031.00	Securities, Commodities, and Financial Services Sales Agents	Summary	Details	Custom
41-3031.01	Sales Agents, Securities and Commodities	Summary	Details	Custom
41-3031.02	Sales Agents, Financial Services	Summary	Details	Custom
41-3041.00	Travel Agents	Summary	Details	Custom
41-3099.99	Sales Representatives, Services, All Other	Summary	Details	Custom
41-4011.00	Sales Representatives, Wholesale and Manufacturing, Technical and Scientific Products	Summary	Details	Custom
41-4011.01	Sales Representatives, Agricultural	Summary	Details	Custom
41-4011.02	Sales Representatives, Chemical and Pharmaceutical	Summary	Details	Custom
41-4011.03	Sales Representatives, Electrical/Electronic	Summary	Details	Custom

B

Updated 2002

Summary Report for:
41-2031.00 - Retail Salespersons

Sell merchandise, such as furniture, motor vehicles, appliances, or apparel in a retail establishment.

Tasks | Knowledge | Skill | Ability | Work Activities | Work Context | Job Zone | Interests | Work Styles | Work Values | Related Occupations | Wages & Employment

Tasks

- Greet customers and ascertain what each customer wants or needs.
- Open and close cash registers, performing tasks such as counting money, separating charge slips, coupons, and vouchers, balancing cash drawers, and making deposits.
- Maintain knowledge of current sales and promotions, policies regarding payment and exchanges, and security practices.
- Compute sales prices, total purchases and receive and process cash or credit payment.
- Maintain records related to sales.
- Watch for and recognize security risks and thefts, and know how to prevent or handle these situations.
- Recommend, select, and help locate or obtain merchandise based on customer needs and desires.
- Answer questions regarding the store and its merchandise.
- Describe merchandise and explain use, operation, and care of merchandise to customers.
- Ticket, arrange and display merchandise to promote sales.

back to top

Knowledge

Customer and Personal Service — Knowledge of principles and processes for providing customer and personal services. This includes customer needs assessment, meeting quality standards for services, and evaluation of customer satisfaction.

Sales and Marketing — Knowledge of principles and methods for showing, promoting, and selling products or services. This includes marketing strategy and tactics, product demonstration, sales techniques, and sales control systems.

Administration and Management — Knowledge of business and management principles involved in strategic planning, resource allocation, human resources modeling, leadership technique, production methods, and coordination of people and resources.

Education and Training — Knowledge of principles and methods for curriculum and training design, teaching and instruction for individuals and groups, and the measurement of training effects.

Mathematics — Knowledge of arithmetic, algebra, geometry, calculus, statistics, and their applications.

English Language — Knowledge of the structure and content of the English language including the meaning and spelling of words, rules of composition, and grammar.

C

Step 4. *Obtain Job Duties from O*NET.* The list of job duties you uncovered through the job analysis in step 3 may or may not be complete. We'll therefore use O*NET to compile a more complete list. (Refer to the A, B, and C examples pictured just above.)

Start by going to http://online.onetcenter.org (A). Here, click on *Find Occupations*. Assume you want to create job descriptions for a retail salesperson. Key *Retail Sales* in the Keyword drop-down box. This brings you to the Occupations matching "retail sales" page (B).

Clicking on the *Retail Salespersons* summary produces the job summary and specific occupational duties for retail salespersons (C). For a small store, you might want to combine the duties of the "retail salesperson" with those of "first-line supervisors/managers of retail sales workers."

Step 5. ***List the Job's Human Requirements from O*NET.*** Next, return to the summary for *Retail Salesperson* (C). Here, click, for example, Knowledge, Skills, and Abilities. Use this information to help develop a job specification for your job. Use this information for recruiting, selecting, and training your employees.

Step 6. ***Finalize the Job Description.*** Finally, perhaps using Figure 4-9 as a guide, write an appropriate job summary for the job. Then use the information obtained previously in steps 4 and 5 to create a complete listing of the tasks, duties, and human requirements of each of the jobs you will need to fill. ■

If your professor has assigned this, go to the Assignments section of **mymanagementlab.com** to complete these discussion questions.

Talk About It 2: Pick a job that someone with whom you are familiar is doing, such as a bus driver, mechanic, and so on. Review the O*NET information for that job. To what extent does the person seem to have what it takes to do that job, based on the O*NET information? How does that correspond to how he or she is actually doing?

Writing Job Specifications

LEARNING OBJECTIVE 4-5

Explain how to write a job specification.

The job specification takes the job description and answers the question, "What human traits and experience are required to do this job effectively?" It shows what kind of person to recruit and for what qualities you should test that person. It may be a section of the job description, or a separate document. Often—as in Figure 4-7 on pages 110–111—it is part of the job description.[45]

Specifications for Trained versus Untrained Personnel

Writing job specifications for trained and experienced employees is relatively straightforward. Here job specifications tend to focus on factors such as length of previous service, quality of relevant training, and previous job performance.

The problems are more complex when you're filling jobs with untrained people (with the intention of training them on the job). Here you must specify qualities such as physical traits, personality, interests, or sensory skills that imply some potential for performing the job or for trainability. Thus, for a job that requires detailed manipulation in a circuit board assembly line, you might want someone who scores high on a test of

Hill Street Studios/Blend Images/Corbis

Filling jobs with untrained employees requires identifying the personal traits that predict performance.

finger dexterity. Employers identify the job's human requirements either through a subjective, judgmental approach or through statistical analysis (or both).

Specifications Based on Judgment

Most job specifications simply reflect the educated guesses of people like supervisors and human resource managers. The basic procedure here is to ask, "What does it take in terms of education, intelligence, training, and the like to do this job well?"

How does one make such "educated guesses"? You could simply review the job's duties, and deduce from those what human traits and skills the job requires. You can also choose human traits and skills from those listed in Web-based job descriptions like those at www.jobdescription.com. (For example, a typical job description there lists "Generates creative solutions" and "Manages difficult or emotional customer situations.") O*NET online is another option. Job listings there include lists of required education and other experience and skills.

In any case, use common sense. Don't ignore the behaviors that may apply to almost any job but that might not normally surface through a job analysis. Industriousness is an example. Who wants an employee who doesn't work hard? One researcher collected supervisor ratings and other information from 18,000 employees in 42 different hourly entry-level jobs.[46] Generic work behaviors that he found to be important to all jobs included thoroughness, attendance, unruliness [lack of], and scheduling flexibility (for instance, offers to stay late when store is busy). Another study, of over 7,000 executives, found that crucial top-leader behaviors included: takes initiative, practices self-development, displays high integrity, drives for results, and develops others.[47]

Job Specifications Based on Statistical Analysis

Basing job specifications on statistical analysis rather than only judgment is the more defensible approach, but it's also more difficult. The aim here is to determine statistically the relationship between (1) some *predictor* (human trait such as height, intelligence, or finger dexterity), and (2) some indicator or *criterion* of job effectiveness, such as performance as rated by the supervisor.

This procedure has five steps: (1) analyze the job and decide how to measure job performance; (2) select personal traits like finger dexterity that you believe should predict performance; (3) test candidates for these traits; (4) measure these candidates' subsequent job performance; and (5) statistically analyze the relationship between the human trait (finger dexterity) and job performance. Your aim is to determine whether the trait predicts performance.

Why is this more defensible than the judgmental approach? First, if the trait does not predict performance, why use it? Second, equal rights laws prohibit using traits that you can't prove distinguish between high and low job performers. But, in practice, most employers rely on judgmental approaches.

The Job-Requirements Matrix

job-requirements matrix
A more complete description of what the worker does and how and why he or she does it; it clarifies each task's purpose and each duty's required knowledge, skills, abilities, and other characteristics.

task statement
Written item that shows *what* the worker does on one particular job task; *how* the worker does it; the *knowledge, skills, and aptitudes required* to do it; and the *purpose of the task*.

Although most employers use job descriptions and specifications to summarize their jobs' duties and responsibilities, the **job-requirements matrix** is also popular.[48] A typical matrix lists the following information, in five columns:

Column 1: Each of the job's four or five *main job duties* (such as Post Accounts Payable)

Column 2: The *task statements* for the main tasks associated with each main job duty

Column 3: The relative *importance* of each main job duty

Column 4: The *time spent* on each main job duty

Column 5: The *knowledge, skills, ability*, and *other* human characteristics (KSAO) related to each main job duty[49]

The main step in creating a job-requirements matrix involves writing the *task statements.* Each **task statement** describes *what* the worker does on each of a main job duty's separate job tasks and *how* the worker does it.

LEARNING OBJECTIVE 4-6

List some human traits and behaviors you would want an employee to bring to a job if employee engagement is important to doing the job well.

Employee Engagement Guide for Managers

How does one identify candidates who have a high likelihood of becoming engaged employees? In terms of the job specification, the question is, "What desirable traits should someone possess to make it more likely that he or she will become an engaged employee?" The human resource consulting company Development Dimensions International conducted a study of 3,800 employees. It identified several personal characteristics that seemed to predict the likelihood someone would be engaged.[50] These traits included adaptability, passion for work, emotional maturity, positive disposition, self-advocacy, and achievement orientation.

A sensible suggestion is to seek out people who already have track records of being engaged employees. Since past behavior is often the best predictor of future behavior one suggestion is that if you want to hire people who are more likely to become engaged employees, "... look for examples of engagement in other areas of life."[51] For example, seek out candidates with a demonstrated commitment to serve others, such as nurses, veterans, and voluntary first responders.

LEARNING OBJECTIVE 4-7

Explain competency-based job analysis, including what it means and how it's done in practice.

Using Competencies Models

Many people still think of a "job" as a set of specific duties someone carries out for pay, but the concept of job is changing. Companies today are flattening their hierarchies, squeezing out managers, and leaving the remaining workers with more jobs to do. Changes like these tend to blur where one job starts and another ends. In situations like these, relying on a list of job duties that itemizes specific things you expect the worker to do is often impractical.[52]

Many employers are therefore using a newer job analysis approach. Instead of listing the job's duties, they are listing, in *competency models* (or profiles), the knowledge, skills, and experience someone needs to do the job. Such models or profiles (see Figure 4-10) list the competencies employees must be able to exhibit to get their jobs done.[53] In creating a competency model for HR managers, the Society for Human

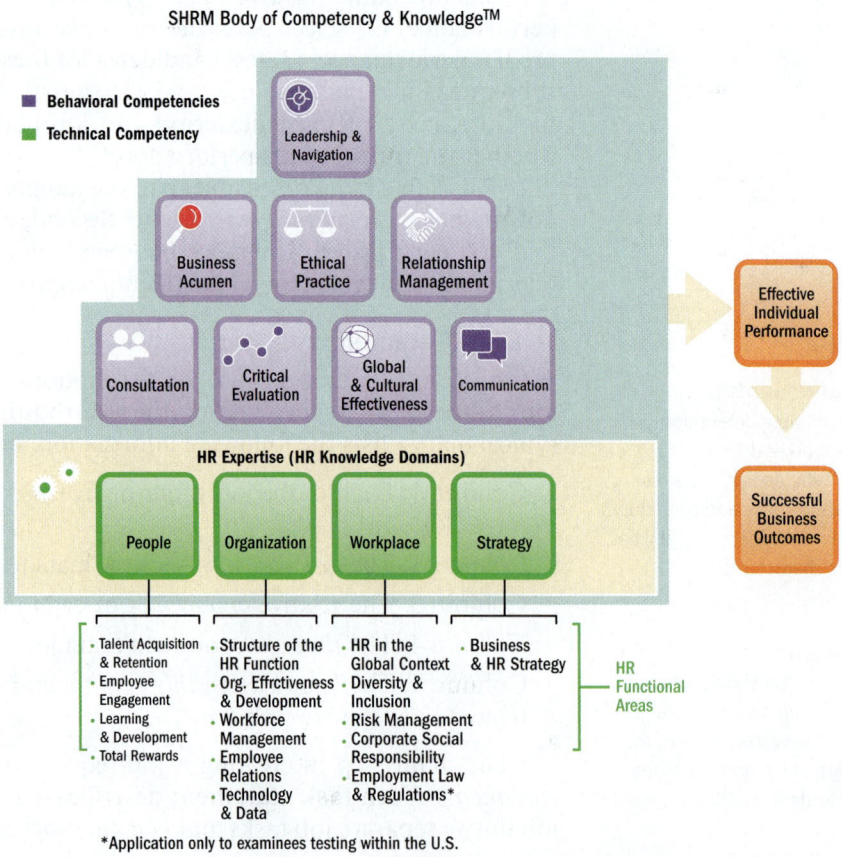

FIGURE 4-10 HR Manager Competency Model

Source: The SHRM Body of Competency and Knowledge. ©2014, Society for Human Resource Management., Alexandria, VA. Used with permission. All rights reserved.

Resource Management describes a competency as a "cluster of highly interrelated attributes" (such as research design knowledge, critical thinking skills, and deductive reasoning abilities) that give rise to the behaviors (such as *critical evaluation*) someone would need to perform a given job (in this case, HR manager) effectively.[54]

The competency model or profile then becomes the guidepost for recruiting, selecting, training, evaluating, and developing employees for each job.[55] For instance, the manager *hires* new employees using tests that measure the profile's list of competencies, *trains* employees with courses that develop these competencies, and *appraises* performance by assessing the worker's competencies. The accompanying Strategic Context feature illustrates.

IMPROVING PERFORMANCE: *The Strategic Context*

Daimler Alabama Example

In planning its Alabama Mercedes-Benz factory, Germany-based Daimler's strategy was to design a high-tech factory.[56] The plant emphasizes *just-in-time* inventory methods, so inventories stay negligible due to the arrival "just in time" of parts. It also organizes employees into *work teams*, and emphasizes that all employees must dedicate themselves to *continuous improvement* (seeking continuously to find better ways to do things).

Such a production strategy requires certain employee competencies (skills and behaviors). For example, it requires multiskilled and flexible employees who are eager to work cooperatively in teams.

Competencies-based job analysis played an important role in this factory. Guidelines here regarding whom to hire and how to train them are based more on the competencies someone needs to do the job (such as "ability to work cooperatively on a team") than on lists of job duties. Because they don't have to follow detailed job descriptions showing what "my job" is, it's easier for employees to move from job to job within their teams. Not being pigeonholed also encourages workers to look beyond their own jobs to find ways to improve things. For instance, one team found a $0.23 plastic prong that worked better than the one for $2.50 the plant was using to keep car doors open during painting. Building its modern "continuous improvement" plant meant Daimler needed employees who thought for themselves. Organizing its jobs around worker competencies and using **competency-based job analysis** helped Daimler achieve its strategic aims here. ■

competency-based job analysis
Describing the job in terms of measurable, observable, behavioral competencies (knowledge, skills, and/or behaviors) that an employee doing that job must exhibit to do the job well.

If your professor has assigned this, go to the Assignments section of **mymanagementlab.com** to complete these discussion questions.

Talk About It 3: Specifically, what competencies would you look for in a prospective Alabama plant employee? Why?

How to Write Competencies Statements

The process for identifying the job's required competencies is similar to traditional job analysis. For example, you might interview job incumbents and their supervisors and ask open-ended questions regarding job responsibilities and activities.

But instead of compiling lists of job duties, your aim is to finish the statement, "*In order to perform this job competently, the employee should be able to….*" Use your knowledge of the job to answer this, or the worker's or supervisor's insights, or use information from a source such as O*NET, or the Department of Labor's Office of Personnel Management (see www.opm.gov). Then, for each competency write a *competency statement*.

The ideal competency statement will include three elements.[57] One is the *name and a brief description* of the competency, such as "Project Management—creating accurate and effective project schedules." The second is a *description of the observable behaviors* that represent proficiency in the competency, such as "continuously manage project risks and dependencies by making timely decisions." Third are *proficiency levels.* For example (for project management from low to high):[58]

- ***Proficiency Level 1.*** *Identifies* project risks and dependencies and communicates routinely to stakeholders
- ***Proficiency Level 2.*** *Develops systems to monitor* risks and dependencies and report changes
- ***Proficiency Level 3.*** Anticipates changing conditions and impact to risks and dependencies and takes preventive action

FIGURE 4-11 Skills Matrix

Note: This is an example of a skills matrix for technical/engineering product development employees. The light blue boxes show the level required for each skill for these product development employees. An accompanying key would provide specific examples for each level of each skill, with difficulty increasing for each skill level starting at Level 1. For example, Level 1 for Technical Expertise/Skills might say "has or is in process of acquiring the basic knowledge necessary to do this type of job," while Level 6 might say, "Capable of conducting and supervising highly complex analytical tasks requiring advanced technical know-how and skills." *Source:* Copyright Gary Dessler PhD.

	Technical Expertise/Skills	Decision Making and Problem Solving Skills	Interpersonal Skills	Leadership Skills	Commercial Awareness Skills
Level 6	6	6	6	6	6
Level 5	5	5	5	5	5
Level 4	4	4	4	4	4
Level 3	3	3	3	3	3
Level 2	2	2	2	2	2
Level 1	1	1	1	1	1

BP EXAMPLE British Petroleum's (BP's) exploration division executives wanted to shift employees from a job duties–oriented "that's-not-my-job" attitude to one that motivated employees to obtain the skills required to accomplish broader responsibilities.[59]

Their solution was a skills matrix like that in Figure 4-11. They had skills matrices for each job or job family (such as drilling managers). As in Figure 4-11, each matrix listed (1) the types of skills required to do that job such as technical expertise, and (2) the minimum skill required for proficiency at each level. The figure's note shows how to actually use the matrix.

BP's skills matrix approach also supported its talent management efforts. Talent management efforts in this unit could now focus on recruiting, hiring, training, appraising, and rewarding employees based on the set of skills employees need to perform the job in question.

Chapter Review

MyManagementLab® Go to mymanagementlab.com to complete the problems marked with this icon. ✪

Chapter Section Summaries

4-1. Employers today often view all the staff–train–reward activities as part of a single integrated ***talent management* process**. We defined talent management as *the holistic, integrated and results and goal-oriented process of planning, recruiting, selecting, developing, managing, and compensating employees*. When a manager takes a talent management perspective, he or she should keep in mind that the talent management tasks are parts of a single interrelated talent management process; make sure talent management decisions such as staffing and pay are goal-directed; use the same "profile" for formulating recruitment plans for a job as you do for making selection, training, appraisal, and payment decisions for it; and integrate/coordinate all the talent management functions.

4-2. All managers should be familiar with **the basics of job analysis**. Job analysis is the procedure through which you determine the duties of the department's positions and the characteristics of the people to hire for them. Job descriptions are a list of what the job entails, while job specifications identify what kind of people to hire for the job. The job analysis itself involves collecting information on matters such as work activities; required human behaviors; and machines, tools, and equipment used. Managers use job analysis information in recruitment and selection, compensation, training, and performance appraisal. The basic steps in job analysis include deciding on the use of the job analysis information, reviewing relevant background information including organization charts, analyzing the job, verifying the information, and developing job descriptions and job specifications.

4-3. There are various **methods for collecting job analysis information**. These include interviews, questionnaires, observation, participant diary/logs, and quantitative techniques such as position analysis questionnaires. Employers increasingly collect information from employees via the Internet.

4-4. Managers should know how to **write job descriptions**. While there is no standard format, most descriptions contain sections that cover job identification, a job summary, a listing of responsibilities and duties, the job incumbent's authority, and performance standards. The job description may also contain information regarding the job's working conditions, and the job specifications. Many employers use Internet sources such as www.jobdescription.com to facilitate writing job descriptions.

4-5. In **writing job specifications**, it's important to distinguish between specifications for trained versus untrained personnel. For trained employees, the process is relatively straightforward, because you're looking primarily for traits like experience. For untrained personnel, it's necessary to identify traits that might predict success on the job. Most job specifications come from the educated guesses of people like supervisors, and are based mostly on judgment. Some employers use statistical analyses to identify predictors or human traits that are related to success on the job.

4-6. Human traits and behaviors that may predict the job candidates' likelihood to be **engaged** and that the manager might therefore want to include in the job specification include adaptability, passion for work, emotional maturity, positive disposition, self-advocacy, achievement orientation, and a work history that includes a demonstrated commitment to serve others.

4-7. Employers are using **competencies models** and profiles in talent management. The aim is to create descriptions of what is required for exceptional performance in a given role or job, in terms of required competencies, personal attributes, knowledge, and experience. Each job's profile then becomes the anchor for creating recruitment, selection, training, and evaluation and development plans for each job. *Competency-based job analysis* means describing the job in terms of measurable, observable, behavioral competencies (such as specific skills) that an employee doing the job must exhibit to do the job well. With the job of, say, a team member possibly changing daily, one should identify the skills the employee may need to move among jobs.

Discussion Questions

4-1. Why, in summary, should managers think of staffing, training, appraising, and paying employees as a talent management process?

✪ **4-2.** What items are typically included in the job description?

4-3. We discussed several methods for collecting job analysis data—questionnaires, the position analysis questionnaire, and so on. Compare and contrast these methods, explaining what each is useful for and listing the pros and cons of each.

4-4. Describe the types of information typically found in a job specification.

4-5. Explain how you would conduct a job analysis.

✪ **4-6.** Do you think all companies can really do without detailed job descriptions? Why or why not?

4-7. Explain how you would create a job-requirements matrix for a job.

4-8. In a company with only 25 employees, is there less need for job descriptions? Why or why not?

Individual and Group Activities

4-9. Working individually or in groups, obtain copies of job descriptions for clerical positions at the college or university where you study, or the firm where you work. What types of information do they contain? Do they give you enough information to explain what the job involves and how to do it? How would you improve on the description?

4-10. Working individually or in groups, use O*NET to develop a job description for your professor in this class. Based on that, use your judgment to develop a job specification. Compare your conclusions with those of other students or groups. Were there any significant differences? What do you think accounted for the differences?

4-11. Appendices A and B at the end of this book (pages 612–629) list the knowledge someone studying for the HRCI (Appendix A) or SHRM (Appendix B) certification exam needs to have in each area of human resource management (such as in Strategic Management, and Workforce Planning). In groups of several students, do four things: (1) review Appendix A and/or B; (2) identify the material in this chapter that relates to the Appendix A and/or Appendix B required knowledge lists; (3) write four multiple-choice exam questions on this material that you believe would be suitable for inclusion in the HRCI exam and/or the SHRM exam; and, (4) if time permits, have someone from your team post your team's questions in front of the class, so that students in all teams can answer the exam questions created by the other teams.

Experiential Exercise

The Instructor's Job Description

Purpose: The purpose of this exercise is to give you experience in developing a job description, by developing one for your instructor.

Required Understanding: You should understand the mechanics of job analysis and be thoroughly familiar with the job analysis questionnaires. (See Figures 4-4 and 4-9.)

How to Set Up the Exercise/Instructions: Set up groups of several students for this exercise. As in all exercises in this book, the groups should be separated and should not converse with each other. Half of the groups in the class will develop the job description using the job analysis questionnaire (Figure 4-4), and the other half of the groups will develop it using the job description questionnaire (Figure 4-9). Each student should review his or her questionnaire (as appropriate) before joining his or her group.

4-12. Each group should do a job analysis of the instructor's job: Half of the groups will use the Figure 4-4 job analysis questionnaire for this purpose, and half will use the Figure 4-9 job description questionnaire.

4-13. Based on this information, each group will develop its own job description and job specification for the instructor.

4-14. Next, each group should choose a partner group, one that developed the job description and job specification using the alternate method. (A group that used the job analysis questionnaire should be paired with a group that used the job description questionnaire.)

4-15. Finally, within each of these new combined groups, compare and critique each of the two sets of job descriptions and job specifications. Did each job analysis method provide different types of information? Which seems superior? Does one seem more advantageous for some types of jobs than others?

Application Case

The Flood

In May 2011, Mississippi River flooding hit Vicksburg, Mississippi, and the Optima Air Filter Company. Many employees' homes were devastated. Optima found that it had to hire almost three completely new crews, one for each shift. The problem was that the "old-timers" had known their jobs so well that no one had ever bothered to draw up job descriptions for them. When about 30 new employees began taking their places, there was general confusion about what they should do and how they should do it.

The flood quickly became old news to the firm's out-of-state customers, who wanted filters, not excuses. Phil Mann, the firm's president, was at his wits' end. He had about 30 new employees, 10 old-timers, and his original factory supervisor, Maybelline. He decided to meet with Linda Lowe, a consultant from the local university's business school. She immediately had the old-timers fill out a job questionnaire that listed all their duties. Arguments ensued almost at once: Both Phil and Maybelline thought the old-timers were exaggerating to make themselves look more important, and the old-timers insisted that the lists faithfully reflected their duties. Meanwhile, the customers clamored for their filters.

Questions

4-16. Should Phil and Linda ignore the old-timers' protests and write the job descriptions as they see fit? Why? Why not? How would you go about resolving the differences?

4-17. How would you have conducted the job analysis? What should Phil do now?

Continuing Case

Carter Cleaning Company

The Job Description

Based on her review of the stores, Jennifer concluded that one of the first matters she had to attend to involved developing job descriptions for her store managers.

As Jennifer tells it, her lessons regarding job descriptions in her basic management and HR management courses were insufficient to convince her of the pivotal role job descriptions actually play in the smooth functioning of an enterprise. Many times during her first few weeks on the job, Jennifer found herself asking one of her store managers why he was violating what she knew to be recommended company policies and procedures. Repeatedly, the answers were either "Because I didn't know it was my job" or "Because I didn't know that was the way we were supposed to do it." Jennifer knew that a job description, along with a set of standards and procedures that specified what was to be done and how to do it, would go a long way toward alleviating this problem.

In general, the store manager is responsible for directing all store activities in such a way that quality work is produced, customer relations and sales are maximized, and profitability is maintained through effective control of labor, supply, and energy costs. In accomplishing that general aim, a specific store manager's duties and responsibilities include quality control, store appearance and cleanliness, customer relations, bookkeeping and cash management, cost control and productivity, damage control, pricing, inventory control, spotting and cleaning, machine maintenance, purchasing, employee safety, hazardous waste removal, human resource administration, and pest control.

The questions that Jennifer had to address follow.

Questions

4-18. What should be the format and final form of the store manager's job description?

4-19. Is it practical to specify standards and procedures in the body of the job description, or should these be kept separate?

4-20. How should Jennifer go about collecting the information required for the standards, procedures, and job description?

4-21. What, in your opinion, should the store manager's job description look like and contain?

Translating Strategy into HR Policies and Practices Case*,§

**The accompanying strategy map for this chapter is in MyManagementLab, and the overall map on the inside back cover of this text outlines the relationships involved.*

Improving Performance at The Hotel Paris

The New Job Descriptions

The Hotel Paris's competitive strategy is "To use superior guest service to differentiate the Hotel Paris properties, and to thereby increase the length of stay and return rate of guests, and thus boost revenues and profitability." HR manager Lisa Cruz must now formulate functional policies and activities that support this competitive strategy and boost performance by eliciting the required employee behaviors and competencies.

As an experienced human resource director, the Hotel Paris's Lisa Cruz knew that recruitment and selection processes invariably influenced employee competencies and behavior and, through them, the company's bottom line. Everything about the workforce—its collective skills, morale, experience, and motivation—depended on attracting and then selecting the right employees.

In reviewing the Hotel Paris's employment systems, she was therefore concerned that virtually all the company's job descriptions were out of date, and that many jobs had no descriptions at all. She knew that without accurate job descriptions, all her improvement efforts would be in vain. After all, if you don't know a job's duties, responsibilities, and human requirements, how can you decide whom to hire or how to train them? To create human resource policies and practices that would produce employee competencies and behaviors needed to achieve the hotel's strategic aims, Lisa's team first had to produce a set of usable job descriptions.

A brief analysis, conducted with her company's CFO, reinforced that observation. They chose departments across the hotel chain that did and did not have updated job descriptions. While they understood that many other factors might be influencing the results, they believed that the statistical relationships they observed did suggest that having job descriptions had a positive influence on various employee behaviors and competencies. Perhaps having the descriptions facilitated the employee selection process, or perhaps the departments with the descriptions just had better managers. In any case, Lisa received the go-ahead to design new job descriptions for the chain.

While the resulting job descriptions included numerous traditional duties and responsibilities, most also included several competencies unique to each job. For example, job descriptions for the front-desk clerks included competencies such as "able to check a guest in or out in five minutes or less." Most service employees' descriptions included the competency, "able to exhibit patience and guest supportiveness even when busy with other activities." Lisa knew that including these competencies would make it easier for her team to devise useful employee selection, training, and evaluation processes.

Questions

In teams or individually:

4-22. Based on the hotel's stated strategy and on what you learned here in Chapter 4 of Dessler Human Resource Management, list at least four more important employee behaviors important for the Hotel Paris's staff to exhibit.

4-23. If time permits, spend some time prior to class observing the front-desk clerk at a local hotel. In any case, create a job description for a Hotel Paris front-desk clerk.

§ Written by and copyright Gary Dessler, PhD.

MyManagementLab

Go to **mymanagementlab.com** for Auto-graded writing questions as well as the following Assisted-graded writing questions:

4-24. What is job analysis? How can you make use of the information it provides?

4-25. Explain what a competencies model is and what the model would look like for the job of university professor.

4-26. MyManagementLab only—comprehensive writing assignment for this chapter.

✪ Try It!

How would you apply the concepts and skills you learned in this chapter? If your professor has assigned this, go to the Assignments section of **mymanagementlab.com** to complete the simulation: *Teams*.

✪ PERSONAL INVENTORY ASSESSMENTS

Personal Assessment of Management Skills

How good are you at sizing up one's skills? Complete this assessment to learn more about your personality.

Key Terms

talent management, 96
job analysis, 97
job description, 97
job specifications, 97
organization chart, 98
process chart, 99
workflow analysis, 99
business process reengineering, 99
job enlargement, 100
job rotation, 100
job enrichment, 100
diary/log, 105
position analysis questionnaire (PAQ), 105
Standard Occupational Classification (SOC), 110
job-requirements matrix, 117
task statement, 117
competency-based job analysis, 119

CHAPTER 4

Endnotes

1. Daimler is now expanding this plant; see www.autoblog.com/2009/03/23/rumormill-mercedes-benz-expected-to-expand-alabama-plant, accessed March 25, 2009; and http://mbusi.com/, accessed August 20, 2011. The plant currently builds Daimler's newly redesigned C-Class car. http://wot.motortrend.com/daimler-invests-in-alabama-plant-for-next-c-class-99493.html, accessed March 21, 2015.
2. See, for example, Toni Hodges DeTuncq and Lynn Schmidt, "Examining Integrated Talent Management," *Training & Development*, September 2013, pp. 31–35.
3. www.talent_management101.com, accessed December 10, 2007; and www.astd.org/Publications/Blogs/ASTD-Blog/2009/05/How-DoYou-Define-Talent-Management, accessed June 16, 2014. See also Nikki Dries, "Talent Management, from Phenomenon to Theory: Introduction to the Special Issue," *Human Resource Management Review*, 23, 2013, pp. 267–271.
4. Ibid.
5. www.silkRoadTech.com, accessed December 10, 2007.
6. For a good discussion of job analysis, see James Clifford, "Job Analysis: Why Do It, and How Should It Be Done?" *Public Personnel Management* 23, no. 2 (Summer 1994), pp. 321–340; and "Job Analysis," www.paq.com/index.cfm?FuseAction=bulletins.job-analysis, accessed February 3, 2009.
7. One writer calls job analysis "the hub of virtually all human resource management activities necessary for the successful functioning organizations." See Parbudyal Singh, "Job Analysis for a Changing Workplace," *Human Resource Management Review* 18 (2008), p. 87.
8. Richard Henderson, *Compensation Management: Rewarding Performance* (Upper Saddle River, NJ: Prentice Hall, 1994), pp. 139–150. See also T. A. Stetz et al., "New Tricks for an Old Dog: Visualizing Job Analysis Results," *Public Personnel Management* 38, no. 1 (Spring 2009), pp. 91–100.
9. Ron Miller, "Streamlining Claims Processing," *eWeek* 23, no. 25 (June 19, 2006), pp. 33, 35.
10. Darin Hartley, "Job Analysis at the Speed of Reality," *Training & Development*, September 2004, pp. 20–22.
11. See Henderson, *Compensation Management*, pp. 148–152.
12. Wayne Cascio, *Applied Psychology in Human Resource Management* (Upper Saddle River, NJ: Prentice Hall, 1998), p. 142. Distortion of information is a potential problem with all self-report methods of gathering information. See, for example, http://apps.opm.gov/ADT/ContentFiles/AssessmentDecisionGuide071807.pdf, accessed October 1, 2011.
13. Frederick Morgeson et al., "Self Presentation Processes in Job Analysis: A Field Experiment Investigating Inflation in Abilities, Tasks, and Competencies," *Journal of Applied Psychology* 89, no. 4 (November 4, 2004), pp. 674–686; and Frederick Morgeson and Stephen Humphrey, "The Work Design Questionnaire (WDQ): Developing and Validating a Comprehensive Measure for Assessing Job Design and the Nature of Work," *Journal of Applied Psychology* 91, no. 6 (2006), pp. 1321–1339.
14. Arthur Martinez et al., "Job Title Inflation," *Human Resource Management Review* 18 (2008), pp. 19–27.
15. Note that the PAQ (and other quantitative techniques) can also be used for job evaluation, which is explained in Chapter 11.
16. We will see that job evaluation is the process through which jobs are compared to one another

and their values determined for pay purposes. Some use the PAQ for job evaluation.

17. Jack Smith and Milton Hakel, "Convergence Among Data Sources, Response Bias, and Reliability and Validity of a Structured Job Analysis Questionnaire," *Personnel Psychology* 32 (Winter 1979), pp. 677–692. See also Frederick Morgeson and Stephen Humphrey, "The Work Design Questionnaire (WDQ): Developing and Validating a Comprehensive Measure for Assessing Job Design and the Nature of Work," *Journal of Applied Psychology* 91, no. 6 (2006), pp. 1321–1339; www.paq.com/index.cfm?FuseAction=bulletins.job-analysis, accessed February 3, 2009.
18. www.paq.com/index.cfm?FuseAction=bulletins.job-analysis, accessed February 3, 2009.
19. Another technique, *functional job analysis,* is similar to the DOL method. However, it rates the job not just on data, people, and things, but also on the extent to which performing the task requires four other things—specific instructions, reasoning and judgment, mathematical ability, and verbal and language facilities.
20. This is based on Dianna Stone et al., "Factors Affecting the Effectiveness and Acceptance of Electronic Selection Systems," *Human Resource Management Review* 23 (2013), pp. 53–54.
21. Ibid.
22. Roni Reiter-Palmon et al., "Development of an O*NET Web-Based Job Analysis and Its Implementation in the U.S. Navy: Lessons Learned," *Human Resource Management Review* 16 (2006), pp. 294–309.
23. Ibid., p. 295.
24. You can access the site at www.onetcenter.org/content.html/4.A#cm_4.A, accessed June 20, 2015.
25. Digitizing the information also enables the employer to quantify, tag, and electronically store and access it more readily. Lauren McEntire et al., "Innovations in Job Analysis: Development and Application of Metrics to Analyze Job Data," *Human Resource Management Review* 16 (2006), pp. 310–323.
26. See, for example, Kathryn Tyler, "Job Worth Doing: Update Descriptions," *HR Magazine*, January 2013, pp. 47–49.
27. This feature is based on Rebecca Ruiz, "Care for the Caregivers: Child-Care Providers Have Long Been Thought of as Full-Time Baby Sitters. The Government Can Help Them Become Well-Paid Professionals." *The American Prospect* 21.8 (2010), A17+. *Academic OneFile*. Web. 26 Mar. 2013.
28. Regarding this discussion, see Henderson, *Compensation Management*, pp. 175–184. See also Louisa Wah, "The Alphabet Soup of Job Titles," *Management Review* 87, no. 6 (June 1, 1998), pp. 40–43.
29. For discussions of writing job descriptions, see James Evered, "How to Write a Good Job Description," *Supervisory Management*, April 1981, pp. 14–19; Roger J. Plachy, "Writing Job Descriptions That Get Results," *Personnel*, October 1987, pp. 56–58; and Jean Phillips and Stanley Gulley, *Strategic Staffing* (Upper Saddle River, New Jersey: Pearson Education, 2012), pp. 89–95.
30. Evered, "How to Write a Good Job Description," p. 16.
31. Ibid.
32. Ibid.
33. http://hiring.monster.com/hr/hr-best-practices/recruiting-hiring-advice/job-descriptions/marketing-and-sales-manager-job-description-sample.aspx, accessed June 25, 2014.
34. http://job-descriptions.careerplanner.com/Marketing-Managers.cfm, accessed June 25, 2014.
35. www.linkedin.com/groups/Best-job-descriptions-40949.S.201279941, accessed March 26, 2013.
36. Ashley Ross, "Job Titles Retailored to Fit," *New York Times*, September 1, 2013, p. 11.
37. http://academicaffairs.ucsd.edu/staffhr/classification/task-statements.html, accessed March 27, 2013.
38. www.eeoc.gov/facts/ada17.html, accessed July 17, 2013.
39. Deborah Kearney, *Reasonable Accommodations: Job Descriptions in the Age of ADA, OSHA, and Workers Comp* (New York: Van Nostrand Reinhold, 1994), p. 9. See also Paul Starkman, "The ADA's Essential Job Function Requirements: Just How Essential Does an Essential Job Function Have to Be?" *Employee Relations Law Journal* 26, no. 4 (Spring 2001), pp. 43–102; and Benjamin Wolkinson and Sarah Wolkinson, "The Pregnant Police Officer's Overtime Duties and Forced Leave Policies under Title VII, the ADA, and FMLA," *Employee Relations Law Journal* 36, no. 1 (Summer 2010), pp. 3–20.
40. Kearney, *Reasonable Accommodations.*
41. O*NET™ is a trademark of the U.S. Department of Labor, Employment, and Training Administration.
42. See, for example, Christelle Lapolice et al., "Linking O*NET Descriptors to Occupational Literacy Requirements Using Job Component Validation," *Personnel Psychology* 61 (2008), pp. 405–441.
43. Mariani, "Replace with a Database."
44. Jorgen Sandberg, "Understanding Competence at Work," *Harvard Business Review*, March 2001, p. 28. Other organization chart software vendors include Nakisa, Aquire, and Human-Concepts. See "Advanced Org Charting," *Workforce Management*, May 19, 2008, p. 34.
45. Based on Ernest J. McCormick and Joseph Tiffin, *Industrial Psychology* (Upper Saddle River, NJ: Prentice Hall, 1974), pp. 56–61.
46. Steven Hunt, "Generic Work Behavior: An Investigation into the Dimensions of Entry-Level, Hourly Job Performance," *Personnel Psychology* 49 (1996), pp. 51–83.
47. "Are the Best People Being Promoted?" *Harvard Business Review*, September 2013, p. 89.
48. Jean Phillips and Stanley Gulley, *Strategic Staffing* (Upper Saddle River, NJ: Pearson Education, 2012), pp. 96–102.
49. Ibid., p. 102.
50. "Hiring engaged and self-motivated new employees is often the intangible ingredient that eludes managers in the selection process," www.HR.com, February 21, 2006, accessed January 21, 2014.
51. Paul Marciano, "How to Hire Engaged Employees," http://www.monster.com/about/b/how-to-hire-engaged-employees accessed June 20, 2015.
52. Jeffrey Shippmann et al., "The Practice of Competency Modeling," *Personnel Psychology* 53, no. 3 (2000), p. 703.
53. Michael Campion et al., "Doing Competencies Well: Best Practices in Competency Modeling," *Personnel Psychology* 64 (2011), pp. 225–262.
54. www.shrm.org/certification/Documents/SHRM-BoCK-FINAL4.pdf, p. 4, accessed March 20, 2015.
55. Richard S. Wellins et al., "Nine Best Practices for Effective Talent Management," DDI Development Dimensions International, Inc. www.ddiworld.com/DDIWorld/media/white-papers/ninebestpracticetalentmanagement_wp_ddi.pdf?extpdf, accessed August 20, 2011. For a discussion of competency modelling, see Campion et al., "Doing Competencies Well."
56. Based on Lindsay Chappell, "Mercedes Factories Embrace a New Order," *Automotive News*, May 28, 2001. See also www.autoblog.com/2009/03/23/rumormillmercedes-benz-expected-to-expandalabama-plant, accessed March 25, 2009, http://mbusi.com, accessed August 20, 2011.
57. This is adapted from Campion et al., "Doing Competencies Well."
58. Ibid.
59. See, for example, Carol Spicer, "Building a Competency Model," *HR Magazine,* April 2009, pp. 34–36.

5

Personnel Planning and Recruiting

Yosuke Tanaka/Aflo Foto Agency/AGE Fotostock

LEARNING OBJECTIVES

5-1 Explain the main techniques used in employment planning and forecasting.

5-2 Explain and give examples for the need for effective recruiting.

5-3 Name and describe the main internal sources of candidates.

5-4 Discuss a workforce planning method you would use to improve employee engagement.

5-5 List and discuss the main outside sources of candidates.

5-6 Explain how to recruit a more diverse workforce.

5-7 Discuss practical guidelines for obtaining application information.

Like most luxury hotel businesses, Four Seasons builds its strategy around offering superior customer service, and doing that requires staffing its hotels with highly motivated and high-morale employees.[1] Therefore, in thinking through how to recruit employees, Four Seasons managers sought a way to use recruitment to encourage the employee motivation and morale that would lead to improved customer service. We will see what they did.

WHERE ARE WE NOW ...

In Chapter 4, we discussed job analysis and the methods managers use to create job descriptions, job specifications, and competency profiles or models. The purpose of this chapter is to improve your effectiveness in recruiting candidates. The topics we discuss include personnel planning and forecasting, using promotion from within to foster engagement, recruiting job candidates, and developing and using application forms. Then, in Chapter 6, we'll turn to the methods managers use to select the best employees from this applicant pool

Introduction

Job analysis identifies the duties and human requirements of each of the company's jobs. The next step is to decide which of these jobs you need to fill, and to recruit and select employees for them.

The recruiting and selecting process can be envisioned as a series of hurdles, as illustrated in Figure 5-1:

1. Decide what positions to fill, through *workforce/personnel planning and forecasting*.
2. Build a pool of candidates for these jobs, by *recruiting* internal or external candidates.
3. Have candidates complete *application forms* and perhaps undergo initial screening interviews.
4. Use *selection tools* like tests, background investigations, and physical exams to screen candidates.
5. Decide who to make an offer to, by having the supervisor and perhaps others *interview* the candidates.

This chapter focuses on personnel planning and on recruiting employees. Chapters 6 and 7 address tests, background checks, physical exams, and interviews.

Workforce Planning and Forecasting

LEARNING OBJECTIVE **5-1**
Explain the main techniques used in employment planning and forecasting.

workforce (or employment or personnel) planning
The process of deciding what positions the firm will have to fill, and how to fill them.

Workforce (or employment or personnel) planning is the process of deciding what positions the firm will have to fill, and how to fill them. Its aim is to identify and address the gaps between the employer's workforce today, and its projected workforce needs. Workforce planning should precede recruitment and selection. After all, if you don't know what your employment needs will be in the next few months or years, why are you hiring?

One consulting firm's approach illustrates workforce planning.[2] First, Towers Watson *reviews the client's business plan and workforce data* (for instance, on how sales influence staffing levels). This helps them better understand how projected business plan changes may influence the client's headcount and skills requirements. Second, they *identify what positions the firm will have to fill and potential workforce gaps,* by making workforce supply and demand projections; this helps them understand what new future positions they'll have to fill, and what current employees may be promotable into those positions. Third, they develop a *workforce strategic plan*; here they prioritize key workforce gaps (such as, what positions will have to be filled, and who do we have who can fill them?) and identify specific (training and other) plans for filling any gaps. Finally, they *implement* the changes (for instance, new recruiting and training programs), and use various metrics to monitor the process. Towers Watson

FIGURE 5-1 Steps in Recruitment and Selection Process

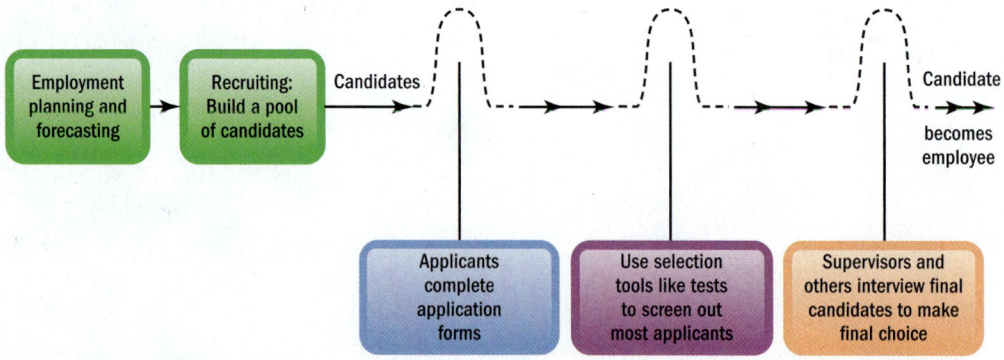

The recruitment and selection process is a series of hurdles aimed at selecting the best candidate for the job.

The dashboards, which are part of Towers Watson's workforce planning Internet software, help clients manage the workforce planning process.

Source: © Towers Watson 2012. Used with permission.

Workforce scan

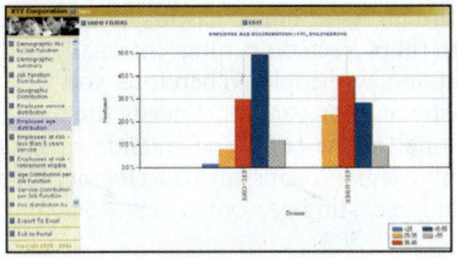

Dashboards

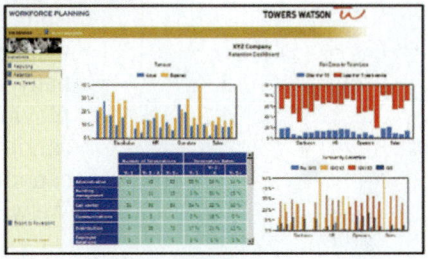

Workforce projection model

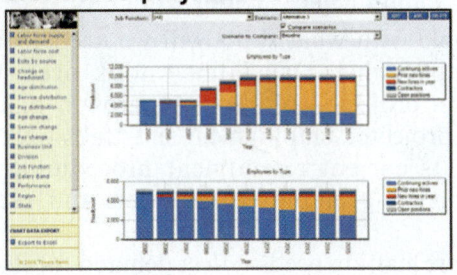

External labour scan

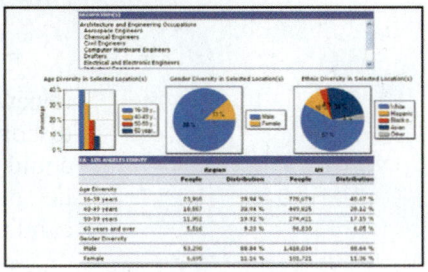

clients can use its special "MAPS" software to facilitate the workforce planning process. MAPS contains dashboards (see the four exhibits above). The manager uses these, for instance, to monitor key recruitment metrics, and to conduct a detailed analysis of the current workforce and historical workforce trends.

Workforce planning embraces all future positions, from maintenance clerk to CEO. However, we'll see that most firms call the process of deciding how to fill executive jobs *succession planning*.[3]

Strategy and Workforce Planning

Workforce planning shouldn't occur in a vacuum. Instead, workforce/employment planning is best understood as an outgrowth of the firm's strategic and business planning. For example, plans to enter new businesses, to build new plants, or to reduce activities will all influence the number of and types of positions to be filled. At the same time, decisions regarding how to fill these positions will impact other HR plans, for instance, training and recruitment plans. The Strategic Context feature illustrates.

IMPROVING PERFORMANCE: *The Strategic Context*

Four Seasons

As noted, Four Seasons builds its strategy around offering superior customer service, and that requires highly motivated and high-morale employees.[4] How can Four Seasons use its recruitment practices to encourage such motivation and morale? One way Four Seasons does this is by filling hotel positions around the world with internal transfers. In one recent year, for instance, about 280 employees relocated from hotels in one country to another within the Four Seasons chain. Employees love it. It gives them a chance for adventure and to see the world, while building a career with a great hotel chain.[5] And it's great for Four Seasons too, because the resulting high morale and motivation supports Four Seasons' strategic goal of superior customer service. In other words, Four Seasons uses recruitment practices that produce the excellent service the chain needs to achieve its strategic goals. ■

Source: Based on Robert Hackett, "a global opportunity," fortune, volume 171, number two, February 1, 2015, page 22.

If your professor has assigned this, go to the Assignments section of **mymanagementlab.com** to complete these discussion questions.

Talk About It 1: Can you think of any other benefits Four Seasons may derive from its policy of transferring employees among its hotels? What are they?

Like any good plans, employment plans are built on forecasts—basic assumptions about the future. As at Four Seasons, one basic employment planning decision will be whether to fill projected openings internally (with current employees) or externally (by bringing in new people). Therefore, you will usually need three sets of employment forecasts: one for personnel needs (demand), one for the supply of inside candidates, and one for the supply of outside candidates. With these, the manager can identify supply–demand gaps, and develop action plans to fill the projected gaps. We will start with forecasting personnel needs/demand.

Forecasting Personnel Needs (Labor Demand)

How many people with what skills will we need? Managers consider several factors.[6] For example, when Dan Hilbert took over staffing at Valero Energy, he reviewed Valero's projected retirements, growth plans, and turnover history. He discovered that projected employment shortfalls were four times more than Valero could fill with its current recruitment procedures. He formulated new personnel plans for boosting employee retention and recruiting and screening more candidates.[7]

A firm's future staffing needs reflect demand for its products or services, adjusted for changes the firm plans to make in its strategic goals and for changes in its turnover rate and productivity. Forecasting workforce demand therefore starts with estimating what the demand will be for your products or services. Short term, management should be concerned with daily, weekly, and seasonal forecasts.[8] For example, retailers track daily sales trends because they know, for instance, that Mother's Day produces a jump in business and a need for additional store staff. Seasonal forecasts are critical for retailers contemplating end-of-year holiday sales, and for many firms such as landscaping and air-conditioning vendors.

Longer term, managers will follow industry publications and economic forecasts closely, to try to get a sense for future demand. Such future predictions won't be precise, but should help you address the potential changes in demand.

The basic process for forecasting personnel needs is to forecast revenues first. Then estimate the size of the staff required to support this sales volume. However, managers must also consider other factors. These include projected turnover, decisions to upgrade (or downgrade) products or services, productivity changes, financial resources, and decisions to enter or leave businesses. The basic tools for projecting personnel needs include trend analysis, ratio analysis, and the scatter plot.

trend analysis
Study of a firm's past employment needs over a period of years to predict future needs.

TREND ANALYSIS **Trend analysis** means studying variations in the firm's employment levels over the past few years. For example, compute the number of employees at the end of each of the last 5 years in each subgroup (like sales, production, secretarial, and administrative) to identify trends.

Trend analysis can provide an initial rough estimate of future staffing needs. However, employment levels rarely depend just on the passage of time. Other factors (like productivity and retirements, for instance), and changing skill needs will influence impending workforce needs.

ratio analysis
A forecasting technique for determining future staff needs by using ratios between, for example, sales volume and number of employees needed.

RATIO ANALYSIS Another simple approach, **ratio analysis**, means making forecasts based on the historical ratio between (1) some causal factor (like sales volume) and (2) the number of employees required (such as number of salespeople). For example, suppose a salesperson traditionally generates $500,000 in sales. If the sales revenue to salespeople ratio remains the same, you would require six new salespeople next year (each of whom produces an extra $500,000) to produce a hoped-for extra $3 million in sales.

Like trend analysis, ratio analysis assumes that things like productivity remain about the same. If sales productivity were to rise or fall, the ratio of sales to salespeople would change.

scatter plot
A graphical method used to help identify the relationship between two variables.

THE SCATTER PLOT A **scatter plot** shows graphically how two variables—such as sales and your firm's staffing levels—are related. If they are, then if you can forecast the business activity (like sales), you should also be able to estimate your personnel needs.

For example, suppose a 500-bed hospital expects to expand to 1,200 beds over the next 5 years. The human resource director wants to forecast how many registered nurses the hospital will need. The human resource director realizes she must determine the relationship between hospital size (in number of beds) and number of nurses required. She calls eight hospitals of various sizes and finds this:

Size of Hospital (Number of Beds)	Number of Registered Nurses
200	240
300	260
400	470
500	500
600	620
700	660
800	820
900	860

Figure 5-2's graph compares hospital size and number of nurses. If the two are related, then the points you plot (from the data above) will tend to fall on a straight line, as here. If you carefully draw in a line to minimize the distances between the line and each one of the plotted points, you will be able to estimate the number of nurses needed for each hospital size. Thus, for a 1,200-bed hospital, the human resource director would assume she needs about 1,210 nurses.

While simple, tools like scatter plots have drawbacks.[9]

1. Historical sales/personnel relationships assume that the firm's existing activities and skill needs will continue as is.
2. They tend to reward managers for adding employees, irrespective of the company's needs.
3. They tend to institutionalize existing ways of doing things, even in the face of change.

Computerized systems and Excel spreadsheets help managers translate estimates of projected productivity and sales levels into forecastable personnel requirements.

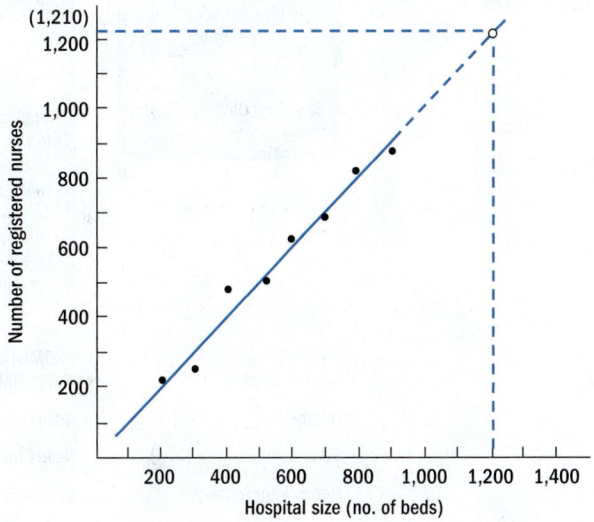

FIGURE 5-2 Determining the Relationship Between Hospital Size and Number of Nurses
Note: After fitting the line, you can project how many employees you'll need, given your projected volume.

Computerized forecasts enable managers to build more variables into their personnel projections. Thus, at Chelan County Public Utility District, the development manager built a statistical model encompassing such things as age, tenure, turnover rate, and time to train new employees.[10] This model helped quickly identify five occupational "hotspots" among 33 occupational groups at the company. This in turn prompted Chelan to focus more closely on creating plans to retain and hire, for instance, more systems operators.[11]

MANAGERIAL JUDGMENT Few historical trends, ratios, or relationships will continue unchanged into the future. Judgment is thus needed to adjust the forecast. Important factors that may modify your initial forecast of personnel requirements include decisions to upgrade quality or enter into new markets; technological and administrative changes resulting in increased productivity; and financial resources available, for instance, a projected budget crunch.

Forecasting the Supply of Inside Candidates

The personnel demand forecast provides only half the staffing equation, by answering the question: "How many employees in what positions will we need?" Next, the manager must forecast the *supply* (availability) of inside and outside candidates.

Most firms start with possible inside candidates. The main task here is determining which current employees are qualified or trainable for the projected openings. Department managers or owners of smaller firms can use manual devices to track employee qualifications (or will simply know who can do what). For example, you can create your own *personnel skills inventory and development record form.*[12] For each current employee, list the person's skills, education, company-sponsored courses taken, career and development interests, languages, desired assignments, and other relevant experiences. Computerized versions of skills inventory systems are also available.[13]

personnel replacement charts
Company records showing present performance and promotability of inside candidates for the most important positions.

position replacement card
A card prepared for each position in a company to show possible replacement candidates and their qualifications.

Personnel replacement charts (Figure 5-3) are another option, particularly for the firm's top positions. They show the present performance and promotability for each position's potential replacement. As an alternative, with a **position replacement card** you create a card for each position, showing possible replacements as well as their present performance, promotion potential, and training.

FIGURE 5-3 Personnel or Management Replacement Chart Showing Development Needs of Potential Future Divisional Vice Presidents

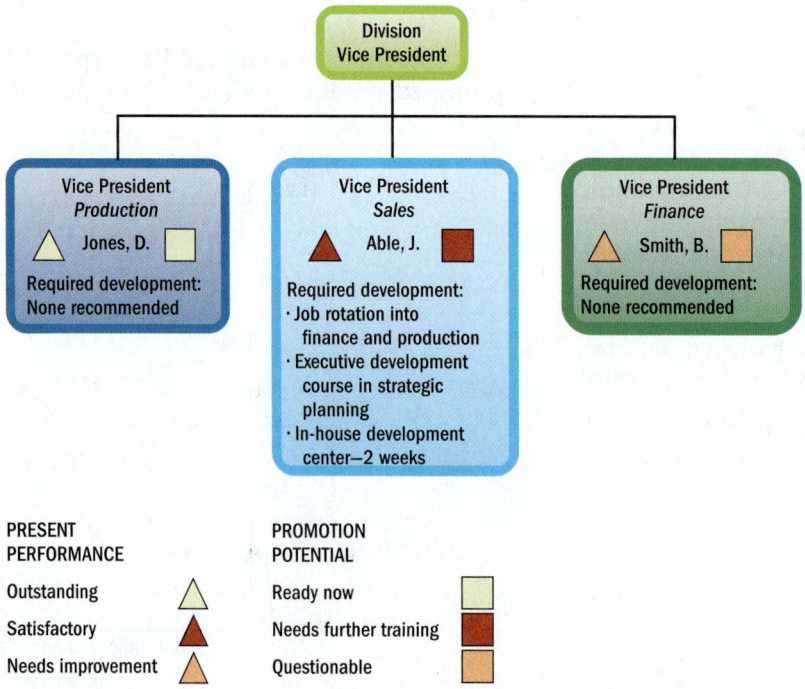

Larger firms obviously can't track the qualifications of hundreds or thousands of employees manually. They therefore computerize this information, using various packaged software systems such as Survey Analytics's Skills Inventory Software. Skills inventory systems such as one from Perceptyx (www.perceptyx.com) enables employers to collect and compile employee skills information in real time via online employee surveys. Skills inventory programs help management anticipate staffing and skills shortages, and facilitate workforce planning, recruitment, and training.[14] They typically include items like *work experience codes, product knowledge*, the employee's *level of familiarity* with the employer's product lines or services, the person's *industry experience, formal education*, industry *experiences*, foreign *language* skills, *relocation* limitations, *career* interests, and *performance* appraisals.

The usual skills inventory process is for the employee, the supervisor, and human resource manager to enter information about the employee's background, experience, and skills via the system. Then, when a manager needs someone for a position, he or she uses key words to describe the position's specifications (for instance, in terms of education and skills). The computerized system then produces a list of qualified candidates. As the user of one such system said, "The [SumTotal] platform allows us to track and assess the talent pool and promote people within the company. ... The succession module helps us to identify who the next senior managers could be and build development plans to help them achieve their potential."[15]

The employer must secure all its employee data.[16] Legislation gives employees legal rights regarding who has access to information about them.[17] Internet access makes it relatively easy for more people to access the firm's computerized files.[18] The U.S. Office of Personnel Management recently lost data on as many as 14 million current and former employees this way.[19] Figure 5-4 summarizes some guidelines for keeping employee data safe.

MARKOV ANALYSIS Employers also use a mathematical process known as *Markov analysis* (or "transition analysis") to forecast availability of internal job candidates. Markov analysis involves creating a matrix that shows the probabilities that employees in the chain of feeder positions for a key job (such as from junior engineer, to engineer, to senior engineer, to engineering supervisor, to director of engineering) will move from position to position and therefore be available to fill the key position.

Forecasting the Supply of Outside Candidates

If there won't be enough skilled inside candidates to fill the anticipated openings (or you want to go outside for another reason), you will turn to outside candidates.

Forecasting workforce availability depends first on the manager's own sense of what's happening in his or her industry and locale. For example, unemployment rates above 7% a few years ago signaled to HR managers that finding good candidates might be easier.[20] The manager then supplements such observations with formal labor market analyses. For example, look for economic projections online from the U.S. Congressional Budget Office (www.cbo.gov) and the Bureau of Labor Statistics (www.bls.gov/emp/ep_pub_occ_projections.htm). You may also want to

FIGURE 5-4 Keeping Data Safe

Source: Reprinted with permission from HR Magazine, November 2005. © SHRM.

Since intruders can strike from outside an organization or from within, HR departments can help screen out potential identity thieves by following four basic rules:

- Perform background checks on anyone who is going to have access to personal information.
- If someone with access to personal information is out sick or on leave, don't hire a temporary employee to replace him or her. Instead, bring in a trusted worker from another department.
- Perform random background checks such as random drug tests. Just because someone passed 5 years ago doesn't mean their current situation is the same.
- Limit access to information such as SSNs, health information, and other sensitive data to HR managers who require it to do their jobs.

forecast specific occupations. O*NET (discussed in Chapter 4) reports projections for most occupations. The U.S. Bureau of Labor Statistics publishes annual occupational projections both online and in the *Monthly Labor Review* and in *Occupational Outlook Quarterly*.

Today's emphasis on technology means many applicants may lack basic skills such as math, communication, creativity, and teamwork.[21] Such needs, too, get factored into the employer's workforce and training plans.

Predictive Workforce Monitoring

Most employers review their workforce plans every year or so, but this isn't always sufficient For instance, having failed to do much formal workforce planning, Valero Energy almost lacked sufficient time to implement a plan to address replacing employees who would soon retire.

Workforce planning therefore often involves *paying continuous attention* to workforce planning issues. Managers call this *predictive workforce monitoring*. For example, Intel Corporation conducts semiannual "Organization Capability Assessments." The staffing department works with the firm's business heads twice a year to assess workforce needs—both immediate and up to 2 years in the future.[22] Boeing Corp. considers various factors when predicting talent gaps as part of its "workforce modeling" process. These include Boeing workforce characteristics such as age, retirement eligibility for employees with various skills, economic trends, anticipated increases or decreases in staffing levels, and internal transfers and promotions.[23] The accompanying HR as a Profit Center feature shows an example.

IMPROVING PERFORMANCE: *HR as a Profit Center*

Predicting Labor Needs

Valero Energy created a "labor supply chain" for improving the efficiency of its workforce planning, recruiting, and hiring process. It includes an analytic tool that predicts Valero's labor needs based on past trends. And, it includes computer screen "dashboards" that show how components in the staffing chain, such as ads placed on job boards, are performing according to cost, speed, and quality. Before implementing the labor supply chain system, it took 41 pieces of paper to bring on board an employee and more than 120 days to fill a position; each hire cost about $12,000. The new system eliminated most of the paper forms needed to hire an employee, time to fill fell below 40 days, and cost per hire dropped to $2,300.[24] ■

Source: Based on Ed Frauenheim, "Valero Energy," Workforce Management, March 13, 2006.

If your professor has assigned this, go to the Assignments section of **mymanagementlab.com** to complete this discussion.

Talk About It 2: Explain how Valero might use the Towers Watson workforce planning process on pages 128–129.

Matching Projected Labor Supply and Labor Demand

Workforce planning should logically culminate in a workforce plan. This plan lays out the employer's projected workforce and skills gaps, as well as staffing plans for filling these gaps. For example, the plan should identify the positions to be filled; potential internal and external candidates or sources for these positions; the training and promotions moving people into the positions will entail; and the resources that implementing the plan will require, for instance, in recruiter fees, estimated training costs, relocation costs, and interview expenses.[25]

succession planning
The ongoing process of systematically identifying, assessing, and developing organizational leadership to enhance performance.

Succession Planning

Succession planning involves developing workforce plans for the company's top positions. **Succession planning** is the ongoing process of systematically identifying, assessing, and developing organizational leadership to enhance performance.[26] It entails three steps: identify key position needs, develop inside candidates, and assess and choose those who will fill the key positions.[27]

First, based on the company's strategic and business plans, top management and the human resource director identify what the company's future key position needs will be. Matters to address here include defining key positions and "high potentials," reviewing the company's current talent, and creating (based on the company's strategy) skills profiles for the key positions.[28]

After identifying future key positions, management turns to creating candidates for these jobs. "Creating" means identifying inside or outside candidates and providing them with the developmental experiences they require to be viable candidates. Employers develop high-potential employees through internal training and cross-functional experiences, job rotation, external training, and global/regional assignments.[29]

Finally, succession planning requires assessing these candidates and selecting those who will actually fill the key positions.[30]

EXAMPLE At Dole Foods, the new president's strategy involved improving financial performance by reducing redundancies and centralizing certain activities, including succession planning.[31] Dole contracted with application system providers (ASPs) to handle things like payroll management.[32] For succession management, Dole chose software from Pilat NAI. The Pilat system keeps all the data on its own servers for a monthly fee. Dole's managers access the program via the Web using a password. They fill out online résumés for themselves, including career interests, and note special considerations such as geographic restrictions.

The managers also assess themselves on four competencies. Once the manager provides his or her input, the program notifies that manager's boss, who assesses his or her subordinate and indicates whether the person is promotable. This assessment and the online résumés then go automatically to the division head and the divisional HR director. Dole's senior vice president for human resources then uses the information to create career development plans for each manager, including seminars and other programs.[33]

Watch It!

How does a company actually do workforce planning? If your professor has assigned this, go to the Assignments section of **mymanagementlab.com** to complete the video exercise titled *Gawker Media: Personnel Planning and Recruiting*.

LEARNING OBJECTIVE **5-2**

Explain and give examples for the need for effective recruiting.

Why Effective Recruiting is Important

Assuming the company authorizes you to fill a position, the next step is to build up, through recruiting, an applicant pool. **Employee recruiting** means finding and/or attracting applicants for the employer's open positions.

employee recruiting
Finding and/or attracting applicants for the employer's open positions.

Recruiting is important. If only two candidates apply for two openings, you may have little choice but to hire them. But if 10 or 20 applicants appear, you can use techniques like interviews and tests to screen out all but the best.

Even when unemployment rates are high, many employers have trouble finding qualified applicants. One survey found that about two-thirds of the manufacturing executives surveyed a few years ago faced a "moderate to severe shortage of skilled labor."[34] With manufacturing jobs increasingly high-tech, the available jobs require more math and science than most applicants possess.[35] A recent Lloyd's of London risk index listed "talent and skill shortages" as the number 2 risk facing businesses today ("loss of customers" was number 1).[36]

Of course, it's not just recruiting but effective recruiting that is important. Consider one study of recruiter effectiveness.[37] Subjects were 41 graduating college

FIGURE 5-5 Recruiting Yield Pyramid

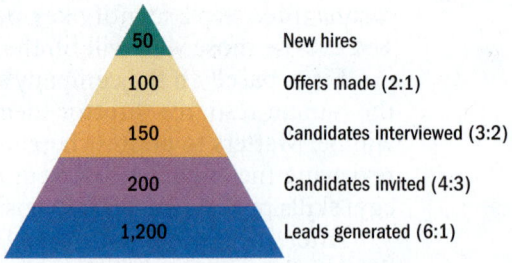

students who'd been on several job interviews. When asked after the initial job interview why they thought a particular company might be a good fit, 39 mentioned the nature of the job, but 23 said they'd been turned off by the recruiters. For example, some were dressed sloppily; others were "barely literate"; some were rude; and some made offensive comments. Also potentially undermining one's recruiting is the fact that some recruiting methods are superior to others, depending on the job, and that recruiting depends on nonrecruitment issues such as pay.[38] We've also seem that employment law prescribes what you can do.[39]

Even the employer's "brand" or reputation will impact recruiting success. Most obviously, it is futile to recruit if the employer's reputation is that it's an awful place to work.

How does the employer want others to see it as a place to work? The branding often focuses on what it's like to work at the company, including company values and the work environment.[40] GE, for instance, stresses innovation (hiring "bright, interesting people working together on new and exciting projects").[41] Others stress being environmentally or socially responsible.[42]

The Recruiting Yield Pyramid

recruiting yield pyramid
The historical arithmetic relationships between recruitment leads and invitees, invitees and interviews, interviews and offers made, and offers made and offers accepted.

Filling a relative handful of positions might require recruiting dozens or hundreds of candidates. Managers therefore use a staffing or **recruiting yield pyramid**, as shown in Figure 5-5, to gauge the staffing issues it needs to address. In Figure 5-5, the company knows it needs 50 new entry-level accountants next year. From experience, the firm also knows the following:

- The ratio of offers made to actual new hires is 2 to 1.
- The ratio of candidates interviewed to offers made is 3 to 2.
- The ratio of candidates invited for interviews to candidates interviewed is about 4 to 3.
- Finally, the firm knows that of six leads that come in from all its recruiting sources, it typically invites only one applicant for an interview—a 6-to-1 ratio.

Therefore, the firm must generate about 1,200 leads to be able to invite in 200 viable candidates of which it interviews about 150, and so on.

KNOW YOUR EMPLOYMENT LAW

Recruiting Employees

As we explained in Chapter 2, numerous federal, state, and local laws and court decisions restrict what employers can and cannot do when recruiting job applicants. In practice, "the key question in all recruitment procedures is whether the method limits qualified applicants from applying."[43] So, for example, gender-specific ads that call for "busboy" or "firemen" would obviously raise red flags. Similarly, courts will often question word-of-mouth recruiting, because workers tend to nominate candidates of the same nationality, race, and religion.[44]

Other laws are relevant. For example, it is illegal for employers to conspire not to hire each other's employees. Yet Apple and Google recently paid over $400 million to settle a claim alleging that they did just that.[45] ■

THE SUPERVISOR'S ROLE Line and staff cooperation in recruitment is essential. The human resource manager charged with filling an open position is seldom very familiar with the job itself. So, for example, the recruiter will want to know from the supervisor what the job really entails and its job specifications, as well as informal things like the supervisor's leadership style and how the team gets along.

HR in Practice at the Hotel Paris As they reviewed the details of the Hotel Paris's current recruitment practices, Lisa Cruz and the firm's CFO became increasingly concerned. They found that the recruitment function was totally unmanaged. To see how they handled this, see the case on page 168 of this chapter.

Internal Sources of Candidates

LEARNING OBJECTIVE 5-3
Name and describe the main internal sources of candidates.

Recruiting typically brings to mind LinkedIn, employment agencies, and classified ads, but internal sources—in other words, current employees or "hiring from within"—are often the best sources of candidates.

Filling open positions with inside candidates has advantages. First, there is really no substitute for knowing a candidate's strengths and weaknesses, as you should after working with him or her for some time. Current employees may also be more committed to the company. Morale and engagement may rise if employees see promotions as rewards for loyalty and competence. And inside candidates should require less orientation and (perhaps) training than outsiders.

There are other advantages. External hires tend to come in at higher salaries than do those promoted internally, and some apparent "stars" hired from outside may turn out to have excelled more because of the company they came from than from their own skills.

One executive recruiter argues that internal candidates are always better than external ones unless the internal candidates simply can't pass muster. One study concluded that firms that hired their CEOs from inside rather than outside performed better. On the other hand, some firms—particularly those facing enormous challenges—such as IBM and Ford Motor Company—did extremely well by bringing in outside managers (respectively, Louis Gerstner and Alan Mullally).[46]

Hiring from within can also backfire. Inbreeding is a potential drawback, if new perspectives are required. The process of posting openings and getting inside applicants can also be a waste of time, since often the department manager already knows whom he or she wants to hire. Rejected inside applicants may become discontented; telling them why you rejected them and what remedial actions they might take is crucial.

There are some practical rules to use in determining whether to go outside or promote from within. For example, if you need specific skills that aren't currently available in your company, or have to embark on a tough turnaround, or face a situation in which your current succession planning or skills inventory systems are inadequate, it may be best to look outside. On the other hand, if your company is thriving and you have effective succession planning and skills inventory systems, have the skills you need internally, and have a unique and strong company culture, then look within.[47]

Finding Internal Candidates

job posting
Publicizing an open job to employees (often by literally posting it on bulletin boards) and listing its attributes, like qualifications, supervisor, working schedule, and pay rate.

In a perfect world, the employer will adhere to formal internal-recruitment policies and procedures. These typically rely heavily on job posting and on the firm's skills inventories. **Job posting** means publicizing the open job to employees (usually by literally posting it on company intranets or bulletin boards). These postings list the job's attributes, like qualifications, supervisor, work schedule, and pay rate. Qualifications skills inventories also play a role. For example, they may reveal to the company's recruiters those employees who have the right background for the open job. Ideally, the employer's system therefore matches the best inside candidate with the job. In practice, this doesn't always happen. For better or worse, internal politics and having the right connections may well lead to placements that seem (and indeed may be) unfair and suboptimal.

Rehiring someone who left your employ has pros and cons. Former employees are known quantities (more or less) and are already familiar with how you do things. On the other hand, employees who you let go may return with negative attitudes.[48] Inquire (before rehiring) about what they did during the layoff and how they feel about returning. After a probationary period, credit them with the years of service they had accumulated before they left.[49]

LEARNING OBJECTIVE 5-4

Discuss a workforce planning method you would use to improve employee engagement.

Employee Engagement Guide for Managers

Promotion from Within

Many employers encourage internal recruiting, on the reasonable assumption that doing so improves employee engagement. Thus, as IBM shifted from supplying mostly hardware to consulting, it assessed its skills gaps and instituted workforce plans to train current employees for new jobs; this assumedly fostered employee engagement. Similarly, International Paper appointed a single person "to provide support to all [business units], Staff Groups and Regions for Workforce Planning and Engagement."[50] Other employers, faced with strategic shifts, simply dismiss employees who don't "fit."

FedEx has had strong internal recruiting and promotion-from-within policies almost from its inception. FedEx's commitment to promotion from within grew out of founder Frederick Smith's belief that "when people are placed first they will provide the highest possible service, and profits will follow" (go to www.fedex.com, then to United States, about FedEx, FedEx overview, and then corporate philosophy).[51] FedEx weaves together promotion from within with other policies—including annual employee attitude surveys, employee recognition and reward programs, a leadership evaluation process, extensive employee communication, and an employee appeals process—to foster employee commitment and engagement. FedEx's approach underscores the need to take an integrated approach to fostering employee engagement. For example, as we will discuss further in Chapter 8 (Careers), promotion-from-within is futile without effective performance appraisal and training practices.

Also, as at FedEx, effective promotion from within requires a system for accessing career records and *posting job openings*, one that guarantees eligible employees are informed of openings and considered for them. FedEx calls its job posting system JCATS (Job Change Applicant Tracking System). Announcements of new job openings via this online system usually take place each Friday. All employees applying for the position get numerical scores based on job performance and length of service. They are then advised as to whether they were chosen as candidates.

A manager interested in fostering his or her employees' engagement can draw several useful guidelines from FedEx's promotion-from-within system: show a genuine interest in your employees' career aspirations; provide career-oriented appraisals; have a formal job-posting system; see that your employees have access to the training they need; and balance your desire to keep good employees with the benefits of helping them learn of and apply for other positions in your company.

Outside Sources of Candidates

Employers can't always get all the employees they need from their current staff, and sometimes they just don't want to. We look at the sources firms use to find outside candidates next.

LEARNING OBJECTIVE 5-5

List and discuss the main outside sources of candidates.

Informal Recruiting and the Hidden Job Market

Many (or most) job openings aren't publicized at all; jobs are created and become available when employers serendipitously encounter the right candidates. The author of *Unlock the Hidden Job Market* estimates that perhaps half of all positions are filled informally (without formal recruiting).[52] Similarly, one survey found that 28% of those surveyed found their most recent job through word of mouth. Nineteen percent used online job boards, 16% direct approaches from employers and employment services, 7% print ads, and only 1% social media sites (although 22% used sites like LinkedIn to *search* for jobs).[53]

Recruiting via the Internet

Most employers recruit through their own websites, or through online job boards such as Indeed and CareerBuilder. For example, the CareerBuilder.com iPhone application lets someone search nearly 2 million jobs on CareerBuilder.com, the largest U.S. job site.[54] Users may search for jobs by keyword, read job descriptions and salaries, save jobs to a list of favorites, and e-mail job links to anyone on their contact list. Employers increasingly use niche job boards such as jobsinsports.com and vetjobs.com.[55]

Online recruiting is getting more sophisticated. One example is the *virtual office tour*.[56] In China the local office of Accountants Deloitte Touche Tohmatsu Limited posted a virtual office tour on Weibo (similar to Twitter's messaging service). People visiting the site can virtually enter each of the company's offices in Asia, walking through meeting rooms and talking virtually with local employees, to get a feel for what working in that office is like.

There are many other such online recruiting tools. For example, ResumePal (see www.jobfox.com) is an online standard universal job application. Job seekers submit it to participating employers, who can then use the standardized application's keywords to identify viable candidates more easily.[57] McDonald's Corp. posted a series of employee testimonials on social networking sites like Second Life to attract applicants.[58] Other employers simply screen through job boards' résumé listings.[59]

Monster helps employers integrate streaming video into their job postings.[60] The *dot-jobs* domain gives job seekers a one-click conduit for finding jobs at the employers who register at www.goto.jobs. For example, applicants seeking a job at Disneyland can go to www.Disneyland.jobs. HireVue "lets candidates create video interviews and send them to employers to review, share, and compare with other applicants."[61]

Virtual (fully online) job fairs are another option. Here online visitors see a similar setup to a regular job fair. They can listen to presentations, visit booths, leave résumés and business cards, participate in live chats, and get contact information from recruiters and even hiring managers.[62] Fairs last about 5 hours.

PROS AND CONS Online recruiting generates more responses quicker and for a longer time at less cost than just about any other method. And, because they are richer and more comprehensive in describing the jobs, web-based ads have a stronger effect on applicant attraction than do printed ads.[63] But, online recruiting has two potential problems.

First, older people and some minorities are less likely to use the Internet, so online recruiting may inadvertently exclude more older applicants (and certain minorities).[64]

The second problem is Internet overload: Employers end up deluged with résumés. Self-screening helps: The Cheesecake Factory posts detailed job duties listings, so those not interested needn't apply. Another approach is to have job seekers complete a short online prescreening questionnaire, then use these to identify those who may proceed in the hiring process.[65]

Most employers also use applicant tracking systems, to which we now turn.

Improving Performance Through HRIS: Using Applicant Tracking

A deluge of applicants means that most employers now use applicant tracking software to screen applications.[66] **Applicant tracking systems (ATS)** are online systems that help employers attract, gather, screen, compile, and manage applicants.[67] They also provide other services, including requisitions management (for monitoring the firm's open jobs), applicant data collection (for scanning applicants' data into the system), and reporting (to create various recruiting-related reports such as cost per hire and hire by source).[68] Most systems are from *application service providers* (ASPs). These

applicant tracking systems (ATS)
Online systems that help employers attract, gather, screen, compile, and manage applicants.

basically redirect applicants from the employer's to the ASP's site. Thus, applicants who log on to take a test at the employer are actually taking the test at the ASP's site.[69] Major suppliers include Automatic Data Processing (ADP.com), HRSmart (hrsmart.com), SilkRoad Technology (silkroad.com), and Monster (monster.com).[70]

As one example, a bank uses its ATS to bump applicants who don't meet the basic job requirements; it then e-mails them suggesting they review the bank's site for more appropriate positions. This bank then uses either phone interviews or automated interview systems to whittle down the applicant pool to a few candidates. Then its recruiters interview those at headquarters and send them through the final selection process.[71] One Ohio-based nursing care facility company arranged to have the recruiting dashboard vendor jobs2Web integrate its dashboard with the employer's applicant tracking system. The recruiting manager now uses the dashboard to monitor recruitment data trends on things like which recruiting sources are doing the best job of attracting applications.[72] ■

TRENDS SHAPING HR: *SCIENCE IN TALENT MANAGEMENT*

Most employers use tools like job boards to produce large numbers of recruits, and then use ATS and screening systems to cut those numbers down. Google's "People Operations" (HR) group is more scientific. When their research showed that tools like job boards weren't cost-effective for them, they created their own in-house recruiting firm. This in-house team uses a proprietary candidate database called gHire. Google's recruiters continually expand and winnow this candidate list, by searching social networking and other sites, by searching who's working where, and by reaching out to prospective hires and maintaining dialogues with them, sometimes for years. These in-house recruiters produce hand-picked candidates and account for about half of Google's yearly hires.[73]

Google's career website is another big source of candidates. Applicants not only apply through it, but can share examples of their skills with Google employees, and through them discover what Google employment is like.

Google also actively solicits employee referrals. Because inside referrals turned out to be great candidates, Google analyzed how to boost employee referrals. It found that higher referral fees weren't the answer, (since Googlers loved recommending great candidates). Instead, Google streamlined the selection process, so more referrals got hired.

Google uses outside recruiters sparingly for special assignments, and dropped job boards several years ago. [74] ■

IMPROVING ONLINE RECRUITING EFFECTIVENESS The employer's online effort needs to be thought out. For example, one survey of Web-based recruiting uncovered these applicant objections: Job openings lacked relevant information (such as job descriptions); and, it was often difficult to format résumés and post them in the form required.[75]

Employers take several steps. Most place employment information one click away from their home pages.[76] Applicants can submit their résumés online at most *Fortune* 500 firms' websites. Fewer companies give job seekers the option of completing online applications, although that's what most applicants prefer.[77] Furthermore, the best Web ads don't just transfer newspaper ads to the Web. As one specialist put it, "Getting recruiters out of the 'shrunken want ad mentality' is a big problem." Figure 5-6 is an example of recycling a print ad to the Web. The ineffective Web ad has needless abbreviations, and doesn't say much about why the job seeker should want that job.[78]

Now look at the effective Web ad in Figure 5-6. It provides good reasons to work for this company. It starts with an attention-grabbing heading and uses the extra space to provide more specific job information. Many employers include the entire

FIGURE 5-6 Ineffective and Effective Web Ads

Ineffective Ad, Recycled from Magazine to the Web	Effective Web Ad (Space Not an Issue)
Process Engineer Pay: $65k–$85k/year	Do you want to help us make this a better world?
Immediate Need in Florida for a Wastewater Treatment Process Engineer. Must have a min. 4–7 years Industrial Wastewater exp. Reply KimGD@WatersCleanX.com	We are one of the top wastewater treatment companies in the world, with installations from Miami to London to Beijing. We are growing fast and looking for an experienced process engineer to join our team. If you have at least 4–7 years' experience designing processes for wastewater treatment facilities and a dedication to make this a better world, we would like to hear from you. Pay range depending on experience is $65,000–$85,000. Please reply in confidence to KimGD@WatersCleanX.com

job description.[79] Ideally, an ad also should provide a way (such as a checklist of the job's human requirements) for potential applicants to gauge if the job is a good fit.[80]

Finally, online recruiting requires caution for *applicants*. Many job boards don't check the legitimacy of the "recruiters" who place ads. Many applicants submit personal details, not realizing who is getting them.[81] U.S. laws generally do not prohibit job boards from sharing your data with other sources. One job board reportedly had personal information on more than 1 million subscribers stolen.[82]

TRENDS SHAPING HR: *DIGITAL AND SOCIAL MEDIA*

Anyone seeking a job should probably sign up with LinkedIn. Accenture predicts that about 80% of new recruits will soon come through prospective employees' social media connections.[83]

Recruiters use social media recruiting in several ways. They dig through social websites and competitors' publications to find applicants who may not even be looking for jobs. They seek passive candidates (people not actively looking for jobs) by using social networking sites such as *LinkedIn Recruiter Lite* (a premium service) to browse members' résumés and to find such candidates.[84] Many firms use Twitter to announce job openings to job seekers who subscribe to their Twitter feeds.[85] Theladders.com's Pipeline™ networking tool lets recruiters maintain a dialogue with prospective job seekers even before they're interested in seeking a job. Others use Facebook's friend-finding search function, and Twitter, to learn more about prospective and actual candidates. TalentBin searches sites such as Pinterest to find qualified tech workers.[86] Many employers have social media strategies and career pages that establish an online presence highlighting the benefits of working for them.[87] At one diversity conference, consultants Hewitt Associates displayed posters asking attendees to text message *hewdiversity* to a specific 5-digit number. Each person texting then became part of Hewitt's "mobile recruiting network," periodically receiving text messages regarding Hewitt openings.[88]

LinkedIn Recruiter Lite not only lets employers post jobs on LinkedIn. The employer can also conduct its own LinkedIn search for talent, by using Recruiter Lite's search filters to search through LinkedIn's database to find the most relevant profiles (including names and profiles). Recruiters can then use LinkedIn's InMail to send short personalized messages to people they're interested in. And by joining relevant LinkedIn groups the recruiter can discover other LinkedIn group members who might be potential hires.[89] This not only helps them generate more relevant applicants, but provides a form of "crowdsourcing," by letting the recruiter mine the applicants' sites for feedback from the person's blog comments and his or her likes/dislikes. Recruiters also post job openings on professional associations and other social networks.[90]

Cloud-based applications such as Oracle Talent Acquisition Cloud enable employers to integrate recruiting with related activities including requisitions management, applicant tracking, and interview management. The Oracle Taleo Social Sourcing Cloud Service is integrated with social sites like LinkedIn, Twitter, and Facebook. It notifies the company's current employees about open positions, and then scans their social connections for referral suggestions that they may want to make to friends, or directly to the employer. With the My Staffing Pro applicant tracking system, applicants can apply on Facebook, share job openings, connect with managers, and log in with the social profile. Recruiters can post job openings on Twitter and Facebook, accept applications via Facebook, and more easily screen out the best applicants. ■

Advertising

While Web-based recruiting is replacing traditional help wanted ads, a glance at almost any paper will confirm that print ads are still popular. To use such help wanted ads successfully, employers should address two issues: the advertising medium and the ad's construction.

THE MEDIA The best medium—the local paper, *The Wall Street Journal, The Economist*, for instance—depends on the positions for which you're recruiting. For example, the local newspaper is often a good source for local blue-collar help, clerical employees, and lower-level administrative employees. On the other hand, if recruiting for workers with special skills, such as furniture finishers, you'd probably want to advertise in places with many furniture manufacturers, such as the Carolinas, even if your plant is in Tennessee. The point is to target your ads where they'll reach your prospective employees.

For specialized employees, advertise in trade and professional journals like *American Psychologist, Sales Management, Chemical Engineering,* and *Women's Wear Daily*. Help wanted ads in papers like *The Wall Street Journal* can be good sources of middle- or senior-management personnel. Most of these print outlets now include online ads with the purchase of print help wanted ads.

Technology lets companies be more creative.[91] For example, Electronic Arts (EA) uses its products to help solicit applicants. EA includes information about its internship program on the back of its video game manuals. Thanks to nontraditional techniques like these, EA has a database of more than 200,000 potential job candidates.

CONSTRUCTING (WRITING) THE AD Experienced advertisers use the guide AIDA (attention, interest, desire, action) to construct ads. First, you must attract attention to the ad, or readers may ignore it. Why does the ad in Figure 5-7 attract attention? The phrase "next key player" helps.

Next, develop interest in the job. For instance, "are you looking to make an impact?"

Create desire by spotlighting words such as *travel* or *challenge*. As an example, having a graduate school nearby may appeal to engineers and professional people.

Finally, the ad should prompt action with a statement like "call today."

Job applicants view ads with more specific job information as more attractive and more credible.[92] If the job has big drawbacks, consider a realistic ad. When the New York City Administration for Children's Services was having problems with employee retention, it began using these ads: "Wanted: men and women willing to walk into strange buildings in dangerous neighborhoods, [and] be screamed at by unhinged individuals...."[93]

Employment Agencies

There are three main types of employment agencies: (1) public agencies operated by federal, state, or local governments; (2) agencies associated with nonprofit organizations; and (3) privately owned agencies.

FIGURE 5-7 Help Wanted Ad That Draws Attention

Source: "Help Wanted Ad That Draws Attention", in Giombetti Associates, Hampden, MA. Reprinted with permission.

Are You Our Next Key Player?

PLANT CONTROLLER

Northern New Jersey

Are you looking to make an impact? Can you be a strategic business partner and team player, versus a classic, "bean counter"? Our client, a growing **Northern New Jersey** manufacturer with two locations, needs a high-energy, self-initiating, technically competent Plant Controller. Your organizational skills and strong understanding of general, cost, and manufacturing accounting are a must. We are not looking for a delegator, this is a hands-on position. If you have a positive can-do attitude and have what it takes to drive our accounting function, read oh!

Responsibilities and Qualifications:

- Monthly closings, management reporting, product costing, and annual budget.
- Accurate inventory valuations, year-end physical inventory, and internal controls.
- 4-year Accounting degree, with 5–8 years experience in a manufacturing environment.
- Must be proficient in Microsoft Excel and have general computer skills and aptitude.
- Must be analytical and technically competent, with the leadership ability to influence people, situations, and circumstances.

If you have what it takes to be our next key player, tell us in your cover letter, *"Beyond the beans, what is the role of a Plant Controller?"* Only cover letters addressing that question will be considered. Please indicate your general salary requirements in your cover letter and email or fax your resume and cover letter to:

Ross Giombetti
Giombetti Associates
2 Allen Street, P.O. Box 720
Hampden, MA 01036
Email: Rossgiombetti@giombettiassoc.com
Fax: (413) 566-2009

PERFORMANCE GIOMBETTI ASSOCIATES INSTITUTE OF LEADERSHIP DYNAMICS

PUBLIC AND NONPROFIT AGENCIES Every state has a public, state-run employment service agency. The U.S. Department of Labor supports these agencies, through grants and through other assistance such as a nationwide computerized job bank. The National Job Bank enables agency counselors to advise applicants about available jobs in other states as well.

Some employers have mixed experiences with public agencies. For one thing, applicants for unemployment insurance are required to register and to make themselves available for job interviews. Some of these people are not interested in returning to work, so employers can end up with applicants who have little desire for immediate employment. And fairly or not, employers probably view some of these local agencies as lethargic in their efforts to fill area employers' jobs.

Yet these agencies are useful. Beyond just filling jobs, counselors will visit an employer's work site, review the employer's job requirements, and even assist the employer in writing job descriptions. Most states have turned their local state employment service agencies into "one-stop" shops—neighborhood training/employment/career assessment centers.[94] At Oregon State's centers, job seekers can use "iMatch" skills assessment software, while employers can get up-to-date local economic news and use the center's online recruitment tools.[95] More employers should be taking advantage of these centers (formerly the "unemployment offices" in many cities).

Most (nonprofit) professional and technical societies, such as the Institute for Electrical and Electronic Engineers (IEEE), have units that help members find jobs. Many special public agencies place people who are in special categories, such as those who are disabled.

PRIVATE AGENCIES Private employment agencies are important sources of clerical, white-collar, and managerial personnel. They charge fees (set by state law and posted in their offices) for each applicant they place. Most are "fee-paid" jobs, in which the employer pays the fee. Use one if:

1. Your firm doesn't have its own human resources department and feels it can't do a good job recruiting and screening.
2. You must fill a job quickly.
3. There is a perceived need to attract more minority or female applicants.
4. You want to reach currently employed individuals, who might feel more comfortable dealing with agencies than with competing companies.
5. You want to reduce the time you're devoting to recruiting.[96]

Yet using employment agencies requires avoiding the potential pitfalls. For example, the employment agency's screening may let poor applicants go directly to the supervisors responsible for hiring, who may in turn naively hire them. Conversely, improper screening at the agency could block potentially successful applicants.

To help avoid problems:

1. Give the agency an accurate and complete job description.
2. Make sure tests, application blanks, and interviews are part of the agency's selection process.
3. Periodically review equal employment data on candidates accepted or rejected by your firm, and by the agency.
4. Screen the agency. Check with other managers to find out which agencies have been the most effective at filling the sorts of positions you need filled. Review the Internet and classified ads to discover the agencies that handle the positions you seek to fill.
5. Supplement the agency's reference checking by checking at least the final candidate's references yourself.

Recruitment Process Outsourcers

Recruitment process outsourcers are special vendors that handle all or most of an employer's recruiting needs. They usually sign short-term contracts with the employer, and receive a monthly fee that varies with the amount of actual recruiting the employer needs done. This makes it easier for an employer to ramp up or ramp down its recruiting expenses, as compared with paying the relatively fixed costs of an in-house recruitment office.[97] Large RPO providers include Manpower Group Solutions, IBM, and Randstad Sourceright.[98]

Temporary Workers and Alternative Staffing

Employers increasingly supplement their permanent workforces by hiring contingent or temporary workers, often through temporary help employment agencies. Also known as *part-time* or *just-in-time workers*, the contingent workforce is big and growing. In the recent recession, about 26% of all jobs private-sector employers added were temporary positions, two to three times the comparable figures for the last two recessions. The contingent workforce isn't limited to clerical or maintenance staff. It includes thousands of engineering, science, and management support occupations, such as temporary chief financial officers, human resource managers, and chief executive officers.[99]

Employers use temps for many reasons. One is continuing weak economic confidence among employers. Another is the trend toward organizing around short-term projects. For example, Makino, which manufactures machine tools, now outsources the installation of large machines to contract firms, who in turn hire temps to do the installations. Flexibility is another concern, with more employers wanting to quickly reduce employment levels if the economic turnaround proves short-lived.[100] Other employers use temp agency–supplied workers to "try out" prospective employees.[101]

Employers have also long used "temps" to fill in for employees who were out sick or on vacation. Productivity in output per hour paid is higher, since temps are generally paid only when they're working—not for days off. However, temps often cost employers more per hour than comparable permanent workers, since the agency gets a fee.[102]

alternative staffing
The use of nontraditional recruitment sources.

Temporary employees are examples of **alternative staffing**—basically, the use of nontraditional recruitment sources. Other alternative staffing arrangements include "in-house temporary employees" (people employed directly by the company, but on an explicit short-term basis) and "contract technical employees" (highly skilled workers like engineers, who are supplied for long-term projects under contract from an outside technical services firm).

THE TEMP AGENCY Employers can hire temp workers either through direct hires or through temporary staff agencies. Direct hiring involves simply hiring workers and placing them on the job. The employer usually pays these people directly, as it does all its employees, but classifies them separately, as casual, seasonal, or temporary employees, and often pays few if any benefits.[103] The other approach is to use a temp agency. Here the agency handles all the recruiting, screening, and payroll administration for the temps. Thus, Nike hired Kelly Services to manage Nike's temp needs.

When working with temporary agencies, understand their policies. For example, with temps, the time sheet is not just a verification of hours worked. Once the worker's supervisor signs it, it's usually an agreement to pay the agency's fees. What is the policy if the client wants to hire one of the agency's temps as a permanent employee? How does the agency plan to recruit employees? And finally, check their references.[104]

TEMP EMPLOYEES' CONCERNS To make temporary relationships successful, those supervising temps should understand their concerns. In one survey, temporary workers said they were:

1. Treated by employers in a dehumanizing and ultimately discouraging way.
2. Insecure about their employment and pessimistic about the future.
3. Worried about their lack of insurance and pension benefits.
4. Misled about their job assignments and in particular about whether temporary assignments were likely to become full-time.
5. "Underemployed" (particularly those trying to return to the full-time labor market).[105]

KNOW YOUR EMPLOYMENT LAW

Contract Employees

Several years ago, federal agents rounded up about 250 illegal "contract" cleaning workers in 60 Walmart stores. The raid underscores the need to understand the status of the contract employees who work on your premises handling activities like security or after-hours store cleaning.[106] The fact that they actually work for another, temp-type company is no excuse. For purposes of most employment laws, with certain limited exceptions, employees of temporary staffing firms working in an employer's workplace will be considered to be employees both of the agency and of the employer.[107] The employer's liability depends on the degree to which its supervisors control the temp employee's activities. Therefore, the more the agency does the better. For example, have the agency handle training. Let it negotiate and set the pay rates and vacation/time-off policies.

Employers can take other steps. Require the agency to follow the employer's background checking process, and to assume the legal risks if the employer and agency are found to be jointly responsible. Carefully track how many temporary employees your company actually has. Screen and supervise temporary employees with care if they may have access to your intellectual property and computer systems.[108] Don't treat temporary workers as "employees," for instance, in terms of business cards, employee handbooks, or employee ID badges.[109] ■

TRENDS SHAPING HR: *THE NEW EXTENDED WORKFORCE*

Many employers today build their staff wholly or in part around an extended workforce consisting, for instance, of freelance programmers, designers, or marketers. Freelancer community websites enable such employers to recruit the right freelance team based on the freelancer's reputation and work product. For example, Elance.com (see www.elance.com/) reports its members' skills assessments, and lists detailed project work experience, making it easier for prospective employers to decide who to hire. Similarly, the TopCoder.com (see www.topcoder.com/how-it-works/) programming community site enables employers to identify top programmers based on the reputations they earned within the community. New hiring sites like these may have a big impact on HR. Some employers may well use them to democratize HR, by letting their line managers recruit and hire new employees directly. ■

If your professor has assigned this, go to the Assignments section of **mymanagementlab.com** to complete these discussion questions.

Talk About It 3: Go to one or more sites like these. If you were a programming manager for a company, could you use the site to find and hire a new employee directly? If not, what else might you need?

Offshoring and Outsourcing Jobs

Rather than bringing people in to do the company's jobs, outsourcing and offshoring send the jobs out. *Outsourcing* means having outside vendors supply services (such as benefits management, market research, or manufacturing) that the company's own employees previously did in-house. *Offshoring* means having outside vendors or employees *abroad* supply services that the company's own employees previously did in-house.

Employees, unions, legislators, and even many business owners feel that "shipping jobs out" (particularly overseas) is ill-advised. That notwithstanding, employers are

The numbers of temporary and freelance workers are increasing all over the world.

Chad Baker/Jason Reed/Ryan McVay/Getty Images

sending jobs out, and not just blue-collar jobs. For example, GE's transportation division shifted some mid-level drafting jobs from Pennsylvania to India.[110]

Sending out jobs, particularly overseas, presents employers with special personnel challenges. One is the likelihood of cultural misunderstandings (such as between your home-based customers and the employees abroad). Others are security and information privacy concerns; the need to deal with foreign contract, liability, and legal systems issues; and the fact that the offshore employees need special training (for instance, in using pseudonyms like "Jim" without discomfort).

Rising wages in China and India, coupled with reputational issues and a desire to invest more in local communities, are prompting employers to bring jobs back. Several U.S. employers including Apple and Microsoft are shifting jobs back to America.[111]

Executive Recruiters

Executive recruiters (also known as *headhunters*) are special employment agencies employers retain to seek out top-management talent for their clients. The percentage of your firm's positions filled by these services might be small. However, these jobs include key executive and technical positions. For executive positions, headhunters may be your only source of candidates. The employer always pays the fees.

There are contingent and retained executive recruiters. Members of the Association of Executive Search Consultants usually focus on executive positions paying $150,000 or more, and on "*retained* executive search." They are paid regardless of whether the employer hires the executive through the search firm's efforts. *Contingency-based recruiters* tend to handle junior- to middle-level management job searches in the $80,000 to $160,000 range. Recruiter fees are dropping from the usual 30% or more of the executive's first-year pay.[112] Top recruiters (all retained) include Heidrick and Struggles, Egon Zehnder International, Russell Reynolds, and Spencer Stuart.

The challenging part of recruiting has always been finding potential candidates. Not surprisingly, Internet-based databases now dramatically speed up such searches. Executive recruiters are also creating specialized units aimed at specialized functions (such as sales) or industries (such as oil products).

Recruiters bring a lot to the table. They have many contacts and are relatively adept at finding qualified candidates who aren't actively looking to change jobs. They can keep your firm's name confidential, and can save top management's time by building an applicant pool. The recruiter's fee might actually turn out to be small when you compare it to the executive time saved.

The big issue is ensuring that the recruiter really understands your needs and then delivers properly vetted candidates. It is essential that the employer explain completely what sort of candidate is required. Some recruiters also may be more interested in persuading you to hire a candidate than in finding one who will really do the job. And one or two of the "final candidates" may actually just be fillers to make the recruiter's one "real" candidate look better.

WORKING WITH RECRUITERS Retaining and working with executive recruiters require some caution. In choosing and working with one, guidelines include:[113]

1. Make sure the firm can conduct a thorough search. Under their ethics code, a recruiter can't approach the executive talent of a former client for a period of 2 years after completing a search for that client. Since former clients are off limits for 2 years, the recruiter must search from a constantly diminishing pool.[114]
2. Meet the individual who will actually handle your assignment.
3. Make sure to ask how much the search firm charges. Get the agreement in writing.[115]
4. Make sure the recruiter and you agree on what sort of individual to hire for the position.

5. Ask if the recruiter has vetted the final candidates. Do not be surprised if the answer is, "No, I just get candidates—we don't really screen them."
6. *Never* rely solely on any recruiter do all the reference checking. Let them check the candidates' references, but get notes of these references in writing from the recruiter (if possible). Recheck at least the final candidates' references yourself.
7. Consider using a recruiter who has a special expertise in your specific industry—he or she may have the best grasp of who's available.

INTERNAL RECRUITING More employers are bringing management recruiting in-house. They still use executive recruiters such as Heidrick and Struggles to conduct top officer (CEO and president) and board member placements, and to conduct confidential searches. But employers ranging from General Electric to Sears now have their own internal executive recruiting offices doing most of their own management recruiting. Time Warner reported saving millions of dollars per year using internal recruiting teams.[116]

With employers increasingly finding new ways of recruiting top management talent, executive search firms are diversifying. For example, the head of Korn/Ferry says his firm is increasingly being asked to investigate prospective candidates' backgrounds, and his firm is also expanding into areas such as employee development.[117] The accompanying HR Tools feature explains what small businesses can do.

IMPROVING PERFORMANCE: *HR Tools for Line Managers and Small Businesses*

Recruiting 101

There comes a time in the life of most small businesses when it dawns on the owner that new blood is needed to take the company to the next level. Should the owner personally recruit this person?

While most large firms don't think twice about hiring executive search firms, small-firm owners will understandably hesitate before committing to a fee that could reach $60,000 or more for a $120,000 marketing manager.

However, engaging in a search like this is not like seeking supervisors or data entry clerks. Chances are, you won't find a top manager by placing ads. He or she is probably not reading the want ads. You'll end up with résumés of people who are, for one reason or another, out of work, unhappy with their work, or unsuited for your job. Many may be capable. But you will have to ferret out the gem by interviewing and assessing them.

You won't know where to place or how to write the ads; or where to search, who to contact, or how to screen out the laggards who may appear to be viable candidates. Even if you do, this process will be time-consuming and will divert your attention from other duties.

If you do decide to do the job yourself, consider retaining an industrial psychologist to spend 4 or 5 hours assessing the problem-solving ability, personality, interests, and energy level of the two or three candidates in which you are most interested. The input can provide a valuable perspective on the candidates.

Exercise special care when recruiting applicants from competing companies. Always check to see if applicants are bound by noncompete or nondisclosure agreements. And (especially when recruiting other firms' higher-level employees) perhaps check with an attorney before asking certain questions—regarding patents or potential antitrust issues, for instance.[118]

If you're a manager with an open position to fill in a *Fortune* 500 company, even you may find you have a dilemma. You may find that your local HR office will do little recruiting, other than, perhaps, placing an ad on CareerBuilder. On the other hand, your firm almost surely will not let you place your own help wanted ads. What to do? Use word of mouth to "advertise" your open position within and outside your company. And contact your colleagues in other firms to let them know you are recruiting. ■

If your professor has assigned this, go to the Assignments section of **mymanagementlab.com** to complete these discussion questions.

Talk About It 4: You own a small chemical engineering company and want to hire a new president. Based on what you read in this chapter, how would you go about doing so, and why?

Referrals and Walk-Ins

Employee referral campaigns are a very important recruiting option. Here the employer posts announcements of openings and requests for referrals on its website, bulletin boards, and/or wallboards. It often offers prizes or cash awards for referrals that lead to hiring. For example, at health-care giant Kaiser Permanente, referring someone for one of its "award-eligible positions" can produce bonuses of $3,000 or more.[119] The Container Store trains employees to recruit candidates from among the firm's customers.

Referral's big advantage is that it tends to generate "more applicants, more hires, and a higher yield ratio (hires/applicants)."[120] Current employees tend to provide accurate information about their referrals because they're putting their own reputations on the line. And the new employees may come with a more realistic picture of what the firm is like. A SHRM survey found that of 586 employer respondents, 69% said employee referral programs are more cost-effective than other recruiting practices and 80% specifically said they are more cost-effective than employment agencies. On average, referral programs cost around $400–$900 per hire in incentives and rewards.[121]

If morale is low, address that prior to asking for referrals. And if you don't hire someone's referral, explain to your employee/referrer why you did not hire his or her candidate. In addition, remember that relying on referrals might be discriminatory where a workforce is already homogeneous.

WALK-INS Particularly for hourly workers, walk-ins—direct applications made at your office—are a big source of applicants. Sometimes, posting a "Help Wanted" sign outside the door may be the most cost-effective way of attracting good local applicants. Treat walk-ins courteously, for both the employer's community reputation and the applicant's self-esteem. Many employers give every walk-in a brief interview, even if it is only to get information on the applicant "in case a position should be open in the future." Employers also typically receive unsolicited applications from professional and white-collar applicants. Good business practice requires answering all applicants' letters of inquiry promptly.

On-Demand Recruiting Services

on-demand recruiting services (ODRS)
Services that provide short-term specialized recruiting to support specific projects without the expense of retaining traditional search firms.

On-demand recruiting services (ODRS) are recruiters who are paid by the hour or project, instead of a percentage fee, to support a specific project. For example, when the human resource manager for a biotech firm had to hire several dozen people with scientific degrees and experience in pharmaceuticals, she used an ODRS firm. A traditional recruiting firm might charge 20% to 30% of each hire's salary. The ODRS firm charged by time, rather than per hire. It handled recruiting and prescreening, and left the client with a short list of qualified candidates.[122]

College Recruiting

college recruiting
Sending an employer's representatives to college campuses to prescreen applicants and create an applicant pool from the graduating class.

College recruiting—sending an employer's representatives to college campuses to prescreen applicants and create an applicant pool from the graduating class—is important. One study several years ago concluded, for instance, that new college graduates filled about 38% of all externally filled jobs requiring a college degree.[123]

One problem is that such recruiting is expensive. Schedules must be set well in advance, company brochures printed, interview records kept, and much time spent on campus. And recruiters are sometimes ineffective. Some are unprepared, show little interest in the candidate, and act superior. Many don't screen candidates effectively. Employers need to train recruiters in how to interview candidates, how to explain what the company has to offer, and how to put candidates at ease. The recruiter should be personable and have a record of attracting good candidates.[124] GE hires 800 to 1,000 students each year from about 40 schools, and uses teams of employees and interns to build GE's brand at each school.[125] Shell Oil reduced the list of schools its recruiters visit, using factors such as quality of academic program, number of students enrolled, and diversity of the student body.[126]

The campus recruiter has two main goals. One is to determine if a candidate is worthy of further consideration. Usual traits to assess include communication skills, education, experience, and technical and interpersonal skills. The other aim is to make the employer attractive to candidates. A sincere and informal attitude, respect for the applicant, and prompt follow-up letters can help sell the employer to the interviewee.

Employers who build relationships with opinion leaders such as career counselors and professors have better recruiting results.[127] Building close ties with a college's career center provides recruiters with useful feedback regarding things like labor market conditions and the effectiveness of one's on- and offline recruiting ads.[128]

Employers generally invite good candidates for an on-site visit. The invitation should be warm but businesslike, and provide a choice of dates. Have a host meet the applicant, preferably at the airport or at his or her hotel. A package containing the applicant's schedule as well as other information—such as annual reports and employee benefits—should be waiting for the applicant at the hotel.

Plan the interviews and adhere to the schedule. Avoid interruptions; give the candidate the undivided attention of each person with whom he or she interviews. Have another recently hired graduate host the candidate's lunch. Make any offer as soon as possible, preferably at the time of the visit. Frequent follow-ups to "find out how the decision process is going" may help to tilt the applicant in your favor.

What else to do? A study of 96 graduating students provides some insights. Fifty-three percent said "on-site visit opportunities to meet with people in positions similar to those applied for, or with higher-ranking persons" had a positive effect. Fifty-one percent mentioned, "impressive hotel/dinner arrangements and having well-organized site arrangements." "Disorganized, unprepared interviewer behavior, or uninformed, useless answers" turned off 41%.[129]

INTERNSHIPS Internships can be win–win situations. For students, they can mean honing business skills, learning more about potential employers, and discovering one's career likes (and dislikes). And employers can use the interns to make useful contributions while evaluating them as possible full-time employees. A recent study found that about 60% of internships turned into job offers.[130]

Unfortunately, some internships turn into nightmares. Many interns, particularly in industries like fashion and media, report long unpaid days doing menial work. The *New York Times* recently quoted one company's manager as saying "we need to hire a 22—22—22," in other words a 22-year-old willing to work 22-hour days for $22,000 a year.[131]

Telecommuters

Telecommuters do all or most of their work remotely, often from home, using information technology. For example, JetBlue Airways uses at-home agents to handle its reservation needs. These JetBlue employee "crewmembers" live in the Salt Lake City area and work out of their homes. They use JetBlue-supplied computers and technology, and receive JetBlue training.[132]

Military Personnel

Returning and discharged U.S. military personnel provide an excellent source of trained and disciplined recruits. Yet all too often they have trouble getting placed. For example, the unemployment rate for veterans of the second Gulf War was about 10% versus 6.4% for nonveterans not too long ago. To help remedy this, the federal government offers tax credits to employers who hire veterans, and many employers including Walmart have special programs to recruit veterans.[133] The military also has programs to facilitate soldiers finding jobs. Thus the U.S. Army's Partnership for

Youth Success enables someone entering the Army to select a post-Army corporate partner as a way to help soldiers find a job after leaving the Army.[134]

Misconceptions about veterans (for instance, that posttraumatic stress disorders influence job performance) are generally not valid.[135] The U.S. Army's Warrior Transition Command website (www.wtc.army.mil) discusses such misconceptions. Walmart has a 5-year program guaranteeing any honorably discharged veteran who left the service in the past year a job.[136] The website www.helmetstohardhats.org puts vets together with building trades employers.

The accompanying Profit Center feature describes how one employer reduced recruiting costs.

IMPROVING PERFORMANCE: *HR as a Profit Center*

Cutting Recruitment Costs

One problem raising recruiting costs is that more applicants is not always better. Realistically, the manager looking to hire five engineers probably won't be twice as selective with 20,000 applicants as with 10,000. Furthermore, the employer needs *qualified, hirable* applicants. An Internet ad may generate thousands of nonviable applicants. The employer's applicant tracking system should help compare recruiting sources, as we said, but many lack the tools to do so.[137]

GE Medical hires about 500 technical workers a year to design sophisticated medical devices such as CT scanners. It has cut its hiring costs by 17%, reduced time to fill the positions by 20% to 30%, and cut in half the percentage of new hires who don't work out.[138]

GE Medical's HR team accomplished this in part by applying its purchasing techniques to its dealings with recruiters. For example, it called a meeting and told 20 recruiters that it would work with only the 10 best. To measure "best," the company created measures inspired by manufacturing techniques, such as "percentage of résumés that result in interviews" and "percentage of interviews that lead to offers." Similarly, GE Medical discovered that current employees are very effective as references. For instance, GE Medical interviews just 1% of applicants whose résumés it receives, while 10% of employee referrals result in actual hires. So GE Medical took steps to double the number of employee referrals. It simplified the referral forms, eliminated bureaucratic submission procedures, and added a small reward like a Sears gift certificate for referring a qualified candidate. GE also upped the incentive—$2,000 if someone referred is hired, and $3,000 if he or she is a software engineer. ■

Source: Based on Thomas Stewart, "In Search of Elusive Tech Workers," Fortune, February 16, 1998, pp. 171–172; and http://www.outsourcing-center.com/2006-10-ge-looks-to-recruitment-process-outsourcer-to-find-meat-and-potatoes-candidates-as-well-as-the-purple-squirrel-article-37479.html, accessed October 5, 2011. Gino Ruiz, "Special Report: Talent Acquisition," Workforce Management, July 23, 2007, p. 39.

If your professor has assigned this, go to the Assignments section of **mymanagementlab.com** to complete this discussion question.

✪ **Talk About It 5:** What other tools described in this chapter could GE Medical use to improve recruiting efficiency?

LEARNING OBJECTIVE **5-6**

Explain how to recruit a more diverse workforce.

Recruiting a More Diverse Workforce

We saw in Chapter 2 that recruiting a diverse workforce isn't just socially responsible. Given the rise in minority, older worker, and women candidates, it is a necessity. The recruiting tools we described to this point are certainly useful for minority and other applicants, too. However, diversity recruiting requires several special steps, to which we now turn.[139]

Recruiting Women

Given the progress women have made in getting and excelling in a wide range of professional, managerial, and military occupations, one might assume that employers need no special recruitment efforts to recruit women, but that's not necessarily the case. For example, women still face headwinds in certain male-dominated occupations such as engineering. Women also carry the heavier burden of child-rearing, fill proportionately fewer high-level managerial posts, and still earn only about 70% of what men earn for similar jobs. Many employers therefore focus particular efforts on recruiting qualified women.

The most effective strategy is top management driven.[140] Here the employer emphasizes the importance of recruiting women (as well as men), identifies gaps in the recruitment and retention of women, and puts in place a comprehensive plan to attract women applicants. The overall aim is to make it clear that the employer is the sort of place in which women want to work, and the details of any such plan needn't be complicated. For example, particularly for "nontraditional" jobs (like engineering) use the company website to highlight women now doing those jobs. Emphasize the effectiveness of the employer's mentoring program in moving women up. Offer real workplace flexibility; for example, not just flexible hours but the option of staying on a partner track even while working part-time. (For example, Yahoo! recently implemented a generous 8-week paid maternity/paternity leave policy.) Focus a portion of the recruiting effort on women's organizations, women's employment websites, and career fairs at women's colleges. Make sure benefits cover matters such as family planning and prenatal care. Maintain a zero-tolerance sexual harassment policy.

Recruiting Single Parents

Recently there were about 10 million single parent families with children under 18 maintained by the mother, about two-thirds of whom were employed. There were about 1.25 million single parent families with children under 18 maintained by the father, three-fourths of whom were employed. Being a single parent isn't easy, and recruiting and keeping them requires understanding the problems they face.[141] (And keep in mind that many of these issues also apply to families in which both parents are struggling to make ends meet.) In one survey,

> Many described falling into bed exhausted at midnight without even minimal time for themselves.... They often needed personal sick time or excused days off to care for sick children. As one mother noted, "I don't have enough sick days to get sick."[142]

Given such concerns, the first step in attracting and keeping single parents is to make the workplace user friendly.[143] Surveys suggest that a supportive attitude on the supervisor's part can go far toward making the single parent's work–home balancing act more bearable.[144] Many firms have *flextime* programs that provide employees some schedule flexibility (such as 1-hour windows at the beginning or end of the day). Unfortunately, for many single parents this may not be enough. CNN even offered a "Work/Life Balance Calculator" to assess how far out of balance one's life may be.[145] We'll discuss other options in Chapter 13, Benefits and Services.

Di Carlo Darsa S/PhotoAlto/AGE Fotostock

Not just single parents, but also their children may occasionally need some extra support.

Older Workers

When it comes to hiring older workers, employers don't have much choice.[146] The fastest-growing labor force segment is those from 45 to 64 years old. On the positive side, a survey by AARP and SHRM concluded that older workers tend to have lower absenteeism rates, more reliability, and better work habits than younger workers.[147] Firms like Home Depot capitalize on this by hiring older employees, who "serve as a powerful draw to baby boomer shoppers by mirroring their knowledge and perspective."[148]

It therefore makes sense for employers to encourage older workers to stay (or to come to work at the company). The big draw is probably to provide opportunities for flexible (and often shorter) work schedules.[149] At one company, workers over 65 can progressively shorten their work schedules; another company uses "mini shifts" to accommodate those interested in working less than full time. Other suggestions include the following: phased retirement that allows workers to ease out of the workforce; portable jobs for "snowbirds" who wish to live in warmer climates in the winter; part-time projects for retirees; and full benefits for part-timers.[150]

As always in recruiting, projecting the right image is crucial. The most effective ads here emphasize schedule flexibility, and accentuate the firm's equal opportunity employment statement, not "giving retirees opportunities to transfer their knowledge" to the new work setting.[151]

Diversity Counts

Older workers are good workers. A study focused on the validity of six common stereotypes about older workers: that they are less motivated, less willing to participate in training and career development, more resistant to change, less trusting, less healthy, and more vulnerable to work–family imbalance.[152] They actually found not a negative but a weakly positive relationship between age and motivation and job involvement (suggesting that as age goes up motivation actually rises). They did find a weak negative relationship between age and trainability. Age was weakly but positively related to willingness to change, and to being more trusting. Older workers were no more likely than younger ones to have psychological problems or day-to-day physical health problems, but were more likely to have heightened blood pressure and cholesterol. Older workers did not experience more work–family imbalance. So there was little support for the common age stereotypes.

What should employers do? First, raise employees', managers', and recruiters' consciousness about incorrect age stereotypes. And provide opportunities for more contacts with older people and for information flows between younger and older workers.[153] ■

Recruiting Minorities

Similar prescriptions apply to recruiting minorities.[154] First, *understand* the barriers that prevent minorities from applying. For example, some minority applicants won't meet the educational or experience standards for the job; many employers therefore offer remedial training. In one retail chain, a lack of role models stopped women from applying. Sometimes (as we saw) it's insufficient schedule flexibility.

After recognizing the impediments, one turns to formulating plans for remedying them and for attracting and retaining minorities and women. This may include, for instance, basic skills training, flexible work options, role models, and redesigned jobs.

Finally, implement these plans. For example, many job seekers check with friends or relatives when job hunting, so encouraging your minority employees to assist in your recruitment efforts makes sense. Diversity recruitment specialists include www.diversity.com, www.2trabajo.com, and http://recruitersnetwork.com/resources/diversity.htm. Other firms collaborate with specialist professional organizations (such as the National Black MBA Association (http://careersuccess.nbmbaa.org/).

Some employers experience difficulty in hiring and assimilating people previously on welfare. Applicants sometimes lack basic work skills, such as reporting for work on time, working in teams, and taking orders. The key to welfare-to-work seems to be the employer's pretraining program. Here, participants get counseling and basic skills training over several weeks.[155]

The Disabled

The research is quite persuasive regarding the fact that in terms of virtually all work criteria, employees with disabilities are capable workers. Thousands of employers in the United States and elsewhere have found that disabled employees provide an excellent and largely untapped source of competent, efficient labor for jobs ranging from information technology to creative advertising to receptionist.[156]

Employers can do several things to tap this huge potential workforce. The U.S. Department of Labor's Office of Disability Employment Policy offers several programs, including one that helps link disabled college undergraduates who are looking for summer internships with potential employers.[157] All states have local agencies (such as "Corporate Connections" in Tennessee) that provide placement services and other recruitment and training tools and information for employers seeking to hire the disabled. Employers also must use common sense. For example, employers who post job openings only in newspapers may miss potential employees who are visually impaired.[158]

LEARNING OBJECTIVE **5-7**

Discuss practical guidelines for obtaining application information.

Developing and Using Application Forms

Purpose of Application Forms

application form
The form that provides information on education, prior work record, and skills.

With a pool of applicants, the prescreening process can begin. The **application form** is usually the first step in this process (some firms first require a brief, prescreening interview or online test).

A filled-in application provides four types of information. First, you can make judgments on *substantive matters*, such as whether the applicant has the education and experience to do the job. Second, you can draw conclusions about the applicant's *previous progress* and growth, especially important for management candidates. Third, you can draw tentative conclusions about the applicant's *stability* based on previous work record (although years of downsizing suggest the need for caution here). Fourth, you may be able to use the data in the application to *predict* which candidates will succeed on the job.

Application Guidelines

Ineffective use of the application can cost the employer dearly. Managers should keep several practical guidelines in mind. In the "Employment History" section, request detailed information on each prior employer, including the name of the supervisor and his or her e-mail address and telephone number; this is essential for reference checking. In signing the application, the applicant should certify that falsified statements may be cause for dismissal, that investigation of credit and employment and driving record is authorized, that a medical examination and drug screening tests may be required, and that employment is for no definite period.

Estimates of how many applicants exaggerate their qualifications range from 40% to 70%.[159] The most common problems concern education and job experience. A majority of graduating seniors reportedly believe that employers expect a degree of exaggeration on résumés. Much of this exaggeration occurs on résumés, but may occur on application forms too. Therefore, make sure applicants complete the form and sign a statement on it indicating that the information is true. The court will almost always support a discharge for falsifying information when applying for work.[160]

Finally, doing a less-than-complete job of filling in the form may reflect poor work habits. Some applicants scribble "see résumé attached" on the application. This is not acceptable. You need the signed, completed form. Some firms no longer ask applicants for résumés at all, but instead request and then peruse Web presence links, such as Twitter or LinkedIn accounts.[161]

Most employers need several application forms. For technical and managerial personnel, the form may require detailed answers to questions about education and training. The form for hourly factory workers might focus on tools and equipment. Figure 5-8 illustrates one employment application.

FIGURE 5-8 FBI Employment Application

Source: From FBI Preliminary Application for Honors Internship Program, Federal Bureau of Investigation.

FIELD OFFICE USE ONLY

HP

Div: Program:

FEDERAL BUREAU OF INVESTIGATION

Preliminary Application for Honors Internship Program (Please Type or Print in Ink)

Date: _____

I. PERSONAL HISTORY

Name in Full (Last, First, Middle, Maiden)

List College(s) attended, Major, Degree (if applicable), Grade Point Average

Birth Date (Month, Day, Year)
Birth Place:

Social Security Number: (Optional)

Current Address

Street Apt. No.

City State Zip Code

Home Phone Area Code Number

Work Phone Area Code Number

Are you: Licensed Driver ☐ Yes ☐ No U. S. Citizen ☐ Yes ☐ No

Have you served on active duty in the Armed Forces of the United States? ☐ Yes ☐ No

Branch of military service and dates of active duty:

Type of Discharge

How did you learn or become interested in the FBI Honors Internship Program?

Do you have a foreign language background? ☐ Yes ☐ No List proficiency for each language on reverse side.

Have you ever been arrested or charged with any violation including traffic, but excluding parking tickets? ☐ Yes ☐ No If so, list all such matters even if found not guilty, not formally charged, no court appearance, or matter settled by payment of fine or forfeiture of collateral. Include date, place, charge, disposition, details, and police agency on reverse side.

II. EMPLOYMENT HISTORY

Identify your most recent three years FULL-TIME work experience, after high school (excluding summer, part-time and temporary employment).

From	To	Description of Work	Name/Location of Employer

III. PERSONAL DECLARATIONS

Persons with a disability who require an accommodation to complete the application process are required to notify the FBI of their need for the accommodation.

Have you used marijuana during the last three years or more than 15 times? ☐ Yes ☐ No

Have you used any illegal drug(s) or combination of illegal drugs, other than marijuana, more than 5 times or during the last 10 years? ☐ Yes ☐ No

All Information provided by applicants concerning their drug history will be subject to verification by a preemployment polygraph examination.

Do you understand all prospective FBI employees will be required to submit to an urinalysis for drug abuse prior to employment? ☐ Yes ☐ No

I am aware that willfully withholding information or making false statements on this application constitutes a violation of Section 1001, Title 18, U.S. Code and if appointed, will be the basis for dismissal from the Federal Bureau of Investigation. I agree to these conditions and I hereby certify that all statements made by me on this application are true and complete, to the best of my knowledge.

Signature of Applicant as usually written. **(Do Not Use Nickname)**

The Federal Bureau of Investigation is an equal opportunity employer.

KNOW YOUR EMPLOYMENT LAW

Application Forms and EEO Law

Application forms must comply with equal employment laws. Problematical items include:

Education. A question on dates of attendance and graduation is a potential violation, since it may reveal the applicant's age.

Arrest record. The courts have usually held that employers violate Title VII by disqualifying applicants from employment because of an arrest. This item has an adverse impact on minorities, and employers usually can't show it's required as a business necessity.

Notify in case of emergency. It is generally legal to require the name, address, and phone number of a person to notify in case of emergency.

However, asking the relationship of this person could indicate the applicant's marital status or lineage.

Membership in organizations. Some forms ask to list memberships in clubs, organizations, or societies. Employers should include instructions not to include organizations that would reveal race, religion, physical handicaps, marital status, or ancestry.

Physical handicaps. It is usually illegal to require the listing of an applicant's physical handicaps or past illnesses unless the application blank specifically asks only for those that "may interfere with your job performance." Similarly, it is generally illegal to ask if the applicant has received workers' compensation.

Marital status. In general, the application should not ask whether an applicant is single, married, divorced, separated, or living with anyone, or the names, occupations, and ages of the applicant's spouse or children.

Housing. Asking whether an applicant *owns, rents*, or *leases* a house may be discriminatory. It can adversely affect minority groups and is difficult to justify on business necessity.

Video résumés. More candidates are submitting video résumés, a practice replete with benefits and threats. To facilitate using video résumés, several websites compile multimedia résumés for applicants.[162] The danger is that a video makes it more likely that rejected candidates may claim discrimination.[163] ■

Using Application Forms to Predict Job Performance

Some employers use analyses of application information ("biodata") to *predict* employee tenure and performance. In one study, the researchers found that applicants who had longer tenure with previous employers were less likely to quit, and also had higher performance within 6 months after hire.[164] Examples of predictive biodata items might include "quit a job without giving notice," "graduated from college," and "traveled considerably growing up."[165]

Choose biodata items with three things in mind. First, equal employment law limits the items you'll want to use (avoid age, race, or gender, for instance). And, noninvasive items are best. In one study, subjects perceived items such as "dollar sales achieved" and "grade point average in math" as not invasive. Items such as "birth order" and "frequent dates in high school" were more invasive. Finally, some applicants will fake biodata answers in an effort to impress the employer.[166]

Mandatory Arbitration

Many employers, aware of the high costs of employment litigation, require applicants to agree on their applications to mandatory arbitration should a dispute arise.

Different federal courts have taken different positions on the enforceability of such "mandatory alternative dispute resolution" clauses. They are generally enforceable, with two caveats. First, it must be a fair process.[167] For example, the agreement should be a signed and dated separate agreement. Use simple wording. Provide for reconsideration and judicial appeal if there is an error of law.[168] The employer must absorb most of the cost of the arbitration process. The process should be reasonably swift. Employees should be eligible to receive the full remedies that they would have had if they had access to the courts.

Second, mandatory arbitration clauses turn some candidates off. In one study, 389 MBA students read simulated employment brochures. Mandatory employment arbitration had a significantly negative impact on the attractiveness of the company as a place to work.[169]

Chapter Review

MyManagementLab® Go to **mymanagementlab.com** to complete the problems marked with this icon. ✪

Chapter Section Summaries

5-1. Recruitment and selection start with **workforce planning and forecasting**. Workforce planning is the process of deciding what positions the firm will have to fill, and how to fill them. This often starts by forecasting personnel needs, perhaps using trend analysis, ratio analysis, scatter plots, or computerized software packages. Next forecast the supply of inside candidates. Here employers use manual systems and replacement charts, and computerized skills inventories. Forecasting the supply of outside candidates is important, particularly when unemployment is low and good candidates are more difficult to come by.

5-2. Managers need to understand why **effective recruiting is important**. Without enough candidates, employers cannot effectively screen the candidates or hire the best. Some employers use a recruiting yield pyramid to estimate how many applicants they need to generate in order to fill predicted job openings.

5-3. Filling open positions with **internal sources of candidates** has several advantages. You are familiar with their strengths and weaknesses, and they require less orientation. Finding internal candidates often utilizes job posting. For filling the company's projected top-level positions, succession planning—the ongoing process of systematically identifying, assessing, and developing organizational leadership to enhance performance—is the process of choice.

5-4. Workforce plans influence **employee engagement**. For example, plans to develop and retain employees and promote from within tend to foster engagement, while contrary policies may erode it. Recognizing this, at some companies such as FedEx, internal recruiting and promotion from within both play central roles in employee engagement. The promotion-from-within policy includes helping employees identify and develop their promotion potential. It also requires a coordinated system for accessing career records and posting job openings, one that guarantees all eligible employees are informed of openings and considered for them.

5-5. Employers use a variety of **outside sources of candidates** when recruiting applicants. These include recruiting via the Internet, advertising and employment agencies (including public and nonprofit agencies, and private agencies), temporary agencies and other alternative staffing methods, executive recruiters, college recruiting, referrals and walk-ins, and military personnel.

5-6. Understanding how to **recruit a more diverse workforce** is important. Whether the target is the single parent, older workers, or minorities, the basic rule is to understand their special needs and to create a set of policies and practices that create a more hospitable environment in which they can work.

5-7. **Employers develop and use application forms** to collect essential background information about the applicant. The application should enable you to make judgments on substantial matters such as the person's education and to identify the person's job references and supervisors. Of course, it's important to make sure the application complies with equal employment laws, for instance, with respect to questions regarding physical handicaps.

Discussion Questions

✪**5-1.** Briefly outline the workforce planning process.

✪**5-2.** Briefly explain each step in the recruitment and selection process.

5-3. What are the four main types of information that application forms provide?

5-4. How, specifically, do equal employment laws apply to personnel recruiting activities?

5-5. What are the five main things you would do to recruit and retain a more diverse workforce?

Individual and Group Activities

5-6. Bring to class several classified and display ads from the Web or the Sunday help wanted ads. Analyze the effectiveness of these ads using the guidelines discussed in this chapter.

5-7. Working individually or in groups, develop a 5-year forecast of occupational market conditions for five occupations such as accountant, nurse, and engineer.

5-8. Working individually or in groups, visit the local office of your state employment agency (or check out its site online). Come back to class prepared to discuss the following questions: What types of jobs seem to be available through this agency, predominantly? To what extent do you think this particular agency would be a good source of professional, technical, and/or managerial applicants? What sorts of paperwork are applicants to the state agency required to complete before their applications are processed by the agency? What other services does the office provide? What other opinions did you form about the state agency?

5-9. Working individually or in groups, find at least five employment ads, either on the Internet or in a local newspaper, that suggest that the company is family friendly and should appeal to women, minorities, older workers, and single parents. Discuss what the firm is doing to be family friendly.

5-10. Working individually or in groups, interview a manager between the ages of 25 and 35 at a local business who manages employees age 40 or older. Ask the manager to describe three or four of his or her most challenging experiences managing older employees.

5-11. Appendices A and B at the end of this book (pages 612–629) list the knowledge someone studying for the HRCI (Appendix A) or SHRM (Appendix B) certification exam needs to have in each area of human resource management (such as in Strategic Management, and Workforce Planning). In groups of several students, do four things: (1) review Appendix A and/or B; (2) identify the material in this chapter that relates to the Appendix A and/or B required knowledge lists; (3) write four multiple-choice exam questions on this material that you believe would be suitable for inclusion in the HRCI exam and/or the SHRM exam; and, (4) if time permits, have someone from your team post your team's questions in front of the class, so that students in all teams can answer the exam questions created by the other teams.

Experiential Exercise

The Nursing Shortage

As of August 2013, U.S. unemployment was still disappointingly high, and employers were still holding back on their hiring. However, while many people were unemployed, that was not the case with nurse professionals. Virtually every hospital was aggressively recruiting nurses. Many were turning to foreign-trained nurses, for example, by recruiting nurses in the Philippines. Experts expect nurses to be in very short supply for years to come.

Purpose: The purpose of this exercise is to give you experience in creating a recruitment program.

Required Understanding: You should be thoroughly familiar with the contents of this chapter, and with the nurse recruitment program of a hospital such as Lenox Hill Hospital in New York (see http://lenoxhillhospital.org/careers_default.aspx).

How to Set Up the Exercise/Instructions:
Set up groups of four to five students for this exercise. The groups should work separately and should not converse with each other. Each group should address the following tasks:

5-12. Based on information available on the hospital's website, create a hard-copy ad for the hospital to place in the Sunday edition of the *New York Times*. Which (geographic) editions of the *Times* would you use, and why?

5-13. Analyze the hospital's current online nurses' ad. How would you improve on it?

5-14. Prepare in outline form a complete nurses' recruiting program for this hospital, including all recruiting sources your group would use.

Application Case

Finding People Who Are Passionate About What They Do

Trilogy Enterprises Inc. of Austin, Texas, is a fast-growing software company, and provides software solutions to giant global firms for improving sales and performance. Many of its approaches to business practice are unusual, but in Trilogy's fast-changing and highly competitive environment, they seem to work.

There is no dress code and employees make their own hours, often very long. They tend to socialize together (the average age is 26), both in the office's well-stocked kitchen and on company-sponsored events and trips to places like local dance clubs and retreats in Las Vegas. Responsibility is heavy and comes early, with a "just do it now" attitude. New recruits get a few weeks of intensive training, described by participants as "more like boot camp than business school." Information is delivered as if with "a fire hose," and new employees are expected to commit their expertise and vitality to everything they do. Jeff Daniel, director of college recruiting, admits the intense and unconventional firm is not the employer for everybody.

The firm employs about 700 people. Trilogy's managers know the rapid growth they seek depends on having a staff of the best people they can find, quickly trained and given broad responsibility and freedom as soon as possible. CEO Joe Liemandt says, "At a software company, people are everything.... Of course, the leaders at every company say, 'People are everything.' But they don't act on it."

Trilogy makes finding the right people a company-wide mission. Recruiters actively scour college career fairs and computer science departments for talented overachievers with ambition and entrepreneurial instincts. Top managers conduct the first rounds of interviews. Employees take top recruits and their significant others out on the town when they fly into Austin for the standard, 3-day preliminary visit. A typical day might begin with grueling interviews but end with mountain biking.

One year, Trilogy reviewed 15,000 résumés, conducted 4,000 on-campus interviews, flew 850 prospects in for interviews, and hired 262 college graduates. The cost per hire was $13,000; Jeff Daniel believes it was worth every penny.

Questions

5-15. Identify some of the established recruiting techniques that apparently underlie Trilogy's unconventional approach to attracting talent.

5-16. What particular elements of Trilogy's culture most likely appeal to the kind of employees it seeks? How does it convey those elements to job prospects?

5-17. Would Trilogy be an appealing employer for you? Why? If not, what would it take for you to accept a job offer from Trilogy?

5-18. What suggestions would you make to Trilogy for improving its recruiting processes?

Sources: Chuck Salter, "Insanity, Inc.," *Fast Company*, January 1999, pp. 101–108; and www.trilogy.com/sections/careers/work, accessed August 24, 2007.

Continuing Case

Carter Cleaning Company

Getting Better Applicants

If you were to ask Jennifer and her father what the main problem was in running their firm, their answer would be quick and short: hiring good people. Originally begun as a string of coin-operated laundromats requiring virtually no skilled help, the chain grew to six stores, each heavily dependent on skilled managers, cleaner/spotters, and pressers. Employees generally have no more than a high school education, and the market for them is very competitive. Over a typical weekend, literally dozens of want ads for experienced pressers or cleaner/spotters can be found in area newspapers. All these people usually are paid around $15 per hour, and they change jobs frequently. Jennifer and her father thus face the continuing task of recruiting and hiring qualified workers out of a pool of individuals they feel are almost nomadic in their propensity to move from area to area and job to job. Turnover in their stores (as in the stores of many of their competitors) often approaches 400%. "Don't talk to me about human resources planning and trend analysis," says Jennifer. "We're fighting an economic war, and I'm happy just to be able to round up enough live applicants to be able to keep my trenches fully manned."

In light of this problem, Jennifer's father asked her to answer the following questions:

Questions

5-19. First, how would you recommend we go about reducing the turnover in our stores?

5-20. Provide a detailed list of recommendations concerning how we should go about increasing our pool of acceptable job applicants so we no longer face the need to hire almost anyone who walks in the door. (Your recommendations regarding the latter should include completely worded online and hard-copy advertisements and recommendations regarding any other recruiting strategies you would suggest we use.)

Translating Strategy into HR Policies and Practices Case*,§

**The accompanying strategy map for this chapter is in the MyManagementLab, and the overall map on the inside back cover of this text outlines the relationships involved.*

Improving Performance at the Hotel Paris

The New Recruitment Process

The Hotel Paris's competitive strategy is "to use superior guest service to differentiate the Hotel Paris properties, and to thereby increase the length of stay and return rate of guests, and thus boost revenues and profitability." HR manager Lisa Cruz must now formulate functional policies and activities that support this competitive strategy and boost performance, by eliciting the required employee behaviors and competencies.

As a longtime HR professional, Lisa Cruz was well aware of the importance of effective employee recruitment. If the Hotel Paris didn't get enough applicants, it could not be selective about who to hire. And, if it could not be selective about who to hire, it wasn't likely that the hotels would enjoy the customer-oriented employee behaviors that the company's strategy relied on. She was therefore disappointed to discover that the Hotel Paris was paying virtually no attention to the job of recruiting prospective employees. Individual hotel managers slapped together help wanted ads when they had positions to fill, and no one in the chain had any measurable idea of how many recruits these ads were producing or which recruiting approaches worked the best (or worked at all). Lisa knew that it was time to step back and get control of the Hotel Paris's recruitment function.

As they reviewed the details of the Hotel Paris's current recruitment practices, Lisa Cruz and the firm's CFO became increasingly concerned. What they found, basically, was that the recruitment function was totally unmanaged. The previous HR director had simply allowed the responsibility for recruiting to remain with each separate hotel, and the hotel managers, not being HR professionals, usually just took the path of least resistance when a job became available by placing help wanted ads in their local papers. There was no sense of direction from the Hotel Paris's headquarters regarding what sorts of applicants the company preferred, what media and alternative sources of recruits its managers should use, no online recruiting, and, of course, no measurement at all of effectiveness of the recruitment process. The company totally ignored recruitment-source metrics that other firms used effectively, such as number of qualified applicants per position, percentage of jobs filled from within, the offer-to-acceptance ratio, acceptance by recruiting source, turnover by recruiting source, and selection test results by recruiting source. This despite the fact, as the CFO put it, "that high performance companies consistently score much higher than low-performing firms on HR practices such as number of qualified applicants per position, and percentage of jobs filled from within."

It was safe to say that achieving the Hotel Paris's strategic aims depended largely on the quality of the people that it attracted to, and then selected for, employment at the firm. "What we want are employees who will put our guests first, who will use initiative to see that our guests are satisfied, and who will work tirelessly to provide our guests with services that exceed their expectations," said the CFO. Lisa and the CFO both knew this process had to start with better recruiting. The CFO gave her the green light to design a new recruitment process.

Lisa and her team had the firm's IT department create a central recruiting link for the Hotel Paris's website, with geographical links that each local hotel could use to publicize its openings. The HR team created a series of standard ads the managers could use for each job title. These standard ads emphasized the company's service-oriented values, and basically said (without actually saying it) that if you were not people oriented you should not apply. They emphasized what it was like to work for the Hotel Paris, and the excellent benefits (which the HR team was about to get started on) the firm provided. It created a new intranet-based job posting system and encouraged employees to use it to apply for open positions. For several jobs, including housekeeping crew and front-desk clerk, applicants must now first pass a short prescreening test to apply. The HR team analyzed the performance (for instance, in terms of applicants/source and applicants hired/source) of the various local newspapers and recruiting firms the hotels had used in the past, and chose the best to be the approved recruiting sources in their local areas.

After 6 months with these and other recruitment function changes, the number of applicants was up on average 40%. Lisa and her team were now set to institute new screening procedures that would help them select the high-commitment, service-oriented, motivated employees they were looking for.

Questions

5-21. Given the hotel's required personnel skills, what recruiting sources would you have suggested it use, and why?

5-22. What would a Hotel Paris help wanted ad look like?

5-23. Based on what you know and on what you learned here in Chapter 5 of Dessler *Human Resource Management*, how would you suggest Hotel Paris measure the effectiveness of its recruiting efforts?

§Written by and copyright Gary Dessler, PhD.

CHAPTER 5

MyManagementLab

Go to **mymanagementlab.com** for Auto-graded writing questions as well as the following Assisted-graded writing questions:

5-24. What are the pros and cons of five sources of job candidates?

5-25. As explained in this chapter, technology is in many ways revolutionizing how employers recruit for employees. You manage a small women's clothing store and need to hire an assistant manager. How would you use social media to recruit candidates?

5-26. MyManagementLab Only—comprehensive writing assignment for this chapter.

✪ Try It!

How would you apply the concepts and skills you learned in this chapter? If your professor has assigned this, go to the Assignments section of **mymanagementlab.com** to complete the simulation: *Plans & Planning Tools*.

Key Terms

workforce (or employment or personnel) planning, 128
trend analysis, 130
ratio analysis, 130
scatter plot, 131
personnel replacement charts, 132
position replacement card, 132
succession planning, 134
employee recruiting, 135
recruiting yield pyramid, 136
job posting, 137
applicant tracking systems (ATS), 139
alternative staffing, 145
on-demand recruiting services (ODRS), 149
college recruiting, 149
application form, 154

Endnotes

1. Robert Hackett, "A Global Opportunity," *Fortune* 171, no. 2 (February 1, 2015), p. 22.
2. This section is quoted or paraphrased from, "Workforce Planning: Translating the Business Plan into the People Plan," Towers Watson, www.towerswatson.com/en-GB/Insights/IC-Types/Survey-Research-Results/2012/11/workforce-planning-translating-the-business-plan-into-the-people-plan?page=0, accessed March 29, 2013.
3. "Transforming Talent Management: Pursuing New Perspectives," 2013 Talent Management Conference & Exposition, Society for Human Resource Management, "Preparing for Tomorrow's Talent Gap: Five Strategies to Start Today" workshop, p. 4. See also "Succession Planning Orientation Guide," *Workforce,* February 2014, pp. 32–34.
4. Hackett, "A Global Opportunity."
5. Ibid.
6. Jones Shannon, "Does HR Planning Improve Business Performance?" *Industrial Management*, January/February 2003, p. 20. See also Michelle Harrison et al., "Effective Succession Planning," *Training & Development*, October 2006, pp. 22–23.
7. Carolyn Hirschman, "Putting Forecasting in Focus," *HR Magazine*, March 2007, pp. 44–49.
8. Jean Phillips and Stanley Gully, *Strategic Staffing* (Upper Saddle River, NJ: Pearson Education, 2012), pp. 116–181.
9. Shannon, "Does HR Planning Improve Business Performance?" p. 16.
10. See, for example, Fay Hansen, "The Long View," *Workforce Management*, April 20, 2008, pp. 1, 14.
11. Bill Roberts, "Can They Keep Our Lights On?" *HR Magazine*, June 2010, pp. 62–68. For an example of a computerized personnel planning system, see www.kronos.com/scheduling-software/scheduling.aspx, accessed October 2, 2011.
12. See, for example, www.shrm.org/TemplatesTools/hrqa/Pages/Howcanaskillsinventorybeused for strategicHRplanning.aspx, accessed February 6, 2014.
13. http://skillsdbpro.com/SkillsDBPROWeb.html; http://skillsdbpro.com/client-list/; and www.surveyanalytics.com/skills-inventory.html, accessed June 22, 2015.
14. www.surveyanalytics.com/skills-inventory-software.html, accessed June 1, 2011.
15. www.sumtotalsystems.com/datasheets/sumt_succession_planning.pdf, accessed June 1, 2011.
16. For a recent discussion see, for example, "Pitfalls Abound for Employers Lacking Electronic Information Retention Policies," *BNA Bulletin to Management*, January 1, 2008, pp. 1–2.
17. The legislation includes the Federal Privacy Act of 1974 (applies to federal workers), the New York Personal Privacy Act of 1985, HIPAA (regulates use of medical records), and the Americans with Disabilities Act.
18. Ibid. See also Bill Roberts, "Risky Business," *HR Magazine,* October 2006, pp. 69–72.
19. www.wired.com/2015/06/opm-breach-security-privacy-debacle/ accessed August 25, 2015.
20. See, for example, Society for Human Resource Management, "HR's Insight into the Economy," *Workplace Visions* 4 (2008), p. 5.
21. www.astd.org/NR/rdonlyres/CBAB6F0D-97FA-4B1F-920C-6EBAF98906D1/0/BridgingtheSkillsGap.pdf, accessed June 1, 2011.
22. "Next Generation Talent Management," www.hewittassociates.com/_MetaBasicCMAssetCache_/Assets/Articles/next_generation.pdf, accessed November 9, 2010.
23. "Boeing Soars Over Potential Talent Gaps with Its Workforce Planning Strategies," *Bloomberg BNA Bulletin to Management,* February 19, 2013, p. 57.
24. Ed Frauenheim, "Valero Energy," *Workforce Management,* March 13, 2006.
25. Phillips and Gully, *Strategic Staffing,* pp. 116–181.
26. See also Soonhee Kim, "Linking Employee Assessments to Succession Planning," *Public Personnel Management* 32, no. 4 (Winter 2003), pp. 533–547; Michael Laff, "Talent Management: From Hire to Retire," *Training & Development*, November 2006, pp. 42–48.
27. See, for example, David Day, "Developing Leadership Talent," SHRM Foundation, www.shrm.org/about/foundation/research/Documents/Developing%20Lead%20Talent-%20FINAL.pdf, accessed October 4, 2011.
28. Quoted in Susan Wells, "Who's Next," *HR Magazine*, November 2003, p. 43. See also Christee Atwood, "Implementing Your Succession Plan," *Training & Development*, November 2007, pp. 54–57; and Day, "Developing Leadership Talent."
29. See "Succession Management: Identifying and Developing Leaders," *BNA Bulletin to Management* 21, no. 12 (December 2003), p. 15; and Day, "Developing Leadership Talent."
30. Kim, "Linking Employee Assessments to Succession Planning."
31. Bill Roberts, "Matching Talent with Tasks," *HR Magazine*, November 2002, pp. 91–96.
32. www.sumtotalsystems.com/datasheets/sumt_succession_planning.pdf, accessed June 1, 2011.
33. Ibid., p. 34.
34. Susan Ladika, "Manufacturers Enroll in Recruiting 101," *Workforce Management*, May 2012.
35. David Ferris, "Ex-Factor for Factories Is Factoring in Recruiting," *Workforce Management*, December 2012, p. 8.
36. Susan Caminiti, "Leveraging Human Capital," Fortune.com/edit sections, 2012, pp. 52–54.
37. Sara Rynes, Robert Bretz Jr., and Barry Gerhart, "The Importance of Recruitment and Job Choice: A Different Way of Looking," *Personnel Psychology* 44, no. 3 (September 1991), pp. 487–521.
38. Tom Porter, "Effective Techniques to Attract, Hire, and Retain 'Top Notch' Employees for Your Company," *San Diego Business Journal* 21, no. 13 (March 27, 2000), p. B36.
39. Jonathan Segal, "Land Executives, Not Lawsuits," *HR Magazine*, October 2006, pp. 123–130.
40. "Recruitment Marketing," www.recruiter.com/recruitment_marketing/, accessed May 1, 2012.
41. www.ge.com/careers/why_ge.html, accessed May 1, 2012.
42. Stanley Gully, Jean Phillips, William Castellano, Khongji Han, and Andrea Kim, "A Mediated Moderation Model of Recruiting Socially and Environmentally Responsible Job Applicants," *Personnel Psychology* 66 (2013), p. 966.
43. Kenneth Sovereign, *Personnel Law* (Upper Saddle River, NJ: Prentice Hall, 1999), pp. 47–49.
44. Ibid., p. 48.
45. "Apple, Google Agree to Pay $415 Million in Settlement of

Antitrust Hiring Charges," *Bloomberg BNA Bulletin to Management*, January 27, 2015, p. 27.
46. Todd Henneman, "The Insiders or the Outsiders?" *Workforce,* March 2014, pp. 29–31, 48.
47. Eric Krell, "Look Outside or Seek Within?" *HR Magazine,* January/February 2015, pp. 61–64.
48. "Hiring Works the Second Time Around," *BNA Bulletin to Management*, January 30, 1997, p. 40; and Issie Lapowsky, "How to Rehire Former Employees," *INC.*, May 18, 2010, www.inc.com/guides/2010/05/rehiring-former-employees.html, accessed October 3, 2011.
49. Ibid.
50. See www.linkedin.com/jobs2/view/10696437, accessed June 22, 2015.
51. www.fedex.com/ma/about/overview/philosophy.html.
52. Lauren Weber and Leslie Kwoh, "Beware the Phantom Job Listing," *Wall Street Journal*, January 9, 2013, page B1.
53. "Many Workers Use Social Networking Sites in Job Hunt, Edit Own Content, Survey Finds," *BNA Bulletin to Management*, May 10, 2011, p. 147.
54. Reprinted from www.careerbuilder.com/MarketingWeb/iPhone/CBJobsApplication.aspx?cbRecursionCnt=1&cbsid=7fd458dafd4a444fb192d9a24ceed771-291142537-wx-6&ns_siteid=ns_us_g_careerbuilder_iphone, accessed March 23, 2009.
55. Deborah Silver, "Niche Sites Gain Monster-Sized Following," *Workforce Management*, March 2011, pp. 10–11.
56. Except as noted, this *Online Recruiting* section is based on Lauren Weber, "Seeking Software Fix for Job-Search Game," *Wall Street Journal*, June 6, 2012, p. B8; and Juro Osawa and Paul Moser, "In China, Recruiting Gets Social," *Wall Street Journal*, August 2, 2012, p. B4.
57. "ResumePal: Recruiter's Friend?" *Workforce Management*, June 22, 2009, p. 28.
58. "Innovative HR Programs Cultivate Successful Employees," *Nation's Restaurant News* 41, no. 50 (December 17, 2007), p. 74.
59. J. De Avila, "Beyond Job Boards: Targeting the Source," *Wall Street Journal* (Eastern Edition), July 2, 2009, pp. D1, D5.
60. Gina Ruiz, "Firms Tapping Web Videos to Lure Jobseekers," *Workforce Management*, October 8, 2007, p. 12.
61. Sarah Fister Gale, "Social Media Transforms a Recruiting Source Software Industry," *Workforce Management,* workforce.com, June 2013, p. 26. See also Thomas Cottereau, "The Future of Live Video Interviews for Recruitment," *HR Magazine,* November 2014, pp. 48–50.
62. Elizabeth Agnvall, "Job Fairs Go Virtual," *HR Magazine*, July 2007, p. 85; Gary Stern, "Virtual Job Fairs Becoming More of a Reality," *Workforce Management*, February 2011, p. 11.
63. Matthias Baum and Rudiger Kabst, "The Effectiveness of Recruitment Advertisements and Recruitment Websites: Indirect and Interactive Effects on Applicant Attraction," *Human Resource Management* 53, no. 3 (May–June 2014), pp. 353–378.
64. "EEOC Issues Much Delayed Definition of 'Applicant,'" *HR Magazine,* April 2004, p. 29; Valerie Hoffman and Greg Davis, "OFCCP's Internet Applicant Definition Requires Overhaul of Recruitment and Hiring Policies," *Society for Human Resources Management Legal Report*, January/February 2006, p. 2.
65. This carries legal risks, particularly if the device disproportionately screens out minority or female applicants. Lisa Harpe, "Designing an Effective Employment Prescreening Program," *Employment Relations Today* 32, no. 3 (Fall 2005), pp. 43–51.
66. Lauren Weber, "Your Resume Versus Oblivion," *Wall Street Journal*, January 24, 2012, pp. B1, B6.
67. William Dickmeyer, "Applicant Tracking Reports Make Data Meaningful," *Workforce*, February 2001, pp. 65–67; and, as an example, www.icims.com/prelude/1101/3009?_vsrefdom=google_ppc&gclid=CPHki_nx1KsCF-cPt7QodmkjLDA, accessed October 4, 2011.
68. Paul Gilster, "Channel the Resume Flood with Applicant Tracking Systems," *Workforce*, January 2001, pp. 32–34; William Dickmeyer, "Applicant Tracking Reports Make Data Meaningful," *Workforce*, February 2001, pp. 65–67; and, as an example, www.icims.com/prelude/1101/3009?_vsrefdom=google_ppc&gclid=CPHki_nx1KsCF-cPt7QodmkjLDA, accessed October 4, 2011.
69. Note also that for EEO purposes, "Feds Want a Look at Online Job Sites," *HR Magazine*, November 2008, p. 12.
70. "E-Recruiting Software Providers," *Workforce Management*, June 22, 2009, p. 14.
71. Weber, "Your Resume Versus Oblivion."
72. Dave Zielinski, "Get to the Source," *HR Magazine*, November 2012, p. 68.
73. (Laszlo Bock, Work Rules! (New York: Twelve: 2015) 81, 82).
74. (Laszlo Bock, Work Rules! (New York: Twelve: 2015) 79 – 86)
75. Daniel Feldman and Brian Klaas, "Internet Job Hunting: A Field Study of Applicant Experiences with Online Recruiting," *Human Resource Management* 41, no. 2 (Summer 2002), pp. 175–192.
76. "Does Your Company's Website Click with Job Seekers?" *Workforce*, August 2000, p. 260.
77. "Study Says Career Web Sites Could Snare More Job Seekers," *BNA Bulletin to Management*, February 1, 2001, p. 36.
78. Sarah Gale, "Internet Recruiting: Better, Cheaper, Faster," *Workforce*, December 2001, p. 75.
79. "Help Wanted—and Found," *Fortune*, October 2, 2006, p. 40.
80. James Breaugh, "Employee Recruitment: Current Knowledge and Important Areas for Future Research," *Human Resource Management Review* 18 (2008), p. 114.
81. "Job Seekers' Privacy Has Been Eroded with Online Job Searchers, Report Says," *BNA Bulletin to Management*, November 20, 2003, p. 369.
82. Breaugh, "Employee Recruitment."
83. Anthony Abbatiello, "The Digital Override," *Workforce,* May 2014, pp. 36–39; "Social Recruiting in 2012, the Ladders.com," Special Advertising Supplement to *Workforce Management*, 2012; and http://cdn.theladders.net/static/recruitladder/pdf/WP%20Social%20Recruiting%20in%202012.pdf, accessed July 2, 2014.
84. Aliah Wright, "Your Social Media Is Showing," *HR Magazine*, March 2012, p. 16.
85. Jennifer Arnold, "Twittering at Face Booking While They Were," *HR Magazine*, December 2009, p. 54.
86. Ibid.
87. *Bloomberg BNA Bulletin to Management*, "Certain Social Media Tools Are Helping HR Connect Swiftly with the Right Job Candidates," July 24, 2012, p. 233.
88. Jennifer Taylor Arnold, "Recruiting on the Run," February 2010, *HR Magazine*, pp. 65–67.
89. https://premium.linkedin.com/premiumhiring/features, accessed April 6, 2015.
90. Jim Lundy, "Research Note," *Aragon Research* 3 (January 31, 2014).
91. Eric Krell, "Recruiting Outlook: Creative HR for 2003," *Workforce*, December 2002, pp. 40–44.
92. Breaugh, "Employee Recruitment," p. 111.
93. Ibid., p. 113.
94. Find your nearest one-stop center at www.servicelocator.org.
95. Lynn Doherty and E. Norman Sims, "Quick, Easy Recruitment Help: From a State?" *Workforce*, May 1998, p. 36.
96. Ibid.
97. Robert Grossman, "How to Recruit a Recruitment Outsourcer," *HR Magazine*, July 2012, pp. 51–54; and Susan Ladika, "A Lot to Process," *Workforce Management*, July 2012, pp. 16–18. See also Max Mihelich, "RPO Is On the Go," *Workforce*, February 2014, pp. 44–47.
98. "Recruitment Process Outsourcing Providers," *Workforce Management*, February 2013, p. 20.
99. One "Wharton MBA and GE alum" manages short-term projects for major companies and served as interim CEO for one firm. See Jodi Greenstone Miller and Matt Miller, "The Best Executive and Professional Jobs May No Longer Be Full-Time Gigs," *Harvard Business Review*, May 2012, p. 51.
100. "As Hiring Falters, More Workers Are Temporary," *New York Times*, December 20, 2010, pp. A1, A4.
101. John Zappe, "Temp-to-Hire Is Becoming a Full-Time Practice at Firms," *Workforce Management*, June 2005, pp. 82–86.
102. Shari Cauldron, "Contingent Workforce Spurs HR Planning," *Personnel Journal*, July 1994, p. 60.
103. Robert Bohner Jr. and Elizabeth Salasko, "Beware the Legal Risks of Hiring Temps," *Workforce*, October 2002, pp. 50–57. See also Fay Hansen, "A Permanent Strategy for Temporary Hires," *Workforce Management*, February 26, 2007, p. 27; and Robert Grossman, "Strategic Temp–Tations," *HR Magazine*, March 2012, pp. 24–34.
104. This is based on or quoted from Nancy Howe, "Match Temp Services to Your Needs," *Personnel Journal*, March 1989, pp. 45–51. See also Stephen Miller, "Collaboration Is Key to Effective Outsourcing," *HR Magazine* 58 (2008), pp. 60–61; and, as an example, www.bbb.org/shreveport/accredited-business-directory/employment-contractors-temporary-help/plain-dealing-la, accessed September 23, 2011.
105. Daniel Feldman, Helen Doerpinghaus, and William Turnley, "Managing Temporary Workers: A Permanent HRM Challenge," *Organizational Dynamics* 23, no. 2 (Fall 1994), p. 49. See also Kathryn Tyler, "Treat Contingent Workers with Care," *HR Magazine*, March 2008, p. 75; and www.employment.oregon.gov/EMPLOY/ES/BUS/index.shtml, accessed October 4, 2011.
106. Carolyn Hirschman, "Are Your Contractors Legal?" *HR*

Magazine, March 2004, pp. 59–63. See also Dori Meinert, "Modern-Day Slavery," *HR Magazine*, May 2012, pp. 22–24.
107. Hirschman, "Are Your Contractors Legal?"
108. Margaret Steen, "More Employers Take on Temps, but Planning Is Paramount," *Workforce Management*, May 2011, p. 14.
109. Heather Jackson and Cary Donham, "Five Things to Know About Working with Staffing Firms," *Workforce Management*, October 2013, p. 47.
110. This section is based on Robyn Meredith, "Giant Sucking Sound," *Forbes*, 172, no. 6, September 29, 2003, p. 158; Jim McKay, "Inevitable Outsourcing, Offshoring Stirred Passions at Pittsburgh Summit," *Knight Ridder/Tribune Business News*, March 11, 2004; Peter Panepento, "General Electric Transportation to Outsource Drafting Jobs to India," *Knight Ridder/Tribune Business News*, May 5, 2004; Julie Harbin, "Recent Survey Charts Execs' Willingness to Outsource Jobs," *San Diego Business Journal* 25, no. 14 (April 5, 2004), pp. 8–10; and Ben W. Heineman Jr, "Why We Can All Stop Worrying About Offshoring and Outsourcing," *The Atlantic*, March 26, 2013, www.theatlantic.com/business/archive/2013/03/whywe-can-all-stop-worrying-about-offshoring-and-outsourcing/274388/, accessed August 20, 2014.
111. Ed Frauenheim, "Homeward Bound," *Workforce Management*, February 2013, pp. 26–31.
112. Susan Wells, "Slow Times for Executive Recruiting," *HR Magazine*, April 2003, pp. 61–67.
113. Michelle Martinez, "Working with an Outside Recruiter? Get It in Writing," *HR Magazine*, January 2001, pp. 98–105.
114. See, for example, Stephenie Overman, "Searching for the Top," *HR Magazine*, January 2008, p. 49.
115. Bill Leonard, "Recruiting from the Competition," *HR Magazine*, February 2001, pp. 78–86. See also G. Anders, "Secrets of the Talent Scouts," *New York Times* (Late New York Edition) (March 15, 2009), pp. 1, 7 (Sec. 3).
116. Carol Hymowitz and Jeff Green, "These Days, Anybody Can Headhunt," *Bloomberg Business Week*, January 27, 2013, pp. 19–20; Joann Lublin, "More Executive Recruiting Ships in House," *Wall Street Journal*, October 10, 2012, p. B8.
117. Lauren Weber, "Here's What Boards Want in Executives," *Wall Street Journal*, December 10, 2014, p. B5.
118. Based on John Wareham, *Secrets of a Corporate Headhunter* (New York: Playboy Press, 1981), pp. 213–225; Chip McCreary, "Get the Most Out of Search Firms," *Workforce*, August 1997, pp. S28–S30.
119. www.kaiserpermanentejobs.org/employee-referral-program.aspx, accessed August 20, 2011.
120. Breaugh, "Employee Recruitment," p. 109.
121. "Tell a Friend: Employee Referral Programs Earn High Marks for Low Recruiting Costs," *BNA Bulletin to Management*, June 28, 2001, p. 201.
122. Martha Frase-Blunt, "A Recruiting Spigot," *HR Magazine*, April 2003, pp. 71–79.
123. Sara Rynes, Marc Orlitzky, and Robert Bretz Jr., "Experienced Hiring Versus College Recruiting: Practices and Emerging Trends," *Personnel Psychology* 50 (1997), pp. 309–339. See also Lisa Munniksma, "Career Matchmakers: Partnering with Collegiate Career Centers Offers Recruiters Access to Rich Source of Applicants," *HR Magazine* 50, no. 2 (February 2005), p. 93.
124. See, for example, Breaugh, "Employee Recruitment," p. 111; "Recruiters Look to Be Big Man on Campus," *Workforce Management*, September 2010, p. 12.
125. Ibid.
126. Joe Mullich, "Finding the Schools That Yield the Best Job Applicant ROI," *Workforce Management*, March 2004, pp. 67–68.
127. Greet Van Hoye and Filip Lievens, "Tapping the Grapevine: A Closer Look at Word-of-Mouth as a Recruitment Source," *Journal of Applied Psychology* 94, no. 2 (2009), pp. 341–352.
128. Munniksma, "Career Matchmakers."
129. Wendy Boswell et al., "Individual Job Choice Decisions and the Impact of Job Attributes and Recruitment Practices: A Longitudinal Field Study," *Human Resource Management* 42, no. 1 (Spring 2003), pp. 23–37. See also Breaugh, "Employee Recruitment," p. 115.
130. Hao Zhao Oh and Robert Liden, "Internship: A Recruitment and Selected Perspective," *Journal of Applied Psychology* 96, no. 1 (2011), pp. 221–229.
131. Teddy Wayne, "The No-Limits Job," *New York Times*, March 3, 2013, Sunday Styles p. 1. Over the past few years, unpaid interns have increasingly sued their employers, and won. See Max Mihelich, "Free Advice on Unpaid Internships," *Workforce*, August 2014, pp. 40–43.
132. Martha Frase-Blunt, "Call Centers Come Home," *HR Magazine*, January 2007, pp. 85–90.
133. Christopher Stone and Dianna Stone, "Factors Affecting Hiring Decisions About Veterans," *Human Resource Management Review* 25, no. 1 (2015), pp. 68–79.
134. Theresa Minton-Eversole, "Mission: Recruitment," *HR Magazine*, January 2009, pp. 43–45.
135. See, for example, Stephanie Castellano, "The Value of Veterans," *Training & Development*, February 2013, p. 16.
136. Wal-Mart to Hire Projected 100,000 Vets Over Five Years," *Bloomberg BNA Bulletin to Management*, January 22, 2013, p. 26, www.humanresourcemetrics.org/recruiting_cost_ratio.html.
137. Gino Ruiz, "Special Report: Talent Acquisition," *Workforce Management*, July 23, 2007, p. 39.
138. Thomas Stewart, "In Search of Elusive Tech Workers," *Fortune*, February 16, 1998, pp. 171–172; and www.outsourcing-center.com/2006-10-ge-looks-to-recruitment-process-outsourcer-to-find-meat-and-potatoes-candidates-as-well-as-the-purple-squirrel-article-37479.html, accessed October 5, 2011.
139. "Internship Programs Help These Recruiters Toward Qualified Students with Disabilities," *BNA Bulletin to Management*, July 17, 2003, p. 225.
140. www.recruitingtrends.com/recruiting-women/; http://online.wsj.com/article/SB10001424127887323764804578314450063914388.html; www.theresumator.com/blog/how-to-recruit-women-for-your-workforce/; http://blogs.kenan-flagler.unc.edu/2012/06/12/the-new-business-imperative-recruiting-and-retaining-women-in-the-workplace/. All accessed May 9, 2013.
141. Judith Casey and Marcie Pitt-Catsouphes, "Employed Single Mothers: Balancing Job and Home Life," *Employee Assistance Quarterly* 9, no. 324 (1994), pp. 37–53; www.catalyst.org/publication/252/working-parents, accessed October 3, 2011.
142. Casey and Pitt-Catsouphes, "Employed Single Mothers," p. 42.
143. "Barclaycard Helps Single Parents to Find Employment," *Personnel Today*, November 7, 2006.
144. Caroline Straub, "Antecedents and Organizational Consequences of Family Supportive Supervisor Behavior: A Multilevel Conceptual Framework for Research," *Human Resource Management Review* 22 (2012), pp. 15–26.
145. Susan Glairon, "Single Parents Need More Flexibility at Work, Advocate in Denver Says," *Daily Camera*, February 8, 2002; www.cnn.com/2008/LIVING/worklife/06/04/balance.calculator, accessed October 5, 2011.
146. Sandra Block and Stephanie Armour, "Many Americans Retire Years Before They Want To," *USA Today*, July 26, 2006, http://usatoday.com, accessed December 23, 2007.
147. Phaedra Brotherton, "Tapping into an Older Workforce," *Mosaics* (Society for Human Resource Management, March/April 2000). See also Thomas Ng and Daniel Feldman, "The Relationship of Age to Ten Dimensions of Job Performance," *Journal of Applied Psychology* 90, no. 2 (2008), pp. 392–423.
148. Sue Shellenbarger, "Gray Is Good: Employers Make Efforts to Retain Older, Experienced Workers," *Wall Street Journal*, December 1, 2005.
149. Alison Wellner, "Tapping a Silver Mine," *HR Magazine*, March 2002, p. 29.
150. Sue Shellenbarger, "Gray Is Good." See also Robert Grossman, "Keep Pace with Older Workers," *HR Magazine*, May 2008, pp. 39–46.
151. Gary Adams and Barbara Rau, "Attracting Retirees to Apply: Desired Organizational Characteristics of Bridge Employment," *Journal of Organizational Behavior* 26, no. 6 (September 2005), pp. 649–660.
152. Thomas NG and Daniel Feldman, "Evaluating Six Common Stereotypes About Older Workers with Meta-analytical Data," *Personnel Psychology* 60, no. 6 (2012), pp. 821–858.
153. Ibid.
154. Abby Ellin, "Supervising the Graybeards," *New York Times*, January 16, 2000, p. B16; Derek Avery and Patrick McKay, "Target Practice: An Organizational Impression Management Approach to Attracting Minority and Female Job Applicants," *Personnel Psychology* 59 (2006), pp. 157–189.
155. Herbert Greenberg, "A Hidden Source of Talent," *HR Magazine*, March 1997, pp. 88–91.
156. Linda Moore, "Firms Need to Improve Recruitment, Hiring of Disabled Workers, EEO Chief Says," *Knight Ridder/Tribune Business News*, November 5, 2003. See also "Recruiting Disabled More Than Good Deed, Experts Say," *BNA Bulletin to Management*, February 27, 2007, p. 71.
157. "Students with Disabilities Available," *HR Briefing*, June 15, 2002, p. 5.
158. Moore, "Firms Need to Improve Recruitment."
159. This paragraph is based on Jennifer L. Wood, James M. Schmidtke, and Diane L. Decker, "Lying on Job Applications: The Effects of Job Relevance, Commission, and Human Resource Management

Experience," *Journal of Business and Psychology* 22 (2007), pp. 1–9.

160. Kenneth Sovereign, *Personnel Law* (Upper Saddle River, NJ: Pearson, 1999), p. 51, 132.
161. Rachel Emma Silverman, "No More Resumes, Say Some Firms," *Wall Street Journal*, January 24, 2012, p. B6.
162. Alina Dizik, "Wooing Job Recruiters with Video Resumes," *Wall Street Journal*, May 20, 2010, p. D4. As of August 20, 2014, these companies included resumebook.tv and optimalresume.com.
163. Kathy Gurchiek, "Video Resumes Spark Curiosity, Questions," *HR Magazine*, May 2007, pp. 28–30; "Video Resumes Can Illuminate Applicants' Abilities, but Pose Discrimination Concerns," *BNA Bulletin to Management*, May 20, 2007, pp. 169–170.
164. Murray Barrick and Ryan Zimmerman, "Hiring for Retention and Performance," *Human Resource Management* 48, no. 2 (March/April 2009), pp 183–206.
165. James Breaugh, "The Use of Biodata for Employee Selection: Test Research and Future Directions," *Human Resource Management Review* 19 (2009), pp. 219–231. Utilizing biodata items presumes that the employer can show that the items predict performance. Biodata items such as "graduated from college" may have an adverse impact on minorities, but studies suggest that employers can avoid that problem through judicious choice of biodata items (p. 229).
166. Fred Mael, Mary Connerley, and Ray Morath, "None of Your Business: Parameters of Biodata Invasiveness," *Personnel Psychology* 49 (1996), pp. 613–650; and Kenneth Law et al., "Impression Management and Faking in Biodata Scores Among Chinese Job-Seekers," *Asia Pacific Journal of Management* 19, no. 4 (December 2002), pp. 541–556.
167. "Supreme Court Denies Circuit City's Bid for Review of Mandatory Arbitration," *BNA Bulletin to Management*, June 6, 2002, p. 177.
168. "Supreme Court Gives the Employers Green Light to Hold Most Employees to Arbitration Pacts," *BNA Bulletin to Management*, March 29, 2001, pp. 97–98.
169. Douglas Mahony et al., "The Effects of Mandatory Employment Arbitration Systems on Applicants Attraction to Organizations," *Human Resource Management* 44, no. 4 (Winter 2005), pp. 449–470; See also H. John Bernardin et al., "Mandatory and Binding Arbitration: Effects on Employee Attitudes and Recruiting Results," *Human Resource Management* 50, no. 2 (March–April 2011), pp. 175–200.

6

Employee Testing and Selection

Lisa Werner/Alamy

LEARNING OBJECTIVES

6-1 Answer the question: Why is it important to test and select employees?

6-2 Explain what is meant by reliability and validity.

6-3 List and briefly describe the basic categories of selection tests, with examples.

6-4 Explain how to use two work simulations for selection.

6-5 Describe four ways to improve an employer's background checking process.

Google job candidates used to have a dozen or more grueling interviews. But, with Google hiring thousands of people annually, this selection process proved too slow.[1] Now Google uses just four to five interviews, but lets all its employees express opinions on each candidate by e-mail, using what it calls "crowdsourcing." The changes speed up hiring and bring Google's hiring policies more in line with its fast-growth strategy.[2]

WHERE ARE WE NOW ...

Chapter 5 focused on how to build an applicant pool. The purpose of Chapter 6 is to explain how to use various tools to select the best candidate for the job. The main topics we'll cover include the selection process, basic testing techniques, types of tests, work samples and simulations, and making background and reference checks. In Chapter 7, we will turn to the techniques you can use to improve your skills at what is probably the most widely used screening tool, the selection interview.

LEARNING OBJECTIVE 6-1

Answer the question: Why is it important to test and select employees?

Why Employee Selection is Important

After reviewing the applicants' résumés, the manager turns to selecting the best candidate for the job. This usually means reducing the applicant pool by using the screening tools we discuss in this and the following chapter: tests, assessment centers, interviews, and background and reference checks. The aim of employee selection is to achieve *person-job fit*. This means matching the knowledge, skills, abilities, and other competencies (KSACs) that are required for performing the job (based on job analysis) with the applicant's KSACs.

Of course, a candidate might be "right" for a job, but wrong for the organization.[3] For example, an experienced airline pilot might excel at American Airlines but perhaps not at Southwest, where the organizational values require that all employees help out, even with baggage handling. Therefore, while person-job fit is usually the main consideration, *person-organization fit* is important too.

In any case, selecting the right employee is important for three main reasons. First, employees with the right skills will perform better for you and the company. Employees without these skills or who are abrasive or obstructionist won't perform effectively, and your own performance and the firm's will suffer. The time to screen out undesirables is before they are in the door.

Second, effective selection is important because it is costly to recruit and hire employees. One survey found that the average cost of hiring an employee who doesn't work out is about $50,000.[4]

Third, it's important because inept hiring has legal consequences. For one thing, we saw in Chapter 2 that equal employment laws require nondiscriminatory selection procedures.[5] **Negligent hiring** is another such problem. It means hiring employees with criminal records or other problems who then use access to customers' homes (or similar opportunities) to commit crimes.[6] In one case, *Ponticas v. K.M.S. Investments*, an apartment manager entered a woman's apartment and assaulted her.[7] The court found the apartment complex's owner negligent for not checking the manager's background properly.[8]

negligent hiring
Hiring workers with questionable backgrounds without proper safeguards.

The Basics of Testing and Selecting Employees

In this chapter, we'll discuss several popular selection tools, starting with tests. A *test* is basically a sample of a person's behavior. Any test or screening tool has two important characteristics, *reliability* and *validity*. We'll start with the former.

LEARNING OBJECTIVE 6-2

Explain what is meant by reliability and validity.

Reliability

Reliability is a selection tool's first requirement and refers to its consistency: "A reliable test is one that yields consistent scores when a person takes two alternate forms of the test or when he or she takes the same test on two or more different occasions."[9] If a person scores 90 on an intelligence test on a Monday and 130 when retested on Tuesday, you probably wouldn't have much faith in the test.

reliability
The consistency of scores obtained by the same person when retested with the identical tests or with alternate forms of the same test.

You can measure reliability in several ways. One is to administer a test to a group one day, re-administer the same test several days later to the same group, and then correlate the first set of scores with the second (called *test-retest reliability estimates*).[10] Or you could administer a test and then administer what experts believe to be an equivalent test later; this would be an *equivalent or alternate form estimate*. (The Scholastic Assessment Test [SAT] is one example.) Or, compare the test taker's answers to certain questions on the test with his or her answers to a separate set of questions on the same test aimed at measuring the same thing. This is an *internal comparison estimate*. For example, a psychologist includes 10 items on a test believing that they all measure interest in working outdoors, and then determines the degree to which responses to these 10 items vary together.

Many things cause a test to be unreliable. These include physical conditions (quiet one day, noisy the next), differences in the test taker (healthy one day,

FIGURE 6-1 Test Score Correlation Examples

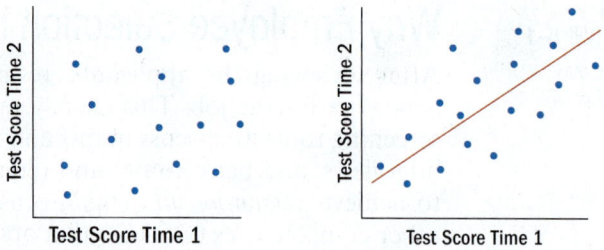

sick the next), and differences in test administration (courteous one day, curt the next). Or the questions may do a poor job of sampling the material; for example, test one focuses more on Chapters 1 and 3, while test two focuses more on Chapters 2 and 4.

Because measuring reliability generally involves comparing two measures that assess the same thing, it is typical to judge a test's reliability in terms of a *reliability coefficient*. This basically shows the degree to which the two measures (say, test score one day and test score the next day) are correlated.

Figure 6-1 illustrates correlation. In both the left and the right scatter plots, the psychologist compared each applicant's time 1 test score (on the *x*-axis) with his or her subsequent (time 2) test score (on the *y*-axis). On the left, the scatter plot points (each point showing one applicant's test score and subsequent test performance) are dispersed. There seems to be no correlation between test scores obtained at time 1 and at time 2. On the right, the psychologist tried a new test. Here the resulting points fall in a predictable pattern. This suggests that the applicants' test scores correlate closely with their previous scores.

Validity

test validity
The accuracy with which a test, interview, and so on, measures what it purports to measure or fulfills the function it was designed to fill.

Reliability, while indispensable, tells you only that the test is measuring something consistently. *Validity* tells you whether the test is measuring what you think it's supposed to be measuring.[11] **Test validity** answers the question "Does this test measure what it's supposed to measure?" Put another way, it refers to the correctness of the inferences that we can make based on the test.[12] For example, if Jane's scores on mechanical comprehension tests are higher than Jim's, can we be sure that Jane possesses more mechanical comprehension than Jim?[13] With employee selection tests, *validity* often refers to evidence that the test is job related—in other words, that performance on the test accurately predicts job performance. A selection test must be valid since, without proof of validity, there is no logical or (under EEO law) legally permissible reason to use it to screen job applicants.

A test, as we said, is a sample of a person's behavior, but some tests are more clearly representative of the behavior being sampled than others. A swimming test clearly corresponds to a lifeguard's on-the-job behavior. On the other hand, there may be no apparent relationship between the test and the behavior. Thus, in Figure 6-2, the psychologist asks the person to interpret the picture, and then draws conclusions about the person's personality and behavior. Here it is more difficult to prove that the tests are measuring what they are said to measure, in this case, some trait of the person's personality—in other words, prove that they're valid.

criterion validity
A type of validity based on showing that scores on the test (predictors) are related to job performance (criterion).

There are several ways to demonstrate a test's validity.[14] **Criterion validity** involves demonstrating statistically a relationship between scores on a selection procedure and job performance of a sample of workers. For example, it means demonstrating that those who do well on the test also do well on the job, and that those who do poorly on the test do poorly on the job. The test has validity to the extent that the people with higher test scores perform better on the job. In psychological measurement, a *predictor* is the measurement (in this case, the test score) that you are trying to relate to a *criterion*, such as performance on the job. The term *criterion validity* reflects that terminology.

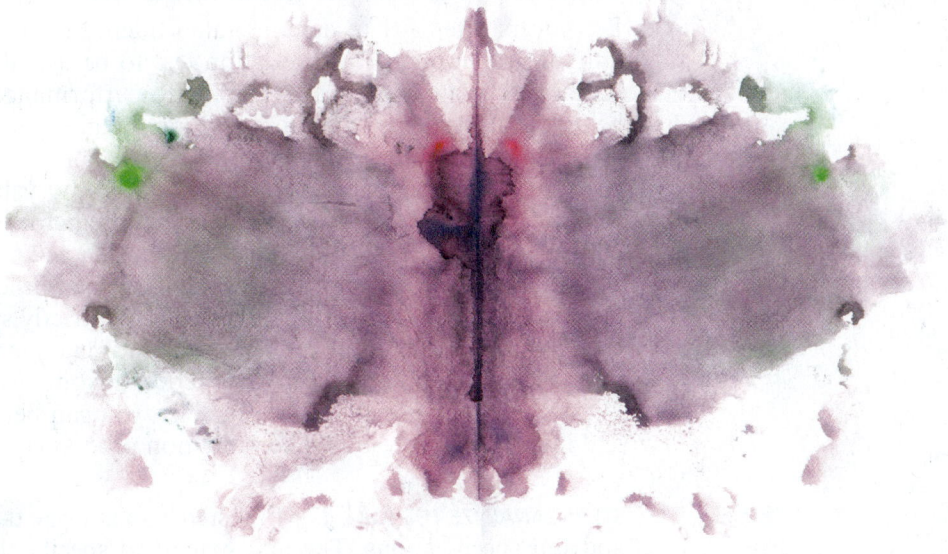

FIGURE 6-2 A Slide from the Rorschach Test
Source: Fotolia LLC.

content validity
A test that is content valid is one that contains a fair sample of the tasks and skills actually needed for the job in question.

Content validity is a demonstration that the content of a selection procedure is representative of important aspects of performance on the job. For example, employers may demonstrate the *content validity* of a test by showing that the test constitutes a fair sample of the job's content. The basic procedure here is to identify job tasks that are critical to performance, and then randomly select a sample of those tasks to test. In selecting students for dental school, one might give applicants chunks of chalk, and ask them to carve something like a tooth. If the content you choose for the test is a representative sample of the job, then the test is probably content valid. Clumsy dental students need not apply. Subject matter experts (SMEs, such as practicing dentists) help choose the tasks.

construct validity
A test that is construct valid is one that demonstrates that a selection procedure measures a construct and that construct is important for successful job performance.

Construct validity means demonstrating that (1) a selection procedure measures a construct (an abstract idea such as morale or honesty) and (2) that the construct is important for successful job performance.

At best, invalid tests are a waste of time; at worst, they are discriminatory. Tests you buy "off the shelf" should include information on their validity.[15] But ideally, you should revalidate the tests for the job(s) at hand. In any case, tests rarely predict performance with 100% accuracy (or anywhere near it). Therefore, don't make tests your only selection tool; also use other tools like interviews and background checks.

TRENDS SHAPING HR: *Digital and Social Media*

Talent analytics is revolutionizing employee selection.[16] Its numbers-crunching data analysis tools including statistical techniques, algorithms, data mining, and problem-solving let employers search through their employee data to identify patterns and correlations that show what types of people succeed or fail. For example, department store chain Bon-Ton Stores Inc. had very high turnover among its cosmetics sales associates.

Bon-Ton chose 450 current cosmetics associates who filled out anonymous surveys aimed at identifying employee traits. By using talent analytics to analyze these and other data, the company identified cosmetics associates' traits that correlated with performance and tenure. Bon-Ton had assumed that the best associates were friendly and enthusiastic about cosmetics. However, the best were actually problem solvers. They take information about what the customer wants and needs, and solve the problem.[17] Talent analysis thereby helped Bon Ton formulate better selection criteria. ■

Evidence-Based HR: How to Validate a Test

Employers often opt to demonstrate evidence of a test's validity using criterion validity. Here, in order for a selection test to be useful, you need evidence that scores on the test relate in a predictable way to performance on the job. Thus, other things being equal, students who score high on the graduate admissions tests also do better in graduate school. Applicants who score high on mechanical comprehension tests perform better as engineers. In other words, you validate the test before using it by ensuring that scores on the test are a good predictor of some *criterion* like job performance—thus demonstrating the test's *criterion validity*.[18]

An industrial psychologist usually conducts the validation study. The human resource department coordinates the effort. Strictly speaking, the supervisor's role is just to make sure that the job's human requirements and performance standards are clear to the psychologist. But in practice, anyone using tests (or test results) should know something about validation. Then you can better understand how to use tests and interpret their results. The validation process consists of five steps:

STEP 1: ANALYZE THE JOB The first step is to analyze the job and write job descriptions and job specifications. The aim here is to specify the human traits and skills you believe are required for job performance. For example, must an applicant be verbal, a good talker? These requirements become the *predictors,* the human traits and skills you believe predict success on the job. For an assembler's job, *predictors* might include manual dexterity and patience.[19]

In this first step, also define "success on the job," since it's this success for which you want predictors. The standards of success are *criteria*. You could use production-related criteria (quantity, quality, and so on), personnel data (absenteeism, length of service, and so on), or worker performance (reported by supervisors).

STEP 2: CHOOSE THE TESTS Once you know the predictors (such as manual dexterity) the next step is to decide how to test for them. Employers usually base this choice on experience, previous research, and "best guesses." They usually don't start with just one test. Instead, they choose several tests and combine them into a test battery. The test battery aims to measure an array of possible predictors, such as aggressiveness, extroversion, and numerical ability.

What tests are available and where do you get them? Ideally, use a professional, such as an industrial psychologist. However, many firms publish tests.[20] Some tests are available to virtually any purchaser, others only to qualified buyers (such as with degrees in psychology). Wonderlic, Inc., publishes a well-known intellectual capacity test and other tests, including aptitude test batteries and interest inventories. G. Neil Company of Sunrise, Florida, offers employment testing materials including, for example, a clerical skills test, telemarketing ability test, service ability test, management ability test, team skills test, and sales abilities test. Figure 6-3 lists several Web sites that provide information about tests or testing programs.

FIGURE 6-3 Examples of Web Sites Offering Information on Tests or Testing Programs

- www.hr-guide.com/data/G371.htm
  Provides general information and sources for all types of employment tests.
- http://ericae.net
  Provides technical information on all types of employment and nonemployment tests.
- www.ets.org/testcoll
  Provides information on more than 20,000 tests.
- www.kaplan.com
  Information from Kaplan test preparation on how various admissions tests work.
- www.assessments.biz
  One of many firms offering employment tests.

However, do not let the widespread availability of tests blind you to this fact: You should use tests in a manner consistent with equal employment laws, and in a manner that is ethical and protects the test taker's privacy.

STEP 3: ADMINISTER THE TEST Next, administer the selected test(s). One option is to administer the tests to employees currently on the job. You then compare their test scores with their current performance; this is *concurrent (at the same time) validation.* Its advantage is that data on performance are readily available. The disadvantage is that current employees may not be representative of new applicants (who, of course, are really the ones for whom you are interested in developing a screening test). Current employees have already had on-the-job training and screening by your existing selection techniques.

Predictive validation is the second and more dependable way to validate a test. Here you administer the test to applicants before you hire them, then hire these applicants using only existing selection techniques, not the results of the new tests. After they've been on the job for some time, measure their performance and compare it to their earlier test scores. You can then determine whether you could have used their performance on the new test to predict their subsequent job performance.

STEP 4: RELATE YOUR TEST SCORES AND CRITERIA Here, ascertain if there is a significant relationship between test scores (the predictor) and performance (the criterion). The usual method is to determine the statistical relationship between (1) scores on the test and (2) job performance using correlation analysis, which shows the degree of statistical relationship.

expectancy chart
A graph showing the relationship between test scores and job performance for a group of people.

If there is a correlation between test and job performance, you can develop an **expectancy chart**. This presents the relationship between test scores and job performance graphically. To do this, split the employees into, say, five groups according to test scores, with those scoring the highest fifth on the test, the second highest fifth, and so on. Then compute the percentage of high job performers in each of these five test score groups and present the data in an expectancy chart like that in Figure 6-4.

In this case, someone scoring in the top fifth of the test has a 97% chance of being a high performer, while one scoring in the lowest fifth has only a 29% chance of being a high performer.[21]

STEP 5: CROSS-VALIDATE AND REVALIDATE Before using the test, you may want to check it by "cross-validating"—in other words, by again performing steps 3 and 4 on a new sample of employees. At a minimum, revalidate the test periodically.

Some tests (such as the 16PF® Personality Profile) are professionally scored and interpreted. Thus Wonderlic, Inc., lets an employer administer the 16PF. The employer then faxes (or scans) the answer sheet to Wonderlic, which scores the candidate's profile

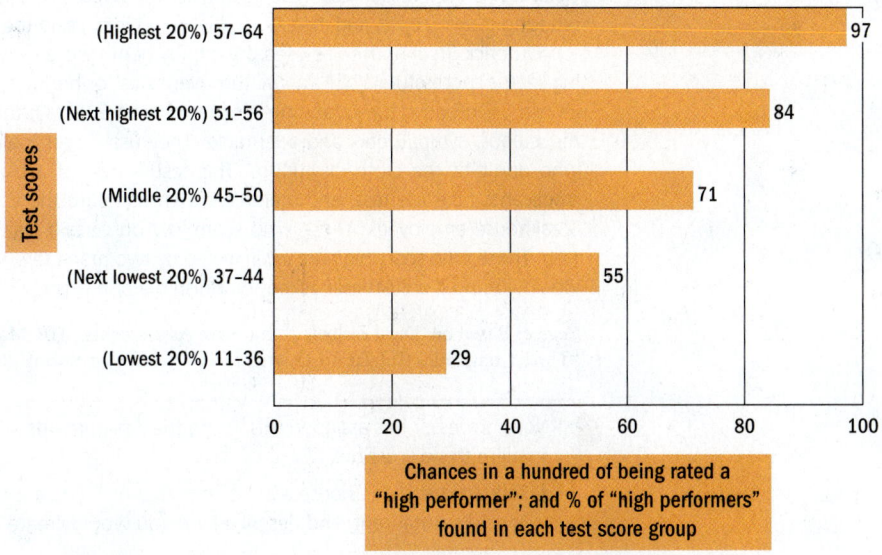

FIGURE 6-4 Expectancy Chart

Note: This expectancy chart shows the relation between scores made on the Minnesota Paper Form Board and rated success of junior draftspersons.

Example: Those who score between 37 and 44 have a 55% chance of being rated high performer and those scoring between 57 and 64 have a 97% chance.

and faxes (or scans) back the interpretive report. Psychologists easily score many psychological tests online or using interpretive Windows-based software. However, managers can easily score many tests, like the Wonderlic Personnel Test, themselves.

Bias

Most employers know they shouldn't use biased tests in the selection process.[22] For example, a particular IQ test may provide a valid measure of cognitive ability for middle-class whites but not for some minorities, if the score depends on familiarity with certain aspects of middle-class culture.[23] Until recently, many industrial psychologists believed they were adequately controlling test bias, but that issue is under review.[24] Employers should therefore redouble their efforts to ensure that the tests they're using aren't producing biased decisions.

Utility Analysis

Knowing that a test predicts performance isn't always of practical use. For example, if it is going to cost the employer $1,000 per applicant for the test, and hundreds of applicants must be tested, the cost of the test may exceed the benefits derived from hiring a few more capable employees.

Answering the question, "Does it pay to use the test?" requires *utility analysis*. Two selection experts say, "Using dollar and cents terms, [utility analysis] shows the degree to which use of a selection measure improves the quality of individuals selected over what would have happened if the measure had not been used."[25] The information required for utility analysis generally includes, for instance, the validity of the selection measure, a measure of job performance in dollars, applicants' average test scores, cost of testing an applicant, and the number of applicants tested and selected.

Prudent employers endeavor to streamline their selection processes, for instance to minimize how long it takes to fill a position. For example, with almost 60,000 job applicants per day, the U.S. federal government was taking about 122 days to fill a position. By reviewing each step in its hiring process, it reduced time to hire to about 105 days by, for instance, eliminating the applicant essay.[26] The accompanying HR as a Profit Center feature shows how employers use tests to improve performance.

IMPROVING PERFORMANCE: *HR as a Profit Center*

Using Tests to Cut Costs and Boost Profits

Financial services firm Key Bank knew it needed a better way to screen and select tellers and call-center employees.[27] The company calculated it cost about $10,000 to select and train an employee, but it was losing 13% of new tellers and call-center employees within the first 90 days. That turnover number dropped to 4% after Key Bank implemented a computerized *virtual job tryout candidate assessment screening tool*. "We calculated a $1.7 million cost savings in teller turnover in one year, simply by making better hiring decisions, reducing training costs and increasing quality of hires," said the firm's human resources director.

Outback Steakhouse has used preemployment tests almost from when the company started. The testing seems successful. While annual turnover rates for hourly employees may reach 200% in the restaurant industry, Outback's turnover ranges from 40% to 60%. Outback wants employees who are highly social, meticulous, sympathetic, and adaptable. They use a personality assessment test to screen out applicants who don't fit the Outback culture. This test is part of a three-step preemployment screening process. Applicants take the test, and managers then compare the candidates' results to the profile for Outback Steakhouse employees. Those who score low on certain traits (like compassion) don't move to the next step. Those who score high are interviewed by two managers, who ask behavioral questions such as "What would you do if a customer asked for a dish we don't have?"[28] ■

Source: Based on Dave Zielinski, "Effective Assessments," HR Magazine, January 2011, pp. 61–64.; Sarah Gale, "Three Companies Cut Turnover with Tests," Workforce, Spring 2002, pp. 66–69.

If your professor has assigned this, go to the Assignments section of **mymanagementlab.com** to complete this discussion.

Talk About It 1: Choose a position with which you are familiar, such as a counterperson at a McDonald's restaurant, and describe how you would create a selection process for it similar to those in this feature.

Watch It!
How does a company actually do testing? If your professor has assigned this, go to the Assignments section of mymanagementlab.com to complete the video exercise titled *Patagonia Employee Testing and Selection*.

Validity Generalization

Many employers, particularly smaller ones, won't find it cost-effective to conduct validity studies for the selection tools they use. These employers must find tests and other screening tools that have been shown to be valid in other settings (companies), and then bring them in-house in the hopes that they'll be valid there, too.[29]

If the test is valid in one company, to what extent can we generalize those validity findings to our own company? *Validity generalization* "refers to the degree to which evidence of a measure's validity obtained in one situation can be generalized to another situation without further study."[30] Factors to consider include existing validation evidence regarding using the test for various specific purposes, the similarity of the subjects with those in your organization, and the similarity of the jobs.[31]

Under the Uniform Guidelines, validation of selection procedures is desirable, but "the Uniform Guidelines require users to produce evidence of validity only when adverse impact is shown to exist. If there is no adverse impact, there is no validation requirement under the Guidelines."[32]

KNOW YOUR EMPLOYMENT LAW

Testing and Equal Employment Opportunity

Suppose a plaintiff shows that one of your selection procedures has an adverse impact on his or her protected class. If so you may have to demonstrate the validity and selection fairness of the allegedly discriminatory test or item. With respect to testing, the EEO laws boil down to two things: (1) You must be able to prove that your tests are related to success or failure on the job, and (2) you must prove that your tests don't unfairly discriminate against either minority or nonminority subgroups. (Also note that the same burden of proving job relatedness falls on interviews and other techniques, including performance appraisals, that falls on tests). ■

Fotosearch/AGE Fotostock

Many employers administer online employment tests to job candidates.

Test Takers' Individual Rights and Test Security

Test takers have rights to privacy and feedback under the American Psychological Association's (APA) standard for educational and psychological tests; these guide psychologists but are *not* legally enforceable. Test takers have rights such as:

- To the confidentiality of test results.
- To informed consent regarding use of these results.
- To expect that only people qualified to interpret the scores will have access to them, or that sufficient information will accompany the scores to ensure their appropriate interpretation.
- To expect the test is fair. For example, no test taker should have prior access to the questions or answers.[33]

The Federal Privacy Act gives federal employees the right to inspect their personnel files, and limits the disclosure of personnel information without the employee's consent, (the recent hacking of federal employees' files notwithstanding) among other things.[34]

Common law provides employees some protection against disclosing information about them to people outside the company. The main application here involves defamation (either libel or slander), but there are privacy issues, too.[35] The bottom line is this:

1. Make sure you understand the need to keep employees' information confidential.
2. Adopt a "need to know" policy. For example, if an employee has been rehabilitated after a period of drug use, the new supervisor may not "need to know."

Diversity Counts: Gender Issues in Testing

Employers using selection tests should know that gender issues may distort results. Some parents and others socialize girls into traditionally female roles and boys into traditionally male roles. For example, they may encourage young boys but not girls to make things with tools, or young girls but not boys to take care of their siblings. Such encouragement may in turn translate into differences in how males and females answer items on and score on, say, tests of vocational interests. And these test score differences may in turn cause counselors and others to nudge men and women into what tend to be largely gender-segregated occupations, for instance, male engineers and female nurses.

The bottom line is that employers and others need to interpret the results of various tests (including of interests and aptitudes) with care. It may often be the case that such results say more about how the person was brought up and socialized than it does about the person's inherent ability to do some task. ■

How Do Employers Use Tests at Work?

About 41% of companies in one survey tested applicants for basic skills (defined as the ability to read instructions, write reports, and do arithmetic).[36] About 67% of the respondents required employees to take job skills tests, and 29% required some form of psychological measurement.[37] To see what such tests are like, try the short test in Figure 6-5.

Tests are not just for lower-level workers. In general, as work demands increase (in terms of skill requirements, training, and pay), employers tend to rely more on

FIGURE 6-5 Sample Test

Source: Based on a sample selection test from the *New York Times.*

CHECK YES OR NO	YES	NO
1. You like a lot of excitement in your life.		
2. An employee who takes it easy at work is cheating on the employer.		
3. You are a cautious person.		
4. In the past three years you have found yourself in a shouting match at school or work.		
5. You like to drive fast just for fun.		

Analysis: According to John Kamp, an industrial psychologist, applicants who answered no, yes, yes, no, no to questions 1, 2, 3, 4, and 5 are statistically likely to be absent less often, to have fewer on-the-job injuries, and, if the job involves driving, to have fewer on-the-job driving accidents. Actual scores on the test are based on answers to 130 questions.

selection testing.[38] And, employers don't use tests just to find good employees, but also to screen out bad ones.[39] For good reason: In retail, employers apprehended about one out of every 28 workers for stealing.[40]

HR in Practice at the Hotel Paris As she considered what to do next to improve the employees' performance in a way that would support the Hotel Paris's strategy, Lisa Cruz, the Hotel Paris's HR director, knew that employee selection had to play a role. The Hotel Paris currently had an informal screening process in which local hotel managers obtained application forms, interviewed applicants, and checked their references. To see how she improved their system, see the case on page 195.

LEARNING OBJECTIVE 6-3
List and briefly describe the basic categories of selection tests, with examples.

Types of Tests

We can conveniently classify tests according to whether they measure cognitive (mental) abilities, motor and physical abilities, personality and interests, or achievement.[41] We'll look at each.

Tests of Cognitive Abilities

Cognitive tests include tests of general reasoning ability (intelligence) and tests of specific mental abilities like memory and inductive reasoning.

INTELLIGENCE TESTS Intelligence (IQ) tests are tests of general intellectual abilities. They measure not a single trait but rather a range of abilities, including memory, vocabulary, verbal fluency, and numerical ability. An adult's IQ score is a "derived" scored; it reflects the extent to which the person is above or below the "average" adult's intelligence score.

Intelligence is often measured with individually administered tests like the Stanford-Binet Test or the Wechsler Test. Employers can administer other IQ tests such as the Wonderlic individually or to groups of people.[42] In one illustrative study of firefighter trainees' performance over 23 years, the researchers found that a measure of general intellectual ability and a physical ability assessment were highly predictive of trainee performance.[43]

SPECIFIC COGNITIVE ABILITIES There are also measures of specific mental abilities, such as deductive reasoning, verbal comprehension, memory, and numerical ability.

Psychologists often call such tests *aptitude tests*, since they purport to measure aptitude for the job in question. Consider the Test of Mechanical Comprehension illustrated in Figure 6-6, which tests applicants' understanding of basic mechanical principles. This may reflect a person's aptitude for jobs—like that of machinist or engineer—that require mechanical comprehension. Other tests of mechanical aptitude include the Mechanical Reasoning Test and the SRA Test of Mechanical Aptitude. The revised Minnesota Paper Form Board Test consists of 64 two-dimensional diagrams cut into separate pieces. It provides insights into an applicant's mechanical spatial ability; you'd use it for screening applicants for jobs such as designers or engineers.

Tests of Motor and Physical Abilities

You might also want to measure motor abilities, such as finger dexterity, manual dexterity, and (if hiring pilots) reaction time. Thus, the Crawford Small Parts Dexterity

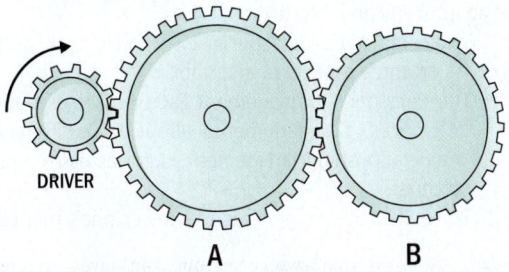

Which gear will turn the same way as the driver?

FIGURE 6-6 Type of Question Applicant Might Expect on a Test of Mechanical Comprehension

Test measures the speed and accuracy of simple judgment as well as the speed of finger, hand, and arm movements. Other tests include the Stromberg Dexterity Test and the Purdue Peg Board.

Tests of physical abilities may also be required. These include static strength (such as lifting weights), dynamic strength (pull-ups), body coordination (jumping rope), and stamina.[44] Applicants for the U.S. Marines must pass its Initial Strength Test (2 pull-ups, 35 sit-ups, and a 1.5-mile run).

Measuring Personality and Interests

A person's cognitive and physical abilities alone seldom explain his or her job performance. As one consultant put it, most people are hired based on qualifications, but are fired because of attitude, motivation, and temperament.[45]

Personality tests measure basic aspects of an applicant's personality, such as introversion, stability, and motivation. Industrial psychologists often focus on the "big five" personality dimensions: extraversion, emotional stability/neuroticism, agreeableness, conscientiousness, and openness to experience.[46]

> Neuroticism represents a tendency to exhibit poor emotional adjustment and experience negative effects, such as anxiety, insecurity, and hostility. Extraversion represents a tendency to be sociable, assertive, active, and to experience positive effects, such as energy and zeal. Openness to experience is the disposition to be imaginative, nonconforming, unconventional, and autonomous. Agreeableness is the tendency to be trusting, compliant, caring, and gentle. Conscientiousness is comprised of two related facets: achievement and dependability.[47]

Some personality tests are *projective*. The psychologist presents an ambiguous stimulus (like an inkblot or clouded picture) and the person reacts. The person supposedly projects into the ambiguous picture his or her attitudes, such as insecurity. Other projective techniques include Make a Picture Story (MAPS) and the Forer Structured Sentence Completion Test.

Other personality tests are *self-reported*: applicants fill them out. Thus, available online,[48] the Myers-Briggs test provides a personality type classification useful for decisions such as career selection and planning. Its DiSC Profile learning instrument enables the user to gain insight into his or her behavioral style.[49]

Personality test results do often correlate with job performance. For example "in personality research, conscientiousness has been the most consistent and universal predictor of job performance."[50] In another study, neuroticism was negatively related to motivation.[51] Extroversion correlates with success in sales and management jobs.[52] The responsibility, socialization, and self-control scales of the California Psychological Inventory predicted dysfunctional job behaviors among law enforcement officers.[53] Emotional stability, extroversion, and agreeableness predicted whether expatriates would leave their overseas assignments early.[54] The HR Practices feature presents an example.

IMPROVING PERFORMANCE: *HR Practices Around the Globe*

Testing for Assignments Abroad

Living and working abroad require some special talents. Not everyone can easily adapt to having one's family far away, and to dealing with colleagues with different cultural values. Doing so requires high levels of adaptability and interpersonal skills.[55]

Employers often use special inventories such as the Global Competencies Inventory (GCI) here. It focuses on three aspects of adaptability.

- ✓ The Perception Management Factor assesses people's tendency to be rigid in their view of cultural differences, to be judgmental about those differences, and to deal with complexity and uncertainty.
- ✓ The Relationship Management Factor assesses a person's awareness of the impact he or she is having on others.
- ✓ The Self-Management Factor assesses one's mental and emotional health. ■

Source: Adapted from www.kozaigroup.com/-inventories.php, accessed March 3, 2008; and http:// ko-zaigroup .com/inventories/the-global competencies-inventory-gci/what is-the-gci/.

If your professor has assigned this, go to the Assignments section of **mymanagementlab.com** to complete this discussion.

Talk About It 2: You are trying to decide if you would be a good candidate for a job abroad, but you don't want to take any formal tests. Discuss another indicator you would use to answer the question, "Would I be a good candidate for a job abroad?"

There are four caveats. *First,* projective personality tests are particularly hard to interpret. An expert must analyze the test taker's interpretations and infer from them his or her personality.

Second, personality tests can trigger legal challenges. For example, one court held that the Minnesota Multiphasic Personality Inventory (MMPI) is a medical test (because it can screen out applicants with psychological impairments), and so might violate the ADA.[56]

Third, a panel of distinguished industrial psychologists said using *self-report* personality tests in selection "should be reconsidered [due to low validity]."[57] Other experts call such concerns "unfounded."[58]

Fourth, people can and will fake responses to personality and integrity tests.[59] The bottom line: make sure the personality tests you use predict performance for the jobs you are testing for.

interest inventory
A personal development and selection device that compares the person's current interests with those of others now in various occupations so as to determine the preferred occupation for the individual.

INTEREST INVENTORIES **Interest inventories** compare one's interests with those of people in various occupations. Thus, the Strong-Campbell Interest Inventory provides a report comparing one's interests to those of people already in occupations like accounting or engineering. Someone taking the Self-Directed Search (SDS) (www.self-directed-search.com) uses it to identify likely high-fit occupations. The assumption is that someone will do better in occupations in which he or she is interested, and indeed such inventories can predict employee performance and turnover.[60] One study found that poor vocational fit correlated with counterproductive work behaviors, perhaps because poor fit frustrates the worker.[61]

Achievement Tests

Achievement tests measure what someone has learned. Most of the tests you take in school are achievement tests. They measure your "job knowledge" in areas like economics, marketing, or human resources. Achievement tests are also popular at work. For example, the Purdue Test for Machinists and Machine Operators tests the job knowledge of experienced machinists with questions like "What is meant by 'tolerance'"? Some achievement tests measure the applicant's abilities; a swimming test is one example.

Improving Performance Through HRIS: Computerization and Online Testing

Computerized and/or online testing is increasingly replacing paper-and-pencil tests. For example, Timken Company uses online assessment of math skills for hourly position applicants.[62] Many employers have applicants take short Web-based tests before reviewing their résumés and holding interviews. This leaves a smaller pool to undergo the more personal and costly testing and interviewing.[63] The applicant tracking systems we discussed in Chapter 5 often include online prescreening tests.[64] Vendors (as in www.iphonetypingtest.com) are making tests available for applicants to take via their smart phones.[65] Employers using automated screening systems should remember that applicants are human beings. Ensure the rejection standards are valid, and inform applicants quickly regarding their status.[66]

Computerized and online tests are increasingly sophisticated. For example, SHL (www.shl.com/us/) offers online adaptive personality tests. As a candidate answers each question, these tests adapt the next question to the test taker's answers to the previous question. This improves test validity and may reduce cheating (since each candidate basically gets a customized test).[67] Service firms like Unicru process and score online preemployment tests from employers' applicants. Most of the tests we describe are available in computerized form. ■

COMPUTERIZED MULTIMEDIA CANDIDATE ASSESSMENT TOOLS Development Dimensions International developed a computerized multimedia skill test that Ford Motor Company uses for hiring assembly workers. "The company can test everything from how people tighten the bolt, to whether they followed a certain procedure correctly, to using a weight-sensitive mat on the floor that, when stepped on at the wrong time, will mark a candidate down in a safety category."[68]

IMPROVING PERFORMANCE: *The Strategic Context*

Crowdsourcing at Google

Google knows that to maintain its fast-growth strategy, it must keep innovating new services. To support that strategy, Google needs its employees engaged and collaborating with each other. Having employees thinking of themselves in isolated "silos" would inhibit the cross-pollination that Google's strategy depends on. In formulating its employee selection practices, Google therefore found a way to foster the employee engagement and collaboration its success depends on. Google uses "crowdsourcing" when it comes to making hiring decisions.[69]

Here's how it works.[70] When a prospective employee applies for a job, his or her information (such as school and previous employers) goes into Google's applicant tracking system (ATS). The ATS then matches the applicant's information with that of current Google employees. When it finds a match, it asks those Google employees to comment on the applicant's suitability for the position. This helps give Google recruiters a valuable insight into how the Google employees actually doing the work think the applicant will do at Google. And it supports Google's strategy, by fostering a sense of community and collaboration among Google employees, who see themselves working together to select new "Googlers." ■

Source: Based on Wright, "At Google, It Takes a Village to Hire an Employee."

If your professor has assigned this, go to the Assignments section of **mymanagementlab.com** to complete these discussion questions.

✪ **Talk About It 3:** Do you think it would really go counter to the sort of culture Google is trying to nurture to have a central HR department simply test candidates and assign them to work teams with just an interview with the team supervisor? Why?

LEARNING OBJECTIVE **6-4**
Explain how to use two work simulations for selection.

Work Samples and Simulations

With **work samples**, you present examinees with situations representative of the job for which they're applying, and evaluate their responses.[71] Experts consider these (and *simulations,* like the assessment centers we also discuss in this section) to be tests. But they differ from most tests because they directly measure job performance.

work samples
Actual job tasks used in testing applicants' performance.

work sampling technique
A testing method based on measuring performance on actual basic job tasks.

Using Work Sampling for Employee Selection

The **work sampling technique** tries to predict job performance by requiring job candidates to perform one or more samples of the job's tasks. For example, work samples for a cashier may include operating a cash register and counting money.[72]

Work sampling has several advantages. It measures actual job tasks, so it's harder to fake answers. The work sample's content—the actual tasks the person must perform—is not as likely to be unfair to minorities (as might a personnel test that possibly emphasizes middle-class concepts and values).[73] Work sampling doesn't delve into the applicant's personality, so there's almost no chance of applicants viewing it as an invasion of privacy. Designed properly, work samples also exhibit better validity than do other tests designed to predict performance.

FIGURE 6-7 Example of a Work Sampling Question

Note: This is one step in installing pulleys and belts.

Checks key before installing against:

—shaft	score 3
—pulley	score 2
—neither	score 1

Note: This is one step in installing pulleys and belts.

The basic procedure is to select a sample of several tasks crucial to performing the job, and then to test applicants on them.[74] An observer monitors performance on each task, and indicates on a checklist how well the applicant performs. For example, in creating a work sampling test for maintenance mechanics, experts first listed all possible job tasks (like "install pulleys and belts"). Four crucial tasks were installing pulleys and belts, disassembling and installing a gearbox, installing and aligning a motor, and pressing a bushing into a sprocket. Since mechanics could perform each task in a slightly different way, the experts gave different weights to different approaches.

Figure 6-7 shows one of the steps required for the task *installing pulleys and belts*—"checks key before installing ..." Here the examinee might choose to check the key against (1) the shaft, (2) the pulley, or (3) neither. The right of the figure lists the weights (scores) reflecting the worth of each method. The applicant performs the task, and the observer checks off and scores the approach used.

Situational Judgment Tests

Situational judgment tests are personnel tests "designed to assess an applicant's judgment regarding a situation encountered in the workplace."[75] For example:

> You are a sales associate at Best Buy in Miami, Florida. The store sells electronics, including smart phones. Competition comes from other neighborhood retailers, and from online firms. Many customers who come to your store check the product with you, and then buy it on Amazon. As a sales associate, you are responsible for providing exceptional customer service, demonstrating product knowledge, and maximizing sales. You get a weekly salary, with no sales incentive. How would you respond to this situation?
>
> **Situation:**
> A customer comes to you with a printout for a Samsung Galaxy phone from Amazon.com, and proceeds to ask you detailed questions about battery life, and how to work the phone, while mentioning that "Amazon's price is $50 less than yours." You have been with this customer for almost an hour, and there are other customers waiting. You would:
>
> 1. Tell the customer to go buy the phone on Amazon.
> 2. Tell the customer to wait 20 minutes while you take care of another customer.
> 3. Tell the customer that the local Sprint Mobility dealer has the phone for even less than Amazon.
> 4. Explain the advantages of similar phones you have that may better fulfill the buyer's requirements.
> 5. Ask your supervisor to come over and try to sell the customer on buying the Galaxy from you.

management assessment center
A simulation in which management candidates are asked to perform realistic tasks in hypothetical situations and are scored on their performance. It usually also involves testing and the use of management games.

Management Assessment Centers

A **management assessment center** is a 2- to 3-day simulation in which 10 to 12 candidates perform realistic management tasks (like making presentations) under the observation of experts who appraise each candidate's leadership potential. For example, The Cheesecake Factory created its Professional Assessment and

Development Center to help select promotable managers. Candidates undergo 2 days of exercises, simulations, and classroom learning to see if they have the skills for key management positions.[76]

Typical simulated tasks include:

- ***The in-basket.*** The candidate gets reports, memos, notes of incoming phone calls, e-mails, and other materials collected in the actual or computerized in-basket of the simulated job he or she is about to start. The candidate must take appropriate action on each item. Trained evaluators review the candidate's efforts.
- ***Leaderless group discussion.*** Trainers give a leaderless group a discussion question and tell members to arrive at a group decision. They then evaluate each group member's interpersonal skills, acceptance by the group, leadership ability, and individual influence.
- ***Management games.*** Participants solve realistic problems as members of simulated companies competing in a marketplace.
- ***Individual oral presentations.*** Here trainers evaluate each participant's communication skills and persuasiveness.
- ***Testing.*** These may include tests of personality, mental ability, interests, and achievements.
- ***The interview.*** Most require an interview with a trainer to assess interests, past performance, and motivation.

Supervisor recommendations usually play a big role in choosing center participants. Line managers usually act as assessors and arrive at their ratings through consensus.[77] Assessment centers are expensive to develop, take longer than conventional tests, require managers acting as assessors, and often require psychologists. However, studies suggest they are worth it.[78]

Situational Testing and Video-Based Situational Testing

situational test
A test that requires examinees to respond to situations representative of the job.

video-based simulation
A situational test in which examinees respond to video simulations of realistic job situations.

Situational tests require examinees to respond to situations representative of the job. Work sampling (discussed earlier) and some assessment center tasks (such as in-baskets) fall in this category. So do video-based tests and miniature job training (described next), and the situational interviews we address in Chapter 7.[79] Some employers, such as Knack, use video games to determine candidates' creativity and ability to multitask.[80]

The **video-based simulation** presents the candidate with several online or computer video situations, each followed by one or more multiple-choice questions. For example, the scenario might depict an employee handling a situation on the job. At a critical moment, the scenario ends and the video asks the candidate to choose from several courses of action. For example:

(*A manager is upset about the condition of the department and takes it out on one of the department's employees.*)

MANAGER: Well, I'm glad you're here.

ASSOCIATE: Why?

MANAGER: I take a day off and come back to find the department in a mess. You should know better.

ASSOCIATE: But I didn't work late last night.

MANAGER: But there have been plenty of times before when you've left this department in a mess.

(*The scenario stops here.*)

If you were this associate, what would you do?

a. Let the other associates responsible for the mess know that you took the heat.
b. Straighten up the department, and try to reason with the manager later.
c. Suggest to the manager that he talk to the other associates who made the mess.
d. Take it up with the manager's boss.[81]

miniature job training and evaluation
Training candidates to perform several of the job's tasks, and then evaluating the candidates' performance prior to hire.

The Miniature Job Training and Evaluation Approach

Miniature job training and evaluation involves training candidates to perform several of the job's tasks, and then evaluating their performance prior to hire. The approach assumes that a person who demonstrates that he or she can learn and perform the sample of tasks will be able to learn and perform the job itself. Like work sampling, *miniature job training and evaluation* tests applicants with actual samples of the job, so it is inherently content relevant and valid.

For example, when Honda built an auto plant in Lincoln, Alabama, it had to hire thousands of new employees. Working with an Alabama industrial development training agency, Honda began running help wanted ads.

Honda and the Alabama agency first eliminated those applicants who lacked the education or experience, and then gave preference to applicants near the plant. About 340 applicants per 6-week session received special training at a new facility about 15 miles south of the plant. It included classroom instruction, watching videos of current Honda employees in action, and actually practicing particular jobs. Some candidates who watched the videos simply dropped out when they saw the work's pace and repetitiveness.

The training sessions serve two purposes. First, job candidates learn the actual skills they'll need to do the Honda jobs. Second, the training sessions provide an opportunity for special assessors from the Alabama state agency to scrutinize the trainees' work and to rate them. They then invite those who graduate to apply for jobs at the plants. Honda teams, consisting of employees from HR and departmental representatives, do the final screening. [82]

Realistic Job Previews

Sometimes, a dose of realism makes the best screening tool. For example, when Walmart began explicitly explaining and asking about work schedules and work preferences, turnover improved.[83] In general, applicants who receive realistic job previews are more likely to turn down job offers, but their employers are more likely to have less turnover.[84]

Choosing a Selection Method

The employer needs to consider several things before choosing to use a particular selection tool (or tools). These include the tool's reliability and validity, its return on investment (in terms of utility analysis), applicant reactions, usability, adverse impact, and the tool's *selection ratio* (does it screen out, as it should, a high

Bi Shanghong/Xinhua Press/Corbis

Employers such as Honda first train and then have applicants perform several of the job tasks, and then evaluate the candidates before hiring them.

TABLE 6-1 Evaluation of Selected Assessment Methods

Assessment Method	Validity	Adverse Impact	Costs (Develop/ Administer)
Cognitive ability tests	High	High (against minorities)	Low/low
Job knowledge test	High	High (against minorities)	Low/low
Personality tests	Low to moderate	Low	Low/low
Integrity tests	Moderate to high	Low	Low/low
Structured interviews	High	Low	High/high
Situational judgment tests	Moderate	Moderate (against minorities)	High/low
Work samples	High	Low	High/high
Assessment centers	Moderate to high	Low to moderate, depending on exercise	High/high
Physical ability tests	Moderate to high	High (against females and older workers)	High/high

Source: From Selection Assessment Methods, SHRM Foundation, 2005. Reprinted by permission from SHRM Foundation.

percentage of applicants or admit virtually all?).[85] Table 6-1 summarizes the validity, potential adverse impact, and cost of several popular assessment methods. The HR Tools feature shows how line managers may devise their own tests.

IMPROVING PERFORMANCE: *HR Tools for Line Managers and Small Businesses*

Employee Testing and Selection

One of the ironies of being a line manager in even the largest of companies is that, when it comes to screening employees, you're often on your own. Some large firms' HR departments may work with the hiring manager to design and administer the sorts of screening tools we discussed in this chapter. But the fact is that in many of these firms, the HR departments do little more than some preliminary prescreening (for instance, arithmetic tests for clerical applicants), and then follow up with background checks and drug and physical exams.

What should you do if you are, say, a marketing manager, and want to screen some of your job applicants more formally? It is possible to devise your own test battery, but caution is required. Purchasing and then using packaged intelligence tests or psychological tests or even tests of marketing ability could be problematical. Doing so may violate company policy, raise questions of validity, and even expose your employer to EEO liability if problems arise.

A preferred approach is to devise and use screening tools, the face validity of which is obvious. The work sampling test we discussed is one example. It's not unreasonable, for instance, for the marketing manager to ask an advertising applicant to spend half an hour designing an ad, or to ask a marketing research applicant to quickly outline a marketing research program for a hypothetical product. Similarly, a production manager might reasonably ask an inventory control applicant to spend a few minutes using a standard inventory control model to solve an inventory problem.

For small business owners, some tests' ease of use makes them particularly good for small firms. One is the *Wonderlic Personnel Test*; it measures general mental ability in about 15 minutes. The tester reads the instructions, and then keeps time as the candidate works through the 50 short problems on two pages. The tester scores the test by totaling the number of correct answers. Comparing the person's score with the minimum scores recommended for various occupations shows whether the person achieved the minimally acceptable score for the type of job in question. The *Predictive Index* measures work-related personality traits on a two-sided sheet. For example, there is the "social interest" pattern for a person who is generally unselfish, congenial, and unassuming. This person would be a good personnel interviewer, for instance. A template makes scoring simple.

As many managers know, for some jobs past performance is a more useful predictor of performance than are formal selection tests. For example, one study of prospective NFL players concluded that collegiate performance was a significantly better predictor of NFL performance than were physical ability tests.[86] ■

Source: Based on Brian J. Hoffman, John W. Michel, and Kevin J. Williams,"On the Predictive Efficiency of Past Performance and Physical Ability: The Case of the National Football League," Human Performance 24, no. 2 (2011), pp. 158–172.

If your professor has assigned this, go to the Assignments section of **mymanagementlab.com** to complete this discussion.

Talk About It 4: You own a small ladies' dress shop in a mall and want to hire a salesperson. Create a test for doing so.

Background Investigations and Other Selection Methods

LEARNING OBJECTIVE **6-5**
Describe four ways to improve an employer's background checking process.

Testing is only part of an employer's selection process. Other tools may include background investigations and reference checks, preemployment information services, honesty testing, and substance abuse screening.

Why Perform Background Investigations and Reference Checks?

One major company was about to announce a new CEO until they discovered he had a wife and two children in one state as well as a wife and two children in another state.[87] More mundanely, the recruiter HireRight found that of the over 600,000 educational verifications they did in one recent 12-month period, 32% had discrepancies.[88]

One of the easiest ways to avoid hiring mistakes is to check the candidate's background thoroughly. Doing so is inexpensive and (if done right) useful. There's usually no reason why even supervisors in large companies can't check the references of someone they're about to hire, as long as they know the rules.

Most employers check and verify the job applicant's background information and references. In one survey of about 700 human resource managers, 87% said they conduct reference checks, 69% conduct background employment checks, 61% check employee criminal records, 56% check employees' driving records, and 35% sometimes or always check credit.[89] Commonly verified data include legal eligibility for employment (in compliance with immigration laws), dates of prior employment, military service (including discharge status), education, identification (including date of birth and address to confirm identity), county criminal records (current residence, last residence), motor vehicle record, credit, licensing verification, Social Security number, and reference checks.[90] Some employers check executive candidates' civil litigation records, with the candidate's prior approval.[91] Massachusetts and Hawaii prohibit private employers from asking about criminal records on initial written applications.[92]

There are two main reasons to check backgrounds—to verify the applicant's information (name and so forth) and to uncover damaging information.[93] Lying on one's application isn't unusual. A survey found that 23% of 7,000 executive résumés contained exaggerated or false information.[94]

Even relatively sophisticated companies fall prey to criminal employees, in part because they haven't conducted proper background checks. In Chicago, a pharmaceutical firm discovered it had hired gang members in mail delivery and computer repair. The crooks were stealing computer parts, and using the mail department to ship them to their own nearby computer store.[95]

How deeply you search depends on the position. For example, a credit check is more important for hiring an accountant than a groundskeeper. In any case, also periodically check the credit ratings of employees (like cashiers) who have easy access to company assets, and the driving records of employees who use company cars.

Yet most managers don't view references as very useful. Few employers will talk freely about former employees. For example, in one poll, the Society for Human Resource Management found that 98% of 433 responding members said their organizations would verify dates of employment for current or former employees. However, 68% said they wouldn't discuss work performance; 82% said they wouldn't discuss character or personality; and 87% said they wouldn't disclose a disciplinary action.[96]

Many supervisors don't want to damage a former employee's chances for a job; others might prefer giving an incompetent employee good reviews to get rid of him or her.

Another reason is legal. Employers providing references generally can't be successfully sued for defamation unless the employee can show "malice"—that is, ill will, culpable recklessness, or disregard of the employee's rights.[97] But many managers and companies understandably still don't want the grief. The following explains this.

KNOW YOUR EMPLOYMENT LAW

Giving References

Federal laws that affect references include the Privacy Act of 1974, the Fair Credit Reporting Act of 1970, the Family Education Rights and Privacy Act of 1974 (and Buckley Amendment of 1974), and the Freedom of Information Act of 1966. They give people the right to know the nature and substance of information in their credit files and files with government agencies, and (Privacy Act) to review records pertaining to them from any private business that contracts with a federal agency. The person may thus see your comments.[98]

Beyond that, common law (and in particular the tort of defamation) applies to any information you supply. Communication is defamatory if it is false and tends to harm the reputation of another by lowering the person in the estimation of the community or by deterring other persons from dealing with him or her.

Truth is not always a defense. In some states, employees can sue employers for disclosing to a large number of people true but embarrassing private facts about the employee. One case involved a supervisor shouting that the employee's wife had been having sexual relations with certain people. The jury found the employer liable for invasion of the couple's privacy and for intentional infliction of emotional distress.[99]

The net result is that most employers and managers restrict who can give references and what they can say. As a rule, only authorized managers should provide information. Other suggestions include "Don't volunteer information," "Avoid vague statements," and "Do not answer trap questions such as, 'Would you rehire this person?'" In practice, many firms have a policy of not providing any information about former employees except for their dates of employment, last salary, and position titles.[100]

(However, *not* disclosing relevant information can be dangerous, too. In one case, a company fired an employee for allegedly bringing a handgun to work. After his next employer fired him for absenteeism, he returned to that company and shot several employees. The injured parties and their relatives sued the previous employer, who had provided the employee with a clean letter of recommendation.)

The person alleging defamation has various legal remedies, including suing the source of the reference for defamation.[101] In one case, a court awarded a man $56,000 after a company turned him down for a job after the former employer called him a "character." Many firms will check references for a small fee.[102] One supervisor hired such a firm. It found that someone at the supervisor's previous company suggested that the employee was "... not comfortable with taking risks, or making big decisions." The former employee sued, demanding an end to defamation and $45,000 in compensation.[103] ■

How to Check a Candidate's Background

There are several things managers and employers can do to get better information.

Most employers at least try to verify an applicant's current (or former) position and salary with his or her current (or former) employer by phone (assuming you cleared doing so with the candidate). Others call the applicant's current and previous supervisors to try to discover more about the person's motivation, technical competence, and ability to work with others (although, again, many employers have policies against providing such information). Figure 6-8 shows one form for phone references. Many employers get background reports from commercial credit rating companies for information about credit standing, indebtedness, reputation, character, and lifestyle. (Others check social network sites, as we will see in a moment.)

FIGURE 6-8 Reference Checking Form

Source: Reprinted with permission of the Society for Human Resource Management (www.shrm.org), Alexandria, VA 22314.

(Verify that the applicant has provided permission before conducting reference checks.)

Candidate Name _____

Reference Name _____

Company Name _____

Dates of Employment From: _____ To: _____

Position(s) Held _____

Salary History _____

Reason for Leaving _____

Explain the reason for your call and verify the above information with the supervisor (including the reason for leaving)

_____

1. Please describe the type of work for which the candidate was responsible.

_____

2. How would you describe the applicant's relationships with coworkers, subordinates (if applicable), and with superiors?

_____

3. Did the candidate have a positive or negative work attitude? Please elaborate.

_____

4. How would you describe the quantity and quality of output generated by the former employee?

_____

5. What were his/her strengths on the job?

_____

6. What were his/her weaknesses on the job?

_____

7. What is your overall assessment of the candidate?

_____

8. Would you recommend him/her for this position? Why or why not?

_____

9. Would this individual be eligible for rehire? Why or why not?

_____

Other comments?

_____

Automated online reference checking can improve the results. With a system such as Pre-Hire 360 (www.skillsurvey.com/pre-hire-360), the hiring employer inputs the applicant's name and e-mail address. Then the person's preselected references rate the applicant's skills anonymously, using a survey. The system then compiles these references into a report for the employer.[104]

TRENDS SHAPING HR: *DIGITAL AND SOCIAL MEDIA*

Digital tools are changing the background-checking process. Employers are Googling applicants or checking Facebook and LinkedIn, and what they're finding isn't always pretty. One candidate described his interests on Facebook as smoking pot and shooting people. The student may have been kidding, but didn't get the job.[105] An article called "Funny, They Don't Look Like My References" notes that the new LinkedIn premium service "Reference Search" lets employers identify people in their own networks who worked for the same company when a job candidate did, and thus use them to get references on the candidate.[106] According to LinkedIn, you just select Reference Search, then enter a company name, candidate's name, and the timeframe, and click search. Employers are integrating such tools with software solutions such as Oracle/Taleo Verify to facilitate obtaining such information and then integrating it into the candidate's dashboard-accessible profile.

Web and social media background searches can be problematical. While applicants usually don't list race, age, disability or ethnic origin on their résumés, their Facebook pages may reveal such information, setting the stage for possible EEOC claims. Or, an overeager supervisor might conduct his or her own Facebook page "background check."[107]

In any case, it's probably best to get the candidate's prior approval for social networking searches.[108] And do not use a pretext or fabricate an identity.[109] Maryland law restricts employer demands for applicant usernames and passwords.[110] Other states will undoubtedly follow.

The solution isn't necessarily to prohibit the legitimate use of social media–based information (unless perusing such information is illegal under the law, as in Maryland). Instead, follow intelligent social media staffing policies and procedures. For example, inform employees and prospective employees ahead of time regarding what information the employer plans to review. Assign one or two specially trained human resource professionals to search social media sites. And warn unauthorized employees (such as prospective supervisors) about accessing such information.[111] ■

If your professor has assigned this, go to the Assignments section of **mymanagementlab.com** to complete this discussion question.

✪ **Talk About It 5:** Review your Facebook or other social media site. How do you think a prospective employer would react to what you've had posted there?

Using Preemployment Information Services

It is easy to have employment screening services check out applicants. Major background checking providers include Automatic Data Processing Inc., First Advantage, HireRight, and Sterling Backcheck.[112] They use databases to access information about matters such as workers' compensation, credit histories, and conviction and driving records. For example, retail employers use First Advantage Corporation's Esteem Database to see if their job candidates have previously been involved in suspected retail thefts.[113] Another firm advertises that for less than $50 it will do a criminal history report, motor vehicle/driver's record report, and (after the person is hired) a workers' compensation claims report history, plus confirm identity, name, and Social Security number. There are thousands of databases, including sex offender registries and criminal and educational histories.

There are three reasons to use caution with such services.[114] First, EEO laws apply. For example, New Jersey recently became the 13th state to pass a "Ban the Box" law prohibiting prospective employees from questioning applicants about convictions until late in the hiring process.[115] So be careful not to use the product of an unreasonable investigation.

Second, various federal and state laws govern how employers acquire and use applicants' and employees' background information. At the federal level, the Fair Credit Reporting Act is the main directive. In addition, at least 21 states impose their own requirements. Authorizing background reports while complying with these laws requires four steps, as follows:

Step 1: Disclosure and authorization. Before requesting reports, the employer must disclose to the applicant or employee that a report will be requested and that the employee/applicant may receive a copy. (Do this on the application form.)

Step 2: Certification. The employer must certify to the reporting agency that the employer will comply with the federal and state legal requirements—for example, that the employer obtained written consent from the employee/applicant.

Step 3: Providing copies of reports. Under federal law, the employer must provide copies of the report to the applicant or employee if adverse action (such as withdrawing a job offer) is contemplated.[116]

Step 4: Notice after adverse action. If the employer anticipates taking an adverse action, the employee/applicant must get an adverse action notice. This contains information such as the name of the consumer reporting agency. The employee/applicant then has various remedies under the laws.[117]

Third, the criminal background information may be flawed. Many return "possible matches" for the wrong person (who happens to be a criminal).[118] One such firm paid a $2.6 million penalty after the Federal Trade Commission sued it for such erroneous reporting.[119]

Making the Background Check More Valuable

There are steps one can take to improve the usefulness of the background information being sought. Specifically:

- Include on the application form a statement for applicants to sign explicitly authorizing a background and credit check, such as:

  > I hereby certify that the facts set forth in the above employment application are true and complete to the best of my knowledge. I understand that falsified statements or misrepresentation of information on this application or omission of any information sought may be cause for dismissal, if employed, or may lead to refusal to make an offer and/or to withdrawal of an offer. I also authorize investigation of credit, employment record, driving record, and, once a job offer is made or during employment, workers' compensation background if required.

- Telephone references tend to produce more candid assessments. Use a form, such as Figure 6-8. Remember that you can get relatively accurate information regarding dates of employment, eligibility for rehire, and job qualifications. It's more difficult to get other background information (such as reasons for leaving a previous job).[120]

- Persistence and attentiveness to possible red flags improve results. For example, if the former employer hesitates or seems to qualify his or her answer, don't go on to the next question. Try to unearth what the applicant did to make the former employer pause. If he says, "Joe requires some special care," say, "Special care?"
- Compare the application to the résumé; people tend to be more creative on their résumés than on their application forms, where they must certify the information.
- Try to ask open-ended questions (such as, "How much structure does the applicant need in his/her work?") to get the references to talk more about the candidate.[121] But in asking for information: Only ask for and obtain information that you're going to use; remember that using arrest information is highly problematical; use information that is specific and job related; and keep information confidential.
- Ask the references supplied by the applicant to suggest other references. You might ask each of the applicant's references, "Could you give me the name of another person who might be familiar with the applicant's performance?" Then you begin getting information from references that may be more objective, because they did not come directly from the applicant (or use LinkedIn's Reference Search service).

The Polygraph and Honesty Testing

The polygraph is a device that measures physiological changes like increased perspiration. The assumption is that such changes reflect changes in emotional state that accompany lying.

Complaints about offensiveness plus grave doubts about the polygraph's accuracy culminated in the Employee Polygraph Protection Act of 1988.[122] With a few exceptions, the law prohibits employers from conducting polygraph examinations of all job applicants and most employees. (Also prohibited are other mechanical or electrical devices that attempt to measure honesty or dishonesty, including voice stress analyzers.) Federal laws don't prohibit paper-and-pencil tests or chemical testing, as for drugs.

Local, state, and federal government employers (including the FBI) can use polygraphs for selection screening and other purposes, but state laws restrict many local and state governments. Private employers can use polygraph testing, but only under strictly limited circumstances.[123] These include firms with national defense or security contracts, nuclear power-related contracts with the Department of Energy, access to highly classified information, counterintelligence-related contracts with the FBI or Department of Justice, and private businesses (1) hiring private security personnel, (2) hiring persons with access to drugs, or (3) doing ongoing investigations involving economic loss or injury to an employer's business, such as a theft.

However, even for ongoing investigations of theft, the law restricts employers' rights. To administer a polygraph test for an ongoing investigation, an employer must meet four standards:

1. It must show that it suffered an economic loss or injury.
2. It must show that the employee in question had access to the property.
3. It must have a reasonable suspicion before asking the employee to take the polygraph.
4. The person to be tested must receive the details of the investigation before the test, as well as the polygraph questions to be asked.

WRITTEN HONESTY TESTS The Polygraph Protection Act triggered a burgeoning market for paper-and-pencil (or computerized or online) honesty tests. These are psychological tests designed to predict job applicants' proneness to dishonesty and other forms of counterproductivity.[124] Most measure attitudes regarding things like tolerance of others who steal and admission of theft-related activities. Tests include the Phase II profile. London House, Inc., and Stanton Corporation publish similar tests.[125]

Psychologists were initially skeptical about paper-and-pencil honesty tests, but studies support these tests' validity.[126] One study involved 111 employees hired by a convenience store chain to work at store or gas station counters.[127] The firm estimated that "shrinkage" equaled 3% of sales, and believed that internal theft accounted for much of this. Scores on an honesty test successfully predicted theft here (as measured by termination for theft). At Hospital Management Corp., an integrity test is the first step in the hiring process, and those who fail go no further. It instituted the test after determining that the test did weed out undesirable applicants. For example, after the test was used for several months, workers compensation claims dropped among new hires.[128]

Testing for Honesty: Practical Guidelines

With or without testing, there's a lot a manager can do to screen out dishonest applicants or employees. Specifically:

- Ask blunt questions.[129] Says one expert, there is nothing wrong with asking the applicant direct questions, such as, "Have you ever stolen anything from an employer?" "Have you recently held jobs other than those listed on your application?" "Is any information on your application misrepresented or falsified?"
- Listen, rather than talk. Thus liars may try to answer direct questions somewhat evasively. For example, ask them if they've ever used drugs, and they might say, "I don't take drugs."[130]
- Watch for telltale body signals. For example, someone who is not telling the truth may move his or her body slightly away from you.[131] Establish a baseline by seeing how the person's body is positioned when he or she is undoubtedly telling the truth. Know that it is *not* true that adult liars won't look you in the eye when they're lying; polished liars may actually do so excessively.[132]
- Do a credit check. Include a clause in your application giving you the right to conduct background checks, including credit checks and motor vehicle reports.
- Check all employment and personal references.
- Use written honesty tests and psychological tests.
- Test for drugs. Devise a drug-testing program and give each applicant a copy of the policy.
- Establish a search-and-seizure policy and conduct searches. Give each applicant a copy of the policy and require each to return a signed copy. The policy should state, "All lockers, desks, and similar property remain the property of the company and may be inspected routinely."

Honesty testing requires caution. Having just taken and "failed" what is fairly obviously an "honesty test," the candidate may leave the premises feeling mistreated. Some "honesty" questions also pose invasion-of-privacy issues. And some states such as Massachusetts and Rhode Island limit paper-and-pencil honesty testing.

Graphology

Graphology is the use of handwriting analysis to determine the writer's basic personality traits. It thus has some resemblance to projective personality tests, although graphology's validity is highly suspect. The handwriting analyst studies an applicant's handwriting and signature to discover the person's needs, desires, and psychological makeup. In one typical example the graphologist notes that a writing sample has small handwriting, a vertical stance, and narrow letters (among other things) and so is indicative of someone with uptight tendencies.

Virtually all scientific studies suggest graphology is not valid, or that when graphologists do accurately size up candidates, it's because they are also privy to other background information. Yet some firms swear by it.[133] One 325-employee firm uses profiles based on handwriting samples to design follow-up interviews.[134] Most experts shun it.

"Human Lie Detectors"

Some employers are using so-called "human lie detectors," experts who may (or may not) be able to identify lying just by watching candidates.[135] One Wall Street firm uses a former FBI agent. He sits in on interviews and watches for signs of candidate deceptiveness. Signs include pupils changing size (fear), irregular breathing (nervousness), crossing legs ("liars distance themselves from an untruth"), and quick verbal responses (scripted statements).

Physical Exams

Once the employer extends the person a job offer, a medical exam is often the next step in selection (although it may also occur after the new employee starts work).

There are several reasons for preemployment medical exams: to verify that the applicant meets the job's physical requirements, to discover any medical limitations you should consider in placement, and to establish a baseline for future workers' compensation claims. Exams can also reduce absenteeism and accidents and detect communicable diseases.

Under the Americans with Disabilities Act, an employer cannot reject someone with a disability if he or she is otherwise qualified and can perform the essential job functions with reasonable accommodation. Recall that the ADA permits a medical exam during the period between the job offer and commencement of work if such exams are standard practice for all applicants for that job category.[136]

Substance Abuse Screening

Most employers conduct drug screenings. The most common practice is to test candidates just before they're formally hired. Many also test current employees when there is reason to believe they've been using drugs—after a work accident, or with obvious behavioral symptoms such as chronic lateness. Some firms routinely administer drug tests on a random or periodic basis, while others require drug tests when they transfer or promote employees to new positions.[137] Most employers that conduct such tests use urine sampling. Numerous vendors provide workplace drug-testing services.[138] Employers may use urine testing to test for illicit drugs, breath alcohol tests to determine amount of alcohol in the blood, blood tests to measure alcohol or drugs in the blood at the time of the test, hair analyses to reveal drug history, saliva tests for substances such as marijuana and cocaine, and skin patches to determine drug use.[139]

Yet drug testing, while ubiquitous, is neither as simple nor as effective as it might appear. First, no drug test is foolproof. Some urine sample tests can't distinguish between legal and illegal substances; for example, Advil can produce positive results for marijuana. Furthermore, "there is a swarm of products that promise to help employees (both male and female) beat drug tests."[140] (Employers should view the presence of adulterants in a sample as a positive test.) One alternative, hair follicle testing, requires a small sample of hair, which the lab analyzes.[141] But here, too, classified ads advertise chemicals to rub on the scalp to fool the test.

There's also the question of what is the point.[142] Unlike roadside breathalyzers for DUI drivers, tests for drugs show only whether drug residues are present; they do not indicate impairment (or, for that matter, habituation or addiction).[143] Some therefore argue that testing is not justifiable on the grounds of boosting workplace safety.[144] Many feel the testing procedures themselves are degrading and intrusive. Many employers reasonably counter that they don't want drug-prone employees on their premises. Employers should choose the lab they engage to do the testing with care.

Drug Testing Legal Issues

Drug testing raises legal issues.[145] As one attorney writes, "It is not uncommon for employees to claim that drug tests violate their rights to privacy under common law or, in some states, a state statutory or constitutional provision."[146] Hair follicle testing is less intrusive than urinalysis but can actually produce more personal information: A 3-inch hair segment could record 6 months of drug use.

Several federal laws affect workplace drug testing. Under the Americans with Disabilities Act, a court would probably consider a former drug user (who no longer uses illegal drugs and has successfully completed or is participating in a rehabilitation program) as a qualified applicant with a disability.[147] Under the Drug Free Workplace Act of 1988, federal contractors must maintain a workplace free from illegal drugs. While this doesn't require contractors to conduct drug testing or rehabilitate affected employees, many do. Under the U.S. Department of Transportation workplace regulations, firms with over 50 eligible employees in transportation industries must conduct alcohol testing on workers with sensitive or safety-related jobs. These include mass transit workers, air traffic controllers, train crews, and school bus drivers.[148] Other laws, including the Federal Rehabilitation Act of 1973 and various state laws, protect rehabilitating drug users or those who have a physical or mental addiction.

What should an employer do when a job candidate tests positive? Most companies will not hire such candidates, and a few will immediately fire current employees who test positive. Current employees have more legal recourse; employers must tell them the reason for dismissal if the reason is a positive drug test.[149]

Particularly where sensitive jobs are concerned, courts tend to side with employers. In one case, a U.S. Court of Appeals ruled that Exxon acted properly in firing a truck driver who failed a drug test. Exxon requires random testing of employees in safety-sensitive jobs. The employee drove a tractor-trailer carrying 12,000 gallons of flammable motor fuel and tested positive for cocaine. The union representing the employee challenged the firing. An arbitrator reduced the penalty to a 2-month suspension, but the appeals court ruled that the employer acted properly in firing the truck driver.[150]

Complying with Immigration Law

Employees hired in the United States must prove they are eligible to work here. The requirement to verify eligibility does not provide any basis to reject an applicant just because he or she is a foreigner, not a U.S. citizen, or an alien residing in the United States, as long as that person can prove his or her identity and employment eligibility. To comply with this law, employers should follow procedures outlined in the so-called I-9 Employment Eligibility Verification form.[151] More than 500,000 employers are using the federal government's voluntary electronic employment verification program, E-Verify.[152] Federal contractors must use it.[153] There is no charge to use E-Verify.[154] Many employers now use automated I-9 verification systems with drop-down menus to electronically compile and submit applicants' I-9 data.[155] The I-9 forms contain a prominent "antidiscrimination notice."[156]

Applicants can prove their eligibility for employment in two ways. One is to show a document (such as a U.S. passport or alien registration card with photograph) that proves both identity and employment eligibility. The other is to show a document that proves the person's identity, along with a second document showing his or her employment eligibility, such as a work permit.[157] In any case, it's always advisable to get two forms of proof of identity.

Identity theft—undocumented workers stealing and using an authorized worker's identity—is a problem even with E-Verify.[158] The federal government is tightening restrictions on hiring undocumented workers. Realizing that many documents are fakes, the government is putting the onus on employers to make sure whom they're hiring. The Department of Homeland Security files criminal charges against suspected employer violators.[159]

You can verify Social Security numbers by calling the Social Security Administration. Employers can avoid accusations of discrimination by verifying the documents of all applicants, not just those they may think suspicious.[160]

Chapter Review

MyManagementLab® Go to **mymanagementlab.com** to complete the problems marked with this icon. ✪

Chapter Section Summaries

6-1. Careful **employee selection is important** for several reasons. Your own performance always depends on your subordinates; it is costly to recruit and hire employees; and mismanaging the hiring process has various legal implications including equal employment, negligent hiring, and defamation.

6-2. Whether you are administering tests or making decisions based on test results, managers need to understand several **basic testing concepts**. Reliability refers to a test's consistency, while validity tells you whether the test is measuring what you think it's supposed to be measuring. Criterion validity means demonstrating that those who do well on the test also do well on the job while content validity means showing that the test constitutes a fair sample of the job's content. Validating a test involves analyzing the job, choosing the tests, administering the test, relating your test scores and criteria, and cross-validating and revalidating. Test takers have rights to privacy and feedback as well as to confidentiality.

6-3. Whether they are administered via paper and pencil, by computer, or online, we discussed several main **types of tests**. Tests of cognitive abilities measure things like reasoning ability and include intelligence tests and tests of specific cognitive abilities such as mechanical comprehension. There are also tests of motor and physical abilities, and measures of personality and interests. With respect to personality, psychologists often focus on the "big five" personality dimensions: extroversion, emotional stability/neuroticism, agreeableness, conscientiousness, and openness to experience. Achievement tests measure what someone has learned.

6-4. With **work samples and simulations**, you present examinees with situations representative of the jobs for which they are applying. One example is the management assessment center, a 2- to 3-day simulation in which 10 to 12 candidates perform realistic management tasks under the observation of experts who appraise each candidate's leadership potential. Video-based situational testing and the miniature job training and evaluation approach are two other examples.

6-5. Testing is only part of an employer's selection process; you also want to conduct **background investigations and other selection procedures**.

- The main point of doing a background check is to verify the applicant's information and to uncover potentially damaging information. However, care must be taken, particularly when giving a reference, that the employee not be defamed and that his or her privacy rights are maintained.
- Given former employers' reluctance to provide a comprehensive report, those checking

references need to do several things. Make sure the applicant explicitly authorizes a background check, use a checklist or form for obtaining telephone references, and be persistent and attentive to potential red flags.

- Given the growing popularity of computerized employment background databases, many or most employers use preemployment information services to obtain background information.
- For many types of jobs, honesty testing is essential and paper-and-pencil tests have proven useful.
- Most employers also require that new hires, before actually coming on board, take physical exams and substance abuse screening. It's essential to comply with immigration law, in particular by having the candidate complete an I-9 Employment Eligibility Verification Form and submit proof of eligibility.

Discussion Questions

6-1. What is the difference between reliability and validity?

6-2. Explain why you think a certified psychologist who is specifically trained in test construction should (or should not) be used by a small business that needs an employment test.

✪ **6-3.** Why is it important to conduct preemployment background investigations? How would you do so?

6-4. Explain how you would get around the problem of former employers being unwilling to give bad references on their former employees.

✪ **6-5.** How can employers protect themselves against negligent hiring claims?

Individual and Group Activities

6-6. Write a short essay discussing some of the ethical and legal considerations in testing.

6-7. Working individually or in groups, develop a list of specific selection techniques that you would suggest your dean use to hire the next HR professor at your school. Explain why you chose each selection technique.

6-8. Working individually or in groups, contact the publisher of a standardized test such as the Scholastic Assessment Test and obtain from it written information regarding the test's validity and reliability. Present a short report in class discussing what the test is supposed to measure and the degree to which you think the test does what it is supposed to do, based on the reported validity and reliability scores.

6-9. Appendices A and B at the end of this book (pages 612–629) list the knowledge someone studying for the HRCI (Appendix A) or SHRM (Appendix B) certification exam needs to have in each area of human resource management (such as in Strategic Management, and Workforce Planning). In groups of several students, do four things: (1) review Appendix A and/or B; (2) identify the material in this chapter that relates to the Appendix A and/or B required knowledge lists; (3) write four multiple-choice exam questions on this material that you believe would be suitable for inclusion in the HRCI exam and/or the SHRM exam; and, (4) if time permits, have someone from your team post your team's questions in front of the class, so that students in all teams can answer the exam questions created by the other teams.

Experiential Exercise

A Test for a Reservation Clerk

Purpose: The purpose of this exercise is to give you practice in developing a test to measure *one specific ability* for the job of airline reservation clerk for a major airline. If time permits, you'll be able to combine your tests into a test battery.

Required Understanding: Your airline has decided to outsource its reservation jobs to Asia. You should be fully acquainted with the procedure for developing a personnel test and should read the following description of an airline reservation clerk's duties:

> Customers contact our airline reservation clerks to obtain flight schedules, prices, and itineraries. The reservation clerks look up the requested information on our airline's online flight schedule systems, which are updated continuously. The reservation clerk must speak clearly, deal courteously and expeditiously with the customer, and be able to find quickly alternative flight arrangements in order to provide the customer with the itinerary that fits his or her needs. Alternative flights and prices must be found quickly, so that the customer is not kept waiting, and so that our reservations operations group maintains its efficiency standards. There may be a dozen or more alternative routes between the customer's starting point and destination.

You may assume that we will hire about one-third of the applicants as airline reservation clerks. Therefore, your objective is to create a test that is useful in selecting a third of those available.

How to Set Up the Exercise/Instructions:

Divide the class into teams of five or six students. The ideal candidate will need to have a number of skills to perform this job well. Your job is to select a single skill and to develop a test to measure that skill. Please use only the materials available in the room. The test should permit quantitative scoring and may be an individual or a group test.

Please go to your assigned groups. As per our discussion of test development in this chapter, each group should make a list of the skills relevant to success in the airline reservation clerk's job. Each group should then rate the importance of these skills on a 5-point scale. Then, develop a test to measure what you believe to be the top-ranked skill. If time permits, the groups should combine the various tests from each group into a test battery. If possible, leave time for a group of students to take the test battery.

Application Case

The Insider

A federal jury convicted a stock trader who worked for a well-known investment firm, along with two alleged accomplices, of insider trading. According to the indictment, the trader got inside information about pending mergers from lawyers. The lawyers allegedly browsed around their law firm picking up information about corporate deals others in the firm were working on. The lawyers would then allegedly pass their information on to a friend, who in turn passed it on to the trader. Such "inside" information reportedly helped the trader (and his investment firm) earn millions of dollars. The trader would then allegedly thank the lawyers, for instance, with envelopes filled with cash.

Things like that are not supposed to happen. Federal and state laws prohibit them. And investment firms have their own compliance procedures to identify and head off shady trades. The problem is that controlling such behavior once the firm has someone working for it who may be prone to engage in inside trading isn't easy. "Better to avoid hiring such people in the first place," said one pundit.

Over lunch at Bouley restaurant in Manhattan's TriBeCa area, the heads of several investment firms were discussing the conviction, and what they could do to make sure something like that didn't occur in their firms. "It's not just compliance," said one. "We've got to keep out the bad apples." They ask you for your advice.

Questions

6-10. We want you to design an employee selection program for hiring stock traders. We already know what to look for as far as technical skills are concerned—accounting courses, economics, and so on. What we want is a program for screening out potential bad apples. To that end, please let us know the following: What screening test(s) would you suggest, and why? What questions should we add to our application form? Specifically how should we check candidates' backgrounds, and what questions should we ask previous employers and references?

6-11. What else (if anything) would you suggest?

Continuing Case

Carter Cleaning Company

Honesty Testing

CHAPTER 6

Jennifer Carter, of the Carter Cleaning Centers, and her father have what the latter describes as an easy but hard job when it comes to screening job applicants. It is easy because for two important jobs—the people who actually do the pressing and those who do the cleaning/spotting—the applicants are easily screened with about 20 minutes of on-the-job testing. As with typists, Jennifer points out, "Applicants either know how to press clothes fast or how to use cleaning chemicals and machines, or they don't, and we find out very quickly by just trying them out on the job." On the other hand, applicant screening for the stores can also be frustratingly hard because of the nature of some of the other qualities that Jennifer would like to screen for. Two of the most critical problems facing her company are employee turnover and employee honesty. Jennifer and her father sorely need to implement practices that will reduce the rate of employee turnover. If there is a way to do this through employee testing and screening techniques, Jennifer would like to know about it because of the management time and money that are now being wasted by the never-ending need to recruit and hire new employees. Of even greater concern to Jennifer and her father is the need to institute new practices to screen out those employees who may be predisposed to steal from the company.

Employee theft is an enormous problem for the Carter Cleaning Centers, and not just cash. For example, the cleaner/spotter often opens the store without a manager present, to get the day's work started, and it is not unusual for that person to "run a route." Running a route means that an employee canvasses his or her neighborhood to pick up people's clothes for cleaning and then secretly cleans and presses them in the Carter store, using the company's supplies, gas, and power. It would also not be unusual for an unsupervised person (or his or her supervisor, for that matter) to accept a 1-hour rush order for cleaning or laundering, quickly clean and press the item, and return it to the customer for payment without making out a proper ticket for the item posting the sale. The money, of course, goes into the worker's pocket instead of into the cash register.

The more serious problem concerns the store manager and the counter workers who actually handle the cash. According to Jack Carter, "You would not believe the creativity employees use to get around the management controls we set up to cut down on employee theft." As one extreme example of this felonious creativity, Jack tells the following story: "To cut down on the amount of money my employees were stealing, I had a small sign painted and placed in front of all our cash registers. The sign said: YOUR ENTIRE ORDER FREE IF WE DON'T GIVE YOU A CASH REGISTER RECEIPT WHEN YOU PAY. CALL 552–0235. It was my intention with this sign to force all our cash-handling employees to give receipts so the cash register would record them for my accountants. After all, if all the cash that comes in is recorded in the cash register, then we should have a much better handle on stealing in our stores. Well, one of our managers found a way around this. I came into the store one night and noticed that the cash register this particular manager was using just didn't look right, although the sign was placed in front of it. It turned out that every afternoon at about 5:00 p.m. when the other employees left, this character would pull his own cash register out of a box that he hid underneath our supplies. Customers coming in would notice the sign and, of course, the fact that he was meticulous in ringing up every sale. But unknown to them, for about 5 months the sales that came in for about an hour every day went into his cash register, not mine. It took us that long to figure out where our cash for that store was going."

Here is what Jennifer would like you to answer:

Questions

6-12. What would be the advantages and disadvantages to Jennifer's company of routinely administering honesty tests to all its employees?

6-13. Specifically, what other screening techniques could the company use to screen out theft-prone and turnover-prone employees, and how exactly could these be used?

6-14. How should her company terminate employees caught stealing, and what kind of procedure should be set up for handling reference calls about these employees when they go to other companies looking for jobs?

Translating Strategy into HR Policies and Practices Case*,§

**The accompanying strategy map for this chapter is in the MyManagementLab, and the overall map on the inside back cover of this text outlines the relationships involved.*

Improving Performance at The Hotel Paris

The New Employee Testing Program

The Hotel Paris's competitive strategy is "To use superior guest service to differentiate the Hotel Paris properties, and to thereby increase the length of stay and return rate of guests, and thus boost revenues and profitability." HR manager Lisa Cruz must now formulate functional policies and activities that support this competitive strategy and boost performance, by eliciting the required employee behaviors and competencies.

As she considered what to do next, Lisa Cruz, the Hotel Paris's HR director, knew that employee selection had to play a role. The Hotel Paris currently had an informal screening process in which local hotel managers obtained application forms, interviewed applicants, and checked their references. However, a pilot project using an employment test for service people at the Chicago hotel had produced startling results. Lisa found consistent, significant relationships between test performance and a range of employee competencies and behaviors such as speed of check-in/out, employee turnover, and percentage of calls answered with the required greeting. She knew that such employee capabilities and behaviors translated into the improved guest service performance the Hotel Paris needed to execute its strategy. She therefore had to decide what selection procedures would be best.

Lisa's team, working with an industrial psychologist, designs a test battery that they believe will produce the sorts of high-morale, patient, people-oriented employees they are looking for. It includes a preliminary, computerized test in which applicants for the positions of front-desk clerk, door person, assistant manager, and security guard must deal with an apparently irate guest; a work sample in which front-desk clerk candidates spend 10 minutes processing an incoming "guest"; a personality test aimed at weeding out applicants who lack emotional stability; the Wonderlic test of mental ability; and the Phase II Profile for assessing candidate honesty. Their subsequent validity analysis shows that scores on the test batteries predict scores on the hotel's employee capabilities and behavior metrics. A second analysis confirmed that, as the percentage of employees hired after testing rose, so too did the hotel's employee capabilities and behaviors scores, for instance (see the strategy map), in terms of speed of check-in/out, and the percent of guests receiving the Hotel Paris required greeting.

Lisa and the CFO also found other measurable improvements apparently resulting from the new testing process. For example, it took less time to fill an open position, and cost per hire diminished, so the HR department became more efficient. The new testing program thus did not only contribute to the hotel's performance by improving employee capabilities and behaviors. It also did so by directly improving profit margins and profits.

Questions

6-15. Provide a detailed example of a security guard work sample test.

6-16. Provide a detailed example of two personality test items you would suggest they use, and why you would suggest using them.

6-17. Based on what you read here in this Dessler *Human Resource Management* Chapter, what other tests would you suggest to Lisa, and why would you suggest them?

6-18. How would you suggest Lisa try to confirm that it is indeed the testing and not some other change that accounts for the improved performance.

§Written by and copyright Gary Dessler, PhD.

MyManagementLab

Go to **mymanagementlab.com** for Auto-graded writing questions as well as the following Assisted-graded writing questions:

6-19. Explain how you would go about validating a test. How can this information be useful to a manager?

6-20. Explain how digital and social media have changed the employee selection process, and the advice you would give an employer about avoiding problems with using such tools for selection.

6-21. MyManagementLab Only—comprehensive writing assignment for this chapter.

✪ Try It!

How would you apply the concepts and skills you learned in this chapter? If your professor has assigned this, go to the Assignments section of mymanagementlab.com to complete the simulation: *Individual Behavior*.

✪ PERSONAL INVENTORY ASSESSMENTS

Are You a Type A Personality?

Personality plays a big role in selection and employee performance. Complete this assessment to learn more about your personality.

Key Terms

negligent hiring, 167
reliability, 167
test validity, 168
criterion validity, 168
content validity, 179
construct validity, 170
expectancy chart, 171
interest inventory, 177
work samples, 178
work sampling technique, 178
management assessment center, 179
situational test, 180
video-based simulation, 180
miniature job training and evaluation, 181

Endnotes

1. Kevin Delaney, "Google Adjusts Hiring Process as Needs Grow," *Wall Street Journal*, October 23, 2006, pp. B1, B8; http://google-blog.blogspot.com/2009/01/changes-to-recruiting.html, accessed March 25, 2009.
2. Aliah D. Wright, "At Google, It Takes a Village to Hire an Employee," *HR Magazine* 56, no. 7 (2009 HR Trendbook supplement).
3. See, for example, Jean Phillips and Stanley Gully, *Strategic Staffing* (Upper Saddle River, NJ: Pearson Education, 2012), pp. 234–235.
4. "Regret That Bad Hire? It's an Expensive Global Problem," *Bloomberg BNA Bulletin to Management*, June 4, 2013, p. 179.
5. Even if they use a third party to prepare an employment test, contractors are "ultimately responsible" for ensuring the tests' job relatedness and EEO compliance. "DOL Officials Discuss Contractors' Duties on Validating Tests," *BNA Bulletin to Management*, September 4, 2007, p. 287. Furthermore, enforcement units are increasing their scrutiny of employers who rely on tests and screening. See "Litigation Increasing with Employer Reliance on Tests, Screening," *BNA Bulletin to Management*, April 8, 2008, p. 119. However, see also C. Tuna et al., "Job-Test Ruling Cheers Employers," *Wall Street Journal*, July 1, 2009, p. B1–B2.
6. See, for example, Ann Marie Ryan and Marja Lasek, "Negligent Hiring and Defamation: Areas of Liability Related to Pre-Employment Inquiries," *Personnel Psychology* 44, no. 2 (Summer 1991), pp. 293–319. See also Jay Stuller, "Fatal Attraction," *Across the Board* 42, no. 6 (November–December 2005), pp. 18–23.
7. For example, Ryan Zimmerman, "Wal-Mart to Toughen Job Screening," *Wall Street Journal*, July 12, 2004, pp. B1–B8. See also Michael Tucker, "Show and Tell," *HR Magazine*, January 2012, pp. 51–52.
8. Negligent hiring highlights the need to think through what the job's human requirements really are. For example, "non-rapist" isn't likely to appear as a required knowledge, skill, or ability in a job analysis of an apartment manager, but in situations like this screening for such tendencies is obviously required. To avoid negligent hiring claims, "make a systematic effort to gain relevant information about the applicant, verify documentation, follow up on missing records or gaps in employment, and keep a detailed log of all attempts to obtain information, including the names and dates for phone calls or other requests." Fay Hansen, "Taking 'Reasonable' Action to Avoid Negligent Hiring Claims," *Workforce Management*, September 11, 2006, p. 31. Similarly, the Employers Liability Act of 1969 holds employers responsible for their employees' health and safety at work. Because personality traits may predict problems such as unsafe behaviors and bullying, this act makes careful employee selection even more advisable.
9. Kevin Murphy and Charles Davidshofer, *Psychological Testing: Principles and Applications* (Upper Saddle River, NJ: Prentice Hall, 2001), p. 73.
10. Ibid., pp. 116–119.
11. W. Bruce Walsh and Nancy Betz, *Tests and Assessment*

(Upper Saddle River, NJ: Prentice Hall, 2001).
12. Murphy and Davidshofer, *Psychological Testing*, p. 74.
13. Ibid.
14. See James Ledvinka, *Federal Regulation of Personnel and Human Resource Management* (Boston: Kent, 1982), p. 113; and Murphy and Davidshofer, *Psychological Testing*, pp. 154–165.
15. www.siop.org/workplace/employment%20testing/information_to_consider_when_cre.aspx, accessed March 22, 2009.
16. Based on Joseph Walker, "Meet the New Boss: Big Data," *Wall Street Journal*, September 20, 2012, p. B1. Also see Josh Bersin, "Big Data in Human Resources: Talent Analytics (People Analytics) Comes of Age," www.forbes.com/sites/joshbersin/2013/02/17/bigdata-in-human-resources-talent-analytics-comes-of-age, accessed March 29, 2015.
17. Bill Roberts, "Hire Intelligence," *HR Magazine*, May 2011, p. 64.
18. The procedure you would use to demonstrate content validity differs from that used to demonstrate criterion validity (as described in steps 1 through 5). Content validity tends to emphasize judgment. Here, you first do a careful job analysis to identify the work behaviors required. Then combine several samples of those behaviors into a test. A typing and computer skills test for a clerk would be an example. The fact that the test is a comprehensive sample of actual, observable, on-the-job behaviors is what lends the test its content validity.
19. Murphy and Davidshofer, *Psychological Testing*, p. 73. See also Chad Van Iddekinge and Robert Ployhart, "Developments in the Criterion-Related Validation of Selection Procedures: A Critical Review and Recommendations for Practice," *Personnel Psychology* 60, no. 1 (2008), pp. 871–925.
20. Psychological Assessment Resources, Inc., in Odessa, Florida, is typical.
21. Experts sometimes have to develop separate expectancy charts and cutting points for minorities and nonminorities if the validation studies indicate that high performers from either group (minority or nonminority) score lower (or higher) on the test.
22. In employment testing, bias has a precise meaning. Specifically, "bias is said to exist when a test makes systematic errors in measurement or prediction." Murphy and Davidshofer, *Psychological Testing*, p. 303.
23. Ibid., p. 305.
24. Herman Aguinis, Steven Culpepper, and Charles Pierce, "Revival of Test Bias Research in Preemployment Testing," *Journal of Applied Psychology* 95, no. 4 (2010), p. 648.
25. Robert Gatewood and Hubert Feild, *Human Resource Selection* (Mason, OH: South-Western, Cengage Learning, 2008), p. 243.
26. Bill Leonard, "Wanted: Shorter Time to Hire," *HR Magazine*, November 2011, pp. 49–52.
27. This is based on Dave Zielinski, "Effective Assessments," *HR Magazine*, January 2011, pp. 61–64.
28. Sarah Gale, "Three Companies Cut Turnover with Tests," *Workforce*, Spring 2002, pp. 66–69.
29. The Uniform Guidelines say, "Employers should ensure that tests and selection procedures are not adopted casually by managers who know little about these processes … no test or selection procedure should be implemented without an understanding of its effectiveness and limitations for the organization, its appropriateness for a specific job, and whether it can be appropriately administered and scored."
30. Phillips and Gully, *Strategic Staffing*, p. 220.
31. Ibid., p. 220.
32. www.uniformguidelines.com/qandaprint.html, accessed July 19, 2013. Conversely, validating a test that suffers from adverse impact may not be enough. Under the Uniform Guidelines, the employer should also find an equally valid *but less adversely impacting* alternative.
33. A complete discussion of the APA's "Ethical Principles of Psychologists and Code of Conduct" is beyond this book's text's scope. But points it addresses include competence, integrity, respect for people's dignity, nondiscrimination, and sexual harassment. From "Ethical Principles of Psychologists and Code of Conduct," *American Psychologist* 47 (1992), pp. 1597–1611; and www.apa.org/ethics/code/index.aspx, accessed September 9, 2011.
34. Mendelsohn and Morrison, "The Right to Privacy in the Work Place," p. 22.
35. Kenneth Sovereign, *Personnel Law* (Upper Saddle River, NJ: Prentice Hall, 1999), pp. 204–206.
36. "One-Third of Job Applicants Flunked Basic Literacy and Math Tests Last Year, American Management Association Survey Finds," *American Management Association*, www.amanet.org/press/amanews/bjp2001.htm, accessed January 11, 2008.
37. Ibid. See also Alison Wolf and Andrew Jenkins, "Explaining Greater Test Use for Selection: The Role of HR Professionals in a World of Expanding Regulation," *Human Resource Management Journal* 16, no. 2 (2006), pp. 193–213.
38. Steffanie Wilk and Peter Capelli, "Understanding the Determinants of Employer Use of Selection Methods," *Personnel Psychology* 56 (2003), p. 117.
39. Kevin Hart, "Not Wanted: Thieves," *HR Magazine*, April 2008, p. 119.
40. Sarah Needleman, "Businesses Say Theft by Their Workers Is Up," *Wall Street Journal*, December 11, 2008, p. B8.
41. Except as noted, this is based on Laurence Siegel and Irving Lane, *Personnel and Organizational Psychology* (Burr Ridge, IL: McGraw-Hill, 1982), pp. 170–185. See also Cabot Jaffee, "Measurement of Human Potential," *Employment Relations Today* 17, no. 2 (Summer 2000), pp. 15–27; Maureen Patterson, "Overcoming the Hiring Crunch; Tests Deliver Informed Choices," *Employment Relations Today* 27, no. 3 (Fall 2000), pp. 77–88; Kathryn Tyler, "Put Applicants' Skills to the Test," *HR Magazine*, January 2000, p. 74; Murphy and Davidshofer, *Psychological Testing*, pp. 215–403; Elizabeth Schoenfelt and Leslie Pedigo, "A Review of Court Decisions on Cognitive Ability Testing, 1992–2004," *Review of Public Personnel Administration* 25, no. 3 (2005), pp. 271–287.
42. See, for example, Paul Agnello, Rachel Ryan, and Kenneth Yusko, "Implications of Modern Intelligence Research for Assessing Intelligence in the Workplace," *Human Resource Management Review* 25, no. 1 (2015), pp. 47–55; and C. A. Scherbaum and H. W. Goldstein, "Intelligence and the Modern World of Work," *Human Resource Management Review* 25, no. 1, March 2015, pp. 1–3.
43. Norman Henderson, "Predicting Long-Term Firefighter Performance from Cognitive and Physical Ability Measures," *Personnel Psychology* 60, no. 3 (2010), pp. 999–1039.
44. As an example, results of meta-analyses in one study indicated that isometric strength tests were valid predictors of both supervisory ratings of physical performance and performance on work simulations. See Barry R. Blakley, Miguel Quinones, Marnie Swerdlin Crawford, and I. Ann Jago, "The Validity of Isometric Strength Tests," *Personnel Psychology* 47 (1994), pp. 247–274; and www.military.com/military-fitness/marine-corps-fitness-requirements/marine-corps-fitness-test, accessed October 4, 2011.
45. William Wagner, "All Skill, No Finesse," *Workforce*, June 2000, pp. 108–116. See also, for example, James Diefendorff and Kajal Mehta, "The Relations of Motivational Traits with Workplace Deviance," *Journal of Applied Psychology* 92, no. 4 (2007), pp. 967–977.
46. See, for example, Joyce Hogan et al., "Personality Measurement, Faking, and Employee Selection," *Journal of Applied Psychology* 92, no. 5 (2007), pp. 1270–1285; Colin Gill and Gerard Hodgkinson, "Development and Validation of the Five Factor Model Questionnaire (FFMQ): An Adjectival-Based Personality Inventory for Use in Occupational Settings," *Personnel Psychology* 60 (2007), pp. 731–766; and Lisa Penney and Emily Witt, "A Review of Personality and Performance: Identifying Boundaries, Contingencies, and Future Research Directions," *Human Resource Management Review* 20, no. 1 (2011), pp. 297–310.
47. Timothy Judge et al., "Personality and Leadership: A Qualitative and Quantitative Review," *Journal of Applied Psychology* 87, no. 4 (2002), p. 765.
48. www.myersbriggsreports.com/?gcli =CK71m6rE-h6ACFVZS2godDEj gkw, accessed August 21, 2014.
49. Ibid.
50. L. A. Witt et al., "The Interactive Effects of Conscientiousness and Agreeableness on Job Performance," *Journal of Applied Psychology* 87, no. 1 (2002), pp. 164–169.
51. Timothy Judge and Remus Ilies, "Relationship of Personality to Performance Motivation: A Meta Analytic Review," *Journal of Applied Psychology* 87, no. 4 (2002), pp. 797–807.
52. Murray Barrick et al., "Personality and Job Performance: Test of the Immediate Effects of Motivation Among Sales Representatives," *Journal of Applied Psychology* 87, no. 1 (2002), p. 43.
53. Charles Sarchione et al., "Prediction of Dysfunctional Job Behaviors Among Law-Enforcement Officers," *Journal of Applied Psychology* 83, no. 6 (1998), pp. 904–912. See also W. A. Scroggins et al., "Psychological Testing in Personnel Selection, Part III: The Resurgence of Personality Testing," *Public Personnel Management* 38, no. 1 (Spring 2009), pp. 67–77.
54. Paula Caligiuri, "The Big Five Personality Characteristics as

Predictors of Expatriate Desire to Terminate the Assignment and Supervisor Rated Performance," *Personnel Psychology* 53 (2000), pp. 67–68. For some other examples, see Ryan Zimmerman, "Understanding the Impact of Personality Traits on Individuals' Turnover Decisions: A Meta-Analytic Path Model," *Personnel Psychology* 60, no. 1 (2008), pp. 309–348.

55. Adapted from www.kozaigroup.com/-inventories.php, accessed March 3, 2008; and http://kozaigroup.com/inventories/the-global competencies-inventory-gci/what is-the-gci/, accessed August 21, 2014.
56. Diane Cadrain, "Reassess Personality Tests After Court Case," *HR Magazine* 50, no. 9 (September 2005), p. 30.
57. Frederick Morgeson et al., "Reconsidering the Use of Personality Tests in Personnel Selection Contexts," *Personnel Psychology* 60 (2007), p. 683; and Frederick Morgeson et al., "Are We Getting Fooled Again? Coming to Terms with Limitations in the Use of Personality Tests for Personnel Selection," *Personnel Psychology* 60 (2007), p. 1046.
58. Robert Tett and Neil Christiansen, "Personality Tests at the Crossroads: A Response to Morgeson, Campion, Dipboye, Hollenbeck, Murphy, and Schmitt," *Personnel Psychology* 60 (2007), p. 967. See also Deniz Ones et al., "In Support of Personality Assessment in Organizational Settings," *Personnel Psychology* 60 (2007), pp. 995–1027.
59. See also Edwin A. J. van Hoot and Marise Ph. Born, "Intentional Response Distortion on Personality Tests: Using Eye Tracking to Understand Response Processes When Thinking," *Journal of Applied Psychology* 97, no. 2 (2012), pp. 301–316.
60. Chad H. Van Iddeking et al., "Are You Interested? A Meta-Analysis of Relations Between Vocational Interests and Employee Performance and Turnover," *Journal of Applied Psychology* 96, no 6 (2011), pp. 1167–1194.
61. Dracos Iliescu et al., "Vocational Fit and Counterproductive Work Behaviors: A Self-Regulation Perspective," *Journal of Applied Psychology* 100, no. 1 (2015), pp. 21–39.
62. Ed Frauenheim, "More Companies Go with Online Test to Fill in the Blanks," *Workforce Management*, May 2011, p. 12.
63. John Bateson et al., "When Hiring, First Test, and Then Interview," *Harvard Business Review*, November 2013, p. 34.
64. Requiring job seekers to complete prescreening questionnaires and screening selected applicants out on this basis carries legal and business consequences. See, for example, Lisa Harpe, "Designing an Effective Employment Prescreening Program," *Employment Relations Today* 32, no. 3 (Fall 2005), pp. 41–43.
65. www.iphonetypingtest.com, accessed March 23, 2009.
66. See, for example, Meg Breslin, "Can You Handle Rejection?" *Workforce Management*, October 2012, pp. 32–36.
67. Ed Frauenheim, "Personality Tests Adapt to the Times," *Workforce Management*, February 2010, p. 4.
68. Except as noted, this is based on Dave Zielinski, "Effective Assessments," *HR Magazine*, January 2011, pp. 61–64.
69. Wright, "At Google, It Takes a Village to Hire an Employee."
70. Ibid.
71. Jeff Weekley and Casey Jones, "Video-Based Situational Testing," *Personnel Psychology* 50 (1997), p. 25.
72. Elaine Pulakos, *Selection Assessment Methods*, SHRM Foundation, 2005, p. 14.
73. However, studies suggest that blacks may be somewhat less likely to do well on work sample tests than are whites. See, for example, Philip Roth, Philip Bobko, and Lynn McFarland, "A Meta-Analysis of Work Sample Test Validity: Updating and Integrating Some Classic Literature," *Personnel Psychology* 58, no. 4 (Winter 2005), pp. 1009–1037; and Philip Roth et al., "Work Sample Tests in Personnel Selection: A Meta-Analysis of Black–White Differences in Overall and Exercise Scores," *Personnel Psychology* 60, no. 1 (2008), pp. 637–662.
74. Siegel and Lane, *Personnel and Organizational Psychology*, pp. 182–183.
75. Quoted from Deborah Whetzel and Michael McDaniel, "Situational Judgment Tests: An Overview of Current Research," *Human Resource Management Review* 19 (2009), pp. 188–202.
76. "Help Wanted—and Found," *Fortune*, October 2, 2006, p. 40. See also Brian Hoffman et al., "Exercises and Dimensions Are the Currency of Assessment Centers," *Personnel Psychology* 60, no. 4 (2011), pp. 351–395.
77. Annette Spychalski, Miguel Quinones, Barbara Gaugler, and Katja Pohley, "A Survey of Assessment Center Practices in Organizations in the United States," *Personnel Psychology* 50, no. 1 (Spring 1997), pp. 71–90. See also Winfred Arthur Jr. et al., "A Meta Analysis of the Criterion Related Validity of Assessment Center Data Dimensions," *Personnel Psychology* 56 (2003), pp. 124–154; and Brian Hoffman et al., "Exercises and Dimensions Are the Currency of Assessment Centers," *Personnel Psychology* 60, no. 4 (2011), pp. 351–395.
78. See, for example, John Meriac et al., "Further Evidence for the Validity of Assessment Center Dimensions: A Meta-Analysis of the Incremental Criterion-Related Validity of Dimension Ratings," *Journal of Applied Psychology* 93, no. 5 (2008), pp. 1042–1052.
79. Weekley and Jones, "Video-Based Situational Testing," p. 26.
80. Catherine Rampell, "Your Next Job Application Could Involve a Video Game," *New York Times*, January 25, 2014.
81. Ibid., p. 30.
82. Robert Grossman, "Made from Scratch," *HR Magazine*, April 2002, pp. 44–53.
83. Coleman Peterson, "Employee Retention, the Secrets Behind Wal-Mart's Successful Hiring Policies," *Human Resource Management* 44, no. 1 (Spring 2005), pp. 85–88. See also Murray Barrick and Ryan Zimmerman, "Reducing Voluntary, Avoidable Turnover Through Selection," *Journal of Applied Psychology* 90, no. 1 (2005), pp. 159–166.
84. James Breaugh, "Employee Recruitment: Current Knowledge and Important Areas for Future Research," *Human Resource Management Review* 18 (2008), pp. 106–107.
85. Phillips and Gully, *Strategic Staffing*, p. 223.
86. Brian J. Hoffman, John W. Michel, and Kevin J. Williams, "On the Predictive Efficiency of Past Performance and Physical Ability: The Case of the National Football League," *Human Performance* 24, no. 2 (2011), pp. 158–172.
87. Lara Walsh, "To Tell the Truth: Catching Tall Tales on Résumés," *Workforce*, December 2014, p. 10.
88. "Resume Fakery Is Rampant, Global; Employer Caution Needed, *Bloomberg BNA Bulletin to Management*, November 4, 2014, p. 351.
89. "Internet, E-Mail Monitoring Common at Most Workplaces," *BNA Bulletin to Management*, February 1, 2001, p. 34. See also "Are Your Background Checks Balanced? Experts Identify Concerns over Verifications," *BNA Bulletin to Management*, May 13, 2004, p. 153.
90. Merry Mayer, "Background Checks in Focus," *HR Magazine*, January 2002, pp. 59–62; and Carroll Lachnit, "Protecting People and Profits with Background Checks," *Workforce*, February 2002, p. 52.
91. Matthew Heller, "Special Report: Background Checking," *Workforce Management*, March 3, 2008, pp. 35–54.
92. Bill Roberts, "Close-up on Screening," *HR Magazine*, February 2011, pp. 23–29.
93. Seymour Adler, "Verifying a Job Candidate's Background: The State of Practice in a Vital Human Resources Activity," *Review of Business* 15, no. 2 (Winter 1993), p. 6.
94. Heller, "Special Report: Background Checking," p. 35.
95. This is based on Samuel Greengard, "Have Gangs Invaded Your Workplace?" *Personnel Journal*, February 1996, pp. 47–48.
96. Dori Meinert, "Seeing Behind the Mask," *HR Magazine* 56, no. 2 (February 2011), www.shrm.org/Publications/hrmagazine/EditorialContent/2011/0211/Pages/0211meinert.aspx, accessed August 20, 2011.
97. Ibid., p. 55.
98. For example, one U.S. Court of Appeals found that bad references might be grounds for a suit when they are retaliations for the employee having previously filed an EEOC claim. "Negative Reference Leads to Charge of Retaliation," *BNA Bulletin to Management*, October 21, 2004, p. 344.
99. *Kehr v. Consolidated Freightways of Delaware*, Docket No. 86–2126, July 15, 1987, U.S. Seventh Circuit Court of Appeals. Discussed in *Commerce Clearing House, Ideas and Trends*, October 16, 1987, p. 165.
100. James Bell, James Castagnera, and Jane Patterson Young, "Employment References: Do You Know the Law?" *Personnel Journal* 63, no. 2 (February 1984), pp. 32–36. In order to demonstrate defamation, several elements must be present: (a) the defamatory statement must have been communicated to another party; (b) the statement must be a false statement of fact; (c) injury to reputation must have occurred; and (d) the employer must not be protected under qualified or absolute privilege. For a discussion, see Ryan and Lasek, "Negligent Hiring and Defamation," p. 307. See also James Burns Jr., "Employment References: Is There a Better Way?" *Employee Relations Law Journal* 23, no. 2 (Fall 1997), pp. 157–168.
101. For additional information, see Lawrence E. Dube Jr., "Employment References and the Law," *Personnel Journal* 65, no.

2 (February 1986), pp. 87–91. See also Mickey Veich, "Uncover the Resume Ruse," *Security Management*, October 1994, pp. 75–76.
102. "Undercover Callers Tip Off Job Seekers to Former Employers' Negative References," *BNA Bulletin to Management*, May 27, 1999, p. 161.
103. Eileen Zimmerman, "A Subtle Reference Trap for Unwary Employers," *Workforce*, April 2003, p. 22.
104. Michelle Goodman, "Reference Checks Go Tech," *Workforce Management*, May 2012, pp. 26–28.
105. Alan Finder, "When a Risqué Online Persona Undermines a Chance for a Job," *New York Times*, June 11, 2006, p. 1.
106. Natasha Singer, "Funny, They Don't Look Like My References," *New York Times*, November 9, 2014, p. 4.
107. "Practitioners Discuss Various Pitfalls of Using Social Media to Vet Job Applicants," *BNA Bulletin to Management*, November 1, 2011, pp. 345–346.
108. Rita Zeidner, "How Deep Can You Probe?" *HR Magazine*, October 1, 2007, pp. 57–62.
109. "Web Searches on Applicants Are Potentially Perilous for Employers," *BNA Bulletin to Management*, October 14, 2008, p. 335.
110. "Maryland Is First State to Restrict Employer Demands for Employee, Applicant Passwords," *BNA Bulletin to Management*, May 8, 2012, p. 145.
111. "Practitioners Discuss Various Pitfalls of Using Social Media to Vet Job Applicants," www.bna.com/practitioners-discuss-various-n12884904116/, accessed July 4, 2014.
112. Max Mihelich, "More Background Noise," *Workforce*, September 2014, pp. 52–55.
113. Stephanie Clifford and Jessica Silver-Greenberg, "Retailers Track Employee Thefts in Vast Databases," *New York Times*, April 4, 2013, pp. A1, A16.
114. Jeffrey M. Hahn, "Pre-Employment Information Services: Employers Beware?" *Employee Relations Law Journal* 17, no. 1 (Summer 1991), pp. 45–69. See also "Pre-Employment Background Screenings Have Evolved, but So Have Liability Risks," *BNA Bulletin to Management*, November 1, 2005, p. 345.
115. "Employer Concerns About Liability Loom as Push for Ban the Box Policies Spread," *Bloomberg BNA Bulletin to Management*, August 19, 2014, pp. 257–258.
116. Under California law, applicants or employees must have the option of requesting a copy of the report regardless of action.
117. Teresa Butler Stivarius, "Background Checks: Steps to Basic Compliance in a Multistate Environment," *Society for Human Resource Management Legal Report*, March–April 2003, pp. 1–8.
118. See, for example, Dori Meinert, "Search and Verify," *HR Magazine*, December 2012, pp. 37–41.
119. "Background Check Firm Pays $2.6 Million Penalty," *Workforce Management*, October 2012, p. 12.
120. See Paul Taylor et al., "Dimensionality and the Validity of a Structured Telephone Reference Check Procedure," *Personnel Psychology* 57 (2004), pp. 745–772, for a discussion of checking other work habits and traits.
121. "Getting Applicant Information Difficult but Still Necessary," *BNA Bulletin to Management*, February 5, 1999, p. 63. See also Robert Howie and Laurence Shapiro, "Pre-Employment Criminal Background Checks: Why Employers Should Look Before They Leap," *Employee Relations Law Journal*, Summer 2002, pp. 63–77.
122. Polygraphs are still widely used in law enforcement and reportedly are quite useful. See, for example, Laurie Cohen, "The Polygraph Paradox," *Wall Street Journal*, March 22, 2008, p. A1.
123. After a tragedy in Manhattan several years ago, more parents began turning to private investigators and industrial psychologists to conduct checks, including polygraph tests, on prospective nannies. Gabrielle Birkner, "Nanny Interviews Get More Aggressive," *Wall Street Journal*, December 15–16, 2012, pp. A19, A21.
124. John Jones and William Terris, "Post-Polygraph Selection Techniques," *Recruitment Today*, May–June 1989, pp. 25–31.
125. Norma Fritz, "In Focus: Honest Answers—Post Polygraph," *Personnel*, April 1989, p. 8. See also Richard White Jr., "Ask Me No Questions, Tell Me No Lies: Examining the Uses and Misuses of the Polygraph," *Public Personnel Management* 30, no. 4 (Winter 2001), pp. 483–493.
126. A recent meta-analysis concluded that "relations between integrity tests and measures of job performance tend to be rather weak." Chad H. Van Iddeking et al., "The Criterion Related Validity of Integrity Tests: An Updated Meta-Analysis," *Journal of Applied Psychology* 97, no. 3 (2012), pp. 499–530, a point disputed by a panel of test publishers. William G. Harris et al., "Test Publishers' Perspective on 'An Updated Meta-Analysis': Comment on Van Iddeking, Ross, Raymark, and Odle-Dusseau (2012)," *Journal of Applied Psychology* 97, no. 3 (2012), pp. 531–536.
127. John Bernardin and Donna Cooke, "Validity of an Honesty Test in Predicting Theft Among Convenience Store Employees," *Academy of Management Journal* 36, no. 5 (1993), pp. 1097–1108.
128. Bill Roberts, "Your Cheating Heart," *HR Magazine*, June 2011, pp. 55–57.
129. These are based on "Divining Integrity Through Interviews," *BNA Bulletin to Management*, June 4, 1987, p. 184; and *Commerce Clearing House, Ideas and Trends*, December 29, 1998, pp. 222–223. See also Bridget A. Styers and Kenneth S. Shultz, "Perceived Reasonableness of Employment Testing Accommodations for Persons with Disabilities," *Public Personnel Management* 38, no. 3 (Fall 2009), pp. 71–91.
130. Ibid.
131. www.clearfit.com/resource-center/hiring-process/how-to-spot-someone-lying-in-an-interview/, accessed February 19, 2014.
132. www.forbes.com/sites/carolkinseygoman/2013/05/20/7-tips-for-spotting-liars-at-work/, accessed February 19, 2014.
133. Bill Leonard, "Reading Employees," *HR Magazine*, April 1999, pp. 67–73.
134. Ibid.
135. This is based on Kyle Stock, "Wary Investors Turn to Lie Pros," *Wall Street Journal*, December 29, 2010, p. C3.
136. Mick Haus, "Pre-Employment Physicals and the ADA," *Safety and Health*, February 1992, pp. 64–65. See also Bridget A. Styers and Kenneth S. Shultz, "Perceived Reasonableness of Employment Testing Accommodations for Persons with Disabilities," *Public Personnel Management* 38, no. 3 (Fall 2009), pp. 71–91.
137. Scott MacDonald, Samantha Wells, and Richard Fry, "The Limitations of Drug Screening in the Workplace," *International Labor Review* 132, no. 1 (1993), p. 98. Not all agree that drug testing is worthwhile. See, for example, Veronica I. Luzzi et al., "Analytic Performance of Immunoassays for Drugs of Abuse Below Established Cutoff Values," *Clinical Chemistry* 50 (2004), pp. 717–722.
138. For example, www.questdiagnostics.com/home/companies/employer/drug-screening/testing-reasons/pre-employment.html, accessed August 22, 2014.
139. Rita Zeidner, "Putting Drug Screening to the Test," *HR Magazine*, November 2010, p. 26.
140. Diane Cadrain, "Are Your Employees' Drug Tests Accurate?" *HR Magazine*, January 2003, pp. 40–45.
141. Chris Berka and Courtney Poignand, "Hair Follicle Testing—An Alternative to Urinalysis for Drug Abuse Screening," *Employee Relations Today*, Winter 1991–1992, pp. 405–409; for an example, see www.americanscreeningcorp.com/default.aspx, accessed October 8, 2011.
142. MacDonald et al., "The Limitations of Drug Screening," pp. 102–104.
143. R. J. McCunney, "Drug Testing: Technical Complications of a Complex Social Issue," *American Journal of Industrial Medicine* 15, no. 5 (1989), pp. 589–600; discussed in MacDonald et al., "The Limitations of Drug Screening," p. 102.
144. MacDonald et al., "The Limitations of Drug Screening," p. 103.
145. This is based on Ann M. O'Neill, "Legal Issues Presented by Hair Follicle Testing," *Employee Relations Today*, Winter 1991–1992, pp. 411–415.
146. Ibid., p. 411.
147. Ibid., p. 413.
148. Richard Lisko, "A Manager's Guide to Drug Testing," *Security Management* 38, no. 8 (August 1994), p. 92. See also Randall Kesselring and Jeffrey Pittman, "Drug Testing Laws and Employment Injuries," *Journal of Labor Research*, Spring 2002, pp. 293–301.
149. Michael A. McDaniel, "Does Pre-Employment Drug Use Predict On-the-Job Suitability?" *Personnel Psychology* 41, no. 4 (Winter 1988), pp. 717–729.
150. *Exxon Corp. v. Esso Workers Union, Inc.*, CA1#96–2241, 7/8/97; discussed in *BNA Bulletin to Management*, August 7, 1997, p. 249.
151. For the form, see www.uscis.gov/files/form/i-9.pdf, accessed October 4, 2011.
152. "More Than 500,000 Employers Are Now Enrolled in E-Verify Program," *Bloomberg BNA*

Bulletin to Management, January 28, 2014, p. 27.

153. "President Bush Signs Executive Order: Federal Contractors Must Use E-Verify," *BNA Bulletin to Management*, June 17, 2008, p. 193.
154. www.dhs.gov/files/programs/gc_1185221678150.shtm, accessed February 21, 2010. Many small business owners in particular find that the new E-Verify system makes it more difficult to fill open positions. Angus Loten, Sarah Needleman, and Adam Janofsky, "Small Business Has a Beef with E-Verify," *Wall Street Journal,* July 25, 2013, p. B6.
155. Davis Zielinski, "Automating I-9 Verification," *HR Magazine*, May 2011, pp. 57–60. Employees themselves can use E-Verify to confirm their U.S. work authorization status. "New Tools Will Aid Employers During Verification Process," *BNA Bulletin to Management*, March 15, 2011.
156. "As E-Verify, No Match Rules, I-9 Evolve, Employers Need to Stay on Top of Issues," *BNA Bulletin Management*, April 15, 2008, p. 121. For the latest I-9 form see www.uscis.gov/files/form/i-9.pdf, accessed September 7, 2013.
157. Note that the acceptable documents on page 3 of the previous I-9 form did not reflect the most current list of acceptable documents for confirming identity and eligibility. For the latest I-9 form see www.uscis.gov/files/form/i-9.pdf, accessed September 7, 2013.
158. "Identity Theft Remains Top Challenge for E-Verify," *BNA Bulletin to Management*, April 19, 2011, p. 121.
159. Susan Ladika, "Trouble on the Hiring Front," *HR Magazine*, October 2006, pp. 56–62.
160. Russell Gerbman, "License to Work," *HR Magazine*, June 2000, pp. 151–160; the I-9 form clearly states that the employer may not discriminate. See www.uscis.gov/files/form/i-9.pdf, accessed October 4, 2011.

7

Interviewing Candidates

Neil Setchfield/Getty Images

LEARNING OBJECTIVES

7-1 List and give examples of the main types of selection interviews.

7-2 List and explain the main errors that can undermine an interview's usefulness.

7-3 Define a structured situational interview and explain how to design and conduct effective selection interviews.

7-4 Discuss how to use employee selection methods to improve employee engagement.

7-5 List the main points to know about developing and extending the actual job offer.

When it comes to hiring, Urban Outfitters knows just what it's looking for.[2] The lifestyle retailer, with over 200 stores in the United States, Canada, and Europe, built its strategy around fostering a culture of creativity and individuality within its stores. That means that maintaining its unique store environment requires employees that match its core values of community, pride, creativity, and respect. The question is, how do you find and attract such applicants, while controlling hiring costs in the competitive retail industry?

WHERE ARE WE NOW ...

Chapter 6 discussed important tools managers use to select employees. Now we'll turn to one of these tools—the employment interview. The main topics we'll cover include types of interviews, things that undermine interviewing's usefulness, designing and conducting effective selection interviews, using a total selection process to improve employee engagement, and making the offer. In Chapter 8, we'll turn to training the new employee.

If the interview is just one of several selection tools, why devote a whole chapter to it? Because interviews are the most widely used selection procedure, and most people aren't nearly as good at interviewing as they think they are.[1]

Basic Types of Interviews

LEARNING OBJECTIVE 7-1
List and give examples of the main types of selection interviews.

Managers use several interviews at work, such as performance appraisal interviews and exit interviews. A *selection interview* (the focus of this chapter) is a selection procedure designed to predict future job performance based on applicants' oral responses to oral inquiries.[3] Many techniques in this chapter also apply to appraisal and exit interviews. However, we'll postpone discussions of those two interviews until later chapters.

There are several ways to conduct selection interviews. For example, we can classify selection interviews according to

1. How *structured* they are
2. Their "content"—the *types of questions* they contain
3. How the firm *administers* the interviews (for instance, one-on-one or via a committee)

Each has pros and cons. We'll look at each.

Structured Versus Unstructured Interviews

unstructured (or nondirective) interview
An unstructured conversational-style interview in which the interviewer pursues points of interest as they come up in response to questions.

structured (or directive) interview
An interview following a set sequence of questions.

First, most interviews vary in the degree to which the interviewer structures the interview process.[4] In **unstructured (or nondirective) interviews**, the manager follows no set format. A few questions might be specified in advance, but they're usually not, and there is seldom a formal guide for scoring "right" or "wrong" answers. Typical questions here might include, for instance, "Tell me about yourself," "Why do you think you'd do a good job here?" and "What would you say are your main strengths and weaknesses?" Some describe this type of interview as little more than a general conversation.[5]

At the other extreme, in **structured (or directive) interviews**, the employer lists questions ahead of time, and may even weight possible alternative answers for appropriateness.[6] McMurray's Patterned Interview was one early example. The interviewer followed a printed form to ask a series of questions, such as "How was the person's present job obtained?" Comments printed beneath the questions (such as "Has he/she shown self-reliance in getting his/her jobs?") then guide the interviewer in evaluating the answers. Some experts still restrict the term *structured interview* to interviews like these, which are based on carefully selected job-related questions with predetermined answers.

In practice, interview structure is a matter of degree. Sometimes the manager may just want to ensure he or she has a set list of questions to ask so as to avoid skipping any questions. Here, he or she might choose questions from a list like that in Figure 7-3 (page 215). The structured interview guide in Figure 7A-1 (pages 227–229) illustrates a more structured approach. As another example, the Department of Homeland Security uses the structured guide in Figure 7-1 to help screen Coast Guard officer candidates. It contains a formal candidate rating procedure, and also enables geographically dispersed interviewers to complete the form via the Web.[7]

Structured interviews are generally best.[8] In such interviews, all interviewers generally ask all applicants the same questions. Partly because of this, these interviews tend to be more consistent, reliable, and valid. Having a standardized list of questions can also help less talented interviewers conduct better interviews. Standardizing the interview also enhances job relatedness (we'll see that the questions chosen tend to provide insights into how the person will actually do the job), reduces overall subjectivity and thus the potential for bias, and may "enhance the ability to withstand legal challenge."[9] However, blindly following a structured format may not provide enough opportunity to pursue points of interest. The interviewer should always have an opportunity to ask follow-up questions and pursue points of interest as they develop. We'll see how to write a structured interview later in this chapter.

FIGURE 7-1 Officer Programs Applicant Interview Form

Source: From Officer Programs Applicant Interview Form CG_5527 from http://www.uscg.mil/forms/cg/CG_5527.pdf accessed August 29, 2015.

U.S. Department of Homeland Security CG-5527 (06-04)	**Officer Programs Applicant Interview Form**	1. Date:

2. Name of Applicant (Last, First, MI)

3. **Overall Impression:** Compare this applicant to others you have interviewed or known. (Note: Scores of 4 through 7 constitute a recommendation for selection.)

NOT RECOMMENDED			RECOMMENDED			
Unsatisfactory 1☐	Limited Potential 2☐	Fair Performer 3☐	Good Performer 4☐	Excellent Performer 5☐	Exceptional Performer 6☐	Distinguished Performer 7☐

Comments:

4. **Performance of Duties:** Measures an applicant's ability to manage and to get things done.

Unsatisfactory	Limited Potential	Fair Performer	Good Performer	Excellent Performer	Exceptional Performer	Distinguished Performer
1☐	2☐	3☐	4☐	5☐	6☐	7☐

Comments:

5. **Communication Skills:** Measures an applicant's ability to communicate in a positive, clear, and convincing manner.

Unsatisfactory	Limited Potential	Fair Performer	Good Performer	Excellent Performer	Exceptional Performer	Distinguished Performer
1☐	2☐	3☐	4☐	5☐	6☐	7☐

Comments:

6. **Names of Board Members**	7. **Rank**	8. **Command/Unit**	9. **Signature**	10. **Career Total of Interviews Conducted**

PREVIOUS EDITIONS ARE OBSOLETE *CONTINUED ON REVERSE*

Reset

Interview Content (What Types of Questions to Ask)

We can also classify interviews based on the "content" or the types of questions interviewers ask. Many interviewers ask relatively unfocused questions, such as "What do you want to be doing in 5 years?" Questions like these generally do not provide much insight into how the person will do on the job. That is why *situational, behavioral*, and *job-related* questions are best.

situational interview
A series of job-related questions that focus on how the candidate would behave in a given situation.

In a **situational interview**, you ask the candidate what his or her behavior *would be* in a given situation.[10] For example, ask a supervisory candidate how he or she would act in response to a subordinate coming to work late 3 days in a row.

behavioral interview
A series of job-related questions that focus on how the candidate reacted to actual situations in the past.

Whereas situational interviews ask applicants to describe how they *would* react to a hypothetical situation today or tomorrow, **behavioral interviews** ask applicants

FIGURE 7-1 *Continued*

Page 2 - CG-5527 (06-04)

11. **Leadership Skills:** Measures an applicant's ability to support, develop, direct, and influence others in performing work.

Unsatisfactory	Limited Potential	Fair Performer	Good Performer	Excellent Performer	Exceptional Performer	Distinguished Performer
1☐	2☐	3☐	4☐	5☐	6☐	7☐

Comments:

12. **Personal and Professional Qualities:** Measures qualities which illustrate the applicant's character.

Unsatisfactory	Limited Potential	Fair Performer	Good Performer	Excellent Performer	Exceptional Performer	Distinguished Performer
1☐	2☐	3☐	4☐	5☐	6☐	7☐

Comments:

Reset

to describe *how they reacted* to actual situations in the past.[11] *Situational* questions start with phrases such as, "Suppose you were faced with the following situation.... What would you do?" *Behavioral* questions start with phrases like, "Can you think of a time when.... What did you do?"[12] In one variant, Vanguard uses an interviewing technique it calls STAR. Vanguard managers ask interviewees about a particular situation (S) or task (T) they faced to uncover the actions (A) the candidates took, and the results (R) of their actions.[13] Behavioral interviews are increasingly used.[14]

When Citizen's Banking Corporation in Flint, Michigan, found that 31 of the 50 people in its call center quit in one year, the center's head switched to behavioral interviews. Many who left did so because they didn't enjoy irate questions from clients. So she no longer tries to predict how candidates will act based on asking them if they want to work with angry clients. Instead, she asks behavioral questions like, "Tell me about a time you were speaking with an irate person, and how you turned the situation around." This makes it harder to fool the interviewer; only four people left in the following year.[15]

Bain & Company uses case interviews as part of its candidate selection process. By having candidates explain how they would address the case "client's" problems, the case interview combines elements of behavioral and situational questioning to provide a more realistic assessment of the candidate's consulting skills.

job-related interview
A series of job-related questions that focus on relevant past job-related behaviors.

stress interview
An interview in which the applicant is made uncomfortable by a series of often rude questions. This technique helps identify hypersensitive applicants and those with low or high stress tolerance.

OTHER TYPES OF QUESTIONS In a **job-related interview**, the interviewer asks applicants questions about job-relevant past experiences. The questions here don't revolve around hypothetical or actual situations or scenarios. Instead, the interviewer asks questions such as, "Which courses did you like best in business school?" The aim is to draw conclusions about, say, the candidate's ability to handle the financial aspects of the job in question.

There are other, lesser-used types of questions. In a **stress interview**, the interviewer seeks to make the applicant uncomfortable with occasionally rude questions. The aim is supposedly to spot sensitive applicants and those with low (or high) stress tolerance. Thus, a candidate for a customer relations manager position who obligingly mentions having had four jobs in the past 2 years might be told that frequent job changes reflect irresponsible and immature behavior. If the applicant then responds with a reasonable explanation of why the job changes were necessary, the interviewer might pursue another topic. On the other hand, if the formerly tranquil applicant reacts explosively, the interviewer might deduce that the person has a low tolerance for stress.

The stress interview's invasive and ethically dubious nature demands that the interviewer be both skilled in its use and sure the job really requires handling stress. This is definitely not an approach for amateur interrogators or for those without the skills to keep the interview under control.

Puzzle questions are popular. Recruiters see how candidates think under pressure. For example, an interviewer at Microsoft asked a tech service applicant this: "Mike and Todd have $21 between them. Mike has $20 more than Todd does. How much money has Mike, and how much money has Todd?"[16] (The answer is two paragraphs below.)

HR in Practice at the Hotel Paris As an experienced HR professional, Lisa knew that the company's new testing program would go only so far. To see how the Hotel Paris created a new interview process, see the case on page 223.

How Should We Conduct the Interview?

Employers also administer interviews in various ways: *one-on-one or by a panel of interviewers, sequentially or all at once, computerized or personally,* or *online.*

unstructured sequential interview
An interview in which each interviewer forms an independent opinion after asking different questions.

structured sequential interview
An interview in which the applicant is interviewed sequentially by several persons; each rates the applicant on a standard form.

Most selection interviews are probably still *one-on-one* and *sequential.* In a one-on-one interview, two people meet alone, and one interviews the other by seeking oral responses to oral inquiries. Employers tend to schedule these interviews *sequentially.* In a *sequential (or serial) interview*, several persons interview the applicant, in sequence, one-on-one, and then make their hiring decision. In an **unstructured sequential interview**, each interviewer generally just asks questions as they come to mind. In a **structured sequential interview**, each interviewer rates the candidates on a standard evaluation form, using standardized questions. The hiring manager then reviews these ratings before deciding whom to hire.[17] (Answer: Mike had $20.50, Todd $0.50.)

panel interview
An interview in which a group of interviewers questions the applicant.

A **panel interview**, also known as a board interview, is an interview conducted by a team of interviewers (usually two to three), who together question each candidate and then combine their ratings of each candidate's answers into a final panel score. This contrasts with the *one-on-one interview* (in which one interviewer meets one candidate) and a *serial interview* (where several interviewers assess a single candidate one-on-one, sequentially).[18]

The panel format enables interviewers to ask follow-up questions, much as reporters do in press conferences. This may elicit more meaningful responses than a series of one-on-one interviews. On the other hand, some candidates find panel interviews more stressful, so they may actually inhibit responses. (An even more stressful variant is the **mass interview**. Here a panel interviews several candidates simultaneously. The panel might pose a problem, and then watches to see which candidate takes the lead in formulating an answer.)

mass interview
A panel interviews several candidates simultaneously.

Whether panel interviews are more or less reliable and valid than sequential interviews depends on how the employer actually does the panel interview. For example, *structured* panel interviews in which members use scoring sheets with descriptive scoring examples for sample answers are more reliable and valid than those that don't. Training panel interviewers may boost interview reliability.[19]

For better or worse, some employers use "speed dating" interviewing. One sent e-mails to all applicants for an advertised position. Four hundred (of 800 applicants) showed up. Over several hours, applicants first mingled with employees, and then (in a so-called "speed dating area") had one-on-one contacts with employees for a few minutes. Based on this, the recruiting team chose 68 candidates for follow-up interviews.[20]

PHONE INTERVIEWS Employers also conduct interviews via phone. Somewhat counterintuitively, these can actually be more useful than face-to-face interviews for judging one's conscientiousness, intelligence, and interpersonal skills. Because they needn't worry about appearance or handshakes, each party can focus on answers. And perhaps candidates—somewhat surprised by an unplanned call from the recruiter—give more spontaneous answers.[21] In one study, interviewers tended to evaluate applicants more favorably in telephone versus face-to-face interviews, particularly where interviewees were less physically attractive. The applicants preferred the face-to-face interviews.[22]

COMPUTER-BASED JOB INTERVIEWS A *computerized selection interview* is one in which a job candidate's oral and/or keyed replies are obtained in response to computerized oral, visual, or written questions and/or situations. Most such interviews present a series of multiple-choice questions regarding background, experience, education, skills, knowledge, and work attitudes. Some confront candidates with realistic scenarios (such as irate customers) to which they must respond.[23]

WEB-BASED VIDEO INTERVIEWS With phone and tablet video functionalities and FaceTime™ and Skype™, Web-based "in-person" interview use is widespread; about 18% of candidates took such interviews in one recent year.[24] With the InterviewStream 360 Video Practice Interview System, college career centers and outplacement firms can have students or job seekers record interviews for their own development and for prospective employers.[25] InterviewStream, Inc., (www.InterviewStream.com) offers employer clients prerecorded and live video interview management systems for prescreening candidates and interviewing remote talent. Or, the client and candidate can use InterviewStream's live videoconference platform for a live interview.[26] Employers including Microsoft use the virtual community Second Life to conduct job interviews. Job seekers create avatars to represent themselves.[27]

For Hilton Worldwide, which recruits in 94 countries, distances often made in-person interviews impractical. Now, online video interviews make it easy for Hilton to do initial screening interviews.[28] Another firm's CEO conducts initial screening interviews via text-only chats or instant messaging because, he says, this reduces potential distractions like gender, ethnicity, and body language.[29]

An online video interview requires little special preparation for employers, but Career FAQs (www.careerfaqs.com.au) lists things that *interviewees* should keep in mind. It's often the obvious things people overlook (for more on how to take interviews, see Appendix 2 to this chapter, page 230):[30]

- ***Look presentable.*** It might seem silly sitting at home wearing a suit, but it could make a difference.
- ***Clean up the room.*** Do not let the interviewer see clutter.
- ***Test first.*** As Career FAQs says, "Five minutes before the video interview is not a good time to realize that your Internet is down…"
- ***Do a dry run.*** Record yourself before the interview to see how you're "coming across."
- ***Relax.*** The golden rule with such interviews is to treat them like face-to-face meetings. Smile, look confident and enthusiastic, make eye contact, and don't shout, but do speak clearly.

TRENDS SHAPING HR: *DIGITAL AND SOCIAL MEDIA*

Today the growing popularity of mobile-based (iPhone or iPad, for instance) interviews is disrupting how job interviewing is done. They enable the interviewee to "do" the interview at his or her leisure from wherever the person wants, and also allow even prescreen interviews to occur directly between hiring managers and job applicants, rather than HR.

The HireVue system is an example.[31] As described at http://hirevue.com/mobile/, the free HireVue tool (available as an app for iPhone, iPad, and iPod) enables interviewees to take their HireVue Interviews

> anytime, anywhere when invited by a potential employer. You can complete your HireVue Digital Interview on your own time, when it works for you, anywhere you have an internet connection....

Candidates, at their convenience, record their responses to the employer's video and written questions. The recruiter then plays back the recorded information and rates the candidate. The employer can arrange for candidates to first respond to several such questions, and then arrange for a set time for a synchronous online interview. Another HireVue tool uses data analysis to examine what the vendor says is more than 15,000 digital interview attributes to predict which candidates are most likely to be top performers and identify which interviewers make the best hiring decisions.[32] The Improving Performance feature illustrates. ■

IMPROVING PERFORMANCE: *The Strategic Context*

Urban Outfitters

Urban Outfitters needs store employees who share its core values of community, pride, creativity, and Respect. The question is, how does it find and attract such applicants, while controlling hiring costs in the competitive retail industry? Because it receives so many applications, the company first used group interviews for selecting sales associates. Retail managers would interview six to eight candidates at once, in a group interview. Store managers didn't think this was a good fit for Urban Outfitter's culture, though.

Urban Outfitters switched to HireVue on-demand interviews in its 200 retail stores. The HireVue system enabled applicants to watch videos about Urban Outfitters and the job, and then to respond in writing and by video to Urban's interview questions and instructions, at their leisure, "on demand." The hiring managers then reviewed the recorded interviews, usually outside of peak business hours when the stores weren't as busy.

The new system reportedly has been a boon to Urban Outfitters. It reduced screening time by 80%, lets store managers process many more applicants, and is preferred by applicants, 90% of whom can do their interviews after hours. The HireVue system also supports Urban Outfitters' strategy. As it says,

> Moving to digital interviewing has transformed our hiring process into a true reflection of the Urban Outfitters culture. Our value in creativity and community and our nonconformist approach now begins with our candidate experience. No other initiative has impacted our hiring teams like digital recruiting has.[33] ■

If your professor has assigned this, go to the Assignments section of **mymanagementlab.com** to complete this discussion.

Talk About It 1: You have to hire dozens of wait staff every year for a new restaurant on Miami Beach. Explain how you would use a HireVue interview, including questions and tasks for candidates.

LEARNING OBJECTIVE **7-2**

List and explain the main errors that can undermine an interview's usefulness.

Avoiding Errors That Can Undermine an Interview's Usefulness

Interviews hold an ironic place in the hiring process: Everyone uses them, but they're generally not particularly valid. The key is to do them properly. If you do, then the interview is generally a good predictor of performance and is comparable with many other selection techniques.[34] Keep three things in mind—use structured interviews, know what to ask, and avoid the common interviewing errors.

First, *structure the interview.*[35] Structured interviews (particularly structured interviews using situational questions) are more valid than unstructured interviews for predicting job performance. They are more valid partly because they are more reliable—for example, the same interviewer administers the interview more consistently from candidate to candidate.[36] Situational structured interviews yield a higher mean validity than do job-related (or behavioral) interviews, which in turn yield a higher mean validity than do "psychological" interviews (which focus more on motives and interests).[37]

Second, interviews are better at revealing some things than others, so know what to focus on. In one study, interviewers were able to size up the interviewee's extroversion and agreeableness. What they could *not* assess accurately were the traits that often matter most on jobs—like conscientiousness and emotional stability.[38] One implication seems to be, focus more on situational and job knowledge questions that help you assess how the candidate will actually respond to typical situations on that job.

Third, whether the interview is in person or online, effective employment interviewers understand and avoid the following common interview errors.

First Impressions (Snap Judgments)

Probably the most widespread error is that interviewers tend to jump to conclusions—make snap judgments—about candidates during the first few minutes of the interview (or even before the interview starts, based on test scores or résumé data). One researcher estimates that in 85% of the cases, interviewers had made up their minds before the interview even began, based on first impressions the interviewers gleaned from candidates' applications and personal appearance.[39] In one typical study, giving interviewers the candidates' test scores biased the ultimate assessment of the candidates. In another study, interviewers judged candidates who they were told formerly suffered from depression more negatively.[40]

First impressions are especially damaging when the prior information about the candidate is negative. In one study, interviewers who previously received unfavorable reference letters about applicants gave those applicants less credit for past successes and held them more personally responsible for past failures after the interview. And the interviewers' final decisions (to accept or reject those applicants) always reflected what they expected of the applicants based on the references, quite aside from the applicants' actual interview performance.[41]

Add to this two more interviewing facts. First, interviewers are more influenced by unfavorable than favorable information about the candidate. Second, their impressions are much more likely to change from favorable to unfavorable than from unfavorable to favorable. Indeed, many interviewers really search more for negative information, often without realizing it.

The bottom line is that most interviews are loaded against the applicant. One who starts well could easily end up with a low rating because unfavorable information tends to predominate. And for the interviewee who starts out poorly, it's almost impossible to overcome that first bad impression.[42] One psychologist interviewed CEOs of 80 top companies. She concluded that you "don't even get to open your mouth."[43] Instead, the interviewer will size up your posture, handshake, smile, and "captivating aura." It's difficult to overcome that first impression.

Not Clarifying What the Job Requires

Interviewers who don't have an accurate picture of what the job entails and what sort of candidate is best for it usually make their decisions based on incorrect impressions or stereotypes of what a good applicant is. They then erroneously match interviewees with their incorrect stereotypes. You should clarify what sorts of traits you're looking for, and why, before starting the interview.

One classic study involved 30 professional interviewers.[44] Half got just this brief job description: "the eight applicants here represented by their application blanks are applying for the position of secretary." The other 15 interviewers got much more explicit job information, including bilingual ability, for instance.

More job knowledge translated into better interviews. The 15 interviewers with more job information generally all agreed among themselves about each candidate's potential; those without it did not. The latter also didn't discriminate as well among applicants—they tended to give them all high ratings.

candidate-order (or contrast) error
An error of judgment on the part of the interviewer due to interviewing one or more very good or very bad candidates just before the interview in question.

Candidate-Order (Contrast) Error and Pressure to Hire

Candidate-order (or contrast) error means that the order in which you see applicants affects how you rate them. In one study, managers had to evaluate a sample candidate who was "just average" after first evaluating several "unfavorable" candidates. They scored the average candidate more favorably than they might otherwise because, in contrast to the unfavorable candidates, the average one looked better than he actually was. This contrast effect can be huge: In some early studies, evaluators based only a small part of the applicant's rating on his or her actual potential.[45]

Pressure to hire accentuates this problem. Researchers told one group of managers to assume they were behind in their recruiting quota. They told a second group they were ahead. Those "behind" rated the same recruits more highly.[46]

Nonverbal Behavior and Impression Management

The applicant's nonverbal behavior (smiling, avoiding your gaze, and so on) can also have a surprisingly large impact on his or her rating. In one study, 52 human resource specialists watched videotaped job interviews in which *the applicants' verbal content was identical*, but their nonverbal behavior differed markedly. Researchers told applicants in one group to exhibit minimal eye contact, a low energy level, and low voice modulation. Those in a second group demonstrated the opposite behavior. Twenty-three of the 26 personnel specialists who saw the high-eye-contact, high-energy-level candidate would have invited him or her for a second interview. None who saw the low-eye-contact, low-energy-level candidate would have recommended a second interview.[47] So, it pays interviewees to "look alive."

Nonverbal behaviors are probably so important because interviewers infer your personality from the way you act in the interview. In one study, 99 graduating college seniors completed questionnaires which included measures of personality, among other things. The students then reported their success in generating follow-up interviews and job offers. The interviewee's personality, particularly his or her level of extroversion, had a pronounced influence on whether he or she received follow-up interviews and job offers.[48] In turn, extroverted applicants seem particularly prone to self-promotion, and self-promotion is strongly related to the interviewer's perceptions of candidate–job fit.[49] Even structuring the interview doesn't seem to cancel out the effects of such nonverbal behavior.[50]

IMPRESSION MANAGEMENT Clever candidates capitalize on that fact. One study found that some used ingratiation to persuade interviewers to like them. For instance, the candidates praised the interviewers or appeared to agree with their opinions, thus signaling they shared similar beliefs. Sensing that a perceived similarity in attitudes may influence how the interviewer rates them, some interviewees try to emphasize (or fabricate) such similarities.[51] Others make self-promoting comments about their accomplishments.[52] Self-promotion means promoting one's own skills and abilities to create the impression of competence.[53] Psychologists call using techniques like ingratiation and self-promotion "impression management." Self-promotion is an effective tactic, but faking or lying generally backfires.[54]

Effect of Personal Characteristics: Attractiveness, Gender, Race

Unfortunately, physical attributes also distort assessments.[55] For example, people usually ascribe more favorable traits and more successful life outcomes to attractive people.[56] Similarly, race can play a role, depending on how you conduct the interview. In one study, for example, the white members of a racially balanced interview panel rated white candidates higher, while the black interviewers rated black candidates higher. But in all cases, *structured* interviews produced less of a difference between minority and white interviewees than did unstructured ones.[57]

Interviewers' reactions to minority stereotypes are complex. In one study, the researchers dressed the "applicants" in either traditional Muslim attire (black scarf and full-length black robe) or simple two-piece black pantsuits. Both applicants got the same number of job offers. However, interactions were shorter and more interpersonally negative when applicants wore the Muslim attire.[58]

In general, candidates evidencing various attributes and disabilities (such as child-care demands, HIV-positive status, or being wheelchair-bound) have less chance of obtaining a positive decision, even when they performed well in the structured interview.[59] The following expands on this.

Diversity Counts: Applicant Disability and the Employment Interview

Researchers surveyed 40 disabled people from various occupations. The disabled people felt that interviewers tend to avoid directly addressing the disability, and therefore make their decisions without all the facts.[60]

What the disabled people prefer is a discussion that lets the employer address his or her concerns and reach a knowledgeable conclusion. Among the questions they said they would like interviewers to ask were these: Is there any kind of setting or special equipment that will facilitate the interview process for you? Is there any specific technology that you currently use or have used in previous jobs that assists the way you work? What other kind of support did you have in previous jobs? Is there anything that would benefit you? Discuss a barrier or obstacle, if any, that you have encountered in any of your previous jobs. How was that addressed? And, Do you anticipate any transportation or scheduling issues with the work schedule expected of this position?

Remember that under the Americans with Disabilities Act, the interviewer must limit his or her questions to whether the applicant has any physical or mental impairment that may interfere with his or her ability to perform the job's essential tasks.[61]

In another study, the researchers manipulated the candidates' appearance, for instance "by placing scar-like marks on the cheeks of some of the applicants for some interviews, but not for others." Results revealed that managers who interviewed a facially stigmatized applicant (versus a non-stigmatized applicant) "rated the applicant lower [and] recalled less information about the interview" (in part, apparently, because staring at the "scars" distracted the interviewers).[62]

Note that the use of employment discrimination "testers" makes nondiscriminatory interviewing even more important. As defined by the EEOC, testers are "individuals who apply for employment which they do not intend to accept, for the sole purpose of uncovering unlawful discriminatory hiring practices."[63] Although not really seeking employment, testers have legal standing with the courts and EEOC.[64]

One civil rights group sent four university students—two white, two black—to an employment agency, supposedly in pursuit of a job. The civil rights group gave the four "testers" backgrounds and training to make their qualifications appear almost indistinguishable from each other. The white tester/applicants got interviews and job offers. The black tester/applicants got neither interviews nor offers.[65] The HR Practices feature shows why care is required abroad too. ■

IMPROVING PERFORMANCE: *HR Practices Around the Globe*

Selection Practices Abroad

In choosing selection criteria abroad, the manager in a multinational subsidiary walks a thin line between using the parent company's selection process and adapting it to local cultural differences. One study focused on Bangladesh.[66] Traditional selection practices there are different from what one might expect in the United States. For example, "age is considered synonymous to wisdom." Therefore, job advertisements for mid- and senior-level positions often set a minimum age as a selection criteria. But managers of multinational subsidiaries there are slowly implementing their corporate headquarters' prescribed HRM practices. As a result, the multinationals are affecting local recruitment and selection practices. That said, a manager would still be wise to understand each country's unique cultural demands before holding an interview there. ■

Source: Based on Monowar Mahmood, "National Culture vs Corporate Culture: Employee Recruitment and Se-lection Practices of Multinationals in a Developing Country Context," Journal of International Management Studies 11, no.1, (Jan. 2011), p. 110. Published by International Academy of Business and Economics, From www.iabe.org/domains/iabe/journal.aspx?journalid.

If your professor has assigned this, go to the Assignments section of **mymanagementlab.com** to complete this discussion.

Talk About It 2: You are interviewing candidates in Bangladesh and you have a great candidate who unfortunately is 25 years old, when the job calls for someone at least 40. List three interview questions you would ask to see if the person is still qualified.

Interviewer Behavior

Finally, the *interviewer's* behavior affects interviewee performance and rating.

For example, some interviewers inadvertently telegraph the expected answers,[67] as in: "This job involves a lot of stress. You can handle that, can't you?" Even subtle cues (like a smile or nod) can telegraph the desired answer.[68] Some interviewers talk so much that applicants have no time to answer questions. At the other extreme, some interviewers let the applicant dominate the interview, and so don't ask all their questions.[69] When interviewers have favorable pre-interview impressions of the applicant, they tend to act more positively toward that person (smiling more, for instance).[70] Other interviewers play interrogator, forgetting that it's uncivil to play "gotcha" by gleefully pouncing on inconsistencies. Some interviewers play amateur psychologist, unprofessionally probing for hidden meanings in what the applicant says. Others ask improper questions, forgetting that discriminatory questions "had a significant negative effect on participant's reactions to the interview and interviewer."[71] Other interviewers just can't conduct interviews.

In summary, interviewing errors to avoid include:

- First impressions (snap judgments)
- Not clarifying what the job involves and requires
- Candidate-order error and pressure to hire
- Nonverbal behavior and impression management
- The effects of interviewees' personal characteristics
- The interviewer's inadvertent behaviors

We'll address what *interviewees* can do to apply these findings and to excel in the interview in Appendix 2 to this chapter.

LEARNING OBJECTIVE **7-3**

Define a structured situational interview and give examples of situational questions, behavioral questions, and background questions that provide structure.

How to Design and Conduct an Effective Interview

There's little doubt that the **structured situational interview**—a series of job-relevant questions with predetermined answers that interviewers ask of all applicants for the job—produces superior results.[72] The basic idea is to (1) write situational (what would you do), behavioral (what did you do), or job knowledge questions, *and* (2) have job experts (like those supervising the job) also write several answers for each of these questions, rating the answers from good to poor. The people who interview the applicants then use rating sheets anchored with these examples of good or bad answers to rate the interviewees' answers.[73]

structured situational interview

A series of job-relevant questions with predetermined answers that interviewers ask of all applicants for the job.

Designing a Structured Situational Interview

The procedure is as follows.[74]

Step 1. **Analyze the job.** Write a job description with a list of job duties; required knowledge, skills, and abilities; and other worker qualifications.

Step 2. **Rate the job's main duties.** Rate each job duty, say from 1 to 5, based on how important it is to doing the job.

Step 3. **Create interview questions.** Create situational, behavioral, and job knowledge interview questions for each of the job duties, with more questions for the important duties.

The people who create the questions usually write them as critical incidents. For example, to probe for conscientiousness, the interviewer might ask this situational question:

> Your spouse and two teenage children are sick in bed with colds. There are no relatives or friends available to look in on them. Your shift starts in 3 hours. What would you do?

Step 4. **Create benchmark answers.** Next, *for each question*, develop ideal (benchmark) answers for good (a 5 rating), marginal (a 3 rating), and poor (a 1 rating) answers. The structured interview guide (pages 227–229) presents an example. Three benchmark answers (from low to high) for the example question above might be, "I'd stay home—my spouse and family come first" (1); "I'd phone my supervisor and explain my situation" (3); and "Since they only have colds, I'd come to work" (5).

Step 5. Appoint the interview panel and conduct interviews. Employers generally conduct structured situational interviews using a panel, rather than one-on-one. The panel usually consists of three to six members, preferably the same ones who wrote the questions and answers. It may also include the job's supervisor and/or incumbent, and a human resources representative. The same panel interviews all candidates for the job.[75]

The panel members review the job description, questions, and benchmark answers before the interview. One panel member introduces the applicant, and asks all questions of all applicants in this and succeeding candidates' interviews (to ensure consistency). However, all panel members record and rate the applicant's answers on the rating sheet (as on pages 228–229). They do this by indicating where the candidate's answer to each question falls relative to the benchmark poor, marginal, or good answers. At the end of the interview, someone answers any questions the applicant has.[76]

Web-based programs help interviewers design and organize behaviorally based selection interviews. For example, SelectPro (www.selectpro.net) enables interviewers to create behavior-based selection interviews, custom interview guides, and automated online interviews. The HR Tools feature presents more guidance.

IMPROVING PERFORMANCE: *HR Tools for Line Managers and Small Businesses*

How to Conduct an Effective Interview

You may not have the time or inclination to create a structured situational interview. However, there is still much you can do to make your interviews systematic and productive.

Step 1: First, know the job. Do not start the interview unless you understand the job's duties and what human skills you're looking for. Study the job description.

Step 2: Structure the interview. Any structuring is better than none. If pressed for time, you can still do several things to ask more consistent and job-relevant questions, without developing a full-blown structured interview.[77] For example:[78]

- Base questions on *actual job duties.* This will minimize irrelevant questions.
- Use *job knowledge, situational, or behavioral questions.* Questions that simply ask for opinions and attitudes, goals and aspirations, and self-descriptions and self-evaluations allow candidates to present themselves in an overly favorable manner or avoid revealing weaknesses.[79] Figure 7-2 illustrates structured questions.
- *Use the same questions* with all candidates. This improves reliability. It also reduces bias by giving all candidates the same opportunity.
- For each question, if possible, *have several ideal answers* and a score for each. Then rate each candidate's answers against this scale.
- If possible, use an *interview form.* Interviews based on structured guides like the ones in Figure 7-1 (pages 204–205) or Figure 7A-1, "structured interview guide" (pages 227–229), usually result in better interviews.[80] At the very least, list your questions before the interview.

Step 3: Get organized. Hold the interview in a private place to minimize interruptions (including text messages). Prior to the interview, review the candidate's application and résumé. Note any areas that are vague or that may indicate strengths or weaknesses.

Step 4: Establish rapport. The main reason for the interview is to find out about the applicant. Start by putting the person at ease. Greet the candidate and start the interview by asking a noncontroversial question, perhaps about the weather that day.

Step 5: Ask questions. Try to follow the situational, behavioral, and job knowledge questions you wrote out ahead of time. You'll find a sampling of other, supplementary

FIGURE 7-2 Examples of Questions That Provide Interview Structure

Job Knowledge Questions

1. What steps would you follow in changing the fan belt on a Toyota Camry?
2. What factors would you consider in choosing a computer to use for work?

Experience Questions

3. What experience have you had actually repairing automobile engines?
4. What experience have you had creating marketing programs for consumer products?

Behavioral (Past Behavior) Questions

5. Tell me about a time when you had to deal with a particularly obnoxious person. What was the situation, and how did you handle it?
6. Tell me about a time when you were under a great deal of stress. What was the situation, and how did you handle it?

Situational (What Would You Do) Questions

7. Suppose your boss insisted that a presentation had to be finished by tonight, but your subordinate said she has to get home early to attend an online class, so she is unable to help you. What would you do?
8. The CEO just told you that he's planning on firing your boss, with whom you are very close, and replacing him with you. What would you do?

questions (such as "Tell me a little about yourself?") in Figure 7-3.

As a rule,

Don't telegraph the desired answer.
Don't interrogate the applicant as if the person is on trial.
Don't monopolize the interview, nor let the applicant do so.
Do ask open-ended questions.
Do encourage the applicant to express thoughts fully.
Do draw out the applicant's opinions and feelings by repeating the person's last comment as a question (e.g., "You didn't like your last job?").
Do ask for examples.[81]
Do ask, "If I were to arrange for an interview with your boss, what would he or she say are your strengths, weaker points, and overall performance?[82]

In its own selection process, Google emphasizes work samples and situational (and behavioral) interviews.[83] For specific questions, Google provides its interviewers with access to its "QDroid" system; this system e-mails each interviewer a list of specific questions to ask the candidate for the specific job.

Step 6: Take brief, unobtrusive notes during the interview. Doing so may help avoid making a snap decision early in the interview, and may also help jog your memory once the interview is complete. Jot down just the key points of what the interviewee says.[84]

Step 7: Close the interview. Leave time to answer any questions the candidate may have and, if appropriate, to advocate your firm to the candidate.

Try to end the interview on a positive note. Tell the applicant whether there is any interest and, if so, what the next step will be. Make rejections diplomatically—"Although your background is impressive, there are other candidates whose experience is closer to our requirements." Remember, as one recruiter says, "An interview experience should leave a lasting, positive impression of the company, whether the candidate receives and accepts an offer or not."[85] If the applicant is still under consideration but you can't reach a decision now, say so.

Step 8: Review the interview. Once the candidate leaves, review your interview notes, score the interview answers (if you used a guide), and make a decision.

In rejecting a candidate, one perennial question is, should you provide an explanation or not? In one study, rejected candidates who received an explanation felt that the rejection process was fairer. Unfortunately, doing so may not be practical. Most employers say little, to avoid pushback and legal problems.[86] ■

If your professor has assigned this, go to the Assignments section of **mymanagementlab.com** to complete this discussion.

✪ **Talk About It 3:** Write a one-paragraph (single-spaced) memo to the people who do your company's recruiting on the topic, "The five most important things an interviewer can do to have a useful selection interview."

Organization and Planning Skills

1. Describe a specific situation which illustrates how you set objectives to reach a goal.
2. Tell me about a time when you had to choose between two or more important opportunities. How did you go about deciding which was most important to you?
3. Tell me how you normally schedule your time in order to accomplish your day-to-day tasks.
4. Describe a situation where you had a major role in organizing an important event. How did you do it?
5. Think about a lengthy term paper or report that you have written. Describe how you organized, researched, and wrote that report.
6. Give an example of how you organized notes and other materials in order to study for an important exam.
7. Describe a time when you reorganized something to be more efficient. How did you do it?
8. Think of a time when you made important plans that were fouled up. How did you react? What did you do?

Interaction and Leadership

1. Tell me about an event in your past which has greatly influenced the way you relate to people.
2. Give a specific example that best illustrates your ability to deal with an uncooperative person.
3. Some people have the ability to "roll with the punches." Describe a time when you demonstrated this skill.
4. Tell me when you had to work with someone who had a negative opinion of you. How did you overcome this?
5. Recall a time when you participated on a team. Tell me an important lesson you learned that is useful to you today.
6. Describe an instance when you reversed a negative situation at school, work, or home. How did you do it?
7. Describe a situation which best illustrates your leadership ability.
8. Think about someone whose leadership you admire. What qualities impress you?

Assertiveness and Motivation

1. Describe several work standards that you have set for yourself in past jobs. Why are these important to you?
2. Tell me a time when you have experienced a lack of motivation. What caused this? What did you do about it?
3. Describe a situation where you had to deal with someone whom you felt was dishonest. How did you handle it?
4. Describe a situation that made you extremely angry. How did you react?
5. Tell me about a time that best illustrates your ability to "stick things out" in a tough situation.
6. Describe a time when you motivated an unmotivated person to do something you wanted them to do.
7. Give me an example of a time when you were affected by organizational politics. How did you react?
8. Give me an example of when someone tried to take advantage of you. How did you react?

Decision Making and Problem Solving

1. Give an example that illustrates your ability to make a tough decision.
2. Tell me about a decision you made even though you did not have all the facts.
3. Describe a situation where you have had to "stand up" for a decision you made, even though it was unpopular.
4. Describe a situation where you changed your mind, even after you publicly committed to a decision.
5. Describe a situation that illustrates your ability to analyze and solve a problem.
6. Tell me about a time where you acted as a mediator to solve a problem between two other people.
7. Describe a problem that seemed almost overwhelming to you. How did you handle it?
8. Tell me about a time where you have used a creative or unique approach to solve a tough problem.

The following general questions will also help you prepare for employment interviews:

1. Tell me a little about yourself.
2. Why did you attend Indiana State University?
3. What led you to choose your major or career field?
4. What college subjects did you like best/least? What did you like/dislike about them?
5. What has been your greatest challenge in college?
6. Describe your most rewarding college experience.
7. Do you think that your grades are a good indication of your academic abilities?
8. If you could change a decision you made while at college, what would you change? Why?
9. What campus involvements did you choose? What did you gain/contribute?
10. What are your plans for continued or graduate study?
11. What interests you about this job? What challenges are you looking for in a position?
12. How have your educational and work experiences prepared you for this position?
13. What work experiences have been most valuable to you and why?
14. Why are you interested in our organization? In what way do you think you can contribute to our company?
15. How would you describe yourself?
16. What do you consider to be your greatest strengths? Weaknesses? Give examples.
17. If I asked the people who know you for one reason why I shouldn't hire you, what would they say?
18. What accomplishments have given you the most satisfaction? Why?
19. What are your long-range career objectives? How do you plan to achieve these?
20. How would you describe your ideal job?
21. What two or three things are most important to you in your job?
22. Do you have a geographical preference? Why?

FIGURE 7-3 Suggested Supplementary Questions for Interviewing Applicants

Source: "Suggested Supplementary Questions for Interviewing Applicants", from Indiana State University Career Center website. copyright © 2012 by Indiana.

Go into the interview with an accurate picture of the traits of an ideal candidate, know what you're going to ask, and be prepared to keep an open mind about the candidate.

Digital Vision/Photodisc/Thinkstock

Profiles and Employee Interviews

Employers using competency models or profiles (which list required skills, knowledge, behaviors, and other competencies) can use the profile for formulating job-related situational, behavioral, and knowledge interview questions. Table 7-1 summarizes illustrative skill, knowledge, trait, and experience profile items for chemical engineer candidates, with sample interview questions.

Watch It!

What do you think of how Zipcar conducts its interviewing candidates program? If your professor has assigned this, go to the Assignments section of mymanagementlab.com to complete the video exercise titled *Interviewing Candidates (Zipcar).*

TABLE 7-1 Asking Profile-Oriented Interview Questions

Profile Component	Example	Sample Interview Question
Skill	Able to use computer drafting software	Tell me about a time you used CAD Pro computerized design software.
Knowledge	How extreme heat affects hydrochloric acid (HCl)	Suppose you have an application where HCl is heated to 400 degrees Fahrenheit at 2 atmospheres of pressure; what happens to the HCl?
Trait	Willing to travel abroad at least 4 months per year visiting facilities	Suppose you had a family meeting to attend next week and we informed you that you had to leave for a job abroad immediately. How would you handle that?
Experience	Designed pollution filter for acid-cleaning facility	Tell me about a time when you designed a pollution filter for an acid-cleaning facility. How did it work? What particular problems did you encounter?

LEARNING OBJECTIVE 7-4

Discuss how to use employee selection methods to improve employee engagement.

Employee Engagement Guide for Managers

Building Engagement: A Total Selection Program

Many employers create a *total selection program* aimed at selecting candidates whose totality of attributes best fits the employer's total requirements. The program Toyota Motor uses to select employees for auto assembly team jobs illustrates this.

Toyota looks for several things in candidates. It wants employees with good interpersonal skills, due to the job's emphasis on teamwork. Toyota's emphasis on *kaizen*—on having the workers improve job processes through worker commitment to top quality—helps explain its emphasis on reasoning and problem-solving skills and on hiring intelligent, educated, and engaged workers.[87] Quality is a Toyota core value, and so Toyota looks for a history of quality commitment in those it hires. This helps explain why Toyota holds group interviews focusing on accomplishments. By asking candidates about what they are proudest of, Toyota gets a better insight into the person's values regarding quality and doing things right. Toyota is also looking for employees who have an eagerness to learn, and who are willing to try things Toyota's way or the team's way. Toyota's production system relies on consensus decision making, job rotation, and flexible career paths, and these also require open-minded, flexible team players, not dogmatists.

The Toyota Way

Toyota's hiring process aims to identify such assembler candidates. The process takes about 20 hours and six phases over several days:[88]

Step 1: an in-depth online application (20–30 minutes)
Step 2: a 2–5-hour computer-based assessment
Step 3: a 6–8-hour work simulation assessment
Step 4: a face-to-face interview
Step 5: a background check, drug screen, and medical check
Step 6: job offer

For example, in step 1, applicants complete an application form summarizing their experience and skills, and often view a video describing Toyota's work environment and selection system. This provides a realistic preview of the work and of the hiring process's extensiveness. Many applicants drop out here.

Step 2 aims to assess the applicant's technical knowledge and potential. Here applicants take tests that help identify problem-solving skills, learning potential, and occupational preferences. Skilled trade applicants (experienced mechanics, for instance) also take tool and die or general maintenance tests.

In step 3, applicants engage in simulated realistic production activities in Toyota's assessment center, under the observation of Toyota screening experts. The production (work sample) test assesses how well each candidate does on an actual assembler task. Also here, group discussion exercises help show how each applicant interacts with others in their group and solves problems.

In one simulation, candidates play the roles of the management and the workers of a firm that makes electrical circuits. During one scenario, the team must decide which circuit should be manufactured and how to effectively assign people, materials, and money to produce them. In another, participants role-play a team responsible for choosing new features for next year's car. Team members first individually rank 12 features based upon market appeal and then suggest one feature not included on the list. They must then come to a consensus on the best rank ordering. As one candidate who went through this process said, "There are three workstations in which you will be required to spend 2 hours at each one. You then have to get in a group and problem solve a special project with them for another hour or so. I left my house at 5 A.M. and did not return until 6:30 P.M.; it was a very long day."[89]

The time and effort applicants must invest in their Toyota visits are no accident. Toyota seeks engaged, flexible, quality-oriented team players, and those who lack these traits and values tend not to make it through the screening process. The rigorousness of the process tends to screen out those who are less engaged.

In summary, Toyota uses a total hiring process to identify and select engaged employees. While other firms do this in various ways, four common themes are apparent from Toyota's process. First, *value-based hiring* means it clarifies its own values before it embarks on an employee selection program. Whether based on excellence, kaizen/continuous improvement, integrity, or some other, value-based hiring begins with clarifying what your firm's values are and what you're looking for in employees.

Second, high-engagement firms such as Toyota commit the time and effort for an *exhaustive screening process*. Eight to ten hours of interviewing even for entry-level employees is not unusual, and firms like this will spend 20 hours or more with someone before deciding to hire. Many are rejected.

Third, the screening process doesn't just identify knowledge and technical skills. In addition, the candidate's *values and skills are matched* with the needs of the firm. Teamwork, kaizen, problem-solving, engagement, and flexibility are essential values at Toyota, so problem-solving skills, interpersonal skills, and engagement with the firm's commitment to quality are crucial human requirements.

Fourth, *self-selection* is an important screening practice here. In some firms this just means realistic previews. At others, practices such as long probationary periods in entry-level jobs help screen out those who don't fit. At Toyota, the screening process itself demands a sacrifice in terms of time and effort.

TRENDS SHAPING HR: *SCIENCE IN TALENT MANAGEMENT*

As another example, Google takes a scientific, evidence-based approach to its selection (and other HR) practices.

In its hiring process, Google starts (as explained in Chapter 4) with strong candidates. Recall that where possible, its internal recruiting group proactively identifies candidates, rather than using job boards to attract unscreened résumés.

The main elements in Google's selection process include work samples, testing, and interviewing. Virtually all of Google's technical hires take work sample tests, such as actually writing algorithms. Work samples are combined with testing of cognitive ability (similar to IQ tests), and of conscientiousness. Early in its evolution Google was known for putting candidates through a dozen or more interviews. However Google's own analysis showed that after the first four interviews the amount of useful information it got was not large. It therefore now generally makes hiring decisions after the fourth interview.

The interview emphasizes situational and behavioral questions. For specific questions, Google provides (as noted) its interviewers with access to its QDroid system; this e-mails each interviewer specific questions to ask the candidate for the specific job. Google interviewers were once known for trick questions, but the emphasis today is on using validated questions (from the QDroid system). The questions aim to assess the candidate's cognitive ability, leadership (particularly willingness to lead projects), "Googleyness" (values such as fun-loving and conscientious), and role-related knowledge (such as in computer science). Who actually does the interviewing? Here Google believes in the "wisdom of crowds": the interviewing "crowd" includes not just the prospective boss but prospective subordinates and representatives of other unrelated departments. Google then averages all the interviewers' interview ratings on a candidate to get a score. Finally, the hiring committee reviews the file, as does a Google senior manager, and then the CEO before an offer is made.[90]

Google is continually analyzing and improving its selection process. For example, it periodically runs experiments using algorithms that identify common keywords so as to analyse résumés of successful Google employees in particular jobs. Google then looks for these keywords in applicants who it *rejected* over the past year, and reevaluates these rejected applicants for these keywords, hiring many of these former "rejects" as a result. Similarly, interviewers get printouts showing how effective they've been as interviewers in terms of candidates hired or not hired. The process is thus analytical, evidence-based, and scientific. ■

Developing and Extending the Job Offer

LEARNING OBJECTIVE 7-5

List the main points to know about developing and extending the actual job offer.

After all the interviews, background checks, and tests, the employer decides to whom to make an offer using one or more approaches. The *judgmental* approach subjectively weighs all the evidence about the candidate. The *statistical* approach quantifies all the evidence and perhaps uses a formula to predict job success. The *hybrid* approach combines statistical results with judgment. Statistical and hybrid are more defensible; judgmental is better than nothing.

The employer will base the actual offer on, for instance, the candidate's apparent attractiveness as a prospective employee, the level of the position, and pay rates for similar positions. Next the employer extends an actual job offer to the candidate verbally. Here, the employer's point person (who might be the person to whom the new employee will report, or the human resource director, for instance) discusses the offer's main parameters. These include, for instance, pay rates, benefits, and actual job duties. There may be some negotiations. Then, once agreement is reached, the employer will extend a written job offer to the candidate.

There are several issues to consider with the written offer. Perhaps most important, understand the difference between a job offer letter and a contract. In a job offer letter, the employer lists the offer's basic information. This typically starts with a welcome sentence. It then includes job-specific information (such as details on salary and pay), benefits information, paid leave information, and terms of employment (including, for instance, successful completion of job testing and physical exams). There should be a strong statement that the employment relationship is "at will." There is then a closing statement. This again welcomes the employee, mentions who the employer's point person is if any questions arise, and instructs the candidate to sign the letter of offer if it is acceptable. It is prudent to have an attorney review the offer before extending it.[91]

For many positions (such as executive) a contract is in order. In contrast to a letter of offer (which should always be "at will"), an employment contract may have a duration (such as 3 years). Therefore, the contract will also describe grounds for termination or resignation, and severance provisions. The contract will almost always also include terms regarding confidentiality, nondisclosure requirements, and covenants not to compete (although some job offer letters for positions such as engineer may include such provisions as well). See www.Shrm.org/template-tools/toolkits for more information.

Depending upon the position, the employment contract (and, occasionally, the offer letter) may include a relocation provision. This lays out what the employer is willing to pay the new employee to relocate, for instance, in terms of moving expenses. State law generally governs enforcement of individual employment contracts. Letter of offer and employment contract samples are available online.[92]

Chapter Review

MyManagementLab® Go to **mymanagementlab.com** to complete the problems marked with this icon. ✪

Chapter Section Summaries

7-1. A selection interview is a selection procedure designed to predict future job performance based on applicants' oral responses to oral inquiries; we discussed several **basic types of interviews**. There are structured versus unstructured interviews. We also distinguished between interviews based on the types of questions and on how you administer the interview.

7-2. One reason selection interviews are often less useful than they should be is that managers make predictable **errors that undermine an interview's usefulness**. They jump to conclusions or make snap judgments based on preliminary information, they don't clarify what the job really requires, they succumb to candidate-order error and pressure to hire, and they let a variety of nonverbal behaviors and personal characteristics undermine the validity of the interview.

7-3. The manager should know how to **design and conduct an effective interview**. The structured situational interview is a series of job-related questions with predetermined answers that interviewers ask of all applicants for the job. Steps in creating a structured situational interview include analyzing the job, rating the job's main duties, creating interview questions, creating benchmark answers, and appointing the interview panel and conducting interviews.

7-4. High-engagement firms like Toyota use total hiring programs to select employees. Activities include clarifying the firm's values, committing the time and effort, matching the applicant's values with the firm's, having realistic previews, and encouraging self-selection.

7-5. After choosing which candidate to hire, the employer turns to **developing and extending the job offer**. Things to keep in mind here include understanding the difference between a job offer letter and a contract. A job offer letter lists the offer's basic information, including details on salary and pay, benefits information, paid leave information, and terms of employment. There should be a strong statement specifying that the employment relationship is "at will." In contrast to a letter of offer, it is not unusual for an employment contract to have a duration (such as 3 years).

Discussion Questions

7-1. There are several ways to conduct a selection interview. Explain and illustrate the basic ways in which you can classify selection interviews.

7-2. Briefly describe each of the following types of interviews: unstructured panel interviews, structured sequential interviews, job-related structured interviews.

7-3. For what sorts of jobs do you think unstructured interviews might be most appropriate? Why?

✪ **7-4.** How would you explain the fact that structured interviews, regardless of content, are generally more valid than unstructured interviews for predicting job performance?

7-5. Briefly discuss what an interviewer can do to improve his or her interviewing performance.

✪ **7-6.** What items should a letter of offer definitely contain?

7-7 What parallels do you see between the Toyota and Google total selection processes? What differences?

Individual and Group Activities

7-8. Prepare and give a short presentation titled "How to Be Effective as a Selection Interviewer."

7-9. Use the Internet to find employers who now do preliminary selection interviews via the Web. Do you think these interviews are useful? Why? How would you improve them?

7-10. In groups, discuss and compile examples of "the worst interview I ever had." What was it about these interviews that made them so bad? If time permits, discuss as a class.

7-11. In groups, prepare an interview (including a sequence of at least 20 questions) you'll use to interview candidates for the job of teaching a course in human resource management. Each group should present its interview questions in class.

7-12. Some firms swear by unorthodox interview methods. For example, Tech Planet, of Menlo Park, California, uses weekly lunches and "wacky follow-up sessions" as substitutes for first-round job interviews. During the informal meals, candidates are expected to mingle, and the Tech Planet employees they meet at the luncheons then review them. One Tech Planet employee asks candidates to ride a unicycle in her office to see if "they'll bond with the corporate culture or not." Toward the end of the screening process, the surviving group of interviewees has to solve brainteasers, and then openly evaluate their fellow candidates' strengths and weaknesses. What do you think of this screening process? What are its pros and cons? What changes, if any, would you recommend?[93]

7-13. Several years ago, Lockheed Martin Corp. sued the Boeing Corp. in Orlando, Florida, accusing it of using Lockheed's trade secrets to help win a multibillion-dollar government contract. Among other things, Lockheed Martin claimed that Boeing had obtained those trade secrets from a former Lockheed Martin employee who switched to Boeing.[94] But in describing methods companies use to commit corporate espionage, one writer says that hiring away the competitor's employees or hiring people to go through its dumpster are just the most obvious methods companies use to commit corporate espionage. As he says, "one of the more unusual scams—sometimes referred to as 'help wanted'—uses a person posing as a corporate headhunter who approaches an employee of the target company with a potentially lucrative job offer. During the interview, the employee is quizzed about his responsibilities, accomplishments, and current projects. The goal is to extract important details without the employee realizing there is no job."[95]

Assume you own a small high-tech company. What would you do (in terms of employee training, or a letter from you, for instance) to try to minimize the chance that one of your employees will fall into that kind of a trap? Also, compile a list of 10 questions that you think such a corporate spy might ask one of your employees.

7-14. Appendices A and B at the end of this book (pages 612–629) list the knowledge someone studying for the HRCI (Appendix A) or SHRM (Appendix B) certification exam needs to have in each area of human resource management (such as in Strategic Management, and Workforce Planning). In groups of several students, do four things: (1) review Appendix A and/or B; (2) identify the material in this chapter that relates to the Appendix A and/or B required knowledge lists; (3) write four multiple-choice exam questions on this material that you believe would be suitable for inclusion in the HRCI exam and/or the SHRM exam; and, (4) if time permits, have someone from your team post your team's questions in front of the class, so that students in all teams can answer the exam questions created by the other teams.

Experiential Exercise

The Most Important Person You'll Ever Hire

Purpose: The purpose of this exercise is to give you practice using some of the interview techniques you learned from this chapter.

Required Understanding: You should be familiar with the information presented in this chapter, and read this: For parents, children are precious. It's therefore interesting that parents who hire "nannies" to take care of their children usually do little more than ask several interview questions and conduct what is often, at best, a perfunctory reference check. Given the often questionable validity of interviews, and the (often) relative inexperience of the father or mother doing the interviewing, it's not surprising that many of these arrangements end in disappointment. You know from this chapter that it is difficult to conduct a valid interview unless you know exactly what you're looking for and, preferably, structure the interview. Most parents simply aren't trained to do this.

How to Set Up the Exercise/Instructions:

- Set up groups of five or six students. Two students will be the interviewees, while the other students in the group will serve as panel interviewers. The interviewees will develop an interviewer assessment form, and the panel interviewers will develop a structured situational interview for a "nanny."

7-15. Instructions for the interviewees: The interviewees should leave the room for about 20 minutes. While out of the room, the interviewees should develop an "interviewer assessment form" based on the information presented in this chapter regarding factors that can undermine the usefulness of an interview. During the panel interview, the interviewees should assess the interviewers using the interviewer assessment form. After the panel interviewers have conducted the interview, the interviewees should leave the room to discuss their notes. Did the interviewers exhibit any of the factors that can undermine the usefulness of an interview? If so, which ones? What suggestions would you (the interviewees) make to the interviewers on how to improve the usefulness of the interview?

7-16. Instructions for the interviewers: While the interviewees are out of the room, the panel interviewers will have 20 minutes to develop a short structured situational interview form for a "nanny." The panel interview team will interview two candidates for the position. During the panel interview, each interviewer should be taking notes on a copy of the structured situational interview form. After the panel interview, the panel interviewers should discuss their notes. What were your first impressions of each interviewee? Were your impressions similar? Which candidate would you all select for the position and why?

Application Case

The Out-of-Control Interview

Maria Fernandez is a bright, popular, and well-informed mechanical engineer who graduated with an engineering degree from State University in June 2014. During the spring preceding her graduation, she went out on many job interviews, most of which she thought were conducted courteously and were reasonably useful in giving both her and the prospective employer a good impression of where each of them stood on matters of importance to both of them. It was, therefore, with great anticipation that she looked forward to an interview with the one firm in which she most wanted to work: Apex Environmental. She had always had a strong interest in the environment and believed that the best use of her training and skills lay in working for a firm like Apex, where she thought she could have a successful career while making the world a better place.

The interview, however, was a disaster. Maria walked into a room where five men—the president of the company, two vice presidents, the marketing director, and another engineer—began throwing questions at her that she felt were aimed primarily at tripping her up rather than finding out what she could offer through her engineering skills. The questions ranged from being unnecessarily discourteous ("Why would you take a job as a waitress in college if you're such an intelligent person?") to being irrelevant and sexist ("Are you planning on starting a family anytime soon?"). Then, after the interview, she met with two of the gentlemen individually (including the president), and the discussions focused on her technical expertise. She thought that these later discussions went fairly well. However, given the apparent aimlessness and even mean-spiritedness of the panel interview, she was astonished when several days later the firm made her a job offer.

The offer forced her to consider several matters. From her point of view, the job itself was perfect. She liked what she would be doing, the industry, and the firm's location. And in fact, the president had been quite courteous in subsequent discussions. She was left wondering whether the panel interview had been intentionally tense to see how she'd stand up under pressure, and, if so, why they would do such a thing.

Questions

7-17. How would you explain the nature of the panel interview Maria had to endure? Specifically, do you think it reflected a well-thought-out interviewing strategy on the part of the firm or carelessness on the part of the firm's management? If it were carelessness, what would you do to improve the interview process at Apex Environmental?

7-18. Would you take the job offer if you were Maria? If you're not sure, what additional information would help you make your decision?

7-19. The job of applications engineer for which Maria was applying requires (a) excellent technical skills with respect to mechanical engineering, (b) a commitment to working in the area of pollution control, (c) the ability to deal well and confidently with customers who have engineering problems, (d) a willingness to travel worldwide, and (e) a very intelligent and well-balanced personality. List 10 questions you would ask when interviewing applicants for the job.

Continuing Case

Carter Cleaning Company

The Better Interview

Like virtually all the other HR-related activities at Carter Cleaning Centers, the company currently has no organized approach to interviewing job candidates. Store managers, who do almost all the hiring, have a few of their own favorite questions that they ask. But in the absence of any guidance from management, they all admit their interview performance leaves something to be desired. Similarly, Jack Carter himself is admittedly most comfortable dealing with what he calls the "nuts and bolts" machinery aspect of his business and has never felt particularly comfortable having to interview management or other job applicants. Jennifer is sure that this lack of formal interviewing practices, procedures, and training account for some of the employee turnover and theft problems. Therefore, she wants to do something to improve her company's performance in this important area.

Questions

7-20. In general, what can Jennifer do to improve her employee interviewing practices? Should she develop interview forms that list questions for management and nonmanagement jobs? If so, how should these look, and what questions should be included? Should she initiate a computer-based interview approach? If so, why and how?

7-21. Should she implement an interview training program for her managers, and if so, specifically what should be the content of such a training program? In other words, if she did decide to start training her management people to be better interviewers, what should she tell them and how should she tell it to them?

Translating Strategy into HR Policies and Practices Case*,§

**The accompanying strategy map for this chapter is in MyManagementLab, and the overall map on the inside back cover of this text outlines the relationships involved.*

Improving Performance at the Hotel Paris

The New Interviewing Program

The Hotel Paris's competitive strategy is "To use superior guest service to differentiate the Hotel Paris properties, and to thereby increase the length of stay and return rate of guests, and thus boost revenues and profitability." HR manager Lisa Cruz must now formulate functional policies and activities that support this competitive strategy, by eliciting the required employee behaviors and competencies.

As an experienced HR professional, Lisa knew that the company's new testing program would go only so far. She knew that, at best, employment tests accounted for perhaps 30% of employee performance. It was essential that she and her team design a package of interviews that her hotel managers could use to assess—on an interactive and personal basis—candidates for various positions. It was only in that way that the hotel could hire the sorts of employees whose competencies and behaviors would translate into the kinds of outcomes—such as improved guest services—that the hotel required to achieve its strategic goals.

Lisa received budgetary approval to design a new employee interview system. She and her team started by reviewing the job descriptions and job specifications for the positions of front-desk clerk, assistant manager, security guard, valet, door person, and housekeeper. Focusing on developing structured interviews for each position, the team set about devising interview questions. For example, for the front-desk clerk and assistant manager, they formulated several *behavioral questions*, including, "Tell me about a time when you had to deal with an irate person, and what you did," and "Tell me about a time when you had to deal with several conflicting demands at once, such as having to study for several final exams at the same time, while working. How did you handle the situation?" They also developed a number of *situational questions*, including "Suppose you have a very pushy incoming guest who insists on being checked in at once, while at the same time you're trying to process the check-out for another guest who must be at the airport in 10 minutes. How would you handle the situation?" For these and other positions, they also developed several *job knowledge* questions. For example, for security guard applicants, one question her team created was, "What are the local legal restrictions, if any, regarding using products like Mace if confronted by an unruly person on the hotel grounds?" The team combined the questions into structured interviews for each job, and turned to testing, fine-tuning, and finally using the new system.

Questions

7-22. For the jobs of security guard and valet, develop five additional situational, five behavioral, and five job knowledge questions, with descriptive good/average/poor answers.

7-23. Combine, (based on what you read in this Dessler, *Human Resource Management* chapter) your questions into a complete interview that you would give to someone who must interview candidates for these jobs.

---

§Written by and copyright Gary Dessler, PhD.

MyManagementLab

Go to **mymanagementlab.com** for Auto-graded writing questions as well as the following Assisted-graded writing questions:

7-24. Briefly discuss and give examples of at least five common interviewing mistakes. What recommendations would you give for avoiding these interviewing mistakes?

7-25. What parallels do you see between the Toyota and Google total selection processes? What differences?

7-26. MyManagementLab only—comprehensive writing assignment for this chapter.

PERSONAL INVENTORY ASSESSMENTS

Work Motivation Indicator

Motivation plays a big role in any job. Complete this assessment to learn more about your personality.

Key Terms

unstructured (or nondirective) interview, 203
structured (or directive) interview, 203
situational interview, 204
behavioral interview, 204
job-related interview, 205
stress interview, 205
unstructured sequential interview, 206
structured sequential interview, 206
panel interview, 206
mass interview, 206
candidate-order (or contrast) error, 209
structured situational interview, 212

Endnotes

1. Derek Chapman and David Zweig, "Developing a Nomological Network for Interview Structure: Antecedents and Consequences of the Structured Selection Interview," *Personnel Psychology* 58 (2005), pp. 673–702.
2. This is adapted from http://learn.hirevue.com/urbanoutfitters-casestudy, accessed March 27, 2015.
3. Michael McDaniel et al., "The Validity of Employment Interviews: A Comprehensive Review and Meta-Analysis," *Journal of Applied Psychology* 79, no. 4 (1994), p. 599. See also Laura Graves and Ronald Karren, "The Employee Selection Interview: A Fresh Look at an Old Problem," *Human Resource Management* 35, no. 2 (Summer 1996), pp. 163–180. For an argument against holding selection interviews, see D. Heath et al., "Hold the Interview," *Fast Company*, no. 136 (June 2009), pp. 51–52.
4. Therese Macan, "The Employment Interview: A Review of Current Studies and Directions for Future Research," *Human Resource Management Review* 19 (2009), pp. 203–218.
5. Duane Schultz and Sydney Schultz, *Psychology and Work Today* (Upper Saddle River, NJ: Prentice Hall, 1998), p. 830. A study found that interview structure "was best described by four dimensions: questioning consistency, evaluation standardization, question sophistication, and rapport building." Chapman and Zweig, "Developing a Nomological Network."
6. McDaniel et al., "The Validity of Employment Interviews," p. 602.
7. We'll see later in this chapter that there are other ways to "structure" selection interviews. Many of them have nothing to do with using structured guides like these.
8. See also Julia Levashina, Christopher Hartwell, Frederick Morageson, and Michael Campion, "The Structured Employment Interview: Narrative and Quantitative Review of the Research Literature," *Personnel Psychology* 67 (2014), pp. 241–293.
9. Laura Gollub Williamson et al., "Employment Interview on Trial: Linking Interview Structure with Litigation Outcomes," *Journal of Applied Psychology* 82, no. 6 (1996), p. 908. As an example, the findings of one recent study "demonstrate the value of using highly structured interviews to minimize the potential influence of applicant demographic characteristics on selection decisions." Julie McCarthy, Chad Van Iddekinge, and Michael Campion, "Are Highly Structured Job Interviews Resistant to Demographic Similarity Effects?" *Personnel Psychology* 60, no. 3 (2010), pp. 325–359.
10. Williamson et al., "Employment Interview on Trial."
11. McDaniel et al., "The Validity of Employment Interviews," p. 602.
12. Paul Taylor and Bruce Small, "Asking Applicants What They Would Do Versus What They Did: A Meta-Analytic Comparison of Situational and Past Behavior Employment Interview Questions," *Journal of Occupational and Organizational Psychology* 75, no. 3 (September 2002), pp. 277–295.
13. Margery Weinstein, "You're Hired!" *Training* 48, no. 4, pp. 34–37; www.trainingmag.com/article/you%E2%80%99re-hired, accessed July 19, 2013.
14. Aparna Nancherla, "Anticipated Growth in Behavioral Interviewing," *Training & Development*, April 2008, p. 20.
15. Bill Stoneman, "Matching Personalities with Jobs Made Easier with Behavioral Interviews," *American Banker*, November 30, 2000, p. 8a.
16. Martha Frase-Blunt, "Games Interviewers Play," *HR Magazine*, January 2001, pp. 104–114.
17. Kevin Murphy and Charles Davidshofer, *Psychological Testing* (Upper Saddle River, NJ: Prentice Hall, 2001), pp. 430–431.
18. Marlene Dixon et al., "The Panel Interview: A Review of Empirical Research and Guidelines for Practice," *Public Personnel Management* 31, no. 3 (Fall 2002), pp. 397–429.
19. Ibid. See also M. Ronald Buckley, Katherine A. Jackson, and Mark C. Bolino, "The Influence of Relational Demography on Panel Interview Ratings: A Field Experiment," *Personnel Psychology* 60, no. 3 (Autumn 2007), pp. 627–646.
20. Emily Maltby, "To Find the Best Hires, Firms Become Creative," *Wall Street Journal*, November 17, 2009, p. B6.
21. "Phone Interviews Might Be the Most Telling, Study Finds," *BNA Bulletin to Management*, September 1998, p. 273; and Lisa M. Moynihan et al., "A Longitudinal Study of the Relationships Among Job Search Self-Efficacy, Job Interviews, and Employment Outcomes," *Journal of Business and Psychology* 18, no. 2 (Winter 2003), pp. 207–233. For phone interview job search suggestions, see, for example, Janet Wagner,

"Can You Succeed in a Phone Interview?" *Strategic Finance* 91, no. 10 (April 2010), pp. 22, 61.

22. Susan Strauss et al., "The Effects of Videoconference, Telephone, and Face-to-Face Media on Interviewer and Applicant Judgments in Employment Interviews," *Journal of Management* 27, no. 3 (2001), pp. 363–381. If the employer records a video interview with the intention of sharing it with hiring managers who don't participate in the interview, it's advisable to first obtain the candidate's written permission. Matt Bolch, "Lights, Camera … Interview!" *HR Magazine*, March 2007, pp. 99–102.
23. Douglas Rodgers, "Computer-Aided Interviewing Overcomes First Impressions," *Personnel Journal*, April 1987, pp. 148–152; see also Linda Thornburg, "Computer-Assisted Interviewing Shortens Hiring Cycle," *HR Magazine*, February 1998, p. 73ff; and http://interviewstream.com/demorequest?gclid=COyxjOqd36sCFUbs7QodMziuOw, accessed August 22, 2014.
24. "LinkedIn Isn't Just for Hiring Anymore; Useful for Branding, Career Growth as Well," *Bloomberg BNA Bulletin to Management*, August 27, 2013, p. 275.
25. http://interviewstream.com/About, accessed August 22, 2014.
26. Job interviewing apps are also available through Apple's App Store. One is from *Martin's iPhone Apps.* For people seeking technical jobs, this app includes hundreds of potential interview questions, such as brain teasers and algorithms. www.martinreddy.net/iphone/interview, accessed August 21, 2014.
27. Anjali Athavaley, "A Job Interview You Don't Have to Show Up For," *Wall Street Journal*, June 20, 2007, http://online.wsj.com/article/SB118229876637841321.html, accessed April 8, 2011.
28. "Video Interviews Used to Connect with Candidates, Reduce Cost," *Bloomberg BNA Bulletin to Management,* March 11, 2014, p. 78.
29. Matt Mullenweg, "The CEO of Automattic on Holding 'Auditions' to Build a Strong Team," *Harvard Business Review*, April 2014, pp. 39–42.
30. These are quoted or adapted from www.careerfaqs.com.au/getthatjob_video_interview.asp, accessed March 2, 2009.
31. The following is largely quoted or abstracted directly from http://hirevue.com/mobile/, accessed June 25, 2015.
32. www.linkedin.com/company/hirevue, and https://www.linkedin.com/company/hirevue, accessed June 25, 2015.
33. http://learn.hirevue.com/urbanoutfitters-casestudy, accessed June 25, 2015.
34. For example, structured employment interviews using either situational questions or behavioral questions tend to yield high criterion-related validities (.63 versus .47). This is particularly so where the raters can use descriptively anchored rating scale answer sheets; these use short descriptors to illustrate good, average, or poor performance. Taylor and Small, "Asking Applicants What They Would Do Versus What They Did." See also McCarthy et al., "Are Highly Structured Job Interviews Resistant to Demographic Similarity Effects?" Some suggest using construct validity to validate employment interviews. Doing so involves showing which constructs (such as conscientiousness) explain interview ratings variations, explaining how these items may relate to job performance, and then testing the statistical relationships. Maria Ambani, Sorin Valcea, and M. Ronald Buckley, "The Relentless Pursuit of Construct Validity in the Design of Employment Interviews," *Human Resource Management Review* 24 (2014), pp. 160–175.
35. Williamson et al., "Employment Interview on Trial," p. 900.
36. Frank Schmidt and Ryan Zimmerman, "A Counterintuitive Hypothesis About Employment Interview Validity and Some Supporting Evidence," *Journal of Applied Psychology* 89, no. 3 (2004), pp. 553–561.
37. This validity discussion and these findings are based on McDaniel et al., "The Validity of Employment Interviews," pp. 607–610; the validities for situational, job-related, and psychological interviews were (.50), (.39), and (.29), respectively.
38. Murray Barrick et al., "Accuracy of Interviewer Judgments of Job Applicant Personality Traits," *Personnel Psychology* 53 (2000), pp. 925–951.
39. McDaniel et al., "The Validity of Employment Interviews," p. 608.
40. Anthony Dalessio and Todd Silverhart, "Combining Biodata Test and Interview Information: Predicting Decisions and Performance Criteria," *Personnel Psychology* 47 (1994), p. 313; and Nora Reilly et al., "Benchmarks Affect Perceptions of Prior Disability in a Structured Interview," *Journal of Business & Psychology* 20, no. 4 (Summer 2006), pp. 489–500.
41. S. W. Constantin, "An Investigation of Information Favorability in the Employment Interview," *Journal of Applied Psychology* 61 (1976), pp. 743–749. It should be noted that a number of the studies discussed in this chapter involve having interviewers evaluate interviews based on written transcripts (rather than face-to-face) and that a study suggests that this procedure may not be equivalent to having interviewers interview applicants directly. See Charles Gorman, William Glover, and Michael Doherty, "Can We Learn Anything About Interviewing Real People from 'Interviews' of Paper People? A Study of the External Validity Paradigm," *Organizational Behavior and Human Performance* 22, no. 2 (October 1978), pp. 165–192; and Frederick P. Morgeson, Matthew H. Reider, Michael A. Campion, and Rebecca A. Bull, "Review of Research on Age Discrimination in the Employment Interview," *Journal of Business Psychology* 22 (2008), pp. 223–232.
42. David Tucker and Patricia Rowe, "Relationship Between Expectancy, Causal Attribution, and Final Hiring Decisions in the Employment Interview," *Journal of Applied Psychology* 64, no. 1 (February 1979), pp. 27–34. See also Robert Dipboye, Gail Fontenelle, and Kathleen Garner, "Effect of Previewing the Application on Interview Process and Outcomes," *Journal of Applied Psychology* 69, no. 1 (February 1984), pp. 118–128; and Reilly et al., "Benchmarks Affect Perceptions of Prior Disability in a Structured Interview."
43. Anita Chaudhuri, "Beat the Clock: Applying for Job? A New Study Shows That Interviewers Will Make Up Their Minds About You Within a Minute," *The Guardian*, June 14, 2000, pp. 2–6.
44. John Langdale and Joseph Weitz, "Estimating the Influence of Job Information on Interviewer Agreement," *Journal of Applied Psychology* 57 (1973), pp. 23–27.
45. R. E. Carlson, "Effect of Applicant Sample on Ratings of Valid Information in an Employment Setting," *Journal of Applied Psychology* 54 (1970), pp. 217–222.
46. R. E. Carlson, "Selection Interview Decisions: The Effect of Interviewer Experience, Relative Quota Situation, and Applicant Sample on Interview Decisions," *Personnel Psychology* 20 (1967), pp. 259–280.
47. See, for example, Scott T. Fleischmann, "The Messages of Body Language in Job Interviews," *Employee Relations* 18, no. 2 (Summer 1991), pp. 161–166; James Westphal and Ithai Stern, "Flattery Will Get You Everywhere (Especially If You're a Male Caucasian): How Ingratiation, Board Room Behavior, and a Demographic Minority Status Affect Additional Board Appointments at U.S. Companies," *Academy of Management Journal* 50, no. 2 (2007), pp. 267–288.
48. David Caldwell and Jerry Burger, "Personality Characteristics of Job Applicants and Success in Screening Interviews," *Personnel Psychology* 51 (1998), pp. 119–136.
49. Amy Kristof-Brown et al., "Applicant Impression Management: Dispositional Influences and Consequences for Recruiter Perceptions of Fit and Similarity," *Journal of Management* 28, no. 1 (2002), pp. 27–46. See also Lynn McFarland et al., "Impression Management Use and Effectiveness Across Assessment Methods," *Journal of Management* 29, no. 5 (2003), pp. 641–661.
50. Timothy DeGroot and Janaki Gooty, "Can Nonverbal Cues Be Used to Make Meaningful Personality Attributions in Employment Interviews?" *Journal of Business Psychology* 24 (2009), p. 179.
51. Richard Posthuma, Frederick Morgeson, and Michael Campion, "Beyond Employment Interview Validity: A Comprehensive Narrative Review of Recent Research and Trends Over Time," *Personnel Psychology*, 2002, 55, pp. 1–87.
52. C. K. Stevens and A. L. Kristof, "Making the Right Impression: A Field Study of Applicant Impression Management During Interviews," *Journal of Applied Psychology* 80, pp. 587–606; Schultz and Schultz, *Psychology and Work Today*, p. 82. See also Jay Stuller, "Fatal Attraction," *Across the Board* 42, no. 6 (November/December 2005), pp. 18–23. See also Allen Huffcutt et al., "Understanding Applicant Behavior in Employment Interviews: A Theoretical Model of Interviewee Performance," *Human Resource Management Review* 20, no. 1 (2011), pp. 350–367.
53. Chad Higgins and Timothy Judge, "The Effect of Applicant Influence Tactics on Recruiter Perceptions of Fit and Hiring Recommendations: A Field Study," *Journal of Applied Psychology* 89, no. 4 (2004), pp. 622–632. Some researchers in this area question results like these. The problem is that much of the interviewing research uses students as raters and hypothetical jobs, so it's not clear that we can apply the findings to the real world. For example, see Frederick P. Morgeson, Matthew H. Reider, Michael A. Campion, and Rebecca A. Bull, "Review of Research on Age Discrimination in the Employment Interview," *Journal of*

Business Psychology 22 (2008), pp. 223–232.

54. Brian Swider et al., "Managing and Creating an Image in the Interview: The Role of Interviewee Initial Impressions," *Journal of Applied Psychology* 96, no. 6 (2011), pp. 1275–1288.
55. See, for example, Madeline Heilmann and Lois Saruwatari, "When Beauty Is Beastly: The Effects of Appearance and Sex on Evaluations of Job Applicants for Managerial and Nonmanagerial Jobs," *Organizational Behavior and Human Performance* 23 (June 1979), pp. 360–372; and Cynthia Marlowe, Sandra Schneider, and Carnot Nelson, "Gender and Attractiveness Biases in Hiring Decisions: Are More Experienced Managers Less Biased?" *Journal of Applied Psychology* 81, no. 1 (1996), pp. 11–21.
56. Marlowe et al., "Gender and Attractiveness Biases," p. 11.
57. Allen Huffcutt and Philip Roth, "Racial Group Differences in Employment Interview Evaluations," *Journal of Applied Psychology* 83, no. 2 (1998), pp. 179–189.
58. Eden King and Afra Ahmad, "An Experimental Field Study of Interpersonal Discrimination Toward Muslim Job Applicants," *Personnel Psychology* 63, no. 4 (2010), pp. 881–906.
59. N. S. Miceli et al., "Potential Discrimination in Structured Employment Interviews," *Employee Responsibilities and Rights* 13, no. 1 (March 2001), pp. 15–38.
60. Andrea Rodriguez and Fran Prezant, "Better Interviews for People with Disabilities," *Workforce*, www.workforce.com, accessed November 14, 2003.
61. Pat Tammaro, "Laws to Prevent Discrimination Affect Job Interview Process," *The Houston Business Journal*, June 16, 2000, p. 48.
62. Juan Madera and Michele Hebl, "Discrimination Against Facially Stigmatized Applicants in Interviews: An Eye Tracking and Face-to-Face Investigation," *Journal of Applied Psychology* 97, no. 2, pp. 317–330.
63. This is based on John F. Wymer III and Deborah A. Sudbury, "Employment Discrimination: 'Testers'—Will Your Hiring Practices 'Pass'?" *Employee Relations Law Journal* 17, no. 4 (Spring 1992), pp. 623–633.
64. Bureau of National Affairs, *Daily Labor Report*, December 5, 1990, p. D1.
65. Wymer and Sudbury, "Employment Discrimination," p. 629.
66. Monowar Mahmood, "National Culture Versus Corporate Culture: Employee Recruitment and Selection Practices of Multinationals in a Developing Country Context," *Journal of International Management Studies* 11, no. 1 (Jan. 2011), p. 110. Published by International Academy of Business and Economics, www.iabe.org/domains/iabeX/journal.aspx?journalid=16, accessed July 19, 2013.
67. Arthur Pell, "Nine Interviewing Pitfalls," *Managers Magazine*, January 1994, p. 20.
68. Thomas Dougherty, Daniel Turban, and John Callender, "Confirming First Impressions in the Employment Interview: A Field Study of Interviewer Behavior," *Journal of Applied Psychology* 79, no. 5 (1994), p. 663.
69. See Pell, "Nine Interviewing Pitfalls," p. 29; Parth Sarathi, "Making Selection Interviews Effective," *Management and Labor Studies* 18, no. 1 (1993), pp. 5–7.
70. Posthuma, Morgeson, and Campion, "Beyond Employment Interview Validity," pp. 1–87.
71. Pell, "Nine Interviewing Pitfalls," p. 30; quote from Alan M. Saks and Julie M. McCarthy, "Effects of Discriminatory Interview Questions and Gender on Applicant Reactions," *Journal of Business and Psychology* 21, no. 2 (Winter 2006), p. 175.
72. This section is based on Elliot Pursell et al., "Structured Interviewing," *Personnel Journal* 59 (November 1980), pp. 907–912; and G. Latham et al., "The Situational Interview," *Journal of Applied Psychology* 65 (1980), pp. 422–427. See also Michael Campion, Elliott Pursell, and Barbara Brown, "Structured Interviewing: Raising the Psychometric Properties of the Employment Interview," *Personnel Psychology* 41 (1988), pp. 25–42; and Paul R. Bernthal, "Recruitment and Selection," www.ddiworld.com/DDIWorld/media/trend-research/recruitment-and-selection_ere_es_ddi.pdf?ext=.pdf, accessed October 10, 2011. For a recent approach, see K. G. Melchers et. al., "Is More Structure Really Better? A Comparison of Frame-of-Reference Training and Descriptively Anchored Rating Scales to Improve Interviewers' Rating Quality," *Personnel Psychology* 64, no. 1 (2011), pp. 53–87.
73. Taylor and Small, "Asking Applicants What They Would Do Versus What They Did." Structured employment interviews using either situational questions or behavioral questions tend to yield high validities. However, structured interviews with situational question formats yield the higher ratings. This may be because interviewers get more consistent (reliable) responses with situational questions (which force all applicants to apply the same scenario) than they do with behavioral questions (which require each applicant to find applicable experiences). However, there is some evidence that for higher-level positions, situational question–based interviews are inferior to behavioral question–based ones, possibly because the situations are "just too simple to allow any real differentiation among candidates for higher level positions." Allen Huffcutt et al., "Comparison of Situational and Behavioral Description Interview Questions for Higher Level Positions," *Personnel Psychology* 54, no. 3 (2001), p. 619.
74. See Phillip Lowry, "The Structured Interview: An Alternative to the Assessment Center?" *Public Personnel Management* 23, no. 2 (Summer 1994), pp. 201–215. See also Todd Maurer and Jerry Solamon, "The Science and Practice of a Structured Employment Interview Coaching Program," *Personnel Psychology* 59, no. 2 (Summer 2006), pp. 433–456.
75. Pursell et al., "Structured Interviewing," p. 910.
76. From a speech by industrial psychologist Paul Green and contained in *BNA Bulletin to Management*, June 20, 1985, pp. 2–3. For additional practical guidance see, for example, www.state.gov/documents/organization/107843.pdf, accessed October 10, 2012.
77. Williamson et al., "Employment Interview on Trial," p. 901; Michael Campion, David Palmer, and James Campion, "A Review of Structure in the Selection Interview," *Personnel Psychology* 50 (1997), pp. 655–702. See also Maurer and Solamon, "The Science and Practice of a Structured Employment Interview."
78. Unless otherwise specified, the following are based on Williamson et al., "Employment Interview on Trial," pp. 901–902.
79. Campion, Palmer, and Campion, "A Review of Structure," p. 668.
80. Carlson, "Selection Interview Decisions."
81. Pamela Kaul, "Interviewing Is Your Business," *Association Management*, November 1992, p. 29. See also Nancy Woodward, "Asking for Salary Histories," *HR Magazine*, February 2000, pp. 109–112. Gathering information about specific interview dimensions such as social ability, responsibility, and independence (as is often done with structured interviews) can improve interview accuracy, at least for more complicated jobs. See also Andrea Poe, "Graduate Work: Behavioral Interviewing Can Tell You If an Applicant Just Out of College Has Traits Needed for the Job," *HR Magazine* 48, no. 10 (October 2003), pp. 95–96.
82. Edwin Walley, "Successful Interviewing Techniques," *The CPA Journal* 63 (September 1993), p. 70; and Randy Myers, "Interviewing Techniques: Tips from the Pros," *Journal of Accountancy* 202, no. 2 (August 2006), pp. 53–55.
83. Laszlo Bock, *Work Rules!* (New York: Twelve, 2015), pp. 93–94.
84. Catherine Middendorf and Therese Macan, "Note Taking in the Employment Interview: Effects on Recall and Judgment," *Journal of Applied Psychology* 87, no. 2 (2002), pp. 293–303.
85. Kristen Weirick, "The Perfect Interview," HR Magazine, April 1, 2008, p. 85.
86. Stephen Gilliland et al., "Improving Applicants' Reactions to Rejection Letters: An Application of Fairness Theory," *Personnel Psychology* 54 (2001), pp. 669–703.
87. See, for example, Gary Dessler, *Winning Commitment* (New York: McGraw-Hill, 1993).
88. "Toyota Looking for 1,500 Outstanding Mississippians from All Backgrounds," www.Mississippi.org/press-room/Toyota-looking-for-1500, accessed February 17, 2014.
89. "Toyota Hiring Process," www.indeed.com/forum/cmp/Toyota/Toyota-Hiring-Process/t31886, accessed August 22, 2014.
90. Bock, *Work Rules!*, pp. 87–127.
91. www.Shrm.org/template-tools/how-to-guides, accessed March 3, 2012.
92. See, for example, www.unh.edu/hr/sites/unh.edu.hr/files/pdfs/offer-letter-template-status-staff.pdf, http://jobsearchtech.about.com/od/jobofferletters/a/jobofferletter.htm, and http://office.microsoft.com/en-us/templates/results.aspx?qu=offer+letter&ex=1.
93. Kris Maher, "New High-Tech Recruiting Tools: Unicycles, Yahtzee and Silly Putty," *Wall Street Journal*, June 6, 2000, p. B14; see also Paul McNamara, "Extreme Interview," *Network World*, June 25, 2001, p. 65.
94. Tim Barker, "Corporate Espionage Takes Center Stage with Boeing Revelation," *Knight Ridder/Tribune Business News*, June 15, 2003.
95. Ibid.
96. See, for example, the classic, excellent discussion of job hunting and interviewing in Richard Payne, *How to Get a Better Job Quickly* (New York: New American Library, 1979).

Appendix 1 for Chapter 7

Structured Interview Guide

STEP 1—Create a Structured Interview Guide

Instructions:
First, here in step 1, create a structured interview guide like this one (including a competency definition, a lead question, and benchmark examples and answers, for instance) *for each of the job's required competencies*:

Competency: Interpersonal Skills

Definition:
Shows understanding, courtesy, tact, empathy, concern; develops and maintains relationships; may deal with people who are difficult, hostile, distressed; relates well to people from varied backgrounds and situations; is sensitive to individual differences.

Lead Questions:
Describe a situation in which you had to deal with people who were upset about a problem. What specific actions did you take? What was the outcome or result?

Benchmark Level	Level Definition	Level Examples
5	Establishes and maintains ongoing working relationships with management, other employees, internal or external stakeholders, or customers. Remains courteous when discussing information or eliciting highly sensitive or controversial information from people who are reluctant to give it. Effectively handles situations involving a high degree of tension or discomfort involving people who are demonstrating a high degree of hostility or distress.	Presents controversial findings tactfully to irate organization senior management officials regarding shortcomings of a newly installed computer system, software programs, and associated equipment.
4		Mediates disputes concerning system design/architecture, the nature and capacity of data management systems, system resources allocations, or other equally controversial/sensitive matters.
3	Cooperates and works well with management, other employees, or customers, on short-term assignments. Remains courteous when discussing information or eliciting moderately sensitive or controversial information from people who are hesitant to give it. Effectively handles situations involving a moderate degree of tension or discomfort involving people who are demonstrating a moderate degree of hostility or distress.	Courteously and tactfully delivers effective instruction to frustrated customers. Provides technical advice to customers and the public on various types of IT such as communication or security systems, data management procedures or analysis.
2		Familiarizes new employees with administrative procedures and office systems.
1	Cooperates and works well with management, other employees, or customers during brief interactions. Remains courteous when discussing information or eliciting non-sensitive or non-controversial information from people who are willing to give it. Effectively handles situations involving little or no tension, discomfort, hostility, or distress.	Responds courteously to customers' general inquiries. Greets and assists visitors attending a meeting within own organization.

FIGURE 7A-1 Structured Interview Guide

Source: From Conducting Effective Structured Interviews Resource Guide for Hiring Managers and Supervisors,2005, United States Department of State Bureau of Human Resources.

STEP 2—INDIVIDUAL EVALUATION FORM

Instructions:
Next, in step 2, create a form for evaluating each job candidate on each of the job's competencies:

Candidate to be assessed: _____

Date of Interview: _____

Competency: Problem Solving

Definition:
Identifies problems; determines accuracy and relevance of information; uses sound judgment to generate and evaluate alternatives, and to make the recommendations.

Question:
Describe a situation in which you identified a problem and evaluated the alternatives to make a recommendation or decision. What was the problem and who was affected?

Probes:
How did you generate and evaluate your alternatives? What was the outcome?

Describe specific behaviors observed: (Use back of sheet, if necessary)

1–Low	2	3–Average	4	5–Outstanding
Uses logic to identify alternatives to solve routine problems. Reacts to and solves problems by gathering and applying information from standard materials or sources that provide a limited number of alternatives.		Uses logic to identify alternatives to solve moderately difficult problems. Identifies and solves problems by gathering and applying information from a variety of materials or sources that provide several alternatives.		Uses logic to identify alternatives to solve complex or sensitive problems. Anticipates problems and identifies and evaluates potential sources of information and generates alternatives to solve problems where standards do not exist.

Final Evaluation:	Printed Name:	Signature:

FIGURE 7A-1 *Continued*

STEP 3—PANEL CONSENSUS EVALUATION FORM

Instructions:
Finally, in step 3, create a panel consensus evaluation form like this one, which the members of the panel who interviewed the candidate will use to evaluate his or her interview performance.

Candidate: _____

Date: _____

Panel Consensus Evaluation Form

Instructions:
Translate each individual evaluation for each competency onto this form. If all of the individual competency evaluations are within one rating scale point, enter the average of the evaluations in the column labeled Group Evaluation. If more than one point separates any two raters, a consensus discussion must occur with each party justifying his/her evaluation. The lead interviewer or his/her designee should take notes on the consensus discussion in the space provided. Any changes in evaluation should be initialed and a final evaluation entered for each competency.

Competency	Final Individual Evaluations			Group Evaluation
	(1)	(2)	(3)	
Interpersonal Skills				
Self-Management				
Reasoning				
Decision Making				
Problem Solving				
Oral Communication				
Total Score				

Consensus Discussion Notes:

Signature Panel Member 1: _____

Signature Panel Member 2: _____

Signature Panel Member 3: _____

FIGURE 7A-1 *Continued*

Appendix 2 for Chapter 7

Interview Guide for Interviewees

Before managers move into positions where they have to interview others, they usually must navigate some interviews themselves. It's therefore useful to apply some of what we discussed in this chapter to navigating one's own interviews.

Beyond trying to determine how you would perform the technical parts of the job, interviewers will try to discover what you are like as a person. In other words, how you get along with other people and your desire to work. They will look here at how you behave. For example, they will note whether you respond concisely, cooperate fully in answering questions, state personal opinions when relevant, and keep to the subject at hand; these are very important elements in influencing the interviewer's decision.

There are six things to do to get an extra edge in the interview.[96]

1. ***Preparation is essential.*** Before the interview, learn all you can about the employer, the job, and the people doing the recruiting. On the Web, using social media, or looking through business periodicals, find out what is happening in the employer's field. Try to unearth the employer's problems. Be ready to explain why you think you would be able to solve such problems, citing some of your *specific accomplishments* to make your case.
2. ***Uncover the interviewer's real needs.*** Spend as little time as possible briefly answering your interviewer's first questions and as much time as possible getting him or her to describe his or her needs. Determine what the person is expecting to accomplish, and the type of person he or she feels is needed. Use open-ended questions such as, "Could you tell me more about that?"
3. ***Relate yourself to the interviewer's needs.*** Once you know the type of person your interviewer is looking for and the sorts of problems he or she wants solved, you are in a good position to describe your own accomplishments *in terms of the interviewer's needs.* Start by saying something like, "One of the problem areas you've said is important to you is similar to a problem I once faced." Then state the problem, describe your solution, and reveal the results.
4. ***Think before answering.*** Answering a question should be a three-step process: Pause—Think—Speak. *Pause* to make sure you understand what the interviewer is driving at, *think* about how to structure your answer, and then *speak.* In your answer, try to emphasize how hiring you will help the interviewer solve his or her problem.
5. ***Remember that appearance and enthusiasm are important.*** Appropriate clothing, good grooming, a firm handshake, and energy are important. Maintain eye contact. In addition, speak with enthusiasm, nod agreement, and remember to take a moment to frame your answer (pause, think, speak) so that you sound articulate and fluent.
6. ***Make a good first impression.*** Remember that in most cases interviewers make up their minds about the applicant early in the interview. A good first impression may turn to bad during the interview, but it's unlikely. Bad first impressions are almost impossible to overcome. Experts suggest paying attention to the following key interviewing considerations:

   - Appropriate clothing
   - Good grooming
   - A firm handshake
   - The appearance of controlled energy
   - Pertinent humor and readiness to smile
   - A genuine interest in the employer's operation and alert attention when the interviewer speaks
   - Pride in past performance
   - An understanding of the employer's needs and a desire to serve them

8

Training and Developing Employees

Andria Patino/Corbis

LEARNING OBJECTIVES

8-1 Summarize the purpose and process of employee orientation.

8-2 Give an example of how to design onboarding to improve employee engagement.

8-3 List and briefly explain each of the steps in the training process.

8-4 Explain how to use five training techniques.

8-5 List and briefly discuss four management development methods.

8-6 List and briefly discuss the importance of the steps in leading organizational change.

8-7 Explain why a controlled study may be superior for evaluating the training program's effects.

For about 6 years after buying May Department Stores Co., Macy's Inc. emphasized consolidation.[1] First it focused on integrating the regional department stores under one Macy's umbrella. Then the recession hit and Macy's turned to cutting costs. Meanwhile, Macy's customer service suffered. Many sales associates failed to provide the service level that customers wanted. With deteriorating service cutting into its sales and profits, the question was, what should Macy's do about it now? We'll see what it did.

WHERE ARE WE NOW ...

Chapters 6 and 7 focused on the methods managers use to interview and select employees. Once employees are on board, the employer must train them. The purpose of this chapter is to increase your effectiveness in training employees. The main topics we'll cover include orienting employees, designing onboarding to improve employee engagement, the training process, analyzing training needs, implementing training and development programs, and evaluating the training effort. Then, in Chapter 9, we'll turn to appraising employees.

Orienting and Onboarding New Employees

LEARNING OBJECTIVE **8-1**
Summarize the purpose and process of employee orientation.

Carefully selecting employees doesn't guarantee they'll perform effectively. Even high-potential employees can't do their jobs if they don't know what to do or how to do it. Making sure your employees do know what to do and how to do it is the purpose of orientation and training. The human resources department usually designs the orientation and training programs, but the supervisor does most of the day-to-day orienting and training. Every manager therefore should know how to orient and train employees. We will start with orientation.

The Purposes of Employee Orientation/Onboarding

employee orientation
A procedure for providing new employees with basic background information about the firm.

Employee orientation (or *onboarding*) provides new employees with the basic background information (such as computer passwords and company rules) they need to do their jobs; ideally it should also help them start becoming emotionally attached to and engaged in the firm.[2] The manager wants to accomplish four things when orienting new employees:

1. Make the new employee feel welcome and at home and part of the team.
2. Make sure the new employee has the basic information to function effectively, such as e-mail access, personnel policies and benefits, and expectations in terms of work behavior.
3. Help the new employee understand the organization in a broad sense (its past, present, culture, and strategies and vision of the future).
4. Start socializing the person into the firm's culture and ways of doing things.[3] For example, the Mayo Clinic's "heritage and culture" onboarding program emphasizes core Mayo Clinic values such as teamwork, personal responsibility, integrity, customer service, and mutual respect.[4]

The Orientation Process

The length of the orientation program depends on what you cover. Most take several hours. The human resource specialist (or, in smaller firms, the office manager) performs the first part of the orientation by explaining basic matters like working hours and benefits. Then the supervisor continues the orientation by explaining the department's organization, introducing the person to his or her new colleagues, familiarizing him or her with the workplace, and reducing first-day jitters. At a minimum, the orientation should provide information on matters such as employee benefits, personnel policies, safety measures and regulations, and a facilities tour;[5] new employees should receive (and sign for) print or Internet-based employee handbooks covering such matters. At the other extreme, the beauty company L'Oreal's onboarding program takes about 2 years. It includes special training and roundtable discussions, meetings with key insiders, on-the-job learning, individual mentoring, and special experiences such as site visits.[6] You'll find a variety of orientation checklists online.[7]

Supervisors should be vigilant. Follow up on and encourage new employees to engage in activities (such as taking breaks with colleagues) that will enable them to "learn the ropes." Especially for new employees with disabilities, integration and socialization are highly influenced by coworkers' and supervisors' behavior.[8]

THE EMPLOYEE HANDBOOK Courts may find that the employee handbook's contents are legally binding commitments. Even apparently sensible handbook policies (such as "the company will not retaliate against employees who raise concerns about important issues in the workplace") can backfire without the proper disclaimers. The handbook should include a disclaimer stating "nothing in this handbook should be taken as creating a binding contract between employer and employees, and all employment is on an at will basis."[9] Say that statements of company policies, benefits, and regulations do not constitute the terms and conditions of an employment contract, either expressed or implied. Do not insert statements such as "No employee will be fired without just cause" or statements that imply or state that employees have tenure.

ORIENTATION TECHNOLOGY Employers use technology to support orientation. For example, at the University of Cincinnati, new employees spend about 45 minutes online learning about their new employer's mission, organization, and policies and procedures. IBM uses virtual environments like Second Life to support orientation, particularly for employees abroad. The new employees choose virtual avatars, for instance, to learn how to enroll for benefits.[10] ION Geophysical uses an online onboarding portal solution called RedCarpet. It includes a streaming video welcome message, and photos and profiles of new colleagues.[11] With Workday's iPhone app, users can search their company's directory for names, images, and contact information; call or e-mail coworkers directly; and view physical addresses on Google Maps.[12] Some employers place scannable QR codes along the orientation tour's stops, to provide information about each department and its role.[13] Other companies "gamify" onboarding, for instance, by offering rewards and recognition for new hires' contributions.[14]

LEARNING OBJECTIVE **8-2**

Give an example of how to design onboarding to improve employee engagement.

Employee Engagement Guide for Managers: Onboarding at Toyota

In many firms today, orientation goes well beyond providing basic information about things like work hours.[15] Onboarding at Toyota Motor Manufacturing USA illustrates this. While it does cover routine topics such as company benefits, its main aim is to engage Toyota's new employees in the firm's ideology of quality, teamwork, personal development, open communication, and mutual respect.[16] The initial program takes about 4 days:[17]

Day 1: The first day begins early and includes an overview of the program, a welcome to the company, and a discussion of the firm's organizational structure and human resource department by the firm's human resources vice president. He or she devotes about an hour and a half to discussing Toyota history and culture, and about 2 hours to employee benefits. Managers then spend several hours discussing Toyota's commitment to quality and teamwork.

Day 2: A typical second day focuses first on the importance of mutual respect, teamwork, and open communication at Toyota. The rest of the day covers topics such as safety, environmental affairs, and the Toyota production system.

Day 3: Given the importance of working in teams at Toyota, this day begins with 2½ to 3 hours devoted to communication training, such as "making requests and giving feedback." The rest of the day covers matters such as Toyota's problem-solving methods, quality assurance, hazard communications, and safety.

Day 4: Topics today include teamwork training and the Toyota suggestion system. This session also covers what work teams are responsible for and how to work together as a team. The afternoon session covers fire prevention and fire extinguisher training. By the end of day 4, new employees should be well on their way to being engaged in Toyota's ideology, in particular its mission of quality and its values of teamwork, continuous improvement, and problem-solving.[18]

The bottom line is that there's more to orienting employees than introducing them to new coworkers. Even without a program like Toyota's, use the onboarding opportunity to start instilling in the new employee the company values and traditions in which you expect the person to become engaged.

LEARNING OBJECTIVE 8-3

List and briefly explain each of the steps in the training process.

Overview of the Training Process

training
The process of teaching new or current employees the basic skills they need to perform their jobs.

Directly after orientation, training should begin. **Training** means giving new or current employees the skills that they need to perform their jobs, such as showing new salespeople how to sell your product. Training might involve having the current jobholder explain the job to the new hire, or multi-week classroom or Internet classes. In one recent year, employers spent about $1,208 per employee on training.[19]

Training is important. If even high-potential employees don't know what to do and how to do it, they will improvise or do nothing useful at all. Furthermore, by one estimate, about three-fourths of 30-something-aged high achievers begin looking for new positions within a year of starting, often due to dissatisfaction with inadequate training.[20] Employers also increasingly capitalize on the fact that training fosters engagement. For example, Coca-Cola UK uses employee development plans, training, and leadership development to attract and retain the best employees and inspire their engagement.[21]

Important though it is, training can't work miracles. To paraphrase Google's head of "People Operations" (HR), there are two ways to build a great workforce. One is to hire top performers (what he calls "90th percentile performers"), and the other is to hire average performers and then use training to try to make them 90th percentilers.[22] He found the former approach worked best for Google.

KNOW YOUR EMPLOYMENT LAW

Training and the Law

Managers should understand the legal implications of their training-related decisions. With respect to *discrimination*, Title VII of the Civil Rights Act of 1964 and related legislation requires that the employer avoid discriminatory actions in all aspects of its human resource management process, and that applies to selecting which employees to train. Employers face much the same consequences for discriminating against protected individuals when selecting candidates for training programs as they would in selecting candidates for jobs, or for promotion or other related decisions.

negligent training
A situation where an employer fails to train adequately, and the employee subsequently harms a third party.

Inadequate training can also expose the employer to liability for **negligent training**. As one expert puts it, "it's clear from the case law that where an employer fails to train adequately and an employee subsequently does harm to third parties, the court will find the employer liable." Among other things, the employer should confirm the applicant/employee's claims of skill and experience, provide adequate training (particularly where employees work with dangerous equipment), and evaluate the training to ensure that it is actually reducing risks.[23] ■

Aligning Strategy and Training

The employer's strategic plans should govern its training goals.[24] In essence, the task is to identify the employee behaviors the firm will need to execute its strategy, and then from that deduce what competencies (for instance, skills and knowledge) employees will need. Then, put in place training goals and programs to instill these competencies.[25] For example, with the health-care landscape in America changing fast, the Walgreens chain had to reformulate its strategy. It broadened its offerings, and today is the second-largest dispenser of flu shots in the United States. Its in-store health clinics provide medical care. It purchased drugstore.com.

Strategic changes like these affected the skills that Walgreens employees required, and therefore its training and other staffing policies. For example, Walgreens established Walgreens University. It offers more than 400 programs that Walgreens employees can take to build their skills (and even get college credit in pharmacy-related topics). For example, some programs develop assistant store manager skills, and Walgreens in-store health clinic nurse practitioners can take courses that expand their medical care expertise. The bottom line is that Walgreens reformulated its training (and other) HR policies to produce the employee skills the company needed to support its new strategy.[26] The accompanying Strategic Context feature provides another example.

IMPROVING PERFORMANCE: *The Strategic Context*

The Training Program That Turned Macy's Around

For about 6 years after buying May Department Stores Co., in the early 2000s, Macy's Inc. was in a consolidation/cost-cutting mode. During these years, with the focus on cost-cutting, Macy's customer service suffered. Many sales associates weren't providing the level of service that customers wanted. The question was, what should Macy's do about it?

Macy's top management turned to a new strategy. As its CEO said, "We are [now] talking about a cultural shift … becoming more of a growth company."[27] However, Macy's top management knew that growth would not occur without a big improvement in how its sales associates treated customers.

To produce the improved customer service Macy's needed to achieve its new strategy, Macy's installed a new training program. Rather than just watching a 90-minute interactive video as they previously did, sales associates now attended 3½-hour training sessions aimed at cultivating higher levels of customer service. Macy's managers believed the training program and resulting customer service improvement would be the biggest factor in driving their company's sales growth. And, indeed, same-store sales rose 5.3% in 2011, 3.7% in 2012, and about 3.5% in 2013, well above many competitors'.[28] ■

Source: Based on Rachel Dodes, "At Macy's, a Makeover on Service," The Wall Street Journal, April 11, 2011, p. B-10.; "Macy's Earnings, Revenue Edge Above Estimates," www.cnbc.com/id/100491292.

If your professor has assigned this, go to the Assignments section of **mymanagementlab.com** to complete this discussion question.

Talk About It 1: What other human resource management steps do you think Macy's should take in order to improve customer service performance?

The ADDIE Five-Step Training Process

The employer should use a rational training process. The gold standard here is still the basic analysis-design-develop-implement-evaluate (ADDIE) training process model that training experts have used for years.[29] As an example, one training vendor describes its training process as follows:[30]

- *Analyze* the training need.
- *Design* the overall training program.
- *Develop* the course (actually assembling/creating the training materials).
- *Implement* training, by actually training the targeted employee group using methods such as on-the-job or online training.
- *Evaluate* the course's effectiveness.

We'll look at each step next.

Conducting the Training Needs Analysis

The training needs analysis may address the employer's *strategic/longer term* training needs and/or its *current* training needs.

STRATEGIC TRAINING NEEDS ANALYSIS Strategic goals (perhaps to enter new lines of business or to expand abroad) often mean the firm will have to fill new jobs. *Strategic training needs analysis* identifies the training employees will need to fill these future jobs. For example, when Wisconsin-based Signicast Corp. decided to build a new high-tech plant, the firm's top managers knew the plant's employees would need new skills to run the computerized machines. They worked closely with their HR team to formulate hiring and training programs to ensure the firm would have the human resources required to populate the new plant.

CURRENT TRAINING NEEDS ANALYSIS Most training efforts aim to improve current performance—specifically training new employees, and those whose performance is deficient.

How you analyze current training needs depends on whether you're training new or current employees. The main task for *new* employees is to determine what the job entails and to break it down into subtasks, each of which you then teach to the new employee.

Analyzing *current* employees' training needs is more complex, because you must also ascertain whether training is the solution. For example, performance may be down due to poor motivation. Managers use *task analysis* to identify new employees' training needs, and *performance analysis* to identify current employees' training needs.

TASK ANALYSIS FOR ANALYZING NEW EMPLOYEES' TRAINING NEEDS Particularly with lower-level workers, it's customary to hire inexperienced personnel and train them. The aim here is to give these new employees the skills and knowledge they need to do the job. **Task analysis** is a detailed study of the job to determine what specific skills (like reading spreadsheets for a clerk) the job requires. For task analysis, job descriptions and job specifications are essential. They list the job's specific duties and skills, which are the basic reference points in determining the training required. Managers also uncover training needs by reviewing performance standards, performing the job, and questioning current jobholders and their supervisors.[31]

task analysis
A detailed study of a job to identify the specific skills required.

Some managers supplement the job description and specification with a *task analysis record form*. This form (see Table 8-1) consolidates information regarding required tasks and skills. As Table 8-1 illustrates, the form contains six columns of information, such as "Skills or knowledge required."

COMPETENCY PROFILES AND MODELS IN TRAINING AND DEVELOPMENT The **competency model** consolidates, usually in one diagram, a precise overview of the competencies someone would need to do the job well. Figure 4-10 (on page 118) was one example.

Many employers therefore design their training programs to foster these competencies. For example, the American Society for Training and Development (ASTD) built a competencies model for the job of training and development professional. It includes 10 core trainer competencies, including *being able to achieve performance improvement, instructional design*, and *training delivery*. As one competency example, the model describes *instructional design* as "designing, creating, and developing formal learning solutions to meet organizational needs; analyzing and selecting the most appropriate strategy, methodologies, and technologies to maximize the learning experience and impact."[32] Training a trainer would thus require, for instance, making sure he or she could, once training is complete, exhibit these skills and knowledge (competencies).[33] Employers increasingly focus on building work-related competencies or skills. For example, AT&T provides its employees with short "mini-degrees." These show readiness for specific jobs.[34]

competency model
A graphic model that consolidates, usually in one diagram, a precise overview of the competencies (the knowledge, skills, and behaviors) someone would need to do a job well.

With many competency-oriented training programs, trainees don't learn just by taking classes but through a mix of real-world exercises, teamwork, and online resources, under a learning coach; the aim is to show mastery of particular competencies.[35] For example, some college degrees (as offered by Western Governors University) start with a list of competencies to be learned, criteria for assessing competencies mastery, and examples of the competencies (such as using a spreadsheet). Students then complete their projects and have their competencies evaluated.

PERFORMANCE ANALYSIS: ANALYZING CURRENT EMPLOYEES' TRAINING NEEDS For underperforming current employees, you can't assume that training is the solution. In other words, is it lack of training, or something else? **Performance analysis** is the process of verifying that there is a performance deficiency and determining whether the employer should correct such deficiencies through training or some other means (like transferring the employee).

performance analysis
Verifying that there is a performance deficiency and determining whether that deficiency should be corrected through training or through some other means (such as transferring the employee).

TABLE 8-1 Sample Task Analysis Record Form

	Task List	When and How Often Performed	Quantity and Quality of Performance	Conditions Under Which Performed	Skills or Knowledge Required	Where Best Learned
1.	Operate paper cutter	4 times per day		Noisy pressroom: distractions		
1.1	Start motor	4 times per day				On the job
1.2	Set cutting distance		± tolerance of 0.007 in.		Read gauge	On the job
1.3	Place paper on cutting table		Must be completely even to prevent uneven cut		Lift paper correctly	On the job
1.4	Push paper up to cutter				Must be even	On the job
1.5	Grasp safety release with left hand		100% of time, for safety		Essential for safety	On the job but practice first with no distractions
1.6	Grasp cutter release with right hand				Must keep both hands on releases	On the job but practice first with no distractions
1.7	Simultaneously pull safety release with left hand and cutter release with right hand				Must keep both hands on releases	On the job but practice first with no distractions
1.8	Wait for cutter to retract		100% of time, for safety		Must keep both hands on releases	On the job but practice first with no distractions
1.9	Retract paper				Wait until cutter retracts	On the job but practice first with no distractions
1.10	Shut off		100% of time, for safety			On the job but practice first with no distractions
2.	Operate printing press					
2.1	Start motor					

Note: Task analysis record form showing some of the tasks and subtasks performed by a printing press operator.

Performance analysis begins with comparing the person's actual performance to what it should be. Doing so helps to confirm that there is a performance deficiency, and (hopefully) helps the manager to identify its cause. Examples of performance deficiencies might be:

I expect each salesperson to make 10 new contracts per week, but John averages only six.
Other plants our size average no more than two serious accidents per month; we're averaging five.

Ways to identify how a current employee is doing include:

- Performance appraisals
- Job-related performance data (including productivity, absenteeism and tardiness, grievances, waste, late deliveries, product quality, downtime, repairs, equipment utilization, and customer complaints)

- Observations by supervisors or other specialists
- Interviews with the employee or his or her supervisor
- Tests of things like job knowledge, skills, and attendance
- Attitude surveys
- Individual employee daily diaries
- Assessment center results
- Special performance gap analytical software, such as from Saba Software, Inc.

CAN'T DO/WON'T DO Uncovering why performance is down is the heart of performance analysis. The aim here is to distinguish between can't-do and won't-do problems. First, determine whether it is a *can't-do* problem and, if so, its specific causes. For example: The employees don't know what to do or what your standards are; there are obstacles in the system such as lack of tools or supplies; there are no job aids (such as color-coded wires that show assemblers which wire goes where); you've hired people who haven't the skills to do the job; or training is inadequate.

Or, it might be a *won't-do* problem. Here employees could do a good job if they wanted to. One expert says, "Perhaps the biggest trap that trainers fall into is [developing] training for problems that training just won't fix."[36] For instance, the better solution might be to change the incentives.

Designing the Training Program

Armed with the needs analysis results, the manager next designs the training program. *Design* means planning the overall training program including training objectives, delivery methods, and program evaluation. Sub-steps include setting performance objectives, creating a detailed training outline (all training program steps from start to finish), choosing a program delivery method (such as lectures or Web), and verifying the overall program design with management. The design should include summaries of how you plan to set a training environment that motivates your trainees both to learn and to transfer what they learn to the job. It is also here that the manager reviews possible training program content (including workbooks, exercises, and activities), and estimates a budget for the training program.[37] If the program is to use technology, the manager should include a review of the technology he or she plans to use as part of the analysis.[38] We'll look more closely next at several specific design issues.

Kim Kulish/Corbis

Most employers can build training programs like this one based on existing online and offline content offered by training content providers.

SETTING LEARNING OBJECTIVES[39] Training, development, learning, or (more generally) *instructional objectives* should specify in measurable terms what the trainee should be able to do after successfully completing the training program.[40] For example:

> *The technical service representative will be able to adjust the color guidelines on this HP Officejet All-in-One printer copier within 10 minutes according to the device's specifications.*

The learning objectives should first address the performance deficiencies that you identified via the needs analysis. Thus, if the sales team's sales are 40% too low, the objectives should focus on ensuring that the team members get the product knowledge, and attitudes they need to boost sales. But at the same time, the learning objectives must be practical, given the constraints.

One constraint is financial. The employer will generally want to see and approve a *training budget* for the program. Typical costs include the development costs (of having, say, a human resource specialist working on the program for a week or two), the direct and indirect (overhead) costs of the trainers' time, participant compensation (for the time they're actually being trained), and the cost of evaluating the program. There are algorithms for estimating training program costs, for instance, in terms of labor hours and direct costs.[41] The question, of course, isn't just "Can we afford this program?" but "Does it pay to spend this much, given the benefits we'll devise—will it improve performance, and if so by how much?" Therefore, prepare to defend the program on a benefits-versus-costs basis.

There are also other constraints to consider. For example, time constraints may require reducing three or four desirable learning objectives to one or two.

CREATING A MOTIVATIONAL LEARNING ENVIRONMENT Municipalities running programs for traffic violators know there's often no better way to get someone's attention than to present a terrifying video accident. In other words, they know the best training starts not with a lecture but by making the material meaningful.

The same is true at work. Learning requires both ability and motivation, and the training program's design should accommodate both. In terms of *ability*, the learner–trainee needs (among other things) the required reading, writing, and mathematics skills. Trainees are rarely homogeneous, for instance, in terms of intellectual capacity. In setting the learning environment, the manager therefore should address several trainee-ability issues. For example, how will our program accommodate differences in trainee abilities? Do we need to provide remedial training?

Second, the learner must also be motivated. No manager should waste his or her time showing a disinterested employee how to do something (even if he or she has the requisite ability).

Many books exist on how to motivate employees, but several specific observations are pertinent here.[42] The training program's effects will be diminished if trainees return to their jobs to snide comments such as, "I hope you liked your little vacation" from colleagues. Therefore, the low-hanging fruit in motivating trainees is to make sure the trainee's peers and supervisor support the training effort. Ideally, particularly for larger programs, top management should visibly support the program. Beyond that, various motivation theories provide useful guidance. From behavior modification, we know that the training should provide opportunities for positive reinforcement. "Expectancy theory" shows us that the trainees need to know they have the ability to succeed in the program, and that the value to them of completing the program is high. Self-efficacy is crucial—trainees must believe they have the capacity to succeed. We can summarize such motivational points as follows.

MAKE THE LEARNING MEANINGFUL Learners are more motivated to learn something that has meaning for them. Therefore:

1. At the start of training, provide a bird's-eye view of the material that you are going to present. For example, show why it's important, and provide an overview.[43]
2. Use familiar examples.

3. Organize the information so you can present it logically, in meaningful units.
4. Use terms and concepts that are already familiar to trainees.
5. Use visual aids.
6. Create a perceived training need in trainees' minds.[44] In one study, pilots who experienced pretraining accident-related events subsequently learned more from an accident-reduction training program than did those experiencing fewer such events.[45] Similarly, "before the training, managers need to sit down and talk with the trainee about why they are enrolled in the class, what they are expected to learn, and how they can use it on the job."[46]

MAKE SKILLS TRANSFER OBVIOUS AND EASY Make it easy to transfer new skills and behaviors from the training site to the job site:

1. Maximize the similarity between the training situation and the work situation.
2. Provide adequate practice.
3. Label or identify each feature of the machine and/or step in the process.
4. Direct the trainees' attention to important aspects of the job. For example, if you're training a customer service rep to handle calls, explain the different types of calls he or she will encounter.[47]
5. Provide "heads-up" information. For example, supervisors often face stressful conditions. You can reduce the negative impact of such events by letting supervisory trainees know they might occur.[48]
6. Trainees learn best at their own pace. If possible, let them pace themselves.

REINFORCE THE LEARNING Make sure the learner gets plenty of feedback. In particular:

1. Trainees learn best when the trainers immediately reinforce correct responses, perhaps with a quick "well done."
2. The learning curve goes down late in the day. Partial-day training is generally superior to full-day training.
3. Provide follow-up assignments at the close of training, so trainees are reinforced by having to apply back on the job what they've learned.[49]
4. Incentivize. Some companies, such as Hudson Trail Outfitters, an outdoor-gear retailer, offer trainees incentives of outdoor gear for completing each training program segment.[50]

ENSURE TRANSFER OF LEARNING TO THE JOB Unfortunately, less than 35% of trainees seem to be transferring what they learned in training to their jobs a year after training. Improving on that sad statistic requires steps at each stage of training. *Prior to training*, get trainee and supervisor input in designing the program, institute a training attendance policy, and encourage employees to participate.

During training, provide trainees with training experiences and conditions (surroundings, equipment) that resemble the actual work environment. Goal-setting is important. In one study, some trainees set goals at the start of the program for the skills they were being taught. After training, they were rated more highly on these skills than were those who hadn't set goals.[51]

After training, reinforce what trainees learned, for instance, by appraising and rewarding employees for using new skills, and by making sure that they have the tools and materials they need to use their new skills.[52]

OTHER TRAINING DESIGN ISSUES Managers address several other issues during the training design stage. Most importantly, they review alternative training methodologies (lectures, Web-based, and so on) and choose likely methods for their program. They also decide how to organize the various training content components, choose how to evaluate the program, develop an overall summary plan for the program, and obtain management's approval to move ahead.

Developing the Program

Program development means actually assembling the program's training content and materials. It means choosing the specific content the program will present, as well as designing/choosing the specific instructional methods (lectures, cases, Web-based, and so on) you will use. Training equipment and materials include (for example) iPads, workbooks, lectures, PowerPoint slides, Web- and computer-based activities, course activities, trainer resources (manuals, for instance), and support materials.

Some employers create their own training content, but there's also a vast selection of online and offline content. The "ATD Education 2015 Program Catalogue" (Association for Talent Development, www.TD.org/education) illustrates the many off-the-shelf training and development offerings available. It includes certificate programs on topics such as coaching, consulting skills, and presentation skills, as well as online workshops on hundreds of topics such as game design, survey design, and developing a mentoring program. (Trainers Warehouse and G.Neil are among thousands of suppliers.)[53] Turnkey training packages often include a trainer's guide, self-study book, video, and other content.

Once you design, approve, and develop the program, management can implement and then evaluate it. *Implement* means actually provide the training, using one or more of the instructional methods (such as lectures) that we discuss next. In general, there are several more practical steps a manager can take before, during, and after the training to improve participants' learning and engagement. *Before* the training, send announcements far in advance, provide directions, provide a point of contact, and make sure participants have pretraining materials. *During* training, make sure all participants have a point of contact in case they have questions or need guidance. *After* training, remember training does not end when the program ends. Instead, periodically ascertain that trainees are transferring their learning to the job.[54]

TRENDS SHAPING HR: *DIGITAL AND SOCIAL MEDIA*

the cloud
Refers to placing software programs and services on vendors' remote servers, from which they can then deliver these programs and services seamlessly to employees' digital devices

In designing and developing its training program, the employer will have to decide how the program will be delivered. Increasingly, this is occurring via "the cloud." Basically, **the cloud** refers to placing software programs and services on vendors' remote servers, from which they can then deliver these programs and services seamlessly to employees' digital devices. For example, you may use Microsoft Office 365, which resides on Microsoft's servers but which you use on your own (or employer's) computer devices. Similarly, when you start watching reruns of *Downton Abbey* on a TV, and then finish watching it on an iPad on the train home, you're using cloud-based services.

Cloud-based training is revolutionizing the training industry, by enabling employers to outsource much or all of their training activities. Because both the courses and the overall learning management system are hosted by the vendor, the employer need not concern itself with setting up or updating the programs on its own computers; the vendor manages the software for it. Furthermore the more advanced cloud-based learning systems let trainees access the training software and courses from wherever they are, using a variety of mobile devices. This not only improves convenience, but facilitates collaboration among employees when, for instance, they're working together on a training-based project. Cloud-based learning systems tend to be cost-effective, since the vendor handles upgrades and maintenance. The employer and vendor can store the on-the-cloud course modules and specific course content (such as PowerPoint slides, lectures, webinars, and photos); this makes it easier to build and modify e-learning courses. Typical cloud-based learning management system features include a course library, assessments and quizzes, reports and dashboards (for monitoring training performance), gamification elements (such as points and badges), messaging and notification systems, and a facility for scheduling and delivering both virtual and classroom training.[55] ■

Watch It!
What do you think of how Wilson Learning conducts its training programs? If your professor has assigned this, go to the Assignments section of mymanagementlab.com to complete the video exercise titled *Wilson Learning: Training.*

LEARNING OBJECTIVE **8-4**
Explain how to use five training techniques.

Implementing the Training Program

HR in Practice at the Hotel Paris As Lisa and the CFO reviewed measures of the Hotel Paris's current training efforts, it was clear that some changes were in order. Most other service companies provided at least 40 hours of training per employee per year, while the Hotel Paris offered, on average, no more than 5 or 6. To see how they handled this, see the case on pages 266–267.

On-the-Job Training

We'll see that much training today takes place online or uses other digital tools such as iPhones or iPads. However, much training is still in-person and interpersonal, as on-the-job training notably illustrates.

on-the-job training (OJT)
Training a person to learn a job while working on it.

On-the-job training (OJT) means having a person learn a job by actually doing it. Every employee, from mailroom clerk to CEO, should get on-the-job training when he or she joins a firm. In many firms, OJT is the only training available.[56]

TYPES OF ON-THE-JOB TRAINING The most familiar on-the-job training is the *coaching or understudy method.* Here, an experienced worker or the trainee's supervisor trains the employee. This may involve simply observing the supervisor, or (preferably) having the supervisor or job expert show the new employee the ropes, step by step. On-the-job training is part of multifaceted training at Men's Wearhouse, which combines on-the-job training with comprehensive initiation programs and continuing-education seminars. Every manager is accountable for developing his or her subordinates.[57] *Job rotation*, in which an employee (usually a management trainee) moves from job to job at planned intervals, is another OJT technique. *Special assignments* similarly give lower-level executives firsthand experience in working on actual problems.

Do not take the on-the-job training effort for granted. Instead, plan out and structure the OJT experience. Train the trainers themselves (often the employees' supervisors), and provide training materials. They should know, for instance, how to motivate learners. Because low expectations may translate into poor trainee performance, supervisor/trainers should emphasize their high expectations.

Many firms use "peer training" for OJT.[58] For example, some adopt "peer to peer development." The employer selects several employees who spend several days per week over several months learning what the technology or change will entail, and then spread the new skills and values to their colleagues back on the job.[59] Others use employee teams to analyze jobs and prepare training materials. They reportedly conduct task analyses more quickly and effectively than do training experts. Figure 8-1 presents steps to help ensure OJT success.[60]

Apprenticeship Training

apprenticeship training
A structured process by which people become skilled workers through a combination of classroom instruction and on-the-job training.

Apprenticeship training is a process by which people become skilled workers, usually through a combination of formal learning and long-term on-the-job training, often under the tutelage of a master craftsperson. When steelmaker Dofasco (now part of ArcelorMittal) discovered that many of its employees would be retiring within 5 to 10 years, it decided to revive its apprenticeship training. New recruits spend about 32 months in an internal apprenticeship training program, learning various jobs under the tutelage of experienced employees.[61]

FIGURE 8-1 Steps in On-the-Job Training

Step 1: Prepare the learner
1. Put the learner at ease. **2.** Explain why he or she is being taught. **3.** Create interest and find out what the learner already knows about the job. **4.** Explain the whole job and relate it to some job the worker already knows. **5.** Place the learner as close to the normal working position as possible. **6.** Familiarize the worker with equipment, materials, tools, and trade terms.
Step 2: Present the operation
1. Explain quantity and quality requirements. **2.** Go through the job at the normal work pace. **3.** Go through the job at a slow pace several times, explaining each step. Between operations, explain the difficult parts, or those in which errors are likely to be made. **4.** Again, go through the job at a slow pace several times; explain the key points. **5.** Have the learner explain the steps as you go through the job at a slow pace.
Step 3: Do a tryout
1. Have the learner go through the job several times, slowly, explaining each step to you. Correct mistakes and, if necessary, do some of the complicated steps the first few times. **2.** Run the job at the normal pace. **3.** Have the learner do the job, gradually building up skill and speed. **4.** Once the learner can do the job, let the work begin, but don't abandon him or her.
Step 4: Follow-up
1. Designate to whom the learner should go for help. **2.** Gradually decrease supervision, checking work from time to time. **3.** Correct faulty work patterns before they become a habit. Show why the method you suggest is superior. **4.** Compliment good work.

The U.S. Department of Labor's National Apprenticeship System promotes apprenticeship programs. More than 460,000 apprentices participate in 28,000 programs, and registered programs can receive federal and state contracts and other assistance.[62] Figure 8-2 lists popular recent apprenticeships.

FIGURE 8-2 Some Popular Apprenticeships

Source: From Available Occupations from www.doleta.gov/OA/occupations.cfm, accessed August 30, 2015. Those offering or seeking apprenticeships will find programs at this site by city and state.

The U.S. Department of Labor's Registered Apprenticeship program offers access to more than 1,000 occupations, such as the following:

- Able seaman
- Carpenter
- Chef
- Child care development specialist
- Construction craft laborer
- Dental assistant
- Electrician
- Elevator constructor
- Fire medic
- Law enforcement agent
- Over-the-road truck driver
- Pipefitter

Informal Learning

Surveys estimate that as much as 80% of what employees learn on the job they learn through informal means, including performing their jobs while interacting every day with their colleagues.[63]

Employers can facilitate informal learning. For example, one Siemens plant places tools in cafeteria areas to take advantage of the work-related discussions taking place. Even installing whiteboards with markers can facilitate informal learning. Sun Microsystems implemented an informal online learning tool it called Sun Learning eXchange. This evolved into a platform containing more than 5,000 informal learning items/suggestions addressing topics ranging from sales to technical support.[64] Cheesecake Factory uses VideoCafé, a YouTube-type platform, to let employees "upload and share video snippets on job-related topics, including customer greetings and food preparation."

Job Instruction Training

job instruction training (JIT)
Listing each job's basic tasks, along with key points, in order to provide step-by-step training for employees.

Many jobs (or parts of jobs) consist of a sequence of steps best learned step-by-step. Such step-by-step training is called **job instruction training (JIT)**. First, list the job's required steps (let's say for using a mechanical paper cutter) each in its proper sequence. Then list a corresponding "key point" (if any) beside each step. The steps in such a *job instruction training sheet* show trainees what to do, and the key points show how it's to be done—and why, as follows:

Steps	Key Points
1. Start motor	None
2. Set cutting distance	Carefully read scale—to prevent wrong-sized cut
3. Place paper on cutting table	Make sure paper is even—to prevent uneven cut
4. Push paper up to cutter	Make sure paper is tight—to prevent uneven cut
5. Grasp safety release with left hand	Do not release left hand—to prevent hand from being caught in cutter
6. Grasp cutter release with right hand	Do not release right hand—to prevent hand from being caught in cutter
7. Simultaneously pull cutter and safety releases	Keep both hands on corresponding releases—avoid hands being on cutting table
8. Wait for cutter to retract	Keep both hands on releases—to avoid having hands on cutting table
9. Retract paper	Make sure cutter is retracted; keep both hands away from releases
10. Shut off motor	None

As another example, the "exit" steps UPS teaches drivers include: Shift into the lowest gear or into park; turn off the ignition; apply the parking brake; release the seatbelt with left hand; open the door; place the key on your ring finger.[65]

Lectures

Lecturing is a quick and simple way to present knowledge to large groups of trainees, as when the sales force needs to learn a new product's features.[66] Here are some guidelines for presenting a lecture:[67]

- Don't start out on the wrong foot, for instance, with an irrelevant joke.
- Speak only about what you know well.
- Give your listeners signals. For instance, if you have a list of items, start by saying something like,"There are four reasons why the sales reports are necessary.... The first...."
- Use anecdotes and stories to show rather than tell.

- Be alert to your audience. Watch body language for negative signals like fidgeting or boredom.
- Maintain eye contact with the audience.
- Make sure everyone can hear. Repeat questions that you get from trainees.
- Leave hands hanging naturally at your sides.
- Talk from notes or PowerPoint slides, rather than from a script.
- Break a long talk into a series of short talks. Don't give a short overview and then spend a 1-hour presentation going point by point through the material. Break the long talk into a series of 10-minute talks, each with its own introduction. Write brief PowerPoint slides, and spend about a minute on each. Each introduction highlights what you'll discuss, why it's important to the audience members, and why they should listen to you.[68]
- Practice. If possible, rehearse under conditions similar to those under which you will actually give your presentation.

Programmed Learning

programmed learning
A systematic method for teaching job skills, involving presenting questions or facts, allowing the person to respond, and giving the learner immediate feedback on the accuracy of his or her answers.

Whether the medium is a textbook, iPad, or the Internet, **programmed learning** is a step-by-step, self-learning method that consists of three parts:

1. Presenting questions, facts, or problems to the learner
2. Allowing the person to respond
3. Providing feedback on the accuracy of answers, with instructions on what to do next

Generally, programmed learning presents facts and follow-up questions frame by frame. What the next question is often depends on how the learner answers the previous question. The built-in feedback from the answers provides reinforcement.

Programmed learning reduces training time. It also facilitates learning by letting trainees learn at their own pace, get immediate feedback, and reduce their risk of error. Some argue that trainees do not learn much more from programmed learning than from a textbook. Yet studies generally support programmed learning's effectiveness.[69] In addition to the usual programmed learning, computerized *intelligent tutoring systems* learn what questions and approaches worked and did not work for the learner, and then adjust the instructional sequence to the trainee's unique needs.

Behavior Modeling

behavior modeling
A training technique in which trainees are first shown good management techniques in a film, are asked to play roles in a simulated situation, and are then given feedback and praise by their supervisor.

Behavior modeling involves (1) showing trainees the right (or "model") way of doing something, (2) letting trainees practice that way, and then (3) giving feedback on the trainees' performance. Behavior modeling is one of the most widely used, well-researched, and highly regarded psychologically based training interventions.[70] The basic procedure is as follows:

1. ***Modeling.*** First, trainees watch live or video examples showing models behaving effectively in a problem situation. Thus, the video might show a supervisor effectively disciplining a subordinate, if teaching "how to discipline" is the aim of the training program.
2. ***Role-playing.*** Next, the trainees get roles to play in a simulated situation; here they are to practice the effective behaviors demonstrated by the models.
3. ***Social reinforcement.*** The trainer provides reinforcement in the form of praise and constructive feedback.
4. ***Transfer of training.*** Finally, trainees are encouraged to apply their new skills when they are back on their jobs.

Audiovisual-Based Training

Although increasingly replaced by Web-based methods, audiovisual-based training techniques like DVDs, films, PowerPoint, and audiotapes are still used.[71] The Ford Motor Company uses videos in its dealer training sessions to simulate problems and reactions to various customer complaints, for example.

Vestibule Training

With vestibule training, trainees learn on the actual or simulated equipment but are trained off the job (perhaps in a separate room or *vestibule*). Vestibule training is necessary when it's too costly or dangerous to train employees on the job. Putting new assembly-line workers right to work could slow production, for instance, and when safety is a concern—as with pilots—simulated training may be the only practical alternative. As an example, UPS uses a life-size learning lab to provide a 40-hour, 5-day realistic training program for driver candidates.[72]

Electronic Performance Support Systems (EPSS)

electronic performance support systems (EPSS)
Sets of computerized tools and displays that automate training, documentation, and phone support; integrate this automation into applications; and provide support that's faster, cheaper, and more effective than traditional methods.

job aid
A set of instructions, diagrams, or similar methods available at the job site to guide the worker.

Electronic performance support systems (EPSS) are computerized tools and displays that automate training, documentation, and phone support.[73] When you call a Dell service rep, he or she is probably asking questions prompted by an EPSS; it takes you both, step by step, through an analytical sequence. Without the EPSS, Dell would have to train its service reps to memorize an unrealistically large number of solutions. Aetna Insurance cut its 13-week instructor-led training course for new call center employees by about 2 weeks by providing employees with performance support tools.[74]

Performance support systems are modern job aids. **Job aids** are sets of instructions, diagrams, or similar methods available at the job site to guide the worker.[75] Job aids work particularly well on complex jobs that require multiple steps, or where it's dangerous to forget a step. For example, airline pilots use job aids (a checklist of things to do prior to takeoff).

Videoconferencing

Videoconferencing involves delivering programs over broadband lines, the Internet, or satellite. Vendors such as Cisco offer videoconference products such as Webex and TelePresence.[76] Cisco's Unified Video Conferencing (CUVC) product line combines Cisco group collaboration and decision-making software with videoconferencing, video telephony, and realistic "TelePresence" capabilities.[77]

Computer-Based Training (CBT)

Computer-based training refers to training methods that use interactive computer-based systems to increase knowledge or skills. For example, employers use CBT to teach employees safe methods for avoiding falls. The system lets trainees replay the lessons and answer questions, and is especially effective when paired with actual practice under a trainer's watchful eye.[78]

Computer-based training is increasingly realistic. For example, *interactive multimedia training* integrates the use of text, video, graphics, photos, animation, and sound to create a complex training environment with which the trainee interacts.[79] In training a physician, for instance, such a system lets a medical student take a hypothetical patient's medical history, conduct an examination, and analyze lab tests. The student can then interpret the sounds and draw conclusions for a diagnosis. *Virtual reality training* takes this realism a step further, by putting trainees into a simulated environment.

Simulated Learning and Gaming

"Simulated learning" means different things to different people. A survey asked training professionals what experiences qualified as simulated learning experiences. The percentages of trainers choosing each experience were: Virtual reality-type games, 19%; Step-by-step animated guide, 8%; Scenarios with questions and decision trees overlaying animation, 19%; Online role-play with photos and videos, 14%; Software training including screenshots with interactive requests, 35%; and Other, 6%.[80]

Virtual reality puts the trainee in an artificial three-dimensional environment that simulates events and situations experienced on the job.[81] Sensory devices transmit how the trainee is responding to the computer, and the trainee "sees, feels and hears" what is going on, assisted by special glasses.[82] Facebook's recent purchase of virtual reality glasses maker Oculus VR Inc. highlights virtual reality's growing potential.[83]

Employers also increasingly use computerized simulations (sometimes called *interactive learning*) to inject realism into their training. Orlando-based Environmental Tectonics Corporation created an Advanced Disaster Management simulation for emergency medical response trainees. One simulated scenario involves a plane crash. So realistic that it's "unsettling," trainees including firefighters and airport officials respond to the simulated crash's sights and sounds via pointing devices and radios.[84] Cisco embedded the learning required to train thousands of Cisco trainees for Cisco certification exams within a video game–like program that includes music, graphics, and sound effects.[85] A Novartis pharmaceuticals division runs about 80 or so clinical trials per year, and must be sure each trial team is trained for this. Novartis uses a custom-made simulation*. For example, the simulation shows trainees "how their decisions affected the quality of the trial and whether their decision saved time or added time to the process."[86] The Cheesecake Factory uses a simulation that shows employees how to build the "perfect hamburger."

Training simulations are expensive to create, but for large companies the cost per employee is usually reasonable.[87] In general, interactive and simulated technologies reduce learning time by an average of 50%.[88] Other advantages include mastery of learning (if the trainee doesn't learn it, he or she generally can't move on to the next step), increased retention, and increased trainee motivation (resulting from responsive feedback).

Specialist multimedia software houses such as Graphic Media of Portland, Oregon, produce much of the content for these programs. They produce both custom titles and generic programs such as a $999 package for teaching workplace safety.

Lifelong and Literacy Training Techniques

lifelong learning
Provides employees with continuing learning experiences over their tenure with the firm, with the aims of ensuring they have the opportunity to learn the skills they need to do their jobs and to expand their occupational horizons.

Lifelong learning means providing employees with continuing learning experiences over their tenure with the firm, with the aim of ensuring they have the opportunity to learn the skills they need to do their jobs and to expand their horizons. Lifelong learning may thus range from basic remedial skills (for instance, English as a second language) to college. For example, one senior waiter at the Rhapsody restaurant in Chicago received his undergraduate degree and began work toward a master of social work using the lifelong learning account (LiLA) program his employer offers. Somewhat similar to 401(k) plans, LiLA plans accept employer and employee contributions (without the tax advantages of 401(k) plans), and the employee can use these funds to better himself or herself.[89]

LITERACY TRAINING By one estimate, about 39 million people in the United States have learning disabilities.[90] Yet today's emphasis on teamwork and quality requires that employees read, write, and understand numbers.[91]

Employers often turn to private firms like Education Management Corporation to provide the requisite education.[92] Another simple approach is to have supervisors teach basic skills by giving employees writing and speaking exercises.[93] For example, if an employee needs to use a manual to find out how to change a part, teach that person how to use the index to locate the relevant section. Some call in teachers from a local high school.

Diversity training can be important, as in the following feature.

IMPROVING PERFORMANCE: *HR Practices Around the Globe*

Diversity Training at ABC Virtual Communications, Inc.

Diversity training aims to improve cross-cultural sensitivity, with the goal of fostering more harmonious working relationships among a firm's employees. Such training typically includes improving interpersonal skills, understanding and valuing cultural differences, improving technical skills, socializing employees into the corporate culture, indoctrinating new workers into the U.S. work ethic, improving English proficiency and basic math skills, and improving bilingual skills for English-speaking employees.[94] For example, IBM has online programs to educate managers regarding diversity, inclusive leadership, and sexual harassment.

Training materials include interactive learning modules that enable trainees to practice what they've learned, testimonials from IBM executives, and self-assessment tools.[95]

Most employers opt for an off-the-shelf diversity training program such as *Just Be F.A.I.R.* from VisionPoint productions. It includes streaming video, a facilitator discussion guide, participant materials and workbook, a DVD with print materials, PowerPoint slides, and two videos (the purchase price for the program is about $1,000). Vignettes illustrate such things as the potential pitfalls of stereotyping people.[96]

ABC Virtual Communications, Inc. (www.abcv.com) is a Des Moines, Iowa, provider of customized software development and other solutions. It therefore requires qualified personnel, particularly software engineers. Recruiting such employees is particularly difficult in Iowa, where many recent graduates move away.

ABC therefore recruits foreign-born individuals. However, hiring these skilled employees wasn't enough: ABC needed a diversity management training program that could turn these new employees—and the firm's current employees—into productive colleagues.

Its program consists of several courses. New ABC employees, representing 14 countries and 45 ethnic groups, take a mandatory 8-hour orientation overview for new employees on the "American workplace." All ABC employees take an "effective communications" training course. Conversational English and accent reduction classes for employees and their families are available through Rosetta Stone language learning software. The company also partnered with Des Moines Area Community College to create specialized classes for individual needs. At ABC Virtual, a globally diverse workforce was the key to improved performance, and diversity training helped the firm manage its diversity.[97] ■

Source: Based on Matthew Reis, "Do-It-Yourself Diversity," Training & Development, March 2004, pp. 80–81.; www.prismdiversity.com/resource /diversity_training.html, accessed June 1, 2011.; Jennifer Salopek, "Trends: Lost in Translation," Training & Development, December 2003, p. 15; www.visionpoint.com/training-solutions/title/just-be-fair-basic-diversity-training, accessed June 17, 2011.; Paraphrased from "Best Practice: Workforce Diversity Training," The Manufacturing Practices Center of Excellence, www.brmpcoe.org/bestpracticea/internal/abev/abcv_15.html.

If your professor has assigned this, go to the Assignments section of **mymanagementlab.com** to complete this discussion.

✪ **Talk About It 2:** List five competencies that you believe such a diversity program should cultivate.

Team Training

Teamwork does not always come naturally. Companies devote many hours to training new employees to listen to each other and to cooperate. For example, a Baltimore Coca-Cola plant suffered from high turnover and absenteeism.[98] The new plant manager decided to address these problems by reorganizing around teams. He then used team training to support and improve team functioning.

Team training focused on technical, interpersonal, and team management issues. In terms of *technical training*, for instance, management encouraged team employees to learn each other's jobs, to encourage flexible team assignments. **Cross training** means training employees to do different tasks or jobs than their own; doing so facilitates flexibility and job rotation, as when you expect team members to occasionally share jobs.

cross training
Training employees to do different tasks or jobs than their own; doing so facilitates flexibility and job rotation.

Interpersonal problems often undermine teamwork. Team training here therefore included *interpersonal skills* training such as in listening, handling conflict, and negotiating.[99] Effective teams also require *team management* skills, for instance, in problem-solving, meetings management, consensus decision making, and team leadership, and the teams received such training as well.

Many employers use team training to build stronger management teams. For example, some use outdoor "adventure" training such as Outward Bound programs to build teamwork. This usually involves taking a firm's management team out into rugged, mountainous terrain.[100] The aim is to foster trust and cooperation among trainees. One chief financial officer for a bank helped organize a retreat for 73 of his firm's financial employees. As he said, "They are very individualistic in their approach to their work.... What I have been trying to do is get them to see the power of acting more like a team."[101]

Internet-Based Training

Employers use Internet-based learning to deliver almost all the types of training we have discussed to this point. For example, ADP trains new salespeople online, using a Blackboard learning management system similar to one used by college students.[102]

The Italian eyewear company Luxottica (whose brands include LensCrafters and Sunglass Hut) provides training to its 38,000 employees worldwide via instant online access to information on new products and regulations.[103] Recently, state-owned postal service China Post created a new center to manage its online training college, which now delivers about 9,000 hours of training annually, offering over 600 programs.[104]

LEARNING PORTALS A *learning portal* is a section of an employer's website that offers employees online access to training courses. Many employers arrange to have an online training vendor make its courses available via the employer's portal. Most often, the employer contracts with application service providers (ASPs). When employees go to their firm's learning portal, they actually access the menu of training courses that the ASP offers for the employer. A Google search for e-learning companies reveals many, such as SkillSoft, Plateau Systems, and Employment Law Learning Technologies.

Learning management systems (LMS) are special software tools that support Internet training by helping employers identify training needs and schedule, deliver, assess, and manage the online training itself. (Blackboard and WebCT are two familiar college-oriented learning management systems.) General Motors uses an LMS to help its dealers in Africa and the Middle East deliver training. The Internet-based LMS includes a course catalog, supervisor-approved self-enrollment, and pre- and post-course tests. The system then automatically schedules the individual's training.[105] Many employers integrate the LMS with the company's talent management systems. That way, skills inventories and succession plans automatically update as employees complete their training.[106]

Online learning doesn't necessarily teach individuals faster or better. In one review, Web-based instruction was a bit more effective than classroom instruction for teaching memory of facts and principles; Web-based instruction and classroom instruction were equally effective for teaching information about how to perform a task or action.[107] But, of course, the need to teach large numbers of students remotely, or to enable trainees to study at their leisure, often makes e-learning the logical choice.[108]

Some employers opt for *blended learning*. Here, trainees use multiple delivery methods (such as manuals, in-class lectures, and Web-based seminars or "webinars") to learn the material.[109] Intuit (which makes TurboTax) uses instructor-led classroom training for getting new distributors up to speed. Then it uses virtual classroom systems (see the following) for things like monthly meetings with distributors, and for classes on special software features.[110]

The Virtual Classroom

virtual classroom
Teaching method that uses special collaboration software to enable multiple remote learners, using their PCs or laptops, to participate in live audio and visual discussions, communicate via written text, and learn via content such as PowerPoint slides.

A **virtual classroom** uses collaboration software to enable multiple remote learners, using their PCs, tablets, or laptops, to participate in live audio and visual discussions, communicate via written text, and learn via content such as PowerPoint slides.

The virtual classroom combines the best of Web-based learning offered by systems like Blackboard and WebCT with live video and audio. Thus, Elluminate Live! lets learners communicate with clear, two-way audio; build communities with user profiles and live video; collaborate with chat and shared whiteboards; and learn with shared applications such as PowerPoint slides.[111]

TRENDS SHAPING HR: *DIGITAL AND SOCIAL MEDIA*

Mobile learning (or "on-demand learning") means delivering learning content, on the learner's demand, via mobile devices like cell phones, laptops, and tablets, wherever and whenever the learner has the time and desire to access it.[112] For example, trainees can take full online courses using dominKnow's (www.dominknow.com) iPhone-optimized Touch Learning Center Portal.[113]

Most large employers distribute internal communications and training via mobile devices.[114] Employees at CompuCom Systems Inc. access instruction manuals through mobile devices; the company subsidizes employee purchases of smart phones or tablets to facilitate this. Natural user interfaces such as Apple's Siri voice recognition system facilitate such training.[115]

Employers use mobile learning to deliver training and downloads on topics "from how to close an important sales deal to optimizing organizational change."[116] IBM uses mobile learning to deliver just-in-time information (for instance, about new product features) to its sales force. To facilitate this, its training department often breaks up, say, an hour program into easier-to-use 10-minute pieces. Some employers use blogs to communicate learning to trainees.[117] J.P. Morgan encourages employees to use instant messaging, for instance, to update colleagues about new products quickly.

Employers also use social media, such as LinkedIn, Facebook, and Twitter, and virtual worlds like Second Life to communicate company news and messages and to provide training.[118] For example, British Petroleum uses Second Life to train new gas station employees. The aim here is to show new gas station employees how to use the safety features of gasoline storage tanks. BP built three-dimensional renderings of the tank systems in Second Life. Trainees use these to "see" underground and observe the effects of using the safety devices.[119]

Web 2.0 learning
Training that uses online technologies such as social networks, virtual worlds (such as Second Life), and systems that blend synchronous and asynchronous delivery with blogs, chat rooms, bookmark sharing, and tools such as 3-D simulations.

Web 2.0 learning is learning that utilizes online technologies such as social networks, virtual worlds (such as Second Life), and systems that blend synchronous and asynchronous delivery with blogs, chat rooms, bookmark sharing, and tools such as 3-D simulations.[120] About 40% of learning professionals surveyed said their companies use Web 2.0 learning, and 86% said they anticipated doing so. One large firm uses Web 2.0 to deliver credit card sales training to its service representatives around the country. *Collaborative peer forums* require teams of six to eight trainees to virtually "sell" their sales problem and solution to an executive.[121]

The accompanying HR Tools feature shows how managers can create their own training programs. ■

IMPROVING PERFORMANCE: *HR Tools for Line Managers and Small Businesses*

Creating Your Own Training Program

While it would be nice if supervisors in even the largest firms could expect their firms to provide packaged training programs to train the new people they hire, many times they cannot. However, you still have many options.

Create Your Own Five-Step Training Program

Remember ADDIE—analyze (is training the problem?), design (including learning objectives, and motivating the trainee), develop (what specific materials and methods will we use?), implement (train the person), and evaluate. For many types of jobs, start by *setting training objectives*—be specific about what your employee should be able to do after training. Write a job description—list of the job's duties—if not already available. Write (see Table 8-1, page 238) a *task analysis record form* showing the steps in each of the employee's tasks. Write a *job instruction training form*; here list a key point (such as "carefully read scale") for each step (such as "set cutting distance"). Finally, compile the objectives, job description, task analysis form, and job instruction form in a *training manual*. Also, include an introduction to the job and an explanation of how the job relates to other jobs in the company.

Use Private Vendors

The small business owner can tap hundreds of suppliers of prepackaged training solutions. These range from self-study programs from the American Management Association (www.amanet.org) and SHRM (www.shrm.org), to specialized programs. For example, the employer might arrange with PureSafety to have its employees take occupational safety courses from www.puresafety.com.

SkillSoft is another example (go to http://skillsoft.com and click "Products"). Its courses include software development, business strategy and operations, professional effectiveness, and desktop computer skills. As an example, the course "interviewing effectively" shows supervisors how to use behavioral questioning to interview candidates.[122]

The buyer's guide from the American Society of Training and Development (www.astd.org) is a good place to start to find a vendor (check under "Resources").

Check the SBA

The government's Small Business Administration (see www.SBA.gov/training) provides a virtual campus that offers online courses, workshops, publications, and learning tools aimed at supporting small businesses.[123] For example, the small business owner can link under "Small Business Planner" to "Writing Effective Job Descriptions," and "The Interview Process: How to Select the Right Person." See the site map at www.sba.gov/sitemap for examples of what it offers.

Check NAM

The National Association of Manufacturers (NAM) is the largest industrial trade organization in the United States. It represents about 14,000 member manufacturers, including 10,000 small and midsized companies.

NAM helps employees maintain and upgrade their work skills and continue their professional development. It offers courses and a skills certification process.[124] There are no long-term contracts to sign. Employers simply pay about $10–$30 per course taken by each employee. The catalog includes OSHA, quality, and technical training as well as courses in areas like customer service. ■

Source: Based on Based on Paul Harris, "Small Businesses Bask in Training's Spotlight," T&D, 59, no. 2, Fall 2005, pp. 46–52; Stephen Covey, "Small Business, Big Opportunity," Training, 43, no. 11, November 2006, p. 40; www.themanufacturinginstitute.org/Skills-Certification/Right-Skills-Now/Right-Skills-Now.aspx, accessed August 24, 2014.

If your professor has assigned this, go to the Assignments section of **mymanagementlab.com** to complete this discussion question.

Talk About It 3: What would you tell the owner of a small restaurant whose employees haven't been trained properly to do?

Implementing Management Development Programs

LEARNING OBJECTIVE 8-5
List and briefly discuss four management development methods.

management development
Any attempt to improve current or future management performance by imparting knowledge, changing attitudes, or increasing skills.

Management development is any attempt to improve managerial performance by imparting knowledge, changing attitudes, or increasing skills. It thus includes in-house programs like courses, coaching, and rotational assignments; professional programs like those given by SHRM; online programs from various sources; and university programs like executive MBAs.

Management development is important for several reasons. For one thing, promotion from within is a major source of management talent, and virtually all promoted managers require some development to prepare them for their new jobs. Furthermore, management development facilitates organizational continuity, by preparing employees and current managers to smoothly assume higher-level positions.

Strategy's Role in Management Development

Management development programs should reflect the firm's strategic plans.[125] For example, strategies to enter new businesses or expand overseas imply that the employer will need succession plans in place to obtain and/or develop managers who have the skills to manage these new businesses. Management development programs then impart the knowledge, attitudes, and skills these managers will need to excel at their jobs.[126]

Some management development programs are company-wide and involve all or most new (or potential) managers. Thus, new MBAs may join GE's management development program and rotate through various assignments and educational experiences. The firm may then slot superior candidates onto a "fast track," a development program that prepares them more quickly for senior-level commands.

Other development programs aim to fill specific top positions, such as CEO. For example, GE will spend years developing, testing, and watching potential replacements for CEO Jeffrey Immelt.

Succession Planning

Management development is often part of the employer's *succession planning process.*[127] *Succession planning* involves developing workforce plans for the company's top positions; it is the ongoing process of systematically identifying, assessing, and developing organizational leadership to enhance performance.[128]

Succession planning programs involve several stages.[129] First, an organization projection is made. Here, based on the company's strategic and business plans, top management and the human resource director identify what the company's future key position needs will be. The employer anticipates its management needs based on factors like plant expansion or contraction. Next, HR and management review the firm's management skills inventory to identify the management talent now employed.[130] These inventories, you may recall, contain data on things like education and work experience, career preferences, and performance appraisals. At this stage, management replacement charts may be drawn (see Figure 5-3, page 132). These summarize potential candidates for each of your management slots, as well as each person's development needs. As in Figure 5-3, the development needs for a future division vice president might include job rotation (to obtain more experience in the firm's finance and production division), executive development programs (to provide training and strategic planning), and assignment for 2 weeks to the employer's in-house management development center. At this stage, management may decide that one or more outside candidates should be recruited as well.

Management then turns to the development stage of the succession planning process. This means providing possible candidates with the developmental experiences they require to be viable candidates. Employers develop high-potential employees through internal training and cross-functional experiences, job rotation, external training, and global/regional assignments.[131]

Finally, succession planning requires assessing all these candidates and selecting those who will actually fill the key positions.[132]

Improving Performance Through HRIS: Succession Systems

At Dole Foods, the new president's strategy involved improving financial performance by reducing redundancies and centralizing certain activities, including succession planning.[133] Web technology helped Dole do this. Dole contracted with application service providers (ASPs) to handle things like payroll management.[134] For succession management, Dole chose software from Pilat NAI. The Pilat system keeps all the data on its own servers for a monthly fee. Dole's managers access the program via the Web using a password. They fill out online résumés for themselves, including career interests, and note special considerations such as geographic restrictions.

The managers also assess themselves on four competencies. Once the manager provides his or her input, the program notifies that manager's boss, who assesses his or her subordinate and indicates whether the person is promotable. This assessment and the online résumés then go automatically to the division head and the divisional HR director. Dole's senior vice president for human resources then uses the information to create career development plans for each manager, including seminars and other programs.[135] ■

Candidate Assessment and the 9-Box Grid

Some high-potential managers fail in their jobs, while some apparently low-potential managers excel. How then does an employer choose who to send through an expensive development program?

The 9-Box Grid is one tool. It shows *Potential* from low to medium to high on the vertical axis, and *Performance* from low to medium to high across the bottom—a total of nine possible boxes.

The grid can simplify, somewhat, the task of choosing development candidates. At the extremes, for instance, low potentials/low performers would not move on. The high-potential/high-performance stars most assuredly would. Most employers focus their development resources on high-performance/high-potential stars, and secondarily on those rated high-potential/moderate-performance, or high-performance/moderate-potential.[136] Other employers focus development resources on the company's "mission-critical employees"—those central to the firm's success and survival. We'll see how later in this section.

In any case, individual assessment should always precede development. At frozen foods manufacturer Schwan, senior executives first whittle 40 or more development candidates down to about 10. Then the program begins with a 1-day assessment by outside consultants of each manager's leadership strengths and weaknesses. This assessment becomes the basis for each manager's individual development plan. Action-learning (practical) projects then supplement individual and group training activities.[137]

We'll look at some popular development activities next.

Managerial On-the-Job Training and Rotation

job rotation
A management training technique that involves moving a trainee from department to department to broaden his or her experience and identify strong and weak points.

Managerial on-the-job training methods include job rotation, the coaching/understudy approach, and action learning. **Job rotation** means moving managers from department to department to broaden their understanding of the business and to test their abilities. The trainee may be a recent college graduate, or a senior manager being groomed for further promotion. In addition to providing a well-rounded training experience, job rotation helps avoid stagnation through the constant introduction of new points of view in each department. It also helps identify the trainee's strong and weak points. Periodic job changing can also improve interdepartmental cooperation; managers become more understanding of each other's problems; rotation also widens the acquaintances among management. The accompanying HR Practices feature illustrates this.

IMPROVING PERFORMANCE: *HR Practices Around the Globe*

Global Job Rotation

As firms expand globally, job rotation takes on a new meaning. At firms like Shell and BP, rotating managers globally is a primary means through which the firms maintain their flexibility and responsiveness even as they grow to an enormous size.

An advantage of global job rotation (rotating managers from, say, Sweden to New York) is that it builds a network of informal ties that ensures superior cross-border communication and mutual understanding as well as tight interunit coordination and control.

Improved communication and understanding stem from the personal relationships that are forged as managers work in the firm's various locations. These activities can also enhance organizational control. When employees from the firm's global locations are rotated or brought together at, say, the Harvard Business School or Europe's INSEAD for a management-training program, the aim is more than just teaching basic skills. It is also to build a stronger identification with the company's culture and values. By creating shared values and a consistent view of the firm and its goals, management development activities like these can facilitate communication. They ensure that through a sense of shared values and purpose the firm's policies are followed, even with a minimal reliance on other forms of control.[138] ■

Source: Based on Paul Evans, Yves Doz and Andre Laurent, Human Resource Management in International Firms, New York: St. Martin's Press, 1990, pp. 122–124; www.sony.net/SonyInfo/csr_report/employees/training/index3.html; www.mckinsey.com/insights/organization/how_multinationals_can_attract_the_talent_they_need.

If your professor has assigned this, go to the Assignments section of **mymanagementlab.com** to complete this discussion.

✪ **Talk About It 4:** Using websites such as www.sony.net (click "Careers") and www.mckinsey.com (insert *how multinationals can attract the talent they need* into their search box), discuss examples of how multinational companies use job rotation and other means to develop their managers.

COACHING/UNDERSTUDY APPROACH Here the trainee works directly with a senior manager or with the person he or she is to replace; the latter is responsible for the trainee's coaching. Normally, the understudy relieves the executive of certain responsibilities, giving the trainee a chance to learn the job.

action learning
A training technique by which management trainees are allowed to work full-time analyzing and solving problems in other departments.

ACTION LEARNING **Action learning** programs give managers released time to work analyzing and solving problems in departments other than their own. It is reportedly the fastest-growing leadership development technique today, used by companies ranging from Wells Fargo to Boeing.[139] Its basics include carefully selected teams of 5 to 25 members, assigning them real-world business problems that extend beyond their usual areas of expertise, and structured learning through coaching and feedback. The employer's senior managers usually choose the projects and decide whether to accept the teams' recommendations.[140]

For example, Pacific Gas & Electric Company's (PG&E) Action-Forum Process has three phases:

1. A 6- to 8-week *framework* phase, during which the team defines and collects data on an issue;
2. The *action forum*—2 to 3 days at PG&E's learning center discussing the issue and developing action-plan recommendations; and
3. *Accountability sessions*, where the teams meet with the leadership group at monthly intervals to review progress.

Off-the-Job Management Training and Development Techniques

There are also many off-the-job techniques for training and developing managers.

case study method
A development method in which the manager is presented with a written description of an organizational problem to diagnose and solve.

As most everyone knows, the **case study method** has trainees solve realistic problems after studying written or video case descriptions. The person then analyzes the case, diagnoses the problem, and presents his or her findings and solutions in a discussion with other trainees. *Integrated case scenarios* create long-term, comprehensive case situations. One FBI Academy scenario starts with"a concerned citizen's telephone call and ends 14 weeks later with a simulated trial. In between is the stuff of a genuine investigation…." Scriptwriters (often training team employees) write the scripts. The scripts include background stories, detailed personnel histories, and role-playing instructions; their aim is to develop specific skills, such as interviewing witnesses.[141]

management game
A development technique in which teams of managers compete by making computerized decisions regarding realistic but simulated situations.

Computerized **management games** enable trainees to learn by making realistic decisions in simulated situations. For example, *Interpret* is a team exercise that "explores team communication, the management of information and the planning and implementation of a strategy. It raises management trainees' communication skills, helps them to better manage the information flow between individuals and the team, and improves planning and problem-solving skills."[142] In other games each team might have to decide how much to spend on advertising, how much to produce, and how much inventory to maintain.

People learn best by being involved, and games gain such involvement. They also help trainees develop problem-solving skills, and focus attention on planning rather than just putting out fires. They can develop leadership skills and foster cooperation and teamwork.

Gamification of such training also reportedly improves learning, engagement, and morale and is fairly easy to achieve. For instance, inject point systems, badges, and leaderboards into the training.[143]

OUTSIDE SEMINARS Numerous companies and universities offer Web-based and traditional classroom management development seminars and conferences. The selection of 1- to 3-day training programs offered by the American Management Association illustrates what's available. Recently, for instance, its offerings ranged from "developing your emotional intelligence" to "assertiveness training," "assertiveness training for managers," "assertiveness training for women in business," "dynamic listening skills for successful communication," and "fundamentals of cost accounting."[144] Specialized groups, such as SHRM, provide specialized seminars for their profession's members.[145]

UNIVERSITY-RELATED PROGRAMS Many universities provide executive education and continuing education programs in leadership, supervision, and the like. These can range from 1- to 4-day programs to executive development programs lasting 1 to 4 months.

In one such program, Hasbro wanted to improve its executives' creativity skills. Dartmouth University's Amos Tuck Business School provided a "custom approach to designing a program that would be built from the ground up to suit Hasbro's specific needs."[146] The Advanced Management Program of Harvard's Graduate School of Business Administration is another such program.[147]

role-playing
A training technique in which trainees act out parts in a realistic management situation.

ROLE-PLAYING The aim of **role-playing** is to create a realistic situation and then have the trainees assume the parts (or roles) of specific persons in that situation. Each trainee gets a role, such as:

> You are the head of a crew of telephone maintenance workers, each of whom drives a small service truck to and from the various jobs. Every so often you get a new truck to exchange for an old one, and you have the problem of deciding to which of your crew members you should give the new truck. Often there are hard feelings, so you have a tough time being fair.[148]

When combined with the general instructions and other roles, role-playing can trigger spirited discussions among the trainees. The aim is to develop trainees' skills in areas like leadership and delegating. For example, a supervisor could experiment with both a considerate and an autocratic leadership style, whereas in the real world this isn't so easy. Role-playing may also help someone to be more sensitive to others' feelings.

in-house development center
A company-based method for exposing prospective managers to realistic exercises to develop improved management skills.

CORPORATE UNIVERSITIES Many firms, particularly larger ones, establish **in-house development centers** (often called *corporate universities*). Employers may collaborate with academic institutions, and with training and development program providers and Web-based educational portals, to create packages of programs and materials for their centers. The best corporate universities (1) actively align offerings with corporate goals, (2) focus on developing skills that support business needs, (3) evaluate learning and performance, (4) use technology to support learning, and (5) partner with academia.[149]

Many employers offer virtual—rather than brick-and-mortar—corporate university services. For example, Cerner offers its employees "Cerner KnowledgeWorks." This offers employees three types of knowledge. *Dynamic knowledge* "is real-time content … such as e-mails, instant messages, or conference calls." *Moderated content* "includes best practices, such as case studies or wikis that capture information about situations where we did well and how we did it." *Codified content* "is more formal documentation of official company practices, and includes installation guides, help files, and formal training or courses."[150]

executive coach
An outside consultant who questions the executive's associates in order to identify the executive's strengths and weaknesses, and then counsels the executive so he or she can capitalize on those strengths and overcome the weaknesses.

EXECUTIVE COACHES Many firms retain executive coaches to help develop their top managers' effectiveness. An **executive coach** is an outside consultant who questions the executive's boss, peers, subordinates, and (sometimes) family in order to identify the executive's strengths and weaknesses, and to counsel the executive so he or she can capitalize on those strengths and overcome the weaknesses.[151] Executive coaching can cost $50,000 per executive. Experts recommend using formal assessments prior to coaching, to uncover strengths and weaknesses and to provide more focused coaching.[152]

Executive coaching can be effective. Participants in one study included about 1,400 senior managers who had received "360-degree" performance feedback from bosses, peers, and subordinates. About 400 worked with an executive coach to review the feedback. About a year later, these and about 400 managers who didn't receive coaching again received multisource feedback. The managers who received coaching were more likely to set more effective goals for their subordinates, and to have improved ratings from subordinates and supervisors.[153]

The coaching field is unregulated, so managers should do their due diligence. Check references, and consult the International Coach Federation, a trade group.

THE SHRM LEARNING SYSTEM The Society for Human Resource Management (SHRM) encourages HR professionals to qualify for certification by taking examinations. The society offers several preparatory training programs.[154] These include self-study, and a college/university option that includes classroom interaction with instructors and other learners.[155]

Leadership Development at GE

General Electric is known for its success in developing its executive talent. GE's current mix of executive development programs illustrates what it offers:[156]

Leadership programs: These multiyear training programs rotate about 3,000 employees per year through various functions with the aim of enabling people to run a large GE business.

Session C: This is GE's intense multilevel performance appraisal process. The CEO personally reviews GE's top 625 officers every year.

Crotonville: This is GE's corporate training campus in New York and offers a mix of conventional classroom learning and team-based training and cultural trips.

Boca Raton: At this annual meeting of GE's top 625 officers, they network, share their best ideas, and get to understand the company's strategy for the coming year.

The next big thing: Whether it's productivity and quality improvement through "Six Sigma" or "innovation," GE focuses its employees on central themes or initiatives.

Monthly dinners: Jeffrey Immelt, GE's CEO, meets periodically at dinners and breakfasts to learn more about his top executives and to "strengthen his connections with his top team."[157]

TRENDS SHAPING HR: *CUSTOMIZED TALENT MANAGEMENT THROUGH DIFFERENTIAL DEVELOPMENT ASSIGNMENTS*

In today's competitive environment, the usual HR practice of allocating development opportunities and other scarce resources across the board or based solely on performance makes less sense. It often makes more sense to focus more of the employer's resources on the "mission-critical employees" who the employer deems most crucial to the its future growth.

We'll look closer at how employers do this in the following chapter, but several examples follow:

- High-potential trainees in Johnson & Johnson's special "LeAD" leadership development program receive advice and regular assessments from coaches brought in from outside the company.[158]
- Some companies share future strategies on a privileged basis with rising leaders. For example, they invite them to quarterly meetings with high-level executives, and let them access an online portal where the rising leaders can review the company's strategy and critical metrics.[159] ■

Managing Organizational Change Programs

LEARNING OBJECTIVE 8-6
List and briefly discuss the importance of the steps in leading organizational change.

Companies often find it necessary to change how they do things. For example, Microsoft changed its CEO a few years ago, then reorganized, changed its strategy to include supplying hardware (tablets, etc.) as well as software, and made other personnel changes. As here, organizational change may impact a company's strategy, culture, structure, technologies, or the attitudes and skills of its employees.

Making changes is never easy, but the hardest part is often overcoming employee resistance. Individuals, groups, and even entire organizations tend to resist change, because they are accustomed to the usual way of doing things or because of perceived threats to their influence, for instance.[160]

Lewin's Change Process

Psychologist Kurt Lewin formulated a model to summarize the basic process for implementing a change with minimal resistance. To Lewin, all behavior in organizations was a product of two kinds of forces: those striving to maintain the status quo and those pushing for change. Implementing change thus means reducing the forces for the status quo or building up the forces for change. Lewin's process consists of three steps:

1. ***Unfreezing*** means reducing the forces that are striving to maintain the status quo, usually by presenting a provocative problem or event to get people to recognize the need for change and to search for new solutions.
2. ***Moving*** means developing new behaviors, values, and attitudes. The manager may accomplish this through organizational structure changes, through conventional training and development activities, and sometimes through the other organizational development techniques (such as team building) we'll discuss later.
3. ***Refreezing*** means building in the reinforcement to make sure the organization doesn't slide back into its former ways of doing things—for instance, change the incentive system.

In practice, to deal with employee intransigence, some experts suggest that the manager use a process such as the following to implement the change:[161]

To bring about a desired organizational change at work:

1. ***Establish a sense of urgency.*** Create a sense of urgency. For example, present employees with a (fictitious) analyst's report describing the firm's imminent demise.

Bloomberg/Contributor/Getty Images

Microsoft appointed Satya Nadella its new CEO a few years ago, then reorganized, changed its strategy, and made other personnel changes.

2. ***Mobilize commitment*** through joint diagnoses of problems. Create a task force to diagnose the problems facing the department or the company. This can help to produce a shared understanding of what can and must be improved.
3. ***Create a guiding coalition.*** It's never easy to implement big changes alone. Therefore, create a "guiding coalition" of influential people. They'll act as missionaries and implementers.
4. ***Develop and communicate a shared vision*** of what you see coming from the change. Keep the vision simple (for example, "We will be faster than anyone at satisfying customer needs."), and lead by example.[162]
5. ***Help employees make the change.*** Eliminate impediments. For example, do current policies or procedures make it difficult to act? Do intransigent managers discourage employees from acting?
6. ***Aim first for attainable short-term accomplishments.*** Use the credibility from these to make additional changes.[163]
7. ***Reinforce the new ways of doing things*** with changes to the company's systems and procedures. For example, use new appraisal systems and incentives to reinforce the desired new behaviors.
8. ***Monitor and assess progress.*** In brief, this involves comparing where the company or department is with where it should be.

Using Organizational Development

Beyond this process, there are many other ways to reduce resistance. Among the many suggestions are that managers impose rewards or sanctions that guide employee behaviors, explain why the change is needed, negotiate with employees, give inspirational speeches, or ask employees to help design the change.[164] Organizational development (OD) taps into the latter. **Organizational development** is a change process through which employees formulate the change that's required and implement it, often with the assistance of trained consultants. OD has several distinguishing characteristics:

organizational development
A special approach to organizational change in which employees themselves formulate and implement the change that's required.

1. It usually involves *action research*, which means collecting data about a group, department, or organization, and feeding the information back to the employees so they can analyze it and develop hypotheses about what the problems might be.
2. It applies behavioral science knowledge to improve the organization's effectiveness.
3. It changes the organization in a particular direction—toward empowerment, improved problem-solving, responsiveness, quality of work, and effectiveness.

For example, according to experts French and Bell, one OD method, *team-building meetings*, begins with the consultant interviewing each of the group members and the leader before the meeting.[165] They are asked what their problems are, how they think the group functions, and what obstacles are keeping the group from performing better. The consultant then categorizes the interview data into themes (such as "inadequate communications") and presents the themes to the group at the start of the meeting. The group ranks the themes in terms of importance, and the most important ones become the agenda for the meeting. The group then explores and discusses the issues, examines the underlying causes of the problems, and begins devising solutions.

Survey research is one of many more OD options (see Table 8-2). It requires having employees throughout the organization complete attitude surveys. The facilitator then uses those data as a basis for problem analysis and action planning. Surveys are a convenient way to unfreeze a company's management and employees. They provide a comparative, graphic illustration of the fact that the organization does have problems to solve.[166]

TABLE 8-2 Categories of OD Interventions

Human Process	Human Resource Management
T-groups	Goal setting
Process consultation	Performance appraisal
Third-party intervention	Reward systems
Team building	Career planning and development
Organizational confrontation meeting	Managing workforce diversity
Survey research	Employee wellness
Technostructural	**Strategic**
Formal structural change	Integrated strategic management
Differentiation and integration	Culture change
Cooperative union–management projects	Strategic change
Quality circles	Self-designing organizations
Total quality management	
Work design	

Evaluating the Training Effort

LEARNING OBJECTIVE **8-7**
Explain why a controlled study may be superior for evaluating the training program's effects.

With today's emphasis on measuring results, it is crucial that the manager evaluate the training program. There are several things you can measure: participants' *reactions* to the program, what (if anything) the trainees *learned* from the program, and to what extent their on-the-job *behavior* or *results* changed as a result of the program. In one survey of about 500 U.S. organizations, 77% evaluated their training programs by eliciting reactions, 36% evaluated learning, and about 10% to 15% assessed the program's behavior and/or results.[167] Computerization facilitates evaluation. For example, Bovis Lend Lease uses learning management system software to monitor which employees are taking which courses, and the extent to which they're improving their skills.[168]

There are two basic issues to address when evaluating training programs. One is the design of the evaluation study and, in particular, whether to use controlled experimentation. The second is, "What should we measure?"

Designing the Study

In deciding how to design the evaluation study, the basic concern is this: How can we be sure that the training (rather than, say, a company-wide wage increase) caused the results that we're trying to measure? The *time series design* is one option. Here, as in Figure 8-3, you take a series of performance measures before and after the training program. This can provide some insight into the program's effectiveness.[169] However, you can't be sure that the training (rather than, say, the raise) caused any change.

controlled experimentation
Formal methods for testing the effectiveness of a training program, preferably with before-and-after tests and a control group.

Controlled experimentation is therefore the gold standard. A controlled experiment uses a training group and a control group that receives no training. Data (for instance, on quantity of sales or quality of service) are obtained both before and after one group is exposed to training and before and after a corresponding period in the control group. This makes it easier to determine the extent to which any change in the training group's performance resulted from the training, rather than from some organizationwide change like a raise in pay. (The pay raise should have affected employees in both groups equally.)[170]

FIGURE 8-3 Using a Time Series Graph to Assess a Training Program's Effects

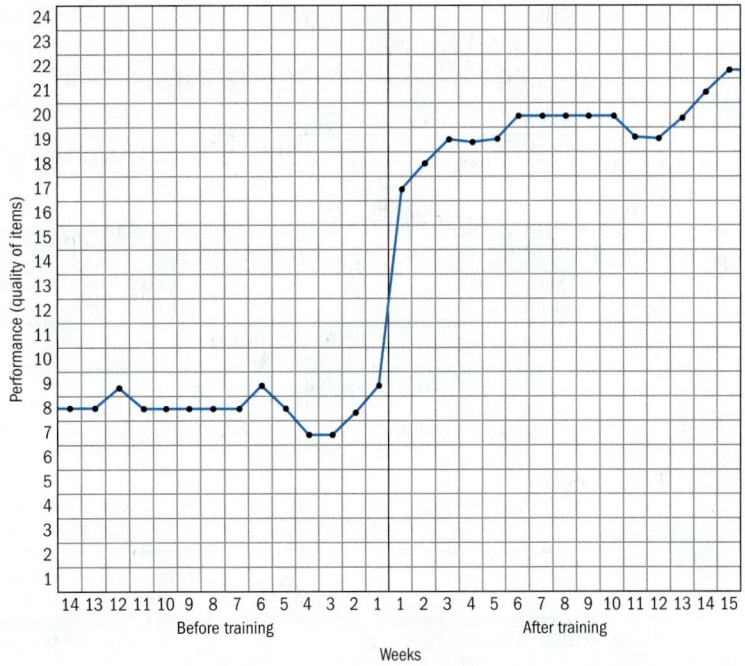

Training Effects to Measure

The manager can measure four basic categories of training outcomes or effects:

1. ***Reaction.*** Evaluate trainees' reactions to the program. Did they like the program? Did they think it worthwhile?
2. ***Learning.*** Test the trainees to determine whether they learned the principles, skills, and facts they were supposed to learn.
3. ***Behavior.*** Ask whether the trainees' on-the-job behavior changed because of the training program. For example, are employees in the store's complaint department more courteous toward disgruntled customers?
4. ***Results.*** Most important, ask, "What results did we achieve, in terms of the training objectives previously set?" For example, did the number of customer complaints diminish? Reactions, learning, and behavior are important. But if the training program doesn't produce measurable performance-related results, then it probably hasn't achieved its goals.[171]

Evaluating these is straightforward. Figure 8-4 presents one page from a sample evaluation questionnaire for assessing *reactions*. Or, you might assess trainees' *learning* by testing their new knowledge. For *behavioral change,* perhaps assess the effectiveness of a supervisory performance appraisal training program by asking that person's subordinates, "Did your supervisor provide you with examples of good and bad performance when he or she appraised your performance most recently?" Finally, directly assess a training program's *results* by measuring, say, the percentage of phone caller questions that call center trainees subsequently answered correctly.

A careful comparison of the training program's costs and benefits can enable the human resource team to compute the program's return on investment. Online calculators are available to facilitate such analyses.[172]

A program at MGM Resorts illustrates training evaluation.[173] In the hospitality industry, how likely guests are to return is a crucial metric, and is measured at MGM by "Net Promoter Scores" (NPS). With MGM's NPS scores not up to par, its training team concluded "guest facing" employees weren't sufficiently engaged. It created an Essentials of Hotel Management Program for front desk and assistant managers. The program emphasized skills like collaboration and communications. At the end of the approximately 1-year program, NPS scores had risen about 2% (which is considered a notable accomplishment).[174]

OPM

INSTRUCTOR HANDOUTS

United States Office of Personnel Management

TRAINING EVALUATION FORM

TITLE OF COURSE: **"Work and Family Issues — A Module for Supervisors and Managers"**
NAME OF INSTRUCTOR:

DATE OF TRAINING
Started:_____
Ended:_____

NAME: (Optional)	**POSITION TITLE/GRADE:**

AGENCY:	**OFFICE PHONE:** (Optional)	**OFFICE ADDRESS:** (Optional)

Rate Your Knowledge and Skill Level
(Circle your rating)

Before this course Low ----------High
1 2 3 4 5

After this course Low ----------High
1 2 3 4 5

Overall, how would you rate this course?

__ Excellent __Very Good __ Good

__ Fair __ Poor

EVALUATION OF COURSE
(Check appropriate box)

ITEMS OF EVALUATION How did the course sharpen your knowledge or skills in:	Excellent	Very Good	Good	Fair	Poor	Not Applicable
1. What work and family programs are	°	°	°	°	°	°
2. Who uses work and family programs	°	°	°	°	°	°
3. How to recognize/solve work/family issues	°	°	°	°	°	°
4. Helping you take practical steps on the job	°	°	°	°	°	°

RATING OF INSTRUCTOR

1. Presentation, organization, delivery	°	°	°	°	°	°
2. Knowledge and command of the subject	°	°	°	°	°	°
3. Use of audio-visuals or other training aids	°	°	°	°	°	°
4. Stimulation of an open exchange of ideas, participation, & group interaction	°	°	°	°	°	°

STRONG POINTS OF THE COURSE
°
°
°

WEAK POINTS OF THE COURSE
°
°
°

ADDITIONAL DATA YOU WOULD LIKE TO HAVE COVERED IN COURSE
°
°
°

ADDITIONAL COMMENTS/OR RECOMMENDATIONS

FIGURE 8-4 A Training Evaluation Form

Source: From Instructor Handouts: Training Evaluation Form, United States Office of Personnel Management.

Chapter Review

MyManagementLab® Go to **mymanagementlab.com** to complete the problems marked with this icon. ✪

Chapter Section Summaries

8-1. Getting your new employee on board and up to speed begins with **orienting and training** him or her. Employee orientation means providing new employees with the information they need to function, and helping them start being emotionally attached to the firm. The four-step training process includes needs analysis, instructional design, implementation, and evaluation. Trainees need to be motivated to learn. Ensuring that they are motivated involves making the learning meaningful, making skills transfer easy, and reinforcing the learning.

8-2. There is more to orienting employees than introducing them to their coworkers. Even without a company-wide program like Toyota's, use the onboarding opportunity to begin instilling in the new employee the company values and traditions in which you expect the person to become **engaged**.

8-3. We used the acronym **ADDIE** to outline the **training process**: analyze, develop, design, implement, and evaluate. Before training employees, it's necessary to analyze their training needs and design the training program. In training new employees, employers use task analysis—basically, a detailed study of the job—to determine what skills the job requires. For current employees, performance analysis is required, specifically to verify that there is performance efficiency and to determine if training is the solution. Distinguishing between can't-do and won't-do problems is the main issue here. Once you understand the issues, you can design a training program, which means identifying specific training objectives, clarifying a training budget, and then actually designing the program in terms of the actual content.

8-4. With this in place, you can turn to **implementing the training program**. Specific training methods include on-the-job training, apprenticeship training, informal learning, job instruction training, lectures, programmed learning, audiovisual-based training, vestibule training, videoconferencing, electronic performance support systems, and computer-based training. Frequently, programs today are Internet-based, with employees accessing packaged online programs, backed up by learning management systems, through their company's learning portals. Employers also increasingly use mobile learning, for instance, delivering short courses and explanations to employees' smart phones. With increasing demands for technologically literate employees, lifelong learning can help ensure employees have the basic educational backgrounds they need to succeed on their jobs. Diversity training aims to create better cross-cultural sensitivity with the goal of fostering more harmonious working relationships.

8-5. Most training methods are useful for all employees, but some are particularly appropriate for **management development programs**. Like all employees, new managers often get on-the-job training, for instance, via job rotation and coaching. In addition, it's usual to supply various off-the-job training and development opportunities—for instance, using the case study method, management games, outside seminars, university-related programs, corporate universities, executive coaches, and (for human resource managers) the SHRM learning system.

8-6. When facing economic, competitive, or other challenges, managers have to execute **organizational change programs**. These may aim at changing the company's strategy, culture, structure, technologies, or the attitudes and skills of the employees. Often, the trickiest part of organizational change is overcoming employees' resistance to it. With that in mind, steps in an effective organizational change program include establishing a sense of urgency, mobilizing commitment, creating a guiding coalition, developing and communicating a shared vision, helping employees make the change, consolidating gains, reinforcing new ways of doing things, and monitoring and assessing progress. Organizational development involves action research, which means collecting data about a group and feeding the information back to the employees so they can analyze it and develop hypotheses about what the problems might be.

8-7. Whatever the training program, it's important to **evaluate the training effort**. You can measure reaction, learning, behavior, or results, ideally using a control group that is not exposed to training, in parallel with the group that you're training.

Discussion Questions

8-1. "A well-thought-out orientation program is essential for all new employees, whether they have experience or not." Explain why you agree or disagree with this statement.

8-2. Explain how you would apply our "motivation points" (pages 240–241) in developing a lecture, say, on orientation and training.

✪ **8-3.** What are some typical on-the-job training techniques? What do you think are some of the main drawbacks of relying on informal on-the-job training for breaking new employees into their jobs? What are some important advantages to using cloud-based training?

✪ **8-4.** Describe the pros and cons of five management development methods.

8-5. Do you think job rotation is a good method to use for developing management trainees? Why or why not?

8-6. What is organizational development, and how does it differ from traditional approaches to organizational change?

8-7. List and briefly explain each of the steps in the training process.

Individual and Group Activities

8-8. You're the supervisor of a group of employees whose task is to assemble disk drives that go into computers. You find that quality is not what it should be and that many of your group's devices have to be brought back and reworked. Your boss says, "You'd better start doing a better job of training your workers."

a. What are some of the staffing factors that could be contributing to this problem?

b. Explain how you would go about assessing whether it is in fact a training problem.

8-9. Choose a task with which you are familiar—mowing the lawn, making a salad, or studying for a test—and develop a job instruction sheet for it.

8-10. Working individually or in groups, develop a short, programmed learning program on the subject "Guidelines for Giving a More Effective Lecture."

8-11. Find three or four actual examples of employers using social media for training purposes. At what levels of managers are the offerings aimed? What seem to be the most popular types of programs? Why do you think that's the case?

8-12. Working individually or in groups, develop several specific examples to illustrate how a professor teaching human resource management could use at least four of the techniques described in this chapter in teaching his or her HR course.

8-13. Working individually or in groups, develop an orientation program for high school graduates entering your university as freshmen.

8-14. Appendices A and B at the end of this book (pages 612–629) list the knowledge someone studying for the HRCI (Appendix A) or SHRM (Appendix B) certification exam needs to have in each area of human resource management (such as in Strategic Management, and Workforce Planning). In groups of several students, do four things: (1) review Appendix A and/or B; (2) identify the material in this chapter that relates to the Appendix A and/or B required knowledge lists; (3) write four multiple-choice exam questions on this material that you believe would be suitable for inclusion in the HRCI exam and/or the SHRM exam; and, (4) if time permits, have someone from your team post your team's questions in front of the class, so that students in all teams can answer the exam questions created by the other teams.

8-15. Perhaps no training task in Afghanistan was more pressing than that involved in creating the country's new army, which is an ongoing task. These were the people who were to help the coalition bring security to Afghanistan. However, many new soldiers and even officers had no experience. There were language barriers between trainers and trainees. And some trainees found themselves quickly under fire from insurgents when they went as trainees out into the field. Based on what you learned about training from this chapter, list the five most important things you would tell the U.S. officer in charge of training to keep in mind as he designs the training program.

Experiential Exercise

Flying the Friendlier Skies

Purpose: The purpose of this exercise is to give you practice in developing a training program for the job of airline reservation clerk for a major airline.

Required Understanding: You should be fully acquainted with the material in this chapter and should read the following description of an airline reservation clerk's duties:

> Customers contact our airline reservation clerks to obtain flight schedules, prices, and itineraries. The reservation clerks look up the requested information on our airline's online flight schedule systems, which are updated continuously. The reservation clerk must deal courteously and expeditiously with the customer, and be able to quickly find alternative flight arrangements in order to provide the customer with the itinerary that fits his or her needs. Alternative flights and prices must be found quickly, so that the customer is not kept waiting, and so that our reservations operations group maintains its efficiency standards. It is often necessary to look under various routings, since there may be a dozen or more alternative routes between the customer's starting point and destination.

You may assume that we just hired 30 new clerks, and that you must create a 3-day training program.

How to Set Up the Exercise/Instructions: Divide the class into teams of five or six students.

Airline reservation clerks obviously need numerous skills to perform their jobs. This airline has asked you to quickly design the outline of a training program for its new reservation clerks.

8-16. You may want to start by listing the job's main duties and by reviewing any work you may have done for the exercise at the end of Chapter 6.

8-17. In any case, please produce the requested outline, making sure to be very specific about what you want to teach the new clerks, and what methods and aids you suggest using to train them.

Application Case*

Reinventing the Wheel at Apex Door Company

Jim Delaney, president of Apex Door, has a problem. No matter how often he tells his employees how to do their jobs, they invariably "decide to do it their way," as he puts it, and arguments ensue between Jim, the employee, and the employee's supervisor. One example is the door-design department, where the designers are expected to work with the architects to design doors that meet the specifications. While it's not "rocket science," as Jim puts it, the designers invariably make mistakes—such as designing in too much steel, a problem that can cost Apex tens of thousands of wasted dollars, once you consider the number of doors in, say, a 30-story office tower.

The order processing department is another example. Jim has a very specific and detailed way he wants the order written up, but most of the order clerks don't understand how to use the multipage order form. They simply improvise when it comes to a detailed question such as whether to classify the customer as "industrial" or "commercial."

The current training process is as follows. None of the jobs has a training manual per se, although several have somewhat out-of-date job descriptions. The training for new people is all on the job. Usually, the person leaving the company trains the new person during the 1- or 2-week overlap period, but if there's no overlap, the new person is trained as well as possible by other employees who have filled in occasionally on the job in the past. The training is the same throughout the company—for machinists, secretaries, assemblers, engineers, and accounting clerks, for example.

Questions

8-18. What do you think of Apex's training process? Could it help to explain why employees "do things their way"? If so, how?

8-19. What role should job descriptions play in training at Apex?

8-20. Explain in detail what you would do to improve the training process at Apex. Make sure to provide specific suggestions, please.

Continuing Case

Carter Cleaning Company

The New Training Program

The Carter Cleaning Centers currently have no formal orientation or training policies or procedures, and Jennifer believes this is one reason why the standards to which she and her father would like employees to adhere are generally not followed.

The Carters would prefer that certain practices and procedures be used in dealing with the customers at the front counters. For example, all customers should be greeted with what Jack refers to as a "big hello." Garments they drop off should immediately be inspected for any damage or unusual stains so these can be brought to the customer's attention, lest the customer later return to pick up the garment and erroneously blame the store. The garments are then supposed to

*Source: Copyright Dr. Gary Dessler.

be placed together in a nylon sack immediately to separate them from other customers' garments. The ticket also has to be carefully written, with the customer's name and telephone number and the date clearly noted on all copies. The counter person is also supposed to take the opportunity to try to sell the customer additional services such as waterproofing, or simply notify the customer that "Now that people are doing their spring cleaning, we're having a special on drapery cleaning all this month." Finally, as the customer leaves, the counter person is supposed to make a courteous comment like "Have a nice day." Each of the other jobs in the stores—pressing, cleaning and spotting, and so forth—similarly contain certain steps, procedures, and, most importantly, standards the Carters would prefer to see upheld.

The company has had problems, Jennifer feels, because of a lack of adequate employee training and orientation. For example, two new employees became very upset last month when they discovered that they were not paid at the end of the week, on Friday, but instead were paid (as are all Carter employees) on the following Tuesday. The Carters use the extra 2 days in part to give them time to obtain everyone's hours and compute their pay. The other reason they do it, according to Jack, is that "frankly, when we stay a few days behind in paying employees it helps to ensure that they at least give us a few days' notice before quitting on us. While we are certainly obligated to pay them anything they earn, we find that psychologically they seem to be less likely to just walk out on us Friday evening and not show up Monday morning if they still haven't gotten their pay from the previous week. This way they at least give us a few days' notice so we can find a replacement."

There are other matters that could be covered during orientation and training, says Jennifer. These include company policy regarding paid holidays, lateness and absences, health benefits (there are none, other than workers' compensation), substance abuse, eating or smoking on the job (both forbidden), and general matters like the maintenance of a clean and safe work area, personal appearance and cleanliness, time sheets, personal telephone calls, and personal e-mail.

Jennifer believes that implementing orientation and training programs would help to ensure that employees know how to do their jobs the right way. And she and her father further believe that it is only when employees understand the right way to do their jobs that there is any hope their jobs will be accomplished the way the Carters want them to be accomplished.

Questions

8-21. Specifically, what should the Carters cover in their new employee orientation program, and how should they convey this information?

8-22. In the HR management course Jennifer took, the book suggested using a job instruction sheet to identify tasks performed by an employee. Should the Carter Cleaning Centers use a form like this for the counter person's job? If so, what should the form look like, say, for a counter person?

8-23. Which specific training techniques should Jennifer use to train her pressers, her cleaner/spotters, her managers, and her counter people? Why should these training techniques be used?

Translating Strategy into HR Policies and Practices Case*,§

**The accompanying strategy map for this chapter is in MyManagementLab, and the overall map on the inside back cover of this text outlines the relationships involved.*

Improving Performance at the Hotel Paris

The New Training Program

The Hotel Paris's competitive strategy is "To use superior guest service to differentiate the Hotel Paris properties, and to thereby increase the length of stay and return rate of guests, and thus boost revenues and profitability." HR manager Lisa Cruz must now formulate functional policies and activities that support this competitive strategy, by eliciting the required employee behaviors and competencies.

As she reviewed her company's training processes, Lisa had many reasons to be concerned. For one thing, the Hotel Paris relied almost exclusively on informal on-the-job training. New security guards attended a 1-week program offered by a law enforcement agency, but all other new hires, from assistant manager to housekeeping crew, learned the rudiments of their jobs from their colleagues and their supervisors, on the job. Lisa noted that the drawbacks of this informality were evident when she compared the Hotel Paris's performance on various training metrics with those of other hotels and service firms. For example, in terms of number of hours training per employee per year, number of hours training for new employees, cost per trainee hour, and percent of payroll spent on training, the Hotel Paris was far from the norm when benchmarked against similar firms.

As Lisa and the CFO reviewed measures of the Hotel Paris's current training efforts, it was clear that (when compared to similar companies) some changes were in order. Most other service companies provided at least 40 hours of training per employee per year, while the Hotel Paris offered, on average, no more than 5 or 6. Similar firms offered at least 40 hours of training per *new* employee, while the Hotel Paris offered, at most, 10. Even the apparently "good" metrics comparisons simply masked poor results. For example, whereas most service firms spend about 8% of their payrolls on training, the Hotel Paris spent less than 1%. The problem, of course, was that the Hotel Paris's training wasn't more efficient, it was simply nonexistent.

Given this and the commonsense links between (1) employee training and (2) employee performance, the CFO gave his go-ahead for Lisa and her team to design a comprehensive package of training programs for all Hotel Paris employees. They retained a training supplier to design a 1-day training program composed of lectures and audiovisual material for all new employees. This program covered the Hotel Paris's history, its competitive strategy, and its critical employee capabilities and behaviors, including the need to be customer oriented. With a combination of lectures and video examples of correct and incorrect behaviors, the behavior-modeling part of this program aimed to cultivate in new employees the company's essential values, including, "we endeavor to do everything we can to make the guests' stay 100% pleasant."

§Written by and copyright Gary Dessler, PhD.

The team developed separate training programs for each of the hotel's other individual job categories. For example, it retained a special vendor to create computer-based training programs, complete with interactive scenarios, for both the front-desk clerks and telephone operators. As with all the new training programs, they had these translated into the languages of the countries in which the Hotel Paris did business. The team chose to stay with on-the-job training for both the housekeeping and valet/door person job categories, but formalized this training with special handbooks for each job category's supervisory staff. For assistant managers, the team developed a new videoconference-based online training and development program. In this way, the new managers could interact with other assistant managers around the chain, even as they were learning the basics of their new jobs. Lisa and the CFO were not at all surprised to find that within a year of instituting the new training programs, scores on numerous employee capabilities and behavior metrics (including speed of check-in/out, percent of employees scoring at least 90% on Hotel Paris's values quiz, and percent room cleaning infractions) improved markedly. They knew from previous analyses that these improvements would, in turn, drive improvements in customer and organizational outcomes, and strategic performance.

Questions

8-24. Based on what you read in this chapter, what would you have suggested Lisa and her team do first with respect to training, particularly in terms of the company's strategy? Why?

8-25. Have Lisa and the CFO sufficiently investigated whether training is really called for? Why? What would you suggest?

8-26. Based on what you read in this Dessler *Human Resource Management* chapter and what you may access via the Web, develop a detailed training program for one of these hotel positions: security guard, housekeeper, or door person.

MyManagementLab

Go to **mymanagementlab.com** for Auto-graded writing questions as well as the following Assisted-graded writing questions:

8-27. John Santos is an undergraduate business student majoring in accounting. He just failed the first accounting course, Accounting 101. He is understandably upset. How would you use performance analysis to identify what, if any, are John's training needs?

8-28. Knowing that you are taking an HR management course, a friend asks you this: I just hired a nanny for my child and I want to make sure she knows what to do; in outline form, what should I cover in the training program I give her?

8-29. MyManagementLab only—comprehensive writing assignment for this chapter.

✪ Try It!

How would you apply the concepts and skills you learned in this chapter? If your professor has assigned this, go to the Assignments section of mymanagementlab.com to complete the simulation: *Change*.

✪ PERSONAL INVENTORY ASSESSMENTS

Leadership Style Indicator

What sort of leadership style do you think you would exhibit in leading an organizational change? Complete this assessment to learn more about your personality.

Key Terms

employee orientation, 233
training, 235
negligent training, 235
task analysis, 237
competency model, 237
performance analysis, 237
the cloud, 242
on-the-job training (OJT), 243
apprenticeship training, 243
job instruction training (JIT), 245
programmed learning, 246
behavior modeling, 246
electronic performance support systems (EPSS), 247
job aid, 247
lifelong learning, 248
cross training, 249
virtual classroom, 250
Web 2.0 learning, 251
management development, 252
job rotation, 254
action learning, 255
case study method, 255
management game, 255
role-playing, 256
in-house development center, 256
executive coach, 256
organizational development, 259
controlled experimentation, 260

Endnotes

1. Rachel Dodes, "At Macy's, a Makeover on Service," *Wall Street Journal*, April 11, 2011, p. B10. See also, http://macysinc.com/macys/m.o.m.strategies/default.aspx, accessed June 28, 2015.
2. Marjorie Derven, "Management Onboarding," *TD*, April 2008, pp. 49–52. See also www.roberthalf.com/onboarding, accessed August 23, 2014.
3. Sabrina Hicks, "Successful Orientation Programs," *Training & Development*, April 2000, p. 59. See also Howard Klein and Natasha Weaver, "The Effectiveness of an Organizational Level Orientation Program in the Socialization of New Hires," *Personnel Psychology* 53 (2000), pp. 47–66; Laurie Friedman, "Are You Losing Potential New Hires at Hello?" *Training & Development*, November 2006, pp. 25–27; and Talya N. Bauer, "Onboarding New Employees: Maximizing Success," *SHRM Foundation*, www.right.com/thought-leadership/research/shrm-foundations-effective-practice-guidelines-series-on-boarding-new-employees-maximizing-success-sponsored-by-right-management.pdf, accessed March 2, 2014.
4. Sheila Hicks et al., "Orientation Redesign," *Training & Development*, July 2006, pp. 43–46.
5. See, for example, John Kammeyer-Mueller and Connie Wanberg, "Unwrapping the Organizational Entry Process: Disentangling Multiple Antecedents and Their Pathways to Adjustments," *Journal of Applied Psychology* 88, no. 5 (2003), pp. 779–794.
6. www.right.com/thought-leadership/research/shrm-foundations-effective-practice-guidelines-series-on-boardingnew-employees-maximizing-success-sponsored-by-right-management.pdf, accessed August 23, 2014.
7. www.shrm.org/templatestools/samples/hrforms/articles/pages/1cms_002153.aspx, http://hrweb.berkeley.edu/guides/managing-hr/recruiting-staff/new-employee/checklist, and www.go2hr.ca/articles/new-hire-orientation-checklist, all accessed March 30, 2015.
8. Mukta Kulkarni and Mark Lengnick–Hall, "Socialization of People with Disabilities in the Workplace," *Human Resource Management* 60, no. 4 (July–August 2011), pp. 521–540.
9. "Drug Rep Claims Handbook Protection from Retaliation," *BNA Bulletin to Management*, December 18, 2012, p. 8.
10. Ed Frauenheim, "IBM Learning Programs Get a 'Second Life,'" *Workforce Management*, December 11, 2006, p. 6. See also J. T. Arnold, "Gaming Technology Used to Orient New Hires," *HR Magazine* (2009 HR Trendbook supp), pp. 36, 38.
11. Jennifer Taylor Arnold, "Ramping Up Onboarding," *HR Magazine*, May 2010, pp. 75–78.
12. www.workday.com/company/news/workdaymobility.php, accessed March 24, 2009.
13. "Four Ways to Use QR Codes to Enliven Your Learning Event," *Training & Development*, January 2013, p. 19.
14. "New Survey Reveals One in Six Companies Using Gaming Techniques to Make Onboarding Fun," *Bloomberg BNA Bulletin to Management*, March 26, 2013, p. 99.
15. For example, IBM's "assimilation process" has three main steps: *affirming* (welcoming the new employee and assigning a coach); *beginning* (he or she is met in person, meets the team, is introduced on the intranet onboarding platform, and learns his or her roles and responsibilities); and *connecting* (which includes having an "ask coach" make sure the employee is on track). www.right.com/thought-leadership/research/shrm-foundations-effective-practice-guidelines-series-onboarding-new-employees-maximizing-success-sponsored-by-right-management.pdf.
16. See, for example, Gary Dessler, *Winning Commitment: How to Build and Keep a Competitive Workforce* (New York: McGraw-Hill, 1993); and Gary Dessler, "How to Earn Your Employees' Commitment," *Academy of Management Executive* 13, no. 2 (1999).
17. Ibid., and see www.autonews.com/article/20050718/SUB/507180713/toyota-seeks-efficiency-training-for-all; http://thetoyotaway.org/excerpts.html; www.toyotageorgetown.com/tps1.asp; http://sloanreview.mit. edu/article/what-really-happened-to-toyota; and www.glassdoor.com/Reviews/Employee-Review-Toyota-Tsusho-America-RVW3553588.htm; all accessed February 28, 2014.
18. Ibid. While long respected for its commitment to these principles—and to the high-quality cars that its employee engagement produced—Toyota ran into problems a few years ago. In pursuing a new faster-growth strategy, Toyota's famed employee selection and on-boarding/training program may have faltered, possibly leading to some employee morale and vehicle quality problems. Soon under new top management, the company seems to have returned to its quality roots.
19. Laurie Miller, "2014 State of the Industry Report," *TD*, November 2014, pp. 30–34.
20. "Lack of Training Fuels Desire to Job Search," *Training & Development*, January 2013, p. 23.
21. Go to www.coca-cola.co.uk, then click "About Us" and "Employment—Our People."
22. Laszlo Bock, *Work Rules!* (New York: Twelve, 2015), p. 60.
23. Ibid., p. 33.
24. Rita Smith, "Aligning Learning with Business Strategy," *Training & Development*, November 2008, pp. 41–43.
25. Christine Ellis and Sarah Gale, "A Seat at the Table," *Training*, March 2001, pp. 90–96.
26. Paul Harris, "The Value Add of Learning," *TD*, October 2014, pp. 53–55.
27. Dodes, "At Macy's, a Makeover on Service." See also, http://macysinc.com/macys/m.o.m.-strategies/default.aspx, accessed June 28, 2015.
28. Ibid. See also "Macy's Earnings, Revenue Edge Above Estimates," **www.cnbc.com/id/100491292**, accessed April 4, 2013.
29. W. Clayton Allen, "Overview and Evolution of the ADDIE Training System," *Advances in Developing Human Resources* 8, no. 4 (November 2006), pp. 430–441.
30. www.intulogy.com/process, accessed April 20, 2011.
31. P. Nick Blanchard and James Thacker, *Effective Training: Systems, Strategies, and Practices* (Upper Saddle River, NJ: Prentice Hall, 1999), pp. 138–139. See also Matthew Casey and Dennis Doverspike, "Training Needs Analysis and Evaluation for New Technologies Through the Use of Problem Based Inquiry," *Performance Improvement Quarterly* 18, no. 1 (2005), pp. 110–124.
32. Justin Arneson et al., "Training and Development Competencies: We Define to Create Competitive Advantage," *Training & Development*, January 2013, p. 45.
33. See also, for example, Jennifer Salopek, "The Power of the Pyramid," *Training & Development*, May 2009, pp. 70–73.
34. "Retooling Vocational Education," *The Economist*, August 23, 2014, p. 66.
35. Pat Galagan, "It's the Competency That Matters, Not the Course," *T + D*, January 2015, pp. 24–27.
36. Tom Barron, "When Things Go Haywire," *Training & Development*, February 1999, pp. 25–27; see also, for example, Bill Stetar, "Training: It's Not Always the Answer," *Quality Progress*, March 2005, pp. 44–49, http://performancetechnology.com/ptg_pdfs/qp0305stetar.pdf, accessed October 11, 2012.
37. Employers increasingly utilize learning content management systems (LCMS) to compile author training content. See, for example, Bill Perry, "Customized Content at Your Fingertips," *Training & Development*, June 2009, pp. 29–30.
38. P. Nick Blanchard and James Thacker, *Effective Training* (Upper Saddle River, NJ: Pearson, 2010), pp. 26–94, 153–199, 285–316; see also Bruno Neal," "e-ADDIE!," *T1D* 65, no. 3 (March 2011), pp. 76–77. Should be T+D.
39. Jay Bahlis, "Blueprint for Planning Learning," *Training & Development*, March 2008, pp. 64–67.
40. P. Nick Blanchard and James Thacker, *Effective Training: Systems, Strategies, and Practices* (Upper Saddle River, NJ: Prentice Hall, 2007), p. 8; and G. Sadri, "Boosting Performance Through Self-Efficacy," *T1D* 65 no. 6 (June 2011), pp. 30–31. Should be T+D.
41. Emily Baumann and Greta Ballentine, "Estimate Training Resources with Precision," *T + D*, February 2014, pp. 20–22.
42. Ibid.
43. Ibid., p. 90.
44. Kenneth Wexley and Gary Latham, *Developing and Training Human Resources in Organizations* (Upper Saddle River, NJ: Prentice Hall, 2002), p. 305.
45. Ibid.
46. Kathryn Tyler, "Focus on Training," *HR Magazine*, May 2000, pp. 94–102.
47. Janice A. Cannon-Bowers et al., "Framework for Understanding Pre-Practice Conditions and Their Impact on Learning," *Personnel Psychology* 51 (1998), pp. 291–320; see also J. S. Goodman et al., "Feedback Specificity, Information Processing, and Transfer of Training," *Organizational Behavior and Human Decision Processes* 115 no. 2 (July 2011), pp. 253–267.
48. Ibid., p. 305.
49. Ibid., and see Kendra Lee, "Reinforce Training," *Training* 48 no. 3 (May/June 2011), p. 24.
50. Eric Krell, "Get Sold on Training Incentives,"*HR Magazine*, February 2013, p. 57.
51. Stefanie Johnson,"Go for the Goal (as): Relationship Between Goal Setting and Transfer of

Training Following Leadership Development," *Academy of Management Learning & Education* 11, no. 4 (2012), pp. 555–569.
52. Alan Saks and Monica Belcourt, "An Investigation of Training Activities and Transfer of Training in Organizations," *Human Resource Management* 45, no. 4 (Winter 2006), pp. 629–648. The percentage of managers transferring behaviors from training to the job may be as low as 10% to 20%. See George Vellios, "On the Level," *Training & Development*, December 2008, pp. 26–29. See also K. Lee, "Implement Training Successfully," *Training* 46, no. 5 (June 2009), p. 16.
53. Large training providers include Element K, Geo Learning, learn.com, Outsmart, Plateau, Saba People Systems, and SumTotal Systems. "Training Providers," *Workforce Management*, January 2011, p. 8. See also Jean Barbazette, "Take the Pain Out of Writing Training Materials," *T + D*, April 2013, pp. 108–110.
54. ASTD Infoline, "Planning and Organizing Training Events," August 2013; and Robert Hewes, "Step-by-Step," *T + D*, February 2014, pp. 56–61.
55. www.litmos.com/learning–management–system; www.talentlms.com; http://money.CNN.com/2014/09/03/technology/enterprise/what-is-the-cloud, both accessed March 31, 2015.
56. Wexley and Latham, *Developing and Training Human Resources in Organizations*, pp. 78–79.
57. Donna Goldwasser, "Me a Trainer?" *Training*, April 2001, pp. 60–66; http://employment.menswearhouse.com/ats/advantageSelector.action;jsessionid=C6EA17158451F5A2902F7195B678CF6A?type=training, accessed June 1, 2011.
58. See, for example, www.aps-online.net/consulting/structured_ojt.htm, accessed June 1, 2011; and Kathryn Tyler, "15 Ways to Train on the Job," *HR Magazine* 53 no. 9 (September 2008), pp. 105–108.
59. Valerie Davis-Howard, "Unleash Change Through a Peer-to-Peer Approach," *T + D*, July 2014, pp. 76–77.
60. The following four steps in on-the-job training based on William Berliner and William McLarney, *Management Practice and Training* (Burr Ridge, IL: McGraw-Hill, 1974), pp. 442–443. For the discussion of employee task analysis, see "Eight Steps to Better On-the-Job Training," *HR Focus* 80, no. 7 (July 2003), pp. 11, 13–14.
61. Cindy Waxer, "Steelmaker Revives Apprentice Program to Address Graying Workforce, Forge Next Leaders," *Workforce Management*, January 30, 2006, p. 40.
62. Kermit Kaleba, "New Changes to Apprenticeship Program Could Be Forthcoming," *Training & Development*, February 2008, p. 14.
63. Robert Weintraub and Jennifer Martineau, "The Just in Time Imperative," *Training & Development*, June 2002, p. 52; Andrew Paradise, "Informal Learning: Overlooked or Overhyped?" *Training & Development*, July 2008, pp. 52–53. In one survey, about one-third of respondents said they did not earmark training dollars for informal learning.
64. Aparna Nancherla, "Knowledge Delivered in Any Other Form Is … Perhaps Sweeter," *Training & Development*, May 2009, pp. 54–60.
65. Nadira Hira, "The Making of a UPS Driver," *Fortune*, November 12, 2007, p. 120.
66. Arthur Winfred Jr. et al., "Effectiveness of Training in Organizations: A Meta Analysis of Design and Evaluation Features," *Journal of Applied Psychology* 88, no. 2 (2003), pp. 234–245.
67. Donald Michalak and Edwin G. Yager, *Making the Training Process Work* (New York: Harper & Row, 1979), pp. 108–111. See also Richard Wiegand, "Can All Your Trainees Hear You?" *Training & Development Journal* 41, no. 8 (August 1987), pp. 38–43; and "Dos and Don'ts at the Podium," *Journal of Accountancy* 200, no. 3 (September 2005).
68. Jacqueline Schmidt and Joseph Miller, "The Five-Minute Rule for Presentations," *Training & Development*, March 2000, pp. 16–17; and "Dos and Don'ts at the Podium," op cit.
69. G. N. Nash, J. P. Muczyk, and F. L. Vettori, "The Role and Practical Effectiveness of Programmed Instruction," *Personnel Psychology* 24 (1971), pp. 397–418; Duane Schultz and Sydney Ellen Schultz, *Psychology and Work Today* (Upper Saddle River, NJ: Prentice Hall, 1998), pp. 181–183; chemistry study based on N. Izzet Kurbanoglu, Yavuz Taskesenligil, and Mustafa Sozbilir, "Programmed Instruction Revisited: A Study on Teaching Stereochemistry," *Chemistry Education Research and Practice* 7, no. 1 (2006), pp. 13–21.
70. Paul Taylor et al., "A Meta-Analytic Review of Behavior Modeling Training," *Journal of Applied Psychology* 90, no. 4 (2005), pp. 692–719.
71. Wexley and Latham, *Developing and Training Human Resources in Organizations*, pp. 131–133. See also Teri O. Grady and Mike Matthews, "Video … Through the Eyes of the Trainee," *Training* 24, no. 7 (July 1987), pp. 57–62; "New ARTBA PPE Video and Laborers' Night Work Suggestions Highlight Construction Safety Advances," *EHS Today* 2, no. 7 (July 2009), p. 51.
72. Paula Ketter, "What Can Training Do for Brown?" *Training & Development*, May 2008, pp. 30–36.
73. Craig Marion, "What Is the EPSS Movement and What Does It Mean to Information Designers?" http://www.smn-web.com/e-hr/letture/perform/EPSS%20Movement.htm, August 20, 1999, accessed June 28, 2015.
74. Josh Bersin and Karen O'Leonard, "Performance Support Systems," *Training & Development*, April 2005, p. 68.
75. Blanchard and Thacker, *Effective Training*, 2010, p. 163.
76. www.cisco.com/en/US/products/ps10352/index.html, accessed June 28, 2015.
77. www.radvision.com/Support/cisco.htm, accessed June 1, 2011.
78. Dina Berta, "Computer-Based Training Clicks with Both Franchisees and Their Employees," *Nation's Restaurant News*, July 9, 2001, pp. 1, 18; and, "Is Online Fall Protection Training Effective?" *EHS Today* 3, no. 7 (July 2010).
79. P. Nick Blanchard and James Thacker, *Effective Training: Systems, Strategies, and Practices* (Upper Saddle River, NJ: Pearson, 2003), p. 247; see also Michael Laff, "Simulations: Slowly Proving Their Worth," *Training & Development*, June 2007, pp. 30–34.
80. Laff, "Simulations."
81. Blanchard and Thacker, *Effective Training*, 2003, p. 248.
82. Ibid., p. 249. See also Kim Kleps, "Virtual Sales Training Scores a Hit," *Training & Development*, December 2006, pp. 63–64.
83. www.reuters.com/article/2014/03/26/us-facebook-acquisition-idUSBREA2O1WX20140326, accessed June 28, 2015.
84. Jenni Jarventaus, "Virtual Threat, Real Sweat." T+D, May 2007, Vol. 61 Issue 5, p. 72
85. Clark Aldrich, "Engaging Mini-Games Find Niche in Training," *Training & Development*, July 2007, pp. 22–24; and "Cisco's Global Training Machine," *Workforce Management*, November 17, 2008, p. 30.
86. Drew Robb, "Let the Games Begin," *HR Magazine*, September 2012, p. 96.
87. "What Do Simulations Cost?" *Training & Development*, June 2007, p. 88; see also Paul Harris, "Immersive Learning Seeks a Foothold," *Training & Development*, January 2009, pp. 40–45; and R. S. Polimeni et al., "Using Computer Simulations to Recruit and Train Generation Y Accountants," *The CPA Journal* 79, no. 5 (May 2009), pp. 64–68.
88. Garry Kranz, "More to Learn," *Workforce Management*, January 2011, p. 27; quote is from Ann Pace, "Spurring Innovation and Engaging the Learners of the 2011 Workplace," *T+D* 65, no. 8 (August 2011), pp. 64–69.
89. Susan Ladika, "When Learning Lasts a Lifetime," *HR Magazine*, May 2008, p. 57.
90. Jeremy Smerd, "New Workers Sorely Lacking Literacy Skills," *Workforce Management*, December 10, 2008, p. 6.
91. Paula Ketter, "The Hidden Disability," *Training & Development*, June 2006, pp. 34–40.
92. Jennifer Salopek, "The Growth of Succession Management," *Training & Development*, June 2007, pp. 22–24; and Kermit Kaleba, "Businesses Continue to Push for Lifelong Learning," *Training & Development*, June 2007, p. 14.
93. Rita Zeidner, "One Workforce—Many Languages," *HR Magazine*, January 2009, pp. 33–37.
94. Matthew Reis, "Do-It-Yourself Diversity," *Training & Development*, March 2004, pp. 80–81.
95. www.prismdiversity.com/resources/diversity_training.html, accessed June 1, 2011.
96. Jennifer Salopek, "Trends: Lost in Translation," *Training & Development*, December 2003, p. 15; www.visionpoint.com/training-solutions/title/just-be-fair-basic-diversity-training, accessed June 17, 2011.
97. Paraphrased from "Best Practice: Workforce Diversity Training," Manufacturing Practices Center of Excellence, www.brm-pcoe.org/bestpracticea/internal/abev/abcv_15.html.
98. Blanchard and Thacker, *Effective Training*, 2003, pp. 403–405.
99. Ibid., p. 404.
100. Holly Dolezalek, "Extreme Training," *Training* 47, no. 1 (January 2010), pp. 26–28.
101. Douglas Shuit, "Sound of the Retreat," *Workforce Management*, September 2003, p. 40.
102. Kevin Alansky, "Blackboard Pays Off for ADP," *T + D* 65, no. 6 (June 2011), pp. 68–69; see also Barbara Carnes, "The Ties That Bind," *Training & Development*, January 2013, pp. 38–40.
103. Greg Wright, "Retailers Buy into Relearning," *HR Magazine*, December 7, 2010, pp. 87–90.
104. Pat Galagan, "Made Fast in China," *Training & Development*, January 2013, p. 30.
105. John Zonneveld, "GM Dealer Training Goes Global," *Training & Development*, December 2006, pp. 47–51. See also "What's Next for the LMS?" *Training*

& Development, September 2011, p. 16.

106. "The Next Generation of Corporate Learning," *Training & Development*, June 2003, p. 47.
107. Ibid.
108. For a list of guidelines for using e-learning, see, for example, Mark Simon, "E-Learning No How," *Training & Development*, January 2009, pp. 34–39. See also Sarah Gilbert, "E-learning Design with Ease," *T + D*, July 2014, pp. 70–71.
109. "The Next Generation of Corporate Learning," *Training & Development*, June 2004, p. 47; Jennifer Hofmann and Nanatte Miner, "Real Blended Learning Stands Up," *Training & Development*, September 2008, pp. 28–31; J. Hofmann, "Top 10 Challenges of Blended Learning," *Training* (Minneapolis, Minn.) 48, no. 2 (March/April 2011), pp. 12–13; and Lee Salz, "Use Webinars for Training and Revenue," *Training* 48, no. 2 (March/April 2011), p. 14.
110. Ruth Clark, "Harnessing the Virtual Classroom," *Training & Development*, November 2005, pp. 40–46.
111. Traci Sitzmann et al., "The Comparative Effectiveness of Web-Based and Classroom Instruction: A Meta-Analysis," *Personnel Psychology* 59 (2006), pp. 623–664.
112. Jennifer Taylor Arnold, "Learning On-the-Fly," *HR Magazine*, September 2007, p. 137; see also M. Donahue, "Mobile Learning Is the Next Generation in Training." *Hotel Management* 226, no. 4 (April 4, 2011), p. 17.
113. www.dominknow.com, accessed March 23, 2009.
114. Bill Roberts, "From IT Learning to Mobile Learning," *HR Magazine*, August 2012, pp. 61–65.
115. Chris Pirie, "Technology Plus Learning Equals Inspiration," *Training & Development*, December 2012, pp. 39–46.
116. Elizabeth Agnvall, "Just-in-Time Training," *HR Magazine*, May 2006, pp. 67–78.
117. For a similar program at Accenture, see Don Vanthournout and Dana Koch, "Training at Your Fingertips," *Training & Development*, September 2008, pp. 52–57. For a discussion of blogs in training see Becky Livingston, "Harnessing Blogs for Learning," *T + D* 65, no. 5 (May 2011), pp. 76–77.
118. Catherine Skrzypinski, "Social Media Changes Employee Expectations Regarding Communication," *HR Magazine*, January 2013, p. 14; see also Dan Steer, "Improve Formal Learning with Social Media," *Training & Development*, December 2012, pp. 31–33.
119. Pat Galagan, "Second That," *Training & Development*, February 2008, pp. 34–37.
120. Paraphrased from Manuel London and M. J. Hall, "Unlocking the Value of Web 2.0 Technologies for Training and Development: The Shift from Instructor-Controlled, Adaptive Learning to Learner-Driven, Generative Learning," *Human Resource Management* 50, no. 6 (November–December 2011), p. 761.
121. This is based on ibid., pp. 763–765.
122. Paul Harris, "Small Businesses Bask in Training's Spotlight," *T + D*, 59, no. 2, Fall 2005, pp. 46–52.
123. Ibid.
124. www.themanufacturinginstitute.org/Skills-Certification/Right-Skills-Now/Right-Skills-Now.aspx, accessed August 24, 2014.
125. For a discussion of leadership development tools, see John Beeson, "Building Bench Strength: A Tool Kit for Executive Development," *Business Horizons* 47, no. 6 (November 2004), pp. 3–9. See also Rita Smith and Beth Bledsoe, "Grooming Leaders for Growth," *T + D*, August 2006, pp. 47–50.
126. Paula Caligiuri, "Developing Global Leaders," *Human Resource Management Review* 16 (2006), pp. 219–228.
127. Ibid.
128. Whereas *succession planning* aims to identify and develop employees to fill specific slots, talent management is a broader activity. *Talent management* involves identifying, recruiting, hiring, and developing high-potential employees. Soonhee Kim, "Linking Employee Assessments to Succession Planning," *Public Personnel Management* 32, no. 4 (Winter 2003), pp. 533–547. See also Michael Laff, "Talent Management: From Hire to Retire," *T + D*, November 2006, pp. 42–48.
129. See, for example, David Day, "Developing Leadership Talent," *SHRM Foundation*, www.shrm.org/about/foundation/research/Documents/Developing%20Lead%20Talent-%20FINAL.pdf, accessed October 4, 2011.
130. Quoted in Susan Wells, "Who's Next," *HR Magazine*, November 2003, p. 43. See also Christee Atwood, "Implementing Your Succession Plan," *T + D*, November 2007, pp. 54–57; and Day, "Developing Leadership Talent."
131. See "Succession Management: Identifying and Developing Leaders," *BNA Bulletin to Management* 21, no. 12 (December 2003), p. 15; and Day, "Developing Leadership Talent."
132. Kim, "Linking Employee Assessments to Succession Planning."
133. Bill Roberts, "Matching Talent with Tasks," *HR Magazine*, November 2002, pp. 91–96.
134. www.sumtotalsystems.com/datasheets/sumt_succession_planning.pdf, accessed June 1, 2011.
135. Ibid., p. 34.
136. Gail Johnson Morris and Kim Rogers, "High Potentials Are Still Your Best Bet," *Training & Development*, February 2013, pp. 58–62.
137. Ann Pomeroy, "Head of the Class," *HR Magazine*, January 2005, p. 57. Of course, traits like cognitive ability and personality also mold job success, not just training. See, for example, Lisa Dragoni et al., "Developing Executive Leaders: The Relative Contribution of Cognitive Ability, Personality, and the Accumulation of Work Experience in Predicting Strategic Thinking Competency," *Personnel Psychology* 60, no. 4 (2011), pp. 829–861.
138. See Paul Evans, Yves Doz, and Andre Laurent, *Human Resource Management in International Firms* (New York: St. Martin's Press, 1990), pp. 122–124; www.sony.net/SonyInfo/csr_report/employees/training/index3.html; accessed March 4, 2014; and www.mckinsey.com/insights/organization/how_multinationals_can_attract_the_talent_they_need, accessed March 4, 2014.
139. Michael Marquardt, "Action Learning Around the World," *TD*, February 2015, pp. 45–49.
140. "Thrown into Deep End, Workers Surface as Leaders," *BNA Bulletin to Management*, July 11, 2002, p. 223. See also Michelle Peters, "Accomplish Two for One with Action Learning," *Training & Development*, February 2013, pp. 52–54.
141. Chris Whitcomb, "Scenario-Based Training at the FBI," *Training & Development*, June 1999, pp. 42–46. See also Michael Laff, "Serious Gaming: The Trainer's New Best Friend," *Training & Development*, January 2007, pp. 52–57.
142. http://teamcommunication.blogspot.com, accessed July 6, 2014.
143. Carol Leaman, "Boost Basic Job Skills Training," *Training & Development*, August 2014, pp. 34–39.
144. American Management Association, www.amanet.org, accessed July 6, 2014.
145. For information on the SHRM learning system, see www.shrm.org/Education/educationalproducts/learning/Pages/default.aspx?utm_campaign=LearningSystem_All_2012&utm_medium=mailing&utm_source=brochure, accessed July 21, 2013.
146. Ann Pomeroy, "Head of the Class," *HR Magazine*, January 2005, p. 57. See also Michael Laff, "Centralized Training Leads to Nontraditional Universities," *Training & Development*, January 2007, pp. 27–29; Chris Musselwhite, "University Executive Education Gets Real," *Training & Development*, May 2006, p. 57; and Ralph Miller and David Abdow, "Executive Education That Works," *Training & Development*, December 2012, pp. 28–30.
147. For a list of Harvard programs, see www.exed.hbs.edu/Pages/default.aspx, accessed July 21, 2013.
148. Norman Maier, Allen Solem, and Ayesha Maier, *The Role Play Technique* (San Diego, CA: University Associates, 1975), pp. 2–3. See also Karen Griggs, "A Role Play for Revising Style and Applying Management Theories," *Business Communication Quarterly* 68, no. 1 (March 2005), pp. 60–65.
149. Martha Peak, "Go Corporate U!" *Management Review* 86, no. 2 (February 1997), pp. 33–37, and Jessica Li and Amy Lui Abel, "Prioritizing and Maximizing the Impact of Corporate Universities," *T + D* 65, no. 5 (May 2011), pp. 54–57.
150. Russell Gerbman, "Corporate Universities 101," *HR Magazine*, February 2000, pp. 101–106; Holly Dolezalek, "University 2.0," *Training* 44, no. 8 (September 2007), pp. 22–23.
151. "Executive Coaching: Corporate Therapy," *The Economist*, November 15, 2003, p. 61. See also Steve Gladis, "Executive Coaching Builds Steam in Organizations," *Training & Development*, December 2007, pp. 59–61.
152. "As Corporate Coaching Goes Mainstream, Key Prerequisite Overlooked: Assessment," *BNA Bulletin to Management*, May 16, 2006, p. 153.
153. James Smither et al., "Can Working with an Executive Coach Improve Multisource Feedback Ratings over Time?" *Personnel Psychology* 56, no. 1 (Spring 2003), pp. 23–44.
154. www.shrm.org/Education/educationalproducts/learning/Pages/default.aspx.
155. For information on the SHRM learning system, see www.shrm.org/Education/educationalproducts/learning/Pages/default.aspx?utm_campaign=LearningSystem_All_2012&utm_medium=mailing&utm_source=brochure, accessed July 21, 2013.
156. This is based on Diane Brady, "Can GE Still Manage?" *Bloomberg Businessweek*, April 25, 2010, p. 29.
157. Ibid.
158. Quoted and abstracted from "Five Rules for Talent

Management in the New Economy," May 2010, www.towerswatson.com/viewpoints/1988, accessed August 22, 2011.
159. Ibid.
160. See, for example, John Austin, "Mapping Out a Game Plan for Change," *HR Magazine*, April 2009, pp. 39–42.
161. The steps are based on Michael Beer, Russell Eisenstat, and Bert Spector, "Why Change Programs Don't Produce Change," *Harvard Business Review*, November–December 1990, pp. 158–166; Thomas Cummings and Christopher Worley, *Organization Development and Change*, Minneapolis, MN: West Publishing Company, 1993; John P. Kotter, "Leading Change: Why Transformation Efforts Fail," *Harvard Business Review*, March–April 1995, pp. 59–66; and John P. Kotter, *Leading Change* (Boston: Harvard Business School Press, 1996). See also Eric Abrahamson, "Change Without Pain," *Harvard Business Review*, July–August 2000, pp. 75–79; and David Herold et al., "Beyond Change Management: A Multilevel Investigation of Contextual and Personal Influences on Employees' Commitment to Change," *Journal of Applied Psychology* 92, no. 4 (2007), p. 949.
162. Kotter, "Leading Change," p. 85.
163. Beer, Eisenstat, and Spector, "Why Change Programs Don't Produce Change," p. 164.
164. Stacie Furst and Daniel Cable, "Employee Resistance to Organizational Change: Managerial Influence Tactics and Leader Member Exchange," *Journal of Applied Psychology* 3, no. 2 (2008), p. 453.
165. Wendell French and Cecil Bell Jr., *Organization Development* (Upper Saddle River, NJ: Prentice Hall, 1995), pp. 171–193. For examples of actual team-building programs, see, for example, www.teambuildinginc.com and www.teamcraft.com, both accessed August 24, 2014.
166. Benjamin Schneider, Steven Ashworth, A. Catherine Higgs, and Linda Carr, "Design Validity, and Use of Strategically Focused Employee Attitude Surveys," *Personnel Psychology* 49 (1996), pp. 695–705.
167. Wexley and Latham, *Developing and Training Human Resources in Organizations*, p. 128.
168. Todd Raphel, "What Learning Management Reports Do for You," *Workforce*, June 2001, pp. 56–58.
169. Wexley and Latham, *Developing and Training Human Resources in Organizations*, p. 153.
170. See, for example, Jack Phillips and Patti Phillips, "Moving From Evidence to Proof," *T + D* 65, no. 8 (August 2011), pp. 34–39, for a discussion of a process for gathering training assessment data.
171. However, see Phyllis Tharenou et al., "A Review and Critique of Research on Training and Organizational Level Outcomes," *Human Resource Management Review* 17 (2007), pp. 251–273.
172. For some examples, see, for instance, http://exceltemplates.net/images/2009/training-cost.jpg, www.tjtaylor.net/resources-tools2.htm, www.redhat.com/resourcelibrary/onlinetools/training-roi-calculator, and www.fastrak-consulting.co.uk/tactix/Features/tngroi/tngroi.htm. See also Tamar Elkeles, Patty Phillips, and Jack Phillips, "ROI Calculations for Technology-Based Learning," *TD*, January 2015, pp. 42–47.
173. Jennifer Salopek, "Showstopping Learning," *TD*, October 2014, pp. 56–59.
174. Ibid.

9

Performance Management and Appraisal

TRW Instruments

LEARNING OBJECTIVES

9-1 Describe the performance appraisal process.

9-2 Discuss the pros and cons of at least eight performance appraisal methods.

9-3 Give examples of potential appraisal problems and how to deal with them.

9-4 List steps to take in the appraisal interview.

9-5 Explain key points in how to use the appraisal interview to boost employee engagement.

9-6 Explain how you would take a performance management approach to appraisal.

TRW supplies automotive steering, braking, and safety and electronic equipment to customers worldwide.[1] Several years ago, TRW was deeply in debt.[2] With over 100,000 employees on five continents, TRW management knew it had to base its new strategy on improving competitiveness and performance. At the time, most of the firm's far-flung departments used their own paper-based performance appraisal systems. Top management decided it needed a new company-wide performance management system to help bring what TRW's employees were doing into synch with the firm's new strategic goals. We'll see what they did.

WHERE ARE WE NOW ...

Chapters 6–8 explained selecting, training, and developing employees. After employees have been on the job for some time, you should appraise their performance. The purpose of this chapter is to show you how to do that. The main topics we cover include the basics of performance appraisal, tools for appraising performance, dealing with rater error appraisal problems, the appraisal interview, employee engagement guide for managers, and performance management. Career planning is a logical consequence of appraisal: We'll turn to career planning in Chapter 10.

Basics of Performance Appraisal

LEARNING OBJECTIVE **9-1**
Describe the performance appraisal process.

Few things supervisors do are fraught with more peril than appraising subordinates' performance. Employees tend to be overly optimistic about their ratings. And they know their raises, careers, and peace of mind may hinge on how you rate them. As if that's not enough, few appraisal processes are as fair as employers think they are. Many obvious and not-so-obvious problems (such as the tendency to rate everyone "average") distort the process.[3] However, the perils notwithstanding, performance appraisal plays a big role in managing people.

The Performance Appraisal Process

performance appraisal
Evaluating an employee's current and/or past performance relative to his or her performance standards.

performance appraisal process
A three-step appraisal process involving (1) setting work standards, (2) assessing the employee's actual performance relative to those standards, and (3) providing feedback to the employee with the aim of helping him or her to eliminate performance deficiencies or to continue to perform above par.

Performance appraisal means evaluating an employee's current and/or past performance relative to his or her performance standards. You may equate appraisal forms like Figure 9-1 with "performance appraisal," but appraisal involves more than forms. It also requires setting performance standards, and assumes that the employee receives the training, feedback, and incentives required to eliminate performance deficiencies. Stripped to its essentials, performance appraisal always involves the three-step **performance appraisal process**: (1) setting work standards; (2) assessing the employee's actual performance relative to those standards (this often involves some rating form); and (3) providing feedback to the employee with the aim of helping him or her to eliminate performance deficiencies or to continue to perform above par.

Effective appraisals actually begin before the actual appraisal, with the manager defining the employee's job and performance criteria. *Defining the job* means making sure that you and your subordinate agree on his or her duties and job standards and on the appraisal method you will use.

Why Appraise Performance?

There are five reasons to appraise subordinates' performance.

- First, most employers base pay, promotion, and retention decisions on the employee's appraisal.[4]
- Appraisals play a central role in the employer's *performance management* process. Performance management means continuously ensuring that each employee's performance makes sense in terms of the company's overall goals.
- The appraisal lets the manager and subordinate develop a plan for correcting any deficiencies, and to reinforce the subordinate's strengths.
- Appraisals provide an opportunity to review the employee's career plans in light of his or her exhibited strengths and weaknesses. We address career planning in Chapter 10.
- Finally, appraisals enable the supervisor to identify if there is a training need, and the remedial steps required.

FIGURE 9-1 Sample Faculty Evaluation Survey
Source: Copyright Gary Dessler, PhD.

Instructions: Thoughtful evaluations help the faculty member better understand and improve his or her teaching practices. For each of the following eight items, please assign a score, giving your highest score of 7 for Outstanding, a score of 4 for Average, your lowest score of 1 for Needs Improvement, and an NA if the question is not applicable:

Evaluation Items

____ 1. The instructor was prepared for his/her lectures.
____ 2. The course was consistent with the course objectives.
____ 3. The instructor was fair in how he/she graded me.
____ 4. The instructor carefully planned and organized this course.
____ 5. The instructor was available during his/her posted office hours.
____ 6. The instructor responded to online inquiries in a timely manner.
____ 7. In terms of knowledge and/or experience, the instructor was competent to teach this course.
____ 8. Overall how would you rate this course?

Defining the Employee's Goals and Performance Standards

The performance appraisal should compare "what should be" with "what is." Therefore, as noted, the first step in performance appraisal and management is to decide what should be—in other words, to let employees know what you expect of them in terms of performance standards. Managers use one or more of three bases—goals, job dimensions or traits, and behaviors or competencies—to establish ahead of time what the person's performance standards will be.

First, the manager can assess to what extent *the employee is attaining his or her numerical goals*. Such goals should derive from the company's overall profitability, cost reduction, or efficiency goals. For example, a company-wide goal of reducing costs by 10% should translate into goals for how individual employees and/or teams will cut costs. The HR as a Profit Center feature shows an example.

IMPROVING PERFORMANCE: *HR as a Profit Center*

Setting Performance Goals at Ball Corporation

Ball Corporation supplies metal packaging to customers such as food processors and paint manufacturers worldwide.[5] The management team at one Ball plant concluded that it could improve plant performance by instituting an improved process for setting goals and for ensuring that the plant's employees' behaviors were in synch with these goals.[6] The new program began by training plant leaders on how to improve performance, and on setting and communicating daily performance goals. They in turn communicated and tracked daily goal attainment by distributing team scorecards to the plant's work teams. Plant employees received special coaching and training to ensure they had the skills required for achieving the goals. According to management, within 12 months the plant increased production by 84 million cans, reduced customer complaints by 50%, and obtained a return on investment of more than $3 million.[7] ■

Source: Based on www.ball.com; "Aligning People and Processes for Performance Improvement," T&D 65, no. 3, March 2011, p. 80.

If your professor has assigned this, go to the Assignments section of **mymanagementlab.com** to complete this discussion.

✪ **Talk About It 1:** Explain what performance appraisal process behaviors the Ball program included.

Managers often say that effective goals should be "SMART." They are *specific*, and clearly state the desired results. They are *measurable*, and answer the question "how much?" They are *attainable*. They are *relevant*, and clearly derive from what the manager and company want to achieve. And they are *timely*, with deadlines and milestones.[8] Research provides insights into setting motivational goals. The accompanying HR Tools feature summarizes these findings.

IMPROVING PERFORMANCE: *HR Tools for Line Managers and Small Businesses*

How to Set Effective Goals

Behavioral science research studies suggest four guidelines for setting performance goals:

1. **Assign specific goals.** Employees who receive specific goals usually perform better than those who do not.
2. **Assign measurable goals.** Put goals in quantitative terms and include target dates or deadlines. If measurable results will not be available, then "satisfactory completion"—such as "satisfactorily attended workshop"—is the next best thing.
3. **Assign challenging but doable goals.** Goals should be challenging, but not so difficult that they appear unrealistic.
4. **Encourage participation.** Managers often face this question: Should I tell my employees what their goals are, or let them participate with me in setting their goals? The evidence suggests that participatively set goals do not consistently result in higher performance than assigned goals, nor do assigned goals consistently result in higher performance than participative ones. It is only when the participatively set goals are set higher than the assigned ones that the participatively set goals produce higher

performance. Because it tends to be easier to set higher standards when your employees participate, participation tends to lead to improved performance.[9] ■

Source: Based on E. A. Locke and G. P. Latham, "Building a Practically Useful Theory of Goal Setting and Task Motivation. A 35-Year Odyssey," American Psychologist 57, no. 9 (2002), pp. 705–717.

If your professor has assigned this, go to the Assignments section of **mymanagementlab.com** to complete this discussion question.

Talk About It 2: "Why is it not a good idea to simply tell employees to 'do their best' when assigning a task?"

A *second* basis upon which to appraise someone is to use a form with *basic job dimensions* or *traits* such as such as "communication" or "teamwork." The assumption is that "good teamwork" is a useful standard for "what should be."

A third option is to appraise employees based *on their mastery of the competencies* (the skills, knowledge, and/or personal behaviors) performing the job requires. For example, we saw in Chapter 4 that BP's exploration division appraises employees' skills using a skills matrix (see Figure 4-11, page 120). This matrix shows the basic skills to be assessed (such as "technical expertise"), and the minimum level of each skill the job requires (what the minimum skill level "should be"). Employees appraised as having the requisite level of each skill are qualified to fill the position.

Who Should Do the Appraising?

Appraisals by the immediate supervisor are still the heart of most appraisal processes. Getting a supervisor's appraisal is relatively straightforward and makes sense. The supervisor is usually in the best position to observe and evaluate the subordinate's performance, and is responsible for that person's performance.

The human resources department serves an advisory role. Generally, they provide the advice on what appraisal tool to use, but leaves final decisions on procedures to operating managers. The human resource team should also train supervisors to improve their appraisal skills, monitor the appraisal system's effectiveness, and ensure that it complies with EEO laws.

However, relying only on supervisors' appraisals isn't advisable. For example, an employee's supervisor may not appreciate how customers and colleagues see the employee's performance. There is also always some danger of bias for or against the employee. If so, managers have several options.

PEER APPRAISALS People often come across differently to their peers than they do to their boss. Peer appraisals—appraisals by one's peers—are therefore increasingly popular. The American military requires generals and admirals to be evaluated by their peers (and subordinates).[10] Facebook has employees compile peer reviews every 6 months.[11] Google employees receive annual feedback from both their supervisor and their peers.[12] (We'll discuss automated "crowd" appraisals later in this chapter.)

Typically, an employee due for a peer appraisal chooses an appraisal chairperson. The latter (perhaps with the employee's input) then selects a supervisor and several peers to evaluate the employee's work.

Peer appraisals can be effective. One's peers see aspects of the person that the boss may never see, so peers' opinions can be useful developmentally. Knowing your colleagues will appraise you can also change behavior. One study involved undergraduates placed into self-managing work groups. The researchers found that instituting peer appraisals had "an immediate positive impact on [improving] perception of open communication, task motivation, social loafing, group viability, cohesion, and satisfaction."[13]

RATING COMMITTEES A rating committee usually consists of the employee's immediate supervisor and three or four other supervisors.[14]

Using multiple raters is advantageous. It helps cancel out problems such as bias on the part of individual raters.[15] It can also provide a way to include in the appraisal the

Many employers use rating committees to appraise employees.

Oliver Eltinger/Fancy/AGE Fotostock

different facets of an employee's performance observed by different appraisers. Studies often find that the ratings obtained from different sources rarely match.[16] It's therefore advisable to obtain ratings from the supervisor, his or her boss, and at least one other manager who is familiar with the employee's work.[17] At a minimum, employers require that the supervisor's boss sign off on any appraisals the supervisor does.

SELF-RATINGS Some employers obtain employees' self-ratings, usually in conjunction with supervisors' ratings. The basic problem, of course, is that employees usually rate themselves higher than do their supervisors or peers.[18] One study found that, when asked to rate their own job performances, 40% of employees in jobs of all types placed themselves in the top 10%, and virtually all remaining employees rated themselves at least in the top 50%.[19] In another study, subjects' self-ratings correlated negatively with their subsequent performance in an assessment center—the higher they appraised themselves, the worse they did in the center. In contrast, an average of the person's supervisor, peer, and subordinate ratings predicted the subjects' assessment center performance.[20]

APPRAISAL BY SUBORDINATES Many employers have subordinates rate their managers, usually for developmental rather than for pay purposes. Anonymity affects the feedback. Managers who receive feedback from subordinates who identify themselves view the upward feedback process more positively. However, subordinates who identify themselves tend to give inflated ratings.[21]

The evidence suggests that upward feedback improves managers' performance. One study focused on 252 managers during five annual administrations of an upward feedback program. Managers who were initially rated poor or moderate "showed significant improvements in [their] upward feedback ratings over the five-year period."[22] And, managers who met with their subordinates to discuss their upward assessment improved more than the managers who did not.[23]

Of course, employees no longer need their employers for upward evaluation systems—sites like Glassdoor and apps like Memo let employees post their own anonymous comments.[24]

360-DEGREE FEEDBACK With 360-degree feedback, the employer collects performance information all around an employee—from his or her supervisors, subordinates, peers, and internal or external customers—generally for developmental rather than pay purposes.[25] The usual process is to have the raters complete online ratee appraisal surveys. Computerized systems then compile this feedback into individualized reports to rates.

Results are mixed. Participants seem to prefer this approach, but one study concluded that multisource feedback led to "generally small" improvements in subsequent ratings by supervisors, peers, and subordinates.[26] Such appraisals are more candid when subordinates know rewards or promotions are not involved. Make sure the feedback the person receives is productive, unbiased, and development oriented.[27] And, it helps to collect multisource feedback by using a Web-based system that lets the rater rate the person along a series of dimensions.[28]

Techniques for Appraising Performance

We will see that many employers use digital tools to automate the appraisal/performance management process. With their digital dashboards, these tools monitor, report, and correct performance deviations in real time. Yet many employers still use traditional performance appraisal tools like those described next.

LEARNING OBJECTIVE **9-2**

Discuss the pros and cons of at least eight performance appraisal methods.

Graphic Rating Scale Method

The **graphic rating scale** is the simplest and most popular method for appraising performance. You'll find several varieties. As in the graphic rating scale in Figure 9-2, the scale may lists several *job dimensions or traits* (such as "communication" or "teamwork") and a range of performance values (from "below expectations" to "role model" or "unsatisfactory" to "outstanding") for each trait. The supervisor rates each subordinate by circling or checking the score that best describes the subordinate's performance for each trait, and totals the ratings.

graphic rating scale
A scale that lists a number of traits and a range of performance for each. The employee is then rated by identifying the score that best describes his or her level of performance for each trait.

Competency- (or skill- or behavior-) based graphic rating scales are another option. For example, Figure 9-3 shows a partial rating form for a pizza chef. This graphic rating form assesses the person's competencies and skills. Here the employer wants to appraise a pizza chef's job-related skills, one of which is: "Be able to maintain adequate inventory of pizza dough." As another example, Section I of Figure 9-4 focuses on behavioral competencies.[29] Here "Effectively leads and motivates nurses" is a required behavioral competency for a nurse supervisor.

Finally, the scale might rate (as in Section II of Figure 9-4) how well the employee did with respect to achieving specific profit, cost, or efficiency *goals*. "Nursing unit experienced zero patient medication errors in period" would be one example.

Alternation Ranking Method

Ranking employees from best to worst on a trait or traits is another option. Since it is usually easier to distinguish between the worst and best employees, an **alternation ranking method** is most popular. First, list all subordinates to be rated, and then cross out the names of any not known well enough to rank. Then, on a form like that in Figure 9-5 (page 282), indicate the employee who is the highest on the performance dimension being measured and the one who is the lowest. Then choose the next highest and the next lowest, alternating between highest and lowest until all employees have been ranked.

alternation ranking method
Ranking employees from best to worst on a particular trait, choosing highest, then lowest, until all are ranked.

Paired Comparison Method

The **paired comparison method** makes the ranking method more precise. For every trait (quantity of work, quality of work, and so on), you compare every employee with every other employee. With, say, five employees to rate, you use a chart as in Figure 9-6 (page 282) of all possible pairs of employees for each trait. Then choose who the better employee of the pair is. In Figure 9-6, Maria ranked highest (has the most + marks) for quality of work, whereas Art was ranked highest for creativity.

paired comparison method
Ranking employees by making a chart of all possible pairs of the employees for each trait and indicating which is the better employee of the pair.

Sample Performance Rating Form

Employee's Name _____ Level: Entry-level employee

Manager's Name _____

Key Work Responsibilities	Results/Goals to Be Achieved
1. _____	1. _____
2. _____	2. _____
3. _____	3. _____
4. _____	4. _____

Communication

1	2	3	4	5
Below Expectations		**Meets Expectations**		**Role Model**
Even with guidance, fails to prepare straightforward communications, including forms, paperwork, and records, in a timely and accurate manner; products require minimal corrections. Even with guidance, fails to adapt style and materials to communicate straightforward information.		With guidance, prepares straightforward communications, including forms, paperwork, and records, in a timely and accurate manner; products require minimal corrections. With guidance, adapts style and materials to communicate straightforward information.		Independently prepares communications, such as forms, paperwork, and records, in a timely, clear, and accurate manner; products require few, if any, corrections. Independently adapts style and materials to communicate information.

Organizational Know-How

1	2	3	4	5
Below Expectations		**Meets Expectations**		**Role Model**
<performance standards appear here>		<performance standards appear here>		<performance standards appear here>

Personal Effectiveness

1	2	3	4	5
Below Expectations		**Meets Expectations**		**Role Model**
<performance standards appear here>		<performance standards appear here>		<performance standards appear here>

Teamwork

1	2	3	4	5
Below Expectations		**Meets Expectations**		**Role Model**
<performance standards appear here>		<performance standards appear here>		<performance standards appear here>

Achieving Business Results

1	2	3	4	5
Below Expectations		**Meets Expectations**		**Role Model**
<performance standards appear here>		<performance standards appear here>		<performance standards appear here>

FIGURE 9-2 Sample Graphic Performance Rating Form with Behavioral Examples

Source: Reproduced with permission of the SHRM Foundation.

FIGURE 9-3 One Item from an Appraisal Form Assessing Employee Performance on Specific Job-Related Skills

Position: Pizza Cheif			
Skill 1: Be able to maintain adequate inventory of pizza dough		Rating	
Each round pizza dough must be between 12 and 14 ounces each, kneaded at least 2 minutes before being placed in the temperature and humidity-controlled cooler, and kept there for at least 5 hours prior to use. There should be enough, but no more for each day's demand.	Needs improvement	Satisfactory	Excellent

Forced Distribution Method

The **forced distribution method** is similar to grading on a curve. With this method, the manager places predetermined percentages of ratees into performance categories. At Lending Tree, the top 15% ratees are "1's," the middle 75% are "2's," and the bottom 10% are "3's" and the "first to go." GE used top 20%, middle 70%, and bottom 10% for its managers, and most of the bottom 10% lost their jobs.[30] (GE no longer strictly adheres to its 20/70/10 split, and today is experimenting with less stressful alternatives.)[31]

forced distribution method
Similar to grading on a curve; predetermined percentages of ratees are placed in various performance categories.

Forced distribution's big advantage is that it prevents supervisors from rating all or most employees "satisfactory" or "high." Forced distribution makes some sense. It reflects the fact that top employees often outperform average or poor ones by as much as 100%.[32] About a fourth of *Fortune* 500 companies use versions of it.[33]

But, as students know, with forced grading you're either in the top 5% or 10% (and get that "A"), or you're not. Forced distribution rating systems may also increase the risk of discriminatory adverse impact.[34] One survey found that 77% of responding employers were at least "somewhat satisfied" with forced ranking, while the remaining 23% were dissatisfied. The biggest complaints: 44% said it damages morale.[35] Some writers refer unkindly to it as "Rank and Yank."[36] Therefore, appoint a committee to review any employee's low ranking. And remember that distinguishing between top and bottom performers is usually not even the problem: "The challenge is to differentiate meaningfully between the other 80%."[37] For many years, Microsoft graded employees against one another in what employees called the "stack," ranking them from 1 to 5.[38] Microsoft recently substituted more frequent and qualitative appraisals.

Critical Incident Method

With the **critical incident method**, the supervisor keeps a log of positive and negative examples (critical incidents) of a subordinate's work-related behaviors. Every 6 months or so, supervisor and subordinate meet to discuss the latter's performance, using the incidents as examples. One study involved 112 first-line supervisors. The conclusion of this and similar studies is that compiling critical incidents as they occur anchors the eventual appraisal in reality and thus improves appraisal outcomes.[39] It's thus advisable to keep a diary of employees' performances.[40]

critical incident method
Keeping a record of uncommonly good or undesirable examples of an employee's work-related behavior and reviewing it with the employee at predetermined times.

Compiling incidents is useful. It provides examples the supervisor can use to explain the person's rating. It makes the supervisor think about the subordinate's appraisal all during the year (so the rating doesn't just reflect the employee's most recent performance). The downside is that it doesn't produce relative ratings for pay raise purposes. In Table 9-1, one of the assistant plant manager's duties was to supervise procurement and minimize inventory costs. The critical incident log shows that he or she let inventory storage costs rise 15%; this provides an example of what performance to improve.

Section I: Competencies: Does this employee exhibit the core competencies the job requires?

Exhibits Leadership Competency

Effectively leads and motivates nurses: Builds a culture that is open and receptive to improved clinical care; Sets clear goals for nurses; Is supportive of nurses; Motivates nurses to achieve their goals.

Generally exceeds expectations	Generally meets expectations	Generally fails to meet expectations
_____	_____	_____

Exhibits Technical Supervisory Competency

Effectively supervises nurses' technical activities: Exhibits the command of technical nursing knowledge and skills required to supervise nurses effectively, such as, assuring that nurses accurately administer medications, treat patients, intervene effectively to patients' expressions of symptoms, and accurately carry out physicians' instructions.

Generally exceeds expectations	Generally meets expectations	Generally fails to meet expectations
_____	_____	_____

Exhibits Managerial Supervisory Competency

Effectively manages unit: Develops annual, monthly, weekly, and daily plans within context of hospital's plans; effectively organizes and assigns nurses' work; maintains required nursing staffing levels and trains nurses; effectively monitors and controls nursing unit performance using hospital-approved metrics.

Generally exceeds expectations	Generally meets expectations	Generally fails to meet expectations
_____	_____	_____

Exhibits Communications Competency

Effectively communicates: Actively listens to and understands what others say; effectively conveys facts and ideas in writing and orally.

Generally exceeds expectations	Generally meets expectations	Generally fails to meet expectations
_____	_____	_____

Exhibits Decision-Making Competency

Effectively recognizes and solves problems and makes decisions: uses data to analyze alternatives and support conclusions; able to solve problems even of moderate to high complexity.

Generally exceeds expectations	Generally meets expectations	Generally fails to meet expectations
_____	_____	_____

Section II: Goals: Did this employee achieve his or her goals for the period you are appraising?

Primary goals employee was to achieve for this period *(Note: list specific goals)*	Rating 5 Exceeded goal 3 Met goal 1 Did not achieve goal	Explanations and/or examples
Goal 1	5 4 3 2 1	
Goal 2	5 4 3 2 1	
Goal 3	5 4 3 2 1	
Goal 4	5 4 3 2 1	
Goal 5	5 4 3 2 1	

Employee name and signature	Person doing appraisal	Date of appraisal

Source: Copyright Gary Dessler PhD

FIGURE 9-4 Pearson Pennsylvania Hospital Competencies and Goals-Based Appraisal Form for a Nurse-Supervisor

Source: Copyright Gary Dessler, PhD.

FIGURE 9-5 Alternation Ranking Method

ALTERNATION RANKING SCALE

Trait: _____

For the trait you are measuring, list all the employees you want to rank. Put the highest-ranking employee's name on line 1. Put the lowest-ranking employee's name on line 20. Then list the next highest ranking on line 2, the next lowest ranking on line 19, and so on. Continue until all names are on the scale.

Highest-ranking employee

1. _____	11. _____
2. _____	12. _____
3. _____	13. _____
4. _____	14. _____
5. _____	15. _____
6. _____	16. _____
7. _____	17. _____
8. _____	18. _____
9. _____	19. _____
10. _____	20. _____

Lowest-ranking employee

Narrative Forms

All or part of the written appraisal may be in narrative form, as in Figure 9-7. Here the person's supervisor assesses the employee's past performance and required areas of improvement. The supervisor's narrative assessment helps the employee understand where his or her performance was good or bad, and how to improve that performance.

FIGURE 9-6 Paired Comparison Method

Note: + means "better than." - means "worse than." For each chart, add up the number of + 's in each column to get the highest ranked employee.

Note: + means "better than." – means "worse than." For each chart, add up the number of +'s in each column to get the highest ranked employee.

FOR THE TRAIT "QUALITY OF WORK"

	Employee rated:				
As Compared to:	A Art	B Maria	C Chuck	D Diane	E José
A Art		+	+	–	–
B Maria	–		–	–	–
C Chuck	–	+		+	–
D Diane	+	+	–		+
E José	+	+	+	–	

Maria ranks highest here

FOR THE TRAIT "CREATIVITY"

	Employee rated:				
As Compared to:	A Art	B Maria	C Chuck	D Diane	E José
A Art		–	–	–	–
B Maria	+		–	+	+
C Chuck	+	+		–	+
D Diane	+	–	+		–
E José	+	–	–	+	

Art ranks highest here

TABLE 9-1 Examples of Critical Incidents for Assistant Plant Manager

Continuing Duties	Targets	Critical Incidents
Schedule production for plant	90% utilization of personnel and machinery in plant; orders delivered on time	Instituted new production scheduling system; decreased late orders by 10% last month; increased machine utilization in plant by 20% last month
Supervise procurement of raw materials and inventory control	Minimize inventory costs while keeping adequate supplies on hand	Let inventory storage costs rise 15% last month; overordered parts "A" and "B" by 20%; underordered part "C" by 30%
Supervise machinery maintenance	No shutdowns due to faulty machinery	Instituted new preventative maintenance system for plant; prevented a machine breakdown by discovering faulty part

FIGURE 9-7 Sample Narrative Appraisal Form

Source: Copyright Gary Dessler, PhD.

Supervisory Appraisal of Employee: Narrative Form

Employee's Name	Department	Present Position
Appraisal Date	Supervisor Name/Title	Performance Period

Supervisor-Appraiser: First, briefly describe results for each of this employee's goals this year. Then, preferably using specific examples, describe the level of the employee's job knowledge, skills, and abilities. Then, jointly set goals for the coming period and describe required employee training and development in each area. Finally, describe your overall assessment of this employee's work this period.

Appraisal Criteria	Narrative Appraisal	Goals, Training, & Development
Job-Related Goals 1. _____ 2. _____ 3. _____	_____ _____ _____	_____ _____ _____
Employee Job Knowledge		
Employee Job Skills		
Employee Job Abilities		
Overall Assessment		

behaviorally anchored rating scale (BARS)
An appraisal method that aims at combining the benefits of narrative critical incidents and quantified ratings by anchoring a quantified scale with specific narrative examples of good and poor performance.

Behaviorally Anchored Rating Scales

A **behaviorally anchored rating scale (BARS)** is an appraisal tool that anchors a numerical rating scale with specific illustrative examples of good or poor performance. Developing a BARS typically involves five steps:

1. ***Write critical incidents.*** Ask the job's jobholders and/or supervisors to write specific illustrations (critical incidents) of effective and ineffective performance on the job.

2. ***Develop performance dimensions.*** Have these people cluster the incidents into 5 or 10 performance dimensions, such as "salesmanship skills."
3. ***Reallocate incidents.*** To verify these groupings, have another team who also knows the job reallocate the original critical incidents to the cluster they think it fits best. Retain a critical incident if most of this second team assigns it to the same cluster as did the first.
4. ***Scale the incidents.*** This second group then rates the behavior described by the incident as to how effectively or ineffectively it represents performance on the dimension.
5. ***Develop a final instrument.*** Choose about six or seven of the incidents as the dimension's behavioral anchors.[41] Figure 9-8 illustrates a BARS, for a car salesperson.

Three researchers developed a BARS for grocery checkout clerks.[42] They collected many checkout clerk critical incidents, and then grouped or clustered these into eight

FIGURE 9-8 Behaviorally Anchored Rating Scale

Automobile Salesmanship Skills

Persuade prospective buyers to buy one of our vehicles; use our vehicles' benefits to encourage people to buy; use salesmanship skills to overcome buyers' stated reasons not to buy; adjust sales pitch to buyer's needs.

10 — A prospect said she would only buy one of our luxury convertibles or would buy a competitor's car. When the finance firm rejected her application, the salesperson compared our lower-priced car to the competitor's and convinced her to buy our lower-priced model.

9

8 — Salesperson asks prospective buyer what he or she is looking for in a vehicle and why, listens carefully to the buyer, and then explains how our vehicle fulfills those needs and why.

7

6 — The prospect said he was looking for a car that he could use to haul his boat and for off-road purposes, and the salesperson emphasized our vehicle's low price and quality in the sales pitch.

5

4 — The prospective buyer said she really wanted to special-order a car with an unusual color and amenities, and the salesperson said she'd be better off not waiting 2 months and should settle for a standard model.

3

2 — The prospect said he didn't "like the looks" of our vehicle, and the salesperson told him "the style is the style" and that he'd probably be happier with a competitor's vehicle.

1

performance dimensions: Knowledge and Judgment; Conscientiousness; Skill in Human Relations; Skill in Operation of Register; Skill in Bagging; Organizational Ability of Checkstand Work; Skill in Monetary Transactions; and Observational Ability.

They then developed behaviorally anchored rating scales *for each of these eight dimensions*. Each contained a vertical scale (ranging from 1 to 9) for rating performance from "extremely poor" to "extremely good." Then they inserted specific critical incidents (such as "by knowing the price of items, this checker would be expected to look for mismarked and unmarked items") to anchor or illustrate each level of performance.

The BARS method has several advantages. Most notably, the critical incidents along the scale illustrate what to look for in terms of superior, average, and poor performance (an idea equally valuable when creating most other types of appraisal tools, including graphic rating scales). The critical incidents make it easier to explain the ratings to appraisees. And, clustering the critical incidents into five or six performance dimensions (such as "salesmanship skills") helps make the performance dimensions more independent of one another. (For example, a rater should be less likely to rate an employee high on all dimensions simply because he or she was rated high in "salesmanship skills.")[43] BARS is similar to another appraisal method, Behavioral Observation Scales (BOS), but the latter involves rating how frequently the ratees exhibit the illustrative behaviors.[44]

Mixed Standard Scales

Mixed standard scales are somewhat similar to behaviorally anchored scales. However they are called mixed scales because the employer "mixes" together sequentially the good and poor behavioral example statements when listing them. The aim is to reduce rating errors by making it less obvious to the appraiser (1) what performance dimensions he or she is rating; and (2) whether the behavioral example statements represent high, medium, or low performance. For each statement the appraiser rates the employee by indicating whether the latter's performance is better than, the same, or worse than the statement.

Management by Objectives

The term *management by objectives (MBO)* usually refers to a multistep company-wide goal-setting and appraisal program. MBO requires the manager to set specific measurable, organizationally relevant goals with each employee, and then periodically discuss the latter's progress toward these goals. The steps are:

1. ***Set the organization's goals.*** Establish a company-wide plan for next year and set goals.
2. ***Set departmental goals.*** Department heads and their superiors jointly set goals for their departments.
3. ***Discuss departmental goals.*** Department heads discuss the department's goals with their subordinates and ask them to develop their own individual goals. They should ask, "How could each employee help the department attain its goals?"
4. ***Define expected results (set individual goals).*** Department heads and their subordinates set short-term performance targets for each employee.
5. ***Conduct performance reviews.*** After a period, department heads compare each employee's actual and expected results.
6. ***Provide feedback.*** Department heads hold periodic performance review meetings with subordinates. Here they discuss the subordinates' performance and make any plans for rectifying or continuing the person's performance.

Formal MBO programs require numerous time-consuming meetings, and their use has diminished.[45] However, some companies successfully use streamlined versions. For example, Google CEO Larry Page sets company-wide "OKRs" (objectives and key results) quarterly. All Google employees then make sure their own goals are more or less in synch with the CEO's. All employees' goals are posted on Google's internal Web site, next to their names.[46]

Computerized and Web-Based Performance Appraisal

Employers increasingly use computerized or Internet-based appraisal systems. Most enable managers to compile computerized notes on subordinates during the year, and then to merge these with ratings for the employee on several performance traits. The software presents written examples to support part of the appraisal. Most such appraisals combine several appraisal tools, usually graphic ratings anchored by critical incidents.[47]

For example, Employee Appraiser (see www.halogensoftware.com) presents a menu of evaluation dimensions, including dependability, initiative, communication, decision making, leadership, judgment, and planning and productivity.[48] Within each dimension (such as communication) are separate performance factors for things like writing, verbal communication, and receptivity to criticism. When the user clicks on a performance factor, he or she is presented with a graphic rating scale. However, instead of numerical ratings, Employee Appraiser uses behaviorally anchored examples. Thus, for *verbal communication* there are six choices, ranging from "presents ideas clearly" to "lacks structure." The manager chooses the phrase that most accurately describes the worker. Then Employee Appraiser generates an appraisal with sample text.

Successfactors, a subsidiary of software giant SAP, offers a Web-based employee appraisal solution. It includes performance review forms and approval processes, 51 competencies for most job types, a built-in writing assistant, and a legal scan.[49]

Electronic Performance Monitoring

Electronic performance monitoring (EPM) systems use computer network technology to allow managers to monitor their employees' computers. They allow managers to monitor the employees' rate, accuracy, and time spent working online.[50]

electronic performance monitoring (EPM)
Having supervisors electronically monitor the amount of computerized data an employee is processing per day, and thereby his or her performance.

EPM can improve productivity, but also seems to raise employee stress. However, one researcher concludes that electronic performance monitoring "represents the future of performance feedback where supervisors can electronically monitor the amount and quality of work an employee is producing and have objective indicators of employee performance immediately available and visible."[51]

Similarly, some employers digitally track workers' performance through wearables. For example, the British retailer Tesco has warehouse workers wear armbands. These track which specific goods each worker is moving and how long the task is taking to complete and quantify and report things like how long it takes each worker to fulfill each order.[52]

Jose Luis Pelaez/Blend Boost/AGE Fotostock

Many employers today make use of computerized or online appraisals for evaluating employee performance.

Conversation Days

When employees at Juniper Networks Inc. expressed concerns about their annual performance reviews and the lack of positive feedback, Juniper changed the process. Instead of once-a-year performance reviews, there are now semiannual "conversation days." The stress in these manager-employee conversations is on areas for improvement and growth, and on setting stretch goals that align with the employee's career interests. There are no explicit performance ratings. In 2015, GE similarly began experimenting with substituting frequent conversations for traditional appraisals.

Appraisal in Practice: Using Multiple Methods

Which appraisal method to use? In practice, the rating form will probably merge several approaches. For example, Figure 9-2 (page 279) has a numerical graphic rating scale anchored with behavioral incidents such as "Even with guidance, fails to...." The Strategic Context feature (page 288) shows how one employer created a new appraisal system.

TRENDS SHAPING HR: *CUSTOMIZED TALENT MANAGEMENT*

There has always been some customizing of appraisals. For example, rating a salesperson based on whether she attained her sales goals assumes she had her own customized goals to meet.

Today, some employers are customizing their appraisal in other ways. For example, it is increasingly common for companies to adapt their appraisals and rewards to how critical the employees are to the company's strategic success—their "mission-critical" employees. For example, GE prioritizes jobs and focuses on what it calls its employee "game changers."[53] Unilever includes 15% of employees per management level in its high-potential list each year.[54] Shell China appoints "career stewards" to meet regularly with "emerging leaders."[55] McKinsey & Co. recommends limiting the "high potential group in whom the company invests heavily to no more than 10 to 20% of managerial and professional staff."[56]

Figure 9-9 illustrates one way to customize appraisals. Accenture uses a 4 × 4 matrix to plot employees by *Performance* (exceptional, high, medium, low) and *Value to the Organization* (mission-critical, core, necessary, nonessential). Consider

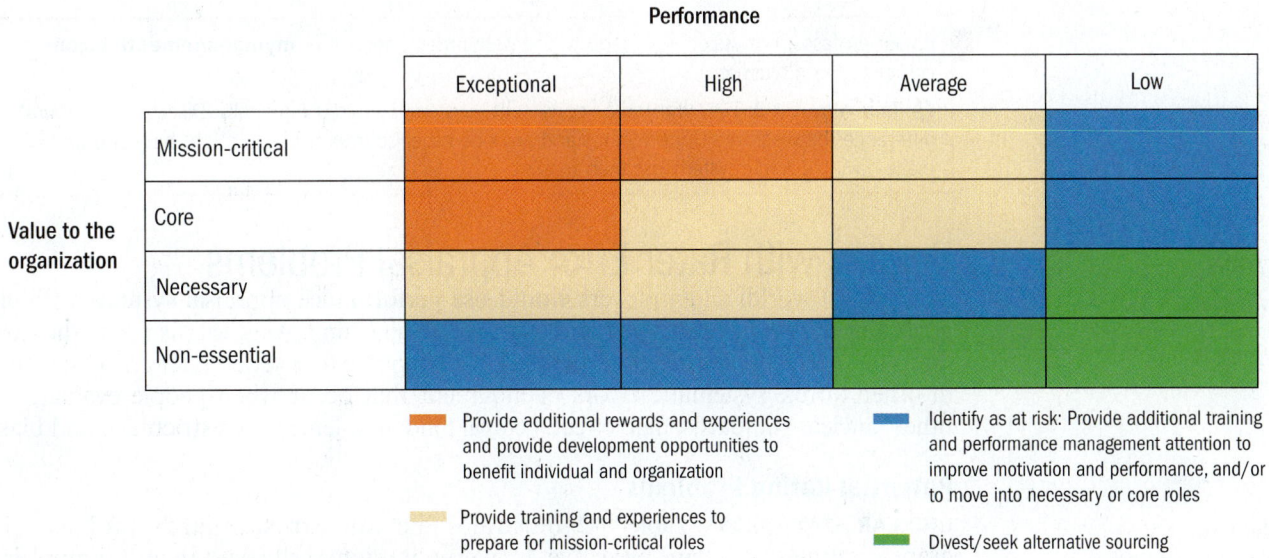

FIGURE 9-9 Accenture's Strategic Role Assessment Matrix

Source: Reprinted by permission from "Accenture's Strategic Role Assessment Matrix", in "The New Talent Equation," Outlook, June 2009. © 2009 Accenture., © 2009.

a chemical engineering company. Here the firm's experienced engineers may be "mission-critical," engineer-trainees "core," sales, accounting, and HR "necessary," and outsourceable employees such maintenance "nonessential."

This company would then tie each employee's pay, development, dismissal, and other personnel decisions to each employee's position in the matrix, in other words to both their performance rating and criticalness to the company (so that, not unreasonably, someone with more critical skills might get more slack and development then would someone who's "nonessential"). Hopefully, this employer would also design its incentives, promotions, and raises to support rather than turn off the mission critical engineers.[57] ■

IMPROVING PERFORMANCE: *The Strategic Context*

TRW's New Global Performance Appraisal/Management System

As a global competitor facing stiff competition, TRW needed a performance appraisal system that was consistent and comprehensive.[58] It had to be *consistent* in that employees in all of TRW's far-flung organization could use the same system. It had to be *comprehensive* in that it consolidated the various components of performance management into a single cost-effective system. For TRW, these components included goal setting, performance appraisal, professional development, and succession planning.

TRW's team created an online system, one in which most TRW employees and supervisors worldwide could input and review their data electronically. (The team subsequently created an equivalent paper-based system, for use by certain employees abroad who didn't have easy access to the Web.) The Web-based performance management system included data such as biographical data, previous year's professional development activities, overall performance, and future potential/positions.

In practice, either the employee or the manager can trigger the process by completing the appraisal and sending it to the other (the employee usually begins the process). Once the employee finishes the online form, a system-generated e-mail notifies the manager that the form is ready for review. Then the two fine-tune the appraisal by meeting in person, and by interacting online.

The new system focuses everyone's attention on goal-oriented performance. It identifies development needs that are important to both TRW and the employee. It gives managers instantaneous access to employee performance-related data (by clicking the "managing employees" function, a manager sees an overview of the assessment status of each of his or her direct reports). It gives all managers access to an employee database so that, for instance, a search for a mechanical engineer with Chinese language skills takes just a few minutes. And the system lets the manager quickly review the development needs of all his or her employees. ■

Source: Based on D. Bradford Neary, "Creating a Company-Wide, Online, Performance Management System: A Case Study at TRW Inc.," Human Resource Management 41, no. 4 (Winter 2002), p. 495.

If your professor has assigned this, go to the Assignments section of **mymanagementlab.com** to complete this discussion.

✪ **Talk About It 3:** TRW wanted a "consistent" system it could use globally. Discuss two cultural differences between the United States and any one other country that you might have thought would make having a single system less than feasible.

LEARNING OBJECTIVE **9-3**
Give examples of potential appraisal problems and how to deal with them.

Dealing with Rater Error Appraisal Problems

In a perfect world, all employers would use performance appraisal systems with clear goals, fair appraisals, swift feedback, and useful coaching. Alas, that is rarely the case.[59] Graphic-type rating forms in particular are susceptible to several "rater error" problems; in other words, systematic errors in judgment that occur when people evaluate each other: unclear standards, halo effect, central tendency, leniency or strictness, and bias.

Potential Rating Problems

unclear standards
An appraisal that is too open to interpretation.

UNCLEAR STANDARDS Table 9-2 illustrates the **unclear standards** problem. This graphic rating scale seems objective. However, it might well result in unfair appraisals, because the traits and degrees of merit are ambiguous. For example, different supervisors might define "good" performance, "fair" performance, and so on, differently. The same is true of traits such as "quality of work."[60]

Supervisors must be familiar with appraisal techniques, understand and avoid problems that can cripple appraisals, and know how to conduct appraisals fairly.

GARO/PHANIE/AGE Fotostock

The way to fix this problem is to include descriptive phrases that define or illustrate each trait, as in Figure 9-2. That form spells out what measures like "Role Model" or "Below Expectations" mean. This specificity results in more consistent and more easily explained appraisals.

halo effect
In performance appraisal, the problem that occurs when a supervisor's rating of a subordinate on one trait biases the rating of that person on other traits.

HALO EFFECT Experts define **halo effect** as "the influence of a rater's general impression on ratings of specific ratee qualities."[61] For example, supervisors often rate unfriendly employees lower on all traits, rather than just on "gets along well with others." Being aware of this problem is a step toward avoiding it. Supervisory training can also alleviate the problem, as can using a BARS (on which, recall, the performance dimensions are usually more independent of each other).

central tendency
A tendency to rate all employees the same way, such as rating them all average.

CENTRAL TENDENCY **Central tendency** means rating all employees average. For example, if the rating scale ranges from 1 to 7, raters tend to avoid the highs (6 and 7) and lows (1 and 2) and rate most of their people between 3 and 5. Doing so distorts the evaluations, making them less useful for promotion, salary, or counseling purposes. Ranking employees instead of using graphic rating scales can reduce this problem, since ranking means you can't rate them all average.

strictness/leniency
The problem that occurs when a supervisor has a tendency to rate all subordinates either high or low.

LENIENCY OR STRICTNESS Other supervisors tend to rate all their subordinates high or low, just as some instructors are notoriously high or low graders. This **strictness/leniency** problem is especially severe with graphic rating scales. *Ranking* forces supervisors to distinguish between high and low performers.

TABLE 9-2 A Graphic Rating Scale with Unclear Standards

	Excellent	Good	Fair	Poor
Quantity of work				
Quality of work				
Creativity				
Integrity				

Note: For example, what exactly is meant by "good," "quantity of work," and so forth?

There are other solutions. One is for the employer to recommend that supervisors avoid giving all their employees high (or low) ratings. A second is to require a distribution—that, say, about 10% of the people should be rated "excellent," 20% "good," and so forth. (But remember it may not be an error at all, as when all subordinates really are superior.)[62]

RECENCY EFFECTS Recency means letting what the employee has done recently blind you to what his or her performance has been over the year. The main solution is to accumulate critical incidents all year long.

Diversity Counts: The Problem of Bias

bias
The tendency to allow individual differences such as age, race, and sex to affect the appraisal ratings employees receive.

Biased appraisals have a variety of causes. One study of **bias** (the tendency for individual differences to affect judgements) focused on rater personality. Raters who scored higher on "conscientiousness" tended to give their peers lower ratings—they were stricter, in other words; those more "agreeable" gave higher ratings—they were more lenient.[63] Managers also tend to be more lenient when appraising subordinates for administrative purposes like pay raises then for development purposes.[64] Furthermore, "performance ratings amplify the quality of the personal relationship between boss and employee. Good relationships tend to create good [appraisal] experiences, bad relationships bad ones."[65]

Unfortunately, subordinates' demographic traits (age, race, gender, and so on) also affect ratings. A 36-year-old supervisor ranked a 62-year-old subordinate at the bottom of the department's rankings, and then fired him. The court held that the younger boss's discriminatory motives might have prejudiced the dismissal decision.[66] In one study, promoted women had to have received higher performance ratings than promoted men to be promoted, "suggesting that women were held to stricter standards for promotion."[67] In another study, raters penalized successful women for their success.[68] The point is that the appraisal often says more about the appraiser than about the appraisee.[69] (Or, as one researcher said, "Rater idiosyncratic biases account for the largest percentage of the observed variances in performance ratings.")[70] Potential bias is one reason to use multiple raters, have the supervisor's boss review the rating, and/or have "calibration" meetings where supervisors discuss their reasons for the appraisals they gave each of their subordinates.[71] ■

The Need for Fairness

So, due to either the supervisor's ineptness or the method's inherent unfairness, many appraisals are unfair. Some managers ignore accuracy and instead use appraisals for political purposes (such as encouraging employees with whom they don't agree to leave the firm).[72] The employees' standards should be clear, employees should understand the basis on which you're going to appraise them, and the appraisal should be objective.[73] Make sure the employee has an opportunity to express his or her opinions.

In practice (as most students probably already know), the quality of the interpersonal relationship between the supervisor and employee will shape the appraisal's impact and worth. Supervisors should be trained in both the technical and interpersonal aspects of appraising employees and giving feedback.[74] They should understand how to build trust through open relationships, engage in continuous performance conversations, diagnose and productively address performance issues, and deliver and react to feedback conversations constructively.[75] To facilitate this, the employer should evaluate and reward supervisors partly based on their effectiveness in managing performance.[76]

FIGURE 9-10 Checklist of Best Practices for Administering Fair Performance Appraisals

- Base the performance review on duties and standards from a job analysis.
- Try to base the performance review on observable job behaviors or objective performance data.
- Make it clear ahead of time what your performance expectations are.
- Use a standardized performance review procedure for all employees.
- Make sure whoever conducts the reviews has frequent opportunities to observe the employee's job performance.
- Either use multiple raters or have the rater's supervisor evaluate the appraisal results.
- Include an appeals mechanism.
- Document the appraisal review process and results.
- Discuss the appraisal results with the employee.
- Let the employees know ahead of time how you're going to conduct the reviews.
- Let the employee provide input regarding your assessment of him or her.
- Indicate what the employee needs to do to improve.
- Train the supervisors who will be doing the appraisals. Make sure they understand the procedure to use, how problems (like leniency and strictness) arise, and how to deal with them.

Figure 9-10 lists best practices for ensuring fair appraisals. Table 9-3 summarizes each appraisal method's pros and cons.

TABLE 9-3 Important Advantages and Disadvantages of Appraisal Tools

Tool	Advantages	Disadvantages
Graphic rating scale	Simple to use; provides a quantitative rating for each employee.	Standards may be unclear; halo effect, central tendency, leniency, bias can also be problems.
BARS	Provides behavioral "anchors." BARS is very accurate.	Difficult to develop.
Alternation ranking	Simple to use (but not as simple as graphic rating scales). Avoids central tendency and other problems of rating scales.	Can cause disagreements among employees and may be unfair if all employees are, in fact, excellent.
Forced distribution method	End up with a predetermined number or % of people in each group.	Employees' appraisal results depend on your choice of cutoff points.
Critical incident method	Helps specify what is "right" and "wrong" about the employee's performance; forces supervisor to evaluate subordinates on an ongoing basis.	Difficult to rate or rank employees relative to one another.
MBO	Tied to jointly agreed-upon performance objectives.	Time-consuming.

KNOW YOUR EMPLOYMENT LAW

Appraising Performance

Courts have often found that an inadequate appraisal system lay at the root of illegal discriminatory actions, particularly in cases concerning layoffs, promotions, discharges, or merit pay.[77] For example, one court held that the firm had violated Title VII when it laid off several Hispanic-surnamed employees based on poor performance ratings. The court concluded that the practice was illegal because: the firm based the appraisals on subjective supervisory observations; it did not administer and score the appraisals in a standardized fashion; and two of the three supervisory evaluators did not have daily contact with the employees they appraised. Personal bias, unreasonably rating everyone high or low, and relying just on recent events are some other reasons courts have given in holding a firm's appraisal processes to have been unfair.[78]

Steps to ensure your appraisals are legally defensible include:

- Base the duties and criteria you appraise on a job analysis.
- Communicate performance standards to employees in writing.
- Using a single overall rating of performance is not acceptable to the courts, which often find doing so vague.[79] Courts generally require combining separate ratings for each performance dimension (quality, quantity, and so on) with some formal weighting system to yield a summary score.
- Include an employee appeals process. Employees should be able to review and make comments about their appraisals before they become final, and should have a formal appeals process.
- One appraiser should never have absolute authority to determine a personnel action.
- Document all information. "Without exception, courts condemn informal performance evaluation practices that eschew documentation."[80]
- Train supervisors. If formal rater training is not possible, at least provide raters with written instructions on how to use the rating scale.[81]
- If such a case gets to court, what will judges look for? In a review of about 300 U.S. court decisions, actions reflecting fairness and due process were most important.[82] ■

LEARNING OBJECTIVE **9-4**

List steps to take in the appraisal interview.

Managing the Appraisal Interview

The traditional periodic appraisal typically culminates in an **appraisal interview**. Here the manager and the subordinate review the appraisal and make plans to remedy deficiencies and reinforce strengths. These interviews are often uncomfortable. Few people like to receive—or give—negative feedback. Adequate preparation and effective implementation are essential. Supervisors face four types of appraisal situations, each with its unique objectives:[83]

appraisal interview
An interview in which the supervisor and subordinate review the appraisal and make plans to remedy deficiencies and reinforce strengths.

- ***Satisfactory—Promotable*** is the easiest interview: The person's performance is satisfactory and promotion looms. Your objective is to develop specific development plans.
- ***Satisfactory—Not promotable*** is for employees whose performance is satisfactory but for whom promotion is not possible. The objective here is to maintain satisfactory performance. The best option is usually to find incentives that are important to the person and sufficient to maintain performance. These might include extra time off, a small bonus, or recognition.
- When the person's performance is *unsatisfactory but correctable*, the interview objective is to lay out an action/development plan for correcting the unsatisfactory performance.
- Finally, the interview where the employee is *unsatisfactory* and the situation is *uncorrectable* may be particularly tense. Dismissal is often the preferred option.

How to Conduct the Appraisal Interview

Useful interviews begin before the interview. Beforehand, review the person's job description, compare performance to the standards, and review any previous appraisals. Give the employee at least a week's notice to review his or her work. Set a time for the interview. Interviews with lower-level personnel like clerical workers should take less than an hour. Interviews with management employees often take 1 or 2 hours. Conduct the interview privately with no interruptions.

An effective interview requires effective coaching skills. Coaching doesn't mean telling someone what to do. Instead, it is a process.[84] *Preparation* means understanding the problem and the employee. Here the manager will watch the employee to see what he or she is doing, review productivity data, and observe the workflow.

Planning the solution is next. This requires reaching agreement on the problem, and laying out a change plan in the form of *steps to take, measures of success,* and *date to complete*.

With agreement on a plan, the manager can start the *actual coaching*. One writer says, "An effective coach offers ideas and advice in such a way that the subordinate can hear them, respond to them, and appreciate their value."[85] Useful guidelines include:

1. ***Talk in terms of objective work data.*** Use examples such as absences, tardiness, and productivity.
2. ***Don't get personal.*** Don't say, "You're too slow producing those reports." Instead, compare the person's performance to a standard. ("These reports should normally be done within 10 days.") Similarly, don't compare the person's performance to that of other people. ("He's quicker than you are.")
3. ***Encourage the person to talk.*** Stop and listen to what the person is saying; ask open-ended questions (such as, "What do you think we can do to improve the situation?"). Use a command such as "Go on." Restate the person's last point as a question, as in, "You don't think you can get the job done?"
4. ***Get agreement.*** Make sure the person leaves knowing specifically what he or she is doing right and doing wrong and with agreement on how things will be improved, and has an action plan with targets and dates.

Whether subordinates express satisfaction with their appraisal interview will depend on several things. These include not feeling threatened, having an opportunity to present their ideas and feelings and to influence the course of the interview, and having a helpful and constructive supervisor conduct the interview.

How to Handle a Defensive Subordinate

When a supervisor tells someone his or her performance is poor, the first reaction is often denial. Denial is a defense mechanism. By denying the fault, the person avoids having to question his or her own competence.

Therefore, dealing with defensiveness is an important appraisal skill. In his book *Effective Psychology for Managers*, psychologist Mortimer Feinberg suggests the following:

1. Recognize that defensive behavior is normal.
2. Never attack a person's defenses. Don't try to "explain someone to themselves" (as in, "You know the reason you're using that excuse is that you can't bear to be blamed."). Instead, concentrate on the fact ("sales are down").
3. Postpone action. Sometimes it's best to do nothing. Employees may react to sudden threats by hiding behind their defenses. Given sufficient time, a more rational reaction takes over.
4. Recognize your limitations. The supervisor is (probably) not a psychologist. Offering understanding is one thing; trying to deal with psychological problems is another.

How to Criticize a Subordinate

When necessary, criticize in a manner that lets the person maintain his or her dignity—in private, and constructively. Provide examples of critical incidents and specific suggestions. Avoid once-a-year "critical broadsides" by giving feedback periodically, so that the formal review contains no surprises. Never say the person is "always" wrong. Criticism should be objective and free of personal bias.

When the employee is not doing well, the manager will have to decide how candid to be. Former GE CEO Jack Welch once said it's cruel to tell someone who's mediocre that their work is satisfactory.[86] Someone who might have changed course may instead waste years in a dead-end job, only to be dismissed when a more demanding boss arrives.

Some managers do take a hard line. Not all employees are salvageable, and not all managers will spend time trying to overcome an employee's faults. For example, when one Netflix manager requested a performance improvement plan for a worker, the then-head of HR said basically, "Don't waste your time." Her position was, why waste time coaching this person if she'll probably never be able to do the job right anyway?[87]

On the other hand, many employers are now emphasizing praise over criticism. One tells its managers not to touch on more than two areas that need improvement but instead to emphasize their subordinates' strengths. In one recent year, almost all the *Fortune* 500 companies used the Gallup StrengthsFinder tool (www.gallupstrengthscenter.com) to help employees identify and build on their strengths. Facebook, for instance, has used StrengthsFinder to help train supervisors in a style that better fits its mostly Millennial-aged staff. It would seem that to attract, motivate, and retain today's new employees, a less critical appraisal approach may be advisable.[88]

GET AGREEMENT ON A PLAN The aim of the appraisal should be to improve unsatisfactory performance (and/or to reinforce exemplary performance). The appraisal should therefore result in a plan (Figure 9-11) for what the employee must do to improve his or her efforts.

How to Handle a Formal Written Warning

The employee's performance may be so weak that it requires a formal written warning. Such warnings serve two purposes: (1) to shake your employee out of his or her bad habits, and (2) to help you defend your rating to your own boss and (if needed) to the courts.

FIGURE 9-11 Sample Employee Development Plan

SAMPLE EMPLOYEE DEVELOPMENT PLAN

Employee's Name	Department	Employee's Job Title	Today's Date
Employee's main Objectives for this period:	Did employee fully achieve objective (include rating from appraisal form, from Poor to Outstanding).	What training or other actions are required for improved performance on this objective?	Completion dates:
➢ 1 _____	_____	_____	_____
➢ 2 _____	_____	_____	_____
➢ 3 _____	_____	_____	_____
➢ 4 _____	_____	_____	_____
➢ 5 _____	_____	_____	_____

Employee Signature _____ Manager Signature _____

Copyright Gary dessler, PhD

FIGURE 9-12 Appraisal Interview Checklist

Source: Copyright Gary Dessler, PhD.

Appraisal Interview Checklist

Interview Item: Did you	Yes	No
1. Review the employee's job description, previous appraisals, goals, and current job standards prior to the interview?		
2. Provide adequate time and a private, cordial, non-threatening environment for the interview?		
3. Focus your discussion and comments on objective work data?		
4. Encourage the appraisee to talk (restate last comment as a question, etc.), and make it clear you are listening (nod, etc.)?		
5. Give the appraisee an opportunity to fully present his or her ideas and feelings?		
6. Consciously avoid attacking the appraisee's defenses?		
7. Criticize in a way that allowed the appraisee to maintain his or her dignity?		
8. Discuss your evaluation of each of the appraisee's job duties and/or goals?		
9. Reach agreement on the training and development required to improve the appraisee's performance?		
10. Discuss, as appropriate, the steps the employer may take if improvement goals are not met?		
11. Discuss the appraisee's performance in light of his or her career aspirations?		

Written warnings should list the employee's standards, make it clear that the employee was aware of the standard, specify any deficiencies relative to the standard, and show the employee had an opportunity to correct his or her performance.

Figure 9-12 provides an appraisal interview checklist.

LEARNING OBJECTIVE **9-5**

Explain key points in how to use the appraisal interview to boost employee engagement.

Employee Engagement Guide for Managers

Use the Appraisal Interview to Build Engagement

Managers can use the appraisal interview to improve their employees' engagement. Here are relevant findings and implications.

1. Employees who understand how they and their departments contribute to the company's success are more engaged.[89] Therefore, *take the opportunity to show the employee how his or her efforts contribute to the "big picture"—to his or her team's and the company's success.*
2. Another study found that employees' engagement rose when they experienced what the researchers called "psychological meaningfulness" (namely, the perception that one's role in the organization is worthwhile and valuable).[90] *Use the interview to emphasize the meaningfulness to the company of what the employee is doing.*
3. Employees who experience "psychological safety" (namely, the perception that it's safe to bring oneself to a role without fear of damage to self-image, status, or career) were more engaged.[91] Therefore, *be candid and objective but do so supportively and without unnecessarily undermining the employee's self-image.*[92]
4. Efficacy drives engagement, so use the interview to make sure your employee *has what he or she needs* to do a good job.[93]
5. Managers should be candid and honest, but don't unnecessarily emphasize the negatives. Doing so undermines employee engagement. In one survey, Gallup asked about 1,000 U.S. employees to respond to two statements: "My supervisor focuses on my strengths or positive characteristics" and "My supervisor focuses

on my weaknesses or negative characteristics." It found that about three times more employees whose *managers focused on strengths* were engaged, compared with those whose managers focused on weaknesses.[94]

6. Research shows that involvement in decision making and letting employees voice their opinions improve employee engagement.[95] Use the interview as an opportunity to *show your employees that you listen to their ideas and value their contributions*.
7. Engagement rises when employees have an opportunity to improve their careers.[96] During the interview discuss the person's evaluation *in the context of where he or she sees himself or herself heading career-wise*.[97]
8. Research shows "a significant positive association between distributive [what rewards people get] and informational [what information they get] justice dimensions, and employee engagement."[98] Bottom line: *Make sure that the interviewee views the appraisal and the rewards or remedial actions as fair*.

Performance Management

LEARNING OBJECTIVE **9-6**

Explain how you would take a performance management approach to appraisal.

Performance appraisal is fine in theory, but in practice, appraisals don't always go smoothly. Goals aren't set, the "appraisal" is a form from an office supply store, and the yearly feedback, if any, may be agonizing, with both participants fleeing before any coaching takes place. This runs counter to common sense. Employees should know what their goals are, performance feedback should be useful, and if there is a problem, the time to take action is right away, not 6 months later.

Total Quality Management and Performance Appraisal

Management experts have long argued that most performance appraisals neither motivate employees nor guide their development.[99] Some proponents of the total quality management (TQM) movement even argued for eliminating performance appraisals altogether.[100] *Total quality management* (TQM) programs are organizationwide programs that integrate all functions and processes of the business such that all aspects of the business including design, planning, production, distribution, and field service are aimed at maximizing customer satisfaction through continuous improvements.[101] TQM programs are built on a philosophy encapsulated by several principles, such as: cease dependence on inspection to achieve quality; aim for continuous improvement; institute extensive training; drive out fear so that everyone may work effectively; remove barriers that rob employees of their pride of workmanship (in particular, the annual merit rating); and institute a vigorous program of self-improvement.[102] Basically, TQM advocates argue that the organization is a system of interrelated parts, and that employees' performance is more a function of things like training, communication, tools, and supervision than of their motivation.

What would performance appraisal look like in such a company? Visitors to Toyota Motor's Lexington, Kentucky, Camry plant would find such a system. Teams of employees monitor their own results, generally without managers' interventions. In frequent meetings, the team members continuously align those results with the work team's standards and with the plant's overall quality and productivity goals. Team members who need coaching and training receive it. Procedures that need changing are changed.

What Is Performance Management?

performance management
The *continuous* process of identifying, measuring, and developing the performance of individuals and teams and *aligning* their performance with the organization's *goals*.

That is performance management in action. In comparing performance management and performance appraisal, "the distinction is the contrast between a year-end event—the completion of the appraisal form—and a process that starts the year with performance planning and is integral to the way people are managed throughout the year."[103] **Performance management** is the *continuous* process of identifying, measuring, and developing the performance of individuals and teams and *aligning* their performance with the organization's *goals*.[104] We can summarize performance management's six basic elements as follows:[105]

- ***Direction sharing*** means communicating the company's goals to all employees and then translating these into doable departmental, team, and individual goals.
- ***Goal alignment*** means having a method that enables managers and employees to *see* the link between the employees' goals and those of their department and company.
- ***Ongoing performance monitoring*** usually means computerized systems to measure the team's and/or employee's progress toward meeting performance goals.
- ***Ongoing feedback*** means providing face-to-face and computerized continuous feedback regarding progress toward goals.
- ***Coaching and developmental support*** should be part of the feedback process.
- ***Recognition and rewards*** should provide the incentives to keep the employee's goal-directed performance on track.

TRENDS SHAPING HR: *DIGITAL AND SOCIAL MEDIA*

Employers increasingly use digital technologies including cloud computing, gaming, and social media to support performance management. For example, with Oracle TBE Performance Management Cloud Service, management would:

- First, *assign financial and nonfinancial goals* to each team's activities, goals which support the company's overall strategic goals. (Thus, an airline might measure ground crew aircraft turnaround time in terms of "improve turnaround time to 26 minutes per plane this year.")
- *Inform all teams and employees* of their goals.
- *Use IT-supported tools* (cloud-based performance management software, HR scorecards, and digital dashboards) to continuously display, monitor, and assess each team's and employee's performance (see Figure 9-13). Oracle TBE Performance Management Cloud Service illustrates this.[106] Because the goals are "in the cloud" rather than embedded in documents, managers needn't wait until the annual or semiannual reviews to revise them. And the system's dashboards enable managers to continuously monitor each team or employee's performance, let employees update progress toward goal achievement, and let employees and managers log comments so the process is real-time and interactive. For more details, see www.oracle.com/taleo-tbe.
- Finally, if exceptions are noted, ensure you've *taken corrective action* before things swing out of control.

Beyond the cloud, employers are also adopting social media and gaming–based performance appraisal and management tools. Social media tools allow almost everyone in the company (the "crowd," as in "crowd appraisals") to continuously appraise

FIGURE 9-13 Summary of Performance Management Report

Source: Based on "Personal Goal Management" from the Active Strategy Web site. Copyright © 2012 by ActiveStrategy, Inc.

PERFORMANCE GOAL MANAGEMENT

Report Card | Link | Edit | Options | Copy

Details - 2013 Performance Goal Scorecard — In Progress (01/01/2013 - 12/31/13)

Goals for Brown, Lisa — Score 4.5

Employee's Individual Performance Goals

Goal	Target	Weight	Score	Date
Achieve 10% Sales Increase	8	45	7.0	June 2013
Improved Customer Satisfaction Rating	4.2	25	4.0	June 2013
Meet Budgetary Constraints	5	15	2.5	June 2013
Improved Leadership Ratings	4.8	15	4.5	June 2013

Departmental Performance Goals

Goal	Target	Weight	Score	Date
Achieve 15% Sales Increase	5	50	3.5	June 2013
Increase Online sales 10%	3.5	25	2.8	June 2013
Meet Budgetary Constraints	5	10	4.2	June 2013
All Employees Cross-Trained on All Products	4.5	15	3.5	June 2013

each other's work. Workforce Rypple (subsequently bought by salesforce.com) is one such "social performance management platform."[107] Basically, it supplements traditional appraisals. Employees and managers use it to set goals, and to provide feedback and recognition as tasks get done.[108] For example, Washington-based LivingSocial employees use Rypple to comment on each other's work. LivingSocial then uses these comments as an input to its formal employee appraisals.[109] Solar energy company Sunrun also uses Rypple. A spokesman says: "It's great for putting ideas out there, you can unveil objectives to the whole team, ask for opinions and suggestions and then work on them together. We do 360 feedback each week."[110] Saba Social Performance Management Software is another such tool.[111] Employers often combine such ongoing reviews with Globoforce (www.globoforce.com) type rewards sites, which automate the process of instantaneously rewarding and recognizing colleagues.[112]

Dissatisfaction with its current performance appraisal process prompted Persistent Systems to have the gaming company eMee create a virtual appraisal game. Every Persistent Systems employee has a virtual avatar. Employees use them to give real-time feedback to each other, including virtual gifts and points (only immediate supervisors can give reprimands). The system apparently reduced turnover and improved performance.[113] ■

✪ Watch It!

Who does this company have doing its appraisals? If your professor has assigned this, go to the Assignments section of mymanagementlab.com to complete the video exercise titled *Hautelook: Appraising.*

The HR Practices Around the Globe feature shows how one company developed a company-wide performance management system.

IMPROVING PERFORMANCE: *HR Practices around the Globe*

Performance Management at General Dynamics Armament Systems (GDAS)

General Dynamics Armament Systems (GDAS) designs, develops, and produces high-performance products for the military, industrial, and commercial markets.[114] GDAS reorganized its various programs around teams. The teams and their team members have individual responsibility for income, sales, deliveries, and customer satisfaction. Organizing its programs around teams meant GDAS needed a better way to track the teams' performances and monitor and manage the company's performance.

Its new performance management reporting system uses a standard set of performance metrics processed and reported through a special business metrics scorecard. The scorecard displays the performance metrics for each team in three ways (actual, baseline plan, and current plan). It then calculates and displays a variance between the actual and the planned performances.

GDAS uses multiple scorecards to display performance metrics, such as for team and for divisional performance. The scorecards allow GDAS to maintain all of its crucial performance data in one system so managers can easily access the information anytime via the firm's intranet. The scorecards provide GDAS with approximately 450 performance reports and charts. To produce these charts manually would require 13 full-time employees. Instead, the performance measures reporting system, at a cost of $1 million, generates the reports and charts automatically. ■

Source: Based on www.gdatp.com/about/; Best Practice: Performance Measures Reporting System," Best Manufacturing Practices Center of Excellence, www.bmpcoe.org/bestpractices/internal/gdas/gdas_11.html.

If your professor has assigned this, go to the Assignments section of **mymanagementlab.com** to complete this discussion.

✪ **Talk About It 4:** Describe three examples of scorecard displays GDAS might show on their performance management system's digital dashboard–type display.

The Manager's Role in Performance Management

Technology, useful though it is, isn't mandatory for managers who want to take a performance management approach. What is mandatory is having the right philosophy and on-the-job behaviors. As a philosophy, performance management reflects nonthreatening TQM principles such as cease dependence on inspection to achieve quality, aim for continuous improvement, institute extensive training, and drive out fear so that everyone may work effectively. Behaviors include linking employees' goals to the company's goals, giving employees continuous feedback, providing required resources and coaching, rewarding good performance, and remembering that employees' performance reflects more than just whether they're "motivated."[115]

HR in Practice at the Hotel Paris Both Lisa and the firm's CFO were concerned by the current disconnect between (1) what their current appraisal process was focusing on and (2) what the company wanted to accomplish in terms of its strategic goals. They wanted the firm's new performance management system to help breathe life into the firm's strategic performance. To see what they did, read the case on pages 302 of this chapter.

Chapter Review

MyManagementLab® Go to **mymanagementlab.com** to complete the problems marked with this icon.

Chapter Section Summaries

9-1. **Performance appraisal** means evaluating an employee's current or past performance relative to his or her performance standards. Managers appraise their subordinates' performance to obtain input on which promotion and salary raise decisions can be made, to develop plans for correcting performance deficiencies, and for career-planning purposes. Supervisory ratings are still at the heart of most appraisal processes.

9-2. The appraisal is generally conducted using one or more popular **appraisal methods or tools**. These include graphic rating scales, alternation ranking, paired comparison, forced distribution, critical incidents, behaviorally anchored rating scales, MBO, computerized performance appraisals, and electronic performance monitoring.

9-3. The appraisal process can be improved by eliminating chronic **problems** that often undermine appraisals and graphic rating scales in particular. These problems include unclear standards, halo effect, central tendency, leniency or strictness, and bias.

9-4. An appraisal typically culminates in an **appraisal interview**. Adequate preparation (including giving the subordinate notice, reviewing his or her job description and past performance, choosing the right place for the interview, and leaving enough time for it) is essential.

9-5. The manager can use the appraisal interview to improve the employees' level of **engagement**. For example, show the employee how his or her efforts contribute to the team's and the company's success; use the interview to emphasize the meaningfulness to the company of what the employee is doing; and emphasize support rather than threats.

9-6. **Performance management** is the *continuous* process of identifying, measuring, and developing the performance of individuals and teams and *aligning* their performance with the organization's *goals*. It means continuous interactions and feedback to ensure continuous improvement in the employee's and team's capacity and performance. Most importantly, it requires remembering that your employee's performance usually reflects more than just whether he or she is "motivated."

Discussion Questions

✪ **9-1.** What is the purpose of a performance appraisal?

9-2. Answer the question, "Who should do the appraising?"

9-3. Discuss the pros and cons of four performance appraisal tools.

9-4. Explain how you would use the alternation ranking method, the paired comparison method, and the forced distribution method.

9-5. Explain in your own words how you would go about developing a behaviorally anchored rating scale.

9-6. Explain the problems to be avoided in appraising performance.

✪ **9-7.** Compare and contrast performance management and performance appraisal.

Individual and Group Activities

9-8. Working individually or in groups, develop a graphic rating scale for the following jobs: secretary, professor, bus driver.

9-9. Working individually or in groups, describe the advantages and disadvantages of using the forced distribution appraisal method for college professors.

9-10. Working individually or in groups, develop, over the period of a week, a set of critical incidents covering the classroom performance of one of your instructors.

9-11. Appendices A and B at the end of this book (pages 612–629) list the knowledge someone studying for the HRCI (Appendix A) or SHRM (Appendix B) certification exam needs to have in each area of human resource management (such as in Strategic Management, and Workforce Planning). In groups of several students, do four things: (1) review Appendix A and/or B; (2) identify the material in this chapter that relates to the Appendix A and/or B required knowledge lists; (3) write four multiple-choice exam questions on this material that you believe would be suitable for inclusion in the HRCI exam and/or the SHRM exam; and, (4) if time permits, have someone from your team post your team's questions in front of the class, so that students in all teams can answer the exam questions created by the other teams.

9-12. When he was doing his show The apprentice, Donald Trump often told apprentices "You're fired!" Review recent (or archived) episodes of Donald Trump's *The Apprentice* and answer this: What performance appraisal system did Mr. Trump use, and do you think it resulted in valid appraisals? What techniques discussed in this chapter did he seem to apply? How would you suggest he might change his appraisal system to make it more effective?

Experiential Exercise

Grading the Professor

Purpose: The purpose of this exercise is to give you practice in developing and using a performance appraisal form.

Required Understanding: You are going to develop a performance appraisal form for an instructor and should therefore be thoroughly familiar with the discussion of performance appraisals in this chapter.

How to Set Up the Exercise/Instructions: Divide the class into groups of four or five students.

9-13. First, based on what you now know about performance appraisal, do you think Figure 9-1 is an effective scale for appraising instructors? Why or why not?

9-14. Next, your group should develop its own tool for appraising the performance of an instructor. Decide which of the appraisal tools (graphic rating scales, alternation ranking, and so on) you are going to use, and then design the instrument itself.

9-15. Next, have a spokesperson from each group post his or her group's appraisal tool on the board. How similar are the tools? Do they all measure the same factors? Which factor appears most often? Which do you think is the most effective tool on the board?

9-16. The class should select the top 10 factors from all of the appraisal tools presented to create what the class perceives to be the most effective tool for appraising the performance of the instructor.

Application Case

Appraising the Secretaries at Sweetwater U

Rob Winchester, newly appointed vice president for administrative affairs at Sweetwater State University, faced a tough problem shortly after his university career began. Three weeks after he came on board in September, Sweetwater's president, Rob's boss, told Rob that one of his first tasks was to improve the appraisal system used to evaluate secretarial and clerical performance at Sweetwater U. The main difficulty was that the performance appraisal was traditionally tied directly to salary increases given at the end of the year. Therefore, most administrators were less than accurate when they used the graphic rating forms that were the basis of the clerical staff evaluation. In fact, what usually happened was that each administrator simply rated his or her clerk or secretary as "excellent." This cleared the way for them to receive a maximum pay raise every year.

But the current university budget simply did not include enough money to fund another "maximum" annual raise for every staffer. Furthermore, Sweetwater's president felt that the custom of providing invalid feedback to each secretary on his or her year's performance was not productive, so he had asked the new vice president to revise the system. In October, Rob sent a memo to all administrators, telling them that in the future no more than half the secretaries reporting to any particular administrator could be appraised as "excellent." This move, in effect, forced each supervisor to begin ranking his or her secretaries for quality of performance. The vice president's memo met widespread resistance immediately—from administrators, who were afraid that many of their secretaries would begin leaving for more lucrative jobs, and from secretaries, who felt that the new system was unfair and reduced each secretary's chance of receiving a maximum salary increase. A handful of secretaries had begun picketing outside the president's home on the university campus. The picketing, caustic remarks by disgruntled administrators, and rumors of an impending slowdown by the secretaries (there were about 250 on campus) made Rob Winchester wonder whether he had made the right decision by setting up forced ranking. He knew, however, that there were a few performance appraisal experts in the School of Business, so he decided to set up an appointment with them to discuss the matter.

He met with them the next morning. He explained the situation as he had found it: The current appraisal system had been set up when the university first opened 10 years earlier. A committee of secretaries had developed it. Under that system, Sweetwater's administrators filled out forms similar to the one shown in Table 9-2. This once-a-year appraisal (in March) had run into problems almost immediately, since it was apparent from the start that administrators varied widely in their interpretations of job standards, as well as in how conscientiously they filled out the forms and supervised their secretaries. Moreover, at the end of the first year it became obvious to everyone that each secretary's salary increase was tied directly to the March appraisal. For example, those rated "excellent" received the maximum increases, those rated "good" received smaller increases, and those given neither rating received only the standard across-the-board cost-of-living increase. Since universities in general—and Sweetwater, in particular—have paid secretaries somewhat lower salaries than those prevailing in private industry, some secretaries left in a huff that first year. From that time on, most administrators simply rated all secretaries excellent in order to reduce staff turnover, thus ensuring each a maximum increase. In the process, they also avoided the hard feelings aroused by the significant performance differences otherwise highlighted by administrators.

Two Sweetwater experts agreed to consider the problem, and in 2 weeks they came back to the vice president with the following recommendations. First, the form used to rate the secretaries was grossly insufficient. It was unclear what "excellent" or "quality of work" meant, for example. They recommended instead a form like that in Figure 9-2. In addition, they recommended that the vice president rescind his earlier memo and no longer attempt to force university administrators to arbitrarily rate at least half their secretaries as something less than excellent. The two consultants pointed out that this was unfair, since it was quite possible that any particular administrator might have staffers who were all or virtually all excellent—or conceivably, although less likely, all below standard. The experts said that the way to get all the administrators to take the appraisal process more seriously was to stop tying it to salary increases. In other words, they recommended that every administrator fill out a form as in Figure 9-2 for each secretary at least once a year and then use this form as the basis of a counseling session. Salary increases would have to be made on some basis other than the performance appraisal, so that administrators would no longer hesitate to fill out the rating forms honestly.

Rob thanked the two experts and went back to his office to ponder their recommendations. Some of the recommendations (such as substituting the new rating form for the old) seemed to make sense. Nevertheless, he still had serious doubts as to the efficacy of any graphic rating form, particularly compared with his original, preferred forced ranking approach. The experts' second recommendation—to stop tying the appraisals to automatic salary increases—made sense but raised at least one very practical problem: If salary increases were not to be based on performance appraisals, on what were they to be based? He began wondering whether the experts' recommendations weren't simply based on ivory tower theorizing.

Questions

9-17. Do you think that the experts' recommendations will be sufficient to get most of the administrators to fill out the rating forms properly? Why or why not? What additional actions (if any) do you think will be necessary?

9-18. Do you think that Vice President Winchester would be better off dropping graphic rating forms, substituting instead one of the other techniques we discussed in this chapter, such as a ranking method? Why or why not?

9-19. What performance appraisal system would you develop for the secretaries if you were Rob Winchester? Defend your answer.

Continuing Case

Carter Cleaning Company

The Performance Appraisal

After spending several weeks on the job, Jennifer was surprised to discover that her father had not formally evaluated any employee's performance for all the years that he had owned the business. Jack's position was that he had "a hundred higher-priority things to attend to," such as boosting sales and lowering costs, and, in any case, many employees didn't stick around long enough to be appraisable anyway. Furthermore, contended Jack, manual workers such as those doing the pressing and the cleaning did periodically get positive feedback in terms of praise from Jack for a job well done, or criticism, also from Jack, if things did not look right during one of his swings through the stores. Similarly, Jack was never shy about telling his managers about store problems so that they, too, got some feedback on where they stood.

This informal feedback notwithstanding, Jennifer believes that a more formal appraisal approach is required. She believes that there are criteria such as quality, quantity, attendance, and punctuality that should be evaluated periodically even if a worker is paid on piece rate. Furthermore, she feels quite strongly that the managers need to have a list of quality standards for matters such as store cleanliness, efficiency, safety, and adherence to budget on which they know they are to be formally evaluated.

Questions

9-20. Is Jennifer right about the need to evaluate the workers formally? The managers? Why or why not?

9-21. Develop a performance appraisal method for the workers and managers in each store.

CHAPTER 9

Translating Strategy into HR Policies and Practices Case*,§

**The accompanying strategy map for this chapter is in the MyManagementLab, and the overall map on the inside back cover of this text outlines the relationships involved.*

Improving Performance at the Hotel Paris

The New Performance Management System

The Hotel Paris's competitive strategy is "To use superior guest service to differentiate the Hotel Paris properties, and to thereby increase the length of stay and return rate of guests, and thus boost revenues and profitability." HR manager Lisa Cruz must now formulate appraisal policies and activities that support this competitive strategy, by eliciting the required employee behaviors and competencies.

Lisa knew that the Hotel Paris's performance appraisal system was inadequate. When the founders opened their first hotel, they went to an office-supply store and purchased a pad of performance appraisal forms. The hotel chain used these. Each form was a two-sided page. Supervisors indicates whether the employee's performance in terms of various standard traits including quantity of work, quality of work, and dependability was excellent, good, fair, or poor. Lisa knew that, among other flaws, this appraisal tool did not force either the employee or the supervisor to focus the appraisal on the extent to which the employee was helping the Hotel Paris to achieve its strategic goals. She wanted a system that focused the employee's attention on taking those actions that would contribute to helping the company achieve its goals, for instance, in terms of improved customer service.

Both Lisa and the firm's CFO were concerned by the current disconnect between (1) what the current appraisal process was focusing on and (2) what the company wanted to accomplish in terms of its strategic goals. They wanted the firm's new performance management system to help breathe life into the firm's strategic performance, by focusing employees' behavior specifically on the performances that would help the Hotel Paris achieve its strategic goals.

Lisa and her team created a performance management system that focused on both competencies and objectives. In designing the new system, their starting point was the job descriptions they had created for the hotel's employees. These descriptions each included required competencies. Consequently, using a form similar to Figure 9-3, the front-desk clerks' appraisals now focus on competencies such as "able to check a guest in or out in 5 minutes or less." Most service employees' appraisals include the competency, "able to exhibit patience and guest support of this even when busy with other activities." There were other required competencies. For example, the Hotel Paris wanted all service employees to show initiative in helping guests, to be customer oriented, and to be team players (in terms of sharing information and best practices). Each of these competencies derives from the hotel's aim of becoming more service-oriented. Each employee now also receives one or more strategically relevant objectives for the coming year. (One, for a housecleaning crewmember, said, "Martha will have no more than three room cleaning infractions in the coming year," for instance.)

In addition to the goals- and competencies-based appraisals, other Hotel Paris performance management forms laid out the development efforts that the employee would undertake in the coming year. Instructions also reminded the supervisors that, in addition to the annual and semiannual appraisals, they should continuously interact with and update their employees. The result was a comprehensive performance management system: The supervisor appraised the employee based on goals and competencies that were driven by the company's strategic needs. And, the actual appraisal resulted in new goals for the coming year, as well as in specific development plans that made sense in terms of the company's and the employees' needs and preferences.

Questions

9-22. Choose one job, such as front-desk clerk. Based on any information you have (including job descriptions you may have created in other chapters), write a list of duties, competencies, and performance standards for that chosen job.

9-23. Based on that, and on what you read in this Dessler *Human Resource Management* chapter, create a performance appraisal form for appraising that job.

---

§Written by and copyright Gary Dessler, PhD.

MyManagementLab

Go to **mymanagementlab.com** for Auto-graded writing questions as well as the following Assisted-graded writing questions:

9-24. Discuss the pros and cons of using different potential raters to appraise a person's performance.

9-25. As a new supervisor, you're about to hold your first-ever appraisal interview with one of your subordinates, someone who has not been performing very well for the past 6 months. What should you keep in mind about managing the appraisal interview as you begin the conversation?

9-26. MyManagementLab Only–comprehensive writing assignment for this chapter.

PERSONAL INVENTORY ASSESSMENTS

Work Performance Assessment

What sort of leadership style do you think you would exhibit in leading an organizational change? Complete this assessment to learn more about your personality.

Key Terms

performance appraisal, 274
performance appraisal process, 274
graphic rating scale, 278
alternation ranking method, 278
paired comparison method, 278
forced distribution method, 280
critical incident method, 280
behaviorally anchored rating scale (BARS), 283
electronic performance monitoring (EPM), 286
unclear standards, 288
halo effect, 289
central tendency, 289
strictness/leniency, 289
bias, 290
appraisal interview, 292
performance management, 296

CHAPTER 9

Endnotes

1. http://trw.com, accessed June 1, 2011.
2. D. Bradford Neary, "Creating a Company-Wide, Online, Performance Management System: A Case at TRW, Inc.," *Human Resource Management* 41, no. 4 (Winter 2002), pp. 491–498. See also http://trw.com, accessed April 5, 2013.
3. See, for example, Howard Risher, "Performance Management Needs to Be Fixed," *Compensation & Benefits Review* 44, no. 4 (2014), pp. 191–194.
4. Experts debate the pros and cons of tying appraisals to pay decisions. One side argues that doing so distorts the appraisals. A recent study concludes the opposite. Mary Jo Ducharme et al., "Exploring the Links Between Performance Appraisals and Pay Satisfaction," *Compensation and Benefits Review,* September/October 2005, pp. 46–52. See also Robert Morgan, "Making the Most of Performance Management Systems," *Compensation and Benefits Review,* September/October 2006, pp. 22–27.
5. www.ball.com, accessed August 28, 2014.
6. "Aligning People and Processes for Performance Improvement," *T + D* 65, no. 3, March 2011, p. 80.
7. Ibid.
8. "Get SMART About Setting Goals," *Asia Africa Intelligence Wire,* May 22, 2005.
9. See, for example, E. A. Locke and G. P. Latham, "Building a Practically Useful Theory of Goal Setting and Task Motivation. A 35-Year Odyssey," *American Psychologist* 57, no. 9 (2002), pp. 705–717.
10. Thom Shanker, "Conduct at Issue as Subordinates Review Officers," *New York Times*, April 14, 2013, pp. A1, A4.
11. www.quora.com/What-does-Facebooks-performance-review-process-look-like, accessed April 2, 2015.
12. Bock, *Work Rules!*, p. 171.
13. Vanessa Druskat and Steven Wolf, "Effects and Timing of Developmental Peer Appraisals in Self-Managing Work-Groups," *Journal of Applied Psychology* 84, no. 1 (1999), pp. 58–74. For a recent review, see Erich Dierdorff and Eric Surface, "Placing Peer Ratings in Context: Systematic Influences beyond Ratee Performance," *Personnel Psychology* 60, no. 1 (Spring 2007), pp. 93–126.
14. See, for example, Brian Hoffman and David Woehr, "Disentangling the Meaning of Multisource Performance Rating Source and Dimension Factors," *Personnel Psychology* 62 (2009), pp. 735–765.
15. As one study concluded, "Far from being a source of nonmeaningful error variance, the discrepancies among ratings from multiple perspectives can in fact capture meaningful variance in multilevel managerial performance." In-Sue Oh and Christopher Berry, "The Five Factor Model of Personality and Managerial Performance: Validity Gains Through the Use of 360° Performance Ratings," *Journal of Applied Psychology* 94, no. 6 (2009), p. 1510.
16. Jeffrey Facteau and S. Bartholomew Craig, "Performance Appraisal Ratings from Different Rating Scores," *Journal of Applied Psychology* 86, no. 2 (2001), pp. 215–227.
17. See also Kevin Murphy et al., "Raters Who Pursue Different Goals Give Different Ratings," *Journal of Applied Psychology* 89, no. 1 (2004), pp. 158–164.
18. Such findings may be culturally related. One study compared self and supervisor ratings in "other-oriented" cultures (as in Asia, where values tend to emphasize teams). It found that self and supervisor ratings were related. M. Audrey Korsgaard et al., "The Effect of Other Orientation on Self: Supervisor Rating Agreement," *Journal of Organizational Behavior* 25, no. 7 (November 2004), pp. 873–891. See also Heike Heidemeier and Klaus Mosar, "Self Other Agreement in Job Performance Ratings: A Meta-Analytic Test of a Process Model," *Journal of Applied Psychology* 94, no. 2 (2009), pp. 353–370.
19. Forest Jourden and Chip Heath, "The Evaluation Gap in Performance Perceptions:

Illusory Perceptions of Groups and Individuals," *Journal of Applied Psychology* 81, no. 4 (August 1996), pp. 369–379. See also Sheri Ostroff, "Understanding Self-Other Agreement: A Look at Rater and Ratee Characteristics, Context, and Outcomes," *Personnel Psychology* 57, no. 2 (Summer 2004), pp. 333–375.

20. Paul Atkins and Robert Wood, "Self Versus Others Ratings as Predictors of Assessment Center Ratings: Validation Evidence for 360 Degree Feedback Programs," *Personnel Psychology* 55, no. 4 (Winter 2002), pp. 871–904.
21. David Antonioni, "The Effects of Feedback Accountability on Upward Appraisal Ratings," *Personnel Psychology* 47 (1994), pp. 349–355. For an anonymous online appraisal method, see, for example, http://work.com/perform, accessed October 12, 2012.
22. Alan Walker and James Smither, "A Five-Year Study of Upward Feedback: What Managers Do with Their Results Matters," *Personnel Psychology* 52 (1999), pp. 393–423; and Austin F. R. Smith and Vincent J. Fortunato, "Factors Influencing Employee Intentions to Provide Honest Upward Feedback Ratings," *Journal of Business Psychology* 22 (2008), pp. 191–207.
23. The evidence from another study suggests also that "upward and peer 360-degree ratings may be biased by rater affect [whether the rater likes the ratee]; therefore, at this point, these ratings should be used for the sole purpose of providing ratees with developmental feedback." David Antonioni and Heejoon Park, "The Relationship Between Rater Affect and Three Sources of 360-Degree Feedback Ratings," *Journal of Management* 27, no. 4 (2001), pp. 479–495.
24. Lindsay Gellman, "Memo Lets Workers Vent Anonymously About the Boss," *Wall Street Journal,* January 21, 2015, p. B7.
25. See, for example, "360-Degree Feedback on the Rise Survey Finds," *BNA Bulletin to Management,* January 23, 1997, p. 31; Leanne Atwater et al., "Multisource Feedback: Lessons Learned and Implications for Practice," *Human Resource Management* 46, no. 2 (Summer 2007), p. 285. However, a small number of employers are beginning to use 360-degree feedback for performance appraisals, rather than just development. See, for example, Tracy Maylett, "360° Feedback Revisited: The Transition from Development to Appraisal," *Compensation & Benefits,* September/October 2009, pp. 52–59.
26. James Smither et al., "Does Performance Improve Following Multi-Score Feedback? A Theoretical Model, Meta Analysis, and Review of Empirical Findings," *Personnel Psychology* 58 (2005), pp. 33–36.
27. Jim Meade, "Visual 360: A Performance Appraisal System That's 'Fun,'" *HR Magazine,* July 1999, pp. 118–119, www.halogensoftware.com/landing/free-trial/360-multiraterfeedback?source=msn&c=Search-e360&kw=360%2520evaluations, accessed August 28, 2014.
28. www.sumtotalsystems.com/performance/index.html?e=001&sitenbr=156896193& keys=visual+360&submit.x=11&submit.y=11&submit=submit, accessed April 20, 2008.
29. Howard Risher, "Getting Serious about Performance Management," *Compensation & Benefits Review*, November/December 2005, pp. 18–26.
30. Leslie Kwoh, "Rank and Yank Retains Vocal Fans," *Wall Street Journal*, January 31, 2012, p. B12.
31. Jena McGregor, "The Struggle to Measure Performance," *BusinessWeek*, January 9, 2006, p. 26.
32. Steve Bates, "Forced Ranking," *HR Magazine*, June 2003, pp. 63–68.
33. Steven Cullen et al., "Forced Distribution Rating Systems and the Improvement of Workforce Potential: A Baseline Simulation," *Personnel Psychology* 58 (2005), p. 1.
34. Gary Giumetti, Amber Schroeder, and Fred Switzer III, "Forced Distribution Rating Systems: When Does 'Rank and Yank" Lead to Adverse Impact?" *Journal of Applied Psychology* 100, no. 1 (2015), pp. 180–193.
35. "Survey Says Problems with Forced Ranking Include Lower Morale and Costly Turnover," *BNA Bulletin to Management*, September 16, 2004, p. 297.
36. Steve Bates, "Forced Ranking: Why Grading Employees on a Scale Relative to Each Other Forces a Hard Look at Finding Keepers, Losers May Become Weepers," *HR Magazine* 48, no. 6 (June 2003), p. 62. See also D. J. Schleicher et al., "Rater Reactions to Forced Distribution Rating Systems," *Journal of Management* 35, no. 4 (August 2009), pp. 899–927.
37. Clinton Wingrove, "Developing an Effective Blend of Process and Technology in the New Era of Performance Management," *Compensation & Benefits Review*, January/February 2003, p. 26.
38. Shira Ovide And Rachel Feintzeig, "Microsoft Abandons Dreaded 'Stack,'" *Wall Street Journal*, November 13, 2013, p. B1.
39. Juan Sanchez and Phillip De La Torre, "A Second Look at the Relationship Between Rating and Behavioral Accuracy in Performance Appraisal," *Journal of Applied Psychology* 81, no. 1 (1996), p. 7. See also "How to … Improve Appraisals," *People Management* 15, no. 3 (January 29, 2009), p. 57.
40. Angelo DeNisi and Lawrence Peters, "Organization of Information in Memory and the Performance Appraisal Process: Evidence from the Field," *Journal of Applied Psychology* 81, no. 6 (1996), pp. 717–737. See also A. Fox, "Curing What Ails Performance Reviews," *HR Magazine* 54, no. 1 (January 2009), pp. 52–56.
41. Based on Donald Schwab, Herbert Heneman III, and Thomas DeCotiis, "Behaviorally Anchored Scales: A Review of the Literature," *Personnel Psychology* 28 (1975), pp. 549–562. For a discussion, see also Uco Wiersma and Gary Latham, "The Practicality of Behavioral Observation Scales, Behavioral Expectation Scales, and Trait Scales," *Personnel Psychology* 30, no. 3 (Autumn 1986), pp. 619–689; and Neil M. A. Hauenstein, Reagan D. Brown, and Andrea L. Sinclair, "BARS and Those Mysterious, Missing Middle Anchors," *Journal of Business and Psychology,* 25, no.4, (2010), pp. 663-672.
42. Lawrence Fogli, Charles Hulin, and Milton Blood, "Development of First Level Behavioral Job Criteria," *Journal of Applied Psychology* 55 (1971), pp. 3–8. See also Joseph Maiorca, "How to Construct Behaviorally Anchored Rating Scales (BARS) for Employee Evaluations," *Supervision*, August 1997, pp. 15–19; and Hauenstein et al., "BARS and Those Mysterious, Missing Middle Anchors."
43. Kevin R. Murphy and Joseph Constans, "Behavioral Anchors as a Source of Bias in Rating," *Journal of Applied Psychology* 72, no. 4 (November 1987), pp. 573–577; Aharon Tziner, "A Comparison of Three Methods of Performance Appraisal with Regard to Goal Properties, Goal Perception, and Ratee Satisfaction," *Group & Organization Management* 25, no. 2 (June 2000), pp. 175–191.
44. See for example, Richard D. Goffin et al., "Criterion Validation of Two Approaches to Performance Appraisal: The Behavioural Observation Scale and the Relative Percentile Scale," *Journal of Business and Psychology* 11, no. 1 (1996), pp. 23–33.
45. Many managers call MBO out of date. They say goal setting is no panacea, and and some jobs, for instance in R&D, may not be well measured by goals. Howard Risher, "Individual Performance Goals Can Be Problematic," *Compensation & Benefits Review* 45, no. 2, pp. 63–66.
46. Laszlo Bock, *Work Rules!* (New York: 12, 2015), p. 155.
47. However, one study concludes that Web-based performance management systems don't seem to improve performance management system effectiveness. Edward Lawler III et al., "What Makes Performance Appraisals Effective?" *Compensation & Benefits Review* 44, no. 4 (2012), p. 196.
48. www.employeeappraiser.com/index.php, accessed January 10, 2008.
49. www.successfactors.com/en_us/lp/ppc/employee-appraisal-software.html?Campaign_CRM=CRM-XJ14-HCM-1DG_GPPCPA&CmpLeadSource=Search%20Engine&source=Google_ppc&kw=Employee%20Appraisals%20Software&ad-%E2%80%90id=48484314803&adgroup=Google&gclid=CN2P2c233cQCFZEdgQodVnUA9w, accessed April 4, 2015.
50. See, for example, Stoney Alder and Maureen Ambrose, "Towards Understanding Fairness Judgments Associated with Computer Performance Monitoring: An Integration of the Feedback, Justice, and Monitoring Research," *Human Resource Management Review* 15, no. 1 (March 2005), pp. 43–67. For a more recent analysis of EPM, see Katherine J. S. Rogers, Michael J. Smith, and Pascale C. Sainfort, "Electronic Performance Monitoring, Job Design and Psychological Stress," paper available at www.igi-global.com/chapter/electronic-performance-monitoring-job-design/45284, accessed October 12, 2012.
51. Alder and Ambrose, "Towards Understanding Fairness Judgments"; and David T. Goomas, "Electronic Performance Self Monitoring and Engineered Labor Standards for 'Man-Up' Drivers in a Distribution Center," *Journal of Business and Psychology* 21 no. 4 (Summer 2007), pp. 541–558. Reprinted by permission from Springer Publishing. Cleared via Copyright Clearance Center.
52. H. James Wilson, "Wearables in the Workplace," *Harvard Business Review*, September 2013, pp. 23–25.
53. Adapted or quoted from "Next Generation Talent Management," Hewitt.com, accessed June 2010.

54. Ibid.
55. Ibid.
56. Adapted or quoted from Gunter Stahl et al., "Global Talent Management: How Leading Multinationals Build and Sustain Their Talent Pipelines," Faculty and Research Working Paper, INSEAD, 2007.
57. Herman Aguinis and Ernest O'Boyle Jr., "Star Performers in 21st-Century Organizations," *Personnel Psychology* 67 (2014), pp. 313–315.
58. D. Bradford Neary, "Creating a Company-Wide, Online, Performance Management System: A Case Study at TRW Inc.," *Human Resource Management* 41, no. 4 (Winter 2002), p. 495.
59. See, for example, Jonathan Segal, "Performance Management Blunders," *HR Magazine*, November 2010, pp. 75–77.
60. See, for example, Adrienne Fox, "Curing What Ails Performance Reviews," *HR Magazine*, January 2009, pp. 52–55.
61. Andrew Solomonson and Charles Lance, "Examination of the Relationship Between True Halo and Halo Effect in Performance Ratings," *Journal of Applied Psychology* 82, no. 5 (1997), pp. 665–674.
62. Manuel London, Edward Mone, and John C. Scott, "Performance Management and Assessment: Methods for Improved Rater Accuracy and Employee Goal Setting," *Human Resource Management* 43, no. 4 (Winter 2004), pp. 319–336.
63. Ted Turnasella, "Dagwood Bumstead, Will You Ever Get That Raise?" *Compensation & Benefits Review*, September–October 1995, pp. 25–27. See also Solomonson and Lance, "Examination of the Relationship Between True Halo and Halo Effect," pp. 665–674.
64. I. M. Jawahar and Charles Williams, "Where All the Children Are Above Average: The Performance Appraisal Purpose Effect," *Personnel Psychology* 50 (1997), p. 921.
65. Annette Simmons, "When Performance Reviews Fail," *Training & Development* 57, no. 9 (September 2003), pp. 47–53.
66. "Flawed Ranking System Revives Workers' Bias Claim," *BNA Bulletin to Management*, June 28, 2005, p. 206.
67. Karen Lyness and Madeline Heilman, "When Fit Is Fundamental: Performance Evaluations and Promotions of Upper-Level Female and Male Managers," *Journal of Applied Psychology* 91, no. 4 (2006), pp. 767–775.
68. Madeleine Heilman et al., "Penalties for Success: Reactions to Women Who Succeed at Male Gender Type Tasks," *Journal of Applied Psychology* 89, no. 3 (2004), pp. 416–427. Managers may not rate successful female managers negatively (for instance, in terms of likability and boss desirability) when they see the woman as supportive, caring, and sensitive to their needs. Madeleine Heilmann and Tyler Okimoto, "Why Are Women Penalized for Success at Male Tasks? The Implied Communality Deficit," *Journal of Applied Psychology* 92, no. 1 (2007), pp. 81–92.
69. Wingrove, "Developing an Effective Blend of Process and Technology," pp. 25–30.
70. Gary Greguras et al., "A Field Study of the Effects of Rating Purpose on the Quality of Multisource Ratings," *Personnel Psychology* 56 (2003), pp. 1–21.
71. Joanne Sammer, "Calibrating Consistency," *HR Magazine*, January 2008, pp. 73–74. As one study recently concludes, "Far from being a source of non-meaningful error variance, the discrepancies among ratings from multiple perspectives can in fact capture meaningful variance in multilevel managerial performance." In-Sue Oh and Christopher Berry, "The Five Factor Model of Personality and Managerial Performance: Validity Gains Through the Use of 360° Performance Ratings," *Journal of Applied Psychology* 94, no. 6 (2009), p. 1510.
72. M. Ronald Buckley et al., "Ethical Issues in Human Resources Systems," *Human Resource Management Review* 11 (2001), pp. 11, 29. See also Ann Pomeroy, "The Ethics Squeeze," *HR Magazine,* March 2006, pp. 48–55; "10 Tips for Avoiding Liability in Conducting Evaluations." *The Legal Intelligencer* May 12, 2010, Academic OneFile, accessed October 13, 2012.
73. G. R Weaver and L. K. Treviño, "The Role of Human Resources in Ethics/Compliance Management: A Fairness Perspective," *Human Resource Management Review*, 2001, pp. 113–134. Also see, Julie McCarthy et al., "Progression Through the Ranks: Assessing Employee Reactions to High Stakes Employment Testing," *Personnel Psychology* 62 (2009), p. 826.
74. This is based on Howard Risher, "Getting Performance Management on Track," *Compensation & Benefits Review* 43, no. 5 (2011), pp. 273–281.
75. E. Pulakos and R. O'Leary, "Why Is Performance Management Broken? *Industrial and Organizational Psychology* 4 (2011), pp. 146–164.
76. Ibid.
77. David Martin et al., "The Legal Ramifications of Performance Appraisal: The Growing Significance," *Public Personnel Management* 29, no. 3 (Fall 2000), pp. 381–383.
78. This is based on Kenneth L. Sovereign, *Personnel Law* (Upper Saddle River, NJ: Prentice Hall, 1994), pp. 113–114. See also "Avoiding HR Lawsuits," *Credit Union Executive*, November–December 1999, p. 6.
79. James Austin, Peter Villanova, and Hugh Hindman, "Legal Requirements and Technical Guidelines Involved in Implementing Performance Appraisal Systems," in Gerald Ferris and M. Ronald Buckley (Eds.), *Human Resources Management*, 3rd ed. (Upper Saddle River, NJ: Prentice Hall, 1996), pp. 271–288.
80. Austin et al., "Legal Requirements and Technical Guidelines," p. 282.
81. But beware: One problem with training raters to avoid rating errors is that, sometimes, what appears to be an error—such as leniency—isn't an error at all, as when all subordinates really are superior performers. Manuel London, Edward Mone, and John Scott, "Performance Management and Assessment: Methods for Improved Rater Accuracy and Employee Goal Setting," *Human Resource Management* 43, no. 4 (Winter 2004), pp. 319–336.
82. Wayne Cascio and H. John Bernardin, "Implications of Performance Appraisal Litigation for Personnel Decisions," *Personnel Psychology*, Summer 1981, pp. 211–212; Gerald Barrett and Mary Kernan, "Performance Appraisal and Terminations: A Review of Court Decisions Since *Brito v. Zia* with Implications for Personnel Practices," *Personnel Psychology* 40, no. 3 (Autumn 1987), pp. 489–504; Elaine Pulakos, *Performance Management*, SHRM Foundation, 2004.
83. Based on Robert Johnson, *The Appraisal Interview Guide* (New York: AMACOM, 1979), pp. 5–50; Judy Block, *Performance Appraisal on the Job: Making It Work for You* (New York: Executive Enterprises Publications, 1981), pp. 58–62.
84. This is based on Richard Luecke, *Coaching and Mentoring* (Boston: Harvard Business School Press, 2004), pp. 8–9.
85. Ibid., p. 9.
86. Jack Welch, broadcast interview at Fairfield University, C-SPAN, May 5, 2001.
87. Patty McCord, "How Netflix Reinvented HR," *Harvard Business Review,* January–February 2014, pp. 71–76.
88. Rachel Feintzeig, "You're Awesome! Firms Scrap Negative Feedback," *Wall Street Journal*, February 11, 2015, pp. B1, B5.
89. "Working Today: Understanding What Drives Employee Engagement," from the 2003 TowersPerrin Talent Report. Copyright TowersPerrin.
90. Jamie Gruman and Alan Saks, "Performance Management and Employee Engagement," *Human Resource Management Review* 21, no. 2 (2011), p. 123.
91. Ibid.
92. Ibid.
93. "Sustainable Employee Engagement," *Training & Development* 67, no. 2 (February 2013), p. 20.
94. "Driving Engagement by Focusing on Strengths," *Gallup Business Journal*: http://BusinessJournal.Gallup.com/content/124214/driving-engagement, accessed March 8, 2014.
95. D. Robinson, S. Perryman, and S. Hayday, "The Drivers of Employee Engagement," Institute for Employment Studies, April 2004.
96. Ibid.
97. Ibid.
98. Vishal Gupta and Sushil Kumar, "Impact of Performance Appraisal Justice on Employee Engagement: A Study of Indian Professionals," *Employee Relations* 35, no. 1, (2013), pp. 61–78.
99. Edward Lawler, "Performance Management: The Next Generation," *Compensation & Benefits Review*, May–June 1994, p. 16.
100. See, for example, Greg Boudreau, "Response: What TQM Says about Performance Appraisal," *Compensation & Benefits Review*, June 1994, pp. 20–24.
101. Based in part on Joel D. Ross, *Total Quality Management: Text, Cases, and Readings* (Delray Beach, FL: St. Lucie Press, 1993), p. 1.
102. Ibid., pp. 2–3, 35–36.
103. Howard Risher, "Getting Serious About Performance Management," *Compensation & Benefits Review*, November/December 2005, p. 19. See also Marie-Helene Budworth, "Performance Management: Where Do We Go from Here?" *Human Resource Management Review* 20, no. 1 (2011), pp. 81–84.
104. Peter Glendinning, "Performance Management: Pariah or Messiah," *Public Personnel Management* 31, no. 2 (Summer 2002), pp. 161–178. See also Herman Aguinis, *Performance Management* (Upper Saddle River, NJ: Prentice Hall, 2007), p. 2; "Performance Management Orientation Guide," *Workforce Management*, July 2012, pp. 20–22; and Angelo Kinicki, Kathryn Jacobson, Suzanne Peterson, and Gregory Prussia, "Development and Validation of the Performance Management Behavior Questionnaire," *Personnel Psychology* 60, no. 6 (2013), p. 4.

105. These are quoted or paraphrased from Risher, "Getting Serious About Performance Management," p. 19.
106. https://go.oracle.com/LP=3174?elqCampaignId=6310&src1=ad:pas:go:dg:tal&src2=wwmk14054343mpp012&SC=sckw=WWMK14054343MPP012, accessed April 4, 2015.
107. Leena Rao, "Salesforce Debuts 'Rypple-Powered Work.com' to Help Companies Manage Talent, Partners with Facebook," September 19, 2012, http://techcrunch.com/2012/09/19/salesforce-debuts-rypple-powered-work-com-to-help-companies-manage-talent/, accessed April 5, 2013; Eric Mosley, "The Power of the Crowd Sourced Performance Review," *Compensation & Benefits Review* 45, no. 6 (2013), pp. 320–323.
108. Rao, "Salesforce Debuts 'Rypple-Powered Work.com.'"
109. Rachel Silverman and Leslie Kwoh, "Performance Reviews Facebook Style," *Wall Street Journal*, August 1, 2012, p. B6.
110. Jenny Hill, "Could Social Media Revolutionise the Performance Appraisal Process?" www.hrmagazine.co.uk/hro/features/1073216/could-social-media-revolutionise-performance-appraisal-process, accessed April 5, 2013.
111. www.saba.com/blogs/2011/03/24/what-is-social-performance-management, accessed July 20, 2013.
112. Toni Veranges, "Held in High Regard," *HR Magazine*, November 2014, pp. 54–56.
113. "Game Changing Performance Management: A Software Company Makes a Game out of Yearly Performance Appraisals," *Training & Development* 68, no. 1 (January 2014), p. 80.
114. www.gdatp.com/about, accessed April 5, 2013.
115. Howard Risher, "Getting Serious About Performance Management," *Compensation & Benefits Review*, November/December 2005, p. 45.

10

Managing Careers and Retention

Stefano Gilera/Cultura/Getty Images

LEARNING OBJECTIVES

10-1 Discuss what employers and supervisors can do to support employees' career development needs.

10-2 Explain why career development can improve employee engagement.

10-3 Describe a comprehensive approach to retaining employees.

10-4 List and briefly explain the main decisions employers should address in reaching promotion and other employee life-cycle career decisions.

10-5 Explain each of the main grounds for dismissal.

Cognizant Corporation creates products for things like managing huge volumes of images and other content in computer systems. Creating such products requires creative and engaged employees. Cognizant therefore takes talent development very seriously, and its managers consciously consider the talent development implications of each of their strategic decisions. We'll see how they do this.[1]

WHERE ARE WE NOW ...

Having invested time and resources in selecting, training, and appraising employees, the employer of course wants its employees to want to stay with the firm. The main purpose of this chapter is to explain how to support your employees' career development needs and improve employee retention. The main topics we'll address are career management, improving employee engagement through career management, managing employee turnover and retention, employee life-cycle management, and managing dismissals.

Career Management

LEARNING OBJECTIVE 10-1
Discuss what employers and supervisors can do to support employees' career development needs.

After appraising performance, it's often necessary to address career-related issues and to discuss these issues with subordinates.

Personnel activities like screening, training, and appraising serve two basic roles in organizations. First, their traditional role is to staff the organization—to fill its positions with employees who have the requisite interests, abilities, and skills. Often, however, these activities take on a second role, of ensuring that the long-run interests of the employees are supported by the organization and that, in particular, the employee is encouraged to grow and realize his or her full career potential. A basic assumption underlying the second role is that the employer has an obligation to utilize its employees' abilities to the fullest and to give all employees a chance to grow and to develop successful careers. Employers do this not just because they think that it's the right thing to do, but because by doing so both gain—the employee by having a more fulfilling career, and the employer by reaping the benefits of improved employee relations, engagement, and retention. One way this trend is manifesting itself is in the increased emphasis many firms are placing on career planning and development. We'll address career planning and related topics in this chapter.

Before proceeding, it would be useful to define some important terms we will be using throughout this chapter. We may define **career** as the occupational positions a person holds over the years. **Career management** is the process for enabling employees to better understand and develop their career skills and interests and to use these skills and interests most effectively both within the company and after they leave the firm. **Career development** is the lifelong series of activities (such as workshops) that contribute to a person's career exploration, establishment, success, and fulfillment. **Career planning** is the deliberate process through which someone becomes aware of personal skills, interests, knowledge, motivations, and other characteristics; acquires information about opportunities and choices; identifies career-related goals; and establishes action plans to attain specific goals.

career
The occupational positions a person has had over many years.

career management
The process for enabling employees to better understand and develop their career skills and interests, and to use these skills and interests more effectively.

career development
The lifelong series of activities that contribute to a person's career exploration, establishment, success, and fulfillment.

career planning
The deliberate process through which someone becomes aware of personal skills, interests, knowledge, motivations, and other characteristics and establishes action plans to attain specific goals.

HR in Practice at the Hotel Paris If the Hotel Paris wanted satisfied guests, they had to have engaged employees who did their jobs as if they owned the company, even when the supervisor was nowhere in sight. But for the employees to be engaged, Lisa knew the Hotel Paris had to make it clear that the company was also committed to its employees. To see what they did, see the case on page 333 of this chapter.

Careers Today

People once viewed careers as a sort of upward stairway from job to job, more often than not with one or at most a few firms. Today, many people do still move up, but many (or most) find themselves having to reinvent themselves. For example, the sales rep, laid off by a publishing firm that's just merged, may reinvent her career as an account executive at a media-oriented advertising firm.[2]

Careers today differ in other ways from a few years ago. With many more women pursuing professional and managerial careers, families must balance the challenges associated with dual career pressures. At the same time, what people want from their careers is changing. Baby boomers—those retiring in the next few years—tended to be job- and employer-focused. People entering the job market now often value more opportunities for balanced work–family lives.

The Psychological Contract

One implication is that what employers and employees expect from each other is changing. What the employer and employee expect of each other is part of what psychologists call a *psychological contract.* This is "an unwritten agreement that exists between employers and employees."[3] The psychological contract identifies each party's mutual expectations. For example, the unstated agreement is that management will treat employees fairly and provide satisfactory work conditions, hopefully in a long-term relationship. Employees are expected to respond "by demonstrating a good attitude, following directions, and showing loyalty to the organization."[4]

The problem is that with today's tumultuous labor markets, neither the employer nor the employee can count on long-term commitments from each other. That changes the psychological contract, and makes career management even more critical for the employee.

The Employee's Role in Career Management

We will see that the employee, the manager, and the employer all have roles in the employee's career development. For example, the manager should provide timely and objective performance feedback, offer developmental assignments and support, and have career development discussions with the employee. He or she should act as a coach, appraiser, advisor, and mentor, listening to and clarifying the employee's career plans, giving feedback, generating career options, and linking the employee to organizational resources and career options. For its part, the employer should provide career-oriented training, development, and promotional opportunities, offer career information and career programs, and give employees a variety of career options.

Ultimately, however, it is the employee who must shoulder responsibility for his or her own career; assess interests, skills, and values; seek out career information resources; and generally take those steps that must be taken to ensure a happy and fulfilling career. For the employee, career planning means matching individual strengths and weaknesses with occupational opportunities and threats. In other words, the person wants to pursue occupations, jobs, and a career that capitalize on his or her interests, aptitudes, values, and skills. He or she also wants to choose occupations, jobs, and a career that make sense in terms of projected future demand for various occupations. Ideally, he or she should create in his or her mind an ideal future "self" to strive for.[5]

As one example, career-counseling expert John Holland says that personality (including values, motives, and needs) is an important career choice determinant. For example, a person with a strong social orientation might be attracted to careers that entail interpersonal rather than intellectual or physical activities and to occupations such as social work. Holland found six basic personality types or orientations. For a nominal fee, individuals can use his Self-Directed Search (SDS) test (available online at www.self-directed-search.com) to assess their occupational orientations and preferred occupations. The SDS has an excellent reputation, but one study of 24 no-cost online career assessment Web sites concluded that they were easy to use but suffered from insufficient validation and confidentiality. However, a number of online career assessment instruments such as Career Key (www.careerkey.org) do reportedly provide validated and useful information.[6] O*NET offers a free comprehensive online "My Next Move" occupations and career assessment system (www.onetcenter.org/mynextmove.html). You will find other useful career tools in the following two exercises, and in the discussion in this chapter's appendix.

EXERCISE 1 One useful exercise for identifying occupational skills is to head a page "The School or Occupational Tasks I Most Enjoyed Doing." Then write a short essay describing the tasks. Provide as much detail as you can about your duties and responsibilities, and what you found enjoyable about each task. (It's not necessarily the most enjoyable *job* you've had, but the most enjoyable *task* you've had to perform within your jobs.) Next, on other pages, do the same thing for two other tasks. Now scrutinize the three essays. Underline the skills that you mentioned the most often. For example, did you especially enjoy the hours you spent on the Internet doing research for your boss when you worked one summer as an intern?[7]

EXERCISE 2 Another exercise can prove enlightening. On a page, answer the question: "If you could have any kind of job, what would it be?" Invent your own job if need be, and don't worry about what you *can* do—just what you want to do.[8]

The Employer's Role in Career Management

Along with the employee, the person's manager and employer have career management responsibilities. These depend partly on how long the employee has been with the firm.

For example, *before hiring*, realistic job interviews can help prospective employees more accurately gauge whether the job is a good fit for them. Especially for recent college graduates, *the first job* can be crucial for building confidence and a more realistic picture of what he or she can and cannot do: providing challenging first jobs and having an experienced mentor who can help the person learn the ropes are important. Some refer to this as preventing **reality shock**, a phenomenon that occurs when a new employee's high expectations and enthusiasm confront the reality of a boring, unchallenging job. Periodic *job rotation* can help the person develop a more realistic picture of what he or she is good at, and thus the career moves that might be best. Thus, Intuit offers new graduates entrée into its Rotational Development Programs.[9] These are comprehensive, 2-year programs in which employees first learn about Intuit's products, customers, employees, strategies, and values. Next the employees complete four 6-month rotations, getting experience in a range of Intuit business units and a variety of functions, for instance, product management, marketing, and human resources. All Rotational Development Program participants are paired with an executive advisor, who provides career coaching and mentoring.

reality shock
Results of a period that may occur at the initial career entry when the new employee's high job expectations confront the reality of a boring or otherwise unattractive work situation.

Finally, we will see that once the person has been *on the job* for a while, career-oriented appraisals are important. Here the manager not only appraises the employee but helps the person to match his or her strengths and weaknesses with a feasible career path.

Employer Career Management Methods

Employers including AFLAC, American Express, and Accenture recognize that it pays to help employees improve their careers. For example, American Express recently opened several career counseling centers for its call-center workers, and both Genentech and AFLAC recently hired career counselors and are better preparing their line managers to give career advice.[10] Google has employees who volunteer to act as career coaches and mentors for other employees, and who Google officially designates "career gurus." In one recent year, over 1,000 Google employees (Googlers) used the gurus' services.[11] Some employers create Web-based or offline libraries of career development materials, and offer career workshops and perhaps individual career coaches for career guidance. One bank had an "Opportunity Knocks" program. In addition to career development training and follow-up support, the program included career development centers at work sites that employees could use on company time.[12]

A *career planning workshop* is "a planned learning event in which participants are expected to be actively involved, completing career planning exercises and inventories and participating in career skills practice sessions."[13] A typical workshop includes self-assessment exercises (skills, interests, values, and so on), an assessment of important occupational trends, and goal-setting and action-planning segments.

Career coaches generally help employees create 1- to 5-year plans showing where their careers with the firm may lead. Then, the employer and employee base the latter's development plans on what he or she will need to move up.[14] The coaches help individual employees identify their development needs and obtain the training, professional development, and networking opportunities that they require to satisfy those needs.[15]

Career development systems needn't be complicated. Even just receiving performance feedback from supervisors, having individual development plans, and having access to training is enough for many employees. Beyond that, job postings, formal career-oriented performance appraisals, formal counseling and mentoring with managers, and individual succession planning for high-potential employees are valuable.[16] Yet few respondents in one survey even had individual development plans.[17] Figure 10-1 illustrates a simple employee career planning form.[18]

FIGURE 10-1 Employee Career Development Plan

Source: "Reproduced with permission from the publisher BLR - Business & Legal Resources (www.HR.BLR.com).

Employee Career Development Plan

Employee: _____ **Position:** _____

Manager: _____ **Department:** _____

Date of Appraisal: _____

1. What is the next logical step up for this employee, and when do you think he or she will be ready for it?

Probable Next Job:	When Ready:			
	Now	6 Months	1 Year	2 Years
1.	☐	☐	☐	☐
2.	☐	☐	☐	☐
3.	☐	☐	☐	☐

2. What is the highest probable promotion within five years?

3. What does this employee need to prepare for promotion?

- Knowledge: _____

  Action Plan: _____

- Still Training: _____

  Action Plan: _____

- Management Training: _____

  Action Plan: _____

Improving Performance Through HRIS: Integrating Talent Management and Career and Succession Planning

Consistent with best talent management practice, the employer should endeavor to integrate its career planning with its other HR activities efforts. As one example, an employee's career planning and development plans should reflect his or her performance appraisal ratings and training plans. Similarly, as explained in Chapter 5 (pages 134–135), succession plans should reflect employees' career interests.

Integrated talent management software helps to achieve such coordination. For example, the company that manages the trans-Alaska pipeline has an online portal that lets employees "see their full training history, development plans and upcoming deadlines, register for courses, or do career planning—usually without having to ask for help."[19] At the same time, "managers can get a quick picture of the training needs for a particular group, or see all the employees who have a specific qualification."[20] Similarly, Halogen eSuccession enables the employer to "identify the skills and competencies required to support your 3–5 year strategic plans and cultivate these in your high—potential employees with career and development planning…."[21] ■

Diversity Counts: Toward Career Success

People with disabilities tend to have less career success than do those without disabilities.[22] Some barriers may be self-imposed. For instance, some with disabilities may have lower career expectations, or may not proactively seek work-related help or the accommodations they are due under EEO law.

However, most such problems reflect unfortunate assumptions and actions by managers and coworkers. Though well meaning, they may view those with disabilities as unable to perform various jobs, negatively evaluate them as being poor occupational fits, and assume that jobs designed for those without disabilities are inappropriate for those with disabilities. Figure 10-2 presents some positive strategies for people with disabilities. ■

The Manager as Mentor and Coach

Do not underestimate the impact that a supervisor can have on his or her employee's career development. With little or no additional effort than realistic performance reviews and candid career advice, a competent supervisor can help the employee get on and stay on the right career track. At the other extreme, an unsupportive supervisor may look back on years of having inhibited his or her employees' career development.

The manager can do several things to support subordinates' career development needs. When the subordinate first starts, make sure he or she develops the skills required to do the job well. Schedule regular performance appraisals, and at these reviews cover whether the employee's current skills and performance are consistent with his or her career aspirations. Provide the employee with an informal development plan like that in Figure 10-1. Keep subordinates informed about how they can use the firm's current career-related benefits, and encourage them to do so.[23]

mentoring
Advising, counseling, and guiding.

In doing so the manager may act as mentor. **Mentoring** means having experienced senior people advising, counseling, and guiding employees' longer-term career development. An employee who agonizes over which career to pursue or how to navigate office politics may need mentoring.

Mentoring may be formal or informal. Informally, mid- and senior-level managers may voluntarily help less-experienced employees—for instance, by giving them career advice and helping them to navigate office politics. Many employers also have formal mentoring programs. For instance, the employer may pair protégés with potential mentors, and provide training to help mentor and protégé better understand their respective responsibilities. Studies show that having a mentor either formally or informally give career-related guidance and act as a sounding board can significantly enhance one's career satisfaction and success.[24]

FIGURE 10-2 Career Guideline Suggestions for Those with Disabilities

Source: "Career Management Strategies of People With Disabilities," Human Resource Management, may - June 2014, volume 53, number three, page 455-456. Reprinted by permission from John Wiley & Sons, Inc. Cleared via Copyright Clearance Center

Strategy	Key Import of Strategy
Espousing a positive mind-set and demonstrating extreme persistence	Overcome worries and tocus on tasks at hand
Sensitizing people to ability over disability: • Signaling ability by learning new skills • Signaling ability by helping coworkers through newly gained skills • Signaling ability by trying to enhance performance through feedback seeking	Trounce stereotypes regarding competence
Engaging in disability advocacy: • Awareness building • Influencing organizational policymaking with regard to accommodation	Sensitize others to performance potential of all PWD and help all PWD perform
Building, leveraging, and contributing to relevant networks: • Forming networks comprising PWD • Seeking mentors who have a disability • Serving as role models or mentors to other PWD	Aid general adjustment and career growth of self and other PWD

coaching
Educating, instructing, and training subordinates.

For the supervisor, mentoring is both valuable and risky. It is valuable insofar as you can influence in a positive way the careers and lives of your less experienced subordinates and colleagues. The danger is it can backfire. **Coaching** focuses on teaching daily tasks that you can easily relearn, so coaching's downside is usually limited. *Mentoring* focuses on relatively hard-to-reverse longer-term career issues, and often touches on the person's psychology (motives, and how one gets along with others, for instance). Because the supervisor is usually not a psychologist or trained career advisor, he or she must be extra cautious in the mentoring advice he or she gives.

Research on what supervisors can do to be better mentors reveals few surprises. Effective mentors *set high standards*, are willing to *invest the time* and effort the mentoring relationship requires, and actively *steer protégés* into important projects, teams, and jobs.[25] Effective mentoring requires *trust*, and the level of trust reflects the mentor's *professional competence, consistency, ability to communicate*, and readiness to *share control*.[26]

However, studies suggest that traditional mentoring is less effective for women than it is for men. For example, in one survey of employees who had "active mentoring relationships" in one recent year, 72% of the men received one or more promotions in the ensuing 2 years, compared with 65% of the women. A CEO or other senior executive mentored 78% of the men, compared with 69% of the women.[27]

Figures like these are prompting employers to assign female employees to mentors who have more organizational clout. For example, when Deutsche Bank discovered that several female managing directors had left the firm for better jobs at competitors, it began pairing them with mentor/sponsors from the bank's executive committee. The latter were in a position to advocate the women for promotion.

IMPROVING PERFORMANCE: *The Strategic Context*

Strategic human resource management means formulating HR policies and practices that produce the employee skills and behaviors the company needs to achieve its strategic aims. Cognizant Corporation requires its managers to enumerate the talent implications of each aspect of their strategic plans.[28] Because of this, it's no surprise that Cognizant has a well-thought-out career and talent development process. Each of Cognizant's 170,000 employees has his or her own development plan. Cognizant's Career Architecture Program enables employees to think through and choose Cognizant career tracks best suited to their capabilities and to the company's needs. Its Cognizant Academy provides training that serves both the company's needs today, as well as its projected longer-term talent and development needs. Cognizant's HR strategy has helped keep Cognizant a leader in its field, in part by ensuring that its employees get the career direction and development they need to be motivated to create the company's great products. ■

Source: Based on Kristen fyfe-mills, "commitment to talent development excellence," TD October 2014, pages 39–41. https://www.td.org/Publications/Magazines/TD/TD-Archive/2014/10/BEST-Cognizant; Http://Businesstoday.Intoday.In/Story/Malcolm-Frank-On-Cognizant-Strategy-Going-Forward/1/200337.Html; Http://Www.Cognizant.Com/Insightswhitepapers/Architecting-An-Enterprise-Content-Management-Strategy-A-Four-Pillar-Approach-Codex975.Pdf; Http://Www.Cognizant.Com/About-Cognizant/Company-Overview/Sustainability/Employee-Development.

If your professor has assigned this, go to the Assignments section of **mymanagementlab.com** to complete this discussion question.

Talk About It 1 What engineering and sales benefits would a company like Cognizant derive from taking the time to work out a career development plan for each of its employees?

LEARNING OBJECTIVE **10-2**
Explain why career development can improve employee engagement.

Employee Engagement Guide for Managers

Career Management

As mentioned earlier in this chapter, labor market turbulence has understandably prompted many people to ask why they should be loyal to their employers. "Why," they might ask, "should I be loyal to you if you're just going to dump me when you decide to cut costs again?" Employers today therefore have to think through how they're going to maintain employee engagement, and thereby minimize voluntary departures, and maximize employee effort. (Cognizant Corporation, above, is one example.)

Commitment-Oriented Career Development Efforts

Given the importance to most people of having a fulfilling and successful career, career planning and development can play an important role in engagement. Managed effectively, the employer's career development process should send the signal that the employer cares about the employee's career success. As mentioned earlier, this doesn't necessarily have to be complicated. For example, the required performance appraisal can provide an easy opportunity to link the employee's performance, career interests, and developmental needs into a coherent career plan. With *career-oriented appraisals*, the supervisor and employee jointly merge the latter's past performance, career preferences, and developmental needs into a formal career plan.

Such appraisals needn't be automated but online systems are available. For example, Halogen eAppraisal™ helps the manager to identify employee development activities that are appropriate given the employee's developmental needs and career preferences. The employer then organizes development activities around the person's needs.

The JCPenney Management Career-Grid approach provides another good example of what is possible (although tumultuous management changes several years ago sidelined much of this effort). Penney's managerial performance appraisal form contained a listing of all the Penney's management and sales jobs by title, function, and level that employees could conceivably want to consider. The company trained its supervisors to consider the employee's performance, career interests, and Penney's needs, and to develop a career plan including development activities for the employee.

Here is how it worked. Prior to the annual appraisal, the associate and his or her manager reviewed Penney's career grid. The grid itemized all supervisory positions at Penney (grouped by operation jobs, merchandise jobs, personnel jobs, and general management jobs); it also included specific job titles such as "regional catalog sales manager." The firm also provided thumbnail job descriptions for all the grid's jobs.

The grid also identified typical promotional routes. For example, when considering the next assignment for a management associate, the supervisor could consider not only merchandise positions but also operations and personnel positions. Promotional projections could cross all four groups, as well as one or two job levels. For example, a senior merchandising manager might be projected for promotion to either assistant buyer or general merchandise manager. In sum, Penney's grid approach shows how employers can use a career-oriented appraisal process to guide the employee and manager to focus on the former's strengths, weaknesses, and career prospects and plans.[29]

Other employers use special training and development programs to facilitate their employees' career development. The accompanying HR Practices Around the Globe feature provides an example.

IMPROVING PERFORMANCE: *HR Practices around the Globe*

Career Development at Medtronic[30]

Medtronic is a global medical technology company with more than 85,000 employees around the world. The company offers a wide range of career planning and development support tools aimed at helping employees understand their occupational strengths and weaknesses and reach their potential. These tools include customized development plans, self-assessment and feedback tools, mentoring programs, comprehensive on-site classes covering business, engineering, and science topics, tuition reimbursement scholarships, and online job listings so the employee can seek out new career opportunities within the company.

In addition, new MBA employees can participate in Medtronic's corporate Leadership Development Rotation Program. This is a 2- to 3-year program. It includes 12- to 18-month assignments in two different geographic locations, thus providing participants with both a broad understanding of Medtronics and in-depth functional experiences. Functional tracks include clinical, corporate development, finance, human resources, information technology, marketing/business development, operations, and regulatory.

In addition to their job assignments, participants engage in other developmental experiences including peer mentoring programs, functional training, and leadership workshops. Among other things, candidates for this program are required to have 3 to 5 years of professional and relevant work experience and an

MBA (or other masters-level degree as appropriate) and to be mobile and willing to pursue opportunities in various geographic locations. ■

Source: Based on www.Medtronic.com/careers/develop-your-potential/, accessed March 12, 2013; http://www.medtronic.com/us-en/about-3/medtronic-plc facts.html?cmpid=mdt_plc_2015_US_about_3_story_panel_featured_company_facts_cta_text_link_learn_more.

If your professor has assigned this, go to the Assignments section of **mymanagementlab.com** to complete this discussion.

Talk About It 2: Look more closely at this program (go to www.Medtronic.com; then click "Careers" and "Career Growth") or a similar program and discuss why it should positively affect employee engagement.

Managing Employee Turnover and Retention

LEARNING OBJECTIVE 10-3
Describe a comprehensive approach to retaining employees.

Not all employees' careers plans will coincide with the company's needs. *Turnover*—the rate at which employees leave the firm—varies markedly among industries. For example, turnover in the accommodation and food services industry is very high, with over half the industry's employees voluntarily leaving each year. In contrast, voluntary turnover in educational services is about 12%.[31]

Furthermore, such figures only reflect employees who leave voluntarily, such as for better jobs. They don't include involuntary separations, such as for poor performance.[32] Combining voluntary and involuntary turnover produces some astounding statistics. For example, the turnover in many food service firms is around 100% per year. In other words, many restaurants need to replace just about all their employees every year! Turnover is expensive, as the HR as a Profit Center feature shows.

IMPROVING PERFORMANCE: *HR as a Profit Center*

Turnover and Performance

What is the link between turnover and organizational performance? Perhaps surprisingly, the issue isn't clear (although it would seem obvious that firing an incompetent employee would be a positive).[33] The problem is that what might be a positive in individual cases becomes a negative when the employer repeatedly loses employees. One study concludes that *all* turnover, voluntary or involuntary, is associated with reduced organizational performance. The researchers say, "Organizations must recognize that when turnover rates rise, their workforce and financial performances are at risk. They should search for strategies to mitigate and eliminate turnover, recognizing that lower turnover [of all types] is always better."[34]

One study analyzed the tangible and intangible costs of turnover in a call center with 31 agents and 4 supervisors.[35] Tangible costs associated with an agent's leaving included the costs of recruiting, screening, interviewing, and testing applicants, as well as the cost of wages while the new agent was oriented and trained. Intangible costs included the cost of lost productivity for the new agent (who is less productive at first), the cost of rework for the new agent's errors, and the supervisory cost for coaching the new agent. The researchers' calculations estimated the cost of an agent leaving at about $21,551. This call center averaged 18.6 vacancies per year (about a 60% turnover rate). Therefore, the researchers estimated the total annual cost of agent turnover at $400,853. Taking steps to cut this turnover rate in, say, half could save this firm about $200,000 per year. How to cut turnover? Another study focused on turnover intentions among government technology workers. It concluded that human resource managers could influence turnover through practices such as promotion opportunities, training and development, pay and reward satisfaction, and family-friendly policies.[36] The bottom line is that HR practices can have a big influence on employee turnover, and thereby on the company's profitability. ■

Source: Based on Tae–Youn Park and Jason Shaw, "Turnover Rates and Organizational Performance: A Meta-analysis," Journal of Applied Psychology 98, no. 2 (2013), pp. 268–309: Jolivette Wallace and Kristena Gaylor, "A Study of the Dysfunctional and Functional Aspects of Voluntary Employee Turnover," SAM Advanced Management Journal 77, no. 3 (Summer 2012), p. 27; Barbara Hillmer, Steve Hillmer, and Gale McRoberts, "The Real Costs of Turnover: Lessons from a Call Center," Human Resource Planning 27, no. 3 (2004), pp. 34–41; Kim Soonhee, "The Impact of Human Resource Management on State Government IT Employee Turnover Intentions," Public Personnel Management 41, no. 2 (Summer 2012), p. 257.

If your professor has assigned this, go to the Assignments section of **mymanagementlab.com** to complete this discussion.

Talk About It 3: Discuss three steps you would take to reduce the need to dismiss employees.

Reducing turnover requires identifying and managing the reasons for both voluntary and involuntary turnover.[37] We address managing voluntary turnover here, and managing involuntary turnover later in the chapter.

Managing Voluntary Turnover

In reducing turnover, the logical place to start is by measuring the number of employees (particularly top performers and high potentials) who leave the company.[38] SHRM recommends computing turnover as follows: "First calculate turnover for each month by dividing the number of [voluntary] separations during the month by the average number of employees during that month and multiplying by 100. Then calculate the annual turnover rate by adding the 12 months of turnover percentages together."[39]

However, identifying *why* employees voluntarily leave is not so easy. People who are dissatisfied with their jobs are more likely to leave, but the sources of dissatisfaction are many and varied. In one survey, the consultants collected data from 262 U.S. organizations having a minimum of 1,000 employees.[40] In this survey, the five top reasons that high-commitment/top-performing employees gave for leaving (ranked from high to low) were pay, promotional opportunities, work–life balance, career development, and health-care benefits. (In contrast, *employers* ranked the top five reasons employees left as promotion, career development, pay, relationship with supervisor, and work–life balance). Other reasons employees voluntarily leave include unfairness, not having their voices heard, and a lack of recognition.[41] Sometimes simply asking, "All things considered, how satisfied are you with your job?" can be as effective as soliciting employees' attitudes toward various facets of the job (such as supervision and pay).[42] Practical considerations also affect turnover. For example, high unemployment reduces voluntary turnover, and some locales have fewer job opportunities (and thus turnover) than do others.

Of course, losing low-performing employees isn't as problematic as losing high-performing ones. The restaurant chain Applebee's gives managers higher incentives for reducing turnover among top-performing employees.[43]

In any case, given the variety of things prompting employees to leave voluntarily, what can one do to manage voluntary turnover? We'll list some tactics next, but there is no silver bullet. The manager should understand that retaining employees is a talent management issue, and that the best retention strategies are therefore multifunctional. For example, employees who aren't interested in their jobs, sense that they're not suited for their jobs, or feel undercompensated are more likely to leave. Employers can address such issues only by instituting effective and coordinated talent management (recruitment, selection, training, appraisal, and compensation) practices. Put another way, turnovers (both voluntary and involuntary) often start with poor selection decisions, compounded by inadequate training, insensitive appraisals, and inequitable pay. Trying to formulate a "retention strategy" without considering all of one's HR practices is futile.

A Comprehensive Approach to Retaining Employees

However identifying the problems is an important first step. Effectively conducted *exit interviews* provide useful insights into turnover problem areas. Many employers routinely administer *attitude surveys* to monitor employees about matters such as supervision and pay. Open-door policies and anonymous "*hotlines*" help management identify and remedy morale problems. Usually conducted by the employee's manager, the aim of a *stay interview* is to head off retention problems by finding out "how the employee is doing." Typical questions include "When you travel to work each day, what are you looking forward to?" and "How can I best support you?" Unlike anonymous group surveys, stay interviews are one on one, and reportedly provide useful information for reducing turnover and improving engagement.[44] Sometimes, analyzing the situation leads to simple solutions. Walmart discovered it could significantly reduce voluntary turnover by providing aggressively *realistic previews* about the job's demands and work hours.[45] Then, having identified potential problems, the employer can take steps like the following to boost employee retention.

RAISE PAY The most obvious explanation for why employees quit is often also the correct one: low pay. Particularly for high performers and key employees, enhanced pay has recently been the retention tool of choice for many employers.[46]

HIRE SMART "Retention starts up front, with the selection and hiring of the right employees."[47] This refers not just to the worker but also to hiring the right supervisors. For example, FedEx conducts periodic employee attitude surveys. The supervisor then meets to review the results with his or her employees to address any leadership problems the surveys raise.

DISCUSS CAREERS One expert says, "Professionals who feel their company cares about their development and progress are much more likely to stay."[48] Periodically discuss with employees their career preferences and prospects, and help them lay out career plans.[49]

PROVIDE DIRECTION People can't do their jobs if they don't know what to do or what their goals are. Therefore, retaining employees requires making it clear what your expectations are regarding their performance and what their responsibilities are.

OFFER FLEXIBILITY In one survey, workers identified "flexible work arrangements" and "telecommuting" as the two top benefits that would encourage them to choose one job over another.

USE HIGH-PERFORMANCE HR PRACTICES In one study, call centers that made more use of high involvement work practices (for instance, employee empowerment, problem-solving groups, and self-directed teams) had lower rates of quits, dismissals, and total turnover. So did those that "invested" more in employees (for instance, in terms of promotion opportunities, high relative pay, pensions, and full-time jobs).[50]

COUNTEROFFER? If a valued employee says he or she is leaving, should you make a counteroffer? Many argue against doing so, calling it a "Band-Aid for a head wound."[51] Employers who do allow counteroffers need a policy that specifies what people and positions are eligible for counteroffers, allowable compensation enhancements, and how to determine the offer.[52]

TRENDS SHAPING HR: *DIGITAL AND SOCIAL MEDIA*

Digital and social media tools can vastly improve the employee engagement/retention process. Software company SAS's employee-retention program sifts through employee data on traits like skills, tenure, performance, education, and friendships. It can predict which high-value employees are more likely to quit in the near future (allowing SAS to try to head that off).[53] Alliant Techsystems created a "flight risk model" to calculate the probability an employee would leave and to take corrective action.[54] Based on its analysis of previous survey results, Google's "Googlegeist" survey contains five questions aimed at identifying Googlers who are more likely to leave; if a team's responses fall below 70% favorable, Google knows to take corrective action.[55] Analytical software from Evolv (now Cornerstone, www.cornerstoneondemand.com/evolv) takes HR data analysis deeper than most. It can crunch more than 500 million data points on a vast array of items ranging from unemployment rates to a person's social media usage to help clients like Xerox improve retention.[56] For example, Evolv discovered that employees with two social media accounts perform much better than those with more or less, and that in call-center work, employees with criminal backgrounds perform better than those never arrested.[57]

Web sites such as Globoforce (www.globoforce.com) enable each employee's colleagues to comment on and to recognize and reward the person's contributions. Vendors assert this leads to "dramatic improvements in employee engagement, retention and measurable adoption of corporate culture."[58]

Social media also enables an otherwise muted layoff to go viral. When UBS bank dismissed 10,000 employees recently, former employees quickly took to Twitter. Some claimed they discovered they were fired when they arrived to work and found their passes deactivated.[59] ■

Job Withdrawal

Unfortunately, voluntary turnover is just one way that employees withdraw. Withdrawal in general means separating oneself from one's current situation—it's a means of escape for someone who is dissatisfied or fearful. At work, *job withdrawal* has been defined as "actions intended to place physical or psychological distance between employees and their work environments."[60]

Absences and voluntary turnover are two obvious types of job withdrawal. Others can be less obvious if no less corrosive. Some examples include "taking undeserved work breaks, spending time in idle conversation and neglecting aspects of the job one is obligated to perform."[61] Other employees stop "showing up" mentally ("psychological withdrawal"), perhaps daydreaming at their desks while productivity suffers.[62] The employee is there, but mentally absent. In fact, the *job withdrawal process* tends to be incremental, often evolving from daydreaming to absences to quitting: "When an employee perceives that temporary withdrawal will not resolve his/her problems, then the employee is apt to choose a more permanent form of withdrawal (i.e., turnover, assuming that alternative work opportunities are available)."[63]

Studies confirm the high costs of job withdrawal behavior, so understanding its causes is important.[64] Many people have experienced the desire to withdraw—to "get away" from some situation—so it's perhaps not difficult to empathize with those who feel they must escape. Some think of it in terms of pain versus pleasure. People tend to move toward situations that make them feel good, and away from those that make them feel bad.[65] People are repelled by situations that produce unpleasant, uncomfortable emotions, and are attracted to those that produce pleasant, comfortable ones.[66]

The manager can therefore think of withdrawal-reducing strategies in terms of reducing the job's negative effects, and/or of raising its positive effects. Because potential negatives and positives are virtually limitless, addressing withdrawal problems again requires a comprehensive human resource management approach. Illustrative potential negatives include, for instance, boring jobs, poor supervision, low pay, bullying, lack of career prospects, and poor working conditions. Potential positives include job enrichment, supportive supervision, equitable pay/family-friendly benefits, disciplinary/appeals processes, career development opportunities, safe and healthy working conditions, and having high-morale colleagues.[67] Interviews, surveys, and observation can help identify issues to address.

With more employees taking their jobs home via smart phones and iPads, employee "detachment" (not withdrawal) isn't always a bad thing. Two researchers found detaching oneself from work improves family life. They advise working out a system for ensuring some quality family time. For example, the employee and his or her partner might "agree on certain rules such as keeping the weekend free of work, or switching off the mobile phone after dinner."[68]

LEARNING OBJECTIVE **10-4**

List and briefly explain the main decisions employers should address in reaching promotion and other employee life-cycle career decisions.

Employee Life-Cycle Career Management

An employee's tenure with a firm tends to follow a life cycle, from employment interview to first job, promotion, transfer, and perhaps retirement. We'll look here at the latter three.

Making Promotion Decisions

promotion
Advancement to a position of increased responsibility.

Promotions traditionally refer to advancements to positions of increased responsibility.

Most people crave promotions, which usually mean more pay, responsibility, and (often) job satisfaction. For employers, promotions can provide opportunities to reward exceptional performance, and to fill open positions with tested and loyal employees. Yet the promotion process isn't always a positive experience. Unfairness or secrecy can devalue the process. Furthermore, with more employers downsizing, some "promotions" take the form of more challenging but not necessarily higher-ranked or better-paid jobs.

KNOW YOUR EMPLOYMENT LAW

Establish Clear Guidelines for Managing Promotions

In general, the employer's promotion processes must comply with all the same anti-discrimination laws as do procedures for recruiting and selecting employees or any other HR actions. For example, Title VII of the 1964 Civil Rights Act covers any "terms, conditions, or privileges of employment." Similarly, the Age Discrimination in Employment Act of 1967 made it unlawful to discriminate against older employees or applicants for employment in any manner, including promotion.

The employer should establish safeguards to ensure that the promotion decision doesn't prompt a discrimination claim, or a claim of retaliation, as it often does. For example, the Fifth U.S. Circuit Court of Appeals allowed a woman's claim of retaliation to proceed when she showed that she was turned down for promotion because a supervisor she had previously accused of sexual harassment persuaded her current supervisor not to promote her.[69]

One way to defend against such claims is to make sure promotion procedures are clear and objective. For example, the Eighth U.S. Circuit Court of Appeals held that a company's failure to set objective guidelines and procedures for promoting current employees may suggest employment discrimination.[70] (In this case, the court found that the organization, a community college, did not consistently use the same procedures for hiring and promotions, and did not clarify when and under what conditions vacant positions were announced, or whether there were application deadlines.) In another case, the employer turned down the 61-year-old employee for a promotion because the person who interviewed him said he did not "get a real feeling of confidence" from the candidate.[71] In this case, "the court made it clear that while subjective reasons can justify adverse employment decisions, an employer must articulate any clear and reasonably specific factual bases upon which it based its decision." In other words, have objective evidence supporting your subjective assessment for promotion. ■

Several decisions therefore loom large in any firm's promotion process.

DECISION 1: IS SENIORITY OR COMPETENCE THE RULE? In setting promotion policies, one decision is whether to base promotion on seniority or competence, or some combination of the two.

Today's focus on performance favors competence. However, this depends on several things. Union agreements sometimes contain clauses emphasizing seniority. Civil service regulations that stress seniority often govern promotions in many public-sector organizations.

DECISION 2: HOW SHOULD WE MEASURE COMPETENCE? If the firm opts for competence, it must define and measure competence. Defining and measuring *past* performance is relatively straightforward. But promotions should rest on procedures for predicting the candidate's future performance.

For better or worse, most employers use prior performance as a guide, and assume that (based on exemplary prior performance) the person will do well on the new job. Many others use tests or assessment centers, or tools such as the 9-Box Grid (Chapter 8, page 253), to evaluate promotable employees and identify those with executive potential.

For example, given the public safety issues involved, police departments and the military tend to be very systematic when evaluating candidates for promotion to command positions. For the police, traditional promotional reviews include a written knowledge test, an assessment center, credit for seniority, and a score based on recent performance appraisal ratings. Most include a personnel records review. This includes evaluation of job-related influences such as supervisory-related education and experience, ratings from multiple sources, and systematic evaluation of behavioral evidence.[72]

DECISION 3: IS THE PROCESS FORMAL OR INFORMAL? Many firms have informal promotion processes. They may or may not post open positions, and key managers may use their own unpublished promotion criteria. Here employees (and courts) may conclude that factors like "who you know" are more important than performance, and that working hard to get ahead—at least in this firm—is futile.

Other employers set formal, published promotion policies and procedures. Employees receive a *formal promotion policy* describing the criteria by which the firm awards promotions. A *job posting policy* states the firm will post open positions and their requirements, and circulate these to all employees. As explained in Chapter 5 (Personnel Planning and Recruiting), many employers also maintain *employee qualification databanks* and use replacement charts and computerized employee information systems to assist in such planning.

DECISION 4: VERTICAL, HORIZONTAL, OR OTHER? Promotions aren't necessarily upward. Thus some employees, such as engineers, may have little or no interest in promotion to managerial roles.

Several options are available. Some firms, such as the exploration division of British Petroleum (BP), create two parallel career paths, one for managers and another for "individual contributors" such as high-performing engineers. At BP, individual contributors can move up to nonsupervisory senior positions, such as "senior engineer." These jobs have most of the financial rewards attached to management-track positions at that level.

Another option is to move the person horizontally. For instance, a production employee may move to human resources to develop his or her skills and to test and challenge his or her aptitudes. In a sense, "promotions" are possible even when leaving the person in the same job. For example, you might enrich the job and provide training to enhance the opportunity for assuming more responsibility.

In any case, there are practical steps to take in formulating promotion policies.[73] Establish eligibility requirements, for instance, in terms of minimum tenure and performance ratings. Require the hiring manager to review the job description, and revise if necessary. Vigorously review all candidates' performance and history. Preferably hire only those who meet the job's requirements. And reach out to employees who may have aspired to a promotion but who were not yet ready to be promoted. To paraphrase Google's chief HR officer, doing so is far better than having them quit or withdraw.[74]

Diversity Counts: The Gender Gap

Women still don't reach the top of the career ladder in numbers proportionate to their numbers in U.S. industry. Women constitute more than 40% of the workforce, but hold less than 2% of top management positions. Blatant or subtle discrimination may account for much of this. In one study, promoted women had to receive higher performance ratings than promoted men to get promoted, "suggesting that women were held to stricter standards for promotion."[75] Women report greater barriers (such as being excluded from informal networks) than do men, and more difficulty getting developmental assignments. Women have to be more proactive than men to get such assignments.

Minority women seem particularly at risk. Women of color hold only a small percentage of professional and managerial private-sector positions. One survey asked minority women what they saw as the barriers to a successful career. The minority women reported that the main barriers to advancement included not having an influential mentor (47%), lack of informal networking with influential colleagues (40%), lack of company role models for members of the same racial or ethnic group (29%), and a lack of high-visibility assignments (28%).[76]

Unfortunately, many career development programs are inconsistent with the needs of minority and nonminority women. For example, many programs underestimate the role played by family responsibilities in many women's (and men's) lives. Similarly, some programs assume that career paths are continuous; yet the need to stop working for a time to attend to family needs often punctuates the career paths of many people of color and women (and perhaps men).[77] Many refer to this totality of subtle and not-so-subtle barriers to women's career progress as the *glass ceiling*. Employers need to eliminate the barriers that impede women's career progress. Some specific steps include the following.

ELIMINATE BARRIERS Many practices (such as required late-night meetings) may seem gender neutral but in fact disproportionately affect women.

IMPROVE NETWORKING AND MENTORING To improve female employees' networking opportunities, Marriott International instituted a series of leadership conferences for women. Speakers offered practical tips for career advancement, and shared their experiences. More important, the conferences provided informal opportunities—over lunch, for instance—for the Marriott women to meet and forge business relationships.

BREAK THE GLASS CEILING As one expert puts it, "The roots of gender discrimination are built into a platform of work practices, cultural norms and images that appear unbiased.... People don't even notice them, let alone question them." These range from late meetings to golf course memberships.

ADOPT FLEXIBLE CAREER TRACKS Inflexible promotional ladders (such as "You must work 8 years of 50-hour weeks to apply for partner") can put women—who often have more responsibility for child-raising chores—at a disadvantage.[78] One solution is to institute career tracks (including reduced hours and more flexible year-round work schedules) that enable women to periodically reduce their time at work, but remain on a partner track. For example, when the accounting firm Deloitte & Touche noticed it was losing female auditors, it instituted a new flexible/reduced work schedule. This enabled many working mothers who might otherwise have left to stay with the firm.[79] ■

Managing Transfers

transfers
Reassignments to similar positions in other parts of the firm.

A **transfer** is a move from one job to another, usually with no change in salary or grade. Employers may transfer a worker to vacate a position where he or she is no longer needed, to fill one where he or she is needed, or more generally to find a better fit for the employee within the firm. Many firms today boost productivity by consolidating positions. Transfers are a way to give displaced employees a chance for another assignment or, perhaps, some personal growth. Employees seek transfers for many reasons, including personal enrichment, more interesting jobs, greater convenience—better hours, location of work, and so on—or to jobs offering greater advancement possibilities. Transfers for the firm's convenience—once widely used—are used less of late.

Managing Retirements

Retirement planning is a significant issue for employers. In the United States, the number of 25- to 34-year-olds is growing relatively slowly, and the number of 35- to 44-year-olds is declining. So, with many employees in their 60s approaching

Employers are transferring employees less often, partly because of family resistance.

Darren Baker/Getty Images

retirement age, employers face a problem: "Companies have been so focused on downsizing to contain costs that they largely neglected a looming threat to their competitiveness … a severe shortage of talented workers."[80]

Many have wisely chosen to fill their staffing gaps in part with current or soon-to-be retirees. Fortuitously, 78% of employees in one survey said they expect to continue working in some capacity after normal retirement age (64% said they want to do so part-time). Only about a third plan to continue work for financial reasons; about 43% just want to stay active.[81]

The bottom line is that "retirement planning" is no longer just about helping current employees slip into retirement.[82] It should also help the employer to retain, in some capacity, the skills and brainpower of those who would normally retire and leave the firm.

A reasonable first step is to conduct numerical analyses of pending retirements. This should include a demographic analysis (including a census of the company's employees), determining the current average retirement age for the company's employees, and assessing how retirements will affect the employer's health-care and pension benefits. The employer can then determine the extent of the "retirement problem," and take fact-based steps to address it.[83]

Employers seeking to attract and/or retain retirees should take several steps. The general idea is to institute human resource policies that encourage and support older workers. Not surprisingly, studies show that employees who are more committed and loyal to the employer are more likely to stay beyond their normal retirement age.[84] It helps to create a culture that honors experience. For example, the CVS pharmacy chain knows that traditional recruiting media might not attract older workers; CVS thus works through the National Council on Aging, city agencies, and community organizations to find new employees. They also welcome older workers: "I'm too young to retire. [CVS] is willing to hire older people. They don't look at your age but your experience," said one dedicated older worker.[85] Others modify selection procedures. For example, one British bank stopped using psychometric tests, replacing them with role-playing exercises to gauge how candidates deal with customers.

Other techniques employers use to keep older workers include offering them part-time positions, hiring them as consultants or temporary workers, offering them flexible work arrangements, encouraging them to work past traditional retirement age, providing training to upgrade skills, and instituting a phased retirement program. The latter lets senior workers ease into retirement with gradually reduced work schedules.[86]

> **Watch It!**
> How would an attorney actually guide a client when it comes to dismissals? If your professor has assigned this, go to the Assignments section of mymanagementlab.com to complete the video exercise titled *Employee Engagement (PTC)*.

Managing Dismissals

LEARNING OBJECTIVE 10-5
Explain each of the main grounds for dismissal.

Not all employee separations are voluntary. Some career plans and appraisals end not in promotion or graceful retirement but in **dismissal**—involuntary termination of an employee's employment with the firm. Many dismissals are avoidable. For example, many dismissals flow from bad hiring decisions. Using assessment tests, background checks, drug testing, and clearly defined jobs can reduce such dismissals.[87]

dismissal
Involuntary termination of an employee's employment with the firm.

Grounds for Dismissal

There are four bases for dismissal: unsatisfactory performance, misconduct, lack of qualifications for the job, and changed requirements of (or elimination of) the job.

Unsatisfactory performance refers to a persistent failure to perform assigned duties or to meet prescribed standards on the job.[88] Specific reasons include excessive absenteeism, tardiness, a persistent failure to meet normal job requirements, or an adverse attitude.

Misconduct is deliberate and willful violation of the employer's rules and may include stealing and rowdy behavior.

Lack of qualifications for the job is an employee's inability to do the assigned work, although he or she is diligent. Because this employee may be trying to do the job, it is reasonable to try to salvage him or her—perhaps through further training or by assigning the employee to another job.

Changed requirements of the job is an employee's incapability of doing the job after the nature of the job has changed. Similarly, you may have to dismiss an employee when his or her job is eliminated. Again, the employee may be industrious, so it is reasonable to retrain or transfer this person, if possible.

insubordination
Willful disregard or disobedience of the boss's authority or legitimate orders; criticizing the boss in public.

Insubordination, a form of misconduct, is sometimes the grounds for dismissal. The two basic categories of insubordination are unwillingness to carry out the manager's orders, and disrespectful behavior toward the manager. (This assumes that the orders were legitimate, and that the manager did not incite the reaction through his or her own extreme behavior.) Examples of insubordination include:[89]

1. Direct disregard of the boss's authority
2. Direct disobedience of, or refusal to obey, the boss's orders, particularly in front of others
3. Deliberate defiance of clearly stated company policies, rules, regulations, and procedures
4. Public criticism of the boss
5. Blatant disregard of reasonable instructions
6. Contemptuous display of disrespect
7. Disregard for the chain of command
8. Participation in (or leadership of) an effort to undermine and remove the boss from power

FAIRNESS SAFEGUARDS Dismissals are never easy. However, the manager can take steps to make them fair.[90] First, allow the employee to explain why he (or she)

FIGURE 10-3 Median Weeks of Severance Pay by Job Level

Source: "Median Weeks of Severance Pay by Job Level", in "Severance Pay: Current Trends and Practices," from Culpepper Compensation Surveys & Services website, July 2007. Copyright © 2012 Culpepper and Associates, Inc., © 2012.

Severance Calculation Method	Median Weeks of Severance		
	Executives	Managers	Professionals
Fixed	26	6	4
Variable Amount by Employment Tenure			
1 year	4	2	2
3 years	7	5	5
5 years	10	7	7
10 years	20	12	10
15 years	26	16	15
Maximum	39	26	24

did what he did. It could turn out, for instance, that the employee "disobeyed" the order because he or she did not understand it. Similarly, people who get *full explanations* of why and how termination decisions were made "were more likely to perceive their layoff as fair … and indicate that they did not wish to take the past employer to court."

Second, have a formal *multistep procedure* (including warning) and an appeal process.

Third, *the person who actually does the dismissing* is important. Employees in one study whose managers informed them of an impending layoff viewed the dismissal fairer than did those told by, say, a human resource manager. Some employers take a less diplomatic approach. About 10% of respondents in one survey said they've used e-mail to fire employees.[91] When JCPenney dismissed thousands of employees in 2012, many were fired in groups of a few dozen to over 100 in an auditorium.[92] Use the right person, and dismiss humanely.

Fourth, dismissed employees who feel they've been treated unfairly financially are more likely to sue. Many employers use severance pay to blunt a dismissal's sting.[93] Figure 10-3 summarizes typical severance policies.

KNOW YOUR EMPLOYMENT LAW

Termination at Will

terminate at will
In the absence of a contract, either the employer or the employee can terminate at will the employment relationship.

For more than 100 years, the prevailing rule in the United States has been that without an employment contract, either the employer or the employee can **terminate at will** the employment relationship. In other words, the employee could resign for any reason, at will, and the employer could similarly dismiss an employee for any reason, at will. Today, however, dismissed employees increasingly take their cases to court, and employers are finding that they no longer have a blanket right to fire.

Three main protections against wrongful discharge eroded the termination-at-will doctrine—*statutory exceptions, common law exceptions,* and *public policy exceptions.*

First, *statutory exceptions* include federal and state equal employment and workplace laws that prohibit certain dismissals. For example, Title VII of the Civil Rights Act of 1964 prohibits discharging employees based on race, color, religion, sex, or national origin.[94] Laws protecting LGBT workers from termination for sexual orientation have been passed in 18 states and the District of Colombia, but in 29 states someone can still be terminated based on sexual orientation.[95] For federal employees, the EEOC has held that Title VII of the Civil Rights Act of 1964 applies to LGBT individuals.[96]

Second, numerous *common law exceptions* exist. Courts create these exceptions based on precedents. For example, courts have held that employee handbooks promising termination only "for just cause" may create an exception to the at-will rule.[97]

Finally, under the *public policy exception,* courts have held a discharge to be wrongful when it was against a well-established public policy. Thus, a public policy exception might prohibit an employer from firing an employee for refusing to break the law. ■

Avoiding Wrongful Discharge Suits

Wrongful discharge (or *termination*) occurs when an employee's dismissal does not comply with the law or with the contractual arrangement stated or implied by the employer. (In a *constructive discharge* claim, the plaintiff argues that he or she quit, but had no choice because the employer made the work situation so intolerable.[98])

Avoiding wrongful discharge suits requires several things.[99] *First*, have employment policies including grievance procedures that help show you treat employees fairly. Here employers can also use severance pay to blunt a dismissal's sting.[100] No termination is pleasant, but the first line of defense is to handle it justly.[101]

Second, review and refine all employment-related policies, procedures, and documents to limit challenges. Procedural steps include:[102]

- Have applicants sign the employment application. Make sure it contains a statement that "the employer can terminate at any time."
- Review your employee manual to delete statements that could undermine your defense in a wrongful discharge case. For example, delete "employees can be terminated only for just cause."
- Have written rules listing infractions that may require discipline and discharge.
- If a rule is broken, get the worker's side of the story in front of witnesses, and preferably get it signed. Then check out the story.
- Be sure that employees get a written appraisal at least annually. If an employee shows evidence of incompetence, give that person a warning. Provide an opportunity to improve.
- Keep careful confidential records of all actions such as employee appraisals, warnings or notices, and so on.
- Finally, ask the questions in Figure 10-4.

Security Measures

Prudence suggests using a checklist to ensure (for instance) that dismissed employees return all keys and company property, and (often) accompanying them out of the building. The employer should disable Internet-related passwords and accounts of

Is the employee covered by any type of written agreement, including a collective bargaining agreement? _____

Is a defamation claim likely? _____

Is there a possible discrimination allegation? _____

Is there any workers' compensation involvement? _____

Have reasonable rules and regulations been communicated and enforced? _____

Has the employee been given an opportunity to explain any rule violations or to correct poor performance? _____

Have all monies been paid within 24 hours after separation? _____

Has the employee been advised of his or her rights under COBRA? _____

FIGURE 10-4 Questions to Ask Before Making the Dismissal Final

Source: Sovereign, Kenneth, Personal Law, 4th Edition., © 1999, p 185. Reprinted and electronically reproduced by permission of Pearson Education, Inc., Upper Saddle River, New Jersey.

former employees, plug holes that could allow an ex-employee to gain illegal online access, and have rules for return of company laptops and handhelds. "Measures range from simply disabling access and changing passwords to reconfiguring the network and changing IP addresses, remote access procedures, and telephone numbers," says one chief technology officer.[103]

Supervisor Liability

Courts may hold managers personally liable for their supervisory actions, including dismissals.[104] For example, the Fair Labor Standards Act defines *employer* to include "any person acting directly or indirectly in the interest of an employer in relation to any employee." This can mean the individual supervisor.

There are several ways to avoid having personal liability become an issue.

- *Follow company policies and procedures.* An employee may initiate a claim against a supervisor who he or she alleges did not follow policies and procedures.
- Administer the dismissal in a manner that does not add to the employee's *emotional hardship* (as would having the employee publicly collect his or her belongings and leave the office).
- *Do not act in anger,* since doing so undermines the appearance of objectivity.
- Finally, *use the HR department* for advice regarding how to handle difficult dismissal situations.

The Exit Process and Termination Interview

Dismissing an employee is one of the most difficult tasks you can face at work.[105] The dismissed employee, even if warned many times in the past, may still react with disbelief or even violence. Guidelines for the **termination interview** itself are as follows:

termination interview
The interview in which an employee is informed of the fact that he or she has been dismissed.

1. ***Plan the interview carefully.*** According to experts at Hay Associates, this includes:
   - Make sure the employee keeps the appointment time.
   - Never inform an employee over the phone.
   - Allow 10 minutes as sufficient time for the interview.
   - Use a neutral site, not your own office.
   - Have employee agreements, the human resource file, and a release announcement prepared in advance.
   - Be available at a time after the interview in case questions or problems arise.
   - Have phone numbers ready for medical or security emergencies.
2. ***Get to the point.*** When the employee enters the office, give the person a moment to get comfortable and then inform him or her of your decision.
3. ***Describe the situation.*** Briefly, in three or four sentences, explain why the person is being let go. For instance, "Production in your area is down 4%, and we are continuing to have quality problems. We have talked about these problems several times in the past 3 months, and the solutions are not being followed through on. We have to make a change." Don't personalize the situation as in, "Your production is just not up to par." Emphasize the decision is irrevocable. Preserving the employee's dignity is crucial.[106]
4. ***Listen.*** Continue the interview until the person appears to be talking freely and reasonably calmly.
5. ***Review the severance package.*** Describe severance payments, benefits, access to office support people, and the way references will be handled. However, under no conditions make any promises of benefits beyond those already in the support package.
6. ***Identify the next step.*** The terminated employee may be disoriented and unsure what to do next. Explain where the employee should go next, upon leaving the interview.

outplacement counseling
A formal process by which a terminated person is trained and counseled in the techniques of self-appraisal and securing a new position.

OUTPLACEMENT COUNSELING With **outplacement counseling** the employer arranges for an outside firm to provide terminated employees with career planning and job search skills. *Outplacement firms* usually provide such outplacement services. Employees (usually managers or professionals) who are let go typically have office space and secretarial services they can use at local offices of such firms, plus the counseling services. The outplacement counseling is part of the terminated employee's support or severance package. Why not just give the person you're dismissing the outplacement fee as additional severance? In general, providing outplacement services seems to have positive effects for both the terminated employee and the employer.[107]

FOR THE EMPLOYEE What should you do if you get fired or passed over for a position?[108] Most people surrender to the usual stages of shock, denial, and anger. However, the better first step is usually to think through why you lost the job. Doing so isn't easy. Actively explore what (if anything) you did to contribute to the problem. Then objectively consider what you might do differently in the future, keeping in mind that you should view the loss (difficult though this may be) as an opportunity. Then evaluate your new options and be ready to seize the right opportunity.

exit interviews
Interviews with employees who are leaving the firm, conducted for obtaining information about the job or related matters, to give the employer insight about the company.

EXIT INTERVIEW Many employers conduct **exit interviews** with employees leaving the firm. These are interviews, usually conducted by a human resource professional just prior to the employee leaving, that elicit information aimed at giving employers insights into their companies. Exit interview questions include: How were you recruited? Was the job presented correctly and honestly? What was your supervisor's management style like? How do the employees on the team get along?[109]

The assumption is that because the employee is leaving he or she will be candid, but this is debatable.[110] Researchers found that at the time of separation, 38% of those leaving blamed salary and benefits, and 4% blamed supervision. Followed up 18 months later, 24% blamed supervision and 12% blamed salary and benefits.

Yet these interviews can be useful. When Blue Cross of Northeastern Pennsylvania laid off employees, many said, in exit interviews, "This is not a stable place to work." The firm took steps to address that concern for those who stayed with Blue Cross.

THE EXIT PROCESS The exit interview is just one part of a rational exit process. The employer should follow a checklist. Again ensure, for example, that the employee returns all keys and company equipment, that all computer and database password access is terminated, that proper communications are sent internally (for instance, to other employees if appropriate, and to payroll) and externally, that the employee leaves the premises in a timely fashion, and that if necessary precautions are followed to ensure security.

Layoffs and the Plant Closing Law

Nondisciplinary separations may be initiated by either employer or employee. For the *employer*, reduced sales or profits or the desire for more productivity may require layoffs. *Employees* (as we've seen) may leave for better jobs, to retire, or for other reasons. The Worker Adjustment and Retraining Notification Act (WARN Act, or the plant closing law) requires employers of 100 or more employees to give 60 days' notice before closing a facility or starting a layoff of 50 or more people.[111]

layoff
An employer sending employees home due to a lack of work; this is typically a temporary situation.

A **layoff**, in which the employer sends workers home for a time for lack of work, is usually not a permanent dismissal (although it may turn out to be). Rather, it is a temporary one, which the employer expects will be short term. However, some employers use the term *layoff* as a euphemism for discharge or termination. In the deep recession years of 2008 and 2009 combined, employers carried out a total of about 51,000 mass layoffs, idling over 5 million workers.[112]

A study illustrates one firm's layoff process. Senior management first met to make strategic decisions about the size and timing of the layoffs. They also debated the relative importance of the skills the firm needed going forward. Supervisors then assessed their subordinates, rating their nonunion employees either A, B, or C (union employees were covered by a union agreement making layoffs dependent on seniority). The supervisors then informed each of their subordinates about his or her A, B, or C rating, and told each that those with C grades were most likely to be laid off.[113]

LAYOFF'S EFFECTS It's not surprising that layoffs often result in "deleterious psychological and physical health outcomes" for those losing their jobs as well as for survivors.[114]

But not just the "victims" and "survivors" suffer. In one study, researchers "found that the more managers were personally responsible for handing out WARN notices to employees … the more likely they were to report physical health problems, to seek treatment for these problems, and to complain of disturbed sleep."[115]

Given all this, many employers try to minimize layoffs and dismissals during downturns. Reducing everyone's work hours and mandating vacations are two options. Others reduce layoffs by offering financial bonuses for improved productivity.[116]

Ironically, when some employees most need employee assistance programs (such as counseling)—after they're laid off—they lose them. More firms are therefore extending these program benefits for a month or two to former employees. For example, Florida's Sarasota County extended employee assistance program benefits for 2 months after it laid off some employees.[117]

Adjusting to Downsizings and Mergers

downsizing
The process of reducing, usually dramatically, the number of people employed by a firm.

Downsizing means reducing, usually dramatically, the number of people employed by a firm. The basic idea is to cut costs and raise profitability. Downsizings (some call them "productivity transformation programs")[118] require careful consideration of several matters.

1. First is making sure *the right people* are let go; this requires having an effective appraisal system in place.
2. Second is *compliance with all applicable laws,* including WARN.
3. Third is executing the dismissals in a manner that is *just and fair*.
4. Fourth is *security,* for instance, retrieving keys and ensuring that those leaving don't take prohibited items with them.
5. Fifth is reducing the remaining *employees' uncertainty* and addressing their concerns. This typically involves a post-downsizing announcement and program, including meetings where senior managers field questions from the remaining employees.

Providing advanced notice regarding the layoff can help cushion the otherwise negative effects. So can interpersonal sensitivity (in terms of the manager's demeanor during layoffs).[119] Layoffs can be more challenging abroad due to special legal obligations, such as requirements for a year's notice in some countries.

Supportiveness and creativity are especially important in high-performance-work-system-type firms. These rely heavily on employee engagement and teamwork.[120] Here, turnover is especially disruptive, so it may be particularly important to avoid layoffs. Options here include: implement pay freezes or cuts; introduce a hiring freeze before reducing the workforce; provide candid communications about the need for the downsizing; give employees an opportunity to express their opinions about the downsizing; and be fair and compassionate in implementing the downsizing.[121]

Chapter Review

MyManagementLab® Go to **mymanagementlab.com** to complete the problems marked with this icon. ✪

Chapter Section Summaries

10-1. Employees are ultimately responsible for their own careers, but employers and managers also have roles in **career management**. These include establishing company-based career centers, offering career planning workshops, providing employee development budgets, and offering online career development programs. Perhaps the simplest is to make the appraisal itself career-oriented, by linking the appraisal feedback to the employee's aspirations and plans.

10-2. The employer's career planning and development process and practices (including career-oriented appraisal) help to foster **employee engagement**. Managed effectively, the employer's career development process should send the signal that the employee cares about the employee's career success.

10-3. Managing voluntary turnover requires identifying its causes and then addressing them. A comprehensive approach to **retaining employees** should be multifaceted, and include improved selection, a well-thought-out training and career development program, assistance in helping employees lay out potential career plans, providing employees with meaningful work and recognition and rewards, promoting work–life balance, acknowledging employees' achievements, and providing all this within a supportive company culture.

10-4. Employers need to address employee **lifecycle career management** issues. Most notably, promotions can provide opportunities to reward exceptional performance, and to fill open positions with tested and loyal employees. Several decisions loom large in any firm's promotion process: Is seniority or competence the rule? How should we measure competence? Is the process formal or informal? Vertical, horizontal, or other? Women and people of color still experience relatively less career progress in organizations, and bias and more subtle barriers are often the cause. In general, the employer's promotion processes must comply with all the same antidiscrimination laws as do procedures for recruiting and selecting employees or any other HR actions. Transfers and retirements are other important career lifecycle issues.

10-5. **Managing dismissals** is an important part of any supervisor's job. Among the reasons for dismissal are unsatisfactory performance, misconduct, lack of qualifications, changed job requirements, and insubordination. In dismissing one or more employees, however, remember that termination at will as a policy has been weakened by exceptions in many states. Furthermore, care should be taken to avoid wrongful discharge suits.

Discussion Questions

✪ **10-1.** Why is it advisable for an employee retention effort to be comprehensive? What activities would you say is involved in such a program?

10-2. What is the employee's role in the career development process? The manager's role? The employer's role?

10-3. What are the main decisions employers should address in reaching promotion decisions?

✪ **10-4.** Discuss at least four procedural suggestions for managing dismissals effectively.

10-5. What would you as a supervisor do to avoid someone accusing you of wrongful dismissal?

Individual and Group Activities

10-6. Many rightfully offer IBM as an example of an employer that works hard to improve employee retention and engagement. Browse through the employment pages of IBM's Web site (such as www-03.ibm.com/employment/build_your_career.html). In this chapter, we discussed actions employers can take to improve employee retention and engagement. From the information on IBM's Web pages, what is IBM doing to support retention and engagement?

10-7. In groups of four or five students, meet with one or two administrators and faculty members in your college or university and, based on this, write a 2-page paper on the topic "the faculty promotion process at our college." What do you think of the process? Based on our discussion in this chapter, could you make any suggestions for improving it?

10-8. Working individually or in groups, choose two occupations (such as management consultant, HR manager, or salesperson) and use sources such as O*NET to size up the future demand for this occupation in the next 10 years or so. Does this seem like a good occupation to pursue? Why or why not?

10-9. In groups of four or five students, interview a small business owner or an HR manager with the aim of writing a 2-page paper addressing the topic "steps our company is taking to reduce voluntary employee turnover." What is this employer's turnover rate now? How would you suggest it improve its turnover rate?

10-10. Appendices A and B at the end of this book (pages 612–629) list the knowledge someone studying for the HRCI (Appendix A) or SHRM (Appendix B) certification exam needs to have in each area of human resource management (such as in Strategic Management, and Workforce Planning). In groups of several students, do four things: (1) review Appendix A and/or B; (2) identify the material in this chapter that relates to the Appendix A and/or B required knowledge lists; (3) write four multiple-choice exam questions on this material that you believe would be suitable for inclusion in the HRCI exam and/or the SHRM exam; and, (4) if time permits, have someone from your team post your team's questions in front of the class, so that students in all teams can answer the exam questions created by the other teams.

10-11. Several years ago, a survey of college graduates in the United Kingdom found that although many hadn't found their first jobs, most were already planning "career breaks" and to keep up their hobbies and interests outside work. As one report of the findings put it, "the next generation of workers is determined not to wind up on the hamster wheel of long hours with no play."[122] Part of the problem seems to be that many already see their friends "putting in more than 48 hours a week" at work. Career experts reviewing the results concluded that many of these recent college grads "are not looking for high-pay, high-profile jobs anymore."[123] Instead, they seem to be looking to "compartmentalize" their lives. They want to keep the number of hours they spend at work down, so they can maintain their hobbies and outside interests. If you were mentoring one of these people at work, what three bits of career advice would you give him or her? Why? What (if anything) would you suggest their employers do to accommodate these graduates' stated career wishes?

10-12. Web sites such as Sporting News occasionally run a story listing what they call the greatest coaches (for example, key "greatest coaches" into Google search).[124] Look at this list, and pick out two of the names. Then research these people online to determine what behaviors they exhibited that seem to account for why they were great coaches. How do these behaviors compare with what this chapter had to say about effective coaching?

what am I good at?
Prospects?
Career plan

Experiential Exercise

Where Am I Going ... and Why?

Purpose: The purpose of this exercise is to provide you with experience in analyzing your career preferences.

Required Understanding: Students should be thoroughly familiar with the "Employee's Role in Career Management" section in this chapter, as well as using O*NET (which we discussed in Chapter 4).

How to Set Up the Exercise/Instructions: Using O*NET and the "Employee's Role in Career Management" section in this chapter, analyze your career-related inclinations (you can also take the Self-Directed Search for about $10 at www.self-directed-search.com). Based on this analysis, answer the following questions (if you wish, you may do this analysis in teams of three or four students).

10-13. What does your research suggest to you about what would be your preferable occupational options?

10-14. What are the prospects for these occupations?

10-15. Given these prospects and your own occupational inclinations, outline a brief, 1-page career plan for yourself, including current occupational inclinations, career goals, and an action plan listing four or five development steps you will need to take in order to get from where you are now career-wise to where you want to be, based on your career goals.

mynextmove.org

Application Case

Google Reacts

On the face of it, Google would seem to be the last company that one would expect to have an employee retention problem. Google usually shows up in "Best Employers to Work For" lists; it's famous for full benefits, from dry cleaning to free Web-enabled transportation from San Francisco to great pensions; it offers great stock options; and, as a fast-growing company, it usually has many job applicants. So when its employee turnover began creeping up a few years ago, Google's human resource team had to decide what to do. Part of the problem is that as attractive as Google is to work for, Silicon Valley is filled with attractive employers, from Apple to Facebook. One of Google's first steps was to boost compensation. It gave all 23,000 Google employees a 10% raise, plus a $1,000 tax-free holiday bonus.[125] But, still, Google management knew that pay was just part of the solution. It had to take other steps.

Questions

10-16. Without doing any research beyond what you learned in this chapter, what other steps would you suggest Google take to improve employee retention?

10-17. Was there any information in previous chapters of this book that would help to illustrate other steps Google took to improve retention?

10-18. Use other Internet sources, including Google.com, to finalize an answer to the question: What other steps should Google take to improve employee retention?

Continuing Case

Carter Cleaning Company

The Career Planning Program

Career planning has always been a pretty low-priority item for Carter Cleaning, since "just getting workers to come to work and then keeping them honest is enough of a problem," as Jack likes to say. Yet Jennifer thought it might not be a bad idea to give some thought to what a career planning program might involve for Carter. Many of their employees had been with them for years in dead-end jobs, and she frankly felt a little bad for them: "Perhaps we could help them gain a better perspective on what they want to do," she thought. And she definitely believed that career support would have an effect on improving Carter's employee retention.

Questions

10-19. What would be the advantages to Carter Cleaning of setting up a career planning program?

10-20. Who should participate in the program? All employees? Selected employees?

10-21. Outline and describe the career development program you would propose for the cleaners, pressers, counter people, and managers at the Carter Cleaning Centers.

Translating Strategy into HR Policies and Practices Case*,§

**The accompanying strategy map for this chapter is in MyManagementLab®, and the overall map on the inside back cover of this text outlines the relationships involved.*

Improving Performance at the Hotel Paris

The New Career Management System

The Hotel Paris's competitive strategy is "To use superior guest service to differentiate the Hotel Paris properties, and to thereby increase the length of stay and return rate of guests, and thus boost revenues and profitability." HR manager Lisa Cruz must now formulate functional policies and activities that support this competitive strategy, by eliciting the required employee behaviors and competencies.

Lisa Cruz knew that, as a hospitality business, the Hotel Paris was uniquely dependent upon having engaged, high-morale employees. In a factory or small retail shop, the employer might be able to rely on direct supervision to make sure that the employees were doing their jobs. But in a hotel, just about every employee is "on the front line." There is usually no one there to supervise the limousine driver when he or she picks up a guest at the airport, or when the valet takes the guest's car, or the front-desk clerk signs the guest in, or the housekeeping clerk needs to handle a guest's special request. If the hotel wanted satisfied guests, they had to have engaged employees who did their jobs as if they owned the company, even when the supervisor was nowhere in sight. But for the employees to be engaged, Lisa knew, the Hotel Paris had to make it clear that the company was also committed to its employees.

From her experience, she knew that one way to do this was to help her employees have successful and satisfying careers, and she was therefore concerned to find that the Hotel Paris had no career management process at all. Supervisors weren't trained to discuss employees' developmental needs or promotional options during the performance appraisal interviews. Promotional processes were informal. And the firm made no attempt to provide any career development services that might help its employees to develop a better understanding of what their career options were, or should be. Lisa was sure that engaged employees were key to improving the experiences of the hotel's guests, and that she couldn't boost employee engagement without doing a better job of attending to her employees' career needs. In two hotels she began encouraging supervisors to at least engage in career-oriented appraisals with their subordinates, on a pilot project basis.

For Lisa and the CFO, their preliminary research left little doubt about the advisability of instituting a new career management system at the Hotel Paris. Based on their pilot project, employees in those Hotel Paris hotels who had been working under the new career management directive were more engaged, received more complimentary letters from guests, and received higher performance appraisal ratings than did employees who did not have career plans. The CFO therefore gave the go-ahead to design and institute a new Hotel Paris career management program.

Lisa and her team knew that they already had most of the building blocks in place, thanks to the new performance management system they had instituted just a few weeks earlier. For example, the new performance management system already required that the supervisor appraise the employee based on goals and competencies that were driven by the company's strategic needs; and the appraisal itself produced new goals for the coming year and specific development plans for the employee. These development plans had to make sense in terms of both the company's and the employee's needs and preferences.

In addition to the new performance management elements already in place, Lisa and her team created an online "Hotel Paris Career Center." With links to a choice of career assessment tools such as the Self-Directed Search (www.self-directed-search.com) and wizard-based templates for developing one's own career plan, the site went far toward providing the Hotel Paris's employees with the career assistance that they required. Also on the site, a new "International Job Openings" link made it easier for Hotel Paris employees to identify positions for which they might be qualified. The results exceeded Lisa and the CFO's expectations. Virtually every employee produced a career plan within the first 6 months. The appraisal interviews often turned into animated, career-oriented development sessions, and soon the various measures of employee commitment and guest service were trending up.

Questions

10-22. "Many hotel jobs are inherently 'dead end'; for example, maids, laundry workers, and valets either have no great aspirations to move up, or are just using these jobs temporarily, for instance, to help out with household expenses." First, do you agree with this statement? Why, or why not? Second, list three more specific career activities you would recommend Lisa implement for these employees.

10-23. Using what you learned in this chapter of Dessler *Human Resource Management*, build on the company's new system by recommending two more specific career development activities the hotel should implement.

10-24. What other specific career development activities would you recommend in light of the fact that the Hotel Paris's hotels and employees are dispersed around the world?

---

§Written by and copyright Gary Dessler, PhD.

MyManagementLab

Go to **mymanagementlab.com** for Auto-graded writing questions as well as the following Assisted-graded writing questions:

10-25. You manage a small restaurant in Columbus, Ohio and keeping good employees is one of your biggest challenges. Most wait staff and kitchen staff last no more than 8-9 months. Explain what you would do to improve employee retention.

10-26. Explain what you as a supervisor can do to support your employees' career management needs.

10-27. MyManagementLab Only–comprehensive writing assignment for this chapter.

Try It!

How would you apply the concepts and skills you learned in this chapter? If your professor has assigned this, go to the Assignments section of mymanagementlab.com to complete the simulation: *Career Management.*

PERSONAL INVENTORY ASSESSMENTS

PERSONAL INVENTORY ASSESSMENT

Communicating Supportively

Communicating plays a big role in coaching and mentoring and is important when dismissing an employee as well. Complete this assessment to learn more about your personality.

CHAPTER 10

Key Terms

career, 309
career management, 309
career development, 309
career planning, 309
reality shock, 311
mentoring, 313
coaching, 314
promotion, 320
transfers, 322
dismissal, 324
insubordination, 324
terminate at will, 325
termination interview, 327
outplacement counseling, 328
exit interviews, 328
layoff, 328
downsizing, 329

Endnotes

1. Kristen Fyfe-Mills, "Commitment to Talent Development Excellence," *TD*, October 2014, pp. 39–41, www.td.org/Publications/Magazines/TD/TD-Archive/2014/10/BEST-Cognizant, accessed April 4, 2015; see also http://businesstoday.intoday.in/story/malcolm-frank-on-cognizant-strategy-going-forward/1/200337.html, www.cognizant.com/InsightsWhitepapers/architecting-an-enterprise-content-management-strategy-a-four-pillar-approach-codex975.pdf, and www.cognizant.com/about-cognizant/company-overview/sustainability/employee-development, all accessed April 9, 2015.
2. For example, see Phyllis Moen and Patricia Roehling, *The Career Mystique* (Boulder, CO: Rowman & Littlefield Publishers, 2005); and Geoff Williams, "3 Steps to Reinventing Your Career," *U.S. News & World Report,* June 5, 2013, http://money.usnews.com/money/personal-finance/articles/2013/06/05/3-steps-to-reinventing-your-career, accessed September 2, 2014.
3. Stephen Robbins and Timothy Judge, *Organizational Behavior* (Upper Saddle River, NJ: Pearson Education, 2011), p. 285.
4. Ibid., p. 284.
5. Karoline Strauss et al., "Future Work Selves: How Salient Hoped-For Identities Motivate Proactive Career Behaviors," *Journal of Applied Psychology* 97, no. 3, pp. 580–598.
6. Edward Levinson et al., "A Critical Evaluation of the Web-Based Version of the Career Key," *Career Development Quarterly* 50, no. 1 (September 1, 2002), pp. 26–36.
7. Richard Bolles, *What Color Is Your Parachute?* (Berkeley, CA: Ten Speed Press, 2003), pp. 5–6.
8. This example is based on Richard Bolles, *The Three Boxes of Life* (Berkeley, CA: Ten Speed Press, 1976). Richard Bolles updates his famous career book *What Color Is Your Parachute?* annually. It contains this and many other career exercises. The 2015 edition is published by Ten Speed Press in Berkeley, California.
9. http://careers.intuit.com/university/new-grads, accessed March 12, 2013.
10. Rachel Silverman, "Workers Get Help Climbing the Career Ladder," *Wall Street Journal,* January 14, 2015, p. B6.
11. Laszlo Bock, *Work Rules!* (New York: Twelve, 2015), pp. 217–218.
12. Patrick Kiger, "First USA Bank, Promotions and Job Satisfaction," *Workforce*, March 2001, pp. 54–56.

13. Fred Otte and Peggy Hutcheson, *Helping Employees Manage Careers* (Upper Saddle River, NJ: Prentice Hall, 1992), p. 143.
14. David Foote, "Wanna Keep Your Staff Happy? Think Career," *Computerworld*, October 9, 2000, p. 38. For an example, the U.S. Homeland Security Department's TSA has a career coaching/planning program. See http://tsacareercoaching.tsa.dhs.gov/index.php/faq-tsa-career-plan, accessed September 2, 2014.
15. Julekha Dash, "Coaching to Aid IT Careers, Retention," *Computerworld*, March 20, 2000, p. 52.
16. Yehuda Baruch, "Career Development in Organizations and Beyond: Balancing Traditional and Contemporary Viewpoints," *Human Resource Management Review* 16 (2006), p. 131.
17. Carla Joinson, "Employee, Sculpt Thyself with a Little Help," *HR Magazine*, May 2001, pp. 61–64.
18. See also Jim Bright, "Career Development: Empowering Your Staff to Excellence," *Journal of Banking and Financial Services* 17, no. 3 (July 2003), p.12.
19. Tim Harvey, "Enterprise Training System Is Trans Alaska Pipeline's Latest Safety Innovation," *Pipeline and Gas Journal* 229, no. 12 (December 2002), pp. 28–32.
20. Ibid.
21. www.halogensoftware.com/products/halogen-esuccession/, accessed August 27, 2012.
22. Mukta Kulkarni and K. V. Gopakumar, "Career Management Strategies of People with Disabilities," *Human Resource Management* 53, no. 3 (May–June 2014), pp. 445–466.
23. Bill Hayes, "Helping Workers with Career Goals Boosts Retention Efforts," *Boston Business Journal* 21, no. 11 (April 20, 2001), p. 38.
24. Michael Doody, "A Mentor Is a Key to Career Success," *Health-Care Financial Management* 57, no. 2 (February 2003), pp. 92–94.
25. Richard Luecke, *Coaching and Mentoring* (Boston: Harvard Business School Press, 2004), pp. 100–101.
26. Ferda Erdem and Janset Özen Aytemur, "Mentoring—A Relationship Based on Trust: Qualitative Research," *Public Personnel Management* 37, no. 1 (Spring 2008), pp. 55–65.
27. Herminia Ibarra, Nancy Carter, and Christine Silva, "Why Men Still Get More Promotions Than Women," *Harvard Business Review*, September 2010, pp. 80–85.
28. Fyfe-Mills, "Commitment to Talent Development Excellence." See also http://businesstoday.intoday.in/story/malcolm-frank-on-cognizant-strategy-going-forward/1/200337.html, www.cognizant.com/InsightsWhitepapers/architecting-an-enterprise-content-management-strategy-a-four-pillar-approach-codex975.pdf, and www.cognizant.com/about-cognizant/company-overview/sustainability/employee-development, all accessed April 9, 2015.
29. This is based on Gary Dessler, *Winning Commitment* (New York: McGraw-Hill, 1993), Chapter 10. See also www.glassdoor.com/Reviews/J-CPenney-Reviews-E361.htm, http://jobs.jcp.com/viewalljobs, and www.glassdoor.com/Reviews/Employee-Review-J-CPenney-RVW479729.htm, all accessed July 7, 2014.
30. www.Medtronic.com/careers/develop-your-potential, accessed March 12, 2013; www.medtronic.com/us-en/about-3/medtronic-plc-facts.html?cmpid=mdt_plc_2015_US_about_3_story_panel_featured_company_facts_cta_text_link_learn_more, accessed April 10, 2015.
31. See, for example, www.nobscot.com/survey/index.cfm and www.bls.gov/jlt, accessed April 27, 2011. For computing turnover, see SHRM, "Executive Brief: Differences in Employee Turnover Across Key Industries," www.shrm.org, accessed August 30, 2012.
32. Jean Phillips and Stanley Gully, *Strategic Staffing* (Upper Saddle River, NJ: Pearson Education, 2012).
33. Tae-Youn Park and Jason Shaw, "Turnover Rates and Organizational Performance: A Meta-analysis," *Journal of Applied Psychology* 98, no. 2 (2013), pp. 268–309.
34. Ibid., p. 283. See also Jolivette Wallace and Kristena Gaylor, "A Study of the Dysfunctional and Functional Aspects of Voluntary Employee Turnover," *SAM Advanced Management Journal* 77, no. 3 (Summer 2012), p. 27.
35. The following example is based on Barbara Hillmer, Steve Hillmer, and Gale McRoberts, "The Real Costs of Turnover: Lessons from a Call Center," *Human Resource Planning* 27, no. 3 (2004), pp. 34–41.
36. Kim Soonhee, "The Impact of Human Resource Management on State Government IT Employee Turnover Intentions," *Public Personnel Management* 41, no. 2 (Summer 2012), p. 257.
37. Park and Shaw, "Turnover Rates and Organizational Performance."
38. Adrienne Fox, "Drive Turnover Down," *HR Magazine*, July 2012, pp. 23–27.
39. SHRM, "Executive Brief."
40. www.worldatwork.org/waw/adimLink?id=17180, accessed April 27, 2011.
41. Phillips and Gully, *Strategic Staffing*, p. 329.
42. Stephen Robbins and Timothy Judge, *Organizational Behavior* (Upper Saddle River, NJ: Pearson Education, 2011), p. 81.
43. Phillips and Gully, *Strategic Staffing*, p. 328.
44. Katherine Tyler, "Who Will Stay and Who Will Go?" *HR Magazine*, December 2011, pp. 101–103.
45. See also David Ernest, David Allen, and Ronald Landis, "Mechanisms Linking Realistic Job Previews with Turnover: A Meta-analytic Path Analysis," *Personnel Psychology* 60, no. 4 (2011), pp. 865–897.
46. "Employers Using Cash to Retain Key Talent," *BNA Bulletin to Management*, June 26, 2012, p. 202.
47. Max Messmer, "Employee Retention: Why It Matters Now," *CPA Magazine*, June/July 2009, p. 28; and "The Employee Retention Challenge," Development Dimensions International, 2009.
48. Messmer, "Employee Retention."
49. Ibid. See also Eric Krell, "Five Ways to Manage High Turnover," *HR Magazine*, April 2012, pp. 63–65.
50. Rosemary Batt and Alexander Colvin, "An Employment Systems Approach to Turnover: Human Resources Practices, Quits, Dismissals, and Performance," *Academy of Management Journal* 54, no. 4 (2011), pp. 695–717.
51. "Counteroffers: Smart Move to Keep a Star or Waste of Time?" *BNA Bulletin to Management*, November 6, 2012, p. 358.
52. Ibid.
53. Baker, op cit. Stephen Baker, "Data Mining Moves to Human Resources" Bloomberg Business, March 11, 2009. See also "HR Analytics," *Workforce Management*, August 2012, p. 24.
54. Ed Frauenheim, "Numbers Game," *Workforce Management* 90, no. 3 (March 2011), p. 21.
55. Bock, *Work Rules!*, p. 142.
56. "The World's Top 10 Most Innovative Companies in Big Data," www.fastcompany.com/most-innovative-companies/2014/industry/big-data, accessed April 24, 2015.
57. Ibid.
58. From www.globoforce.com, accessed April 7, 2013. Used by permission from Globoforce
59. "Shocked UBS Staff Take to Twitter," www.CNBC.com/ID/49617998/, accessed October 21, 2012.
60. David Wilson, "Comparative Effects of Race/Ethnicity and Employee Engagement on Withdrawal Behavior," *Journal of Managerial Issues* 21, no. 2 (Summer 2009), pp. 165–166, 195–215.
61. Paul Eder and Robert Eisenberger, "Perceived Organizational Support: Reducing the Negative Influence of Coworker Withdrawal Behavior," *Journal of Management* 34, no. 1 (February 2008), pp. 55–68.
62. Wilson, "Comparative Effects of Race/Ethnicity and Employee Engagement."
63. Lisa Hope Pelled and Katherine R. Xin, "Down and Out: An Investigation of the Relationship Between Mood and Employee Withdrawal Behavior," *Journal of Management* 25, no. 6 (1999), pp. 875–895.
64. Ibid.
65. Ibid.
66. Ibid.
67. See, for example, Margaret Shaffer and David Harrison, "Expatriates' Psychological Withdrawal from International Assignments: Work, Nonwork, and Family Influences," *Personnel Psychology* 51, no. 1 (Spring 1998), pp. 87–118; Karl Pajo, Alan Coetzer, and Nigel Guenole, "Formal Development Opportunities and Withdrawal Behaviors by Employees in Small and Medium-Sized Enterprises," *Journal of Small Business Management* 48, no. 3 (July 2010), pp. 281–301; and P. Eder et al., "Perceived Organizational Support: Reducing the Negative Influence of Coworker Withdrawal Behavior," *Journal of Management* 34 no. 1 (February 2008), pp. 55–68.
68. Verena Hahn and Christian Dormann, "The Role of Partners and Children for Employees' Psychological Detachment from Work and Well-Being," *Journal of Applied Psychology* 98, no. 1 (2013), pp. 26–36.
69. *Gee v. Pincipi*, 5th Cir., number 01-50159, April 18, 2002, "Alleged Harasser's Comments Tainted Promotion Decision," www.shrm.org, accessed March 2, 2004.
70. Maria Danaher, "Unclean Promotion Procedures Smack of Discrimination," www.shrm.org, accessed March 2, 2004.
71. Elaine Herskowitz, "The Perils of Subjective Hiring and Promotion Criteria," www.shrm.org, accessed January 1, 2009.
72. George Thornton III and David Morris, "The Application of Assessment Center Technology to the Evaluation of Personnel Records," *Public Personnel Management* 30, no. 1 (Spring 2001), p. 55.
73. Pamela Babcock, quoting Terry Henley, SPHR, in "Promotions: Is There a 'New Normal'?" www.shrm.org/hrdisciplines/employeereltions/articles/Pages/PromotionsIsThereaNewNormal.aspx, accessed June 1, 2011.

74. Bock, *Work Rules!*, p. 358.
75. Karen Lyness and Madeline Heilman, "When Fit Is Fundamental: Performance Evaluations and Promotions of Upper-Level Female and Male Managers," *Journal of Applied Psychology* 91, no. 4 (2006), pp. 777–785.
76. "Minority Women Surveyed on Career Growth Factors," *Community Banker* 9, no. 3 (March 2000), p. 44.
77. In Ellen Cook et al., "Career Development of Women of Color and White Women: Assumptions, Conceptualization, and Interventions from an Ecological Perspective," *Career Development Quarterly* 50, no. 4 (June 2002), pp. 291–306.
78. Kathleen Melymuka, "Glass Ceilings & Clear Solutions," *Computerworld*, May 29, 2000, p. 56.
79. Robin Shay, "Don't Get Caught in the Legal Wringer When Dealing with Difficult to Manage Employees," www.shrm.org, http://moss07.shrm.org/Publications/hrmagazine/EditorialContent/Pages/0702toc.aspx, accessed July 28, 2009.
80. Ken Dychtwald et al., "It's Time to Retire Retirement," *Harvard Business Review*, March 2004, p. 49.
81. "Employees Plan to Work Past Retirement, but Not Necessarily for Financial Reasons," *BNA Bulletin to Management*, February 19, 2004, pp. 57–58. See also Mo Wang, "Profiling Retirees in the Retirement Transition and Adjustment Process: Examining the Longitudinal Change Patterns of Retirees' Psychological Well-Being," *Journal of Applied Psychology* 92, no. 2 (2007), pp. 455–474.
82. See, for example, Matt Bolch, "Bidding Adieu," *HR Magazine*, June 2006, pp. 123–127; and Claudia Deutsch, "A Longer Goodbye," *New York Times*, April 20, 2008, pp. H1, H10.
83. Luis Fleites and Lou Valentino, "The Case for Phased Retirement," *Compensation & Benefits Review*, March/April 2007, pp. 42–46.
84. Andrew Luchak et al., "When Do Committed Employees Retire? The Effects of Organizational Commitment on Retirement Plans Under a Defined Benefit Pension Plan," *Human Resource Management* 47, no. 3 (Fall 2008), pp. 581–599.
85. Dychtwald et al., "It's Time to Retire Retirement," p. 52.
86. Eric Krell, "Ways to Phased Retirement," *HR Magazine*, October 2010, p. 90.
87. Andrea Poe, "Make Foresight 20/20," *HR Magazine*, February 20, 2000, pp. 74–80. See also Nancy Hatch Woodward, "Smoother Separations," *HR Magazine*, June 2007, pp. 94–97.
88. Joseph Famularo, *Handbook of Modern Personnel Administration* (New York: McGraw Hill, 1982), pp. 65.3–65.5. See also Carolyn Hirschman, "Off Duty, Out of Work," *HR Magazine*, www.shrm.org/hrmagazine/articles/0203/0203hirschman.asp, accessed January 10, 2008.
89. Kenneth Sovereign, *Personnel Law* (Upper Saddle River, NJ: Prentice Hall, 1999), p. 148; "Disciplinary Issues: What Constitutes Insubordination?" www.shrm.org/TemplatesTools/hrqa/Pages/CMS_020144.aspx, accessed September 11, 2013.
90. C. R. Wanberg, L. W. Bunce, & M. B. Gavin, "Perceived fairness of layoffs among individuals who have been laid off: A longitudinal study" *Personnel Psychology*, 52, 1999, 59-84; Brian Klaas and Gregory Dell'omo, "Managerial Use of Dismissal: Organizational Level Determinants," *Personnel Psychology* 50 (1997), pp. 927–953; Nancy Hatch Woodward, "Smoother Separations," *HR Magazine*, June 2007, pp. 94–97.
91. "E-Mail Used for Layoffs, Humiliation," *BNA Bulletin to Management*, October 2, 2007, p. 315.
92. Donna Mattioli et al., "Penney Wounded by Deep Staff Cuts," *Wall Street Journal*, April 15, 2013.
93. "Fairness to Employees Can Stave Off Litigation," *BNA Bulletin to Management*, November 27, 1999, p. 377.
94. Robert Lanza and Morton Warren, "United States: Employment at Will Prevails Despite Exceptions to the Rule," *Society for Human Resource Management Legal Report*, October/November 2005, pp. 1–8.
95. Max Mihelich, "The Changing Landscape of LGBT Discrimination Laws," *Workforce*, October 2014, pp. 22–24.
96. "Facts about Discrimination in Federal Government Employment Based on Marital Status, Political Affiliation, Status as a Parent, Sexual Orientation, or Transgender (Gender Identity) Status," www.eeoc.gov/federal/otherprotections.cfm, accessed July 9, 2015. See also, http://employment.findlaw.com/employment-discrimination/sexual-orientation-discrimination-in-the-workplace.html, accessed July 9, 2015.
97. Mihelich, op. cit.
98. Paul Falcon, "Give Employees the (Gentle) Hook," *HR Magazine*, April 2001, pp. 121–128.
99. James Coil III and Charles Rice, "Three Steps to Creating Effective Employee Releases," *Employment Relations Today*, Spring 1994, pp. 91–94; Richard Bayer, "Termination with Dignity," *Business Horizons* 43, no. 5 (September 2000), pp. 4–10; Betty Sosnin, "Orderly Departures," *HR Magazine* 50, no. 11 (November 2005), pp. 74–78; "Severance Pay: Not Always the Norm," *HR Magazine*, May 2008, p. 28.
100. See, for example, Richard Hannah, "The Attraction of Severance," *Compensation & Benefits Review*, November/December 2008, pp. 37–44.
101. Jonathan Segal, "Severance Strategies," *HR Magazine*, July 2008, pp. 95–96.
102. Coil and Rice, "Three Steps to Creating Effective Employee Releases"; "Fairness to Employees Can Stave Off Litigation"; Bayer, "Termination with Dignity"; Sosnin, "Orderly Departures"; "Severance Pay: Not Always the Norm."
103. Jaikumar Vijayan, "Downsizings Leave Firms Vulnerable to Digital Attacks," *Computerworld* 25 (2001), pp. 6–7.
104. Edward Isler et al., "Personal Liability and Employee Discipline," *Society for Human Resource Management Legal Report*, September/October 2000, pp. 1–4.
105. Based on Coil and Rice, "Three Steps to Creating Effective Employee Releases." See also Martha Frase-Blunt, "Making Exit Interviews Work," *HR Magazine*, August 2004, pp. 9–11.
106. William J. Morin and Lyle York, *Outplacement Techniques* (New York: AMACOM, 1982), pp. 101–131; F. Leigh Branham, "How to Evaluate Executive Outplacement Services," *Personnel Journal* 62 (April 1983), pp. 323–326; Sylvia Milne, "The Termination Interview," *Canadian Manager*, Spring 1994, pp. 15–16; and Matthew S. Wood and Steven J. Karau, "Preserving Employee Dignity During the Termination Interview: An Empirical Examination," *Journal of Business Ethics* 86, no. 4 (2009), pp. 519–534.
107. Bram Lowsky, "Inside Outplacement," *Workforce*, June 2014, pp. 36–39, 48.
108. Mitchell Lee Marks et al., "Rebounding from Career Setbacks," *Harvard Business Review*, October 2014, pp. 105–108.
109. Marlene Piturro, "Alternatives to Downsizing," *Management Review*, October 1999, pp. 37–42; "How Safe Is Your Job?" *Money*, December 1, 2001, p. 130.
110. Joseph Zarandona and Michael Camuso, "A Study of Exit Interviews: Does the Last Word Count," *Personnel* 62, no. 3 (March 1981), pp. 47–48. For another point of view, see "Firms Can Profit from Data Obtained from Exit Interviews," *Knight-Ridder/Tribune Business News*, February 13, 2001, Item 0104 4446.
111. See Rodney Sorensen and Stephen Robinson, "What Employers Can Do to Stay Out of Legal Trouble When Forced to Implement Layoffs," *Compensation & Benefits Review*, January/February 2009, pp. 25–32.
112. "Mass Layoffs at Lowest Level Since July 2008, BLS Says," *BNA Bulletin to Management*, January 12, 2010, p. 13.
113. Leon Grunberg, Sarah Moore, and Edward Greenberg, "Managers' Reactions to Implementing Layoffs: Relationship to Health Problems and Withdrawal Behaviors," *Human Resource Management* 45, no. 2 (Summer 2006), pp. 159–178.
114. Ibid.
115. Ibid.
116. "Adopting Laid-Off Alternatives Could Help Employers Survive, Even Thrive, Analysts Say," *BNA Bulletin to Management*, February 24, 2009, p. 57.
117. Joann Lublin, "Employers See Value in Helping Those Laid Off," *Wall Street Journal*, September 24, 2007, p. B3.
118. "Calling a Layoff a Layoff," *Workforce Management*, April 21, 2008, p. 41.
119. "Communication Can Reduce Problems, Litigation After Layoffs, Attorneys Say," *BNA Bulletin to Management*, April 14, 2003, p. 129.
120. Roderick Iversen and Christopher Zatzick, "The Effects of Downsizing of Labor Productivity: The Value of Showing Consideration for Employees' Morale and Welfare and High Performance Work Systems," *Human Resource Management* 50, no. 1 (January/February 2011), pp. 29–44.
121. Ibid., p. 40.
122. "New Trend in Career Hunt," *Europe Intelligence Wire*, February 10, 2004.
123. Ibid.
124. See, for example, http://aol.sportingnews.com/ncaabasketball/story/2009-07-29/sporting-news-50-greatest-coaches-all-time, accessed July 7, 2014.
125. http://abclocal.go.com/kgo/story?section=news/business&id=7775524, accessed June 1, 2011.
126. Brett Arends, "How Summer Can Change Your Future," *Wall Street Journal*, May 17–18, 2014, p. B8.
127. John Holland, *Making Vocational Choices: A Theory of Careers* (Upper Saddle River, NJ: Prentice Hall, 1973).
128. Bart Wille and Filip De Fruyt, "Vocations as a Source of Identity: Reciprocal Relations Between Big Five Personality Traits and RIASEC Characteristics Over 15 Years," *Journal of Applied Psychology* 99, no. 2 (2014), pp. 262–281.

129. Ibid., p. 5. Researchers and career specialists are working with the U.S. government's O*NET to devise a methodology that will enable individuals to make better use of O*NET in identifying and choosing career paths. See, for example, Patrick Converse et al., "Matching Individuals to Occupations Using Abilities and the O*NET: Issues and an Application in Career Guidance," *Personnel Psychology* 57 (2004), pp. 451–57.
130. Quoted or paraphrased from www.onetcenter.org/mynextmove.html, accessed April 8, 2013.
131. This is based on Edgar Schein, *Career Dynamics* (Reading, MA; Addison Wesley, 1978), pp. 128–129; and Edgar Schein, "Career Anchors Revisited: Implications for Career Development in the 21st Century," *Academy of Management Executive* 10, no. 4 (1996), pp. 80–88.
132. Ibid., pp. 257–262. For a test of Schein's career anchor concept, see Yvon Martineau et al., "Multiple Career Anchors of Québec Engineers: Impact on Career Path and Success," *Relations Industrielles/Industrial Relations* 60, no. 3 (Summer 2005), pp. 45, 455–482.
133. Deb Koen, "Revitalize Your Career," *Training and Development*, January 2003, pp. 59–60.
134. See John Wareham, "How to Make a Headhunter Call You," *Across-the-Board* 32, no. 1 (January 1995), pp. 49–50; and Deborah Wright Brown and Alison Konrad, "Job Seeking in a Turbulent Environment: Social Networks and the Importance of Cross-Industry Ties to an Industry Change," *Human Relations* 54, no. 8 (August 2001), p. 1018.
135. Erica Fry, "How to Land Your Dream Job," *Fortune*, September 22, 2014, pp. 104–105.
136. Dan Klamm, "3 Ways to Ace Your Job Interview with Social Media," http://mashable.com/2010/06/01/job-interview-social-media/, accessed April 1, 2013.
137. Rachel Silverman, "New Year, New Job? Read This First," *Wall Street Journal*, January 2, 2015, pp. B1, B4.
138. Erica Fry, "Start Up: You," *Fortune,* January 1, 2015, pp. 84–87.
139. Based on Phyllis Korkke, "How to Say 'Look at Me!' to an Online Recruiter," *New York Times*, January 20, 2013, p. 8; and Eilene Zimmerman, "Recruiting a Recruiter for Your Next Job," *New York Times*, April 7, 2013, p. 10.
140. Sheryl Jean, "Say Goodbye to Paper, Hello to Social Resume," *Miami Herald*, March 4, 2013, p. 19.
141. Susan Adams, "The 10 Best Websites for Your Career," *Forbes*, www.forbes.com/sites/susanadams/2012/09/14/the-10-best-websites-for-your-career, accessed April 10, 2015.
142. "Resume Banks Launched," *Financial Executives* 17, no. 6 (September 2001), p. 72; James Siegel, "The ACCA Launches Online Career Center," *A/C, Heating & Refrigeration News*, June 16, 2003, p. 5.
143. See, for example, "Job Search Tips" *The America's Intelligence Wire*, May 17, 2004; and "What to Do When Your Job Search Stalls," *BusinessWeek* online, March 16, 2004.
144. A classic but still one of the most useful job search guides available: Richard Payne, *How to Get a Better Job Quicker* (New York: Mentor, 1987), pp. 54–87.
145. "Read This Before You Put a Resume Online," *Fortune*, May 24, 1999, pp. 290–291.
146. Sara Needleman, "Posting a Job Profile Online? Keep It Polished," August 29, 2006, *Wall Street Journal*, p. B7.
147. Payne, *How to Get a Better Job Quicker*.

Appendix for Chapter 10

Managing Your Career and Finding a Job

The individual must be responsible for creating and managing his or her own career. And, in today's job marketplace, knowing how to find and get a job is crucial.

Making Career Choices

It is unfortunate but true that many people don't put much thought into their careers. Some choose majors based on class scheduling preferences, favorite professors, or unstated psychological motives. Others stumble into jobs because "that's all that was available." If there was ever anything that cried out for fact-based decisions, it is choosing your career. The first and essential step is to learn as much as possible about your interests, aptitudes, and skills. The most direct way to do this is through experience, preferably a roster of jobs, internships, and experiences that will help you crystallize what it is you like to do and are great at. Getting experience doesn't just help career planning: In one study, the researchers sent out 9,400 fictitious resumes for "applicants" that differed in things like grade point average, major, and university. On-the-job experience—for instance, via internships—seemed to be the single most important factor in getting a job interview.[126] Beyond that, there are career tests and exercises you can use.

Identify Your Occupational Orientation Career-counseling expert John Holland says that personality (including values, motives, and needs) is one career choice determinant. For example, a person with a strong social orientation on Holland's Self-Directed Search (SDS) might be attracted to careers that entail interpersonal rather than intellectual or physical activities and to occupations such as social work. Based on research with his earlier Vocational Preference Test (VPT), Holland found six basic personality types or orientations (see www.self-directed-search.com).[127]

1. ***Realistic orientation.*** These people are attracted to occupations that involve physical activities requiring skill, strength, and coordination. Examples include forestry, farming, and agriculture.
2. ***Investigative orientation.*** Investigative people are attracted to careers that involve cognitive activities (thinking, organizing, understanding) rather than affective activities (feeling, acting, or interpersonal and emotional tasks). Examples include biologist, chemist, and college professor.
3. ***Artistic orientation.*** People here are attracted to careers that involve self-expression, artistic creation, expression of emotions, and individualistic activities. Examples include artists, advertising executives, and musicians.

4. ***Social orientation.*** These people are attracted to careers that involve interpersonal rather than intellectual or physical activities. Examples include clinical psychology, foreign service, and social work.
5. ***Enterprising orientation.*** Verbal activities aimed at influencing others characterize enterprising personalities. Examples include managers, lawyers, and public relations executives.
6. ***Conventional orientation.*** A conventional orientation favors careers that involve structured, rule-regulated activities, as well as careers in which it is expected that the employee subordinate his or her personal needs to those of the organization. Examples include accountants and bankers.

Most people have more than one "RIASEC" occupational orientation (they might be social, realistic, and investigative, for example), and Holland believes that the more similar or compatible these orientations are, the less internal conflict or indecision a person will face in making a career choice. You can take Holland's SDS online for a small fee (see www.self-directed-search.com). Of course, as someone gains experience, it is possible (or likely) that his or her RIASEC scores will change over time.[128]

Identify Your Skills You may have a "conventional" orientation, but whether you have *the skills* to be an accountant, banker, or credit manager will affect which occupation you ultimately choose. Therefore, you have to identify your skills. We presented some exercises for this earlier in this chapter, on page 310.

Aptitudes and Special Talents For career planning purposes, a person's aptitudes are usually measured with a test battery such as the general aptitude test battery (GATB), which most state one-stop career centers make available. This instrument measures various aptitudes including intelligence and mathematical ability. You can also use specialized tests, such as for mechanical comprehension. Holland's Self-Directed Search will also provide some insights into your aptitudes, as will O*NET.[129]

O*NET O*NET offers a free online "My Next Move" occupation and career assessment system (www.onetcenter.org/mynextmove.html). It includes *O*NET Interest Profiler*, a tool that offers customized career suggestions on over 900 different careers based on a person's interests and level of education and work experience. Users obtain important information including skills, tasks, salaries, and employment outlook for occupations.[130]

Identify Your Career Anchors Professor Edgar Schein says that career planning is a continuing process of

CHAPTER 10

As noted in the accompanying text, O*NET offers a free comprehensive online "My Next Move" occupation and career assessment system for building your future career (www.onetcenter.org/mynextmove.html).

Source: From O*NET website, www.onetonline.org.

discovery—one in which a person slowly develops a clearer occupational self-concept in terms of what his or her talents, abilities, motives, needs, attitudes, and values are. Schein also says that as you learn more about yourself, it becomes apparent that you have a dominant *career anchor*, a concern or value that you will not give up if a [career] choice has to be made.

Career anchors, as their name implies, are the pivots around which a person's career swings; a person becomes conscious of them because of learning, through experience, about his or her talents and abilities, motives and needs, and attitudes and values. Based on his research at the Massachusetts Institute of Technology, Schein believes that career anchors are difficult to predict because they are evolutionary and a product of a process of discovery. Some people may never find out what their career anchors are until they have to make a major choice—such as whether to take the promotion to the headquarters staff or strike out on their own by starting a business. It is at this point that all the person's past work experiences, interests, aptitudes, and orientations converge into a meaningful pattern that helps show what (career anchor) is the most important factor in driving the person's career choices. Based on his study of MIT graduates, Schein identified five career anchors.[131]

Technical/Functional Competence People who had a strong technical/functional career anchor tended to avoid decisions that would drive them toward general management. Instead, they made decisions that would enable them to remain and grow in their chosen technical or functional fields.

Managerial Competence Other people showed a strong motivation to become managers, and their career experience enabled them to believe they had the skills and values required. A management position of high responsibility is their ultimate goal. When pressed to explain why they believed they had the skills necessary to gain such positions, many in Schein's research sample answered that they were qualified because of what they saw as their competencies in a combination of three areas: (1) *analytical competence* (ability to identify, analyze, and solve problems under conditions of incomplete information and uncertainty); (2) *interpersonal competence* (ability to influence, supervise, lead, manipulate, and control people at all levels); and (3) *emotional competence* (the capacity to be stimulated by emotional and interpersonal crises rather than exhausted or debilitated by them, and the capacity to bear high levels of responsibility without becoming paralyzed).

Creativity Some of the graduates had become successful entrepreneurs. To Schein these people seemed to have a need "to build or create something that was entirely their own product—a product or process that bears their name, a company of their own, or a personal fortune that reflects their accomplishments." For example, one graduate had become a successful purchaser, restorer, and renter of townhouses in a large city; another had built a successful consulting firm.

Autonomy and Independence Some seemed driven by the need to be on their own, free of the dependence that can arise when a person elects to work in a large organization where promotions, transfers, and salary decisions make them subordinate to others. Many of these graduates also had a strong technical/functional orientation. Instead of pursuing this orientation in an organization, they had decided to become consultants, working either alone or as part of a relatively small firm. Others had become professors of business, freelance writers, and proprietors of a small retail business.

Security A few of the graduates were mostly concerned with long-run career stability and job security. They seemed willing to do what was required to maintain job security, a decent income, and a stable future in the form of a good retirement program and benefits. For those interested in *geographic security*, maintaining a stable, secure career in familiar surroundings was generally more important than pursuing superior career choices, if choosing the latter meant injecting instability or insecurity into their lives by forcing them to pull up roots and move to another city. For others, security meant *organizational security*. They might today opt for government jobs, where tenure still tends to be a way of life. They were much more willing to let their employers decide what their careers should be.

Assessing Career Anchors To help you identify career anchors, take a few sheets of blank paper and write out your answers to the following questions:[132]

1. What was your major area of concentration (if any) in high school? Why did you choose that area? How did you feel about it?
2. What is (or was) your major area of concentration in college? Why did you choose that area? How did you feel about it?
3. What was your first job after school? (Include military if relevant.) What were you looking for in your first job?
4. What were your ambitions or long-range goals when you started your career? Have they changed? When? Why?
5. What was your first major change of job or company? What were you looking for in your next job?
6. What was your next major change of job, company, or career? Why did you initiate or accept it? What were you looking for? (Do this for each of your major changes of job, company, or career.)

7. As you look back over your career, identify some times you have especially enjoyed. What was it about those times that you enjoyed?
8. As you look back, identify some times you have not especially enjoyed. What was it about those times you did not enjoy?
9. Have you ever refused a job move or promotion? Why?
10. Now review all your answers carefully, as well as the descriptions for the five career anchors (technical/functional competence, managerial competence, creativity and independence, autonomy, security). Based on your answers to the questions, rate, for yourself, each of the anchors from 1 to 5. 1 equals low importance, 5 equals high importance.

    Technical/functional competence _____
    Managerial competence _____
    Creativity and independence _____
    Autonomy _____
    Security _____

What Do You Want to Do?

Identify High-Potential Occupations Learning about your skills and interests is only step one in choosing an occupation. You also have to identify those occupations that fit your occupational orientations, skills, career anchors, and occupational preferences, and that are (preferably) in high demand in the years to come.

Here, use the Internet. The U.S. Department of Labor's online *Occupational Outlook Handbook* (www.bls.gov/oco) is updated each year, and provides detailed descriptions and information on hundreds of occupations. O*NET (www.onetonline.org/) provides occupational demand projections. Figure 10A-1 lists some other sites to use both for occupational information and for information on where to turn to when searching for a job—the subject to which we now turn.

Selected Online Sources of Occupational Information

- All Star Jobs
- CampusCareeerCenter
- CareerBliss.com
- CareerOneSto
- CareerExplorer
- CareerOverview
- CityTownInfo
- College Central Network
- CollegeGrad.com
- Construct My Future (information about construction careers)
- Cool Works
- EducationPlanner
- eMedicalAssistants
- Explore Health Careers
- Green Jobs Ready
- hotjobs.com
- International Jobs
- Job Search Intelligence
- MyArtsCareer
- Occupational Outlook Handbook
- Professional Development for Teachers
- Quintessential Careers
- ResumeINDEX
- SalaryList
- Science Buddies—Careers
- Simply Hired
- Snag a Job

FIGURE 10A-1 Selected Online Sources of Occupational Information

Source: Based on http://mappingyourfuture.org/planyourcareer/careerresources.htm, accessed October 8, 2015.

Finding the Right Job

Your next step is to find a job that you want in the company and locale where you want to work.

Before leaving a current job, however, make sure leaving is what you want. Many people, dissatisfied at work, assume it must be the job or the occupation. But why switch from being a lawyer to a teacher, when it's not the profession but that law firm's 80-hour weeks that are the problem?

One must use a process of elimination. For example, you may like your occupation and employer, but not how your specific job is structured. Others may find their employers' ways of doing things are the problem. Or, it may in fact be the occupation.

In any case, the solution should fit the cause. For example, if, after thinking it through, you are satisfied with your occupation and where you work, but not with your job as it's organized now, try reconfiguring it. For example, consider alternative work arrangements such as flexible hours or telecommuting; delegate or eliminate the job functions you least prefer; and seek out a "stretch assignment" that will let you work on something you find more challenging.[133] If it's the specific employer, look elsewhere.

Job Search Techniques In Chapter 5 (Personnel Planning and Recruiting), we saw that employers use various tools to find recruits, so it shouldn't be surprising that job seekers should use basically the same tools.

Personal Contacts Generally, the most popular way to seek job leads and interviews is to rely on personal contacts (networking) such as friends and relatives.[134] So, let as many responsible people as possible know that you are looking for a job and also what kind of job you want. (Beware, though, if you don't want your job search getting back to your current boss. If that is the case, then just pick out two or three very close friends and ask them to be discreet in seeking a job for you.)

No matter how close your friends or relatives are to you, by the way, you do not want to impose too much on them. It is usually best to ask them for the name of someone they think you should talk to in the kind of firm in which you'd like to work, and then do the digging yourself.

Trends Shaping HR: Digital and Social Media Job searching is the flip side of recruiting, so for anyone who wants to attract recruiters, social media is obviously important. For example, it's been estimated that over 90% of recruiters use LinkedIn, so use this source wisely.[135] Don't turn off recruiters with sloppy photos or writing. Do include recommendations, document your accomplishments, and (if possible) send well-crafted updates and position statements on important issues to the members of your LinkedIn groups.

Once you get an interview, acing it means knowing as much as possible about the prospective employer and what it's looking for in employees, and here social media tools are excellent sources of such information.[136] For example, you will find lists of new hires and demographic information about employees on the employer's LinkedIn site. Following the employer's official Twitter accounts and blogs can reveal things like changes in the company's strategies, as well as show you did your homework. Its executives may also have their own "unofficial" Twitter accounts and blogs. Use these for insights into the issues they face. Similarly, use other social media including Twitter to help establish your brand, for instance, by sharing relevant news.

New Web sites aim to help employers find "passive candidates," plausible candidates who aren't actively looking for jobs.[137] For example, Poacht gleans employment information from people's LinkedIn profiles (without their names or other identifying information), and asks them if they're willing to switch jobs. Switch is an app that suggests jobs to users who then swipe right or left depending on whether they're interested in the jobs.

And remember that the head of Elance (which places millions of short-term professionals via its site) says those on its site are viewed as "mobile, independent bundles of skills," so keep updating your skills and remain adaptable.[138]

Employers scour social media, so make sure your name stands out. For example, job seekers can enhance their professional reputations by creating a Twitter presence. Those "Liking" a company on Facebook may receive early notice of job openings. Spend a few minutes every day on LinkedIn making new connections, and share links and advice with those in your LinkedIn network.[139] Join LinkedIn industry groups to build visibility. Make sure your résumé is in PDF format and readable on a smart phone screen. To bring yourself to recruiters' attention, follow up on comments they make on their blogs or in industry Web sites. Fewer job searchers are using paper résumés and are instead using social résumés. *Social résumés* provide snapshots of who the job searcher is by combining text material, photos, and samples of a person's work in infographic résumés posted on social media such as Twitter, LinkedIn, and blogs.[140] Finally, remember that the prospective employer will probably Google you before extending the offer, and may ask for access to your Facebook and LinkedIn pages. ■

Online Job Boards and Employer Web Sites Most large job search sites such as Monster.com have local-area search capabilities. Useful open-job aggregator sites include Indeed.com and SimplyHired.com. Idealist.com is good for nonprofit jobs, and there's USAJobs for federal jobs.[141] Use the *Wall Street Journal*'s career Web site (www.careerjournal.com) to search for jobs by occupation and location. Most big-city newspapers also have their own (or links to) online local job listings. In addition to job boards like Monster and specialized ones (like www.theladder.com), virtually all large companies, industries, and crafts have their own specialized sites.[142] For example, the Air Conditioning Contractors in America (www.acca.org/careers) and Financial Executives International (www.fei.org) make it easy for industry employers and prospective employees to match their needs. Remember to use mobile services, for instance, accessing jobs via the Careerbuilder iPhone portal.

Answering Advertisements Answering ads tends to be a low-probability way to get a job, and this is particularly so as the level of jobs increases. Furthermore, automated applicant tracking services now crunch through thousands of résumés in seconds, making it even harder to stand out by answering ads. Nevertheless, good sources of classified ads for professionals and managers include the *New York Times*, the *Wall Street Journal*, and specialized journals in your field that list job openings. All these sources also post the positions online, of course.

Many employers don't even accept application letters or résumés anymore. For those who do, be sure to create the right impression with the materials you submit; check the style, grammar, neatness, and so forth, and check your résumé to make sure it's geared to the job for which you are applying. In your cover letter or email, be sure to specifically address why your background and accomplishments are appropriate to the advertised position; you must respond clearly to the company's identified needs.[143]

Be careful in replying to blind ads, however (such as those with just a post office box). Some executive search firms and employers will run ads even when no position exists just to gauge the market, and there is some risk that you blunder into responding to your own firm.

Employment Agencies Agencies are especially good at placing people in jobs paying up to about $80,000, but they can be useful for higher-paying jobs as well. The employer usually pays the fees for professional and management jobs. Assuming you know the job you want, review a few back issues of your paper's Sunday classified ads and sites like LinkedIn to identify agencies that handle the positions you want. Approach three or four initially, preferably in response to specific ads, and avoid signing any contract that gives an agency the exclusive right to place you.

States' one-stop career centers can be helpful. In them, job seekers can not only apply for unemployment benefits, but also register with the state job service, talk to career counselors, use computers to write résumés and access the Internet, take tests, and use career libraries offering books and videos on various employment topics. In some centers job hunters can make use of free computers and photocopiers to facilitate job searches.

Executive Recruiters We've seen that employers retain executive recruiters to seek out top talent for their clients; employers always pay any fees. They do not do career counseling, but if you know the job you want, it pays to contact a few (keeping in mind however that most use LinkedIn to find passive candidates). Send/email your résumé and a cover note summarizing your objective in precise terms, including job title and the size of company desired, work-related accomplishments, current salary, and salary requirements. (Beware, because some firms call themselves executive search or career consultants but do no searches: In return for an (often hefty) fee they help you manage your search. Remember that with a search firm you never pay a fee.)

Career Counselors Career counselors will not help you find a job per se; rather, they specialize in aptitude testing, career counseling, and resume preparation. They are listed under "Career Counseling" or "Vocational Guidance." Their services usually cost $450 or so and include psychological testing and interviews with an experienced career counselor. Check the firm's services, prices, and history as well as the credentials of the person you will be dealing with.

Executive Search Consultants Executive marketing consultants manage your job-hunting campaign. They generally are not recruiters and do not have jobs to fill. Depending on the services you choose, your cost will range from $600 to $5,000 or more. The process may involve months of weekly meetings. Services include résumé and letter writing, interview skill building, and developing a full job-hunting campaign. Before approaching a consultant, it's advisable to do your own self-appraisal (as explained in this appendix) and read books like Richard Bolles's *What Color Is Your Parachute?*

Also make sure to do your due diligence, and remember these consultants are not recruiters and will not get you a job—you must do the legwork. Then check the Better Business Bureau, and decide which of these firms (if any) is for you.

Writing Your Résumé Your résumé is often still an important selling document, one that can determine whether you get offered a job interview. Of course, you should not produce a slipshod résumé: Avoid overcrowded pages, difficult-to-read copies, typographical errors, and other problems of this sort. And do not use a make-do résumé. Produce a new résumé for each job you are applying for, gearing your job objective and accomplishments to the job you want. Here are some résumé pointers, as offered by employment counselor Richard Payne and other experts.[144]

Start your résumé with your name, home and e-mail address, and home or cell phone number. Next, state your *job objective*. This should summarize in one sentence the specific position you want, where you want to do it (type and size of company), and a special reason an employer might have for wanting you to fill the job. For example, "Marketing manager in a medium-size e-commerce company in a situation in which strong creative skills would be valuable."

For each of your previous jobs, write a paragraph that shows job title, whom you reported to directly and indirectly, who reported to you, how many people reported to you, the operational and human resource budgets you controlled, and what your job entailed (in one sentence).

Your accomplishments should be the heart of your résumé. These show for each of your previous jobs: (1) a concrete action you took and why you took it and (2) the specific result of your action—the "payoff." For example, "As production supervisor, I introduced a new process to replace costly hand soldering of component parts. The new process reduced assembly time per unit from 30 to 10 minutes and reduced labor costs by over 60%." Use several of these statements for each job.

Keep your résumé to 2 pages or less, and list education, military service (if any), and personal background (hobbies, interests, associations) on the last page. For most job applications today, it's important to write a résumé that is electronically readable. Many applicant tracking systems use software to scan through large numbers of résumés, screening out those that don't seem to match (often based on the absence of certain key words). Therefore present your qualifications using powerful key words appropriate to the job or jobs for which you are applying. For example, a trainer might use key words and phrases such as: *computer-based training, interactive video*, and *group facilitator*.

If you post your résumé on the Web, experts suggest taking precautions. At a minimum, date your résumé (in case it lands on your boss's desk 2 years from now). Also insert a disclaimer forbidding unauthorized transmission by headhunters; check ahead of time to see who has access to the database on which you're posting your résumé; and consider cloaking your identity by listing your capabilities but not your name or employer—just an anonymous e-mail account to receive inquiries.[145]

Online Bios Employers often encourage or require their professionals and managers to post brief biographies on corporate intranets or Web sites. These bios let other employees know about their colleagues' expertise; they can also attract recruiters' inquiries. Tips for writing such bios include:[146]

Fill it with details. "The more information you enter, the more likely a person seeking someone with your background will find you...."
Avoid touchy subjects. For example, avoid religion and politics.
Look the part. Your profile may require posting photos. If so, dress in professional attire.
Make it search friendly. Make sure your profile contains the key words you think someone searching for someone with your background and expertise would be looking for, such as *manager, supervisor*, or *engineer*.
Use abbreviations. Abbreviations are important. For example, someone searching the site might more readily punch in "MBA" than "Masters in Business Administration."
Say it with numbers. Describe specifically how your work has contributed to your current employer's and past employer's bottom lines.
Proofread. Carefully proofread your online profile, as you would your résumé.

Handling the Interview

You have done all your homework, and now you have an interview scheduled with the person who is responsible for hiring for the job you want. What must you do to excel in the interview? Here are some suggestions.

Prepare, Prepare, Prepare First, preparation is essential. Before the interview, learn all you can about the employer, the job, and the people doing the recruiting. Search the Internet (or your library) to find out what is happening in the employer's field. Who is the competition? How are they doing?

Uncover the Interviewer's Needs Spend as little time as possible answering your interviewer's first questions and as much time as possible getting the person to describe his or her needs—what the person is looking to get accomplished and the type of person needed. Use open-ended questions, such as "Could you tell me more about that?"

Relate Yourself to the Person's Needs Once you understand the person your interviewer is looking for and the sorts of problems he or she needs solved, you are in a good position to describe your own accomplishments in terms of the interviewer's needs.[147] Start by saying something like, "One of the problem areas you've indicated is important to you is similar to a problem I once faced." Then state the problem, describe your solution, and reveal the results.

Make a Good Appearance and Show Enthusiasm Appearance, a firm handshake, and visual cues such as looking the interviewer in the eyes are crucial. Remember that studies of interviews show that in almost 80% of the cases, interviewers make up their minds about the applicant during the first few moments of the interview. A good first impression may turn bad during the interview, but it is unlikely. Bad first impressions, however, are almost impossible to overcome.

11

Establishing Strategic Pay Plans

Ariel Skelley/Getty Images

LEARNING OBJECTIVES

11-1 List the basic factors determining pay rates.

11-2 Define and give an example of how to conduct a job evaluation.

11-3 Explain in detail how to establish a market-competitive pay plan.

11-4 Explain how to price managerial and professional jobs.

11-5 Explain the difference between competency-based and traditional pay plans.

11-6 Describe the importance of total rewards for improving employee engagement.

In the grocery business, when Walmart opens a store, the other stores' usual reaction is to cut costs, particularly wages and benefits. So as Wegmans Food Markets, Inc., adds more stores and increasingly competes with Walmart, its management needs to decide this: Should we cut pay to better compete based on cost, or pursue a different compensation policy?[1] We'll see how Wegmans boosted profits by raising pay.

WHERE ARE WE NOW ...

Once you've appraised and coached your employees, they of course expect to be paid. Prudent employers don't set pay rates arbitrarily. Each employee's pay should make sense in terms of what other employees earn, and this requires a pay plan. The main purpose of this chapter is to show you how to establish a pay plan. The main topics we cover are basic factors in determining pay rates; job evaluation methods; how to create a market-competitive pay plan; pricing managerial and professional jobs; contemporary topics in compensation; and total rewards for employee engagement. The next chapter focuses specifically on pay-for-performance and incentive plans.

LEARNING OBJECTIVE 11-1
List the basic factors determining pay rates.

employee compensation
All forms of pay or rewards going to employees and arising from their employment.

direct financial payments
Pay in the form of wages, salaries, incentives, commissions, and bonuses.

indirect financial payments
Pay in the form of financial benefits such as insurance.

Basic Factors in Determining Pay Rates

Employee compensation includes all forms of pay going to employees and arising from their employment. It has two main components, **direct financial payments** (wages, salaries, incentives, commissions, and bonuses) and **indirect financial payments** (financial benefits like employer-paid insurance and vacations).

In turn, employers can make direct financial payments to employees based on increments of time or based on performance. Time-based pay still predominates. Blue-collar and clerical workers receive hourly or daily wages, for instance. Others, like managers or Web designers, tend to be salaried and paid weekly, monthly, or yearly.

The second direct payment option is to pay for performance. For example, piecework ties compensation to the amount of production (or number of "pieces") the worker turns out. Sales commissions tie pay to sales. Many employers' pay plans combine time-based pay and incentives.

In this chapter, we explain how to formulate plans for paying employees a time-based wage or salary. Subsequent chapters cover performance-based financial incentives and bonuses (Chapter 12) and employee benefits (Chapter 13).

Several factors should influence any pay plan's design. These include strategic policy considerations, as well as equity, legal, and union considerations.

Aligning Total Rewards with Strategy

The compensation plan should first advance the firm's strategic aims—management should produce an *aligned reward strategy.* This means creating a compensation package that produces the employee behaviors the firm needs to achieve its competitive strategy.[2] Put another way, the rewards should provide a clear pathway between each reward and specific business goals.[3]

We will see that many employers formulate a total rewards strategy to support their strategic aims. *Total rewards* encompass traditional pay, incentives, and benefits, but also "rewards" such as more challenging jobs (job design), career development, and recognition.

Table 11-1 lists illustrative questions to ask when crafting a strategy-oriented pay policy.

HR in Practice at the Hotel Paris Even a casual review by Lisa Cruz and the CFO made it clear that the Hotel Paris's compensation plan wasn't designed to support the firm's new strategic goals. To see how they handled this, see the case on page 380 of this chapter.

Equity and Its Impact on Pay Rates

In studies at Emory University, researchers investigated how capuchin monkeys reacted to inequitable pay. Some monkeys got sweet grapes in return for trading pebbles; others got cucumber slices. If a monkey receiving a cucumber slice saw a neighbor get grapes, it slammed down the pebble or refused to eat.[4] It seems even lower primates may demand fair treatment in pay.

Among humans, too, *the equity theory of motivation* postulates that people are motivated to maintain a balance between what they perceive as their contributions and their rewards. Equity theory states that if a person perceives an inequity,

TABLE 11-1 Do Our Compensation Policies Support Our Strategic Aims?

- What are our strategic aims?
- What employee behaviors and skills do we need to achieve our strategic aims?
- What compensation policies and practices—salary, incentive plans, and benefits—will help to produce the employee behaviors we need to achieve our strategic aims?

a tension or drive will develop that motivates him or her to reduce the tension and perceived inequity. Research tends to support equity theory, particularly as it applies to those underpaid.[5] For example, in one study turnover of retail buyers was significantly lower when the buyers perceived fair treatment in rewards and in how employers allocated rewards.[6] Overpaying can sometimes backfire, too, perhaps "due to feelings of guilt or discomfort."[7]

In compensation, one can address *external, internal, individual*, and *procedural* equity.[8]

- ***External equity*** refers to how a job's pay rate in one company compares to the job's pay rate in other companies.
- ***Internal equity*** refers to how fair the job's pay rate is when compared to other jobs within the same company (for instance, is the sales manager's pay fair, when compared to what the production manager earns?).
- ***Individual equity*** refers to the fairness of an individual's pay as compared with what his or her coworkers are earning for the same or very similar jobs within the company, based on each person's performance.
- ***Procedural equity*** refers to the "perceived fairness of the processes and procedures used to make decisions regarding the allocation of pay."[9]

Managers use various means to address such equity issues. For example, they use salary surveys (surveys of what other employers are paying) to monitor and maintain external equity. They use job analysis and comparisons of each job ("job evaluation") to maintain internal equity. They use performance appraisal and incentive pay to maintain individual equity. And they use communications, grievance mechanisms, and employees' participation to help ensure that employees view the pay process as procedurally fair. Some firms administer attitude surveys to monitor employees' pay satisfaction. Questions typically include, "How satisfied are you with your pay?" and "What factors do you believe are used when your pay is determined?"[10]

To head off discussions that might prompt feelings of internal inequity, some firms maintain strict secrecy over pay rates, while others publicize them.[11] However, "open pay" policies can backfire. In one firm, employees vigorously opposed paying a high salary to a great candidate unless everyone else's pay went up, too, for instance.[12] As of now, the research concerning pay secrecy is inconclusive, and most employers don't have open pay policies.[13] For external equity, online pay sites like Salary.com make it easy to see what one could earn elsewhere.

Davis-Bacon Act (1931)
A 1931 law that sets wage rates for laborers employed by contractors working for the federal government.

Walsh-Healey Public Contract Act (1936)
A 1936 law that requires minimum wage and working conditions for employees working on any government contract amounting to more than $10,000.

Legal Considerations in Compensation

Employers do not have free reign in designing pay plans. Various laws specify things like minimum wages, overtime rates, and benefits.[14] For example, the **1931 Davis-Bacon Act** lets the secretary of labor set wage rates for laborers and mechanics employed by contractors working for the federal government. The **1936 Walsh-Healey Public Contract Act** sets basic labor standards for employees working on any government contract that amounts to more than $10,000. It contains minimum wage, maximum hour, and safety and health provisions, and requires time-and-a-half pay for work over 40 hours a week. **Title VII of the 1964 Civil Rights Act** makes it unlawful for employers to discriminate against any individual with respect to hiring, compensation, terms, conditions, or privileges of employment because of race, color, religion, sex, or national origin.[15] We'll look next at other important compensation-related laws.

Title VII of the 1964 Civil Rights Act
This act makes it unlawful for employers to discriminate against any individual with respect to hiring, compensation, terms, conditions, or privileges of employment because of race, color, religion, sex, or national origin.

Fair Labor Standards Act (1938)
This 1938 act provides for minimum wages, maximum hours, overtime pay, and child labor protection. The law, amended many times, covers most employees.

THE 1938 FAIR LABOR STANDARDS ACT The **Fair Labor Standards Act**, originally passed in **1938** and since amended many times, contains minimum wage, maximum hours, overtime pay, equal pay, record-keeping, and child labor provisions that are familiar to most working people.[16] It covers virtually all U.S. workers engaged in the production and/or sale of goods for interstate and foreign commerce. In addition, agricultural workers and those employed by certain larger retail and service companies are included. State fair labor standards laws cover most employers not covered by the Fair Labor Standards Act (FLSA).[17]

One familiar provision governs *overtime pay.* It says employers must pay overtime at a rate of at least one-and-a-half times normal pay for any hours worked over 40 in a workweek. Thus, if a worker covered by the act works 44 hours in one week, he or she must be paid for 4 of those hours at a rate equal to one-and-a-half times the hourly or weekly base rate the person would have earned for 40 hours.[18] For example, if the person earns $12 an hour (or $480 for a 40-hour week), he or she would be paid at the rate of $18 per hour ($12 times 1.5) for each of the 4 overtime hours worked, or $72 ($18 times 4) for the extra 4 hours. If the employee instead receives time off for the overtime hours, the employer must compute the number of hours granted off at the one-and-a-half-times rate (6 hours off for the 4 hours of overtime in our case), in lieu of overtime pay. LinkedIn recently paid $5.8 million in overtime violation damages to 359 former and current employees.[19]

KNOW YOUR EMPLOYMENT LAW

The Workday

Employers need to be vigilant about employees who arrive early or leave late, lest the extra time spent on the employer's property obligate the employer to compensate the employee for that time. For example, a diligent employee may get dropped off at work early and spend, say, 20 minutes before his or her day actually starts doing work-related chores such as compiling a list of clients to call that day. While there is no hard and fast rule, some courts follow the rule that employees who arrive 15 or more minutes early are presumed to be working unless the employer can prove otherwise.[20] If using time clocks, employers should always instruct employees not to clock in more than 5–10 minutes early (or out 5–10 minutes late). Smart phones give employers further reason to meticulously record workers' hours. An app from the Department of Labor lets employees track their work hours.[21] The Chicago Police Department distributed smart phones to its officers in the field. One police officer subsequently sued, claiming that he wasn't paid overtime for the hours he spent using his smart phone off the clock. Vendors such as Pacific Timesheet (www.pacifictimesheet.com) provide mobile payroll time sheets.[22] Outside the office, employees can fill these in via their iPhones or similar devices.[23] Newer time clocks have iPad-like touch screens and reduce "buddy punching" with instant photos and biometric sensors.[24] ■

The FLSA also sets a *minimum wage*. This sets a floor for employees covered by the act (and usually bumps up wages for practically all workers when Congress raises the minimum). The minimum wage was $7.25 in 2015. Many states have their own minimum wage. For example, the minimum wage as of 2016 is $10.00 in California and Massachusetts.[25] New York state is debating raising its minimum wage to $15 per hour. Various cities have set their own (higher) minimum wages.[26] Under new federal rules, workers on federal contracts earn a minimum of $10.10 per hour.[27]

FLSA *child labor provisions* prohibit employing minors between 16 and 18 years old in hazardous occupations, and carefully restrict employment of those under 16.

A great many employers today pay people as "independent contractors" rather than as employees. Strictly speaking, these people are like consultants, and therefore are not covered by the FLSA. The Know Your Employment Law feature nearby explains about paying this type of worker.

EXEMPT/NONEXEMPT Specific categories of employees are *exempt* from the FLSA or certain provisions of the act, and particularly from the act's overtime provisions.

FIGURE 11-1 Some Typical Exempt, Nonexempt Job Titles

EXEMPT	NONEXEMPT
Lawyers	Paralegals
Medical doctors	Accounting clerks
Dentists	Bookkeepers
Engineers (with degrees)	Licensed practical nurses
Teachers	Clerical employees
Scientists	Most secretaries (although some, such as the CEO's secretary, might be exempt)
Registered nurses	Lab technicians
General managers	
Pharmacists	
Administrative employees*	

* The administrative exemption is designed for relatively high-level employees whose main job is to "keep the business running." Examples of administrative functions, whose high level employees may typically be exempt, include labor relations and personnel (human resources employees), payroll and finance (including budgeting and benefits management), records maintenance, accounting and tax, marketing and advertising (as differentiated from direct sales), quality control, public relations (including shareholder or investment relations, and government relations), legal and regulatory compliance, and some computer-related jobs (such as network, internet and database administration).

They are "exempt employees." A person's exemption depends on his or her responsibilities, duties, and salary. Bona fide executive, administrative (like office managers), and professional employees (like architects) are generally exempt from the minimum wage and overtime requirements of the act.[28] A white-collar worker earning more than $100,000 and performing any one exempt administrative, executive, or professional duty is automatically ineligible for overtime pay. Other employees can generally earn up to $23,660 per year and still automatically get overtime pay (so most employees earning less than $455 per week are nonexempt and earn overtime).[29] Figure 11-1 lists some examples of typically exempt and nonexempt jobs. In 2014 President Obama instructed the U.S. Labor Department to devise policies to raise the exempt threshold from $455 per week to $984 per week, or about $50,000 per year.[30] And in 2015 his administration proposed setting the threshold at $50,440 a year, which would include many workers classified as managers.[31]

If an employee is exempt from the FLSA's minimum wage provisions, then he or she is also exempt from its overtime pay provisions. However, certain employees are *always* exempt from overtime pay provisions. They include, among others, agricultural employees, live-in household employees, taxi drivers, and motion picture theater employees.[32]

Identifying exemptions is tricky. As noted, some jobs—for example, top managers and lawyers—are clearly exempt, while others—such as office workers earning less than $23,660 per year—are clearly nonexempt (although again, that may have risen to $50,440 when you read this). But beyond that, one should review the job before classifying it as exempt or nonexempt. Figure 11-2 presents a procedure for making this decision. Make sure, for instance, that the job currently does in fact require, say, an exempt-type supervisory duty.[33]

FLSA exemption lawsuits are on the rise. "Supervisors" are saying they don't really supervise two or more employees.[34] And the U.S. Supreme Court held that drug company sales reps that call on doctors are FLSA-exempt outside salespersons.[35]

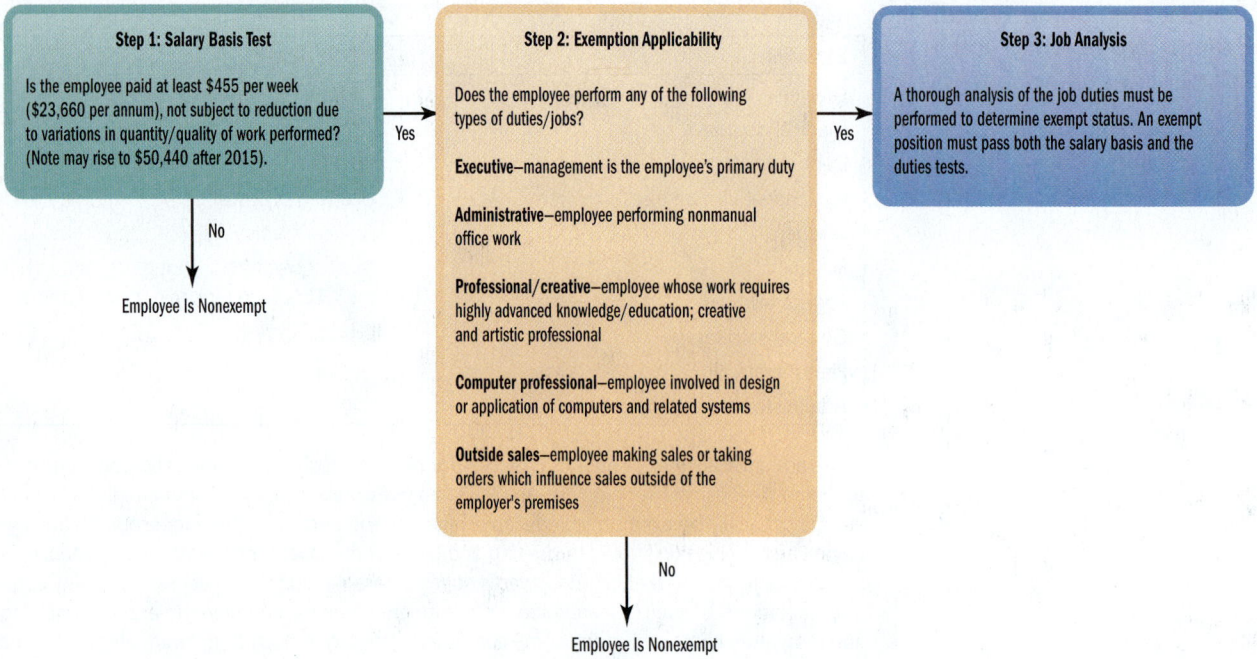

FIGURE 11-2 Who is Exempt?; Who is Not Exempt?

Source: Based on www.flsa.com/coverage.html, accessed August 5, 2011; and www.dol.gov/elaws/esa/flsa/screen75.asp, accessed September 12, 2015.

KNOW YOUR EMPLOYMENT LAW

The Independent Contractor

Whether someone is an employee or an *independent contractor* is a continuing concern for employers.[36] For example, a federal court ruled that most of FedEx's roughly 15,000 owner-operator delivery people were independent contractors, not employees.[37]

Why claim that someone is an independent contractor? Because the FLSA's overtime and most other requirements do not apply, and the employer need not pay unemployment compensation; payroll taxes; Social Security taxes; or city, state, and federal income taxes or compulsory workers' compensation for that worker.

The problem is that many so-called independent contractor relationships aren't independent contractor relationships. In general, an individual is an independent contractor if the payer has the right to control or direct only the result of the work and not what will be done and how it will be done.[38] However, there is no single rule or test. Instead, the courts will look at the total situation. The major consideration is this: The more the employer controls what the worker does and how he or she does it, the more likely it is that the courts will find the worker to be an employee. Figure 11-3 lists some factors courts will consider. The IRS lists rules at its Web site.[39] Uber faces lawsuits that its drivers are employees, not independent contractors.

To minimize the risks of independent contractor misclassification, employers should execute written agreements with all independent contractors; you'll find samples online.[40] Furthermore, employers should not impose work rules on or attempt to prohibit independent contractors from working for others. They should require independent contractors to provide their own tools and to be separately incorporated business entities.[41]

Because the Affordable Care Act covers employers with 50 or more employees, government agencies will be looking more closely at employers' independent contractors. To minimize problems, some employers are having staffing companies supply more of their workforce, thus staying below the 50-employee limit.[42] ■

FIGURE 11-3 Independent Contractor

Source: Reproduced with permission from the publisher BLR—Business & Legal Resources (www.HR.BLR.com)

Independent Contractor

Managers are to use the following checklist to classify individuals as independent contractors. If more than three questions are answered "yes," the manager will confer with human resources regarding the classification. (EE = Employees, IC = Independent Contractors)

Factors which show control :

	Yes/EE	No/IC	N/A
1. Worker must comply with instructions.	☐	☐	☐
2. Worker is trained by person hired.	☐	☐	☐
3. Worker's services are integrated in business.	☐	☐	☐
4. Worker must personally render services.	☐	☐	☐
5. Worker cannot hire or fire assistants.	☐	☐	☐
6. Work relationship is continuous or indefinite.	☐	☐	☐
7. Work hours are present.	☐	☐	☐
8. Worker must devote full time to this business.	☐	☐	☐
9. Work is done on the employer's premises.	☐	☐	☐
10. Worker cannot control order or sequence.	☐	☐	☐
11. Worker submits oral or written reports.	☐	☐	☐
12. Worker is paid at specific intervals.	☐	☐	☐
13. Worker's business expenses are reimbursed.	☐	☐	☐
14. Worker is provided with tools or materials.	☐	☐	☐
15. Worker has no significant investment.	☐	☐	☐
16. Worker has no opportunity for profit/loss.	☐	☐	☐
17. Worker is not engaged by many different firms.	☐	☐	☐
18. Worker does not offer services to public.	☐	☐	☐
19. Worker may be discharged by employer.	☐	☐	☐
20. Worker can terminate without liability.	☐	☐	☐

Equal Pay Act
A 1963 amendment to the Fair Labor Standards Act designed to require equal pay for women doing the same work as men.

1963 EQUAL PAY ACT The **Equal Pay Act**, an amendment to the Fair Labor Standards Act, states that employees of one sex may not be paid wages at a rate lower than that paid to employees of the opposite sex for doing roughly equivalent work. Specifically, if the work requires equal skills, effort, and responsibility and involves similar working conditions, employees of both sexes must receive equal pay, unless the differences in pay stem from a seniority system, a merit system, the quantity or quality of production, or "any factor other than sex."

Employee Retirement Income Security Act (ERISA)
The 1974 law that provides government protection of pensions for all employees with company pension plans. It also regulates vesting rights (employees who leave before retirement may claim compensation from the pension plan).

1974 EMPLOYEE RETIREMENT INCOME SECURITY ACT Aimed at protecting employees' pensions, the **Employee Retirement Income Security Act (ERISA)** provides for the creation of government-run, employer-financed corporations to protect employees against the failure of their employers' pension plans. It also sets regulations regarding vesting rights (*vesting* refers to the equity or ownership the employees build up in their pension plans should their employment terminate before retirement). ERISA also regulates *portability rights* (the transfer of an employee's vested rights from one organization to another). It also contains fiduciary standards to prevent dishonesty in pension plan funding.

OTHER LEGISLATION AFFECTING COMPENSATION Various other laws influence compensation decisions. For example, the *Age Discrimination in Employment Act* prohibits age discrimination against employees who are 40 years of age and older in all aspects of employment, including compensation.[43] The *Americans with Disabilities*

Act prohibits discrimination against qualified persons with disabilities in all aspects of employment. The *Family and Medical Leave Act* aims to entitle eligible employees, both men and women, to take up to 12 weeks of unpaid, job-protected leave for the birth of a child or for the care of a child, spouse, or parent. And various executive orders require employers that are federal government contractors or subcontractors to not discriminate in certain employment areas, including compensation.

Each state has its own *workers' compensation laws.* Among other things, these aim to provide prompt, sure, and reasonable income to victims of work-related accidents. The *Social Security Act of 1935* (as amended) provides for unemployment compensation for workers unemployed through no fault of their own for up to 26 weeks (and recently extended), and for retirement benefits. (We'll discuss Social Security benefits in a later chapter.) The federal wage garnishment law limits the amount of an employee's earnings that employers can withhold (garnish) per week, and protects the worker from discharge due to garnishment.

Union Influences on Compensation Decisions

Unions and labor relations laws also influence pay plan design. The National Labor Relations Act of 1935 (Wagner Act) granted employees the right to unionize and to bargain collectively. Historically, the wage rate has been the main issue in collective bargaining. However, unions also negotiate other pay-related issues, including time off with pay, income security (for those in industries with periodic layoffs), cost-of-living adjustments, and health care benefits.

The Wagner Act created the National Labor Relations Board (NLRB) to oversee employer practices and ensure that employees receive their rights. For example, the NLRB says that employers must give the union a written explanation of the employer's "wage curves"—the graph that relates job to pay rate. The union is also entitled to know members' salaries.[44]

Pay Policies

The employer's compensation strategy will manifest itself in *pay policies.* For example, a top hospital like Johns Hopkins might have a policy of paying nurses 20% above the prevailing market wage. Pay policies can influence the employer's performance and profitability, as the accompanying feature on Wegmans Food Markets illustrates.

Javier Larrea/Pixtal/AGE Fotostock

Two executives discuss a print layout; one happens to be in a wheelchair. Federal law prohibits discrimination against qualified persons with disabilities in all aspects of employment, including compensation.

Managers need pay policies on a range of issues. One is whether to emphasize *seniority* or *performance.* For example, it takes 18 years for a U.S. federal employee to progress from step 1 to step 9 of the government's pay scale. Such seniority-based pay may be advantageous to the extent that seniority is an objective standard. One disadvantage is that top performers may get the same raises as poor ones. Seniority-based pay might seem to be a relic reserved for some government agencies and unionized firms. However, one survey found that 60% of employees responding thought high-seniority employees got the most pay. Only about 35% said their companies paid high performers more.[45]

How to distinguish between *high and low performers* is another policy issue. For example, for many years Payless ShoeSource gave everyone the same raise. However, after seeing its market share drop over several years, management decided on a turnaround strategy. This necessitated revising the firm's compensation policies, to differentiate more aggressively between top performers and others.[46] Other pay policies cover how to award salary increases and promotions, overtime pay, probationary pay, leaves for military service, jury duty, and holidays.

IMPROVING PERFORMANCE: *The Strategic Context*

Wegmans Food Markets

Strategic compensation management means formulating a total rewards package that produces the employee skills and behaviors that the company needs to achieve its strategic goals.

Wegmans exemplifies this. It competes in the retail food sector, where profit margins are thin and where online competitors and giants like Walmart drive costs and prices down. The usual competitor's reaction is to cut employee benefits and costs.[47] Wegmans takes a different approach. It views its workforce as an integral part of achieving Wegmans's strategic aims of *optimizing service while controlling costs by improving systems and productivity*. For example, one dairy department employee designed a new way to organize the cooler, thus improving ordering and inventory control.[48] The firm offers above-market pay rates, affordable health insurance, and a full range of employee benefits.[49] Wegmans's pay policies thus aim to produce exactly the sorts of high-productivity employee behaviors the company needs to achieve its strategic aims.

It's likely that its pay policies are one reason for Wegmans's exceptional profitability. For example, its employee turnover (about 38% for part-timers, 6%–7% for full-timers) is well below the industry's overall average of about 47%.[50] Its stores (which at about 120,000 square feet are much larger than competitors') average about $950,000 a week in sales (compared to a national average of $361,564), or about $49 million in sales annually, compared with a typical Walmart store's grocery sales of $23.5 million in sales.[51] As Wegmans's human resource head has said, good employees assure higher productivity, and that translates into better bottom-line results.[52] ■

Source: Based on Demby, "Two Stores Refused to Join the Race."; www.wegmans.com; Demby, "Two Stores Refuse to Join the Race," www.hoovers.com/company/Wegmans_Food_Markets_Inc/cfhtji-1.Html.

If your professor has assigned this, go to the Assignments section of **mymanagementlab.com** to complete this discussion question.

Talk About It 1: If Wegmans does so well with a high-pay policy, why don't more employers do this as well?

GEOGRAPHY How to account for geographic differences in cost of living is another big pay policy issue. For example, the average base pay for an office supervisor ranges from about $49,980 in Florida to $60,980 in New York.[53]

Employers handle cost-of-living differentials for transferees in several ways. One is to pay a differential for ongoing costs in addition to a one-time allocation. For example, one employer pays a differential of $6,000 per year to people earning $35,000 to $45,000 whom it transfers from Atlanta to Minneapolis. Others simply raise the employee's base salary. The accompanying feature on compensating expatriate employees expands on this.

IMPROVING PERFORMANCE: *HR Practices Around the Globe*

Compensating Expatriate Employees

The question of cost-of-living differentials has particular significance to multinational firms, where pay rates range widely from, say, France to Zambia.

How should multinationals compensate expatriate employees—those it sends overseas? Two basic international compensation policies are popular: home-based and host-based plans.[54]

With a *home-based salary plan*, an international transferee's base salary reflects his or her home country's salary. The employer then adds allowances for cost-of-living differences—housing and schooling costs, for instance. This is a reasonable approach for short-term assignments, and avoids the problem of having to change the employee's base salary every time he or she moves.

In the *host-based plan*, the firm ties the international transferee's base salary to the host country's salary structure. In other words, the manager from New York who is sent to France would have his or her base salary changed to the prevailing base salary for that position in France, rather than keep the New York base salary. The firm usually tacks on cost-of-living, housing, schooling, and other allowances here as well.

Most multinational enterprises set expatriates' salaries according to the *home-based salary plan*. (Thus, a French manager assigned to Kiev by a U.S. multinational will generally have a base salary that reflects the salary structure in the manager's home country, in this case France.) In addition, the person typically gets allowances including cost-of-living, relocation, housing, education, and hardship allowances (for more challenging countries). The employer also usually pays any extra tax burdens resulting from taxes the manager is liable for over and above those he or she would have to pay in the home country. ■

Source: Based on Compensation Management.

If your professor has assigned this, go to the Assignments section of **mymanagementlab.com** to complete this discussion question.

Talk About It 2: Why do you think most employers opt for the home-based salary plan?

Job Evaluation Methods

LEARNING OBJECTIVE **11-2**
Define and give an example of how to conduct a job evaluation.

Employers use two basic approaches to setting pay rates: *market-based approaches* and *job evaluation methods*. Many firms, particularly smaller ones, simply use a *market-based* approach. Doing so involves conducting formal or informal salary surveys to determine what others in the relevant labor markets are paying for particular jobs. They then use these figures to price their own jobs. *Job evaluation methods* involve assigning values to each of the company's jobs. This process helps produce a pay plan in which each job's pay is equitable based on what other employers are paying for these jobs *and* based on each job's value to the employer.[55]

job evaluation
A systematic comparison done in order to determine the worth of one job relative to another.

Job evaluation is a formal and systematic comparison of jobs to determine the worth of one job relative to another. Job evaluation aims to determine a job's relative worth. Job evaluation eventually results in a *wage* or *salary structure* or hierarchy (this shows the pay rate for various jobs or groups of jobs). The basic principle of job evaluation is this: Jobs that require greater qualifications, more responsibilities, and more complex job duties should receive more pay than jobs with lesser requirements.[56] The basic job evaluation procedure is to compare jobs in relation to one another—for example, in terms of required effort, job complexity, and skills. Suppose you know (based on your job evaluation) the relative worth of the key jobs in your firm. You then conduct a salary survey to see what others are paying for similar jobs. By combining the information from the job evaluation and from the salary survey, you are on your way to being able to create a **market-competitive pay plan**—one where your pay rates are equitable both internally (based on each job's relative value) and externally (in other words when compared with what other employers are paying).

market-competitive pay plan
Pay plan where pay rates are equitable both internally (based on each job's relative value) and externally (in other words when compared with what other employers are paying).

Compensable Factors

You can use two basic approaches to compare the worth of several jobs. First, you might decide that one job is more important than another is, and not dig any deeper. As an alternative, you could compare the jobs by focusing on certain basic factors the jobs have in

The job evaluation committee typically includes at least several employees, and has the important task of evaluating the worth of each job using compensable factors.

Noel Hendrickson/Blend Images/AGE Fotostock

compensable factor
A fundamental, compensable element of a job, such as skills, effort, responsibility, and working conditions.

common. Compensation management specialists call these **compensable factors**. They are the factors that establish how the jobs compare to one another, and that determine the pay for each job.

Some employers develop their own compensable factors. However, most use factors popularized by packaged job evaluation systems or by federal legislation. For example, the Equal Pay Act uses four compensable factors—skills, effort, responsibility, and working conditions. The method popularized by the Hay consulting firm emphasizes three factors: know-how, problem solving, and accountability. Walmart uses knowledge, problem-solving skills, and accountability requirements.

Choosing compensable factors plays a big role in job evaluation. You usually compare each job with all comparable jobs using the same compensable factors. However, the compensable factors you use depend on the job and the job evaluation method. For example, "decision making" might make sense for a manager's job, but not for a cleaner's job.[57]

Preparing for the Job Evaluation

Job evaluation is a judgmental process and demands close cooperation among supervisors, HR specialists, and employees and union representatives. The initial steps include identifying the need for the program, getting cooperation, and then choosing an evaluation committee. The committee then performs the actual evaluation.

Identifying the need for job evaluation shouldn't be difficult. For example, dissatisfaction reflected in high turnover, work stoppages, or arguments may result from paying employees different rates for similar jobs. Managers may express uneasiness with an informal way of assigning pay rates.

Employees may fear that a systematic evaluation of their jobs may reduce their pay rates, so *getting employees to cooperate* in the evaluation is important. For example, you can tell employees that because of the impending job evaluation program, pay rate decisions will no longer be made just by management whim, and that no current employee's rate will be adversely affected because of the job evaluation.

Finally, *choose a job evaluation committee.* The committee usually consists of about five members, most of whom are employees. Management has the right to serve on such committees, but employees may view this with suspicion. However, a human resource specialist can usually be justified to provide expert assistance. Union representation is possible. In most cases, though, the union's position is that it is accepting the results of the job evaluation only as an initial decision and is reserving the right to appeal actual job pricing decisions through grievance or bargaining channels.[58] Once appointed, each committee member should receive a manual explaining both the job evaluation process and how to conduct the job evaluation.

benchmark job
A job that is used to anchor the employer's pay scale and around which other jobs are arranged in order of relative worth.

The evaluation committee then performs three main functions. First, it usually identifies 10 or 15 key **benchmark jobs**. These will be the first jobs they'll evaluate and will serve as the anchors or benchmarks against which the relative importance or value of all other jobs is compared. Next, the committee may select *compensable factors* (although the human resources department will usually choose these). Finally, the committee performs its most important function—actually *evaluating the worth of each job.* For this, the committee will probably use one of the following methods: ranking, job classification, or point method.

Job Evaluation Methods: Ranking

ranking method
The simplest method of job evaluation that involves ranking each job relative to all other jobs, usually based on overall difficulty.

The simplest job evaluation method ranks each job relative to all other jobs, usually based on some overall factor like "job difficulty." There are several steps in the job **ranking method**.

1. ***Obtain job information.*** Job analysis is the first step. Here job descriptions for each job are prepared, and the information they contain about the job's duties is usually the basis for ranking jobs. (Sometimes job specifications are also prepared. However, the ranking method usually ranks jobs based on the whole job, rather than on several compensable factors. Therefore, job specifications, which tend to list job demands in terms of compensable factors such as problem solving, decision making, and skills, are not as important with ranking as they are for other job evaluation methods.)
2. ***Select and group jobs.*** It is usually not practical to make a single ranking for all jobs in an organization. The usual procedure is to rank jobs by department or in clusters (such as factory workers or clerical workers). This removes the need for direct comparison of, say, factory jobs and clerical jobs.
3. ***Select compensable factors.*** In the ranking method, it is common to use just one factor (such as job difficulty) and to rank jobs based on the whole job. However regardless of the number of factors you choose, explain the definition of the factor(s) to the evaluators carefully so that they all evaluate the jobs consistently.
4. ***Rank jobs.*** For example, each rater gets a set of index cards, each of which contains a brief description of a job. Then they arrange these cards from lowest to highest. Some managers use an "alternation ranking method" to make this procedure more accurate. Here you take the cards, first choosing the highest and the lowest, then the next highest and next lowest, and so forth, until you've ranked all the cards. Table 11-2 illustrates such a job ranking. Jobs in this small health facility rank from orderly up to office manager. The corresponding current pay scales are shown in the column following the job titles. (After ranking, it is possible to slot additional jobs based on their difficulty between those already ranked and to assign each an appropriate wage rate.) The ranked listing of jobs enables us to compare each job's rank with its current pay, and decide if what we are currently paying is internally equitable; we may adjust a job's pay up or down, based on this. Online programs (for example, go to www.hr-guide.com, click under "Job Evaluation, Ranking," and then click "Interactive Ranking Program") can help you rank (and check the rankings of) your positions.[59]
5. ***Combine ratings.*** Usually, several raters rank the jobs independently. Then the rating committee (or the employer) can simply average the raters' rankings.
6. ***Compare current pay with what others are paying based on salary survey.*** Next, we show on the same table (in the middle column) what others in the community

TABLE 11-2 Job Ranking at Jackson Hospital

Ranking Order	Our Current Annual Pay Scale	What Others Pay: Salary Survey Pay	Our Final Assigned Pay
1. Office manager	$43,000	$45,000	$44,000
2. Chief nurse	42,500	43,000	42,750
3. Bookkeeper	34,000	36,000	35,000
4. Nurse	32, 500	33,000	32,750
5. Cook	31,000	32,000	31,500
6. Nurse's aide	28,500	30,500	29,500
7. Orderly	25,500	27,000	27,000

Note: After ranking, it becomes possible to slot additional jobs (based on overall job difficulty, for instance) between those already ranked and to assign each an appropriate wage rate.

are paying for similar jobs, based on a salary survey that we conduct. This helps us ensure that our pay will be *externally* equitable.

7. ***Assign a new pay scale.*** Finally, we compare what we are currently paying for each job with what others are paying, and decide (in this case) to adjust our pay scale by raising what we pay for each job. The last column therefore shows our new pay scale.

This is the simplest job evaluation method, as well as the easiest to explain. And it usually takes less time than other methods.

Drawbacks derive more from how managers use ranking than from the method itself. For example, there's a tendency to rely too heavily on "guesstimates" (of things like overall difficulty), since ranking usually does not use compensable factors. Similarly, ranking provides no yardstick for quantifying the value of one job relative to another. For example, job number 4 may in fact be five times "more valuable" than job number 5, but with the ranking method all you know is that one job ranks higher than the other. Ranking is usually more appropriate for small employers that can't afford the time or expense of a more elaborate method.

The *factor comparison method* is a special ranking method. It requires ranking each of a job's "factors" (such as education required, experience, and complexity), and then adding up the points representing the number of "degrees" of each factor each job has. Employers seldom use it today.

job classification (or job grading)
A method for categorizing jobs into groups.

classes
Grouping jobs based on a set of rules for each group or class, such as amount of independent judgment, skill, physical effort, and so forth, required. Classes usually contain similar jobs.

grades
A job classification system like the class system, although grades often contain dissimilar jobs, such as secretaries, mechanics, and firefighters. Grade descriptions are written based on compensable factors listed in classification systems.

Job Evaluation Methods: Job Classification

Job classification (or job grading) is a simple, widely used job evaluation method in which raters categorize jobs into groups; all the jobs in each group are of roughly the same value for pay purposes. We call these groups **classes** if they contain similar jobs, or **grades** if they contain jobs that are similar in difficulty but otherwise different. Thus, in the federal government's pay grade system, a "press secretary" and a "fire chief" might both be graded "GS-10" (GS stands for "General Schedule"). On the other hand, in its job class system, the state of Florida might classify all "secretary IIs" in one class, all "maintenance engineers" in another, and so forth.

In practice, there are several ways to categorize jobs. One is to write class or grade summaries or descriptions (similar to job descriptions); you then place jobs into the classes or grades based on how well they fit these descriptions. Another is to write a set of compensable factor-based rules for each class (for instance, how much independent judgment, skill, and physical effort does the class of jobs require?). Then categorize each job according to these rules.

The usual procedure blends these two: the analysts choose compensable factors and then develop short class or grade descriptions that describe each class (or grade) in terms of the amount or level of the factors in those jobs. For example, the

FIGURE 11-4 Example of a Grade Definition

Source: From "Grade Level Guide for Clerical and Assistance Work" from U.S. Office of Personnel Management, June 1989.

Grade	Nature of Assignment	Level of Responsibility
GS-7	Performs specialized duties in a defined functional or program area involving a wide variety of problems or situations; develops information, identifies interrelationships, and takes actions consistent with objectives of the function or program served.	Work is assigned in terms of objectives, priorities, and deadlines; the employee works independently in resolving most conflicts; completed work is evaluated for conformance to policy; guidelines, such as regulations, precedent cases, and policy statements require considerable interpretation and adaptation.

U.S. government's classification system uses eight compensable factors: (1) difficulty and variety of work, (2) supervision received and exercised, (3) judgment exercised, (4) originality required, (5) nature and purpose of interpersonal work relationships, (6) responsibility, (7) experience, and (8) knowledge required. Based on these compensable factors, raters write a **grade definition** like that in Figure 11-4. This one shows one grade description (for grade GS-7) for the federal government's pay grade system. Then the evaluation committee reviews all job descriptions and slots each job into its appropriate grade, by comparing each job description to the rules in each grade description. Thus, the federal government system classifies the positions *automotive mechanic, welder, electrician*, and *machinist* in grade GS-10.

grade definition
Written descriptions of the level of, say, responsibility and knowledge required by jobs in each grade. Similar jobs can then be combined into grades or classes.

The classification method has several advantages. The main one is that most employers usually end up grouping jobs into classes or grades anyway, regardless of the evaluation method they use. They do this to avoid having to price separately dozens or hundreds of jobs. Of course, the job classification automatically groups the employer's jobs into classes. The disadvantages are that it isn't easy to write the class or grade descriptions, and considerable judgment is required to apply them. Yet many employers use this method with success.

Job Evaluation Methods: Point Method

point method
The job evaluation method in which a number of compensable factors are identified and then the degree to which each of these factors is present on the job is determined.

The **point method**'s overall aim is to determine the degree to which the jobs you're evaluating contain selected compensable factors. It involves identifying several compensable factors for the jobs, as well as the degree to which each factor is present in each job. Assume there are five degrees of the compensable factor "responsibility" a job could contain. Further, assume you assign a different number of points to each degree of each compensable factor. Once the evaluation committee determines the degree to which each compensable factor (like "responsibility" and "effort") is present in a job, it can calculate a total point value for the job by adding up the corresponding degree points for each factor. The result is a quantitative point rating for each job. The point method of job evaluation is the most popular job evaluation method today.[60]

"PACKAGED" POINT PLANS A number of groups (such as the Hay Group, the National Electrical Manufacturer's Association, and the National Trade Association) have developed standardized point plans. Many thousands of employers use these systems. They contain ready-made factor and degree definitions and point assessments for a wide range of jobs. Employers can often use them with little or no modification.

Computerized Job Evaluations

Using job evaluation methods such as the point method can be time-consuming. Accumulating the information about "how much" of each compensable factor the job contains is a tedious process. The evaluation committees must debate the level of each compensable factor in each job. They then write down their consensus judgments and compute each job's point values or rankings. Many employers therefore turn to computerized systems.

Computer-aided job evaluation can streamline the job evaluation process

Source: Reprinted by permission from Computer-aided job evaluation can streamline the job evaluation process, in Screen capture: www.hrsoftware.netcgi/JobEvaluation.cgi.

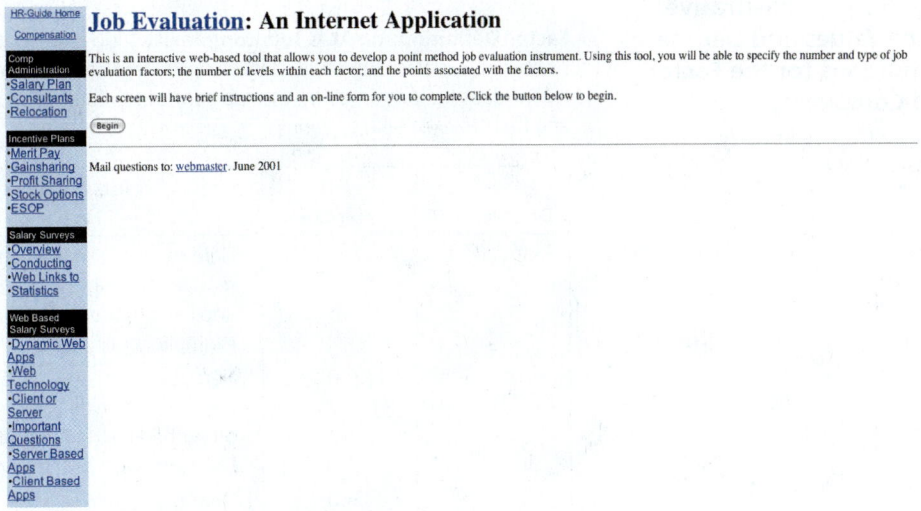

Most such computerized systems have two main components.[61] There is, first, a structured questionnaire. This contains items such as "enter total number of employees who report to this position." Second, such systems may use statistical models. These allow the computer program to price jobs more or less automatically, by assigning points based on the questionnaire responses.

How to Create A Market-Competitive Pay Plan

LEARNING OBJECTIVE 11-3
Explain in detail how to establish a market-competitive pay plan.

As we said, many firms simply price their jobs based on what other employers are paying—they just use a market-based approach. However, most employers also base their pay plans on job evaluation methods like those just described. These evaluations assign values (such as point values) to each job. This helps to produce a pay plan in which each job's pay is internally equitable, based, as it is, on the job's value to the employer (as measured, for instance, by how many points it warrants). However, even with the job evaluation approach, managers must adjust pay rates to fit the market.[62] After all, you want employees' pay to be equitable internally—relative to what their colleagues in the firm are earning—but also competitive externally—relative to what *other employers* are paying. In a *market-competitive pay plan* a job's compensation reflects the job's value in the company, as well as what other employers are paying for similar jobs in the marketplace. Because the point method (or "point-factor method") is so popular, we'll use it as the centerpiece of our step-by-step example for creating a market-competitive pay plan.[63] The 16 steps in creating a market-competitive pay plan begin with choosing benchmark jobs.

1. Choose Benchmark Jobs

Particularly when an employer has dozens or hundreds of different jobs, it's impractical and unnecessary to evaluate each of them separately. Therefore, the first step in the point method is to select benchmark jobs. Benchmark jobs are representative of the jobs the employer needs to evaluate. Like "accounting clerk" they should be common among employers (thus making it easier to survey what competitors are paying for similar jobs).[64]

2. Select Compensable Factors

The choice of compensable factors depends on tradition (as noted, the Equal Pay Act of 1963 uses four compensable factors: skill, effort, responsibility, and working conditions), and on strategic and practical considerations. For example, if your firm's competitive advantage is quality, you might substitute "responsibility for quality"

FIGURE 11-5 Illustrative Point Values and Degree Definitions for the Factor Job Complexity

Source: Copyright Gary Dessler, PhD.

Factor Definition: What Is Job Complexity? Job complexity generally refers to the amount of judgment, initiative, ingenuity, and complex data analysis that doing the job requires. To what extent does the person doing this job confront unfamiliar problems, deal with complex decisions, and have to exercise discretion?

Degree	Points	Job Complexity Degree Definitions: What to Look for in the Job
First	120	Here the job is routine and consists of repetitive operations requiring little or no choice of action and the automatic application of easily understood rules and procedures. For example, a filing clerk.
Second	240	Here the employee follows detailed instructions but may have to make limited decisions based on previously prescribed instructions which lay our prescribed alternatives. For example, a billing clerk or a receptionist.
Third	360	Here the employee again follows detailed instructions but because the number of matters to consider is more varied the employee needs to exhibit initiative and independent judgment, under direct supervision. For example, a nurse's aide.
Fourth	480	Here the employee can generally follow standard practices but the presence of nonroutine problems requires that the employee be able to use initiative and judgment to analyze and evaluate situations, possibly modifying the standard procedures to adjust to the new situations. For example, a nurse.
Fifth	600	On this job, the employee needs to use independent judgment and plan and perform complex work under only general supervision, often working independently toward achieving overall results. For example, medical intern.

for working conditions, or simply add it as a fifth factor.[65] Similarly, using "working conditions" makes little practical sense for evaluating executive jobs.

The employer should carefully define each factor. This is to ensure that the evaluation committee members will each apply the factors with consistency. Figure 11-5 shows (on top) one such definition, in this case for the factor job complexity. The human resource specialist often draws up the definitions.

3. Assign Weights to Compensable Factors

Having selected compensable factors, the next step is to determine the relative importance (or weighting) of each factor (for instance, how much more important is "skill" than "effort"?). This is important because for each cluster of jobs some factors are bound to be more important than others are. Thus, for executive jobs the "mental requirements" factor would carry far more weight than would "physical requirements." To assign weights, we assume we have a total 100 percentage points to allocate for each job. Then (as an illustration), assign percentage weights of 60% for the factor job complexity, 30% for effort, and 10% for working conditions.[66]

4. Convert Percentages to Points for Each Factor

Next, we want to convert the percentage weights assigned to each compensable factor into point values for each factor (this is, after all, the point method). It is traditional to assume we are working with a total of 1,000 points (although one could use some other figure). To convert percentages to points for each compensable factor, *multiply the percentage weight for each compensable factor (from the previous step) by 1,000.*[67] This will tell you the *maximum number of points* for each compensable factor. Doing so in this case would translate into 1,000 × 0.60 = 600 possible points for job complexity, 1,000 × 0.30 = 300 points for effort, and 1,000 × 0.10 = 100 points for working conditions.

5. Define Each Factor's Degrees

Next, split each factor into degrees, and define (write degree definitions for) each degree so that raters may judge the amount or degree of a factor existing in a job. Thus, for a compensable factor such as "job complexity" you might choose to have five degrees, ranging from "here the job is routine" to "uses independent judgment." (Our definitions for each degree are shown in Figure 11-5 under "Job Complexity Degree Definitions: What to Look For in the Job.") The number of degrees usually does not exceed five or six, and the actual number depends mostly on judgment. Thus, if all employees work either in a quiet, air-conditioned office or in a noisy, hot factory, then two degrees would probably suffice for the factor "working conditions." You need not have the same number of degrees for each factor, and you should limit degrees to the number necessary to distinguish among jobs.

6. Determine for Each Factor Its Factor Degrees' Points

The evaluation committee must be able to determine the number of points each job is worth. To do this, the committee must be able to examine each job and (from each factor's degree definitions) *determine what degree of each compensable factor* that job has. For them to do this, we must first assign points to *each degree of each compensable factor*. For example, in our illustration, we have five possible degrees of job complexity, and the job complexity compensable factor is worth up to 600 points maximum. In our case, we simply decide that the first degree level of job complexity is worth 120 (or one-fifth of 600) points, the second degree level is worth 240 points, the third degree level is worth 360 points, the fourth degree level is worth 480 points, and the fifth degree is worth the maximum 600 points (see Figure 11-5).[68] Do this for each factor (as in Table 11-3).

7. Review Job Descriptions and Job Specifications

The heart of job *evaluation* involves determining the amount or degree to which the job contains the selected compensable factors such as effort, job complexity, and working conditions. The team conducting the job evaluation will frequently do so by first reviewing each job's job description and job specification. As we explained in Chapter 4 (Job Analysis), it is through the job analysis that the manager identifies the job's duties and responsibilities and writes the job description and job specification. Ideally therefore, the job analyst included in the job description and specification information about the compensable factors (such as job complexity) around which the employer plans to build its compensation plan.[69]

TABLE 11-3 Points Assigned to Factors and to Their Degrees (Revised)

Factors	First-Degree Points	Second-Degree Points	Third-Degree Points	Fourth-Degree Points	Fifth-Degree Points
Job complexity (Total maximum points equal 600)	120	240	360	480	600
Effort (Total maximum points equal 300)	60	120	180	240	300
Working conditions (Total maximum points equal 100 points)	20	40	60	80	100

8. Evaluate the Jobs

Steps 1–7 provide us with the information (for instance, on points and degrees) based on which we can evaluate the jobs. The committee has now gathered the job descriptions and job specifications for the benchmark jobs they will focus on.

Then, from their review of each job description and job specification, the committee *determines the degree to which each compensable factor is present in each job.* Thus for, say, a job of master mechanic, the team might conclude (after studying the job description and job specification) that the master mechanic's job deserves the third degree level of *job complexity* points, the first degree level of *effort*, and the first degree level of *working conditions*.

Knowing the job complexity, effort, and working conditions degrees for each job, *and knowing the number of points we previously assigned to each degree* of each compensable factor, we can now determine how many job complexity, effort, and working conditions points each benchmark job should contain. (We know the degree level for each factor for each job, so we merely check the corresponding points (see Table 11-3) that we previously assigned to each of these degrees.)

Finally, we add up these degree points for each job to determine each job's total number of points.[70] The master mechanic job gets 360 + 60 + 20 = 440 points from Table 11-3. This enables us to list a hierarchy of jobs, based upon each job's points. We can soon turn to assigning wage rates to each job (step 9). But first, we should define market-competitive pay plan and wage curve.

What should the pay rate be for each job? Of course, jobs with more points should command higher pay. The question is what pay rate to use. Our company's current, "internal" pay rates? Or pay rates based on what the "external" market is paying?[71]

market-competitive pay system
A pay system in which the employer's actual pay rates are competitive with those in the relevant labor market.

With a **market-competitive pay system**, the employer's actual pay rates are competitive with those in the relevant labor market, as well as equitable internally.[72] Put simply, the basic approach is to compare what the employer is *currently* paying for each job ("internal pay") with what the market is paying for the same or similar job ("external pay"), and then to combine this information to produce a market-competitive pay system.

wage curve
Shows the relationship between the value of the job and the average wage paid for this job.

WAGE CURVES **Wage curves** play a central role in assigning wage rates to jobs. The wage curve typically shows the pay rates paid for jobs, relative to the points or rankings assigned to each job by the job evaluation. Figure 11-6 presents an example. Note that it shows pay rates for jobs on the vertical axis, and point values for these jobs along the horizontal axis. The purpose of the wage curve is to show the relationships between (1) the value of the job (expressed in points) as determined by

FIGURE 11-6 Plotting a Wage Curve

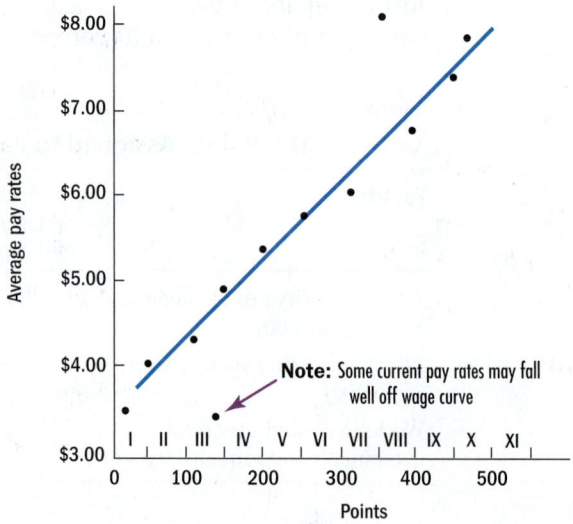

one of the job evaluation methods and (2) the pay rates for the job. (We'll see that many employers may combine jobs into classes or grades. Here the wage curve would show the relationship between average pay rates for each grade, and each grade's average point value.) The pay rates on the wage curve are traditionally those now paid by the employer. However, if there is reason to believe the current pay rates are out of step with the market rates for these jobs, the employer will have to adjust them. One way to do this is to compare a wage curve that shows the jobs' *current* wage rates relative to the jobs' points, with a second curve that shows *market* wage rates relative to points. We do this as follows.

9. Draw the Current (Internal) Wage Curve

First, to study how each job's points relates to its current pay rate, we start by drawing an *internal wage curve.* Plotting each job's points and the wage rate the employer is now paying for each job (or wage rates, if there are several for each job) produces a scatter plot as in Figure 11-7 (left). We now draw a wage curve (on the right) through these plots that shows how point values relate to current wage rates. We can draw this wage line by just estimating a line that best fits the plotted points (by minimizing the distances between the plots and the curve). Or we can use regression, a statistical technique. Using the latter will produce a current/internal wage curve that best fits the plotted points. In any case, we show the results in Figure 11-7 (right).[73]

10. Conduct a Market Analysis: Salary Surveys

salary survey
A survey aimed at determining prevailing wage rates. A good salary survey provides specific wage rates for specific jobs. Formal written questionnaire surveys are the most comprehensive, but telephone surveys and newspaper ads are also sources of information.

Next, we must compile the information needed to draw an *external wage curve* for our jobs, based on what other employers are paying for similar jobs. **Salary surveys**—surveys of what others are paying—play a big role in pricing jobs.[74] Employers use salary surveys in three ways. First, they use survey data to price benchmark jobs. Benchmark jobs are the anchor jobs around which they slot their other jobs, based on each job's relative worth to the firm. Second, employers typically price 20% or more of their positions directly in the marketplace (rather than relative to the firm's benchmark jobs), based on a survey of what comparable firms are paying for comparable jobs. (Google might do this for jobs like systems engineer, whose salaries fluctuate widely and often.) Third, surveys also collect data on benefits like insurance, sick leave, and vacations for decisions regarding employee benefits.

Salary surveys can be formal or informal. *Informal* phone or Internet surveys are good for checking specific issues, such as when a bank wants to confirm the salary at which to advertise a newly open teller's job, or whether some banks are really paying tellers an incentive. Some large employers can afford to send out their own *formal* surveys to collect compensation information from other employers. These ask about things like number of employees, overtime policies, starting salaries, and paid vacations.

Many employers use surveys published by consulting firms, professional associations, or government agencies. For example, the U.S. Department of Labor's Bureau of Labor Statistics' (BLS) *National Compensation Survey (NCS)* provides comprehensive reports of occupational earnings, compensation cost trends, and benefits (www.bls.gov/bls/wages.htm).

FIGURE 11-7 The Current/Internal Wage Curve

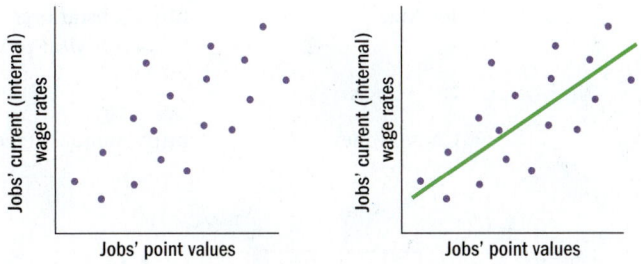

Detailed occupational earnings are available from the national compensation survey for over 800 occupations in the United States, calculated with data from employers in all industry sectors in every State and the District of Columbia (http://stats.bls.gov/oes/current/oes_nat.htm). The *Current Employment Statistics Survey* is a monthly survey of the payroll records of business establishments that provides data on earnings of production and nonsupervisory workers at the national level. This provides information about earnings as well as production bonuses, commissions, and cost-of-living increases. The *National Compensation Survey—Benefits* provides information on the share of workers who participate in specified benefits, such as health care, retirement plans, and paid vacations. These data also show the details of those benefits, such as amounts of paid leave. Internationally, the BLS reports comparative hourly compensation costs in local currencies and U.S. dollars for production workers and all employees in manufacturing in its international labor comparisons tables.

Private consulting and/or executive recruiting companies like Hay & Associates, Towers Watson Global Data Services, and Aon/Hewitt (www.aon.com) publish data covering compensation for top and middle management and members of boards of directors. Professional organizations like the Society for Human Resource Management and the Financial Executives Institute publish surveys of compensation practices among members of their associations.[75]

USING THE INTERNET TO DO COMPENSATION SURVEYS Internet-based options makes it easy for anyone to access published compensation survey information. Table 11-4 shows some popular salary survey Web sites.

Many of these sites, such as Salary.com, provide national salary levels for jobs that the site then arithmetically adjusts to each locale based on cost-of-living formulas. To get a real-time picture of what employers in your area are actually paying for, say, accounting clerks, it's useful to access the online Internet sites of one or two of your local newspapers. For example, the *South Florida Sun-Sentinel* (and many papers) uses a site called Careerbuilder.com. It lists just about all the job opportunities listed in the newspaper by category and, in many instances, their wage rates (www.careerbuilder.com).

11. Draw the Market (External) Wage Curve

The current/internal wage curve from step 9 is helpful. For example showing, as it does, how a job's current pay rate compares with its points helps the employer identify jobs for which pay rates are currently too high or too low, relative to other jobs

TABLE 11-4 Some Pay Data Web Sites

Sponsor	Internet Address	What It Provides	Downside
Salary.com	www.salary.com	Salary by job and ZIP code, plus job and description, for hundreds of jobs	Adapts national averages by applying local cost-of-living differences
U.S. Office of Personnel Management	www.opm.gov/oca/09Tables/index.asp	Salaries and wages for U.S. government jobs, by location	Limited to U.S. government jobs
Job Star	http://jobstar.org/tools/salary/sal-prof.php	Profession-specific salary surveys	Necessary to review numerous salary surveys for each profession
CNN Money	http://money.cnn.com	Input your current salary and city; for comparable salary in destination city	Based on national averages adapted to cost-of-living differences

FIGURE 11-8 The Market/External Wage Curve

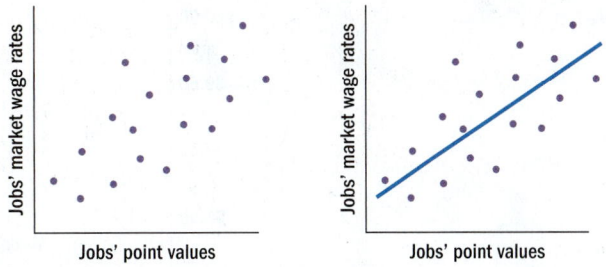

in the company. (For example, if a job's current wage rate is well above the internal wage curve, it suggests that the present wage rate for that job is inequitably high, given the number of points we've assigned to that job.)

What the current (internal) wage curve does *not* reveal is whether our pay rates are too high, too low, or just right relative to what other firms are paying. For this, we need to draw a *market* or *external wage* curve.

To draw the market/external wage curve, we produce a scatter plot and wage curve as in Figure 11-8 (left and right). However, instead of using our firm's current wage rates, we use market wage rates (obtained from salary surveys). The market/external wage curve thereby compares our jobs' points with market pay rates for our jobs.

12. Compare and Adjust Current and Market Wage Rates for Jobs

How different are the market rates other employers are paying for our jobs and the current rates we are now paying for our jobs? To determine this, we combine both the current/internal and market/external wage curves on one graph, as in Figure 11-9. The market wage curve might be higher than our current wage curve (suggesting that our current pay rates may be too low), or below our current wage curve (suggesting that our current wage rates might be too high). Or perhaps market wage rates are higher for some of our jobs and lower for others.[76]

Based on comparing the current/internal wage curve and market/external wage curve in Figure 11-9, we must decide whether to adjust the current pay rates for our jobs, and if so how. This calls for a policy decision by management. Strategic considerations influence this decision. Do our strategic aspirations suggest we should pay more, the same, or less than competitors? For example, we might decide to move our current internal wage curve up (and thereby give everyone a raise), or down (and thereby perhaps withhold pay increases for some time), or adjust the slope of the internal wage curve to increase what we pay for some jobs and decrease what we pay for

FIGURE 11-9 Plotting Both the Market and Internal Wage Curves

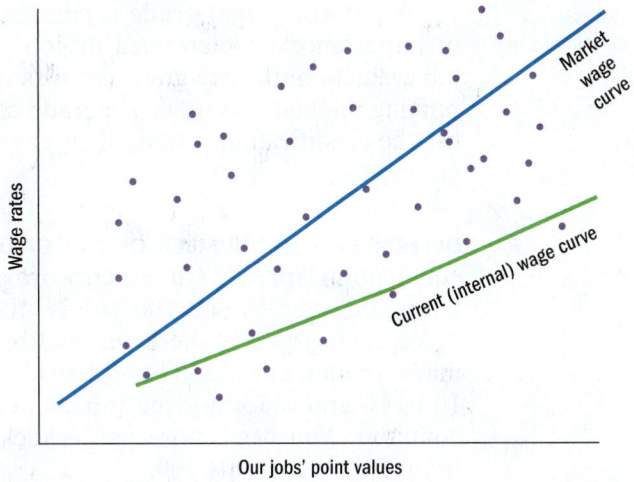

FIGURE 11-10 Wage Structure

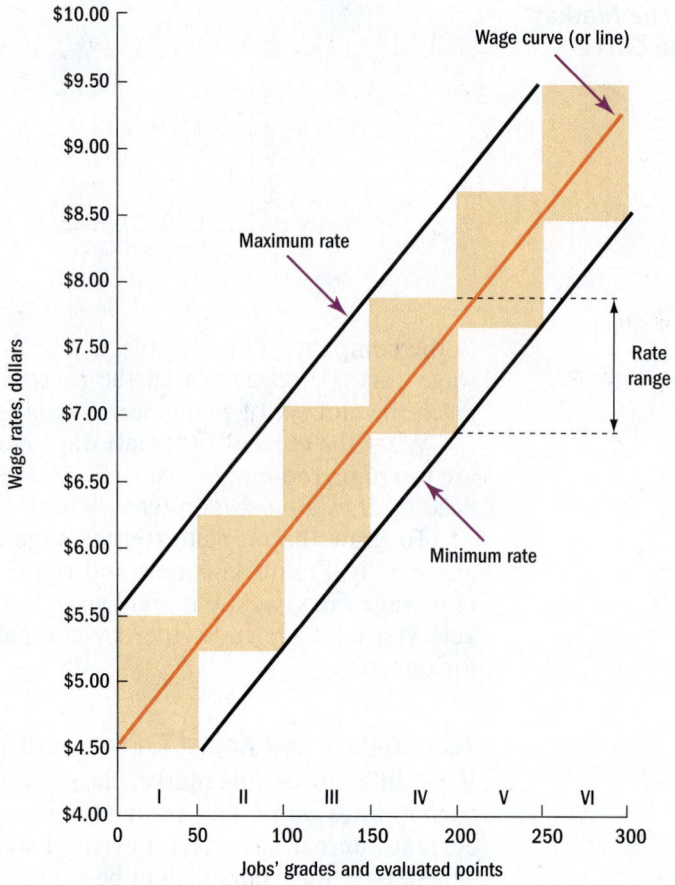

others. In any case, the wage curve we end up with (the orange line in Figure 11-10) should now be equitable internally (in terms of the point value of each job) and equitable externally (in terms of what other firms are paying).[77]

13. Develop Pay Grades

Employers typically group similar jobs (in terms of points) into grades for pay purposes. Then, instead of having to deal with hundreds of job rates, you might only have to focus on, say, pay rates for 10 or 12 pay grades. For example, Serco, a services firm which operates a London, England, light railway system, set up pay grades after ranking jobs using a system based on knowledge, management complexity, and the job's magnitude and impact on the organization.[78]

pay (or wage) grade
A pay grade is composed of jobs of approximately equal difficulty.

A **pay (or wage) grade** is composed of jobs of approximately equal difficulty or importance as determined by job evaluation. If you used the point method of job evaluation, the pay grade consists of jobs falling within a range of points. If the ranking method was used, the grade consists of a specific number of ranks. If you use the classification system, then your jobs are already categorized into classes (or grades).

DETERMINING THE NUMBER OF PAY GRADES It is standard to establish grades of equal point spread. (In other words, each grade might include all those jobs falling between 50 and 100 points, 100 and 150 points, 150 and 200 points, etc.) Since each grade is the same width, the main issue involves determining how many grades to have. There doesn't seem to be any optimal number, although 10 to 16 grades for a given job cluster (shop jobs, clerical jobs, etc.) seems to be common. You need more pay grades if there are, say, 1,000 jobs to be graded than if there are only 100.

14. Establish Rate Ranges

pay (or rate) ranges
A series of steps or levels within a pay grade, usually based upon years of service.

Most employers do not pay just one rate for all jobs in a particular pay grade. For example, GE Medical won't want to pay all its accounting clerks, from beginners to long tenure, at the same rate, even though they may all be in the same pay grade. Instead, employers develop vertical pay (or "rate") ranges for each of the horizontal pay grades (or pay classes). These **pay (or rate) ranges** often appear as vertical boxes within each grade, showing minimum, maximum, and midpoint pay rates for that grade, as in Figure 11-10. (Specialists call this graph a *wage structure.* Figure 11-10 graphically depicts the range of pay rates—in this case, per hour—paid for each pay grade.) Alternatively, you may depict the pay range for each class or grade as steps in a table, as in Table 11-5. Here you will have specific corresponding pay rates for each step within each grade in tabular form. Thus, Table 11-5 shows the pay rates and steps for most federal government grades. As of the time of this pay schedule, for instance, employees in positions classified in grade GS-10 could be paid annual salaries between $46,691 and $60,695, depending on the level or step at which they were hired into the grade, the amount of time they were in the grade, and any merit increases they've received.

DEVELOPING RATE RANGES As in Figure 11-10, the wage curve usually anchors the average pay rate for each vertical pay range. The firm might then arbitrarily decide on a maximum and minimum rate for each grade, such as 15% above and below the wage curve. As an alternative, some employers allow the pay range for each grade to become taller (they include more pay rates) for the higher pay ranges, reflecting the greater demands and performance variability inherent in more complex jobs. As in Figure 11-10, most employers structure their rate ranges to overlap a bit, so an employee in one grade who has more experience or seniority may earn more than would someone in an entry-level position in the next higher pay grade.[79]

There are several reasons to use pay ranges for each pay grade. First, it lets the employer take a more flexible stance in the labor market. For example, it makes

TABLE 11-5

SALARY TABLE 2015-GS
INCORPORATING THE 1% GENERAL SCHEDULE INCREASE
EFFECTIVE JANUARY 2015

Annual Rates by Grade and Step

Grade	Step 1	Step 2	Step 3	Step 4	Step 5	Step 6	Step 7	Step 8	Step 9	Step 10	Within Grade Amounts
1	$ 18,161	$ 18,768	$ 19,372	$ 19,973	$ 20,577	$ 20,931	$ 21,528	$ 22,130	$ 22,153	$ 22,712	Varies
2	20,419	20,905	21,581	22,153	22,403	23,062	23,721	24,380	25,039	25,698	Varies
3	22,279	23,022	23,765	24,508	25,251	25,994	26,737	27,480	28,223	28,966	743
4	25,011	25,845	26,679	27,513	28,347	29,181	30,015	30,849	31,683	32,517	834
5	27,982	28,915	29,848	30,781	31,714	32,647	33,580	34,513	35,446	36,379	933
6	31,192	32,232	33,272	34,312	35,352	36,392	37,432	38,472	39,512	40,552	1,040
7	34,662	35,817	36,972	38,127	39,282	40,437	41,592	42,747	43,902	45,057	1,155
8	38,387	39,667	40,947	42,227	43,507	44,787	46,067	47,347	48,627	49,907	1,280
9	42,399	43,812	45,225	46,638	48,051	49,464	50,877	52,290	53,703	55,116	1,413
10	46,691	48,247	49,803	51,359	52,915	54,471	56,027	57,583	59,139	60,695	1,556
11	51,298	53,008	54,718	56,428	58,138	59,848	61,558	63,268	64,978	66,688	1,710
12	61,486	63,536	65,586	67,636	69,686	71,736	73,786	75,836	77,886	79,936	2,050
13	73,115	75,552	77,989	80,426	82,863	85,300	87,737	90,174	92,611	95,048	2,437
14	86,399	89,279	92,159	95,039	97,919	100,799	103,679	106,559	109,439	112,319	2,880
15	101,630	105,018	108,406	111,794	115,182	118,570	121,958	125,346	128,734	132,122	3,388

Source: From Salary table 2015-gs Incorporating the 1% general schedule increase Effective january 2015, from http://www.opm.gov/policy-data-oversight/pay-leave/salaries-wages/salary-tables/pdf/2015/GS.pdf.

it easier to attract experienced, higher-paid employees into a pay grade at the top of the range, since the starting salary for the pay grade's lowest step may be too low to attract them. Pay ranges also let companies provide for performance differences between employees within the same grade or between those with different seniorities.

compa ratio
Equals an employee's pay rate divided by the pay range midpoint for his or her pay grade.

Compensation experts sometimes use *compa ratios.* The **compa ratio** equals an employee's pay rate divided by the pay range midpoint for his or her pay grade. A compa ratio of 1 means the employee is being paid exactly at the pay range midpoint. If the compa ratio is above 1 then the person's pay rate exceeds the midpoint pay for the job. If it is below then the pay rate is less than the midpoint. The compa ratio can help reveal how many jobs in each pay grade are paid above and below competitive market pay rates.[80]

15. Address Remaining Jobs

To this point, we have focused our job evaluation on a limited number of benchmark jobs, as is traditional. We now want to add our remaining jobs to the wage structure. We can do this in two ways. We can evaluate each of the remaining jobs using the same process we just went through. Or we can simply slot the remaining jobs into the wage structure where we feel they belong, without formally evaluating and assigning points to these jobs. Jobs similar enough to our benchmark jobs we can easily slot into the wage structure. Jobs we're not sure about should undergo the same job evaluation process; we assign points to them and precisely slot them into the wage structure.[81]

16. Correct Out-of-Line Rates

Finally, the wage rate the firm is now paying for a particular job may fall well off the wage curve or well outside the rate range for its grade, as illustrated in Figure 11-6 (page 362). This means that the average pay for that job is currently too high or too low, relative to other jobs in the firm. For underpaid jobs, the solution is clear: Raise the wages of underpaid employees to the minimum of the rate range for their pay grade.

Current pay rates falling above the rate range are a different story. These are "red circle," "flagged," or "overrates." There are several ways to cope with this problem. One is to freeze the rate paid to these employees until general salary increases bring the other jobs into line. A second option is to transfer or promote the employees involved to jobs for which you can legitimately pay them their current pay rates. The third option is to freeze the rate for 6 months, during which time you try to transfer or promote the overpaid employees. If you cannot, then cut the rate you pay these employees to the maximum in the pay range for their pay grade. The accompanying HR Tools feature explains a streamlined pay plan procedure for small businesses.

IMPROVING PERFORMANCE: *HR Tools for Line Managers and Small Businesses*

Developing a Workable Pay Plan

Pay plans are as important for small firms as a large ones. Pay that is too high wastes money; too low triggers turnover; and internally inequitable causes endless demands for raises. The owner who wants to concentrate on major issues like sales needs a rational pay plan.

Surveying market rates come first. Sites like LinkedIn and Salary.com will show localized average pay rates for jobs in your geographic area. The Sunday newspaper classified ads (online and offline) will contain information on wages offered for jobs similar to those you're trying to price. Local job service "one-stop" offices can provide a wealth of information, as they compile extensive information on pay ranges and averages for many jobs. Employment agencies, always anxious to form ties with employers, will provide good data. Local college and university career centers will reveal prevailing pay rates for many jobs. Professional associations (such as the careers link for civil engineers at www.asce.org) are good sources of professionals' pay rates.

Smaller firms are making use of the Internet in other ways. StockHouse Media Corp (www.stockhouse.com) uses the Web for determining salaries for all the firm's personnel. For example, the HR manager surfs the Web to monitor rates and trends by periodically checking job boards, company Web sites, LinkedIn, and industry associations.[82]

If you employ more than 20 employees or so, conduct at least a rudimentary job evaluation (probably using the ranking method we covered on pages 356–357). You will need job descriptions (see, for example O*NET and jobdescription.com), since these will be the source of data regarding the nature and worth of each job.

You may find it easier to split your employees into three clusters—say, managerial/professional, office/clerical, and plant personnel. For each of the three groups, choose one or more compensable factors. Then rank (or assign points to) each job in that cluster based on, say, a ranking job evaluation. For each job you will then want to create a pay range. In general, you might choose as the midpoint of that range the average market salary for that job, or an average of the market rate and what you are currently paying. Then produce a total range of about 30% around this average, broken into five steps. (Thus, assemblers, one of the plant personnel jobs, might earn from $8.00 to $12.60 per hour, in five steps.)

Required compensation policies will include amount of holiday and vacation pay (as we explain in Chapter 13), overtime pay policy, method of pay (weekly, biweekly, monthly), garnishments, and time card or sign-in sheet procedures. Many examples are available online.[83] ■

If your professor has assigned this, go to the Assignments section of **mymanagementlab.com** to complete these discussion questions.

Talk About It 3: What type of job evaluation method would you use in a company with 15 employees? Why?

Pricing Managerial and Professional Jobs

LEARNING OBJECTIVE **11-4**
Explain how to price managerial and professional jobs.

Developing compensation plans for managers or professionals is similar in many respects to developing plans for any employee. The basic aim is the same: to attract, motivate, and retain good employees. And job evaluation is about as applicable to managerial and professional jobs (below the top executive levels) as to production and clerical ones.

There are some big differences though. Managerial jobs tend to stress harder-to-quantify factors like judgment and problem solving more than do production and clerical jobs. There is also more emphasis on paying managers and professionals based on their performance or on what they can do, rather than on static job demands like working conditions. And one must compete in the marketplace for executives who sometimes have rock star pay. So, job evaluation, although still important for management jobs, usually plays a secondary role to issues like bonuses, incentives, market rates, and benefits.

What Determines Executive Pay?

The traditional wisdom is that company size and performance significantly affect top managers' salaries. Yet early studies showed that these explained only about 30% of CEO pay: "In reality, CEO pay is set by the board taking into account a variety of factors such as the business strategy, corporate trends, and most importantly where they want to be in a short and long term."[84] One study concluded that three main factors, *job complexity* (span of control, the number of functional divisions over which the executive has direct responsibility, and management level), the employer's *ability to pay* (total profit and rate of return), and the executive's *human capital* (educational level, field of study, work experience), accounted for about two-thirds of executive compensation variance.[85] In practice, CEOs exercise influence over their boards of directors, so their pay sometimes doesn't reflect strictly arms-length negotiations.[86]

Many employers do use job evaluation for pricing managerial jobs (at least, below the top jobs). The basic approach is to classify executive and management positions into grades, each with a salary range.

As with nonmanagerial jobs, one alternative is to rank the executive and management positions in relation to each other, then group into classes those of similar value. However, firms also use the job classification and point methods, with compensable factors like position scope, complexity, and difficulty. As with any jobs, job analysis, salary surveys, and the fine-tuning of salary levels around wage curves play roles.

Shareholder activism and government oversight have tightened the restrictions on what companies pay top executives. For example, the banking giant HSBC shelved plans to raise its CEO's pay by over a third after shareholders rejected the proposals.[87]

Compensating Executives

Compensation for a company's top executives usually consists of four main elements.[88] *Base pay* includes the person's fixed salary as well as, often, guaranteed bonuses such as "10% of pay at the end of the fourth fiscal quarter, regardless of whether the company makes a profit." *Short-term incentives* are usually cash or stock bonuses for achieving short-term goals, such as year-to-year sales revenue increases. *Long-term incentives* aim to encourage the executive to take actions that drive up the value of the company's stock and include things like stock options; these generally give the executive the right to purchase stock at a specific price for a specific period. Finally, *executive benefits and perks* include things such as supplemental executive retirement pension plans. With so many complicated elements, employers must also be alert to the tax and securities law implications of their executive compensation decisions.[89]

Salary is traditionally the cornerstone of executive compensation. On it, employers layer benefits, incentives, and perquisites—all normally conferred in proportion to base pay. Procter & Gamble Co.'s CEO was paid $15.2 million recently, including a base salary of $1.6 million, a cash-based bonus of $2.4 million, stock options valued at $4.4 million, stock awards of $6.45 million, plus perks such as air travel.[90] Top executive compensation packages can be whoppers. The CEO of Oracle earned just over $96 million in one recent year, and the CEO of Walt Disney Corporation $37.1 million.[91] But overpaid as many critics may think they are, one expert says CEOs with the highest 20% of compensation produced stock returns 60% greater than those of other firms in their industries.[92]

Executive compensation emphasizes performance (discussed in Chapter 12) more than do other employees' pay plans, since organizational results reflect executives' contributions more directly than those of lower-echelon employees.[93] Indeed, boards are boosting the emphasis on performance-based pay (in part due to shareholder activism). The big issue here is identifying the appropriate performance measures. Typical short-term measures include revenue growth and operating profit margin. Long-term measures include rate of return above some predetermined base.

Compensating Professional Employees

In compensating professionals, employers should first ensure that the person is actually a "professional" under the law. The Fair Labor Standards Act "provides an exemption from both minimum wage and overtime pay for employees employed as bona fide executive, administrative, professional and outside sales employees."[94] However, calling someone a professional doesn't make him or her one. In addition to earning at least $455 per week, the person's main duty must "be the performance of work requiring advanced knowledge," and "the advanced knowledge must be customarily acquired by a prolonged course of specialized intellectual instruction."[95] One company hired a high school graduate as an exempt "product design specialist II," earning $62,000 per year. The job required 12 years of relevant experience, but no particular education. The court ruled the job was nonexempt.[96]

Beyond that, compensating professional employees like engineers presents unique problems.[97] Analytical jobs emphasize compensable factors such as creativity and problem solving, ones not easily compared or measured. Furthermore, how do you measure performance? For example, the success of an engineer's design depends on how the firm develops and markets it.

Employers can use job evaluation for professional jobs. Compensable factors here tend to focus on problem solving, creativity, job scope, and technical knowledge and expertise. Firms use the point method and job classification.

Yet, in practice, firms rarely rely on just job evaluation for pricing professional jobs. Factors like creativity (as noted) are hard to measure, and non-pay issues often influence professionals' job decisions. For example, a few years ago Google raised its employees' salaries by 10% in the face of defections by even their highest-paid professionals, such as the head of its Chrome OS team, to Facebook.[98] Many of these Google professionals, although well paid by most standards, still felt underpaid. Some moved to jobs they hoped would have more challenges. Others may have sought younger firms with new stock options.

Most employers therefore emphasize a market-pricing approach for these jobs. They price professional jobs in the marketplace as best they can, to establish the values for benchmark jobs. Then they slot these benchmark jobs and their other professional jobs into a salary structure. Each professional discipline (such as engineer) usually ends up having four to six grade levels, each with a broad salary range. This helps employers remain competitive when bidding for professionals who literally have global employment possibilities.[99]

Improving Performance Through HRIS: Payroll Administration

Payroll administration is one of the first functions most employers computerize or outsource, and for good reason. Administering the payroll system—keeping track of each employee's FLSA worker status, wage rate, dependents, benefits, overtime, tax status, and so on; computing each paycheck; and then directing the actual printing of checks or direct deposits is a time-consuming task, one complicated by the need to comply with many federal, state, and local wage, hour, and other laws.

Many employers do perform this function in-house, usually with a payroll processing software package. Intuit's *Basic Payroll* lets the employer "enter hours worked and get instant paycheck calculations, including earnings, payroll taxes, and deductions. Then print paychecks yourself. *Basic Payroll* calculates federal and state payroll taxes for you, so you can easily e-pay federal taxes and write a check for state taxes."[100] Kronos's *Workforce Payroll* automates the payroll process, and offers self-service features. For example (see www.kronos.com/HR/Payroll-Software/Payroll-Software.aspx), *Workforce Payroll* will "let your employees see pay stubs and earning histories, make changes to direct deposit and W-4 forms, print W-2s, and even check out how changes to their deductions will affect their paychecks."

On the other hand, many employers do outsource payroll administration to vendors such as ADP. These vendors offer a range of payroll processing options. For instance, smaller employers may opt to call in their payroll data to the vendor's specialists, while larger ones may have this data processed automatically online. In deciding which vendor to use, the employer should consider its goals and the potential economic benefits, as well as factors such as the vendor's reputation. SHRM recommends evaluating the initial list of prospective vendors based on the employer's goals for the relationship. Don't just consider the relative economic benefits of outsourcing the function (rather than doing it in-house), but also the desirability of integrating the employer's internal systems with the vendor's, streamlining tax compliance and filings, and increasing employee self-service.[101] ■

LEARNING OBJECTIVE **11-5**

Explain the difference between competency-based and traditional pay plans.

Contemporary Topics in Compensation

In this final section, we'll look at five important contemporary compensation topics: competency-based pay, broadbanding, comparable worth, board oversight of executive pay, and total rewards.

Many employers, such as General Mills, pay certain workers based on attained skill levels.

Mark Richard/PhotoEdit, Inc.

Competency-Based Pay

Some managers question whether job evaluations that slot jobs into narrow cubbyholes ("Machinist I," "Machinist II," and so on) might not actually be counterproductive. For example, high-performance work systems depend on flexible multiskilled job assignments and on teamwork, and there's no place here for employees to say, "That's not my job."

competency-based pay
Where the company pays for the employee's range, depth, and types of skills and knowledge, rather than for the job title he or she holds.

Competency-based pay aims to avoid that problem.[102] With competency (generally skill or knowledge-based) pay, you pay the employee for the skills and knowledge he or she is capable of using rather than for the responsibilities or title of the job currently held.[103] Experts variously call this competence-, knowledge-, or skill-based pay. With competency-based pay, an employee in a class I job who could (but may not have to at the moment) do class II work gets paid as a class II worker, not a class I. *Competencies* are demonstrable personal characteristics such as knowledge, skills, and personal behaviors such as leadership. Why pay employees based on the skill levels they achieve, rather than based on the jobs they're assigned to? With more companies organizing around teams, you want to encourage employees to get and to use the skills required to rotate among jobs.

In practice, competency-based pay usually comes down to pay for knowledge, or skill based pay.[104] Most such pay programs generally contain five elements. The employer *defines* specific required skills and chooses a *method* for basing the person's pay on his or her skills. A *training* system lets employees acquire skills. There is a formal competency *testing* system. And, the work is *designed* so that employees can easily move among jobs of varying skill levels. As an example, review Chapter 4's Figure 4-11 on page 120. For this job, BP lists the minimum level for each skill (such as Technical Expertise, and Problem Solving) someone holding this job must attain. As an employee achieves each level of each skill, he or she would receive a bump in pay. The accompanying JLG program feature shows another example.

IMPROVING PERFORMANCE: *HR Practices Around the Globe*

JLG's Skill-Based Pay Program

JLG industries supplies access equipment such as aerial work platforms and mast booms.[105] The firm instituted a skill-based pay program to reward employees for the number of basic skills they can perform rather than for the jobs to which they are assigned.[106] JLG integrated the skill pay program into its existing payroll system, and supported it with a computerized reporting system.

As an employee acquires and masters a new skill, JLG increases his or her pay on a scheduled basis. Pay increases are directly proportional to employee "value" based on skill acquisition. Pay adjustment increments are $0.30 per hour and can be in addition to regularly scheduled merit increases. Qualified employees are eligible to receive a skill-based wage adjustment at three times. The first increase is available at the completion of an initial 6-month probationary employment period. An additional skill-based adjustment may come in conjunction with the employee's annual merit review. Other skill-based adjustments are allowed yearly and 6 months after the annual merit review.

JLG assigns hourly production and maintenance workers to a particular "job family." A job family consists of a group of employees performing similar activities and requiring similar skills. *Each job family has a set of required skills,* including certain job-related skills as well as skills related to quality and safety.

Skill assessment is ongoing. Formal evaluation begins at the end of the 6-month probationary period, at which time the employee is tested for mastery of *the minimum skills* required for the job family. (A 100% mastery of these minimum skills is required for successful completion of the probationary period.) Then, twice a year, the company analyzes the employee's progress toward more *advanced skills*, and sets training objectives. Overall responsibility for skills acquisition and career development rests with the employee. The employee determines his/her level of participation in acquiring new or additional skills. Supervisors assist by helping the employee identify and plan for new skills to be acquired, and by creating opportunities for cross-training and certifying the skills training.

To determine if an employee is qualified for a skill-based pay raise, a comparison is made between the employee's current wage rate and the skill-based target rate within the job family to which the employee is assigned. If the current wage rate is equal to or greater than the target rate, no pay adjustment is made. If the current rate is below the target rate, a skill-based adjustment is authorized for employees who mastered the job family's skills.

In place since the 1990s, JLG reports that the program is producing benefits. The skill mastery it fosters permits faster adaptation to technology and product mix changes. With a greater skill range, workers are better able to focus on problem areas and avoid idle time waiting for problems to be fixed, or for work done by others. Employees participate more actively in problem solving because of their wider perspective on total workflow. The program permits lower overall staffing levels by incorporating into job family skill requirements specialized tasks others might otherwise be hired to perform. The company has been able to raise minimum hiring qualifications. Overall increases in productivity have enabled expansion of capacity. ■

Source: From "JLG Industries, Inc., "Information: Skill-Based Pay Program," www.bmpcoe.org/bestpractices/internal/jlg/jlg_14.html.

If your professor has assigned this, go to the Assignments section of **mymanagementlab.com** to complete this discussion.

Talk About It 4: Review our discussion of competencies in Chapter 4; then write three competency statements for one job you believe they would have at a company such as JLG. A useful competency statement includes three elements: the *name and a brief description* of the competency, a *description of the observable behaviors* that represent proficiency in the competency, and *proficiency levels*.

Broadbanding

Most firms end up with pay plans that slot jobs into classes or grades, each with its own vertical pay rate range. For example, the U.S. government's pay plan consists of 15 main grades (GS-1 to GS-15), each with its own pay range. For an employee whose job falls in one of these grades, the pay range for that grade dictates his or her minimum and maximum salary.

The question is, "How wide should the salary grades be, in terms of the number of job evaluation points they include?" (For example, should the U.S. government collapse its 15 salary grades into 5 or 6 broader bands.) There is a downside to having (say, 15) narrow grades. For instance, if you want someone whose job is in grade 2 to fill in for a time in a job that happens to be in grade 1, it's difficult to reassign that person without lowering his or her salary. Similarly, if you want the person to learn about a job that happens to be in grade 3, the employee might first want a corresponding raise to grade 3 pay. Traditional grade pay plans thus may tend to breed inflexibility.

broadbanding
Consolidating salary grades and ranges into just a few wide levels or "bands," each of which contains a relatively wide range of jobs and salary levels.

That is why some firms broadband their pay plans.[107] **Broadbanding** means collapsing salary grades into just a few wide levels or bands, each of which contains a relatively wide range of jobs and pay levels. Figure 11-11 illustrates this. Here, the company's previous six pay grades are consolidated into two broad grades or "broadbands."

FIGURE 11-11
Broadbanded Structure and How It Relates to Traditional Pay Grades and Ranges

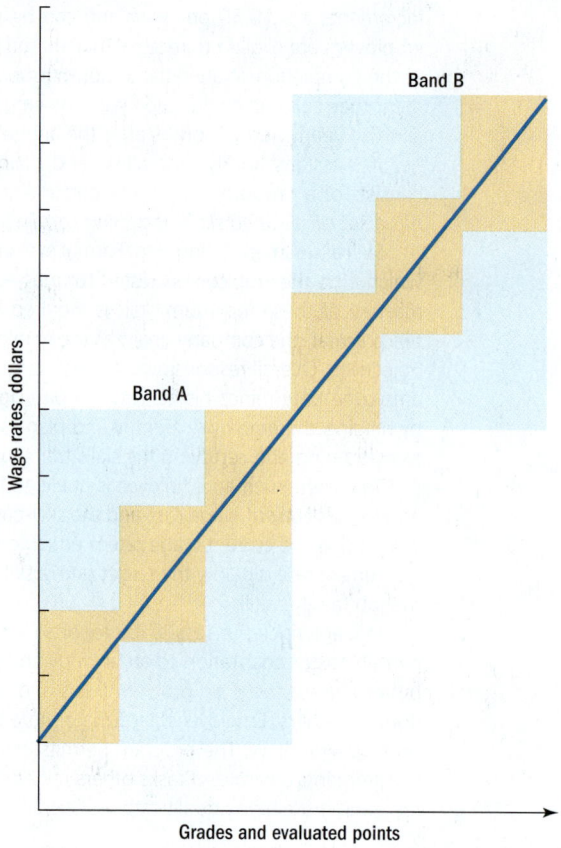

A company may create broadbands for all its jobs, or for specific groups such as managers or professionals. The (vertical) pay rate range of each broadband is relatively large, since it ranges from the minimum pay of the lowest grade the firm merged into the broadband up to the maximum pay of the highest merged grade. Thus, for example, instead of having 10 salary grades, each of which contains a salary range of $15,000, the firm might collapse the 10 grades into three broadbands, each with a set of jobs such that the difference between the lowest- and highest-paid jobs might be $40,000 or more. For the jobs that fall in this broadband, there is therefore a much wider range of pay rates. You can move an employee from job to job within the broadband more easily, without worrying about the employee's moving outside the relatively narrow rate range associated with a traditional narrow pay grade.

Broadbanding injects greater flexibility into employee pay.[108] For example, "the employee who needs to spend time in a lower-level job to develop a certain skill set can receive higher-than-usual pay for the work, a circumstance considered impossible under traditional pay systems."[109] Conversely, employees assigned to traditional narrowly defined pay grades may take a "that's not my job" attitude and focus on their usual assigned duties.[110]

comparable worth
The concept by which women who are usually paid less than men can claim that men in comparable rather than in strictly equal jobs are paid more.

Comparable Worth

Comparable worth refers to the requirement to pay men and women equal wages for jobs that are dissimilar but of comparable value (for instance measured in points) to the employer. This may mean comparing dissimilar jobs, such as nurses to truck mechanics. The question "comparable worth" seeks to address is this: Should you pay women who are performing jobs *equal* to men's or just *comparable* to men's the same as men?

County of Washington v. Gunther (1981) was a pivotal case. It involved Washington County, Oregon, prison matrons who claimed sex discrimination. The county had evaluated roughly comparable (but different) men's jobs as having 5%

more "job content" (based on a point evaluation system) than the women's jobs, but paid the men 35% more.[111] Why should there be such a pay discrepancy for roughly comparable jobs? After moving through the courts to the U.S. Supreme Court, Washington County finally agreed to pay 35,000 employees in female-dominated jobs almost $500 million in pay raises over 7 years to settle.

Comparable worth has implications for job evaluation. Virtually every comparable worth case that reached court involved the point method of job evaluation. By assigning points to dissimilar jobs, point plans facilitate comparability ratings among different jobs. Should employers still use point plans? Perhaps the wisest approach is for employers to price their jobs as they see fit (with or without point plans), but to also ensure that women have equal access to all jobs. In other words, eliminate sex-segregated jobs.

Diveristy Counts: The Pay Gap

All this notwithstanding, women in the United States earn only about 81% as much as men.[112] In general, education may reduce the wage gap somewhat.[113] But gaps remain, even among the most highly trained. For example, new female medical doctors recently earned about $17,000 per year less than their male counterparts did.[114] Reasons put forward for the male-female gap range from the outdated notion that employers view women as having less leverage, to the fact that professional men change jobs more often (gaining more raises in the process) and that women tend to end up in departments that pay less.[115] In any case, it's a problem employers should recognize and address. ■

✪ Watch It!

How do companies actually adjust salaries and raises? If your professor has assigned this, go to the Assignments section of mymanagementlab.com to complete the video exercise titled *Compensation (Focus Pointe).*

Board Oversight of Executive Pay

There are various reasons why boards are scrutinizing their executives' pay more than in the past. The Dodd-Frank Law of 2010 requires that American companies give shareholders a "say on pay." Law firms are filing class-action suits demanding information from companies about their senior executive pay decisions.[116] The Financial Accounting Standards Board requires that most public companies recognize as an expense the fair value of the stock options they grant.[117] The Sarbanes-Oxley Act makes executives personally liable, under certain conditions, for corporate financial oversight lapses. The chief justice of Delaware's Supreme Court said that governance issues, shareholder activism, and other changes have "created a new set of expectations for directors."[118] The Securities and Exchange Commission (SEC) requires filing detailed compensation-related information, including a listing of all individual "perks" or benefits if they total more than $100,000.[119]

The net result is that lawyers specializing in executive pay suggest that boards of directors (whose compensation committees usually make these pay decisions in large firms) ask themselves these questions:[120]

- Has our compensation committee identified its duties and processes?
- Is our compensation committee using the appropriate compensation advisors?
- Are there particular executive compensation issues that our committee should address?[121]
- Do our procedures demonstrate diligence and independence (including careful deliberations and records)?
- Is our committee appropriately communicating its decisions? How will shareholders react?[122]

LEARNING OBJECTIVE **11-6**

Describe the importance of total rewards for improving employee engagement.

Employee Engagement Guide For Managers

Total Rewards Programs

Total rewards is an important concept in compensation management. People bring to their jobs many needs—for challenging work and for respect and appreciation, for instance—not all of which are satisfied by pay or bonuses. "'Total rewards' encompass not only compensation and benefits but also personal and professional growth opportunities and a motivating work environment."[123] It includes not just traditional financial rewards (wages and incentives plus benefits and perks), but also nonfinancial and intangible rewards such as recognition, the nature of the job/quality of work, career development opportunities,[124] good relationships with managers and colleagues, organizational justice, trust in employees, feeling of being valued and involved, opportunities for promotion,[125] and a great work climate.[126] Total rewards also include recognition programs and redesigned jobs (discussed in Chapter 4), telecommuting programs, health and well-being programs, and training and career development.

TRENDS SHAPING HR: *DIGITAL AND SOCIAL MEDIA*

Noncash recognition/appreciation rewards such as gift cards, merchandise, and recognition are important parts of such total compensation.[127]

New digital and social media tools enable employees to recognize and reward each other. For example, a West Virginia DuPont plant installed an online system that enabled employees to give each other recognition; 95% were soon using it.[128] International Fitness Holdings lets employees use a Facebook-type application to recognize peers by posting messages and sending private e-mails.[129] Employers contract with sites like Globoforce.com to provide online recognition systems. ■

Total Rewards and Employee Engagement

When it comes to employee engagement, both material and non-material rewards—total rewards—seem essential. [130] For example, one study found that base pay and benefits alone were weakly related to engagement.[131] However, intangible rewards (such as the nature of the job/quality of work and career development opportunities) had high or very high impacts on engagement and performance, when combined with base salary and short-term incentives or bonuses.[132]

It's therefore not surprising that many high-engagement employers do emphasize total rewards. For example, the values laid out in Toyota's famous "The Toyota Way" include mutual trust and respect, stable employment, helping employees to develop their technical skills, and "support for production staff combining work with childcare, career design support, and raising of corporate awareness." Disney emphasizes providing employees/cast members with a total rewards package that includes pay plus various benefits and career development opportunities.[133] Similarly, many "Best Companies to Work For" emphasize intangible rewards. For example, one top executive at NetApp takes an opportunity to call and thank several employees each day for their efforts, and Whole Foods emphasizes employee involvement, for instance letting employees vote on new hires and see what all Whole Foods employees earn.[134] At SAS there is stimulating work, an empowering management philosophy, flexible work, and an emphasis on being happy at work.[135]

In addition to encouraging such rewards, the employer should issue total reward statements periodically. List all the rewards—financial and nonfinancial—the company offers, and note their importance to the employees' overall well-being.[136] Doing so increases their impact.

Chapter Review

MyManagementLab® Go to **mymanagementlab.com** to complete the problems marked with this icon. ✪

Chapter Section Summaries

11-1. In establishing strategic pay plans, managers first need to understand some **basic factors in determining pay rates**. Employee compensation includes both direct financial payments and indirect financial statements. The factors determining the design of any pay plan include legal, union, company strategy/policy, and equity. Legal considerations include, most importantly, the Fair Labor Standards Act, which governs matters such as minimum wages and overtime pay. Specific categories of employees are exempt from the act or certain provisions of the act, particularly its overtime provisions. The Equal Pay Act of 1963 and the Employee Retirement Income Security Act are other important laws.

11-2. Employers use two basic approaches to setting pay rates: *market-based approaches* and **job evaluation methods**. Many firms, particularly smaller ones, simply use a *market-based* approach. Job evaluation methods involve assigning values to each of the company's jobs. This helps to produce a pay plan in which each job's pay is equitable based on its value to the employer. Popular job evaluation methods include ranking, job classification, and the point method.

11-3. We said the process of **creating a market-competitive pay plan** while ensuring external, internal, and procedural equity consists of 16 steps as follows: (1) Choose benchmark jobs; (2) Select compensable factors; (3) Assign weights to compensable factors; (4) Convert percentages to points for each factor; (5) Define each factor's degrees; (6) Determine for each factor its factor degrees' points; (7) Review job descriptions and job specifications; (8) Evaluate the jobs; (9) Draw the current (internal) wage curve; (10) Conduct a market analysis: Salary surveys; (11) Draw the market (external) wage curve; (12) Compare and adjust current and market wage rates for jobs; (13) Develop pay grades; (14) Establish rate ranges; (15) Address remaining jobs; and (16) Correct out-of-line rates.

11-4. **Pricing managerial and professional jobs** involves some special issues. Managerial pay typically consists of base pay, short-term incentives, long-term incentives, and executive benefits and, particularly at the top levels, doesn't lend itself to job evaluation but rather to understanding the job's complexity, the employer's ability to pay, and the need to be competitive in attracting top talent.

11-5. We addressed five important **special topics in compensation**. More employers are moving from paying jobs based on their intrinsic duties toward paying jobs based on the competencies the job requires. Broadbanding means consolidating several rates and ranges into a few wide levels or "bands," each of which contains a relatively wide range of jobs in salary levels. Comparable worth refers to the requirement to pay men and women equal pay for jobs that are of comparable rather than strictly equal value to the employee. With many stockholders concerned with excessive executive remuneration, board oversight of executive pay has become an important issue, and boards of directors should use qualified advisors and exercise diligence and independence in formulating executive pay plans.

11-6. Research shows that if **employee engagement** is the aim, it makes sense to emphasize total rewards, not just financial rewards. For example, one study found that base pay and benefits alone had a weak relationship with employee engagement. However, total rewards including intangible rewards such as the nature of the job/quality of work, and career development opportunities had a high or very high impact on engagement and performance, when combined with base salary and short-term incentives or bonuses.

Discussion Questions

✪ **11-1.** What is the difference between exempt and nonexempt jobs?

11-2. Should the job evaluation depend on an appraisal of the jobholder's performance? Why? Why not?

11-3. What is the relationship between compensable factors and job specifications?

✪ **11-4.** Define and give an example of how to conduct a job evaluation.

11-5. The average pay for most university presidents is around $300,000 per year, but many earn much more. For example, the president of NYU received about $1 million in 1 year. Discuss why you would (or would not) pay university presidents as much as or more than many corporate CEOs.

11-6. Do small companies need to develop a pay plan? Why or why not?

Individual and Group Activities

11-7. Working individually or in groups, conduct salary surveys for the following positions: entry-level accountant and entry-level chemical engineer. What sources did you use, and what conclusions did you reach? If you were the HR manager for a local engineering firm, what would you recommend that you pay for each job?

11-8. Working individually or in groups, develop compensation policies for the teller position at a local bank. Assume that there are four tellers: two were hired in May and the other two were hired in December. The compensation policies should address the following: appraisals, raises, holidays, vacation pay, overtime pay, method of pay, garnishments, and time cards.

11-9. Working individually or in groups, access relevant Web sites to determine what equitable pay ranges are for these jobs: chemical engineer, marketing manager, and HR manager, all with a bachelor's degree and 5 years' experience. Do so for the following cities: New York, New York; San Francisco, California; Houston, Texas; Denver, Colorado; Miami, Florida; Atlanta, Georgia; Chicago, Illinois; Birmingham, Alabama; Detroit, Michigan; and Washington, D.C. For each position in each city, what are the pay ranges and the average pay? Does geographical location impact the salaries of the different positions? If so, how?

11-10. Appendices A and B at the end of this book (pages 612–629) list the knowledge someone studying for the HRCI (Appendix A) or SHRM (Appendix B) certification exam needs to have in each area of human resource management (such as in Strategic Management, and Workforce Planning). In groups of several students, do four things: (1) review Appendix A and/or B; (2) identify the material in this chapter that relates to the Appendix A and/or B required knowledge lists; (3) write four multiple-choice exam questions on this material that you believe would be suitable for inclusion in the HRCI exam and/or the SHRM exam; and, (4) if time permits, have someone from your team post your team's questions in front of the class, so that students in all teams can answer the exam questions created by the other teams.

11-11. Working individually or in groups, use the point system described in steps 1 to 16 in this chapter. Do so for a job description that you find online—a list like that at http://hiring.monster.com/hr/hr-best-practices/recruiting-hiring-advice/job-descriptions/sample-job-descriptions.aspx is useful. To simplify things, assume there is only one compensable factor you have to use, and that it is job complexity, so that you can use Figure 11-5.

Experiential Exercise

Ranking the College's Administrators

Purpose: The purpose of this exercise is to give you experience in performing a job evaluation using the ranking method.

Required Understanding: You should be thoroughly familiar with the ranking method of job evaluation and obtain job descriptions for your college's dean, department chairperson, director of admissions, library director, registrar, and your professor.

How to Set Up the Exercise/Instructions: Divide the class into groups of four or five students. The groups will perform a job evaluation of the positions of dean, department chairperson, and professor using the ranking method.

Perform a job evaluation by ranking the jobs. You may use one or more compensable factors.

11-12. If time permits, a spokesperson from each group can put his or her group's rankings on the board. Did the groups end up with about the same results? How did they differ? Why do you think they differed?

Application Case

Salary Inequities at AstraZeneca

More than 50 years after passage of the Equal Pay Act, women in America still earn about 80 cents for every dollar earned by a man. That adds up to a loss for the average female worker of about $380,000 over a lifetime.

Recently, the U.S. Department of Labor's Office of Federal Contract Compliance Programs (OFCCP) entered into an agreement with AstraZeneca, a large international pharmaceuticals firm, for the company to pay some of its female sales associates a total of $250,000.[137] AstraZeneca had a contract valued at over $2 billion with the U.S. Department of Veterans Affairs to provide drugs to hospitals around the country. That made it subject to Executive Order 11246, which aims to ensure that employees of U.S. contractors and subcontractors with federal contracts pay their employees fairly without regard to sex, race, color, religion, and national origin.

After conducting a compliance review, the OFCCP concluded that AstraZeneca violated Executive Order 11246 by failing to ensure certain women employees were paid fairly. According to the OFCCP lawsuit, an AstraZeneca Business Center had routinely paid some of its female "primary care" and "specialty care" level III pharmaceutical sales specialists an average of $1,700 less than men with the same positions. Because of the company's pay secrecy policies, many of the women didn't know they were being paid less. In addition to the financial settlement, AstraZeneca and OFCCP will review records of the firm's female employees in 14 states. If they find additional statistical evidence of wage discrimination, the company must remedy it.

Questions

AstraZeneca has brought you in as a compensation consultant. Here are the questions they would like you to answer for them:

11-13. Although the case with OFCCP is closed, we wonder if there are any less discriminatory explanations possible for why our women sales reps on average earned less than men. If so, what are they?

11-14. Our own company now uses a point method to evaluate jobs for pay purposes, and each resulting job class also has a rate range associated with it. Sales associates are now paid a salary that is not based on incentive pay. List three specific things we can do to ensure that a similar problem (inequitable pay based on gender) does not arise again, assuming they continue using the point plan.

11-15. What sort of compensation plan would you recommend for us, and why?

Continuing Case

Carter Cleaning Company

The New Pay Plan

Carter Cleaning Centers does not have a formal wage structure nor does it have rate ranges or use compensable factors. Wage rates are based mostly on those prevailing in the surrounding community and are tempered with an attempt on the part of Jack Carter to maintain some semblance of equity between what workers with different responsibilities in the stores are paid.

Carter does not make any formal surveys when determining what his company should pay. He peruses the want ads almost every day and conducts informal surveys among his friends in the local chapter of the laundry and cleaners trade association. While Jack has taken a "seat-of-the-pants" approach to paying employees, his salary schedule has been guided by several basic pay policies. Although many of his colleagues adhere to a policy of paying minimum rates, Jack has always followed a policy of paying his employees about 10% above what he feels are the prevailing rates, a policy that he believes reduces turnover while fostering employee loyalty. Of somewhat more concern to

Jennifer is her father's informal policy of paying men about 20% more than women for the same job. Her father's explanation is, "They're stronger and can work harder for longer hours, and besides they all have families to support."

Questions

11-16. Is the company at the point where it should be setting up a formal salary structure based on a complete job evaluation? Why?

11-17. Is Jack Carter's policy of paying 10% more than the prevailing rates a sound one, and how could that be determined?

11-18. Similarly, is Carter's male–female differential wise? If not, why not?

11-19. Specifically, what would you suggest Jennifer do now with respect to her company's pay plan?

Translating Strategy into HR Policies and Practices Case*,§

**The accompanying strategy map for this chapter is in MyManagementLab, and the overall map on the inside back cover of this text outlines the relationships involved.*

Improving Performance at the Hotel Paris

The New Compensation Plan

The Hotel Paris's competitive strategy is "To use superior guest service to differentiate the Hotel Paris properties, and to thereby increase the length of stay and return rate of guests, and thus boost revenues and profitability." HR manager Lisa Cruz must now formulate functional policies and activities that support this competitive strategy by eliciting the required employee behaviors and competencies.

Like several other HR systems at the Hotel Paris, the compensation program was unplanned and unsophisticated. The company has a narrow target range for what it will pay employees in each job category (front-desk clerk, security guard, and so forth). Each hotel manager decides where to start a new employee within that narrow pay range. The company has given little thought to tying general pay levels or individual employees' pay to the company's strategic goals. For example, the firm's policy is simply to pay its employees a "competitive salary," by which it means about average for what other hotels in the city are paying for similar jobs. Lisa knows that pay policies like these may actually run counter to what the company wants to achieve strategically, in terms of creating an extraordinarily service-oriented workforce. How can you hire and retain a top workforce, and channel its behaviors toward high-quality guest services, if you don't somehow link performance and pay? She and her team therefore turn to the task of assessing and redesigning the company's compensation plan.

Even the most casual review by Lisa Cruz and the CFO made it clear that the company's compensation plan wasn't designed to support the firm's new strategic goals. For one thing, they knew that they should pay somewhat more on average than did their competitors if they expected employees to exceed expectations when it came to serving guests. Yet their review of a variety of metrics (including the Hotel Paris's salary/competitive salary ratios, the total compensation expense per employee, and the target percentile for total compensation) suggested that in virtually all job categories the Hotel Paris paid no more than average and, occasionally, paid somewhat less.

The current compensation policies had also bred what one hotel manager called an "I don't care" attitude on the part of most employees. What she meant was that most Hotel Paris employees quickly learned that regardless of what their performance was, they always ended up getting paid about the same as employees who performed better and worse than they did. So, the firm's compensation plan actually created a disconnect between pay and performance: It was not channeling employees' behaviors toward those required to achieve the company's goals. In some ways, it was doing the opposite.

Lisa and the CFO knew they had to institute a new, strategic compensation plan. They wanted a plan that improved employee morale, contributed to employee engagement, reduced employee turnover, and rewarded (and thus encouraged) the sorts of service-oriented behaviors that boosted guest satisfaction. After meeting with the company's CEO and the board, the CFO gave Lisa the go-ahead to redesign the company's compensation plan, with the overall aim of creating a new plan that would support the company's strategic aims.

Lisa and her team (which included a consulting compensation expert) set numerous new measurable compensation policies for the Hotel Paris, and these new policies formed the heart of the new compensation plan. A new job evaluation study provided a more rational and fair basis upon which the company could assign pay rates. A formal compensation survey by the consultant established, for the first time at the Hotel Paris, a clear picture of what competitive hotels and similar businesses were paying in each geographic area, and enabled the Hotel Paris team to more accurately set targets for what each position at the hotel should be paying. Rather than just paying at the industry average, or slightly below, the new policy called for the Hotel Paris to move all its salaries into the 75th percentile over the next 3 years.

As they instituted the new compensation policies, Lisa and the CFO were pleased to learn from feedback from the hotel managers that they were already noting several positive changes. The number of applicants for each position had increased by over 50% on average, turnover dropped by 80%, and surveys of morale and commitment were producing higher results. Lisa and her team now began to consider how to inject more of a "pay for performance" element into the company's compensation plan, perhaps by instituting new bonuses and incentives. We will see what she did in Chapter 12.

Questions

11-20. Lisa knew little about setting up a new compensation plan. Based on what you learned here in Dessler *Human Resource Management*, what would you tell her if she asked, "How do I set up a new compensation plan for the Hotel Paris?"

11-21. Would you suggest that Hotel Paris implement a competency-based pay plan for its nonmanagerial staff? Why or why not? Outline what they need to do for one.

11-22. Devise a ranking job evaluation system for the Hotel Paris's nonmanagerial employees (housekeepers, valets, front-desk clerks, phone operators, waitstaff, groundskeepers, and security guards) and use it to show the worth of these jobs relative to one another.

§ Written and copyright by Gary Dessler, PhD.

MyManagementLab

Go to **mymanagementlab.com** for Auto-graded writing questions as well as the following Assisted-graded writing questions:

11-23. You want to hire a new salesperson for the small dress shop you own in Columbus, Ohio, but first need to decide what sort of pay package to offer whomever you eventually hire. How would you conduct a salary survey to determine what the pay should be?

11-24. Compare and contrast the following methods of job evaluation: ranking, classification, factor comparison, and point method.

11-25. MyManagementLab Only–comprehensive writing assignment for this chapter.

✪ Try It!

How would you use pay or other components of a total rewards program to solve a "motivation problem" in a company? If your professor has assigned this, go to the Assignments section of mymanagementlab.com to complete the simulation: *Motivation.*

Key Terms

employee compensation, 346
direct financial payments, 346
indirect financial payments, 346
Davis-Bacon Act (1931), 347
Walsh-Healey Public Contract Act (1936), 347
Title VII of the 1964 Civil Rights Act, 347
Fair Labor Standards Act (1938), 347
Equal Pay Act, 351
Employee Retirement Income Security Act (ERISA), 351
job evaluation, 354
market-competitive pay plan, 354
compensable factor, 355
benchmark job, 356
ranking method, 356
job classification (or job grading), 357
classes, 357
grades, 357
grade definition, 358
point method, 358
market-competitive pay system, 362
wage curve, 362
salary survey, 363
pay (or wage) grade, 366
pay (or rate) ranges, 367
compa ratio, 368
competency-based pay, 372
broadbanding, 373
comparable worth, 374

Endnotes

1. Elayne Robertson Demby, "Two Stores Refused to Join the Race to the Bottom for Benefits and Wages," *Workforce Management*, February 2004, pp. 57–59; www.wegmans.com/webapp/wcs/stores/servlet/CategoryDisplay?categoryId=284278&storeId=10052&langId=-1, accessed July 13, 2015.
2. Richard Henderson, *Compensation Management* (Reston, VA: Reston Publishing, 1980), pp. 101–127; and Stacey L. Kaplan, "Total Rewards in Action: Developing a Total Rewards Strategy," *Benefits & Compensation Digest* 42, no. 8 (August 2005), pp. 32–37.
3. Duncan Brown, "The Future of Reward Management: From Total Reward Strategies to Smart Rewards," *Compensation & Benefits Review* 46, no. 3, pp. 147–151.
4. Nicholas Wade, "Play Fair: Your Life May Depend on It," *New York Times*, September 12, 2003, p. 12.
5. Robert Bretz and Stephen Thomas, "Perceived Inequity, Motivation, and Final Offer Arbitration in Major League Baseball," *Journal of Applied Psychology*, June 1992, pp. 280–282; Reginald Ell, "Addressing Employees' Feelings of Inequity: Capitalizing on Equity Theory in Modern Management," *Supervision* 72, no. 5 (May 2011), pp. 3–6.
6. James DeConinck and Duane Bachmann, "An Analysis of Turnover Among Retail Buyers," *Journal of Business Research* 58, no. 7 (July 2005), pp. 874–882.
7. Michael Harris et al., "Keeping Up with the Joneses: A Field Study of the Relationships Among Upward, Lateral, and Downward Comparisons and Pay Level Satisfaction," *Journal of Applied Psychology* 93, no. 3 (2008), pp. 665–673.
8. David Terpstra and Andre Honoree, "The Relative Importance of External, Internal, Individual, and Procedural Equity to Pay Satisfaction," *Compensation & Benefits Review*, November/December 2003, pp. 67–74.
9. Ibid., p. 68.
10. Millicent Nelson et al., "Pay Me More: What Companies Need to Know About Employee Pay Satisfaction," *Compensation & Benefits Review*, March/April 2008, pp. 35–42.
11. Pay inequities manifest in unexpected ways. In one study, the researchers studied the impact of keeping pay rates secret, rather than publicizing them. They found that individuals with lower levels of tolerance for inequity reacted particularly harshly to pay secrecy in terms of weaker individual test performance. Peter Bamberger and Elena Belogolovsky, "The Impact of Pay Secrecy on Individual Test Performance," *Personnel Psychology* 60, no. 3 (2010), pp. 965–996.
12. Rachel Emma Silverman, "Psst.... This Is What Your Coworker Is Paid," *Wall Street Journal*, January 30, 2013, p. B6. Pay confidentiality may also violate the National Labor Relations Act, which permits workers to engage in concerted activities for collective bargaining "or other mutual aid or protection." Howard Risher, "Pay Transparency Is Coming," *Compensation & Benefits Review* 46, no. 1 (2014), pp. 3–5.
13. Frank Giancola, "What the Research Says About the Effects of Open Pay Policies on Employees' Pay Satisfaction and Job Performance," *Compensation & Benefits Review* 46, no. 3 (May/June 2014), pp. 161–168.
14. Henderson, *Compensation Management*; see also Barry Gerhart and Sara Rynes, *Compensation: Theory, Evidence, and Strategic Implications* (Thousand Oaks, CA: Sage Publications, 2003); and Joseph Martocchio, *Strategic Compensation* (Upper Saddle River, NJ: Prentice Hall, 2006), pp. 67–94.
15. In a recent case, *Ledbetter v. Goodyear Tire & Rubber Co.*, the U.S. Supreme Court notably restricted the amount of time (to 180 or 300 days) after each allegedly discriminatory pay decision under Title VII to file or forever lose the claim.

Congress subsequently passed and President Obama signed a new law significantly expanding the amount of time to file such claims.
16. The Genetic Information Nondiscrimination Act amended the Fair Labor Standards Act to increase penalties for the death or serious injury of employees under age 18. Allen Smith, "Penalties for Child Labor Violations Increase," *HR Magazine*, July 2008, p. 19.
17. States including Alaska, Arkansas, California, Colorado, Connecticut, Hawaii, Illinois, Kentucky, Maryland, Minnesota, Montana, New Jersey, North Dakota, Oregon, Pennsylvania, Washington, West Virginia, and Wisconsin have their own overtime laws.
18. We'll see that the federal government is pressing to expand employment overtime eligibility. See, for example, "Obama Signs Memo Telling Labor Department to Expand Employee Overtime Eligibility," *Bloomberg BNA Bulletin to Management*, March 18, 2014, pp. 81–82.
19. "LinkedIn to Pay $5.8 Million in Overtime, Damages to 359 Employees in Four States," *Bloomberg BNA Bulletin to Management*, August 12, 2014, p. 251.
20. Ibid., p. 215.
21. James Coleman, "App Provides Reminder to Ensure Recordkeeping Is in Order," *BNA Bulletin to Management*, June 14, 2011, p. 191.
22. www.pacifictimesheet.com/timesheet_products/pacific_timesheet_handheld_pda_field_data_entry_software.htm, accessed March 23, 2009.
23. Coleman, "App Provides Reminder."
24. Dave Zielinski, "On the Clock," *HR Magazine*, April 2012, pp. 67–68. "Time stealing" is a serious problem. One study concluded that about 21% of hourly employees may be stealing company time, mostly by punching in and out earlier or later than scheduled. To deal with this problem, employers are increasingly utilizing biometric technology to track attendance. For example, one company uses a facial recognition device to identify who is punching in or out. Sarah Fister Gale, "Employers Punching in Biometric Technology to Track Attendance," *Workforce Management*, May 2013, p. 14.
25. www.ncsl.org/research/labor-and-employment/state-minimum-wage-chart.aspx, accessed April 12, 2015.
26. www.nbcnews.com/feature/in-plain-sight/minimum-wage-hikes-where-voters-gave-themselves-raise-n241616, accessed April 12, 2015.
27. *Bloomberg BNA Bulletin to Management*, "The DOL Releases Proposed Rule Setting $10.10 as Minimum Wage for Federal Contractors," June 17, 2014, pp. 185–186.
28. For a description of exemption requirements, see Jeffrey Friedman, "The Fair Labor Standards Act Today: A Primer," *Compensation*, January/February 2002, pp. 51–54. See also www.shrm.org/issues/FLSA, accessed August 12, 2007; and www.dol.gov/whd/flsa, accessed September 3, 2014.
29. "Employer Ordered to Pay $2 Million in Overtime," *BNA Bulletin to Management*, September 26, 1996, pp. 308–309. See also "Restaurant Managers Awarded $2.9 Million in Overtime Wages for Nonmanagement Work," *BNA Bulletin to Management*, August 30, 2001, p. 275.
30. www.govdocs.com/salaried-employees- to-get-overtime-pay-with-executive-order, accessed March 24, 2014.
31. www.latimes.com/business/la-fi-overtime-rules-20150701-story.html, and www.huffingtonpost.com/2015/07/01/obama-overtime-proposal_n_7704908.html, both accessed July 11, 2015.
32. How to apply these rules is not an exact science. If there's doubt about exemption eligibility, it's probably best to check with the local Department of Labor Wage and Hour office. See, for example, "Attorneys Say FLSA Draws a Fine Line Between Exempt/Nonexempt Employees," *BNA Bulletin to Management*, July 5, 2005, p. 219; Tim Watson and Barry Miller, "Tightening a White Collar Exemption," *HR Magazine*, December 2010, p. 95.
33. See, for example, Friedman, "The Fair Labor Standards Act Today: A Primer."; Andre Honoree, "The New Fair Labor Standards Act Regulations and the Sales Force: Who Is Entitled to Overtime Pay?" *Compensation & Benefits Review*, January/February 2006, p. 31; www.shrm.org/issues/FLSA, accessed August 12, 2007; www.dol.gov/esa/whd/flsa, accessed August 12, 2007; and www.dol.gov/whd/flsa, accessed September 3, 2014.
34. Diane Cadrain, "Guard Against FLSA Claims," *HR Magazine*, April 2008, pp. 97–100.
35. "Justices 5–4 Reject Labor Department View, Find Pharmaceutical Sales Reps FLSA-Exempt," *BNA Bulletin to Management*, June 19, 2012, p. 193.
36. Several state legislatures have moved to tighten regulations regarding misclassifying workers as independent contractors, some going so far as adding criminal penalties for violations. "Misclassification Cases Draw More Attention, Attorneys Say," *BNA Bulletin to Management*, December 15, 2009, p. 399. The U.S. Department of Labor is working with state agencies to challenge independent contractor worker misclassifications. "DOL, State Agencies, and Litigants Proceed with Challenges to Worker Misclassification," *BNA Bulletin to Management*, August 14, 2012, p. 257.
37. "Federal Court Mostly Rules for FedEx Ground in Driver Lawsuits Alleging Misclassification," *BNA Bulletin to Management*, December 21, 2010, p. 403. Different countries classify independent contractors in different ways, which requires knowledge of the specific local requirements. Eric Krell, "Status Check," *HR Magazine*, November 2011, pp. 63–66.
38. www.irs.gov/Businesses/Small-Businesses-&-Self-Employed/Independent-Contractor-Defined, accessed March 19, 2014.
39. http://www.irs.gov/Businesses/Small-Businesses-&-Self-Employed/Independent-Contractor-Self-Employed-or-Employee, accessed July 13, 2015.
40. See, for instance, www.uschambersmallbusinessnation.com/toolkits/tool/indcon_m.
41. This is based on Matthew Simpson, "Five Steps to Reduce the Risks of Miscalculation," *BNA Bulletin to Management*, February 21, 2012, p. 63.
42. Conrad De Aenlle, "Employee or Contractor? Healthcare Law Raises Stakes," *New York Times*, February 15, 2015, p. BU 11.
43. Robert Nobile, "How Discrimination Laws Affect Compensation," *Compensation & Benefits Review*, July/August 1996, pp. 38–42.
44. See, for example, www.bls.gov/opub/cwc/cm20030124ar01p1.htm, accessed October 9, 2011. See also Barry Hirsch and Edward Schumacher, "Unions, Wages, and Skills," *Journal of Human Resources* 33, no. 1 (Winter 1998), p. 115.
45. Peg Buchenroth, "Driving Performance: Making Pay Work for the Organization," *Compensation & Benefits Review*, May/June 2006, pp. 30–35.
46. Jessica Marquez, "Raising the Performance Bar," *Workforce Management*, April 24, 2006, pp. 31–32.
47. Demby, "Two Stores Refused to Join the Race."
48. Ibid.
49. www.wegmans.com, accessed June 1, 2011.
50. Demby, "Two Stores Refuse to Join the Race"; www.hoovers.com/company/Wegmans_Food_Markets_Inc/cfhtji-1.Html, accessed June 1, 2011.
51. Ibid.
52. Demby, "Two Stores Refuse to Join the Race."
53. www.bls.gov/oes/current/oes431011.htm, accessed July 27, 2013.
54. This is based on compensation management.
55. See, for example, Joseph Martocchio, *Strategic Compensation* (Upper Saddle River, NJ: Pearson Education, 2011), p. 140; John Kilgour, "Job Evaluation Revisited: The Point-Factor Method," *Compensation & Benefits Review*, July/August 2008, pp. 37–46; and www.shrm.org/TemplatesTools/Toolkits/Pages/PerformingJobEvaluations.aspx, accessed April 5, 2014.
56. Martocchio, *Strategic Compensation*, 2006, p. 138. See also Nona Tobin, "Can Technology Ease the Pain of Salary Surveys?" *Public Personnel Management* 31, no. 1 (Spring 2002), pp. 65–78.
57. Job analysis (Chapter 4) can be a useful source of information on compensable factors, as well as on job descriptions and job specifications. For example, a quantitative job analysis technique like the position analysis questionnaire generates quantitative information on the degree to which the following five basic factors are present in each job: having decision-making/communication/social responsibilities, performing skilled activities, being physically active, operating vehicles or equipment, and processing information. As a result, a job analysis technique like the PAQ is actually as (or some say, more) appropriate as a job evaluation technique (than for job analysis) in that jobs can be quantitatively compared to one another on those five dimensions and their relative worth thus ascertained.
58. Michael Carrell and Christina Heavrin, *Labor Relations and Collective Bargaining* (Upper Saddle River, NJ: Prentice Hall, 2004), pp. 300–303.
59. www.hr-guide.com/data/G909.htm, accessed July 10, 2014.
60. Kilgour, "Job Evaluation Revisited," p. 40.
61. See, for example, http://pristina.usembassy.gov/uploads/images/TPAyt1xR9zbj_JQ2iG1tpw/caje1.pdf.
62. Martocchio, *Strategic Compensation*, 2011, p. 140.
63. For a discussion, see Roger Plachy, "The Point Factor Job Evaluation System: A Step-by-Step Guide, Part I," *Compensation & Benefits Review*, July/August 1987, pp. 12–27; Roger Plachy, "The Case for Effective Point-Factor Job Evaluation, Viewpoint I," *Compensation & Benefits Review*, March/April 1987, pp. 45–48; Roger Plachy, "The Point-Factor Job Evaluation System: A Step-by-Step

Guide, Part II," *Compensation & Benefits Review*, September/October 1987, pp. 9–24; and particularly Kilgour, "Job Evaluation Revisited," pp. 37–46.
64. Martocchio, *Strategic Compensation*, 2011, p. 141.
65. Kilgour, "Job Evaluation Revisited," pp. 37–46.
66. Ibid.
67. Ibid.
68. Ibid.
69. Ibid.
70. Ibid.
71. Ibid. Of course, the level of economic activity influences compensation expectations. Fay Hansen, "Currents in Compensation and Benefits," *Compensation & Benefits Review* 42, no. 6 (2010), p. 435.
72. Martocchio, *Strategic Compensation*, 2011, p. 151.
73. Kilgour, "Job Evaluation Revisited," pp. 37–46.
74. Henderson, *Compensation Management*, pp. 260–269. See also "Web Access Transforms Compensation Surveys," *Workforce Management*, April 24, 2006, p. 34.
75. See Judy Canavan, "Compensation Surveys: The Good, the Bad, and the Ugly," *Compensation & Benefits Review* 46, no. 2 (2014), pp. 74–79.
76. Kilgour, "Job Evaluation Revisited," pp. 37–46. See also William Liccione, "Linking the Market and Internal Values of Jobs: Rethinking the Market Line," *Compensation & Benefits Review* 46, no. 2 (2014), pp. 80–88.
77. Kilgour, "Job Evaluation Revisited," pp. 37–46.
78. David W. Belcher, *Compensation Administration* (Englewood Cliffs, NJ: Prentice Hall, 1974), pp. 257–276; and Nicola Sulliva, "Serco Introduces Pay Grade Structure for Senior Staff," *Employee Benefits*, July 2010, p. 5.
79. Martocchio, *Strategic Compensation,* 2011, p. 185.
80. Ibid., p. 189.
81. Kilgour, "Job Evaluation Revisited," pp. 37–46.
82. Susan Marks, "Can the Internet Help You Hit the Salary Mark?" *Workforce*, January 2001, pp. 86–93.
83. For sources of sample policies see, for example, sites such as http://hr.blr.com/timesavers?type=54 and the HR systems discussionon pages 000–000.
84. James Reda, "Executive Pay Today and Tomorrow," *Corporate Board* 22, no. 126 (January 2001), p. 18.
85. Syed Tahir Hijazi, "Determinants of Executive Compensation and Its Impact on Organizational Performance," *Compensation & Benefits Review* 39, no. 2 (March–April 2007), p. 58(9).
86. For example, some authors argue that executives of large companies use their power to have themselves compensated in ways that are not sufficiently related to performance. Lucian Bebchuk and Jesse Fried, *Pay Without Performance: The Unfulfilled Promise of Executive Compensation* (Boston: Harvard University Press, 2004).
87. http://uk.reuters.com/article/2010/02/23/uk-hsbc-idUKTRE61M6FT20100223, accessed June 23, 2011.
88. Mark Meltzer and Howard Goldsmith, "Executive Compensation for Growth Companies," *Compensation & Benefits Review*, November/December 1997, pp. 41–50; Martocchio, *Strategic Compensation,* 2011, pp. 421–428. See also Martin J. Conyon, "Executive Compensation and Incentives," *The Academy of Management Perspectives* 20, no. 1 (February 2006), p. 25(20); and "Realities of Executive Compensation—2006/2007 Report on Executive Pay and Stock Options," www.watsonwyatt.com/research/resrender.asp?id=2006-US-0085&page=1, accessed May 20, 2007.
89. Douglas Tormey, "Executive Compensation: Creating a 'Legal' Checklist," *Compensation & Benefits Review*, July/August 1996, pp. 12–36. See also Bruce Ellig, "Executive Pay: A Primer," *Compensation & Benefits Review*, January/February 2003, pp. 44–50.
90. http://finance.yahoo.com/news/p-gs-ceo-pay-slips-200307540.html, accessed February 8, 2013.
91. "At the Top of Their Industries," *New York Times*, April 7, 2013, p. B.8.
92. "American Chief Executives Are Not Overpaid," *The Economist*, September 8, 2012, p. 67.
93. See, for example, Fay Hansen, "Current Trends in Compensation and Benefits," *Compensation & Benefits Review* 36, no. 2 (March/April 2004), pp. 7–8.
94. www.dol.gov/whd/regs/compliance/fairpay/fs17d_professional.pdf, accessed June 1, 2011.
95. Ibid.
96. Roger S. Achille, "FLSA Requires Education for Professional Exemption," www.shrm.org/LegalIssues/FederalResources/Pages/2ndFLSAProfessionalExemption.Aspx, accessed August 28, 2011.
97. See, for example, Martocchio, *Strategic Compensation* 2006; and Patricia Zingheim and Jay Schuster, "Designing Pay and Rewards in Professional Services Companies," *Compensation & Benefits Review*, January/February 2007, pp. 55–62.
98. Farhad Manjoo, "Engineers to the Valley: Pay Up," *Fast Company* 153, no. 38 (March 2011).
99. Dimitris Manolopoulos, "What Motivates Research and Development Professionals? Evidence from Decentralized Laboratories in Greece," *International Journal of Human Resource Management* 17, no. 4 (April 2006), pp. 616–647.
100. www.bing.com/shopping/quickbooks-basic-payroll-2012-complete-package/p/F0EBDFF1F6F276B60004?q=payroll+software&lpf=0&lpq=payroll%2bsoftware&FORM=ENCA&lppc=16, accessed May 20, 2012.
101. www.shrm.org/HRdisciplines/pages/CMS_012013.aspx, accessed May 20, 2012.
102. See, for example, Robert Heneman and Peter LeBlanc, "Development of and Approach for Valuing Knowledge Work," *Compensation & Benefits—Review*, July/August 2002, p. 47. A survey found that only about 12% of employers use skill-based pay, and 13% use competency-based pay. Frank Giancola, "Skill-Based Pay: Fad or Classic?" *Compensation & Benefits Review* 43, no. 4 (2011), pp. 220–226.
103. Gerald Ledford Jr., "Paying for the Skills, Knowledge, and Competencies of Knowledge Workers," *Compensation & Benefits Review*, July/August 1995, p. 56; see also P. K. Zingheim et al., "Competencies and Rewards: Substance or Just Style?" *Compensation and Benefits Review* 35, no. 5 (September/October 2003), pp. 40–44.
104. Martocchio, *Strategic Compensation*, 2011, p. 168.
105. www.jlg.com/en-US/Industries.html, accessed April 9, 2013.
106. Quoted or paraphrased from "JLG Industries, Inc., "Information: Skill-Based Pay Program," www.bmpcoe.org/bestpractices/internal/jlg/jlg_14.html, accessed April 9, 2013.
107. See, for example, www.shrm.org/hrdisciplines/compensation/articles/pages/salarystructures.aspx, accessed September 27, 2013.
108. David Hofrichter, "Broadbanding: A 'Second Generation' Approach," *Compensation & Benefits Review*, September/October 1993, pp. 53–58. See also "The Future of Salary Management," *Compensation & Benefits Review*, July/August 2001, pp. 7–12.
109. Ibid., p. 55.
110. For example, see Sandra Emerson, "Job Evaluation: A Barrier to Excellence?" *Compensation & Benefits Review*, January/February 1991, pp. 39–52; Nan Weiner, "Job Evaluation Systems: A Critique," *Human Resource Management Review* 1, no. 2 (Summer 1991), pp. 119–132; and Brian Klaas, "Compensation in the Jobless Organization," *Human Resource Management Review* 12, no. 1 (Spring 2002), pp. 43–62.
111. *County of Washington v. Gunther*, U.S. Supreme Court, no. 80–426, June 8, 1981.
112. Laura Fitzpatrick, "Why Do Women Still Earn Less Than Men?" www.time.com/time/nation/article/0,8599,1983185,00.html, accessed September 4, 2014.
113. Christopher Dougherty, "Why Are the Returns to Schooling Higher for Women Than for Men?" *Journal of Human Resources* 40, no. 4 (Fall 2005), pp. 969–988.
114. Rachel Silverman, "Women Doctors Face Pay Disparity," *Wall Street Journal*, February 8, 2011, p. D4.
115. "Women Still Earned Less Than Men, BLS Data Show," *BNA Bulletin to Management*, June 8, 2000, p. 72. See also E. Frazier, "Raises for Women Executives Match Those for Men, but Pay Gap Persists," *The Chronicle of Philanthropy* 20, no. 24 (October 2, 2008), p. 33.
116. "The Say on Pay Payday," *The Economist*, February 16, 2013, p. 65.
117. Mark Poerio and Eric Keller, "Executive Compensation 2005: Many Forces, One Direction," *Compensation & Benefits Review*, May/June 2005, pp. 34–40.
118. Ibid., p. 38.
119. Jennifer Dudley, "The New Executive Compensation Rule: The Tough Disclosures," *Compensation & Benefits Review*, July/August 2007, pp. 28–34.
120. Society for Human Resource Management, "Changing Leadership Strategies," *Workplace Visions*, no. 1 (2008), p. 3.
121. For a discussion of some of the issues that go into hammering out an executive employment agreement, see, for example, Jonathan Cohen and Laura Clark, "Is the Executive Employment Agreement Dead?" *Compensation & Benefits Review*, July/August 2007, pp. 50–55.
122. Ibid. See also Brent Longnecker and James Krueger, "The Next Wave of Compensation Disclosure," *Compensation & Benefits Review*, January/February 2007, pp. 50–54.
123. Robert L. Heneman, "Implementing Total Rewards Strategies," www.shrm.org/hrdisciplines/benefits/Documents/07RewardsStratReport.pdf, accessed March 24, 2014.
124. Dow Scott and Tom McMullen, "The Impact of Rewards Programs on Employee Engagement," *WorldatWork: Survey of*

Rewards and Employee Engagement, June 2010, www.worldatwork.org.
125. Duncan Brown and Peter Reilly, "Reward and Engagement: The New Realities," *Compensation & Benefits Review*, 45, no. 3, 2013, pp. 145–157.
126. Tom McMullen, "Eight Recommendations to Improve Employee Engagement," *Journal of Compensation and Benefits*, July/August 2013, p. 23.
127. Melissa Van Dyke and Mike Ryan, "Changing the Compensation Conversation on the Growing Utility of Non-Cash Rewards and Recognition," *Compensation & Benefits Review* 44, no. 5 (2013), pp. 276–279.
128. Meg Breslin, "Solid Rewards Program Can Be Rewarding for Businesses," *Workforce Management*, January 2013, p. 8.
129. Dave Zielinski, "Giving Praise," *HR Magazine*, October 2012, p. 77.
130. Scott and McMullen, "The Impact Rewards Programs on Employee Engagement."
131. Ibid.
132. While some total rewards elements contribute to engagement and performance, it is not clear that others do. For example, it's not clear that "programs such as pet insurance and working at home add anything to the business success of our organization." See Jay Schuster and Patricia Zingheim, "Recalibrating Best Practice," *Compensation & Benefits Review* 45, no. 3 (2013), pp. 134–135.
133. http://disneycareers.com/en/working-here/total-rewards, accessed March 24, 2014.
134. This is based on George Bradt, "How the Best Big Companies to Work for Drive Appreciation, Access and Rewards," www.forbes.com/sites/georgebradt/2014/03/12/how-the-best-fortune-500-companies-to-work-for-drive-appreciation- access-rewards-2, accessed March 24, 2014.
135. www.sas.com/en_us/careers.html, accessed March 24, 2014.
136. McMullen, "Eight Recommendations to Improve Employee Engagement."
137. This case based on www.nature.com/scitable/forums/women-in-science/astrozeneca-settles-women-s-pay-inequality-20334719; www.dol.gov/opa/media/press/ofccp/OFCCP20110829.htm; and http://social.dol.gov/blog/astrazeneca-what-we-learned/, all accessed August 31, 2012.

12

Pay for Performance and Financial Incentives

Tom Cockrem/Getty Images

LEARNING OBJECTIVES

12-1 Explain how you would apply four motivation theories in formulating an incentive plan.

12-2 Discuss the main incentives for individual employees.

12-3 Discuss the pros and cons of commissions versus straight pay for salespeople.

12-4 Describe the main incentives for managers and executives.

12-5 Name and describe the most popular organization-wide incentive plans.

12-6 Explain how to use incentives to improve employee engagement.

The owners of a 21-store fast-food franchise in the Midwest knew that their stores' performance and profits depended on their employees' performance. They hoped a new employee incentive program could boost their employees' and their stores' performance. We'll see that they did.

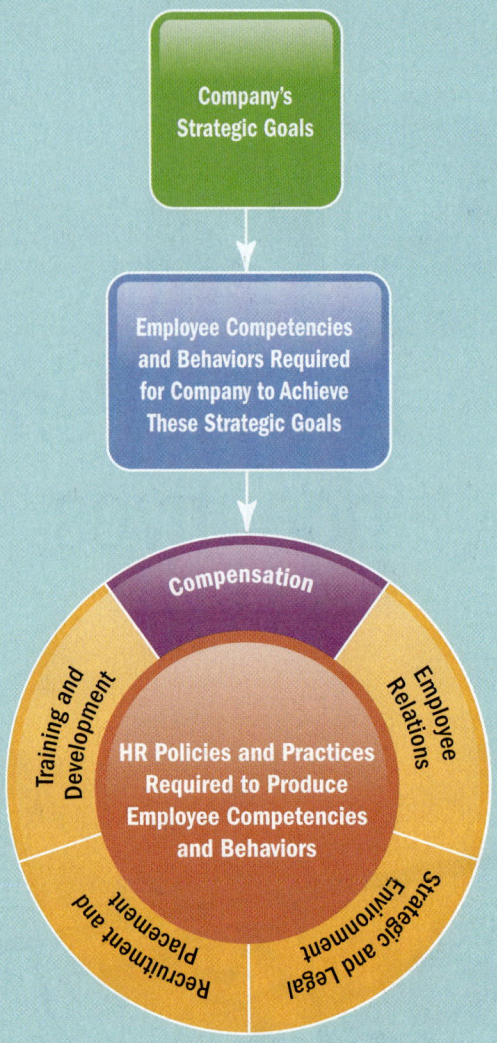

WHERE ARE WE NOW ...

Chapter 11 focused on developing pay plans and on salaries and wages. Incentives are important in any pay plan. The main purpose of this chapter is to explain how managers use incentives to motivate employees. The main topics we'll discuss are money's role in motivation, individual employee incentive and recognition programs, incentives for salespeople, incentives for managers and executives, team and organization-wide incentive plans, and incentives and employee engagement. In Chapter 13, we'll turn to the financial and nonfinancial benefits that comprise the third component of employee compensation packages.

LEARNING OBJECTIVE **12-1**

Explain how you would apply four motivation theories in formulating an incentive plan.

financial incentives
Financial rewards paid to workers whose production exceeds some predetermined standard.

productivity
The ratio of outputs (goods and services) divided by the inputs (resources such as labor and capital).

fair day's work
Output standards devised based on careful, scientific analysis.

scientific management movement
Management approach based on improving work methods through observation and analysis.

variable pay
Any plan that ties pay to productivity or profitability, usually as one-time lump payments.

Money's Role In Motivation

Frederick Taylor popularized using **financial incentives**—financial rewards paid to workers whose production exceeds some predetermined standard—in the late 1800s. As a supervisor at the Midvale Steel Company, Taylor was concerned with what he called "systematic soldiering"—the tendency of employees to produce at the minimum acceptable level. Some workers had the energy to run home and work on their houses after a 12-hour day. Taylor knew that if he could harness this energy at work, Midvale could achieve huge productivity gains. **Productivity** "is the ratio of outputs (goods and services) divided by the inputs (resources such as labor and capital)."[1]

In pursuing that aim, Taylor turned to financial incentives. At the time, primitive incentive plans were in use, but were generally ineffective (because employers arbitrarily changed incentive rates).

Taylor made three contributions. He saw the need for formulating a "**fair day's work**," namely precise output standards for each job. He spearheaded the **scientific management movement**, which emphasized improving work through observation and analysis. And he popularized using incentive pay to reward employees who produced over standard.

Incentive Pay Terminology

Managers often use two terms synonymously with incentive plans.[2] Traditionally, all incentive plans are *pay-for-performance* plans. They all tie employees' pay to the employees' performance. **Variable pay** is more specific: It is usually an incentive plan that ties a group's or team's pay to some measure of the firm's (or the unit's) overall profitability;[3] *profit-sharing plans* (discussed later) are one example.[4] However, confusing as it may be, some experts use the term *variable pay* to include incentive plans for individual employees.[5]

Linking Strategy, Performance, and Incentive Pay

In any case, incentive pay—tying workers' pay to their performance—is widely popular.[6] The problem is that linking pay to performance is easier said than done. (One plan, at Levi Strauss, is widely assumed to have been the last nail in the coffin of Levi's U.S.-based production.) As logical as it seems to link pay to performance, about 83% of companies with such programs say their programs are at best somewhat successful. One study found that just 28% of the 2,600 U.S. workers it surveyed said their companies' incentive plans motivated them. "Employees don't see a strong connection between pay and performance, and their performance is not particularly influenced by the company's incentive plan," said one expert.[7] Equally problematical is the fact that some incentives incentivize the wrong behavior.[8] Thus, incentivizing "number of cars sold" in a dealership might produce high performance (in numbers of cars sold) but low per-car profit, inadvertently undermining its strategy to boost dealer profits.

Another big reason for incentive plans' often-dismal results is the fact that incentives that may motivate some people won't motivate others.[9] Compensation experts therefore argue that managers should understand the motivational bases of incentive plans.[10] We'll review some motivation background next, and then go on to explain various incentive plans.

Motivation and Incentives

Several motivation theories have particular relevance to designing incentive plans.

MOTIVATORS AND FREDERICK HERZBERG Frederick Herzberg said the best way to motivate someone is to organize the job so that doing it provides the challenge and recognition we all need to help satisfy "higher-level" needs for things like accomplishment and recognition. These needs are relatively insatiable, says Herzberg, so challenging work provides a sort of built-in motivation generator. Doing things to satisfy a worker's "lower-level" needs for things like better pay and working conditions just keeps the person from becoming dissatisfied.

Herzberg says the factors ("hygienes") that satisfy lower-level needs are different from those ("motivators") that satisfy or partially satisfy higher-level needs. If *hygiene* factors (factors outside the job itself, such as working conditions, salary, and incentive pay) are inadequate, employees become dissatisfied. However, adding more of these hygienes (like incentives) to the job (supplying what Herzberg calls "extrinsic motivation") is an inferior way to try to motivate someone, because lower-level needs are quickly satisfied. Inevitably the person says, in effect, "I want another raise."

Instead of relying on hygienes, says Herzberg, managers interested in creating a self-motivated workforce should emphasize "job content" or *motivator* factors. Managers do this by enriching workers' jobs so that the jobs are more challenging, and by providing feedback and recognition—by making doing the job intrinsically motivating, in other words. In organizational psychology, **intrinsic motivation** is motivation that derives from the pleasure someone gets from doing the job or task. It comes from "within" the person, rather than from externally, such as from a financial incentive plan. Intrinsic motivation means that just doing the task provides the motivation. Herzberg makes the point that relying exclusively on financial incentives is risky. The employer should also provide the recognition and challenging work that most people desire.

intrinsic motivation
Motivation that derives from the pleasure someone gets from doing the job or task.

DEMOTIVATORS AND EDWARD DECI Psychologist Edward Deci's work highlights another potential downside to relying too heavily on extrinsic rewards: They may backfire. Deci found that extrinsic rewards could at times actually detract from the person's intrinsic motivation.[11] The point may be stated thusly: Be cautious in devising incentive pay for highly motivated employees, lest you inadvertently demean and detract from the desire they have to do the job out of a sense of responsibility.

EXPECTANCY THEORY AND VICTOR VROOM In general, people won't pursue rewards they find unattractive, or where the odds of success are very low. Psychologist Victor Vroom's expectancy motivation theory echoes these commonsense observations. He says a person's motivation to exert some level of effort depends on three things: the person's **expectancy** (in terms of probability) that his or her effort will lead to performance;[12] **instrumentality**, or the perceived connection (if any) between successful performance and actually obtaining the rewards; and **valence**, which represents the perceived value the person attaches to the reward.[13] In Vroom's theory:

expectancy
A person's expectation that his or her effort will lead to performance.

instrumentality
The perceived relationship between successful performance and obtaining the reward.

valence
The perceived value a person attaches to the reward.

$$\text{Motivation} = (E \times I \times V),$$

where E represents expectancy, I instrumentality, and V valence. If E or I or V is zero or inconsequential, there will be no motivation.

Vroom's theory has three implications for how managers design incentive plans.

- First, if employees don't *expect* that effort will produce performance, no motivation will occur. So, managers must ensure that their employees have the skills to do the job, and believe they can do the job. Thus, training, job descriptions, and confidence building and support are important in using incentives.
- Second, Vroom's theory suggests that employees must see the *instrumentality* of their efforts—they must believe that successful performance will in fact lead to getting the reward. Managers can accomplish this, for instance, by creating easy to understand incentive plans.
- Third, the reward itself must be of *value* to the employee. Ideally, the manager should take into account individual employee preferences.

BEHAVIOR MODIFICATION/REINFORCEMENT AND B. F. SKINNER Using incentives also assumes the manager understands how consequences affect behavior.[14] Psychologist B.F. Skinner's findings are useful here. Managers apply Skinner's principles by using *behavior modification.* **Behavior modification** means changing behavior through rewards or punishments that are contingent on performance. For managers, behavior modification boils down to two main principles. First, that behavior that appears to lead to a positive

behavior modification
Using contingent rewards or punishment to change behavior.

consequence (reward) tends to be repeated, whereas behavior that appears to lead to a negative consequence (punishment) tends not to be repeated; and second, that managers can therefore get someone to change his or her behavior by providing the properly scheduled rewards (or punishment).

To arrange our discussion, we will organize the following sections around individual employee incentive and recognition programs, sales compensation programs, management and executive incentive compensation programs, and team- and organization-wide incentive programs. First, however, we look at some legal aspects of incentive plan design.

KNOW YOUR EMPLOYMENT LAW

Employee Incentives and the Law

Various laws affect incentive pay. Under the Fair Labor Standards Act, if the incentive the worker receives is in the form of a prize or cash award, the employer generally must *include the value of that award* when calculating the worker's overtime pay for that pay period.[15] So, unless you structure the incentive bonuses properly, the bonus itself becomes part of the week's wages. For example, suppose someone who earns $10 per hour for a 40-hour week also earns, in one week, performance incentive pay (a performance bonus) of $80 for the week, or $480 total pay for the week. Further, assume she *also* works 2 hours overtime that week. The overtime rate for each of the 2 hours she works overtime is not simply 1.5 times her regular $10-per-hour pay. Instead, it is 1.5 times $12 per hour. Why? Because with her performance bonus she earned $480 for the 40-hour week, and $480 divided by 40 hours is $12 per hour. Therefore she actually earned in total that week $480 plus the overtime pay of $12 per hour for the two extra hours, or $480 + $24 = $504 total for the week.

Certain bonuses are excludable from overtime pay calculations. For example, Christmas and gift bonuses that are not based on hours worked, or are so substantial that employees don't consider them a part of their wages, do not have to be included in overtime pay calculations. Similarly, purely discretionary bonuses in which the employer retains discretion over how much if anything to pay are excludable.

However, other types of incentive pay *must* be included. Under the Fair Labor Standards Act (FLSA), bonuses to include in overtime pay computations include those promised to newly hired employees; those provided for in union contracts or other agreements; and those announced to induce employees to work more productively or efficiently or to induce them to remain with the company. Such bonuses would include many of those we turn to next, such as individual and group production bonuses. ■

Individual Employee Incentive and Recognition Programs

Several incentive plans are particularly suited for use with individual employees.

LEARNING OBJECTIVE **12-2**
Discuss the main incentives for individual employees.

Piecework

piecework
A system of pay based on the number of items processed by each individual worker in a unit of time, such as items per hour or items per day.

Piecework is the oldest incentive plan and still the most commonly used. Earnings are tied directly to what the worker produces; the person is paid a piece rate for each unit he or she produces. Thus, if Tom Smith gets $0.40 apiece for stamping out doorjambs, then he would get, say, $80 for stamping out 200.

Developing a workable piece rate plan requires both job evaluation and (strictly speaking) industrial engineering. Job evaluation enables you to assign an hourly wage rate to the job in question. But the crucial issue in piece rate planning is the production standard, and this standard is often developed by industrial engineers. The engineers state production standards in terms of a standard number of minutes per unit or a standard number of units per hour. In Tom Smith's case, the job evaluation indicated that his doorjamb stamping job was worth $8.00 an hour. The industrial engineer determined that 20 jambs per hour was the standard production rate. Therefore, the engineered piece rate (for each doorjamb) was $8.00 divided by 20, which equals $0.40 per doorjamb.

straight piecework
An incentive plan in which a person is paid a sum for each item he or she makes or sells, with a strict proportionality between results and rewards.

With a **straight piecework** plan, Tom Smith would be paid based on the number of doorjambs he produced; there would be no guaranteed minimum wage. However, today most employers must guarantee their workers a minimum wage. With a guaranteed piecework plan, Tom Smith would be paid $7.25 per hour (the 2015 minimum wage) whether or not he stamped out 18 doorjambs per hour (at $0.40 each). But he would also get $0.40 for each unit over 18.

Piecework generally implies straight piecework, a strict proportionality between results and rewards regardless of the level of output. Thus, in Smith's case, he continues to get $0.40 apiece for stamping out doorjambs, even if he stamps out more than planned, say, 500 per day. However, certain piecework plans call for a sharing of productivity gains between worker and employer. Typically, the worker here receives reduced credit for all production above standard—perhaps $0.35 per piece over 400 units per day, for instance.[16] Conversely, some such plans boost the employee's share once a threshold is met—such as paying Tom $0.45 each once he reached 400 units per day.

standard hour plan
A plan by which a worker is paid a basic hourly rate but is paid an extra percentage of his or her rate for production exceeding the standard per hour or per day. Similar to piecework payment but based on a percent premium.

The **standard hour plan** is like the piecework plan, with one difference. Instead of getting a rate per piece, the worker gets a pay premium equal to the percent by which his or her performance exceeds the standard. So if Tom's standard is 160 doorjambs per day ($64 per day), and he brings in 200 jambs, he'd get an extra 25% (40/160), or $80. Using this approach may reduce workers' tendency to link their production standard (18 jambs per hour) to pay. This makes it easier to change the standard.

ADVANTAGES AND DISADVANTAGES Piecework incentive plans have several advantages. They are simple to calculate and easily understood by employees. Piecework plans appear equitable in principle, and their incentive value can be powerful since they tie pay directly to performance.

Piecework also has disadvantages. The main one is its unsavory reputation, based on some employers' habit of arbitrarily raising production standards whenever they found their workers earning "excessive" wages. A more subtle disadvantage is that since piece rates are quoted on a per piece basis, in worker's minds the production standard (in pieces per hour) becomes tied inseparably to the amount of money earned.

Piecework systems thus risk engendering rigidity. When the employer tries to revise production standards, resistance ensues.[17] Employees become preoccupied with producing the number of units needed. They can become less focused on quality and may resist switching jobs (since doing so could reduce productivity). Attempts to introduce new processes may more likely fail, insofar as they require adjusting engineered standards. Equipment maintenance tends to decline as employees focus on maximizing quantity.[18]

For such reasons, more employers are moving to other plans, such as those on the following pages.[19]

Merit Pay as an Incentive

merit pay (merit raise)
Any salary increase awarded to an employee based on his or her individual performance.

Merit pay or a **merit raise** is a salary increase the firm awards to an individual employee based on individual performance. It is different from a bonus in that it usually becomes part of the employee's base salary, whereas bonuses are generally one-time payments. Although the term *merit pay* can apply to the incentive raises given to any employee, the term is more often used for professional, office, and clerical employees.

Merit pay is the subject of much debate. Advocates argue that awarding pay raises across the board (without regard to individual merit) may detract from performance by showing employees they'll be rewarded regardless of how they perform.

Detractors present good reasons why merit pay can backfire. Most notably, since many appraisals are unfair, so too are the merit decisions you base them on.[20]

The evidence, while mixed, tends to support using merit pay. One study focused on 218 workers in a nuclear waste facility. The researchers found a "very modest relationship between merit pay increase and performance rating."[21] Research into tying merit pay increases to teachers' or faculty members' research and/or teaching performance suggest that merit pay is more clearly linked with research productivity than with teaching effectiveness.[22]

When they're not working, the solution is not to throw out merit raises, but to improve them. This starts with establishing effective appraisal procedures and ensuring that managers do in fact tie merit pay awards to performance.

Merit plan effectiveness also depends on differentiating among employees. In one survey, the highest-paid office clerical employees got short-term incentive payouts of about 13%, the lowest-rated got 3%, and mid-rated employees got 8%.[23]

Employers are experimenting with using crowdsourcing for awarding bonuses. For example, one small San Francisco–based company asked each employee to allocate 1,200 stock options among coworkers however they chose.[24] Allowing everyone to "vote" on each other's performance this way can help identify employees who are helpful team contributors but might otherwise slip under management's radar.

HR in Practice at the Hotel Paris Based on their analysis, Lisa Cruz and the CFO concluded that, by any measure, their company's incentive plan was inadequate. The percentage of the workforce whose merit increase was tied to performance was effectively zero, because managers awarded merit pay across the board. To see how they handled this, see the case on page 411.

MERIT PAY OPTIONS Two adaptations of merit pay plans are popular. One awards merit raises in a lump sum once a year and does *not* make the raise part of the employee's salary (making them, in effect, short-term bonuses for lower-level workers). Traditional merit increases are cumulative, but these *lump-sum merit raises* are not. This produces two potential benefits. First, the merit raise is not baked into the employee's salary, so you need not pay it year after year. Lump-sum merit increases can also be more dramatic motivators than a traditional merit raise. For example, a 5% lump-sum merit payment to a $30,000 employee is $1,500 cash, as opposed to a weekly merit payout of $29 for 52 weeks.

The other adaptation ties merit awards to both individual and organizational performance. Table 12-1 presents an example. In this example, you might measure the company's performance by, say, profits. Here, company performance and the employee's performance (using his or her performance appraisal) receive equal weight in computing the merit pay. In Table 12-1 an outstanding performer would receive 70% of his or her maximum lump-sum award even when the organization's performance was marginal. However, employees with marginal or unacceptable performance would get no lump-sum awards even when the firm's performance was outstanding. For example, at Discovery Communications executive assistants can receive bonuses of up to 10% of their salaries. The boss's evaluation of the assistant's individual performance accounts for 80% of the potential bonus, 10% is based on how the division does, and 10% on how the company does.[25]

Incentives for Professional Employees

Professional employees are those whose work involves the application of learned knowledge to the solution of the employer's problems, such as lawyers and engineers.

Making incentive pay decisions for professional employees is challenging. For one thing, firms usually pay professionals well anyway. For another, they're already driven by the desire to produce high-caliber work.

However, it is unrealistic to assume that people like Google engineers work only for professional gratification. Few firms, therefore, work harder to maintain competitive incentives for professionals. For example, Google reportedly pays higher

TABLE 12-1 Merit Award Determination Matrix (an Example)

The Employee's Performance Rating (Weight = 0.50)	*The Company's Performance (Weight = 0.50)*				
	Outstanding	Excellent	Good	Marginal	Unacceptable
Outstanding	1.00	0.90	0.80	0.70	0.00
Excellent	0.90	0.80	0.70	0.60	0.00
Good	0.80	0.70	0.60	0.50	0.00
Marginal	—	—	—	—	—
Unacceptable	—	—	—	—	—

Note: To determine the dollar value of each employee's award: (1) multiply the employee's annual, straight-time wage or salary as of June 30 times his or her maximum incentive award (as determined by management or the board—such as, "10% of each employee's pay") and (2) multiply the resultant product by the appropriate percentage figure from this table. For example, if an employee had an annual salary of $40,000 on June 30 and a maximum incentive award of 7% and if her performance and the organization's performance were both "excellent," the employee's award would be $2,240: ($40,000 × 0.07 × 0.80 = $2,240).

incentives to engineers working on important projects. Those who choose the intrinsic motivation of working on more theoretical long-term projects are rewarded if their research pays off.[26] As at most Silicon Valley firms, Google's professionals also bask in the light of potentially millionaire-making stock option grants.

Dual-career ladders are another way to manage professionals' pay. At many employers, higher pay requires rerouting from, say, engineering into management. However, not all professionals want management. Therefore, many employers institute one path for managers, and another for technical experts, allowing the latter to earn higher pay without switching to management.[27]

Nonfinancial and Recognition-Based Awards

Employers often supplement financial incentives with various nonfinancial and recognition-based awards. The term *recognition program* usually refers to formal programs, such as employee-of-the-month programs. *Social recognition program* generally refers to informal manager–employee exchanges such as praise, approval, or expressions of appreciation for a job well done. *Performance feedback* means providing quantitative or qualitative information on task performance so as to change or maintain performance; showing workers a graph of how their performance is trending is an example.[28]

TRENDS SHAPING HR: *DIGITAL AND SOCIAL MEDIA*[29]

Employers are bulking up their recognition programs with digital support. For example, Baudville, a workplace recognition vendor, offers an e-card service called ePraise. Employers use this to tell employees they're appreciated. Intuit shifted its employee recognition, years of service, patent awards, and wellness awards programs to Globoforce, an online awards vendor. This "allowed us to build efficiencies and improved effectiveness" into the programs, says Intuit's vice president of performance, rewards, and workplace.[30] Management consultant Hewitt Associates uses www.bravanta.com to help its managers more easily recognize exceptional employee service with special awards. Other recognition sites include www.premierechoiceaward.com/secure/home.asp, and www.giveanything.com.

Various new apps let employees showcase their awards, contributions, and praise from coworkers. For example, go to http://quickbooks.intuit.com/r/, and key "7 mobile apps for recognizing and rewarding employees" into the search box, and click "search."[31] Apps also enable employees to praise each other.[32] For example, one lets employees "give recognition by picking out a badge and typing in a quick note to thank the people who matter most...." Others let users post the positive feedback they receive to their LinkedIn profiles.

Mobile technology is also changing how employers incentivize front-line service people. For example, pay for a $4.00 espresso in some New York coffeehouses with a credit card and the iPad screen will ask how big a tip you want to leave—from $1.00 to $3.00.[33] ■

Most employers combine financial and nonfinancial awards. At American Skandia, which provides insurance and financial planning products and services, customer service reps who exceed standards receive a plaque, a $500 check, their photo and story on the firm's internal Web site, and a dinner for themselves and their teams.[34] One survey of 235 managers found that the most-used financial and nonfinancial rewards to motivate employees (from most used to least) were:[35] employee recognition, gift certificates, special events, cash rewards, merchandise incentives, e-mail/print communications, training programs, work/life benefits, variable pay, group travel, individual travel, and sweepstakes. The HR Tools feature elaborates.

IMPROVING PERFORMANCE: *HR Tools for Line Managers and Small Businesses*

The supervisor should not rely just on the employer's financial incentive plans for motivating subordinates. Those plans may not be complete, plus there are simply too many opportunities to motivate employees every day to let those opportunities pass. What to do?

First, the best option for motivating an employee is also the simplest—*make sure the employee has a doable goal* and that he or she agrees with it. It makes little sense to try to motivate employees with financial incentives if they don't know their goals or don't agree with them. Psychologist Edwin Locke and his colleagues have consistently found that specific, challenging goals lead to higher task performance than do specific, unchallenging goals; vague goals; or no goals.

Second, *recognizing an employee's contribution* is a powerful motivation tool. Studies (and theories like those of Herzberg) show that recognition has a positive impact on performance, either alone or in combination with financial rewards. For example, in one study, combining financial rewards with recognition produced a 30% performance improvement in service firms, almost twice the effect of using each reward alone.

Third, use *social recognition* (such as compliments) as positive reinforcement on a day-to-day basis. Figure 12-1 presents a list.[36] ■

If your professor has assigned this, go to the Assignments section of **mymanagementlab.com** to complete this discussion question.

Talk About It 1: You have decided to verify that recognition does in fact improve performance. To that end, you will use an honest observation to praise someone's performance today. What was the effect of your experiment?

- Challenging work assignments
- Freedom to choose own work activity
- Having fun built into work
- More of preferred task
- Role as boss's stand-in when he or she is away
- Role in presentations to top management
- Job rotation
- Encouragement of learning and continuous improvement
- Being provided with ample encouragement
- Being allowed to set own goals
- Compliments
- Expression of appreciation in front of others
- Note of thanks
- Employee-of-the-month award
- Special commendation
- Bigger desk
- Bigger office or cubicle

FIGURE 12-1 Social Recognition and Related Positive Reinforcement Managers Can Use

Source: Based on Bob Nelson, *1001 Ways to Reward Employees* (New York: Workman Pub, 1994), p. 19; Sunny C. L. Fong and Margaret A. Shaffer, "The Dimensionality and Determinants of Pay Satisfaction: A Cross-Cultural Investigation of a Group Incentive Plan," *International Journal of Human Resource Management* 14, no. 4 (June 2003), p. 559 (22).

Job Design

Although not usually considered an "incentive," job design (discussed in Chapter 4) can significantly impact employee motivation and retention. A study by Harvard Business School researchers concluded that job design is a primary driver of employee engagement. A study by Sibson Consulting concluded that job responsibility and feedback were the fifth- and seventh-most important drivers of employee engagement. A study by Towers Watson concluded that challenging work ranked as the seventh-most important driver for attracting employees.[37] Job design is thus a useful part of an employer's total rewards program.

The Strategic Context feature illustrates how employers combine incentives to boost profits.

IMPROVING PERFORMANCE: *The Strategic Context*

The Fast-Food Chain

The heart of just about any fast-food chain's strategy is to control performance: One chain wanted to know, "Can financial and nonfinancial incentives boost performance in our fast-food chain?"

Two researchers studied the impact of financial and nonfinancial incentives on business performance in 21 stores of a fast-food franchise in the Midwest.[38] The researchers compared performance over time in stores that did and did not use financial and nonfinancial incentives. Each store had about 25 workers and two managers. The researchers trained the managers to identify measurable employee behaviors that were currently deficient but that could influence store performance. Example behaviors included "keeping both hands moving at the drive-through window" and "repeating the customer's order back to him or her."[39] Then the researchers instituted financial and nonfinancial incentive plans. They measured store performance in terms of gross profitability (revenue minus expenses), drive-through time, and employee turnover.

Financial Incentives

Some employees in some of the stores received financial incentives for exhibiting the desired behaviors. The financial incentives consisted of lump-sum bonuses in the workers' paychecks. For example, if the manager observed a work team exhibiting up to 50 behaviors (such as "working during idle time") during the observation period, he or she added $25 to the paychecks of all store employees that period; 50 to 100 behaviors added $50 per paycheck, and more than 100 behaviors added $75 per paycheck. Payouts eventually rose over time as the employees learned to enact the behaviors they were to exhibit.

Nonfinancial Incentives

The researchers trained the managers in some stores to use nonfinancial incentives such as feedback and recognition. For example, for *performance feedback* managers maintained charts showing the drive-through times at the end of each day. They placed the charts by the time clocks. Thus, these store employees could keep track of their store's performance on measures like drive-through times. The researchers also trained managers to administer *recognition* to employees. For instance, "I noticed that today the drive-through times were really good."[40]

Results

Both the financial and nonfinancial incentives improved employee and store performance.[41] For example, store profits rose 30% for those units where managers used financial rewards. Store profits rose 36% for those units where managers used nonfinancial rewards. During the same 9-month period, drive-through times decreased 19% for the financial incentives group, and 25% for the nonfinancial incentives groups. Turnover improved 13% for the financial incentives group, and 10% for the nonfinancial incentives group.

Implications for Managers

Here is what these findings mean for managers designing incentive plans:[42]

1. Link the incentive to behavior that is crucial for achieving strategic goals.[43] For example, this chain wanted to boost store performance and profits. Incentivizing employees to work faster and smarter accomplished that.

2. The point of an incentive is to motivate the person to work better. Therefore, it makes more sense to use an incentive plan when (1) motivation (not ability) is the problem; (2) when the employee's effort and results are directly related; and (3) when the employee can actually control the results you plan to incentivize. Put another way, make sure there is a clear link between the person's *effort and performance* and between the *performance and reward*, that the incentive is *attractive* to the employee, and that the employee *has the skills* to do the job.
3. Don't just rely on material rewards. Support the incentive plan with performance feedback (as in the form of performance graphs) and with recognition.[44]
4. Set complete standards. For example, don't just pay for "repeating the customer's order" if speed is important too.
5. Be scientific. As in this study, *gather evidence* and analyze the effects of the incentive plan over time.[45] ■

If your professor has assigned this, go to the Assignments section of **mymanagementlab.com** to complete this discussion question.

✪ **Talk About It 2:** The dean has asked you to design an incentive plan for your professor. How would you apply what you learned in this feature to do so?

LEARNING OBJECTIVE **12-3**

Discuss the pros and cons of commissions versus straight pay for salespeople.

Incentives for Salespeople

As one survey said, "the performance metrics given to the sales team must drive behaviors that will help the company's … strategy to be successful."[46]

Unfortunately, the same survey also found that "30% of respondents believe their sales compensation program rewarded the right behaviors 'not well' or 'very poorly.'"[47]

Employers are therefore moving to align (1) how they measure and reward their salespeople with (2) their firms' strategic goals.[48]

Salary Plan

Sales compensation plans may focus on salary, commissions, or some combination to drive sales objectives.[49] Some firms pay salespeople fixed salaries (perhaps with occasional incentives in the form of bonuses, sales contest prizes, and the like).[50] Straight salary makes sense when the main task involves prospecting (finding new clients) or account servicing. Turnover is another reason. Faced with the difficulty of attracting and keeping good salespeople, a Buick–GMC dealership in Lincolnton, North Carolina, offers straight salary as an option to salespeople who sell an average of at least eight vehicles a month (plus a small "retention bonus" per car sold).[51]

The straight salary approach also makes it easier to switch salespersons' territories, and it can foster sales staff loyalty. The main disadvantage, of course, is that straight salary may demotivate potentially high-performing salespeople.[52]

Commission Plan

Straight commission plans pay salespeople for results, and only for results. Commission plans tend to attract high-performing salespeople who see that effort clearly produces rewards. Sales costs are proportionate to sales rather than fixed, and the company's fixed sales costs are thus lower. Such plans are easy to understand and compute. Commission plan alternatives include straight commissions, quota bonuses (for meeting particular quotas), management by objectives programs (pay is based on specific metrics), and ranking programs (these reward high achievers but pay little or no bonuses to the lowest-performing salespeople).[53]

However, problems abound. In poorly designed plans, salespeople may focus on making the sale, and neglect nonselling duties such as servicing small accounts and pushing hard-to-sell items. Wide variations in pay may occur; this can make some feel the plan is inequitable. Misjudging sales potential can lead to excessively high commissions and to the need to cut commission rates. Salespersons' pay may be excessive in boom times and low in recessions. Furthermore, sales performance—like any performance—reflects not just motivation, but ability. If the person can't sell, commissions won't produce sales.[54]

Combination Plan

Most companies pay salespeople a combination of salary and commissions, usually with a sizable salary component. An incentive mix of about 70% base salary/30% incentive seems typical; this cushions the salesperson's downside risk (of earning nothing), while limiting the risk that the commissions could get out of hand from the firm's point of view.[55]

Combination plans have pros and cons.[56] They give salespeople a floor to their earnings, let the company specify what services the salary component is for (such as servicing current accounts), and still provide an incentive for superior performance. However, the salary component isn't tied to performance, so the employer trades away some incentive value.

Combination plans also tend to become complicated, and misunderstandings can result. This might not be a problem with a simple salary-plus-commission plan, but most plans are not so simple. For example, in a "commission-plus-drawing-account" plan, the salesperson is paid based on commissions. However, he or she can draw on future earnings during low sales periods. In the "commission-plus-bonus" plan, the firm pays its salespeople mostly based on commissions. However, they also get a small bonus for directed activities like selling slow-moving items.

Maximizing Sales Results

In setting sales quotas and commission rates, the goal is to motivate sales activity but avoid excessive commissions. Unfortunately, the tendency to set commission rates informally often reduces plans' effectiveness.[57]

Setting effective quotas is an art. Questions to ask include: Are quotas communicated to the sales force within 1 month of the start of the period? Does the sales force know how their quotas are set? Do you combine bottom-up information (like account forecasts) with top-down requirements (like the company business goals)? Are returns and de-bookings reasonably low?[58]

One expert suggests this rule as to whether the sales incentive plan is effective: 75% or more of the sales force achieving quota or better, 10% of the sales force achieving higher performance level (than previously), and 5% to 10% of the sales force achieving below-quota performance and receiving performance development coaching.[59] The employer should also consider the effect of sales carryover. In most firms, a significant portion of the sales in one year reflects a "carryover" (sales that would repeat even without any efforts by the sales force) of sales from the prior year. Paying the sales force a commission on all the current year's sales means the employer has paid a commission on last year's carryover sales, which the sales force had little or no role in bringing in this year.[60]

A survey of sales effectiveness reveals that salespeople at high-performing companies:

- Receive 38% of their total cash compensation in the form of *sale incentive pay* (compared with 27% for salespeople at low-performing companies)
- Are twice as likely to receive stock, *stock options*, or other equity pay as their counterparts at low-performing companies (36% versus 18%)
- Spend 264 more hours per year on *high-value sales activities* (e.g., prospecting, making sales presentations, and closing) than salespeople at low-performing companies

- Spend 40% more time each year with their *best potential customers*—qualified leads and prospects they know—than salespeople at low-performing companies
- Spend nearly 25% *less time on administration*, allowing them to allocate more time to core sales activities, such as prospecting leads and closing sales[61]

Distinguishing among performers is also important. For example, some companies distinguish among stars, laggards, and core performers. Some companies limit how much their salespeople can earn in commissions, but doing so can perversely encourage stars to quit selling when they reach their quotas. Laggards seem to do better with more frequent, quarterly bonuses and social pressure to improve their performance. Core performers—the vast midrange of the sales force—should have multitier targets. The first tier target is what sales agents historically attain. The second tier reflects what a small percentage of the sales force attains. The third tier target is usually only attained by the company's star salespeople.[62]

Sales Incentives in Action

Car salespersons' compensation ranges from 100% commission to a small base salary with commission accounting for most of total compensation. Traditionally, the car salesperson's commission is based on a percentage of the difference between the dealer's invoice cost and the amount the car is sold for, minus an amount to cover the "pack" or dealer overhead (the pack being perhaps $300 for a new car to $800 for a used car, and rising for pricier cars).[63]

This approach encourages the salesperson to hold firm on the retail price, and to push "after-sale products" like floor mats and side moldings. There may also be extra incentives to sell packages such as rustproofing. For selling slow-moving vehicles, the salesperson may get a "spiff"—an extra incentive bonus over commission. And there are bonuses, such as Salesperson of the Month (perhaps $300 for most cars sold).[64]

Commission plans like these still dominate, but not as much. Many dealers are substituting salary plus bonus plans for commissions. This reflects the growing emphasis on "one price no hassle" pricing.[65] But in either case, the pay plan's aim is to produce the salesperson behaviors the dealership needs to support its strategic aims.

TRENDS SHAPING HR: *DIGITAL AND SOCIAL MEDIA*

Somewhat astonishingly, given the amount of money employers pay out in commissions, about 60% of employers track sales performance and sales commissions much as they did decades ago, using spreadsheets.[66] But to maximize performance, the sales manager typically needs evidence, such as: Do the salespeople know how we measure and reward performance? And, does our commission plan maximize sales of our most profitable products?[67] Spreadsheets don't easily support such analyses.[68] For example, with more than 1,000 sales representatives, First Tennessee Bank had problems managing its sales incentive programs.[69] Bank employees had to enter by hand sales information for each of the 1,000 sales reps onto Excel spreadsheets. The process "had begun to spiral out of control." Switching to an *enterprise incentive management* (EIM) software system solved the problem.[70]

Many employers therefore use such EIM software to track and control sales commissions.[71] Several vendors supply these. For example, Oracle Sales Cloud enables management to easily create scorecard metrics such as number of prospecting calls and sales contracts, and to monitor these in real-time on the system's dashboards.[72] Users can also gamify the sales incentive process with Oracle Sales Cloud, by creating rewards such as points or badges based on each salesperson's performance. ■

LEARNING OBJECTIVE 12-4
Describe the main incentives for managers and executives.

Incentives for Managers and Executives

Managers play a crucial role in divisional and company-wide profitability, and employers therefore put considerable thought into how to reward them. Most managers get short-term and long-term incentives in addition to salary.[73] Of firms offering short-term incentive plans, virtually all—96% in one study—provided those incentives in cash. For those offering long-term incentives, about 48% offer them as stock options. The options aim to reward management for long-term growth in shareholder value.[74]

Strategy and the Executive's Long-Term and Total Rewards Package

Whether consolidating operations or pursuing growth, firms can't fully implement most strategies in just 1 or 2 years. Therefore, the long-term signals you send managers via their long-term incentives can determine whether the firm's strategy succeeds.

The executives' reward components—base salary, short- and long-term incentives, and benefits—must align with each other and with the company's strategic aims. Compensation experts suggest first specifying the strategic aims—"What is our strategy and what are our strategic goals?"—and then deciding what long-term behaviors (boosting sales, cutting costs, and so on) are important for achieving these strategic aims. Next shape each component of the executive total compensation package (base salary, short- and long-term incentives, and benefits) to encourage these required behaviors; then group the components into a balanced plan that makes sense in terms of motivating the executive to achieve the firm's aims. The point is this: Each pay component should help focus the manager's attention on the behaviors required to achieve the company's strategic goals.[75]

Using multiple, strategy-based performance criteria for incentivizing executives is best. Criteria include financial performance, number of strategic goals met, employee productivity measures, customer satisfaction surveys, and employee morale surveys.[76]

One expert estimates that the typical CEO's salary accounts for about one-fifth of his or her pay. A bonus based on explicit performance standards accounts for another fifth, and long-term incentive awards such as stock options and long-term performance plans account for the remaining three-fifths.[77] Ideally, the plan's performance standards should include a combination of market benchmarks (such as performance against competitors) as well as business performance standards (such as earnings per share growth).

SARBANES-OXLEY The Sarbanes-Oxley Act of 2002 affects how employers formulate their executive incentive programs. Congress passed Sarbanes-Oxley to inject a higher level of responsibility into executives' and board members' decisions. It makes them personally liable for violating their fiduciary responsibilities to their shareholders. The act also requires CEOs and CFOs of a public company to repay any bonuses, incentives, or equity-based compensation received from the company during the 12-month period following the issuance of a financial statement that the company must restate due to material noncompliance with a financial reporting requirement stemming from misconduct.[78]

Short-Term Incentives and the Annual Bonus

For better or worse, employers are shifting away from long-term incentives to put more emphasis on short-term performance and incentives.[79] Most firms have **annual bonus** plans for motivating managers' short-term performance. Such short-term incentives can easily produce plus-or-minus adjustments of 25% or more to total pay. Three factors influence one's bonus: eligibility, fund size, and individual performance.

annual bonus
Plans that are designed to motivate short-term performance of managers and that are tied to company profitability.

ELIGIBILITY Employers first decide eligibility. Traditionally, most based annual bonus eligibility on job level/title, base salary, and/or officer status. Some simply based eligibility on job level or job title, or salary.[80] Recently, more employers are offering a broader range of employee annual incentive plans "... in which both executives and other employees participate."[81]

The trend is evident from surveys of what determines bonus plan eligibility. Rather than job title or officer status, *salary grade or band* was the most common eligibility determinant, reported by 42% of employers in one survey. This was followed by *title/reporting relationship* (24%), *officer status* (13%), *compensation committee approval* (11%), *discretionary* (6%), and *base salary* (2%).[82]

The percentage size of any bonus is typically greater for top executives. Thus, an executive earning $250,000 in salary may be able to earn another 80% of his or her salary as a bonus, while a manager in the same firm earning $100,000 can earn only another 30%. Recently, Microsoft's CEO was eligible for an annual bonus of up to 100% of his salary (but collected only half). A typical bonus percentage might be executives, 45% of base salary; managers, 25%; and supervisory personnel, 12%.

FUND SIZE Second, one must determine how big the annual bonus fund should be. Most employers (33% in one survey) traditionally use the sum of targets approach.[83] This means they estimate the likely bonus for each eligible ("target") employee, and total these to arrive at the bonus pool's size.

However, more employers are funding the short-term bonus based on financial results. Here there are no fixed rules about the proportion of profits to pay out. One alternative is to reserve a minimal amount of the profits, say, 10%, for safeguarding stockholders' investments. Then establish a fund for bonuses equal to, say, 20% of the operating profit (profit from the company's core business) before taxes in excess of this safeguard amount. Suppose the operating profits were $200,000 (after putting away 10% to safeguard stockholders). Then the management bonus fund might be 20% of $200,000 or $40,000. Most employers use more than one financial measure on which to base the bonus fund, with sales, earnings per share, and cash flow the most popular.[84] Other illustrative formulas include:

- Twelve percent of net earnings after deducting 6% of net capital
- Ten percent of the amount by which net income exceeds 5% of stockholders' equity

Employers also use formulas to build their bonus pools on other measures they wish to emphasize. For example, Transocean Ltd., the firm that managed the Deepwater Horizon Gulf oil rig that sank in 2010, uses a formula that includes "safety" as 25% of the formula. After the Gulf explosion, senior Transocean executives donated any safety bonuses to the victims' families.[85]

Some firms don't use a formula to determine fund size at all, but make that decision on a discretionary basis.[86] Others, again, determine fund size by simply summing up the likely awards.

Ken Fisher/Getty Images

Even in retail stores, it's not unusual to compensate managers partly based on short-term sales and profits.

THE INDIVIDUAL AWARDS Finally, one must decide the actual individual awards. Typically, the employer sets a target bonus (as well as maximum bonus, perhaps double the target bonus) for each eligible position. The actual bonus then reflects the manager's performance. For example, having previously decided which financial performance measures (return on assets, revenue growth, and so on) to use to measure each manager's performance, the employer computes preliminary total company bonus estimates, and compares the total amount of money required with the bonus fund available.[87] If necessary, it then adjusts the individual bonus estimates. In any case, outstanding managers should receive at least their target bonuses, and marginal ones should receive at best below-average awards. Use what you save on the marginal employees to supplement the outstanding employees.

One question is whether to give managers bonuses based on individual performance, corporate performance, or both. Firms usually tie top-level executive bonuses mostly to overall corporate results (or divisional results if the executive heads a major division). But as one moves farther down, corporate profits become a less accurate gauge of a manager's contribution. For supervisors or the heads of functional departments, it often makes more sense to gear the bonus more closely to individual performance. A study of CEOs of Standard & Poor's 1500 companies for one 3-year period found that 57% of the CEOs received pay increases although company performance (in terms of total shareholder return) did not improve.[88]

Many firms do end up tying short-term bonuses to both organizational and individual performance. Perhaps the simplest method is the *split-award plan.* This makes the manager eligible for two bonuses, one based on his or her individual effort and one based on the organization's overall performance. Thus, a manager might be eligible for an individual performance bonus of up to $10,000, but receive only $2,000 at the end of the year, based on his or her individual performance evaluation. But the person might also receive a second bonus of $3,000, based on the firm's profits for the year.

One drawback to this approach is that it may give marginal performers too much—for instance, someone could get a company-based bonus, even if his or her own performance is mediocre. One way to avoid this is to use the *multiplier method.* As Table 12-2 illustrates, multiply the person's target bonus by 1.00, 0.80, or zero (if the firm's performance is excellent, and the person's performance is excellent, good, fair, or poor). A manager whose own performance is poor does not even receive the company-based bonus.

Employers use *long-term incentives* to inject a long-term perspective into their executives' decisions. With only short-term criteria to shoot for, a manager could conceivably boost profitability by reducing plant maintenance, for instance; this tactic might catch up with the company 3 or 4 years later. Popular long-term incentives include cash, stock options, stock, stock appreciation rights, and phantom stock.[89] PepsiCo's CEO was paid $13.2 million recently, including a base salary of $1.6 million, stock awards of $7.5 million, and a performance-based bonus of $4 million, plus perks such as air travel.[90]

Long-term incentives such as stock options, if well-designed, should only pay off if the firm achieves its strategic goals (such as "double our rate of return"), because the owners and investors should also benefit from the executives' efforts. Long-term

TABLE 12-2 Multiplier Approach to Determining Annual Bonus

Individual Performance (Based on Appraisal, Weight = 0.50)	*Company Performance (Based on Sales Targets, Weight = 0.50)*			
	Excellent	Good	Fair	Poor
Excellent	1.00	0.90	0.80	0.70
Good	0.80	0.70	0.60	0.50
Fair	0.00	0.00	0.00	0.00
Poor	0.00	0.00	0.00	0.00

Note: To determine the dollar amount of a manager's award, multiply the maximum possible (target) bonus by the appropriate factor in the matrix.

incentives may also be "golden handcuffs," motivating executives to stay by letting them accumulate capital (usually options to buy company stock) that they can cash in only after a certain period. Again, popular long-term incentives include cash, stock, stock options, stock appreciation rights, and phantom stock.[91] We'll look at each.

stock option
The right to purchase a stated number of shares of a company stock at today's price at some time in the future.

STOCK OPTIONS A **stock option** is the right to purchase a specific number of shares of company stock at a specific price during a specific period. The executive thus hopes to profit by exercising his or her option to buy the shares in the future but at today's price. This assumes the stock will go up. Unfortunately, this depends partly on considerations outside the manager's control.[92] When stock markets dropped a few years ago, many employers including Intel and Google modified option plans to boost the likely payout.[93] The HR Practices Around the Globe feature addresses one aspect of this.

IMPROVING PERFORMANCE: *HR Practices Around the Globe*

"International human resource management" is important because cultural, political, legal, and economic differences mean that employees in one country often react differently to an HR practice than would employees in other countries.

For example, until January 2006, China basically prohibited publicly listed companies from offering stock incentive plans to their managers. At that point better economic conditions and an evolving political philosophy led to new regulations. Soon 42 Chinese-listed companies were permitting such plans.

A study focused on those 42 companies. It sought to determine how the new incentive plans affected company performance. To understand the findings it's important to know that managing in China still has unique characteristics. For example, prior to becoming publicly listed firms, the big firms were usually owned by the government. Furthermore, the government may well continue to retain certain ownership control rights even after the firms go on the stock market. In such cases, the goals of the owners and the management may diverge. For example, government owners might want to maximize employment, rather than profitability. The question is, given such cultural and political realities, do management stock option plans in China translate into improved company performance, as they often do in the United States?

The researchers compared the performance of the 42 Chinese companies that did adopt management stock-option plans with a control group of firms without such plans. One thing they found was that the stock-option plans did improve firm performance *in companies controlled by private shareholders*, but not in companies controlled by the government. In the latter, goals such as maximizing employment may have outweighed boosting profits, thus limiting managers' profit-boosting efforts.

The findings highlight why managing globally is challenging. In this case, a stock option plan that might improve financial performance in the United States might fail in China, where the government owners' goals may well differ from the desire of managers to boost profits. ■

Source: Based on Robert Boylan, Maggie Foley, and Yu-Jun Lian, "Are Equity Incentives Effective in Chinese Listed Firms? New Evidence from Propensity Score Matching (PSN)," *International Journal of Business Strategy* 10, no. 3 (September 2010).

If your professor has assigned this, go to the Assignments section of **mymanagementlab.com** to complete these discussion questions.

Talk About It 3: Given these findings, would it make sense for managers in government-controlled companies to receive stock options tied to something other than profitability, such as "no employees lose their jobs in this company"? Why?

The chronic problem with stock options is that they often reward even managers who have lackluster performance, but there are also other issues. Several years ago some executives allegedly lied about the dates they received their options to boost their returns. Options may also encourage executives to take perilous risks in pursuit of higher (at least short-term) profits.[94] Stock options provide an incentive to go for spectacular results, but since the managers haven't actually bought the stock yet, they don't risk their own money. One solution is to simply draft the option plan so it forces recipients to convert their options to stock more quickly.[95]

OTHER STOCK PLANS Beyond that, the trend is toward tying rewards more explicitly to performance goals. Instead of stock options, more firms are granting various types of performance-based shares. With *performance-contingent restricted stock* the executive receives his or her shares only if he or she meets the preset performance targets.[96] With (time-based) *restricted stock plans*, the firm usually awards rights to the shares without cost to the executive but the employee is restricted from acquiring (and selling) the shares for, say, 5 years. The employer's aim is to retain the employee's services during that time.[97] With *indexed options*, the option's exercise price fluctuates with the performance of, say, a market index. Then, if the company's stock does no better than the index, the manager's options are worthless. With *premium priced options*, the exercise price is higher than the stock's closing price on the date of the grant, so the executive can't profit from the options until the stock makes significant gains.[98]

Stock appreciation rights (SARs) let the recipient exercise the stock option (by buying the stock) or to take any appreciation in the stock price in cash, stock, or some combination of these. Under *phantom stock plans*, executives receive not shares but "units" that are similar to shares of company stock. Then at some future time, they receive value (usually in cash) equal to the appreciation of the "phantom" stock they own. Both SARs and phantom stock essentially "are bonus plans that grant not stock but rather the right to receive an award based on the value of the company's stock."[99] A *performance achievement plan* awards shares of stock for the achievement of predetermined financial targets, such as profit or growth in earnings per share. Most employees seem to prefer cash bonuses to either stock options or restricted stocks. Due to differences in employee preferences, when possible, enable each employee to choose whether to receive stock options or restricted stock.[100]

ETHICS AND INCENTIVES Anyone designing a long-term incentive plan should keep in mind the management truism "People put their efforts where they know they'll be rewarded." The problem is that simplistic incentives that focus on just one factor (such as cost-cutting) may inadvertently encourage managers to ignore other important factors (such as long-term investment). Similarly, in the absence of strong ethical standards, incentives may breed unethical behavior.[101] Examples are depressingly familiar. For example, *Forbes* alleged that one firm's culture now "rewards hard-nosed aggressiveness and doesn't put the client's interests before those of the firm."[102] For stock-option plan designers, the solution is to include a sufficient array of bonus-able criteria in the incentive plan, while fostering an ethical culture.

Some Other Executive Incentives

golden parachute
A payment companies make in connection with a change in ownership or control of a company.

Companies also offer other executive incentives. Some incentivize executives to stay with the firm. This is especially important when executives might flee because another company is stalking the firm with intentions to buy it. **Golden parachutes** are extraordinary (large) payments companies make to executives in connection with a change in company ownership or control.[103]

Some firms use loans as incentives, for example by guaranteeing large loans to directors and officers to buy company stock. Thus, directors and officers of Conseco owed the company more than $500 million in loans when company shares tanked.[104]

> **Watch It!**
> How does a company actually go about creating an incentive plan? If your professor has assigned this, go to the Assignments section of mymanagementlab.com to complete the video exercise titled *Joie de Vivre Hospitality: Pay for Performance and Financial Incentives.*

LEARNING OBJECTIVE 12-5
Name and describe the most popular organization-wide incentive plans.

Team and Organization-Wide Incentive Plans

We've focused so far on individual employee incentives (such as piecework, commissions, and executive bonuses). Let's look now at incentives for teams, and for all employees company-wide.

How to Design Team Incentives

team (or group) incentive plan
A plan in which a production standard is set for a specific work group, and its members are paid incentives if the group exceeds the production standard.

Firms increasingly rely on teams to manage their work. They therefore need incentive plans that encourage teamwork and focus teams on performance. **Team (or group) incentive plans** pay incentives to the team based on the team's performance.

The main question here is how to reward the team's performance, and the wrong choice can prove lethal. Levi Strauss switched from an individual to a team incentive plan, one that rewarded the team as a whole for its output. Unfortunately, they neglected the fact that some employees worked harder than others. The slower ones (economists sometimes call them "free riders" because they take a free ride on others' efforts) were paid the same as the faster ones. The faster ones, no longer individually incentivized, slowed down, production declined, and Levi's closed its U.S. factories.

So, the main aim is to have all your team pulling together. Free riders notwithstanding, the usual approach is still to tie rewards to some overall standard (goal) of group performance, such as "20 total labor hours per car."[105] One company established such an overall standard for its teams. If the firm reached 100% of its goal, the employees would share in about 5% of the improvement (in labor costs saved). The firm divided the resulting bonus pool by the number of employees to compute the value of a "share." If the firm achieved less than 100% of its goal, the bonus pool was less. The results of this plan in terms of focusing teams on the firm's strategic goals were reportedly "extraordinary."[106] Firms such as Toyota that use team plans rely on employee selection, training, and peer pressure to minimize free riding.

While most employers just use experience to estimate what the team goal or standard should be ("20 total labor hours per car"), others carefully engineer their production standards. If so, the employer will typically base the team incentive on either the piece rate or standard hour plan. All team members then typically receive the same share of the team's incentive pay. Thus, the team might receive say, $5 for each wheel installed above the industrially engineered "standard" 10 wheels per hour.

Occasionally, the employer may want to pay team members according to some other formula. For instance, instead of paying each team member based on how well the team as a whole does, pay everyone based on how well the *best* team member does. This counterintuitive option may make sense when an employer has reason to believe the new team incentive plan might demotivate high-performing team members. That's what happened at Levi's, for instance.

Team incentives can foster a sense of cooperation and unanimity.

vgajic/Getty Images

Team incentives often make sense. They reinforce team planning and problem solving, and can help ensure cooperation. Team incentives also facilitate training, since each member has an interest in getting new members up to speed fast. The main disadvantage is the demotivating effects of free rider workers who share in the team-based pay but who don't put their hearts into it.

Evidence-Based HR: Inequities That Undercut Team Incentives

Although about 85% of large employers reportedly use some type of group- or team-based incentives, studies suggest that team incentives are often counterproductive. Why?

A researcher studied business students enrolled in a graduate online MBA program.[107] She devised a method for categorizing how they said they reacted to the team incentives they'd experienced in the past.

Inequity was the big problem.[108] Sometimes all team members' financial compensation was the same, although one or two people "did the lion's share of the work." In other cases, the employer chose one or two team members for promotion, leaving others to feel they'd worked hard to support someone else's career. The bottom line is that unless you take steps to minimize inequities, it may be best to pay employees based on their individual contributions, rather than on collective team performance.

organization-wide incentive plan
Incentive plan in which all or most employees can participate.

Many employers take the team incentive idea to the next logical level and institute incentive plans in which all or most employees participate. **Organization-wide incentive plans** are plans in which all or most employees can participate, and which generally tie the reward to some measure of company-wide performance. Also called *variable pay plans*, we'll look at them next.

Profit-Sharing Plans

profit-sharing plan
A plan whereby employees share in the company's profits.

Profit-sharing plans are plans in which all or most employees receive a share of the firm's annual profits. Research is sketchy. One study concluded that there is ample evidence that profit-sharing plans boost productivity and morale, but that their effect on profits is insignificant, once you factor in the costs of the plans' payouts.[109] A more recent study, conducted in Spain, concluded that profit-sharing plans improve employee commitment.[110]

There are several types of profit-sharing plans. With *current profit-sharing* or cash plans, employees share in a portion of the employer's profits quarterly or annually. Here the firm simply distributes a percentage of profits (usually 15% to 20%) as profit shares to employees at regular intervals. The Home Depot instituted such a cash program for all its store workers. It started paying store associates a bonus if their stores met certain financial goals. In one recent year, it distributed $90 million under that company-wide incentive plan.[111]

With *deferred profit-sharing* plans, the employer puts cash awards into trust accounts for the employees' retirement.[112] Employees' income taxes on the distributions are deferred until the employee retires or withdraws funds from the plan (thus "deferred profit sharing-plans"). Such plans are essentially pension plans "in which the employer has discretion to determine when and how much the company pays into the plan."[113] The employer generally distributes such awards based on a percentage of the employee's salary, or some measure of the employee's contribution to company profits.[114]

Scanlon Plans

Scanlon plan
An incentive plan developed in 1937 by Joseph Scanlon and designed to encourage cooperation, involvement, and sharing of benefits.

Few would argue with the idea that one of the best ways of ensuring that employees are engaged and committed is to ensure that by pursuing his or her goals, the worker pursues the employer's goals as well. Experts have proposed many ways to achieve this. However, few have been as successful as the **Scanlon plan**, developed in 1937 by Joseph Scanlon, a United Steel Workers Union official.[115] It is still popular today.

The Scanlon plan is remarkably progressive, considering that it is now more than 75 years old. Scanlon plans have five basic features.[116] The first is Scanlon's *philosophy of cooperation.* This philosophy assumes that managers and workers must rid themselves of the "us" and "them" attitudes that normally inhibit employees from developing a sense of ownership in the company.

A second feature is what its practitioners call *identity.* This means that in order to focus employee involvement, the company must articulate its mission or purpose, and employees must understand how the business operates in terms of customers, prices, and costs. *Competence* is a third basic feature. The program, say three experts, "explicitly recognizes that a Scanlon plan demands a high level of competence from employees at all levels."[117] This suggests careful selection and training.

The fourth feature of the plan is the *involvement system.* Employees present improvement suggestions to the appropriate departmental-level committees, which transmit the valuable ones to the executive-level committee. It then decides whether to implement the suggestion.

The fifth element of the plan is the *sharing of benefits formula.* If a suggestion is implemented and successful, all employees usually share in 75% of the savings. For example, assume that the normal monthly ratio of payroll costs to sales is 50%. (Thus, if sales are $600,000, payroll costs should be $300,000.) Assume the firm implements suggestions that result in payroll costs of $250,000 in a month when sales were $550,000 and payroll costs therefore should have been $275,000 (50% of sales). The savings attributable to these suggestions is $25,000 ($275,000 minus $250,000). Workers would typically split 75% of this ($18,750), while $6,250 would go to the firm. In practice, the firm sets aside about one-quarter of the $18,750, for months when payroll costs exceed the standard.

Other Gainsharing Plans

gainsharing plan
An incentive plan that engages employees in a common effort to achieve productivity objectives and share the gains.

The Scanlon plan is one early version of today's **gainsharing plans**. Gainsharing is an incentive plan that engages many or all employees in a common effort to achieve a company's productivity objectives, with any resulting cost-savings gains shared among employees and the company.[118] In addition to the Scanlon plan, other popular gainsharing plans include the Lincoln, Rucker, and Improshare plans.

The basic difference among these plans is how employers determine employee bonuses. The Scanlon formula divides payroll expenses by total sales (or, sometimes, by total sales plus increases in inventory). In one version of the *Lincoln incentive system*, first instituted at the Lincoln Electric Company of Ohio, employees work on a guaranteed piecework basis. The company then distributes total annual profits (less taxes, 6% dividends to stockholders, and a reserve) each year among employees based on their merit rating. Most firms customize their gainsharing plans.

Results—from programs in hospitals, as well as manufacturing plants—suggest that gainsharing improves productivity and patient care, and reduce grievances, but may also entail considerable implementation costs.[119] Based on positive results, the U.S. Department of Health and Human Services approved certain hospital gainsharing plans. Here the hospital pays physicians a share of any cost savings attributable in part to the physicians' efforts.[120]

At-Risk Pay Plans

earnings-at-risk pay plan
Plan that puts some portion of employees' normal pay at risk if they don't meet their goals, in return for possibly obtaining a much larger bonus if they exceed their goals.

Pay for performance can support an employer's cost control efforts. Base pay and benefits represent the lion's share of labor costs, and normally neither varies much even when sales plummet.[121] (Pay cuts adversely affect morale, and if sales fall one year, it's generally hard to cut labor costs without downsizing.) Variable pay plans are one way around this. For example, in an **earnings-at-risk pay plan**, employees agree to put some portion (say, 10%) of their normal pay at risk (forego it) if they don't meet their goals, in return for possibly obtaining a much larger bonus if they exceed their goals. For example, put part of the employees' pay "at risk" by replacing (1) 10% of each worker's wages with (2) a 10% bonus if the company meets its goals plus an additional 3% bonus if it exceeds these goals.

employee stock ownership plan (ESOP)
A corporation contributes shares of its own stock to a trust in which additional contributions are made annually. The trust distributes the stock to employees on retirement or separation from service.

Employee Stock Ownership Plans

Employee stock ownership plans (ESOPs) are company-wide plans in which the employer contributes shares of its own stock (or cash to be used to purchase such stock) to a trust established to purchase shares of the firm's stock for employees. The firm generally makes these contributions annually in proportion to total employee compensation, with a limit of 15% of compensation. The trust holds the stock in individual employee accounts. It then distributes the stock to employees upon retirement (or other separation from service), assuming the person has worked long enough to earn ownership of the stock. (*Stock options*, as discussed earlier in this chapter, go directly to the employees individually to use as they see fit, rather than into a retirement trust.)

ESOPs are popular. The company receives a tax deduction equal to the fair market value of the shares it transfers to the trustee, and can claim an income tax deduction for dividends paid on ESOP-owned stock. Employees, as noted, aren't taxed until they receive a distribution from the trust, usually at retirement. The Employee Retirement Income Security Act (ERISA) allows a firm to borrow against employee stock held in trust and then repay the loan in pretax rather than after-tax dollars, another tax incentive for using such plans.[122]

ESOPs can also help the shareholders of closely held corporations (for instance, a family owns all the shares) to diversify their assets. They place some of their own shares of the company's stock into the ESOP trust and (with the company compensating them for the shares they put in the trust) then purchase other marketable securities for themselves in their place.[123]

Studies suggest that ESOPs probably do encourage employees to develop a sense of ownership in and commitment to the firm, but their effects on motivation and performance are questionable. In any case, those responsible for the funds—usually, the firm's top executives—must be fastidious in executing their fiduciary responsibilities for the fund.[124]

BROAD-BASED STOCK OPTIONS Some companies offer "broad-based stock option plans" in which all or most employees can participate. The basic thinking is that sharing ownership in the company with employees makes motivational and practical sense.[125]

Employers seem to be cutting back on these. For example, Time Warner, Microsoft, Aetna, and Charles Schwab discontinued distributing stock options to most employees. Some of them, including Microsoft, are instead awarding stock. With current tax laws, companies must show the options as an expense when awarded, reducing their attractiveness as a "costless" reward. Microsoft and others apparently feel awarding stock instead of stock options is a more direct and immediate way to link pay to performance.[126]

Incentive Plans in Practice: Nucor

Nucor Corp. is the largest steel producer in the United States. It also has the highest productivity and lowest labor cost per ton.[127] Employees can earn bonuses of 100% or more of base salary, and all Nucor employees participate in one of four performance-based incentive plans. With the *production incentive plan*, operating and maintenance employees and supervisors get weekly bonuses based on their work groups' productivity. The *department manager incentive plan* pays department managers annual incentive bonuses based mostly on the ratio of net income to dollars of assets employed for their division. With the *professional and clerical bonus plan*, employees who are not in one of the two previous plans get bonuses based on their divisions' net income return on assets.[128] Finally, under the *senior officer incentive plan*, Nucor senior managers (whose base salaries are lower than those in comparable firms) get bonuses based on Nucor's annual overall percentage of net income to stockholders equity.[129] Nucor also divides 10% of its operating profits yearly among all employees (except senior officers). Depending on company performance, this may be from 1% to over 20% of an employee's pay.

LEARNING OBJECTIVE **12-6**
Explain how to use incentives to improve employee engagement.

Employee Engagement Guide for Managers

Incentives and Engagement

A survey provides some insights into the role of incentive pay in fostering employee engagement. Of approximately 6,300 compensations professionals the researchers solicited, 736 responded to the survey.[130] Here's what the researchers found.

First, although the compensation professionals believed that total rewards programs can influence employee engagement, many of them did *not* specifically include employee engagement as one of the goals of their compensation plans. About 60% agreed or strongly agreed that "employee engagement and performance metrics are incorporated into variable pay programs in our organization." Only 37% agreed or strongly agreed that "in the organization, engagement levels fostered by line managers are important factor in evaluating performance."

Second, they concluded that the most direct ways to encourage employee engagement with incentives are (1) to measure the extent to which *supervisors are encouraging their subordinates to be engaged,* and (2) to *use incentives to reward supervisors for improving employee engagement.*

Third, even more important than the rewards themselves, getting employees involved in developing the rewards programs was the "gold standard" for building employee cooperation and commitment.

So in brief: Make improving employee engagement a formal target of your compensation plan; appraise and incentivize your supervisors partly based on whether they take steps to improve their subordinates' engagement; and if possible let employees participate in devising the compensation plan.

Chapter Review

MyManagementLab® Go to **mymanagementlab.com** to complete the problems marked with this icon. ✪

Chapter Section Summaries

12-1. In designing an effective financial incentive plan, it's important to understand the relationship between **money and motivation**. Hertzberg said the best way to motivate someone is to organize the job so that it provides the feedback and challenge that help satisfy the person's higher-level needs. Deci found that extrinsic rewards may actually detract from a person's intrinsic motivation. Vroom's expectancy motivation theory says a person's motivation depends on expectancy, instrumentality, and valence. Skinner's behavior modification–based approach means changing behavior through rewards or punishments that are contingent on performance.

12-2. Piecework is an **individual employee incentives and recognition program** incentive plan in which a person is paid a sum for each item he or she makes. Merit pay is a salary increase awarded based on individual performance. Nonfinancial and recognition-based awards include awards in the form of employee recognition, gift certificates, and individual travel. Many employers use enterprise incentive management systems to automate the planning, analysis, and management of their incentive plans.

12-3. **Incentives for salespeople** are typically sales commissions. Although the percentage of pay in the form of sales commission may vary, a survey found that salespeople at high-performing companies receive about 38% of their total cash compensation in sales-related variable pay.

12-4. Managers take many things into consideration when formulating **incentives for managers and executives**. Most firms have annual bonus plans aimed at motivating managers' short-term performance. The actual award often depends on some combination of individual performance and organizational performance, so that, for instance, high-performing managers get a bonus even if the company itself underperforms. Long-term incentives include stock options, "golden parachutes," and stock appreciation rights.

12-5. With more employers organizing their efforts around teams, **team and organization-wide incentive plans are more important**. With team incentive plans, the main question is whether to reward members based on individual or team performance; both have pros and cons. Organization-wide incentive plans are plans in which all or most employees can participate. These include profit-sharing plans in which employees share in the company's profits; gainsharing plans, including the Scanlon plan, engage employees in a common effort to achieve productivity objectives and thereby share the gains. Employee stock ownership plans are company-wide plans in which the employer contributes shares of its own stock to a trust established to purchase shares of the firm's stock for employees.

12-6. Consciously make **employee engagement** a target of your compensation plan; appraise and incentivize supervisors partly based on their effectiveness in improving their subordinates' engagement; and if possible enable employees to participate in devising the compensation plan.

Discussion Questions

12-1. Compare and contrast six types of incentive plans.

✪ 12-2. Explain five reasons why incentive plans fail.

12-3. Describe the nature of some important management incentives.

12-4. You are applying for a job as a manager and are at the point of negotiating salary and incentives. What questions would you ask your prospective employer concerning incentives? Describe the incentives package you would try to negotiate for yourself.

12-5. In this chapter, we listed a number of guidelines for instituting a pay-for-performance plan. Do you think these points make sense in terms of motivation theory? Why or why not?

12-6. What is merit pay? Do you think it's a good idea to award employees merit raises? Why or why not?

✪ 12-7. Give four examples of when you would suggest using team or group incentive programs rather than individual incentive programs.

Individual and Group Activities

12-8. Working individually or in groups, create an incentive plan for the following positions: chemical engineer, plant manager, used-car salesperson. What factors did you have to consider in reaching your conclusions?

12-9. A state university system in the Southeast instituted a "Teacher Incentive Program" (TIP) for its faculty. Faculty committees within each of the university's colleges were told to award $5,000 raises (not bonuses) to about 40% of their faculty members based on how good a job they did teaching undergraduates, and how many courses they taught per year. What are the potential advantages and pitfalls of such an incentive program? How well do you think it was accepted by the faculty? Do you think it had the desired effect?

12-10. Appendices A and B at the end of this book (pages 612–629) list the knowledge someone studying for the HRCI (Appendix A) or SHRM (Appendix B) certification exam needs to have in each area of human resource management (such as in Strategic Management, and Workforce Planning). In groups of several students, do four things: (1) review Appendix A and/or B; (2) identify the material in this chapter that relates to the Appendix A and/or B required knowledge lists; (3) write four multiple-choice exam questions on this material that you believe would be suitable for inclusion in the HRCI exam and/or the SHRM exam; and, (4) if time permits, have someone from your team post your team's questions in front of the class, so that students in all teams can answer the exam questions created by the other teams.

12-11. Several years ago, the pension plan of the Utility Workers Union of America proposed that shareholders change the corporate bylaws of Dominion Resources, Inc., so that in the future management had to get shareholder approval of executive pay exceeding $1 million, as well as detailed information about the firm's executive incentive plans. The union pointed out that, usually, under IRS regulations, corporations can't deduct more than $1 million in pay for any of a company's top five paid executives. Under the new rules the Utility Workers Union is pushing, boards of directors will no longer be able to approve executive pay above $1 million; instead, shareholders would have to vote on it. In terms of effectively running a company, what do you think are the pros and cons of the union's recommendations? Would you vote for or against the union's recommendation? Why?

Experiential Exercise

Motivating the Sales Force at Express Auto

Purpose: The purpose of this exercise is to give you practice developing an incentive plan.

Required Understanding: Be thoroughly familiar with this chapter, and read the following:

Express Auto, an automobile mega-dealership with more than 600 employees that represents 22 brands, has just received a very discouraging set of survey results. Customer satisfaction scores have fallen for the ninth straight quarter. Customer complaints include:

- It was hard to get prompt feedback from mechanics by phone.
- Salespeople often did not return phone calls.
- The finance people seemed "pushy."
- New cars were often not properly cleaned or had minor items that needed immediate repair or adjustment.
- Cars often had to be returned to have repair work redone.

Table 12-3 describes Express Auto's current compensation system.

How to Set Up the Exercise/Instructions: Divide the class into groups of four to five students. One or more groups should analyze each of the five teams in column one. Each student group should analyze the compensation package for its Express Auto team. Each group should address these questions:

12-12. In what ways might your team's compensation plan contribute to the customer service problems?

12-13. What recommendations would you make to improve the compensation system in a way that would likely improve customer satisfaction?

TABLE 12-3 Express Auto Compensation System

Express Auto Team	Responsibility of Team	Current Compensation Method
1. Sales force	Persuade buyer to purchase a car.	Very small salary (minimum wage) with commissions. Commission rate increases with every 20 cars sold per month.
2. Finance office	Help close the sale; persuade customer to use company finance plan.	Salary, plus bonus for each $10,000 financed with the company.
3. Detailing	Inspect cars delivered from factory, clean, and make minor adjustments.	Piecework paid on the number of cars detailed per day.
4. Mechanics	Provide factory warranty service, maintenance, and repair.	Small hourly wage, plus bonus based on (1) number of cars completed per day and (2) finishing each car faster than the standard estimated time to repair.
5. Receptionists/phone service personnel	Primary liaison between customer and sales force, finance, and mechanics.	Minimum wage.

Application Case

Inserting the Team Concept into Compensation—or Not

In his new position at Hathaway Manufacturing, one of the first things Sandy Caldwell wanted to do was improve productivity through teamwork at every level of the firm. As the new human resource manager for this plant, Sandy set out to change the culture to accommodate the team-based approach he had become so enthusiastic about in his most recent position.

Sandy started by installing the concept of team management at the highest level, to oversee the operations of the entire plant. The new management team consisted of manufacturing, distribution, planning, technical, and human resource plant managers. Together they developed a new vision for the 500-employee facility, which they expressed in the simple phrase "Excellence Together." They drafted a new mission statement for the firm that focused on becoming customer driven and team based, and that called upon employees to raise their level of commitment and begin acting as "owners" of the firm.

The next step was to convey the team message to employees throughout the company. The communication process went surprisingly well, and Sandy was happy to see his idea of a "workforce of owners" begin to take shape. Teams trained together, developed production plans together, and embraced the technique of 360-degree feedback, in which an employee's performance evaluation is obtained from supervisors, subordinates, peers, and internal or external customers. Performance and morale improved, and productivity began to tick upward. The company even sponsored occasional celebrations to reward team achievements, and the team structure seemed firmly in place.

Sandy decided to change one more thing. Hathaway's long-standing policy had been to give all employees the same annual pay increase. But Sandy felt that in the new team environment, outstanding performance should be the criterion for pay raises. After consulting with CEO Regina Cioffi, Sandy sent a memo to all employees announcing the change to team-based pay for performance.

The reaction was immediate and 100% negative. None of the employees was happy with the change, and among their complaints, two stood out. First, because the 360-degree feedback system made everyone responsible in part for someone else's performance evaluation, no one was comfortable with the idea that pay raises might also be linked to peer input. Second, there was a widespread perception that the way the change was decided upon, and the way it was announced, put the firm's commitment to team effort in doubt. Simply put, employees felt left out of the decision process.

Sandy and Regina arranged a meeting for early the next morning. Sitting in her office, they began a painful debate. Should the new policy be rescinded as quickly as it was adopted, or should it be allowed to stand?

Questions

12-14. Does the pay-for-performance plan seem like a good idea? Why or why not?

12-15. What advice would you give Regina and Sandy as they consider their decision?

12-16. What mistakes did they make in adopting and communicating the new salary plan? How might Sandy have approached this major compensation change a little differently?

12-17. Assuming the new pay plan is eventually accepted, how would you address the fact that in the new performance evaluation system, employees' input affects their peers' pay levels?

Note: The incident in this case is based on an actual event at Frito-Lay's Kirkwood, New York, plant, as reported in C. James Novak, "Proceed with Caution When Paying Teams," *HR Magazine,* April 1997, p. 73.

Continuing Case

Carter Cleaning Company

The Incentive Plan

The question of whether to pay Carter Cleaning Center employees an hourly wage or an incentive of some kind has always intrigued Jack Carter.

His basic policy has been to pay employees an hourly wage, except that his managers do receive an end-of-year bonus depending, as Jack puts it, "on whether their stores do well or not that year."

However, he is considering using an incentive plan in one store. Jack knows that a presser should press about 25 "tops" (jackets, dresses, blouses) per hour. Most of his pressers do not attain this ideal standard, though. In one instance, a presser named Walt was paid $8 per hour, and Jack noticed that regardless of the amount of work he had to do, Walt always ended up going home at about 3:00 P.M., so he earned about $300 at the end of the week. If it was a holiday week, for instance, and there were a lot of clothes to press, he might average 22 to 23 tops per hour (someone else did pants) and so he'd earn perhaps $300 and still finish each day in time to leave by 3:00 P.M. so he could pick up his children at school. But when things were very slow in the store, his productivity would drop to perhaps 12 to 15 pieces an hour, so that at the end of the week he'd end up earning perhaps $280, and in fact not go home much earlier than he did when it was busy.

Jack spoke with Walt several times, and while Walt always promised to try to do better, it gradually became apparent to Jack that Walt was simply going to earn his $300 per week no matter what. Though Walt never told him so directly, it dawned on Jack that Walt had a family to support and was not about to earn less than his "target" wage, regardless of how busy or slow the store was. The problem was that the longer Walt kept pressing each day, the longer the steam boilers and compressors had to be kept on to power his machines, and the fuel charges alone ran close to $6 per hour. Jack clearly needed some way short of firing Walt to solve the problem, since the fuel bills were eating up his profits.

His solution was to tell Walt that, instead of an hourly $8 wage, he would henceforth pay him $0.33 per item pressed. That way, said Jack to himself, if Walt presses 25 items per hour at $0.33 he will in effect get a small raise. He'll get more items pressed per hour and will therefore be able to shut the machines down earlier.

On the whole, the experiment worked well. Walt generally presses 25 to 35 pieces per hour now. He gets to leave earlier and, with the small increase in pay, he generally earns his target wage. Two problems have arisen, though. The quality of Walt's work has dipped a bit, plus his manager has to spend a minute or two each hour counting the number of pieces Walt pressed that hour. Otherwise, Jack is fairly pleased with the results of his incentive plan, and he's wondering whether to extend it to other employees and other stores.

Questions

12-18. Should this plan be extended to pressers in the other stores?

12-19. Should other employees (cleaner/spotters, counter people) be put on a similar plan? Why or why not? If so, how, exactly?

12-20. Is there another incentive plan you think would work better for the pressers? Describe it.

12-21. A store manager's job is to keep total wages to no more than 30% of sales and to maintain the fuel bill and the supply bill at about 9% of sales each. Managers can also directly affect sales by ensuring courteous customer service and by ensuring that the work is done properly. What suggestions would you make to Jennifer and her father for an incentive plan for store managers or front-desk clerks?

Translating Strategy into HR Policies and Practices Case*,§

**The accompanying strategy map for this chapter is in MyManagementLab; the overall map in the inside back cover of this text outlines the relationships involved.*

Improving Performance at the Hotel Paris

The New Incentive Plan

The Hotel Paris's competitive strategy is "To use superior guest service to differentiate the Hotel Paris properties, and to thereby increase the length of stay and return rate of guests, and thus boost revenues and profitability." HR manager Lisa Cruz must now formulate functional policies and activities that support this competitive strategy by eliciting the required employee behaviors and competencies.

One of Lisa Cruz's biggest pay-related concerns is that the Hotel Paris compensation plan does not link pay to performance in any effective way. Because salaries were historically barely competitive, supervisors tended to award merit raises across the board. So, employees who performed well got only about the same raises as did those who performed poorly. Similarly, there was no bonus or incentive plan of any kind aimed at linking employee performance to strategically relevant employee capabilities and behaviors such as greeting guests in a friendly manner or providing expeditious check-ins and check-outs. The bottom line for Lisa and the CFO was that the company's financial rewards system—potentially, the single-biggest tool they had for channeling employee performance toward accomplishing the Hotel Paris's goals—was totally inadequate. She and her team thus turned to the job of deciding what sort of incentive-based reward systems to install.

Based on their analysis, Lisa Cruz and the CFO concluded that, by any metric, their company's incentive plan had to be changed. The percentage of the workforce whose merit increase or incentive pay was tied to performance was effectively zero, because managers awarded merit pay across the board. No more than 5% of the workforce (just the managers) was eligible for incentive pay. And, the percentage difference in incentive pay between a low-performing and a high-performing employee was less than 2%. Lisa knew from industry studies that in top firms, over 80% of the workforce had merit pay or incentive pay tied to performance. She also knew that in high-performing firms, there was at least a 5% or 6% difference in incentive pay between a low-performing and a high-performing employee. The CFO authorized Lisa to design a new strategy-oriented incentive plan for the Hotel Paris's employees. Their overall aim was to incentivize the pay plans of just about all the company's employees.

Lisa and the company's CFO laid out three measurable criteria that the new incentive plan had to meet. First, at least 90% (and preferably all) of the Hotel Paris's employees must be eligible for a merit increase or incentive pay that is tied to performance. Second, there must be at least a 10% difference in incentive pay between a low-performing and high-performing employee. Third, the new incentive plan had to include specific bonuses and evaluative mechanisms that linked employee behaviors in each job category with strategically relevant employee capabilities and behaviors. For example, front-desk clerks were to be rewarded in part based on the friendliness and speed of their check-ins and check-outs, and the housecleaning crew was to be evaluated and rewarded in part based on the percentage of room cleaning infractions.

With these criteria in mind, Lisa and her team turned to designing the new merit and incentive pay plan. They created a larger merit pay pool, and instructed supervisors that employees scoring in the lower 10% of performance were to receive no merit pay, while the difference in merit pay between the top category and medium category employees was to be 10%. They contracted with an online employee recognition firm and instituted a new "Hotel Paris instantaneous thank-you award program." Under this program, any guest or any supervisor could recommend any hotel employee for an instantaneous recognition award; if approved by the department manager, the employee could choose the recognition award by going to the company's Web site. The incentive structure for all the company's managers, including hotel managers, assistant managers, and departmental managers, now ties at least 10% of each manager's annual pay to the degree to which his or her hotel achieves its strategic aims. The plan measures this in terms of ratings on the guest satisfaction index, average length of guest stay, and frequency of guest returns. Ratings on all these metrics soon began to rise.

Questions

12-22. Discuss what you think of the measurable criteria that Lisa and the CFO set for their new incentive plan.

12-23. Given what you know about the Hotel Paris's strategic goals, list three or four specific behaviors you would incentivize for each of the following groups of employees: front-desk clerks, hotel managers, valets, housekeepers.

12-24. Based on what you learned in this chapter of Dessler *Human Resource Management*, lay out a complete incentive plan (including all long- and short-term incentives) for the Hotel Paris's hotel managers.

---

§ Written and copyright by Gary Dessler, PhD.

MyManagementLab

Go to **mymanagementlab.com** for Auto-graded writing questions as well as the following Assisted-graded writing questions:

12-25. When and why would you pay a salesperson based solely on commission? Based on a combined salary and commission?

12-26. Explain the role recognition and other non-material incentives play in an effective incentive plan.

12-27. MyManagementLab Only–comprehensive writing assignment for this chapter.

✪ PERSONAL INVENTORY ASSESSMENTS

Diagnosing Poor Performance and Enhancing Motivation

Incentives play a big role in employee motivation. Complete this assessment to learn more about your personality.

Key Terms

financial incentives, 387
productivity, 387
fair day's work, 387
scientific management movement, 387
variable pay, 387
intrinsic motivation, 388
expectancy, 388
instrumentality, 388
valence, 388
behavior modification, 388
piecework, 389
straight piecework, 390
standard hour plan, 390
merit pay (merit raise), 390
annual bonus, 398
stock option, 401
golden parachute, 402
team (or group) incentive plan, 403
organization-wide incentive plan, 404
profit-sharing plan, 404
Scanlon plan, 404
gainsharing plan, 405
earnings-at-risk pay plan, 405
employee stock ownership plan (ESOP), 406

Endnotes

1. Jay Heizer and Barry Render, *Operations Management* (Upper Saddle River, NJ: Pearson, 2001), p. 15.
2. See, for example, Mary Ducharme and Mark Podolsky, "Variable Pay: Its Impact on Motivation and Organisation Performance," *International Journal of Human Resources Development and Management* 6 (May 9, 2006), p. 68.
3. Ibid.
4. "Employers Use Pay to Lever Performance," *BNA Bulletin to Management*, August 21, 1997, p. 272; and "Variable Pay Is Superior to Bonus," *People Management*, February 24, 2011, p. 14.
5. See, for example, Kenan Abosch, "Variable Pay: Do We Have the Basics in Place?" *Compensation & Benefits Review*, July/August 1998, pp. 2–22.
6. Even the traditional holiday bonus is being replaced by performance-based pay. "Cash Bonuses Are Ghosts of Holidays Past, Survey Says," *BNA Bulletin to Management*, December 13, 2005, p. 396.
7. "Few Employees See the Pay for Performance Connection," *Compensation & Benefits Review* 17, no. 2 (June 2003); "Most Workers Not Motivated by Cash," *Incentive Today*, July–August 2004, p. 19; and "Pay-for-Performance Plans' Impact Uncertain: Study," *Modern Healthcare*, May 24, 2004, p. 34.
8. Kathy Chu, "Employers See Lackluster Results Linking Salary to Performance," *Wall Street Journal*, June 15, 2004, p. D2.
9. Ted Turnasella, "Pay and Personality," *Compensation & Benefits Review*, March/April 2002, pp. 45–59.
10. Jason Shaw et al., "Reactions to Merit Pay Increases: A Longitudinal Test of a Signal Sensitivity Perspective," *Journal of Applied Psychology* 88, no. 3 (2003), pp. 538–544.
11. See, for example, Edward Deci, *Intrinsic Motivation* (New York: Plenum, 1975).
12. Ruth Kanfer, "Motivation Theory," in Harry C. Triandis, Marvin D. Dunnette, and Leaetta M. Hough, *Handbook of Industrial and Organizational Psychology* (Palo Alto, CA: Consulting Psychologists Press, 1994), p. 113. For a discussion about applying Vroom's principles, see B. Schaffer, "Leadership and Motivation." *Supervision* 69, no. 2 (February 2008), pp. 6–9.
13. For a discussion, see John P. Campbell and Robert Prichard, "Motivation Theory in Industrial and Organizational Psychology," in Marvin Dunnette (ed.), *Industrial and Organizational Psychology* (Chicago: Rand McNally, 1976), pp. 74–75; Kanfer, "Motivation Theory," pp. 115–116; and B. Schaffer, "Leadership and Motivation," op cit.
14. See, for example, Aubrey Daniels et al., "The Leader's Role in Pay Systems and Organizational Performance," *Compensation & Benefits Review*, May/June 2006, pp. 58–60; and Suzanne Peterson and Fred Luthans, "The Impact of Financial and Nonfinancial Incentives on Business Unit Outcomes Over Time," *Journal of Applied Psychology* 91, no. 1 (2006), pp. 156–165.
15. See, for example, Diane Cadrain, "Cash Versus Non-Cash Rewards," *HR Magazine*, April 2003, pp. 81–87.
16. Richard Henderson, *Compensation Management* (Reston, VA: Reston, 1979), p. 363.
17. David Belcher, *Compensation Administration* (Englewood Cliffs, NJ: Prentice Hall, 1973), p. 314.
18. These problems have been long known. See, for example, Thomas Wilson, "Is It Time to Eliminate the Piece Rate Incentive System?" *Compensation and Benefits Review*, March–April 1992, pp. 43–49.
19. William Atkinson, "Incentive Pay Programs That Work in Textile," *Textile World* 151, no. 2 (February 2001), pp. 55–57.
20. See, for example, "Bias Creeps into Bonus Process, MIT Study Finds," *Workforce Management*, September 20, 2008, pp 8–9
21. Michael Harris et al., "A Longitudinal Examination of a Merit Pay System: Relationships Among Performance Ratings, Merit Increases, and Total Pay Increases," *Journal of Applied Psychology* 83, no. 5 (1998), pp. 825–831. See also H. Risher, "Add Merit Pay for Performance," *Compensation and Benefits Review* 40, no. 6 (November/December 2008), pp. 22–29.
22. Eric R. Schulz and Denise Marie Tanguay, "Merit Pay in a Public Higher Education Institution: Questions of Impact and Attitudes," *Public Personnel Management* 35, no. 1 (Spring 2006), p. 71(18); Thomas S. Dee and Benjamin J. Keys, "Does Merit Pay Reward Good Teachers? Evidence from a Randomized Experiment," *Journal of Policy Analysis & Management* 23, no. 3 (Summer 2004), pp. 471–488. See also Sanghee Park and Michael Sturman, "How and What You Pay Matters: The Relative Effectiveness of Merit Pay, Bonuses and Long-Term Incentives on Future Job Performance," *Compensation & Benefits Review* 44, no. 2 (2012), pp. 80–85.
23. Fay Hansen, "Wage and Salary Trends," *Compensation & Benefits Review* 40, no. 5 (November/December 2008), p. 5.
24. Rachel Silverman, "My Colleague, My Paymaster," *Wall Street Journal*, April 4, 2012, pp. B1, B8.
25. Jonathan Glater, "Varying the Recipe Helps TV Operations Solve Morale Problem," *New York Times*, March 7, 2001, p. C1.
26. Steve Yegge, quoted in http://glinden.blogspot.com/2006/09/management-and-incentives-at-google.html, accessed June 1, 2011. See also Franck Giancola, "Should HR Professionals Devote More Time to Intrinsic Rewards?" *Compensation & Benefits Review* 46, no. 1 (2014), pp. 25–31.
27. Brian Skelton, "Dual-Career Tracks: Rewarding and Maintaining Technical Expertise," www.todaysengineer.org/2003/May/dual-ladder.asp, accessed September 8, 2014.
28. Peterson and Luthans, "The Impact of Financial and Nonfinancial Incentives."
29. "WorkSimple 'Praise' App Boosts Employee Recognition," *T+D* (January 2012), p. 21, *Academic OneFile*, accessed March 17, 2013.
30. Michelle V. Rafter, "Back in a Giving Mood," *Workforce Management* 88, no. 10 (September 14, 2009), pp. 25–29.
31. http://blog.intuit.com/employees/6-mobile-apps-for-recognizing-and-rewarding-employees, accessed July 11, 2014.
32. Like those at http://blog.intuit.com/employees/6-mobile-apps-for-recognizing-and-rewarding-employees.
33. Hilary Stout, "3 Dollar Tip on a 4-Dollar Cup of Coffee? Gratuities Grow, Automatically," *New York Times*, February 1, 2015, pp. 1, 4.
34. See, for example, Leslie Yerkes, *Fun Works: Creating Places Where People Love to Work* (San Francisco, CA: Berrett-Koehler Publishers, 2007).

35. Charlotte Huff, "Recognition That Resonates," *Workforce Management*, September 11, 2006, pp. 25–29. A survey of executives concluded that three nonfinancial incentives—praise and commendation from immediate managers, attention from leaders, and opportunities to lead project or task forces—all ranked higher in motivational effectiveness than did financial incentives including stock options. Daniel Morrell, "Employee Perceptions and the Motivation of Non-Monetary Incentives," *Compensation & Benefits Review* 43, no. 5 (September/October 2011), pp. 318–323.
36. Bob Nelson, *1001 Ways to Reward Employees* (New York: Workman Pub., 1994), p. 19. See also Sunny C. L. Fong and Margaret A. Shaffer, "The Dimensionality and Determinants of Pay Satisfaction: A Cross-Cultural Investigation of a Group Incentive Plan," *International Journal of Human Resource Management* 14, no. 4 (June 2003), p. 559(22).
37. www.deloitte.com/assets/DcomUnitedStates/Local%20Assets/Documents/us_consulting_ 2010StrategicSalesCompensationSurvey_072910.pdf, accessed September 8, 2014.
38. Peterson and Luthans, "The Impact of Financial and Nonfinancial Incentives," pp. 156–165.
39. Ibid., p. 159.
40. Ibid., p. 159.
41. Ibid., p. 162. See also "Delivering Incentive Compensation Plans That Work," *Financial Executive* 25, no. 7 (September 2009), pp. 52–54, and "Survey Finds Many Employers Not Satisfied with Their Pay-for-Performance Programs," *BNA Bulletin to Management*, January 7, 2014, p. 3.
42. For a checklist for determining when pay for performance is advisable, see Myron Glassman et al., "Evaluating Pay for Performance Systems: Critical Issues for Implementation," *Compensation & Benefits Review* 42, no. 4 (2010), p. 236.
43. "Two Frameworks for a More ROI-Minded Rewards Plan," *Pay for Performance Report,* February 2003, p. 1, www.ioma.com/issues/PFP/2003_02/518132-1.html, accessed November 3, 2009; and Alan Robinson and Dean Schroeder, "Rewards That Really Work," *Security Management*, July 2004, pp. 30–34. See also Patricia Zingheim and Jay Schuster, "What Are Key Pay Issues Right Now?" *Compensation & Benefits Review*, May/June 2007, pp. 51–55.
44. Reed Taussig, "Managing Cash Based Incentives," *Compensation & Benefits Review*, March/April 2002, pp. 65–68. See also Nigel Nicholson, "How to Motivate Your Problem People," *Harvard Business Review*, January 2003, pp. 57–65; and "Incentives, Motivation and Workplace Performance," Incentive Research Foundation, www.incentivescentral.org/employees/whitepapers, accessed May 19, 2007.
45. Theodore Weinberger, "Evaluating the Effectiveness of an Incentive Plan Design Within Company Constraints," *Compensation & Benefits Review*, November/December 2005, pp. 27–33; and Howard Risher, "Adding Merit to Pay for Performance," *Compensation & Benefits Review*, November/December 2008, pp. 22–29.
46. www.deloitte.com/assets/DcomUnitedStates/Local%20Assets/Documents/us_consulting_ 2010StrategicSalesCompensationSurvey_ 072910.pdf, accessed June 1, 2011.
47. Ibid.
48. Deloitte Varicent, 2010 Strategic Sales Compensation Survey, p. 6, at www.deloitte.com/assets/Dcom-UnitedStates/Local%20Assets/Documents/us_consulting_2010Strategic SalesCompensationSurvey_072910.pdf, accessed August 29, 2011.
49. www.deloitte.com/assets/DcomUnitedStates/Local%20Assets/Documents/us_consulting_2010 StrategicSalesCompensationSurvey_ 072910.pdf, accessed September 8, 2014. See also Pankaj Madhani, "Managing Salesforce Compensation: A Lifecycle Perspective," *Compensation & Benefits Review* 44, no. 6, pp. 315–326.
50. Straight salary by itself is not, of course, an incentive compensation plan as we use the term in this chapter.
51. Donna Harris, "Dealers Rethink How They Pay Salespeople," *Automotive News*, June 14, 2010, www.autonews.com/article/20100614/RETAIL07/306149932?CSAuthResp=1%3A37354836327014 7%3A423310%3A4129%3A24%3Aapproved%3A06E323F6579E1FCB5665B3CC4B7C6C0B&=, accessed September 8, 2014.
52. Sonjun Luo, "Does Your Sales Incentive Plan Pay for Performance?" *Compensation & Benefits Review*, January/February 2003, pp. 18–24.
53. Scott Ladd, "May the Sales Force Be with You," *HR Magazine*, September 2010, p. 105.
54. Luo, "Does Your Sales Incentive Plan Pay for Performance," pp. 331–345. See also James M. Pappas and Karen E. Flaherty, "The Moderating Role of Individual-Difference Variables in Compensation Research," *Journal of Managerial Psychology* 21, no. 1 (January 2006), pp. 19–35; and T. B. Lopez, C. D. Hopkins, and M. A. Raymond, "Reward Preferences of Salespeople: How Do Commissions Rate?" *Journal of Personal Selling & Sales Management* 26, no. 4 (Fall 2006), p. 381(10).
55. Bill O'Connell, "Dead Solid Perfect: Achieving Sales Compensation Alignment," *Compensation & Benefits Review*, March/April 1996, pp. 46–47. See also C. Albrech, "Moving to a Global Sales Incentive Compensation Plan," *Compensation & Benefits Review* 41, no. 4 (July/August 2009), p. 52.
56. See, for example, Pankaj Madhani, "Realigning Fixed and Variable Pay in Sales Organizations: An Organizational Lifestyle Approach," *Compensation & Benefits Review* 42, no. 6, pp. 488–498.
57. Leslie Stretch, "From Strategy to Profitability: How Sales Compensation Management Drives Business Performance," *Compensation & Benefits Review*, May/June 2008, pp. 32–37.
58. S. Scott Sands, "Ineffective Quotas: The Hidden Threat to Sales Compensation Plans," *Compensation & Benefits Review* (March/April 2000), pp. 35–42. See also "Driving Profitable Sales Growth: 2006/2007 Report on Sales Effectiveness," www.watsonwyatt.com/research/resrender.asp?id=2006-US-0060&page=1, accessed May 20, 2007.
59. Peter Gundy, "Sales Compensation Programs: Built to Last," *Compensation & Benefits Review* (September/October 2002), pp. 21–28. See also T. B. Lopez, C. D. Hopkins, and M. A. Raymond, "Reward Preferences of Salespeople: How Do Commissions Rate?" *Journal of Personal Selling & Sales Management* 26, no. 4 (Fall 2006), p. 381(10).
60. Pankaj Madhani, "Reallocating Fixed and Variable Pay in Sales Organizations: a Sales Carryover Perspective," *Compensation & Benefits Review* 43, no. 6, (2011) pp. 346–360.
61. "Driving Profitable Sales Growth: 2006/2007 Report on Sales Effectiveness," www.watsonwyatt.com/research/resrender.asp?id=2006-US-0060&page=1, accessed May 20, 2007.
62. Thomas Steenburgh and Michael Ahearne, "Motivating Salespeople: What Really Works," *The Harvard Business Review*, July–August 2012, pp. 71–75.
63. "Car Salesman Commission the Way It Works," http://carsalesprofessional.com/carsalesman-commission/, accessed June 26, 2011.
64. Ibid.
65. Peter Glendinning, "Kicking the Tires of Automotive Sales Compensation," *Compensation & Benefits Review*, September/October 2000, pp. 47–53; and Michele Marchetti, "Why Sales Contests Don't Work," *Sales and Marketing Management* 156 (January 2004), p. 19. See also "Salary and Bonus Gain Favor in Sales Pay (for Motor Vehicle Salespeople)," *Automotive News* 75, no. 5915 (February 5, 2001), p. 50.
66. Varicent, "2010 Strategic Sales."
67. Bob Conlin, "Best Practices for Designing New Sales Compensation Plans," *Compensation & Benefits Review*, March/April 2008, p. 51.
68. Ibid., p. 53.
69. Jeremy Wuittner, "Plenty of Incentives to Use E.I.M. Software Systems," *American Banker* 168, no. 129 (July 8, 2003), p. 680.
70. Nina McIntyre, "Using EIM Technology to Successfully Motivate Employees," *Compensation & Benefits Review*, July/August 2001, pp. 57–60.
71. www.vuesoftware.com/Product/Compensation_Management.aspx, accessed September 8, 2014.
72. Oracle Fusion Incentive Compensation Data Sheet, http://www.oracle.com/us/products/applications/fusion/hcm-workforce-compensation–1543936.pdf, accessed July 14, 2015.
73. Mark Meltzer and Howard Goldsmith, "Executive Compensation for Growth Companies," *Compensation & Benefits Review*, November/December 1997, pp. 41–50; and Barbara Kiviat, "Everyone into the Bonus Pool," *Time* 162, no. 24 (December 15, 2003), p. A5.
74. www.mercer.com/pressrelease/details.jhtml/dynamic/idContent/1263210, accessed January 2, 2007.
75. Meltzer and Goldsmith, "Executive Compensation for Growth Companies," pp. 41–50. See also Patricia Zingheim and Jay Schuster, "Designing Pay and Rewards in Professional Companies," *Compensation & Benefits Review*, January/February 2007, pp. 55–62; and Ronald Bottano and Russell Miller, "Making Executive Compensation Count: Tapping into the New Long-Term Incentive Portfolio," *Compensation & Benefits Review*, July/August 2007, pp. 43–47.
76. George Yancey, "Aligning the CEO's Incentive Plan with Criteria That Drive Organizational Performance," *Compensation & Benefits Review* 42, no. 3 (2010), pp. 190–196.
77. Richard Ericson, "Benchmarking for Executive Incentive Pay: The Importance of Performance

Standards," *Compensation & Benefits Review* 43, no. 2, (2010), pp. 92–99.
78. See "The Impact of Sarbanes-Oxley on Executive Compensation," www.thelenreid.com, accessed December 11, 2003. See also Brent Longnecker and James Krueger, "The Next Wave of Compensation Disclosure," *Compensation & Benefits Review*, January/February 2007, pp. 50–54.
79. James Reda, "Executive Compensation: Balancing Risk, Performance and Pay," *Financial Executive* 25, no. 9 (November 2009), pp. 46–50. See also Bruce Ellig, "Short-Term Incentives: Top-Down or Bottom-Up?" *Compensation & Benefits Review* 43, no 3, (May/June 2011), pp. 179–183.
80. Meltzer and Goldsmith, "Executive Compensation for Growth Companies," pp. 44–45; See also Jennifer Wynter-Palmer, "Is the Use of Short-Term Incentives Good Organization Strategy?" *Compensation & Benefits Review* 44, no. 5, 2013, pp. 254–265.
81. Max Smith and Ben Stradley, "New Research Tracks the Evolution of Annual Incentive Plans," *Executive Compensation*, Towers Watson, 2010, Towerswatson.com, accessed August 28, 2011.
82. Ibid.
83. Ibid.
84. Ibid.
85. Dionne Searcey, "Transocean Executives to Donate Bonuses," *Wall Street Journal*, April 6, 2011, p. B1.
86. Meltzer and Goldsmith, "Executive Compensation for Growth Companies," p. 44. Fay Hansen, "Salary and Wage Trends," *Compensation & Benefits Review*, March/April 2004, pp. 9–10.
87. Bruce Ellig, "Executive Pay Financial Measurements," *Compensation & Benefits Review*, September/October 2008, pp. 42–49.
88. "Study: CEO Compensation Not Tied to Company Performance," *BNA Bulletin to Management*, March 22, 2011, p. 92.
89. See for example Bruce Ellig, "Long-Term Incentive Plan Combinations," *Compensation & Benefits Review* 46, no. 1 (2014), pp. 10–15.
90. www.usatoday.com/story/money/business/2014/03/21/pepsico-ceospay-bumped-to-132-million/6717929/, accessed April 3, 2014.
91. See, for example, Bruce Ellig, "Stock Awards Can Be a Powerful Executive Pay Element," *Compensation & Benefits Review* 45, no. 6 (2013), pp. 309–319.
92. Benjamin Dunford et al., "Underwater Stock Options and Voluntary Executive Turnover: A Multidisciplinary Perspective Integrating Behavioral and Economic Theories," *Personnel Psychology* 61 (2008), pp. 687–726.
93. Phred Dvorak, "Slump Yields Employee Rewards," *Wall Street Journal*, October 10, 2008, p. B2; Don Clark and Jerry DiColo, "Intel to Let Workers Exchange Options," *Wall Street Journal*, March 24, 2009, p. B3.
94. Wm. Gerard Sanders and Donald Hambrick, "Swinging for the Fences: The Effects of CEO Stock Options on Company Risk-Taking and Performance," *Academy of Management Journal* 50, no. 5 (2007), pp. 1055–1078.
95. "Study Finds That Directly Owning Stock Shares Leads to Better Results," *Compensation & Benefits Review*, March/April 2001, p. 7. See also Lucian A. Bebchuk and Jesse M. Fried, "Pay Without Performance: Overview of the Issues," *Academy of Management Perspective* 20, no. 1 (February 2006), p. 5(20).
96. www.mercer.com/pressrelease/details.jhtml/dynamic/idContent/1263210, accessed January 2, 2007.
97. www.nceo.org/main/article.php/id/43/, accessed June 1, 2011.
98. Louis Lavelle, "How to Halt the Options Express," *BusinessWeek*, September 9, 2002.
99. www.ncco.org/main/article.plip/id/43/, accessed June 1, 2011.
100. Menahchem Abudy and Efrat Shust, "Employee's Attitudes Toward Equity-Based Compensation," *Compensation & Benefits Review* 44, no. 5 (2013), pp. 246–253.
101. Christine Bevilacqua and Parbudyal Singh, "Pay for Performance—Panacea or Pandora's Box? Revisiting an Old Debate in the Current Economic Environment," *Compensation & Benefits Review*, September/October 2009, pp. 21–26.
102. www.forbes.com/2010/06/14/goldman-sachs-paulson-markets-lloyd-blankfein.html, accessed May 21, 2011.
103. Under IRS regulations, companies cannot deduct all golden parachute payments made to executives, and the executive must pay a 20% excise tax on the golden parachute payments. "Final Regs Issued for Golden Parachute Payments," *Executive Tax and Management Report* 66, no. 17 (September 2003), p. 1.
104. "Conseco Not Alone on Executive Perks," *Knight-Ridder/Tribune Business News*, August 28, 2003, item 03240015. See also "Realities of Executive Compensation—2006/2007 Report on Executive Pay and Stock Options," www.watsonwyatt.com/research/resrender.asp?id=2006-US-0085&page=1, accessed May 20, 2007.
105. Other suggestions are as follows: equal payments to all members on the team; differential payments to team members based on their contributions to the team's performance; and differential payments determined by a ratio of each group member's base pay to the total base pay of the group. See Kathryn Bartol and Laura Hagmann, "Team Based Pay Plans: A Key to Effective Team Work," *Compensation & Benefits Review*, November–December 1992, pp. 24–29. See also Charlotte Garvey, "Steer Teams with the Right Pay," *HR Magazine*, May 2002, pp. 70–71; and K. Merriman, "On the Folly of Rewarding Team Performance, While Hoping for Teamwork," *Compensation & Benefits Review* 41, no. 1 (January/February 2009), pp. 61–66.
106. Richard Seaman, "The Case Study: Rejuvenating an Organization with Team Pay," *Compensation & Benefits Review*, September/October 1997, pp. 25–30. See also Peter Wright, Mark Kroll, Jeffrey A. Krug, and Michael Pettus, "Influences of Top Management Team Incentives on Firm Risk Taking," *Strategic Management Journal* 28, no. 1 (January 2007), pp. 81–89.
107. K. Merriman, "On the Folly of Rewarding Team Performance, While Hoping for Teamwork," *Compensation & Benefits Review*, January/February 2009, pp. 61–66.
108. As another example, see Bernd Irlenbusch and Gabriele K. Lünser, "Relative Rewards Within Team-Based Compensation," November 2006. IZA Discussion Paper No. 2423. Available at SSRN: http://ssrn.com/abstract=947075, accessed May 21, 2011.
109. Seongsu Kim, "Does Profit Sharing Increase Firms' Profits?" *Journal of Labor Research,* Spring 1998, pp. 351–371. See also Jacqueline Coyle-Shapiro et al., "Using Profit-Sharing to Enhance Employee Attitudes: A Longitudinal Examination of the Effects on Trust and Commitment," *Human Resource Management* 41, no. 4 (Winter 2002), pp. 423–449.
110. Alberto Bayo-Moriones and Martin Larraza-Kintana, "Profit Sharing Plans and Effective Commitment: Does the Context Matter?" *Human Resource Management* 48, no. 2 (March–April 2009), pp. 207–226.
111. Kaja Whitehouse, "More Companies Offer Packages Linking Pay Plans to Performance," *Wall Street Journal*, December 13, 2005, p. B4.
112. Under the U.S. tax code, "any arrangement that provides for the deferral of compensation in a year later than the year in which the compensation was earned may be considered a deferred compensation arrangement." Steven Friedman, "2008 Compliance Strategies for Employers in Light of Final 409A Regulations," *Compensation & Benefits Review*, March/April 2008, p. 27.
113. www.axa-equitable.com/retirement/how-do-company-profit-sharing-plans-work.html, accessed June 1, 2011.
114. Joseph Martocchio, *Strategic Compensation* (Upper Saddle River, NJ: Prentice Hall, 2006), pp. 163–165.
115. Brian Graham-Moore and Timothy Ross, *The Scanlon Way to Improved Productivity: A Practical Guide* (New York: Wiley, 1978), p. 2. For a review of potential problems, see Denis Collins, "Death of a Gainsharing Plan: Power Politics and Participatory Management," *Organizational Dynamics* 24 (Summer 1995), pp. 23–37. For an historical perspective on gainsharing's effectiveness, see Alexander Gardner, "Goal Setting and Gainsharing: The Evidence of Effectiveness," *Compensation & Benefits Review* 43, no 4 (July/August 2011), pp. 236–244.
116. These are based in part on Steven Markham, K. Dow Scott, and Walter Cox Jr., "The Evolutionary Development of a Scanlon Plan," *Compensation & Benefits Review*, March/April 1992, pp. 50–56. See also Woodruff Imberman, "Are You Ready to Boost Productivity with a Gainsharing Plan? To Survive and Prosper in Our Hyper-competitive Environment, Board Converters Must Motivate Employees at All Levels," *Official Board Markets* 82, no. 47 (November 25, 2006), p. 5(2); and James Reynolds and Daniel Roble, "Combining Pay for Performance with Gainsharing," *Healthcare Financial Management* 60, no. 11 (November 2006), p. 50(6).
117. Markham et al., "The Evolutionary Development of a Scanlon Plan," p. 51.
118. Barry W. Thomas and Madeline Hess Olson, "Gainsharing: The Design Guarantees Success," *Personnel Journal*, May 1998, pp. 73–79; and A. C. Gardner, "Goal Setting and Gainsharing: The Evidence on Effectiveness," *Compensation and Benefits Review* 43, no. 4 (July/August 2011), pp. 236–244.
119. Paraphrased from Woodruff Imberman, "Boosting Plant

Performance with Gainsharing," *Business Horizons*, November–December 1992, p. 77. See also Max Reynolds and Joane Goodroe, "The Return of Gainsharing: Gainsharing Appears to Be Enjoying a Renaissance," *Healthcare Financial Management* 59, no. 11 (November 2005), p. 114(6); and hospital gainsharing discussion in Anjana Patel, "Gainsharing: Past, Present, and Future," *Healthcare Financial Management* 60, no. 9 (September 2006), pp. 124–128, 130.

120. Paul Rossler and C. Patrick Koelling, "The Effect of Gainsharing on Business Performance at a Paper Mill," *National Productivity Review,* Summer 1993, pp. 365–382; and Anjana Patel, "Gainsharing: Past, Present, and Future," *Healthcare Financial Management* 60, no. 9 (September 2006), pp. 124–128, 130.
121. Robert Greene, "Variable Compensation: Good Fit to Turbulent Environments," *Compensation & Benefits Review* 44, no. 6, November/December 2012, p. 308.
122. See, for example, www.dol.gov/dol/topic/health-plans/erisa.htm, accessed October 2, 2011.
123. Steven Etkind, "ESOPs Create Liquidity for Share Holders and Help Diversify Their Assets," *Estate Planning* 24, no. 4 (May 1998), pp. 158–165. See also S. Coomes, "Employee Stock Plans Can Save Taxes, Attract Talent," *Nation's Restaurant News* 42, no. 36 (September 15, 2008), p. 12.
124. William Smith, Harold Lazarus, and Harold Murray Kalkstein, "Employee Stock Ownership Plans: Motivation and Moral Issues," *Compensation & Benefits Review*, September/October 1990, pp. 37–46. See also "ESOP Trustees Breached Their Fiduciary Duties Under ERISA by Failing to Make Prudent Investigation into Value of Stock Purchased by ESOP," *Tax Management Compensation Planning Journal* 30, no. 10 (October 4, 2002), p. 301(1); and J. D. Mamorsky, "Court Approves ERISA Action Against ENRON Executives, Trustee, and Plan Auditor for Retirement Plan Losses," *Journal of Compensation and Benefits* 20, no. 1 (January–February 2004), p. 46(7).
125. James Sesil et al., "Broad-Based Employee Stock Options in U.S. New Economy Firms," *British Journal of Industrial Relations* 40, no. 2 (June 2002), pp. 273–294.
126. Eric Dash, "Time Warner Stops Granting Stock Options to Most of Staff," *New York Times*, February 19, 2005, item 128921996.
127. Janet Wiscombe, "Can Pay for Performance Really Work?" *Workforce*, August 2001, p. 30.
128. Susan Marks, "Incentives That Really Reward and Motivate," *Workforce*, June 2001, pp. 108–114.
129. Although not an issue at Nucor, the employer needs to beware of instituting so many incentive plans (cash bonuses, stock options, recognition programs, and so on) that employees don't have a clear priority of the employer's priorities. See, for example, Stephen Rubenfeld and Jannifer David, "Multiple Employee Incentive Plans: Too Much of a Good Thing?" *Compensation & Benefits Review*, March/April 2006, pp. 35–43.
130. This is based on Dow Scott and Tom McMullen, "The Impact of Rewards Programs on Employee Engagement," Worldat-Work, June 2010.

13

Benefits and Services

Maridav/Shutterstock

LEARNING OBJECTIVES

13-1 Name and define each of the main pay for time not worked benefits.

13-2 Describe each of the main insurance benefits.

13-3 Discuss the main retirement benefits.

13-4 Outline the main employees' services benefits.

13-5 Explain the main flexible benefit programs.

13-6 Explain how to use benefits to improve engagement, productivity, and performance.

About 25 years ago, Gary Erickson was biking through California and got an idea that changed his life—to create tastier and healthier health bars than those then available.[1] That was the beginning of Clif Bar, a company Erickson started as a small bakery and then grew into one with hundreds of employees selling healthy foods and drinks. He wanted an employee benefits plan for his employees that highlighted Clif Bar's healthy/sustainable focus; we'll see what he did.

WHERE ARE WE NOW ...

Chapters 11 and 12 addressed salaries (or wages) and incentives. The main purpose of this chapter is to explain the third major pay component: employee benefits. The main topics we discuss are pay for time not worked benefits, insurance benefits, retirement benefits, employees' services benefits, flexible benefits, and using benefits to improve engagement and performance. This chapter completes our discussion of employee compensation. The next chapter starts a new part of this book, and focuses on managing employee relations.

Introduction: The Benefits Picture Today

benefits
Indirect financial and nonfinancial payments employees receive for continuing their employment with the company.

"What are your benefits?" is the first thing many applicants ask. **Benefits**—indirect financial and nonfinancial payments employees receive for continuing their employment with the company—are an important part of just about everyone's compensation.[2] They include things like health and life insurance, pensions, paid time off, and child-care assistance.[3] Employee benefits account for about 37% of wages and salaries (or about 30% of total payrolls). Figure 13-1 summarizes the breakdown of benefits as a percentage of employee compensation.

For most employees, *health benefits* are the 800-pound gorilla of the benefits package. In one survey, 78% of employees cited health-care benefits as most crucial to retaining them; 75% cited compensation. But the same survey found that only 34% are satisfied with their health-care benefits.[4] Even human resource managers sometimes underestimate benefits' attractiveness. One survey concluded that many human resource managers erroneously assume that things like job security and autonomy and independence are more important to employees than are benefits.[5]

Policy Issues

Employers therefore should design benefits packages carefully. The list of policy issues includes what benefits to offer, who receives coverage, whether to include retirees in the plan, whether to deny benefits to employees during initial "probationary" periods, how to finance benefits, cost-containment procedures, and how to communicate benefits options to employees.[6]

Legal issues loom large. Federal laws mandate some benefits (such as Social Security) while other benefits are at the employer's discretion (see Table 13-1). However, federal law still affects discretionary benefits such as vacation leave. And employers must adhere to the laws of the states in which they do business. For example, California requires most state contractors to provide domestic partner benefits for employees.[7]

There are many benefits and ways to classify them. We will classify them as (1) pay for time not worked (such as vacations), (2) insurance benefits, (3) retirement benefits, (4) personal services benefits, and (5) flexible benefits. We will start our discussion with pay for time not worked.

HR in Practice at the Hotel Paris As they reviewed the benefits numbers, Lisa Cruz and the CFO became increasingly concerned. They computed several benefits-related metrics for their firm, including *benefits costs as a percentage of payroll* and *sick days per full-time equivalent employee per year.* The results were not what they should have been. They had to change their benefits plan. To see how they handled this, read the case on pages 444.

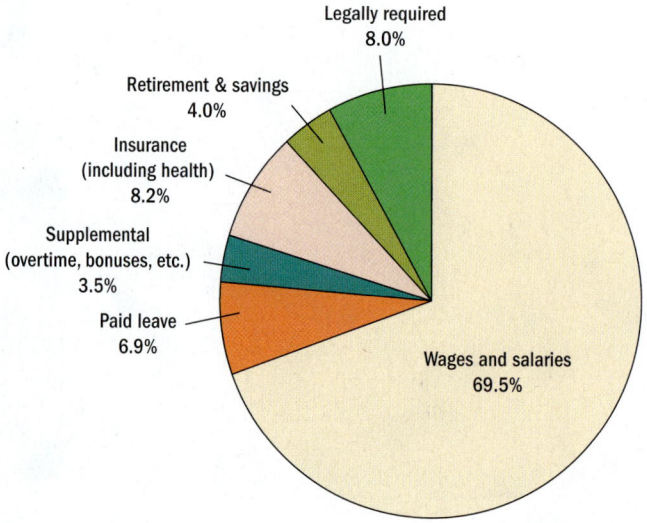

FIGURE 13-1 Relative Importance of Employer Costs for Employee Compensation (private industry), June 2015

Source: Based on Employer Costs For Employee Compensation—June 2015, http://www.bls.gov/news.release/pdf/ecec.pdf accessed September 17, 2015.

TABLE 13-1 Some Required and Discretionary Benefits

Benefits Required by Federal or Most State Laws	Benefits Discretionary on Part of Employer*
Social Security	Disability, health, and life insurance
Unemployment insurance	Pensions
Workers' compensation	Paid time off for vacations, holidays, sick leave, personal leave, jury duty, etc.
Leaves under Family and Medical Leave Act	Employee assistance and counseling programs; "family-friendly" benefits for child care, elder care, flexible work schedules, etc.; executive perquisites

Note: *Although not required under federal law, all these benefits are regulated in some way by federal law, as explained in this chapter.

Pay For Time Not Worked

LEARNING OBJECTIVE **13-1**

Name and define each of the main pay for time not worked benefits.

Pay for time not worked—also called **supplemental pay benefits**—is a very costly benefit, because of the large amount of time off most employees receive. Common time-off-with-pay benefits include holidays, vacations, jury duty, funeral leave, military duty, personal days, sick leave, sabbatical leave, maternity leave, and unemployment insurance payments for laid-off or terminated employees.

supplemental pay benefits
Benefits for time not worked such as unemployment insurance, vacation and holiday pay, and sick pay.

unemployment insurance (or compensation)
Provides benefits if a person is unable to work through some fault other than his or her own.

Unemployment Insurance

All states have their own **unemployment insurance (or compensation)** laws. These provide benefits to eligible workers who become unemployed through no fault of their own. The benefits derive from a tax on employers that can range from 0.1% to 5% of taxable payroll in most states. An employer's unemployment tax rate reflects its rate of employee terminations. Unemployment tax rates are rising in many states. For example, prior to the 2007–2008 recession, Maryland's unemployment insurance tax rate was 0.3% or lower, but now ranges from 0.6% to 9.0% per employee.[8] All states follow federal unemployment insurance guidelines.

Firms aren't required to let everyone they dismiss receive unemployment benefits—only those released through no fault of their own. Thus, strictly speaking, a worker fired for chronic lateness can't legitimately claim benefits. But many managers are lackadaisical in protecting their employers. Employers therefore spend thousands of dollars on unemployment taxes unnecessarily.

The main rule is to keep a list of written warnings to demonstrate that poor performance caused the dismissal. The checklist in Table 13-2 can help. (Those fired during their initial "90-day probation" *are* eligible for unemployment, so follow that checklist for them, too.)

Vacations and Holidays

Most firms offer vacation and holiday benefits. About 90% of full-time workers and 40% of part-timers get paid holidays, an average of eight paid holidays off.[9] Common U.S. paid holidays include New Year's Day, Memorial Day, Independence Day, Labor Day, Thanksgiving Day, and Christmas Day.[10] On average, American workers get about 9 days of vacation leave after 1 year's employment, 14 days after 5 years, and 17 after 10 years.[11]

Firms should address several holiday- and vacation-related policy issues, such as how many vacation days employees get, and which days (if any) are paid holidays. Other vacation policy decisions include: Are employees paid for accrued vacation time if they quit before taking their vacations? Will you pay employees for a holiday if they don't come to work the day before and the day after the holiday? And, should we pay some premium—such as time and a half—when employees must work on holidays?

Unemployment insurance/compensation laws provide short-term benefits to people who lose their jobs through no fault of their own.

Mark Peterson/Corbis

More firms are taking a more flexible vacation leave approach. For example, IBM gives each employee at least 3 weeks' vacation, but doesn't track how much vacation each takes. Employees just make informal arrangements with supervisors.[12]

In contrast, some employers emphasize centralized absence oversight (called "integrated absence management"). This starts with collecting data. For instance, how many people are on leave; how many days of work is the employer losing; how much is the employer spending to replace absent workers; and what units have the attendance problems?[13] These employers then closely monitor all aspects of their employees' leaves and absences. Wage surveys and Web sites[14] provide sample vacation policies for inclusion in the firm's employee manual.

TABLE 13-2 An Unemployment Insurance Cost-Control Checklist

Do You:

- ✓ Keep documented history of lateness, absence, and warning notices
- ✓ Warn chronically late employees before discharging them
- ✓ Have a rule that 3 days' absence without calling in is reason for automatic discharge
- ✓ Request doctor's note on return to work after absence
- ✓ Make written approval for personal leave mandatory
- ✓ Stipulate date for return to work from leave
- ✓ Obtain a signed resignation statement
- ✓ Mail job abandonment letter if employee fails to return on time
- ✓ Document all instances of poor performance
- ✓ Require supervisors to document the steps taken to remedy the situation
- ✓ Document employee's refusal of advice and direction
- ✓ Require all employees to sign a statement acknowledging acceptance of firm's policies and rules
- ✓ File the protest against a former employee's unemployment claim on time (usually within 10 days)
- ✓ Use proper terminology on claim form and attach documented evidence regarding separation
- ✓ Attend hearings and appeal unwarranted claims
- ✓ Check every claim against the individual's personnel file
- ✓ Routinely conduct exit interviews to produce information for protesting unemployment claims

KNOW YOUR EMPLOYMENT LAW

Some Legal Aspects of Vacations and Holidays

Although federal law doesn't require vacation benefits, the employer must still formulate its vacation policy with care. As an example, many employers' vacation policies say vacation pay accrues, say, on a biweekly basis. By doing so, these employers obligate themselves to pay new employees pro rata vacation pay if they leave the firm during their first year. But if the employer's vacation policy requires that a new employee pass his or her first employment anniversary *before becoming entitled* to a vacation, the employee gets no vacation pay if he or she leaves during that first year.

Another frequent question is whether the employer can cancel an employee's scheduled vacation, for instance, due to a rush of orders. Here it's important that the employer formulate its vacation policy so it's clear that the employer reserves the right to require vacation cancellation and rescheduling if production so demands. ■

Sick Leave

sick leave
Provides pay to an employee when he or she is out of work because of illness.

Sick leave provides pay to employees when they're out of work due to illness. Most policies grant full pay for a specified number of sick days—perhaps 12 per year, usually accumulating at the rate of, say, 1 day per month of service.

The problem is that while many employees use their sick days only when sick, others use them whether they're sick or not. In one survey, personal illnesses accounted for about 45% of unscheduled sick leave absences. Family issues (27%), personal needs (13%), and "entitlement" (9%) were other reasons cited.[15] Such absenteeism costs U.S. employers perhaps $100 billion per year, with personal illness accounting for about a third of the absences.[16]

COST-REDUCTION TACTICS Employers use several tactics to reduce excessive sick leave absence. Some repurchase unused sick leave at the end of the year by paying their employees a sum for each unused sick day. The problem is that legitimately sick employees may come to work. Others hold monthly lotteries in which only employees with perfect monthly attendance are eligible for a cash prize. At Marriott, employees can trade the value of some sick days for other benefits. Others aggressively investigate all absences, calling absent employees at home.[17]

Many employers use *pooled paid leave plans* (or *"banks"*).[18] These plans lump together sick leave, vacation, and personal days into a single leave pool. For example, one hospital previously granted new employees 25 days off per year (10 vacation days, 3 personal days, and 12 sick days). Employees used, on average, 5 of those 12 sick days (as well as all vacations and personal days).[19] The pooled paid leave plan allowed new employees to accrue 18 days to use as they saw fit. (Special absences like serious short-term illnesses and bereavement leave were handled separately.) The pooled plan reduced absences. Most firms don't include federal holidays in their paid time off "banks."[20] The accompanying Profit Center feature shows how one employer cut costs.

IMPROVING PERFORMANCE: *HR as a Profit Center*

Controlling Sick Leave

Sick leave often gets out of control because employers don't measure it. In one survey, only 57% of employers formally tracked sick days for their exempt employees.[21] Three-fourths of the employers couldn't provide an estimate of what sick pay was costing them. Therefore, the employer should first have a system for monitoring sick leaves and for measuring their financial impact.[22]

As an example, when she became director of the United Kingdom's Driver and Vehicle Licensing Agency, the new director knew steps were needed to address its absence rate.[23] The rate had peaked at 14 days out per employee in 2005, at a cost of about $20 million per year (then £10.3 million).

The new director organized a human resource absence initiative.[24] The agency set a goal of reducing absences by 30% by 2010. Agency directors received absence-reduction goals, and their progress was tracked. The agency introduced new policies on special leave, rehabilitation support, and monitoring absentees. They made it easier for employees to swap work shifts, and introduced a guaranteed leave day policy.

By 2010, the sickness absence rate was down to 7.5 days per employee and productivity was up, for multiyear savings of about $48 million dollars (£24.4 million). ■

Source: Based on "Creating Holistic Time Off Programs Can Significantly Reduce Expenses," Compensation & Benefits Review, July/August 2007, pp. 18–19; Rita Zeidner, "Strategies for Saving in a Down Economy," HR Magazine, February 2009, p. 28. Judith Whitaker, "How HR Made a Difference," People Management 27 (October 28, 2010).

If your professor has assigned this, go to the Assignments section of **mymanagementlab.com** to complete this discussion question.

Talk About It 1: A note on this agency in Wikipedia refers to "amazingly high" levels of sick leave among staff at the DVLA [around 2007], with employees having an average of three weeks a year sick leave."[25] What sorts of inaction on the part of previous managers could help explain such poor attendance?

Leaves and the Family and Medical Leave Act

Parental leave is an important benefit. About half of workers are women, about 80% will become pregnant during their work lives, and many workers are single parents. Under the Pregnancy Discrimination Act, employers must treat women applying for pregnancy leave as they would any other employee requesting a leave under the employer's sick leave policies. Furthermore, the Family and Medical Leave Act of 1993 (FMLA) (see www.dol.gov/whd/regs/compliance/posters/fmlaen.pdf) stipulates that:[26]

1. Private employers of 50 or more employees must provide eligible employees (women or men) up to 12 weeks of unpaid leave for their own serious illness, the birth or adoption of a child, or the care of a seriously ill child, spouse, or parent.
2. Employers may require employees to take their paid sick leave or annual leave as part of the 12-week leave provided in the law.
3. Employees taking leave are entitled to receive health benefits while they are on unpaid leave, under the same terms and conditions as when they were on the job.
4. Employers must guarantee most employees the right to return to their previous or equivalent position with no loss of benefits at the end of the leave.

In a survey of 416 human resource professionals, about half said they had approved FMLA leaves they believed were not legitimate, due to vague interpretations of the law.[27] Others find tracking leaves problematic.[28] Furthermore, though the leaves are usually unpaid, the costs associated with hiring and training temporary replacements are high.

Other laws govern sick leaves. For example, under the Americans with Disabilities Act (ADA), a qualified employee with a disability may be eligible for a leave if it's necessary to accommodate the employee.[29]

KNOW YOUR EMPLOYMENT LAW

FMLA Guidelines

Managers who want to avoid granting nonrequired FMLA leaves need to understand the FMLA. For example, to be eligible for leave under the FMLA, the employee must have worked for the employer for at least a total of 12 months and have worked (not just been paid, as someone might be if on leave) for 1,250 or more hours in the past 12 consecutive months.[30] If these conditions do not apply, no leave is required.

Employers should have procedures for all leaves of absence (including those under the FMLA). In particular:

- Give no employee a leave until the reason for the leave is clear.
- If the leave is for medical or family reasons, the employer should obtain medical certification.
- Use a standard form to record both the employee's expected return date and the fact that, without an authorized extension, the firm may terminate his or her employment (see Figure 13-2).
- One employment lawyer says employers should "kind of bend over backward" when deciding if an employee is eligible for leave based on an FMLA situation.[31] However, employers can require independent medical assessments before approving FMLA disability leaves.[32] ■

FIGURE 13-2 Online Request for Leave Form

Source: From Request for Leave or Approved Absence, http://www.opm.gov/FORMS/PDF_FILL/opm71.pdf.

Request for Leave or Approved Absence

1. **Name** *(Last, first, middle)*

2. **Employee or Social Security Number (Enter only the last 4 digits of the Social Security Number (SSN))**

3. **Organization**

4. **Type of Leave/Absence** *(Check appropriate box(es) below)*	Date From	Date To	Time From	Time To	Total Hours
☐ **Accrued Annual Leave**					
☐ **Restored Annual Leave**					
☐ **Advanced Annual Leave**					
☐ **Accrued Sick Leave**					
☐ **Advanced Sick Leave**					
☐ **Compensatory Time Off**					
☐ **Other Paid Absence** *(Specify in Remarks)*					
☐ **Leave Without Pay**					

Purpose:
- ☐ Illness/injury/incapacitation of requesting employee
- ☐ Medical/dental/optical examination of requesting employee
- ☐ Care of family member, including medical/dental/optical examination of family member, or bereavement
- ☐ Care of family member with a serious health condition
- ☐ Other

5. **Family and Medical Leave**

If annual leave, sick leave, or leave without pay will be used under the Family and Medical Leave Act of 1993, please provide the following information:

☐ **I hereby invoke my entitlement to Family and Medical Leave for:**
- ☐ Birth/Adoption/Foster Care
- ☐ Serious health condition of spouse, son, daughter, or parent
- ☐ Serious health condition of self

Contact your supervisor and/or your personnel office to obtain additional information about your entitlements and responsibilities under the Family and Medical Leave Act. Medical certification of a serious health condition may be required by your agency.

6. **Remarks:**

7. **Certification:** I hereby request leave/approved absence from duty as indicated above and certify that such leave/absence is requested for the purpose(s) indicated. I understand that I must comply with my employing agency's procedures for requesting leave/approved absence (and provide additional documentation, including medical certification, if required) and that falsification on this form may be grounds for disciplinary action, including removal.

7a. **Employee Signature** 7b. **Date**

8a. **Official Action on Request:** ☐ **Approved** ☐ **Disapproved** *(If disapproved, give reason. If annual leave, initiate action to reschedule.)*

8b. **Reason for Disapproval:**

8c. **Supervisor Signature** 8d. **Date**

PRIVACY ACT STATEMENT
Section 6311 of Title 5, United States Code, authorizes collection of this information. The primary use of this information is by management and your payroll office to approve and record your use of leave. Additional disclosures of the information may be: to the Department of Labor when processing a claim for compensation regarding a job connected injury or illness; to a State unemployment compensation office regarding a claim; to Federal Life Insurance or Health Benefits carriers regarding a claim; to a Federal, State, or local law enforcement agency when your agency becomes aware of a violation or possible violation of civil or criminal law; to a Federal agency when conducting an investigation for employment or security reasons; to the Office of Personnel Management or the General Accounting Office when the information is required for evaluation of leave administration; or the General Services Administration in connection with its responsibilities for records management.

Public Law 104-134 (April 26, 1996) requires that any person doing business with the Federal Government furnish a social security number or tax identification number. This is an amendment to Title 31, Section 7701. Furnishing the social security number, as well as other data, is voluntary, but failure to do so may delay or prevent action on the application. If your agency uses the information furnished on this form for purposes other than those indicated above, it may provide you with an additional statement reflecting those purposes.

Office of Personnel Management
5 CFR 630

Local Reproduction Authorized

OPM Form 71
Rev. September 2009
Formerly Standard Form (SF) 71
Previous editions usable

Print Form | Clear Form | Save Form

Many employers are enriching their parental leave plans to make it more attractive for mothers to return from maternity leave. Tactics include keeping in touch during maternity leave, offering flexible jobs with reduced travel and hours, and longer leaves.[33]

Severance Pay

severance pay
A one-time payment some employers provide when terminating an employee.

Many employers provide **severance pay**, a one-time separation payment when terminating an employee. Most managers expect employees to give them 1 or 2 weeks' notice if they plan to quit, so it seems appropriate to provide severance pay when dismissing an employee. Reducing the chances of litigation from disgruntled former employees is another reason. Severance pay also helps reassure employees who stay on after a downsizing that they'll receive some financial help if they're let go, too.

The reason for the dismissal affects the employer's severance pay policy. About 95% of employees dismissed due to downsizings got severance pay, but only about a third of employers offer severance when terminating for poor performance. It is uncommon to pay when employees quit. The average maximum severance is 39 weeks for executives and about 30 weeks for other dismissed employees.[34] However severance pay usually depends on tenure with the employer. Thus, about half of employers surveyed give white-collar and exempt employees 1 week of severance pay per year of service, and about one-third do the same for blue-collar workers.[35] If the employer obligates itself (for instance, in its employee handbook) to pay severance, then its "voluntary" plan must comply with additional rules under ERISA.[36]

GUIDELINES In any event, keep several things in mind when designing the severance plan:

- List the situations for which the firm will pay severance, such as layoffs resulting from reorganizations.
- Require signing of a knowing and voluntary waiver/general release prior to remittance of any severance pay, absolving the employer from employment-related liability.
- Reserve the right to terminate or alter the severance policy.
- Make it clear that any continuing severance payments continue until only the stated deadline or until the employee gets a new job, whichever occurs first.
- Remember that, as with all personnel actions, employers must make severance payments, if any, equitably.[37]

supplemental unemployment benefits
Provide for a "guaranteed annual income" in certain industries where employers must shut down to change machinery or due to reduced work. These benefits are paid by the company and supplement unemployment benefits.

Supplemental Unemployment Benefits

In some industries such as auto making, shutdowns to reduce inventories or change machines are common. **Supplemental unemployment benefits** are cash payments that supplement the employee's unemployment compensation, to help the person maintain his or her standard of living while out of work.

Insurance Benefits

Most employers also provide a number of required or voluntary insurance benefits, such as workers' compensation and health insurance.

LEARNING OBJECTIVE **13-2**
Describe each of the main insurance benefits.

Workers' Compensation

Workers' compensation laws aim to provide sure, prompt income and medical benefits to work-related accident victims or their dependents, regardless of fault. Every state has its own workers' compensation law and commission, and some run their own insurance programs. However, most require employers to carry workers' compensation insurance with private, state-approved insurance companies. Neither the state nor the federal government contributes any funds for workers' compensation.

workers' compensation
Provides income and medical benefits to work-related accident victims or their dependents regardless of fault.

HOW BENEFITS ARE DETERMINED Workers' compensation can be monetary or medical. In the event of a worker's death or disablement, the person's dependents receive a cash benefit based on prior earnings—usually one-half to two-thirds the worker's average weekly wage, per week of employment. Most states have a time limit—such as 500 weeks—for which benefits can be paid. If the injury causes a specific loss (such as an arm), the employee may receive additional benefits based on a statutory list of losses, even though he or she may return to work. In addition to these cash benefits, employers must furnish medical, surgical, and hospital services as required for the employee.

For workers' compensation to cover an injury or work-related illness, one must only prove that it arose while the worker was on the job. It doesn't matter that he or she may have been at fault. Suppose you instruct employees to wear safety goggles at their machines. One worker doesn't and has an eye injury on the job. The company must still provide workers' compensation benefits.

Keep in mind that ADA provisions generally prohibit employers from inquiring about an applicant's workers' compensation history. Furthermore, failing to let an employee who was on injury-related workers' compensation return to work, or not accommodating him or her, could trigger ADA lawsuits.

CONTROLLING WORKERS' COMPENSATION COSTS It is important to control workers' compensation claims (and therefore costs). The employer's insurance company usually pays the claim, but the employer's premiums reflect the amount of claims.[38] Fewer claims also imply fewer accidents.

There are several ways to reduce workers' compensation claims. For example, screen out accident-prone workers. Reduce accident-causing conditions. And reduce the health problems that sometimes trigger these claims—for instance, by instituting effective safety and health programs, and complying with safety standards laws. Furthermore, some workers' compensation claims are not legitimate. Red flags include vague accident details, minor accidents resulting in major injuries, lack of witnesses, injuries occurring late Friday, and late reporting.[39]

Case management is a popular cost-control method. It is "the treatment of injured workers on a case-by-case basis by an assigned manager, usually a registered nurse, who coordinates with the physician and health plan to determine which care settings are the most effective for quality care and cost."[40]

Moving aggressively to support the injured employee and to get him or her back to work quickly is important too. The involvement of an attorney and the duration of the claim both influence the workers claim cost.[41] Many firms have programs such as physical therapy nursing assistance to help reintegrate claim recipients. Also, monitor health-care providers to confirm they're complying with their fee schedules.[42]

Hospitalization, Health, and Disability Insurance

Health insurance looms large in many people's choice of employer, because it's so expensive.[43] Hospitalization, health, and disability insurance helps protect employees against hospitalization costs and the income loss arising from off-the-job accidents or illness. Many employers purchase insurance from life insurance companies, casualty insurance companies, or Blue Cross (for hospital expenses) and Blue Shield (for physician expenses) organizations. Others contract with health maintenance organizations or preferred provider organizations. The employer and employee usually both contribute to the plan. Health insurance costs rose about 4% in one recent year, to a total of $15,745 for family coverage. And of course employers are racing to deal with implementing the Patient Protection and Affordable Care ("Obamacare") Act, as we will see.[44]

Table 13-3 illustrates the prevalence of health-related benefits.

TABLE 13-3 Percentage of Employers Offering Some Popular Health Benefits

Prescription drug program coverage	98%
Dental insurance	96%
Mail-order prescription program	90%
Mental health coverage	89%
Preferred provider organization (PPO)	86%
Accidental death and dismemberment insurance (AD&D)	83%
Vision insurance	82%
Contraceptive coverage	82%
Chiropractic coverage	80%
Employee assistance plan	77%
Long-term disability	77%

Source: Employee Benefits An Overview of Employee Benefits Offerings in the U.S (2013). www.shrm.org/Research/SurveyFindings/Articles/Documents/13-0245%202013_EmpBenefits_FNL.pdf, accessed April 4, 2014. SHRM Foundation.

COVERAGE Under the Patient Protection and Affordable Care Act, employers with at least 50 full-time-equivalent employees are to offer minimum levels of affordable health-care coverage or pay a penalty. Most employer health plans provide at least basic hospitalization and surgical and medical insurance for all eligible employees at group rates. Insurance is generally available to all employees—including new nonprobationary ones—regardless of health or physical condition. Most basic plans pay for hospital room and board, surgery charges, and medical expenses (such as doctors' visits to the hospital). Some also provide "major medical" coverage to meet the medical expenses resulting from serious illnesses.

Most employers' health plans also cover health-related expenses like doctors' visits, eye care, and dental services. Other plans pay for general and diagnostic visits to the doctor's office, vision care, hearing aids, and prescription drugs. *Disability insurance* provides income protection for salary loss due to illness or accident, and may continue until age 65 or beyond. Disability benefits usually range from 50% to 75% of the employee's base pay if he or she is disabled.

health maintenance organization (HMO)
A prepaid health-care system that generally provides routine round-the-clock medical services as well as preventive medicine in a clinic-type arrangement for employees, who pay a nominal fee in addition to the fixed annual fee the employer pays.

HMOS Many employers offer membership in a **health maintenance organization (HMO)**, a medical organization consisting of specialists (surgeons, psychiatrists, and so on), often operating out of a health-care center. It provides routine medical services to employees who pay a nominal fee. Employees often have "gatekeeper" doctors who must approve appointments with specialist doctors. The HMO receives a fixed annual fee per employee from the employer (or employer and employee), regardless of whether it provides that person service.

PPOS Preferred provider organizations (PPOs) are a cross between HMOs and the traditional doctor–patient arrangement: They are "groups of health care providers that contract with employers, insurance companies, or third-party payers to provide medical care services at a reduced fee."[45] Unlike HMOs, PPOs let employees select providers (such as doctors) from a relatively wide list, and see them in their offices, often without gatekeeper doctor approval. Providers agree to discounts and to certain controls, for example, on testing.[46]

MENTAL HEALTH BENEFITS The World Health Organization estimated that more than 34 million people in the United States between the ages of 18 and 64 suffer from mental illness.[47] Mental illnesses represent about 24% of all reported disabilities, more than disabling injuries, cardiovascular diseases, and cancer combined.

Mental health costs are rising. Reasons include widespread drug and alcohol problems, an increase in states that require employers to offer minimum mental health benefits, and the fact that mental health claims tend to trigger other health-care claims. The Mental Health Parity Act of 1996 (as amended in 2008) sets minimum mental health-care benefits; it also prohibits employer group health plans from adopting mental health benefits limitations without comparable limitations on medical and surgical benefits.[48]

KNOW YOUR EMPLOYMENT LAW

Patient Protection and Affordable Care Act of 2010

As noted, under the Patient Protection and Affordable Care Act, employers with at least 50 full-time-equivalent employees are to offer minimum levels of affordable health-care coverage or pay a penalty. To be eligible, an employee must work at least 30 hours per week or a total of 130 hours in a calendar month.[49] The bill was signed into law by President Obama in 2010, and employers face a number of other deadlines under the act.[50] By 2018, employers with health-care plans that cost more than the threshold the law sets (for instance, $27,500 for family coverage) have to pay a 40% tax on the amount of coverage over $27,500. Individual and group health plans that already provide dependent coverage must expand eligibility up to age 26.[51]

Again, employers with 50 or more employees must either offer full-time employees coverage or risk paying an excise tax.[52] So at one extreme employers might offer a certain minimum level of insurance affordable to at least 95% of its full-time employees and dependents; or at the other extreme not offer minimum essential coverage and pay a penalty of $167 per month for each full-time employee.

Under the law, each state (or, when necessary, the federal government) may run public health insurance exchanges—in effect, marketplaces for buying and selling insurance. In part to discourage employers from dropping their health-care plans and sending employees to the health exchanges, the law imposes those fines of $2,000 per worker on any employer with more than 50 workers who doesn't offer a health insurance plan.

The act's deadlines are changing. Back in 2013 the administration put several Affordable Care Act elements on hold. And it issued new rules allowing states that planned to offer exchanges to have 2 extra years, until 2015, to verify eligibility.

Because employers have to pay a 40% surcharge beginning in 2018 on health insurance plans exceeding $27,500 for a family (or $10,200 for an individual), many employers are moving to reduce their health-care benefits, for instance by increasing employee co-pays and deductibles.[53] To avoid penalties that could reach $2,000 per employee, some employers are directing employees who qualify for Medicaid to sign up for it, instead of employer-supplied insurance.[54] Some employers are considering eliminating their health plans, or turning more full-time workers into part-timers working less than 30 hours per week.[55] About 43% of employers surveyed say their workers will have to pay more for their health-care plans.[56] Others are considering reducing their coverage.[57] Other employers calculate that it may be cheaper to pay the penalty than supply the insurance.[58]

COBRA

COBRA—the Consolidated Omnibus Budget Reconciliation Act—requires most private employers to continue to make health benefits available to separated employees and their families for a time, generally 18 months after separation.[59] The former employee must pay for the coverage.

Employers ignore COBRA's regulations at their peril. The employer does not want separated employees to leave and be injured, and then claim it never told them they could have continued their insurance coverage. Therefore, when a new employee first becomes eligible for the company's insurance plan, the person *must* receive (and acknowledge receiving) an explanation of his or her COBRA rights. And all employees separated from the company should sign a form acknowledging that they received and understand those rights. (See Figure 13-3 for a checklist.)

Other Laws

Other federal laws are pertinent. For example, among other things, the *Employee Retirement Income Security Act* of 1974 (ERISA) sets minimum standards for most voluntarily established pension and health plans in private industry.[60] *The Newborn Mother's Protection Act of 1996* prohibits employers' health plans from using incentives to encourage employees to leave the hospital after childbirth after less than the legislatively determined minimum stay. Employers who provide health-care services must follow the privacy rules of the *Health Insurance Portability and Accountability Act of 1996 (HIPAA)*.[61] Employers must provide the same health-care benefits to employees over the age of 65 that they do to younger workers, even though the older workers are eligible for federal Medicare health insurance. Under the *Americans with Disabilities Act,* the health plan generally shouldn't make distinctions based on disability. Under the *Genetic Information Nondiscrimination Act* of 2008 (GINA), even innocent actions can be problems. For example, if a health plan administrator writes down that a member's mother passed away from breast cancer, making the note could conceivably violate the act.[62] States such as California have their own FMLAs.[63]

FIGURE 13-3 COBRA Record-Keeping Compliance Checklist

Reproduced with permission from the publisher BLR - Business and Legal Resources.

Detailed record keeping is crucial for COBRA compliance. The following checklist is designed to ensure that the proper records are maintained for problem-free COBRA compliance.

	Yes	No
• Do you maintain records so that it is easily determined who is covered by your group health care plan?	☐	☐
• Do you record terminations of covered employees as soon as terminations occur?	☐	☐
• Do you track reduction of hours of employees covered by group health care plans?	☐	☐
• Do you track deaths of employees covered by group health care plans?	☐	☐
• Do you track leaves of absence of employees covered by group health care plans?	☐	☐
• Do you track Medicare eligibility of employees covered by group health care plans?	☐	☐
• Do you track the disability status of employees covered by group health care plans?	☐	☐
• Do you track retirees covered by group health care plans?	☐	☐
• Do you maintain current addresses of employees?	☐	☐
• Do you maintain current addresses of individuals receiving COBRA benefits?	☐	☐
• Do you require employees to provide a written acknowledgment that they have received notice of their COBRA rights?	☐	☐
• Do you have a system to determine who has paid COBRA premiums on time?	☐	☐
• Do you have a system to determine who has obtained other group health coverage so that they are no longer eligible for COBRA under your plan?	☐	☐
• Do you maintain a telephone log of calls received about COBRA?	☐	☐
• Do you maintain a record of changes in your plan?	☐	☐
• Do you maintain a record of how premiums are calculated?	☐	☐
• Do you maintain a log of those employees who are denied COBRA coverage?	☐	☐
• Do you maintain a log of why employees are denied COBRA coverage?	☐	☐

Global employers must account for multinational legal, cultural, and programmatic insurance-related differences. For example, the most prevalent supplemental employee benefits in the United States are pension, medical, and life and long-term disability insurance; in the United Kingdom (with its national health program) they are pension, car benefit, and life and long-term disability.[64] ■

Trends in Employer Health-Care Cost Control

A business with 50 employees might pay $1 million or more just for insurance coverage, before accounting for things like sick days. Health-care cost control is therefore one big way the HR department can improve profits.

Employers are endeavoring to rein in health-care costs.[65] Most cost-control efforts should start by instituting methods for measuring and auditing health-care costs.[66] It makes little sense to initiate cost cuts when employers are paying out thousands or millions of dollars in erroneous claims. One survey found that although the industry standard for percentage of claims errors is 3%, the *actual* percentage of claims with errors was about 6.3%. The industry standard for percentage of claims dollars actually paid in error was 1%; the *actual* percentage of claims dollars paid in error was 3.4%. So, setting standards for errors and then auditing all claims may be the most direct way to reduce employer health-care expenses.[67]

Beyond that, for many employers, deductibles and co-pays are the low-hanging fruit in health-care cost control. For example, at least 20% of employees were enrolled in high-deductible plans recently.[68]

WELLNESS PROGRAMS Because various illnesses are preventable, many employers offer preventive programs.[69] For example, the top three health-care priorities of employers in a recent Aon Hewitt Health Care Survey report were, "Offer incentives or disincentives to motivate sustained health-care behavior change"; "Promote a culture of health in the workplace (e.g., healthy cafeteria, flexible schedules to allow time for physical activity)"; and "Move to rewarding improved health results or outcomes."[70] In one study "employers who undertook prevention programs aimed at cardiovascular disease … reported an average 28% reduction in sick leave, [and] a 26% reduction in direct health-care costs."[71]

Employers offer a variety of preventive services and incentives.[72] Some *link each employee's health-care premiums* to his or her healthy behaviors.[73] *Clinical prevention* programs include things like mammograms and routine checkups. Walgreens owns companies that provide *on-site health-care services* such as mammograms for employers.[74] *Health promotion and disease prevention* programs include seminars and incentives aimed at improving unhealthy behaviors.[75] Other wellness program trends include obesity management, stress management, senior health improvement, and tobacco cessation programs.[76] Incentives, for instance, $50–$100, can boost wellness program participation, but may backfire.[77] Whirlpool gives nonsmoker discounts on health-care premiums worth about $500. It suspended 39 workers it caught smoking outside the plant after claiming on their benefits enrollment forms that they were nonsmokers.

OTHER COST-CONTROL OPTIONS Employers are taking other cost-control steps. *Consumer-driven health plans (CDHPs)* are increasingly popular. These are high-deductible plans that give employees access to, for instance, a health savings account. (The Medicare Modernization Act of 2003 allows employers to establish tax-free health savings accounts [HSAs].)[78] After the employer, employee, or both deposit pretax (and thus tax-sheltered) pay in the employees' HSAs, employees or their families can use their HSA funds to pay for "low dollar" (not catastrophic) medical expenses.[79] The assumption is that this will motivate employees to utilize less expensive health-care options, and thus avoid big deductibles.[80] More employers are offering limited-benefit health-care insurance plans. Unlike health-care plans that may have lifetime coverage of $1 million or more, these "mini" medical plans have annual caps of about $2,000–$10,000 per year, and correspondingly lower premiums.[81]

Some employers offer *defined contribution health insurance plans*. Like 401(k) pension plans, these defined contribution health insurance plans tie each employee's health-care benefits to what he or she and the employer contributes, rather than providing health-care benefits (for instance, hospital care limits) that are defined in advance.[82] Many employers are reducing health benefits for their future *retirees.*[83] IBM moved retirees from their company-supported plan, substituting a *stipend* to buy insurance at *private exchange* insurance marketplaces.[84] Other employers are hiring "patient advocates," for instance, registered nurses who review employees' medications and (with the consultation of independent physicians) recommend reduced medication regimes.[85] Small firms are joining *benefits purchasing alliances,* banding together to purchase health-care benefits. Other employers encourage *medical tourism*, which means asking employees to have non-urgent medical procedures abroad, where costs are lower.[86] Some, such as Viking Range Corp., have *self-funded* or self-insured health plans.[87] About 19% of almost 600 employers surveyed had some form of health-care plan *spousal exclusion policies*, such as excluding a spouse when similar coverage was available from the spouse's employer.[88] Employers are demanding insurers use *accountable care organizations* (ACO), special vendors who help insurers, health-care providers, and others with the goal of improving costs and outcomes.[89] About 34% of employers with over 500 employees offer some type of on-site or nearby health clinics, sometimes managed through third parties.[90] Many others retain *cost-containment specialists* to help reduce such costs. And most negotiate more aggressively with their health-care insurance providers.[91] Also important, *make sure employees know the costs* of their medical benefits.[92] So, for example, periodically send a statement to each employee listing the employer's costs for each health benefit. *Online selection* lets employees choose the best of the employer's health-care offerings, based on input from other employees concerning matters like doctor visits and specialists. Outsourcing is important.[93] In one survey, 94% outsourced management of flexible spending accounts, 89% outsourced defined contribution plans, 72% outsourced defined benefit plans, and 68% outsourced the auditing of dependents.[94] The accompanying Profit Center feature shows how one employer cut costs.

IMPROVING PERFORMANCE: *HR as a Profit Center*

The Doctor Is on the Phone

With more than 12,000 employees in its health plan, Rent-A-Center was looking for a better way to get its employees the medical advice they required, while also reducing health plan costs. The company signed an agreement with Teladoc, Inc. Teladoc's doctors provide medical consultations over the phone. In the first 16 months the new telemedicine program was in effect, Rent-A-Center saved more than $770,000 in doctor and hospital visits and in employee productivity that would have been lost.

The program seems to be win-win. The Teladoc consultation is free to employees, compared to a $20 office co-payment, and the doctors are available 24 hours per day, usually within 30 minutes. If necessary, they call in antibiotics prescriptions. And for Rent-A-Center, there's that extra $770,000 in their bottom line.[95] ■

Source: Based on Susan Galactica, "There's a Doctor on the Phone? Employers Dial-Up Telemedicine," Workforce Management, September 2012, p. 8. See also, "Speakers tout advantages, $6 billion potential of telemedicine," Bloomberg BNA bulletin to management, December 16, 2014, page 399.

If your professor has assigned this, go to the Assignments section of **mymanagementlab.com** to complete these discussion questions.

Talk About It 2: Would you recommend this program to your employer? Why or why not?

Long-Term Care

Long-term care insurance—for things like nursing assistance to former employees in their old age—is a key employee benefit. The Health Insurance Portability and Accountability Act of 1996 lets employers and employees deduct the cost of long-term care insurance premiums from their annual income taxes, making this benefit more attractive.[96] Employers can also provide insurance benefits for several types of long-term care, such as adult day care, assisted living, and custodial care.

Life Insurance

group life insurance
Provides lower rates for the employer or employee and includes all employees, including new employees, regardless of health or physical condition.

In addition to hospitalization and medical benefits, most employers provide **group life insurance** plans. Such plans generally offer lower rates than individual plans, and usually accept all employees regardless of health or physical condition.

In general, there are three key personnel policies to address: the benefits-paid schedule (the amount of life insurance benefits is usually tied to the employee's annual earnings), supplemental benefits (continued life insurance coverage after retirement, for instance), and financing (the amount and percent the employee contributes).

Accidental death and dismemberment coverage provides a lump-sum benefit in addition to life insurance benefits when death is accidental. It also provides benefits in case of accidental loss of limbs or sight.

Benefits for Part-Time and Contingent Workers

About 19 million people work part-time (less than 35 hours a week).[97] The recession, more phased retirements, and a desire to better balance work and family life help explain this phenomenon. In any case, many firms provide holiday, sick leave, and vacation benefits to part-timers, and more than 70% offer some form of health-care benefits to them.[98]

Retirement Benefits

The first contingent of baby boomers turned 65 a few years ago. This presents two challenges for employers. First (as we explained in Chapter 10 (Careers and Retention)), employers are taking steps to entice older workers to keep working in some capacity.[99] Second, retirement benefits such as federal Social Security and employer pension/retirement plans like the 401(k) are big issues.

LEARNING OBJECTIVE **13-3**
Discuss the main retirement benefits.

Social Security

Most people assume that **Social Security** provides income only when they are older than 62, but it actually provides three types of benefits. The familiar *retirement benefits* provide an income if you retire at age 62 or thereafter and are insured under the Social Security Act. Second are *survivor's* or *death benefits.* These provide monthly payments to your dependents regardless of your age at death (assuming you're insured under Social Security). Finally, *disability payments* provide monthly payments to employees who become disabled totally (and to their dependents) if they meet certain requirements. The Social Security system also administers the Medicare program, which provides health services to people age 65 or older. "Full retirement age" for nondiscounted Social Security benefits traditionally was 65—the usual age for retirement. It is now 67 for those born 1960 or later.[100]

Social Security
Federal program that provides three types of benefits: retirement income at the age of 62 and thereafter, survivor's or death benefits payable to the employee's dependents regardless of age at time of death, and disability benefits payable to disabled employees and their dependents. These benefits are payable only if the employee is insured under the Social Security Act.

A tax on the employee's wages funds Social Security (technically, "Federal Old Age and Survivor's Insurance"). Recently, the maximum amount of earnings subject to Social Security tax was $118,500; the employer pays 7.65% (including Medicare) and the employee 7.65%.[101]

Pension Plans

Pension plans provide income to individuals in their retirement, and just over half of full-time workers participate in some type of pension plan at work.

pension plans
Plans that provide a fixed sum when employees reach a predetermined retirement age or when they can no longer work due to disability.

We can classify pension plans as contributory versus noncontributory plans, qualified versus nonqualified plans, and defined contribution versus defined benefit plans.[102] The employee contributes to the contributory pension plan, while the employer makes all contributions to the noncontributory pension plan. Employers derive certain tax benefits (such as tax deductions) for contributing to qualified pension plans (they are "qualified" for preferred tax treatment by the IRS); nonqualified pension plans get less favorable tax treatment. As with all pay plan components, employers should ensure retirement benefits support their strategic needs. For example, set guiding principles such as "assist in attracting employees."[103]

With **defined benefit pension plans**, the employee's pension is specified ("defined"), in that the person knows in advance his or her pension benefits. A formula usually ties the pension to a percentage of the person's preretirement pay (for example, to an average of his or her last 5 years of employment), multiplied by the years he or she worked for the company. Due to tax law changes and other reasons, defined benefit plans now represent a minority of pension benefit plans.[104] However, even younger employees now express a strong preference for defined benefit plans.[105] Some companies, such as Union Pacific, offer them as employee retention tools.[106]

defined benefit pension plan
A plan that contains a formula for determining retirement benefits.

Defined contribution pension plans specify ("define") what *contribution* the employee and employer will make to the employee's retirement or savings fund. Here the contribution is defined, not the pension. With a *defined benefit* plan, the employee can compute what his or her retirement *benefits* will be upon retirement.

defined contribution pension plan
A plan in which the employer's contribution to employees' retirement savings funds is specified.

With a *defined contribution* plan, the actual pension will depend on the amounts contributed to the fund *and* on the success of the fund's investment earnings. Defined contribution plans are popular among employers due to their relative ease of administration, favorable tax treatment, and other factors. **Portability**—making it easier for employees who leave the firm prior to retirement to take their accumulated pension funds with them—is easier with defined contribution plans.

portability
Instituting policies that enable employees to easily take their accumulated pension funds when they leave an employer.

In any case, CEO retirement packages tend to dwarf the average employee's.[107] For example, when Target's CEO stepped down recently after a huge credit card breach, he walked away with retirement plans worth more than $47 million, plus a $7.2 million severance payment and $4.1 million from vested stock awards.

401(K) PLANS The most popular defined contribution plans are based on section 401(k) of the Internal Revenue Code, and called **401(k) plans**. The employee authorizes the employer to deduct a sum from his or her paycheck before taxes, and to invest it in the bundle of investments in his or her 401(k) account. The deduction is pretax, so the employee pays no tax on those dollars until after he or she retires (or removes the money from the 401(k) plan). The person can deduct annually an amount up to the IRS maximum (about $15,000). Employers often match employee's 401(k) contributions dollar for dollar up to a set percentage. The employer arranges, usually with an investment company such as Fidelity Investments, to administer the 401(k) plan and to make investment options (typically mutual stock funds and bond funds) available to the plan. In the recent downturn, more employees made "hardship withdrawals" from their 401(k) plans.[108]

401(k) plan
A defined contribution plan based on section 401(k) of the Internal Revenue Code.

savings and thrift plan
Plan in which employees contribute a portion of their earnings to a fund; the employer usually matches this contribution in whole or in part.

deferred profit-sharing plan
A plan in which a certain amount of profits is credited to each employee's account, payable at retirement, termination, or death.

Employers must choose 401(k) providers with care. The employer has a fiduciary responsibility to its employees and must monitor the fund and its administration.[109] In addition to trustworthiness, the 401(k) plan provider should make it easy to enroll and participate in the plan.[110] Firms such as Vanguard, Fidelity, and others establish Web-based 401(k) plans with online tools such as an "asset allocation planner"—even for small firms. Employers must also monitor 401(k) housekeeping issues such as late deposits and incorrect employer matching contributions.[111]

Under the Pension Protection Act of 2006, employers who sponsor plans that facilitate both *automatic enrollment* and allocation to *default investments* (such as age-appropriate "lifestyle funds") reduce their compliance burdens.[112]

Jitalia17/Getty Images

Firms such as Vanguard, Fidelity, and others can establish online, fully Web-based 401(k) plans even for small firms with 10 to 50 employees.

OTHER PLANS The 401(k) plan is one example of a **savings and thrift plan**.[113] In any savings and thrift plan, employees contribute a portion of their earnings to a fund, and the employer usually matches this contribution completely or in part.

As discussed in Chapter 12 (Incentives), employers use a **deferred profit-sharing plan** to contribute a portion of their profits in cash to a pension fund, regardless of the level of employee contribution (personal income taxes on those contributions are deferred until the employee retires or leaves the employer). An **employee stock ownership plan (ESOP)** is a qualified, tax-deductible defined contribution plan in which employers contribute stock to a trust for eventual use by employees who retire.

CASH BALANCE PENSION PLANS With *defined benefits* plans, to get your maximum pension, you generally must stay with your employer until you retire—the formula takes the number of years you work into consideration. With *defined contribution* plans, your pension is more portable—you can leave with it at any time, perhaps rolling it over into your next employer's pension plan. Without delving into the details, **cash balance plans** are a hybrid; they have defined benefit plans' more predictable benefits, but the portability advantages of defined contribution plans.[114] The employer contributes a percentage of employees' current pay to the employees' pension plans every year, and employees earn interest on this amount.[115]

KNOW YOUR EMPLOYMENT LAW

Pension Planning and the Law

Federal law regulates pension planning and administration. As a rule, pension planning requires expert help.[116]

The **Employee Retirement Income Security Act of 1975 (ERISA)** is the basic law. It requires that employers have written pension plan documents and adhere to certain guidelines, such as regarding eligibility.[117] ERISA protects the employer's pension or health plans' assets by requiring that those who control the plans act responsibly. The *fiduciary's* responsibility is to run the plan solely in the interest of participants and beneficiaries.

Employers (and employees) also want their pension contributions to be "qualified," or tax deductible, so they must adhere to the *income tax codes.* Under *labor relations laws*, the employer must let its unions participate in pension plan administration. The *Job Creation and Worker Assistance Act* provides guidelines regarding what rates of return employers should use in computing their pension plan values. ■

employee stock ownership plan (ESOP)
A qualified, tax-deductible stock bonus plan in which employers contribute stock to a trust for eventual use by employees.

cash balance plans
Plans under which the employer contributes a percentage of employees' current pay to employees' pension plans every year, and employees earn interest on this amount.

Employee Retirement Income Security Act of 1975 (ERISA)
Signed into law by President Ford to require that pension rights be vested and protected by a government agency, the PBGC.

Pension Benefits Guarantee Corporation (PBGC)
Established under ERISA to ensure that pensions meet vesting obligations; also insures pensions should a plan terminate without sufficient funds to meet its vested obligations.

ERISA established the **Pension Benefits Guarantee Corporation (PBGC)** to oversee and insure a pension if a plan terminates without sufficient funds. Thousands of benefits plans, both private and public, are worryingly underfunded.[118] However, the PBGC guarantees only defined benefit plans, not defined contribution plans. And it will only pay a pension of up to about $60,000 per year for someone 65 years of age with a plan terminating as of 2015.[119] So, high-income workers still face reduced pensions if their employers go bankrupt.

MEMBERSHIP REQUIREMENTS When does the employee become eligible for a pension? Under the Tax Reform Act of 1986, an employer can require that an employee complete a period of no more than 2 years' service to the company before becoming eligible to participate in the plan. However, if it requires more than 1 year of service before eligibility, the plan must grant employees full and immediate vesting rights at the end of that period.

VESTING *Vested funds* are the money employer and employee have placed in the latter's pension fund that cannot be forfeited for any reason. The employees' contributions are always theirs, of course. However, until ERISA, the *employers'* contribution in many pension plans didn't vest until the employee retired. Someone could have worked for a company for 30 years and been left with no pension if the company went bust 1 year before the person retired.

Employers can choose one of two minimum vesting schedules (employers can allow funds to vest faster if they wish). With *cliff vesting*, the period for acquiring a nonforfeitable right to employer matching contributions (if any) is 3 years. So, the employee must have nonforfeitable rights to these funds by the end of 3 years. With the second (*graded vesting*) option, pension plan participants must receive nonforfeitable rights to the matching contributions as follows: 20% after 2 years, and then 20% for each succeeding year, with a 100% nonforfeitable right by the end of 6 years.

Pensions and Early Retirement

early retirement window
A type of offering by which employees are encouraged to retire early, the incentive being liberal pension benefits plus perhaps a cash payment.

To trim their workforces or for other reasons, some employers encourage employees to retire early. Many such plans take the form of **early retirement window** arrangements for specific employees (often age 50+). The "window" means that for a limited time, the employees can retire early, generally with a combination of improved or liberalized pension benefits plus a cash payment.

Early retirement programs can backfire, however. When Verizon offered enhanced pension benefits to encourage what it hoped would be 12,000 employees to retire, more than 21,000 took the plan. Verizon had to replace 16,000 managers.[120]

Furthermore, unless structured properly, older employees can challenge early retirement programs as de facto ways for forcing them to retire against their will. Although it is generally legal to use incentives to encourage individuals to choose early retirement, the employee's decision must be voluntary. Under the Older Workers' Benefit Protection Act (OWBPA), the employee's waiver must be knowing and voluntary, and give the employee ample time to consider the agreement and to seek legal advice.

Improving Performance Through HRIS: Online Benefits Management Systems

Benefits administration can require devoting hundreds of hours to answering employees' questions (such as "If I retire in 2 years, what will be my monthly retirement income?") about benefits and updating employees' benefits information.[121] Tasks like that cry out for online self-service benefits management applications.

For example, when the organization that assists Pennsylvania school districts with their insurance needs decided to help the school boards automate their benefits administration, they chose a company called Benelogic.[122] The solution, called the "Employee Benefit Electronic Service Tool," lets users manage all aspects of benefits administration, including enrollment, plan descriptions, eligibility, and premium reconciliation, via their browsers.[123]

Benelogic hosts and maintains the Web application on its servers, and creates customized, Web-based applications for each school district. The system facilitates online employee benefit enrollment, and provides centralized call center support for benefit-related questions. It even handles benefits-related payroll and similar functions by collaborating with companies like ADP (for payroll). Each school board employee accesses the Benelogic site via a link on his or her own board's Web site.

Employers are also adding new services to their own benefits Web sites. In addition to offering things like self-enrollment, the insurance company USAA's Web site (www.usaa.com) helps employees achieve better work–life balance. For example, employees can respond to a list of words (such as *stressed*), and see suggestions for dealing with stress.[124] Boeing's Pay & Benefits Profile site gives employees real-time information about their salary and bonuses, benefits, pension, and even special services such as child-care referrals.[125] ■

TRENDS SHAPING HR: *DIGITAL AND SOCIAL MEDIA*

There was a time not too long ago when communicating with employees about their benefits required a ponderous and expensive process involving communiqués from the central HR office, but with digital and social media that's no longer the case.[126] First, as just noted, employers are using benefits systems such as Benelogic, and in-house benefits Web sites. Others are pulling their Twitter feeds into their benefits Web sites to keep those Web sites up-to-date. Others use their company blogs to communicate employee perks and benefits. Some use their Facebook and LinkedIn pages to publicize their benefits to a wider audience. Recently, Siemens created an internal social media Web site for its 13,000 UK employees. Among other things, Siemens UK uses it to keep its employees up-to-date about its latest employee benefits offerings, to run real-time employee feedback polls about Siemens benefits, and to remind employees about the availability of various benefits. (For example, that each employee has points to use as part of the Siemens employee recognition program.)

To facilitate employee benefits self-management, other employers provide workers with mobile apps (see, for example, http://appfinder.lisisoft.com/tag/employee-benefits.html). For example, clients of Discovery Benefits Inc., a benefits administrator, reportedly logged in through its app about 25,000 times in one recent year, saving Discovery the time it would have spent dealing with call-ins.[127]

On the other hand, social media sites get some workers in trouble. In one case, an employee took a sick day, saying that chronic pain prevented her from coming to work. Unfortunately, she posted pictures of herself drinking at a festival the day she was supposed to be home sick. One of her Facebook "friends" got the photo and showed it to a company supervisor. The company fired her for absence, and an appeals court upheld the employer's decision.[128] ■

Personal Services and Family-Friendly Benefits

LEARNING OBJECTIVE **13-4**
Outline the main employees' services benefits.

Although time off, insurance, and retirement account for the lion's share of benefits costs, most employers also provide various services benefits. These include personal services (such as legal and personal counseling), "family-friendly" services (such as child-care facilities), educational subsidies, and executive perquisites (such as company cars for its executives).

Challenging economic times mean employers are revamping their personal services benefits. Among the most-*dropped* benefits have been educational assistance, long-term care insurance, and job sharing. "Most-added" benefits included legal counseling, lactation rooms, work-at-home policies, and paid or subsidized off-site fitness.[129] For example, when the Dallas/Fort Worth International Airport found that its employee fitness and wellness facility wasn't producing the expected health cost savings, it instituted incentives to get employees to use it more regularly.[130]

Personal Services

Personal services benefits include credit unions, legal services, counseling, and social and recreational opportunities. (Some employers use the term *voluntary benefits* to cover personal services benefits that range from things like pet insurance to automobile insurance.[131]) We'll look at some of these.

employee assistance program (EAP)
A formal employer program for providing employees with counseling and/or treatment programs for problems such as alcoholism, gambling, or stress.

Employee assistance programs (EAPs) provide counseling and advisory services, such as personal legal and financial services, child- and elder care referrals, adoption assistance, mental health counseling, and life event planning.[132] EAPs are popular, with more than 60% of larger firms offering them. One study found that personal mental health was the most common problem addressed by employee assistance programs, followed by family problems.[133]

Diego Cervo/Shutterstock

Software giant SAS Institute, Inc., is one company that offers generous employee benefits. The North Carolina firm keeps turnover at 4% in an industry where 20% is typical, partly by offering family-friendly benefits like paid maternity leave, day care on site, lunchtime piano concerts, massages, and yoga classes like this one.

For employers, EAPs produce advantages, not just costs. For example, sick family members and problems like depression account for many sick days. Employee assistance programs can reduce such absences by providing expert advice on issues like elder care referrals.[134] Few but the largest employers establish their own EAPs. Most contract with vendors such as Ceridian Life Works, Comps Sync, and Integrated Behavioral Health.[135]

In either case, everyone involved including supervisors and EAP staff must respect *confidentiality.* Also, keep files locked, limit access, and minimize identifying information. *Be aware of legal issues.* For example, in most states counselors must disclose suspicions of child abuse to state agencies. *Define* the program's purpose, employee eligibility, the roles and responsibilities of EAP and employer personnel, and procedures for using the plan. Ensure your EAP vendors fulfill *professional and state licensing requirements.*

Family-Friendly (Work–Life) Benefits

Several trends have changed the benefits landscape. There are more households where both adults work, more one-parent households, more women in the workforce, and more workers over age 65.[136]

family-friendly (or work–life) benefits
Benefits such as child-care and fitness facilities that make it easier for employees to balance their work and family responsibilities.

Such trends lead many employers to bolster their **family-friendly (or "work–life") benefits.**[137] These include child care, elder care, fitness facilities, and flexible work schedules—benefits that help employees balance their family and work lives.[138] We'll look at some examples.

SUBSIDIZED CHILD CARE Most working people make private provisions to take care of their children. Employers who want to reduce the distractions associated with finding reliable child care can help. Some employers simply investigate the day care facilities in their communities and recommend certain ones to employees. Others set up company-sponsored and subsidized day care facilities. For example, Abbott Laboratories built a $10 million child-care center at its headquarters north of Chicago, daytime home to about 400 children of Abbott employees.[139]

By establishing subsidized day care, employers assumedly can benefit in several ways. These include improved recruiting results, lower absenteeism, improved morale, favorable publicity, and lower turnover. But, good planning is required. This often starts with a questionnaire to employees to answer questions like, "What would you be willing to pay for care for one child in a child-care center near work?"

SICK CHILD BENEFITS Unexpected absences accounted for a cost per absence to employers of about $700 per episode (for temp employees and reduced productivity, for instance). More employers are thus offering emergency child-care benefits, for example, when an employee's babysitter is a no-show. Texas Instruments built a Web database its employees use to find last-minute child-care providers. Others, like Canada's CIBC, are expanding their on-site child-care centers to handle last-minute emergencies.[140]

ELDER CARE The responsibility for caring for aging relatives can affect employee performance.[141] One study found that, to care for an older relative, 64% of employees took sick days or vacation time, 33% decreased work hours, 22% took leaves of absence, 20% changed their job status from full- to part-time, 16% quit their jobs, and 13% retired early.

More employers are therefore providing elder care services. For example, the United Auto Workers and Ford provide elder care referral services for Ford's salaried employees, including assessments and recommendations on the best care.[142] The National Council on Aging has a Web site to help find benefit programs: www.benefitscheckup.org.

EDUCATIONAL SUBSIDIES The percentage of employers offering education benefits is diminishing.[143] Such programs are expensive, and the employer may also be paying its best employees to leave. Researchers studied how the U.S. Navy's part-time college education reimbursements influenced job mobility. Taking tuition assistance decreased the probability the person stayed in the Navy.[144]

Payments may range from all tuition and expenses down to a fixed several hundred dollars per year. Many employers also reimburse non–job-related courses (such as a Web designer taking an accounting class) that pertain to company business.[145] Many employers provide college programs on the employer's premises, or remedial work in basic literacy.

Other Personal Services Benefits

Employers provide other personal services benefits.[146] Google, perennially one of the "100 best companies to work for," is famous for its personal services benefits, and the remarkable thing is that most of them cost Google nothing. This is because Google arranges with local vendors to provide on-Google site programs such as ATMs, mobile libraries, bike repair, car wash and oil change, dry cleaning, haircuts and salons, and organic grocery delivery.[147] Free though they are to Google, why does Google even bother? Largely because their on-site availability boosts employees' efficiency by reducing the need for them to seek services off-site. (It also offers the Google Child Care Center, and free shuttle service from San Francisco, for instance.)[148] CVS Caremark, seeking to retain older employees, offers various elder-friendly benefits. Its "snowbird" program lets pharmacists winter in Florida and work in the Northeast when it's warmer, for instance.[149] Nestlé Purina Pet Care's St. Louis headquarters lets employees bring their dogs to work.[150]

Nonmonetary benefits are another option.[151] In one survey, the nonmonetary benefits most desired by employees were: allowing more flexibility with one's work schedule, making available additional training and development opportunities, offering additional paid time off, and providing opportunities to work abroad.[152]

Unfortunately, it's not easy to evaluate the "profitability" of personal services-type programs.[153] The bottom line is that employers are reviewing (and often reducing) these benefits. Even Google, long known for offering benefits that blow most other employers away, cut back a bit of late.

Diversity Counts

DOMESTIC PARTNER BENEFITS When employers provide *domestic partner benefits* to employees, the employees' same-sex or opposite-sex domestic partners are eligible to receive the same benefits (health care, life insurance, and so forth) as do the husband, wife, or legal dependent of one of the firm's employees. Many employers offer domestic partner benefits. For instance, Northrop Grumman Corp. extends domestic partner benefits to the 9,500 salaried workers at its Newport News shipyard.[154]

The Defense of Marriage Act provided that employers may not treat same-sex domestic partners the same as employees' spouses for purposes of federal law. However, in 2013, the U.S. Supreme Court struck down part of the Defense of Marriage Act. Under that ruling, gay couples married in states where it is legal must receive the same federal health, tax, Social Security, and other benefits heterosexual couples receive.[155] In 2013, the United States Labor Secretary announced that the spousal leave provisions of the family and medical leave act apply to married gay couples.[156] In 2015, the U.S. Supreme Court held that same-sex couples can marry nationwide.[157] ■

The Strategic Context feature illustrates how one employer uses benefits to support its strategic goals.

IMPROVING PERFORMANCE: *The Strategic Context*

Gary Erickson started Clif Bar as a small bakery and grew it into a company that's been growing 20% per year. Central to his "healthy foods" strategy is the idea that his hundreds of employees should live the values of sustainability, healthiness, and eco-friendliness.[158] Therefore, he put together a benefits package that encouraged just such values. For example, the company encourages eco-friendliness by reimbursing employees up to $6,500 if they buy hybrid or electric vehicles. Those who bike or walk to work receive $1,500 per year. Clif Bar's subsidized cafeteria serves meals cooked with local organic ingredients. Employees become eligible for 6-week paid sabbaticals after 7 years working for the company. With employee turnover only 3%, in one recent year Clif Bar received over 7,500 applications for 114 open jobs, so his benefits plan also seems to be helping keep workforce costs under control. ■

Source: Based on JP Mangalindan, "a healthier, more rewarding workplace," fortune, October 6, 2014, pages 49–50.

If your professor has assigned this, go to the Assignments section of **mymanagementlab.com** to complete this discussion question.

Talk About It 3: How do you think offering benefits like these affects Clif Bar's recruiting and selection process and helps the company to keep costs down?

Executive Perquisites

When you reach the pinnacle of the organizational pyramid—or close to the top—you will find, waiting for you, the "executive perk." Perquisites (perks for short) are special benefits for top executives. They range from company planes to private bathrooms.

Most fall between these extremes. Perks include *management loans* (typically to exercise executives' stock options); *financial counseling*; and *relocation benefits*, often including subsidized mortgages, purchase of the executive's current house, and payment for the move. Publicly traded companies must itemize all executives' perks (if they total more than $100,000).

LEARNING OBJECTIVE **13-5**

Explain the main flexible benefit programs.

Flexible Benefits Programs

Employees prefer choice in their benefits plans. In one survey of working couples, 83% took advantage of flexible hours (when available); 69% took advantage of the flexible-style benefits we'll discuss next; and 75% said that they prefer flexible benefits plans.[159]

Given this, it is prudent to survey employees' benefits preferences, perhaps using a form like that in Figure 13-4. In any case, employers should provide for choice when designing benefits plans.

The Cafeteria Approach

flexible benefits plan/ cafeteria benefits plan

Individualized plans allowed by employers to accommodate employee preferences for benefits.

One way to provide a choice is with an aptly named *cafeteria benefits plan.* (Pay specialists use **flexible benefits plan** and **cafeteria benefits plan** synonymously.) A *cafeteria plan* is one in which the employer gives each employee a benefits fund budget, and lets the person spend it on the benefits he or she prefers, subject to two constraints. First, the employer must of course limit the total cost for each employee's benefits package. Second, each employee's benefits plan must include certain required items such as Social Security, workers' compensation, and unemployment insurance. Employees can often make midyear changes to their plans if, for instance, their dependent care costs rise and they want to divert contributions.[160] IRS regulations require formal written plans describing the employer's cafeteria plan, including benefits and procedures for choosing them.[161]

TYPES OF PLANS Cafeteria plans come in several varieties. To give employees more flexibility in what benefits they use, about 70% of employers offer *flexible spending accounts* for medical and other expenses. This option lets employees pay for certain benefits expenses with pretax dollars (so the IRS, in effect, subsidizes some of the employee's expense). To encourage employees to use this option, some firms are offering *debit cards* that employees can use at their medical provider or pharmacy.[162] *Core plus option plans* establish a core set of benefits (such as medical insurance), which are usually mandatory for all employees. Beyond the core, employees can then choose various benefits options.[163]

FIGURE 13-4 One Page from Online Survey of Employees' Benefits Preferences

Reprinted with permission from GrapeVine solutions.

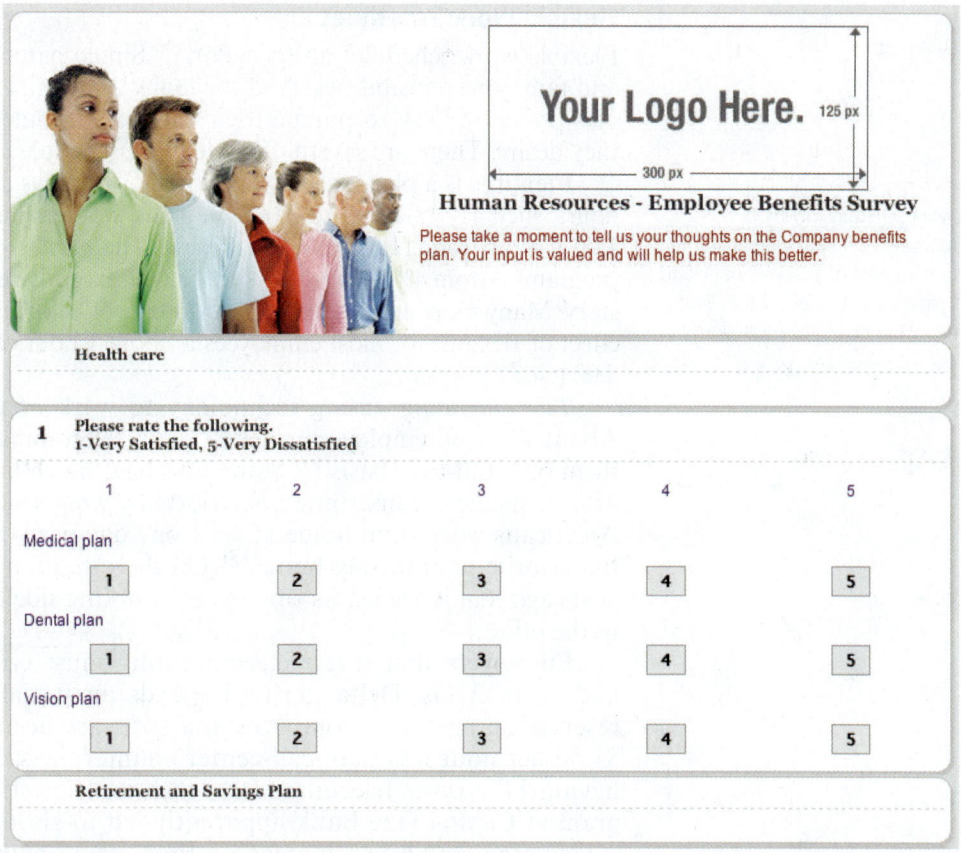

The accompanying HR Tools feature explains how many smaller employers manage the costs of their various benefits.

IMPROVING PERFORMANCE: *HR Tools for Line Managers and Small Businesses*

Benefits and Employee Leasing

Many businesses—particularly smaller ones—don't have the resources or employee base to support the cost of many of the benefits we've discussed in this chapter. That's one big reason they turn to "employee leasing."

In brief, employee leasing firms (also called *professional employer organizations* or *staff leasing firms*) assume all or most of the employer's human resources chores. In doing so, they also become the employer of record for the employer's employees, by transferring them all to the employee leasing firm's payroll. The leasing firm thus becomes the employees' legal employer, and usually handles employee-related activities such as recruiting, hiring (with client firms' supervisors' approvals), and paying taxes (Social Security payments, unemployment insurance, and so on).

Insurance and benefits are usually the big attraction. Even group rates for life or health insurance can be quite high when only 20 or 30 employees are involved. That's where leasing comes in. Remember that the leasing firm is now the legal employer. The employees are thus part of a larger insurable group, along with other employers' former employees. The small business owner may get insurance it couldn't otherwise afford.

As in dealing with all vendors, the employer should have a detailed negotiated agreement with the employee leasing firm. Define what the services will be; include priorities, responsibilities, and warranties.[164] Understand that if the leasing firm merges into another firm, the new parent may require you to change your systems once the contract period expires.[165] ■

Source: Based on Bill Roberts, "Good Vendor Relations," HR Magazine, September 2011, p. 110.

If your professor has assigned this, go to the Assignments section of **mymanagementlab.com** to complete this discussion.

Talk About It 4: Explain how you believe you'd react to having your employer switch you to a leasing firm, and why.

Flexible Work Schedules

Flexible work schedules are popular.[166] Single parents use them for balancing work and family responsibilities. And for many millennial employees, flexible work schedules provide a way to pursue their careers without surrendering the quality of life they desire. There are several flexible work schedule options.

flextime
A work schedule in which employees' workdays are built around a core of midday hours, and employees determine, within limits, what other hours they will work.

Flextime is a plan whereby employees' workdays are built around a core of midday hours, such as 11:00 A.M. to 2:00 P.M. Thus, workers may opt to work from 7:00 A.M. to 3:00 P.M. or from 11:00 A.M. to 7:00 P.M. The number of employees in formal flextime programs—from 4% of operators to 17% of executive employees—doesn't tell the whole story. Many more employees take advantage of informal flexible work schedules.[167] The effect of flextime for most employees is about 1 hour of leeway before 9:00 A.M. or after 5:00 P.M.[168]

Telecommuting—using technology to work away from the office—is popular. About 48% of employers offer ad hoc telecommuting options, while 17% offer them on a full-time basis.[169] Some jobs have much higher rates. For example, almost 45% of medical transcription is reportedly work from home.[170] Just over 13 million Americans work from home at least one day per week, with Fridays and Mondays the favorite days to stay home.[171] On the other hand, Yahoo! famously said a few years ago that it needed its employees "working side by side" and brought them back to the office.[172]

Employers that offer telecommuting must calculate the program's benefits and costs. Thus, Delta Airlines spends an initial $2,500 for each home-based reservation agent for computer and software licenses, but pays each such agent $1.50 per hour less than call-center counterparts. Less obvious expenses include having IT answer telecommuters' technical questions.[173] A telecommuting program at Capital One Bank apparently led to about a 41% increase in workplace satisfaction, and a 53% increase in those who say their workplace enhances group productivity.[174]

compressed workweek
Schedule in which employee works fewer but longer days each week.

COMPRESSED WORKWEEKS Many employees, like airline pilots, don't work conventional 5-day, 40-hour workweeks. Workers like these typically have **compressed workweek** schedules—they work fewer days each week, but each day they work longer hours. Some firms have four 10-hour day workweeks. Some workers—in hospitals, for instance—work three 12-hour shifts, and then take off for 4 days.[175] Some experts argue that 12-hour shifts increase fatigue and accidents. To reduce potential side effects, some employers install treadmills, exercise bikes, and special lights that mimic daylight.

job sharing
Allows two or more people to share a single full-time job.

work sharing
Refers to a temporary reduction in work hours by a group of employees during economic downturns as a way to prevent layoffs.

OTHER FLEXIBLE WORK ARRANGEMENTS **Job sharing** allows two or more people to share a single full-time job. For example, two people may share a 40-hour-per-week job, with one working mornings and the other working afternoons. About 22% of the firms questioned in one survey indicated that they allow job sharing.[176] Job sharing can be particularly useful for retirement-aged employees. It allows them to reduce their hours while the company retains their expertise.[177] **Work sharing** refers to a temporary reduction in work hours by a group of employees during economic downturns as a way to prevent layoffs. Thus, 400 employees may all agree to work (and be paid for) only 35 hours per week, to avoid a layoff of 30 workers.

EFFECTIVENESS OF FLEXIBLE WORK SCHEDULE ARRANGEMENTS Studies show that flexible work schedules have positive effects on employee productivity, job satisfaction, and employee absenteeism; the effect on absenteeism is generally greater than on productivity. Highly flexible programs were less effective than less flexible ones.[178]

LEARNING OBJECTIVE 13-6
Explain how to use benefits to improve engagement, productivity, and performance.

Employee Engagement Guide For Managers

Costco's Compensation Plan

Costco's HR strategy is to deflect Walmart's famously low costs and wages by paying employees more, and thereby producing improved employee engagement, productivity, and customer service.[179]

For example, Costco pays its employees on average about $21 per hour (not including overtime,) almost triple the federal minimum wage.[180] That compares with Walmart's average wage for full-time employees in the United States of $12.67 an hour.[181] Costco's *starting* pay is $11.50 per hour, again far above the minimum wage.[182]

Costco's employee benefits are also highly competitive, particularly compared with the typically sparse offerings in the retail industry.[183] For example, Costco pays about 90% of the health insurance costs of its over 90,000 domestic employees.[184] Its other benefits include (as examples) dental care, a pharmacy/prescriptions program, a vision program, a 401(k) plan, a dependent care assistance plan, an external network of professional counselors, voluntary short-term disability, long-term disability, and life insurance.[185] Costco also extends these benefits to employees' spouses, children, and domestic partners. To get the most from these plans, Costco employees can use www.costcobenefits.com, for instance, to find physicians in their areas.

Costco doesn't directly measure employee engagement; it says it tracks engagement by "byproducts," such as turnover and productivity.[186] By those criteria, Costco's engagement efforts seem to be working. Its sales per employee are about $500,000 a year versus $340,000 at Walmart's Sam's Club.[187] Costco's turnover is far below the retail industry average, and employee retention is higher.[188] Costco, by the way, is not alone. Other large chains with traditionally excellent customer service, like Nordstrom and the Container Store, also do well financially, in part by treating employees well and keeping engagement up.[189]

Chapter Review

MyManagementLab® Go to **mymanagementlab.com** to complete the problems marked with this icon. ✪

Chapter Section Summaries

13-1. Employers provide numerous **pay for time not worked benefits**. These include unemployment insurance, vacation and other leave days, and sick pay. Minimizing sick leave pay is important, and here cost reduction tactics include paid leave plans that lump sick leave, vacation, and holidays into one leave pool. The Family and Medical Leave Act requires larger employers to provide up to 12 weeks of unpaid leave for family-related issues.

13-2. Most employers also provide required or voluntary **insurance benefits**. Workers' compensation laws aim to provide sure, prompt medical benefits to work-related accident victims or their dependents, regardless of fault. Most employer health plans provide at least basic hospitalization and surgical and medical insurance for eligible employees. When an employee is terminated or terminates his or her employment, it is essential that the employer make the person aware of his or her COBRA rights. Employers generally work hard to keep the rising cost of health-care insurance under control.

13-3. **Retirement benefits** are important to employees today. Social Security is a federal program that provides retirement income at the age of 62 and thereafter, as well as other benefits. Many employers make available pension plans; these provide an income when employees reach retirement age or when they can no longer work due to disability. Defined benefit plans contain a formula for determining retirement benefits, while defined contribution plans are plans in which the contribution to employees' retirement savings plans is specified. 401(k) plans are the most well-known of the latter. The Employee Retirement Income Security Act of 1975 requires that employers have written pension plan documents, and established the Pension Benefits Guarantee Corporation to oversee employers' pension plans. Key pension policy issues include membership requirements and testing.

13-4. Most employers also provide various **personal services and family-friendly benefits**. These include credit unions, employee assistance programs, and subsidized child care and elder care.

13-5. Employees prefer choice in their benefits plans, so **flexible benefits programs** are important. Flexible benefits or cafeteria benefits plans are individual plans that accommodate employee preferences for benefits. Some employers turn to employee leasing companies to capitalize on the advantage of the leasing firm's large employee base to get better employee benefits for their employees. Employers also are implementing various types of flexible work schedules, including flextime, compressed workweeks, and other flexible work arrangements such as job sharing.

13-6. Costco's HR strategy is to deflect Walmart's low wages by paying employees more, thereby producing more **employee engagement**, higher productivity, and better customer service. As one example, Costco pays about 90% of the health insurance costs of its over 90,000 domestic employees.

Discussion Questions

13-1. What is unemployment insurance? Is an organization required to pay unemployment benefits to all dismissed employees? Explain how you would go about minimizing your organization's unemployment insurance tax.

13-2. Explain how ERISA protects employees' pension rights.

13-3. Describe the main retirement benefits.

13-4. What are the main provisions of the FMLA?

Individual and Group Activities

13-5. Working individually or in groups, research the unemployment insurance rate and laws of your state. Write a summary detailing your state's unemployment laws. Assuming Company X has a 30% rate of annual personnel terminations, calculate Company X's approximate unemployment tax rate in your state.

13-6. Assume you run a small business. Working individually or in groups, visit the Web site www.dol.gov/elaws. See the Small Business Retirement Savings Advisor. Write a two-page summary explaining: (1) the various retirement savings programs available to small business employers, and (2) which retirement savings program you would choose for your small business and why.

13-7. You are the HR consultant to a small business with about 40 employees. Now the firm offers only 5 days of vacation, 5 paid holidays, and legally mandated benefits such as unemployment insurance payments. Develop a list of other benefits you believe it should offer, along with your reasons for suggesting them.

13-8. Appendices A and B at the end of this book (pages 612–629) list the knowledge someone studying for the HRCI (Appendix A) or SHRM (Appendix B) certification exam needs to have in each area of human resource management (such as in Strategic Management, and Workforce Planning). In groups of several students, do four things: (1) review Appendix A and/or B; (2) identify the material in this chapter that relates to the Appendix A and/or B required knowledge lists; (3) write four multiple-choice exam questions on this material that you believe would be suitable for inclusion in the HRCI exam and/or the SHRM exam; and, (4) if time permits, have someone from your team post your team's questions in front of the class, so that students in all teams can answer the exam questions created by the other teams.

Experiential Exercise

Revising the Benefits Package

Purpose: The purpose of this exercise is to provide practice in developing a benefits package for a small business.

Required Understanding: Be very familiar with the material presented in this chapter. In addition, review Chapter to reacquaint yourself with sources of compensation survey information, and come to class prepared to share with your group the benefits package for the small business in which you work or in which someone with whom you're familiar works.

How to Set Up the Exercise/Instructions: Divide the class into groups of four or five students. Your assignment is as follows: Maria Cortes runs a small personnel recruiting office in Miami and has decided to start offering an expanded benefits package to her 25 employees. At the current time, the only benefits are 7 paid holidays per year and 5 sick days per year. In her company, there are 2 other managers, as well as 17 full-time recruiters and 5 secretarial staff members. Your assignment is as follows:

- In the time allotted, your group should create a benefits package in keeping with the size and requirements of this firm.

Application Case

Striking for Benefits

A few years ago, the strike by Southern California grocery workers against the state's major supermarket chains was almost 5 months old. The main issue was employee benefits, and specifically how much (if any) of the employees' health-care costs the employees should pay themselves. Based on their existing contract, Southern California grocery workers had unusually good health benefits. For example, they paid nothing toward their health insurance premiums, and paid only $10 co-payments for doctor visits. However, supporting these excellent health benefits cost the big Southern California grocery chains over $4 per hour per worker.

The big grocery chains were not proposing cutting health-care insurance benefits for their existing employees. Instead, they proposed putting any new employees hired after the new contract went into effect into a separate insurance pool, and contributing $1.35 per hour for their health insurance coverage. That meant new employees' health insurance would cost each new employee perhaps $10 per week. And, if that $10 per week wasn't enough to cover the cost of health care, then the employees would have to pay more, or do without some of their benefits.

It was a difficult situation for all involved. For the grocery chain employers, skyrocketing health-care costs were undermining their competitiveness; the current employees feared any step down the slippery slope that might eventually mean cutting their own health benefits. The unions didn't welcome a situation in which they'd end up representing two classes of employees, one (the existing employees) who had excellent health insurance benefits, and another (newly hired employees) whose benefits were relatively meager, and who might therefore be unhappy from the moment they took their jobs and joined the union.

Questions

13-9. Assume you are mediating this dispute. Discuss five creative solutions you would suggest for how the grocers could reduce the health insurance benefits and the cost of their total benefits package without making any employees pay more.

13-10. From the grocery chains' point of view, what is the downside of having two classes of employees, one of which has superior health insurance benefits? How would you suggest they handle the problem?

13-11. Similarly, from the point of view of the union, what are the downsides of having to represent two classes of employees, and how would you suggest handling the situation?

Source: Based on "Settlement Nears for Southern California Grocery Strike," *Knight-Ridder/Tribune Business News*, February 26, 2004, item 04057052.

Continuing Case

Carter Cleaning Company

The New Benefit Plan

Carter Cleaning Centers has traditionally provided only legislatively required benefits for its employees. These include unemployment compensation, Social Security, and workers' compensation (which is provided through the same insurance carrier that insures the stores for such hazards as theft and fire). The principals of the firm—Jack, Jennifer, and their families—have individual, family-supplied health and life insurance.

Jennifer can see several potential problems with the company's policies regarding benefits and services. One is turnover. She wants to study whether similar companies' experiences with providing health and life insurance benefits enable these firms to reduce employee turnover and perhaps pay lower wages. Jennifer is also concerned that her company has no formal vacation or paid days off or sick leave policies. Informally, at least, it is understood that employees get 1 week's vacation after 1 year's work, but in the past the policy regarding paid vacations for days such as New Year's Day and Thanksgiving Day has been very inconsistent. Sometimes employees who had been on the job only 2 or 3 weeks were paid fully for one of these holidays, while at other times employees who had been with the firm for 6 months or more had been paid for only half a day.

She also wonders whether it would be advisable to establish some type of day care center for the employees' children. Many of them have no place to go during the day (they are preschoolers) or have no place to go after school; she wonders whether a day care benefit would be in the best interests of the company.

Questions

13-12. Draw up a policy statement regarding vacations, sick leave, and paid days off for Carter Cleaning Centers.

13-13. What would you tell Jennifer are the advantages and disadvantages to Carter Cleaning Centers of providing its employees with health, hospitalization, and life insurance programs?

13-14. Would you advise establishing some type of day care center for the Carter Cleaning employees? Why or why not?

Translating Strategy into HR Policies and Practices Case*, §

**The accompanying strategy map for this chapter is in MyManagementLab, and the overall map on the inside back cover of this text outlines the relationships involved.*

Improving Performance at the Hotel Paris

The New Benefits Plan

The Hotel Paris's competitive strategy is "To use superior guest service to differentiate the Hotel Paris properties, and to thereby increase the length of stay and return rate of guests, and thus boost revenues and profitability." HR manager Lisa Cruz must now formulate functional policies and activities that support this competitive strategy by eliciting the required employee behaviors and competencies.

While the Hotel Paris's benefits (in terms of things like holidays and health care) were comparable to other hotels', Lisa knew they weren't good enough to support the high-quality service behaviors her company sought. Indeed, the fact that they were roughly comparable to those of similar firms didn't seem to impress the Hotel Paris's employees. Sixty percent of them consistently said they were dissatisfied with their benefits. Lisa's concern (with which the CFO concurred) was that dissatisfaction with benefits contributed to low morale and engagement, and thus to inhibiting the Hotel Paris from achieving its strategic aims. Lisa therefore turned to the task of assessing and redesigning the company's benefits plans.

As they reviewed the benefits numbers, Lisa and the CFO became concerned. They computed several benefits-related metrics for their firm, including benefits costs as a percentage of payroll, sick days per full-time-equivalent employee per year, benefits cost/competitor's benefits cost ratio, and workers' compensation experience ratings. The results, said the CFO, offered a "good news–bad news" situation. On the good side, as noted, the ratios were similar to most competing hotels'. The bad news was that the measures were well below those for high-performing service businesses. The CFO authorized Lisa to design and propose a new benefits plan.

Lisa knew there were several things she wanted to accomplish. She wanted a plan that contributed to improved employee morale and engagement. And, she wanted the plan to include elements that made it easier for her employees to do their jobs—so that, as she put it, "they could come to work and give their full attention to giving our guests great service, without worrying about child care and other family distractions."

The new plan's centerpiece was a proposal for much better family-friendly benefits. Because so many of each hotel's employees were single parents, and because each hotel had to run 24 hours a day, Lisa's team proposed, and the board approved, setting aside a room in each hotel for an on-site child-care facility and for hiring a trained professional attendant. They considered instituting a flexible work schedule program, but for most of the jobs, this was impractical, because each front-line employee simply had to be there at his or her appointed hour. However, they did institute a new job-sharing program. Now two people could share one housekeeping or front-desk clerk job, as long as the job was covered.

One of the metrics Lisa and her team specifically wanted to address was the relatively high absence rate at the Hotel Paris. Because so many of these jobs are front-line jobs—valets, limousine drivers, and front-desk clerks, for instance—absence had a particularly serious effect on metrics like overtime pay and temporary help costs. Here, at the urging of her compensation consultant, Lisa decided to opt for a system similar to Marriott's BENETRADE. With this benefit program, employees can trade the value of some sick days for other benefits. As Lisa put it, "I'd rather see our employees using their sick day pay for things like additional health-care benefits, if it means they'll think twice before taking a sick day to run a personal errand."

After just less than a year, Lisa and the CFO believe the new program is successful. Their studies suggest that the improved benefits are directly contributing to improved employee morale and commitment, sick days have diminished by 40%, and employee turnover is down 60%. And when they advertise for open positions, over 60% of the applicants cite "family-friendly benefits" as a top reason for applying to work at the Hotel Paris.

Questions

13-15. What is your opinion of the new Hotel Paris benefits plan?

13-16. Because employers typically make benefits available to all employees, they may not have the motivational effects of incentive plans. Given this, list five employee behaviors you believe Hotel Paris could try to improve through an enhanced benefits plan, and explain why you chose them.

13-17. Given your answer to question 13-16 and what you read in this chapter of Dessler *Human Resource Management,* explain specifically what other benefits you would recommend the Hotel Paris implement to achieve these behavioral improvements.

---

§Written by and copyright Gary Dessler, PhD.

MyManagementLab

Go to **mymanagementlab.com** for Auto-graded writing questions as well as the following Assisted-graded writing questions:

13-18. You are applying for a job as a manager and are at the point of negotiating salary and benefits. What questions would you ask your prospective employer concerning benefits? Describe the benefits package you would try to negotiate for yourself.

13-19. Your clients want to know how they can use their employee benefits package to improve employee engagement. What would you tell them?

13-20. MyManagementLab Only–comprehensive writing assignment for this chapter.

Key Terms

benefits, 418
supplemental pay benefits, 419
unemployment insurance (or compensation), 419
sick leave, 421
severance pay, 423
supplemental unemployment benefits, 424
workers' compensation, 424
health maintenance organization (HMO), 426
group life insurance, 430
Social Security, 431
pension plans, 431
defined benefit pension plan, 431
defined contribution pension plan, 431
portability, 432
401(k) plan, 432
savings and thrift plan, 432
deferred profit-sharing plan, 432
employee stock ownership plan (ESOP), 433
cash balance plans, 433
Employee Retirement Income Security Act 1975 (ERISA), 433
Pension Benefits Guarantee Corporation (PBGC), 433
early retirement window, 433
employee assistance program (EAP), 435
family-friendly (or work–life) benefits, 436
flexible benefits plan/cafeteria benefits plan, 438
flextime, 440
compressed workweek, 440
job sharing, 440
work sharing, 440

Endnotes

1. J. P. Mangalindan, "A Healthier, More Rewarding Workplace," *Fortune*, October 6, 2014, pp. 49–50.
2. Based on Frederick Hills, Thomas Bergmann, and Vida Scarpello, *Compensation Decision Making* (Fort Worth, TX: The Dryden Press, 1994), p. 424. See also Fay Hansen, "The Cutting Edge of Benefit Cost Control," *Workforce*, March 2003, pp. 36–42; Crain's Benefits Outlook 2009, www.crainsbenefit.com/news/survey-finds-nearly-20-percent-of-employers-plan-to-drop-health-benefits.php, accessed July 28, 2009.
3. "Survey Finds 99 Percent of Employers Providing Health-Care Benefits," *Compensation & Benefits Review*, September/October 2002, p. 11. See also "National Compensation Survey: Employee Benefits in Private Industry in the United States, March 2006," U.S. Department of Labor, U.S. Bureau of Labor Statistics, August 2006.
4. "Trouble Ahead? Dissatisfaction with Benefits, Compensation," *HR Trendbook*, 2008, p. 16.
5. Frank Giancola, "Are Employee Benefit Programs Being Given Enough Credit for Their Effect on Employee Attitudes?" *Compensation & Benefits Review* 44, no. 5 (2012), pp. 291–297.
6. Joseph Martocchio, *Strategic Compensation* (Upper Saddle River, NJ: Prentice Hall, 2001), p. 262.
7. "California Domestic Partner Benefits Mandate Carries Likely Impact Beyond State's Borders," *BNA Bulletin to Management*, November 6, 2003, p. 353.
8. "HR Plays a Major Role in Curbing Company Unemployment Insurance Costs, Analysts Say," *BNA Bulletin to Management*, August 3, 2010, pp. 241–242; www.dllr.state.md.us/employment/uitrustfundpoints.shtml, accessed July 15, 2015.
9. www.bls.gov/opub/perspectives/issue2.pdf, accessed September 8, 2014.
10. Ibid.
11. www.bls.gov/opub/perspectives/issue2.pdf, accessed June 1, 2011.
12. Ken Belson, "At IBM, a Vacation Anytime, or Maybe No Vacation at All," *New York Times*, August 31, 2007, pp. A1–A18.
13. Robert Grossman, "Gone But Not Forgotten," *HR Magazine*, September 2011, p. 44; then put in place solutions such as rigorous absenteeism claims reviews.
14. See for instance, www.insperity.com/products/performance-management/policies.
15. "National Compensation Survey: Employee Benefits in Private Industry in the United States, March 2006," U.S. Bureau of Labor Statistics, August 2006, p. 116. See also "Spurious Sick-Notes Spiral Upwards," *The Safety and Health Practitioner* 22, no. 6 (June 2004), p. 3.
16. "Unscheduled Employee Absences Cost Companies More Than Ever," *Compensation & Benefits Review*, March/April 2003, p. 19; Robert Grossman, "Gone but Not Forgotten," *HR Magazine* 56, no. 9 (September 2011), pp. 34–46.
17. "Making Up for Lost Time: How Employers Can Curb Excessive Unscheduled Absences," *BNA Human Resources Report*, October 20, 2003, p. 1097. See also W. H. J. Hassink et al., "Do Financial Bonuses Reduce Employee Absenteeism? Evidence from a Lottery," *Industrial and Labor Relations Review* 62, no. 3 (April 2009), pp. 327–342.
18. "SHRM Benefits Survey Finds Growth in Employer Use of Paid Leave Pools," *BNA Bulletin to Management*, March 21, 2002, p. 89.
19. See M. Michael Markowich and Steve Eckberg, "Get Control of the Absentee-Minded," *Personnel Journal*, March 1996, pp. 115–120; "Exploring the Pluses, Minuses, and Myths of Switching to Paid Time Off Banks," *BNA Bulletin to Management* 55, no. 25 (June 17, 2004), pp. 193–194.
20. Society for Human Resource Management 2009 Employee Benefits Survey, quoted in Martha Frase, "Taking Time Off to the Bank," *HR Magazine*, March 2010, p. 42. See also Marissa Warford, "Does Paid Time Off Pay Off?" *Workforce*, August 2014, pp. 26–29, 48.
21. "Creating Holistic Time Off Programs Can Significantly Reduce Expenses," *Compensation & Benefits Review*, July/August 2007, pp. 18–19.
22. See, for example, Rita Zeidner, "Strategies for Saving in a Down Economy," *HR Magazine*, February 2009, p. 28.
23. Judith Whitaker, "How HR Made a Difference," *People*

Management 27 (October 28, 2010).
24. Ibid.
25. http://en.wikipedia.org/wiki/Driver_and_Vehicle_Licensing_Agency, accessed April 13, 2013.
26. In 2008, Congress amended the family and medical leave act to include, among other things, leave rights particularly for military families. See Sarah Martin, "FMLA Protection Recently Expanded to Military Families: Qualifying Exigency and Service Member Family Leave," *Compensation & Benefits Review*, September/October 2009, pp. 43–51.
27. "Ten Years After It Was Signed into Law, FMLA Needs Makeover, Advocates Contend," *BNA Bulletin to Management*, February 20, 2003, p. 58.
28. "HR Professionals Face Sundry Challenges Administering FMLA Leave, Survey Asserts," *BNA Bulletin to Management*, July 20, 2007, p. 233.
29. Jill Fisher, "Reconciling the Family Medical Leave Act with Overlapping or Conflicting State Leave Laws," *Compensation & Benefits Review*, September/October 2007, pp. 39–44.
30. Based on Dennis Grant, "Managing Employee Leaves: A Legal Primer," *Compensation & Benefits Review* 35, no. 4 (2003), p. 41. See also Daniel Ritter et al., "Recent Developments Under the Family and Medical Leave Act," *Compensation & Benefits Review*, September/October 2007, p. 33.
31. Gillian Flynn, "Employers Need an FMLA Brush-Up," *Workforce*, April 1997, pp. 101–104. See also "Worker Who Was Employee for Less Than One Year Can Pursue FMLA Claim, Federal Court Determines," *BNA Fair Employment Practices*, April 26, 2001, p. 51.
32. "Workers Who Come and Go Under FMLA Complicate Attendance Policies, Lawyer Says," *BNA Bulletin to Management*, March 16, 2000, p. 81; see for example, https://www.mls-ime.com/services.html, accessed July 15, 2015.
33. Sue Shellenbarger, "The Mommy Drain: Employers Beef Up Perks to Lure New Mothers Back to Work," *Wall Street Journal*, September 28, 2006, p. D1.
34. "Severance Pay," July 2007, *Culpepper Compensation & Benefits Surveys*.
35. Terry Baglieri, "Severance Pay," www.shrm.org, accessed December 23, 2006. See also www.shrm.org/hrdisciplines/compensation/articles/pages/cms_022345.aspx, accessed July 15, 2015.
36. Baglieri, op. cit.
37. Baglieri, op. cit.
38. "Workers' Compensation Costs Are Rising Faster Than Wages," *BNA Bulletin to Management*, July 31, 2003, p. 244.
39. "Workers' Comp Claims Rise with Layoffs, but Employers Can Identify, Prevent Fraud," *BNA Bulletin to Management*, October 4, 2001, p. 313.
40. "Using Case Management in Workers' Compensation," *BNA Bulletin to Management*, June 6, 1996, p. 181; for other tactics, see, for example, H. Jorgensen, "Overhauling Claims Management." *Risk Management* 54, no. 7 (July 2007), p. 50. See also Donna Owens, "Back to Work," *HR Magazine*, November 2012, pp. 49–51.
41. "Workers Comp Research Provides Insight into Curbing Health Care Costs," *EHS Today*, February 2010, p. 18.
42. "Firms Cite Own Efforts as Key to Controlling Costs," *BNA Bulletin to Management*, March 21, 1996, p. 89. See also "Workers' Compensation Outlook: Cost Control Persists," *BNA Bulletin to Management*, January 30, 1997, pp.33–44; and Annmarie Lipold, "The Soaring Costs of Workers' Comp," *Workforce*, February 2003, p. 42ff.
43. In one recent survey, 53% of workers said they would trade some pay for better retirement benefits: "Employees Willing to Trade Pay for More Benefits, Survey Finds," *BNA Bulletin to Management*, March 6, 2012, p. 78.
44. Emily Jane Fox, "Health Insurance Premiums Climb 4% in 2012," http://money.cnn.com/2012/09/11/pf/insurance/health-insurance-premiums/index.html, accessed April 12, 2013. See also "Costs This Year Increased at Highest Rate Since 2004, Survey Reveals," *HR Focus* 88, no. 1 (January 10, 2011); "Health Costs," http://kff.org/health-costs/, accessed April 20, 2015.
45. Hills, Bergmann, and Scarpello, *Compensation Decision Making*, p. 137.
46. "Costs This Year Increased at Highest Rate Since 2004, Survey Reveals," *HR Focus* 88, no. 1 (January 10, 2011); "Health Costs," http://kff.org/health-costs/, accessed April 20, 2015.
47. Society for Human Resource Management, "Mental Health Trends," *Workplace Visions*, no. 2, http://moss07.shrm.org/Research/FutureWorkplaceTrends/Pages/0303.aspx, accessed July 28, 2009.
48. "Mental-Health Parity Measure Enacted as Part of Financial Rescue Signed by Bush," *BNA Bulletin to Management*, October 7, 2008, p. 321. Because the act requires employers who offer mental health coverage to make that coverage similar to their medical and surgical health coverage benefits, some employers drop health care coverage. Alice Andors, "This Parity Pay Off?" *HR Magazine*, September 2012, pp. 45–46.
49. "IRS Unveils Proposed Rules of 'Shared Responsibility,'" *BNA Bulletin to Management*, January 18, 2013, p. 12. See also Wendy Voss and Jesse Noa, "The ACA's Employer Mandate: What Are the Implications?" *Bloomberg BNA Bulletin to Management*, June 17, 2014, pp. S1–S12.
50. "Deadlines Vary for Implementing Provisions of Health Care Law," *BNA Bulletin to Management*, May 4, 2010, p. 143; "Ruling Means Employers Now Face Various PPACA Deadlines," *BNA Bulletin to Management*, August 10, 2012, p. 222.
51. "Regulation Will Allow Young Adults Up to Age 26 to Retain Dependent Coverage," *BNA Bulletin to Management*, May 18, 2010, p. 153.
52. Patricia Moran, "2015 Healthcare Compliance: A Checklist for Employers," *Bloomberg BNA Bulletin to Management*, February 10, 2015, pp. S1–S4.
53. "Lavish Cadillac Health Plans Dying Out as ACA Tax Looms Three Years Hence," *Bloomberg BNA Bulletin to Management*, January 13, 2015, p. 9.
54. Anna Mathews and Julie Jargon, "Firms Try to Escape Health Penalties," *Wall Street Journal*, October 22, 2014, pp. A1, A2.
55. Ibid.
56. "The Insured and the Unsure," *The Economist* 6 (January 20, 2013), p. 59.
57. Mark Lutes and Adam Solander, "Cadillac Tax Could Jeopardize Viability of Employer-Based Plans," *BNA Bulletin to Management*, November 27, 2012, p. 382.
58. Joanne Sammer, "How to Choose Health Insurance Exchanges," *HR Magazine*, October 2012, pp. 47–52.
59. See, for example, Karli Dunkelberger, "Avoiding COBRA's Bite: Three Keys to Compliance," *Compensation & Benefits Review*, March/April 2005, pp. 44–48. See also Patrick Muldowney, "Cobra and the Stimulus Act: A Sign of Things to Come?" *Compensation & Benefits Review* 42, no. 1 (January/February 2010), pp. 24–49.
60. www.DOL.gov, accessed December 23, 2006.
61. Larri Short and Eileen Kahanar, "Unlocking the Secrets of the New Privacy Rules," *Occupational Hazards*, September 2002, pp. 51–54.
62. Kevin Maroney, "Prognosis Negative? GINA's Interim Incentives Ruling a Concern for Wellness Programs," *Compensation & Benefits Review* 42, no. 2 (2010), pp. 94–101.
63. Joanne Deschenaux, "Managing Leaves of Absence in California Is Complicated," *HR Magazine*, June 2011, p. 23.
64. David Tobenkin, "Learn the Landscape," *HR Magazine*, May 2011, pp. 51–53.
65. http://insight.aon.com/?elqPURLPage=6567, accessed April 11, 2013.
66. James Curcio, "Creating Standardized Metrics and Benchmarking for Health, Absence and Productivity Management Programs: The EMPAQ Initiative," *Compensation & Benefits Review* 42, no. 2 (2010), pp. 109–126.
67. Vanessa Fuhrmanns, "Oops! As Health Plans Become More Complicated, They're Also Subject to a Lot More Costly Mistakes," *Wall Street Journal*, January 24, 2005, p. R4.
68. Jerry Geisel, "Employers Accelerate Health Care Cost-Shifting," *Business Insurance* 45, no. 21 (May 23, 2011), pp. 3, 21; http://kff.org/report-section/ehbs-2014-summary-of-findings/, accessed July 15, 2015.
69. "Employer Partners to Launch a Three-Year Wellness Initiative," *BNA Bulletin to Management*, August 7, 2007, p. 255.
70. http://insight.aon.com/?elqPURLPage?6567, accessed April 11, 2013.
71. Ron Finch, "Preventive Services: Improving the Bottom Line for Employers and Employees," *Compensation & Benefits Review*, March/April 2005, p. 18.
72. "Employer Partners to Launch a Three-Year Wellness Initiative," *BNA Bulletin to Management*, August 7, 2007, p. 255. See also Drew Robb, "Benefits Choices: Educating the Consumer," *HR Magazine*, March 2011, pp. 29–30.
73. Susan Wells, "Wellness Rewards," *HR Magazine*, February 2012, pp. 67–69.
74. "On-Site Clinics Aimed at Cutting Costs, Promoting Wellness," *BNA Bulletin to Management*, March 25, 2008, p. 103. See also Susan Wells, "Navigating the Expanding Wellness Industry," *HR Magazine*, March 2011, pp. 45–50.
75. Ibid. See also Josh Cable, "The Road to Wellness," *Occupational Hazards*, April 2007, pp. 23–27.
76. George DeVries, "The Top 10 Wellness Trends for 2008 and Beyond," *Compensation & Benefits Review*, July/August 2008, pp. 60–63.
77. Susan Wells, "Getting Paid for Staying Well," *HR Magazine*, February 2010, p. 59.

78. Christine Keller and Christopher Condeluci, "Tax Relief and Health Care Act Should Prompt Re-Examination of HSAs," *SHRM Legal Report*, July–August 2007, p. 1.
79. In contrast, with health reimbursement arrangements (HRA) only the employer makes contributions. See "Types of Tax Favored Health Accounts," *HR Magazine*, August 2008, p. 76.
80. Michael Bond et al., "Using Health Savings Accounts to Provide Low-Cost Health-Care," *Compensation & Benefits Review*, March/April 2005, pp. 29–32.
81. Martha Frase, "Minimalist Health Coverage," *HR Magazine*, June 2009, pp. 107–112.
82. "To Cut Costs, Employers Considering Defined Contribution Health Insurance Plans," *BNA Bulletin to Management*, November 20, 2011, p. 377.
83. "One in Five Big Firms May Drop Coverage for Future Retirees, Health Survey Finds," *BNA Bulletin to Management*, December 12, 2002, p. 393. Reducing retiree benefits requires a preliminary legal review. See James McElligott Jr., "Retiree Medical Benefit Developments in the Courts, Congress, and EEOC," *Compensation & Benefits Review*, March/April 2005, pp. 23–28; and Joanne Sammer, "Exit Strategy: Ending Retiree Medical Benefits," *HR Magazine*, September 2011, pp. 57–62.
84. Kathleen McGrory, "Big Shift May Come in Retirees' Coverage," *Miami Herald*, September 16, 2013, pp. 1B, 6B.
85. Sandra Yin, "A New Breed," *American Way*, May 1, 2013, pp. 40–41.
86. Robert Christadore, "Benefits Purchasing Alliances: Creating Stability in an Unstable World," *Compensation & Benefits Review*, September/October 2001, pp. 49–53; Betty Liddick, "Going the Distance for Health Savings," *HR Magazine*, March 2007, pp. 51–55; J. Wojcik, "Employers Consider Short-Haul Medical Tourism," *Business Insurance* 43, no. 29 (August 24, 2009), pp. 1, 20.
87. Rita Pyrillis, "Self-Thought: Companies Ponder Bringing Insurance In-House," *Workforce Management*, April 2012, pp. 3–4.
88. David Tobenkin, "Spousal Exclusions on the Rise," *HR Magazine*, November 2011, pp. 55–56.
89. Rebecca Vesely, "A New Remedy Emerges for Spiraling Health Costs," *Workforce Management*, June 2012, p. 14.
90. Susan Ladika, "Some Firms Find In-House Clinics Just What the Doctor Ordered," *Workforce Management*, March 2011, pp. 6–7.
91. "Hewitt Says Employer Measures to Control Increases in Health Care Costs Are Working," *BNA Bulletin to Management*, October 7, 2008, p. 323.
92. Alan Cohen, "Decision-Support in the Benefits Consumer Age," *Compensation & Benefits Review*, March/April 2006, pp. 46–51.
93. "HR Outsourcing: Managing Costs and Maximizing Provider Relations," *BNA, Inc.* 21, no. 11 (Washington, DC: November 2003), p. 10.
94. Bill Roberts, "Outsourcing in Turbulent Times," *HR Magazine*, November 2009, p. 45.
95. Susan Galactica, "There's a Doctor on the Phone? Employers Dial-Up Telemedicine," *Workforce Management*, September 2012, p. 8. See also "Speakers Tout Advantages, $6 Billion Potential of Telemedicine," *Bloomberg BNA Bulletin to Management*, December 16, 2014, p. 399.
96. Carolyn Hirschman, "Will Employers Take the Lead in Long-Term Care?" *HR Magazine*, March 1997, pp. 59–66; see also A. D. Postal, "Industry Ramps Up Opposition to LTC Program in Senate Health Bill," *National Underwriter* (Life & Health/Financial Services Edition) 113, no. 14 (July 20, 2009), pp. 10, 32.
97. http://www.bls.gov/news.release/empsit.t08.htm, accessed September 17, 2015.
98. See, for example, Nancy Woodward, "Part-Time Benefits: A Moving Target," *HR Magazine*, November 2012, pp. 61–64.
99. Brenda Sunoo, "Millions May Retire," *Workforce*, December 1997, p. 48. See also "Many Older Workers Choose to 'Un-Retire' or Not Retire at All," *Knight Ridder/Tribune Business News*, September 28, 2003, item 03271012; and "For Many Seniors, a Job Beats Retirement," *Knight Ridder/Tribune Business News*, February 9, 2003, item 3040001.
100. The U.S. Treasury has reportedly spent most of the trust fund on other government programs, so that changes (for instance, in terms of reducing benefits, making people wait longer for benefits, or making some people pay more for benefits) will be necessary. John Kilgour, "Social Security in the 21st Century," *Compensation & Benefits Review* 42, no. 6 (2010), pp. 459–469.
101. http://www.ssa.gov/policy/docs/quickfacts/prog_highlights/index.html, accessed September 17, 2015.
102. Martocchio, *Strategic Compensation*, pp. 245–248; and Lin Grensing-Pophal, "A Pension Formula That Pays Off," *HR Magazine* (February 2003), pp. 58–62.
103. For one recent example of how to do this, see Gail Nichols, "Reviewing and Redesigning Retirement Plans," *Compensation & Benefits Review*, May/June 2008, pp. 40–47.
104. Many employers are considering terminating their plans, but most employers are considering instead either ceasing benefits accruals for all participants or just for future participants. Michael Cotter, "The Big Freeze: The Next Phase in the Decline of Defined Benefit Plans," *Compensation & Benefits Review*, March/April 2009, pp. 44–53.
105. Patty Kujawa, "The Young and Not So Restless," *Workforce Management*, May 2012, p. 6. See also Joanne Sammer, "Are Defined Benefit Plans Dead?" *HR Magazine*, July 2012, pp. 29–32.
106. Patty Kujawa, "Young Workers Craving Defined Benefit Plans," *Workforce Management*, March 2011, p. 16.
107. "Target CEO's $47 Million Package Shows Gap with Workers," *Bloomberg BNA Bulletin to Management*, January 13, 2015, p. 12.
108. Jessica Marquez, "More Workers Yanking Money Out of 401(k)s," *Workforce Management*, August 11, 2008, p. 4.
109. Nancy Pridgen, "The Duty to Monitor Appointed Fiduciaries Under ERISA," *Compensation & Benefits Review*, September/October 2007, pp. 46–51; "Individual 401(k) Plan Participant Can Sue Plan Fiduciary for Losses, Justices Rule," *BNA Bulletin to Management*, February 20, 2008, p. 65.
110. "Benefit Trends: Automatic Enrollment Takes Off," *Compensation & Benefits Review*, September/October 2008, p. 14.
111. For a discussion, see Jewel Esposito, "Avoiding 401(k) ERISA Disasters," *Compensation & Benefits Review* 42, no. 1 (January/February 2010), pp. 39–45.
112. Jack VanDerhei, "The Pension Protection Act and 401(k)s," *Wall Street Journal*, April 20, 2008, p. 12.
113. Wyatt, "401(k) Conversion," p. 20.
114. "New Pension Law Plus a Recent Court Ruling Doom Age-Related Suits, Practitioners Say," *BNA Bulletin to Management* 57, no. 36 (September 5, 2006), pp. 281–282; and www.dol.gov/ebsa/FAQs/faq_consumer_cashbalanceplans.html, accessed January 9, 2010.
115. Harold Burlingame and Michael Gulotta, "Cash Balance Pension Plan Facilitates Restructuring the Workforce at AT&T," *Compensation & Benefits Review*, November/December 1998, pp. 25–31; Jerry Geisel, "IRS Releases Long-Awaited Cash Balance Guidance," *Pensions & Investments* 38, no. 22 (November 1 2010), p. 22.
116. Rita Pyrillis, "Picking a PBM for'13," *Workforce Management*, June 2012, p. 8.
117. This is based on Eric Parmenter, "Employee Benefit Compliance Checklist," *Compensation & Benefits Review*, May/June 2002, pp. 29–38.
118. John Kilgour, "Public Pension Underfunding in California: A Perfect Storm Likely to Sweep the Nation," *Compensation & Benefits Review* 44, no. 6 (2013), pp. 345–351.
119. www.pbgc.gov/wr/benefits/guaranteed-benefits.html, accessed July 15, 2015.
120. Patrick Kiger, "Early-Retirement Plans Backfire, Driving Up Costs Instead of Cutting Them," *Workforce Management*, January 2004, pp. 66–68.
121. "Benefits Cost Control Solutions to Consider Now," *HR Focus* 80, no. 11 (November 2003), p. 1.
122. Johanna Rodgers, "Web Based Apps Simplify Employee Benefits," *Insurance and Technology* 28, no. 11 (November 2003), p. 21. See also www.benelogic.com, accessed June 28, 2011.
123. Ibid.
124. Scott Harper, "Online Resources System Boosts Worker Awareness," *BNA Bulletin to Management*, April 10, 2007, p. 119.
125. Drew Robb, "A Total View of Employee Records," *HR Magazine*, August 2007, pp. 93–96.
126. The following is based on www.tlnt.com/2012/04/26/the-5-best-social-media-tools-for-employee-benefits-communication/, www.abenity.com/celebrate/how-to-use-social-media-to-communicate-employee-perks-benefits/, www.benefitspro.com/2013/04/19/social-media-a-tool-to-boost-employee-engagement-p, and www.employeebenefits.co.uk/benefits/communication/siemens-launches-social-media-website/105812.article, all accessed April 20, 2015.
127. Michelle Rafter, "Mobile Apps for Benefits Go from Luxury to Necessity," *Workforce Management*, June 2012, p. 3.
128. "Employee Who's Facebook Photos Suggested Fraud Lacks FMLA Claims, Sixth Circuit Rules," *BNA Bulletin to Management*, November 20, 2012, p. 371.
129. Brad Reagan, "Perks with a Payoff," *Wall Street Journal*, October 24, 2011, p. r3.
130. Ibid.
131. Carolyn Hirschman, "Employees' Choice," *HR Magazine*, February 2006, pp. 95–99.
132. Joseph O'Connell, "Using Employee Assistance Programs to Avoid Crises," *Long Island Business News*, April 19, 2002, p. 10.

133. See Scott MacDonald et al., "Absenteeism and Other Workplace Indicators of Employee Assistance Program Clients and Matched Controls," *Employee Assistance Quarterly* 15, no. 3 (2000), pp. 51–58. See also Paul Courtis et al., "Performance Measures in the Employee Assistance Program," *Employee Assistance Quarterly* 19, no. 3 (2005), pp. 45–58.
134. See, for example, Donna Owens, "EAPs for a Diverse World," *HR Magazine*, October 2006, pp. 91–96.
135. Rita Pyrillis, "Devoid of Data," *Workforce*, June 2014, pp. 48–50.
136. "Fathers Fighting to Keep Work–Life Balance Are Finding Employers Firmly in their Corner," *BNA Bulletin to Management* 56, no. 24 (June 14, 2005), p. 185.
137. Susan Wells, "Are You Too Family-Friendly?" *HR Magazine*, October 2007, pp. 35–39.
138. Maureen Hannay and Melissa Northam, "Low-Cost Strategies for Employee Retention," *Compensation & Benefits Review*, July/August 2000, pp. 65–72. See also Roseanne Geisel, "Responding to Changing Ideas of Family," *HR Magazine*, August 2004, pp. 89–98.
139. Patrick Kiger, "A Case for Childcare," *Workforce Management*, April 2004, pp. 34–40.
140. www.shrm.org/rewards/library, accessed December 23, 2006. See also Kathy Gurchiek, "Give Us Your Sick," *HR Magazine*, January 2007, pp. 91–93.
141. Kelli Earhart, R. Dennis Middlemist, and Willie Hopkins, "Elder Care: An Emerging Assistance Issue," *Employee Assistance Quarterly* 8, no. 3 (1993), pp. 1–10. See also "Finding a Balance Between Conflicting Responsibilities: Work and Caring for Aging Parents," *Monday Business Briefing*, July 7, 2004; and "Employers Feel Impact of Eldercare: Some Expanded Benefits for Workers," *Knight Ridder/Tribune Business News*, June 13, 2004, item 04165011.
142. Rudy Yandrick, "Elder Care Grows Up," *HR Magazine*, November 2001, pp. 72–77.
143. Jennifer Schramm, "Undereducated," *HR Magazine*, September 2011, p. 136.
144. Richard Buddin and Kanika Kapur, "The Effect of Employer-Sponsored Education on Job Mobility: Evidence from the U.S. Navy," *Industrial Relations* 44, no. 2 (April 2005), pp. 341–363.
145. Mary Burke, Euren Esen, and Jessica Cullison, "2003 Benefits Survey," SHRM/SHRM Foundation, 1800 Duke Street, Alexandria VA, 2003, p. 30. See also Michael Laff, "U.S. Employers Tighten Reins on Tuition Reimbursement," *Training & Development*, July 2006, p. 18.
146. "Rising Gas Prices Prompting Employers to Consider Varied Computer Benefit Options," *BNA Bulletin to Management*, June 20, 2008, p. 201.
147. Laszlo Bock, *Work Rules!* (New York: 12, 2015), p. 274.
148. See "The 100 Best Companies to Work For," *Fortune*, February 6, 2012, p. 117.
149. Tamera Lionel, "Benefits for Older Workers," *HR Magazine*, March 2012, pp. 53–58.
150. "Perks at Work," *Workforce*, September 2014, pp. 40–43.
151. Michael Custers, "Rethinking Existing HR Technologies for New Games in Employee Engagement and Benefits," *Compensation & Benefits Review* 44, no. 6, 2013, pp. 332–335.
152. Ibid.
153. Marcus Butts et al., "How Important Are Work-Family Support Policies? A Meta-Analytic Investigation of Their Effects on Employee Outcomes," *Journal of Applied Psychology* 98, no. 1 (2013), pp. 1–25.
154. Carolyn Shapiro, "More Companies Cover Benefits for Employees' Domestic Partners," *KnightRidder/Tribune Business News*, July 20, 2003.
155. http://articles.washingtonpost.com/2013-06-26/politics/40195683_1_gay-couples-edith-windsor-doma, accessed August 1, 2013.
156. "FMLA Protection Extends to Gay Spouses as BOOL Updates Policies Following Windsor," *Bloomberg BNA Bulletin to Management*, August 20, 2013, p. 265.
157. www.cnn.com/2015/06/26/politics/supreme-court-same-sex-marriage-ruling/index.html; www.nytimes.com/2015/06/27/us/supreme-court-same-sex-marriage.html?_r=0, both accessed July 15, 2015.
158. Mangalindan, "A Healthier, More Rewarding Workplace."
159. "Couples Want Flexible Leave, Benefits," *BNA Bulletin to Management*, February 19, 1998, p. 53; SHRM, "2003 Benefits Survey," p. 14. See also Paul Harris, "Flexible Work Policies Mean Business," *Training & Development*, April 2007, pp. 32–36.
160. Carolyn Hirshman, "Kinder, Simpler Cafeteria Rules," *HR Magazine*, January 2001, pp. 74–79.
161. "Employers Should Update Cafeteria Plans Now Based on Proposed Regs, Experts Say," *BNA Bulletin to Management*, September 4, 2007, pp. 281–282.
162. "Debit Cards for Health-Care Expenses Receive Increased Employer Attention," *BNA Bulletin to Management*, September 25, 2003, p. 305.
163. Martocchio, *Strategic Compensation*, p. 263.
164. Bill Roberts, "Good Vendor Relations," *HR Magazine*, September 2011, p. 110.
165. Ibid.
166. Elka Maria Torpey, "Flexible Work: Adjusting the When and Where of Your Job," *Occupational Outlook Quarterly*, Summer 2007, pp. 14–27.
167. "Slightly More Workers Are Skirting 9–5 Tradition," *BNA Bulletin to Management*, June 20, 2002, p. 197.
168. The percentage of employers with flextime programs actually dropped from 2007 to 2011, from 58% to 53%. Joseph Coombs, "Flexibility Still Meeting Resistance," *HR Magazine*, July 2011, p. 72.
169. Dori Meinert, "Make Telecommuting Pay Off," *HR Magazine*, June 2011, pp. 33–37. See also Donna Dennis et al., "Effective Leadership in a Virtual Workforce," *Training & Development*, February 2013, pp. 47–49.
170. "Telework Among Full-Time Employees Almost Doubled in the Last Decade, Study Says," *BNA Bulletin to Management*, June 12, 2012, p. 187.
171. "13.4 Million Work from Home in 2010, Census Bureau Reports," *BNA Bulletin to Management*, October 16, 2012, p. 330.
172. Martha White, "One Part Gone: Yahoo Says No to Telecommuting," www.CNBC.com/ID/100492123, accessed February 25, 2013.
173. Dori Meinert, "Make Telecommuting Pay Off," *HR Magazine*, June 2011, pp. 33–37.
174. Ann Pomeroy, "The Future Is Now," *HR Magazine*, September 2007, pp. 46–52. See also "Telework Among Full-Time Employees Almost Doubled in the Last Decade, Study Says," *BNA Bulletin to Management*, June 12, 2012, p. 187.
175. See, for example, "Compressed Workweeks Gain Popularity, but Concerns Remain About Effectiveness," *BNA Bulletin to Management*, September 16, 2008, p. 297.
176. SHRM, "2003 Benefits Survey," p. 2.
177. "With Job Sharing Arrangements, Companies Can Get Two Employees for the Price of One," *BNA Bulletin to Management* 56, no. 47 (November 22, 2005), pp. 369–370.
178. Boris Baltes et al., "Flexible and Compressed Workweek Schedules: A Meta-Analysis of Their Effects on Work-Related Criteria," *Journal of Applied Psychology* 84, no. 4 (1999), pp. 496–513. See also Charlotte Hoff, "With Flextime, Less Can Be More," *Workforce Management*, May 2005, pp. 65–66.
179. http://articles.moneycentral.msn.com/Investing/Extra/CostcoTheAntiWalMart.aspx?page?1, accessed September 15, 2011; and, Hamilton Nolan, "The Anti-Wal-Mart," http://gawker.com/costco-the-anti-wal-mart-511739135, accessed August 7, 2013.
180. Tavia Grant, "How One Company Levels the Pay Slope of Executives and Workers," *Globe and Mail*, November 16, 2013, www.the GlobeandMail.com/news/national, accessed April 1, 2014.
181. Stone, "Costco CEO Craig Jelinek Leads the Cheapest, Happiest Company in the World."
182. Kevin Short, "11 Reasons to Love Costco That Have Nothing to Do with Shopping," November 19, 2013, www.HuffingtonPost.com/2013/11/19/reasons-love-Costco, accessed April 1, 2014.
183. www.Costco.com/benefits.HTML, accessed April 1, 2014.
184. Ibid.
185. Ibid.
186. Garry Kranz, "Special Report on Employee Engagement Losing Lifeblood," *Workforce*, July 21, 2011, www.workforce.com/articles/special-report-on-employee-engagement-losing-lifeblood, accessed April 10, 2014.
187. http://articles.moneycentral.msn.com/Investing/Extra/CostcoThe AntiWalMart.aspx?page?1, accessed September 15, 2011; and Hamilton Nolan, "The Anti-Wal-Mart," http://gawker.com/costco-the-anti-wal-mart-511739135, accessed August 7, 2013.
188. Ibid. See also Brad Stone, "Costco CEO Craig Jelinek Leads the Cheapest, Happiest Company in the World," *Bloomberg BusinessWeek*, June 6, 2013, www.BusinessWeek.com/articles/2013-06-06/Costco-CEO-Craig-Jelinek-leads-the-cheapest-happiest-company-in-the-world, accessed March 31, 2014.
189. Ibid.

14

Building Positive Employee Relations

Qilai Shen/In Pictures/Corbis

LEARNING OBJECTIVES

14-1 Define *employee relations.*

14-2 Discuss at least four methods for managing employee relations.

14-3 Explain what is meant by ethical behavior.

14-4 Explain what is meant by fair disciplinary practices.

14-5 Answer the question, "How do companies become 'Best Companies to Work For'?"

After a worker uprising over pay and work rules at Apple Inc.'s Foxconn iPhone assembly plant in Shenzhen, China, Apple asked the plant's owner to have the Fair Labor Association (FLA) survey the plant's workers. The FLA found "tons of issues."[1] We'll see what they found and what Foxconn's management did to improve the situation.

WHERE ARE WE NOW ...

Although people tend to view recruitment, selection, appraisal, training, and compensation as the heart of human resource management, most employees expect something more. For example, they expect to be treated fairly, and to have a safe work environment. Now, in Part Five, we therefore turn to ethics, employee fairness, safety, and union relations. The main purpose of this chapter is to explain the building blocks of positive employee relations. Our topics include what is employee relations, managing employee relations, using human resource management tools to promote ethics and fair treatment, managing employee discipline, and developing employee engagement and great places to work for.

What Is Employee Relations?

LEARNING OBJECTIVE 14-1
Define *employee relations.*

employee relations
The activity that involves establishing and maintaining the positive employee–employer relationships that contribute to satisfactory productivity, motivation, morale, and discipline, and to maintaining a positive, productive, and cohesive work environment.

Anyone who has worked knows that some companies are better to work for than are others. Some companies we've touched on in this book—Wegmans, SAS, and Google, for instance—show up repeatedly on "Best Companies to Work For" lists, while others always seem to have labor problems and negative press. This common-sense observation reflects the fact that some companies do have better employee relations than do others.

Employee relations is the managerial activity that involves establishing and maintaining the positive employee–employer relationships that contribute to satisfactory productivity, motivation, morale, and discipline, and to maintaining a positive, productive, and cohesive work environment.[2] Whether you're recruiting employees, managing union organizing campaigns, asking employees to work overtime, or doing some other task, it obviously makes sense to have employees "on your side." Many employers therefore endeavor to build positive employee relations, on the sensible assumption that doing so beats building negative ones. Managing employee relations is usually assigned to HR, and is a topic that both the SHRM and HRCI exams address.

Employers can do many things to build positive employee relations. Some examples include providing good training, fair appraisals, and competitive pay and benefits (all of which we discussed in previous chapters). However, most employers also institute special "employee relations programs" to maintain positive employee relations. These include employee fair treatment programs, improving employee relations through improved communications, developing employee recognition/relations programs, and having fair and predictable disciplinary procedures.

Employee Relations Programs For Building And Maintaining Positive Employee Relations

LEARNING OBJECTIVE 14-2
Discuss at least four methods for managing employee relations.

We'll begin with how to ensure fair treatment.

Ensuring Fair Treatment

fair treatment
Reflects concrete actions, such as "employees are treated with respect," and "employees are treated fairly."

Anyone who has suffered unfair treatment at work knows it is demoralizing. Unfair treatment reduces morale, poisons trust, and negatively impacts employee relations and performance.[3] Employees of abusive supervisors are more likely to quit, and to report lower job and life satisfaction and higher stress.[4] The effects on employees of such abusiveness are particularly pronounced where the abusive supervisors seem to have support from higher-ups.[5] Even when someone just witnesses abusive supervision—for instance, seeing a coworker abused—it triggers adverse reactions including further unethical behavior.[6] At work, **fair treatment** reflects concrete actions such as "employees are treated with respect," and "employees are treated fairly" (see Figure 14-1).[7]

There are many reasons why managers should be fair. The golden rule is one obvious reason. What may not be so obvious is that unfairness can backfire on the company. For example, victims of unfairness exhibit more workplace deviance, such as theft and sabotage.[8] Victims of unfairness also suffer a range of ill effects including poor health, strain, and psychological conditions.[9] Unfairness leads to increased tensions between the employee and his or her family or partner.[10] Abusive supervisors undermine their subordinates' effectiveness and may prompt them to act destructively.[11] In terms of employee relations, employees' perceptions of fairness relate positively to enhanced employee commitment; enhanced satisfaction with the company, job, and leader; and enhanced organizational citizenship behaviors.[12]

The employer and the manager are responsible for ensuring that the employee is treated fairly and with respect (and that its employees treat each other respectfully).[13] Techniques for minimizing unfairness (discussed in previous chapters) include hire competent and well-balanced employees and supervisors, ensure equitable pay,

FIGURE 14-1 Perceptions of Fair Interpersonal Treatment Scale

Source: "The Perceptions of Their Interpersonal Treatment Scale: Development and Validation of a Measure of Interpersonal Treatment in the Workplace" by Michelle A. Donovan, from *Journal of Applied Psychology* 83, no. 5 (1998).

What is your organization like most of the time? Circle yes if the item describes your organization, No if it does not describe your organization, and ? if you cannot decide.

IN THIS ORGANIZATION:

1. Employees are praised for good work	Yes	?	No
2. Supervisors yell at employees (R)	Yes	?	No
3. Supervisors play favorites (R)	Yes	?	No
4. Employees are trusted	Yes	?	No
5. Employees' complaints are dealt with effectively	Yes	?	No
6. Employees are treated like children (R)	Yes	?	No
7. Employees are treated with respect	Yes	?	No
8. Employees' question and problems are responded to quickly	Yes	?	No
9. Employees are lied to (R)	Yes	?	No
10. Employees' suggestions are ignored (R)	Yes	?	No
11. Supervisors swear at employees (R)	Yes	?	No
12. Employees' hard work is appreciated	Yes	?	No
13. Supervisors threaten to fire or lay off employees (R)	Yes	?	No
14. Employees are treated fairly	Yes	?	No
15. Coworkers help each other out	Yes	?	No
16. Coworkers argue with each other (R)	Yes	?	No
17. Coworkers put each other down (R)	Yes	?	No
18. Coworkers treat each other with respect	Yes	?	No

Note: R = the item is reverse scored

institute fair performance appraisal systems, and have policies requiring fair treatment of all employees. Communications systems (such as periodic attitude surveys), and disciplinary appeals programs (both discussed later in this chapter) can also reduce unfairness.

procedural justice
Refers to just procedures in the allocation of rewards or discipline, in terms of the actual procedures being evenhanded and fair.

distributive justice
Refers to a system of distributing rewards and discipline in which the actual results or outcomes of are evenhanded and fair.

RESEARCH INSIGHT A study illustrates the effects of unfairness. College instructors first completed surveys concerning the extent to which they saw their colleges as treating them with *procedural* and *distributive* justice. (**Procedural justice** refers to justice in the allocation of rewards or discipline, in terms of the procedures being evenhanded and fair; **distributive justice** refers to a system for distributing rewards and discipline in which *the actual results* or outcomes are evenhanded and fair.) Procedural justice items included, for example, "In general, the department/college's procedures allow for requests for clarification or for additional information about a decision." Distributive justice items included, "I am fairly rewarded considering the responsibilities I have."

Then the instructors completed organizational commitment questionnaires, with items such as "I am proud to tell others that I am part of this department/college." Their students then completed surveys, with items such as "The instructor was sympathetic to my needs," and "The instructor treated me fairly."

The results were impressive. Instructors who perceived high distributive and procedural justice were more committed. Furthermore, these instructors' students reported higher levels of instructor effort, prosocial behaviors, and fairness, and had more positive reactions to their instructors.[14] So in this case, treating some professors badly backfired on the university. Treating others fairly produced improved employee commitment and results.

The accompanying Strategic Context feature shows how one employer in China improved the fairness with which it treated employees.

IMPROVING PERFORMANCE: *The Strategic Context*

A New HR Strategy at the Foxconn Plant in Shenzhen, China

social responsibility
Refers to the extent to which companies should and do channel resources toward improving one or more segments of society other than the firm's owners or stockholders.

The phrase *social responsibility* tends to trigger images of charitable contributions and helping the homeless, but it actually refers to much more. For example, it refers to the honesty of the company's ads; to the quality of the parts it builds into its products; and to the honesty, ethics, fairness, and "rightness" of its dealings with customers, suppliers, and, of course, employees. The basic question is always whether the company is serving all its constituencies (or "stakeholders") fairly and honestly. Corporate **social responsibility** thus refers to the extent to which companies should and do channel resources toward improving one or more segments of society other than the firm's owners or stockholders.[15]

A worker uprising at Apple's Foxconn iPhone assembly plant in Shenzhen, China, shows that workers around the globe want their employers to treat them in a fair and socially responsible manner.

Producing quality products as efficiently as possible was long the strategy at this plant. However, after the uprising over pay and work rules at the Foxconn plant, Apple asked the plant's owner to have the Fair Labor Association (FLA) survey the plant's workers. The FLA found "tons of issues."[16] For example, employees faced "overly strict" product-quality demands without adequate training: "Every job is tagged to time, there are targets on how many things must be completed within an hour," said Xie Xiaogang, 22, who worked at Foxconn's Shenzhen plant. "In this environment, many people cannot take it."[17] Heavy overtime work requirements and having to work through a holiday week were other examples.

To foster the improved behaviors that the plant's performance required, Hon Hai, the Foxconn plant's owner, tweaked its efficiency-first strategy and changed its plant human resource strategy and practices, for instance, by raising salaries and cutting mandatory overtime. Those changes were among 284 made at Foxconn after the audits uncovered violations of Chinese regulations.[18] The changes show that fair treatment is a global obligation. ■

Source: Based on Daniel Denison, Corporate Culture and Organizational Effectiveness, New York: Wiley, 1990, p. 155; "When the Jobs Inspector Calls," Economist, March 31, 2012, p. 73; Alexandra Ho and Tim Culpan, with assistance from Jun Yang in Seoul, Andrea Wong in Taipei, Tian Ying in Beijing, and Jasmine Wang in Hong Kong. "Foxconn Labor Disputes Disrupt IPhone Output for 2nd Time," Bloomberg News, October 8, 2012, www.bloomberg.com/news/ 2012-10-07/foxconn-labor-disputes-disrupt-iphone-output-for-2nd-time.html.

If your professor has assigned this, go to the Assignments section of **mymanagementlab.com** to complete this discussion question.

Talk About It 1: How would you explain the fact that workers in such diverse cultures as America and China seem to crave fair treatment?

Bullying and Victimization

Some workplace unfairness, such as bullying, is blatant. Bullying and victimization—singling out someone to harass and mistreat—is a serious problem. For example, one survey of 1,000 U.S. employees concluded that about 45% said they had worked for abusive bosses.[19] The U.S. government (www.stopbullying.gov) says most would agree that bullying involves three things:

- ***Imbalance of power.*** People who bully use their power to control or harm, and the people being bullied may have a hard time defending themselves.
- ***Intent to cause harm.*** Actions done by accident are not bullying; the person bullying has a goal to cause harm.
- ***Repetition.*** Incidents of bullying happen to the same person over and over by the same person or group, and that bullying can take many forms, such as:
  - ***Verbal:*** name-calling, teasing
  - ***Social:*** spreading rumors, leaving people out on purpose, breaking up friendships
  - ***Physical:*** hitting, punching, shoving
  - ***Cyberbullying:*** using the Internet, mobile phones, or other digital technologies to harm others

Undoubtedly, the perpetrator is to blame for bullying. However, how some people behave does make them more likely victims.[20] Those "more likely" include submissive victims (who seem more anxious, cautious, quiet, and sensitive), provocative victims (who show more aggressive behavior), and victims low in self-determination (who seem to leave it to others to make decisions for them). High performers can earn colleagues' envy and thus suffer victimization.[21] Building team cohesion through teambuilding training, social gatherings, and friendly inter-team competition can head off such envy and victimization.[22]

Beyond fairness, maintaining positive employee relations requires having special communications programs in place that let employees express their opinions, and let management know if there's a problem. We turn to these programs next.

Improving Employee Relations Through Communications Programs

Many employers use communications programs to bolster their employee relations efforts, on the reasonable assumption that employees feel better about their employers when they're "kept in the loop." Therefore, for example, one university's Web site says, "We believe in keeping our employees fully informed about our policies, procedures, practices and benefits."[23] This employer uses an *open-door policy* to encourage communication between employees and managers, an *employee handbook* covering basic employment information, and "the opportunity to keep abreast of University events and other information of interest through the *website, e-mail* and *hard copy memoranda*."[24]

Two-way communication also helps management know what's bothering employees. To paraphrase one writer, no one likes getting complaints, but soliciting complaints is vital for employers who want to short-circuit inequitable treatment and maintain positive employee relations.[25] Approaches may include hosting employee *focus groups*, making available *ombudsman* and *suggestion boxes*, and implementing telephone, messaging, and Web-based *hotlines*. (Some employers use hotline providers to manage their hotlines. A vendor sets up the hotlines for the employer; it also receives the employees' comments, and provides ongoing feedback to the employer about employees' concerns, as well as periodic summaries of comments and trends.) *Exit interviews*, discussed in an earlier chapter, provide another opportunity to sample the quality of one's employee relations.[26] Managers also use *open-door policies* and "management by walking around" to informally ask employees "how things are going."

USING ORGANIZATIONAL CLIMATE SURVEYS Similarly, employers use attitude, morale, or *climate surveys* to support employee relations efforts. They use the surveys to "take the pulse" of their employees' attitudes toward a variety of organizational issues including leadership, safety, role clarity, fairness, and pay, and to thereby get a sense of whether their employee relations need improvement. The dividing lines between attitude surveys, satisfaction or morale surveys, and climate surveys are somewhat arbitrary; several experts define **organizational climate** as the perceptions a company's employees share about the firm's psychological environment, for instance, in terms of things like concern for employees' well-being, supervisory behavior, flexibility, appreciation, ethics, empowerment, political behaviors, and rewards.[27]

organizational climate
The perceptions a company's employees share about the firm's psychological environment, for instance, in terms of things like concern for employees' well-being, supervisory behavior, flexibility, appreciation, ethics, empowerment, political behaviors, and rewards.

Many employers use online surveys from firms like Know Your Company (http://knowyourcompany.com), focusing on questions such as "Are you proud to work here?"[28] Google conducts an annual "Googlegeist" survey. This focuses not on engagement per se but on its markers such as willingness to leave.[29] Other surveys are available off the shelf. For instance, one SHRM sample survey has employees use a scale from 1 ("to a very little extent") to 5 ("to a very great extent") to answer survey questions. Questions include, "Overall, how satisfied are you with your supervisor?," "Overall, how satisfied are you with your job?," and "Does doing your job well lead to things like recognition and respect from those you work with?"[30]

Develop Employee Recognition/Relations Programs

Opportunities for two-way communications like these improve employee relations, but there are other employee relations programs. Most notable here are the employee recognition and award programs we touched on in Chapters 10 and 11, particularly formal company-wide programs such as employee-of-the-month awards. For example, one trade journal notes how the Murray Supply Co. held a special dinner for all its employees, at which it gave out special awards for things like safe driving, tenure with the company, and branch employee of the year.[31] As here, employers often distribute such awards with much fanfare at special events such as awards dinners. One SHRM survey found that 76% of organizations surveyed had such employee recognition programs, and another 5% planned to implement one soon.[32]

Instituting recognition and service award programs requires planning.[33] For example, instituting a *service award program* requires reviewing the tenure of existing employees and establishing meaningful award periods (1 year, 5 years, etc.). It also requires establishing a budget, selecting awards, having a procedure for monitoring what awards to actually award, having a process for giving awards (such as special dinners or staff meetings), and periodically assessing program success. Similarly, instituting a *recognition program* requires developing criteria for recognition (such as customer service, cost savings, etc.), creating forms and procedures for submitting and reviewing nominations, selecting meaningful recognition awards, and establishing a process for actually awarding the recognition awards.

Use Employee Involvement Programs

Employee relations also tend to improve when employees become involved with the company in positive ways, and so *employee involvement* is another useful employee relations strategy.

Employers encourage employee involvement in various ways. Some organize focus groups. A *focus group* is a small sample of employees who are presented with a specific question or issue and who interactively express their opinions and attitudes on that issue with the group's assigned facilitator.

TRENDS SHAPING HR: *DIGITAL AND SOCIAL MEDIA*

Many employers use *social media* such as the pinboard-style photo-sharing Web site Pinterest to encourage involvement.[34] One survey found that just over half of employers use social media tools to communicate with employees and to help develop a sense of community.[35] For example, Red Door Interactive used a Pinterest-based project it called "San Diego Office Inspiration." This encouraged employees to contribute interior design and decor ideas for its new offices.[36] ■

suggestion teams
Temporary teams whose members work on specific analytical assignments, such as how to cut costs or raise productivity.

problem-solving teams
Teams that identify and research work processes and develop solutions to work-related problems.

quality circle
A special type of formal problem-solving team, usually composed of 6 to 12 specially trained employees who meet once a week to solve problems affecting their work area.

self-managing/self-directed work team
A small (usually 8 to 10 members) group of carefully selected, trained, and empowered employees who basically run themselves with little or no outside supervision, usually for the purpose of accomplishing a specific task or mission.

USING EMPLOYEE INVOLVEMENT TEAMS Employers also use special teams to gain employees' involvement. **Suggestion teams** are temporary teams whose members work on specific analytical assignments, such as how to cut costs or raise productivity. One airline split employees (such as baggage handlers and ground crew) into separate teams, linking team members via its Web site for brainstorming and voting on ideas.[37] Some employers formalize this process by appointing semipermanent **problem-solving teams**. These identify and research work processes and develop solutions to work-related problems.[38] They usually consist of the supervisor and five to eight employees from a common work area.[39]

A **quality circle** is a type of formal problem-solving team, usually composed of 6 to 12 specially trained employees who meet weekly to solve problems affecting their work area.[40] The team gets training in problem-analysis techniques (including basic statistics). Then it applies these techniques to solve problems in its work area.[41]

In many facilities, specially trained teams of self-managing employees do their jobs with little or no oversight from supervisory personnel. A **self-managing/self-directed work team** is a small (usually 8 to 10 members) group of carefully selected, trained, and empowered employees who basically run themselves with little or no outside supervision, usually for the purpose of accomplishing a specific task or mission.[42] The task or mission might be an auto dashboard installed or a fully processed insurance claim. For example, the GE aircraft engine plant in Durham, North Carolina, is a self-managing team-based facility. Employees work in teams, all of which report to the factory manager.[43] In such teams, employees "train one another, formulate and track their own budgets, make capital investment proposals as needed, handle quality control and inspection, develop their own quantitative standards, improve every process and product, and create prototypes of possible new products."[44]

USING SUGGESTION SYSTEMS Most employers understand that employee suggestions can produce significant savings (and, through involvement and rewards, improved employee relations). For example, one study several years ago of 47 companies concluded that the firms had saved more than $624 million in one year from their suggestion programs; more than 250,000 suggestions were submitted, of which employers adopted over 93,000 ideas.[45] Furthermore, employees like these programs. In one survey, 54% of the 497 employees surveyed said they made more than 20 suggestions per year, while another 24% said they made between 10 and 20 suggestions per year.[46] The accompanying HR as a Profit Center feature provides an example.

IMPROVING PERFORMANCE: *HR As A Profit Center*

The Cost-Effective Suggestion System[47]

A Lockheed Martin unit in Oswego, New York, developed its "Cost-Effectiveness Plus" suggestion program to encourage and recognize employees for streamlining processes. With the Cost-Effectiveness Plus program, employees electronically submit their ideas. These are then evaluated and approved by the local manager and the program's coordinator (and by higher management when necessary). This program reportedly saves this facility about $77,000 per implemented idea, or more than $100 million each year.

Today's suggestion systems are more sophisticated than the "suggestion boxes" of years ago.[48] The main improvements are in how the manager formalizes and communicates the suggestion process. The head of one company that designs and installs suggestion systems for employers lists the essential elements of an effective employee suggestion system as follows:[49]

- ✓ Senior staff support
- ✓ A simple, easy process for submitting suggestions
- ✓ A strong process for evaluating and implementing suggestions
- ✓ An effective program for publicizing and communicating the program
- ✓ A program focus on key organizational goals ■

Source: Based on Wells, "From Ideas to Results", HR Magazine.

If your professor has assigned this, go to the Assignments section of **mymanagementlab.com** to complete this discussion.

Talk About It 2: Based on this, write a one-page outline describing an employee suggestion system for a small department store.

LEARNING OBJECTIVE 14-3

Explain what is meant by ethical behavior.

The Ethical Organization

People face ethical choices every day. Is it wrong to use a company credit card for personal purchases? Is a $50 gift to a client unacceptable? Compare your answers by doing the quiz in Figure 14-2.

Most everyone reading this book rightfully views themselves as ethical people, so why include ethics in a human resource management book? For three reasons: First, ethics is not theoretical. Instead, it greases the wheels that make businesses work. Managers who promise raises but don't deliver, salespeople who say "The order's coming" when it's not, production managers who take kickbacks from suppliers—they all corrode the trust that day-to-day business transactions depend on.

Second, it is hard to even imagine an *un*ethical company with good employee relations.

Third, ethical dilemmas are part of human resource management. For example, your team shouldn't start work on the new machine until all the safety measures are checked, but your boss is pressing you start: What should you do? One survey found that 6 of the 10 most serious ethical work issues—workplace safety, employee records security, employee theft, affirmative action, comparable work, and employee privacy rights—were HR-related.[50] Another found that 54% of human resource professionals surveyed had observed misconduct ranging from violations of Title VII to violations of the Occupational Safety and Health Act.[51]

The spread of technology into the workshop has raised a variety of new ethical questions and many old ones still linger. Compare your answers with those of other Americans surveyed, on page 475.

Office Technology

1. Is it wrong to use company e-mail for personal reasons?
   ☐ Yes ☐ No
2. Is it wrong to use office equipment to help your children or spouse do schoolwork?
   ☐ Yes ☐ No
3. Is it wrong to play computer games on office equipment during the workday?
   ☐ Yes ☐ No
4. Is it wrong to use office equipment to do Internet shopping?
   ☐ Yes ☐ No
5. Is it unethical to blame an error you made on a technological glitch?
   ☐ Yes ☐ No
6. Is it unethical to visit pornographic Web sites using office equipment?
   ☐ Yes ☐ No

Gifts and Entertainment

7. What's the value at which a gift from a supplier or client becomes troubling?
   ☐ $25 ☐ $50 ☐ $100
8. Is a $50 gift to a boss unacceptable?
   ☐ Yes ☐ No
9. Is a $50 gift *from* the boss unacceptable?
   ☐ Yes ☐ No
10. Of gifts from suppliers: Is it OK to take a $200 pair of football tickets?
    ☐ Yes ☐ No
11. Is it OK to take a $120 pair of theater tickets?
    ☐ Yes ☐ No
12. Is it OK to take a $100 holiday food basket?
    ☐ Yes ☐ No
13. Is it OK to take a $25 gift certificate?
    ☐ Yes ☐ No
14. Can you accept a $75 prize won at a raffle at a supplier's conference?
    ☐ Yes ☐ No

Truth and Lies

15. Due to on-the-job pressure, have you ever abused or lied about sick days?
    ☐ Yes ☐ No
16. Due to on-the-job pressure, have you ever taken credit for someone else's work or idea?
    ☐ Yes ☐ No

FIGURE 14-2 The *Wall Street Journal* Workplace Ethics Quiz

Source: Ethics and Compliance Officer Association, Waltham, MA, and the Ethical Leadership Group, Global Compliance's Expert Advisors, Wilmette, IL. (printed in the *Wall Street Journal,* October 21, 1999, pp. B1–B4). © 1999 by Ethics and Compliance Officer Association. Reprinted by permission. All rights reserved.

ethics
The study of standards of conduct and moral judgment; also the standards of right conduct.

Ethics are "the principles of conduct governing an individual or a group"—the principles people use to decide what their conduct should be.[52] Of course, not all conduct involves ethics.[53] For example, buying an iPad usually isn't an ethical decision. Instead, ethical decisions are rooted in *morality*. Morality refers to society's accepted standards of behavior. To be more precise, morality (and therefore ethical decisions) always involves the most fundamental questions of what is right and wrong, such as stealing, murder, and how to treat other people.

Ethics and Employee Rights

Societies don't rely on employers' ethics or sense of fairness or morality to ensure that they do what's right. Societies also institute various laws and procedures for enforcing these laws. These laws lay out what employers can and cannot do, for instance, in terms of discriminating based on race. In so doing, these laws also carve out explicit rights for employees. For example, Title VII of the Civil Rights Act gives employees the right to bring legal charges against an employer who they believe discriminated against them due to race.

Protecting employee rights is thus part and parcel of all the employment laws we discuss in this book. As just a few examples, the National Labor Relations Act established the right of employees to engage in collective bargaining. And, the Fair Labor Standards Act gave employees the right to a minimum wage and overtime pay. The bottom line is that although ethics, fairness, and morality help govern how employers treat their employees, the enforceable rights embedded in employment law also govern what employers and employees can do.

What Shapes Ethical Behavior at Work?

Why do people do bad things? It's complicated. However, one review of over 30 years of ethics research concluded that three factors combine to determine the ethical choices we make.[54] The authors titled their paper "Bad Apples, Bad Cases, and Bad Barrels." This title highlighted their conclusion that when

> "Bad apples" (people who are inclined to make unethical choices), must deal with "Bad cases" (ethical situations that are ripe for unethical choices), while working in "Bad barrels" (company environments that foster or condone unethical choices), … then people tend to act unethically.

Here's a closer look at what they found.

The Person (What Makes Bad Apples?)

First, because people bring to their jobs their own ideas of what is morally right and wrong, each person must shoulder much of the credit (or blame) for his or her ethical choices.

For example, researchers surveyed CEOs to study the CEOs' intentions to engage in two questionable practices: soliciting a competitor's technological secrets, and making illegal payments to foreign officials. The researchers concluded that the CEOs' personal predispositions more strongly affected their decisions than did outside pressures or characteristics of their firms.[55] The most principled people, with the highest level of "cognitive moral development," think through the implications of their decisions and apply ethical principles. How would you rate your own ethics? Figure 14-2 (page 457) presented a short self-assessment survey (you'll find typical survey takers' answers on page 475).

Which Ethical Situations Make for Ethically Dangerous Situations (Bad Cases)?

But, it's not just the person but the situation that's important. For example, the researchers found that "smaller" ethical dilemmas prompt more bad choices. What determines "small"? Basically, how much harm can befall victims of the choice, or the number of people potentially affected. People seemed more likely to "do the wrong thing" in "less serious" situations, in other words. That obviously doesn't mean that some people don't do bad things when huge consequences are involved; it just means that people cut more ethical corners on small things. The problem is that one thing leads to another; people start by doing small bad things and then "graduate" to larger ones.[56] And employees who worry about being excluded from a group may support the group's unethical behavior to stay in the group, compounding a bad situation.[57]

What Are the "Bad Barrels"?—The Outside Factors That Mold Ethical Choices

Finally, the study found that some companies produce more poisonous social environments (outside factors or "barrels") than do others; these bad environments in turn foster unethical choices.[58] For example, companies that promoted an "everyone for him- or herself" culture were more likely to suffer more unethical choices. Those that encouraged employees to consider the well-being of everyone had more ethical choices. Most importantly, companies whose managers put in place "a strong ethical culture that clearly communicates the range of acceptable and unacceptable behavior" suffered fewer unethical decisions.[59]

We can translate finding like these into the following specific steps managers can take to create more ethical environments.

How Managers Can Create More Ethical Environments

REDUCE JOB-RELATED PRESSURES If people did unethical things at work solely for personal gain or because they were "bad people," it perhaps would be understandable (though inexcusable). The scary thing is that it's often not personal interests but the pressures of the job. As one former executive said at his trial, "I took these actions, knowing they were wrong, in a misguided attempt to preserve the company to allow it to withstand what I believed were temporary financial difficulties."[60]

One study illustrates this. It asked employees to list their reasons for taking unethical actions at work.[61] For most of these employees, "meeting schedule pressures," "meeting overly aggressive financial or business objectives," and "helping the company survive" were the three top causes. "Advancing my own career or financial interests" ranked about last.[62] In any case, reducing such "outside" pressures helps head off ethical lapses.

"WALK THE TALK" It's hard to resist even subtle pressure from one's boss. So it's not surprising that in one report, "the level of misconduct at work dropped dramatically when employees said their supervisors exhibited ethical behavior."[63] Examples of how supervisors lead subordinates astray ethically include:

- Tell staffers to do whatever is necessary to achieve results.
- Overload top performers to ensure that work gets done.
- Look the other way when wrong doing occurs.
- Take credit for others' work or shift blame.[64]

Managers therefore have to walk the talk—not just talk ethics but behave ethically. Here some managers urge employees to apply a quick "ethics test" to evaluate whether what they're about to do fits the company's code of conduct. For example, Raytheon Co. asks employees who face ethical dilemmas to ask:

Is the action legal?
Is it right?
Who will be affected?
Does it fit Raytheon's values?
How will it "feel" afterward?
How will it look in the newspaper?
Will it reflect poorly on the company?[65]

How Human Resource Managers Can Create More Ethical Environments

There are also steps the HR group can take.

INSTITUTE ETHICS POLICIES AND CODES Employers use ethics policies and codes to signal that their companies are serious about ethics. For example, IBM's code of ethics says, in part:

> Neither you nor any member of your family may, directly or through others, solicit or accept from anyone money, a gift, or any amenity that could influence or could reasonably give the appearance of influencing IBM's business relationship with that person or organization. If you or your family members receive a gift (including money), even if the gift was unsolicited, you must notify your manager and take appropriate measures, which may include returning or disposing of what you received.[66]

ENFORCE THE RULES Codifying such rules without enforcing them is futile. To paraphrase one study, managers' statements can reduce unethical behavior on the part of employees, but knowing that behavior is actually being monitored and enforced has the biggest impact.[67] *Ethics audits* address topics like conflicts of interest, giving and receiving gifts, employee discrimination, and access to company information.[68] One study found that fraud controls such as hotlines, surprise audits, fraud training for employees, and mandatory vacations can each reduce internal theft by around 50%.[69] More firms, such as Lockheed Martin Corp., also appoint chief ethics officers.[70]

ENCOURAGE WHISTLEBLOWERS Some companies encourage employees to use hotlines and other means to "blow the whistle" on the company when they discover fraud. In complying with the Dodd-Frank Act, the SEC established a whistleblower reward for people who report unethical corporate behavior to it.[71] It is also tracking possible incidents of retaliation against whistleblowers.[72]

> **Watch It!**
> What steps did an actual company take to tighten its ethics processes after confronting accusations of corporate misdeeds? If your professor has chosen to assign this, go to **www.mymanagementlab.com** to complete the video exercise titled *Global Ethics and Siemens*.

organizational culture
The characteristic values, traditions, and behaviors a company's employees share.

FOSTER THE RIGHT CULTURE[73] **Organizational culture** is the "characteristic values, traditions, and behaviors a company's employees share." A *value* is a basic belief about what is right or wrong, or about what you should or shouldn't do. ("Honesty is the best policy" would be a value.) Managing people and shaping their behavior depends on shaping the values they use as behavioral guides. For example, if management really believes "honesty is the best policy," the actions it takes should reflect this value. Managers therefore have to think through how to send the right signals to their employees—in other words, create the right culture. Doing so includes:

- ***Clarifying expectations.*** First, make clear what values you want subordinates to follow. For example, the IBM ethics statement shows the company takes ethics seriously.
- ***Using signs and symbols.*** *Symbolism*—what the manager actually does—ultimately does the most to create and sustain the company's culture. As we said earlier, managers need to "walk the talk." They can't say "don't falsify the financials" and then do so themselves.
- ***Providing physical support.*** The physical signs of the employer's values—its incentive plan, appraisal system, and disciplinary procedures, for instance—send strong signals regarding what employees should and should not do. For example, do the promotions employees get reward ethical behavior or penalize it?[74]

The accompanying HR Tools feature illustrates ethics management in small businesses.

IMPROVING PERFORMANCE: *HR Tools For Line Managers And Small Businesses*

Small Business Ethics

When people think of unethical corporate behavior, big companies come to mind, because they're usually in the headlines. Yet studies show that small and midsize enterprises are prone to the same unethical corporate behavior as big firms.

For example, one study of 20 small to midsize firms found that bribery, corrupt dealings, payoffs to local gangsters, and a general tone of dishonesty were all "business as usual" at many of these firms.[75] Some were clever about their corrupt dealings. When doing business abroad, one U.S. business tried to keep its hands clean by forming a "strategic alliance" with a local firm. The latter then did the dirty work, for example, handling the local bribes, while the U.S. firm's managers looked the other way.

There are several reasons why smaller firms should be particularly alert to unethical behavior. Small firms don't have the resources for ethics officers, ethics hotlines, or the ethics training that big firms have. Furthermore, having an unethical accountant in a billion-dollar firm embezzle $10 million is a nuisance. Having the sales manager of a $10 million firm walk off with $1 million cash could be the end.

Small business owners can take several steps to establish a useful ethics program. First, *size up your company's current ethics-related activities.*[76] Even a self-audit based on guidelines like those in this chapter (the availability of an ethics code, ethics training, internal controls to monitor ethical behavior, and so on) can be worthwhile. Second, *create a code of conduct (Googling "code of conduct" will reveal thousands of examples)*, and make it clear that you take it seriously. Third, *train your people*. Training needn't be complicated. For example, one expert suggests having your managers develop scenarios, relevant to your business, illustrating which behaviors are ethical and which are not; then meet to discuss these. Fourth, make it easier to *solicit feedback* from your employees, so that they can more easily report suspicions of unethical behavior. ("Open door" polices and anonymous suggestion boxes are examples.) And, perhaps most importantly, *walk the talk*. In a small business, the owner is so visible that employees will take their ethical signals from him or her. ■

If your professor has assigned this, go to the Assignments section of **mymanagementlab.com** to complete this discussion.

Talk About It 3: Create a 50-word ethics code for a small business. Then, explain how the owner might use an ethics code to help avoid mistreatment of employees.

HIRE RIGHT As one writer says, "The simplest way to tune up an organization, ethically speaking, is to hire more ethical people."[77] Start by using recruitment materials that emphasize your firm's commitment to honest dealings and ethics. Then use screening tools like honesty tests, background checks, and interview questions (such as "Have you ever observed someone stretching the rules at work? What did you do about it?") to screen out problematical people.[78] Finally, treat job applicants fairly. "If prospective employees perceive that the hiring process does not treat people fairly, they may assume that ethical behavior is not important in the company."[79] Here, keep several things in mind:

- Applicants tend to view the *formal procedure* (such as the interview) as fair to the extent that it tests job-related criteria and provides an opportunity to demonstrate competence.
- Applicants expect respect. *Interpersonal treatment* reflects such things as the propriety of the questions, the politeness of interviewer, and the degree of two-way communication.
- Applicants see a selection system as fair to the extent that the employer provides *useful feedback* about the employee's or candidate's own performance.[80]

USE ETHICS TRAINING Ethics training usually involves showing employees how to recognize ethical dilemmas, how to apply codes of conduct to resolve problems, and how to use personnel activities like disciplinary practices in ethical ways.[81] The training should emphasize the moral underpinnings of the ethical choice and the company's deep commitment to integrity and ethics. Include participation by top managers in the program to emphasize that commitment.[82]

Ethics training is basically mandatory. Since 1991, federal sentencing guidelines have prescribed reduced penalties for employers accused of misconduct who implement codes of conduct and ethics training.[83] The Sarbanes-Oxley Act of 2002 makes ethics training even more important.

Ethics training is often Internet-based. Online ethics training tools include *Business Ethics for Managers* from SkillSoft (www.skillsoft.com).[84] Lockheed Martin's 160,000 employees take ethics and legal compliance training via the firm's intranet. Lockheed's online ethics program software also keeps track of how well the company and its employees are doing in terms of maintaining high ethical standards.[85] Some employers are switching from packaged ethics training to more company-relevant customized programs. For example, Yahoo! had a vendor produce an animated package containing ethical scenarios set in Yahoo! company offices around the world. The 45-minute program covers Yahoo!'s code of conduct as well as issues like the Foreign Corrupt Practices Act.[86]

USE REWARDS AND DISCIPLINE Employees expect you to punish unethical conduct and to reward ethical conduct.[87] The employer should discipline executives, not just underlings, who misbehave.[88]

INSTITUTE EMPLOYEE PRIVACY POLICIES[89] Most employees probably view invasions of their privacy by their employers as unethical. At work, employee privacy violations include *intrusion* (such as locker room and e-mail surveillance), *publication* of private matters, *disclosure* of medical records, and *appropriation* of an employee's name or likeness for commercial purposes.[90] In practice, background checks, monitoring off-duty conduct and lifestyle, drug testing, workplace searches, and workplace monitoring trigger most privacy violations.[91]

KNOW YOUR EMPLOYMENT LAW

Electronic Monitoring

Electronic Communications Privacy Act (ECPA)
The ECPA is a federal law intended to help restrict interception and monitoring of oral and wire communications.

What can the employer do to balance privacy concerns with its need to protect itself? There are two main restrictions on workplace monitoring: the **Electronic Communications Privacy Act (ECPA)**, and *common-law protections* against invasion of privacy (protections that have evolved from court decisions, for instance, decisions against defaming employees by publicizing highly personal matters about them without their permission). The ECPA is a federal law intended to help restrict interception and monitoring of oral and wire communications. It contains two exceptions. The "business purpose exception" permits employers to monitor communications if they can show a legitimate business reason for doing so. The second, "consent exception," lets employers monitor communications if they have their employees' consent to do so.[92]

Electronic eavesdropping is thus legal—up to a point. For example, federal law and most state laws allow employers to monitor employees' phone calls in the ordinary course of business. However, they must stop listening when it becomes clear the conversation is personal. You can also intercept e-mail to protect the property rights of the e-mail provider. However, court cases suggest employers may have fewer rights to monitor e-mail than previously assumed.[93]

More employers are using iris scanning to verify employee identity.

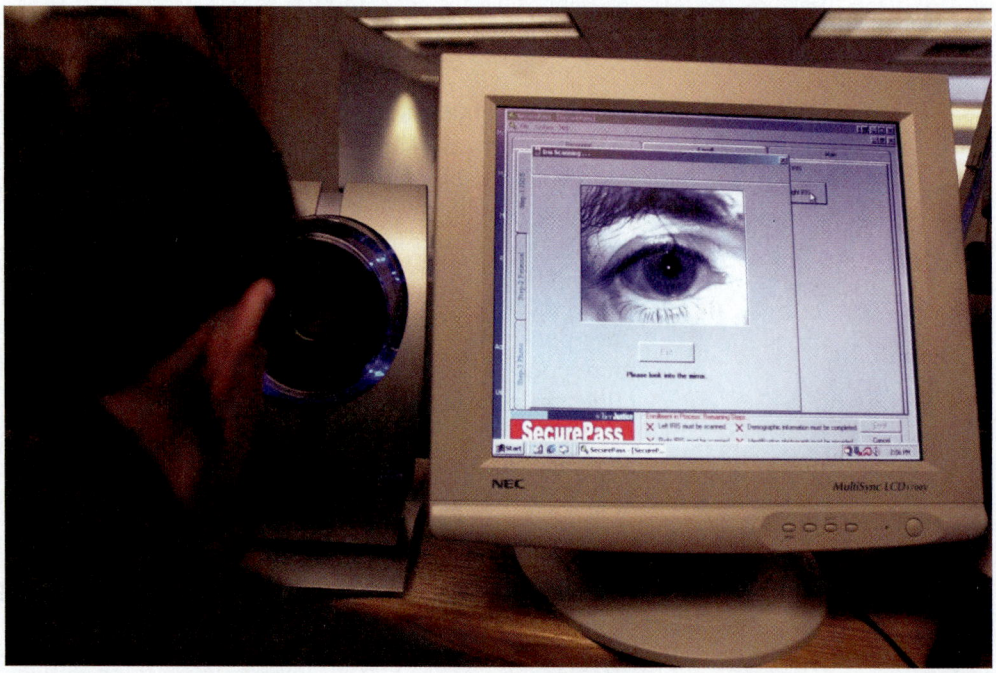

Jacob Silberberg/Stringer/Getty Images

To be safe, employers issue e-mail and online service usage policies, which warn employees that those systems should be used for business only. Employers also have employees sign e-mail and telephone monitoring acknowledgment statements like that in Figure 14-3. Many employees probably assume that their communications using the corporate e-mail system are open to review, but that e-mails they send via the employer's system but using personal e-mail accounts such as Gmail aren't. However, that's not necessarily true. An attorney should review the company's e-mail policy, but, at a minimum, make it clear that employees should have no expectation of privacy in their e-mail and Internet usage.[94] Also emphasize that all messages sent and received on the employer's e-mail system are company property and not confidential.[95]

Videotaped workplace monitoring requires more caution. Continuous video surveillance of employees in an office setting may not be a problem. But a Boston employer had to pay over $200,000 to five workers it secretly videotaped in an employee locker room, after they sued.[96] ■

In one survey 41% of employers with more than 20,000 employees had someone reading employee e-mails.[97] Ninety-six percent block access to adult Web sites, 61% to game sites.[98] Some check employees' personal blogs or Facebook sites to see if they're publicizing work-related matters.[99]

TRENDS SHAPING HR: *DIGITAL AND SOCIAL MEDIA*

Monitoring reflects in part a proliferation of online and smart devices and social media tools.[100] For example, a New Jersey court found one employer liable when one of its employees used his company computer at work to distribute child pornography.[101] Security is another problem: One "4-gigabyte MP3 player, such as the first generation of iPod Mini … can take home a lot of corporate data," said one employer (a process some graphically describe as "podslurping").[102] And, increasingly, disgruntled employees are using their companies' cloud services to hack into and undermine their employers' computer systems.[103]

Monitoring today therefore goes far beyond listening in on phone lines. New York's Bronx Lebanon Hospital uses biometric scanners to ensure that employees who clock in really are who they say they are.[104] Iris scanning tends to be the most accurate authorization device. Some organizations like the Federal Aviation Administration use it to control employees' access to their network information systems.[105] UPS uses GPS to monitor their drivers' whereabouts—and therefore productivity.[106] One restaurant in Dallas digitally monitors most everything waiters do, for instance, tracking every ticket, dish, and drink that they process.[107] This not only makes it easier to track employee theft, but also helps identify exceptionally conscientious waiters. To keep productivity up, the British grocery chain Tesco has some

FIGURE 14-3 Sample E-Mail Monitoring Acknowledgment Statement

I understand that XYZ Company periodically monitors any e-mail communications created, sent, or retrieved using this company's e-mail system. Therefore, I understand that my e-mail communications may be read by individuals other than the intended recipient. I also understand that XYZ Company periodically monitors telephone communications, for example to improve customer service quality.

Signature _____ Date _____

Print Name _____ Department _____

distribution center employees wear "Motorola arm-mounted terminals" (armbands) that keep track of how quickly employees are unloading and scanning goods.[108]

Such monitoring, as we said, raises privacy issues.[109] The dilemma is that it can also boost profits. For example, employers routinely use software to monitor (usually secretly) what their employees are doing online. When one employer noticed high employee overtime claims, they installed new software, and discovered many employees spent hours each day shopping online instead of working.

Physicians often say that "every medicine contains a little poison," since anything, even aspirin, becomes dangerous if misused. For employers, the dilemma is to obtain the profit advantages of monitoring, while minimizing the ethical and privacy issues that it raises. ■

If your professor has assigned this, go to the Assignments section of **mymanagementlab.com** to complete these discussion questions.

Talk About It 4: How would you feel if your employer told you to wear an armband monitor? Why? How would you react?

Managing Employee Discipline

LEARNING OBJECTIVE 14-4

Explain what is meant by fair disciplinary practices.

The purpose of *discipline* is to encourage employees to behave sensibly at work (where *sensible* means adhering to rules and regulations). Discipline is necessary when an employee violates a rule.[110]

Proper disciplinary procedures are important for several reasons. For one thing, positive employee relations requires trust, and few personnel actions will undermine trust as will arbitrary discipline. Legal concerns are another reason. One study surveyed 45 published arbitration awards in which tardiness had triggered discipline and/or discharge. When arbitrators overturned employers' decisions, it was usually because of inadequate disciplinary procedures—for example, the employer had failed to clarify what "tardy" meant. Unfair disciplinary procedures can backfire in other ways. For example, unfair discipline can trigger retaliatory employee misbehavior. And, of course, it is hard to be seen as ethical when disciplinary actions are unfair.[111]

The Three Pillars of Fair Discipline

Disciplining employees is often unavoidable, but any such discipline should be rooted in the need to be fair. The manager builds a fair discipline process on three pillars: rules and regulations, a system of progressive penalties, and an appeals process.[112]

RULES AND REGULATIONS An acceptable disciplinary process begins with a set of clear disciplinary rules and regulations. The rules should cover problems such as theft, destruction of company property, drinking on the job, and insubordination. Examples of rules include:

Poor performance is not acceptable. Each employee is expected to perform his or her work properly and efficiently and to meet established standards of quality.

Alcohol and drugs do not mix with work. The use of either during working hours and reporting for work under the influence of either are both strictly prohibited.

The purpose of the rules is to inform employees ahead of time what is and is not acceptable behavior. Tell employees, preferably in writing, what is not permitted. The employee orientation handbook should contain the rules and regulations.

PENALTIES A system of progressive penalties is the second pillar of effective discipline. The severity of the penalty usually depends on the offense and the number of times it has occurred. For example, most companies issue warnings for the first unexcused lateness. However, for a fourth offense, discharge is the usual disciplinary action.

APPEALS PROCESS Third, an appeals process should be part of the disciplinary process. The aim here is to ensure that supervisors mete out discipline fairly. FedEx's *guaranteed fair treatment* multistep program illustrates this. We'll look at it in a moment.

An appeals process is essential but is no panacea. The employer can sometimes mitigate the effects of unfair discipline by catching it during an appeal. However, some supervisory behavior may be impossible to overcome. For example, behaviors that attack the employee's personal and/or social identity are difficult to remedy.[113]

Diversity Counts

COMPARING MALES AND FEMALES IN A DISCIPLINE SITUATION What several researchers sadly call the "Evil Woman Thesis" argues that when a woman doesn't act the way other men and women expect she should act, they tend to treat her more harshly than they might if a man acted unexpectedly.[114]

While such a thesis might seem preposterous, the research seems to support it. In one study, 360 graduate and undergraduate business school students reviewed a labor arbitration case. The case involved two employees, one male and one female, with similar work records and tenure with their employers. Both were discharged for violation of company rules related to alcohol and drugs. The case portrays one worker's behavior as a more serious breach of company rules: The more culpable worker (a male in half the study and a female in the other half) had brought the intoxicant to work. The students had to express their agreement with two alternative approaches (tough or not-so-tough) to settling the dispute that arose after the discharge.

The researchers found bias against the female "employee" by both the male and female students. Both the male and female students recommended harsher treatment for the "culpable" female employee in the case than they did for the "culpable" man. As the researchers conclude, "women, as decision makers, appear to be as willing as men to impose harsher discipline on women than upon men." ■

How to Discipline an Employee

Even if you're a manager in a *Fortune* 500 company, you may find yourself without company guidelines when you have to discipline an employee for violating company rules. An error could trigger a costly appeal, or even litigation. To help head off errors, fair discipline guidelines would include:[115]

- Make sure the evidence supports the charge of employee wrongdoing.
- Make sure to protect the employees' due process rights.[116] For example, did the person have a chance to defend himself or herself?
- Adequately warn the employee of the disciplinary consequences of his or her alleged misconduct. Have the employee sign a form as in Figure 14-4
- The rule that allegedly was violated should be "reasonably related" to the efficient and safe operation of the particular work environment.
- Objectively investigate the matter before administering discipline.
- The investigation should produce substantial evidence of misconduct.
- Apply applicable rules, orders, or penalties *without discrimination*.
- Maintain the employee's right to counsel. For example, all union employees generally have the right to bring a representative to an interview that they reasonably believe might lead to disciplinary action.
- Don't rob your subordinate of his or her dignity, for instance by disciplining the person in public.
- Listen to what the person has to say.
- Remember that the burden of proof is on you. In U.S. society, a person is considered innocent until proven guilty.
- Get the facts. Don't base your decision on hearsay evidence or on your general impression.
- Don't act while angry.
- Adhere to your company's disciplinary appeals process.[117]

FIGURE 14-4 Report of Employee Discipline

Apex Telecommunications Corporation
Report of Disciplinary Action and Warning

Employee's Name_____
Employee's Department_____
Date of Misconduct_____ Today's Date_____

Description of Incident and misconduct (including witnesses, if any)_____

Witnesses to Incident_____

If the misconduct violated an Apex Co. policy or rule, state the policy or rule_____

Employee's explanation for misconduct, if any_____

Disciplinary action taken, if any_____

The employee was warned today that if misconduct such as this reoccurs at any time during the next_____ weeks, he or she may be subject to the following disciplinary action_____

Supervisor's signature Employee's signature

Print name Print name

Discipline Without Punishment

Traditional discipline processes have two main drawbacks. First, no one likes being punished. Second, punishment tends to gain short-term compliance, but not long-term cooperation.

Discipline without punishment (or alternative or nonpunitive discipline) aims to avoid these drawbacks by reducing the punitive nature of the discipline. Steps include:[118]

1. ***Issue an oral reminder for a first infraction.***
2. ***Should another incident arise within 6 weeks, issue a formal written reminder, and place a copy in the employee's personnel file.*** Also, hold a second private discussion with the employee.
3. ***Give a paid, one-day "decision-making leave."*** If another incident occurs in the next 6 weeks or so, tell the employee to take a 1-day leave with pay, and to consider whether he or she wants to abide by the company's rules. When the employee returns to work, he or she meets with you and gives you a decision.
4. ***If no further incidents occur in the next year or so, purge the 1-day paid suspension from the person's file.*** If the behavior is repeated, the next step is dismissal.

The process would not apply to exceptional circumstances. Criminal behavior or in-plant fighting might be grounds for immediate dismissal, for instance.

Employee Engagement Guide For Managers

LEARNING OBJECTIVE 14-5

Answer the question, "How do companies become 'Best Companies to Work For'?"

How Companies Become "Best Companies to Work For"

We began this chapter by noting that some companies are better to work for than are others, and we therefore focused on programs managers use to cultivate the positive employee relations that contribute to being a best place to work. This final section zeroes in on three companies that are known in part for actually being best places to work.

The "Best Companies to Work For"

Each year, several organizations publish "Best Companies to Work For" lists, the most notable of which is probably "Fortune Magazine's 100 Best Companies to Work For®."[119] Based on an extensive multinational survey of employees by the Great Place to Work® Institute (www.greatplacetowork.com), the survey seeks to identify the best companies to work for based on how the employees working in them actually feel about working there. The Great Place to Work Institute defines a great workplace "as one where employees trust the people they work for, have pride in the work they do, and enjoy the people they work with."[120] They say that the companies on their great companies list "have the highest levels of trust, strongest evidence of employee engagement and demonstrate the best applied management practices and programs" as defined by the institute's proprietary models.[121] We'll look at three recent "Fortune Magazine's 100 Best Companies to Work For"—SAS, Google, and FedEx.

SAS: Great Benefits, Trust, and Work-Life Balance

SAS, headquartered in Cary, North Carolina, is a leader in providing business analytics software and services to companies that include 90 of the top 100 companies on the *Fortune* global 500 list.[122] Founded in the 1970s, the company is privately owned and has long been known for the quality of its benefits and for the support it provides for its employees' work–life balance. It has annual revenues of over $2.3 billion, and a worldwide workforce of over 13,000 people, about half of whom work at the company's North Carolina campus.

When most people think about employee relations at SAS, the first thing that comes to mind is probably the company's employee benefits, which are extraordinary. They include (for example) 3 to 4 weeks per year company-paid vacations, paid sick days, flexible work schedules, 11 paid holidays, competitive pay, company-paid life insurance and accidental death and dismemberment insurance, retirement plans, an on-site recreation and fitness center, employee assistance programs, domestic partner benefits, and subsidized on-site child-care centers in Cary (eligibility is based on seniority).[123]

As impressive as these benefits are, they are in some respects just a symbol of SAS's approach to employee relations. While many employers talk about "putting their employees first," SAS has long put its money where its mouth is. For example, late in 2008, as the recession was gaining speed, most employers were laying off employees. SAS's founder and CEO, Dr. Jim Goodnight, held a special global webcast to announce to his employees that none of SAS's 13,000 worldwide employees would lose their jobs.[124] They have reportedly never laid off an employee.[125] SAS goes to great lengths to foster its employees' trust in other ways, for instance by giving them abundant freedom in the hours they work. They also have the Great Place to Work Institute independently survey SAS workers on important characteristics of trust including open communication, respect, career paths, and being treated as a human being.[126]

What does all this do for SAS? As one long-term employee put it, "I just can't imagine leaving SAS, and I felt that way for a very long time … if somebody offered to double my salary, I wouldn't even think about it."[127] Employee turnover, about 20% in software companies, is about 3% at SAS, which highlights another important facet of the SAS benefits programs.[128] One person who has studied SAS estimates that the lower turnover alone saves SAS $60 million to $80 million a year. As another example, letting employees visit on-campus health professionals (as SAS does) can cut hours out of the average employee's time away from work for doctors' visits.[129] And, of course, the effect on engagement, morale, and productivity may be priceless.

Google: Happiness and People Analytics

When Google founders Larry Page and Sergey Brin began building Google, they wanted to make it a great place to work, and in doing so, they turned to SAS. They met with SAS executives and sent a team there to better understand what made SAS consistently a "Best Company to Work For."[130]

It's therefore not surprising that Google is one of the few employers whose employee benefits equal or exceed those at SAS. In addition to things like health-care benefits and flexible work hours (and the possibility of making millions on stock options), its benefits include on-site dry cleaners, bowling alleys, cafés, transportation to and from campus, and nap pods.[131] As Google puts it, "It's all about removing barriers so Googlers can focus on the things they love, both inside and outside of work. We're constantly searching for unique ways to improve the health and happiness of our Googlers."[132]

Aside from the breadth and depth of its benefits, what sets Google apart is the scientific way it goes about deciding how to "improve the health and happiness" of Google employees. At Google, maintaining positive employee relations is highly analytical (one writer calls Google "The Happiness Machine."[133] Google calls its human resource department, "People Operations" (employees call it "POPS"). It has hired social scientists to create what they call the People & Innovation Lab, with a Google "people analytics team" charged with finding out how to make Googlers happy.[134] Google "monitors its employees well-being to a degree that can seem absurd to those who work outside [Google's headquarters in] Mountain View [California]."[135] The social scientists run little experiments, for instance, to determine if successful middle managers have certain skills, and what's the best way to remind people to contribute to their 401(k)s.[136] In one case, when the analytics team found that women staffers' turnover was too high, they concluded that new mothers were leaving at twice Google's average departure rate.[137] The study led to a redesigned maternity leave plan that includes 5 months off at full pay and full benefits. The new plan cut female Googler turnover in half.[138] To support its analytical approach, Google "solicits employee feedback on everything from how they prefer to be compensated, to the design of new bicycles used throughout the expansive headquarters campus."[139] So, it's little wonder why Googlers are happy.

FedEx: Guaranteed Fair Treatment

FedEx has been one of the "Fortune Magazine's 100 Best Companies to Work For" for 12 of the past 15 years. Several things—excellent benefits, competitive salaries, and (as we discussed in Chapter 5) a focus on promoting from within (as embodied by its Job Change Applicant Tracking System [JCATS]) help to explain this; however, it may be FedEx's emphasis on building trust through communications that most sets it apart.

SURVEY FEEDBACK ACTION (SFA) The FedEx survey feedback action (SFA) program is one example. SFA includes an anonymous survey that allows employees to express feelings about the company and their managers, and to some extent about service, pay, and benefits. Each manager then has an opportunity to use the results to help design a blueprint for improving workgroup engagement and commitment.[140]

SFA has three phases. First, the survey itself is a standard, anonymous questionnaire given each year to every employee. The questions are designed to gather information about what helps and hinders employees in their work environment. Sample items include: "I can tell my manager what I think" and "My manager tells me what was expected." A workgroup's survey results are compiled and sent anonymously to the manager.

The second phase is a feedback session between the manager and his or her workgroup. The goal here is to identify specific concerns or problems, examine causes for these problems, and devise action plans to correct the problems.

The feedback meeting should lead to a third, "action plan" phase. This produces a list of actions that the manager will take to address employees concerns and boost results. It includes: What is the concern? What's your analysis? What's the cause? and What should be done?

THE FEDEX GUARANTEED FAIR TREATMENT PROCESS FedEx's Guaranteed Fair Treatment Process (GFTP) is a sort of turbocharged grievance process. It goes beyond most grievance procedures in several ways, perhaps most notably in that an appeal can go all the way to FedEx's top executives. The effect is twofold: Complaints don't get a chance to accumulate; and all managers think twice before acting unfairly.[141] GFTP is available to all permanent FedEx employees. It covers concerns regarding matters such as disputed performance reviews, disciplinary actions, and terminations.[142]

Employees use Guaranteed Fair Treatment Process packets, available from the HR department, to file GFTP complaints. These include a fact sheet listing the complainant's name and work history; a GFTP tracking sheet to track the complaint at each step; management's rationale (for instance, in terms of applicable policies and procedures); a write-up from the HR department; space for key documents (termination letters, and so on); and space for backup information including witness statements. The employee must try to resolve the problem with his or her supervisor before filing a GFTP appeal.

GFTP contains three steps.[143] In step one, *management review*, the complainant submits a written complaint to a manager, senior manager, or managing director, within seven calendar days of the occurrence of the eligible issue. Then the manager, senior manager, and managing director of the employee's group review all relevant information; hold a telephone conference and/or meeting with the complainant; make a decision to either uphold, modify, or overturn management action; and communicate their decision in writing to the complainant.

If turned down in step one, then in step two, *officer complaint*, the complainant submits a written complaint to an officer (VP or senior vice president) of the division within 7 calendar days of the step one decision.

Finally (if necessary), in step three, *executive appeals review*, the complainant submits a written complaint within seven calendar days of the step two decision to the employee relations department. This department investigates and prepares a GFTP case file for the appeals board executive review. The appeals board—the CEO, the COO, the chief personnel officer, and senior vice presidents—then reviews all relevant information and makes a decision to either uphold, overturn, or initiate a board of review or to take other appropriate action; the appeals board's decision is final.

A "Best Company" Human Resource Philosophy?

SAS, Google, and FedEx are different from each other, and from other companies, and so there's no guarantee that what works for them will work for other firms. For example, SAS is privately owned. Its owners can therefore more easily absorb the short-term fluctuations in profits that great benefits and no layoffs engender than can most publicly traded companies. Google has grown fast through a series of smart strategic moves, and, when the economy turns down, its managers generally still have to focus more on retaining great employees than on laying them off. FedEx, still a "Best Company to Work For," has run into some labor relations problems recently, for instance, from drivers who don't want to be independent contractors.

However, there are several things that any manager intent on building positive employee relations can learn from studying any of these three companies. For example, their managers work hard to cultivate trust and to ensure—for instance, by monitoring employees' attitudes and by instituting open-door and guaranteed fair treatment–type grievance processes—that employees are treated fairly. And, in numerous ways (such as in their recognition programs, involvement programs, ethical standards, benefits, and climate surveys and other two-way communications programs), they all exhibit a deep and evident respect for their employees and to "putting employees first."

But perhaps the single most important thing a manager can glean from these three companies is the human resource philosophy on which they built their human resource management practices. In Chapter 1, we said that people's actions are always based in part on the basic assumptions they make, and that this is especially true in regard to human resource management. The basic assumptions you make about people—Can they be trusted? Do they dislike work? Why do they act as they do? How should they be treated?—together comprise your philosophy of human resource management. And every personnel decision you make—the people you hire, the training you provide, your leadership style, and the like—reflects (for better or worse) this basic philosophy.

One of the things molding your own philosophy is that of your organization's top management. While it may or may not be stated, it is usually communicated by their actions and permeates every level and department. Google's founders want their employees to be happy, and they've worked since Google's founding to make sure that they are. FedEx founder and CEO Frederick Smith is famous for (among many other things) his P-S-P mantra, namely that when you treat your People well they will provide great Service and Profits will follow.[144] Similarly, the founder and CEO of SAS has said, "We've worked hard to create a corporate culture that is based on trust between our employees and the company … a culture that rewards innovation, encourages employees to try new things and yet doesn't penalize them for taking chances, and a culture that cares about employees' personal and professional growth."[145] Such HR philosophies may well be the "magic sauce" that explains why great companies to work for are great.

Chapter Review

MyManagementLab® Go to **mymanagementlab.com** to complete the problems marked with this icon ✪.

Chapter Section Summaries

14-1. **Employee relations** is the activity that involves establishing and maintaining the positive employee–employer relationships that contribute to satisfactory productivity, motivation, morale, and discipline, and to maintaining a positive, productive, and cohesive work environment.

14-2. Managers and HR management use **programs to develop positive employee relations**. Unfair treatment reduces morale, increases stress, and has negative effects on employees and should be weeded out. Managers also use communications programs, recognition programs, and employee involvement programs to build positive employee relations.

14-3. **Ethics** refers to the principles of conduct governing an individual or a group, and specifically to the standards you use to decide what your conduct should be. Numerous factors shape ethical behavior at work. These include individual factors, organizational factors, the boss's influence, ethics policies and codes, and the organization's culture. HR management can influence ethical behavior. Having a fair and open selection process, establishing special ethics training programs, and rewarding (or disciplining) ethical (or unethical) work-related behavior are some examples.

14-4. A fair and just **discipline** process is based on rules and regulations, a system of progressive penalties, and an appeals process. A number of discipline guidelines are important, including discipline should be in line with the way management usually responds to similar incidents, management must adequately investigate the matter, and do not rob a subordinate of his or her dignity.

14-5. There are several things that any manager intent on building positive employee relations and **employee engagement** can draw from studying "Best Companies to Work For" such as SAS, Google, and FedEx. Their managers cultivate trust and ensure that employees are treated fairly. They all exhibit a deep and evident respect for their employees and to "putting employees first." Their human resource philosophy emphasizes trust, respect, and caring about their employees' personal and professional growth.

Discussion Questions

14-1. Explain how you would ensure fairness in disciplining, discussing particularly the prerequisites to disciplining, disciplining guidelines, and the discipline without punishment approach.

14-2. Why is it important in our litigious society to manage electronic monitoring properly?

14-3. Provide two examples of behaviors that would probably be unethical but legal, and three that would probably be illegal but ethical.

14-4. List 10 things your college or university does to encourage ethical behavior by students and/or faculty.

14-5. You need to select a nanny for your or a relative's child, and want someone ethical. What would you do to help ensure you ended up hiring someone ethical?

14-6. You believe your coworker is being bullied. How would you verify this, and what would you do about it if it is true?

14-7. Define *employee relations* and discuss at least four methods for managing it.

Individual and Group Activities

14-8. Working individually or in groups, interview managers or administrators at your employer or college in order to determine the extent to which the employer or college endeavors to build two-way communication, and the specific types of programs used. Do the managers think they are effective? What do the employees (or faculty members) think of the programs in use at the employer or college?

14-9. Working individually or in groups, obtain copies of the student handbook for your college and determine to what extent there is a formal process through which students can air grievances. Based on your contacts with other students, has it been an effective grievance process? Why or why not?

14-10. Working individually or in groups, determine the nature of the academic discipline process in your college. Do you think it is effective? Based on what you read in this chapter, would you recommend any modifications?

14-11. Appendices A and B at the end of this book (pages 612–629) list the knowledge someone studying for the HRCI (Appendix A) or SHRM (Appendix B) certification exam needs to have in each area of human resource management (such as in Strategic Management, and Workforce Planning). In groups of several students, do four things: (1) review Appendix A and/or B; (2) identify the material in this chapter that relates to the Appendix A and/or B required knowledge lists; (3) write four multiple-choice exam questions on this material that you believe would be suitable for inclusion in the HRCI exam and/or the SHRM exam; and, (4) if time permits, have someone from your team post your team's questions in front of the class, so that students in all teams can answer the exam questions created by the other teams.

14-12. In a research study at Ohio State University, a professor found that even honest people, left to their own devices, would steal from their employers.[146] In this study, the researchers gave financial services workers the opportunity to steal a small amount of money after participating in an after-work project for which the pay was inadequate. Would the employees steal to make up for the underpayment? In most cases, yes. Employees who scored low on an honesty test stole whether or not their office had an ethics program that said stealing from the company was illegal. Employees who scored high on the honesty test also stole, but only if their office did not have such an employee ethics program—the "honest" people didn't steal if there was an ethics policy.

Individually or in groups, answer these questions: Do you think findings like these are generalizable? In other words, would they apply across the board to employees in other types of companies and situations? If your answer is yes, what do you think this implies about the need for and wisdom of having an ethics program?

Experiential Exercise

Discipline or Not?

Purpose: The purpose of this exercise is to provide you with some experience in analyzing and handling an actual disciplinary action.

Required Understanding: Students should be thoroughly familiar with the facts of the following incident, titled "Botched Batch." **Do not read the "award" or "discussion" sections until after the groups have completed their deliberations.**

How to Set Up the Exercise/Instructions: Divide the class into groups of four or five students. Each group should take the arbitrator's point of view and assume that they are to analyze the case and make the arbitrator's decision. Review the case again at this point, but please do not read the award and discussion sections.

Each group should answer the following questions:

14-13. Based on what you read in this chapter, including all relevant guidelines, what would your decision be if you were the arbitrator? Why?

14-14. Do you think that after their experience in this arbitration the parties involved will be more or less inclined to settle grievances by themselves without resorting to arbitration?

Botched Batch

Facts: A computer department employee made an entry error that botched an entire run of computer reports. Efforts to rectify the situation produced a second set of improperly run reports. Because of the series of errors, the employer incurred extra costs of $2,400, plus a weekend of overtime work by other computer department staffers. Management suspended the employee for 3 days for negligence, and revoked a promotion for which the employee had previously been approved.

Protesting the discipline, the employee stressed that she had attempted to correct her error in the early stages of the run by notifying the manager of computer operations of her mistake. Maintaining that the resulting string of errors could have been avoided if the manager had followed up on her report and stopped the initial run, the employee argued that she had been treated unfairly because the manager had not been disciplined even though he compounded the problem, whereas she was severely punished. Moreover, citing her "impeccable" work record and management's acknowledgment that she had always been a "model employee," the employee insisted that the denial of her previously approved promotion was "unconscionable."

(*Please do* **not** *read beyond this point until after you have answered the two questions.*)

Award: The arbitrator upholds the 3-day suspension, but decides that the promotion should be restored.

Discussion: "There is no question," the arbitrator notes, that the employee's negligent act "set in motion the train of events that resulted in running two complete sets of reports reflecting improper information." Stressing that the employer incurred substantial cost because of the error, the arbitrator cites "unchallenged" testimony that management had commonly issued 3-day suspensions for similar infractions in the past. Thus, the arbitrator decides, the employer acted with just cause in meting out an "evenhanded" punishment for the negligence.

Turning to the denial of the already approved promotion, the arbitrator says that this action should be viewed "in the same light as a demotion for disciplinary reasons." In such cases, the arbitrator notes, management's decision normally is based on a pattern of unsatisfactory behavior, an employee's inability to perform, or similar grounds. Observing that management had never before reversed a promotion as part of a disciplinary action, the arbitrator says that by tacking on the denial of the promotion in this case, the employer substantially varied its disciplinary policy from its past practice. Because this action on management's part was not "evenhanded," the arbitrator rules, the promotion should be restored.[147]

Application Case

Enron, Ethics, and Organizational Culture

For many people, a company called Enron Corp. still ranks as one of history's classic examples of ethics run amok. During the 1990s and early 2000s, Enron was in the business of wholesaling natural gas and electricity. Enron made its money as the intermediary (wholesaler) between suppliers and customers. Without getting into all the details, the nature of Enron's business—and the fact that Enron didn't actually own the assets—meant that its profit statements and balance sheets listing the firm's assets and liabilities were unusually difficult to understand.

It turned out that the lack of accounting transparency enabled the company's managers to make Enron's financial performance look much better than it actually was. Outside experts began questioning Enron's financial statements in 2001. In fairly short order, Enron collapsed, and courts convicted several of its top executives of things like manipulating Enron's reported assets and profitability. Many investors (including former Enron employees) lost all or most of their investments in Enron. In Enron's case, this breakdown is perhaps more perplexing than usual. As one writer said,

> Enron had all the elements usually found in comprehensive ethics and compliance programs: a code of ethics, a reporting system, as well as a training video on vision and values led by [the company's top executives].[148]

Experts subsequently put forth many explanations for how a company that was apparently so ethical outwardly could actually have been making so many bad ethical decisions without other managers (and the board of directors) noticing. The explanations ranged from a "deliberate concealment of information by officers," to more psychological explanations (such as employees not wanting to contradict their bosses) and the "surprising role of irrationality in decision-making."[149]

But perhaps the most persuasive explanation of how an apparently ethical company could go so wrong concerns organizational culture. The reasoning here is that it's not the rules but what employees feel they should do that determines ethical behavior. For example (speaking in general, not specifically about Enron), the executive director of the Ethics Officer Association put it this way:

> We're a legalistic society, and we've created a lot of laws. We assume that if you just knew what those laws meant that you would behave properly. Well, guess what? You can't write enough laws to tell us what to do at all times every day of the week in every part of the world. We've got to develop the critical thinking and critical reasoning skills of our people because most of the ethical issues that we deal with are in the ethical gray areas.

Questions

14-15. Based on what you read in this chapter, summarize in one page or less how you would explain Enron's ethical meltdown.

14-16. It is said that when one securities analyst tried to confront Enron's CEO about the firm's unusual accounting statements, the CEO publicly used vulgar language to describe the analyst, and that Enron employees subsequently thought doing so was humorous. If true, what does that say about Enron's ethical culture?

14-17. This case and chapter had something to say about how organizational culture influences ethical behavior. What role do you think culture played at Enron? Give five specific examples of things Enron's CEO could have done to create a healthy ethical culture.

Continuing Case

Carter Cleaning Company

Guaranteeing Fair Treatment

Being in the laundry and cleaning business, the Carters feel strongly about not allowing employees to smoke, eat, or drink in their stores. Jennifer was therefore surprised to walk into a store and find two employees eating lunch at the front counter. There was a large pizza in its box, and the two of them were sipping colas and eating slices of pizza and submarine sandwiches off paper plates. Not only did it look messy, but there were grease and soda spills on the counter and the store smelled from onions and pepperoni, even with the exhaust fan pulling air out through the roof. In addition to being a turnoff to customers, the mess on the counter meant that a customer's order might actually become soiled in the store.

Although this was a serious matter, Jennifer didn't feel that what the counter people were doing was grounds for dismissal (partly because the store manager had apparently condoned their actions). It seemed to her that the matter called for more than just a warning but less than dismissal.

Questions

14-18. What would you do if you were Jennifer, and why?

14-19. Should a disciplinary system be established at Carter Cleaning Centers?

14-20. If so, what should it cover? How would you suggest it deal with a situation such as the one with the errant counter people?

14-21. How would you deal with the store manager?

Translating Strategy into HR Policies and Practices Case*, §

** The accompanying strategy map for this chapter is in MyManagementLab; the overall map in the inside back cover of this text outlines the relationships involved.*

Improving Performance at the Hotel Paris

The Hotel Paris's New Ethics, Justice, and Fair Treatment Process

The Hotel Paris's competitive strategy is "To use superior guest service to differentiate the Hotel Paris properties, and to thereby increase the length of stay and return rate of guests, and thus boost revenues and profitability." HR manager Lisa Cruz must now formulate functional policies and activities that support this competitive strategy, by eliciting the required employee behaviors and competencies.

As the head of HR for the Hotel Paris, Lisa Cruz was especially concerned about her company maintaining the highest ethical standards. Her concerns were twofold. First, there are, in any single hotel each day, at least a dozen people (including housekeepers, front-desk clerks, security guards, and so on) with easy access to guests' rooms, and to their personal belongings. Guests—many younger, and many unwary—are continually walking the halls unprotected. So, in a service company like this, there is simply no margin for ethical errors.

But she was concerned about ethics for a second reason. She knew that employees do not like being treated unfairly, and that unfairness in any form could manifest itself in low morale and in diminished performance. She wondered if her employees' low morale and engagement—as measured by her firm's attitude surveys—stemmed, in part, from what they perceived as unjust treatment. Lisa therefore turned to the task of assessing and redesigning the Hotel Paris's ethics, justice, and fair treatment practices.

---

§ Written by and copyright Gary Dessler, PhD.

When she sat with the CFO to discuss her proposal for the Hotel Paris's fairness, justice, and ethics system, Lisa came armed with some research. In 2003, the *Journal of Applied Psychology* published a study that showed how improving the level of interpersonal and procedural justice in a service company can lead to improved employee attitudes and performance and thus to improved hotel performance.[150] And the study was done in a hotel chain.

In this study, the researchers collected employee survey data from a hotel chain's 111 different hotels in the United States and Canada. The employee services department of this hotel chain obtained completed surveys from 8,832 of the hotel's employees. The researchers also obtained data on employee turnover as well as on the employees' commitment, employees' intentions to remain with the organization, and guest satisfaction.

Clearly, having fair and just procedures in place affected these hotels' employee morale and behavior, and thus company performance—they could even measure the links. For example, procedural justice and interpersonal justice were related to increased levels of employees' satisfaction with supervision.

For Lisa and the CFO, these results supported, in a measurably defensible way, the idea that spending the money required to improve procedural and interpersonal justice would likely improve employee attitudes and behaviors (employee commitment, discretionary service behavior, and employee turnover), and, thereby, improve guest satisfaction and company performance.

Lisa and her HR team took steps to institute new ethics, justice, and fair treatment practices at the Hotel Paris. Working with the company's general counsel, they produced and presented to the CEO a new Hotel Paris code of ethics, as well as a more complete set of ethical guidelines. These now appear on the Hotel Paris's careers Web site link, and are part of each new employee's orientation packet. They contracted with a vendor to provide a customized, Web-based ethics training program, and made it clear that the first employees to participate in it were the company's top executives.

Lisa and her team then proceeded methodically through the company's entire HR process, starting with recruitment and selection. The selection process now includes an honesty test. New guidelines ensure an open and fair performance appraisal process. The team completely revamped the hotel's disciplinary process. They instituted a new appeals process that included appeals to each hotel's manager, and then to Lisa Cruz, and finally to a top management executive appeals committee. They instituted a new discipline without punishment system.

After 6 months of operating under the new system, several changes are evident. Surveys Lisa took before the new program, and now, indicate a significant upward movement in the employees' perceptions of "consistent and equitable treatment of all employees." Grievances are down by 80%, 95% of employees are able to quote the ethics code, employee morale and commitment are up, and, in general, employee service–type behaviors (such as greeting guests in a friendly manner) have increased, too. Lisa and the CFO are pleased with the new system, and are optimistic it will also help to improve customer service satisfaction.

Questions

14-22. Based on what you learned in this chapter of Dessler *Human Resource Management*, what do you think of the adequacy and effectiveness of the steps Lisa has taken so far?

14-23. List three more specific steps Hotel Paris should take with respect to each individual human research function (selection, training, and so on) to improve the level of ethics in the company.

14-24. Based on what you learned in this chapter, write a short (less than one page) explanation Lisa can use to sell to top management the need to further improve the hotel chain's fairness and justice processes.

MyManagementLab

Go to **mymanagementlab.com** for Auto-graded writing questions as well as the following Assisted-graded writing questions:

14-25. What techniques would you use as alternatives to traditional discipline? Why do you think alternatives like these are important, given industry's need today for highly engaged and committed employees?

14-26. Using several "Best Companies to Work For" as examples, explain what you would do to improve employee relations in an organization.

14-27. MyManagementLab Only–comprehensive writing assignment for this chapter.

✪ Try It!

How would you apply the concepts and skills you learned in this chapter? If your professor has assigned this, go to the Assignments section of **mymanagementlab.com** to complete the simulation: *Management & Ethics*.

PERSONAL INVENTORY ASSESSMENTS

Ethical Leadership Assessment

Leadership plays a role in fostering ethics. Complete this assessment to learn more about your personality.

Key Terms

employee relations, 451
fair treatment, 451
procedural justice, 452
distributive justice, 452
social responsibility, 453
organizational climate, 454
suggestion teams, 455
problem-solving teams, 455
quality circle, 455
self-managing/self-directed work team, 455
ethics, 457
organizational culture, 460
Electronic Communications Privacy Act (ECPA), 462

Ethics Quiz Answers

Quiz is on page 457.

1. 34% said personal e-mail on company computers is wrong.
2. 37% said using office equipment for schoolwork is wrong.
3. 49% said playing computer games at work is wrong.
4. 54% said Internet shopping at work is wrong.
5. 61% said it's unethical to blame your error on technology.
6. 87% said it's unethical to visit pornographic sites at work.
7. 33% said $25 is the amount at which a gift from a supplier or client becomes troubling, while 33% said $50, and 33% said $100.
8. 35% said a $50 gift to the boss is unacceptable.
9. 12% said a $50 gift from the boss is unacceptable.
10. 70% said it's unacceptable to take the $200 football tickets.
11. 70% said it's unacceptable to take the $120 theater tickets.
12. 35% said it's unacceptable to take the $100 food basket.
13. 45% said it's unacceptable to take the $25 gift certificate.
14. 40% said it's unacceptable to take the $75 raffle prize.
15. 11% reported they lie about sick days.
16. 4% reported they take credit for the work or ideas of others.

Endnotes

1. "When the Jobs Inspector Calls," *The Economist,* March 31, 2012, p. 73.
2. "Workforce Compensation and Performance Service, Office of Performance and Compensation Systems Design, Classification Programs Division," July 1999, HRCD-7; "Employee Relations," *HR Magazine* 55, no. 7 (July 2010), p. SS-4.
3. See, for example, Chris Long et al., "Fairness Monitoring: Linking Managerial Controls and Fairness Judgments in Organizations," *Academy of Management Journal* 54, no. 3 (2012), pp. 1045–1068.
4. Bennett Tepper, "Consequences of Abusive Supervision," *Academy of Management Journal* 43, no. 2 (2000), pp. 178–190. See also Samuel Aryee et al., "Antecedents and Outcomes of Abusive Supervision: A Test of a Trickle-Down Model," *Journal of Applied Psychology* 92, no. 1 (2007), pp. 191–201.
5. Mindy Shoss et al., "Blaming the Organization for Abusive Supervision: The Roles of Perceived Organizational Support and Supervisors Organizational Embodiment," *Journal of Applied Psychology* 98, no. 1 (2013), pp. 158–168.
6. Sean Hannah et al., "Joint Influences of Individual and Work Unit of Abusive Supervision on Ethical Intentions and Behaviors: A Moderated Mediation Model," *Journal of Applied Psychology* 98, no. 4 (2013), pp. 579–592.
7. Michelle Donovan et al., "The Perceptions of Fair Interpersonal Treatment Scale: Development and Validation of a Measure of Interpersonal Treatment in the Workplace," *Journal of Applied Psychology* 83, no. 5 (1998), pp. 683–692.
8. Bennett Tepper et al., "Abusive Supervision and Subordinates Organization Deviance," *Journal of Applied Psychology* 93, no. 4 (2008), pp. 721–732.
9. Jordan Robbins et al., "Perceived Unfairness and Employee Health: A Meta-Analytic Integration," *Journal of Applied Psychology* 97, no. 2 (2012), pp. 235–272.
10. Dawn Carlson et al., "The Fallout from Abusive Supervision: An Examination of Subordinates and Their Partners," *Personnel Psychology* 60, no. 4 (2011), pp. 937–961.
11. Marie Mitchell and Maureen Ambrose, "Employees Behavioral Reactions to Supervisor Aggression: An Examination of Individual and Situational Factors," *Journal of Applied Psychology* 97, no. 6 (2012), pp. 1148–1170.
12. Gary Weaver and Linda Treviño, "The Role of Human Resources in Ethics/Compliance Management: A Fairness Perspective," *Human Resource Management Review* 11 (2001), p. 117.
13. For example, monitor social media sites for evidence that one employee is harassing another. "Facebook Harassment: Social Websites May Prompt Need for New Policies, Procedures," *BNA Bulletin to Management*, July 20, 2010, p. 225.
14. Suzanne Masterson, "A Trickle-Down Model of Organizational Justice: Relating Employees' and Customers' Perceptions of and Reactions to Fairness," *Journal of Applied Psychology* 86, no. 4 (2001), pp. 594–601.
15. Based on Daniel Denison, *Corporate Culture and Organizational Effectiveness* (New York: Wiley, 1990), p. 155.
16. "When the Jobs Inspector Calls," *Economist,* March 31, 2012, p. 73.
17. Alexandra Ho and Tim Culpan, with assistance from Jun Yang in Seoul, Andrea Wong in Taipei, Tian Ying in Beijing, and Jasmine Wang in Hong Kong, "Foxconn Labor Disputes Disrupt IPhone Output for 2nd Time," *Bloomberg News*, October 8, 2012, www.bloomberg.com/news/2012-10-07/foxconn-labor-disputes-disrupt-iphone-output-for-2nd-time.html, accessed April 14, 2013.
18. Ibid.
19. Teresa Daniel, "Tough Boss or Workplace Bully?" *HR Magazine*, June 2009, pp. 83–86.
20. Eugene Kim and Theresa Glomb, "Get Smarty-Pants: Cognitive Ability, Personality, and Victimization," *Journal of Applied Psychology* 95, no. 3 (2010), pp. 889–901. See also Jaclyn Jensen et al., "Is It Better to Be Average? High and Low Performance as Predictors of Employee Victimization," *Journal of Applied Psychology* 90, no. 2 (2014), pp. 296–309.
21. Eugene Kim and Teresa Glomb, "Victimization of High Performers: The Roles of Envy and Work Group Identification," *Journal of Applied Psychology* 9, no. 4 (2014), pp. 619–634.
22. Ibid.
23. http://view.fdu.edu/default.aspx?id?3529, accessed September 6, 2012.
24. Ibid.
25. Carolyn Hirschman, "Giving Voice to Employee Concerns: Encouraging Employees to Speak Out Requires Respectful Treatment and Appropriate Action," *HR Magazine* 53, no. 8 (August 2008), pp. 50–54.

26. Tschanen Niederkohr, "Use the Exit Interview to Gain Valuable Insight," *Aftermarket Business* 117, no. 11 (November 2007), p. 8.
27. J. G. Carr, A. M. Schmidt, J. K. Ford, and R. P. DeShon, "Climate Perceptions Matter: A Meta-Analytic Path Analysis Relating Molar Climate, Cognitive and Affective States, and Individual Level Work Outcomes," *Journal of Applied Psychology* 88 (2003), pp. 605–619; quoted in Stephen Robbins and Timothy Judge, *Organizational Behavior* (Upper Saddle River, NJ: Prentice Hall, 2011), p. 524; and www.yourerc.com/blog/post/What-is-OrganizationalClimate.aspx, accessed September 8, 2014.
28. Rachel Silverman, "Are You Happy in Your Job? Bosses Push Weekly Surveys," *Wall Street Journal*, December 3, 2014, pp. B1, B4.
29. Laszlo Bock, *Work Rules!* (New York: 12, 2015), pp. 140–142.
30. "Survey: Employee Survey Number One," www.shrm.org/templatestools/samples/HR-forms, accessed April 11, 2012.
31. Pat Lenius, "Murray Supply Host Recognition Dinner," *Supply House Times*, May 2011, p. 70.
32. SHRM Survey Findings: Employee Recognition Programs, Winter 2012. In collaboration with and commissioned by Globoforce (www.globoforce.com).
33. This is based on "Recognition: Service Award Checklist," www.shrm.org/templatestools/samples/HR-forms, November 5, 2010, accessed April 14, 2012.
34. http://mashable.com/follow/topics/pinterest, accessed April 15, 2012.
35. "Over Half of Employers Use Social Media for Internal Communications, Survey Reveals," *Bloomberg BNA Bulletin to Management*, June 4, 2013, p. 179.
36. http://mashable.com/2012/04/06/pinterest-employee-engagement/, accessed April 15, 2012.
37. Tamara Lytle, "Giving Employees a Say: Getting—and Acting on—Ideas Offered by Employees Can Save Employers Money and Build a Sense of Ownership among Workers," *HR Magazine* 56, no. 10 (October 2011), pp. 69–74.
38. James H. Shonk, *Team-Based Organizations* (Chicago: Irwin, 1997), pp. 27–33.
39. Ibid., p. 28.
40. John Katzenbach and Douglas Smith, "The Discipline of Teams," *Harvard Business Review*, March/April 1993, pp. 116–118.
41. Everett Adams Jr., "Quality Circle Performance," *Journal of Management* 17, no. 1 (1991), pp. 25–39.
42. See for example, Jack Orsburn et al., *Self-Directed Teams*, Homewood, IL: Business One Irwin, 1990, p. 8; http://sloanreview.mit.edu/article/how-to-lead-a-selfmanaging-team/, accessed July 14, 2014.
43. Charles Fishman, "Engines of Democracy," *Fast Company*, October 1999, pp. 173–202.
44. Tom Peters, *Liberation Management* (New York: Alfred A. Knopf, 1992), pp. 238–239.
45. Susan Wells, "From Ideas to Results: To Get the Most from Your Company's Suggestion System, Move Ideas up the Ladder through a Formal Process," *HR Magazine* 50, no. 2 (February 2005), pp. 54–59.
46. Rebecca Hastings, "Survey: Employees Have Plenty of Suggestions," www.shrm.org/HR-disciplines/employeerelations/articles, February 29, 2012, accessed April 15, 2012.
47. Based on Wells, "From Ideas to Results."
48. Ibid.
49. This is quoted from ibid.
50. Kevin Wooten, "Ethical Dilemmas in Human Resource Management: An Application of a Multidimensional Framework, A Unifying Taxonomy, and Applicable Codes," *Human Resource Management Review* 11 (2001), p. 161. See also Sean Valentine et al., "Employee Job Response as a Function of Ethical Context and Perceived Organization Support," *Journal of Business Research* 59, no. 5 (2006), pp. 582–588.
51. Paul Schumann, "A Moral Principles Framework for Human Resource Management Ethics," *Human Resource Management Review* 11 (2004), p. 94. See also, *2005 National Business Ethics Survey: How Employees Perceive Ethics at Work*, 2005, p. 25. Copyright © 2006, Ethics Resource Center (ERC). In O. C. Ferrell, John Fraedrich, and Linog Ferrell, *Business Ethics* (Boston: Houghton Mifflin, 2008), p. 61.
52. Manuel Velasquez, *Business Ethics: Concepts and Cases* (Upper Saddle River, NJ: Prentice Hall, 1992), p. 9. See also O. C. Ferrell, John Fraedrich, and Linda Ferrell, *Business Ethics* (Boston: Houghton Mifflin, 2008).
53. For further discussion of ethics and morality, see Tom Beauchamp and Norman Bowie, *Ethical Theory and Business* (Upper Saddle River, NJ: Prentice Hall, 2001), pp. 1–19.
54. Jennifer Kish-Gephart, David Harrison, and Linda Trevino, "Bad Apples, Bad Cases, and Bad Barrels: Meta-Analytic Evidence about Sources of Unethical Decisions at Work," *Journal of Applied Psychology* 95, no. 1 (2010), pp. 1–31.
55. Sara Morris et al., "A Test of Environmental, Situational, and Personal Influences on the Ethical Intentions of CEOs," Business and Society, August 1995, pp. 119–147. See also Dennis Moberg, "Ethics Blind Spots in Organizations: How Systematic Errors in Person's Perception Undermine Moral Agency," Organization Studies 27, no. 3 (2006), pp. 413–428; and Scott Reynolds et al., "Automatic Ethics: The Effects of Implicit Assumptions and Contextual Cues on Moral Behavior," Journal of Applied Psychology 95, no. 5 (2010), pp. 752–760.
56. David Welsh, Deidre Snyder, Michael Christian, and Lisa Ordonez, "The Slippery Slope: How Small Ethical Transgressions Pave the Way for Larger Future Transgressions," *Journal of Applied Psychology* 100, no. 1 (2015), pp. 114–127.
57. Stefan Thau et al., "Unethical for the Sake of the Group: Risk of Social Exclusion and Pro-group Unethical Behavior," *Journal of Applied Psychology* 100, no. 1 (2015), pp. 98–113.
58. Ibid., p. 21.
59. Ibid.
60. "Former CEO Joins WorldCom's Indicted," *Miami Herald*, March 3, 2004, p. 4C.
61. Ferrell and Fraedrich, *Business Ethics*, p. 28; adapted from Rebecca Goodell, *Ethics in American Business: Policies, Programs, and Perceptions* (Washington, DC: Ethics Resource Center, 1994), p. 54. For other insights into unethical behavior's causes, see, for example, F. Gino et al., "Nameless + Harmless = Blameless: When Seemingly Irrelevant Factors Influence Judgment of (Un)ethical Behavior," *Organizational Behavior and Human Decision Processes* 111, no. 2 (March 2010), pp. 93–101; and J. Camps et al., "Learning Atmosphere and Ethical Behavior, Does It Make Sense?" *Journal of Business Ethics* 94, no. 1 (June 2010), pp. 129–147.
62. A recent study suggests that people may not be so selfless. Elizabeth Umphress, John Bingham, and Marie Mitchell, "Unethical Behavior in the Name of the Company: The Moderating Effect of Organizational Identification and Positive Reciprocity Beliefs on Unethical Pro-organizational Behavior," *Journal of Applied Psychology* 95, no. 4 (2010), pp. 769–770.
63. "Ethics Policies Are Big with Employers, but Workers See Small Impact on the Workplace," *BNA Bulletin to Management*, June 29, 2000, p. 201.
64. Guy Brumback, "Managing Above the Bottom Line of Ethics," *Supervisory Management*, December 1993, p. 12. See also E. E. Umphress et al., "The Influence of Distributive Justice on Lying for and Stealing from a Supervisor," *Journal of Business Ethics* 86, no. 4 (June 2009), pp. 507–518; and S. Chen, "The Role of Ethical Leadership Versus Institutional Constraints: A Simulation Study of Financial Misreporting by CEOs," *Journal of Business Ethics* 93, part supplement 1 (June 2010), pp. 33–52.
65. Dayton Fandray, "The Ethical Company," *Workforce* 79, no. 12 (December 2000), pp. 74–77.
66. IBM Business Conduct Guidelines, www.ibm.com/investor/pdf/BCG 2012.pdf, accessed August 2, 2013.
67. Richard Beatty et al., "HR's Role in Corporate Governance: Present and Prospective," *Human Resource Management* 42, no. 3 (Fall 2003), p. 268.
68. Eric Krell, "How to Conduct an Ethics Audit," *HR Magazine*, April 2010, pp. 48–51.
69. Betsy Shepherd, "Occupational Fraud," *Workforce Management*, April 2012, p. 18.
70. Dale Buss, "Corporate Compasses," *HR Magazine*, June 2004, pp. 127–132.
71. www.sec.gov/news/press/2011/2011116.htm, accessed September 6, 2012.
72. "SEC Actively Tracking Conduct That Might Constitute Retaliation," *BNA Bulletin to Management*, October 23, 2012, p. 342.
73. David Mayer et al., "Who Displays Ethical Leadership, and Why Does It Matter? An Examination of Antecedents and Consequences of Ethical Leadership," *Academy of Management Journal* 55, no. 1 (2012), p. 167.
74. Sometimes the most straightforward way of changing a company's culture is to move fast to change its top management. See Jeremy Smerd, "A Stalled Culture Change?" *Workforce Management*, December 14, 2009, pp. 1, 3.
75. "Ethics: It Isn't Just the Big Guys," *The American Intelligence Wire*, July 28, 2003, p. 10.
76. Based on "Ethics: It Isn't Just the Big Guys," *The American Intelligence Wire*, July 28, 2003, p. 10.
77. J. Krohe Jr., "The Big Business of Business Ethics," *Across the Board* 34 (May 1997), pp. 23–29; Deborah Wells and Marshall Schminke, "Ethical Development and Human Resources Training: An Integrator Framework," *Human Resource Management Review* 11 (2001), pp. 135–158.
78. "Ethical Issues in the Management of Human Resources," *Human Resource Management Review* 11 (2001), p. 6; Joel Lefkowitz, "The Constancy of Ethics amidst the Changing World of Work," *Human*

Resource Management Review 16 (2006), pp. 245–268; William Byham, "Can You Interview for Integrity?" *Across the Board* 41, no. 2 (March/April 2004), pp. 34–38; Evan Offstein and Ronald Dufresne, "Building Strong Ethics and Promoting Positive Character Development: The Influence of HRM at the United States Military Academy at West Point," *Human Resource Management* 46, no. 1 (Spring 2007), pp. 95–114.

79. Gary Weaver and Linda Treviño, "The Role of Human Resources in Ethics/Compliance Management: A Fairness Perspective," *Human Resource Management Review* 11 (2001), p. 123. See also Linda Andrews, "The Nexus of Ethics," *HR Magazine*, August 2005, pp. 53–58.
80. Russell Cropanzano and Thomas Wright, "Procedural Justice and Organizational Staffing: A Tale of Two Paradigms," *Human Resource Management Review* 13, no. 1 (2003), pp. 7–40.
81. "Ethical Issues in the Management of Human Resources," p. 6.
82. Weaver and Treviño, "The Role of Human Resources in Ethics/Compliance Management," p. 123.
83. Kathryn Tyler, "Do the Right Thing: Ethics Training Programs Help Employees Deal with Ethical Dilemmas," *HR Magazine*, February 2005, pp. 99–102.
84. Tom Asacker, "Ethics in the Workplace," *Training & Development*, August 2004, p. 44; www.skillsoft.com/catalog/detail.asp?CourseCode=pd_18_a01_bs_ enus, accessed September 8, 2014.
85. M. Ronald Buckley et al., "Ethical Issues in Human Resources Systems," *Human Resource Management Review* 11, no. 1, 2 (2001), pp. 11, 29. See also Ann Pomeroy, "The Ethics Squeeze," *HR Magazine*, March 2006, pp. 48–55.
86. Ed Finkel, "Yahoo Takes New Road on Ethics Training," *Workforce Management*, July 2010, p. 2.
87. Ibid., p. 125.
88. Robert Grossman, "Executive Discipline," *HR Magazine*, August 2005, pp. 46–51. See also Jean Thilmany, "Supporting Ethical Employees," *HR Magazine* 52, no. 9 (September 2007), pp. 105–106, 108, 110, 112.
89. Milton Zall, "Employee Privacy," *Journal of Property Management* 66, no. 3 (May 2001), p. 16.
90. Morris Attaway, "Privacy in the Workplace on the Web," *Internal Auditor* 58, no. 1 (February 2010, p. 30.
91. Declam Leonard and Angela France, "Workplace Monitoring: Balancing Business Interests with Employee Privacy Rights," *Society for Human Resource Management Legal Report*, May–June 2003, pp. 3–6.
92. *Vega-Rodriguez v. Puerto Rico Telephone Company*, CA1, #962061, 4/8/97, discussed in "Video Surveillance Withstands Privacy Challenge," *BNA Bulletin to Management*, April 17, 1997, p. 121. Also see, J. Greenwald, "Monitoring Communications? Know Legal Pitfalls," *Business Insurance* 45, no. 6 (February 7, 2011), pp. 1, 17.
93. *Quon v. Arch Wireless Operating Co.*, 529 F.3d 892 (9th Cir. 2008); "Employers Should Re-Examine Policies in Light of Ruling," *BNA Bulletin to Management*, August 12, 2008, p. 263.
94. Dionne Searcey, "Some Courts Raise Bar on Reading Employee E-mail," *Wall Street Journal*, November 19, 2009, p. A17.
95. "When Can an Employer Access Private E-Mail on Its System?" *BNA Bulletin to Management*, July 14, 2009, p. 224; one employment lawyer says that courts look to whether the employer's process is reasonable when determining if the employer's monitoring practices are acceptable. Electronic monitoring is generally reasonable "where there is a legitimate business purpose, where policies exist to set the privacy expectations of employees, and where employees are informed of the rules and understand the methods used to monitor the workplace." Nicole Kamm, "Bodyguard for Electronic Information," *HR Magazine*, January 2010, pp. 57–58.
96. Bill Roberts, "Are You Ready for Biometrics?" *HR Magazine*, March 2003, pp. 95–96.
97. Fredric Leffler and Lauren Palais, "Filter Out Perilous Company E-Mails," *Society for Human Resource Management Legal Report*, August 2008, p. 3. A survey of 220 large U.S. firms suggests that about 38% of them have people reading or otherwise analyzing employees' outgoing e-mail. See Searcey, "Some Courts Raise Bar on Reading Employee Email."
98. Bill Roberts, "Stay Ahead of the Technology Use Curve," *HR Magazine*, October 2008, pp. 57–61.
99. One attorney notes that problems can arise with the Federal Stored Communications Act if the employer uses illicit or coercive means to access the employee's private social media accounts. *BNA Bulletin to Management*, July 21, 2009, p. 225.
100. "Twitter Is Latest Electronic Tool to Pose Challenges and Opportunities for Employers," *BNA Bulletin to Management*, June 16, 2009, p. 185. See also Sean Valentine et al., "Exploring the Ethicality of Firing Employees Who Blog," *Human Resource Management* 49, no. 1 (January/February 2010), pp. 87–108.
101. "After Employer Found Liable for Worker's Child Porn, Policies May Need to Be Revisited," *BNA Bulletin to Management*, March 21, 2006, p. 89.
102. Ibid.
103. "Disgruntled Workers' Hacking of Employers Is on the Rise, FBI–DHS Public Alert Says," *Bloomberg BNA Bulletin to Management*, October 7, 2014, p. 315.
104. "Time Clocks Go High Touch, High Tech to Keep Workers from Gaming the System," *BNA Bulletin to Management*, March 25, 2004, p. 97.
105. Andrea Poe, "Make Foresight 20/20," *HR Magazine*, February 2000, pp. 74–80.
106. Gundars Kaupin et al., "Recommended Employee Location Monitoring Policies," www.shrm.org, accessed January 2, 2007.
107. Steve Lohr, "Unblinking Eyes Track Employees," *New York Times*, June 22, 2014, pp. 1, 15.
108. Claire Suddath, "Tesco Monitors Employees with Motorola on Bands," www.BusinessWeek.com/articles/2013-02-13/Tescomonitors_employees-with-Motorola-arm-bands, accessed February 14, 2013.
109. Rita Zeidner, "New Face in the C-Suite," *HR Magazine*, January 2010, p. 39.
110. Lester Bittel, *What Every Supervisor Should Know* (New York: McGraw-Hill, 1974), p. 308; and Thomas Salvo, "Practical Tips for Successful Progressive Discipline," SHRM White Paper July 2004, www.shrm.org/hrresources/whitepapers_published/CMS_009030 asp, accessed January 5, 2008.
111. David Campbell et al., "Discipline Without Punishment—At Last," *Harvard Business Review*, July/August 1995, pp. 162–178; J. F. Mason, "Myspace, Yourspace: What Employers Must Know About Social-Media Risks," *National Underwriter* (P & C) 115, no. 11 (March 28, 2011), pp. 18, 20.
112. For fair discipline guidelines, see Bittel, *What Every Supervisor Should Know*, p. 308; Paul Falcone, "Fundamentals of Progressive Discipline," *HR Magazine*, February 1997, pp. 90–92; and "How to Discipline and Fire Employees," www.entrepreneur.com/article/79928, accessed May 3, 2012.
113. David Mayer et al., "When Do Fair Procedures Not Matter? A Test of the Identity Violation Effect," *Journal of Applied Psychology*, 94, no. 1, 2009, pp. 142–161.
114. Grossman, "Executive Discipline," pp. 46–51; "The Evil Women Theses," based on Sandra Hartman et al., "Males and Females in a Discipline Situation Exploratory Research on Competing Hypotheses," *Journal of Managerial Issues* 6, no. 1 (Spring 1994), pp. 57, 64–68; "A Woman's Place," *Economist* (August 19, 2000), p. 56.
115. For fair discipline guidelines, see Bittel, *What Every Supervisor Should Know*, p. 308; Falcone, "Fundamentals of Progressive Discipline," pp. 90–92; and "How to Discipline and Fire Employees."
116. George Bohlander, "Why Arbitrators Overturn Managers in Employee Suspension and Discharge Cases," *Journal of Collective Negotiations* 23, no. 1 (1994), pp. 76–77.
117. "Employers Turn to Corporate Ombuds to Defuse Internal Ticking Time Bombs," *BNA Bulletin to Management*, August 9, 2005, p. 249.
118. Dick Grote, "Discipline without Punishment," *Across the Board* 38, no. 5 (September 2001), pp. 52–57.
119. http://money.cnn.com/magazines/fortune/best-companies/2014/list/ accessed July 17, 2015.
120. http://www.greatplacetowork.com/best-companies#sthash.ECoNqRRH.dpbs, accessed July 17, 2015.
121. Ibid.
122. http://www.sas.com/en_us/company-information/great-workplace.html, accessed July 17, 2015.
123. www.sas.com/content/dam/SAS/en_us/doc/other1/benefits-brochure.pdf; also see www.sas.com/en_us/news/pressreleases/2014/january/greatworkplace-US-Fortune-2014.html, accessed September 8, 2014.
124. Mark Crowley, "How SAS Became the World's Best Place to Work," www.fastcompany.com/300-4953/how-SAS-became-worlds-best-place-to-work, accessed April 8, 2014.
125. Rebecca Leung, "Working the Good Life," www.CBSnews.com/news/working-the-good-life/, accessed July 17, 2015.
126. Ibid.
127. Ibid.
128. Ibid.
129. Ibid.
130. Mark Crowley, "Not a Happy Accident: How Google Deliberately Designed Workplace Satisfaction," www.fastcompany.com/300-7268/where-are-they-now, accessed April 8, 2014.
131. http://US.Greatrated.com/Googlean, accessed April 6, 2014.

132. From "Benefits", Google Careers, https://www.google.co.in/about/careers/lifeatgoogle/benefits/, accessed April 7, 2014. Used by permission from Google Press.
133. Farhad Manjoo, "The Happiness Machine," January 21, 2013, www.slate.com, accessed April 6, 2014.
134. Ibid.; and Greta Roberts, "Why Google's Employee Engagement Programs Are Bad for Your Business," www.talentanalytics.com/blog, accessed April 5, 2014.
135. Manjoo, "The Happiness Machine."
136. Ibid.
137. Ibid.
138. Ibid.
139. Crowley, "Not a Happy Accident: How Google Deliberately Designs Workplace Satisfaction."
140. This is based on Gary Dessler, *Winning Commitment*, New York: McGraw-Hill, 1993, pp. 37–51; "The Federal Express Employee Handbook," August 7, 1989, p. 89; and "FedEx Attributes Success to People-First Philosophy," www.fedex.com/ma/about/overview/philosophy.html, accessed July 18, 2015.
141. Ibid.
142. Ibid.
143. Ibid.
144. http://www.fedex.com/cz_english/about/overview/philosophy.html, accessed July 14, 2014.
145. "Working at SAS: An Ideal Environment for New Ideas," SAS Web site, April 20, 2012. Copyright © SAS Institute Inc., Cary, NC, USA. All Rights Reserved. Used with permission.
146. Based on "Theft Is Unethical," *HR Solutions* 34 (October 2002), p. 66.
147. Bureau of National Affairs, *Bulletin to Management*, September 13, 1985, p. 3.
148. David Gebler, "Is Your Culture a Risk Factor?" *Business and Society Review* 111, no. 3 (Fall 2006), pp. 337–362.
149. John Cohan, "'I Didn't Know' and 'I Was Only Doing My Job': Has Corporate Governance Careened Out of Control? A Case Study of Enron's Information Myopia," *Journal of Business Ethics* 40, no. 3 (October 2002), pp. 275–299.
150. Tony Simons and Quinetta Roberson, "Why Managers Should Care About Fairness: The Effects of Aggregate Justice Perceptions on Organizational Outcomes," *Journal of Applied Psychology* 88, no. 3 (2003), p. 432

15

Labor Relations and Collective Bargaining

Oleksiy Maksymenko/AGE Fotostock

LEARNING OBJECTIVES

15-1 Give a brief history of the American labor movement.

15-2 Discuss the main features of at least three major pieces of labor legislation.

15-3 Present examples of what to expect during the union drive and election.

15-4 Illustrate with examples bargaining that is not in good faith.

15-5 Develop a grievance procedure.

15-6 Describe a strategy for cooperative labor relations.

Some people call Costco "The Anti-Walmart," because Costco treats its workers and unions so well.[1] Whereas Walmart is known for difficult labor relations (it said, for instance, it was eliminating health insurance for future employees working under 24 hours per week),[2] Costco actually keeps profits up in part with positive labor relations policies.[3] We'll see how they do it.

WHERE ARE WE NOW ...

Chapter 14 focused on employee relations, ethics and justice—important issues in determining employees' tendencies to join unions. The main purpose of this chapter is to help you deal effectively with unions and grievances. After briefly discussing the history of the American labor movement, we describe the basic labor law, including unfair labor practices. We explain labor negotiations, including the union actions you can expect during the union campaign and election. And we explain what you can expect during the actual bargaining sessions, and how to handle grievances.

LEARNING OBJECTIVE 15-1
Give a brief history of the American labor movement.

The Labor Movement

Today, over 14 million U.S. workers belong to unions—about 11% of the total number of men and women working in America—and another 1.5 million work in places covered by union agreements but don't report being union members.[4] Almost 36% of public-sector workers belong to unions, including heavily unionized occupations such as teachers, police officers, and firefighters. In some private sector industries such as utilities (22.3 % unionization), transportation and warehousing (19.6 percent), and telecommunications (14.8 %), it can still be hard to get jobs without joining unions. And unionization also ranges widely by state, from a high of 24.6% in New York down to 1.9% in North Carolina.[5]

Furthermore, it's a mistake to assume that unions affect employers only negatively. For example, perhaps by professionalizing the staff and/or systematizing practices, heart attack mortality among patients in hospitals with unionized registered nurses was 5% to 9% lower than in nonunion hospitals.[6] The accompanying Strategic Context feature provides another example of the potential benefits of good union-management relations.

IMPROVING PERFORMANCE: *The Strategic Context*

The "Anti-Walmart's" Revenues

It's not easy competing with Walmart's low prices, but Walmart Stores' Sam's Club is actually second in sales to Costco. How does Costco stay ahead? In part with a strategy based on "strong labor relations, low employee turnover, and liberal benefits."[7] For example, Costco's relations with labor unions are comparatively gentle. When California grocery store workers picketed several chains a few years ago, "Costco Wholesale Corp. avoided the fray, quietly renegotiating a separate contract with its union employees there." The new contract boosted Costco workers' wages and the firm's contribution to their pension plans.

Costco's HR strategy is to fend off Walmart's low wages and labor costs by eliciting higher productivity and better service from engaged employees. The strategy seems to be working. Costco's sales per employee are about $500,000 a year versus $340,000 at Sam's Club.[8] Having a positive labor relations strategy that supports Costco's overall aim of boosting profits through better productivity and service is working for Costco. ■

Source: Based on Hamilton Nolan, "The Anti-Wal-Mart," http://gawker.com/costco-the-anti-wal-mart-511739135; 2013.http://articles.moneycentral.msn.com/Investing/Extra/CostcoTheAntiWalMart.aspx?page 1

If your professor has assigned this, go to the Assignments section of **mymanagementlab.com** to complete this discussion question.

Talk About It 1: If supportive labor relations works so well for Costco, why do you think Walmart doesn't use it too?

Support for unions has always ebbed and flowed in America, and today pressures are building against unions. For example, critical budget problems following the recent recession prompted several states to reduce public employees' numbers, pensions, and pay.

We'll look at unions and dealing with them in this chapter.

Why Do Workers Organize?

Experts have spent much time and money trying to figure out why workers unionize, and they've proposed many theories. Yet there is no simple answer.

It's not just about better pay or working conditions, though these are important. For example, recent median weekly wages for union workers was $970, versus $763 for nonunion workers.[9] Union workers also generally receive more holidays, sick leave, unpaid leave, insurance plan benefits, long-term disability benefits, and other benefits—about $14.50 per hour in benefits compared with about $7.50 per hour for nonunion workers.[10]

Library of Congress Prints and Photographs Division

Making fenders at an early Ford factory in Ypsilanti, Michigan. In addition to heavy physical labor, workers faced health hazards—poor lighting, dust, and dangerous machinery.

But it's not just money. The urge to unionize often comes down to the belief on the part of workers that it's only through unity that they can get their fair share of the "pie" and also protect themselves from the arbitrary whims of management. The bottom line is that low morale, fear of job loss, and poor communication (in other words, poor employee relations) also foster unionization. When Kaiser Permanente cut back on vacation and sick leave for its pharmacists, the Guild for Professional Pharmacists won back the lost vacation days. Said one, "Kaiser is a pretty benevolent employer, but there's always the pressure to squeeze a little."[11] One labor relations lawyer says, "The one major thing unions offer is making you a 'for cause' instead of an 'at will' employee, which guarantees a hearing and arbitration if you're fired."[12] So, in practice, low morale, fear of job loss, and arbitrary management actions help foster unionization.

In some respects, things have not changed in decades. Here is how one writer describes the motivation behind the early (1900s) unionization of automobile workers:

> In the years to come, economic issues would make the headlines when union and management met in negotiations. But in the early years, … the principal grievances of the autoworkers were the speed-up of production and the lack of any kind of job security. As production tapered off, the order in which workers were laid off was determined largely by the whim of foremen and other supervisors.… Generally, what the workers revolted against was the lack of human dignity and individuality, and a working relationship that was massively impersonal, cold, and nonhuman. They wanted to be treated like human beings—not like faceless clock card numbers.[13]

Employee Engagement and Unionization

Why else do workers unionize? *Modern Survey* conducted a study that measured items such as employees' interest in being represented by a union, confidence in senior management, and employee engagement. It concluded that 50% of "actively disengaged" employees would vote "yes" to unionization, while only 20% of such employees would vote "no union." It concludes that "paying attention to employee engagement levels within your organization helps to foster positive relationships between employees and management and decreases the likelihood of a workforce seeking union representation."[14]

Gallup conducts its own surveys that complements these conclusions. For example, among the over 500 organizations in which Gallup measures employee engagement, 45% of *non*union employees were engaged, while fewer—38%—of unionized employees were engaged.[15]

Findings like these don't prove that engaged employees are less likely to support a unionization effort in their companies, or that unionized employees are less engaged. The findings are correlational, so they only "prove" that when employee engagement goes up unionization goes down. It could be that the same management policies (such as guaranteed fair treatment systems) affect both employee engagement and non-unionization. But on the whole such findings do suggest that the same sorts of policies (such as good benefits, building trust, and guaranteeing fair treatment) that improve employee engagement may also reduce the likelihood of being unionized.

What Do Unions Want?

We can generalize by saying that unions have two sets of aims, for *union security* and for *improved wages, hours, working conditions*, and *benefits* for their members.

closed shop
A form of union security in which the company can hire only union members. This was outlawed in 1947 but still exists in some industries (such as printing).

union shop
A form of union security in which the company can hire nonunion people, but they must join the union after a prescribed period of time and pay dues. (If they do not, they can be fired.)

agency shop
A form of union security in which employees who do not belong to the union must still pay union dues on the assumption that union efforts benefit all workers.

preferential shop
Union members get preference in hiring, but the employer can still hire nonunion members.

right to work
A term used to describe state statutory or constitutional provisions banning the requirement of union membership as a condition of employment.

UNION SECURITY First and probably foremost, unions seek security for themselves. They fight hard for the right to represent a firm's workers, and to be the exclusive bargaining agent for all employees in the unit. (As such, they negotiate contracts for all employees, including those not members of the union.) Five types of union security are possible:

1. **Closed shop.**[16] The company can hire only current union members. Congress outlawed closed shops in interstate commerce, but they still exist in some states for particular industries (such as printing). They account for fewer than 5% of union contracts.
2. **Union shop**. The company can hire nonunion people, but they must join the union after a prescribed period and pay dues. (If not, they can be fired.) These account for about 73% of union contracts.
3. **Agency shop**. Employees who do not belong to the union still must pay the union an amount equal to union dues (on the assumption that the union's efforts benefit *all* the workers).
4. **Preferential shop**. Union members get preference in hiring, but the employer can still hire nonunion members.
5. **Maintenance of membership arrangement.** Employees do not have to belong to the union. However, union members employed by the firm must maintain membership in the union for the contract period. These account for about 4% of union agreements.

Not all states give unions the right to require union membership as a condition of employment. **Right to work** is a term used to describe "state statutory or constitutional provisions banning the requirement of union membership as a condition of employment."[17] *Right-to-work laws* don't outlaw unions. They do outlaw (within those states) any form of union security. Recently, there were 23 right-to-work states.[18] Right to work adversely affects union membership levels.[19] After Oklahoma became the 22nd state to pass right-to-work legislation, Oklahoma's union membership dropped dramatically in the next three years.[20]

IMPROVED WAGES, HOURS, AND BENEFITS Once the union ensures its security at the employer, it fights to improve its members' wages, hours, working conditions, and benefits. The typical labor agreement also gives the union a role in other human resource activities, including recruiting, selecting, compensating, promoting, training, and discharging employees.

The AFL-CIO and the SEIU

The American Federation of Labor and Congress of Industrial Organizations (AFL-CIO) is a voluntary federation of about 57 national and international labor unions in the United States. For many people in the United States, the AFL-CIO is still synonymous with the word *union.*

There are three layers in the AFL-CIO and most other U.S. unions. The worker joins the local union, to which he or she pays dues. The local is in turn a single chapter in the national union. For example, if you were a teacher in Detroit, you would belong to the local union there, which is one of hundreds of local chapters of the American Federation of Teachers, their national union (most unions actually call themselves international unions). The third layer is the national federation, in this case, the AFL-CIO.

The Service Employees International Union (SEIU) is a federation of more than 2.2 million members. It includes the largest health-care union, with more than 1.1 million members, including nurses, LPNs, and doctors, and the second-largest public employees union, with more than 1 million local and state government workers.[21]

Union federation membership is in flux. Some years ago, the SEIU, the International Brotherhood of Teamsters, and UNITE HERE left the AFL-CIO and established their own federation, called the Change to Win Coalition. Together, the departing unions represented over a quarter of the AFL-CIO's membership and budget. Change to Win plans to be more aggressive about organizing workers than they say the AFL-CIO was.[22] Then the UNITE HERE union left Change to Win and rejoined the AFL-CIO.

Unions And The Law

LEARNING OBJECTIVE 15-2

Discuss the main features of at least three major pieces of labor legislation.

The history of the American labor movement is one of expansion and contraction in response to public policy changes. Until about 1930, there were no special labor laws. Employers were not required to engage in collective bargaining with employees and were virtually unrestrained in their behavior toward unions; the use of spies and firing of union agitators were widespread. "Yellow dog" contracts, whereby management could require nonunion membership as a condition for employment, were widely enforced. Most union weapons—even strikes—were illegal.

This situation lasted until the Great Depression (around 1930).[23] Since then, in response to changing public attitudes and economic conditions, labor law has gone through three clear periods: from "strong encouragement" of unions, to "modified encouragement coupled with regulation," and finally to "detailed regulation of internal union affairs."[24]

Norris-LaGuardia Act of 1932
This law marked the beginning of the era of strong encouragement of unions and guaranteed to each employee the right to bargain collectively "free from interference, restraint, or coercion."

National Labor Relations (or Wagner) Act
This law banned certain types of unfair practices and provided for secret-ballot elections and majority rule for determining whether a firm's employees want to unionize.

Period of Strong Encouragement: The Norris-LaGuardia (1932) and National Labor Relations (or Wagner) Acts (1935)

The **Norris-LaGuardia Act of 1932** set the stage for a new era in which union activity was encouraged. It guaranteed to each employee the right to bargain collectively "free from interference, restraint, or coercion." It declared yellow dog contracts unenforceable. And it limited the courts' abilities to issue injunctions (stop orders) for activities such as peaceful picketing and payment of strike benefits.

Yet this act did little to restrain employers from fighting labor organizations. So, in 1935, Congress passed the **National Labor Relations (or Wagner) Act** to add teeth to Norris LaGuardia. It did this by (1) banning certain unfair labor practices, (2) providing for secret-ballot elections and majority rule for determining whether a firm's employees would unionize, and (3) creating the **National Labor Relations Board (NLRB)** to enforce these two provisions.

National Labor Relations Board (NLRB)
The agency created by the Wagner Act to investigate unfair labor practice charges and to provide for secret-ballot elections and majority rule in determining whether a firm's employees want a union.

UNFAIR EMPLOYER LABOR PRACTICES The Wagner Act deemed "statutory wrongs" (but not crimes) five unfair labor practices used by employers:

1. It is unfair for employers to "interfere with, restrain, or coerce employees" in exercising their legally sanctioned right of self-organization.
2. It is unfair for company representatives to dominate or interfere with either the formation or the administration of labor unions. Among other specific management actions found to be unfair under these first two practices are bribing employees, using company spy systems, moving a business to avoid unionization, and blacklisting union sympathizers.
3. Employers are prohibited from discriminating in any way against employees for their legal union activities.
4. Employers are forbidden to discharge or discriminate against employees simply because the latter file unfair practice charges against the company.
5. Finally, it is an unfair labor practice for employers to refuse to bargain collectively with their employees' duly chosen representatives.

Unions file an unfair labor practice charge (see Figure 15-1) with the National Labor Relations Board. (For example, the American Guild of Musical Artists said it would file an unfair labor charge against the New York City Opera if it cut staff and moved.) The board then decides whether to take action. Possible actions include dismissal of the complaint, request for an injunction against the employer, or an order that the employer cease and desist.

FIGURE 15-1 NLRB Form 501: Filing an Unfair Labor Practice

Source: From Unfair Labor Practice (ULP) Case Forms, National Labor Relations Board, www.nlrb.gov.

FORM NLRB 501
(2 81)

FORM EXEMPT UNDER
44 U.S.C. 3512

UNITED STATES OF AMERICA
NATIONAL LABOR RELATIONS BOARD

CHARGE AGAINST EMPLOYER

INSTRUCTIONS: File an original and 4 copies of this charge with NLRB Regional Director for the region in which the alleged unfair labor practice occurred or is occurring.

DO NOT WRITE IN THIS SPACE

CASE NO. | DATE FILE

1. EMPLOYER AGAINST WHOM CHARGE IS BROUGHT

a. NAME OF EMPLOYER | b. NUMBER OF WORKERS EMPLOYED

c. ADDRESS OF ESTABLISHMENT (*street and number, city, State, and ZIP code*) | d. EMPLOYER REPRESENTATIVE TO CONTACT | e. PHONE NO.

f. TYPE OF ESTABLISHMENT (*factory, mine, wholesaler, etc.*) | g. IDENTIFY PRINCIPAL PRODUCT OR SERVICE

h. THE ABOVE-NAMED EMPLOYER HAS ENGAGED IN AND IS ENGAGING IN UNFAIR LABOR PRACTICES WITHIN THE MEANING OF SECTION 8(a), SUBSECTIONS (1) AND _____ OF THE NATIONAL
(*list subsections*)
LABOR RELATIONS ACT, AND THESE UNFAIR LABOR PRACTICES ARE UNFAIR LABOR PRACTICES AFFECTING COMMERCE WITHIN THE MEANING OF THE ACT.

2. BASIS OF THE CHARGE (*be specific as to facts, names, addresses, plants involved, dates, places, etc.*)

BY THE ABOVE AND OTHER ACTS, THE ABOVE-NAMED EMPLOYER HAS INTERFERED WITH, RESTRAINED, AND COERCED EMPLOYEES IN THE EXERCISE OF THE RIGHTS GUARANTEED IN SECTION 7 OF THE ACT.

3. FULL NAME OF PARTY FILING CHARGE (*if labor organization, give full name, including local name and number*)

4a. ADDRESS (*street and number, city, State, and ZIP code*) | 4b. TELEPHONE NO.

5. FULL NAME OF NATIONAL OR INTERNATIONAL LABOR ORGANIZATION OF WHICH IT IS AN AFFILIATE OR CONSTITUENT UNIT (*to be filled in when charge is filed by a labor organization*)

6. DECLARATION

I declare that I have read the above charge and that the statements therein are true to the best of my knowledge and belief.

By _____
(signature of representative or person filing charge) (title, if any)

Address _____
(telephone number) (date)

WILLFULLY FALSE STATEMENTS ON THIS CHARGE CAN BE PUNISHED BY FINE AND IMPRISONMENT
(*U.S. CODE, TITLE 18, SECTION 1001*)

FROM 1935 TO 1947 Union membership increased quickly after passage of the Wagner Act. Other factors such as an improving economy and aggressive union leadership contributed to this rise. But by the mid-1940s, largely due to massive postwar strikes, public policy began to shift against what many viewed as union excesses. The stage was set for passage of the Taft-Hartley Act.

Taft-Hartley Act of 1947
Also known as the *Labor Management Relations Act*, this law prohibited unfair union labor practices and enumerated the rights of employees as union members. It also enumerated the rights of employers.

Period of Modified Encouragement Coupled with Regulation: The Taft-Hartley Act (1947)

The **Taft-Hartley** *(or Labor Management Relations)* **Act of 1947** reflected the public's less enthusiastic attitude toward unions. It amended the National Labor

Relations (Wagner) Act by limiting unions in four ways: (1) prohibiting unfair union labor practices, (2) enumerating the rights of employees as union members, (3) enumerating the rights of employers, and (4) allowing the president of the United States to bar temporarily national emergency strikes.

Unfair Union Labor Practices

The Taft-Hartley Act enumerated several labor practices that unions were prohibited from engaging in:

1. First, it banned *unions* from *restraining or coercing employees* from exercising their guaranteed bargaining rights. (Some union actions that courts have held illegal include telling an anti-union employee that he or she will lose his or her job once the union gains recognition, and issuing patently false statements during union organizing campaigns.)
2. It is also an unfair labor practice for a union to *cause an employer to discriminate* in any way against an employee so as to encourage or discourage his or her union membership. For example, the union cannot try to force an employer to fire a worker because he or she doesn't attend union meetings or refuses to join a union. There is one exception: Suppose a closed or union shop prevails (and union membership is therefore a prerequisite to employment). Then the union may demand the discharge of someone who fails to pay his or her initiation fees and dues.
3. It is an unfair labor practice for a union to *refuse to bargain in good faith* with the employer about wages, hours, and other employment conditions.
4. It is an unfair labor practice for a union to engage in *featherbedding* (requiring an employer to pay an employee for services not performed).

RIGHTS OF EMPLOYEES The Taft-Hartley Act protected the rights of employees against their unions in other ways. For example, many people felt that compulsory unionism violated the right of freedom of association. Legitimized by Taft-Hartley, new right-to-work laws sprung up in 19 (now 23) states (mainly in the South and Southwest). In New York, for example, in many printing firms you can't work as a press operator unless you belong to a printers' union. In Florida, a right-to-work state, printing shops typically employ both union and nonunion operators. Even today, union membership varies widely by state, from a high of 26.8% in New York to a low of 3.2% in North Carolina.[25] The Taft-Hartley act also required the employee's authorization before the union could subtract dues from his or her paycheck.

In general, the Labor Relations (Taft-Hartley) Act does not restrain unions from unfair labor practices to the extent that the law does employers. It says unions may not restrain or coerce employees. However, "violent or otherwise threatening behavior or clearly coercive or intimidating union activities are necessary before the NLRB will find an unfair labor practice."[26] Examples include physical assaults or threats, economic reprisals, and mass picketing that restrains lawful entry or leaving.

RIGHTS OF EMPLOYERS The Taft-Hartley Act also explicitly gave *employers* certain rights. First, it gave them full freedom to express their views concerning union organization. For example, as a manager you can tell your employees that in your opinion unions are worthless, dangerous to the economy, and immoral. You can even (generally) hint that unionization and high-wage demands might result in the permanent closing of the plant (but not its relocation). Employers can set forth the union's record concerning violence and corruption, if appropriate. In fact, the only major restraint is that employers must avoid threats, promises, coercion, and direct interference with workers who are trying to reach a decision. There can be no threat of reprisal or force or promise of benefit.[27]

Furthermore, the employer (1) cannot meet with employees on company time within 24 hours of an election or (2) suggest to employees that they vote against the union while they are at home or in the employer's office (although he or she can do so while in their work area or where they normally gather).

national emergency strikes
Strikes that might "imperil the national health and safety."

NATIONAL EMERGENCY STRIKES The Taft-Hartley Act also allows the U.S. president to intervene in **national emergency strikes**. These are strikes (for example, by railroad workers) that might "imperil the national health and safety." The president may appoint a board of inquiry and, based on its report, apply for an injunction restraining the strike for 60 days. If the parties don't reach a settlement during that time, the president can have the injunction extended for another 20 days. During this last period, employees take a secret ballot to ascertain their willingness to accept the employer's last offer.

Landrum-Griffin Act of 1959
Also known as the *Labor Management Reporting and Disclosure Act*, this law aimed at protecting union members from possible wrongdoing on the part of their unions.

PERIOD OF DETAILED REGULATION OF INTERNAL UNION AFFAIRS: THE LANDRUM-GRIFFIN ACT (1959) In the 1950s, Senate investigations revealed unsavory practices on the part of some unions, and the result was the **Landrum-Griffin Act (officially, the *Labor Management Reporting and Disclosure Act*) of 1959**. An overriding aim of this act was to protect union members from possible union wrongdoing. Like Taft-Hartley, it also amended the National Labor Relations (Wagner) Act.

First, the act contains a *bill of rights* for union members. It provides for certain rights in the nomination of candidates for union office. It also affirms a member's right to sue his or her union and ensures that the union cannot fine or suspend a member without due process.

This act also laid out rules regarding union elections. For example, national and international unions must elect officers at least once every 5 years, using a secret-ballot mechanism. And the act regulates the kind of person who can serve as a union officer. For example, it bars for a time persons convicted of felonies from holding union officer positions.

Senate investigators also discovered flagrant examples of employer wrongdoing. Employers and their "labor relations consultants" had bribed union agents and officers, for example. Landrum-Griffin therefore expanded the list of unlawful employer actions. For example, companies can no longer pay their own employees to entice them not to join the union.

LABOR LAW TODAY As we'll see toward the end of this chapter, it isn't quite clear whether the pressures toward a more encouraging or a more discouraging climate for labor law will prevail for the next few years. On the one hand, we'll see that unions are pushing for new legislation that would substantially improve unions' efforts. On the other hand, economic realities (shrinking state budgets, for instance) have undoubtedly reduced union membership.[28]

The Union Drive and Election

LEARNING OBJECTIVE 15-3
Present examples of what to expect during the union drive and election.

It is through the union drive and election that a union tries to be recognized to represent employees. To protect themselves and their employers, supervisors need to understand this process. It has five basic steps.[29]

Step 1. Initial Contact

During the initial contact stage, the union determines the employees' interest in organizing, and establishes an organizing committee.

The initiative for the first contact between the employees and the union may come from the employees, from a union already representing other employees of the firm, or from another union. In any case, there is an initial contact.

Once an employer becomes a target, a union official usually assigns a representative to assess employee interest. The representative visits the firm to determine if enough employees are interested in a campaign, identifies employees who would make good leaders in the organizing campaign, and creates an organizing committee. The aim is to educate the committee about the benefits of forming a union and the law and procedures for forming a local union.

The union must follow certain rules when it starts contacting employees. The law allows organizers to solicit employees for membership as long as the effort doesn't endanger the performance or safety of the employees. Therefore, much contact takes place off the job, perhaps at home or at places near work. Organizers can also safely contact employees on company grounds during off hours (such as lunch or break time). Yet, in practice, there will be much informal organizing going on at the workplace as employees debate organizing. Sometimes the first inkling management has is the distribution of handbills soliciting union membership.

Much soliciting will be via e-mail, but prohibiting employees from sending pro-union e-mail messages using company e-mail isn't easy. You can't discriminate against union activities. Therefore, prohibiting only union e-mail may violate NLRB rules. And barring workers from using e-mail for all non–work-related topics may be futile if the company actually does little to stop it.

LABOR RELATIONS CONSULTANTS Both management and unions typically use "labor relations consultants." These may be law firms, researchers, psychologists, labor relations specialists, or public relations firms. Some are former union organizers.[30]

For the employer, the consultant's services may range from ensuring that the firm properly fills out routine labor relations forms to managing the union campaign. Unions may use public relations firms to improve their image, or specialists to manage corporate campaigns. (These pressure shareholders and creditors to get management to agree to the union's demands.)

Some say consultants encourage questionable tactics. One tactic is to delay the union vote with lengthy hearings at the NLRB. The longer the delay in the vote, they argue, the more time the employer has to drill anti-union propaganda into the employees.

union salting
A union organizing tactic by which workers who are in fact employed full-time by a union as undercover organizers are hired by unwitting employers.

UNION SALTING Unions are not without creative ways to win elections. The National Labor Relations Board defines **union salting** as "placing of union members on nonunion job sites for the purpose of organizing." Critics claim that "salts" interfere with business operations and harass employees.[31] The U.S. Supreme Court ruled that union salts are "employees" under the National Labor Relations Act; the NLRB will require that employers pay salts if they fire them for trying to organize.[32] The solution is to know whom you're hiring. However, not hiring someone solely because he or she might be pro-union or a union salt would be discriminatory.[33]

Step 2. Obtaining Authorization Cards

authorization cards
In order to petition for a union election, the union must show that at least 30% of employees may be interested in being unionized. Employees indicate this interest by signing authorization cards.

For the union to petition the NLRB for the right to hold an election, it must show that a sizable number of employees may be interested in organizing. Therefore, the next step for union organizers is to try to get the employees to sign **authorization cards** (see Figure 15-2). Among other things, these usually authorize the union to seek a representation election and state that the employee has applied to join the union. Thirty percent of the eligible employees in an appropriate bargaining unit must sign before the union can petition the NLRB for an election (although that figure may rise to over 50 percent if the employer has agreed with the union to recognize the union if a majority of employees sign the authorization cards).

This is a dangerous time for supervisors. During this stage, both union and management use propaganda. The union claims it can improve working conditions, raise wages, increase benefits, and generally get the workers better deals. Management can attack the union on ethical and moral grounds and cite the cost of union membership. Management can also explain its accomplishments, express facts and opinions, and explain the law applicable to organizing campaigns. However, neither side can threaten, bribe, or coerce employees. And an employer (or supervisor) may not make promises of benefits to employees or make unilateral changes in terms and conditions of employment that were not planned to be implemented prior to the onset of union organizing activity.

FIGURE 15-2 Sample Authorization Card

SAMPLES UNIONS of AMERICA

Authorization for Representation

I hereby authorize Local 409 of the SAMPLES union to be my exclusive representative for the purposes of collective bargaining with my employer. I understand that my signature on this card may be used to obtain certification of Local 409 as our exclusive bargaining representative without an election.

This card will verify that I have applied for union membership and that effective _____ I hereby authorize you to deduct each pay period from my earnings an amount equal to the regular current rate of monthly union dues and initiation fee.

Employer:_____ **Worksite:** _____

Date:_____ **Name:** _____

Street Address:_____ **City:** _____ **Zip code:** _____

Home Phone: _____ **Cell Phone:** _____ **Home E-mail:** _____

Department: _____

Job Title/Classification: _____

Signature: _____

You must print and mail in this authorization card for it to be recognized. Only original cards are valid and should be submitted. Mail to:

SAMPLES Unions of America, Local 409
301 Samples Way
Miami, FL 33101

STEPS TO TAKE Management can take several steps with respect to the authorization cards. For example, the NLRB ruled an employer might lawfully inform employees of their right to revoke their authorization cards, even when employees have not asked for such information. The employer can also distribute pamphlets that explain just how employees can revoke their cards. However, the law prohibits any material assistance to employees such as postage or stationery.

Similarly, it is an unfair labor practice to tell employees they can't sign a card. What you *can* do is prepare supervisors so they can explain what the card actually authorizes the union to do—including subjecting the employee to union rules. The union, for instance, may force the employee to picket and fine any member who does not comply. Such explanations can be an effective weapon.

One thing managers should *not* do is look through signed authorization cards if confronted with them by union representatives. The NLRB could construe that as an unfair labor practice, as spying on those who signed. Doing so could also later form the basis of a charge alleging discrimination due to union activity, if the firm subsequently disciplines someone who signed a card.

During this stage, unions can picket the company, subject to three constraints: (1) The union must file a petition for an election within 30 days after the start of picketing; (2) the firm cannot already be lawfully recognizing another union; and (3) there cannot have been a valid NLRB election during the past 12 months.

Step 3. Hold a Hearing

Once the union collects the authorization cards, one of three things can occur. If the employer chooses *not to contest union recognition* at all, then the parties need no hearing, and a special "consent election" is held. If the employer chooses not to contest the union's *right to an election*, and/or the scope of the bargaining unit, and/or which employees are eligible to vote in the election, no hearing is needed and the parties can stipulate an election. If an employer *does* wish to contest the union's right, it can insist on a hearing to determine those issues. An employer's decision about whether to insist on a hearing is a strategic one. Management bases it on the facts of each case, and on whether it feels it needs more time to try to persuade employees not to elect a union.

Most companies do contest the union's right to represent their employees, claiming that a significant number don't really want the union. It is at this point that the NLRB gets involved. The union usually contacts the NLRB, which requests a hearing. It then sends a hearing officer to investigate. The examiner sends both management and union a notice of representation hearing (NLRB Form 852) that states the time and place of the hearing.

The hearing addresses several issues. First, does the record indicate there is enough evidence to hold an election? (For example, did 30% or more of the employees in an appropriate bargaining unit sign the authorization cards?) Second, the examiner decides what the bargaining unit will be. The **bargaining unit** is the group of employees that the union will be authorized to represent and bargain for collectively. If the entire organization is the bargaining unit, the union will represent all nonsupervisory, nonmanagerial, and nonconfidential employees, even though the union may be oriented mostly toward blue-collar workers. (Professional and nonprofessional employees can be included in the same bargaining unit only if the professionals agree.) If your firm disagrees with the examiner's bargaining unit decision, it can challenge the decision. This will require a separate NLRB ruling.

bargaining unit
The group of employees the union will be authorized to represent.

The NLRB hearing addresses other issues. These include, "Does the employer qualify for coverage by the NLRB?" and "Is the union a labor organization within the meaning of the National Labor Relations Act?"

If the results of the hearing are favorable for the union, the NLRB will order holding an election. It will issue a Notice of Election (NLRB Form 707) to that effect for the employer to post.

Step 4. The Campaign

During the campaign that precedes the election, union and employer appeal to employees for their votes. The union will emphasize that it will prevent unfairness, set up grievance and seniority systems, and improve wages. Union strength, they'll say, will give employees a greater voice in disciplinary matters and in determining wages and working conditions. Management will stress that improvements like those don't require unions and that wages are equal to or better than with a union. Management will also emphasize the cost of union dues; the fact that the union is an "outsider"; and that if the union wins, a strike may follow. It can even attack the union on ethical and moral grounds, while insisting that employees will not be as well off and may lose freedom. But neither side can threaten, bribe, or coerce employees.

Step 5. The Election

The election occurs within 30 to 60 days after the NLRB issues its Decision and Direction of Election. The election is by secret ballot; the NLRB provides the ballots (see Figure 15-3), voting booth, and ballot box; counts the votes; and certifies the results.

The union becomes the employees' representative if it wins the election, and winning means getting a majority of the votes *cast*, not a majority of the total workers in the bargaining unit. (Also keep in mind that if an employer commits an unfair labor practice, the NLRB may reverse a "no union" election. Supervisors must therefore be careful not to commit unfair practices.)

Several things influence whether the union wins the certification election. Unions have a higher probability of success in geographic areas with a higher percentage of union workers. High unemployment seems to lead to poorer results for the union, perhaps because employees fear that unionization efforts might result in reduced job security or employer retaliation. Unions usually carefully pick the size of their bargaining unit (all clerical employees in the company, only those at one facility, and so on) because the larger the bargaining unit, the smaller the probability of union victory. The more workers vote, the less likely a union victory, probably because more workers who are not strong supporters vote.

FIGURE 15-3 Sample NLRB Ballot

UNITED STATES OF AMERICA

National Labor Relations Board

OFFICIAL SECRET BALLOT

FOR CERTAIN EMPLOYEES OF

Do you wish to be represented for purposes of collective bargaining by —

MARK AN "S" IN THE SQUARE OF YOUR CHOICE

YES ☐ NO ☐

DO NOT SIGN THIS BALLOT.Fold and drop in ballot box.
If you spoil this ballot return it to the Board Agent for a new one.

How to Lose an NLRB Election

In recent years, unions have won about 69% of elections held each year (and as we'll see, somewhat fewer decertifications).[34] According to expert Matthew Goodfellow, there is no sure way employers can win elections, but several sure ways to lose one.[35]

Reason 1. Asleep at the switch. In one study, in 68% of the companies that lost to the union, executives were caught unaware. In these companies, turnover and absenteeism had increased, productivity was erratic, and safety was poor. Grievance procedures were rare. But ironically when the first reports of authorization cards began trickling in, management usually responded with letters describing the company as "one big family."[36]

Reason 2. Appointing a committee. Of the losing companies, 36% formed a committee to manage the campaign. The problems here are that: (1) Promptness is essential in an election situation, and committees move slowly. (2) Most committee members are NLRB neophytes, whose views reflect hope rather than experience. (3) A committee's decision is usually a compromise decision, not necessarily the most effective one. This expert suggests giving full responsibility to one decisive executive. A human resource director and a consultant or advisor with broad experience in labor relations should assist this person.

Reason 3. Concentrating on money and benefits. In 54% of the elections studied, the company lost because top management concentrated on money and benefits. As Goodfellow says:

> Employees may want more money, but quite often, if they feel the company treats them fairly, decently, and honestly, they are satisfied with reasonable, competitive rates and benefits. It is only when they feel ignored, uncared for, and disregarded that money becomes a major issue to express their dissatisfaction.[37]

Reason 4. Delegating too much to divisions. For companies with plants scattered around the country, unionizing one plant tends to lead to unionizing others. The solution is, don't abdicate all personnel and industrial relations decisions to plant managers.[38] Dealing effectively with unions—monitoring employees' attitudes, reacting properly when the union appears, and so on—requires centralized guidance from the main office and its human resources staff.

Evidence-Based HR: What to Expect the Union to Do to Win the Election

The other side of the coin is this: What can unions do to boost their chances they'll win the election? A researcher analyzed data from 261 NLRB elections. She found that the best way for unions to win is a "rank-and-file strategy." It includes union tactics such as the following:[39]

1. "Reliance on a slow, underground, person-to-person campaign using house calls, small group meetings, and pre-union associations to develop leadership and union commitment, and prepare workers for employer anti-union strategies before the employer becomes aware of the campaign."
2. The union will focus on building active rank-and-file participation, including an organizing committee reflecting the different interest groups in the bargaining unit.
3. The union will press for a first contract early in the organizing process.
4. The union will use "inside and outside pressure tactics to build worker commitment and compel the employer to run a fair campaign."
5. There will be an emphasis during the organizing campaign on issues such as respect, dignity, and fairness, not just traditional bread-and-butter issues like wages.

The Supervisor's Role

Target recently won a unionization election at a New York store, but a federal judge overturned it and required a new election. The judge found that Target managers had violated labor law by telling employees they couldn't wear union buttons or distribute flyers, and by threatening to discipline workers who discussed union matters.[40]

Supervisors are an employer's first line of defense in the unionizing effort. They are often in the best position to sense employee attitude problems, and to discover the first signs of union activity. However, supervisors can also inadvertently undermine their employer's union efforts. Supervisory unfair labor practices could then (1) cause the NLRB to hold a new election after your company has won a previous election, or (2) cause your company to forfeit the second election and go directly to contract negotiation.

For example, one plant superintendent reacted to a union's initial organizing attempt by prohibiting distribution of union literature in the plant's lunchroom. Since solicitation of off-duty workers in nonwork areas is generally legal, the company subsequently allowed the union to post literature on the company's bulletin board and to distribute literature in nonworking areas inside the plant. However, the NLRB still ruled that the initial act of prohibiting distribution of the literature was an unfair labor practice, one not "made right" by the company's subsequent efforts. The NLRB used the superintendent's action as one reason for invalidating an election that the company had won.[41] (Today certain "supervisors" may no longer be excluded from the bargaining unit. The employer could trigger an unfair labor practice charge if it tries to use those people to assist in its campaign.)[42]

SOME TIPS Supervisors can use the acronym TIPS to remember what *not* to do during the campaigns.[43] *Do not* Threaten, Interrogate, make Promises to, or Spy on employees (for instance, do not threaten that you will close or move the business, cut wages, reduce overtime, or lay off employees). FORE outlines what you may do. *You may* give employees Facts (like what signing the authorization card means), express your Opinion about unions, explain factually correct Rules (such as that the law permits permanently replacing striking employees), and share your Experiences about unions. The Know Your Employment Law feature expands on this.

KNOW YOUR EMPLOYMENT LAW

Rules Regarding Literature and Solicitation

To avoid legal problems, employers need rules governing distribution of literature and solicitation of workers and show supervisors how to apply them.[44] For example:

1. Employers can always bar nonemployees from soliciting employees when the employee is on duty and not on a break.
2. Employers can usually stop employees from soliciting other employees for any purpose if one or both employees are on paid-duty time and not on a break.
3. Most employers (generally not including retail stores, shopping centers, and certain other employers) can bar nonemployees from the building's interiors and work areas as a right of private property owners.[45]
4. Employers can deny on- or off-duty employees access to interior or exterior areas only if they can show the rule is required for reasons of production, safety, or discipline.

Again, such restrictions are valid only if the employer doesn't discriminate against the union. Thus, if the employer lets employees collect money for baby gifts, to sell products, or to engage in other solicitation during their working time, it may not be able lawfully to prohibit them from union soliciting during work time. Here is one example of a specific rule aimed at limiting union organizing or activity:

> Solicitation of employees on company property during working time interferes with the efficient operation of our business. Nonemployees are not permitted to solicit employees on company property for any purpose. Except in break areas where both employees are on break or off the clock, no employee may solicit another employee during working time for any purpose.[46] ■

Decertification Elections: Ousting the Union

Winning an election and signing an agreement don't necessarily mean that the union is in the company to stay. The same law that grants employees the right to unionize also gives them a way to terminate legally (decertify) their union's right to represent them. There are around 450 to 500 **decertification** elections each year, of which unions usually win around 30%.[47] That's actually a more favorable win rate for management than the rate for the original, representation elections.

decertification
Legal process for employees to terminate a union's right to represent them.

Decertification campaigns are similar to certification campaigns.[48] The union organizes membership meetings and house-to-house visits, mails literature into the homes, and uses phone calls, e-mails, NLRB appeals, and (sometimes) threats and harassment to win the election. Employers can't legally start the decertification process, but once started management uses meetings—including one-on-one meetings, small-group meetings, and meetings with entire units—as well as legal or expert assistance, letters, improved working conditions, and subtle or not-so-subtle threats to try to influence the votes.[49]

Globalization complicates the employer's union relations challenges, as the accompanying HR Practices Around the Globe feature shows.

IMPROVING PERFORMANCE: *HR Practices Around The Globe*

France Comes to the Workers' Aid

Employers planning to expand abroad should ponder the recent experience of drug maker Sanofi SA, in France. Because of the relatively high cost of running its research facility in southwestern France, Sanofi told its researchers there it was closing their facility.[50] Employees began staging weekly protests, supported by the French government, which opposes profitable companies slashing jobs. After 9 months, the company was still waiting for a government report on the situation so it could finish negotiating with its unions and try to get some of them other jobs elsewhere. As one Sanofi manager said, "In France, the politics, the labor laws are extremely different than in any other regions.... It means that for sites like Toulouse ... anything you want to do differently gets to be a confrontational issue."[51] ■

Source: Based on Nick Wingfield and Melissa Eddy, "In Germany, Union Culture Clashes with Amazons' Labor Practices," New York Times, August 5, 2013, pp. B1, B4.

If your professor has assigned this, go to the Assignments section of **mymanagementlab.com** to complete this discussion question.

Talk About It 2: With government policies like this, how do you think French companies remain competitive with those, say, in the United States?

The Collective Bargaining Process

What Is Collective Bargaining?

LEARNING OBJECTIVE 15-4

Illustrate with examples of bargaining that is not in good faith.

collective bargaining
The process through which representatives of management and the union meet to negotiate a labor agreement.

When and if the union becomes your employees' representative, a day is set for management and labor to meet and negotiate a labor agreement. This agreement will contain specific provisions covering wages, hours, and working conditions.

What exactly is **collective bargaining**? According to the National Labor Relations Act:

> For the purpose of [this act,] to bargain collectively is the performance of the mutual obligation of the employer and the representative of the employees to meet at reasonable times and confer in good faith with respect to wages, hours, and terms and conditions of employment, or the negotiation of an agreement, or any question arising thereunder, and the execution of a written contract incorporating any agreement reached if requested by either party, but such obligation does not compel either party to agree to a proposal or require the making of a concession.

In plain language, this means that both management and labor are required by law to negotiate wage, hours, and terms and conditions of employment "in good faith."

What Is Good Faith?

good faith bargaining
Both parties are making every reasonable effort to arrive at agreement; proposals are being matched with counterproposals.

Good faith bargaining is the cornerstone of effective labor–management relations. It means that both parties communicate and negotiate, match proposals with counterproposals, and make a reasonable effort to arrive at an agreement. It does not mean that one party compels another to agree. Nor does it require that either party make any specific concessions (although some may be necessary).[52]

How can you tell if bargaining is *not* in good faith? Here are some examples.[53]

Surface bargaining. Going through the motions of bargaining without any real intention of completing an agreement.

Inadequate concessions. Unwillingness to compromise.

Inadequate proposals and demands. The NLRB considers the advancement of proposals to be a positive factor in determining overall good faith.

Dilatory tactics. The law requires that the parties meet and "confer at reasonable times and intervals." Obviously, refusal to meet with the union does not satisfy the positive duty imposed on the employer.

Imposing conditions. Attempts to impose conditions that are so onerous or unreasonable as to indicate bad faith.

Making unilateral changes in conditions. This is a strong indication that the employer is not bargaining with the required intent of reaching an agreement.

Bypassing the representative. The duty of management to bargain in good faith involves, at a minimum, recognition that the union representative is the one with whom the employer must deal in conducting negotiations.

Withholding information. An employer must supply the union with information, upon request, to enable it to discuss the collective bargaining issues intelligently.

Of course, requiring good faith bargaining doesn't mean that negotiations can't grind to a halt. For example, a few years ago the National Football League accused the Players Association of not bargaining in good faith, using delays to "run out the clock" so that the players could bring suit against the NFL.[54]

The Negotiating Team

Both union and management send negotiating teams to the bargaining table, and both go into the bargaining sessions having "done their homework."

First, they acquire data on which to build their bargaining positions.[55] From compensation surveys they compile data on pay and benefits, including comparisons with local pay rates and to rates for similar jobs in the industry. Data on the distribution of the workforce (in terms of age, sex, and seniority, for instance) are important, because it determines benefits. Internal economic data regarding benefits, earnings, and the cost of overtime are important too. Union representatives will have sounded out union members on their desires and conferred with representatives of related unions.

Management will also "cost" the current labor contract and determine the increased cost—total, per employee, and per hour—of the union's demands. It will use information from grievances and feedback from supervisors to determine what the union's demands might be, and prepare counteroffers and arguments.[56] Other popular tactics include attitude surveys to test employee reactions to various sections of the contract that management may feel require change, and informal conferences with local union leaders to discuss the operational effectiveness of the contract and to send up trial balloons on management ideas for change.

Costing the Contract

Collective bargaining experts emphasize the need to cost the union's demands carefully. One says,

> The mistake I see most often is [HR professionals who] enter the negotiations without understanding the financial impact of things they put on the table. For example, the union wants three extra vacation days. That doesn't sound like a lot, except that in some states, if an employee leaves, you have to pay them for unused vacation time. [So] now your employer has to carry that liability on their books at all times.[57]

voluntary (or permissible) bargaining items
Items in collective bargaining over which bargaining is neither illegal nor mandatory—neither party can be compelled against its wishes to negotiate over those items.

illegal bargaining items
Items in collective bargaining that are forbidden by law; for example, a clause agreeing to hire "union members exclusively" would be illegal in a right-to-work state.

mandatory bargaining items
Items in collective bargaining that a party must bargain over if they are introduced by the other party—for example, pay.

Bargaining Items

Labor law sets out categories of specific items that are subject to bargaining: These are mandatory, voluntary, and illegal items.

Voluntary (or permissible) bargaining items are neither mandatory nor illegal; they become a part of negotiations only through the joint agreement of both management and union. Neither party can compel the other to negotiate over voluntary items. You cannot hold up signing a contract because the other party refuses to bargain on a voluntary item, such as benefits for retirees.

Illegal bargaining items are forbidden by law. A clause agreeing to hire union members exclusively would be illegal in a right-to-work state, for example.

Table 15-1 presents some of the 70 or so **mandatory bargaining items** over which bargaining is mandatory under the law. They include wages, hours, rest periods, layoffs, transfers, benefits, and severance pay. Others, such as drug testing, are added as the law evolves.

TABLE 15-1 Bargaining Items

Mandatory	Permissible	Illegal
Rates of pay	Indemnity bonds	Closed shop
Wages	Management rights as to union affairs	Separation of employees based on race
Hours of employment	Pension benefits of retired employees	Discriminatory treatment
Overtime pay	Scope of the bargaining unit	
Shift differentials	Including supervisors in the contract	
Holidays	Additional parties to the contract such as the international union	
Vacations	Use of union label	
Severance pay	Settlement of unfair labor charges	
Pensions	Prices in cafeteria	
Insurance benefits	Continuance of past contract	
Profit-sharing plans	Membership of bargaining team	
Christmas bonuses	Employment of strikebreaker	
Company housing, meals, and discounts		
Employee security		
Job performance		
Union security		
Management–union relationship		
Drug testing of employees		

Source: Michael R. Carrell and Christina Heavrin, *Labor Relations and Collective Bargaining: Cases, Practices, and Law*, 6th edition, © 2001. Reprinted by permission of Pearson Education, Inc. Upper Saddle River, NJ.

Building Negotiating Skills

Hammering out a satisfactory labor agreement requires negotiating skills. Experienced negotiators use *leverage, desire, time, competition, information, credibility*, and *judgment* to improve their bargaining positions.[58] Things you can *leverage* include *necessity, desire, competition*, and *time*.[59] For example, the union knows that an employer who must fill a big order fast (*necessity*) is at a disadvantage.

Similarly, the employer who makes its *desires* too obvious undercuts its position. *Competition* is important too. There is no more convincing ploy than subtly hinting you've got an alternative (like shifting services abroad). *Time* (particularly deadlines) can also tilt things for or against you.

"Knowledge is power" when negotiating, so having *information* is advantageous, as is *credibility*. Finally, good negotiators need *judgment:* the ability to "strike the right balance between gaining advantages and reaching compromises, in the substance as well as in the style of [their] negotiating technique."[60]

Bargaining Hints

Expert Reed Richardson has the following advice for bargainers:

1. Be sure to set clear objectives for every bargaining item, and be sure you understand the reason for each.
2. Do not hurry.
3. When in doubt, caucus with your associates.
4. Be well prepared with firm data supporting your position.
5. Strive to keep some flexibility in your position.
6. Don't concern yourself just with what the other party says and does; find out why.
7. Respect the importance of face saving for the other party.
8. Be alert to the real intentions of the other party—not only for goals, but also for priorities.
9. Be a good listener.
10. Build a reputation for being fair but firm.

11. Learn to control your emotions and use them as a tool.
12. As you make each bargaining move, be sure you know its relationship to all other moves.
13. Measure each move against your objectives.
14. Remember that collective bargaining is a compromise process. There is no such thing as having all the pie.
15. Try to understand the people and their personalities.[61]
16. Remember that excessive bargainer transparency and openness can backfire.[62]

impasse
Collective bargaining situation that occurs when the parties are not able to move further toward settlement, usually because one party is demanding more than the other will offer.

Impasses, Mediation, and Strikes

In collective bargaining, an **impasse** (or stalemate) occurs when the parties are not able to move further toward settlement. This usually occurs because one party is demanding more than the other will offer. Sometimes a third party, such as a mediator, can resolve an impasse. If the impasse is not resolved, the union may call a work stoppage, or strike.[63]

mediation
Intervention in which a neutral third party tries to assist the principals in reaching agreement.

fact finder
A neutral party who studies the issues in a dispute and makes a public recommendation for a reasonable settlement.

arbitration
The most definitive type of third-party intervention, in which the arbitrator usually has the power to determine and dictate the settlement terms.

interest arbitration
Arbitration enacted when labor agreements do not yet exist or when one or both parties are seeking to change the agreement.

rights arbitration
Arbitration that interprets existing contract terms, for instance, when an employee questions the employer's right to have taken some disciplinary action.

strike
A withdrawal of labor.

economic strike
A strike that results from a failure to agree on the terms of a contract that involves wages, benefits, and other conditions of employment.

unfair labor practice strike
A strike aimed at protesting illegal conduct by the employer.

wildcat strike
An unauthorized strike occurring during the term of a contract.

sympathy strike
A strike that takes place when one union strikes in support of the strike of another.

THIRD-PARTY INVOLVEMENT Negotiators use three types of third-party interventions to overcome an impasse. With **mediation**, a neutral third party tries to assist the principals in reaching agreement. The mediator meets with each party to determine where each stands, and then uses this information to find common ground for bargaining. When Hostess Brands couldn't reach agreement with its unions, its bankruptcy judge had them join him for a mediation session, where he tried (unsuccessfully) to broker a new contract.[64]

In certain situations, as in a national emergency dispute, a **fact finder** is a neutral party who studies the issues in a dispute and makes a public recommendation for a reasonable settlement.[65] Presidential emergency fact-finding boards resolved impasses in certain critical transportation disputes.

Arbitration is the most definitive third-party intervention, because the arbitrator may have the power to determine and dictate the settlement terms. With *binding arbitration*, both parties are committed to accepting the arbitrator's award. With *nonbinding arbitration*, they are not. Arbitration may also be voluntary or compulsory (imposed by a government agency). In the United States, voluntary binding arbitration is the most prevalent.

There are two main topics of arbitration. **Interest arbitration** centers on working out a labor agreement; the parties use it when such agreements do not yet exist or when one or both parties are seeking to change the agreement. **Rights arbitration** really means "contract interpretation arbitration." It usually involves interpreting existing contract terms, for instance, when an employee questions the employer's right to have taken some disciplinary action.[66]

SOURCES OF THIRD-PARTY ASSISTANCE Various public and professional agencies make arbitrators and mediators available. For example, the American Arbitration Association (AAA) represents and provides the services of thousands of arbitrators and mediators to employers and unions. The U.S. government's Federal Mediation and Conciliation Service provides both arbitrators and mediators see (Figure 15-4).[67] In addition, most states provide arbitrator and mediation services.

STRIKES A **strike** is a withdrawal of labor. There are four main types of strikes. An **economic strike** results from a failure to agree on the terms of a contract. Unions call **unfair labor practice strikes** to protest illegal conduct by the employer. A **wildcat strike** is an unauthorized strike occurring during the term of a contract. A **sympathy strike** occurs when one union strikes in support of the strike of another union.[68] For example, in sympathy with South Korean Hyundai workers, the United Auto Workers organized a rally outside of Hyundai's technical center in Superior Township, Michigan, and took steps to hold other rallies.[69]

The likelihood of and severity of a strike depend partly on the parties' willingness to "take a strike."[70] The number of major work stoppages (strikes involving

FIGURE 15-4 Form to Request Mediation Services

Source: Federal Mediation and Conciliation Service.

FMCS Form F-53
Revised 5-92

Form Approved
OMB No. 3076-0005

FEDERAL SECTOR LABOR RELATIONS
NOTICE TO FEDERAL MEDIATION AND CONCILIATION SERVICE

Mail To:
Notice Processing Unit
FEDERAL MEDIATION AND CONCILIATION SERVICE
2100 K Street, N.W.
Washington, D.C. 20427

THIS NOTICE IS IN REGARD TO: (MARK"X")

(1) ☐ AN INITIAL CONTRACT (INCLUDED FLRA CERTIFICATION NUMBER) #
☐ A CONTRACT REOPENER REOPENER DATE
☐ THE EXPIRATION OF AN EXISTING AGREEMENT EXPIRATION DATE:

(2) ☐ ***OTHER REQUESTS FOR THE ASSISTANCE OF FMCS IN BARGAINING*** ***(MARK "X")***
SPECIFY TYPE OF ISSUE(S)

(3) ☐ ***REQUEST FOR GRIEVANCE MEDIATION (SEE ITEM #10)*** ***(MARK "X")***
ISSUE(S)

(4) NAME OF FEDERAL AGENCY NAME OF SUBDIVISION OR COMPONENT, IF ANY
STREET ADDRESS OF AGENCY CITY STATE ZIP
AGENCY OFFICIAL TO BE CONTACTED AREA CODE & PHONE NUMBER

(5) NAME OF NATIONAL UNION OR PARENT BODY NAME AND/OR LOCAL NUMBER
STREET ADDRESS CITY STATE ZIP
UNION OFFICIAL TO BE CONTACTED AREA CODE & PHONE NUMBER

LOCATION OF NEGOTIATIONS OR WHERE MEDIATION WILL BE HELD

(6) STREET ADDRESS CITY STATE ZIP

(7) APPROX. # OF EMPLOYEES IN BARGAINING UNIT(S) >> IN ESTABLISHMENT>>

(8) THIS NOTICE OR REQUEST IS FILED ON BEHALF OF ***(MARK "X")*** ☐UNION ☐AGENCY

(9) NAME AND TITLE OF OFFICIAL(S) SUBMITTING THIS NOTICE OR REQUEST AREA CODE AND PHONE NUMBER
STREET ADDRESS CITY STATE ZIP

FOR GRIEVANCE MEDIATION, THE SIGNATURES OF BOTH PARTIES ARE REQUIRED:*

(10) SIGNATURE (AGENCY) DATE | SIGNATURE (UNION) DATE

*Receipt of this form does not commit FMCS to offer its services. Receipt of this form will not be acknowledged in writing by FMCS. While use of this form is voluntary, its use will facilitate FMCS service to respondents. Public reporting burden for this collection of information is estimated to average 10 minutes per response, including time for reviewing the collection of information. Send comments regarding this burden estimate or any other aspect of this collection of information, including suggestions for reducing this burden, to FMCS Division of Administrative Services, Washington, D.C. 20427, and to the Office of Management and Budget, Paperwork Reduction Project. Washington, D.C. 20603

For Instructions, See Back

1,000 workers or more) peaked at about 400 per year between 1965 and 1975, and today average around 20.

picketing
Having employees carry signs announcing their concerns near the employer's place of business.

Picketing, or having employees carry signs announcing their concerns near the employer's place of business, is one of the first activities to appear during a strike. Its purpose is to inform the public about the existence of the labor dispute and often to encourage them to refrain from doing business with the struck employer.

Employers have several options when employees strike. One is to temporarily shut down the affected area and halt operations. A second is to contract out work to blunt the effects of the strike. A third is to continue operations, perhaps using supervisors and other nonstriking workers. A fourth alternative is hiring replacements for the strikers.

Diminished union influence plus competitive pressures now prompt more employers to replace (or consider replacing) strikers with permanent replacement workers. When the United Steel Workers struck refineries recently, BP quickly began training replacement workers.[71] And in a labor dispute a few years ago, the NFL implied even they might use replacement players.[72]

Employers generally can replace strikers. In one case known as *Mackay*, the U.S. Supreme Court ruled that although the National Labor Relations Act does prohibit employers from interfering with employees' right to strike, employers still have the right to continue their operations and to replace strikers. Subsequent decisions by the National Labor Relations Board put some limitations on *Mackay.* For example, employers cannot permanently replace strikers who are protesting unfair labor practices; they must rehire strikers who unconditionally apply for reinstatement.

STRIKE GUIDELINES FOR EMPLOYERS As negotiations between the Hibbing Taconite Steel Plant in Minnesota and the United Steelworkers of America headed toward a deadline, the firm brought in security workers and trailers to house them.

Two experts say that, with a strike imminent, following these guidelines is advisable:

- Pay all striking employees what you owe them on the first day of the strike.
- Secure the facility. Management should control access to the property. Some employers make preparations with special strike security companies to provide security during the strike.[73]
- Notify all customers, and prepare a standard official response to all queries.
- Contact all suppliers and others who will have to cross the picket line. Establish alternative methods of obtaining supplies.
- Arrange for overnight stays in the facility, and for delivered meals, if necessary.
- Notify the local unemployment office of your need for replacement workers.
- Photograph the facility before, during, and after picketing. If necessary, install video equipment to monitor picket lines.
- Record all facts concerning strikers' demeanor and activities and such incidents as violence, threats, mass pickets, property damage, or problems.
- Gather the following evidence: number of pickets and their names; time, date, and location of picketing; wording on every sign carried by pickets; and descriptions of picket cars and license numbers.[74]

corporate campaign
An organized effort by the union that exerts pressure on the corporation by pressuring the company's other unions, shareholders, directors, customers, creditors, and government agencies, often directly.

OTHER "WEAPONS" Management and labor each have other weapons to break an impasse. The union, for example, may resort to a corporate campaign. A **corporate campaign** is an organized effort by the union to exert pressure on the employer by

Picketing is one of the first activities to occur during a strike. The purpose is to inform the public about the labor dispute.

Stacy Walsh Rosenstock/Alamy

boycott
The combined refusal by employees and other interested parties to buy or use the employer's products.

pressuring the company's other unions, shareholders, corporate directors, customers, creditors, and government agencies.[75] Thus, the union might surprise members of the board of directors by picketing their homes and organizing a **boycott** of the company's banks.[76] The United Auto Workers recently began trying to organize hourly factory workers at foreign-owned car plants in the United States. The union commenced picketing U.S. Hyundai, Daimler, Toyota, and Nissan dealerships.[77]

TRENDS SHAPING HR: *DIGITAL AND SOCIAL MEDIA*

UNIONS GO DIGITAL When it comes to organizing just about any sort of campaign, communication is king, a fact that hasn't been lost on unions. For example, in one survey, 49% of unions said they used Facebook to communicate with members and employees, 23% used Twitter, and 13% used YouTube.[78] About 92% of unions have a Web site, while 78.1% use e-mail newsletters.[79] The group trying to organize Starbucks workers (the *Starbucks Workers' Union*) started their own Web site (www.starbucksunion.org).[80] In another recent campaign, the employer restricted the use of its electronic systems (including e-mail) to "business purposes only." The union filed objections. The NLRB held that nonmanagement employees who normally have access to an employer's e-mail system as part of their jobs may use the system to communicate about union matters when not working, such as during lunch or break times.[81] ■

inside games
Union efforts to convince employees to impede or to disrupt production—for example, by slowing the work pace.

lockout
A refusal by the employer to provide opportunities to work.

Inside games are union efforts to convince employees to impede or to disrupt production—for example, by slowing the work pace or refusing to work overtime.[82] Inside games are basically strikes—albeit "strikes" in which the company continues to pay the employees. In one inside game at a Caterpillar plant, UAW grievances rose from 22 to 336. This tied up workers and management in unproductive endeavors on company time.[83]

For their part, employers can try to break an impasse with lockouts. A **lockout** is a refusal by the employer to provide opportunities to work. It (sometimes literally) locks out employees and prohibits them from doing their jobs (and being paid). Faced with a new contract that might slash their wages by 50%, Canadian Auto Workers Union employees from one Caterpillar plant found themselves locked out after 6 months of negotiations failed to produce a settlement.[84]

The NLRB views lockouts as an unfair labor practice only when the employer acts for a prohibited purpose. Trying to bring about a settlement on terms favorable to the employer is not a prohibited purpose. Lockouts are not widely used; employers are usually reluctant to cease operations when employees are willing to continue working.

Employers exert other pressure. When Boeing's union resisted accepting new labor concessions at its assembly facility in Washington, Boeing began actively considering moving the planned assembly of its new Boeing 777X long-range jet to South Carolina. Boeing's Washington state workers subsequently approved a new agreement.[85]

injunction
A court order compelling a party or parties either to resume or to desist from a certain action.

Both employers and unions can seek a court injunction if they believe the other side is causing irreparable harm to the other party. An **injunction** is a court order compelling a party or parties either to resume or to desist from a certain action.[86]

The Contract Agreement

The actual contract agreement may be a 20- or 30-page document, or longer. It may contain just general declarations of policy, or detailed rules and procedures. The tendency today is toward the longer contract.

The main sections of a typical contract cover subjects such as these: (1) management rights; (2) union security and automatic payroll dues deduction; (3) grievance procedures; (4) arbitration of grievances; (5) disciplinary procedures; (6) compensation rates; (7) hours of work and overtime; (8) benefits: vacations, holidays, insurance, pensions; (9) health and safety provisions; (10) employee security seniority provisions; and (11) contract expiration date.

Watch It!
What is it like to actually work out problems with the union? If your professor has assigned this, go to the Assignments section of **mymanagementlab.com** to complete the video exercise titled *UPS: Union Management.*

Dealing With Disputes And Grievances

LEARNING OBJECTIVE 15-5
Develop a grievance procedure.

Signing the labor agreement is not the last step in collective bargaining. No labor contract can cover all contingencies and answer all questions. For example, suppose the contract says you can only discharge an employee for "just cause." You subsequently discharge someone for speaking back to you. Was speaking back to you "just cause"?

The *grievance process* is the process or steps that the employer and union agreed to follow to ascertain whether some action violated the collective bargaining agreement. It is the vehicle for administering the contract day to day. However, this usually involves interpretation only, not negotiating new terms or altering existing ones. The aim is to clarify what those contract points really mean, in the context of addressing grievances regarding things like time off, disciplinary action, and pay. When the Cleveland Browns' head coach fined one of his players $1,701 for not paying the hotel's bill for a $3 bottle of water, players quickly filed grievances with the NFL.[87]

Sources of Grievances

In practice, it is probably easier to list those items that *don't* precipitate grievances than the ones that do. Employees may use just about anything involving wages, hours, or conditions of employment as the basis of a grievance.

Discipline cases and seniority problems including promotions, transfers, and layoffs would top this list. Others would include grievances growing out of job evaluations and work assignments, overtime, vacations, incentive plans, and holidays.[88] Here are three examples of grievances:

- ***Absenteeism.*** An employer fired an employee for excessive absences. The employee filed a grievance stating that there had been no previous warnings related to excessive absences.
- ***Insubordination.*** An employee on two occasions refused to obey a supervisor's order to meet with him, unless a union representative was present at the meeting. As a result, the employee was discharged and subsequently filed a grievance protesting the discharge.
- ***Plant rules.*** The plant had a posted rule barring employees from eating or drinking during unscheduled breaks. The employees filed a grievance claiming the rule was arbitrary.[89]

Grievances are often symptoms of underlying problems. Sometimes bad relationships between supervisors and subordinates are to blame: This is often the cause of grievances over "fair treatment," for instance. Organizational factors like ambiguous instructions also cause frustration and grievances. Union activism is another cause; the union may solicit grievances from workers to underscore ineffective supervision. Some individuals are by their nature negative, dissatisfied, and prone to complaints. Discipline and dismissal are two major sources of grievances.

The Grievance Procedure

grievance procedure
Formal process for addressing any factor involving wages, hours, or conditions of employment that is used as a complaint against the employer.

Most collective bargaining contracts contain a **grievance procedure**. It lists the steps in the procedure, time limits associated with each step, and specific rules such as "all charges of contract violation must be reduced to writing." Nonunionized employers need such procedures, too.

Grievance procedures differ from firm to firm. Some contain simple, two-step procedures. Here, the grievant, union representative, and company representative

EMPLOYEE GRIEVANCE FORM

Aggrieved employee _____ Date_____

Department_____ Employee's job title _____

Employee's work email address and/or other contact information _____

_____

Statement of grievance: Briefly state what happened to lead you to grieve, including for instance situation leading to the complaint, who was involved (names and titles), when the occurrence/situation took place (date and time), and where it took place

_____

_____

_____

_____

_____

_____

_____

_____

Why do you consider this a grievance? (please check one) __Contract violation __Unfair treatment

If you checked contract violation, please list contract articles and sections you believe apply

_____

What remedy are you seeking?

_____

_____

_____

Aggrieved employee's signature_____ Date _____

HR officer signature _____ Date

FIGURE 15-5 Sample Online Grievance Form

meet to discuss the grievance. If they don't find a satisfactory solution, the grievance goes before a third-party arbitrator who hears the case, writes it up, and makes a decision. Figure 15-5 shows a grievance record form.

At the other extreme, the grievance procedure may contain six or more steps. The first step might be for the grievant and shop steward to meet informally with the supervisor of the grievant to try to find a solution. The next steps involve the grievant and union representatives meeting with higher-level managers. Finally, if top management and the union can't reach agreement, the grievance may go to arbitration.

Guidelines for Handling Grievances

The best way for a supervisor to handle a grievance is to develop a work environment in which grievances don't arise in the first place. Hone your ability to avoid, recognize, diagnose, and correct the causes of potential employee dissatisfaction (such as unfair appraisals or poor communications) before they become grievances.

Given that many factors including union pressures prompt grievances, it would be naïve to think that grievances arise only due to supervisor unfairness. However, there's little doubt that the quality of the interpersonal relations among you and your subordinates will influence your team's grievance rate. The supervisor is on the firing line and must steer a course between treating employees fairly and maintaining management's rights and prerogatives. The HR Tools feature presents some guidelines.

IMPROVING PERFORMANCE: ***HR Tools For Line Managers And Small Businesses***

How to Handle a Grievance Situation

Grievances cost money, in terms of lost work time, productivity, and (possibly) arbitrators' fees. One expert has developed a list of supervisor do's and don'ts as useful guides in handling grievances.[90] Some critical ones include:

Do:

1. Investigate and handle each case as though it may eventually result in arbitration.
2. Talk with the employee about his or her grievance; give the person a full hearing.
3. Require the union to identify specific contractual provisions allegedly violated.
4. Comply with the contractual time limits for handling the grievance.
5. Visit the work area of the grievance.
6. Determine whether there were any witnesses.
7. Examine the grievant's personnel record.
8. Fully examine prior grievance records.
9. Treat the union representative as your equal.
10. Hold your grievance discussions privately.
11. Fully inform your own supervisor of grievance matters.

Don't:

1. Discuss the case with the union steward alone—the grievant should be there.
2. Make arrangements with individual employees that are inconsistent with the labor agreement.
3. Hold back the remedy if the company is wrong.
4. Admit to the binding effect of a past practice.
5. Relinquish to the union your rights as a manager.
6. Settle grievances based on what is "fair." Instead, stick to the labor agreement.
7. Bargain over items not covered by the contract.
8. Treat as subject to arbitration claims demanding the discipline or discharge of managers.
9. Give long written grievance answers.
10. Trade a grievance settlement for a grievance withdrawal.
11. Deny grievances because "your hands have been tied by management."
12. Agree to informal amendments in the contract. ■

If your professor has assigned this, go to the Assignments section of **mymanagementlab.com** to complete this discussion.

Talk About It 3: Write a 30-word guide that summarizes the essence of these dos and don'ts.

LEARNING OBJECTIVE 15-6

Describe a strategy for cooperative labor relations.

The Union Movement Today And Tomorrow

Union membership has gradually declined in America from about 20% of the workforce in 1983 (when 17.8 million workers belonged to unions), to about 11% (just over 14 million workers) recently.[91]

Several factors contributed to the decline in union membership over the past 50 or so years. Unions traditionally appealed mostly to blue-collar workers, and the proportion of blue-collar jobs has been decreasing. Globalization increased competition and pressures on employers to cut costs and boost productivity, further squeezing unions. Other factors pressuring employers and unions include the deregulation of trucking, airlines, and communications; outdated equipment and factories; mismanagement; new technology; and laws (such as occupational safety) that somewhat substituted

Tomas Abad/AGE Fotostock

One union's aims include making "... it our first priority to help millions more workers form unions so we can build a strong movement for rewarding work in America...".

for and reduced the need for unions. As noted, the recent recession triggered budget cuts in both the public and private sectors, prompting anti-union public policy attitudes, and the loss of about 1 million public sector union jobs. Bankruptcies, such as those that swept the U.S. airline industry, often end with courts imposing less favorable contract terms on union employees.[92] For example, a bankruptcy court judge recently gave Patriot Coal Corp. the right to drastically reduce pay and benefits for thousands of miners, retirees, and dependents.[93]

The net effect has been the permanent layoff of hundreds of thousands of union members, the permanent closing of company plants, the relocation of companies to nonunion settings (either in the United States or abroad), and mergers and acquisitions that eliminated union jobs and affected collective bargaining agreements. That's why union membership as a percentage of people working has actually dropped by about two-thirds over 50 years, to about 11%.[94]

What Are Unions Doing About It?

Of course, unions aren't sitting idly by. For example, the priorities of the Change to Win Coalition (whose members broke off from the AFL-CIO) include making "... it our first priority to help millions more workers form unions so we can build a strong movement for rewarding work in America [and] unite the strength of everyone who works in the same industry so we can negotiate with today's huge global corporations for everyone's benefit."[95]

In practice, they'll do several things. Change to Win will be very aggressive about trying to organize workers, will focus on organizing women and minority workers, will focus more on organizing temporary or contingent workers, and will target specific multinational companies for international campaigns.[96]

Unions are in fact becoming more aggressive. For example, they are pushing Congress to pass the *Employee Free Choice Act*. This would make it easier for employees to unionize. Instead of secret-ballot elections, the act would institute a "card check" system. Here the union would win recognition when a majority of workers signed authorization cards saying they want the union. Several large companies, including Cingular Wireless, have already agreed to the card check process.[97] The act would also require binding arbitration to set a first contract's terms if the company and union can't negotiate an agreement within 120 days.[98] Unions are also using *class action lawsuits* to support employees in nonunionized companies to pressure employers.[99] And, unions are cooperating more with so-called alternative labor groups, which advocate for improved worker benefits and working conditions, but are not unions themselves.[100]

Finally, unions are becoming more proactive in coordinating their efforts.[101] For example, in its "Union Cities" campaigns, AFL-CIO planners work with local labor councils and individual unions to gain the support of a target city's elected officials. In Los Angeles, this helped the service workers' union organize janitors in that city.

Similarly, unions are extending their efforts abroad. For example, UNITE (now part of UNITE HERE) used a campaign to coordinate 800 workers at one foreign employer's distribution center with other workers at the employer's New York City headquarters, and with local activists and international unions throughout Europe. This forced the employer's parent company, a French conglomerate, to cease resisting the union's organizing efforts. To support its efforts to unionize autoworkers in the United States, the UAW enlisted thousands of union members in Brazil to picket Nissan dealerships there.[102] The same is happening in reverse. When Daimler said it was going to phase out producing its "C" cars in Germany and begin producing them in the United States, its German union, IG Metall, began cooperating with the UAW to unionize Daimler's American plants.[103]

RECENT TRENDS IN LABOR LAWS Several recent NLRB decisions support union efforts. A recent NLRB ruling may make it easier for unions to organize by letting them focus on small "micro" groups within the employer's workforce.[104] Also favoring unions, in late 2014 the NLRB published its Final Rule permitting what many call "quickie" union elections. By allowing unions to call elections in as little as 13 days after filing a representation petition, this new rule is expected by labor experts to make it more difficult for employers to present their argument against the union.[105] The NLRB also lengthened the amount of time that employees who organized under a card check process (see above) had to wait to start a decertification process. And after being exempted for many years from having to disclose their participation with each other in a union campaign, employers and their union campaign-related consultants and attorneys now must report their relationship.[106]

Cooperative Clauses

When AT&T's workers threatened to strike if the company insisted on raising workers' health-care premiums, AT&T began training managers to fill in for workers.[107]

However, labor–management relations history is also sprinkled with cooperation. For example, more than 50 years ago, General Motors and Toyota created a joint venture they called New United Motor Manufacturing Inc. (NUMMI). The partners hoped to merge GM's marketing expertise with Toyota's famous team-based management system.[108] NUMMI and the United Auto Workers (UAW) agreed that management and labor would work together as a team, give workers a voice in decision making, and build high-quality cars at low cost. NUMMI and the UAW installed a new labor–management system in their plant. NUMMI's 2,400 hourly workers were organized around teams of 5 to 10 members. NUMMI reduced the number of supervisors.[109] The plant was soon very successful (although both parties eventually ended their joint venture).

Since then, many labor–management agreements have included so-called cooperative agreements. These agreements generally commit union and management to adopt one or more cooperative themes. One analysis of labor contracts expiring between 1997 and 2007 found that roughly half of the 1,041 contracts studied contained cooperative clauses. Parties commit to adhere to one or more of these cooperative themes (in descending order of frequency-of-mention in the agreements):[110]

- Intent to cooperate
- A statement of commitment to cooperate
- Committees to review mutual concerns that arise
- Decisions on traditional issues
- Guarantees of employment security
- Commitments to high-performance practices
- Decisions on strategic issues
- Full cooperation

At one extreme, for example, Alcoa's agreement contained a full "Cooperative Partnership Clause." This included provisions for joint management–labor decision-making committees, and a commitment to maintain employee security under catastrophic market conditions.[111] At the other extreme, many contain only a statement of intent to cooperate, such as on traditional issues like drug abuse, health care, and safety. The HR Around The Globe feature illustrates cooperation abroad.

There's little doubt, as a study argues, that unions "that have a cooperative relationship with management can play an important role in overcoming barriers to the effective adoption of practices that have been linked to organizational competitiveness."[112] But employers who want to capitalize on that potential must change how they think, by emphasizing a cooperative partnership.[113]

IMPROVING PERFORMANCE: *HR Around The Globe*

Labor-Management Cooperation and Works Councils in America

When the United Auto Workers lost an effort to unionize the Volkswagen plant outside Chattanooga, Tennessee, the vote of 712 to 626 against joining the UAW surprised even Volkswagen management.

Perhaps the biggest reason for the surprise was that Volkswagen actually supported unionizing the plant. Part of the reason Volkswagen supported unionization is because it said it wanted to bring to Chattanooga the works councils that it uses successfully in Germany. A *works council* is an employee committee that elects representatives who work with management to establish policies on things like work hours and dismissal procedures.[114] The works councils meet monthly with managers to discuss topics ranging from no-smoking policies to layoffs.[115] (*Co-determination* is also the rule in Germany and several other countries. **Co-determination** means employees have the legal right to a voice in setting company policies. Workers elect their own representatives to the supervisory board of the employer.)[116] As the CEO of Volkswagen Chattanooga said, works councils are the "key to our success and productivity."[117]

Co-determination
An employee representation system in which workers elect their own representatives to the supervisory (management) board of the employer and have the legal right to a voice in setting company policies on matters such as company organization, hiring, and performance appraisal.

Volkswagen still hopes to bring works councils to its Chattanooga plant, but U.S. labor law may stand in the way, unless the plant's workers vote for a union. Many years ago, some employers tried to neutralize legitimate unions by setting up company backed "faux unions," a practice Congress soon outlawed. While works councils are legitimate, most experts believe that having nonunion employee representatives bargaining on matters such as pay and dismissals won't pass muster with American labor law. ■

If your professor has assigned this, go to the Assignments section of **mymanagementlab.com** to complete this discussion question.

✪ **Talk About It 4:** What do you think accounts for the fact that German labor relations seem to be more cooperative than in America?

CHAPTER 15

Chapter Review

MyManagementLab® Go to **mymanagementlab.com** to complete the problems marked with this icon. ✪

Chapter Section Summaries

15-1. The **labor movement** is important. About 14 million U.S. workers belong to unions—about 11% of the total. Workers unionize not just to get more pay or better working conditions; employer unfairness and the union's power are also important. Unions aim for union security, and then for improved wages, hours, and working conditions and benefits for their members. Union security options include the closed shop, union shop, agency shop, preferential shop, and maintenance of membership arrangement.

15-2. To understand unions and their impact, one should understand the interplay between **unions and the law**. In brief, labor law has gone through periods of strong encouragement of unions, to modified encouragement coupled with regulation, and finally to detailed regulation of internal union affairs. Historically, the laws encouraging the union movement included the Norris-LaGuardia and National Labor Relations (Wagner) Acts of the 1930s. These outlawed certain unfair employer labor practices and made it easier for unions to organize. The Taft-Hartley or Labor Management Relations Act of 1947 addressed keeping unions from restraining or coercing employees, and listed certain unfair union labor practices. In the 1950s, the Landrum-Griffin Act (the Labor Management Reporting and Disclosure Act) further protected union members from possible wrongdoing on the part of their unions.

15-3. When unions begin organizing, all managers and supervisors usually get involved, so it's essential to understand the mechanics of **the union drive and election**. The main steps include initial contact, obtaining authorization cards, holding a hearing, the campaign itself, and the election. Supervisors need to understand their role at each step in this process. Follow the acronym TIPS—do not Threaten, Interrogate, make Promises, or Spy. And follow FORE—provide Facts, express your Opinions, explain factually correct Rules, and share your Experiences.

15-4. The employer and union hammer out an agreement via the **collective bargaining process**. The heart of collective bargaining is good faith bargaining, which means both parties must make reasonable efforts to arrive at agreement, and proposals are matched with counterproposals. In the actual bargaining sessions, there are mandatory bargaining items such as pay, illegal bargaining items, and voluntary bargaining items such as benefits for retirees. If things don't go smoothly during collective bargaining, the parties may utilize third-party intermediaries, including mediators, fact finders, and arbitrators. Strikes represent a withdrawal of labor.

15-5. Most managers become involved with **disputes and grievances** during their careers. Collective bargaining agreements contain a specific grievance procedure listing the steps in the procedure. In general, the best way to handle a grievance is to create an environment in which grievances don't occur. However, if a grievance does occur, things to do include investigate, handle each case as though it may eventually result in arbitration, talk with the employee about the grievance, and comply with the contractual time limits for handling the grievance.

15-6. Membership is down but unions are still influential today, so it's important to understand the **union movement today and tomorrow**. For example, new union federations, such as Change to Win, are being more aggressive about organizing workers, and unions are going global, for instance, with German unions helping Daimler's U.S. employees organize.

Discussion Questions

✪ **15-1.** Why do employees join unions? What are the advantages and disadvantages of being a union member?

15-2. Discuss four sure ways to lose an NLRB election.

✪ **15-3.** Briefly illustrate how labor law has gone through a cycle of repression and encouragement.

15-4. Explain in detail each step in a union drive and election.

15-5. Define impasse, mediation, and strike, and explain the techniques that are used to overcome an impasse.

Individual and Group Activities

15-6. You are the manager of a small manufacturing plant. The union contract covering most of your employees is about to expire. Working individually or in groups, discuss how to prepare for union contract negotiations.

15-7. Working individually or in groups, use Internet resources to find situations where company management and the union reached an impasse at some point during their negotiation process, but eventually resolved the impasse. Describe the issues on both sides that led to the impasse. How did they move past the impasse? What were the final outcomes?

15-8. Appendices A and B at the end of this book (pages 612–629) list the knowledge someone studying for the HRCI (Appendix A) or SHRM (Appendix B) certification exam needs to have in each area of human resource management (such as in Strategic Management, and Workforce Planning). In groups of several students, do four things: (1) review Appendix A and/or B; (2) identify the material in this chapter that relates to the Appendix A and/or B required knowledge lists; (3) write four multiple-choice exam questions on this material that you believe would be suitable for inclusion in the HRCI exam and/or the SHRM exam; and, (4) if time permits, have someone from your team post your team's questions in front of the class, so that students in all teams can answer the exam questions created by the other teams.

15-9. Several years ago, 8,000 Amtrak workers agreed not to disrupt service by walking out, at least not until a court hearing was held. Amtrak had asked the courts for a temporary restraining order, and the Transport Workers Union of America was actually pleased to postpone its walkout. The workers were apparently not upset at Amtrak, but at Congress for failing to provide enough funding for Amtrak. What, if anything, can an employer do when employees threaten to go on strike, not because of what the employer did, but what a third party—in this case, Congress—has done or not done? What laws would prevent the union from going on strike in this case?

Experiential Exercise

The Organizing Campaign at Sam's Cupcake Shop

Purpose: The purpose of this exercise is to give you practice in dealing with some of the elements of a union-organizing campaign.[118]

Required Understanding: You should be familiar with the material covered in this chapter, as well as the following incident, "The Organizing campaign at Sam's Cupcake Shop."

Incident: Sam's Cupcake Shop sells baked goods (croissants, cupcakes, rolls, cakes, etc.) and serves light meals such as breakfast and salads through its chain of ten small retail stores in the borough of Manhattan, in New York City. Each store is staffed with about 9 employees (plus one manager), some of whom do the cooking and some of whom staff the counter and sell the food items. As with Sam's other stores, the Sam's Cupcake Shop on First Avenue is staffed primarily with recent (legal) immigrants to America, all of whom are paid at or just above the minimum wage. It was no secret that at least one New York City agency was pressing (in 2015) for food service owners to raise the minimum wage for food service employees to $15 per hour.[119] Everything at the First Avenue store seemed to be going smoothly, but that apparent tranquility ended abruptly in July 27, 2015. That was the day that Anesha, the First Avenue store's manager called Taylor Brooke, Sam's Cupcake's human resource manager, to tell her that they had "an employee problem."

The problem, Anesha said, was that she'd heard from a few employees that the Service Employees International Union was trying to organize Sam's Cupcake Stores employees. Taylor's first reaction was one of caution, particularly because food service employees are historically difficult to organize—"they don't stay in their jobs long enough to unionize them," to paraphrase one union leader.[120] Unfortunately, Anesha said she had already taken what she called "sensible steps" to blunt the unionization effort. She had, first, explained to her employees that if costs went up because they unionized, then "we'd probably have to close this shop." She said she also promised better work schedules if they "ignored" the union, and told them they were prohibited from discussing union matters during work time. "And don't worry" she said to Taylor, "I've got a list of the employees who are pushing for the union."

The more Anesha talked, the more concerned Taylor became, not just with the union but with the possible consequences of Anesha's efforts. She wondered particularly if Anesha's actions could cause problems down the road for Sam's Cupcakes with the NLRB.

As it turned, she didn't have long to wait for an answer. The following week pickets from the union and its supporters appeared in front of the First Avenue store carrying signs decrying the company's "unfair labor practices." At that point Sam came into Taylor's office and said, "If they think they can railroad me into giving them big raises they are wrong; I am closing that store down." Taylor was in a quandary as to how to reply to Sam, and in general, what she should do.

How to Set Up the Exercise/Instructions: Divide the class into groups of several students. Assume that you are labor relations consultants retained by Taylor to identify the problems and issues involved and to advise Taylor and Sam of the company's rights and obligations, as well as the implications of what's transpired so far, add finally what to do next. Each group will spend the time allotted discussing the issues. Then, outline those issues, as well as an action plan for Taylor and Sam. What should they do next? Can Sam really close the store down?

If time permits, a spokesperson from each group should list on the board the issues involved and the group's recommendations.

Application Case

Negotiating with the Writers Guild of America

The talks between the Writers Guild of America (WGA) and the Alliance of Motion Picture & Television Producers (producers) began tense, and then got tenser.[121]

The biggest issue was how to split revenue from new media, such as when television shows move to the Internet. The producers said they wanted a profit-splitting system rather than the current residual system. Under the residual system, writers continue to receive "residuals" or income from shows they write every time they're shown (such as when *Seinfeld* appears in reruns). Writers Guild executives argued producers' revenues from advertising and subscription fees had recently jumped by about 40%.[122]

The situation grew tenser.[123] Even after meeting six times, it seemed that the parties had made no progress in resolving the dispute.[124]

Soon, the Writers Guild asked its members for strike authorization, and the producers were claiming that the guild was just trying to delay negotiations until the current contract expired (at the end of October). To paraphrase the president of the producers' group said, the WGA leadership seemed unwilling to bargain in good faith.[125] As evidence, the producers claimed that the WGA negotiating committee left one meeting after less than an hour.

Both sides knew timing was very important. During the fall and spring, television series production is in full swing. So, a writers' strike now would have a bigger impact than waiting until, say, the summer to strike. Perhaps not surprisingly, some movement was soon discernible.[126] Then the WGA and producers reached agreement. The new contract was signed soon after the two sides—including top union and industry officials like the head of Walt Disney Co.—began marathon bargaining sessions.[127]

Questions

15-10. The producers said the WGA was not bargaining in good faith. What did they mean by that, and do you think the evidence is sufficient to support the claim?

15-11. The WGA did eventually strike. What tactics could the producers have used to fight back once the strike began? What tactics do you think the WGA used?

15-12. This was a conflict between professional and creative people (the WGA) and TV and movie producers. Do you think the conflict was therefore different in any way than are the conflicts between, say, the Autoworkers or Teamsters unions against auto and trucking companies? Why?

15-13. What role (with examples) did negotiating skills seem to play in the WGA producers' negotiations?

Continuing Case

Carter Cleaning Company

The Grievance

On visiting one of Carter Cleaning Company's stores, Jennifer was surprised to be taken aside by a long-term Carter employee, who met her as she was parking her car. "Murray (the store manager) told me I was suspended for 2 days without pay because I came in late last Thursday," said George. "I'm really upset, but around here the store manager's word seems to be law, and it sometimes seems like the only way anyone can file a grievance is by meeting you or your father like this in the parking lot." Jennifer was very disturbed by this revelation and promised the employee she would look into it and discuss the situation with her father. In the car heading back to headquarters, she began mulling over what Carter Cleaning Company's alternatives might be.

Questions

15-14. Do you think it is important for Carter Cleaning Company to have a formal grievance process? Why or why not?

15-15. Based on what you know about the Carter Cleaning Company, outline the steps in what you think would be the ideal grievance process for this company.

15-16. In addition to the grievance process, can you think of anything else that Carter Cleaning Company might do to make sure grievances and gripes like this one are expressed and are heard by top management?

Translating Strategy into HR Policies and Practices Case*,§

** The accompanying strategy map for this chapter is in MyManagementLab; the overall map on the inside back cover of this text outlines the relationships involved.*

Improving Performance At The Hotel Paris

The Hotel Paris's New Labor Relations Practices

The Hotel Paris's competitive strategy is "To use superior guest service to differentiate the Hotel Paris properties, and to thereby increase the length of stay and return rate of guests, and thus boost revenues and profitability." HR manager Lisa Cruz must now formulate functional policies and activities that support this competitive strategy and boost performance by eliciting the required employee behaviors and competencies.

Lisa Cruz's parents were union members, and she had no strong philosophical objections to unions, per se. However, as the head of HR for the Hotel Paris, she did feel very strongly that her employer should do everything legally possible to remain union-free. She knew that this is what the hotel chain's owners and top executives wanted, and that achieving their strategic goals would be best accomplished by staying union free. Furthermore, the evidence seemed to support their position. At least one study that she'd seen concluded that firms with 30% or more of their eligible workers in unions were in the bottom 10% in terms of performance, while those with 8% to 9% of eligible workers in unions scored in the top 10%.[128] The problem was that the Hotel Paris really had no specific policies and procedures in place to help its managers and supervisors deal with union activities. With all the laws regarding what employers and their managers could and could not do to respond to a union's efforts, Lisa knew her company was "a problem waiting to happen." She turned her attention to deciding what steps she and her team should take with regard to labor relations and collective bargaining.

Lisa and the CFO knew that unionization was a growing reality for the Hotel Paris. Some of the hotel chain's U.S. employees were already unionized, and unions in this industry were quite active. For example, as they were surfing the Internet to better gauge the situation, Lisa and the CFO came across the Web site from the Hotel Employees Restaurant Union, local 26. It describes their success in negotiating a contract at several local hotels including ones managed by the Westin and Hilton chains. The CFO and Lisa agreed that it was important that she and her team develop and institute a new set of policies and practices that would enable the Hotel Paris to deal more effectively with unions.

Together with a labor–management attorney, the team developed a 20-page "What You Need to Know When the Union Calls" manual for Hotel Paris managers and supervisors. This contained three sets of information. First, it provided a succinct outline of *labor relations law*, particularly as it relates to the company's managers. Second, it laid a *detailed set of guidelines* regarding what supervisors could and could not do with respect to union organizing activities. Third, it identified all line supervisors as the company's "*front-line eyes and ears*" with respect to union organizing activity. Here, the manual provided examples of activities that might suggest that a union was trying to organize the hotel's employees, and whom the supervisor should notify.

Lisa and her team also decided to ensure that the company was responsive to its employees' concerns. Lisa and her team believed that

§ Written and copyright by Gary Dessler, PhD.

many of the steps they'd taken earlier should help. For example, improving salaries and wages, providing financial incentives, and instituting the new ethics, justice, and fairness programs already seemed to be having a measurable effect on employee morale.

Questions

15-17. List and briefly describe what you believe are the three most important steps Hotel Paris management can take now to reduce the likelihood unions will organize more of its employees.

15-18. Write a detailed two-page outline for a "What You Need to Know When the Union Calls" manual. Lisa will distribute this manual to her company's supervisors and managers, telling them what they need to know about looking out for possible unionizing activity, and how to handle actual organizing process–related supervisory tasks.

MyManagementLab

Go to **mymanagementlab.com** for Auto-graded writing questions as well as the following Assisted-graded writing questions:

15-19. Describe important tactics you would expect the union to use during the union drive and election.

15-20. Why, would you say, workers join unions and what would you as a manager do to make it less likely your employees would want to join a union at your workplace?

15-21. MyManagementLab only—comprehensive writing assignment for this chapter.

PERSONAL INVENTORY ASSESSMENTS

Strategies for Handling Conflict

Complete this assessment to learn more about your personality.

Key Terms

closed shop, 483
union shop, 483
agency shop, 483
preferential shop, 483
right to work, 483
Norris-LaGuardia Act of 1932, 484
National Labor Relations (or Wagner) Act, 484
National Labor Relations Board (NLRB), 484
Taft-Hartley Act of 1947, 485
national emergency strikes, 487
Landrum-Griffin Act of 1959, 487
union salting, 488
authorization cards, 488
bargaining unit, 490
decertification, 493
collective bargaining, 494
good faith bargaining, 494
voluntary (or permissible) bargaining items, 495
illegal bargaining items, 495
mandatory bargaining items, 495
impasse, 497
mediation, 497
fact finder, 497
arbitration, 497
interest arbitration, 497
rights arbitration, 497
strike, 497
economic strike, 497
unfair labor practice strike, 497
wildcat strike, 497
sympathy strike, 497
picketing, 498
corporate campaign, 499
boycott, 500
inside games, 500
lockout, 500
injunction, 500
grievance procedure, 501
Co-determination, 506

Endnotes

1. For example, see http://articles.moneycentral.msn.com/Investing/Extra/CostcoTheAntiWalMart.aspx?page=1, accessed June 29, 2011; and Hamilton Nolan, "The Anti-Wal-Mart," http://gawker.com/costco-the-anti-wal-mart-511739135, accessed August 7, 2013.
2. Christine Frey, "Costco's Love of Labor: Employees' Well-Being Key to Its Success," www.seattlepi.com/default/article/Costco-s-love-of-labor-Employees-well-being-key-1140722.php, accessed June 29, 2011; Steven Greenhouse and Reed Abelson, "Wal-Mart Cuts Some Health Care Benefits," *New York Times*, October 21, 2011, pp. B1, B5.
3. See, for example, www.costcobenefits.com/cms/what-you-need-to-know-about-costco-benefits/, accessed April 25, 2015.
4. Steven Greenhouse, "Share of the Workforce in a Union Falls to a 97 Year Low, 11.3%," *New York Times*, January 24, 2013, B1; www.bls.gov/news.release/union2.nr0.htm, accessed July 22, 2015.
5. www.bls.gov/news.release/union2.nr0.htm, accessed July 22, 2015.
6. Michael Ash and Jean Seago, "The Effect of Registered

Nurses' Unions on Heart Attack Mortality," *Industrial and Labor Relations Review* 57, no. 3 (April 2004), pp. 422–442.
7. http://articles.moneycentral.msn.com/Investing/Extra/CostcoTheAntiWalMart.aspx?page=1, accessed September 15, 2011; Nolan, "The Anti-Wal-Mart."
8. Ibid.
9. www.bls.gov/news.release/union2.nr0.htm, accessed July 22, 2015.
10. "Union Benefit Costs Prevailing," *Bloomberg BNA Bulletin to Management*, May 14, 2013, p. 156.
11. Kris Maher, "The New Union Worker," *Wall Street Journal*, September 27, 2005, pp. B1, B11.
12. Robert Grossman, "Unions Follow Suit," *HR Magazine*, May 2005, p. 49.
13. Warner Pflug, *The UAW in Pictures* (Detroit: Wayne State University Press, 1971), pp. 11–12.
14. "Employee Engagement: A New Union Avoidance Strategy," June 28, 2011, www.modernsurvey.com, accessed April 12, 2014.
15. This is based on Jessica Tyler, "Employee Engagement and Labor Relations," *Gallup Business Journal*. http://businessJournal.Gallup.com, accessed April 9, 2014.
16. Arthur Sloane and Fred Witney, *Labor Relations* (Upper Saddle River, NJ: Prentice Hall, 2007), pp. 335–336.
17. Benjamin Taylor and Fred Witney, *Labor Relations Law* (Upper Saddle River, NJ: Prentice Hall, 1992), pp. 170–171; www.dol.gov/whd/state/righttowork.htm, accessed June 5, 2010.
18. www.dol.gov/whd/state/righttowork.htm, accessed September 11, 2014. Indiana's law applies only to school teachers; without Indiana, there are 22 right-to-work states.
19. "Research Inconclusive About Effective Right to Work on Economy," *BNA Bulletin to Management*, January 8, 2013, p. 14.
20. "Unions Hit Hard by Job Losses, Right to Work," *Daily Oklahoman* (via *Knight Ridder/Tribune Business News*), February 1, 2005. See also www.dol.gov/whd/state/righttowork.htm, accessed September 11, 2014.
21. www.seiu.org/our-union/, accessed June 1, 2011.
22. Steven Greenhouse, "4th Union Quits AFL-CIO in a Dispute Over Organizing," *New York Times*, September 15, 2005, p. A14.
23. Some trace early U.S. labor relations legislation back to a fire at the Triangle Shirtwaist factory in 1911. Following that tragedy, New York City and New York State soon adopted 36 new laws, and many view these laws as the basis for and precursor to the U.S. labor legislation efforts that began in earnest in the 1930s. "The Birth of the New Deal," *The Economist*, March 19, 2011, p. 39.
24. The following material is based on Sloane and Witney, *Labor Relations*, pp. 46–124.
25. www.bls.gov/news.release/union2.nr0.htm, accessed June 1, 2011.
26. Michael Carrell and Christina Heavrin, *Labor Relations and Collective Bargaining* (Upper Saddle River, NJ: Prentice Hall, 2004), p. 180.
27. Sloane and Witney, *Labor Relations*, p. 121.
28. See, for example, Steven Greenhouse, "High Court to Weigh Union Cases," *New York Times*, November 11, 2013, pp. B1, B2.
29. For organizing examples from the unions' point of view, see www.twu.org/international/steps, accessed June 29, 2011; www.opeiu.org/NeedAUnion/StepstoCreatingaUnionWorkplace/tabid/71/Default.aspx, accessed June 29, 2011; and particularly http://ufcwone.org/steps-form-union, accessed August 7, 2013.
30. Kris Maher, "Unions' New Foe: Consultants," *Wall Street Journal*, August 15, 2005, p. B1.
31. "Some Say Salting Leaves Bitter Taste for Employers," *BNA Bulletin to Management*, March 4, 2004, p. 79; www.nlrb.gov/global/search/index.aspx?mode=s&qt=salting&col=nlrb&gb=y, accessed January 14, 2008. For a management lawyer's perspective, see www.fklaborlaw.com/union_salt-objectives.html, accessed May 25, 2007.
32. "Spurned Union Salts Entitled to Back Pay, D.C. Court Says, Affirming Labor Board," *BNA Bulletin to Management*, June 21, 2001, p. 193.
33. D. Diane Hatch and James Hall, "Salting Cases Clarified by NLRB," *Workforce*, August 2000, p. 92. See also www.fklaborlaw.com/union_salt-objectives.html, accessed May 25, 2007.
34. http://www.laborandcollectivebargaining.com/2014/11/articles/unions-and-organizing/unions-winning-more-elections-but-facing-diminishing-returns/, accessed September 20, 2015.
35. This section is based on Matthew Goodfellow, "How to Lose an NLRB Election," *Personnel Administrator* 23 (September 1976), pp. 40–44. See also Matthew Goodfellow, "Avoid Unionizing: Chemical Company Union Election Results for 1993," *Chemical Marketing Reporter* 246 (July 18, 1994), p. SR14; Gillian Flynn, "When the Unions Come Calling," *Workforce*, November 2000, pp. 82–87.
36. Ibid.
37. Ibid.
38. Harry Katz, "The Decentralization of Collective Bargaining: A Literature Review and Comparative Analysis," *Industrial and Labor Relations Review* 47, no. 1 (October 1993), p. 11; F. Traxler, "Bargaining (De) centralization, Macroeconomic Performance and Control over the Employment Relationship," *British Journal of Industrial Relations* 41, no. 1 (March 2003), pp. 1–27.
39. The following are adapted and/or quoted from Kate Bronfenbrenner, "The Role of Union Strategies in NLRB Certification Elections," *Industrial and Labor Relations Review* 50 (January 1997), pp. 195–212; see also J. Fiorito et. al., "Understanding Organising Activity Among US National Unions," *Industrial Relations Journal* 41, no. 1 (January 2010), pp. 74–92.
40. Stephen Greenhouse, "Union Gets New Election at a Target," *New York Times*, May 22, 2012, B3.
41. Frederick Sullivan, "Limiting Union Organizing Activity Through Supervisors," *Personnel* 55 (July/August 1978), pp. 55–65. See also Edward Young and William Levy, "Responding to a Union-Organizing Campaign: Do You and Your Supervisors Know the Legal Boundaries in a Union Campaign?" *Franchising World* 39, no. 3 (March 2007), pp. 45–49.
42. www.hreonline.com/HRE/view/story.jhtml?id=534358235, accessed April 25, 2015.
43. Carrell and Heavrin, *Labor Relations and Collective Bargaining*, pp. 167–168.
44. Jonathan Segal, "Unshackle Your Supervisors to Stay Union Free," *HR Magazine*, June 1998, pp. 62–65. See also www.nlrb.gov/rights-we-protect/employerunion-rights-and-obligations, accessed September 11, 2014.
45. Whether employers must give union representatives permission to organize on employer-owned property at shopping malls is a matter of legal debate. See, for example, "Union Access to Employer's Customers Restricted," *BNA Bulletin to Management*, February 15, 1996, p. 49; "Workplace Access for Unions Hinges on Legal Issues," *BNA Bulletin to Management*, April 11, 1996, p. 113.
46. "Union Access to Employer's Customers Restricted," pp. 4–65. The appropriateness of these sample rules may be affected by factors unique to an employer's operation, and they should therefore be reviewed by the employer's attorney before implementation.
47. Clyde Scott and Edwin Arnold, "Deauthorization and Decertification Elections: An Analysis and Comparison of Results," *Working USA* 7, no. 3 (Winter 2003), pp. 6–20; http://www.laborandcollectivebargaining.com/2014/11/articles/unions-and-organizing/unions-winning-more-elections-but-facing-diminishing-returns/, accessed September 20, 2015.
48. Carrell and Heavrin, *Labor Relations and Collective Bargaining*, pp. 120–121.
49. See, for example, David Meyer and Trevor Bain, "Union Decertification Election Outcomes: Bargaining Unit Characteristics and Union Resources," *Journal of Labor Research* 15, no. 2 (Spring 1994), pp. 117–136; Sloane and Witney, *Labor Relations*, p. 96.
50. Mimosa Spencer and Jeanne Whalen, "Change France? Sanofi Find It Can't," *Wall Street Journal*, April 11, 2013, pp. B1, D5.
51. Ibid., B1. Similarly, workers in Germany are resisting what they call Amazon's American-style business practices. Nick Wingfield and Melissa Eddy, "In Germany, Union Culture Clashes with Amazons' Labor Practices," *New York Times*, August 5, 2013, pp. B1, B4.
52. www.nlrb.gov/nlrb/shared_files/brochures/basicguide.pdf, accessed January 14, 2008.
53. Carrell and Heavrin, *Labor Relations and Collective Bargaining*, pp. 176–177.
54. www.bloomberg.com/news/2011-02-14/nfl-files-unfair-labor-practice-charge-against-union.html, accessed June 1, 2011.
55. John Fossum, *Labor Relations* (Dallas: BPI, 1982), pp. 246–250; Sloane and Witney, *Labor Relations*, pp. 197–205.
56. *Boulwareism* is the name given to a strategy, now held in disfavor, by which the company, based on an exhaustive study of what it believed its employees wanted, made but one offer at the bargaining table and then refused to bargain any further unless convinced by the union on the basis of new facts that its original position was wrong. Fossum, *Labor Relations*, p. 267.
57. Kathryn Tyler, "Good-Faith Bargaining," *HR Magazine*, January 2005, p. 52.
58. These are based on James C. Freund, *Smart Negotiating* (New York: Simon & Schuster, 1992), pp. 42–46.
59. James C. Freund, *Smart Negotiating* (New York: Simon & Schuster, 1992), pp. 42–46.
60. Ibid., 33. One interesting observation: Communicating threats is more effective than communicating anger. See Marwan Sineceure et al., "Hot or Cold: Is Communicating Anger or Threats More Effective in Negotiation?" *Journal of Applied Psychology* 96, no. 5 (2011), pp. 1019–1032.
61. Reed Richardson, *Collective Bargaining by Objectives* (Upper Saddle River, NJ: Prentice

Hall, 1977), p. 150. Both sides will try to manipulate the media to jockey for better positions; for example, see J. McCafferty, "Labor-Management Dispute Resolution and the Media," *Dispute Resolution Journal* 56, no. 3 (August/October 2001), pp. 40–47.
62. Many negotiators pride themselves on being open, honest, and straightforward in their negotiations, but at least one study suggests that this can lead to excessive concessions. D. Scott DeRue et al., "When Is Straightforwardness a Liability in Negotiations? The Role of Integrative Potential and Structural Power," *Journal of Applied Psychology* 94, no. 4 (2009), pp. 1032–1047.
63. With or without reaching a solution, impasses and union–management conflict can leave union members demoralized. See, for example, Jessica Marquez, "Taking Flight," *Workforce,* June 9, 2008, pp. 1, 18.
64. Jacqueline Palank et al., "Last Chance to Save the Twinkie," *Wall Street Journal*, November 20, 2012, p. B1.
65. Fossum, *Labor Relations*, p. 312.
66. Carrell and Heavrin, *Labor Relations and Collective Bargaining*, p. 501.
67. http://fmcs.gov/assets/files/annual%20reports/FY2006_Annual_Report.pdf, accessed January 14, 2008.
68. Fossum, *Labor Relations*, p. 317.
69. www.autoblog.com/2010/12/06/report-uaw-to-hold-sympathy-strike-for-hyundai-workers-in-korea/, accessed June 1, 2011.
70. This is based on Sloane and Whitney, *Labor Relations*, p. 213.
71. http://fuelfix.com/blog/2015/02/18/strike-update-bp-training-additional-replacement-workers/#30249101=0, accessed July 24, 2015.
72. http://profootballtalk.nbcsports.com/2011/03/21/league-doesnt-rule-out-replacement-players-during-lockout/, accessed June 29, 2011.
73. See for example, www.afimac-us.com/what-we-do/labor-disputes-and-plant-closures/strike-security/, accessed April 11, 2014.
74. Stephen Cabot and Gerald Cuerton, "Labor Disputes and Strikes: Be Prepared," *Personnel Journal* 60 (February 1981), pp. 121–126. See also Brenda Sunoo, "Managing Strikes, Minimizing Loss," *Personnel Journal* 74, no. 1 (January 1995), p. 50ff.
75. Some labor lawyers report an increase in the use by unions of corporate campaigns. Janet Walthall, "Unions Increasingly Using Corporate Campaigns," *BNA Bulletin to Management*, February 16, 2010, p. 55.
76. For a discussion, see Herbert Northrup, "Union Corporate Campaigns and Inside Games as a Strike Form," *Employee Relations Law Journal* 19, no. 4 (Spring 1994), pp. 507–549.
77. Matthew Dolan, "UAW Targets Foreign Car Plants in US," *Wall Street Journal*, December 23, 2010, p. B3. See also Rachel Feintzeig, "Teamsters Act Tough with Twinkies Maker," *Wall Street Journal*, February 14, 2012, p. B-4.
78. www.blogging4jobs.com/wp-content/uploads/2012/02/unions-social-media.png, accessed April 25, 2015.
79. www.bna.com/social-media-new-b17179923064/, accessed April 25, 2015.
80. www.starbucksunion.org, accessed August 7, 2013.
81. www.hreonline.com/HRE/view/story.jhtml?id=534358235, accessed April 25, 2015.
82. Northrup, "Union Corporate Campaigns and Inside Games," p. 513.
83. Ibid., p. 518.
84. James Hagerty and Caroline Van Hasselt, "Lockout Tests Union's Clout," *Wall Street Journal,* January 30, 2012, p. B-1.
85. Jon Ostrower, "Boeing Considers Nonunion Plant for 777X," *Wall Street Journal*, October 20, 2013, p. B3; Jon Ostrower, "Boeing Prods Unions on Pact," *Wall Street Journal*, November 9–10, 2013, p. B3.
86. Clifford Koen Jr., Sondra Hartman, and Dinah Payne, "The NLRB Wields a Rejuvenated Weapon," *Personnel Journal*, December 1996, pp. 85–87; D. Silverman, "The NLRA at 70: A New Approach to Processing 10(j)s [NLRA at Seventy conference in New York City, 2005]," *Labor Law Journal* 56, no. 3 (Fall 2005), pp. 203–206.
87. http://sports.espn.go.com/nfl/news/story?id=4508545, accessed November 17, 2009.
88. Carrell and Heavrin, *Labor Relations and Collective Bargaining*, pp. 417–418.
89. Richardson, *Collective Bargaining by Objectives.*
90. Based on M. Gene Newport, *Supervisory Management* (St. Paul, MN: West Group, 1976), p. 273; see also Walter Baer, "Grievance Handling: 101 Guides for Supervisors" (New York: American Management Association, 1970); and Mark Lurie, "The Eight Essential Steps in Grievance Processing," *Dispute Resolution Journal* 54, no. 4 (November 1999), pp. 61–65.
91. www.bls.gov/news.release/pdf/union2.pdf, accessed April 11, 2014.
92. Susan Carey and Jack Nicas, "AMR Will Ask the Judge to Toss Labor Pacts," *Wall Street Journal,* March 23, 2012, p. B3.
93. Kris Maher and Jacqueline Palank, "Patriot Coal Allowed to Win Union PACs," *Wall Street Journal*, May 30, 2013, p. B1.
94. www.bls.gov/news.release/union2.nr0.htm, accessed April 2, 2009.
95. Jennifer Schramm, "The Future of Unions," *Society for Human Resource Management, Workplace Visions* 4 (2005), pp. 1–8.
96. Ibid. See also www.changetowin.org/about-us.html, accessed February 13, 2010.
97. "The Limits of Solidarity," *Economist*, September 23, 2006, p. 34.
98. Chris Maher, "Specter Won't Support Union-Backed Bill," *Wall Street Journal*, March 25, 2009, p. A3.
99. "Unions Using Class Actions to Pressure Nonunion Companies," *BNA Bulletin to Management*, August 22, 2006, p. 271. See also Robert Grossman, "We Organized Labor and Code," *HR Magazine,* January 2008, pp. 37–40.
100. "New labour, alt–labour," *Economist*, September 14, 2013, pp. 33–34.
101. Dean Scott, "Unions Still a Potent Force," *Kiplinger Business Forecasts*, March 26, 2003.
102. Steven Greenhouse, "At a Nissan Plant in Mississippi, a Battle to Shape the UAW's Future," *New York Times*, October 7, 2013, pp. B1, B3.
103. Neal Boudette, "A New Alliance: UAW in Germany," *Wall Street Journal*, November 8, 2013, pp. B1, B2.
104. Max Mihelich, "Labor Daze," *Workforce*, April 2014, pp. 22–24, 31.
105. www.littler.com/publication-press/publication/nlrb-issues-its-long-anticipated-quickie-election-rule-making-union-or, accessed April 25, 2015.
106. Ibid.
107. Shalini Rankchandran and Anton Troianovski, "AT&T's Strike Camp," *Wall Street Journal,* April 5, 2012, pp. B1–B2.
108. Carrell and Heavrin, *Labor Relations and Collective Bargaining*, pp. 62–63.
109. Ibid.
110. George Gray, Donald Myers, and Phyllis Myers, "Cooperative Provisions in Labor Agreements: A New Paradigm?" *Monthly Labor Review,* January 1, 1999. See also Mark Schoeff Jr., "Labor on the March," *Workforce Management*, February 2010, pp. 1, 18–19.
111. Gray et al., "Cooperative Provisions in Labor Agreements."
112. Carol Gill, "Union Impact on the Effective Adoption of High Performance Work Practices," *Human Resource Management Review* 19 (2009), pp. 39–50.
113. See also Thomas Kochan, "A Jobs Compact for America's Future," *Harvard Business Review*, March 2012, pp. 64–70.
114. Based on ibid.
115. See, for example, www.fedee.com/ewc1.html, accessed November 4, 2009.
116. This is discussed in Eduard Gaugler, "HR Management: An International Comparison," *Personnel* 65, no. 8 (1988), p. 28. See also E. Poutsma et al., "The Diffusion of Calculative and Collaborative HRM Practices in European Firms," *Industrial Relations* 45, no. 4 (October 2006), pp. 513–546.
117. Steven Greenhouse, "Labor Regroups in South after Volkswagen Vote," *New York Times*, February 17, 2004, p. B3.
118. © Gary Dessler, Ph.D. For information on what employers should not do see https://www.nlrb.gov/rights-we-protect/whats-law/employers/interfering-employee-rights-section-7-8a1, accessed July 26, 2015.
119. http://www.nytimes.com/2015/07/27/nyregion/proposed-minimum-wage-increase-for-fast-food-employees-divides-low-wage-workers.html?_r=0, accessed July 26, 2015.
120. Ibid.
121. Chris Pursell, "Rhetoric Flying in WGA Talks," *TelevisionWeek,* July 23, 2007, pp. 3, 35; Peter Sanders, "In Hollywood, a Tale of Two Union Leaderships," *Wall Street Journal*, January 7, 2008, p. B2.
122. Pursell, "Rhetoric Flying in WGA Talks."
123. Ibid.
124. James Hibberd, "Guild Talks Break with No Progress," *TVWeek* 26, no. 38 (October 8, 2007), pp. 1, 30.
125. Ibid.
126. "DGA Deal Sets the Stage for Writers," *TelevisionWeek,* January 21, 2008, pp. 3, 33.
127. "WGA, Studios Reach Tentative Agreement," *UPI NewsTrack*, February 3, 2008.
128. Brian Becker et al., *The HR Scorecard* (Boston: Harvard Business School Press, 2001), p. 16.

16

Safety, Health, and Risk Management

Coco Robicheaux/Alamy

LEARNING OBJECTIVES

16-1 Explain the supervisor's role in safety.

16-2 Explain the basic facts about safety law and OSHA.

16-3 Answer the question, "What causes accidents?"

16-4 List and explain five ways to prevent accidents at work.

16-5 Describe how one company uses employee engagement to improve workplace safety.

16-6 List five workplace health hazards and how to deal with them.

16-7 Discuss the prerequisites for a security plan and how to set up a basic security program.

When it comes to safety strategy, the, explosion and fire on British Petroleum's (BP's) Deepwater Horizon rig in the Gulf of Mexico back in 2010 still stands out for what can go wrong. The blast took the lives of 11 workers.[2] Reports from the scene said a malfunctioning blowout preventer failed to activate, causing the disaster. Past critics of BP's safety practices weren't so sure.

WHERE ARE WE NOW ...

Over 80% of the workers in one survey ranked workplace safety more important than minimum wages, sick days, and maternity leave.[1] The main purpose of this chapter is to provide you with knowledge managers need to reduce workplace safety and health problems. The main topics we discuss are safety and the manager; manager's briefing on occupational safety law; what causes accidents; how to prevent accidents; employee engagement–based safety programs; workplace health hazards—problems and remedies; and occupational security and risk management.

LEARNING OBJECTIVE **16-1**

Explain the supervisor's role in safety.

Introduction: Safety and the Manager

Why Safety Is Important

Safety and accident prevention concern managers for several reasons, one of which is the staggering number of workplace accidents. In one recent year, 4,405 U.S. workers died in workplace events,[3] and workplace accidents caused about 3 million occupational injuries and illnesses.[4] Such figures probably underestimate injuries and illnesses by two or three times.[5] And they ignore the suffering the accidents cause the employee and his or her loved ones. Safety also affects costs and profits, as the accompanying Profit Center feature illustrates.

IMPROVING PERFORMANCE: *HR as a Profit Center*

Improving Safety Boosts Profits

Many people assume that when employers economize on safety programs the money they save improves profits, but that's not the case. For one thing, poor safety practices raise wage rates, because wage rates are higher on jobs with riskier working conditions, other things equal.[6] And poor safety and the injuries and illnesses it begets actually drive up costs, including medical expenses, workers' compensation, and lost productivity.[7]

Consider the evidence. One study found a 9.4% drop in injury claims and a 26% average savings on workers' compensation costs over 4 years in companies inspected by California's occupational safety and health agency.[8] A survey of chief financial officers concluded that for every one dollar invested in injury prevention, the employer earns two dollars; 40% said "productivity" was the top benefit of effective workplace safety.[9] One forest products company saved over $1 million over 5 years by investing only about $50,000 in safety improvements and employee training. In the United States, work-related hearing loss costs employers about $242 million a year in workers' compensation claims alone, costs that are probably avoidable through earmuffs, earplugs, and training.[10] So one of the easiest ways to cut costs and boost profits is to spend money improving safety. ■

Source: Based on Russell Sobel, "Occupational Safety and Profit Maximization: Friends or Foes?," The Journal of Socioeconomics 30, no. 9 (2010), pp. 429–433; David Levine et al., "Randomized Government Safety Inspections Reduce Worker Injuries with No Detectable Job Loss," Science 336 (May 18, 2012), pp. 907–911; Chief Financial Officer Survey, Liberty Mutual Insurance Co., 2005; Mike Rich, "Preventing Hearing Loss," www.adhesivesmag.com, January 2012, pp. 40–41.

If your professor has assigned this, go to the Assignments section of **mymanagementlab.com** to complete this discussion question.

Talk About It 1: Assuming this is true, why do so many employers apparently cut corners on safety?

Injuries aren't just a problem in dangerous industries like construction. For example, computers contribute to airtight "sick building" symptoms like headaches. And office work is susceptible to problems like repetitive trauma injuries.

Management's Role in Safety

We will see that reducing accidents often boils down to reducing accident-causing conditions and accident-causing acts. However, telling employees to "work safely" is futile unless everyone knows management is serious about safety.[11] Management's attitude is crucial.

Historically, for instance, DuPont's accident rate has been much lower than that of the chemical industry as a whole. This good safety record is partly due to an organizational commitment to safety, which is evident in the following description:

> One of the best examples I know of in setting the highest possible priority for safety takes place at a DuPont Plant in Germany. Each morning at the DuPont Polyester and Nylon Plant, the director and his assistants meet at 8:45 to review the past 24 hours. The first matter they discuss is not production, but safety. Only after they have examined reports of accidents and near misses and satisfied themselves that corrective action has been taken do they move on to look at output, quality, and cost matters.[12]

Safety therefore starts at the top.[13] The Strategic Context feature illustrates this.

IMPROVING PERFORMACE: *The Strategic Context*

Deepwater Horizon

To critics of BP's safety practices, the Deepwater Horizon disaster in the Gulf wasn't just due to a malfunctioning blowout preventer. To them, rightly or wrongly, the accident reflected the fact that BP's corporate strategy had long emphasized cost-cutting and profitability at the expense of safety. For example, 5 years earlier, a report by the Chemical Safety Board blamed a huge blast at BP's Texas City, Texas, oil refinery on cost-cutting, and on a safety strategy that aimed to reduce accidents but left in place "unsafe and antiquated equipment." To the board and to some others who studied BP's safety practices, Deepwater was another example of how encouraging safe employee behavior must start at the top, and how top management's strategy can trump even earnest efforts to improve employee safety behaviors.[14] ■

Source: Based on Chip Cummins, U.S. Cites Cost Cuts' Role In BP Refinery Blast, Safety Board Lays Blame With Top-Level Decisions, Raising Firm's Legal Risks, www.wsj.com/articles/SB116222460245007872.

If your professor has assigned this, go to the Assignments section of **mymanagementlab.com** to complete these discussion questions.

Talk About It 2: How would you make the case to BP's management that boosting safety can actually support an "improve profits" strategy? What evidence could you offer?

In sum, employers should institutionalize their commitment with a safety policy, publicize it, and give safety matters high priority. Louisiana-Pacific Corp. starts all meetings with a brief safety message.[15] Georgia-Pacific reduced its workers' compensation costs by requiring that managers halve accidents or forfeit 30% of their bonuses. ABB Inc. requires its top executives to make safety observation tours of the company's facilities, sites, and projects at least quarterly.[16]

The Supervisor's Role in Accident Prevention

After inspecting a work site in which workers were installing sewer pipes in a 4-foot trench, the Occupational Safety & Health Administration (OSHA) inspector cited the employer for violating the OSHA rule requiring employers to have a "stairway, ladder, ramp or other safe means of egress."[17] In the event the trench caved in, workers needed a quick way out.

As in most such cases, the employer had the primary responsibility for safety, but the local supervisor was responsible for day-to-day inspections. Here, the supervisor did not properly do his daily inspection. The trench did cave in, injuring workers (and, secondarily, costing his company many thousands of dollars).

Whether you're the manager in the IT department of a *Fortune* 500 company or managing an excavation or dry cleaning store, daily safety inspections should be part of your routine. As one safety recommendation put it, "a daily walk-through of your workplace—whether you are working in outdoor construction, indoor manufacturing, or any place that poses safety challenges—is an essential part of your work."[18]

What to look for depends on the workplace for which you're responsible. For example, construction sites and dry cleaning stores have hazards all their own. But in general you can use a checklist of unsafe conditions such as the one in Figure 16-6 (pages 525–527) to spot problems. We present another, more extensive checklist in Figure 16-8 (pages 549–552) at the end of this chapter. (Note: Please stop what you are reading and look around where you are now: Can you list four potential safety hazards?)

Occupational Safety and Health Act of 1970
The law passed by Congress in 1970 "to assure so far as possible every working man and woman in the nation safe and healthful working conditions and to preserve our human resources."

Manager's Briefing on Occupational Safety Law

LEARNING OBJECTIVE **16-2**
Explain the basic facts about safety law and OSHA.

Congress passed the **Occupational Safety and Health Act of 1970**[19] "to assure so far as possible every working man and woman in the nation safe and healthful working conditions and to preserve our human resources."[20] The only employers it doesn't cover are self-employed persons, farms in which only immediate members of the employer's family work, and some workplaces already protected by other federal agencies or under other statutes. The act covers federal agencies, but usually not state and local governments.

Occupational Safety and Health Administration (OSHA)
The agency created within the Department of Labor to set safety and health standards for almost all workers in the United States.

The act created the **Occupational Safety and Health Administration (OSHA)** within the Department of Labor. OSHA's basic purpose is to administer the act and to set and enforce the safety and health standards that apply to almost all workers in the United States. Recently, OSHA had about 2,200 inspectors working from branch offices around the country.[21] With a limited number of inspectors, OSHA recently has focused on "fair and effective enforcement," combined with outreach, education and compliance assistance, and various cooperative programs (such as its Voluntary Protection Program).[22]

OSHA Standards and Record Keeping

OSHA operates under the "general" standard clause that each employer:

> ... shall furnish to each of his [or her] employees employment and a place of employment which are free from recognized hazards that are causing or are likely to cause death or serious physical harm to his [or her] employees.

To carry out this basic mission, OSHA promulgates detailed legally enforceable standards. (Figure 16-1 presents a small part of the standard governing guardrails for scaffolds.) The regulations don't just list standards to which employers should adhere, but "how." For example, OSHA's respiratory protection standard also covers employee training.

occupational illness
Any abnormal condition or disorder caused by exposure to environmental factors associated with employment.

Under OSHA, employers with 11 or more employees must maintain records of and report certain occupational injuries and occupational illnesses. An **occupational illness** is any abnormal condition or disorder caused by exposure to environmental factors associated with employment. This includes acute and chronic illnesses caused by inhalation, absorption, ingestion, or direct contact with toxic substances or harmful agents.

WHAT THE EMPLOYER MUST REPORT As in Figure 16-2, employers must report all occupational illnesses.[23] They must also report most occupational injuries, specifically those that result in medical treatment (other than first aid), loss of consciousness, restriction of work (one or more lost workdays), restriction of motion, or transfer to another job.[24] If an on-the-job accident results in the death of an employee, all employers, regardless of size, must report the accident to the nearest OSHA office. As of 2015, if even one employee is hospitalized for inpatient treatment because of a work-related incident, the employer must notify OSHA within 24 hours.[25]

OSHA's current record-keeping rules allow the employer to conclude that an event needn't be reported if the facts so warrant—such as if a worker slips and falls after catching his foot on his car's seat belt when not at work on the company lot.[26]

However, OSHA's record-keeping requirements are still broad.[27] Examples of recordable conditions include food poisoning suffered by an employee in the employer's cafeteria and ankle sprains that occur during voluntary participation in a company softball game at a picnic the employee was required to attend. Figure 16-3 shows the OSHA form for reporting occupational injuries or illness.

FIGURE 16-1 OSHA Standards Example

Source: From Occupational Safety and Hazard Administration (OSHA). Retrieved from https://www.osha.gov/pls/oshaweb/owadisp.show_document?p_table=STANDARDS&p_id=9720.

> Guardrails not less than 2″ × 4″ or the equivalent and not less than 36″ or more than 42″ high, with a midrail, when required, of a 1″ × 4″ lumber or equivalent, and toeboards, shall be installed at all open sides on all scaffolds more than 10 feet above the ground or floor. Toeboards shall be a minimum of 4″ in height. Wire mesh shall be installed in accordance with paragraph [a] (17) of this section.

FIGURE 16-2 What Accidents Must Be Reported Under the Occupational Safety and Health Act (OSHA)?

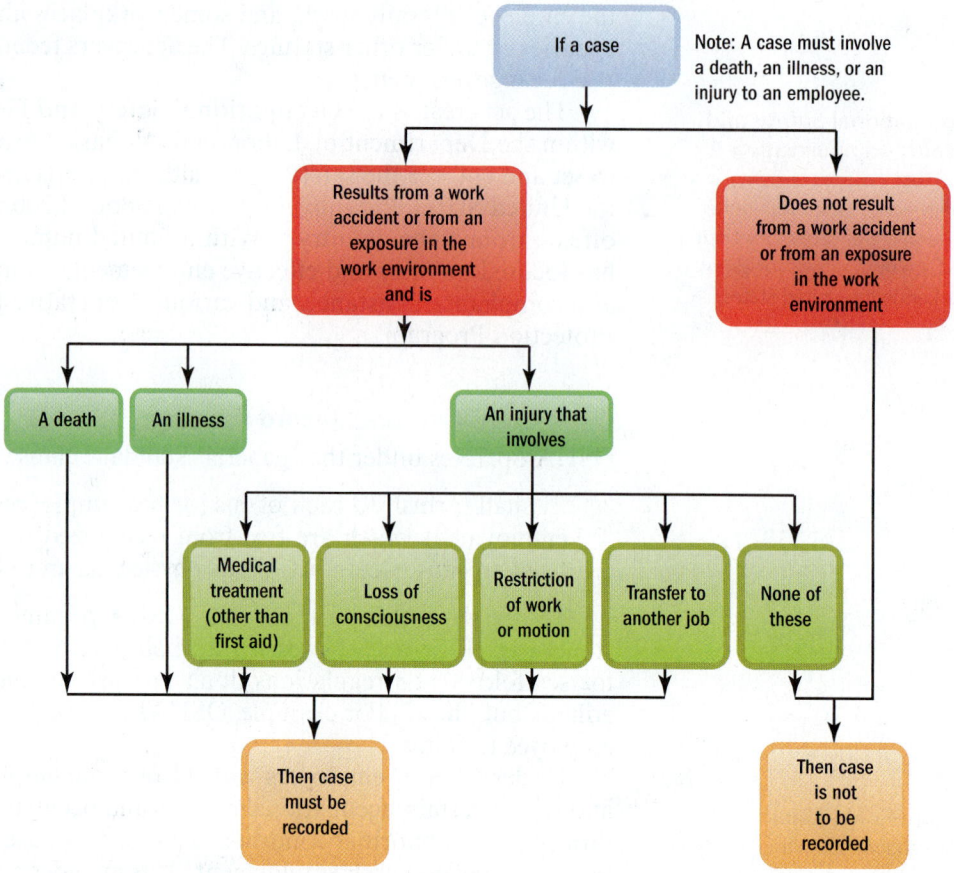

Inspections and Citations

OSHA enforces its standards through inspections and (if necessary) citations. The inspection is usually unannounced. OSHA may not conduct warrantless inspections without an employer's consent. It may inspect with an authorized search warrant or its equivalent.[28] With a limited number of inspectors, OSHA recently has focused on "fair and effective enforcement," combined with outreach, education and compliance assistance, and various OSHA–employer cooperative programs (such as its Voluntary Protection Programs).[29]

OSHA takes a "worst-first" approach in setting inspection priorities. Priorities include, from highest to lowest, imminent dangers, catastrophes and fatal accidents, employee complaints, high-hazard industries inspections, and follow-up inspections.[30] In one recent year, OSHA conducted about 40,600 inspections,[31] and accepted more than 3,000 whistle-blower cases.[32]

OSHA conducts an inspection within 24 hours when a complaint indicates an immediate danger, and within 3 working days when a serious hazard exists. For a "nonserious" complaint filed in writing by a worker or a union, OSHA will respond within 20 working days. OSHA handles other nonserious complaints by writing to the employer and requesting corrective action. OSHA recently told almost 15,000 U.S. employers that because of their higher-than-average injury and illness rates, they may be subject to inspections.[33]

THE INSPECTION The inspection begins when the OSHA officer arrives at the workplace.[34] He or she displays credentials and asks to meet an employer representative. (The credentials must include photograph and serial number.) The officer explains the visit's purpose, the scope of the inspection, and the standards that apply. An authorized employee representative accompanies the officer during the inspection. The inspector can also stop and question workers (in private, if necessary). The act protects each employee from discrimination for exercising his or her disclosure rights.[35]

OSHA's FORM 301

Injury and Illness Incident Report

Attention: This form contains information relating to employee health and must be used in a manner that protects the confidentiality of employees to the extent possible while the information is being used for occupational safety and health purposes.

U.S. Department of Labor
Occupational Safety and Health Administration

Form approved OMB no. 1218-0176

This *Injury and Illness Incident Report* is one of the first forms you must fill out when a recordable work-related injury or illness has occurred. Together with the *Log of Work-Related Injuries and Illnesses* and the accompanying *Summary*, these forms help the employer and OSHA develop a picture of the extent and severity of work-related incidents.

Within 7 calendar days after you receive information that a recordable work-related injury or illness has occurred, you must fill out this form or an equivalent. Some state workers' compensation, insurance, or other reports may be acceptable substitutes. To be considered an equivalent form, any substitute must contain all the information asked for on this form.

According to Public Law 91-596 and 29 CFR 1904, OSHA's recordkeeping rule, you must keep this form on file for 5 years following the year to which it pertains.

If you need additional copies of this form, you may photocopy and use as many as you need.

Completed by _____

Title _____

Phone (_____)_____-_____ **Date** ___/___/___

Information about the employee

1) Full name _____

2) Street _____

City _____ State _____ ZIP _____

3) Date of birth _____/_____/_____

4) Date hired _____/_____/_____

5) ☐ Male
☐ Female

Information about the physician or other health care professional

6) Name of physician or other health care professional _____

_____

7) If treatment was given away from the worksite, where was it given?

Facility _____

Street _____

City _____ State _____ ZIP _____

8) Was employee treated in an emergency room?
☐ Yes
☐ No

9) Was employee hospitalized overnight as an in-patient?
☐ Yes
☐ No

Information about the case

10) Case number from the *Log* _____ *(Transfer the case number from the Log after you record the case.)*

11) Date of injury or illness _____/_____/_____

12) Time employee began work _____ AM/PM

13) Time of event _____ AM/PM
☐ Check if time cannot be determined

14) ***What was the employee doing just before the incident occurred?*** Describe the activity, as well as the tools, equipment, or material the employee was using. Be specific. *Examples:* "climbing a ladder while carrying roofing materials"; "spraying chlorine from hand sprayer"; "daily computer key-entry."

15) ***What happened?*** Tell us how the injury occurred. *Examples:* "When ladder slipped on wet floor, worker fell 20 feet"; "Worker was sprayed with chlorine when gasket broke during replacement"; "Worker developed soreness in wrist over time."

16) ***What was the injury or illness?*** Tell us the part of the body that was affected and how it was affected; be more specific than "hurt," "pain," or sore." *Examples:* "strained back"; "chemical burn, hand"; "carpal tunnel syndrome."

17) ***What object or substance directly harmed the employee?*** *Examples:* "concrete floor"; "chlorine"; "radial arm saw," *If this question does not apply to the incident, leave it blank.*

18) ***If the employee died, when did death occur?*** Date of death _____/_____/_____

Public reporting burden for this collection of information is estimated to average 22 minutes per response, including time for reviewing instructions, searching existing data sources, gathering and maintaining the data needed, and completing and reviewing the collection of information. Persons are not required to respond to the collection of information unless it displays a current valid OMB control number. If you have any comments about this estimate or any other aspects of this data collection, including suggestions for reducing this burden, contact: US Department of Labor, OSHA Office of Statistical Analysis, Room N-3644, 200 Constitution Avenue, NW, Washington, DC 20210. Do not send the completed forms to this office.

FIGURE 16-3 Form Used to Record Occupational Injuries and Illnesses

Source: U.S. Department of Labor.

FIGURE 16-4 OSHA Inspection Tips for Managers

Initial Contact

- Refer the inspector to your OSHA coordinator.
- Check the inspector's credentials.
- Ask why he or she is inspecting. Is it a complaint? Programmed visit? Fatality or accident follow-up? Imminent danger investigation?
- If the inspection is the result of a complaint, the inspector won't identify the complainant, but you are entitled to know whether the person is a current employee.
- Notify your OSHA counsel, who should review all requests from the inspector for documents and information. Your counsel also should review the documents and information you provide to the inspector.

Opening Conference

- Establish the focus and scope of the planned inspection: Does the inspector want to inspect the premises or simply study your records?
- Discuss the procedures for protecting trade-secret areas, conducting employee interviews, and producing documents.
- Show the inspector that you have safety programs in place. He or she may not go to the work floor if paperwork is complete and up-to-date.

Walk-Around Inspection

- Accompany the inspector and take detailed notes.
- If the inspector takes a photo or video, you should too.
- Ask the inspector for duplicates of all physical samples and copies of all test results.
- Be helpful and cooperative, but don't volunteer information.
- To the extent possible, immediately correct any violation the inspector identifies.

OSHA inspectors look for all types of violations, but some areas grab more attention. The five most frequent OSHA inspection violation areas are scaffolding, fall protection, hazard communication, lockout/tagout (electrical disengagement), and respiratory problems.[36]

Finally, the inspector holds a closing conference with the employer's representative. Here the inspector discusses apparent violations for which OSHA may issue or recommend a **citation** and penalty. At this point, the employer can produce records to show compliance efforts. Figure 16-4 lists a manager's inspection guidelines.

citation
Summons informing employers and employees of the regulations and standards that have been violated in the workplace.

PENALTIES OSHA can impose penalties. These generally range from $5,000 up to $150,000 for willful or repeat serious violations but can be far higher—$13 million after a tragedy at BP's Texas City plant, for instance.[37] The parties settle many OSHA cases before litigation, in "precitation settlements."[38] OSHA then issues the citation and agreed-on penalties simultaneously, after the employers initiate negotiation settlements.[39] Nonserious violations may carry no penalties.

In general, OSHA calculates penalties based on the gravity of the violation and usually takes into consideration things like the size of the business, the firm's compliance history, and the employer's good faith.[40] In practice, OSHA must have a final order from the independent Occupational Safety and Health Review Commission (OSHRC) to enforce a penalty.[41] An employer who files a notice of contest can drag out an appeal for years.[42] OSHA publicizes its inspection results online. Its Web site (www.osha.gov) provides easy access to most companies' (or competitors') OSHA enforcement history.[43]

Responsibilities and Rights of Employers and Employees

Both employers and employees have responsibilities and rights under the Occupational Safety Health Act. *Employers* are responsible for providing "a workplace free from recognized hazards," for being familiar with mandatory OSHA standards, and for examining workplace conditions to make sure they conform to OSHA standards.[44] Employers have the right to seek advice and off-site consultation from OSHA, request

Employees have rights and responsibilities under OSHA standards, such as to wear their hard hats, but OSHA can't cite them if they violate their responsibilities.

Hybrid Images/Cultura/AGE Fotostock

and receive proper identification of the OSHA compliance officer before inspection, and to be advised by the compliance officer of the reason for an inspection.

Employees also have rights and responsibilities, but OSHA can't cite them for violations of their responsibilities. Employees are responsible, for example, for complying with all applicable OSHA standards, for following all employer safety and health rules and regulations, and for reporting hazardous conditions to the supervisor. They have the right to demand safety and health on the job without fear of punishment. Retaliating against employees for reporting injuries or safety problems is illegal (see the OSHA safety poster in Figure 16-5).[45] The HR Tools feature explains one OSHA service for small businesses.

IMPROVING PERFORMANCE: *HR Tools for Line Managers and Small Businesses*

Free On-Site Safety and Health Services

OSHA provides free on-site safety and health services for small businesses.[46] This service uses safety experts from state agencies and provides consultations, usually at the employer's workplace. According to OSHA, this safety and health consultation program is completely separate from the OSHA inspection effort, and no citations are issued or penalties proposed.

The employer triggers the process by requesting a voluntary consultation. There is then an opening conference with a safety expert, a walk-through, and a closing conference at which the employer and safety expert discuss the latter's observations. The consultant provides a detailed report explaining the findings. The employer's only obligation is to commit to correcting serious job safety and health hazards in a timely manner.

OSHA also has a Web site called "OSHA's $afety Pays Program" (www.osha.gov/dcsp/smallbusiness/safetypays/estimator.html). Use its pull-down window and choose a potential injury or illness such as "Burns." After you enter other data (such as potential number of injuries), this tool will reveal the estimated cost of the specific occupational injury or illness, and the estimated impact on your company's profits. ■

Source: Based on Sean Smith, "OSHA Resources Can Help Small Businesses with Hazards," Westchester County Business Journal, August 4, 2003, p. 4; www.osha.gov/dcsp/smallbusiness/consult.html.

If your professor has assigned this, go to the Assignments section of **mymanagementlab.com** to complete this discussion.

Talk About It 3: Write a short description on this theme: "How a small business owner can make use of OSHA's $afety Pays Web site."

FIGURE 16-5 OSHA Safety Poster

Source: From You Have the Right to a Safe and Healthy Workplace: Its the Law, U.S. Department of Labor

You Have a Right to a Safe and Healthful Workplace.

IT'S THE LAW!

- You have the right to notify your employer or OSHA about workplace hazards. You may ask OSHA to keep your name confidential.
- You have the right to request an OSHA inspection if you believe that there are unsafe and unhealthful conditions in your workplace. You or your representative may participate in the inspection.
- You can file a complaint with OSHA within 30 days of discrimination by your employer for making safety and health complaints or for exercising your rights under the *OSH Act*.
- You have a right to see OSHA citations issued to your employer. Your employer must post the citations at or near the place of the alleged violation.
- Your employer must correct workplace hazards by the date indicated on the citation and must certify that these hazards have been reduced or eliminated.
- You have the right to copies of your medical records or records of your exposure to toxic and harmful substances or conditions.
- Your employer must post this notice in your workplace.

The *Occupational Safety and Health Act of 1970 (OSH Act)*, P.L. 91-596, assures safe and healthful working conditions for working men and women throughout the Nation. The Occupational Safety and Health Administration, in the U.S. Department of Labor, has the primary responsibility for administering the *OSH Act*. The rights listed here may vary depending on the particular circumstances. To file a complaint, report an emergency, or seek OSHA advice, assistance, or products, call 1-800-321-OSHA or your nearest OSHA office: • Atlanta (404) 562-2300 • Boston (617) 565-9860 • Chicago (312) 353-2220 • Dallas (214) 767-4731 • Denver (303) 844-1600 • Kansas City (816) 426-5861 • New York (212) 337-2378 • Philadelphia (215) 861-4900 • San Francisco (415) 975-4310 • Seattle (206) 553-5930. Teletypewriter (TTY) number is 1-877-889-5627. To file a complaint online or obtain more information on OSHA federal and state programs, visit OSHA's website at www.osha.gov. If your workplace is in a state operating under an OSHA-approved plan, your employer must post the required state equivalent of this poster.

1-800-321-OSHA

www.osha.gov

U.S. Department of Labor • Occupational Safety and Health Administration • OSHA 3165

DEALING WITH EMPLOYEE RESISTANCE Although employees are responsible to comply with OSHA standards, they often resist; the employer usually remains liable for any penalties. The refusal of some workers to wear hard hats typifies this problem.

Employers have attempted to defend themselves by citing worker intransigence. In most cases, courts still hold employers liable for workplace safety violations. The independent three-member Occupational Safety and Health Review Commission says employers must make "a diligent effort to discourage, by discipline if necessary, violations of safety rules by employees."[47] Cited for a workplace injury, the employer may claim employee misconduct. The key here is to provide documented evidence that the employee was properly trained to do the job the right way but did not.[48] But the only sure way to eliminate liability is to make sure that no accidents occur.

TRENDS SHAPING HR: *DIGITAL AND SOCIAL MEDIA*

SITEDOCS DIGITAL WORKPLACE SAFETY Safety compliance usually has been managed centrally, by human resource managers or by a specialized safety unit. However, new digital mobile device–based safety systems now give managers and even employees more influence over safety. For example, the SiteDocs digital safety management system lets the employer digitize, move, store, work with, and access safety documents via mobile devices (iPad) and the Web.[49] Employees can login via the mobile device and view and complete their safety documentation (such as OSHA reports). These become available immediately to management.

A system such as SiteDocs produces many benefits. For example, it enables management to monitor in real time whether employees are completing their documentation and to identify almost at once workplace hazards and incidents. It facilitates due diligence—for example, management knows at once who signed a document and when, and what corrective action was taken. Safety documents can be updated online, without the time and cost of updating hard copies. And the system gives employees instant access to available safety procedures, and automatically files safety forms. ■

What Causes Accidents?

LEARNING OBJECTIVE **16-3**
Answer the question, "What causes accidents?"

There are three basic causes of workplace accidents: chance occurrences, unsafe conditions, and employees' unsafe acts. Chance occurrences (such as walking past a tree just when a branch falls) are more or less beyond management's control. We will therefore focus on unsafe conditions and unsafe acts.

What Causes Unsafe Conditions?

unsafe conditions
The mechanical and physical conditions that cause accidents.

Unsafe conditions are a main cause of accidents. They include:

- Improperly guarded equipment
- Defective equipment
- Hazardous procedures around machines or equipment
- Unsafe storage—congestion, overloading
- Improper illumination—glare, insufficient light
- Improper ventilation.[50]

The solution here is to identify and eliminate the unsafe conditions. The main aim of the OSHA standards is to address such mechanical and physical accident-causing conditions. The employer's safety department (if any) and its human resource managers and top managers should take responsibility for identifying unsafe conditions.

While accidents can happen anywhere, there are some high-danger zones. About one-third of industrial accidents occur around forklift trucks, wheelbarrows, and other handling and lifting areas. The most serious accidents usually occur by metal and woodworking machines and saws, or around transmission machinery like gears, pulleys, and flywheels.[51] Construction accounts for a disproportionate share of accidents, with falls the major problem.[52]

SAFETY CLIMATE Work schedules and fatigue also affect accident rates. Accident rates usually don't increase too noticeably during the first 5 or 6 hours of the workday. But after that, the accident rate increases faster. This is due partly to fatigue and partly to the fact that accidents occur more often during night shifts. With reduced headcount and more people with second jobs, employee fatigue is a growing problem today.[53] Many employers are therefore taking steps to reduce employee fatigue, such as banning mandatory overtime.

The workplace "climate" or psychology is very important. One researcher reviewed the fatal accidents offshore oil workers suffered in the British North Sea.[54] A strong pressure to complete the work as quickly as possible, employees who are under stress, and a poor safety climate—for instance, supervisors who never mentioned safety—were some of the psychological conditions leading to accidents. Similarly, accidents occur more frequently in plants with high seasonal layoff rates, hostility among employees, many garnished wages, and blighted living conditions.

What Causes Unsafe Acts?

Unsafe employee acts (such as running) will undo your efforts to banish unsafe conditions, but there are no easy answers to what causes people to act that way.

It may seem obvious that some people are simply accident prone, but the research isn't clear.[55] On closer inspection it turns out some "accident repeaters" were just unlucky, or may have been more meticulous about reporting their accidents.[56] However, there is evidence that people with specific traits may indeed be accident prone. For example, people who are impulsive, sensation seeking, extremely extroverted, and less conscientious (in terms of being less fastidious and dependable) have more accidents.[57]

Furthermore, the person who is accident prone on one job may not be so on another. For example, personality traits that correlate with filing vehicular insurance claims include *entitlement* ("think there's no reason they should not speed"), *impatience* ("were 'always in a hurry'"), *aggressiveness* ("the first to move when the light turns green"), and *distractibility* ("frequently distracted by cell phones, eating, and so on").[58]

HR in Practice at the Hotel Paris Lisa and the CFO reviewed their company's safety records, and what they found disturbed them deeply. In terms of every safety-related metric they could find, including accident costs per year, lost time due to accidents, workers' compensation per employee, and number of safety training programs per year, the Hotel Paris compared unfavorably with most other hotel chains and service firms. To see how they handled this, see the case on page 553–554 of this chapter.

How to Prevent Accidents

LEARNING OBJECTIVE 16-4
List and explain five ways to prevent accidents at work.

In practice, accident prevention boils down to reducing unsafe conditions and reducing unsafe acts. In large firms, the chief safety officer (often called the "environmental health and safety officer") is responsible.[59] In smaller firms, managers, including those from human resources, plant management, and first-line managers, share these responsibilities.

Reducing Unsafe Conditions

Reducing unsafe conditions like the ones OSHA addresses is the employer's first line of defense. Safety engineers should design jobs to remove or reduce physical hazards. Supervisors play a role here. Checklists like those in Figure 16-6 and Figure 16-8 (pages 525–527 and 549–552 respectively) can help identify and remove potential hazards.

Employers also use computerized tools to design safer equipment. For example, Designsafe helps to automate hazard analysis, risk assessment, and safety options identification. Designsafe helps the safety designer choose the most appropriate safety control device for keeping the worker safe, such as adjustable enclosures, presence-sensing devices, and personal protective equipment.[60]

Sometimes the solution for an unsafe condition is obvious, and sometimes it's not. For example, slippery floors often cause slips and falls.[61] Obvious remedies include floor mats and better lighting. Perhaps less obviously, personal safety gear, like slip-resistant footwear with grooved soles, can also reduce slips and falls. Cut-resistant gloves reduce the hazards of working with sharp objects.[62] (Hand injuries account for about 1 million emergency department visits annually by U.S. workers.)[63] Wearable digital devices such as motion monitors present new safety challenges.[64] The employer should determine the device's usability and ascertain that it won't cause an unanticipated safety problem.

Reducing unsafe conditions is important in offices too.[65] For example, get written confirmation that the space meets all building codes; make sure the builder, contractors, and/or landlord follow OSHA standards in the design and construction of facilities (for instance, unblocked exits); make sure the lease lets you compel the landlord to fix safety problems if ones surface; and make sure air ducts are cleaned of dust and allergens.

FIGURE 16-6 Supervisor's Safety Checklist

Source: Office of the Chief Information Officer, United States Department of Commerce, http://ocio.os.doc.gov/s/groups/public/@doc/@os/@ocio/@oitpp/documents/content/dev01_002574.pdf, assessed October 15, 2013.

FORM **CD-574**
(9/02)

U.S. Department of Commerce
Office Safety Inspection Checklist for
Supervisors and Program Managers

Name:	**Division:**
Location:	**Date:**
Signature:	

This checklist is intended as a guide to assist supervisors and program managers in conducting safety and health inspections of their work areas. It includes questions relating to general office safety, ergonomics, fire prevention, and electrical safety. Questions which receive a "**NO**" answer require corrective action. If you have questions or need assistance with resolving any problems, please contact your safety office. More information on office safety is available through the Department of Commerce Safety Office website at http://ohrm.doc.gov/safetyprogram/safety.htm.

Work Environment

Yes	No	N/A	
○	○	⊙	Are all work areas clean, sanitary, and orderly?
○	○	⊙	Is there adequate lighting?
○	○	⊙	Do noise levels appear high?
○	○	⊙	Is ventilation adequate?

Walking / Working Surfaces

Yes	No	N/A	
○	○	⊙	Are aisles and passages free of stored material that may present trip hazards?
○	○	⊙	Are tile floors in places like kitchens and bathrooms free of water and slippery substances?
○	○	⊙	Are carpet and throw rugs free of tears or trip hazards?
○	○	⊙	Are hand rails provided on all fixed stairways?
○	○	⊙	Are treads provided with anti-slip surfaces?
○	○	⊙	Are step ladders provided for reaching overhead storage areas and are materials stored safely?
○	○	⊙	Are file drawers kept closed when not in use?
○	○	⊙	Are passenger and freight elevators inspected annually and are the inspection certificates available for review on-site?
○	○	⊙	Are pits and floor openings covered or otherwise guarded?
○	○	⊙	Are standard guardrails provided wherever aisle or walkway surfaces are elevated more than 48 inches above any adjacent floor or the ground?
○	○	⊙	Is any furniture unsafe or defective?
○	○	⊙	Are objects covering heating and air conditioning vents?

Ergonomics

Yes	No	N/A	
○	○	⊙	Are employees advised of proper lifting techniques?
○	○	⊙	Are workstations configured to prevent common ergonomic problems? (Chair height allows employees' feet to rest flat on the ground with thighs parallel to the floor, top of computer screen is at or slightly below eye level, keyboard is at elbow height. Additional information on proper configuration of workstations is available through the Commerce Safety website at http://ohrm.doc.gov/safetyprogram/safety.htm)
○	○	⊙	Are mechanical aids and equipment, such as; lifting devices, carts, dollies provided where needed?
○	○	⊙	Are employees surveyed annually on their ergonomic concerns?

(Continued)

FIGURE 16-6 (Continued)

FORM **CD-574**
(9/02)

Emergency Information (Postings)

Yes	No	N/A	
○	○	⊙	Are established emergency phone numbers posted where they can be readily found in case of an emergency?
○	○	⊙	Are employees trained on emergency procedures?
○	○	⊙	Are fire evacuation procedures/diagrams posted?
○	○	⊙	Is emergency information posted in every area where you store hazardous waste?
○	○	⊙	Is established facility emergency information posted near a telephone?
○	○	⊙	Are the OSHA poster, and other required posters displayed conspicuously?
○	○	⊙	Are adequate first aid supplies available and properly maintained?
○	○	⊙	Are an adequate number of first aid trained personnel available to respond to injuries and illnesses until medical assistance arrives?
○	○	⊙	Is a copy of the facility fire prevention and emergency action plan available on site?
○	○	⊙	Are safety hazard warning signs/caution signs provided to warn employees of pertinent hazards?

Fire Prevention

Yes	No	N/A	
○	○	⊙	Are flammable liquids, such as gasoline, kept in approved safety cans and stored in flammable cabinets?
○	○	⊙	Are portable fire extinguishers distributed properly (less than 75 feet travel distance for combustibles and 50 feet for flammables)?
○	○	⊙	Are employees trained on the use of portable fire extinguishers?
○	○	⊙	Are portable fire extinguishers visually inspected monthly and serviced annually?
○	○	⊙	Is the area around portable fire extinguishers free of obstructions and properly labeled ?
○	○	⊙	Is heat-producing equipment used in a well ventilated area?
○	○	⊙	Are fire alarm pull stations clearly marked and unobstructed?
○	○	⊙	Is proper clearance maintained below sprinkler heads (i.e., 18" clear)?

Emergency Exits

Yes	No	N/A	
○	○	⊙	Are doors, passageways or stairways that are neither exits nor access to exits and which could be mistaken for exits, appropriately marked "NOT AN EXIT," "TO BASEMENT," "STOREROOM," etc.?
○	○	⊙	Are a sufficient number of exits provided?
○	○	⊙	Are exits kept free of obstructions or locking devices which could impede immediate escape?
○	○	⊙	Are exits properly marked and illuminated?
○	○	⊙	Are the directions to exits, when not immediately apparent, marked with visible signs?
○	○	⊙	Can emergency exit doors be opened from the direction of exit travel without the use of a key or any special knowledge or effort when the building is occupied?
○	○	⊙	Are exits arranged such that it is not possible to travel toward a fire hazard when exiting the facility?

FIGURE 16-6 (Continued)

FORM **CD-574**
(9/02)

Electrical Systems
(Please have your facility maintenance person or electrician accompany you during this part of the inspection)

Yes	No	N/A	
○	○	⊙	Are all cord and cable connections intact and secure?
○	○	⊙	Are electrical outlets free of overloads?
○	○	⊙	Is fixed wiring used instead of flexible/extension cords?
○	○	⊙	Is the area around electrical panels and breakers free of obstructions?
○	○	⊙	Are high-voltage electrical service rooms kept locked?
○	○	⊙	Are electrical cords routed such that they are free of sharp objects and clearly visible?
○	○	⊙	Are all electrical cords grounded?
○	○	⊙	Are electrical cords in good condition (free of splices, frays, etc.)?
○	○	⊙	Are electrical appliances approved (Underwriters Laboratory, Inc. (UL), etc)?
○	○	⊙	Are electric fans provided with guards of not over one-half inch, preventing finger exposures?
○	○	⊙	Are space heaters UL listed and equipped with shutoffs that activate if the heater tips over?
○	○	⊙	Are space heaters located away from combustibles and properly ventilated?
○	○	⊙	In your electrical rooms are all electrical raceways and enclosures securely fastened in place?
○	○	⊙	Are clamps or other securing means provided on flexible cords or cables at plugs, receptacles, tools, equipment, etc., and is the cord jacket securely held in place?
○	○	⊙	Is sufficient access and working space provided and maintained about all electrical equipment to permit ready and safe operations and maintenance? (This space is 3 feet for less than 600 volts, 4 feet for more than 600 volts)

FORM **CD-574**
(9/02)

Material Storage

Yes	No	N/A	
○	○	⊙	Are storage racks and shelves capable of supporting the intended load and materials stored safely?
○	○	⊙	Are storage racks secured from falling?
○	○	⊙	Are office equipment stored in a stable manner, not capable of falling?

job hazard analysis
A systematic approach to identifying and eliminating workplace hazards before they occur.

JOB HAZARD ANALYSIS A Yale University science student, working late in a lab, was critically injured when her hair became caught in a spinning lathe. **Job hazard analysis** involves a systematic approach to identifying and eliminating such hazards before they cause accidents. According to OSHA, job hazard analysis "focuses on the relationship between the worker, the task, the tools, and the work environment," and ends by reducing the potential risks to acceptable levels.[66]

Consider a safety analyst looking at the Yale science lab, with the aim of identifying potential hazards. Performing a job hazard analysis here might involve looking at the situation and asking these questions:

- ***What can go wrong?*** A student's hair or clothing could become caught in the lathe, a rotating object that "catches" it and pulls it into the machine.
- ***What are the consequences?*** The student could receive a severe injury as his or her body part or hair is caught and drawn into the spinning lathe.
- ***How could it happen?*** The accident could happen as a result of the student leaning too close to the lathe while working at the bench, or walking too close to the lathe, or bending to reach for an article that fell close to the lathe.

- ***What are other contributing factors?*** Speed is one contributing factor. The problem would occur so quickly that the student would be unable to take evasive action once the lathe ensnarled the hair.

The job hazard analysis should provide the basis for creating countermeasures. For example, given the speed with which such a lathe accident would occur, it's unlikely that training by itself would suffice. Instead, the lathe area here should be ensconced in its own protective casing, and changes made to ensure that the lathe can't spin unless the student takes action via a foot pedal to keep the lathe power on.

operational safety reviews
Reviews conducted by agencies to ascertain whether units under their jurisdiction are complying with all the applicable safety laws, regulations, orders, and rules.

OPERATIONAL SAFETY REVIEWS After Japan's Fukushima nuclear power plant exploded several years ago, many wondered if the International Atomic Energy Agency (IAEA) had conducted the necessary operational safety reviews. **Operational safety reviews** (or safety operations reviews) are conducted by agencies to ascertain whether units under their jurisdiction are complying with all the applicable safety laws, regulations, orders, and rules. For example, under IAEA's Operational Safety Review Program, "international teams of experts conduct in-depth reviews of operational safety performance at a nuclear power plant."[67]

PERSONAL PROTECTIVE EQUIPMENT Getting employees to wear personal protective equipment (PPE) like hard hats is famously difficult.[68] Wearability is important. In addition to providing reliable protection, protective gear should fit properly; be easy to care for, maintain, and repair; be flexible and lightweight; provide comfort and reduce heat stress; have rugged construction; be relatively easy to put on and take off; and be easy to clean, dispose of, and recycle.[69] Many employers, such as Kimberly-Clark and MCR Safety, are tapping into new fibers and fabrics to design easier-wearing high-tech solutions.[70] Including employees in planning the safety program and addressing comfort issues contribute to employees' willingness to use the protective gear.[71]

Of course, the manager should require wearing the protective equipment before the accident, not just after it. For example, a combustible dust explosion at a sugar refinery killed 14 employees and burned many others. The employer subsequently required that all employees wear fire-resistant clothing, unfortunately too late for the victims.[72]

Similarly, cold weather means employers must help protect their outdoor workers.[73] This should include, among other things, monitoring temperature and wind chill conditions, making sure workers are supplied with adequate cold-weather apparel, monitoring workers for signs of frostbite, and providing adequate indoor breaks.

But again, reducing unsafe conditions is always the first line of defense. Next use administrative controls (such as job rotation to reduce long-term exposure to the hazard). Only then turn to PPE.[74]

Diversity Counts: Protecting Vulnerable Workers

In designing safe and healthy environments, employers should pay special attention to vulnerable workers, such as young, immigrant, aging, and women workers.[75] (The Fair Labor Standards Act strictly limits young people's exposure to dangerous jobs, but about 64 workers under age 18 died from work-related injuries a few years ago.)[76] For example, as the CEO of one safety engineering company said, "For decades, women essentially were ignored when it came to designing eye and face protection." Today, more products are available in smaller sizes.[77]

Similarly, with more workers postponing retirement, older workers are doing more manufacturing jobs.[78] They can do these jobs effectively. However, there are numerous potential physical changes associated with aging, including loss of strength, loss of muscular flexibility, and reduced reaction time.[79] This means that employers should make special provisions such as designing jobs to reduce heavy lifting, and boosting lighting levels.[80] The fatality rate for older workers is about three times that of younger workers.[81] ■

Reducing Unsafe Acts

While reducing unsafe conditions is the first line of defense, human misbehavior will short-circuit even the best safety efforts.[82]

Sometimes the misbehavior is intentional, but often it's not. For example, distractions contribute to at least half of all car accidents. The National Safety Council recently estimated that cell phone use was involved in 24% of all motor vehicle crashes.[83] (Drivers of commercial motor vehicles on interstate routes are banned from using handheld mobile telephones while driving.)[84] At work, not noticing moving or stationary objects or that a floor is wet often causes accidents.[85] And, ironically, "making a job safer with machine guards or PPE lowers people's risk perceptions and thus can lead to an increase in at-risk behavior."[86]

Unfortunately, just telling employees to "pay attention" usually isn't enough. First identify and try to eliminate potential risks, such as unguarded equipment. Next, reduce potential distractions, such as noise, heat, and stress. Then, carefully screen and train employees, as we explain next.

Reducing Unsafe Acts Through Screening

Proper employee screening and placement reduce unsafe acts. Here the employer's aim is to identify the traits that might predict accidents on the job in question, and then screen candidates for this trait. For example, the Employee Reliability Index (ERI)[87] measures reliability dimensions such as emotional maturity, conscientiousness, and safe job performance.[88] Though not definitive, using the ERI in selection did seem to be associated with reductions in work-related accidents in one study. Others use *job simulation tests* (which attempt to assess the applicant by simulating physically demanding work activities) and *physical capabilities tests* (which measure muscle strength and motion) to predict who will have more accidents.[89]

Similarly, behavioral interview questions can be revealing. For example, ask, "What would you do if you saw another employee working in an unsafe way?" and "What would you do if your supervisor gave you a task, but didn't provide any training on how to perform it safely?"[90]

Reducing Unsafe Acts Through Training

Safety training reduces unsafe acts, especially for new employees. You should instruct employees in safe practices and procedures, warn them of potential hazards, and

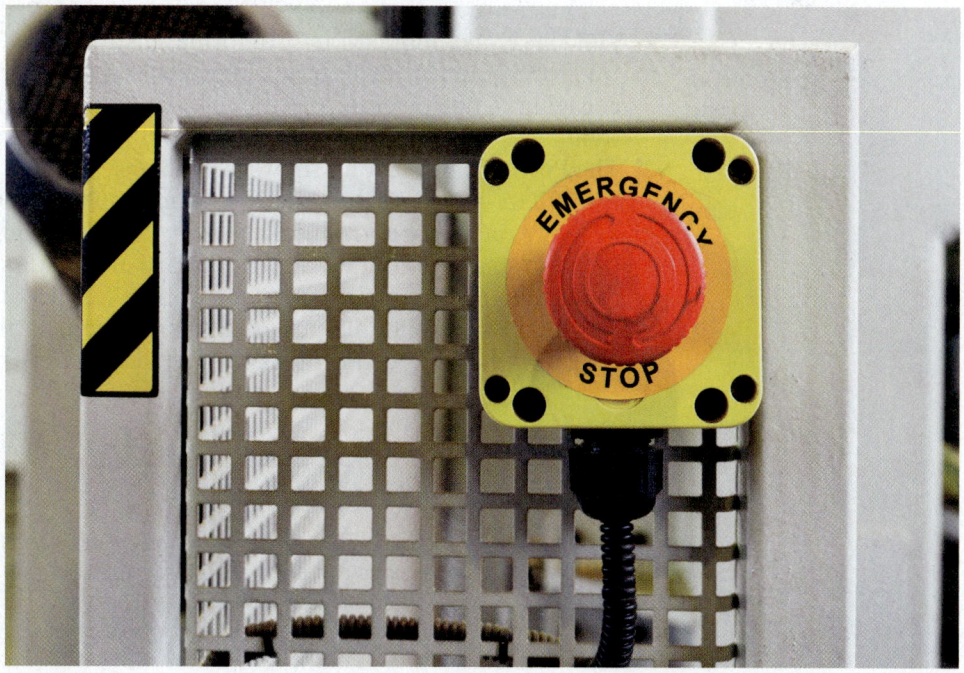

Valery Voennyy/Alamy

Emergency stop devices, such as buttons, override other machine controls to remove power from hazardous machine motion.

work on developing a safety-conscious attitude. OSHA's standards require more than training. Employees must demonstrate that they actually learned what to do. (For example, OSHA's respiratory standard requires that each employee demonstrate how to inspect, put on, and remove respirator seals.[91] OSHA has two booklets, *Training Requirements Under OSHA* and *Teaching Safety and Health in the Workplace*.) Because temporary workers account for a disproportionate share of workplace accidents, the employer should take particular care to train them.[92]

The main aim of safety training is not to meet OSHA training standards; it is to impart the knowledge and skills required to reduce accidents. OSHA, the National Institute for Occupational Safety and Health (NIOSH), and numerous private vendors provide online safety training solutions.[93]

The nature of the safety training is important. One study found that the most effective safety training demanded high employee engagement.[94] In this study, the "least engaging" programs included lectures, films, reading materials, and video-based training. Moderately engaging programs included computer interface instruction with feedback. "Engaging" ones included behavioral modeling, simulation, and hands-on training.

Improving Performance Through HRIS Online Safety Training

Employers also turn to the Web to support their safety training programs.[95] For example, PureSafety (www.ulworkplace.com) enables firms to create their own training Web sites, complete with a "message from the safety director." Once an employer installs the PureSafety Web site, it can populate the site with courses from companies that supply health and safety courses via that site.[96] When the University of California system wanted to deliver mandated safety training to its 50,000 employees on 10 different campuses, it developed a program with the vendor Vivid Learning Systems to deliver online. The 2-hour custom online lab safety fundamentals course covers OSHA regulations as well as interactive exercises and feedback opportunities for participants.[97] ■

Reducing Unsafe Acts Through Posters, Incentives, and Positive Reinforcement

Employers also use various tools to motivate worker safety.[98] Safety posters are one, but are no substitute for comprehensive safety programs. Employers should combine them with other techniques (like screening and training) to reduce unsafe conditions and acts, and change the posters often. Posters should be easily visible, legible, and well-lit.[99]

Incentive programs are also useful.[100] Management at Tesoro Corporation's Golden Eagle refinery in California instituted one such plan. Employees earn "WINGS" (an acronym for Willing Involvement Nurtures Greater Safety) points for engaging in one or more specific safety activities, such as taking emergency response training. Employees can each earn up to $20 per month by accumulating points.[101] The Profit Center feature shows another example.

OSHA has argued that such programs don't cut down on actual injuries or illnesses, but only on injury and illness *reporting*. OSHA might question any safety incentive payment that is so high that the award might dissuade reasonable workers from reporting safety problems.[102] One option (see accompanying Profit Center feature) is to emphasize nontraditional incentives, like recognition.[103] In any case, the incentive program needs to be part of a comprehensive safety program.[104]

IMPROVING PERFORMANCE: *HR as a Profit Center*

Using Positive Reinforcement

Many employers successfully use *positive reinforcement programs* to improve safety. Such programs provide workers with continuing positive feedback, usually in the form of graphical performance reports and supervisory support, to shape the workers' safety-related behavior.

Researchers introduced one program in a wholesale bakery.[105] The new safety program included training and positive reinforcement. The researchers set and communicated a reasonable safety goal (in terms of observed incidents performed safely). Next, employees participated in a 30-minute training session by viewing pairs of slides depicting scenes that the researchers staged in the plant. One slide, for example, showed the supervisor climbing over a conveyor; the parallel slide showed the supervisor walking around the conveyor. After viewing an unsafe act, employees had to describe, "What's unsafe here?" Then the researchers demonstrated the same incident again but performed in a safe manner, and explicitly stated the safe-conduct rule ("go around, not over or under, conveyors").

At the conclusion of the training phase, supervisors showed employees a graph with their pretraining safety record (in terms of observed incidents performed safely) plotted. Supervisors then encouraged workers to consider increasing their performance to the new safety goal for their own protection, to decrease costs, and to help the plant get out of its last-place safety ranking. Then the researchers posted the graph and a list of safety rules.

Whenever observers walked through the plant collecting safety data, they posted on the graph the percentage of incidents they had seen performed safely by the group as a whole, thus providing the workers with positive feedback. Workers could compare their current safety performance with both their previous performance and their assigned goal. In addition, supervisors praised workers when they performed selected incidents safely. Safety in the plant subsequently improved markedly. ■

If your professor has assigned this, go to the Assignments section of **mymanagementlab.com** to complete this discussion.

Talk About It 4: List six more unsafe incidents you believe might occur in a bakery, and a "safe manner" for doing each.

Particularly in situations like this where employees are relatively unsupervised, employers should create a safety-conscious culture by showing that they take safety seriously.

John Panella/Shutterstock

Reducing Unsafe Acts by Fostering a Culture of Safety

Employers and supervisors should create a safety-conscious culture by showing that they take safety seriously. One study measured safety culture in terms of questions like "my supervisor says a good word whenever he sees the job done according to the safety rules" and "my supervisor approaches workers during work to discuss safety issues."[106]

According to one safety expert, a workplace with a safety-oriented culture exhibits:

1. *Teamwork,* in the form of management and employees both involved in safety;
2. Highly visible and interactive *communication and collaboration* on safety matters;
3. A *shared vision* of safety excellence (specifically, an overriding attitude that all accidents and injuries are preventable);
4. *Assignment* of critical safety functions to specific individuals or teams;
5. A *continuous effort* toward identifying and correcting workplace safety problems and hazards;[107] and,
6. *Encouragement* of incident reporting.[108]

Reducing Unsafe Acts by Creating a Supportive Environment

Supportive supervisors' teams seem to have better safety records. "Organizations can develop a supportive environment by training supervisors to be better leaders, emphasizing the importance of teamwork and social support, and establishing the value of safety."[109]

Reducing Unsafe Acts by Establishing a Safety Policy

The company's written safety policy should emphasize that accident prevention is of the utmost importance at your firm, and that the firm will do everything practical to eliminate or reduce accidents and injuries.

Reducing Unsafe Acts by Setting Specific Loss Control Goals

Set specific safety goals to achieve. For example, set safety goals in terms of frequency of lost-time injuries per number of full-time employees.

Reducing Unsafe Acts Through Behavior-Based Safety and Safety Awareness Programs

behavior-based safety
Identifying the worker behaviors that contribute to accidents and then training workers to avoid these behaviors.

Behavior-based safety means identifying the worker behaviors that contribute to accidents and then training workers to avoid these behaviors. Tenneco Corporation (which manufactures Monroe shock absorbers) implemented one such program. The firm selected internal consultants from among its quality managers, training managers, engineers, and production workers. After training, the internal consultants identified five critical behaviors for Tenneco's first safety program, such as *Eyes on task: Does the employee watch his or her hands while performing a task?* The consultants made observations and collected data on the behaviors. Then they instituted training programs to get employees to perform these five behaviors properly.[110]

safety awareness program
Program that enables trained supervisors to orient new workers arriving at a job site regarding common safety hazards and simple prevention methods.

Employers also use *safety awareness* programs to improve employee safe behavior. A **safety awareness program** means trained supervisors orient new workers arriving at a job site regarding common safety hazards and simple prevention methods. For example, the Roadway Safety Awareness Program covers trucker safety issues such as stopping distances required at various speeds (see the accompanying screen grab).

Reducing Unsafe Acts Through Employee Participation

Employees are an excellent source of insights about safety problems and solutions. For example, when the International Truck and Engine Corp. began designing a new robot-based plant, management appointed joint labor–management safety teams for each department.[111] The teams worked with project engineers to design

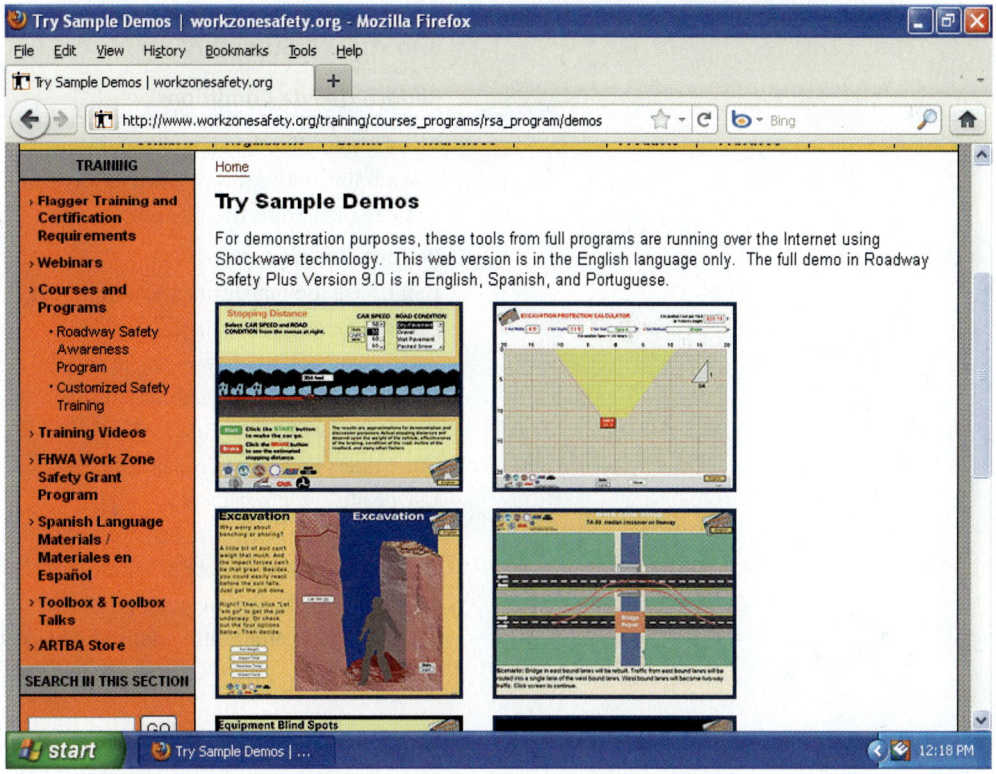

The Roadway Safety Awareness Program covers trucker safety issues such as stopping distances required at various speeds.

Source: National Work Zone Safety Information Clearinghouse, a project of the American Road & Transportation Builders Association—Transportation Development Foundation.

safeguards for the robot equipment. The company sent one safety team to Japan to watch the robot machines in action, and to identify items teams needed to address. This team worked with employees to identify possible hazards and to develop new devices (such as color-coded locks) to protect the employees.[112]

TRENDS SHAPING HR: *DIGITAL AND SOCIAL MEDIA*

Conducting Safety and Health Audits and Inspections

Safety-conscious managers know that good intentions aren't enough: the employer must audit safety compliance. Companies (such as Milliken, discussed pages 534–535) therefore create safety committees to evaluate safety adequacy, to conduct and monitor safety audits, and to suggest ways for improving safety.[113] Line managers should routinely inspect for problems using safety audit/checklists (as in Figure 16-6, page 525–527), including investigating all accidents and "near misses."

Employers expedite and enable employee-generated "distributed" safety audits by using mobile digital tools. For example, managers and employees use iAuditor—Safety Audit and Checklist App,[114] available via iTunes from SafetyCulture Pty Ltd., to facilitate safety audits. iAuditor contains numerous safety checklists and tools that let employers create actions depending on the checklist response.[115] As another example, AssessNET is cloud-based safety software that lets employers remotely manage risk assessments, accident records, and safety audits.[116] Employees use AssessNET from their desktops and mobile devices. It provides them with quick access to safety records, lets them quickly report hazards, and alerts management of safety incidents.[117] With both tools, security-related metrics would include, for instance, injury and illness rates, workers' compensation cost per employee, at-risk behavior reduction, and safety training exercises.[118] To ensure that audits result in improvements, *trend the audit data* (for instance, to see if accident rates are rising or falling or steady), and *track the corrective actions* through to completion.[119] ■

TABLE 16-1 Reducing Unsafe Conditions and Acts: A Summary

Reduce Unsafe Conditions
Identify and eliminate unsafe conditions.
Use administrative means, such as job rotation.
Use personal protective equipment.
Reduce Unsafe Acts
Emphasize top management commitment.
Emphasize safety.
Establish a safety policy.
Reduce unsafe acts through selection.
Provide safety training.
Use posters and other propaganda.
Use positive reinforcement.
Set specific safety goals to achieve.
Use behavior-based safety programs.
Encourage worker participation.
Conduct safety and health audits and inspections regularly.

Table 16-1 summarizes suggestions for reducing unsafe conditions and acts.[120]

LEARNING OBJECTIVE **16-5**

Describe how one company uses employee engagement to improve workplace safety.

Employee Engagement Guide for Managers

Milliken & Company—World-Class Safety Through Employee Engagement

Milliken & Company, founded in 1865, designs, manufactures, and markets chemicals, floor coverings, protective fabrics, and textiles. The company has about 7,000 employees in more than 39 facilities around the world. The privately owned Milliken has received widespread recognition for the quality of its innovative products, for its high employee engagement, and for its world-class employee engagement-based occupational safety program; it's also the only company to consistently rank as a "most ethical company" for 15 years running.[121] A survey of Milliken's employees found an 80% positive engagement level, based on questions concerning employees' commitment, pride in company, and empowerment efforts.[122] Its extraordinarily low workplace illness and injury rates mean it consistently rates as one of the safest companies in which to work.[123]

Involvement-Based Employee Engagement

The centerpiece of Milliken's safety process is its *involvement-based employee engagement* program. For example, employees staff the safety steering and safety subcommittee system, submit "opportunity for improvement" suggestions weekly, review each of these suggestions, and provide feedback on every suggestion.[124] The safety process depends on *cascading goals* deriving from federal, state, and Milliken-based safety guidelines. These goals are translated through weekly meetings into specific metrics (for instance, "accidents per employee hour worked") to be achieved by each plant's subcommittees. Each safety subcommittee then performs weekly *audits,* to ensure compliance and to ensure the plant's safety activities are continuously improved.

The Milliken safety program quantifies each employee's involvement, for instance, in terms of serving on safety subcommittees, being a trainer or safety subject matter expert, or conducting safety audits.[125] Also to help win engagement, the program *empowers* employees, for instance, by training each to do his or her "safety job" (such as being knowledgeable about OSHA safety regulations). All plant employees are also trained to give and receive peer-to-peer safety comments. Each is authorized to act on what he or she observes by providing "constructive feedback" or "appreciative feedback" when observing another employee doing something safely (or not). Each employee is also trained to use Milliken's safety tracking mechanism. This tool helps employees make sure that safety suggestions, safety audit findings, or other safety agenda items are tracked and finalized, by giving each item a number, date, and the name of the responsible Milliken employee.[126]

Members of each plant's employee safety steering committee investigate all safety incidents to help discover the causes.[127] Milliken recognizes employees' safety efforts in formal celebratory events throughout the year, such as having "cheerleaders" provide safety cheers as engineers enter the plant.[128]

LEARNING OBJECTIVE **16-6**

List five workplace health hazards and how to deal with them.

Workplace Health Hazards: Problems and Remedies

Most workplace hazards aren't as obvious as unguarded equipment or slippery floors. Many are unseen hazards that the company inadvertently produces as part of its production processes. Typical workplace exposure hazards include chemicals and other hazardous materials, temperature extremes, biohazards (including naturally occurring, such as mold, and manmade, such as anthrax), and ergonomic hazards (such as uncomfortable equipment).[129]

Chemicals and Industrial Hygiene

OSHA standards list exposure limits for about 600 chemicals, such as asbestos, lead, cadmium, and formaldehyde. Hazardous substances like these require air sampling and other preventive and precautionary measures.

Managing such hazards comes under the area of *industrial hygiene* and involves recognition, evaluation, and control. First, the facility's health and safety officers (possibly working with teams of supervisors and employees) must *recognize* possible exposure hazards. This typically involves conducting plant/facility walk-around surveys, employee interviews, records reviews, and reviews of government (OSHA) and nongovernmental standards.

Once the manager identifies a possible hazard, *evaluation* involves determining how severe the hazard is. This requires measuring the exposure, comparing the measure to some benchmark (such as 0.10 fibers per cubic centimeter for asbestos), and determining if the risk is within standard.[130]

Hazard *control* involves eliminating or reducing the hazard. Note that personal protective gear is generally the *last* option for dealing with such problems. The employer must first install engineering controls (such as process enclosures or ventilation) and administrative controls (including training and improved housekeeping).

The accompanying HR Practices Around the Globe feature shows one safety program abroad.

IMPROVING PERFORMANCE: *HR Practices Around the Globe*

Safety at Saudi Petrol Chemical

The industrial safety and security manager for the Saudi Petrol Chemical Co., in Jubail City, Saudi Arabia, says that his company's excellent safety record results from the fact that "our employees are champions of safety."[131] Employees serve on safety committees, develop and lead daily and monthly safety meetings, and conduct job safety analyses, for instance.

Safety begins with top management. Senior management representatives serve on the company's Management Health and Safety Committee. This committee meets monthly to review incident reports, establish health and safety goals, review safety statistics, and endorse and sponsor safety programs.

The firm cultivates its "safety first" culture from the day a new employee arrives at work. For example, new employees are encouraged to participate in the safety process during orientation. Then (about 6 weeks later) they attend a one-day orientation where company officials emphasize the importance of the company's health, safety, and environmental policies and programs. Employees also participate in monthly departmental training sessions to discuss departmental safety issues and safety suggestions. They work with their departmental committees to conduct monthly safety audits, to review and document departmental job safety, and to submit safety suggestions (about 60 suggestions are submitted per month). Employees are required to report every safety incident and near miss, and more than 600 reports are submitted each year. ■

If your professor has assigned this, go to the Assignments section of **mymanagementlab.com** to complete this discussion.

Talk About It 5: Expand on this statement: "Based on what I've read so far in this chapter, here is why I would say this facility has a good safety program."

Ashley Cooper/Corbis

Exposure to asbestos is a major potential source of occupational respiratory disease. This worker wears protective clothing and a respirator to remove asbestos from ceiling panels in a classroom.

KNOW YOUR EMPLOYMENT LAW

Hazard Communication

In, say, a dry cleaning store, it might not be apparent just by looking at it that the clear cleaning chemical hydrofluoric acid will eat through glass and blind an unsuspecting worker. Under OSHA's regulations, employers must communicate the presence and nature of hazards to which workers might be exposed. OSHA's *hazard communication standard,* recently revised, states that "in order to ensure chemical safety in the workplace, information about the identities and hazards of the chemicals must be available and understandable to workers." In line with this, says OSHA, chemical manufacturers and importers must label and provide hazard safety data sheets to their customers. All employers must have labels and safety data sheets available for their exposed workers, and train workers to handle the chemicals appropriately.[132] ■

Asbestos Exposure at Work and Air Quality

Asbestos is a major source of occupational respiratory disease. Efforts are still under way to rid old buildings of the substance.

OSHA standards require several actions with respect to asbestos. Employers must monitor the air whenever they expect the level of asbestos to rise to one-half the allowable limit (0.10 fibers per cubic centimeter). Engineering controls—walls, special filters, and so forth—are required to maintain an asbestos level that complies with OSHA standards. Only then can employers use respirators if additional efforts are required to achieve compliance.

Alcoholism and Substance Abuse

About two-thirds of people with an alcohol disorder work full-time.[133] Some estimate that almost 13 million workers use drugs illicitly.[134] About 15% of the U.S. workforce "has either been hung over at work, been drinking shortly before showing up for work, or been drinking or impaired while on the job at least once during the previous year."[135] Employee alcoholism may cost U.S. employers about $226 billion per year, for instance, in higher absenteeism and accidents.[136]

For many employers, dealing with substance abuse begins with substance abuse testing.[137] It's unusual to find employers who don't at least test job candidates for substance abuse before formally hiring them. And many states are instituting mandatory random drug testing for high-hazard workers. For example, New Jersey now requires random drug testing of electrical workers.[138]

DEALING WITH SUBSTANCE ABUSE Ideally, a drug-free workplace program includes five components:[139]

1. A drug-free workplace policy
2. Supervisor training
3. Employee education
4. Employee assistance
5. Drug testing

The policy should state, at a minimum, "The use, possession, transfer, or sale of illegal drugs by employees is prohibited." It should also explain the policy's rationale, and the disciplinary consequences. Supervisors should be trained to monitor employees' performance, and to stay alert to drug-related performance problems.

Several tools are available to screen for alcohol or drug abuse. The most widely used self-reporting screening instruments for alcoholism are the 4-item CAGE and the 25-item Michigan Alcoholism Screening Test (MAST). The former asks questions like these: Have you ever (1) attempted to Cut back on alcohol, (2) been Annoyed by comments about your drinking, (3) felt Guilty about drinking, (4) had an Eye-opener first thing in the morning to steady your nerves?[140]

TABLE 16-2 Observable Behavior Patterns Indicating Possible Alcohol-Related Problems

Alcoholism Stage	Some Possible Signs of Alcoholism Problems	Some Possible Alcoholism Performance Issues
Early	Arrives at work late	Reduced job efficiency
	Untrue statements	Misses deadlines
	Leaves work early	
Middle	Frequent absences, especially Mondays	Accidents
	Colleagues mentioning erratic behavior	Warnings from boss
	Mood swings	Noticeably reduced performance
	Anxiety	
	Late returning from lunch	
	Frequent multi-day absences	
Advanced	Personal neglect	Frequent falls, accidents
	Unsteady gait	Strong disciplinary actions
	Violent outbursts	Basically incompetent performance
	Blackouts and frequent forgetfulness	
	Possible drinking on job	

Source: Based on Gopal Patel and John Adkins Jr., "The Employer's Role in Alcoholism Assistance," *Personnel Journal* 62, no. 7 (July 1983), p. 570; Mary-Anne Enoch and David Goldman, "Problem Drinking and Alcoholism: Diagnosis and Treatment," *American Family Physician*, February 1, 2002, www.aafp.org/afp/20020201/441.html, accessed July 20, 2008; and Ken Pidd et al., "Alcohol and Work: Patterns of Use, Workplace Culture, and Safety," www.nisu.flinders.edu.au/pubs/reports/2006/injcat82.pdf, accessed July 20, 2008.

As in Table 16-2, alcohol-related symptoms range from tardiness in the earliest stages of alcohol abuse to prolonged, unpredictable absences in its later stages.[141]

Preemployment drug testing discourages those on drugs from applying for jobs or coming to work for employers who do testing.[142] (For instance, one study found that over 30% of regular drug users employed full-time said they were less likely to work for a company that conducted preemployment screening.)[143] Some applicants or employees may try to evade the test by purchasing "clean" specimens. Several states—including New Jersey, North Carolina, Virginia, Oregon, South Carolina, Pennsylvania, Louisiana, Texas, and Nebraska—have laws making drug-test fraud a crime.[144] The oral fluid drug test eliminates the "clean specimen" problem and is much less expensive to administer.[145]

Preemployment tests pick up only about half the workplace drug users, so ongoing random testing is advisable. One study concluded that preemployment drug testing had little effect on workplace accidents. However, a combination of preemployment and random ongoing testing was associated with a significant reduction in workplace accidents.[146]

Disciplining, discharge, in-house counseling, and referral to an outside agency are the four traditional prescriptions when a *current* employee tests positive. Most professionals seem to counsel treatment rather than outright dismissal, at least initially. Employers often make available employee assistance programs (EAPs) to provide the counseling necessary to support employees with alcohol or drug abuse problems.

Whether the alcohol abuse reflects a "disability" under the ADA depends on several things.[147] In general, employers can hold alcohol-dependent employees to the same performance standards as they hold nonalcoholics. However, there are legal risks. Employees have sued for invasion of privacy, wrongful discharge, defamation, and illegal searches. Therefore, before implementing a drug control program, employers should use employee handbooks and the like to publicize their substance abuse plans. Make sure to explain the conditions under which testing might occur and what accommodations you made for employees who voluntarily seek treatment.

Stress, Burnout, and Depression

Problems such as alcoholism sometimes reflect stress and depression. In turn, a variety of workplace factors can lead to stress. These include work schedule, pace of work, job security, route to and from work, workplace noise, poor supervision, and the number and nature of customers or clients.[148]

Personal factors also influence stress. For example, Type A personalities—workaholics who feel driven to be on time and meet deadlines—normally place themselves under greater stress. Add to job stress the stress caused by nonjob problems like divorce, and many workers are problems waiting to happen.

Human consequences of job stress include anxiety, depression, anger, cardiovascular disease, headaches, accidents, and even early onset Alzheimer's disease.[149] A Danish study found that nurses working under excessive pressure had double the risk for heart attacks.[150]

For the employer, consequences include diminished performance and increased absenteeism and turnover. A study of 46,000 employees concluded that high-stress workers' health-care costs were 46% higher than those of their less-stressed coworkers.[151] Yet only 5% of surveyed U.S. employers say they're addressing workplace stress.[152]

REDUCING JOB STRESS There are a number of ways to alleviate dysfunctional stress. These range from commonsense remedies (getting more sleep) to remedies like biofeedback and meditation. Finding a more suitable job, getting counseling, and planning and organizing each day's activities are other sensible responses.[153] In his book *Stress and the Manager*, Dr. Karl Albrecht suggests the following ways for a person to reduce job stress:[154]

- Build rewarding, pleasant, cooperative relationships with colleagues and employees.
- Don't bite off more than you can chew.
- Build an especially effective and supportive relationship with your boss.
- Negotiate with your boss for realistic deadlines on important projects.
- Learn as much as you can about upcoming events and get as much lead time as you can to prepare for them.
- Find time every day for detachment and relaxation.
- Take a walk around the office to keep your body refreshed and alert.
- Find ways to reduce unnecessary noise.
- Reduce the amount of trivia in your job; delegate routine work when possible.
- Limit interruptions.
- Don't put off dealing with distasteful problems.
- Make a constructive "worry list" that includes solutions for each problem.
- Get more and better quality sleep.[155]

Meditation is an option. Choose a quiet place with soft light and sit comfortably. Then meditate by focusing your thoughts (for example, count breaths or visualize a calming location such as a beach). When your mind wanders, bring it back to focusing your thoughts on your breathing or the beach.[156]

WHAT THE EMPLOYER CAN DO The employer and its supervisors play roles in reducing stress. Supportive supervisors and fair treatment are important; reign in bullying-prone supervisors. Other steps include reducing personal conflicts on the job and encouraging open communication between management and employees. Huntington Hospital in Pasadena, California, introduced an on-site concierge service to help its employees reduce work-related stress. It takes care of tasks like making vacation plans for the employees.[157] Some employers use "resilience training" to help employees deal with stress. As one example, "participants consider previous stressful situations in their lives that they have overcome and identify factors that made the situations manageable."[158]

One British firm has a three-tiered employee stress-reduction program.[159] First is *primary prevention.* This focuses on ensuring that things like job designs and workflows are correct. Second is *intervention.* This includes individual employee assessment, attitude surveys to find sources of stress, and supervisory intervention. Third is *rehabilitation*, which includes employee assistance programs and counseling.

burnout
The total depletion of physical and mental resources caused by excessive striving to reach an unrealistic work-related goal.

BURNOUT Experts define **burnout** as the total depletion of physical and mental resources caused by excessive striving to reach an unrealistic work-related goal. Burnout manifests itself in symptoms such as irritability, discouragement, exhaustion, cynicism, entrapment, and resentment.[160]

Employers can head off burnout, for instance, by monitoring employees in potentially high-stress jobs.[161] What can a burnout candidate do? In his book *How to Beat the High Cost of Success*, Dr. Herbert Freudenberger suggests:

- ***Break your patterns.*** First, the more well-rounded your life is, the better protected you are against burnout.
- ***Get away from it all periodically.*** Schedule occasional periods of introspection where you can get away from your usual routine. Another way to reduce burnout is to (try to) put your job aside once you go home.[162]
- ***Reassess your goals in terms of their intrinsic worth.*** Are the goals you've set for yourself attainable? Are they really worth the sacrifices?
- ***Think about your work.*** Could you do as good a job without being so intense?
- ***Stay active.*** One recent study concluded that "the increase in job burnout and depression was strongest among employees who did not engage in physical activity and weakest to the point of non-significance among those engaging in high physical activity."[163]

EMPLOYEE DEPRESSION *Employee depression* is a serious problem at work. Experts estimate that depression results in about 68 million lost workdays in the United States annually, and may cost U.S. businesses $23 billion or more per year just in absenteeism and lost productivity.[164] Depressed people also tend to have worse safety records.[165]

Employers should work harder to ensure that depressed employees utilize available support services. One survey found that while about two-thirds of large firms offered employee assistance programs covering depression, only about 14% of employees with depression said they ever used one.[166]

Employers therefore need to train supervisors to identify depression's warning signs and to counsel those who may need such services to use the firm's employee assistance program.[167] Depression is a disease. It does no more good to tell a depressed person to "snap out of it" than it would to tell someone with a heart condition to stop acting tired. Typical depression warning signs (if they last for more than 2 weeks) include persistent sad, anxious, or "empty" moods; sleeping too little; reduced appetite; loss of interest in activities once enjoyed; restlessness or irritability; and difficulty concentrating.[168]

Solving Computer-Related Ergonomic Problems

OSHA has no specific standards for computer workstations. It does have general standards that might apply, regarding, for instance, radiation, noise, and electrical hazards.[169]

NIOSH provided general recommendations. Most relate to *ergonomics* or design of the worker–equipment interface. These include:

- Employees should take a 3- to 5-minute break from working at the computer every 20–40 minutes, and use the time for other tasks.
- Design maximum flexibility into the workstation so it can be adapted to the individual operator. For example, use adjustable chairs with midback supports. Don't stay in one position for long periods.

- Reduce glare with devices such as shades over windows and indirect lighting.
- Give workers a complete preplacement vision exam to ensure properly corrected vision for reduced visual strain.[170]
- Allow the user to position his or her wrists at the same level as the elbow.
- Put the screen at or just below eye level, at a distance of 18 to 30 inches from the eyes.
- Let the wrists rest lightly on a pad for support.
- Put the feet flat on the floor or on a footrest.[171]

Repetitive Motion Disorders

Repetitive motion disorders include disorders such as carpal tunnel syndrome and tendonitis, and result from too many uninterrupted repetitions of an activity or motion, or from unnatural motions such as twisting the arm or wrist. It affects people who perform repetitive tasks such as assembly line or computer work. Employers can reduce the problem, for instance, with programs to help workers adjust their pace of work.[172]

Infectious Diseases

With many employees traveling to and from international destinations, monitoring and controlling infectious diseases is an important safety issue.[173]

Employers can take steps to prevent the entry or spread of infectious diseases. These steps include:

1. Closely monitor the Centers for Disease Control and Prevention (CDC) travel alerts. Access this information at www.cdc.gov.
2. Provide daily medical screenings for employees returning from infected areas.
3. Deny access for 10 days to employees or visitors who have had contact with suspected infected individuals.
4. Tell employees to stay home if they have a fever or respiratory system symptoms.
5. Clean work areas and surfaces regularly. Make sanitizers containing alcohol easily available.
6. Stagger breaks. Offer several lunch periods to reduce overcrowding.[174]

Workplace Smoking

Smoking is a serious health and cost problem. For employers, these costs derive from higher health and fire insurance, increased absenteeism, and reduced productivity (as when a smoker takes a 10-minute break behind the store). The California Environmental Protection Agency estimated that each year in the United States, secondhand smoke causes 3,000 deaths due to lung cancer and 35,000 to 62,000 illnesses due to heart problems (not all work-related).[175]

The manager can probably deny a job to a smoker as long as smoking isn't used as a surrogate for other discrimination.[176] Federal laws don't expressly prohibit discrimination against smokers. However, if a majority of a company's smokers also happen to be minorities, antismoking activities could be viewed as discriminatory. Seventeen states and the District of Columbia ban discriminating against smokers.[177] Most employers these days ban indoor smoking, often designating small outdoor areas where smoking is permitted. Many states and municipalities now ban indoor smoking in public areas.[178] With vaping laws in flux, employers should check the status of their local and state laws.[179]

Watch It!

If your professor has assigned this, go to the Assignments section of **mymanagementlab.com** to complete the video exercise titled *City of Los Angeles: Safety*.

Occupational Security and Risk Management

LEARNING OBJECTIVE **16-7**
Discuss the prerequisites for a security plan and how to set up a basic security program.

Workplace safety relates to risks of injury or illness to employees. *Workplace security* relates to protecting employees from internal and external security risks such as criminal acts by outside perpetrators and terrorism.[180] An employer's workplace security plans should address things like establishing a formal security function, protecting the firm's intellectual property (for instance, through noncompete agreements), developing crisis management plans, establishing theft and fraud prevention procedures, preventing workplace violence, and installing facility security systems.[181] A SHRM survey found that about 85% of responding organizations now have some type of formal disaster plan.[182] Many firms of course also have special handling procedures for mail packages and hold regular emergency evacuation drills.

Enterprise Risk Management

Enterprise risk management is "the process of assessing exposures to loss within an operation and determining how best to eliminate, manage or otherwise reduce the risk of an adverse event from having a negative impact on the business."[183]

Companies face a wide variety of risks, only some of which are OSHA-type direct risks to employees' health and safety. Specific risks include, for instance, natural disaster risks, financial risks, and risks to the firm's computer systems. *Human capital risks* would rank high. These include not just safety risks like those we discussed earlier in this chapter but also for instance, "risks" from unionization and from inadequate staffing plans.[184]

How the employer manages a specific risk depends on the class of risk it falls in. For example, *internal preventable* risks arise from actions within the company and include things like employees' illegal conduct or workplace accidents.[185] Employers manage these risks with methods such as codes of conduct, disciplinary procedures, and safety rules. *Strategy risks* are risks that managers accept as part of executing their strategies, such as the risk a banker takes that a borrower defaults. Employers manage some strategy risks with independent experts (like those who assess insurance risks) and with internal experts, like the risk managers who help to oversee banks' loan portfolios. *External risks* come from outside the company and include things like political and natural disasters and terrorism. Managing external risks might involve methods like scenario planning, in which the company endeavors to identify, analyze, and plan for multiple possible eventualities.

Preventing and Dealing with Violence at Work

Violence against employees is one internal preventable enterprise risk, and a huge problem.[186] Customers are often the perpetrators.[187] However, many assaults involve coworkers or a current or former partner or spouse.[188]

Workplace violence incidents by coworkers are predictable and avoidable. *Risk Management Magazine* estimates that about 86% of past workplace violence incidents were anticipated by coworkers, who had brought them to management's attention prior to the incidents actually occurring. Yet management usually did little or nothing.[189] Human resource managers can take several steps to reduce workplace violence risks.

HEIGHTEN SECURITY MEASURES Heightened security measures are the first line of defense, whether the violence is from coworkers, customers, or outsiders. According to OSHA, measures should include those in Figure 16-7.

IMPROVE EMPLOYEE SCREENING With about 30% of workplace attacks committed by coworkers, screening out potentially violent applicants is the employer's next line of defense.

FIGURE 16-7 How to Heighten Security in Your Workplace

Source: Based on "Creating a Safer Workplace: Simple Steps Bring Results," *Safety Now, September 2002,* pp. 1–2. See also www.osha.gov/SLTC/etools/hospital/hazards/workplaceviolence/ checklist.html, and www.osha.gov/Publications/osha3153.pdf, both accessed September 6, 2013.

- Improve external lighting.
- Use drop safes to minimize cash on hand.
- Post signs noting that only a limited amount of cash is on hand.
- Install silent alarms and surveillance cameras.
- Increase the number of staff on duty.
- Provide staff training in conflict resolution and nonviolent response.
- Close establishments during high-risk hours late at night and early in the morning.
- Issue a weapons policy; for instance, "firearms or other dangerous or deadly weapons cannot be brought onto the facility either openly or concealed."

Source: see "Creating a Safer Workplace: Simple Steps Bring Results," *Safety Now September 2002,* pp. 1–2. See also www.osha.gov/OshDoc/data_General_Facts/factsheet-workplace-violence.pdf, accessed September 22, 2015.

Personal and situational factors correlate with workplace aggression. Men and individuals scoring higher on "trait anger" (the predisposition to respond to situations with hostility) are more likely to exhibit aggression. In terms of the situation, interpersonal injustice and poor leadership predict aggression against supervisors.[190]

Employers can screen out potentially violent workers before they're hired. Obtain an employment application, and check the applicant's employment history, education, and references.[191] Sample interview questions include "What frustrates you?" and "Who was your worst supervisor and why?"[192] Certain background circumstances, such as the following, may call for a more in-depth background checking:[193]

- An unexplained gap in employment
- Incomplete or false information on the résumé or application
- A negative, unfavorable, or false reference
- Prior insubordinate or violent behavior on the job[194]
- A criminal history involving harassing or violent behavior
- A prior termination for cause with a suspicious (or no) explanation
- History of drug or alcohol abuse
- Strong indications of instability as indicated, for example, by frequent job changes or geographic moves
- Lost licenses or accreditations[195]

USE WORKPLACE VIOLENCE TRAINING You can also train supervisors to notice the clues that typify potentially violent current employees. Common clues include:[196]

- An act of violence on or off the job
- Erratic behavior evidencing a loss of perception or awareness of actions
- Overly confrontational or antisocial behavior
- Sexually aggressive behavior
- Isolationist or loner tendencies
- Insubordinate behavior with a threat of violence
- Tendency to overreact to criticism
- Exaggerated interest in war, guns, violence, mass murders, catastrophes, and so on
- Commission of a serious breach of security
- Possession of weapons, guns, knives, or like items in the workplace
- Violation of privacy rights of others, such as searching desks or stalking
- Chronic complaining and the raising of frequent, unreasonable grievances
- A retributory or get-even attitude

GUIDELINES FOR FIRING A HIGH-RISK EMPLOYEE When firing a high-risk employee:

- Plan all aspects of the meeting, including its time, location, the people to be present, and agenda.
- Involve security enforcement personnel.
- Advise the employee that he or she is no longer permitted onto the employer's property.
- Conduct the meeting in a room with a door leading to the outside of the building.
- Keep the termination brief and to the point.
- Make sure he or she returns all company-owned property at the meeting.
- Don't let the person return to his or her workstation.
- Conduct the meeting early in the week and early in the morning so he or she has time to meet with employment counselors or support groups.
- Offer as generous a severance package as possible.
- Protect the employee's dignity by not advertising the event.[197]

VIOLENCE TOWARD WOMEN AT WORK Men have more fatal occupational injuries than do women, but the proportion of women who are victims of assault is much higher. The Gender-Motivated Violence Act (part of the Violence Against Women Act) imposes liabilities on employers whose women employees become violence victims.[198] Of all females murdered at work, more than three-fourths are victims of random criminal violence carried out by an assailant unknown to the victim. Family members, coworkers, or acquaintances commit the rest. Tangible security improvements including better lighting, cash-drop boxes, and similar steps can help. Women (and men) should have access to domestic crisis hotlines,[199] and to employee assistance programs.

Securing the Facility

In simplest terms, instituting a basic facility security program requires four steps: analyzing the current *level* of risk, and then installing *mechanical, natural*, and *organizational* security systems.[200] Many employers establish cross-functional threat assessment teams.[201] At one university, for instance, team members meet periodically to review potential threats to university students and employees.[202]

Such teams ideally start with an analysis of the facility's *current level of risk.* Here, start with the obvious. For example, what is the neighborhood like? Does your facility (such as the office building you're in) house other businesses or individuals that might bring unsafe activities to your doorstep? As part of this initial threat assessment, also review these six matters:

1. ***Reception area access***, including need for a "panic button";
2. ***Interior security***, including secure restrooms, and better identification of exits;
3. ***Authorities' involvement***, in particular emergency procedures developed with local law enforcement;
4. ***Mail handling***, including screening and opening mail;
5. ***Evacuation***, including evacuation procedures and training; and
6. ***Backup systems***, such as storing data off site.

Having assessed the potential current level of risk, the employer then turns to assessing and improving natural, mechanical, and organizational security.[203]

Natural security means capitalizing on the facility's natural or architectural features to minimize security problems. For example, do too many entrances hamper controlling facility access?

Mechanical security is the utilization of security systems such as locks, intrusion alarms, access control systems, and surveillance systems to reduce the need for continuous human surveillance.[204]

Finally, *organizational security* means using good management to improve security. For example, it means properly training and motivating security staff and lobby attendants. Ensure that the security staff has written orders that define their duties, especially in situations such as fire, elevator entrapment, hazardous

Many employers install video security cameras to monitor areas in and around their premises.

Andrey Popov/Shutterstock

materials spills, medical emergencies, hostile intrusions, suspicious packages, civil disturbances, and workplace violence.[205] Also ask, "Are you properly investigating the backgrounds of new hires and contractors?"

As one corporate security summary put it, "workplace security involves more than … installing an alarm system."[206] Ideally, a comprehensive corporate anticrime program should start with the following:[207]

1. ***Company philosophy and policy on crime.*** Make sure employees understand that the employer has a zero-tolerance policy with respect to workers who commit any crimes.
2. ***Investigations of job applicants.*** Always conduct full background checks.
3. ***Crime awareness training.*** Make it clear during training and orientation that the employer is tough on workplace crime.
4. ***Crisis management.*** Establish and communicate what to do in the event of a bomb threat, fire, or other emergency.

KNOWLEDGE BASE

Company Security and Employee Privacy

Security programs often entail monitoring employee communications and workplace activities. Ideally, employers should get employees' consent for monitoring. However, the employer may also monitor if it's clear from existing policies and notices that employees should have known monitoring might take place. Steps include:[208]

1. Distribute a policy that (a) says the company reserves the right to inspect and search employees as well as their personal property, electronic media, and files; and (b) that lockers and desks remain the property of the company and are subject to search.
2. Train investigators to focus on the facts and avoid making accusations.
3. Remember that employees can request that an employee representative be present during the investigative interview.
4. Make sure all investigations and searches are evenhanded and nondiscriminatory.

Business Continuity and Emergency Plans

One source estimates that 40% of companies never reopen after suffering business disruptions from a major catastrophe, so putting a disaster plan in place is imperative.[209] Emergency preparedness resources include www.ready.gov and the National Institute for Occupational Safety and Health (www.cdc.gov/niosh/).[210] To help the organization prepare for potential disasters, the human resource department should develop a plan and identify key responsibilities, make sure all employees are aware of the plan, and train employees regularly.[211] Such plans should cover *early detection of a problem, methods for communicating the emergency externally*, and *communications plans for initiating an evacuation.* The initial alarm should come first. The employer should then follow that with an announcement providing specific information about the emergency and letting employees know what action they should take.[212]

One also needs plans for dealing with health issues.[213] Thus, in the case of a cardiac arrest emergency, early CPR and an automated external defibrillator are essential. These devices should be available and one or more local employees trained in their use.[214]

Plans are also required for *business continuity* in the event of a disaster. The employer can designate a secure area of the company Web site for emergency employee communications, listing such things as expected hours of operation, facilities opening schedules, and alternative work locations.[215] The disaster plans should include establishing a command center and identifying employees considered essential in the event of a disaster, including responsibilities for each. Business continuity information is available at www.preparemybusiness.org.

TRENDS SHAPING HR: *DIGITAL AND SOCIAL MEDIA*

Twitter Notifications

Social media such as Twitter are obvious choices for quickly communicating emergency information to large numbers of dispersed individuals. When a tornado hit Bridgeport, Connecticut, a few years ago, the city's administrators used Twitter to tell citizens about things like power outages and blocked roads. The Canadian Red Cross uses social media to publicize preparedness information and respond to questions from affected communities. And emergency managers, utility companies, and the public used social media to share updates on things like shelter locations when Hurricane Sandy struck the Northeast.[216] ■

Terrorism

The employer can take several steps to protect its employees and physical assets from the risk of terrorist attack. These steps, now familiar at many workplaces, include:

- Screen the identities of everyone entering the premises.[217]
- Check mail carefully.
- Identify ahead of time a lean interim "crisis organization" that can run the company after a terrorist threat.
- Identify in advance under what conditions you will close the company down, as well as the shutdown process.
- Institute a process to put a crisis management team together.
- Prepare evacuation plans and make sure exits are well marked and unblocked.
- Designate an employee who will communicate with families and off-site employees.
- Identify an upwind, off-site location near your facility as a staging area for all evacuated personnel.
- Designate in advance several employees who will do headcounts at the staging area.
- Establish an emergency text-messaging procedure to notify affected individuals that an emergency may exist.[218]

Chapter Review

MyManagementLab® Go to **mymanagementlab.com** to complete the problems marked with this icon ✪.

Chapter Section Summaries

16-1. The subject **safety and the manager** concerns managers for several reasons, one of which is the number of workplace accidents. Reducing accidents often boils down to reducing accident-causing conditions and accident-causing acts. However, safety always starts at the top.

16-2. Because of this, all managers need to be familiar with **occupational safety law**. The Occupational Safety and Health Act was passed by Congress in 1972 to assure so far as possible every working man and woman in the nation has safe and healthful working conditions, and to preserve human resources. The act created the Occupational Safety and Health Administration (OSHA).

16-3. There are three basic **causes of workplace accidents**: chance occurrences, unsafe conditions, and employees' unsafe acts. Unsafe conditions include things like improperly guarded equipment and hazardous procedures. Unsafe acts sometimes reflect personality traits such as impatience and distractibility.

16-4. In practice, **how to prevent accidents** boils down to reducing unsafe conditions and reducing unsafe acts. Reducing unsafe conditions is always the first line of defense and includes using checklists and following OSHA standards. There are then several basic approaches to reducing unsafe acts, for instance, through proper selection and placement, training, motivation and positive reinforcement, behavior-based safety, employee participation, and conducting safety and health audits.

16-5. The centerpiece of Milliken's safety process is its *involvement-based* employee engagement **program**. Milliken's employees staff the steering and safety subcommittee system, submit "opportunity for improvement" suggestions weekly, review each of these suggestions, and provide feedback on every suggestion.

16-6. Most **workplace health hazards** aren't obvious, like unguarded equipment. Typical exposure hazards include, for instance, chemicals, biohazards, and improperly designed equipment. Managing exposure hazards like these comes under the area of industrial hygiene, and involves recognition, evaluation, and control. Stress, burnout, and depression are more serious at work than many people realize, and both the employee and employer can take steps to deal with them. Employers especially need to train supervisors to identify depression's warning signs and to counsel those who may need special services.

16-7. Most employers today have **occupational security and risk management programs**. Heightened security measures are an employer's first line of defense against attacks on workers, and include, for instance, improving external lighting. Screening can reduce the risk of hiring potentially violent employees. Instituting a basic facility security program involves analyzing the current level of risk, and then installing mechanical, natural, and organizational security systems.

Discussion Questions

✪ **16-1.** Explain how to reduce the occurrence of unsafe acts on the part of your employees.

16-2. Explain the supervisor's role in safety.

16-3. Explain what causes unsafe acts.

16-4. Describe at least five techniques for reducing accidents.

✪ **16-5.** Explain how you would reduce stress at work.

Individual and Group Activities

16-6. Working individually or in groups, answer the question, "Is there such a thing as an accident-prone person?"

16-7. Working individually or in groups, compile a list of the factors at work or in school that create stress for you. What methods do you use for dealing with the stress?

16-8. Appendices A and B at the end of this book (pages 612–629) list the knowledge someone studying for the HRCI (Appendix A) or SHRM (Appendix B) certification exam needs to have in each area of human resource management (such as in Strategic Management, and Workforce Planning). In groups of several students, do four things: (1) review Appendix A and/or B; (2) identify the material in this chapter that relates to the Appendix A and/or B required knowledge lists; (3) write four multiple-choice exam questions on this material that you believe would be suitable for inclusion in the HRCI exam and/or the SHRM exam; and, (4) if time permits, have someone from your team post your team's questions in front of the class, so that students in all teams can answer the exam questions created by the other teams.

16-9. A safety journal presented some information about what happens when OSHA refers criminal complaints about willful violations of OSHA standards to the U.S. Department of Justice (DOJ). In one 20-year period, of the 119 cases OSHA referred to the DOJ, only 9 resulted in prison time for at least one of the defendants. "The Department of Justice is a disgrace," charged the founder of an organization for family members of workers killed on the job. One possible explanation for this low conviction rate is that the crime in cases like these is generally a misdemeanor, not a felony, and the DOJ generally tries to focus its attention on felony cases. Given this information, what implications do you think this has for how employers and their managers should manage their safety programs, and why do you take that position?

16-10. A 315-foot-tall, 2-million-pound crane collapsed on a construction site in East Toledo, Ohio, killing four ironworkers. Do you think catastrophic failures like this are avoidable? If so, what steps would you suggest the general contractor take to avoid a disaster like this?

Experiential Exercise

How Safe Is My University?

Purpose: The purpose of this exercise is to give you practice in identifying unsafe conditions.

Required Understanding: You should be familiar with material covered in this chapter, particularly that on unsafe conditions and that in Figures 16-6 and 16-8.

How to Set Up the Exercise/Instructions: Divide the class into groups of four. Assume that each group is a safety committee retained by your college's or university's safety engineer to identify and report on any possible unsafe conditions in and around the school building. Each group will spend about 45 minutes in and around the building you are now in for the purpose of identifying and listing possible unsafe conditions. (Make use of the checklists in Figures 16-6 and 16-8.)

Return to the class in about 45 minutes. A spokesperson for each group should list on the board the unsafe conditions you have identified. How many were there? Do you think these also violate OSHA standards? How would you go about checking?

GENERAL

	OK	ACTION NEEDED
1. Is the required OSHA workplace poster displayed in your place of business as required where all employees are likely to see it?	☐	☐
2. Are you aware of the requirement to report all workplace fatalities and any serious accidents (where five or more are hospitalized) to a federal or state OSHA office within 48 hours?	☐	☐
3. Are workplace injury and illness records being kept as required by OSHA?	☐	☐
4. Are you aware that the OSHA annual summary of workplace injuries and illnesses must be posted by February 1 and must remain posted until March 1?	☐	☐
5. Are you aware that employers with 10 or fewer employees are exempt from the OSHA record-keeping requirements, unless they are part of an official BLS or state survey and have received specific instructions to keep records?	☐	☐
6. Have you demonstrated an active interest in safety and health matters by defining a policy for your business and communicating it to all employees?	☐	☐
7. Do you have a safety committee or group that allows participation of employees in safety and health activities?	☐	☐
8. Does the safety committee or group meet regularly and report, in writing, its activities?	☐	☐
9. Do you provide safety and health training for all employees requiring such training, and is it documented?	☐	☐
10. Is one person clearly in charge of safety and health activities?	☐	☐
11. Do all employees know what to do in emergencies?	☐	☐
12. Are emergency telephone numbers posted?	☐	☐
13. Do you have a procedure for handling employee complaints regarding safety and health?	☐	☐

WORKPLACE

ELECTRICAL WIRING, FIXTURES, AND CONTROLS

	OK	ACTION NEEDED
1. Are your workplace electricians familiar with the requirements of the National Electrical Code (NEC)?	☐	☐
2. Do you specify compliance with the NEC for all contract electrical work?	☐	☐
3. If you have electrical installations in hazardous dust or vapor areas, do they meet the NEC for hazardous locations?	☐	☐
4. Are all electrical cords strung so they do not hang on pipes, nails, hooks, etc.?	☐	☐
5. Is all conduit, BX cable, etc., properly attached to all supports and tightly connected to junction and outlet boxes?	☐	☐
6. Is there no evidence of fraying on any electrical cords?	☐	☐
7. Are rubber cords kept free of grease, oil, and chemicals?	☐	☐
8. Are metallic cable and conduit systems properly grounded?	☐	☐
9. Are portable electric tools and appliances grounded or double insulated?	☐	☐
10. Are all ground connections clean and tight?	☐	☐
11. Are fuses and circuit breakers the right type and size for the load on each circuit?	☐	☐
12. Are all fuses free of "jumping" with pennies or metal strips?	☐	☐
13. Do switches show evidence of overheating?	☐	☐
14. Are switches mounted in clean, tightly closed metal boxes?	☐	☐
15. Are all electrical switches marked to show their purpose?	☐	☐
16. Are motors clean and kept free of excessive grease and oil?	☐	☐
17. Are motors properly maintained and provided with adequate overcurrent protection?	☐	☐
18. Are bearings in good condition?	☐	☐
19. Are portable lights equipped with proper guards?	☐	☐
20. Are all lamps kept free of combustible material?	☐	☐
21. Is your electrical system checked periodically by someone competent in the NEC?	☐	☐

Develop your own checklist.

These are only sample questions.

(Continued)

FIGURE 16-8 Self-Inspection Safety and Health Checklist

Source: From OSHA Self-Inspection Checklist for General Industry, from http://www.safetyhouse.ir/safetyhouse/file/OSHA%20Self-Inspection%20Checklist%20for%20General%20Industry.pdf.

Note: For a much more extensive checklist, see "Self-Inspection Checklists," www.osha.gov/Publications/smallbusiness/small-business.html#check, accessed September 6, 2013.

Develop your own checklist.

These are only sample questions.

EXITS AND ACCESS	OK	ACTION NEEDED
1. Are all exits visible and unobstructed?	☐	☐
2. Are all exits marked with a readily visible sign that is properly illuminated?	☐	☐
3. Are there sufficient exits to ensure prompt escape in case of emergency?	☐	☐
4. Are areas with restricted occupancy posted and is access/egress controlled by persons specifically authorized to be in those areas?	☐	☐
5. Do you take special precautions to protect employees during construction and repair operations?	☐	☐

FIRE PROTECTION	OK	ACTION NEEDED
1. Are portable fire extinguishers provided in adequate number and type?	☐	☐
2. Are fire extinguishers inspected monthly for general condition and operability and noted on the inspection tag?	☐	☐
3. Are fire extinguishers recharged regularly and properly noted on the inspection tag?	☐	☐
4. Are fire extinguishers mounted in readily accessible locations?	☐	☐
5. If you have interior standpipes and valves, are these inspected regularly?	☐	☐
6. If you have a fire alarm system, is it tested at least annually?	☐	☐
7. Are employees periodically instructed in the use of extinguishers and fire protection procedures?	☐	☐
8. If you have outside private fire hydrants, were they flushed within the last year and placed on a regular maintenance schedule?	☐	☐
9. Are fire doors and shutters in good operating condition?	☐	☐
Are they unobstructed and protected against obstruction?	☐	☐
10. Are fusible links in place?	☐	☐
11. Is your local fire department well acquainted with your plant, location, and specific hazards?	☐	☐
12. Automatic sprinklers:		
Are water control valves, air, and water pressures checked weekly?	☐	☐
Are control valves locked open?	☐	☐
Is maintenance of the system assigned to responsible persons or a sprinkler contractor?	☐	☐
Are sprinkler heads protected by metal guards where exposed to mechanical damage?	☐	☐
Is proper minimum clearance maintained around sprinkler heads?	☐	☐

HOUSEKEEPING AND GENERAL WORK ENVIRONMENT	OK	ACTION NEEDED
1. Is smoking permitted in designated "safe areas" only?	☐	☐
2. Are NO SMOKING signs prominently posted in areas containing combustibles and flammables?	☐	☐
3. Are covered metal waste cans used for oily and paint-soaked waste?	☐	☐
Are they emptied at least daily?	☐	☐
4. Are paint spray booths, dip tanks, etc., and their exhaust ducts cleaned regularly?	☐	☐
5. Are stand mats, platforms, or similar protection provided to protect employees from wet floors in wet processes?	☐	☐
6. Are waste receptacles provided and are they emptied regularly?	☐	☐
7. Do your toilet facilities meet the requirements of applicable sanitary codes?	☐	☐
8. Are washing facilities provided?	☐	☐
9. Are all areas of your business adequately illuminated?	☐	☐
10. Are floor load capacities posted in second floors, lofts, storage areas, etc.?	☐	☐
11. Are floor openings provided with toe boards and railings or a floor hole cover?	☐	☐
12. Are stairways in good condition with standard railings provided for every flight having four or more risers?	☐	☐
13. Are portable wood ladders and metal ladders adequate for their purpose, in good condition, and provided with secure footing?	☐	☐
14. If you have fixed ladders, are they adequate, and are they in good condition and equipped with side rails or cages or special safety climbing devices, if required?	☐	☐
15. For loading docks:		
Are dockplates kept in serviceable condition and secured to prevent slipping?	☐	☐
Do you have means to prevent car or truck movement when dockplates are in place?	☐	☐

FIGURE 16-8 **(Continued)**

MACHINES AND EQUIPMENT

	OK	ACTION NEEDED
1. Are all machines or operations that expose operators or other employees to rotating parts, pinch points, flying chips, particles, or sparks adequately guarded?	☐	☐
2. Are mechanical power transmission belts and pinch points guarded?	☐	☐
3. Is exposed power shafting less than 7 feet from the floor guarded?	☐	☐
4. Are hand tools and other equipment regularly inspected for safe condition?	☐	☐
5. Is compressed air used for cleaning reduced to less than 30 psi?	☐	☐
6. Are power saws and similar equipment provided with safety guards?	☐	☐
7. Are grinding wheel tool rests set to within 1/8 inch or less of the wheel?	☐	☐
8. Is there any system for inspecting small hand tools for burred ends, cracked handles, etc.?	☐	☐
9. Are compressed gas cylinders examined regularly for obvious signs of defects, deep rusting, or leakage?	☐	☐
10. Is care used in handling and storing cylinders and valves to prevent damage?	☐	☐
11. Are all air receivers periodically examined, including the safety valves?	☐	☐
12. Are safety valves tested regularly and frequently?	☐	☐
13. Is there sufficient clearance from stoves, furnaces, etc., for stock, woodwork, or other combustible materials?	☐	☐
14. Is there clearance of at least 4 feet in front of heating equipment involving open flames, such as gas radiant heaters, and fronts of firing doors of stoves, furnaces, etc.?	☐	☐
15. Are all oil and gas fired devices equipped with flame failure controls that will prevent flow of fuel if pilots or main burners are not working?	☐	☐
16. Is there at least a 2-inch clearance between chimney brickwork and all woodwork or other combustible materials?	☐	☐
17. For welding or flame cutting operations:		
Are only authorized, trained personnel permitted to use such equipment?	☐	☐
Have operators been given a copy of operating instructions and asked to follow them?	☐	☐
Are welding gas cylinders stored so they are not subjected to damage?	☐	☐
Are valve protection caps in place on all cylinders not connected for use?	☐	☐
Are all combustible materials near the operator covered with protective shields or otherwise protected?	☐	☐
Is a fire extinguisher provided at the welding site?	☐	☐
Do operators have the proper protective clothing and equipment?	☐	☐

Develop your own checklist.

These are only sample questions.

MATERIALS

	OK	ACTION NEEDED
1. Are approved safety cans or other acceptable containers used for handling and dispensing flammable liquids?	☐	☐
2. Are all flammable liquids that are kept inside buildings stored in proper storage containers or cabinets?	☐	☐
3. Do you meet OSHA standards for all spray painting or dip tank operations using combustible liquids?	☐	☐
4. Are oxidizing chemicals stored in areas separate from all organic material except shipping bags?	☐	☐
5. Do you have an enforced NO SMOKING rule in areas for storage and use of hazardous materials?	☐	☐
6. Are NO SMOKING signs posted where needed?	☐	☐
7. Is ventilation equipment provided for removal of air contaminants from operations such as production grinding, buffing, spray painting and/or vapor degreasing, and is it operating properly?	☐	☐
8. Are protective measures in effect for operations involved with x-rays or other radiation?	☐	☐
9. For lift truck operations:		
Are only trained personnel allowed to operate forklift trucks?	☐	☐
Is overhead protection provided on high lift rider trucks?	☐	☐
10. For toxic materials:		
Are all materials used in your plant checked for toxic qualities?	☐	☐
Have appropriate control procedures such as ventilation systems, enclosed operations, safe handling practices, proper personal protective equipment (such as respirators, glasses or goggles, gloves, etc.) been instituted for toxic materials?	☐	☐

(Continued)

FIGURE 16-8 (Continued)

Develop your own checklist.

These are only sample questions.

EMPLOYEE PROTECTION	OK	ACTION NEEDED
1. Is there a hospital, clinic, or infirmary for medical care near your business?	☐	☐
2. If medical and first-aid facilities are not nearby, do you have one or more employees trained in first aid?	☐	☐
3. Are your first-aid supplies adequate for the type of potential injuries in your work-place?	☐	☐
4. Are there quick water flush facilities available where employees are exposed to corrosive materials?	☐	☐
5. Are hard hats provided and worn where any danger of falling objects exists?	☐	☐
6. Are protective goggles or glasses provided and worn where there is any danger of flying particles or splashing of corrosive materials?	☐	☐
7. Are protective gloves, aprons, shields, or other means provided for protection from sharp, hot, or corrosive materials?	☐	☐
8. Are approved respirators provided for regular or emergency use where needed?	☐	☐
9. Is all protective equipment maintained in a sanitary condition and readily available for use?	☐	☐
10. Where special equipment is needed for electrical workers, is it available?	☐	☐
11. When lunches are eaten on the premises, are they eaten in areas where there is no exposure to toxic materials, and not in toilet facility areas?	☐	☐
12. Is protection against the effect of occupational noise exposure provided when the sound levels exceed those shown in the OSHA noise standard?	☐	☐

FIGURE 16-8 (Continued)

Application Case

CHAPTER 16

The New Safety and Health Program

At first glance, a dot-com company is one of the last places you'd expect to find potential safety and health hazards—or so the owners of LearnInMotion.com thought. There's no danger of moving machinery, no high-pressure lines, no cutting or heavy lifting, and certainly no fork-lift trucks. However, there are safety and health problems.

In terms of accident-causing conditions, for instance, the one thing dot-com companies have are cables and wires. Even with extensive use of Wi-Fi and Bluetooth, there are cables connecting computers to screens and to servers, and in many cases cables running from some computers to separate printers. There are 10 telephones in this particular office, all on 15-foot power lines that always seem to be snaking around chairs and tables. There is, in fact, an astonishing amount of cable considering this is an office with so-called wireless connections and with fewer than 10 employees. When the installation specialists wired the office (for electricity, high-speed cable, phone lines, burglar alarms, and computers), they estimated they used well over 5 miles of cables of one sort or another. Most of these are hidden in the walls or ceilings, but many of them snake their way from desk to desk, and under and over doorways. Several employees have tried to reduce the nuisance of having to trip over wires whenever they get up by putting their plastic chair pads over the wires closest to them. However, that still leaves many wires unprotected. In other cases, they brought in their own packing tape and tried to tape down the wires in those spaces where they're particularly troublesome, such as across doorways.

The cables and wires are only one of the more obvious potential accident-causing conditions. The firm's programmer, before he left the firm, had tried to repair the main server while the unit was still electrically alive. To this day, they're not sure exactly where he stuck the screwdriver, but the result was that he was "blown across the room," as one manager put it. He was all right, but it was still a scare. And while they haven't received any claims yet, every employee spends hours at his or her computer, so carpal tunnel syndrome is a risk, as are a variety of other problems such as eyestrain and strained backs.

One recent accident particularly scared the owners. The firm uses independent contractors to deliver the firm's books and DVD-based courses in New York and two other cities. A delivery person was riding his bike east at the intersection of Second Avenue and East 64th Street in New York when he was struck by a car going south on Second Avenue. Luckily, he was not hurt, but the bike's front wheel was wrecked, and the narrow escape got the firm's two owners, Mel and Maria, thinking about their lack of a safety program.

It's not just the physical conditions that concern the two owners. They also have some concerns about potential health problems such as job stress and burnout. Although the business may be (relatively) safe with respect to physical conditions, it is also relatively stressful in terms of the demands it makes in hours and deadlines. It is not unusual for employees to get to work by 7:30 or 8 in the morning and to work through until 11 or 12 at night, at least 5 and sometimes 6 or 7 days per week.

The bottom line is that both Maria and Mel feel quite strongly that they need to do something about implementing a health and safety plan. Now, they want you, their management consultants, to help them do it. Here's what they want you to do for them.

Questions

16-11. Based upon your knowledge of health and safety matters and your actual observations of operations that are similar to theirs, make a list of the potential hazardous conditions employees and others face at LearnInMotion.com. What should they do to reduce the potential severity of the top five hazards?

16-12. Would it be advisable for them to set up a procedure for screening out stress-prone or accident-prone individuals? Why or why not? If so, how should they screen them?

16-13. Write a short position paper on the subject, "What should we do to get all our employees to behave more safely at work?"

16-14. Based on what you know and on what other dot-coms are doing, write a short position paper on the subject, "What can we do to reduce the potential problems of stress and burnout in our company?"

Continuing Case

Carter Cleaning Company

The New Safety Program

Employees' safety and health are very important matters in the laundry and cleaning business. Each facility is a small production plant in which machines, powered by high-pressure steam and compressed air, work at high temperatures washing, cleaning, and pressing garments, often under very hot, slippery conditions. Chemical vapors are produced continually, and caustic chemicals are used in the cleaning process. High-temperature stills are almost continually "cooking down" cleaning solvents in order to remove impurities so that the solvents can be reused. If a mistake is made in this process—like injecting too much steam into the still—a boilover occurs, in which boiling chemical solvent erupts out of the still and over the floor, and on anyone who happens to be standing in its way.

As a result of these hazards and the fact that chemically hazardous waste is continually produced in these stores, several government agencies (including OSHA and the Environmental Protection Agency) have instituted strict guidelines regarding the management of these plants. For example, posters have to be placed in each store notifying employees of their right to be told what hazardous chemicals they are dealing with and what the proper method for handling each chemical is. Special waste-management firms must be used to pick up and properly dispose of the hazardous waste.

A chronic problem the Carters (and most other laundry owners) have is the unwillingness on the part of the cleaning/spotting workers to wear safety goggles. Not all the chemicals they use require safety goggles, but some—like the hydrofluoric acid used to remove rust stains from garments—are very dangerous. The latter is kept in special plastic containers, since it dissolves glass. The problem is that wearing safety goggles can be troublesome. They are somewhat uncomfortable, and they become smudged easily and thus cut down on visibility. As a result, Jack has always found it almost impossible to get these employees to wear their goggles.

Questions

16-15. How should the firm go about identifying hazardous conditions that should be rectified? Use checklists such as those in Figures 16-6 and 16-8 to list at least 10 possible dry cleaning store hazardous conditions.

16-16. Would it be advisable for the firm to set up a procedure for screening out accident-prone individuals? How should they do so?

16-17. How would you suggest the Carters get all employees to behave more safely at work? Also, how would you advise them to get those who should be wearing goggles to do so?

Translating Strategy into HR Policies and Practices Case*,§

**The accompanying strategy map for this chapter is in MyManagementLab®; the overall map on the inside back cover of this text outlines the relationships involved.*

Improving Performance at the Hotel Paris

The New Safety and Health Program

The Hotel Paris's competitive strategy is "To use superior guest service to differentiate the Hotel Paris properties, and to thereby increase the length of stay and return rate of guests, and thus boost revenues and profitability." HR manager Lisa Cruz must now formulate functional policies and activities that support this competitive strategy and boost performance, by eliciting the required employee behaviors and competencies.

While "hazardous conditions" might not be the first thing that comes to mind when you think of hotels, Lisa Cruz knew that hazards and safety were in fact serious issues for the Hotel Paris. Indeed, everywhere you look—from the valets leaving car doors open on the driveways to slippery areas around the pools, to thousands of pounds of ammonia, chlorine, and other caustic chemicals that the hotels use each year for cleaning and laundry, hotels provide a fertile environment for accidents. Obviously, hazardous conditions are bad for the Hotel Paris. They are inhumane for the workers. High accident rates probably reduce employee morale and thus service. And accidents raise the company's costs and reduce its profitability, for instance, in terms of workers' compensation claims and absences. Lisa knew that she had to clean up her firm's occupational safety and health systems, for its employees' well-being, and to achieve the company's strategic goals.

Lisa and the CFO reviewed their company's safety records, and what they found disturbed them. In terms of every safety-related metric they could find, including accident costs per year, lost time due to accidents, workers' compensation per employee, and number of safety training programs per year, the Hotel Paris compared unfavorably with most

§Written by and copyright Gary Dessler, PhD.

other hotel chains and service firms. "Just in terms of extra workers' compensation costs, the Hotel Paris must be spending $500,000 a year more than we should be," said the CFO. And that didn't include lost time due to accidents, or the negative effect accidents had on employee morale, or the cost of litigation (as when, for instance, one guest accidentally burned himself with chlorine that a pool attendant had left unprotected). The CFO authorized Lisa to develop a new safety and health program.

Lisa and her team began by hiring a safety and health consultant, someone who had been an inspector and then manager with OSHA. Based on the analysis, the team then took numerous steps, including the following. First, specially trained teams consisting of someone from Lisa's HR group, the local hotel's assistant manager, and three local hotel employees went through each local hotel "with a fine tooth comb," as Lisa put it. They used an extensive checklist to identify and eliminate unsafe conditions.

Lisa's team took other steps. They convinced the Hotel Paris's board of directors and chairman and CEO to issue a joint statement emphasizing the importance of safety, and the CEO, during a one-month period, visited each hotel to meet with all employees and emphasize safety. The Hotel Paris also contracted with a safety training company. This firm created special online safety programs for the company's managers, and developed five-day training seminars for the hotels' staffs.

The new programs seem to be effective. Lisa and the CFO were pleased to find, after about a year, that accident costs per year, lost time due to accidents, and workers' compensation expenses were all down at least 40%. And anecdotal evidence from supervisors suggested that employees feel better about the company's commitment to them and were providing better service as a result.

Questions

16-18. Based on what you read in this chapter of Dessler *Human Resource Management*, what's the first step you would have advised the Hotel Paris to take as part of its new safety and health program, and why?

16-19. List 10 specific high-risk areas in a typical hotel you believe Lisa and her team should look at now, including examples of the safety or health hazards that they should look for there.

16-20. Give three specific examples of how Hotel Paris can use HR practices to improve its safety efforts.

16-21. Write a one-page summary addressing the topic, "How improving safety and health at the Hotel Paris will contribute to us achieving our strategic goals."

MyManagementLab

Go to **mymanagementlab.com** for Auto-graded writing questions as well as the following Assisted-graded writing questions:

16-22. Based on everything you read in this chapter, what is Milliken doing "right" that you believe helps to explain why they have such a good safety record?

16-23. Describe the steps employers can take to reduce workplace violence.

16-24. MyManagementLab only—comprehensive writing assignment for this chapter.

CHAPTER 16

PERSONAL INVENTORY ASSESSMENTS

Stress Management

Controlling one's stress is important. Complete this assessment to learn more about your personality.

Key Terms

Occupational Safety and Health Act of 1970, 516
Occupational Safety and Health Administration (OSHA), 517
occupational illness, 517
citation, 520
unsafe conditions, 523
job hazard analysis, 527
operational safety reviews, 528
behavior-based safety, 532
safety awareness program, 532
burnout, 540

Endnotes

1. "Workers Rate Safety Most Important Workplace Issue," *EHS Today*, October 2010, p. 17.
2. "BP Oil Spill Timeline," July 22, 2010, www.guardian.co.uk/environment/2010/jun/29/bp-oil-spill-timeline-deepwater-horizon, accessed June 29, 2011.
3. Preliminary figures for 2013; http://stats.bls.gov/iif/oshwc/cfoi/cftb0277.pdf, accessed September 11, 2014.
4. Figures for 2012; www.bls.gov/news.release/archives/osh_11072013.pdf, accessed September 11, 2014.
5. "BLS Likely Underestimating Injury and Illness Estimates," *Occupational Hazards*, May 2006, p. 16; Tahira Probst et al., "Organizational Injury Rate Underreporting: The Moderating Effect of Organizational Safety Climate," *Journal of Applied Psychology* 93, no. 5 (2008), pp. 1147–1154.
6. Russell Sobel, "Occupational Safety and Profit Maximization: Friends or Foes?" *The Journal of Socioeconomics* 30, no. 9 (2010), pp. 429–433.

7. www.osha.gov/dcsp/products/topics/businesscase/, accessed April 16, 2013.
8. David Levine et al., "Randomized Government Safety Inspections Reduce Worker Injuries with No Detectable Job Loss," *Science* 336 (May 18, 2012), pp. 907–911.
9. Chief Financial Officer Survey, Liberty Mutual Insurance Co., 2005.
10. Mike Rich, "Preventing Hearing Loss," www.adhesivesmag.com, January 2012, pp. 40–41.
11. One study recently concluded that "employee perceptions of the extent to which managers and supervisors are committed to workplace safety likely influence employee safety behavior and, subsequently, injuries." Jeremy Beus et al., "Safety Climate and Juries: An Examination of Theoretical and Empirical Relationships," *Journal of Applied Psychology* 95, no. 4 (2010), pp. 713–727.
12. Willie Hammer, *Occupational Safety Management and Engineering* (Upper Saddle River, NJ: Prentice Hall, 1985), pp. 62–63. See also "DuPont's 'STOP' Helps Prevent Workplace Injuries and Incidents," *Asia Africa Intelligence Wire*, May 17, 2004.
13. F. David Pierce, "Safety in the Emerging Leadership Paradigm," *Occupational Hazards*, June 2000, pp. 63–66. See also, for example, Josh Williams, "Optimizing the Safety Culture," *Occupational Hazards*, May 2008, pp. 45–49.
14. See the BP case in the Appendix for further discussion.
15. Sandy Smith, "Louisiana-Pacific Corp. Builds Safety into Everything It Does," *Occupational Hazards*, November 2007, pp. 41–42.
16. Sandy Smith, "ABB Inc. Relies on Leadership and Accountability for Safety Performance," *EHS Today*, November 2012, p. 38.
17. "Did This Supervisor Do Enough to Protect Trench Workers?" *Safety Compliance Letter*, October 2003, p. 9.
18. Ibid.
19. Based on "All About OSHA," rev. ed. (Washington, DC: U.S. Department of Labor, 1980), www.osha.gov/law-regs.html, accessed September 11, 2014.
20. Ibid.
21. www.osha.gov/oshstats/commonstats.html, accessed September 11, 2014.
22. www.osha.gov/dcsp/vpp/index.html, accessed September 11, 2014; Edwin Foulke Jr., "OSHA's Evolving Role in Promoting Occupational Safety and Health," *EHS Today*, November 2008, pp. 44–49; www.osha.gov/dcsp/compliance_assistance/index_programs.html, accessed July 15, 2014.
23. "OSHA Hazard Communication Standard Enforcement," *BNA Bulletin to Management*, February 23, 1989, p. 13. See also William Kincaid, "OSHA vs. Excellence in Safety Management," *Occupational Hazards*, December 2002, pp. 34–36. Flow diagram based on *What Every Employer Needs to Know About OSHA Recordkeeping* (Washington, DC: U.S. Department of Labor, 1978), p. 3.
24. "What Every Employer Needs to Know about OSHA Record Keeping," U.S. Department of Labor, Bureau of Labor Statistics, Washington, DC, report 412–413, p. 3, www.osha.gov/recordkeeping/index.html, accessed September 11, 2014.
25. "New OSHA Recordkeeping Rule in Effect with the New Year," *Bloomberg BNA Bulletin to Management*, January 6, 2015, p. 2.
26. Arthur Sapper and Robert Gombar, "Nagging Problems Under OSHA's New Record Keeping Rule," *Occupational Hazards*, March 2002, p. 58.
27. Brian Jackson and Jeffrey Myers, "Just When You Thought You Were Safe: OSHA Record-Keeping Violations," *Management Review*, May 1994, pp. 62–63; www.osha.gov/recordkeeping/index.html, accessed October 26, 2011.
28. "Supreme Court Says OSHA Inspectors Need Warrants," *Engineering News Record*, June 1, 1978, pp. 9–10; W. Scott Railton, "OSHA Gets Tough on Business," *Management Review* 80, no. 12 (December 1991), pp. 28–29; Steve Hollingsworth, "How to Survive an OSHA Inspection," *Occupational Hazards*, March 2004, pp. 31–33.
29. www.osha.gov/as/opa/oshafacts.html, accessed January 19, 2008; Edwin Foulke Jr., "OSHA's Evolving Role in Promoting Occupational Safety and Health," *EHS Today*, November 2008, pp. 44–49; www.osha.gov/dcsp/compliance_assistance/index_programs.html, accessed August 8, 2013.
30. www.osha.gov/dep/index.html, accessed September 11, 2014. OSHA has a program for whistle-blower complaints. Arthur Sapper and William Friedman, "Whistle-Blower Complaints: Avoiding Discrimination Charges Through Documentation," *EHS Today*, May 2013, pp. 22–23.
31. www.osha.gov/oshstats/commonstats.html, accessed April 18, 2013.
32. "Safety OSHA Has Record Number of Whistleblower Investigations, 51% Dismissal Rate," *Bloomberg BNA Bulletin to Management* 66, no. 3 (2015), p. 19.
33. See "Site-Specific Targeting Program Letters Mailed to High Injury/Illness Rate Employers," *BNA Bulletin to Management*, April 10, 2012, p. 113.
34. This section is based on "All About OSHA," pp. 23–25. See also "OSHA Final Rule Expands Employees' Role in Consultations, Protects Employer Records," *BNA Bulletin to Management*, November 2, 2000, p. 345.
35. D. Diane Hatch and James Hall, "A Flurry of New Federal Regulations," *Workforce*, February 2001, p. 98.
36. www.osha.gov/dcsp/compliance_assistance/frequent_standards.html, accessed May 28, 2012.
37. It was not until July 12, 2012, that British Petroleum and the U.S. government agreed on $13 million in OSHA fines and resolving outstanding citations against the company for the Texas City explosion. "BP to Pay $13 Million in OSHA Penalties," *EHS Today*, August 2012, p. 12.
38. www.osha.gov/Publications/osha2098.pdf+OSHA+inspection+priorities&hl=en&ct=clnk&cd=1&gl=us, accessed January 19, 2008.
39. www.osha.gov/Publications/osha2098.pdf, accessed April 27, 2008; www.osha.gov/ooc/citations/Cits330085.pdf, accessed September 11, 2014.
40. "Enforcement Activity Increased in 1997," *BNA Bulletin to Management*, January 29, 1998, p. 28. See also www.osha.gov/as/opa/osha-faq.html, accessed May 26, 2007.
41. "Enforcement Activity Increased."
42. For a discussion of how to deal with citations and proposed penalties, see, for example, Michael Taylor, "OSHA Citations and Proposed Penalties: How to Beat the Rap," *EHS Today*, December 2008, pp. 34–36.
43. Employers with high injury rates may also be subject to additional monitoring. For example, OSHA recently sent about 15,000 letters to employers telling them that their injury and illness rates were much higher than the national average. "OSHA Sends 15,000 Letters to Employers with High Injury Rates and Offers Assistance," *BNA Bulletin to Management*, March 16, 2010, p. 83.
44. Knowing OSHA's rules is not enough. The employer should develop and communicate its own written safety and health rules to employees, monitor violations, and discipline employees who violate the rules. Michael Taylor, "OSHA Compliance Mistakes," *EHS Today*, July 2012, pp. 29–31.
45. "New OSHA Enforcement Memo Target Safety Incentive Programs, Retaliation," BNA *Bulletin to Management*, March 27, 2012, p. 99.
46. Sean Smith, "OSHA Resources Can Help Small Businesses with Hazards," *Westchester County Business Journal*, August 4, 2003, p. 4.
47. Arthur Sapper, "The Oft-Missed Step: Documentation of Safety Discipline," *Occupational Hazards*, January 2006, p. 59.
48. Courtney Malveaux and J. A. Rodriguez Jr., "Can You Claim Employee Misconduct? Take the Legal Test," *EHS Today*, November 2014, pp. 37–41.
49. The following is based on www.sitedocs.com, accessed May 5, 2015.
50. "A Safety Committee Man's Guide," Aetna Life and Casualty Insurance Company, Catalog 87684. See also Dan Petersen, "The Barriers to Safety Excellence," *Occupational Hazards*, December 2000, pp. 37–39.
51. "Did This Supervisor Do Enough to Protect Trench Workers?" *Safety Compliance Letter*, October 2003, p. 9.
52. "Four Ways a Construction Job Can Kill You," *EHS Today*, February 2015, pp. 23–24.
53. "The Dawning of a New Era," *Workforce Management*, December 2010, p. 3.
54. For a discussion, see David Hofmann and Adam Stetzer, "A Cross-Level Investigation of Factors Influencing Unsafe Behaviors and Accidents," *Personnel Psychology* 49 (1996), pp. 307–308. See also David Hofman and Barbara Mark, "An Investigation of the Relationship Between Safety Climate and Medication Errors as Well as Other Nurse and Patient Outcomes," *Personnel Psychology* 50, no. 9 (2006), pp. 847–869.
55. Duane Schultz and Sydney Schultz, *Psychology and Work Today* (Upper Saddle River, NJ: Prentice Hall, 2002), p. 332.
56. Robert Pater and Robert Russell, "Drop That 'Accident Prone' Tag: Look for Causes Beyond Personal Issues," *Industrial Safety and Hygiene News* 38, no. 1 (January 2004), p. 50, http://findarticles.com/p/articles/mi_hb5992/is_200401/ai_n24195869/, accessed August 11, 2009.
57. Discussed in Douglas Haaland, "Who's the Safest Bet for the Job? Find Out Why the Fun Guy in the Next Cubicle May Be the Next Accident Waiting to Happen," *Security Management* 49, no. 2 (February 2005), pp. 51–57.
58. "Thai Research Points to Role of Personality in Road Accidents," www.driveandstayalive.com/info%20section/news/individual%20news%20

articles/x_050204_personality-in-crash-causation_thailand.htm, February 2, 2005, accessed August 11, 2009; Donald Bashline et al., "Bad Behavior: Personality Tests Can Help Underwriters Identify High-Risk Drivers," *Best's Review* 105, no. 12 (April 2005), pp. 63–64.

59. Todd Nighswonger, "Threat of Terror Impacts Workplace Safety," *Occupational Hazards*, July 2002, pp. 24–26.
60. Michael Blotzer, "Safety by Design," *Occupational Hazards*, May 1999, pp. 39–40; www.designsafe.com/dsesoftware.php, accessed May 26, 2007.
61. Susannah Figura, "Don't Slip Up on Safety," *Occupational Hazards*, November 1996, pp. 29–31. See also Russ Wood, "Defining the Boundaries of Safety," *Occupational Hazards*, January 2001, pp. 41–43.
62. See, for example, Laura Walter, "What's in a Glove?" *Occupational Hazards*, May 2008, pp. 35–36.
63. Donald Groce, "Keep the Gloves On!" *Occupational Hazards*, June 2008, pp. 45–47.
64. Tracy Moon Junior, "Wearable Technology in the Workplace," *EHS Today*, December 2014, pp. 28–29.
65. Howard Mavity, "What Should Be Your Safety Concerns When Buying or Leasing Office Space?" *EHS Today*, July 2014, pp. 20–22.
66. www.osha.gov/Publications/osha3071.pdf, accessed April 21, 2011.
67. www-ns.iaea.org/reviews/op-safety-reviews.asp, accessed April 21, 2011.
68. For example, when asked what accounted for injuries such as cuts and lacerations, contusions, and chemical exposure at their facilities, most employees concluded either that workers were not wearing the proper protective equipment or had been given the wrong protection for the task. Brian Perry, "Don't Invite an OSHA Citation with Lower Quality PPE," *EHS Today*, January 2011, p. 23.
69. James Zeigler, "Protective Clothing: Exploring the Wearability Issue," *Occupational Hazards*, September 2000, pp. 81–82. See also Judy Smithers, "Use OSHA's Compliance Directive to Evaluate Your PPE Program," *EHS Today*, January 2012, pp. 43–45.
70. Sandy Smith, "Protective Clothing and the Quest for Improved Performance," *Occupational Hazards*, February 2008, pp. 63–66. Note that the vast array of available personal protective equipment makes choosing the appropriate equipment what one expert calls "complex and sometimes confusing." See Scott Larsen, "Integrated Use of Personal Protective Equipment," *EHS Today*, June 2012, p. 31.
71. Tim Andrews, "Getting Employees Comfortable with PPE," *Occupational Hazards*, January 2000, pp. 35–38. However, "Making a job safer with machine guards or PPE lowers people's risk perceptions and thus can lead to an increase in at-risk behavior." E. Scott Geller, "The Thinking and Seeing Components of People-Based Safety," *Occupational Hazards*, December 2006, pp. 38–40.
72. Laura Walter, "FR Clothing: Leaving Hazards in the Dust," *EHS Today*, January 2010, pp. 20–22.
73. Roger Paquette, "Staying Safe and Warm in Cold Weather Environments," *EHS Today*, January 2015, pp. 19–22.
74. "The Complete Guide to Personal Protective Equipment," *Occupational Hazards*, January 1999, pp. 49–60. See also Edwin Zalewski, "Noise Control: It's More Than Just Earplugs: OSHA Requires Employers to Evaluate Engineering and Administrative Controls Before Using Personal Protective Equipment," *Occupational Hazards* 68, no. 9 (September 2006), p. 48(3). You can find videos about personal protective products at "SafetyLive TV" at www.occupationalhazards.com, accessed March 14, 2009.
75. Sandy Smith, "Protecting Vulnerable Workers," *Occupational Hazards*, April 2004, pp. 25–28.
76. Katherine Torres, "Challenges in Protecting a Young Workforce," *Occupational Hazards*, May 2006, pp. 24–27.
77. J. P. Sankpill, "A Clear Vision for Eye and Face Protection," *EHS Today*, November 2010, p. 29.
78. See, for instance, Laura Walter, "Training the Older Worker," *EHS Today*, February 2011, p. 39.
79. Robert Pater, "Boosting Safety with an Aging Workforce," *Occupational Hazards*, March 2006, p. 24.
80. Michael Silverstein, M.D., "Designing the Age Friendly Workplace," *Occupational Hazards*, December 2007, pp. 29–31.
81. Elizabeth Rogers and William Wiatrowski, "Injuries, Illnesses, and Fatalities Among Older Workers," *Monthly Labor Review* 128, no. 10 (October 2005), pp. 24–30.
82. Bill Sims Jr., "Employee Engagement and Commitment: The Super Bowl of Safety," *EHS Today*, July 2014, pp. 28–29.
83. "Cell Phone Use Contributes to 24% of Crashes," *EHS Today*, May 2012, p. 22.
84. "DOT Final Rule Bans Cell Phone Use by Commercial Bus Drivers, Truckers," *BNA Bulletin to Management*, December 6, 2011, p. 387.
85. Robert Pater and Ron Bowles, "Directing Attention to Boost Safety Performance," *Occupational Hazards*, March 2007, pp. 46–48.
86. E. Scott Geller, "The Thinking and Seeing Components of People-Based Safety," *Occupational Hazards*, December 2006, pp. 38–40.
87. See www.ramsaycorp.com/catalog/view/?productid=208.
88. Gerald Borofsky, Michelle Bielema, and James Hoffman, "Accidents, Turnover, and the Use of a Preemployment Screening Inventory: Further Contributions to the Validation of the Employee Reliability Inventory," *Psychological Reports*, 1993, pp. 1067–1076; www.ramsaycorp.com/catalog/view/?productid=208, accessed October 26, 2011.
89. Ibid., p. 1072. See also Keith Rosenblum, "The Companion Solution to Ergonomics: Pretesting for the Job," *Risk Management* 50, no 11 (November 2003), p. 26(6).
90. Dan Hartshorn, "The Safety Interview," *Occupational Hazards*, October 1999, pp. 107–111.
91. John Rekus, "Is Your Safety Training Program Effective?" *Occupational Hazards*, August 1999, pp. 37–39; see also www.osha.gov/Publications/osha2254.pdf, accessed October 25, 2011.
92. Kathryn Tyler, "Better Safe Than Sorry," *HR Magazine*, December 2014, pp. 44–45.
93. Laura Walter, "Surfing for Safety," *Occupational Hazards*, July 2008, pp. 23–29.
94. Michael Burke et al., "The Dread Factor: How Hazards and Safety Training Influence Learning and Performance," *Journal of Applied Psychology* 96, no. 1 (2011), pp. 46–70.
95. See, for example, Ron Bruce, "Online from Kazakhstan to California," *Occupational Hazards*, June 2008, pp. 61–65.
96. Michael Blotzer, "PDA Software Offers Auditing Advances," *Occupational Hazards*, December 2001, p. 11. See also Erik Andersen, "Automating Health & Safety Processes Creates Value," *Occupational Hazards*, April 2008, pp. 53–63.
97. Dave Zielinski, "Putting Safety Training Online," *HR Magazine*, January 2013, p. 51.
98. In a survey of about 2,600 employees, roughly one-fourth said they would not intervene if they saw a coworker acting unsafely, for fear the coworker would be defensive or angry. Phillip Ragain et al., "The Causes and Consequences of Employees' Silence," *EHS Today*, July 2011, pp. 36–38.
99. Jack Rubinger, "Signs, Labels and Lighting for a Safe and Productive Workplace," *EHS Today*, October 2012, p. 67.
100. See, for example, Josh Cable, "Seven Suggestions for a Successful Safety Incentive Program," *EHS Today*, March 23, 2005: http://ehstoday.com/safety/incentives/ehs_imp_37488, accessed July 24, 2015. See also J. M. Saidler, "Gift Cards Make Safety Motivation Simple," *Occupational Health & Safety* 78, no. 1 (January 2009), pp. 39–40.
101. Don Williamson and Jon Kauffman, "From Tragedy to Triumph: Safety Grows Wings at Golden Eagle," *Occupational Hazards*, February 2006, pp. 17–25; www.tsocorp.com/TSOCorp/SocialResponsibility/HealthandSafety/Healthand-Safety, accessed June 30, 2011.
102. "Are Traditional Incentive Programs Illegal?" *EHS Today*, April 2012, p. 12. See also Howard Mavity, "OSHA: Don't Get Caught in the Trap of Rewarding Employees for Reducing Recordables!" *EHS Today*, September 2012, pp. 39–41; and James Stanley, "OSHA's Warning on Safety Incentive Programs Are Wide of the Mark," *EHS Today*, October 2012, p. 63.
103. James Nash, "Construction Safety: Best Practices in Training Hispanic Workers," *Occupational Hazards*, February 2004, pp. 35–38.
104. Ibid., p. 37.
105. Based on Judi Komaki, Kenneth Barwick, and Lawrence Scott, "A Behavioral Approach to Occupational Safety: Pinpointing and Reinforcing Safe Performance in a Food Manufacturing Plant," *Journal of Applied Psychology* 63 (August 1978), pp. 434–445. See also Anat Arkin, "Incentives to Work Safely," *Personnel Management* 26, no. 9 (September 1994), pp. 48–52; Sandy Smith, "Why Cash Isn't King," *Occupational Hazards*, March 2004, pp. 37–38.
106. Dov Zohar, "A Group Level Model of Safety Climate: Testing the Effect of a Group Climate on Students in Manufacturing Jobs," *Journal of Applied Psychology* 85, no. 4 (2000), pp. 587–596. See also Steven Yule, Rhona Flin, and Andy Murdy, "The Role of Management and Safety Climate in Preventing Risk-Taking at Work," *International Journal of Risk Assessment and Management* 7, no. 2 (December 20, 2006), p. 137; and Judy Agnew, "Building the Foundation for a Sustainable Safety Culture," *EHS Today*, February 2013, pp. 41–43.
107. Quoted from Sandy Smith, "Breakthrough Safety

Management," *Occupational Hazards*, June 2004, p. 43. For a discussion of developing a safety climate survey, see also Sara Singer et al., "Workforce Perceptions of Hospital Safety Culture: Development and Validation of the Patient Safety Climate in Healthcare Organizations Survey," *Health Services Research* 42, no. 5 (October 2007), pp. 19–23.

108. "Encourage Incident Reporting to Improve Safety Culture," *EHS Today*, December 2012, p. 16.
109. Jennifer Nahrgang et al., "Safety at Work: A Meta-Analytic Investigation of the Link Between Job Demands, Job Resources, Burnout, Engagement, and Safety Outcomes," *Journal of Applied Psychology* 96, no. 1 (2011), p. 86.
110. Stan Hodson and Tim Gordon, "Tenneco's Drive to Become Injury Free," *Occupational Hazards*, May 2000, pp. 85–87. For another example, see Terry Mathis, "Lean Behavior-Based Safety," *Occupational Hazards*, May 2005, pp. 33–34.
111. Tim McDaniel, "Employee Participation: A Vehicle for Safety by Design," *Occupational Hazards*, May 2002, pp. 71–76.
112. For another good example, see Christopher Chapman, "Using Kaizen to Improve Safety and Ergonomics," *Occupational Hazards*, February 2006, pp. 27–29.
113. Lisa Cullen, "Safety Committees: A Smart Business Decision," *Occupational Hazards*, May 1999, pp. 99–104. See also www.osha.gov/Publications/osha2098.pdf, accessed May 26, 2007; and D. Kolman, "Effective Safety Committees," *Beverage Industry* 100, no. 3 (March 2009), pp. 63–65.
114. https://itunes.apple.com/us/app/iauditor-safety-audit-checklist/id499999532?mt=8, accessed May 6, 2015.
115. http://download.cnet.com/iAuditor-Safety-Audit-and-Checklist/3000-2064_4-75728239.html, accessed May 6, 2015.
116. www.digitalmarketplace.service.gov.uk/service/5-g1-0377-007, accessed May 6, 2015.
117. www.assessnet.co.uk, accessed May 6, 2015.
118. John Garber, "Introduction to the Human Resource Discipline of Safety and Security," www.shrm.org/templates_tools/toolkits, accessed May 27, 2012.
119. Mike Powell, "Sustaining Your Safety Sweep Audit Process," *EHS Today*, December 2012, pp. 35–36.
120. Note that the vast majority of workers' injury-related deaths occur not at work, but when the employees are off the job, often at home. More employers are therefore implementing safety campaigns encouraging employees to apply safe practices at home. Katherine Torres, "Safety Hits Home," *Occupational Hazards*, July 2006, pp. 19–23.
121. "World-Class Safety: DuPont and Milliken Share Their Proven Successes," BLR, August 23, 2013, http://safety.blr.com/, accessed April 15, 2014.
122. Carey Tebbetts and Robert Allen, "Milliken's Keys to Employee Engagement, Increased Workplace Safety and Productivity," *EHS Today*, January 9, 2013: http://ehstoday.com/safety/millikens-keys-employee-engagement-increased-workplace-safety-and-productivity, accessed July 24, 2015.
123. Ibid
124. Ibid.
125. Ibid.
126. Ibid.
127. Mike Powell, "Harness the Full Power of Your Incident Investigation Process," *EHS Today*, September 2013, p. 71.
128. www.performancesolutionsbymilliken.com, accessed April 15, 2014. As part of its safety program, Milliken has partnered with the Occupational Safety and Health Administration and follows the latter's voluntary protection program's (VPP's) guidelines to help it reach its safety goals. "Milliken and Company VPP Star Site Elm Facility Receiving VPP Recognition," www.osha.gov, accessed April 14, 2014. For another example of how employee engagement impacts occupational safety, see "How Employee Engagement Can Improve the Hospital's Health," *Gallup Business Journal*, http://businessjournal.gallup.com, accessed April 14, 2014.
129. This is based on Paul Puncochar, "The Science and Art to Identifying Workplace Hazards," *Occupational Hazards*, September 2003, pp. 50–54.
130. Ibid., p. 52. See also David Wagner, "The Role of Real-Time Detection in Industrial Hygiene," *EHS Today*, August 2014, pp. 29–30.
131. Based on S. L. Smith, "Sadaf Drives for Safety Excellence," *Occupational Hazards*, November 1998, p. 41. For further discussion, see also Kathy Seabrook, "10 Strategies for Global Safety Management," *Occupational Hazards*, June 1999, pp. 41–43.
132. "Hazard Communication," www.osha.gov/dsg/hazcom/index.HTML, accessed May 26, 2012.
133. Based on the report "Workplace Screening and Brief Intervention: What Employers Can and Should Do About Excessive Alcohol Use," www.ensuringsolutions.org/resources/resources_show.htm?doc_id=673239, accessed August 11, 2009.
134. "Employers Can Play Key Role in Preventing Painkiller Abuse, but Many Remain Reluctant," *BNA Bulletin to Management*, February 15, 2011, p. 49.
135. "15% of Workers Drinking, Drunk, or Hungover While at Work, According to New University Study," *BNA Bulletin to Management*, January 24, 2006, p. 27.
136. Samuel Bacharach et al., "Alcohol Consumption and Workplace Absenteeism: The Moderating Effect of Social Support," *Journal of Applied Psychology* 95, no. 2 (2010), pp. 334–348.
137. See, for example, L. Claussen, "Can You Spot the Meth Addict?" *Safety & Health* 179, no. 4 (April 2009), pp. 48–52.
138. "New Jersey Union Takes on Mandatory Random Drug Tests," *Record* (Hackensack, NJ), January 2, 2008.
139. See for example, http://workplacedrugpolicy.com/program-components.htm; http://www.workingpartners.com/understanding-dfwp/elements-of-dfwp.asp; and http://www.dol.gov/elaws/asp/drugfree/drugs/screen15.asp, accessed July 27, 2015.
140. www.dol.gov/asp/programs/drugs/workingpartners/sab/screen.asp, accessed April 27, 2008; www.dol.gov/whd/FOH/ch64/64a01.htm, accessed September 11, 2014.
141. Gopal Pati and John Adkins Jr., "The Employer's Role in Alcoholism Assistance," *Personnel Journal* 62, no. 7 (July 1983), p. 570. See also Commerce Clearing House, "How Should Employers Respond to Indications an Employee May Have an Alcohol or Drug Problem?" *Ideas and Trends*, April 6, 1989, pp. 53–57; "The Employer's Role in Alcoholism Assistance," *Personnel Journal* 62, no. 7 (July 1983), pp. 568–572.
142. William Current, "Pre-Employment Drug Testing," *Occupational Hazards*, July 2002, p. 56. See also William Current, "Improving Your Drug Testing ROI," *Occupational Health & Safety* 73, no. 4 (April 2004), pp. 40, 42, 44.
143. Ibid.
144. Diane Cadrain, "Are Your Employees' Drug Tests Accurate?" *HR Magazine*, January 2003, pp. 41–45.
145. Sally Roberts, "Random Drug Testing Can Help Reduce Accidents for Construction Companies; Drug Abuse Blamed for Heightened Risk in the Workplace," *Business Insurance* 40 (October 23, 2006), p. 6.
146. Frank Lockwood et al., "Drug Testing Programs and Their Impact on Workplace Accidents: A Time Series Analysis," *Journal of Individual Employment Rights* 8, no. 4 (2000), pp. 295–306; Roberts, "Random Drug Testing Can Help Reduce Accidents."
147. Beth Andrus, "Accommodating the Alcoholic Executive," *Society for Human Resource Management Legal Report*, January 2008, pp. 1, 4.
148. Eric Sundstrom et al., "Office Noise, Satisfaction, and Performance," *Environment and Behavior* no. 2 (March 1994), pp. 195–222; "Stress: How to Cope with Life's Challenges," *American Family Physician* 74, no. 8 (October 15, 2006).
149. "Failing to Tackle Stress Could Cost You Dearly," *Personnel Today*, September 12, 2006; www.sciencedaily.com/releases/2007/06/070604170722.htm, accessed November 3, 2009.
150. Tara Parker-Pope, "Time to Review Workplace Reviews?" *New York Times*, May 18, 2010, p. D5.
151. "Drug-Free Workplace: New Federal Requirements," *BNA Bulletin to Management*, February 9, 1989, pp. 1–4. Note that the Drug-Free Workplace Act does not mandate or mention testing employees for illegal drug use. See also www.dol.gov/elaws/drugfree.htm and www.dot.gov/ost/dapc (this site contains detailed guidelines on urine sampling, who's covered, etc.), both accessed May 26, 2007.
152. "Few Employers Addressing Workplace Stress, Watson Wyatt Surveys Find," *Compensation & Benefits Review*, May/June 2008, p. 12.
153. See, for example, Elizabeth Bernstein, "When a Coworker Is Stressed Out," *Wall Street Journal*, August 26, 2008, pp. B1, B2.
154. Karl Albrecht, *Stress and the Manager* (Englewood Cliffs, NJ: Spectrum, 1979). For a discussion of the related symptoms of depression, see James Krohe Jr., "An Epidemic of Depression?" *Across-the-Board*, September 1994, pp. 23–27; and Todd Nighswonger, "Stress Management," *Occupational Hazards*, September 1999, p. 100.
155. Sabine Sonnentag et al., "'Did You Have a Nice Evening?' A Day-Level Study on Recovery Experiences, Sleep, and Affect," *Journal of Applied Psychology* 93, no. 3 (2008), pp. 674–684.
156. "Meditation Gives Your Mind Permanent Working Holiday; Relaxation Can Improve Your Business Decisions and Your Overall Health," discussed in *Investors Business Daily*, March 24, 2004, p. 89. See also "Meditation Helps Employees Focus, Relieve Stress," *BNA Bulletin to Management*, February 20, 2007, p. 63.

157. Kathryn Tyler, "Stress Management," *HR Magazine*, September 2006, pp. 79–82.
158. William Atkinson, "Turning Stress into Strength," *HR Magazine*, January 2011, p. 51.
159. "Going Head to Head with Stress," *Personnel Today*, April 26, 2005, p. 1.
160. See, for example, Christina Maslach and Michael Leiter, "Early Predictors of Job Burnout and Engagement," *Journal of Applied Psychology* 93, no. 3 (2008), pp. 498–512.
161. Christina Maslach and Michael Leiter, "Early Predictors of Job Burnout and Engagement," *Journal of Applied Psychology* 93, no. 3 (2008), pp. 498–512.
162. Sabine Sonnentag et al., "Staying Well and Engaged When Demands Are High: The Role of Psychological Detachment," *Journal of Applied Psychology* 95, no. 5 (2010), pp. 965–976.
163. Sharon Toker and Michael Biron, "Job Burnout and Depression: Unraveling Their Temporal Relationship and Considering the Role of Physical Activity," *Journal of Applied Psychology* 97, no. 3 (2012), p. 699.
164. Todd Nighswonger, "Depression: The Unseen Safety Risk," *Occupational Hazards*, April 2002, pp. 38–42; http://www.huffingtonpost.com/2013/07/25/depression-missed-work-days-absent_n_3652888.html, accessed July 27, 2015.
165. Ibid., p. 40.
166. "Employers Must Move from Awareness to Action in Dealing with Worker Depression," *BNA Bulletin to Management*, April 29, 2004, p. 137.
167. See, for example, Felix Chima, "Depression and the Workplace: Occupational Social Work Development and Intervention," *Employee Assistance Quarterly* 19, no. 4 (2004), pp. 1–20.
168. Ibid.
169. www.osha.gov, accessed May 28, 2005. See also Jennifer Sinkwitts, "Five Steps to Improve Ergonomics in the Office," *EHS Today*, January 2014, pp. 33–34.
170. Anne Chambers, "Computer Vision Syndrome: Relief Is in Sight," *Occupational Hazards*, October 1999, pp. 179–184; www.osha.gov/etools/computerworkstations/index.html, accessed May 28, 2005.
171. Sandra Lotz Fisher, "Are Your Employees Working Ergosmart?," *Personnel Journal*, December 1996, pp. 91–92. See also www.cdc.gov/od/ohs/Ergonomics/compergo.htm, accessed May 26, 2007.
172. www.ninds.nih.gov/disorders/repetitive_motion/repetitive_motion.htm, accessed February 28, 2010.
173. Sandy Smith, "SARS: What Employers Need to Know," *Occupational Hazards*, July 2003, pp. 33–35.
174. "CDC Recommends Respirators in Revised H1N1 Flu Guidance for Healthcare Workers," *BNA Bulletin to Management*, October 20, 2009, pp. 329–336; Pamela Ferrante, "H1N1: Spreading the Message," *EHS Today*, January 2010, pp. 25–27.
175. Ronald Davis, "Exposure to Environmental Tobacco Smoke: Identifying and Protecting Those at Risk," *Journal of the American Medical Association*, December 9, 1998, pp. 147–148; see also Al Karr, "Lighting Up," *Safety and Health* 162, no. 3 (September 2000), pp. 62–66.
176. However, note that some experts believe that in some circumstances the EEOC might see a smoking addiction as similar to use of illegal drugs, and thus possibly covered by the ADA. "Policies to Not Hire Smokers Raise Privacy, Bias Issues," *BNA Bulletin to Management*, December 14, 2010, p. 399.
177. Joan Deschenauxh, "Is a 'Smoker–Free' Workplace Right for You?" *HR Magazine*, July 2011, pp. 43–45.
178. See http://en.wikipedia.org/wiki/List_of_smoking_bans#United_States for a list.
179. Sarah Sipek, "Vaping Decision Up in the Air, but Some Fuming About Potential ecigarette Regulation," *Workforce*, November 2014, p. 15.
180. Garber, "Introduction to the Human Resource Discipline of Safety and Security."
181. Ibid. See also, "New Challenges for Health and Safety in the Workplace," *Workplace Visions* (Society for Human Resource Management), no. 3 (2003), pp. 2–4, and J. L. Nash, "Protecting Chemical Plants from Terrorists: Opposing Views," *Occupational Hazards*, February 2004, pp. 18–20.
182. "Survey Finds Reaction to September 11 Attacks Spurred Companies to Prepare for Disasters," *BNA Bulletin to Management*, November 29, 2005, p. 377.
183. Garber, "Introduction to the Human Resource Discipline of Safety and Security."
184. "Study: Don't Silo Human Capital Risk," www.shrm.org/hrdisciplines/ethics/articles, accessed May 27, 2012.
185. Robert Kaplan and Anette Mikes, "Managing Risks: A New Framework," *Harvard Business Review*, June 2012, pp. 48–60.
186. "Workplace Violence Takes a Deadly Toll," *EHS Today*, December 2009, p. 17; "Workplace Violence," www.osha.gov/SLTC/workplaceviolence, accessed September 11, 2014.
187. Jerry Hoobler and Jennifer Swanberg, "The Enemy Is Not Us," *International Personnel Management Association for HR* 35, no. 3 (Fall 2006), pp. 229–246.
188. www.cdc.gov/ncipc/dvp/ipv_factsheet.pdf, accessed August 8, 2013.
189. Paul Viollis and Doug Kane, "At-Risk Terminations: Protecting Employees, Preventing Disaster," *Risk Management Magazine* 52, no. 5 (May 2005), pp. 28–33.
190. M. Sandy Hershcovis et al., "Predicting Workplace Aggression: A Meta-Analysis," *Journal of Applied Psychology* 92, no. 1 (2007), pp. 228–238.
191. Alfred Feliu, "Workplace Violence and the Duty of Care: The Scope of an Employer's Obligation to Protect Against the Violent Employee," *Employee Relations Law Journal* 20, no. 3 (Winter 1994/95), p. 395.
192. Dawn Anfuso, "Deflecting Workplace Violence," *Personnel Journal*, October 1994, pp. 66–77.
193. Feliu, "Workplace Violence and the Duty of Care," p. 395.
194. See, for example, James Thelan, "Is That a Threat?" *HR Magazine*, December 2009, pp. 61–63.
195. Feliu, "Workplace Violence and the Duty of Care."
196. Ibid., pp. 401–402.
197. Viollis and Kane, "At-Risk Terminations," pp. 28–33.
198. Kenneth Diamond, "The Gender-Motivated Violence Act: What Employers Should Know," *Employee Relations Law Journal* 25, no. 4 (Spring 2000), pp. 29–41; "Bush Signs 'Violence Against Women Act'; Funding Badly Needed Initiatives to Prevent Domestic & Sexual Violence, Help Victims," *The America's Intelligence Wire*, January 5, 2006.
199. For example, see www.womenshealth.gov/violence-against-women/get-help-for-violence/violence-help-hotlines.html.
200. Unless otherwise noted, the following including the six matters to address is based on Richard Maurer, "Keeping Your Security Program Active," *Occupational Hazards*, March 2003, pp. 49–52.
201. Ibid.
202. http://view.fdu.edu/default.aspx?id=3705, accessed February 28, 2010.
203. Maurer, "Keeping Your Security Program Active," p. 50.
204. Ibid.
205. Maurer, "Keeping Your Security Program Active," p. 52.
206. "Focus on Corporate Security," *BNA HR Executive Series*, Fall 2001, p. 4.
207. Ibid.
208. Louis Obdyke, "Investigating Security Breaches, Workplace Theft, and Employee Fraud," *Society for Human Resource Management Legal Report*, January/February 2003, pp. 1–2.
209. Craig Schroll, "Evacuation Planning: A Matter of Life and Death," *Occupational Hazards*, June 2002, pp. 49–51. See also "Thorough Preparation for Natural Disasters Is Most Effective Way to Reduce Risks, Costs," *BNA Bulletin to Management*, November 20, 2012, p. 369.
210. Sandy Smith, "Are You Prepared?" *EHS Today*, March 2012, pp. 33–36.
211. "HR Plays Key Role in Preparing Organizations for Disasters," *Bloomberg BNA Bulletin to Management*, June 25, 2013, p. 206.
212. Maurer, "Keeping Your Security Program Active," p. 52; Li Yuan et al., "Texting When There's Trouble," *Wall Street Journal*, April 18, 2007, p. B1.
213. "Swine Flu Tests Employer Emergency Plan; Experts Urge Communicating Best Practices," *BNA Bulletin to Management*, May 5, 2009, pp. 137–144.
214. Sandy Devine, "Are You Ready for a Sudden Cardiac Arrest Emergency?" *EHS Today*, April 2009, pp. 26–29.
215. "Business Continuity: What Is the Best Way to Plan for Disasters That May Affect Our Business, Like the Gulf Oil Spill?" www.shrm.org/templates_tools, accessed May 27, 2012.
216. *PR Newswire*, April 2, 2013 pNA; "Get Tips on Using Social Media for Disaster Recovery," *The Public Manager* 42, no. 1 (Spring 2013), p. 35(3); Joseph Porcelli, "How FEMA Drove 23,000 People to Join Its Online Community," *The America's Intelligence Wire*, October 28, 2012; "Officials Take to Social Media to Share Emergency Information: Canadians Tapped into Social Networks, Expect Emergency Responders to Use Social Media: New Red Cross Survey," *CNW Group*, October 9, 2012.
217. See also Shari Lau, "Terrorist Screening, Bonus Pay, Labor Department Audits," *HR Magazine*, October 2012, p. 28.
218. Lloyd Newman, "Terrorism: Is Your Company Prepared?" *Business and Economic Review* 48, no. 2 (February 2002), pp. 7–10; Yuan et al., "Texting When There's Trouble."

17

Managing Global Human Resources

Iain Masterton/Alamy

LEARNING OBJECTIVES

17-1 List the HR challenges of international business.

17-2 Illustrate with examples how intercountry differences affect HRM.

17-3 List and briefly describe the main methods for staffing global organizations.

17-4 Discuss some important issues to keep in mind in training, appraising, and compensating international employees.

17-5 Discuss similarities and differences in employee engagement around the globe.

17-6 Explain with examples how to implement a global human resource management program.

A few years ago the Japanese industrial giant Hitachi embarked on a strategy to streamline its business into six market-based but integrated groups around the world, and to meld these into what it called "One Hitachi."[1] Its HR group needed a new human resource strategy to support this. We'll see what they did.

WHERE ARE WE NOW ...

More managers today are managing people internationally. The purpose of this chapter is to improve your effectiveness at applying your human resource knowledge and skills when global challenges are involved. The topics we'll discuss include the manager's global challenge, adapting human resource activities to intercountry differences, staffing the global organization, training and maintaining employees abroad, employee engagement globally, and managing HR locally: how to implement a global HR system.

LEARNING OBJECTIVE 17-1
List the HR challenges of international business.

The Manager's Global Challenge

You don't have to dig very far to see how important international business is to companies here and abroad. For example, the total sum of U.S. imports and exports rose about nine times in the past 30 years, to about $4.7 trillion recently.[2] That growth has been great for all sorts of businesses, but also confronts managers with special challenges. For one thing, managers have to formulate and execute their market, product, and production plans on a global basis. Ford Motor, for instance, has a "One Ford" strategy aimed at offering similar Ford cars globally.

"Going global" also means employers must address international human resource management issues. For example, "Should we staff our local offices in Europe with local or U.S. managers?" And, "How should we appraise and pay our Asia employees?"[3]

The challenging thing about managing globally is that what works in one country may not work in another. The employer faces an array of political, social, legal, and cultural differences among countries and people abroad. Therefore, for instance, an incentive plan may work in the United States, but backfire in some Eastern European country where workers need a predictable weekly wage to buy necessities. However, in spite of such intercountry differences, the employer must create, for each country's local facility and for the company as a whole, a workable set of human resource policies and practices.[4] Distance adds to the challenge. For example, how should Starbucks' chief HR officer, based in Seattle, monitor Starbucks' HR managers in China?

What Is International Human Resource Management?

international human resource management (IHRM)
The human resource management concepts and techniques employers use to manage the human resource challenges of their international operations.

Employers rely on **international human resource management (IHRM)** to deal with global HR challenges like these. We can define IHRM as the human resource management concepts and techniques employers use to manage the human resource challenges of their international operations. IHRM generally focuses on three main topics:[5]

1. ***Managing human resources in global companies*** (for example, selecting, training, and compensating employees who work abroad)
2. ***Managing expatriate employees*** (those the employer sends abroad)
3. ***Comparing human resource management practices*** in different countries

Adapting Human Resource Activities to Intercountry Differences

LEARNING OBJECTIVE 17-2
Illustrate with examples how intercountry differences affect HRM.

As we said, the challenges of international human resource management don't just stem from the distances involved (though this is important). The bigger issue is dealing with the cultural, political, legal, and economic differences among countries and their people. Their result is that what works in one country might fail in another.

Companies operating only within the United States generally have the luxury of dealing with a relatively limited set of economic, cultural, and legal variables. Economically the United States is a capitalist, competitive society. And while the U.S. workforce reflects a multitude of cultural and ethnic backgrounds, shared values (such as an appreciation for democracy) help to blur cultural differences. Different states and municipalities certainly have their own employment laws. However, a basic federal framework helps produce a predictable set of legal guidelines regarding matters such as employment discrimination and labor relations.

A company operating multiple units abroad doesn't face such homogeneity. For example, minimum legally mandated holidays range from none in the United Kingdom to 5 weeks in Luxembourg. Italy has no formal requirements for employee representatives on boards of directors, but they're usually required in

FIGURE 17-1 Critical Intercountry Differences That Influence International HR Practices

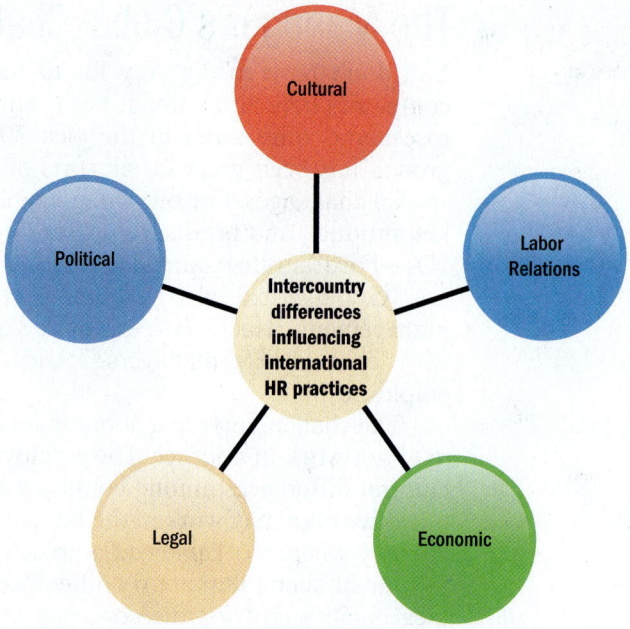

Denmark. The point is that managers have to adapt their human resource policies and practices to the countries in which they're operating. Figure 17-1 sums up critical intercountry differences.

Cultural Factors

For example countries differ widely in their *cultures*—in other words, in the basic values their citizens adhere to, and in how these values manifest themselves in the nation's arts, social programs, and ways of doing things.[6] Cultural differences manifest themselves in differences in how people from different countries think, act, and expect others to act. For example, the head of group purchasing at Michelin says that when he gives performance feedback in France employees don't think it's necessary to mention what's right because they know what they've done right. He focuses instead on what's wrong.[7] That approach would surprise most U.S. employees, so there's a tendency for U.S. managers to sugarcoat what's wrong. In China, heads of companies are inclined to see employees as members of their family, but in turn demand much of them.[8]

THE HOFSTEDE STUDY Studies by Professor Geert Hofstede illustrate international cultural differences. Hofstede says societies differ in five values, which he calls *power distance, individualism, masculinity, uncertainty avoidance,* and *long-term orientation.* For example, power distance represents the degree to which less powerful people accept the unequal distribution of power in society.[9] He concluded that acceptance of such inequality was higher in some countries (such as Mexico) than in others (such as Sweden).[10] In turn, such differences manifest themselves in different behaviors. To see how your country's culture compares with others, go to www.geert-hofstede.com/hofstede_dimensions.php.

Such cultural differences influence human resource policies and practices. For example, Americans' emphasis on individuality may help explain why European managers have more constraints, such as in dismissing workers.[11] As another example, in countries with a history of autocratic rule, employees often had to divulge information. Here, whistle-blower rules are less popular.[12]

LEGAL FACTORS Employers expanding abroad must also be familiar with the labor laws in the countries they're entering. For example, in India, companies with more

Employers need to adapt their HR practices to the cultures of the countries where they do business.

McPHOTOs/Blickwinkel/AGE Fotostock

than 100 workers need government permission to fire anyone.[13] In Brazil, firing someone without "just cause" could trigger a fine of 4% of the total amount the worker ever earned.[14]

Similarly, the U.S. practice of employment at will doesn't exist in Europe, where firing or laying off workers is usually expensive. And in many European countries, **works councils**—formal, employee-elected groups of worker representatives—meet monthly with managers on topics ranging from no-smoking policies to layoffs.[15]

works councils
Formal, employee-elected groups of worker representatives.

Codetermination is the rule in Germany and several other countries. **Codetermination** means employees have the legal right to a voice in setting company policies. Workers elect their own representatives to the supervisory board of the employer.[16]

codetermination
Employees have the legal right to a voice in setting company policies.

Economic Systems

Similarly, differences in *economic systems* translate into differences in intercountry HR practices. In *market* economies (such as the United States), governments play a relatively restrained role in deciding what will be produced and sold at what prices. In *planned* economies (such as North Korea), the government decides and plans what to produce and sell at what price. In *mixed* economies (such as China), many industries are still state-owned, while others make decisions based on market demand.

Differences in economic systems tend to translate into differences in human resource management policies. For instance, dismissing employees in China or Europe is more difficult than in the United States. Labor costs also vary widely. For example, hourly compensation costs (in U.S. dollars) for production workers range from $2.01 in the Philippines to $9.34 in Taiwan, $35.53 in the United States, $47.38 in Germany, to $64.15 in Norway.[17]

HR Abroad Example: The European Union

To appreciate the employment effects of cultural, economic, and legal differences like these, consider Europe and China. The separate countries of the former European Community (EC) unified into a common market for goods, services, capital, and even labor called the *European Union (EU)*. Tariffs for goods moving across borders from one EU country to another generally disappeared, and employees generally move freely between jobs in EU countries. The introduction of a single currency (the euro) by a subset of EU countries further blurred differences. Despite (or perhaps partly because of) Greece's recent fiscal problems, EU countries today are moving towards increased economic integration.

Companies doing business in Europe must adjust their human resource policies and practices to EU directives (laws), as well as to country-specific employment laws. The directives are binding on all member countries, but each country can implement them as they wish. For example, the EU directive on confirmation of employment requires employers to provide employees with written terms and conditions of their employment.[18] In England, a detailed written statement is required, including things like rate of pay, date employment began, and hours of work. Germany doesn't require a written contract.

This interplay of EU directives and country laws means that an employer's human resource practices must vary from country to country. For example:[19]

- ***Minimum EU wages.*** Most EU countries have minimum wage systems. Some set national limits. Others allow employers and unions to work out their own minimum wages.
- ***Working hours.*** The EU sets the workweek at 48 hours, but most EU countries set it at 40 hours.
- ***Termination of employment.*** Required notice periods in Europe impede dismissals (which from employees' perspective is a good thing). For example, Whirlpool Corporation spent more than 3 years trying to eliminate 500 jobs in Italy, while (for better or worse) it took them less than a year to dismiss 1,000 people in Arkansas.[20]

HR Abroad Example: China

For years, employers relied on China's huge workforce to provide products and services at low cost. Part of the reason for the low labor cost was the dearth of labor laws on things like severance pay, minimum wages, and benefits.

But things are changing. For one thing, China's workforce, while still huge, is growing less quickly. For another, China has a new labor contract law. This adds many new employment protections for employees, and makes it more expensive for employers in China to implement personnel actions such as layoffs. Multinational companies doing business in China argue that the new law will raise labor costs and make it difficult to lay off employees, by instituting new severance package rules.[21] Local firms, including the remaining state-owned enterprises, tend to use fewer modern human resource management tools than do private Chinese multinationals like Lenovo, but must also deal with the fallout of the new labor law. There are therefore wide variations in how companies in China deal with HR issues such as the following.[22]

RECRUITING Compared to some Western countries, it is relatively difficult to recruit, hire, and retain good employees. China's employment contract law requires, among many other things, that employers report the names, sexes, identification numbers, and contract terms for all employees they hire within 30 days of hiring to local labor bureaus.[23]

In China, recruiting effectiveness depends on nonrecruitment human resource management issues. Employees gravitate toward employers that provide the best career advancement training and opportunities.[24] Firms like Siemens China, with impressive training and development programs, have the least difficulty attracting good candidates. Poaching employees is a serious matter in China. The employer must verify that the applicant is free to sign a new employment agreement.

SELECTION The dominant employee selection method involves analyzing the applicant's résumé and then interviewing him or her. The ideal way to do this is to institute a structured interview process, as many of the foreign firms in China have done.

COMPENSATION Although many managers endorse performance-based pay in China, other employers, to preserve group harmony, make incentive pay a small part of the pay package. And, as in other parts of Asia, team incentives are advisable.[25]

LABOR UNIONS Recently, Chinese facilities of IBM, PepsiCo, Walmart, and others have seen extensive strikes by Chinese workers.[26] Several things may be contributing to the strikes. China's new labor law expands workers' rights. An aging population in China means a diminishing supply of factory workers. And China's government may see the strikes as a way of raising workers' incomes and thus supporting its desire to boost consumer spending.

The accompanying HR Around the Globe feature compares how smaller U.S. and Chinese employers deal with various HR issues.

IMPROVING PERFORMANCE: *HR Practices Around the Globe*

Comparing Small Businesses, HR Practices in the United States and China

Cross-country differences tend to manifest themselves in small businesses, too. For example, one study compared practices in 248 small U.S. companies with those in 148 small Chinese companies.[27] First, in terms of *job analysis*, jobs in small Chinese companies tend to be more narrowly defined and set in stone than those in small U.S. businesses. For example, the small Chinese firms have more up-to-date job descriptions, their employees deviate from their assigned job duties less frequently, their job descriptions tend to cover all the job's duties, and the job descriptions shape what the workers do.

Similarly, the researchers found significant differences in *performance appraisal practices* between U.S. and Chinese firms. In Chinese firms, compared to the United States, performance appraisals more often focus on the bottom line; appraisal feedback is evaluative rather than developmental; the appraisal focuses on objective, quantifiable results; and the main objective is to improve performance (rather than to develop the employee). Perhaps surprisingly, therefore, performance appraisals in small Chinese companies tend to be more hard-nosed than are those in the United States.

Finally (perhaps surprisingly given China's communist roots), there's more emphasis on incentive pay than guaranteed salaries in China's small businesses. Employees in the Chinese firms are more likely to receive bonuses based on the company's profits, to receive bonuses based on company-wide gainsharing plans, to get stock or stock options as incentives, and to be paid based mostly on an incentive plan rather than on a guaranteed income plan. On the other hand, there tends to be less variation among Chinese employees in pay, and more emphasis on seniority. ■

If your professor has assigned this, go to the Assignments section of **mymanagementlab.com** to complete this discussion question.

Talk About It 1: Why do you think appraisal in these Chinese firms seems to be tougher than in the United States?

Staffing the Global Organization

LEARNING OBJECTIVE 17-3
List and briefly describe the main methods for staffing global organizations.

Employers' focus today is increasingly on managing human resource activities locally. In other words, their main concern is on selecting, training, appraising, and managing the in-country employees where they do business.

However, deciding whether to fill local positions with local versus expatriate ("imported") employees remains a major concern.

HR in Practice at the Hotel Paris On reviewing the data, it was apparent to Lisa and the CFO that the company's global human resource practices were probably inhibiting the Hotel Paris from being the world-class guest services company that it sought to be. To see how they handled this, see the case on page 583 of this chapter.

International Staffing: Home or Local?

expatriates (expats)
Noncitizens of the countries in which employees are working.

home-country nationals
Citizens of the country in which the multinational company has its headquarters.

locals
Citizens of the countries in which employees are working; also called *host-country nationals*.

third-country nationals
Citizens of a country other than the parent or the host country.

In general, we can classify an international company's employees as *expatriates, home-country nationals, locals (host-country nationals),* or *third-country nationals*.[28] **Expatriates (expats)** are noncitizens of the countries in which they are working. Expatriates may also be **home-country nationals**, citizens of the country in which the company is headquartered. **Locals** (also known as *host-country nationals*) work for the company abroad and are citizens of the countries where they are working. **Third-country nationals** are citizens of a country other than the parent or the host country—for example, a French executive working in the Shanghai branch of a U.S. multinational bank.[29]

USING LOCALS Most employees will be locals, for good reason. First, the cost of using expatriates is usually far greater than the cost of using local workers.[30] Some companies are surprised at the cost of posting someone abroad. Agilent Technologies estimated that it cost about three times the expatriate's annual salary to keep the person abroad for 1 year. When it outsourced its expatriate program, it discovered the costs were much higher. The firm then dramatically reduced the number it sent abroad, from about 1,000 to 300 per year.[31]

There are other reasons. In one survey, employers reported a 21% attrition rate for expatriate employees, compared with 10% for their general employee populations.[32] Local people may view the multinational as a "better citizen" if it uses local management talent; some governments even press for staffing with local management.[33] Some expatriates overemphasize short-term results (knowing they will soon move on).[34] It's also more difficult to bring workers into the United States from abroad. U.S. employers must vigorously recruit U.S. workers before filing foreign labor certification requests with the Department of Labor.[35]

USING EXPATS Yet there are also reasons for using expatriates—either home-country or third-country nationals. Employers often can't find local candidates with the required qualifications. Multinationals also view a successful stint abroad as a required step in developing top managers. Furthermore, the assumption is that home-country managers are already steeped in the firm's policies and culture, and thus more likely to apply headquarters' ways of doing things.

However, the trend has been toward using locals or other (non-expat) solutions. Posting expatriates abroad is expensive, security problems give potential expatriates' pause, returning expatriates often leave for other employers within a year or two, and educational facilities are turning out top-quality candidates abroad. As a result, new expatriate postings tend to be down, and many employers are bringing them home early.[36] A survey found that about 47% of U.S. multinationals were maintaining the size of their expat workforces, 18% were increasing it, and 35% were decreasing it.[37] However about half the global companies in one recent survey said they were doubling the number of expats they send to countries like China.[38]

OTHER SOLUTIONS The choice is not just between expatriate versus local employees. For example, there are "commuter" solutions, involving frequent international travel but no formal relocation.[39]

One survey found that about 78% of surveyed employers had some form of "localization" policy. This is a policy of transferring a home-country national employee to a foreign subsidiary as a "permanent transferee."[40] For example, U.S. IBM employees originally from India eventually filled many of the 5,000 jobs that IBM recently shifted from the United States to India. These employees elected to move back to India, albeit at local India pay rates. The human resource team needs to control expat expenses, as the accompanying Profit Center feature explains.

IMPROVING PERFORMANCE: *HR as a Profit Center*

Reducing Expatriate Costs

Given the expense of sending employees abroad for overseas assignments, the employer's human resource team plays a big role in controlling and reducing expatriate costs. A survey shows some of the steps HR managers are taking to reduce these expenses.[41] First, companies are upping the numbers of short-term assignments they make. This lets them use short-term expats to replace some long-term expats (and their families) who the company must maintain abroad for extended periods. Fifty percent of the companies surveyed are also replacing some expatriate postings with local hires. With an eye on cutting costs, many employers were also reviewing their firms' policies regarding such things as housing, education, and home leave, along with expatriate allowances and premiums (cost-of-living allowance and mobility/quality-of-living premiums).[42] The bottom line is that there's a lot human resource managers can do to cut costs and boost profits by better managing expat assignments. ■

Source: Based on "Mercer's International Assignments Survey 2010," www.imercer.com/products/2010/intl-assignments-survey.aspx, accessed June 2, 2011; "Companies Juggle Cost Cutting with Maintaining Competitive Benefits for International Assignments, www.amanet.org/training/articles/Companies-Juggle-cost-cutting-with-Maintaining-Competitive-Benefits-for-International-Assignments.aspx.

If your professor has assigned this, go to the Assignments section of **mymanagementlab.com** to complete this discussion question.

Talk About It 2: What else would you do to cut expat expenses?

OFFSHORING As we explained in Chapter 5, *offshoring*—moving business processes such as manufacturing or call-center operations abroad, and thus having local employees abroad do jobs that the firm's domestic employees previously did in-house—is another globalization option.[43]

IBM Business Consulting Services surveyed employers to see what roles HR was playing in offshoring decisions.[44] Here, human resource managers help top management:[45]

- To understand the *local labor markets*, for example, in terms of their size, education levels, and unions.
- To understand how the firm's current *employment-related reputation* in the locale may affect outsourcing to here.
- To decide how much the firm should *integrate the local workforce* into the parent firm's corporate organization. For example, engineers might best become employees. Others (such as call centers) might best remain employees of vendor firms.
- To deal with skill shortages.[46] This often requires using signing bonuses, higher wages, and improved promotion opportunities.
- To identify how to reduce attrition. This might include more training and development, better compensation, and improved career opportunities.

TRENDS SHAPING HR: *DIGITAL AND SOCIAL MEDIA*

USING TRANSNATIONAL AND VIRTUAL TEAMS Managing internationally may also involve organizing "transnational" teams, composed of employees located in various countries.[47]

virtual teams
Groups of geographically dispersed coworkers who interact using a combination of telecommunications and information technologies to accomplish an organizational task.

Such teams of course often "meet" in virtual environments. **Virtual teams** are groups of geographically dispersed coworkers who interact using a combination of telecommunications and information technologies to accomplish an organizational task. To facilitate the merger of Marion Laboratories and Merrell Dow Pharmaceuticals, the companies created a transnational virtual team composed of members from production sites in Asia, Europe, and North America.[48] The team helped deal with potential merger integration problems.[49]

In a Skype and FaceTime world, virtual teams are both practical and popular. Collaborative software systems such as Microsoft NetMeeting conference system,[50] Cisco WebEx,[51] and GoToMeeting[52] enable virtual teams to hold live project reviews and discussions, share documents and exhibits, and store the sessions on the project's

Web site. Cloud-based tools such as Huddle[53] allow team members to attend from wherever they are using mobile devices, Microsoft Project lets project team members manage tasks and flag issues and risks,[54] and Dropbox[55] facilitates cloud-based document storage. If necessary, large-screen tools such as Cisco Immersive TelePresence [56] make it seem as if team members are together in the same room, although they may be thousands of miles apart.

The main challenges virtual teams face are often people related. Challenges include building trust, cohesion, and team identity, and overcoming the isolation among team members.

Success therefore depends on human resource management actions. In particular, *train* virtual team members in leadership, conflict management, and meetings management, and to respond swiftly to virtual teammates.[57] Be scrupulous about answering e-mails and being positive.[58] *Select* virtual team members using behavioral and situational interviews, where they describe how they'd respond to illustrative virtual team situations. Use current virtual team members to help *recruit* and select new team members.[59] ■

Management Values and International Staffing Policy

It's not just hard facts that influence international staffing decisions. The top executives' personal inclinations and values also play a role. Some executives are just more "expat-oriented." Experts classify top executives' values as *ethnocentric, polycentric*, or *geocentric.*

In an ethnocentrically oriented corporation, "the prevailing attitude is that home-country attitudes, management style, knowledge, evaluation criteria, and managers are superior to anything the host country might have to offer."[60]

ethnocentric
The notion that home-country attitudes, management style, knowledge, evaluation criteria, and managers are superior to anything the host country has to offer.

Such values translate into employment practices. With an **ethnocentric** staffing policy, the firm fills key management jobs with parent-country nationals.[61] Reasons given for ethnocentric staffing policies include lack of qualified host-country management talent, a desire to maintain a unified corporate culture and tighter control, and the desire to transfer the parent company's core competencies (such as a specialized manufacturing skill) to a foreign subsidiary more expeditiously.[62]

polycentric
A conscious belief that only the host-country managers can ever really understand the culture and behavior of the host-country market.

In the **polycentric** corporation, "there is a conscious belief that only host-country managers can ever really understand the culture and behavior of the host-country market; therefore, the foreign subsidiary should be managed by local people."[63]

A polycentric-oriented firm staffs its foreign subsidiaries with host-country nationals, and its home office with parent-country nationals. Such policies may reduce the local cultural misunderstandings that might occur if it used expatriate managers, and be less expensive.[64]

geocentric
The belief that the firm's whole management staff must be scoured on a global basis, on the assumption that the best manager of a specific position anywhere may be in any of the countries in which the firm operates.

A **geocentric** staffing policy "seeks the best people for key jobs throughout the organization, regardless of nationality."[65] This global firm will transfer the best person to the open job, wherever he or she may be. This can optimize placements and help build a more consistent culture among the global management team members.

Ethics and Codes of Conduct

Employers also need to make sure their employees abroad are adhering to their firm's ethics codes. However, exporting a firm's ethics rules requires more than giving employees abroad versions of a U.S. employee handbook. For example, few countries abroad adhere to "employment at will." Therefore, even handbooks that say, "We can fire employees at will" won't enable one to dismiss employees.[66] Instead of exporting the employee handbook, some distribute and publicize a global code of conduct.

Often, the employer's main concern is establishing global standards for adhering to U.S. laws that have cross-border impacts. For example, IBM paid $10 million to settle accusations that it had bribed Chinese and South Korean officials to get $54 million in government contracts.[67] Global employers need global codes of conduct on things like discrimination, harassment, bribery, and Sarbanes-Oxley.

Selecting International Managers

In most respects, screening managers for jobs abroad is similar to screening them for domestic jobs. For either assignment, candidates need the technical knowledge and skills to do the job, and the intelligence and people skills to be successful managers.[68] Testing, interviewing, and background checks are as applicable for selecting expatriates as for domestic assignments.

However, selection for foreign assignments is different. For example, there is the problem of being alone in a foreign land. Furthermore, the person's adaptability is important. Some people adapt anywhere; others fail to adapt anywhere.[69]

How do firms select global managers? Analyses of expatriate practices suggest several things. Traditionally, most selection of expatriates was done "... solely on the basis of successful records of job performance in the home country."[70] Today, however, best practices in international assignee selection include providing *realistic previews* to prospective assignees, facilitating *self-selection* to enable expatriate candidates to decide for themselves if the assignments are right for them, and using *traditional selection procedures* focusing on personal traits such as openness.[71] Employers now also use more expatriate selection criteria. Selection criteria include technical/professional skills, expatriates' willingness to go, experience in the country, personality factors (including flexibility), leadership skills, the ability to work with teams, and previous performance appraisals in the selection process. There seems to be a decline in U.S. companies' premature return rates, suggesting that employers are more successful at sending expatriates abroad.[72]

TESTING As noted, employers can take steps to improve the expat selection process, and testing is an obvious tool. For example, Brookfield Global Relocation Services Intercultural Group has used its Overseas Assignment Inventory (OAI) for over 40 years to help employers do a better job of selecting candidates for assignments abroad. It says, "Proper assessment and selection of employees for international assignments can mean the difference between success and a missed opportunity. The Overseas Assignment Inventory (OAI)—our proprietary assessment tool—can be used for: assessment and selection of candidates, development of chosen expatriates, self-assessment, and building candidate pools." The OAI is an online assessment that measures nine attributes and six context factors crucial for successful adaptation to another culture. Brookfield Global Relocation Services establishes global norms and conducts ongoing validation studies of the OAI.[73]

In terms of personality, successful expatriate employees tend to be extroverted, agreeable, and emotionally stable.[74] So not surprisingly, sociable, outgoing, conscientious people seem more likely to fit into new cultural settings.[75]

Intentions are important, too: For example, people who want expatriate careers try harder to adjust to such a life.[76] Similarly, expatriates who are more satisfied with their jobs abroad are more likely to adapt to the foreign assignment.[77]

REALISTIC PREVIEWS Even in familiar foreign postings there will be language barriers, bouts of homesickness, and new friends. Realistic previews about the problems as well as about the country's cultural benefits are thus an important part of screening. The rule is always "spell it all out" ahead of time.[78]

adaptability screening
A process that aims to assess the assignees' (and spouses') probable success in handling a foreign transfer.

ADAPTABILITY SCREENING With flexibility and adaptability very important, **adaptability screening** should be part of the screening process. Such screening aims to assess the assignee's (and spouse's) probable success in handling the foreign transfer, and to alert them to issues (such as the impact on children) the move may involve. Employers often use specially trained psychologists for this.

Here, companies often look for overseas candidates whose work and nonwork experience, education, and language skills already demonstrate ability for living and working with different cultures. Even several successful summers spent traveling overseas or in foreign student programs might provide some basis to believe the potential transferee can adjust abroad.

Diversity Counts: Sending Women Managers Abroad

While women represent about 50% of the middle management talent in U.S. companies, they represent only about 20% of managers sent abroad.[79] That's up from about 3% in the 1980s and 15% in 2005, but still low.[80] What accounts for this?

Many misperceptions still exist.[81] Line managers make these assignments, and many assume that women don't want to work abroad, are reluctant to move their families abroad, or can't get their spouses to move.[82] In fact, this survey found, women do want international assignments, they are not less inclined to move their families, and their male spouses are not necessarily reluctant.

Safety is another issue. Employers tend to assume that women abroad are more likely to become crime victims. However, most surveyed women expats said that safety was no more an issue with women than it was with men.[83]

Fear of cultural prejudices against women is another issue. In some cultures, women do have to follow different rules, for instance, in terms of attire. But as one expat said, "Even in the more harsh cultures, once they recognize that the women can do the job … it becomes less of a problem."[84]

Employers take several steps to identify more women to assign abroad. For example, *formalize a process* for identifying employees who are willing to take assignments abroad. (At Gillette, for instance, supervisors use the performance review to identify the subordinate's career interests, including for assignments abroad.) *Train managers* to understand how employees really feel about going abroad, and what the real safety and cultural issues are. Let successful female expats *help recruit* prospective female expats. And provide the expat's spouse with *employment assistance*.[85] ■

LEGAL ISSUES In selecting employees for international assignments, managers should consider the legal issues. As we explained in Chapter 2 (Equal Opportunity), American equal employment opportunity laws, including Title VII, the ADEA, and the ADA, does affect qualified employees of U.S. employers doing business abroad, and foreign firms doing business in the United States or its territories.[86] If equal employment opportunity laws conflict with the laws of the country in which the U.S. employer is operating, the laws of the local country generally take precedence.[87]

Avoiding Early Expatriate Returns

You know the expatriate's assignment probably failed when he or she makes an early, unplanned return.

Systematizing the entire expatriate management process is one way to avoid such early returns. For example, employers should have an expatriate policy covering matters such as compensation and travel costs. Include procedures, for instance, requiring that the manager responsible for the expat's costs obtain all chain of command approvals.[88] Another step in avoiding early returns is to test and select people who have the necessary traits and adaptability (as discussed earlier). And perhaps most importantly consider the expat's family situation.

FAMILY PRESSURES In one study, U.S. managers listed, in descending order of importance, reasons for expatriates leaving early: inability of spouse to adjust, managers' inability to adjust, other family problems, managers' personal or emotional immaturity, and inability to cope with larger overseas responsibility.[89]

Such findings underscore a truism about selecting international assignees: The problem is usually not incompetence, but family and personal problems. Yet, many employers still often select expatriates mostly based on technical competence.[90]

Given the role of family problems in expatriate failures, the employer should understand just how unhappy and cut off the expatriate manager's spouse can feel abroad. As one spouse said,[91]

> It's difficult to make close friends. So many expats have their guard up, not wanting to become too close. Too many have been hurt, too many times already, becoming emotionally dependent on a friend only to have the inevitable

happen—one or the other gets transferred. It's also difficult to watch your children get hurt when their best friend gets transferred.[92]

Three things make it easier. First is *language fluency*, since spouses will feel even more cut off if they can't communicate. Second, having *preschool-age children* seemed to make it easier for the spouse to adjust. "This suggests that younger children, perhaps because of their increased dependency, help spouses retain that part of their social identities ..."[93] Third, it helps if there is a *strong bond of closeness* between spouse and expat partner. This provides the continuing emotional support many spouses find lacking abroad.

Keep in mind that it's usually not how different culturally the host country is from the person's home country that causes problems; it's the person's ability to adapt.[94] As noted earlier, some people are so culturally at ease that they're fine transferred anywhere; others will fail anywhere.[95] The HR Tools feature sums up some suggestions.

IMPROVING PERFORMANCE: *HR Tools for Line Managers and Small Businesses*

Some Practical Solutions to the Expatriate Challenge

Expat failure is expensive; managers can take several practical steps to improve the expat's success abroad.

- ✓ *Provide realistic previews* of what to expect abroad, *careful screening* (of both the prospective expat and his or her spouse), *improved orientation,* and *improved benefits* packages.
- ✓ *Shorten the length* of the assignment.
- ✓ Use Internet-based *video technologies* and group decision-making software to enable global virtual teams to conduct business without relocation.[96]
- ✓ Form *"global buddy"* programs. Here local managers assist new expatriates with advice on things such as office politics, norms of behavior, and where to receive emergency medical assistance.[97]
- ✓ *Use executive coaches* to mentor and work with expatriate managers.[98] ■

Source: Based on M. Harvey et al., "Global Virtual Teams: A Human Resource Capital Architecture," International Journal of Human Resource Management 16, no. 9 (September 2005), pp. 1583–1599; Eric Krell, "Budding Relationships," HR Magazine 50, no. 6 (June 2005), pp. 114–118.

If your professor has assigned this, go to the Assignments section of **mymanagementlab.com** to complete this discussion topic.

Talk About It 3: Choose one country abroad and write 200 words on this topic: "Here is what we should cover in our realistic preview to someone we are sending to this country."

Social media such as www.linkedin.com (see their global expat network) and www.expatfinder.com are excellent sources of information, suggestions, support, and employment leads and connections for expats or for those considering a job abroad. A typical link you'll find at those sites is www.linkedin.com/title/expatriate+transfer+advisor.[99]

Training and Maintaining Employees Abroad

LEARNING OBJECTIVE 17-4
Discuss some important issues to keep in mind in training, appraising, and compensating international employees.

Orienting and Training Employees on International Assignment

When it comes to the orientation and training required for expatriate success abroad, the practices of many U.S. employers reflect more talk than substance. Executives agree that international assignees do best when they receive the special training (in things like language and culture) that they require. Few provide it.

Many vendors offer packaged pre-departure training. In general, the programs use on-and offline lectures, simulations, videos, and readings to prepare trainees. Their offerings illustrate the aim and content of such programs. One program aims to provide the trainee with (1) the basics of the new country's history, politics, business norms, education system, and demographics; (2) an understanding of how cultural values affect perceptions, values, and communications; and (3) examples of why moving to a new country can be difficult, and how to manage these challenges.[100] Others aim to boost self-awareness and cross-cultural understanding, and to reduce stress and provide coping strategies.[101] A third prepares individuals and their families "to interact successfully in daily life and business situations abroad; understand the impact various factors have on cultural behaviors and attitudes to make the most of the living abroad experience; and to raise awareness of the challenges of moving abroad, culture shock and how to deal with exposure to new cultural experiences."[102]

Some employers use returning managers to cultivate the global mind-sets of those departing. For example, Bosch holds regular seminars, where new arrived returnees pass on their experience to managers and their families going abroad.

ONGOING TRAINING Beyond such pre-departure training, more firms provide continuing, in-country cross-cultural training during the early stages of an overseas assignment.

For example, managers abroad (both expats and locals) continue to need traditional skills-oriented development. At many firms, including IBM, such development includes rotating assignments to help overseas managers grow professionally. IBM and other firms also have management development centers around the world where executives can hone their skills. And classroom programs (such as those at the London Business School or at INSEAD in France) provide overseas executives the educational opportunities (to acquire MBAs, for instance) that stateside colleagues have.

PepsiCo encourages expatriates to engage in local social activities, such as table tennis tournaments in China, to help them become acclimated faster to local cultures.[103]

International development activities hopefully have other, less tangible benefits. For example, rotating assignments can help managers form bonds with colleagues around the world. These can help the managers form the informal networks they need to make cross-border decisions more expeditiously.

Performance Appraisal of International Managers

Several things complicate appraising an expatriate's performance. Cultural differences are one. For example, a candid exchange is often the norm in the United States, but sometimes less so in China, where "face" is a concern.

Monkey Business Images/Thinkstock

Many global employers bring their international managers together periodically for training seminars.

Furthermore, who does the appraisal? Local management must have some input, but, again, cultural differences may distort the appraisals. (Thus, host-country bosses in Peru might evaluate a U.S. expatriate manager there somewhat negatively if they find his or her use of participative decision making culturally inappropriate.) On the other hand, home-office managers may be so out of touch that they can't provide useful appraisals. In one survey, the managers knew that having appraisers from both the host and home countries produced the best appraisals. But, in practice, most didn't. Instead, they had raters from the host or the home countries do them.[104]

Suggestions for improving the expatriate appraisal process include:

1. Adapt the performance criteria to the local job and situation.
2. Weigh the evaluation more toward the on-site manager's appraisal than toward the home-site manager's.
3. If the home-office manager does the actual written appraisal, have him or her use a former expatriate from the same overseas location for advice.

Compensating Managers Abroad

In compensating those it transfers abroad, an employer such as accounting and advisory firm KPMG has basically three choices—continue paying based on the person's current home-country pay, pay based on what locals in the new country are paid, or pay so the person's home—country standard of living stays the same. [105]

There is some logic in maintaining the person's *home country pay*, particularly if the assignment will be brief. On the other hand paying the new expat based solely on what his or her new *local peers* are earning could be a shock if it means the person's former home-country standard of living (for children's schools, and so forth) can't be maintained under strictly local pay rates. The fact is it can be enormously more expensive to live in some countries (like Japan) than others (like India); if these cost-of-living differences aren't considered, it will be almost impossible to get managers to take "high-cost" assignments. Therefore the more popular approach is to use the third option, namely by paying expats so that on their new jobs their pay is sufficient to maintain their former home-country *standard of living*; here most employers use what is called the balance sheet approach.

THE BALANCE SHEET APPROACH The most common approach to formulating expatriate pay is to equalize purchasing power across countries, a technique known as the *balance sheet approach.*[106]

The basic idea is that each expatriate should enjoy the same standard of living he or she would have had at home. The balance sheet approach addresses four groups of expenses—income taxes, housing, goods and services, and discretionary expenses (child support, car payments, and the like). The employer estimates each of these four expenses in the expat's home country, and in the host country. The employer then pays any differences—such as additional income taxes or housing expenses. (Multiple-nation taxation can be a problem. Respondents often list "tax compliance" as the top challenge in sending employees abroad.)[107]

The base salary will normally be in the same range as the manager's home-country salary. In addition, however, there might be an overseas or foreign service salary premium. The executive receives this as a percentage of base salary, to compensate for the adjustments he or she will have to make.[108] There may also be several allowances, including a housing allowance and an education allowance for the expatriate's children. To help the expatriate manage his or her home and foreign financial obligations, most employers use a *split pay* approach; they pay, say, half a person's actual pay in home-country currency and half in the local currency.[109]

Table 17-1 illustrates the balance sheet approach. In this case, the manager's annual earnings are $160,000, and she faces a U.S. income tax rate of 28%. Other costs are based on the index of living costs abroad published in the "U.S. Department of State Indexes of Living Costs Abroad, Quarters Allowances, and Hardship Differentials," available via the www.state.gov Web site.[110]

TABLE 17-1 The Balance Sheet Approach (Assumes U.S. Base Salary of $160,000)

Annual Expense	Chicago, U.S.	Shanghai, China (US$ Equivalent)	Allowance
Housing & utilities	$35,000	$44,800	$9,800
Goods & services	6,000	7,680	1,680
Taxes	44,800	57,344	12,544
Discretionary income	10,000	12,800	2,800
Total	$95,800	$122,624	$26,824

Determining rates abroad isn't always easy. Although there is a wealth of packaged compensation survey data available in the United States, such data are not quite as easy to come by overseas. Some multinational companies therefore conduct their own local annual compensation surveys. For example, Kraft has conducted one of total compensation in Belgium, Germany, Italy, Spain, and the United Kingdom. Realistically, however, most employers abroad do probably purchase one or more of various international salary surveys such as the Call Centre Remuneration Report – Australia, from Aon Hewitt, or the International Salary Survey Database—United Arab Emirates, from Executive Resources Limited.[111]

EXPATRIATE PAY EXAMPLE As one expat pay example, those working for the company CEMEX (a multinational building supplies company)

> … get foreign service premium equal to a 10% increase in salary. Some get a hardship premium, depending on the country; it ranges from zero in a relatively comfortable posting to, for example, 30% in Bangladesh. We pay for their housing. We pay for their children's schooling up to college. There's home leave—a ticket back to their home country for the entire family once a year. There are language lessons for the spouse. And we gross up the pay of all expats, to take out the potential effects of local tax law. Say you have an executive earning $150,000. This person would cost close to $300,000 as an ex-pat.[112]

foreign service premiums
Financial payments over and above regular base pay, typically ranging between 10% and 30% of base pay.

hardship allowances
Payments that compensate expatriates for exceptionally hard living and working conditions at certain locations.

mobility premiums
Typically, lump-sum payments to reward employees for moving from one assignment to another.

INCENTIVES Employers pay various incentives to encourage the employee to take the job abroad. For example, **foreign service premiums** are financial payments over and above regular base pay. These typically range from 10% to 30% of base pay, and appear as weekly or monthly salary supplements. **Hardship allowances** compensate expatriates for hard living and working conditions at certain foreign locations. (U.S. diplomats posted to Iraq receive about a 70% boost in base salary, among other incentives.)[113] **Mobility premiums** are typically lump-sum payments to reward employees for moving from one assignment to another. In at least one way, executive compensation systems around the world are becoming more similar.[114] U.S. firms that offer overseas managers long-term incentives often use overall corporate performance criteria (like worldwide profits) when awarding incentive pay.

STEPS IN ESTABLISHING A GLOBAL PAY SYSTEM Balancing global consistency in compensation with local considerations starts with establishing a rewards program that makes sense in terms of the employer's strategic aims.[115] Then the employer turns to more micro issues, such as, is how we're paying our employees abroad competitive?[116] Steps to follow in creating a global pay system include these:[117]

Step 1. **Set strategy.** First, formulate longer term strategic goals, for instance, in terms of improving productivity or boosting market share.

Step 2. **Identify crucial executive behaviors.** Next, list the actions you expect your executives to exhibit in order to achieve these strategic goals.

Step 3. **Global philosophy framework.** Next, step back and ask how you want *each pay component* (salary, bonus, incentives, and so forth) to contribute to prompting those executive actions.

Step 4. **Identify gaps.** Next, ask, "To what extent do our pay plans around the world now support these actions and what changes if any are required?"

Step 5. **Systematize pay systems.** Next, create more consistent performance assessment practices, and establish consistent job requirements and performance expectations for similar jobs worldwide.

Step 6. **Adapt pay policies** Finally, review your global pay policies (for setting salary levels, incentives, and so forth). Conduct surveys and analyses to assess local pay practices. Then fine-tune the firm's global pay policies so they make sense for each location.

Union Relations Abroad

Firms opening subsidiaries abroad face differing union-management relations practices among countries and regions. Walmart successfully neutralized unionization attempts in the United States, but had to accept unions in China.

As another example, the 2007–2009 recession and ongoing sovereign-debt crises in countries like Greece pushed up unemployment and understandably reduced unions' clout throughout Europe.[118] However, unions in Europe are still comparatively influential, and labor–management bargaining and relations reflect this.[119] For example, collective bargaining in Western Europe tends to be industry-wide, whereas in the United States it generally occurs at the company or plant level. And, union recognition in Europe is less restrictive than in the United States. For example, even if one union represents 80% of an employer's workers, another union in Europe can try to organize the other 20%.

Terrorism, Safety, and Global HR

Terrorism abroad is a serious issue. Even stationing employees in assumedly safe countries is no guarantee. A few years ago workers in French factories of Sony Corp. and 3M Co. took their managers hostage to negotiate better benefits.[120] When protests erupted in Egypt in February 2011, Medex Global Solutions evacuated more than 500 of its clients' people from Egypt; Medex had already been advising their clients about the possibilities for political unrest.[121]

TAKING PROTECTIVE MEASURES Employers have thus had to institute more comprehensive safety plans abroad, including, for instance, evacuation plans to get employees to safety. (Legally, employers also have a duty of care for protecting international assignees and their dependents and international business travelers.)[122] Many employers use intelligence services for monitoring potential terrorist threats abroad. The head of one intelligence firm estimates such services cost $6,000–$10,000 per year.[123] Some employers retain crisis management teams' services. They then call on these teams, for instance, when criminals kidnap one of their managers. As one executive said, "When you have a specialist, there's a better chance to get the person back."[124]

KIDNAPPING AND RANSOM (K&R) INSURANCE Hiring crisis teams and paying ransoms can be prohibitively expensive for all but the largest firms, so many employers buy kidnapping and ransom (K&R) insurance. Various events may trigger payments under such policies. The obvious ones are kidnapping (for instance, the employee is a hostage until the employer pays a ransom), extortion (threatening bodily harm), and detention (holding an employee without any ransom demand).

The insurance typically covers several costs associated with kidnappings, abductions, or extortion. These include hiring a crisis team, the actual ransom payment, insuring the ransom money in transit, legal expenses, and employee death or dismemberment.[125] The HR Practices Around the Globe feature provides some practical examples.

IMPROVING PERFORMANCE: *HR Practices Around The Globe*

Business Travel

Keeping business travelers safe is a specialty all its own, but suggestions here include:[126]

- ✓ Provide expatriates with training about the place they're going to, so they're more oriented.
- ✓ Tell them not to draw attention to the fact they're Americans—by wearing T-shirts with American names, for instance.
- ✓ Have travelers arrive at airports as close to departure time as possible and wait in areas away from the main flow of traffic.
- ✓ Equip the expatriate's car and home with security systems.
- ✓ Tell employees to vary their departure and arrival times and take different routes.
- ✓ Keep employees current on crime and other problems by regularly checking, for example, the State Department's travel advisories and warnings at http://travel.state.gov.[127] Click on "Travel Alerts" and "Country Information."
- ✓ Advise employees to act confident at all times. Body language can attract perpetrators, and those who look like victims often become victimized.[128]

Increased terrorism worldwide is causing more employers to use special travel safety tools to track and communicate with workers in real time.[129] For example, International SOS provides its clients with online and smart phone tools. These let the client quickly notify employees traveling abroad of potential problems and what to do about them. ■

If your professor has assigned this, go to the Assignments section of **mymanagementlab.com** to complete these discussion questions.

Talk About It 4: Have you traveled abroad and violated any of these rules? Which? Would you do things differently now, knowing what you know?

Squaredpixels/Getty Images

AT&T makes sure that the employee always feels that he or she is still "in the loop" with what's happening back at the home office.

Repatriation: Problems and Solutions

One of the most worrisome facts about sending employees abroad is that 40% to 60% of them will probably quit within 3 years of returning home.[130] Given the investment the employer makes in training and sending these high-potential people abroad, it makes sense to try to retain them. For this, formal repatriation programs can be useful.[131] One study found that about 5% of returning employees resigned if their firms had formal repatriation programs, while about 22% of those left if their firms had no such programs.[132]

Probably the simplest way to improve retention is to value their experience. As one returnee put it: "My company was, in my view, somewhat indifferent to my experience in China as evidenced by a lack of monetary reward, positive increase, or leverage to my career in any way."[133]

The guiding principle of any repatriation program is this: Make sure the expatriate and his or her family don't feel the company has forgotten them. To that end, AT&T has a three-part repatriation program.[134] First, AT&T *matches the expat and his or her family with a psychologist* trained in repatriation issues. The psychologist meets with the family before they go abroad. The psychologist discusses the challenges they will face, assesses with them how well he or she thinks they will adapt, and stays in touch with them throughout their assignment.

Second, AT&T makes sure *the employee always feels that he or she is still "in the loop"* with the home office. For example, AT&T assigns the expatriate a mentor. It also periodically brings the expat back to the home office to meet with and to socialize with colleagues.

Third, AT&T *provides formal repatriation services.* About 6 months before the overseas assignment ends, the psychologist and an HR representative meet with the expat and the family, to start preparing them. For example, they help plan the employee's next career move, help the person update his or her résumé, and begin putting the person in contact with supervisors back home. They work with the person's family on the logistics of the move back. Then, about a month after returning home, the expat and family attend a "welcome home" seminar to discuss matters like the stress of repatriation.[135]

LEARNING OBJECTIVE **17-5**

Discuss similarities and differences in employee engagement around the globe.

Employee Engagement Guide for Managers

Engagement Around the Globe

A recent survey of employee engagement around the globe provides some useful observations.[136]

On average, the percent of engaged employees (including highly engaged and moderately engaged) was 70% in Latin America, 65% in North America, 61% in Asia/Pacific and Africa/Middle East, and 57% in Europe. The percentage of actively disengaged employees was highest in Europe (19%), lowest in Latin America (12%), and 15%–16% in North America, Asia/Pacific, and Africa/Middle East. Recently, the trend was for employee engagement (highly and moderately engaged) in all regions of the world to be converging around the current global average of about 61% of employees engaged. So, workers everywhere are becoming about equally engaged.

What are the top drivers of employee engagement around the globe? Career opportunities was the number-one key driver of employee engagement in all regions of the world, underscoring the universal importance of providing such opportunities. But beyond that point of agreement, the other key drivers varied by geographic area. For example, setting goals/managing performance was the number two key driver of employee engagement in North America but was much less important in Europe; the reputation of the organization was number two in Europe, pay was number two in Asia/Pacific, and recognition was number two in Latin America. So, the management actions that drive engagement vary somewhat by region.

One thing that did not seem to vary much was the global importance of employee engagement. The best performing companies' employees were in the top quartile in employee engagement.

LEARNING OBJECTIVE **17-6**

Explain with examples how to implement a global human resource management program.

Managing HR Locally: How to Put into Practice a Global HR System

Years ago international businesses often ran their international operations from "international" units within their corporate headquarters.[137] That structure evolved into a "multinational" structure; here subsidiary units (often with their own HR units) abroad largely controlled themselves. Now the trend is toward the "global" company. Global companies seek to be fully integrated. For example, a car to be sold in the United States might be designed in France and manufactured in China with parts from Japan.

This global approach has at least two big implications for human resource management. For one thing, it generally means that the company as a whole will want to be able to redeploy their best employees anywhere the firm does business (although most employers still rely most heavily on local employees). For example, one bank has a sort of global SWAT team of employees who are willing to be assigned to work anywhere on short notice. Hilton Worldwide's databanks contain information on every employee's skills, affiliations, language proficiency, and local market connections. Hilton can therefore easily transfer willing employees wherever necessary.

Second, being "global" also affects how the company organizes and manages its human resource management function, with the emphasis often on standardizing HR practices worldwide. The Strategic Context feature shows how one company did this.

IMPROVING PERFORMANCE: *The Strategic Context*

Hitachi

A few years ago, the Japanese conglomerate Hitachi embarked on a strategy to streamline its business into six market-based but integrated groups around the world, and to meld them into what the company called "One Hitachi."[138] Takeo Yamaguchi, Hitachi's top human resource officer, knew Hitachi needed a new human resource strategy to support the One Hitachi strategy. He therefore set out to standardize Hitachi's human resource practices around the world. For example, he built a global HR database including data on things like employee name and performance history. To further support One Hitachi, he also standardized appraisal and compensation policies worldwide. So, for instance, now a manager in one region of the world is graded and compensated using the same processes and standards as a comparable manager in another region. ■

Source: Based on "Voices from the front lines," Harvard business review, September 2014, pages 77–83.

If your professor has assigned this, go to the Assignments section of **mymanagementlab.com** to complete these discussion questions.

Talk About It 5: What problems would you expect Mr. Yamaguchi to face in achieving standardization? How would you suggest he handle them?

However, given cross-cultural and other differences, one could reasonably ask, "Is it realistic for a company to try to institute a standardized human resource management system in its facilities around the world, particularly since doing so usually means transferring one's selection, training, appraisal, pay, and other human resource practices abroad?"

A study suggests "yes." In brief, the study's results show that employers may have to defer to local managers on some specific human resource management policy issues. However, they also suggest that big intercountry HR differences are often not necessary. The important thing is how you implement the global human resource management system.

In this study, the researchers interviewed human resource personnel from six global companies—Agilent, Dow, IBM, Motorola, Procter & Gamble, and Shell Oil Co.—as well as international human resources consultants.[139] The study's overall conclusion was that employers who successfully implement global HR systems do so by applying several best practices. The basic idea is to *develop* systems that are *acceptable* to employees in units around the world, and ones that the employers can *implement* more effectively. Figure 17-2 summarizes this.

FIGURE 17-2 Best Practices for Creating Global HR Systems

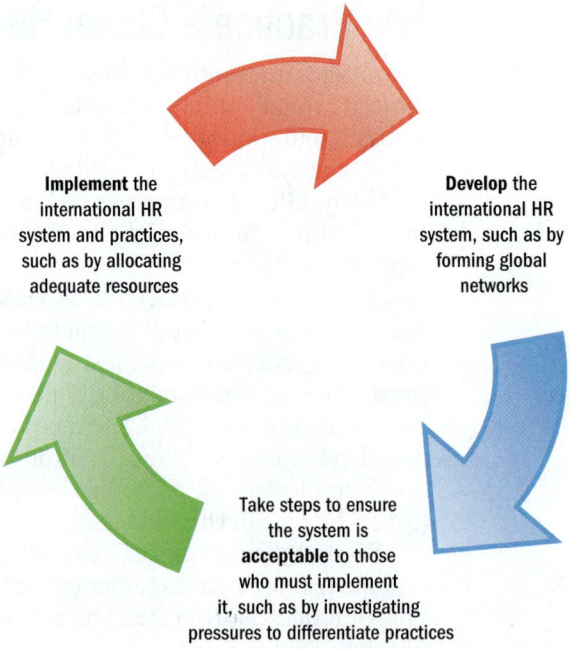

Developing a More Effective Global HR System

First, these employers engage in two best practices in developing their worldwide human resource policies and practices.

Form global HR networks. To head off resistance, human resource managers around the world should feel part of the firm's global human resource management team. Treat the local human resource managers as equal partners. For instance, form global teams to develop the new human resources system. Create "an infrastructure of partners around the world that you use for support, for buy-in, for organization of local activities, and to help you better understand their own systems and their own challenges."[140]

Remember that it's more important to standardize ends and competencies than specific methods. For example, IBM uses a basically standardized recruitment and selection process worldwide. However, "details such as who conducts the interview (hiring manager vs. recruiter), or whether the prescreen is by phone or in person, differ by country."[141]

Making the Global HR System More Acceptable

Next, employers engage in three best practices so that the global human resource systems they develop will be *acceptable* to local managers around the world. These practices are:

Remember that truly global organizations find it easier to install global systems. For example, their managers work on global teams, and the firms identify, recruit, and place employees globally. As one Shell manager said, "If you're truly global, then you are hiring here [the United States] people who are going to immediately go and work in the Hague, and vice versa."[142] Doing so makes it easier for managers everywhere to accept the wisdom of having a standardized human resource management system.

Investigate pressures to differentiate and determine their legitimacy. Local managers will insist, "You can't do that here, because we are different culturally." These "differences" aren't usually persuasive. For example, when Dow wanted to implement an online recruitment and selection tool abroad, the hiring managers there said that their managers would not use it. After investigating the supposed cultural roadblocks, Dow successfully implemented the new system.[143]

However, first carefully assess whether the local culture or other differences might in fact undermine the new system. Be knowledgeable about local legal issues, and be willing to differentiate where necessary.

Try to work within the context of a strong corporate culture. Companies that do so find it easier to obtain agreement among far-flung employees. For example, because of how P&G recruits, selects, trains, and rewards them, its managers have a strong sense of shared values. For instance, new recruits quickly learn to think in terms of "we" instead of "I." They learn to value thoroughness, consistency, self-discipline, and a methodical approach. Having such global unanimity makes it easier to implement standardized human resource practices.

Implementing the Global HR System

Finally, two best practices helped ensure success in actually *implementing* the globally consistent human resource policies and practices.

"You can't communicate enough." "There's a need for constant contact with the decision makers in each country, as well as the people who will be implementing and using the system."[144]

Dedicate adequate resources. For example, don't require the local human resource management offices to implement new job analysis procedures unless the head office provides adequate resources for these additional activities.

Watch It!
How does a company actually go about managing its international human resource management function? If your professor has assigned this, go to the Assignments section of **mymanagementlab.com** to complete the video exercise titled *Joby: Global HR Management*.

Chapter Review

MyManagementLab® Go to **mymanagementlab.com** to complete the problems marked with this icon.

Chapter Section Summaries

17-1. Dealing with **global human resource challenges as a manager** isn't easy. The employer faces an array of political, social, legal, and cultural differences among countries abroad. What works in one country may not work in another.

17-2. **The need for adapting human resource activities to intercountry differences** influences employers' HR processes. For example, citizens of different countries adhere to different values, and countries have differing economic systems as well as different legal, political, and labor relations systems.

17-3. **Staffing the global organization** is a major challenge. Companies may use expatriates, home-country nationals, locals, or third-country nationals. Ethnocentric companies tend to emphasize home-country attitudes, polycentric companies focus more on host-country employees, and geocentric employers try to pick the best candidates from wherever they might be. Selecting employees to successfully work abroad depends on several things, most importantly on adaptability screening and on making sure that each employee's spouse and family get the realistic previews and support necessary to make the transition.

17-4. After selecting the employees to send abroad, attention turns to **training and maintaining your expatriate employees**.

In terms of pre-departure preparation, training efforts ideally first cover the impact of cultural differences; then, the focus moves to getting participants to understand how attitudes influence behavior, providing factual knowledge about the target country, and developing skills in areas like language and adjustment.

In compensating expatriates, most employers use the balance sheet approach; this focuses on four groups of expenses: income taxes, housing, goods and services, and discretionary expenses, and aims to ensure that the employee's standard of living abroad is about what it would have been at home.

With terrorism a threat, most employers today take protective measures, including buying kidnapping and ransom insurance.

Well-thought-out repatriation programs emphasize keeping employees in the loop as far as what's happening in their home offices, bringing them back to the office periodically, and providing formal repatriation services for the expatriate and his or her family to start preparing them for the return.

17-5. The worldwide trend is for employee engagement to converge around the current global average of about 61% of employees engaged. Career opportunities was the number-one key driver of employee engagement in all regions of the world, underscoring its universal importance.

17-6. With employers increasingly relying on local rather than expatriate employees, it's important for managers to understand **how to implement a global HR system**. The basic approach involves: (1) Develop a more effective global HR system; (2) Make the global HR system more acceptable; and (3) Implement the global system.

Discussion Questions

17-1. You are the president of a small business. What are some of the ways you expect "going international" will affect HR activities in your business?

17-2. What are some of the specific, uniquely international activities an international HR manager typically engages in?

17-3. What intercountry differences affect HRM? Give several examples of how each may affect HRM.

17-4. You are the HR manager of a firm that is about to send its first employees overseas to staff a new subsidiary. Your boss, the president, asks you why such assignments often fail, and what you plan to do to avoid such failures. How do you respond?

17-5. As an HR manager, what program would you establish to reduce repatriation problems of returning expatriates and their families?

Individual and Group Activities

17-6. Working individually or in groups, outline an expatriation and repatriation plan for your professor, whom your school is sending to Bulgaria to teach HR for the next 3 years.

17-7. Give three specific examples of multinational corporations in your area. Check on the Internet or with each firm to determine in what countries these firms have operations. Explain the nature of some of their operations, and summarize whatever you can find out about their international employee selection and training HR policies.

17-8. Choose three traits useful for selecting international assignees, and create a straightforward test to screen candidates for these traits.

17-9. Use a library or Internet source to determine the relative cost of living in five countries as of this year, and explain the implications of such differences for drafting a pay plan for managers being sent to each country.

17-10. Appendices A and B at the end of this book (pages 612–629) list the knowledge someone studying for the HRCI (Appendix A) or SHRM (Appendix B) certification exam needs to have in each area of human resource management (such as in Strategic Management, and Workforce Planning). In groups of several students, do four things: (1) review Appendix A and/or B; (2) identify the material in this chapter that relates to the Appendix A and/or B required knowledge lists; (3) write four multiple-choice exam questions on this material that you believe would be suitable for inclusion in the HRCI exam and/or the SHRM exam; and, (4) if time permits, have someone from your team post your team's questions in front of the class, so that students in all teams can answer the exam questions created by the other teams.

17-11. An issue of *HR Magazine* contained an article titled "Aftershocks of War," which said that soldiers returning to their jobs from Iraq would likely require HR's assistance in coping with "delayed emotional trauma." The term *delayed emotional trauma* refers to the personality changes such as anger, anxiety, or irritability that exposure to the traumatic events of war sometimes triggers in returning veterans. Assume you are the HR manager for the employer of John Smith, who is returning to work next week after 1 year in Iraq. Based on what you read in this chapter, what steps would you take to help smooth John's reintegration into your workforce?

Experiential Exercise

A Taxing Problem for Expatriate Employees

Purpose: The purpose of this exercise is to give you practice identifying and analyzing some of the factors that influence expatriates' pay.

Required Understanding: You should be thoroughly familiar with this chapter and with the Web site www.irs.gov.

How to Set Up the Exercise/Instructions: Divide the class into teams of four or five students. Each team member should read the following: One of the trickiest aspects of calculating expatriates' pay relates to the question of the expatriate's U.S. federal income tax liabilities. Go to the Internal Revenue Service's Web site, www.irs.gov. Scroll down to "Individuals," and go to "Overseas Taxpayers." Your team is the expatriate-employee compensation task force for your company, and your firm is about to send several managers and engineers to Japan, England, and Hong Kong. What information did you find on the site that will help your team formulate expat tax and compensation policies? Based on that, what are the three most important things your firm should keep in mind in formulating a compensation policy for employees you're about to send to Japan, England, and Hong Kong?

Application Case*

"Boss, I Think We Have a Problem"

Central Steel Door Corporation has been in business for about 20 years, successfully selling a line of steel industrial-grade doors.[145] The company had gradually increased its presence from the New York City area, first into New England and then down the Atlantic Coast, then through the Midwest and West, and finally into Canada. The company's basic expansion strategy was always the same: Choose an area, open a distribution center, hire a regional sales manager, and then let that regional sales manager help staff the distribution center and hire local sales reps.

Unfortunately, the company's traditional success in finding sales help did not extend to its overseas operations, when Mel Fisher, president of Central Steel Door, decided to expand his company into Europe. He tried for 3 weeks to find a sales manager by advertising in the *International New York Times*, which is read by businesspeople in Europe and by American expatriates living and working in Europe. Although the ads placed in the *Times* also ran for about a month on the *Times*'s Web site, Mr. Fisher so far has received only five applications. One came from a possibly viable candidate, whereas four came from candidates whom Mr. Fisher refers to as "lost souls"—people who seem to have spent most of their time traveling aimlessly from country to country, sipping espresso in sidewalk cafés. When asked what he had done for the last 3 years, one told Mr. Fisher he'd been on a "walkabout."

Other aspects of his international HR activities have been equally problematic. Fisher alienated two of his U.S. sales managers by sending them to Europe to temporarily run the European operations, but neglecting to work out a compensation package that would cover their relatively high living expenses in Germany and Belgium. One ended up staying the better part of the year, and Mr. Fisher was rudely surprised to be informed by the Belgian government that his sales manager owed thousands of dollars in local taxes. The two managers had hired about 10 local people to staff each of the two distribution centers. However, the level of sales was disappointing, so Fisher decided to fire about half the distribution center employees. That's when he got an emergency phone call from his temporary sales manager in Germany: "I've just been told that all these employees should have had written employment agreements and that in any case we can't fire anyone without at least 1 year's notice, and the local authorities here are really up in arms. Boss, I think we have a problem."

Questions

17-12. Based on this chapter and the case incident, compile a list of 10 international HR mistakes Mr. Fisher has made so far.

17-13. How would you have gone about hiring a European sales manager? Why?

17-14. What would you do now if you were Mr. Fisher?

Continuing Case

Carter Cleaning Company

Going Abroad

Jack Carter decided to take his first long vacation in years and go to Mexico for a month a few years ago. What he found surprised him: He spent time in Mexico City and was surprised at the dearth of cleaning stores, particularly considering the amount of air pollution. Traveling north, he passed through Juarez, Mexico, and was similarly surprised at the relatively few cleaning stores he found there. As he drove back into Texas, and back toward home, he began to think about whether it would be advisable to consider expanding his chain of stores into Mexico.

Aside from the possible economic benefits, he liked what he saw in Mexico. Starting a new business again also appealed to him. "I guess entrepreneurship is in my blood," is the way he put it.

As he drove home to have dinner with Jennifer, he began to formulate the questions he would have to ask before deciding whether to expand abroad.

Questions

17-15. Assuming they began by opening just one or two stores in Mexico, what do you see as the main HR-related challenges Jack and Jennifer would have to address?

17-16. How would you go about choosing a manager for a new Mexican store if you were Jack or Jennifer? For instance, would you hire someone locally or send someone from one of your existing stores? Why?

17-17. The cost of living in Mexico is substantially below that of where Carter is now located: How would you go about developing a pay plan for your new manager if you decided to send an expatriate to Mexico?

17-18. Present a detailed explanation of the factors you would look for in your candidate for expatriate manager to run the stores in Mexico.

*Copyright Gary Dessler PhD.

Translating Strategy into HR Policies and Practices Case*,§

**The accompanying strategy map for this chapter is in MyManagementLab; the overall map on the inside back cover of this text outlines the relationships involved.*

Improving Performance at The Hotel Paris

Managing Global Human Resources

The Hotel Paris's competitive strategy is, "To use superior guest service to differentiate the Hotel Paris properties, and to thereby increase the length of stay and return rate of guests, and thus boost revenues and profitability." HR manager Lisa Cruz must now formulate functional policies and activities that support this competitive strategy and boost performance by eliciting the required employee behaviors and competencies.

With hotels in 11 cities in Europe and the United States, Lisa knew that the company had to do a better job of managing its global human resources, Lisa knew. For example, there were no formal means of identifying or training management employees for duties abroad (for those going either to the United States or to Europe). As another example, recently, after spending upward of $200,000 on sending a U.S. manager and her family abroad, they had to return her abruptly when the family complained of missing their friends back home. Lisa knew this was no way to run a multinational business. She turned her attention to developing the HR practices her company required to do business more effectively internationally.

On reviewing the data, it was apparent to Lisa and the CFO that the company's global human resource practices were probably inhibiting the Hotel Paris from being the world-class guest services company that it sought to be. For example, high-performing service and hotel firms had formal departure training programs for at least 90% of the employees they sent abroad; the Hotel Paris had no such programs. Similarly, with each city's hotel operating its own local hotel HR information system, there was no easy way for Lisa, the CFO, or the company's CEO to obtain reports on metrics like turnover, absences, or workers' compensation costs across all the different hotels. As the CFO summed it up, "If we can't measure how each hotel is doing in terms of human resource metrics like these, there's really no way to manage these activities, so there's no telling how much lost profits and wasted efforts are dragging down each hotel's performance." Lisa received approval to institute new global human resources programs and practices.

In instituting these new programs and practices, Lisa had several goals in mind. She wanted an integrated human resource information system (HRIS) that allowed her and the company's top managers to monitor and assess, on an ongoing basis, the company's global performance on strategically required employee competencies and behaviors such as attendance, morale, commitment, and service-oriented behavior. To address this need, she received approval to contract with a company that integrated, via the Internet, the separate hotels' HR systems, including human resource and benefits administration, applicant tracking and résumé scanning, and employee morale surveys and performance appraisals.

She also contracted with an international HR training company to offer expatriate training for Hotel Paris employees and their families before they left for their foreign assignments, and to provide short-term support after they arrived. That training company also helped create a series of weeklong "Managers' Seminars." Held once every 6 months at a different hotel in a different city, these gave selected managers from throughout the Hotel Paris system an opportunity to meet and to learn more about the numerous new HR programs and practices that Lisa and her team had been instituting for the purpose of supporting the company's strategic aims. With the help of their compensation specialist, Lisa and her team also instituted a new incentive program for each of the company's local managers, to focus their attention more fully on the company's service-oriented strategic aims. By the end of the year, the Hotel Paris's performance on metrics such as percent of expatriates receiving pre-departure screening, training, and counseling were at or above those of high-performing similar companies. She and the CFO believed, rightly, that they had begun to get their global HR system under control.

Questions

17-19. Provide a one-page summary of what individual hotel managers should know in order to make it more likely incoming employees from abroad will adapt to their new surroundings.

17-20. In previous chapters of Dessler *Human Resource Management* you recommended various human resource practices the Hotel Paris should use. Choose one of these, and explain why you believe they could take this program abroad, and how you suggest they do so.

17-21. Choose one Hotel Paris human resource practice that you believe is essential to the company specifically for achieving its high-quality-service goal, and explain how you would implement that practice in the firm's various hotels worldwide.

§Written by and copyright Gary Dessler, PhD.

MyManagementLab

Go to **mymanagementlab.com** for Auto-graded writing questions as well as the following Assisted-graded writing questions:

17-22. What special training do overseas candidates need? In what ways is such training similar to and different from traditional diversity training?

17-23. Your boss wants you to transfer from headquarters in Columbus, Ohio to the firm's Moscow, Russia office. You're pretty sure you're suited to work abroad, but to be sure you decide to write a short essay based on what you learned in this chapter titled "Why I think I would be successful in an overseas assignment", What would you say in your essay?

17-24. MyManagementLab only—comprehensive writing assignment for this chapter.

Try It!

How would you apply the concepts and skills you learned in this chapter? If your professor has assigned this, go to the Assignments section of **mymanagementlab.com** to complete the simulation: *Managing in a Global Environment*.

PERSONAL INVENTORY ASSESSMENTS

Intercultural Sensitivity Scale

Expat managers should be interculturally sensitive. Take this PIA to learn more about your personality.

Key Terms

international human resource management (IHRM), 561
works councils, 563
codetermination, 563
expatriates (expats), 566
home-country nationals, 566
locals, 566
third-country nationals, 566
virtual teams, 567
ethnocentric, 568
polycentric, 568
geocentric, 568
adaptability screening, 569
foreign service premiums, 574
hardship allowances, 574
mobility premiums, 574

Endnotes

1. "Voices from the Front Lines," *Harvard Business Review,* September 2014, pp. 77–83.
2. www.census.gov/foreign-trade/statistics/historical/gands.pdf, accessed September 16, 2014.
3. See, for example, Helen Deresky, *International Management* (Upper Saddle River, NJ: Pearson, 2008); and Anne Marie Francesco and Barry Allen Gold, *International Organizational Behavior* (Upper Saddle River, NJ: Pearson, 2005).
4. Nancy Wong, "Mark Your Calendar! Important Task for International HR," *Workforce,* April 2000, pp. 72–74.
5. Anne Marie Francesco and Barry Gold, *International Organizational Behavior* (Upper Saddle River, NJ: Prentice Hall, 2004), p. 145.
6. A. L. Lytle, J. M. Brett, Z. Barsness, C. H. Tinsley, and M. Janssens, "A Paradigm for Quantitative Cross-Cultural Research in Organizational Behavior," in B. M. Staw and L. L. Cummings (Eds), *Research in Organizational Behavior* 17 (1995), pp. 167–214. See also, as an example, Alsoruodan Shao and Daniel Skarlicki, "Service Employees' Reactions to Mistreatment by Customers: A Comparison Between North America and East Asia," *Personnel Psychology 67* (2014), pp. 23–59.
7. "Voices from the Front Lines."
8. Thomas Hout and David Michael, "A Chinese Approach to Management," *Harvard Business Review,* September 2014, pp. 103–107.
9. www.geert-hofstede.com/, accessed August 12, 2013.
10. See Vas Taras, Bradley Kirkman, and Piers Steel, "Examining the Impact of Culture's Consequences: A Three-Decade, Multilevel, Multi-Analytic Review of Hofstadter's Cultural Value Dimensions," *Journal of Applied Psychology* 95, no. 3 (2010), pp. 405–439.
11. Chris Brewster, "European Perspectives on Human Resource Management," *Human Resource Management Review* 14 (2004), pp. 365–382.
12. "SOX Compliance, Corporate Codes of Conduct Can Create Challenges for U.S. Multinationals," *BNA Bulletin to Management*, March 28, 2006, p. 97.
13. "In India, 101 Employees Pose Big Problems," *Bloomberg Businessweek,* January 17–23, 2011, p. 13.
14. "Employer Beware," *The Economist,* March 12, 2011, p. 43.
15. See, for example, www.fedee.com/ewc1.html, accessed August 12, 2013. Similarly, the European Union is in the process of introducing a stronger and more consistent data protection directive for all of its 28 nations. See Bill Roberts, "Tougher Data Privacy Law on EU Horizon," *HR Magazine,* January/February 2015, pp. 68–70.
16. This is discussed in Eduard Gaugler, "HR Management: An International Comparison," *Personnel* 65, no. 8 (1988), p. 28. See also E. Poutsma et al., "The Diffusion of Calculative and Collaborative HRM Practices in European Firms," *Industrial Relations* 45, no. 4 (October 2006), pp. 513–546.
17. 2011 figures, www.bls.gov/news.release/pdf/ichcc.pdf, accessed August 12, 2013.
18. Phillips Taft and Cliff Powell, "The European Pensions and Benefits Environment: A Complex Ecology," *Compensation & Benefits Review*, January/February 2005, pp. 37–50.
19. Ibid.
20. Deborah Ball and James Haggerty, "How to Cut a Job in Italy? Wait, and Wait Some More," *Wall Street Journal*, May 21, 2013, pp. B1, B2.
21. Lisbeth Claus, "What You Need to Know About the New Labor Contract Law of China," *SHRM Global Law Special Report,* October–November 2008.
22. See, for example, Syed Akhtar et al., "Strategic HRM Practices and Their Impact on Company Performance in Chinese Enterprises," *Human Resource Management* 47, no. 1 (Spring 2008), pp. 15–32.
23. Andreas Lauffs, "Chinese Law Spurs Reforms," *HR Magazine*, June 2008, pp. 92–98.
24. See, for example, Kathryn King-Metters and Richard Metters, "Misunderstanding the Chinese Worker," *Wall Street Journal*, July 7, 2008, p. R11.
25. Gary Dessler, "Expanding into China? What Foreign Employers Entering China Should Know About Human Resource Management Today," *SAM Advanced Management Journal*, August 2006. See also Joseph Gamble, "Introducing Western-Style HRM Practices to China: Shop Floor Perceptions in a British Multinational," *Journal of World Business* 41, no. 4 (December 2006), pp. 328–340; and Adrienne Fox, "China: Land of Opportunity and Challenge," *HR Magazine*, September 2007, pp. 38–44.
26. "Striking Chinese Workers Are Headache for Nike, IBM, Secret Weapon for Beijing," *Bloomberg News,* May 6, 2014.
27. Based on Robert Heneman et al., "Compensation Practices in Small Entrepreneurial and High-Growth Companies in the United States and China," *Compensation and Benefits Review*, July/August 2002, pp. 15–16.
28. Francesco and Gold, *International Organizational Behavior,* 2005, p. 145.
29. Ibid., p. 106.
30. Ibid., p. 769; Arvind Phatak, *International Dimensions of Management*, (South-Western College Publishing, 1995) p. 106.
31. Leslie Klass, "Fed Up with High Costs, Companies Winnow the Ranks of Career Expats," *Workforce Management*, October 2004, pp. 84–88.
32. "Survey Says Expatriates Twice as Likely to Leave Employer as Home-Based Workers," *BNA Bulletin to Management*, May 9, 2006, p. 147.

33. Phatak, *International Dimensions of Management*, p. 108.
34. John Daniels and Lee Radebaugh, *International Business*, (Upper Saddle River, NJ: 2001) p. 769.
35. "DOL Releases Final Rule Amending Filing, Processing of Foreign Labor Certifications," *BNA Bulletin to Management*, January 11, 2005, p. 11.
36. Michelle Rafter, "Return Trip for Expats," *Workforce*, March 16, 2009, pp. 1, 3.
37. See "Workforce Trends: Companies Continue to Deploy Ex-Pats," *Compensation & Benefits Review* 42, no. 1 (January/February 2010), p. 6.
38. "Expatriate Assignments in Growth Markets to Soar," *HR Magazine*, January 2013, p. 20.
39. Helene Mayerhofer et al., "Flexpatriate Assignments: A Neglected Issue in Global Staffing," *International Journal of Human Resource Management* 15, no. 8 (December 2004), pp. 1371–1389; and Martha Frase, "International Commuters," *HR Magazine*, March 2007, pp. 91–96.
40. Timothy Dwyer, "Localization's Hidden Costs," *HR Magazine*, June 2004, pp. 135–144.
41. "Mercer's International Assignments Survey 2010," www.imercer.com/products/2010/intl-assignments-survey.aspx, accessed June 2, 2011; "Companies Juggle Cost Cutting with Maintaining Competitive Benefits for International Assignments," www.amanet.org/training/articles/Companies-Juggle-cost-cutting-with-Maintaining-Competitive-Benefits-for-International-Assignments.aspx, accessed June 2, 2011.
42. "Mercer's International Assignments Survey 2010"; "Companies Juggle Cost Cutting with Maintaining Competitive Benefits for International Assignments."
43. Based on Pamela Babcock, "America's Newest Export: White Collar Jobs," *HR Magazine,* April 2004, pp. 50–57.
44. The following is based on "Back-Office and Customer Care Centers in Emerging Economies: A Human Capital Perspective," IBM Business Consulting Services, www-935.ibm.com/services/us/imc/pdf/ge510-3967-back-office-asiapac.pdf, accessed September 16, 2014.
45. Ibid., pp. 3, 4.
46. Ibid., pp. 5, 6.
47. Charles Snow, Scott Snell, Sue Canney Davison, and Donald Hambrick, "Use Transnational Teams to Globalize Your Company," *Organizational Dynamics*, Spring 1996, pp. 50–67.
48. Anthony Townsend, Samuel DiMarie, and Anthony Hendrickson, "Virtual Teams: Technology and the Workplace of the Future," *Academy of Management Executive* 12, no. 3 (1998), pp. 17–29; Christina Gibson and Susan Cohen, *Virtual Teams That Work: Creating Conditions for Virtual Team Effectiveness* (Jossey-Bass: San Francisco, 2004), provides practicing managers with valuable insights into organizing and managing virtual teams. See also Bjorn Ambos and Bodo Schlemglmich, "The Use of International R&D Teams: An Empirical Investigation of Selected Contingency Factors," *Journal of World Business* 39, no. 1 (February 2004), pp. 37–48.
49. Michael Harvey et al., "Challenges to Staffing Global Virtual Teams," *Human Resource Management Review* 14 (2004), p. 281.
50. www.microsoft.com/en-us/download/details.aspx?id=23745, accessed May 6, 2015.
51. https://signup.webex.com/webexmeetings/US/sem_acquisition.html?CPM=KNC-sem&TrackID=1031986&country=US&psearchID=webex%20collaboration%20meeting%20room, accessed May 6, 2015.
52. www1.gotomeeting.com/m/g2msem3.tmpl?Portal=www.gotomeeting.com&c_name=msns&c_mark=NAPPC&c_kwd=go_to_meeting_software_download-Broad&c_prod=GTM&c_cmp=sf-70150000000add7&c_date=CATnumber&c_cell=CMjwmL3KrcUCFUIZ7AodlRIAgQ&gclid=CMjwmL3KrcUCFUIZ7AodlRIAgQ&gclsrc=ds, accessed May 6, 2015.
53. www.huddle.com, accessed May 6, 2015.
54. https://products.office.com/en-us/project?legRedir=true&CorrelationId=20cd3b87-4cc5-4e30-ad86-c713d2a47abd, accessed May 6, 2015.
55. www.dropbox.com, accessed May 6, 2015.
56. www.cisco.com/c/en/us/products/collaboration-endpoints/immersive-telePresence/index.html, accessed May 6, 2015.
57. Except as noted, this is based on information in Bradley Kirkman et al., "Five Challenges to Virtual Team Success: Lessons from Sabre, Inc.," *Academy of Management Executive* 16, no. 3 (2002), p. 70.
58. Paul Berry, "Communication Tips for Global Virtual Teams," *Harvard Business Review*, October 30, 2014, https://hbr.org/2014/10/communication-tips-for-global-virtual-teams, accessed April 30, 2015.
59. This item is based on Bradley Kirkman et al., "The Impact of Team Empowerment on Virtual Team Performance: The Moderating Role of Face-To-Face Interaction," *Academy of Management Journal* 47, no. 2 (2004), pp. 175–192.
60. Phatak, *International Dimensions of Management*, p. 129.
61. Charles Hill, *International Business: Competing in the Global Marketplace* (Burr Ridge, IL: Irwin, 1994), p. 507.
62. Ibid., pp. 507–510.
63. Ibid.
64. Ibid., p. 509.
65. Ibid. See also M. Harvey et al., "An Innovative Global Management Staffing System: A Competency-Based Perspective," *Human Resource Management* 39, no. 4 (Winter 2000), pp. 381–394.
66. Donald Dowling Jr., "Export Codes of Conduct, Not Employee Handbooks," *Society for Human Resource Management Legal Report*, January/February 2007, pp. 1–4.
67. www.nytimes.com/2011/03/19/business/global/19blue.html, accessed June 30, 2011.
68. Mason Carpenter et al., "International Assignment Experience at the Top Can Make a Bottom-Line Difference," *Human Resource Management* 30, no. 223 (Summer–Fall 2000), pp. 277–285. See also Gunter Stahl and Paula Caligiuri, "The Effectiveness of Expatriate Coping Strategies: The Moderating Role of Cultural Distance, Position Level, and Time on the International Assignment," *Journal of Applied Psychology* 90, no. 4 (2005), pp. 603–615.
69. Sunkyu Jun and James Gentry, "An Exploratory Investigation of the Relative Importance of Cultural Similarity and Personal Fit in the Selection and Performance of Expatriates," *Journal of World Business* 40, no. 1 (February 2005), pp. 1–8. See also Jan Selmer, "Cultural Novelty and Adjustment: Western Business Expatriates in China," *International Journal of Human Resource Management* 17, no. 7 (2006), pp. 1211–1222.
70. Mary G. Tye and Peter Y. Chen, "Selection of Expatriates: Decision-Making Models Used by HR Professionals," *Human Resource Planning* 28, no. 4 (December 2005), p. 15(6).
71. Paula Caligiuri et al., "Selection for International Assignments," *Human Resource Management Review* 19 (2009), pp. 251–262.
72. Zsuzsanna Tungli and Maury Peiperl, "Expatriate Practices in German, Japanese, UK and US Multinational Companies: A Comparative Survey of Changes," *Human Resource Management* 48, no. 1 (January–February 2009), pp. 153–171. See also Zsuzsanna Tungli and Maury Peiperl, "Expatriate Practices in German, Japanese, UK and US Multinational Companies: A Comparative Survey of Changes," *Human Resource Management* 48, no. 1 (January/February 2009), pp. 153–171.
73. www.brookfieldgrs.com/intercultural, accessed September 7, 2013.
74. P. Caligiuri, "The Big Five Personality Characteristics as Predictors of Expatriates' Desire to Terminate the Assignment and Supervisor-Rated Performance," *Personnel Psychology* 53, no. 1 (Spring 2000), pp. 67–88. See also Margaret A. Shaffer et al., "You Can Take It with You: Individual Differences and Expatriate Effectiveness," *Journal of Applied Psychology* 91, no. 1 (January 2006), pp. 109–125.
75. Quoted in Meredith Downes, Iris I. Varner, and Luke Musinski, "Personality Traits as Predictors of Expatriate Effectiveness: A Synthesis and Reconceptualization," *Review of Business* 27, no. 3 (Spring/Summer 2007), p. 16.
76. Jan Selmer, "Expatriation: Corporate Policy, Personal Intentions and International Adjustment," *International Journal of Human Resource Management* 9, no. 6 (December 1998), pp. 997–1007. See also Barbara Myers and Judith K. Pringle, "Self-Initiated Foreign Experience as Accelerated Development: Influences of Gender," *Journal of World Business* 40, no. 4 (November 2005), pp. 421–431.
77. Hung-Wen Lee and Ching-Hsing, "Determinants of the Adjustment of Expatriate Managers to Foreign Countries: An Empirical Study," *International Journal of Management* 23, no. 2 (2006), pp. 302–311.
78. P. Blocklyn, "Developing the International Executive," *Personnel,* March 1989, p. 45. See also Paula M. Caligiuri and Jean M. Phillips, "An Application of Self-Assessment Realistic Job Previews to Expatriate Assignments," *International Journal of Human Resource Management* 14, no. 7 (November 2003), pp. 1102–1116.
79. "More Women, Young Workers on the Move," *Workforce Management,* August 20, 2007, p. 9; Andy Smailes, "Women Abroad – How to Get the Most from an International Assignment", *Living Abroad*, January 18, 2013, www.livingabroad.com/women-abroad-how-to-get-the-most-from-an-international-assignment/, accessed July 28, 2015.
80. "More Women…", op. cit.; Tina Vasquez, "Women Abroad: How to Get the Most from an International Assignment," May 31, 2012, www.theglasshammer.

com/news/2012/05/31/women-abroad-%E2%80%93-how-to-get-the-most-from-an-international-assignment/, accessed July 17, 2014.
81. For a good discussion of this, see Yochanan Altman and Susan Shortland, "Women and International Assignments: Taking Stock—A 25 Year Review," *Human Resource Management* 47, no. 2 (Summer 2008), pp. 199–216.
82. Kathryn Tyler, "Don't Fence Her In," *HR Magazine* 46, no. 3 (March 2001), pp. 69–77.
83. Ibid.
84. Ibid.
85. See Nancy Napier and Sully Taylor, "Experiences of Women Professionals Abroad," *International Journal of Human Resource Management* 13, no. 5 (August 2002), pp. 837–851; Iris Fischlmayr, "Female Self-Perception as a Barrier to International Careers?" *International Journal of Human Resource Management* 13, no. 5 (August 2002), pp. 773–783; Wolfgang Mayrhofer and Hugh Scullion, "Female Expatriates in International Business: Evidence from the German Clothing Industry," *International Journal of Human Resource Management* 13, no. 5 (August 2002), pp. 815–836; and Altman and Shortland, "Women and International Assignments."
86. U.S. Equal Employment Opportunity Commission, "The Equal Employment Opportunity Responsibilities of Multinational Employers," www.EEOC.gov/facts/multi-employers.html, accessed February 9, 2004.
87. See Donald Dowling Jr., "Choice of Law Contract Clauses May Not Fly Abroad," *Society for Human Resource Management Legal Report,* October–November 2008, pp. 1–2.
88. Chuck Csizmar, "Does Your Expatriate Program Follow the Rules of the Road?" *Compensation & Benefits Review*, January/February 2008, pp. 61–69.
89. Discussed in Hill, *International Business*, pp. 511–515.
90. Barbara Anderson, "Expatriate Selection: Good Management or Good Luck?" *International Journal of Human Resource Management* 16, no. 4 (April 2005), pp. 567–583.
91. Margaret Shaffer and David Harrison, "Forgotten Partners of International Assignments: Development and Test of a Model of Spouse Adjustment," *Journal of Applied Psychology* 86, no. 2 (2001), pp. 238–254.
92. Ibid., p. 251.
93. Ibid., p. 250.
94. Deresky, *International Management*, p. 90.
95. Sunkyu Jun and James Gentry, "An Exploratory Investigation of the Relative Importance of Cultural Similarity and Personal Fit in the Selection and Performance of Expatriates," *Journal of World Business* 40, no. 1 (February 2005), pp. 1–8. See also Jan Selmer, "Cultural Novelty and Adjustment: Western Business Expatriates in China," *International Journal of Human Resource Management* 17, no. 7 (2006), pp. 1211–1222.
96. M. Harvey et al., "Global Virtual Teams: A Human Resource Capital Architecture," *International Journal of Human Resource Management* 16, no. 9 (September 2005), pp. 1583–1599.
97. Eric Krell, "Budding Relationships," *HR Magazine* 50, no. 6 (June 2005), pp. 114–118. See also Jill Elswick, "Worldly Wisdom: Companies Refine Their Approach to Overseas Assignments, Emphasizing Cost-Cutting and Work–Life Support for Expatriates," *Employee Benefit News,* June 15, 2004, Item 0416600B.
98. Geoffrey Abbott et al., "Coaching Expatriate Managers for Success: Adding Value Beyond Training and Mentoring," *Asia-Pacific Journal of Human Resources* 44, no. 3 (December 2006), pp. 295–317.
99. For others, see www.linkedin.com/groups/Global-Expat-Professional-Network-4763493 and www.linkedin.com/groups/Forum-Expatriate-Management-1056387, both accessed July 29, 2015.
100. Adapted from www.interchangeinstitute.org/html/cross_cultural.htm, accessed July 1, 2011.
101. Adapted from www.kwintessential.co.uk/cultural-services/articles/expat-cultural training.html, accessed July 1, 2011. See also www.global-lt.com/en/us/cultural-training/expatriate-training.html#60Countries, accessed July 28, 2015.
102. www.global-lt.com/en/us/cultural-training/cultural-training-expatriate-training-courses.html#60Countries, accessed July 1, 2011.
103. Lynette Clemetson, "The Pepsi Challenge: Helping Ex-Pats Feel at Home," *Workforce Management*, December 2010, p. 36.
104. Hal Gregersen et al., "Expatriate Performance Appraisal in U.S. Multinational Firms," *Journal of International Business Studies* 27, no. 4 (Winter 1996), pp. 711–739. See also Hsi-An Shih, Yun-Hwa Chiang, and In-Sook Kim, "Expatriate Performance Management from MNEs of Different National Origins," *International Journal of Manpower* 26, no. 2 (February 2005), pp. 157–175; and Francesco and Gold, *International Organizational Behavior,* 2004, pp. 152–153.
105. See for example, www.kpmg.com/Global/en/IssuesAndInsights/ArticlesPublications/Documents/your-assignment-abroad.pdf?sf11313026=1, page 5, accessed July 29, 2015.
106. Stephenie Overman, "Focus on International HR," *HR Magazine*, March 2000, pp. 87–92; Sheila Burns, "Flexible International Assignee Compensation Plans," *Compensation & Benefits Review*, May/June 2003, pp. 35–44; Thomas Shelton, "Global Compensation Strategies: Managing and Administering Split Pay for an Expatriate Workforce," *Compensation & Benefits Review*, January/February 2008, pp. 56–59.
107. "Expatriate Assignments in Growth Markets to Soar," *HR Magazine*, January 2013, p. 20.
108. Phatak, *International Dimensions of Management*, p. 134. See also "China to Levy Income Tax on Expatriates," *Asia Africa Intelligence Wire,* August 3, 2004, Item A120140119.
109. Shelton, "Global Compensation Strategies."
110. http://aoprals.state.gov/content.asp?content_id=186&menu_id=81, accessed May 8, 2014.
111. www.erieri.com/SurveySources/International, accessed July 28, 2015.
112. Luis Hernandez, "On Why Ex-Pat Assignments Succeed—or Fail," *Harvard Business Review*, March 2011, p. 73.
113. Mark Schoeff Jr., "Danger and Duty," *Workforce*, November 19, 2007, pp. 1, 3.
114. See, for example, "More Multinational Organizations Are Taking a Global Approach to Compensation," *Compensation & Benefits Review*, May/June 2008, p. 5.
115. Robin White, "A Strategic Approach to Building a Consistent Global Rewards Program," *Compensation & Benefits Review*, July/August 2005, p. 25.
116. "Recommendations for Managing Global Compensation Clause in a Changing Economy," Hewitt Associates, www.hewittassociates.com/_MetaBasicCMAssetCache_/Assets/Articles/2009/hewitt_pov_globalcomp_0109.pdf, accessed March 22, 2009.
117. White, "A Strategic Approach," pp. 23–40.
118. Asbjørn Wahl, "Political and Ideological Crisis in an Increasingly More Authoritarian European Union," *Monthly Review* 65, no. 8 (January 2014).
119. Robert Sauer and Keith Voelker, *Labor Relations: Structure and Process* (New York: Macmillan, 1993), pp. 510–525; see also Marino Regini, "Human Resource Management and Industrial Relations in European Companies," *International Journal of Human Resource Management* 4, no. 3 (September 1993), pp. 555–568 and www.worker-participation.eu/National-Industrial-Relations/Across-Europe/Trade-Unions2, accessed April 30, 2015.
120. Jessica Marquez, "Hostage-Taking in France Has U.S. Observers on Their Guard," *Workforce Management*, April 20, 2009, p. 10.
121. "Unrest in Egypt Highlights Importance of Crisis Management Plans, Experts Say," *BNA Bulletin to Management,* February 8, 2011, pp. 41–42.
122. Lisbeth Claus, "International Assignees at Risk," *HR Magazine*, February 2010, p. 73.
123. Fay Hansen, "Skirting Danger," *Workforce Magazine*, January 19, 2009, pp. 1, 3.
124. Frank Jossi, "Buying Protection from Terrorism," *HR Magazine*, June 2001, pp. 155–160.
125. Frank Jossi, "Buying Protection from Terrorism," op cit.
126. Based on Samuel Greengard, "Mission Possible: Protecting Employees Abroad," *Workforce,* August 1997, pp. 30–32. See also Z. Phillips, "Global Firms Consider Additional Cover for Overseas Execs," *Business Insurance* 43, no. 23 (June 15–22, 2009), pp. 4, 22.
127. http://travel.state.gov/content/passports/english/alertswarnings.html, accessed September 11, 2014.
128. Greengard, "Mission Possible," p. 32.
129. Jane Levere, "Putting Safety First," *New York Times*, January 27, 2015, p. B4.
130. Carla Joinson, "Save Thousands per Expatriate," *HR Magazine*, July 2002, p. 77. A survey by accountants KPMG found that only about 4% of the 430 human resource executives surveyed believed they were effectively managing the repatriation process. Tanya Mohn, "The Long Trip Home," *New York Times*, March 10, 2009, www.nytimes.com/2009/03/10/business/worldbusiness/10iht-10home.20715091.html, accessed October 15, 2013.
131. Kathryn Tyler, "Retaining Repatriates," *HR Magazine*, March 2006, pp. 97–102.
132. Quoted in Leslie Klaff, "The Right Way to Bring Expats Home," *Workforce*, July 2002, p. 43.

133. Maria Kraimer et al., "The Influence of Expatriate and Repatriate Experiences on Career Advancement and Repatriate Retention," *Human Resource Management* 48, no. 1 (January–February 2009), pp. 27–47.
134. Ibid., p. 43.
135. Ibid.
136. "2014 Global Trends in Employee Engagement," Aon Hewitt, www.aon.com/attachments/human-capital-consulting/2014-trends-in-global-employee-engagement-report.pdf, accessed May 5, 2015.
137. Yaarit Silverstone, Claira Yang, Colin Sloman, and Susan Cantrell, "Trends Reshaping the Future of HR: Reconfiguring the Global Talent Landscape," *Top Trends That Will Reshape the Future of HR: The Future of HR,* Accenture, www.Accenture.com/us-en/Pages/insight-future-HR.aspx, accessed March 6, 2015.
138. "Voices from the Front Lines."
139. Ann Marie Ryan et al., "Designing and Implementing Global Staffing Systems: Part 2—Best Practices," *Human Resource Management* 42, no. 1 (Spring 2003), pp. 85–94.
140. Ibid., p. 89.
141. Ibid., p. 90.
142. Ibid., p. 86. See also M. Schoeff, "Adopting an HR Worldview," *Workforce Management* 87, no. 19 (November 17, 2008), p. 8.
143. Ryan et al., "Designing and Implementing Global Staffing Systems," p. 87.
144. Ibid., p. 92.
145. Written by and copyrighted by Gary Dessler, PhD.

18

Managing Human Resources in Small and Entrepreneurial Firms

Jetta Productions/Getty Images

LEARNING OBJECTIVES

18-1 Explain why HRM is important to small businesses and how small business HRM is different from that in large businesses.

18-2 Give four examples of how entrepreneurs can use Internet and government tools to support the HR effort.

18-3 List five ways entrepreneurs can use their small size to improve their HR processes.

18-4 Discuss how you would choose and deal with a professional employer organization.

18-5 Describe how you would create a start-up human resource system for a new small business.

City Garage is an expanding auto servicing company in Texas.[1] One way they distinguish themselves is with a strategy based on letting customers interact directly with City Garage's mechanics in what it calls its "open service area"—as they say, "We are all about customers."[2] But fast growth and hiring sociable employees require effective hiring. We'll see what they did.

WHERE ARE WE NOW ...

Small businesses have special human resource management needs. The main purpose of this chapter is to help you apply what you know about human resource management to running a small business. The main topics we'll address include the small business challenge; using Internet and government tools to support the HR effort; leveraging small size with familiarity, flexibility, fairness, and informality; using professional employer organizations; and managing HR systems, procedures, and paperwork.

LEARNING OBJECTIVE **18-1**

Explain why HRM is important to small businesses and how small business HRM is different from that in large businesses.

The Small Business Challenge

There's nothing small about *small business*. About 99% of U.S. firms are small businesses, and more than half the people working in the United States work for small firms.[3] Small businesses as a group also account for most of the 600,000 or so new businesses created each year, as well as for most business growth (small firms grow faster than big ones). And small firms create most of the new jobs in the United States.[4]

Statistically speaking, therefore, most people graduating from college in the next few years will work for small businesses—those with less than about 200 employees. So, most everyone reading this book should know something about human resource management in small businesses.

How Small Business Human Resource Management Is Different

Managing human resources in small firms is different for four main reasons: *size, priorities, informality*, and the nature of the *entrepreneur*.

SIZE For one thing, it's very unusual to find a business under 90 or so employees with a dedicated human resource management professional.[5] As a rule, it's not until a company reaches the 100-employee milestone that it can afford an HR specialist. Yet even five- or six-person retail shops must recruit, select, train, and compensate employees. So it's the owner or his or her assistant that does the HR paperwork and tasks. SHRM found, for instance, that even firms with under 100 employees often spend the equivalent of two or so people's time each year addressing human resource management issues.[6] That time usually comes out of the owner's long workday.

PRIORITIES It's not just size but business realities that drive many small business managers and entrepreneurs (the men and women who provide the vision and "spark" that starts a new business) to focus on non-HR issues. After studying small e-commerce firms in the United Kingdom, one researcher concluded that, as important as human resource management is, it just wasn't a high priority for these firms:

> Given their shortage of resources in terms of time, money, people and expertise, a typical SME [*small- and medium-size enterprise*] manager's organizational imperatives are perceived elsewhere, in finance, production and marketing, with HR of diminished relative importance.[7]

INFORMALITY One effect of this is that human resource management tends to be more informal in smaller firms. Thus, one study analyzed training practices in about 900 family and nonfamily small companies.[8] Training tended to be informal, with an emphasis on methods like coworker and supervisory on-the-job training.

Such informality isn't just due to a lack of resources, it's a "matter of survival." Entrepreneurs must react fast to changing competitive conditions. So, there's logic in keeping things like compensation policies flexible. The need for small businesses to adapt quickly often means handling matters like raises, appraisals, and time off "on an informal, reactive basis with a short time horizon."[9]

THE ENTREPRENEUR *Entrepreneurs* are people who create businesses under risky conditions. Researchers believe that small firms' relative informality partly stems from entrepreneurs' tendency to want to control things. "Owners tend to want to impose their stamp and personal management style on internal matters, including the primary goal and orientation of the firm, its working conditions and policies, and the style of internal and external communication and how this is communicated to the staff."[10]

IMPLICATIONS What does all this mean for the typical small firm's human resource management practices?

- First, rudimentary human resource practices may put small business owners at a *competitive disadvantage*. A small business owner not using tools like Web-based recruiting is incurring unnecessary costs, and probably deriving inferior results.
- Second, there is a *lack of specialized HR expertise*.[11] Even in larger small businesses, there are at most one or two human resource management people. This makes missing problems in specific areas such as equal employment law more likely. For example, managers in the smaller firm may not have the expertise to understand the legal implications of inappropriately asking a female job candidate if she's thinking of "starting a family."
- Third, the small business owner may not be fully complying with *compensation regulations and laws.* Examples include paying for overtime hours worked, and distinguishing between employees and independent contractors.
- Fourth, paperwork duplication creates *data entry errors*. Small businesses often don't use human resource information systems. That means employee data (name, address, marital status, and so on) often appears on multiple human resource forms (medical enrollment forms, W-4 forms, and so on). Any personal data change then requires manually changing all forms. This is inefficient, and triggers errors.

Diversity Counts: Necessity and the Entrepreneur

More men than women start new businesses, but according to one study, about 100 million women in 59 countries still started new businesses in one recent year.[12] Interestingly, most of the women who did start businesses were not in the developed world. The most likely countries for women to start businesses were in Latin America and sub-Saharan Africa. This may be because in developed economies, women have more career options. In developing economies such as Ghana, necessity infuses a confidence that drives more women to make it on their own. ■

Why HRM Is Important to Small Businesses

Recently, a small software start-up experienced turmoil when social media postings from one employee accused another of harassment. The moral, says one expert, is that start-ups can't assume that all they need is an employee handbook; they also need a functioning HR system.[13]

Indeed, small firms that have effective HR practices do better than those that don't.[14] For example, researchers studied 168 family-owned high-growth SMEs. They concluded that successful high-growth SMEs placed more stress on training and development, performance appraisals, recruitment packages, maintaining morale, and setting competitive compensation levels than did less successful ones: "These findings suggest that these human resource activities do in fact have a positive impact on performance [in smaller businesses]."[15]

For many small firms, effective human resource management is also required for getting and keeping big customers. For example, to comply with international ISO-9000 quality standards, many large customers check that their small vendors follow the necessary HR standards.[16]

We devote this chapter to methods small business managers can use to improve their human resource management practices, starting with Internet and government tools.

LEARNING OBJECTIVE **18-2**

Give four examples of how entrepreneurs can use Internet and government tools to support the HR effort.

Using Internet and Government Tools to Support the HR Effort

No small business need cede the "HR advantage" to big competitors. Knowledgeable small business managers can level the terrain by using Internet-based HR resources, including free online resources from the U.S. government. We'll look at how.

Complying with Employment Laws

Complying with federal (and state and local) employment law is a thorny issue for entrepreneurs. For example, the entrepreneur needs to know, "Must I pay this person overtime?" and, "Must I report this injury?"

Start by knowing which federal employment laws apply. For example, Title VII of the 1964 Civil Rights Act applies to employers with 15 or more employees, while the Age Discrimination in Employment Act of 1967 applies to those with 20 or more.[17] Small business owners will find the legal answers they need to answer questions like these online at federal agencies' Web sites like the following.

THE DOL The U.S. Department of Labor's "*FirstStep* Employment Law Advisor" (see www.dol.gov/elaws/firststep) helps small business managers determine which laws apply to their businesses. First, the elaws wizard takes the owner through questions such as "What is the maximum number of employees your business or organization employs or will employ during the calendar year?" (See Figure 18-1.)

Proceeding through the wizard, the small business owner arrives at a "results" page. This says, "Based on the information you provided in response to the questions in the Advisor, the following employment laws administered by the Department of Labor (DOL) may apply to your business or organization."[18] For a typical small firm, these laws might include the Consumer Credit Protection Act, Employee Polygraph Protection Act, Fair Labor Standards Act, Immigration and Nationality Act, Occupational Safety and Health Act, Uniformed Services Employment and Reemployment Rights Act, and Whistleblower Act.

A linked DOL site (www.dol.gov/whd/flsa/index.htm) provides information on the Fair Labor Standards Act (FLSA). It's elaws Advisors provide practical guidance on questions such as when to pay overtime. Figure 18-2 presents, from this Web site, a list of elaws Advisors.

THE EEOC The U.S. Equal Employment Opportunity Commission administers Title VII of the Civil Rights Act of 1964 (Title VII), the Age Discrimination in Employment Act of 1967 (ADEA), Title I of the Americans with Disabilities Act

FIGURE 18-1 *FirstStep* Employment Law Advisor

Source: From "elaws - FirstStep Employment Law Advisor", U.S. Department of Labor, http://www.dol.gov/elaws/FirstStep/, accessed September 24, 2015.

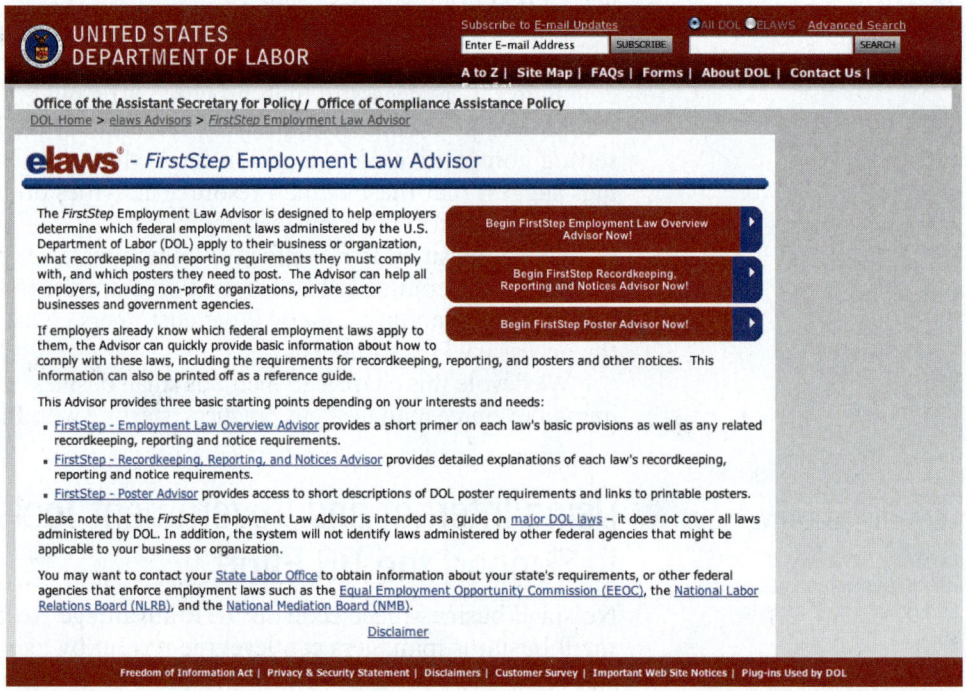

FIGURE 18-2 Sample DOL Elaws Advisors

Source: From "Wage and Hour Related elaws Advisors", http://www.dol.gov/whd/resources/elaws_advisors.htm, accessed September 24, 2015.

- The *Coverage and Employment Status Advisor* helps identify which workers are employees covered by the FLSA.
- The *Hours Worked Advisor* provides information to help determine which hours spent in work-related activities are considered FLSA "hours worked" and, therefore, must be paid.
- The *Overtime Security Advisor* helps determine which employees are exempt from the FLSA minimum wage and overtime pay requirements under the Part 541 overtime regulations.
- The *Overtime Calculator Advisor* computes the amount of overtime pay due in a sample pay period based on information from the user.
- The *Child Labor Rules Advisor* answers questions about the FLSA's youth employment provisions, including at what age young people can work and the jobs they can perform.
- The *Section 14(c) Advisor* helps users understand the special minimum wage requirements for workers with disabilities.

of 1990 (ADA), and the Equal Pay Act of 1963 (EPA). Its Web site (www.eeoc.gov/employers) contains important information regarding matters such as:

- How do I determine if my business is covered by EEOC laws?
- Who may file a charge of discrimination with the EEOC?
- Can a small business resolve a charge without undergoing an investigation or facing a lawsuit?

As the EEOC says, "While the information in this section of our website applies to all employers, it has been specifically designed for small businesses which may not have a human resources department or a specialized EEO staff" (www.eeoc.gov/employers). The site provides small business owners with practical advice. For example, "What should I do when someone files a charge against my company?"

OSHA The DOL's Occupational Safety and Health Administration site (www.osha.gov) similarly supplies small business guidance (see Figure 18-3). OSHA's site provides, among other things, easy access to the *OSHA Small Business Handbook.* This contains practical information, including industry-specific safety and accident checklists.

Employment Planning and Recruiting

Online tools can make small business owners as effective as their large competitors at writing job descriptions and recruiting applicants. As we saw in Chapter 4 (Job Analysis), the Department of Labor's O*NET (http://online.onetcenter.org) illustrates this. It enables business owners to create accurate job descriptions and job specifications quickly.

WEB-BASED RECRUITING Similarly, small business owners can use the online recruiting tools we discussed in Chapter 5. For example, it's easy to scour LinkedIn.com, and to post jobs on Careerbuilder.com, and on professional associations' job boards.

TRENDS SHAPING HR: *DIGITAL AND SOCIAL MEDIA*[19]

Many small businesses use social media to recruit applicants. For example, LinkedIn lets employers post job openings and facilitates business networking. One recruiter reportedly looks for LinkedIn members with compelling summaries, excellent recommendations, and memberships in industry groups. On Twitter, recruiters see if a potential candidate has an appropriate username and photos. But also check Twitter for things like the person's status updates and retweets, to see (for instance) if he or she shares useful information. Small business recruiters should also focus on the social media that makes sense for them. For example, if you're looking for a Facebook marketing expert, look on Facebook. Or look for a photographer on Instagram. And on

FIGURE 18-3 OSHA Web Site

Source: U.S. Department of Labor, www.osha.gov/dcsp/smallbusiness/index.html, accessed September 24, 2015.

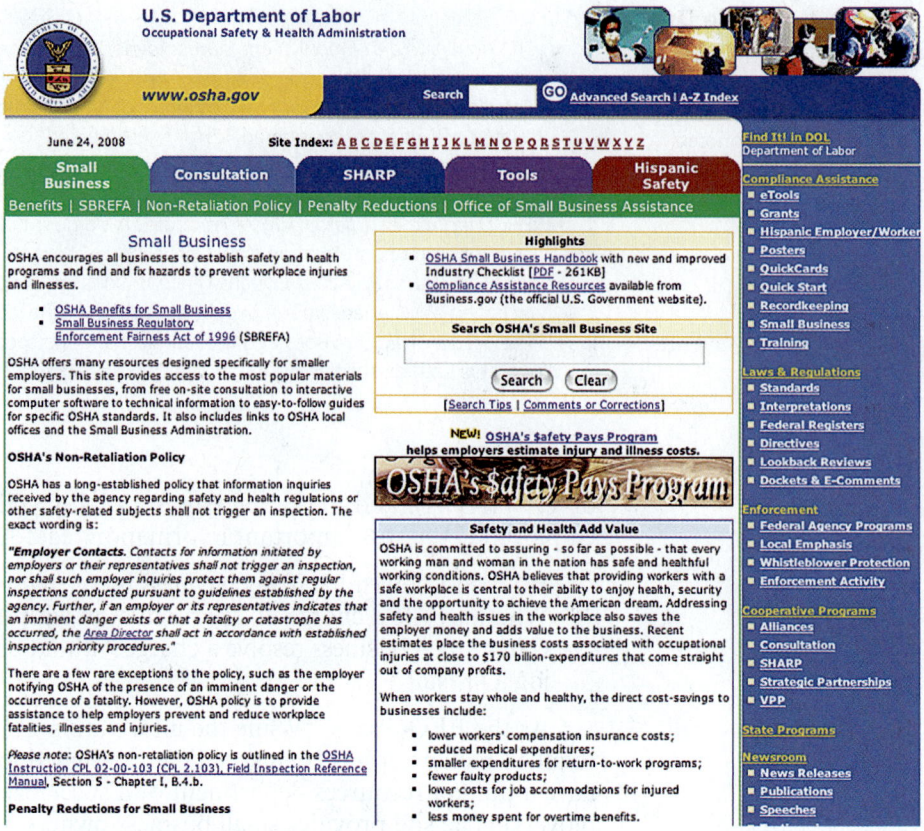

Facebook and LinkedIn, focus recruiting efforts on industry groups that make sense for your company. Check to see how your competitors use social media, and which communities they use.

Social media recruiting entails risks. For example, conversing with someone whose Facebook profile reveals ethnic background could expose the employer to a discrimination suit if that applicant isn't hired. And many agree that at the end of the day, social media recruiting can't substitute for in-person interactions. ■

Employment Selection

Some tests are so easy to use they are particularly good for smaller firms. An example is the *Wonderlic Personnel Test*, which measures general mental ability. With questions somewhat similar to the SAT, it takes less than 15 minutes to administer the four-page booklet. The tester reads the instructions, and then keeps time as the candidate works through the 50 problems. The tester scores the test by totaling the number of correct answers. Comparing the person's score with the minimum scores recommended for various occupations shows whether the person achieved the minimally acceptable score for the job in question.

The *Predictive Index* is another example. It measures work-related personality traits, drives, and behaviors—in particular, dominance, extroversion, patience, and blame avoidance. A template makes scoring simple. The Predictive Index program includes 15 standard benchmark personality patterns. For example, there is the "social interest" pattern, for a person who is generally unselfish, congenial, persuasive, patient, and unassuming. This person would be a good personnel interviewer, for instance.

Many vendors, including Wonderlic and the Predictive Index, offer online applicant testing and screening services. Wonderlic's service (which costs about $8,500 per year for a small firm) first provides job analyses for the employer's jobs. Wonderlic

Use online tests, for instance, to test an applicant's typing speed, proficiency at QuickBooks, or even ability to sell over the phone.

Troels Graugaard/Getty Images

then provides a Web site the small business applicants can log into to take one or several selection tests (including the Wonderlic Personnel Test).

The following are suggestions from *Inc.* magazine for supercharging a small business's recruiting and screening processes.

- ***Keep it in the industry.*** Use online job boards that target a particular industry or city to minimize irrelevant applicants.[20] For example, Jobing.com maintains city-specific job sites in over 19 states.[21] Beyond.com hosts more than 15,000 industry-specific communities.
- ***Automate the process.*** Automated applicant processing systems are inexpensive enough for small employers. For example, systems from Taleo, NuView Systems, and Accolo accept résumés and help automate the screening process. NuView, which costs about $6 to $15 per month per user, asks applicants questions, and bumps out those without, for instance, the required education.[22]
- ***Test online.*** Use online tests, for instance, to test an applicant's proficiency at QuickBooks, or even ability to sell over the phone. Vendors include (as a small sample) IBM's Kenexa, eskill.com/, selectivehiring.com, and berkeassessment.com.[23]
- ***Poll your inner circle.*** Tap friends and employees for recommendations and use social networking sites such as LinkedIn, Facebook, and Twitter. Many employers announce job openings through LinkedIn. One says, "I get people vouching for each applicant, so I don't have to spend hours sorting through résumés."[24]
- ***Send a recording.*** InterviewStream records online video interviews for about $30 to $60.[25] It sends the candidate an e-mail invitation with a link. When he or she clicks the link, a video interviewer asks the company's prerecorded questions. A Webcam captures the candidate's answers. Employers can allow candidates to rerecord their answers. Hiring managers can review the videos at their leisure.[26]

COMPLYING WITH THE LAW Given the time pressures facing most small business owners, confirming the validity of tests one buys online or through office supply stores is probably the exception, not the rule. Many test providers will assist the employer in establishing a testing procedure. For example, as noted, Wonderlic will review your job descriptions as part of its process.

Employment Training

Online training can provide employee training that used to be beyond most small employers' reach.

PRIVATE VENDORS The small business owner can tap hundreds of suppliers of prepackaged training solutions. These range from self-study programs from the American Management Association (www.amanet.org) and SHRM (www.shrm.org), to specialized programs. For example, the employer might arrange with PureSafety to have its employees take occupational safety courses from www.puresafety.com.[27]

SkillSoft is another example (http://skillsoft.com/catalog/default.asp). Its courses include business strategy and operations, professional effectiveness, and computer skills. For example, the course "interviewing effectively" is for managers, team leaders, and human resource professionals. About 2 1/2 hours long, it shows trainees how to use behavioral questioning to interview candidates.[28]

The buyer's guide from the American Society of Training and Development (www.astd.org) is a good place to start to find a vendor (check under "Resources").

THE SBA The federal government's Small Business Administration (www.sba.gov/training) virtual campus offers online courses, workshops, publications, and learning tools aimed at supporting entrepreneurs.[29] For example, under "Small Business Planner," link to "Writing Effective Job Descriptions," "Employees versus Contractors: What's the Difference?," and "How to Select the Right Person"

NAM The National Association of Manufacturers (NAM) is the largest industrial trade organization in the United States. It represents about 14,000 member manufacturers, including 10,000 small and mid-sized companies.

NAM's Virtual University (www.namvu.com) helps employees maintain and upgrade their work skills and continue their professional development. It offers almost 650 courses.[30] There are no long-term contracts to sign. Employers simply pay about $10 to $30 per course taken by each employee. The catalog includes OSHA, quality, and technical training as well as courses in areas like business and finance, personal development, and customer service.

Employment Appraisal and Compensation

Small employers have easy access to computerized and online appraisal and compensation services. For example, Oracle Corporation's ePerformance[31] facilitates performance management by enabling managers to formalize the employee's goals and then assess progress toward meeting those goals. The eAppraisal system from Halogen Software[32] is another example.

Similarly, lack of easy access to high-priced salary surveys once made it difficult and time-consuming for smaller businesses to fine-tune their pay scales. Today, sites like www.salary.com makes it easy to determine local pay rates.

Employment Safety and Health

Safety is an important issue for small employers. One European study found that the majority of all workplace accidents occur in firms with less than 50 employees.[33] (Which is not surprising, since most people work for smaller businesses.) As explained in Chapter 16 (Safety), OHSA provides free services for small employers.[34] These include free on-site safety and health services for small businesses, and its OSHA Sharp program, a certification process through which OSHA certifies that small employers have achieved commendable levels of safety awareness.[35]

LEARNING OBJECTIVE **18-3**

List five ways entrepreneurs can use their small size to improve their HR processes.

Leveraging Small Size with Familiarity, Flexibility, Fairness, and Informality

Because small businesses need to capitalize on their strengths, it makes sense for them to capitalize on their smallness when dealing with employees. For example, smallness can mean more personal *familiarity* with each employee's strengths, needs, and family situation. And it can mean being *flexible* and *informal* in its human resource management policies and practices.[36]

Simple, Informal Employee Selection Procedures

In addition to online recruitment and selection tools,[37] small business managers shouldn't forget simple, low-tech selection aids. For example, the Work Sampling Test we explained in Chapter 6 involves having the candidate show how he or she would actually do one of the job's tasks—such as a marketing candidate spending 30 minutes outlining an ad for a product. The accompanying HR Tools feature presents a more informal selection interview procedure the small business manager may find useful.

IMPROVING PERFORMANCE: *HR Tools for Line Managers and Small Businesses*

A Streamlined Interviewing Process

The small business owner, pressed for time, may use the following practical, streamlined employment interview process.[38] One way to do so is to focus on four basic required factors: knowledge and experience, motivation, intellectual capacity, and personality. To proceed this way, interviewing expert John Drake suggests asking the following questions:

- ✓ **Knowledge and experience.** What must the candidate know to perform the job? What experience is necessary to perform the job? For example, ask a combination of situational questions plus open-ended questions to probe the candidate's suitability for the job, such as "How would you organize such a sales effort?" or "How would you design that kind of Web site?"
- ✓ **Motivation.** What should the person like doing to enjoy this job? Is there anything the person should not dislike? Are there any essential goals or aspirations the person should have? For example, probe such areas as the person's likes and dislikes (for each thing done, what he or she liked or disliked about it).
- ✓ **Intellectual capacity.** Are there any specific intellectual aptitudes required (mathematical, mechanical, and so on)? How complex are the problems the person must solve? What must a person be able to demonstrate intellectually? For example, ask questions that judge such things as complexity of tasks the person has performed, and grades in school.
- ✓ **Personality.** What are the critical personality qualities needed for success on the job (ability to withstand boredom, decisiveness, stability, and so on)? How must the job incumbent handle stress, pressure, and criticism? What kind of interpersonal behavior is required in the job? For example, probe by looking for self-defeating behaviors (aggressiveness, compulsive fidgeting, and so on) and by exploring the person's past interpersonal relationships, such as leading the work team on the last job. Is the candidate personable? Shy? Outgoing?

How to Organize the Interview

- ✓ Have a plan. Devise and use a plan to guide the interview. Drake says that significant areas to touch on include the candidate's:
  - ✓ College experiences
  - ✓ Work experience—summer, part-time
  - ✓ Work experience—full-time (one by one)
  - ✓ Goals and ambitions
  - ✓ Reactions to the job you are interviewing for
  - ✓ Self-assessments (by the candidate of his or her strengths and weaknesses)
  - ✓ Military experiences
  - ✓ Present outside activities[39]
- ✓ Follow your plan. Start with an open-ended question for each topic, such as "Could you tell me about what you did in college?" Then probe for information about the person's knowledge and experience, motivation, intelligence, and personality.

Match the Candidate to the Job

You should now be able to draw conclusions about the person's knowledge and experience, motivation, intellectual capacity, and personality, and to summarize the candidate's strengths and limits. This should provide a rational basis for matching the candidate to the job—one based on the traits and aptitudes the job actually requires. ■

Source: Based on John Drake, Interviewing for Managers: A Complete Guide to Employment Interviewing (New York, AMACOM, 1982).

If your professor has assigned this, go to the Assignments section of **mymanagementlab.com** to complete these discussion questions.

Talk About It 1: List two situational questions (what would you do ...?) and two behavioral questions (what did you do ...?) that you might ask to unearth insights into the candidate's motivation.

Flexibility in Training

One study of 191 small and 201 large firms in Europe found that the small firms were relatively informal in their training and development.[40] Many didn't systematically monitor their managers' skill needs, and fewer than 50% (as opposed to 70% of large firms) had career development programs. The smaller firms also tended to focus any management development they did on teaching specific firm-related competencies (such as how to sell the firm's products).[41] The simplified training process we explained on pages 251–252 (Chapter 8) is one good option for the small business. Informal methods such as the following work well, too.

INFORMAL TRAINING METHODS Training expert Stephen Covey says small businesses can do many things to provide job-related training without establishing expensive formal training programs. His suggestions include:[42]

- Offer to cover the tuition for special classes
- Identify online training opportunities
- Provide a library of tapes and DVDs for systematic, disciplined learning during commute times
- Encourage the sharing of best practices among associates
- When possible, send people to special seminars and association meetings for learning and networking
- Create a learning ethic by having everyone teach each other what they are learning

Source: Questions for Covey: Small Business, Big Opportunity, Nov 2006, Training Magazine. www.Trainingmag.com. Used by permission from Lakewood Media Group.

Flexibility in Benefits and Rewards

The Family and Work Institute surveyed the benefits practices of about 1,000 small and large companies.[43] Not surprisingly, they found that large firms offer more *extensive* benefits packages than do smaller ones. However, many small firms overcame this by offering more flexibility. "They've discovered how to turn tiny into tight-knit, earning employees' trust by keeping them in the loop on company news and financials, and their loyalty by providing frequent feedback on performance."[44] At ID Media, with 90 employees, CEO Lynn Fantom gives all new employees a welcome breakfast on their first day. Internet start-up appssavvy Inc.'s CEO foregoes PowerPoint presentations in favor of humorous YouTube videos.[45]

Basically, the study found that small business owners, by personally interacting with all employees each day, did a better job of "understanding when work/life issues emerge."[46] Wards Furniture in Long Beach, California, exemplifies this. Many of its 17 employees have been with the firm for 10 to 20 years. Brad Ward, an owner, attributes this partly to his firm's willingness to adapt to its workers' needs. For example, workers can share job responsibilities and work part-time from home. As a result, Wards Furniture is a good example of using small size to create valuable work life

At Wards Furniture, workers can share job responsibilities and work part-time from home.

bikeriderlondon/Shutterstock

benefits such as extra time off, compressed workweeks, schedule flexibility, and recognition for employees.

Here are other examples of what Wards and other small employers can offer:[47]

- ***Extra time off.*** For example, Friday afternoons off in the summer.
- ***Compressed workweeks.*** For example, compressed summer workweeks.
- ***Bonuses at critical times.*** Small business owners are more likely to know what's happening in their employees' lives. Use this knowledge to provide special bonuses, for instance, if an employee has a new baby.
- ***Flexibility.*** For example, "If an employee is having a personal problem, help create a work schedule that allows the person to solve problems without feeling like they're going to be in trouble."[48]
- ***Sensitivity to employees' strengths and weaknesses.*** The small business owner should stay attuned to his or her employees' strengths, weaknesses, and aspirations. For example, give them an opportunity to train for and move into the jobs they desire.
- ***Help them better themselves.*** For example, pay employees to take a class to help them develop their job skills.
- ***Feed them.*** Provide free meals occasionally, perhaps by taking your employees to lunch.
- ***Make them feel like owners.*** For example, give employees input into major decisions, let them work directly with clients, get them client feedback, share company performance data with them, and let them share in the company's financial success.
- ***Make sure they have what they need to do their jobs.*** Having motivated employees is only half the challenge. Also ensure they have the necessary training, procedures, computers, and so on.
- ***Constantly recognize a job well done.*** Capitalize on your day-to-day interactions with employees to "never miss an opportunity to give your employees the recognition they deserve."[49]

SIMPLE RETIREMENT BENEFITS Access to retirement benefits is more prevalent in large firms than small ones. About 75% of large firms offer them, while only about 35% of small ones do.[50]

There are several ways for small firms to provide retirement plans. The Pension Protection Act of 2006 provides for a retirement benefit that combines traditional defined benefit and 401(k) (defined contribution) plans.[51] Only available to employers with less than 500 employees, it exempts employers from the complex pension rules to which large employers must adhere. The employees get a retirement plan that blends a defined pension, plus returns on the part of the investment that plan participants contributed.[52]

An easy way for small businesses to provide retirement benefits is through a SIMPLE IRA plan.[53] With the SIMPLE (for Savings Incentive Match Plan for Employees) IRA, employers must (and employees may) make contributions to traditional employee IRAs. These plans are for employers or small businesses with 100 or fewer employees and no other retirement plan.

SIMPLE IRAs are inexpensive and simple. The owner contacts an eligible financial institution and fills out several IRS forms. Most banks, mutual funds, and insurance companies that issue annuity contracts are generally eligible.[54] The plan has very low administrative costs. Employer contributions are tax-deductible.[55] A typical employer contribution might match employee contributions dollar for dollar up to 3% of pay. The financial institution usually handles the IRS paperwork and reporting.

Fairness and the Family Business

Most small businesses are "family businesses," since the owner (and often one or more employees) are family members.

Being a nonfamily employee here isn't easy. The tendency is to treat family and nonfamily employees differently. If so, as one writer puts it, "It's a sure bet that their lower morale and simmering resentments are having a negative effect on your operations and sapping your profits."[56] Reducing such "fairness" problems involves several steps, including:[57]

- ***Set the ground rules.*** One family business consultant says, During the hiring process the [management] applicant should be informed as to whether he or she will be essentially a placeholder, or whether there will be potential for promotion. At a minimum, make the expectations clear, regarding matters such as the level of authority and decision-making the person can expect to attain.[58]
- ***Treat people fairly.*** Work hard to avoid "any appearance that family members are benefiting unfairly from the sacrifice of others."[59]
- ***Confront family issues.*** Discord and tension among family members distract and demoralize employees. Family members must confront and work out their differences.
- ***Erase privilege.*** Family members "should avoid any behavior that would lead people to the conclusion that they are demanding special treatment in terms of assignments or responsibilities."[60] Family employees should come in earlier, work harder, and stay later than other employees stay.

LEARNING OBJECTIVE **18-4**

Discuss how you would choose and deal with a professional employer organization.

Using Professional Employer Organizations

As we explained in Chapter 13 (Benefits and Services), many small business owners look at the issues involved with managing personnel, and decide to outsource most of their human resource functions to vendors.[61] These vendors go by the names *professional employer organizations* (PEOs), *human resource outsourcers* (HROs), or sometimes *employee* or *staff leasing firms*.

How Do PEOs Work?

These vendors range from specialized payroll companies to those that handle all an employer's human resource management requirements.[62] At a minimum, these firms take over the employer's payroll tasks.[63] Usually, however, PEOs assume most of the employer's human resources chores. By transferring the client firm's employees to the

PEO's payroll, PEOs become co-employers of record for the employer's employees. The PEO can then fold the client's employees into the PEO's insurance and benefits program, usually at a lower cost. The PEO usually handles employee-related activities such as recruiting, hiring (with client firms' supervisors' approvals), and payroll and taxes. Most PEOs focus on employers with under 100 employees, and charge fees of 2% to 4% of a company's payroll. HROs usually handle these functions on an "administrative services only"—they're basically your "HR office," but your employees still work for you.[64]

Why Use a PEO?

Employers turn to PEOs for several reasons.

LACK OF SPECIALIZED HR SUPPORT Small firms with fewer than about 100 employees typically have no dedicated HR managers. The owner has most of the human resource management burden on his or her shoulders.

PAPERWORK The Small Business Administration estimates that small business owners spend up to 25% of their time on personnel-related paperwork, such as background checks and benefits sign-ups.[65] Because the PEO takes over most of this, many small businesses conclude that it's cheaper for them just to pay the employee leasing firm's fees.

LIABILITY Legally, PEOs generally "contractually share liability with clients and have a vested interest in preventing workplace injuries and employee lawsuits."[66] The PEO should thus help ensure the small business fulfills its Title VII, OSHA, COBRA, and Fair Labor Standards Act responsibilities.[67]

BENEFITS Insurance and benefits are often the big PEO attraction. Getting health and other insurance is a problem for smaller firms. That's where leasing comes in. Leasing may get a small business insurance for its people that it couldn't otherwise.[68]

PERFORMANCE Finally, the professionalism that the PEO brings to recruiting, screening, training, compensating, and maintaining employee safety and welfare will hopefully translate into improved employee and business results.

Caveats

There are several potential downsides. "If your PEO is poorly managed, or goes bankrupt, you could find yourself with an office full of uninsured workers."[69] Many employers view their human resource management practices (like training new engineers) as strategic, and aren't inclined to turn over such tasks to outsiders. Another potential problem is determining who's responsible. For example, who is responsible for an employee's injuries, the PEO or the employer? The contract should address this.[70]

WARNING SIGNS Several things may signal problems with the prospective PEO. One is *lax due diligence*. For example, because they share liability with the employer, they should question you extensively about your firm's workplace safety and human resource policies and practices.[71] Figure 18-4 summarizes guidelines for finding and working with PEOs.

Watch It!

How does a small company actually carry out its human resource management tasks? If your professor has assigned this, go to the Assignments section of mymanagementlab.com to complete the video exercise titled *Blackbird Guitars: Managing Human Resources in Entrepreneurial Firms*.

FIGURE 18-4 Guidelines for Finding and Working with PEOs

Source: Based on Robert Beck and J. Starkman, "How to Find a PEO That Will Get the Job Done," *National Underwriter* 110, no. 39 (October 16, 2006), pp. 39, 45; Lyle DeWitt, "Advantages of Human Resource Outsourcing," *The CPA Journal* 75, no. 6 (June 2005), p. 13; www.peo.com/dmn, accessed April 28, 2008; Layne Davlin, "Human Resource Solutions for the Franchisee," *Franchising World* 39, no. 10 (October 2007), p. 27; and see for example, www.adp.com/solutions/employer-services/totalsource/what-is-a-peo.aspx, accessed September 24, 2015.

Employers should choose and manage the PEO relationship carefully. Guidelines for doing so include:

- *Conduct a needs analysis.* Know ahead of time exactly what human resource concerns your company wants to address.
- *Review the services* of all PEO firms you're considering. Determine which can meet all your requirements.
- *Determine if the PEO is accredited.* There is no rating system. However, the Employer Services Assurance Corporation of Little Rock, Arkansas (www.Escorp.org), imposes higher financial, auditing, and operating standards on its members. Also check the National Association of Professional Employer Organizations (www.NAPEO.org), and www.PEO.com.
- Check the provider's bank, credit, insurance, and professional references.
- Understand how the *employee benefits will be funded.* Is it fully insured or partially self-funded? Who is the carrier? Confirm that employers will receive first-day coverage.
- See if the contract assumes the *compliance liabilities in the applicable states.*
- *Review the service agreement carefully.* Are the respective parties' responsibilities and liabilities clear?
- Investigate how long the *PEO has been in business.*
- *Check out the prospective PEO's staff. Do they seem to have the expertise to deliver on its* promises?
- Ask, *how will the firm deliver its services?* In person? By phone? Via the Web?
- Ask about upfront fees and how these are determined.
- *Periodically get proof that payroll taxes and insurance premiums are being paid properly* and that any legal issues are handled correctly.

LEARNING OBJECTIVE **18-5**

Describe how you would create a start-up human resource system for a new small business.

Managing HR Systems, Procedures, and Paperwork

Introduction

Consider the paperwork required to run a five-person retail shop. Just to start with, recruiting and hiring an employee might require a help wanted advertising listing, an employment application, an interviewing checklist, various verifications—of education and immigration status, for instance—and a telephone reference checklist. You then might need an employment agreement, confidentiality and noncompetition agreements, and an employer indemnity agreement. To process the new employee you might need a background verification, a new employee checklist, and forms for withholding tax and to obtain new employee data. And to keep track of the employee once on board, you'd need—just to start—a personnel data sheet, daily and weekly time records, an hourly employee's weekly time sheet, and an expense report. Then come all the performance appraisal forms, a disciplinary notice, an employee orientation record, separation notice, and employment reference response.

In fact, this list barely scratches the surface of the policies, procedures, and paperwork you'll need to run the human resource management part of your business. Perhaps with just one or two employees you could track everything in your head, or just write a separate memo for each HR action, placing it in a folder for each worker. But with more employees, you'll need a human resource system comprised of standardized forms. Then as the company grows, you'll computerize various parts of the HR system—payroll, or appraising, for instance. The Strategic Context feature illustrates this.

IMPROVING PERFORMANCE: *The Strategic Context*

City Garage

City Garage's hiring system was inconsistent with its fast-growth strategy.[72] The firm's managers needed mechanics who were comfortable interacting directly with customers in City Garage's "open service area" format (where customers could watch and interact with their mechanics). The old hiring process was a paper-and-pencil application and one interview, followed by a hire/don't hire decision. The process ate up management time and was ineffective. City Garage's solution was to purchase the Personality Profile

Analysis (PPA) online test from Thomas International USA. Now, after a quick application and background check, candidates take the 10-minute, 24-question PPA. City Garage staff then enter the answers into the PPA Software system, and receive test results almost at once. These show whether the applicant is right for the job, based on four personality characteristics. Computerizing its testing system improved City Garage's performance and profits, and helped it achieve its fast-growth "open service area" strategic goals. ■

Source: Based on Gilbert Nicholson, "Automated Assessments for Better Hires," Workforce (December 2000), pp. 102–107; http://www.citygaragedfw.com/.

If your professor has assigned this, go to the Assignments section of **mymanagementlab.com** to complete this discussion question.

Talk About It 2: What other tools and techniques discussed in this chapter would you recommend city Garage try, and why?

Basic Components of Manual HR Systems

Very small employers (say, with 10 employees or less) will probably start with a manual human resource management system. From a practical point of view, this generally means obtaining and organizing a set of standardized personnel forms covering each important aspect of the HR process—recruitment, selection, training, appraisal, compensation, safety—as well as some means for organizing all this information for each of your employees.

The number of forms you would conceivably need even for a small firm is quite large, as the illustrative list in Table 18-1 shows.[73] One simple way to obtain the basic forms of a manual HR system is from Web sites (such as www.hr.com/en/free_forms) or books or CDs that provide compilations of HR forms. The forms you want can then be adapted from these sources for your particular situation. Office supply stores also sell packages of personnel forms. For example, Office Depot sells packages of individual personnel forms, and a "Human Resource Kit" containing 10 copies of each of the following: Application, Employment Interview, Reference Check, Employee Record, Performance Evaluation, Warning Notice, Exit Interview, and Vacation Request, plus a Lawsuit-Prevention Guide.[74] Also available is a package of Employee Record Folders. Use the folders to maintain a file on each individual employee; on the outside of the pocket is printed a form for recording information such as name, start date, company benefits, and so on.

TABLE 18-1 Some Important Employment Forms

New Employee Forms	Current Employee Forms	Employee Separation Forms
Application	Employee Status Change Request	Retirement Checklist
New Employee Checklist	Employee Record	Termination Checklist
Employment Interview	Performance Evaluation	COBRA Acknowledgment
Reference Check	Warning Notice	Unemployment Claim
Telephone Reference Report	Vacation Request	Employee Exit Interview
Employee Manual Acknowledgment	Probation Notice	
Employment Agreement	Job Description	
Employment Application Disclaimer	Probationary Evaluation	
Employee Secrecy Agreement	Direct Deposit Acknowledgment	
	Absence Report	
	Disciplinary Notice	
	Grievance Form	
	Expense Report	
	401(k) Choices Acknowledgment	
	Injury Report	

OTHER SOURCES Several direct-mail catalog companies similarly offer HR materials. For example, HRdirect (www.hrdirect.com) offers packages of personnel forms. These include, for instance, Short- and Long-Form Employee Applications, Applicant Interviews, Employee Performance Reviews, and Absentee Calendars and Reports. Also available are various legal-compliance forms, including standardized Harassment Policy and FMLA Notice forms, as well as posters (for instance, covering legally required postings for matters such as the Americans with Disabilities Act).

G. Neil Company, of Sunrise, Florida (www.gneil.com), is another direct-mail personnel materials source. In addition to a complete line of personnel forms, documents, and posters, it also carries manual systems for matters like attendance history, job analyses and for tracking vacation requests and safety records. It has a complete HR "start-up" kit containing 25 copies of each of the basic components of a manual HR system. These include, for instance, Long-Form Application for Employment, Attendance History, Payroll/Status Change Notice, Absence Report, and Vacation Request & Approval, all organized in a file box.

Automating Individual HR Tasks

As the small business grows, it becomes impractical to rely on manual HR systems. It is at this point that most small- to medium-sized firms begin computerizing individual human resource management tasks.

HR in Practice at the Hotel Paris Lisa had managed to install several separate information systems, such as for performance appraisals. However, as she discussed one day over lunch with the CFO, these systems were not integrated. To see how she handled this, see the case on pages 608–609 of this chapter.

PACKAGED SYSTEMS Here again, there are many resources available. For example, various Web sites contain categorical lists of HR software vendors.[75] These vendors provide software solutions for virtually all personnel tasks, ranging from benefits management to compensation, compliance, employee relations, outsourcing, payroll, and time and attendance systems.

The G. Neil Company sells software packages for monitoring attendance, employee record keeping, writing employee policy handbooks, and conducting computerized employee appraisals. www.hrdirect.com, www.effortlesshr.com, and others offer software and online solutions for writing employee policy manuals, maintaining employee records (including name, address, marital status, number of dependents, emergency contact and phone numbers, hire date, and job history), writing performance reviews, creating job descriptions, tracking attendance and hours worked for each employee, employee scheduling, writing organizational charts, managing payroll, conducting employee surveys, scheduling and tracking employee training activities, and managing OSHA compliance, often cloud-based.[76] Websites such as www.capterra.com/ provide guidance on what HR software is available from vendors such as Zenefits, Halogen TalentSpace, Fairsail HRIS, and Cezanne HR.[77]

Human Resource Information Systems (HRIS)

As the company grows, a more comprehensive system becomes necessary. We can define an integrated human resource information system (HRIS) as interrelated components working together to collect, process, store, and disseminate information to support decision making, coordination, control, analysis, and visualization of an organization's human resource management activities.[78] There are several reasons for installing an HRIS. The first is improved transaction processing.

Improved Transaction Processing

The day-to-day minutiae of maintaining and updating employee records take an enormous amount of time. One study found that 71% of HR employees' time was devoted to transactional tasks like checking leave balances, maintaining address records, and monitoring employee benefits distributions.[79] HRIS packages substitute powerful computerized processing for a wide range of the firm's HR transactions.

Online Self-Processing

HR information systems also facilitate employee self-processing. For example, at Provident Bank, the benefits system Benelogic lets employees self-enroll in all their desired benefits programs over the Internet at a secure site. It also "support[s] employees' quest for 'what if' information relating to, for example, the impact on their take-home pay of various benefits options."[80] That's all work that HR employees would previously have had to do for Provident's employees.

Improved Reporting Capability

By integrating numerous individual HR tasks (training records, appraisals, employee personal data, and so on), the HRIS improves HR's reporting capabilities. For example, reports might be available (company-wide and by department) for health-care cost per employee, pay and benefits as a percent of operating expense, cost per hire, report on training, volunteer turnover rates, turnover costs, time to fill jobs, and return on human capital invested (in terms of training and education fees, for instance).

HR System Integration

Because the HRIS's software components (record keeping, payroll, appraisal, and so forth) are integrated, they enable the employer to reengineer its HR function. For example, PeopleSoft's HRIS electronically routes salary increases, transfers, and other e-forms through the organization to the proper managers for approval. As one person signs off, it's routed to the next. If someone forgets to process a document, a smart agent issues reminders. The HRIS thus automates what might otherwise be a time-consuming manual process.

HRIS Vendors

Many firms today offer HRIS packages. Capterra.com, mentioned earlier, is one good source. The Web site for the International Association for Human Resource Information Management (www.ihrim.org), lists vendors such as Automatic Data Processing, Inc., Business Information Technology, Inc., Human Resource Microsystems, Lawson Software, Oracle Corporation, SAP America, Inc., and many other HRIS vendors.

TRENDS SHAPING HR: *DIGITAL AND SOCIAL MEDIA*

HR on the Cloud

Most suppliers of human resource management systems, such as ADP, Ceridian, Kronos, Oracle, and SAP, offer totally cloud-based systems. For small business owners particularly, the advantages of cloud systems are that the vendors can more easily update them with the latest features—saving the small business owner much time and expense—and that the owner and employees can easily access the information from wherever they are.[81]

BambooHR illustrates an HR system especially designed for small and medium-sized businesses (www.bamboohr.com). A dramatic improvement over spreadsheets and other paper-based systems, bambooHR enables authorized managers and employees to securely and remotely access company information on matters like time off and personal information, and to produce reports and/or follow trends on the system's customizable dashboards. Furthermore, the bambooHR system was designed to be integrated with compatible applications. It can therefore be seamlessly integrated with the small business' payroll systems, applicant tracking systems, benefits enrollment systems, and performance review systems.[82] ■

Chapter Review

MyManagementLab® Go to **mymanagementlab.com** to complete the problems marked with this icon. ✪

Chapter Section Summaries

18-1. Many people reading this book will work for or own their own small businesses, so it's important to understand **the small business challenge**. Without effective human resource management, small business owners run the risk that they'll be at a competitive disadvantage or that without the necessary HR expertise they may commit mistakes that lead to litigation.

18-2. Being small, small businesses can particularly capitalize on freely available **Internet and government tools to support their HR efforts**. For example, you can use Department of Labor elaws Advisors to answer overtime questions, the EEOC's Web sites for answers on questions like "How can we resolve the charge?" and the Department of Labor's OSHA Web site to review, for instance, your small business handbook. To better compete, small business owners can also use online recruiting tools like those we discussed in Chapter 5 and training programs available online from companies such as PureSafety.

18-3. Small businesses need to capitalize on their strengths, and in this case, it means capitalizing on **familiarity, flexibility, and informality**. For example, be flexible about extra time off, compressed workweeks, and job enrichment. They can also use relatively informal but still effective employee selection procedures such as a work-sampling test. Informal training methods include online training opportunities, encouraging the sharing of best practices among associates, and sending employees to seminars. Because small businesses are often family businesses, it's important to treat nonfamily members fairly.

18-4. After reviewing all the challenges of managing human resources, many small business owners turn to **using professional employer organizations**. Also called *human resource outsourcers* or *employee or staff leasing firms*, these firms generally transfer the client firm's employees to the PEO's own payroll and thus become the employer of record for the employer's employees.

18-5. Small business managers need to understand how their **HR systems, procedures, and paperwork** will evolve. At first, there may be a simple manual human resource management system, for instance, with employee records compiled on forms from office supply companies and maintained in manual files. The employer then may purchase one or more packaged systems for automating individual HR tasks, for instance, such as applicant tracking and performance appraisal. As companies grow, they will look to integrate the separate systems with a human resource information system.

Discussion Questions

18-1. How and why is HR in small businesses different than that in large firms?

✪ **18-2.** Explain why HRM is important to small businesses.

18-3. Explain and give at least five examples of ways entrepreneurs can use small size—familiarity, flexibility, and informality—to improve their HR processes.

✪ **18-4.** Describe with examples how you would create a start-up, paper-based human resource system for a new small business.

Individual and Group Activities

18-5. Form teams of five or six persons, each with at least one person who owns or has worked for a small business. Based on their experiences, make a list of the "inadequate-HR risks" the business endured, in terms of competitive disadvantage, lack of specialized HR expertise, workplace litigation, compensation laws compliance, and paperwork/data-entry errors.

18-6. You own a small business, and you are confused about which of your employees is eligible for overtime pay. The employees in question include your secretary, two accounting clerks, one engineer, and two inside salespeople. Individually or in groups of four or five students, use the DOL's Overtime Security Advisor and DOL's Calculator to determine who gets overtime pay.

18-7. You have about 32 employees working in your factory. Working individually or in teams of four or five students, find and create a list of five online sources you could use to provide training to them, at no cost to you or to them.

18-8. Appendices A and B at the end of this book (pages 612–629) list the knowledge someone studying for the HRCI (Appendix A) or SHRM (Appendix B) certification exam needs to have in each area of human resource management (such as in Strategic Management, and Workforce Planning). In groups of several students, do four things: (1) review Appendix A and/or B; (2) identify the material in this chapter that relates to the Appendix A and/or B required knowledge lists; (3) write four multiple-choice exam questions on this material that you believe would be suitable for inclusion in the HRCI exam and/or the SHRM exam; and, (4) if time permits, have someone from your team post your team's questions in front of the class, so that students in all teams can answer the exam questions created by the other teams.

Experiential Exercise

Building an HRIS

Purpose: The purpose of this exercise is to give you practice in creating a human resource management system (HRIS).

Required Understanding: You should be fully acquainted with the material in this chapter.

How to Set Up the Exercise/Instructions: Divide the class into teams of several students. Each team will need access to the Internet.

Assume that the owners of a small business come to you with the following problem. They have a company with less than 40 employees. They have been taking care of all HR paperwork informally, mostly on slips of paper and with memos. They want you to supply them with a human resource management information system—how computerized it is will be up to you, but they can only afford a budget of $5,000 upfront (not counting your consulting), and then about $500 per year for maintenance. You know from your HR training that there are various sources of paper-based and online systems. Write a two-page proposal telling them exactly what your team would suggest, based on its accumulated existing knowledge, and from online research.

Application Case

Netflix Breaks the Rules[83]

Why did Netflix survive as a start-up when the dot-com bubble burst in the late 1990s? Probably because, from the day he started Netflix, founder Reed Hastings believed in breaking the rules. His direct-to consumer mail and video streaming business model certainly helped Netflix to survive. But the firm's unorthodox human resource management practices helped the company to attract and keep the high producers who design the products that are the firm's lifeblood. Hastings knew that top Silicon Valley workers could choose where they worked, and high pay is pretty much standard throughout the Valley's industries. How to set oneself apart? Hastings and his start-up colleagues believed that a culture that balanced a flexible work environment with few constraints and high responsibility was the answer. They called the policy "Freedom and Responsibility."

Just how unorthodox are the Netflix HR practices? Consider this: As a Netflix professional you get unlimited vacations. One engineer takes 5-week vacations to Europe, because he likes (as he says) to take his time off in big chunks. (An HR officer must approve time off in excess of 30 days annually.) As a Netflix employee, your pay isn't tied to performance appraisals, or even to a compensation plan. Frequent market salary surveys and pay hikes keep everyone's pay aligned with Silicon Valley competitors'. Each employee decides whether to take his or her pay in cash or in Netflix stock. Options vest immediately. Netflix doesn't recruit much at college job fairs, instead hiring mostly highly experienced professionals. There's no training, professional development, or career planning at Netflix (except for legally required training, such as diversity training). You're in charge of your own career.

But with freedom like that comes responsibilities. The company expects its salaried employees to work hard—to "do the jobs of three or four people," as one report put it. And Netflix doesn't have the "frat party" free-wheeling atmosphere that many dot-coms do. It's an adult environment. Netflix does not coddle underperformers. Yearly 360-degree performance reviews provide "direct and honest feedback." Those that aren't cutting it are quickly let go, but (whenever possible) amicably. Rather than the sorts of litigiousness that often characterizes dismissals in other firms (having to prove the person was incompetent, for instance), Netflix writes a check. The company believes that a handsome severance payment helps maintain the person's dignity, makes it easier for supervisors to make tough calls with underperformers, and, of course, minimizes blowback from those it dismisses. It's more like a "no-fault divorce," as one observer put it.

Questions

In many respects, the Netflix HR strategy seems like a dream come true for small businesses. You don't need a pay plan; instead, you just update each person's pay every few months based on market surveys. You offer no training and development. And you don't track vacation time, more or less. If someone's not doing well, you just pay him or her to leave, with no hassles. Netflix seems to have hit upon its own version of "Netflix High-Performance Work Practices." Given that, answer the following questions (please be specific).

18-9. What (if anything) is it about Netflix that makes its HR practices work for it?

18-10. Would you suggest using similar practices in other businesses, such as, say, a new restaurant? Why?

18-11. List the criteria you would use for deciding whether another company is right for Netflix-type HR practices.

18-12. What argument would you make in response to the following: "Netflix just lucked out; they'd have done even better with conventional HR practices."

Source: Based on information in Michelle Conlin, "Netflix: Flex to the Max," September 24, 2007, www.businessweek.com/magazine/content/07_39/b4051059.htm, accessed July 3, 2011; Robert J. Grossman, "Tough Love at Netflix," April 1, 2010, www.shrm.org/Publications/hrmagazine/EditorialContent/2010/0410/Pages/0410grossman3.aspx, accessed July 3, 2011; and David F. Larcker, Allan McCall, and Brian Tayan, "Equity on De-mand: The Netflix Approach to Compensation," January 15, 2010, http://hbr.org/product/equity-on-demand-the-netflix-approach-to-compensat/an/CG19-PDF-ENG.

Continuing Case

Carter Cleaning Company

Cleaning in Challenging Times

As the economic downturn worsened a few years ago, revenues at the Carter stores fell steeply. Many of their customers were simply out of work and didn't need (or couldn't afford) dry cleaning. The Carters actually found themselves giving away some free cleaning services. They started a new program wherein existing customers could get one suit or dress cleaned free each month if they needed it for a job interview.

In the midst of this downturn, the Carters knew they had to get their employment costs under control. The problem was that, realistically, there wasn't much room for cutting staffing in a store. Of course, if a store got very slow, they could double up by having a cleaner/spotter spend some time pressing, or having the manager displace the counter person. But if sales only fell 15% to 20% per store, there really wasn't much room for reducing employee head count because each store never employed many people in the first place.

The question therefore naturally arose as to whether the Carters could cut their employment expenses without dismissing too many people. Jennifer Carter has several questions for you.

Questions

18-13. Assume that we don't want to terminate any of our employees. What work-scheduling-related changes could we make that would reduce our payrolls by, say, 20% per week but still keep all our employees on board?

18-14. We are currently handling most of our personnel-related activities, such as sign-ons, benefits administration, and appraisals, manually. What specific suggestions would you have for us in terms of using software systems to automate our HR processes?

18-15. Suggest at least five free Internet-based sources we could turn to for helping us to lower our total employment costs.

Translating Strategy into HR Policies and Practices Case*,§

**The accompanying strategy map for this chapter is in MyManagementLab; the overall map on the inside back cover of this text outlines the relationships involved.*

Improving Performance at the Hotel Paris

The New HRIS

The Hotel Paris's competitive strategy is "To use superior guest service to differentiate the Hotel Paris properties, and to thereby increase the length of stay and return rate of guests, and thus boost revenues and profitability." HR manager Lisa Cruz must now formulate functional policies and activities that support this competitive strategy and boost performance by eliciting the required employee behaviors and competencies.

Challenging economic times in the past few years brought the drawbacks of the Hotel Paris's relatively small size into sharp relief. Large chains like Marriott had vast online reservations capabilities with huge centralized systems that easily and economically handled reservations requests from throughout the world. By comparison, the Hotel Paris still handled reservations much as hotels did 15 years ago, either with separate Web sites for each of their hotel locations, e-mail, or an 800 number.

Their human resource management information systems were similarly primitive. Lisa had managed to install several separate information systems, such as for performance appraisals. However, as she discussed one day over lunch with the CFO, the HR systems were not integrated. Therefore, if an employee changed his or her name, for instance, through marriage, people in Lisa's office had to execute all those name changes manually on all the various employee rosters and benefits plans.

This lack of integration was bad enough in boom times, but was worse as the economy soured. The CFO pointed out to her that the amount of money they were spending on human resource management administration was about 30% higher than it was at larger chains such as Marriott. He understood that large size brings economies of scale. But he believed there had to be something they could do to reduce the cost of administering human resource management.

Lisa's solution was to get the CFO's approval to have several software consulting firms including IBM, Accenture, and Oracle provide

§Written by and copyright Gary Dessler, PhD.

proposals for how to integrate the hotel's HR information systems. After getting the CFO's and CEO's approval, they contracted with one vendor and installed the system.

Questions

18-16. Using any benchmark data that you can find, including information from this textbook, what are some benchmark metrics that Lisa could be using to assess the efficiency of her human resource management operations? To what extent does the Hotel Paris's quality service orientation enter into how Lisa's metrics should compare?

18-17. Throughout this textbook, we've discussed various specific examples of how human resource management departments have been reducing the cost of delivering their services. Keeping in mind the Hotel Paris's quality service orientation, please list and explain with examples how Lisa Cruz could use at least five of these.

18-18. Focusing only on human resource information systems for a moment, what sorts of systems would you suggest Lisa consider recommending for the Hotel Paris? Why?

18-19. Explain with detailed examples how Lisa can use free online and governmental sources to accomplish at least part of what you propose in your previous answers.

18-20. Give three examples of fee-based online tools you suggest Lisa use.

18-21. Based on what you read in this chapter of Dessler, *Human Resource Management*, do you suggest Lisa use a PEO? Why?

MyManagementLab

Go to **mymanagementlab.com** for Auto-graded writing questions as well as the following Assisted-graded writing questions:

18-22. Explain and give at least four examples of how entrepreneurs can use Internet and government tools to support the HR effort.

18-23. This chapter explained that to compete with larger employers, the small business owner should capitalize on familiarity, flexibility, and informality. What does this mean and how as a small business owner would you do that?

18-24. MyManagementLab only—comprehensive writing assignment for this chapter.

Try It!

How would you apply the concepts and skills you learned in this chapter? If your professor has assigned this, go to the Assignments section of **mymanagementlab.com** to complete the simulation: *Entrepreneurship*.

PERSONAL INVENTORY ASSESSMENTS

Delegation Self Assessment

Running one's own business requires a knack for knowing how to delegate. Complete this assessment to learn more about your personality.

Endnotes

1. Gilbert Nicholson, "Automated Assessments for Better Hires," *Workforce* (December 2000), pp. 102–107. See also www.citygaragedfw.com, accessed May 5, 2015.
2. www.citygaragedfw.com, accessed May 5, 2015.
3. "Statistics of U.S. Businesses and Non-Employer Status," www.sba.gov/advo/research/data.html, accessed November 5, 2009; www.census.gov/econ/smallbus.html, accessed May 13, 2014.
4. "Small Business Economic Indicators 2000," Office of Advocacy, U.S. Small Business Administration (Washington, DC, 2001), p. 5. See also "Small Business Laid Foundation for Job Gains," www.sba.gov/advo, accessed March 9, 2006.
5. Business size affects human resource activities such as executive compensation. Peter Hausdorf and Dale Duncan, "Firm Size and Internet Recruiting in Canada: A Preliminary Investigation," *Journal of Small-Business Management* 42, no. 3 (July 2004), pp. 325–334.
6. *SHRM Human Capital Benchmarking Study 2009*, Society for Human Resource Management, p. 12, www.shrm.org/research/surveyfindings/articles/documents/09-0620_human_cap_benchmark_full_fnl.pdf, accessed July 17, 2014.
7. Graham Dietz et al., "HRM Inside UK E-commerce Firms," *International Small Business Journal* 24, no. 5 (October 2006), pp. 443–470.
8. Bernice Kotey and Cathleen Folker, "Employee Training in SMEs: Effect of Size and Firm Type—Family and Nonfamily," *Journal of Small-Business Management* 45, no. 2 (April 2007), pp. 14–39.
9. Dietz et al., "HRM Inside UK E-commerce Firms."
10. Ibid. See also Wasserman, "Planning a Start-Up? Seize the Day … Then Expect to Work All Night," *Harvard Business Review* 87, no. 1 (January 2009), pp. 27.

11. Points 2–5 based on Kathy Williams, "Top HR Compliance Issues for Small Businesses," *Strategic Finance* (February 2005), pp. 21–23.
12. "Entrepreneurs: The Gender Gap," http://diversitywoman.com/entrepreneurs-the-gender-gap, accessed April 20, 2013.
13. Evelyn Rusli, "Torment Claims Make GitHub Grow Up," *Wall Street Journal*, July 18, 2014, pp. B1, B5.
14. However, see Luc Sels et al., "Unraveling the HRM–Performance Link: Value Creating and Cost Increasing Effects of Small-Business HRM," *Journal of Management Studies* 43, no. 2 (March 2006), pp. 319–342. For supporting evidence of HR's positive effects on small companies, see also Andrea Rauch et al., "Effects of Human Capital and Long-Term Human Resources Development and Utilization on Employment Growth of Small-Scale Businesses: A Causal Analysis," *Entrepreneurship Theory and Practice* 29, no. 6 (November 2005), pp. 681–698; Andre Grip and Inge Sieben, "The Effects of Human Resource Management on Small Firms' Productivity and Employee's Wages," *Applied Economics* 37, no. 9 (May 20, 2005), pp. 1047–1054.
15. Dawn Carlson et al., "The Impact of Human Resource Practices and Compensation Design on Performance: An Analysis of Family-Owned SMEs," *Journal of Small Business Management* 44, no. 4 (October 2006), pp. 531–543. See also Jake Messersmith and James Guthrie, "High Performance Work Systems in Emergent Organizations: Implications for Firm Performance," *Human Resource Management* 49, no. 2 (March–April 2010), pp. 241–264.
16. Dietz et al., "HRM Inside UK E-commerce Firms." See also, Diana Wicks, "Checklist of Audit Questions for ISO Internal Audits of Human Resources", http://smallbusiness.chron.com/checklist-audit-questions-iso-internal-audits-human-resources-12265.html, accessed July 30, 2015.
17. www.eeoc.gov/employers/overview.html, accessed February 10, 2008.
18. www.dol.gov/elaws, accessed September 16, 2014; www.dol.gov/elaws/firststep/results.htm?fs=AA0000000C0NN0000000YYYYYB00Y00Y0NY, accessed July 30, 2015.
19. "Six Common Mistakes Small Businesses Make When Incorporating Social Media into Their Recruiting Efforts," www.roberthalf.us/SocialMediaRecruitingMistakes; Rieva Lesonsky, "Find the Perfect Hire by Tapping into Social Media," *Employment Trends*, January 30, 2013, http://smallbiztrends.com/2013/01/3-ways-find-perfect-hire-social-media.html; and Emily Bennington, "Social Media Recruitment: Social Media Platforms and Your Next Hire," http://hiring.monster.com/hr/hr-best-practices/small-business/social-media-trends/social-media-recruitment.aspx, all accessed April 20, 2013.
20. Daren Dahl, "Recruiting: Tapping the Talent Pool … Without Drowning in Resumes," *Inc.* 31, no. 3 (April 2009), pp. 121–122.
21. http://miamidade.jobing.com/jobs, accessed July 30, 2015.
22. Dahl, op. cit.
23. All accessed July 30, 2015.
24. Dahl, op. cit.
25. http://interviewstream.com/, accessed July 30, 2015.
26. Dahl, op. cit.
27. Puresafety is a division of Underwriters Laboratories.
28. Paul Harris, "Small Businesses Bask in Training's Spotlight," T&D 59, no. 2 (Fall 2005), pp. 46–52.
29. Ibid.
30. www.themanufacturinginstitute.org/Education-Workforce/Skills-Certification-System/Skills-Certification-System.aspx, accessed September 10, 2012.
31. www.oracle.com/us/products/applications/peoplesoft-enterprise/hcm-resource-library/051027.pdf Accessed July 29, 2015.
32. www.halogensoftware.com/products/halogen-eappraisal, accessed August 17, 2013.
33. Jan de Kok, "Precautionary Actions within Small-and Medium-Sized Enterprises," *Journal of Small Business Management* 43, no. 4, October 2005, pp. 498–516.
34. Sean Smith, "OSHA Resources Can Help Small Businesses Spot Hazards," *Westchester County Business Journal*, August 4, 2003, p. 4. See also www.osha.gov/dcsp/smallbusiness/index.html, accessed September 16, 2014.
35. www.osha.gov/dcsp/smallbusiness/sharp.html, accessed February 17, 2010.
36. Dietz et al., "HRM Inside UK E-commerce Firms."
37. Adrienne Fox, "McMurray Scouts Top Talent to Produce Winning Results," *HR Magazine* 51, no. 7 (July 2006), pp. 57.
38. This is based on John Drake, *Interviewing for Managers: A Complete Guide to Employment Interviewing* (New York: AMACOM, 1982).
39. Ibid.
40. Colin Gray and Christopher Mabey, "Management Development: Key Differences Between Small and Large Businesses in Europe," *International Small Business Journal* 23, no. 5 (October 2005), pp. 467–485.
41. Ibid. See also Essi Saru, "Organizational Learning and HRD: How Appropriate Are They for Small Firms?" *Journal of European Industrial Training* 31, no. 1 (January 2007), pp. 36–52.
42. From Stephen Covey, "Small Business, Big Opportunity," *Training* 43, no. 11 (November 2006), p. 40 www.Trainingmag.com. Used by permission from Lakewood Media Group.
43. Gina Ruiz, "Smaller Firms in Vanguard of Flex Practices," *Workforce Management* 84, no. 13 (November 21, 2005), p. 10.
44. Kira Bindrum, "Little Firms Redefine Culture of Work," *Crain's New York Business* 25, no. 49 (December 7–13, 2009), p. 20.
45. Ibid., pp. 7–13.
46. Ruiz, "Smaller Firms in Vanguard of Flex Practices."
47. These are from Ty Freyvogel, "Operation Employee Loyalty," *Training Media Review,* September–October 2007.
48. Ibid.
49. Ibid.
50. Jeffrey Marshall and Ellen Heffes, "Benefits: Smaller Firm Workers Often Getting Less," *Financial Executive* 21, no. 9 (November 1, 2005), p. 10.
51. www.dol.gov/ebsa/pdf/ppa2006.pdf, accessed February 18, 2008.
52. Bill Leonard, "New Retirement Plans for Small Employers," *HR Magazine* 51, no. 12 (December 2006), p. 30.
53. See for example, www.irs.gov/Retirement-Plans/Plan-Sponsor/SIMPLE-IRA-Plan, accessed July 30, 2015.
54. Kristen Falk, "The Easy Retirement Plan for Small Business Clients," *National Underwriter* 111, no. 45 (December 3, 2007), pp. 12–13.
55. Ibid. www.irs.gov/Retirement-Plans/Plan-Sponsor/SIMPLE-IRA-Plan, accessed August 17, 2013.
56. Phillip Perry, "Welcome to the Family," *Restaurant Hospitality* 90, no. 5 (May 2006), pp. 73, 74, 76, 78. Used by permission from Phillip Perry.
57. Ibid.
58. Ibid.
59. Ibid.
60. Ibid.
61. Jane Applegate, "Employee Leasing Can Be a Savior for Small Firms," *Business Courier Serving Cincinnati–Northern Kentucky* (January 28, 2000), p. 23.
62. Robert Beck and Jay Starkman, "How to Find a PEO That Will Get the Job Done," *National Underwriter* 110, no. 39 (October 16, 2006), pp. 39, 45.
63. Layne Davlin, "Human Resource Solutions for the Franchisee," *Franchising World* 39, no. 10 (October 2007), pp. 27–28.
64. Beck and Starkman, "How to Find a PEO."
65. Lyle DeWitt, "Advantages of Human Resources Outsourcing," *The CPA Journal* 75, no. 6 (June 2005), p. 13.
66. Max Chafkin, "Fed Up with HR?" *Inc.* 28, no. 5 (May 2006), pp. 50–52.
67. Ibid.
68. Ibid.
69. Ibid. For a useful summary of PEOs' pros and cons, see the discussion at www.proformative.com/questions/peo-pros-and-cons, accessed July 30, 2015.
70. Diana Reitz, "Employee Leasing Breeds Liability Questions," *National Underwriter Property and Casualty Risk and Benefits Management* 104, no. 18 (May 2000), p. 12.
71. Chafkin, "Fed Up with HR?"
72. Gilbert Nicholson, "Automated Assessments for Better Hires," *Workforce* (December 2000), pp. 102–107. See also www.citygaragedfw.com, accessed May 5, 2015.
73. For a more complete list, see, for example, Sondra Servais, *Personnel Director* (Deerfield Beach, FL: Made E-Z Products, 1994); www.hr.com/en/free_forms/, accessed September 10, 2012; and www.entrepreneur.com/formnet/hrcareers.html, accessed September 10, 2012.
74. www.officedepot.com/a/browse/business-forms-tax-forms-andrecordkeeping/N=5+516208/;jsession id=0000zlVADjXrV18WJcAFM0Ped0:13ddq0u44, accessed July 18, 2014.
75. www.ihrim.org, accessed April 28, 2008; www.pmihrm.com/hr_software_ vendors.html, accessed July 18, 2014.
76. See, for example, www.effortlesshr.com/hr-software/online-employee-management-software and www.capterra.com/human-resource-software, both accessed July 18, 2014.
77. www.capterra.com/human-resource-software/, accessed July 30, 2015.
78. Adapted from Kenneth Laudon and Jane Laudon, *Management Information Systems: New Approaches to Organization and Technology* (Upper Saddle River, NJ: Prentice Hall, 1998), p. G7. See also Michael Barrett and Randolph Kahn, "The Governance of Records Management," *Directors and Boards* 26, no. 3 (Spring 2002), pp. 45–48; Anthony Hendrickson, "Human Resource Information Systems: Backbone Technology of Contemporary Human Resources," *Journal of Labor Research* 24, no. 3 (Summer 2003), pp. 381–395; and Mike Harmer, "10 Secrets of Successful

Software Implementations," *HR Magazine,* November 2014, pp. 40–43.

79. "HR Execs Trade Notes on Human Resource Information Systems," *BNA Bulletin to Management* (December 3, 1998), p. 1. See also Brian Walter, "But They Said Their Payroll Program Complied with the FLSA," *Public Personnel Management* 31, no. 1 (Spring 2002), pp. 79–94.
80. "HR Execs Trade Notes on Human Resource Information Systems," *BNA Bulletin to Management* (December 3, 1998), p. 2. See also Ali Velshi, "Human Resources Information," *The Americas Intelligence Wire* (February 11, 2004).
81. www.comparehris.com/BambooHR and www.bamboohr.com/tour.php, both accessed May 4, 2015; Sarah Fister Gale, "Hey, You, Get Onto My Cloud…," *Workforce*, August 2014, pp. 44–45.
82. "HR Execs Trade Notes on Human Resource Information Systems," *BNA Bulletin to Management* (December 3, 1998), p. 2. See also Ali Velshi, "Human Resources Information," *The Americas Intelligence Wire* (February 11, 2004).
83. Copyright Gary Dessler, PhD, 2011; based on information in Michelle Conlin, "Netflix: Flex to the Max," September 24, 2007, www.businessweek.com/magazine/content/07_39/b4051059.htm, accessed July 3, 2011; Robert J. Grossman, "Tough Love at Netflix," April 1, 2010, www.shrm.org/Publications/hrmagazine/EditorialContent/2010/0410/Pages/0410grossman3.aspx, accessed July 3, 2011; and David F. Larcker, Allan McCall, and Brian Tayan, "Equity on Demand: The Netflix Approach to Compensation," January 15, 2010, http://hbr.org/product/equity-on-demand-the-netflix-approach-to-compensat/an/CG19-PDF-ENG, accessed July 3, 2011.

APPENDIX A

HRCI PHR® and SPHR® Certification Body of Knowledge

ABOUT THE HR CERTIFICATION INSTITUTE PHR AND SPHR BODY OF KNOWLEDGE

The HRCI PHR (Professional in Human Resources) and SPHR (Senior Professional in Human Resources) exams are created using the Institute's PHR and SPHR Body of Knowledge, which outlines the responsibilities of, and knowledge needed by, today's HR professional. The PHR and SPHR Body of Knowledge is updated periodically to ensure it is consistent with current practices in the HR field. All questions appearing on the exams are linked to the Body of Knowledge's responsibility and knowledge statements. The HRCI organizes its PHR and SPHR Body of Knowledge into six functional areas (such as Functional Area 01: Business Management and Strategy), each listing various responsibilities and knowledge statements. For brevity, we list just the required knowledge items here, alongside the corresponding chapters in this book that address each particular knowledge area. To see the entire Body of Knowledge (including responsibilities), please go to certification-handbook at HRCI.org.[1]

You'll find two numbers after each functional area heading. The first number is the percentage of the PHR exam that is about that topic. The second number is the percentage of the SPHR exam that is about that topic.

Functional Area 01: Business Management and Strategy (PHR: 11%, SPHR: 30%)

Developing, contributing to and supporting the organization's mission, vision, values, strategic goals and objectives; formulating policies; guiding and leading the change process; and evaluating organizational effectiveness as an organizational leader.

ADDRESSED IN THIS BOOK IN CHAPTER(S):	KNOWLEDGE OF	
1, 3	01	The organization's mission, vision, values, business goals, objectives, plans and processes
2, 11, 14, 15, 16, and Know Your Employment Law features in Chapters 2–16	02	Legislative and regulatory processes
1, 3, strategic Hotel Paris cases in Chapters 3–18 with in-chapter call-outs, "strategic" chapter openers, and *Improving Performance: The Strategic Context* features in most chapters	03	Strategic planning process, design, implementation and evaluation
1, 3	04	Management functions, including planning, organizing, directing and controlling
12, 14	05	Corporate governance procedures and compliance (for example: Sarbanes-Oxley Act)
1, 3, 5	06	**SPHR only* Due diligence processes (for example: M&A, divestitures)

[1] The exact URL is https://www.hrci.org/docs/default-source/web-files/phrsphrbodyofknowledge.pdf?sfvrsn=2, accessed September 30, 2015.

1, 3, 5	07	**SPHR only* Transition techniques for corporate restructuring, M&A off-shoring and divestitures
	08	Elements of a cost-benefit analysis during the life cycle of the business (such as scenarios for growth, including expected, economic stressed and worst-case conditions) and the impact to net worth/earnings for short-, mid- and long-term horizons
3, 12, 14	09	Business concepts (for example: competitive advantage, organizational branding, business case development, corporate responsibility)
3, 14, 16, 18	10	Business processes (for example: operations, sales and marketing, data management)

Functional Area 02: Workforce Planning and Employment (PHR: 24%, SPHR: 17%)

Developing, implementing and evaluating sourcing, recruitment, hiring, orientation, succession planning, retention and organizational exit programs necessary to ensure a workforce's ability to achieve the organization's goals and objectives.

ADDRESSED IN THIS BOOK IN CHAPTER(S):		KNOWLEDGE OF
2, 4, 5, 6, 7, and Know Your Employment Law features in Chapters 1–17	11	Applicable federal laws and regulations related to workforce planning and employment activities (for example: Title VII, ADA, EEOC Uniform Guidelines on Employee Selection Procedures, Immigration Reform and Control Act)
3, 4, 5, 6, 7, and HR as a Profit Center features in Chapters 1–17	12	Methods to assess past and future staffing effectiveness (for example: costs per hire, selection ratios, adverse impact)
5	13	Recruitment sources (for example: employee referral, social networking/ social media) for targeting passive, semi-active and active candidates
5	14	Recruitment strategies
1, 5	15	Staffing alternatives (for example: outsourcing, job sharing, phased retirement)
3, 4, 5	16	Planning techniques (for example: succession planning, forecasting)
2, 6, 7	17	Reliability and validity of selection tests/tools/ methods
6	18	Use and interpretation of selection tests (for example: psychological/personality, cognitive, motor/physical assessments, performance, assessment center)
7	19	Interviewing techniques (for example: behavioral, situational, panel)
5, 10, 11, 12, 13, 14	20	Impact of compensation and benefits on recruitment and retention
5, 17, and HR Practices Around the Globe features in Chapters 4–17	21	**SPHR only* International HR and implications of global workforce for workforce planning and employment.
5, 10, 14	22	Voluntary and involuntary terminations, downsizing, restructuring and out-placement strategies and practices
4, 5, 6, 7, 8, 9, 10	23	Internal workforce assessment techniques (for example: skills testing, skills inventory, workforce demographic analysis)
3, 8, 10, 18	24	Employment policies, practices and procedures (for example: orientation, on-boarding and retention)
5	25	Employer marketing and branding techniques
15	26	Negotiation skills and techniques

Functional Area 03: Human Resource Development (PHR: 18%, SPHR: 19%)

Developing, implementing and evaluating activities and programs that address employee training and development, performance appraisal and talent and performance management to ensure that the knowledge, skills, abilities and performance of the workforce meet current and future organizational and individual needs.

ADDRESSED IN THIS BOOK IN CHAPTER(S):	KNOWLEDGE OF	
8 and in Know Your Employment Law features in this chapter and Chapters 2–18	27	Applicable federal laws and regulations related to HR development activities (for example: Title VII, ADA, Title 17 [Copyright law])
5, 8, 9, 10	28	Career development and leadership development theories and applications (for example: succession planning, dual career ladders)
8	29	Organizational development (OD) theories and applications
8	30	Training program development techniques to create general and specialized training programs
8	31	Facilitation techniques, instructional methods and program delivery mechanisms
4, 8	32	Task/process analysis
9	33	Performance appraisal methods (for example: instruments, ranking and rating scales)
9, 11, 12	34	Performance management methods (for example: goal setting, relationship to compensation, job placements/promotions)
HR Practices Around the Globe features in most chapters and Chapter 17 (Global HR)	35	**SPHR only* Applicable global issues (for example: international law, culture, local management approaches/practices, societal norms).
8	36	Techniques to assess training program effectiveness, including use of applicable metrics (for example: participant surveys, pre- and post-testing)
8, 10	37	Mentoring and executive coaching

Functional Area 04: Compensation and Benefits (PHR: 19%, SPHR: 13%)

Developing/selecting, implementing/administering and evaluating compensation and benefits programs for all employee groups in order to support the organization's goals, objectives and values.

ADDRESSED IN THIS BOOK IN CHAPTER(S):	KNOWLEDGE OF	
2, 11, 12, 13, 15, and Know Your Employment Law features	38	Applicable federal laws and regulations related to compensation, benefits, and tax (for example: FLSA, ERISA, FMLA, USERRA)
11, 12, 13	39	Compensation and benefits strategies
	40	Budgeting and accounting practices related to compensation and benefits
11	41	Job evaluation methods
11	42	Job pricing and pay structures
5, 11	43	External labor markets and/or economic factors
11, 12	44	Pay programs (for example: variable, merit)
11, 12, 13	45	**SPHR only* Executive compensation methods.
11, 12, 13, 14	46	Noncash compensation methods (for example: equity programs, noncash rewards)
13	47	Benefits programs (for example: health and welfare, retirement, Employee Assistance Programs [EAPs])
11, 12, 13, 17, and HR Around the Globe features	48	**SPHR only* International compensation laws and practices (for example: expatriate compensation, entitlements, choice of law codes).
11, 12, 13	49	Fiduciary responsibilities related to compensation and benefits

Functional Area 05: Employee and Labor Relations (PHR: 20%, SPHR: 14%)

Developing, implementing/administering and evaluating the workplace in order to maintain relationships and working conditions that balance employer/employee needs and rights in support of the organization's goals and objectives.

ADDRESSED IN THIS BOOK IN CHAPTER(S):	KNOWLEDGE OF	
2, 10, 14, 15	50	Applicable federal laws affecting employment in union and nonunion environments, such as laws regarding antidiscrimination policies, sexual harassment, labor relations, and privacy (for example: WARN Act, Title VII, NLRA)
14 (Maintaining Positive Employee Relations), 15	51	Techniques and tools for facilitating positive employee relations (for example: employee surveys, dispute/ conflict resolution, labor/management cooperative strategies)
3, 4, 14	52	Employee involvement strategies (for example: employee management committees, self-directed work teams, staff meetings)
10, 14	53	Individual employment rights issues and practices (for example: employment at will, negligent hiring, defamation)
9, 10, 14, 15	54	Workplace behavior issues/practices (for example: absenteeism and performance improvement)
15	55	Unfair labor practices
15	56	The collective bargaining process, strategies and concepts (for example: contract negotiation, costing and administration)
10, 14, including Know Your Employment Law features	57	Legal disciplinary procedures
11, 12, 13, 14	58	Positive employee relations strategies and non-monetary rewards
3, 14, 15	59	Techniques for conducting unbiased investigations
10, 14, 15, including Know Your Employment Law features	60	Legal termination procedures

Functional Area 06: Risk Management (PHR: 8%, SPHR: 7%)

Developing, implementing/administering and evaluating programs, procedures and policies in order to provide a safe, secure working environment and to protect the organization from potential liability.

ADDRESSED IN THIS BOOK IN CHAPTER(S):	KNOWLEDGE OF	
2, 14, 16, including Know Your Employment Law features	61	Applicable federal laws and regulations related to workplace health, safety, security and privacy (for example: OSHA, Drug-Free Workplace Act, ADA, HIPAA, Sarbanes-Oxley Act)
16	62	Occupational injury and illness prevention (safety) and compensation programs
16	63	Investigation procedures of workplace safety, health and security enforcement agencies
13, 16	64	Return to work procedures (for example: interactive dialog, job modification, accommodations)
16	65	Workplace safety risks (for example: trip hazards, blood-borne pathogens)
16	66	Workplace security risks (for example: theft, corporate espionage, sabotage)
14, 16	67	Potential violent behavior and workplace violence conditions

16	68	General health and safety practices (for example: evacuation, hazard communication, ergonomic evaluations)
16	69	Organizational incident and emergency response plans
14, 16	70	Internal investigation, monitoring and surveillance techniques
13, 14, 16	71	Employer/employee rights related to substance abuse
16, 18	72	Business continuity and disaster recovery plans (for example: data storage and backup, alternative work locations, procedures)
14, 16, 18	73	Data integrity techniques and technology (for example: data sharing, password usage, social engineering)
3, 4, 5, 18, and *Trends Shaping HR: Digital and Social Media and Improving Performance Through HRIS* features in Chapters 3–16	74	Technology and applications (for example: social media, monitoring software, biometrics)
	75	Financial management practices (for example: procurement policies, credit card policies and guidelines, expense policies)

CORE KNOWLEDGE

3, 8	76	Needs assessment and analysis
13, 18	77	Third-party or vendor selection, contract negotiation and management, including development of requests for proposals (RFPs)
9, 10, 14	78	Communication skills and strategies (for example: presentation, collaboration, sensitivity)
2, 4, 6, 9, 15, 16, 18, and Know Your Employment Law features in Chapters 2–16	79	Organizational documentation requirements to meet federal and state guidelines
8	80	Adult learning processes
8, 12, 13, 14	81	Motivation concepts and applications
8	82	Training techniques (for example: virtual, classroom, on-the-job)
	83	Leadership concepts and applications
	84	Project management concepts and applications
2 and The New Workforce features in most chapters	85	Diversity concepts and applications (for example: generational, cultural competency, learning styles)
14	86	Human relations concepts and applications (for example: emotional intelligence, organizational behavior)
1, 14	87	Ethical and professional standards
3–18 plus Trends Shaping HR: Digital and Social Media and Improving Performance Through HRIS features in most chapters	88	Technology to support HR activities (for example: HR Information Systems, employee self-service, E-learning, applicant tracking systems)
1, 3, and *HR as a Profit Center* features in most chapters	89	Qualitative and quantitative methods and tools for analysis, interpretation and decision-making purposes (for example: metrics and measurements, cost/benefit analysis, financial statement analysis)
8	90	Change management theory, methods and application
4	91	Job analysis and job description methods
4, 5, 18	92	Employee records management (for example: electronic/paper, retention, disposal)
3, 4, *Improving Performance: The Strategic Context* features in most chapters, a continuing strategic *Hotel Paris* case with in-chapter callouts in Chapters 3–16, and "strategic" chapter openers	93	Techniques for forecasting, planning and predicting the impact of HR activities and programs across functional areas

1, 4	94	Types of organizational structures (for example: matrix, hierarchy)
3	95	Environmental scanning concepts and applications (for example: Strengths, Weaknesses, Opportunities and Threats [SWOT], and Political, Economic, Social and Technological [PEST])
8, 14	96	Methods for assessing employee attitudes, opinions and satisfaction (for example: surveys, focus groups/panels)
	97	Budgeting, accounting and financial concepts
16	98	Risk-management techniques

APPENDIX B

About the Society for Human Resource Management (SHRM) Body of Competency and Knowledge™ Model and Certification Exams

SHRM recently introduced the SHRM Body of Competency and Knowledge™, and announced that it would offer its own certification exams for human resource management professionals.[1] In brief, the SHRM Body of Competency and Knowledge™ model is built on a foundation of 15 functional "HR Expertise (HR Knowledge)" areas such as talent acquisition and retention, which SHRM in turn divides into four main domains—people, workplace, organization, and strategy. The SHRM Body of Competency and Knowledge™ (SHRM) model then layers, on top of these 15 functional knowledge areas, eight HR manager required competencies, such as leadership and navigation, and ethical practice.

SECTION 1: SHRM COMPETENCIES:[2]

The SHRM exams test for these eight managerial competencies as well as for the items in its 18 functional HR knowledge functional areas. Many students will hopefully develop many of these eight competencies as part of their other experiences and courses (management, strategic management, quantitative methods, OB, etc.) as well as in their HR courses. However, Dessler, *Human Resource Management*, 15th ed., touches on many of these competencies. For some examples, see the following table:

Full List of SHRM Competencies	Examples of Pages in Dessler, *Human Resource Management*, 15th ed.
Leadership & Navigation	2, 255, Improving Performance: The Strategic Context features throughout book, as on pages 15–16.
Ethical Practice	19, 456–458, 460, 462.
Business Acumen	68–84, Improving Performance: The Strategic Context features throughout book.
Relationship Management	256, 290, 292–296, 311, 313, 314
Consultation	For example, Employee Engagement Guide for Managers features as on pages 84–87 illustrate how HR managers provide data-based guidance to change organizations.
Critical Evaluation	72–84, 100, 181, 260–264 (HR metrics and evidence-based HR and the scientific way of doing things), 100, 181, 260–264
Global & Cultural Effectiveness	Chapter 17, and Improving Performance: HR Practices Around the Globe features as on page 401 throughout book
Communication	Chapter 14, (employee relations tools), 454, 537

[1] http://shrm.org/certification/Documents/SHRM-BoCK-FINAL4.pdf

[2] Source: Competencies and HR Knowledge from The SHRM Body of Competency and Knowledge, http://shrm.org/certification/Documents/SHRM-BoCK-FINAL4.pdf, accessed February 13, 2015.

SECTION 2: SHRM HR FUNCTIONAL HR AREAS

SHRM's 15 functional areas each include required HR expertise (HR Knowledge) as well as HR manager responsibilities. For brevity, we list below just the required knowledge items, alongside the corresponding chapters in this book that address each particular knowledge area. To see the entire SHRM Body of Competency and Knowledge™ (including Responsibilities), please go to http://shrm.org/certification/Documents/SHRM-BoCK-FINAL4.pdf

DOMAIN 1: PEOPLE

Functional Area #1: Talent Acquisition & Retention

Definition: *Talent Acquisition & Retention* encompasses the activities involved in building and maintaining a workforce. HR demonstrates value by developing, implementing, and measuring the individual and organizational success of activities and programs for sourcing, recruiting, hiring, onboarding, orientation, and retention.

KNOWLEDGE TOPICS	ADDRESSED IN THIS BOOK IN CHAPTER(S):
• Employee lifecycle phases	10
• Employee retention techniques	10, 14
• Employer value proposition techniques	3 and Improving Performance: HR as a Profit Center features in many chapters
• Employment branding approaches	5
• External labor market PEST factors	5
• External and internal recruitment approaches	5
• Evaluation techniques	3, 9
• Formal assessment methods and tools	9
• Identification of bona fide occupational qualifications (BFOQs)	2, 4, 6
• Interviewing techniques	7, 9
• Job analysis, evaluation, and design of job descriptions	4
• Job offer contingencies	7
• Metrics (e.g., cost per hire, days to fill)	1, 3
• Recruitment approaches	5
• Selection approaches	6, 7
• Sourcing approaches	5
• Staffing projection approaches	5

Functional Area #2: Employee Engagement

Definition: *Employee Engagement* solidifies the connection among employee, manager, and the organization's mission, vision, values, and goals. HR demonstrates value by understanding and leveraging the employer employee relationship from both individual and organizational perspectives, developing effective strategies to address appropriate expectations for performance and behavior from employees at all levels.

KNOWLEDGE TOPICS	ADDRESSED IN THIS BOOK IN CHAPTER(S):
• Alternative dispute resolution techniques	2
• Analysis of organizational culture and climate	10, 14
• Coaching and counseling	9, 10

9	• Cognitive biases (e.g., halo bias, similar-to-me bias)
9, 10, 14	• Complaint resolution procedures
	• Conflict management theory and approaches
9, 14, 15	• Disciplinary procedures and approaches
10	• Employee lifecycle phases
5, 18	• Employee recordkeeping and retention
14	• Investigation techniques
1,3,7,9,10,12,14,17	• Management of people
3 and HR as a Profit Center features in many chapters	• Metrics
12	• Motivational theories
8, 14	• Organizational culture influences
8	• Organizational change management
9	• Performance management systems
9	• Principles of effective performance appraisal techniques (e.g., goal-setting, giving feedback)
14	• Principles of survey creation, administration, and evaluation
11, 12, 14	• Recognition approaches
14, 16	• Retaliation prevention approaches
4, 13, 14	• Workplace flexibility

Functional Area #3: Learning & Development

Definition: *Learning & Development* aligns organizational business needs with employees' competencies, knowledge, and skills, effectively closing the gap between them. HR demonstrates value by identifying and creating learning opportunities that increase employee capability and organizational knowledge.

ADDRESSED IN THIS BOOK IN CHAPTER(S):	KNOWLEDGE TOPICS
10	• Career development techniques
10	• Career management philosophies
8, 10	• Change management approaches
9, 10	• Coaching styles and approaches
1, 3–7	• Competency models
10	• Employee lifecycle phases
8	• Knowledge-sharing techniques
8	• Learning evaluation approaches
10	• Mentoring options
3 and HR as a Profit Center features in many chapters	• Metrics
8	• Organizational intervention design and implementation approaches
8	• Leadership development techniques
8	• Learning theories
8	• Needs assessment techniques (e.g., organizational, training)
8	• Skill and competency development approaches
8	• Training design and implementation (e.g., ADDIE model)
8	• Training and development techniques and solutions

Functional Area #4: Total Rewards

Definition: *Total Rewards* encompasses direct and indirect remuneration approaches that employers use to attract, recognize, and retain workers. HR demonstrates value by designing and administering systems and programs (e.g., base pay, benefits, incentive pay, leave, perquisites, retirement) that support recruitment and retention efforts.

ADDRESSED IN THIS BOOK IN CHAPTER(S):	KNOWLEDGE TOPICS
13	• Accounting practices and principles
	• Benefits (e.g., disability insurance, domestic partners, education, employee assistance programs, families, life insurance, retirement plans, unemployment insurance, wellness programs, workers' compensation)
10	• Employee lifecycle phases
5, 11	• External labor markets PEST factors
10, 11, 12	• Fiduciary responsibilities
11, 12, 13	• Income replacement programs
4	• Job analysis, job design, job descriptions
3	• Metrics
13	• Perquisites
11	• Pay practices, policies, approaches, systems, and issues (e.g., base pay, minimum wage determinations, pay compression, pay equity, pay increases, pay levels and banding), and special provisions (e.g., overtime)
11, 12, 13	• Remuneration data analysis (collecting, analyzing, making recommendations)
11, 12, 13	• Time-off plans and approaches (e.g., paid and unpaid leave, vacation/

DOMAIN 2: ORGANIZATION

Functional Area #5: Structure of the HR Function

Definition: *Structure of the HR Function* encompasses the people-related processes, theories, and activities used to deliver HR services that create and drive organizational effectiveness. HR demonstrates value by selecting the appropriate delivery model (e.g. Center of Excellence/COE, generalist, shared services) with an understanding of stakeholder needs and the impact of decisions on the overall workforce.

ADDRESSED IN THIS BOOK IN CHAPTER(S):	KNOWLEDGE TOPICS
3	• Balanced scorecard philosophy
1	• Centralization versus decentralization
1	• Defined approaches to roles and functions for generalists and specialists
3	• Due diligence methodologies
1, 4	• HR organizational structure and design
1	• HR functional integration approaches
15	• Negotiation and influence techniques
	• Stakeholder analysis techniques
1, 3, strategic Hotel Paris cases in Chapters 3–18 with in-chapter call-outs, "strategic" chapter openers, and *Improving Performance: The Strategic Context* features in most chapters	• Strategy design and implementation
1	• Structural model approaches to HR (e.g., Center of Excellence/COE, HR business partner, shared services)

Functional Area #6: Organizational Effectiveness & Development

Definition: *Organizational Effectiveness & Development* deals with the overall structure and functionality of the organization — that is, measuring the effectiveness and growth of people and processes from long- and short-term perspectives, and leading necessary organizational change initiatives. HR demonstrates value by aligning the organization's vision, mission, and goals with day-to-day Operational activities, including organizational design, development, performance measures, and standards.

ADDRESSED IN THIS BOOK IN CHAPTER(S):	KNOWLEDGE TOPICS
3	• Business solution and performance analysis
3	• Change and culture metrics
8	• Change management theories and approaches
	• Consulting techniques
4, 12	• Design approaches for a motivational work environment
4	• Design approaches for work activity
	• Group dynamics
14	• How employees learn culture
14	• How organizational cultures are created
	• Influence techniques
	• Knowledge management approaches (e.g., organizational storytelling techniques)
4, 5	• Labor supply and demand analysis
12	• Motivational theories
	• Organizational behavior theories
	• Organizational culture versus national culture
	• Organizational design structures and approaches (e.g., customer, functional, geographic, matrix, program)
8	• Organizational learning approaches
8	• Organizational needs analysis techniques
9	• Performance management theories, structures, and approaches
	• Project management approaches
4	• Roles and responsibilities (e.g., chain of command, span of control)
1, 3, strategic Hotel Paris cases inchapters 3–18 with in-chapter callouts, "strategic" chapter openers, and *Improving Performance: The Strategic Context* features in most chapters	• Strategic-tactical alignment
14	• Types of cultures (e.g., authoritarian, dominant cultures, mechanistic, participative, subcultures)
6, 7	• Understanding individual differences and Perceptions

Functional Area #7: Workforce Management

Definition: *Workforce Management* enables the organization to meet its talent needs and close critical skill gaps using data-driven processes (e.g., workforce planning, succession planning) that inform HR initiatives. HR demonstrates value by facilitating financial and operational growth, continuity, or stability.

ADDRESSED IN THIS BOOK IN CHAPTER(S):	KNOWLEDGE TOPICS
9, 10, 14	• Communication techniques
8	• Employee development techniques and approaches
8	• Knowledge management, retention, and transfer techniques
8	• Learning theories and philosophies
8	• Needs assessment techniques (e.g., organizational, training)
8	• Restructuring approaches
5, 8	• Succession planning techniques
5	• Workforce planning techniques and analyses (e.g., gap and solution, implementation and evaluation, supply and demand, workforce profile)

Functional Area #8: Employee Relations

Definition: *Employee Relations* refers to any dealings between the organization and its employees regarding the terms and conditions of employment. HR demonstrates value by ensuring that the appropriate framework, mindset, and practices are in place to embrace or react or respond to the employment relationship, including relationships with employee representatives.

ADDRESSED IN THIS BOOK IN CHAPTER(S):	KNOWLEDGE TOPICS
2	• Alternative dispute resolution techniques
15	• Causes of strikes, boycotts, and work stoppages
2, 11	• Child labor
15	• Collective bargaining process
9, 10, 14	• Communication approaches
15	• Contract administration techniques
15	• Contract negotiation approaches
10, 14	• Disciplinary techniques
11	• Standard workday
14 and Employee Engagement Guide for Managers features in Chapters 3–16	• Employee engagement approaches
	• Governmental labor parties and party relations by nation
10, 14	• Grievance, complaint, and conflict resolution techniques
15	• Industrial relations
	• International Labor Organization (ILO) core labor standards
15, 17	• International labor practices
14, 16	• Investigation techniques
	• Labor economics
	• Labor environments (e.g., pluralism, radicalism, unitarianism)
2, 14, 15, 16	• Labor rights
	• Living and fair wage concepts
	• People-management techniques
15	• Positive union/management relations approaches
11–14	• Recognition approaches
13	• Service award approaches
	• Social movement unionism, new unionism, proletariat

- Socialism, syndicalism, anarcho-syndicalism
- Strike actions, secondary actions, general strikes, sit-down strikes, work-to-rule — 15
- Survey techniques — 14
- Trade unions by nation — 15
- Trade union federations — 15
- Unfair labor practices — 15
- Union acceptance and avoidance approaches — 15
- Union attractiveness — 15
- Union membership — 15
- Union structures
- Unionized labor history — 15
- Works councils structures and approaches — 15, 17
- World Trade Organization — 17

Functional Area #9: Technology & Data

Definition: *Technology & Data* deals with the use of tools, technologies, and systems that support the gathering, analysis, and reporting of workforce information, as well as effective and efficient collaboration and communication throughout the organization. HR demonstrates value by developing knowledge about technology uses, trends, and innovations applicable to HR's strategic goals.

KNOWLEDGE TOPICS	ADDRESSED IN THIS BOOK IN CHAPTER(S):
Business process integration approaches	4
Data analytic techniques	3 and Trends Shaping HR: Digital and Social Media features in many chapters
Data management protection approaches	14, 16
Electronic recordkeeping approaches	
Electronic signature acceptance	
HR information systems and sources	18 and Improving Performance Through HRIS features in many chapters
HR management and information system design	18 and Improving Performance Through HRIS features in many chapters
Information management theory	18 and Improving Performance Through HRIS features in many chapters
Procurement approaches	13, 18
Product development	
Project management theories	
Social media practices and usage	5 and Trends Shaping HR: Digital and Social Media features in most chapters
Systems integration approaches	18
Technology use policies and practices	

DOMAIN 3: WORKPLACE

Functional Area #10: HR in the Global Context

Definition: *HR in the Global Context* focuses on organizational growth and workforce-related issues and impacts, viewed from domestic, multinational, transnational, and global perspectives. HR demonstrates value by understanding how global PEST factors influence business decisions, and by applying this knowledge to day-to-day HR activities, policy creation, and business solution recommendations.

ADDRESSED IN THIS BOOK IN CHAPTER(S):	KNOWLEDGE TOPICS
17	• Creating a global organizational culture
17	• Cross-border HR management techniques
17	• Cultural models (e.g., Hall, Hofstede, Schein, Trompenaars)
2, 17	• Global discrimination prevention practices
17	• Global legal systems (e.g., different nations' approaches to government-mandated, government provided, and voluntary benefits, extra-territoriality of laws and legislation)
17,3, and Improving Performance: HR Around the Globe features in many chapters	• Global mindset techniques (e.g., communication barrier removal, cultural awareness training and assimilation, understanding PEST factors)
17 and Improving Performance: HR Around the Globe features	• Global trends in benefits, compensation, diversity and inclusion, employment laws, ethics and sustainability, labor markets, labor relations, safety and security, staffing management
17	• Managing international assignments (e.g., approaches and trends, effective performance, compensation adjustments, employee repatriation)
1, 5, 17	• Moving work (e.g., co-sourcing, near-shoring, offshoring, on-shoring)
11,17	• Taxation approaches
	• Totalization agreements
5, 17	• Visa and work permit considerations

Functional Area #11: Diversity & Inclusion

Definition: *Diversity & Inclusion* encompasses the qualities, life experiences, personalities, education, skills, competencies, and collaboration of the many different types of people who are necessary to propel an organization to success. HR demonstrates value by creating opportunities that leverage the human experience to address organizational needs or solve issues on a global basis.

ADDRESSED IN THIS BOOK IN CHAPTER(S):	KNOWLEDGE TOPICS
1, 2, 5, and The New Workforce features in many chapters	• Approaches to a multi-generational workforce
2, 17, 18, and The New Workforce features in many chapters	• Developing cross-cultural relationships
2, 14	• Effective approaches to building trust and relationships
	• Emotional intelligence
2, 10, 17, and The New Workforce features	• Glass-ceiling prevention
	• High- and low-context cultures
2	• Inclusive leadership
	• Influence of the 4 T's (travel, training, transfers, and teams)
	• Intercultural wisdom
2, 4–13, 16, and The New Workforce features	• Issues related to disability, ethnicity, gender, language, race, sexual orientation
17 and The New Workforce features	• Level of global acceptance of diversity (e.g., disability, ethnicity, gender, language, race, religion, sexual orientation)
	• Mindful communication
2	• Religious influences and accommodation
2, 17, and The New Workforce features	• Techniques for cultural awareness and respect

Functional Area #12: Risk Management

Definition: *Risk management* is the identification, assessment, and prioritization of risks (defined in ISO 31000 as the effect of uncertainty on objectives), followed by the coordinated and economical application of resources to minimize, monitor, and control the probability and/or impact of unfortunate events or to maximize the realization of opportunities.

ADDRESSED IN THIS BOOK IN CHAPTER(S):	KNOWLEDGE TOPICS
16	• Business recovery planning
16	• Continuity of operations planning
16	• Corporate espionage and sabotage prevention
16	• Data integrity mechanisms and practices
	• Data management protection and disclosure approaches
13, 16	• Drug prevention
16, 17	• Duty of care
16	• Emergency/incident response plans
16	• Health and safety practices and procedures
18 and Improving Performance Through HRIS features	• Information management theory
16	• Kidnapping and ransom prevention
16	• Natural disaster and severe weather emergency preparation
16	• Occupational injury and illness prevention, compensation, and accommodations
16	• Public health preparedness and response
16	• Safety auditing techniques
16	• Terrorism prevention and responses
16	• Theft and fraud prevention approaches
14, 16	• Whistleblower protection approaches
16	• Workplace incident investigations
16	• Workplace safety risks and hazards
14, 16	• Workplace violence prevention techniques

Functional Area #13: Corporate Social Responsibility

Definition: *Corporate Social Responsibility* represents the organization's commitment to operate its business in an ethical and sustainable manner. HR demonstrates value by understanding the societal impacts to business decisions and using this insight to improve the quality of life for the community—people, organization, and planet—through philanthropy, ethics and governance, and environmentally sound practices, respectively.

ADDRESSED IN THIS BOOK IN CHAPTER(S):	KNOWLEDGE TOPICS
14, 17	• Anti-bribery approaches
	• Caux principles
	• Charitable/community giving approaches
14	• Code of conduct development

- Community inclusion approaches
- Compliance program evaluation (2, 3, 9, 15, 16, 17, 18)
- Confidentiality measures and approaches (2, 6, 10, 11, 13, 18)
- Conflicts-of-interest avoidance (10, 13, 14, 15)
- Corporate citizenship and governance programs and legislation
- Corporate philanthropy approaches
- Corporate social responsibility best practices (14)
- Economic trend analysis (3, 5)
- Ethical decision-making in a global context (14, 17)
- Ethical employee management practices (14)
- Investigation techniques (14)
- ISO standards (18)
- Key performance indicators (1, 3, and Improving Performance: HR as a Profit Center features)
- PEST factors (3)
- Privacy concerns (14)
- Social auditing techniques
- Social media usage (5 and Trends Shaping HR: Digital and Social Media features in most chapters)
- Transparent decision making
- Volunteer programming

Functional Area #14: U.S. Employment Law & Regulations

Important Note: This Area is applicable only to examinees testing within the United States; examinees outside the U.S. will not be tested on it.

Definition: *U.S. Employment Law & Regulations* deals with the knowledge and application of all relevant laws and regulations in the United States relating to employment. These provisions set the parameters and limitations for each HR Functional Area and for organizations overall. HR demonstrates value by ensuring the organization's compliance with laws and regulations domestically and globally (including extraterritorially).

KNOWLEDGE TOPICS

Listed below are six broad categories of U.S. laws, regulations, and cases relating to employment, together with examples. (This is *not* an exhaustive list of categories *or* examples.) Local laws and regulations, such as those on the state or municipal level, are not included.

ADDRESSED IN THIS BOOK IN CHAPTER(S):

- ***Compensation*** *Examples*: Employee Retirement Income Security Act of 1974 (ERISA); Fair Labor Standards Act of 1938 (FLSA; Wage-Hour Bill; Wagner-Connery Wages and Hours Act) and amendments; Equal Pay Act of 1963 (amending FLSA); Lilly Ledbetter Fair Pay Act of 2009; *Ledbetter v. Goodyear Tire & Rubber Co.* (2007). (2, 11, 12, 13, and Know Your Employment Law features in most chapters)
- ***Employee relations*** *Examples*: Labor Management Relations Act of 1947 (LMRA; Taft-Hartley Act); National Labor Relations Act of 1935 (NLRA; Wagner Act; Wagner-Connery Labor Relations Act); *NLRB v. Weingarten* (1975); *Lechmere, Inc. v. NLRB* (1992). (2, 3, 14, 15, and Know Your Employment Law features in most chapters)
- ***Equal employment opportunity*** *Examples*: Age Discrimination in Employment Act of 1967 (ADEA) and amendments; Americans with Disabilities Act of 1990 (ADA) and ADA Amendments Act of 2008; Civil Rights Acts; Equal (2, 4, 5, 6, 7, 8, 9, 10, and Know Your Employment Law features in most chapters)

Employment Opportunity Act of 1972 (amending Civil Rights Act); Uniform Guidelines on Employee Selection Procedures (1978) (29 CFR Part 1607); *Griggs v. Duke Power Co.* (1971); *Phillips v. Martin Marietta Corp.* (1971).

2, 13,16, and Know Your Employment Law features in most chapters

- ***Job safety and health*** *Examples*: Drug-Free Workplace Act of 1988; Guidelines on Sexual Harassment; Occupational Safety and Health Act of 1970.

2, 11,13, and Know Your Employment Law features in most chapters

- ***Leave and benefits*** *Examples*: Family and Medical Leave Act of 1993 (FMLA; expanded 2008, 2010); Patient Protection and Affordable Care Act (PPACA; ACA; "Obamacare"); *National Federation of Independent Business v. Sebelius* (2012).

2, 4–16, and Know Your Employment Law features in most chapters

- ***Miscellaneous protection laws*** *Examples*: Employee Polygraph Protection Act of 1988; Genetic Information Nondiscrimination Act of 2008 (GINA).

DOMAIN 4: STRATEGY

Functional Area #15: Business & HR Strategy

Definition: *Business & HR Strategy* involves organizational planning to achieve success and create value for stakeholders. HR demonstrates value by contributing its perspective and expertise to development of the enterprise strategy, and by developing, implementing, and evaluating an HR strategy aligned with the organization's goals, values, and tactics, as defined in the enterprise strategy.

ADDRESSED IN THIS BOOK IN CHAPTER(S):	KNOWLEDGE TOPICS
1, 3, strategic Hotel Paris cases in chapters 3–18, with in-chapter callouts, "strategic" chapter openers, and *Improving Performance: The Strategic Context* features in most chapters	• Approaches for linking organizational and HR strategies
3	• Balanced scorecard utilization
3, 5	• Business intelligence factors
3, 8	• Change management techniques
3	• Competitive analysis techniques
8, 13, 14	• Conflict management techniques
3	• Due diligence techniques
7, 8, 9, 10, 14, 15	• Effective communication techniques
1, 14	• Ethical decision-making framework
3, 9	• Goal-setting approaches
18 and Improving Performance Through HRIS features in most chapters	• HR systems integration approaches
4, 5, 11, 15	• Labor market analysis
	• Leadership theories, approaches, and evaluation
	• Leading and lagging indicators
1, 3	• Mission, vision, and values creation
1, 3, strategic Hotel Paris cases in Chapters 3–18 with in-chapter call-outs, "strategic" chapter openers, and *Improving Performance: The Strategic Context* features in most chapters	• Organizational growth strategies, evolution stages, and success factors
	• Project management methods

3, 14	• Quality assurance techniques
1, 3, strategic Hotel Paris cases in Chapters 3–18 with in-chapter call-outs, "strategic" chapter openers, and *Improving Performance: The Strategic Context* features in most chapters	• Strategic management considerations
3	• Strategic planning stages (i.e., strategy formulation, development, implementation, and evaluation)
3	• PEST factors
3	• SWOT and environmental scanning techniques

APPENDIX C

Comprehensive Cases

BANDAG AUTOMOTIVE*

Jim Bandag took over his family's auto supply business in 2012, after helping his father, who founded the business, run it for about 10 years. Based in Illinois, Bandag employs about 300 people, and distributes auto supplies (replacement mufflers, bulbs, engine parts, and so on) through two divisions, one that supplies service stations and repair shops, and a second that sells retail auto supplies through five "Bandag Automotive" auto supply stores.

Jim's father, and now Jim, have always endeavored to keep Bandag's organization chart as simple as possible. The company has a full-time controller, managers for each of the five stores, a manager who oversees the distribution division, and Jim Bandag's executive assistant. Jim (along with his father, working part-time) handles marketing and sales.

Jim's executive assistant administers the firm's day-today human resource management tasks, but the company outsources most HR activities to others, including an employment agency that does its recruiting and screening, a benefits firm that administers its 401(k) plan, and a payroll service that handles its paychecks. Bandag's human resource management systems consist almost entirely of standardized HR forms purchased from an HR supplies company. These include forms such as application and performance appraisal forms, as well as an "honesty" test Bandag uses to screen the staff that works in the five stores. The company performs informal salary surveys to see what other companies in the area are paying for similar positions, and use these results for awarding annual merit increases (which in fact are more accurately cost-of-living adjustments).

Jim's father took a fairly paternal approach to the business. He often walked around speaking with his employees, finding out what their problems were, and even helping them out with an occasional loan—for instance, when he discovered that one of their children was sick, or for part of a new home down payment. Jim, on the other hand, tends to be more abrupt, and does not enjoy the same warm relationship with the employees as did his father. Jim is not unfair or dictatorial. He's just very focused on improving Bandag's financial performance, and so all his decisions, including his HR-related decisions, generally come down to cutting costs. For example, his knee-jerk reaction is usually to offer fewer days off rather than more, fewer benefits rather than more, and to be less flexible when an employee needs, for instance, a few extra days off because a child is sick.

It's therefore perhaps not surprising that over the past few years Bandag's sales and profits have increased markedly, but that the firm has found itself increasingly enmeshed in HR/equal employment–type issues. Indeed, Jim now finds himself spending a day or two a week addressing HR problems. For example, Henry Jaques, an employee at one of the stores, came to Jim's executive assistant and told her he was "irate" about his recent firing and was probably going to sue. Henry's store manager stated on his last performance appraisal that Henry did the technical aspects of his job well, but that he had "serious problems interacting with his coworkers." He was continually arguing with them, and complaining to the store manager about working conditions. The store manager had told Jim that he had to fire Henry because he was making "the whole place poisonous,"

*© Gary Dessler, PhD.

and that (although he felt sorry because he'd heard rumors that Henry suffered from some mental illness) he felt he had to go. Jim approved the dismissal.

Gavin was another problem. Gavin had worked for Bandag for 10 years, the last two as manager of one of the company's five stores. Right after Jim Bandag took over, Gavin told him he had to take a Family and Medical Leave Act medical leave to have hip surgery, and Jim approved the leave. When Gavin returned from leave, Jim told him that his position had been eliminated. Bandag had decided to close his store and open a new, larger store across from a shopping center about a mile away, and had appointed a new manager in Gavin's absence. However, the company did give Gavin a (nonmanagerial) position in the new store as a counter salesperson, at the same salary and with the same benefits as he had before. Even so, "This job is not similar to my old one," Gavin insisted. "It doesn't have nearly as much prestige." His contention is that the FMLA requires that the company bring him back in the same or equivalent position, and that this means a supervisory position, similar to what he had before he went on leave. Jim said no, and they seem to be heading toward litigation.

In another sign of the times at Bandag, the company's controller, Miriam, who had been with the company for about six years, went on pregnancy leave for 12 weeks in 2012 (also under the FMLA), and then received an additional three weeks' leave under Bandag's extended illness days program. Four weeks after she came back, she asked Jim Bandag if she could arrange to work fewer hours per week, and spend about a day per week working out of her home. He refused, and about two months later fired her. Jim Bandag said, "I'm sorry, it's not anything to do with your pregnancy-related requests, but we've got ample reasons to discharge you—your monthly budgets have been several days late, and we've got proof you may have forged documents." She replied, "I don't care what you say your reasons are; you're really firing me because of my pregnancy, and that's illegal."

Jim felt he was on safe ground as far as defending the company for these actions, although he didn't look forward to spending the time and money that he knew it would take to fight each. However, what he learned over lunch from a colleague undermined his confidence about another case that Jim had been sure would be a "slam dunk" for his company. Jim was explaining to his friend that one of Bandag's truck maintenance service people had applied for a job driving one of Bandag's distribution department trucks, and that Jim had turned him down because the worker was deaf. Jim (whose wife has occasionally said of him, "No one has ever accused Jim of being politically correct") was mentioning to his friend the apparent absurdity of a deaf person asking to be a truck delivery person. His friend, who happens to work for UPS, pointed out that the U.S. Court of Appeals for the Ninth Circuit had recently decided that UPS had violated the Americans with Disabilities Act by refusing to consider deaf workers for jobs driving the company's smaller vehicles.

Although Jim's father is semiretired, the sudden uptick in the frequency of such EEO-type issues troubled him, particularly after so many years of labor peace. However, he's not sure what to do about it. Having handed over the reins of the company to his son, he was loath to inject himself back into the company's operational decision making. On the other hand, he was afraid that in the short run these issues were going to drain a great deal of Jim's time and resources, and that in the long run they might be a sign of things to come, with problems like these eventually overwhelming Bandag Automotive. He comes to you, who he knows consults in human resource management, and asks you the following questions.

Questions

1. Given Bandag Automotive's size, and anything else you know about it, should we reorganize the human resource management function, and if so, why and how?
2. What, if anything, would you do to change and/or improve upon the current HR systems, forms, and practices that we now use?

3. Do you think that the employee whom Jim fired for creating what the manager called a poisonous relationship has a legitimate claim against us, and if so, why and what should we do about it?
4. Is it true that we really had to put Gavin back into an equivalent position, or was it adequate to just bring him back into a job at the same salary, bonuses, and benefits as he had before his leave?
5. Miriam, the controller, is basically claiming that the company is retaliating against her for being pregnant, and that the fact that we raised performance issues was just a smokescreen. Do you think the EEOC and/or courts would agree with her, and, in any case, what should we do now?
6. An employee who is deaf has asked us to be one of our delivery people and we turned him down. He's now threatening to sue. What should we do, and why?
7. In the previous 10 years, we've had only one equal employment complaint, and now in the last few years we've had four or five. What should I do about it? Why?

Based generally on actual facts, but Bandag is a fictitious company. Bandag source notes: "The Problem Employee: Discipline or Accommodation?" *Monday Business Briefing*, March 8, 2005; "Employee Says Change in Duties after Leave Violates FMLA," *BNA Bulletin to Management*, January 16, 2007, p. 24; "Manager Fired Days After Announcing Pregnancy," *BNA Bulletin to Management*, January 2, 2007, p. 8; "Ninth Circuit Rules UPS Violated ADA by Barring Deaf Workers from Driving Jobs," *BNA Bulletin to Management*, October 17, 2006, p. 329.

ANGELO'S PIZZA*

Angelo Camero was brought up in the Bronx, New York, and basically always wanted to be in the pizza store business. As a youngster, he would sometimes spend hours at the local pizza store, watching the owner knead the pizza dough, flatten it into a large circular crust, fling it up, and then spread on tomato sauce in larger and larger loops. After graduating from college as a marketing major, he made a beeline back to the Bronx, where he opened his first Angelo's Pizza store, emphasizing its clean, bright interior; its crisp green, red, and white sign; and his all-natural, fresh ingredients. Within five years, Angelo's store was a success, and he had opened three other stores and was considering franchising his concept.

Eager as he was to expand, his four years in business school had taught him the difference between being an entrepreneur and being a manager. As an entrepreneur/small business owner, he knew he had the distinct advantage of being able to personally run the whole operation himself. With just one store and a handful of employees, he could make every decision and watch the cash register, check in the new supplies, oversee the takeout, and personally supervise the service.

When he expanded to three stores, things started getting challenging. He hired managers for the two new stores (both of whom had worked for him at his first store for several years) and gave them only minimal "how to run a store"–type training, on the assumption that, having worked with him for several years, they already knew pretty much everything they needed to know about running a store. However, he was already experiencing human resource management problems, and he knew there was no way he could expand the number of stores he owned, or (certainly) contemplate franchising his idea, unless he had a system in place that he could clone in each new store to provide the managers (or the franchisees) with the necessary management knowledge and expertise to run their stores. Angelo had no training program in place for teaching his store managers how to run their stores. He simply (erroneously, as it turned out) assumed that by working with him they would learn how to do things on the job. Since Angelo had no system in place, the new managers were, in a way, starting off below zero when it came to how to manage a store.

*© Gary Dessler, PhD.

There were several issues that particularly concerned Angelo. Finding and hiring good employees was number one. He'd read the new National Small Business Poll from the National Federation of Independent Business Education Foundation. It found that 71% of small business owners believed that finding qualified employees was "hard." Furthermore, "the search for qualified employees will grow more difficult as demographic and education factors" continue to make it more difficult to find employees. Similarly, reading the *Kiplinger Letter* one day, he noticed that just about every type of business couldn't find enough good employees to hire. Small firms were particularly in jeopardy; the *Letter* said that giant firms can outsource many (particularly entry-level) jobs abroad, and larger companies can also afford to pay better benefits and to train their employees. Small firms rarely have the resources or the economies of scale to allow outsourcing or to install the big training programs that would enable them to take untrained new employees and turn them into skilled ones.

Although finding enough employees was his biggest problem, finding enough honest ones scared him even more. Angelo recalled from one of his business school courses that companies in the United States are losing a total of well over $400 billion a year in employee theft. As a rough approximation, that works out to about $9 per employee per day and about $12,000 lost annually for a typical company. Furthermore, it was small companies like Angelo's that were particularly in the crosshairs, because companies with fewer than 100 employees are particularly prone to employee theft. Why are small firms particularly vulnerable? Perhaps they lack experience dealing with the problem. More importantly: Small firms are more likely to have a single person doing several jobs, such as ordering supplies and paying the delivery person. This undercuts the checks and balances managers often strive for to control theft. Furthermore, the risk of stealing goes up dramatically when the business is largely based on cash. In a pizza store, many people come in and buy just one or two slices and a cola for lunch, and almost all pay with cash, not credit cards.

And, Angelo was not just worried about someone stealing cash. They can steal your whole business idea, something he learned from painful experience. He had been planning to open a store in what he thought would be a particularly good location, and was thinking of having one of his current employees manage the store. Instead, it turned out that this employee was, in a manner of speaking, stealing Angelo's brain: what Angelo knew about customers, suppliers, where to buy pizza dough, where to buy tomato sauce, how much everything should cost, how to furnish the store, where to buy ovens, store layout—everything. This employee soon quit and opened up his own pizza store, not far from where Angelo had planned to open his new store.

That he was having trouble hiring good employees, there was no doubt. The restaurant business is particularly brutal when it comes to turnover. Many restaurants turn over their employees at a rate of 200% to 300% per year—so every year, each position might have a series of two to three employees filling it. As Angelo said, "I was losing two to three employees a month," adding, "We're a high-volume store, and while we should have about six employees per store [to fill all the hours in a week], we were down to only three or four, so my managers and I were really under the gun."

The problem was bad at the hourly employee level: "We were churning a lot at the hourly level," said Angelo. "Applicants would come in, my managers or I would hire them and not spend much time training them, and the good ones would leave in frustration after a few weeks, while often it was the bad ones who'd stay behind." But in the last two years, Angelo's three company-owned stores also went through a total of three store managers—"They were just blowing through the door," as Angelo put it, in part because, without good employees, their workday was brutal. As a rule, when a small business owner or manager can't find enough employees (or an employee doesn't show up for work), about 80% of the time the owner or manager does the job himself or herself. So, these managers often ended up working seven days a week, 10 to 12 hours a day, and many just burned out in the end. One night, working three jobs himself with customers leaving in anger, Angelo decided he'd never just hire someone because he was desperate again, but would start doing his hiring more rationally.

Angelo knew he should have a more formal screening process. As he said, "If there's been a lesson learned, it's much better to spend time up front screening out candidates who don't fit than to hire them and have to put up with their ineffectiveness." He also knew that he could identify many of the traits that his employees needed. For example, he knew that not everyone has the temperament to be a waiter (he has a small pizza/Italian restaurant in the back of his main store). As Angelo said, "I've seen personalities that were off the charts in assertiveness or overly introverted, traits that obviously don't make a good fit for a waiter or waitress."

As a local business, Angelo recruits by placing help wanted ads in two local newspapers, and he's been "shocked" at some of the responses and experiences he's had in response to the ads. Many of the applicants left voicemail messages (Angelo or the other workers in the store were too busy to answer), and some applicants Angelo "just axed" on the assumption that people without good telephone manners wouldn't have very good manners in the store, either. He also quickly learned that he had to throw out a very wide net, even if hiring only one or two people. Many people, as noted, he eliminated from consideration because of the messages they left, and about half the people he scheduled to come in for interviews didn't show up. He'd taken courses in human resource management, so (as he said) "I should know better," but he hired people based almost exclusively on a single interview (he occasionally made a feeble attempt to check references). In total, his HR approach was obviously not working. It wasn't producing enough good recruits, and the people he did hire were often problematic.

What was he looking for? Service-oriented courteous people, for one. For example, he'd hired one employee who used profanity several times, including once in front of a customer. On that employee's third day, Angelo had to tell her, "I think Angelo's isn't the right place for you," and he fired her. As Angelo said, "I felt bad, but also knew that everything I have is on the line for this business, so I wasn't going to let anyone run this business down." Angelo wants reliable people (who'll show up on time), honest people, and people who are flexible about switching jobs and hours as required. He calls his management style "trust and track." "I coach them and give them goals, and then carefully track results."

Angelo's Pizza business has only the most rudimentary human resource management system. Angelo bought several application forms at a local Office Depot, and rarely uses other forms of any sort. He uses his personal accountant for reviewing the company's books, and Angelo himself computes each employee's paycheck at the end of the week and writes the checks. Training is entirely on-the-job. Angelo personally trained each of his employees. For those employees who go on to be store managers, he assumes that they are training their own employees the way that Angelo trained them (for better or worse, as it turns out). Angelo pays "a bit above" prevailing wage rates (judging by other help wanted ads), but probably not enough to make a significant difference in the quality of employees whom he attracts. If you asked Angelo what his reputation is as an employer, Angelo, being a candid and forthright person, would probably tell you that he is a supportive but hard-nosed employer who treats people fairly, but whose business reputation may suffer from disorganization stemming from inadequate organization and training. He approaches you to ask you several questions.

Questions

8. My strategy is to (hopefully) expand the number of stores and eventually franchise, while focusing on serving only high-quality fresh ingredients. What are three specific human resource management implications of my strategy (including specific policies and practices)?
9. Identify and briefly discuss five specific human resource management errors that I'm currently making.

10. Develop a structured interview form that we can use for hiring (1) store managers, (2) wait staff, and (3) counter people/pizza makers.
11. Based on what you know about Angelo's, and what you know from having visited pizza restaurants, write a one-page outline showing specifically how you think Angelo's should go about selecting employees.

Based generally on actual facts, but Angelo's Pizza is a fictitious company. Angelo's Pizza source notes: Dino Berta, "People Problems: Keep Hiring from Becoming a Crying Game," *Nation's Business News*, 36, no. 20, May 20, 2002, pp. 72–74; Ellen Lyon, "Hiring, Personnel Problems Can Challenge Entrepreneurs," *Patriot-News*, October 12, 2004; Rose Robin Pedone, "Businesses' $400 Billion Theft Problem," *Long Island Business News*, 27, July 6, 1998, pp. 1B–2B; "Survey Shows Small-Business Problems with Hiring, Internet," *Providence Business News*, 16, September 10, 2001, pp. 1B; "Finding Good Workers Is Posing a Big Problem as Hiring Picks Up," *Kiplinger Letter*, 81, February 13, 2004; Ian Mount, "A Pizzeria Owner Learns the Value of Watching the Books," *New York Times*, October 25, 2012, p. B8.

GOOGLE*

Fortune magazine named Google the best of the 100 best companies to work for, and there is little doubt why. Among the benefits it offers are free shuttles equipped with Wi-Fi to pick up and drop off employees from San Francisco Bay Area locations, unlimited sick days, annual all-expense-paid ski trips, free gourmet meals, five on-site free doctors, $2,000 bonuses for referring a new hire, free flu shots, a giant lap pool, on-site oil changes, on-site car washes, volleyball courts, TGIF parties, free on-site washers and dryers (with free detergent), Ping-Pong and foosball tables, and free famous people lectures. For many people, it's the gourmet meals and snacks that make Google stand out. For example, human resources director Stacey Sullivan loves the Irish oatmeal with fresh berries at the company's Plymouth Rock Cafe, near Google's "people operations" group. "I sometimes dream about it," she says. Engineer Jan Fitzpatrick loves the raw bar at Google's Tapis restaurant, down the road on the Google campus. Then, of course, there are the stock options—each new employee gets about 1,200 options to buy Google shares (recently worth about $480 per share). In fact, dozens of early Google employees ("Googlers") are already multimillionaires thanks to Google stock. The recession that began back in 2008 did prompt Google and other firms to cut back on some of these benefits (cafeteria hours are shorter today, for instance), but Google still pretty much leads the benefits pack.

For their part, Googlers share certain traits. They tend to be brilliant, team oriented (teamwork is the norm, especially for big projects), and driven. *Fortune* describes them as people who "almost universally" see themselves as the most interesting people on the planet, and who are happy-go-lucky on the outside, but type A—highly intense and goal directed—on the inside. They're also super-hardworking (which makes sense, since it's not unusual for engineers to be in the hallways at 3 A.M. debating some new mathematical solution to a Google search problem). They're so team oriented that when working on projects, it's not unusual for Google team members to give up their larger, more spacious offices and to crowd into a small conference room, where they can "get things done." Historically, Googlers generally graduate with great grades from the best universities, including Stanford, Harvard, and MIT. For many years, Google wouldn't even consider hiring someone with less than a 3.7 average—while also probing deeply into the why behind any B grades. Google also doesn't hire lone wolves, but wants people who work together and people who also have diverse interests (narrow interests or skills are a turnoff at Google). Google also wants people with growth potential. The company is expanding so fast that it needs to hire people who are capable of being promoted five or six times—it's only, the company says, by hiring such overqualified people that it can be sure that the employees will be able to keep up as Google and their own departments expand.

*© Gary Dessler, PhD.

The starting salaries are highly competitive. Experienced engineers start at about $130,000 a year (plus about 1,200 shares of stock options, as noted), and new MBAs can expect between $80,000 and $120,000 per year (with smaller option grants). Most recently, Google had about 10,000 staff members, up from its beginnings with just three employees in a rented garage.

Of course, in a company that's grown from 3 employees to 10,000 and from zero value to hundreds of billions of dollars, it may be quibbling to talk about "problems," but there's no doubt that such rapid growth does confront Google's management, and particularly its "people operations" group, with some big challenges. Let's look at these.

For one, Google, as noted earlier, is a 24-hour operation, and with engineers and others frequently pulling all-nighters to complete their projects, the company needs to provide a package of services and financial benefits that supports that kind of lifestyle, and that helps its employees maintain an acceptable work–life balance.

As another challenge, Google's enormous financial success is a two-edged sword. Although Google usually wins the recruitment race when it comes to competing for new employees against competitors like Microsoft or Yahoo!, Google does need some way to stem a rising tide of retirements. Most Googlers are still in their 20s and 30s, but many have become so wealthy from their Google stock options that they can afford to retire. One 27-year-old engineer received a million-dollar founder's award for her work on the program for searching desktop computers, and wouldn't think of leaving "except to start her own company." Similarly, a former engineering vice president retired (with his Google stock profits) to pursue his love of astronomy. The engineer who dreamed up Gmail recently retired (at the age of 30).

Another challenge is that the work involves not only long hours but can also be very tense. Google is a very numbers-oriented environment. For example, consider a typical weekly Google user interface design meeting. Marisa Meyer, the company's vice president of search products and user experience, runs the meeting, where her employees work out the look and feel of Google's products. Seated around a conference table are about a dozen Googlers, tapping on laptops. During the 2-hour meeting, Meyer needs to evaluate various design proposals, ranging from minor tweaks to a new product's entire layout. She's previously given each presentation an allotted amount of time, and a large digital clock on the wall ticks off the seconds. The presenters must quickly present their ideas, but also handle questions such as "what do users do if the tab is moved from the side of the page to the top?" Furthermore, it's all about the numbers—no one at Google would ever say, for instance, "the tab looks better in red"—you need to prove your point. Presenters must come armed with usability experiment results, showing, for instance, that a certain percentage preferred red or some other color. While the presenters are answering these questions as quickly as possible, the digital clock is ticking, and when it hits the allotted time, the presentation must end, and the next team steps up to present. It is a tough and tense environment, and Googlers must have done their homework.

Growth can also undermine the "outlaw band that's changing the world" culture that fostered the services that made Google famous. Even cofounder Sergi Brin agrees that Google risks becoming less "zany" as it grows. To paraphrase one of its top managers, the hard part of any business is keeping that original innovative, small business feel even as the company grows.

Creating the right culture is especially challenging now that Google is truly global. For example, Google works hard to provide the same financial and service benefits every place it does business around the world, but it can't exactly match its benefits in every country because of international laws and international taxation issues. Offering the same benefits everywhere is more important than it might initially appear. All those benefits make life easier for Google staff, and help them achieve a work–life balance. Achieving the right work–life balance is the centerpiece of Google's culture, but this also becomes more challenging as the company grows. On the one hand, Google does expect all of its employees to work super hard; on the other hand, it realizes that it needs to help them maintain some sort of balance. As one manager says, Google acknowledges "that we work hard but that work is not everything."

Recruitment is another challenge. While Google certainly doesn't lack applicants, attracting the right applicants is crucial if Google is to continue to grow successfully. Working at Google requires a special set of traits, and screening employees is easier if it recruits the right people to begin with. For instance, Google needs to attract people who are super-bright, love to work, have fun, can handle the stress, and who also have outside interests and flexibility.

As the company grows internationally, it also faces the considerable challenge of recruiting and building staff overseas. For example, Google now is introducing a new vertical market–based structure across Europe to attract more business advertisers to its search engine. (By vertical market–based structure, Google means focusing on key vertical industry sectors such as travel, retail, automotive, and technology.) To build these industry groupings abroad from scratch, Google promoted its former head of its U.S. financial services group to be the vertical markets director for Europe; he moved there recently. Google is thus looking for heads for each of its vertical industry groups for all of its key European territories. Each of these vertical market heads will have to educate their market sectors (retailing, travel, and so on) so Google can attract new advertisers. Google already has offices across Europe, and its London office had tripled in size to 100 staff in just two years.

However, one of the biggest challenges Google still faces is gearing up its employee selection system, given that the company must hire thousands of people per year. When Google started in business, job candidates typically suffered through a dozen or more in-person interviews, and the standards were so high that even applicants with years of great work experience often got turned down if they had just average college grades. But a few years ago, even Google's cofounders acknowledged to security analysts that setting such an extraordinarily high bar for hiring was holding back Google's expansion. For Google's first few years, one of the company's cofounders interviewed nearly every job candidate before he or she was hired, and even today one of them still reviews the qualifications of everyone before he or she gets a final offer.

The experience of one candidate illustrates what Google was up against. A 24-year-old was interviewed for a corporate communications job at Google. Google first made contact with the candidate in May, and then, after two phone interviews, invited him to headquarters. There he had separate interviews with about six people and was treated to lunch in a Google cafeteria. They also had him turn in several "homework" assignments, including a personal statement and a marketing plan. In August, Google invited the candidate back for a second round, which it said would involve another four or five interviews. In the meantime, he decided he'd rather work at a start-up, and accepted another job at a new Web-based instant messaging provider.

Google's head of human resources, a former GE executive, says that Google is trying to strike the right balance between letting Google and the candidate get to know each other while also moving quickly. To that end, Google administered a survey to all Google's current employees in an effort to identify the traits that correlate with success at Google. In the survey, employees responded to questions relating to about 300 variables, including their performance on standardized tests, how old they were when they first used a computer, and how many foreign languages they speak. The Google survey team then went back and compared the answers against the 30 or 40 job performance factors they keep for each employee. They thereby identified clusters of traits that Google might better focus on during the hiring process. Google is also moving from the free-form interviews it used in the past to a more structured process.

Questions

12. What do you think of the idea of Google correlating personal traits from the employees' answers on the survey to their performance, and then using that as the basis for screening job candidates? In other words, is it or is it not a good idea? Please explain your answer.
13. The benefits that Google pays obviously represent an enormous expense. Based on what you know about Google and on what you read in this text, how would you defend all these benefits if you're making a presentation to the security analysts who were analyzing Google's performance?
14. If you wanted to hire the brightest people around, how would you go about recruiting and selecting them?
15. To support its growth and expansion strategy, Google wants (among other traits) people who are super-bright and who work hard, often round-the-clock, and who are flexible and maintain a decent work–life balance. List five specific HR policies or practices that you think Google has implemented or should implement to support its strategy, and explain your answer.
16. What sorts of factors do you think Google will have to take into consideration as it tries transferring its culture and reward systems and way of doing business to its operations abroad?
17. Given the sorts of values and culture Google cherishes, briefly describe four specific activities you suggest it pursue during new-employee orientation.

Source: Notes for Google: "Google Brings Vertical Structure to Europe," *New Media Age*, August 4, 2005, p. 2; Debbie Lovewell, "Employer Profile—Google: Searching for Talent," *Employee Benefits*, October 10, 2005, p. 66; "Google Looking for Gourmet Chefs," *Internet Week*, August 4, 2005; Douglas Merrill, "Google's 'Googley' Culture Kept Alive by Tech," *eWeek*, April 11, 2006; Robert Hof, "Google Gives Employees Another Option," *BusinessWeek Online*, December 13, 2005; Kevin Delaney, "Google Adjusts Hiring Process as Needs Grow," *Wall Street Journal*, October 23, 2006, pp. B1, B8; Adam Lishinsky, "Search and Enjoy," *Fortune*, January 22, 2007, pp. 70–82; www.nypost.com/seven/10302008/business/frugal_google_cuts_perks_136011.htm, accessed July 12, 2009; Adam Bryant, "The Quest to Build a Better Boss," *New York Times,* March 13, 2011, pp. 1, 7; Mark C. Crowley, "Not a Happy Accident: How Google Deliberately Designs Workplace Satisfaction", www.fastcompany.com/3007268/where-are-they-now/not-happy-accident-how-google-deliberately-designs-workplace-satisfaction, accessed September 16, 2014; Laszlo Bock, Work Rules!: Insights from Inside Google That Will Transform How You Live and Lead (New York, NY: Twelve, 2015).

MUFFLER MAGIC*

Muffler Magic is a fast-growing chain of 25 automobile service centers in Nevada. Originally started 20 years ago as a muffler repair shop by Ronald Brown, the chain expanded rapidly to new locations, and as it did so Muffler Magic also expanded the services it provided, from muffler replacement to oil changes, brake jobs, and engine repair. Today, one can bring an automobile to a Muffler Magic shop for basically any type of service, from tires to mufflers to engine repair.

Auto service is a tough business. The shop owner is basically dependent upon the quality of the service people he or she hires and retains, and the most qualified mechanics find it easy to pick up and leave for a job paying a bit more at a competitor down the road. It's also a business in which productivity is very important. The single largest expense is usually the cost of labor. Auto service dealers generally don't just make up the prices that they charge customers for various repairs; instead, they charge based on standardized industry rates for jobs like changing spark plugs or repairing a leaky radiator. Therefore, if someone brings a car in for a new alternator and the standard number of hours for changing the alternator is an hour, but it takes the mechanic 2 hours, the service center's owner may end up making less profit on the transaction.

*© Gary Dessler, PhD.

Quality is a persistent problem as well. For example, "rework" has recently been a problem at Muffler Magic. A customer recently brought her car to a Muffler Magic to have the car's brake pads replaced, which the service center did for her. Unfortunately, when she left she drove only about two blocks before she discovered that she had no brake power at all. It was simply fortuitous that she was going so slowly she was able to stop her car by slowly rolling up against a parking bumper. It subsequently turned out that the mechanic who replaced the brake pads had failed to properly tighten a fitting on the hydraulic brake tubes and the brake fluid had run out, leaving the car with no braking power. In a similar problem the month before that, a (different) mechanic replaced a fan belt, but forgot to refill the radiator with fluid; that customer's car overheated before he got four blocks away, and Muffler Magic had to replace the whole engine. Of course problems like these not only diminish the profitability of the company's profits, but, repeated many times over, have the potential for ruining Muffler Magic's word-of-mouth reputation.

Organizationally, Muffler Magic employs about 300 people, and Ron runs his company with eight managers, including himself as president, a controller, a purchasing director, a marketing director, and the human resource manager. He also has three regional managers to whom the eight or nine service center managers in each area of Nevada report. Over the past two years, as the company has opened new service centers, company-wide profits have diminished rather than increased. In part, these diminishing profits probably reflect the fact that Ron Brown has found it increasingly difficult to manage his growing operation. ("Your reach is exceeding your grasp" is how Ron's wife puts it.)

The company has only the most basic HR systems in place. It uses an application form that the human resource manager modified from one that he downloaded from the Web, and the standard employee status change request forms, sign-on forms, I-9 forms, and so on, that it purchased from a human resource management supply house. Training is entirely on-the-job. Muffler Magic expects the experienced technicians that it hires to come to the job fully trained; to that end, the service center managers generally ask candidates for these jobs basic behavioral questions that hopefully provide a window into these applicants' skills. However, most of the other technicians hired to do jobs like rotating tires, fixing brake pads, and replacing mufflers are untrained and inexperienced. They are to be trained by either the service center manager or by more experienced technicians, on-the-job.

Ron Brown faces several HR-type problems. One, as he says, is that he faces the "tyranny of the immediate" when it comes to hiring employees. Although it's fine to say that he should be carefully screening each employee and checking his or her references and work ethic, from a practical point of view, with 25 centers to run, the centers' managers usually just hire anyone who seems to be breathing, as long as he or she can answer some basic interview questions about auto repair, such as, "What do you think the problem is if a 2001 Camry is overheating, and what would you do about it?"

Employee safety is also a problem. An automobile service center may not be the most dangerous type of workplace, but it is potentially dangerous. Employees are dealing with sharp tools, greasy floors, greasy tools, extremely hot temperatures (for instance, on mufflers and engines), and fast-moving engine parts including fan blades. There are some basic things that a service manager can do to ensure more safety, such as insisting that all oil spills be cleaned up immediately. However, from a practical point of view, there are few ways to get around many of the problems—such as when the technician must check out an engine while it is running.

With Muffler Magic's profits going down instead of up, Brown's human resource manager has taken the position that the main problem is financial. As he says, "You get what you pay for" when it comes to employees, and if you compensate technicians better than your competitors do, then you get better technicians, ones who do their jobs better and stay longer with the company—and then profits will rise. So, the HR manager scheduled a meeting between himself, Ron Brown, and a professor of business who teaches compensation management at a local university. The HR manager has asked this professor to spend about a week looking at each of the service centers, analyzing the situation, and coming up with a compensation plan that will address Muffler Magic's quality and productivity problems. At this meeting, the professor makes three basic recommendations for changing the company's compensation policies.

Number one, she says that she has found that Muffler Magic suffers from what she calls "presenteeism"—in other words, employees drag themselves into work even when they're sick, because the company does not pay them if they are out; the company offers no sick days. In just a few days the professor couldn't properly quantify how much Muffler Magic is losing to presenteeism. However, from what she could see at each shop, there are typically one or two technicians working with various maladies like the cold or flu, and it seemed to her that each of these people was probably really only working about half of the time (although they were getting paid for the whole day). So, for 25 service centers per week, Muffler Magic could well be losing 125 or 130 personnel days per week of work. The professor suggests that Muffler Magic start allowing everyone to take three paid sick days per year, a reasonable suggestion. However, as Ron Brown points out, "Right now, we're only losing about half a day's pay for each employee who comes in and who works unproductively; with your suggestion, won't we lose the whole day?" The professor says she'll ponder that one.

Second, the professor recommends putting the technicians on a skill-for-pay plan. Basically, she suggests the following. Give each technician a letter grade (A through E) based upon that technician's particular skill level and abilities. An "A" technician is a team leader and needs to show that he or she has excellent diagnostic troubleshooting skills, and the ability to supervise and direct other technicians. At the other extreme, an "E" technician would typically be a new apprentice with little technical training. The other technicians fall in between those two levels, based on their individual skills and abilities.

In the professor's system, the "A" technician or team leader would assign and supervise all work done within his or her area but generally not do any mechanical repairs himself or herself. The team leader does the diagnostic troubleshooting, supervises and trains the other technicians, and test drives the car before it goes back to the customer. Under this plan, every technician receives a guaranteed hourly wage within a certain range, for instance:

A tech = \$25–\$30 an hour
B tech = \$20–\$25 an hour
C tech = \$15–\$20 an hour
D tech = \$10–\$15 an hour
E tech = \$8–\$10 an hour

Third, to directly address the productivity issue, the professor recommends that each service manager calculate each technician-team's productivity at the end of each day and at the end of each week. She suggests posting the running productivity total conspicuously for daily viewing. Then, the technicians as a group get weekly cash bonuses based upon their productivity. To calculate productivity, the professor recommends dividing the total labor hours billed by the total labor hours paid to technicians; in other words, total labor hours billed *divided by* total hours paid to technicians.

Having done some homework, the professor says that the national average for labor productivity is currently about 60%, and that only the best-run service centers achieve 85% or greater. By her rough calculations, Muffler Magic was attaining about industry average (about 60%—in other words, they were billing for only about 60 hours for each 100 hours that they actually had to pay technicians to do the jobs). (Of course, this was not entirely the technicians' fault. Technicians get time off for breaks and for lunch, and if a particular service center simply didn't have enough business on a particular day or during a particular week, then several technicians may well sit around idly waiting for the next car to come in.) The professor recommends setting a labor efficiency goal of 80% and posting each team's daily productivity results in the workplace to provide them with additional feedback. She recommends that if at the end of a week the team is able to boost its productivity ratio from the current 60% to 80%, then that team would get an additional 10% weekly pay bonus. After that, for every 5% boost of increased productivity above 80%, technicians would receive an additional 5% weekly bonus. So, if a technician's normal weekly pay is $400, that employee would receive an extra $40 at the end of the week when his team moves from 60% productivity to 80% productivity.

After the meeting, Ron Brown thanked the professor for her recommendations and told her he would think about it and get back to her. After the meeting, on the drive home, Ron was pondering what to do. He had to decide whether to institute the professor's sick leave policy, and whether to implement the professor's incentive and compensation plan. Before implementing anything, however, he wanted to make sure he understood the context in which he was making his decision. For example, did Muffler Magic really have an incentive pay problem, or were the problems more broad? Furthermore, how, if at all, would the professor's incentive plan impact the quality of the work that the teams were doing? And should the company really start paying for sick days? Ron Brown had a lot to think about.

Questions

18. Write a one-page summary outline listing three or four recommendations you would make with respect to each HR function (recruiting, selection, training, and so on) that you think Ron Brown should be addressing with his HR manager.

19. Develop a 10-question structured interview form Ron Brown's service center managers can use to interview experienced technicians.

20. If you were Ron Brown, would you implement the professor's recommendation addressing the presenteeism problem—in other words, start paying for sick days? Why or why not?

21. If you were advising Ron Brown, would you recommend that he implement the professor's skill-based pay and incentive pay plan as is? Why? Would you implement it with modifications? If you would modify it, please be specific about what you think those modifications should be, and why.

Based generally on actual facts, but Muffler Magic is a fictitious company. This case is based largely on information in Drew Paras, "The Pay Factor: Technicians' Salaries Can Be the Largest Expense in a Server Shop, as Well as the Biggest Headache. Here's How One Shop Owner Tackled the Problem," *Motor Age*, November 2003, pp. 76–79; see also Jennifer Pellet, "Health Care Crisis," *Chief Executive*, June 2004, pp. 56–61; "Firms Press to Quantify, Control Presenteeism," *Employee Benefits*, December 1, 2002.

BP TEXAS CITY*

When British Petroleum's (BP) Horizon oil rig exploded in the Gulf of Mexico in 2010, it triggered tragic reminders for experts in the safety community. In March 2005, an explosion and fire at BP's Texas City, Texas, refinery killed 15 people and injured 500 people in the worst U.S. industrial accident in more than 10 years. That disaster triggered three investigations: one internal investigation by BP, one by the U.S. Chemical Safety Board, and an independent investigation chaired by former U.S. Secretary of State James Baker and an 11-member panel that was organized at BP's request.

To put the results of these three investigations into context, it's useful to understand that under its current management, BP had pursued, for the past 10 or

*© Gary Dessler, PhD.

so years before the Texas City explosion, a strategy emphasizing cost-cutting and profitability. The basic conclusion of the investigations was that cost-cutting helped compromise safety at the Texas City refinery. It's useful to consider each investigation's findings.

The Chemical Safety Board's (CSB) investigation, according to Carol Merritt, the board's chair, showed that "BP's global management was aware of problems with maintenance, spending, and infrastructure well before March 2005." Apparently, faced with numerous earlier accidents, BP did make some safety improvements. However, it focused primarily on emphasizing personal employee safety behaviors and procedural compliance, and thereby reducing safety accident rates. The problem (according to the CSB) was that "catastrophic safety risks remained." For example, according to the CSB, "unsafe and antiquated equipment designs were left in place, and unacceptable deficiencies in preventive maintenance were tolerated." Basically, the CSB found that BP's budget cuts led to a progressive deterioration of safety at the Texas City refinery. Said Merritt, "In an aging facility like Texas City, it is not responsible to cut budgets related to safety and maintenance without thoroughly examining the impact on the risk of a catastrophic accident."

Looking at specifics, the CSB said that a 2004 internal audit of 35 BP business units, including Texas City (BP's largest refinery), found significant safety gaps they all had in common, including, for instance, a lack of leadership competence, and "systemic underlying issues" such as a widespread tolerance of noncompliance with basic safety rules and poor monitoring of safety management systems and processes. Ironically, the CSB found that BP's accident prevention effort at Texas City had achieved a 70% reduction in worker injuries in the year before the explosion. Unfortunately, this simply meant that individual employees were having fewer accidents. The larger, more fundamental problem was that the potentially explosive situation inherent in the depreciating machinery remained.

The CSB found that the Texas City explosion followed a pattern of years of major accidents at the facility. In fact, there had apparently been an average of one employee death every 16 months at the plant for the last 30 years. The CSB found that the equipment directly involved in the most recent explosion was an obsolete design already phased out in most refineries and chemical plants, and that key pieces of its instrumentation were not working. There had also been previous instances where flammable vapors were released from the same unit in the 10 years prior to the explosion. In 2003, an external audit had referred to the Texas City refinery's infrastructure and assets as "poor" and found what it referred to as a "checkbook mentality," one in which budgets were not sufficient to manage all the risks. In particular, the CSB found that BP had implemented a 25% cut on fixed costs between 1998 and 2000 and that this adversely impacted maintenance expenditures and net expenditures, and refinery infrastructure. Going on, the CSB found that in 2004, there were three major accidents at the refinery that killed three workers.

BP's own internal report concluded that the problems at Texas City were not of recent origin, and instead were years in the making. It said BP was taking steps to address them. Its investigation found "no evidence of anyone consciously or intentionally taking actions or making decisions that put others at risk." Said BP's report, "The underlying reasons for the behaviors and actions displayed during the incident are complex, and the team has spent much time trying to understand them—it is evident that they were many years in the making and will require concerted and committed actions to address." BP's report concluded that there were five underlying causes for the massive explosion:

- A working environment had eroded to one characterized by resistance to change, and a lack of trust.
- Safety, performance, and risk reduction priorities had not been set and consistently reinforced by management.
- Changes in the "complex organization" led to a lack of clear accountabilities and poor communication.

- A poor level of hazard awareness and understanding of safety resulted in workers accepting levels of risk that were considerably higher than at comparable installations.
- Adequate early warning systems for problems were lacking, and there were no independent means of understanding the deteriorating standards at the plant.

The report from the BP-initiated but independent 11-person panel chaired by former U.S. Secretary of State James Baker contained specific conclusions and recommendations. The Baker panel looked at BP's corporate safety oversight, the corporate safety culture, and the process safety management systems at BP at the Texas City plant as well as at BP's other refineries.

Basically, the Baker panel concluded that BP had not provided effective safety process leadership and had not established safety as a core value at the five refineries it looked at (including Texas City).

Like the CSB, the Baker panel found that BP had emphasized personal safety in recent years and had in fact improved personal safety performance, but had not emphasized the overall safety process, thereby mistakenly interpreting "improving personal injury rates as an indication of acceptable process safety performance at its U.S. refineries." In fact, the Baker panel went on, by focusing on these some what misleading improving personal injury rates, BP created a false sense of confidence that it was properly addressing process safety risks. It also found that the safety culture at Texas City did not have the positive, trusting, open environment that a proper safety culture required. The Baker panel's other findings included the following.

- BP did not always ensure that adequate resources were effectively allocated to support or sustain a high level of process safety performance.
- BP's refinery personnel are "overloaded" by corporate initiatives.
- Operators and maintenance personnel work high rates of overtime.
- BP tended to have a short-term focus and its decentralized management system and entrepreneurial culture delegated substantial discretion to refinery plant managers "without clearly defining process safety expectations, responsibilities, or accountabilities."
- There was no common, unifying process safety culture among the five refineries.
- The company's corporate safety management system did not make sure there was timely compliance with internal process safety standards and programs.
- BP's executive management either did not receive refinery-specific information that showed that process safety deficiencies existed at some of the plants, or did not effectively respond to any information it did receive.[1]
- These findings and the following suggestions are based on "BP Safety Report Finds Company's Process Safety Culture Ineffective," *Global Refining & Fuels Report*, January 17, 2007.

The Baker panel made several safety recommendations for BP, including the following.

1. The company's corporate management must provide leadership on process safety.
2. The company should establish a process safety management system that identifies, reduces, and manages the process safety risks of the refineries.
3. The company should make sure its employees have an appropriate level of process safety knowledge and expertise.
4. The company should involve "relevant stakeholders" in developing a positive, trusting, and open process safety culture at each refinery.
5. BP should clearly define expectations and strengthen accountability for process safety performance.
6. BP should better coordinate its process safety support for the refining line organization.

7. BP should develop an integrated set of leading and lagging performance indicators for effectively monitoring process safety performance.
8. BP should establish and implement an effective system to audit process safety performance.
9. The company's board should monitor the implementation of the panel's recommendations and the ongoing process safety performance of the refineries.
10. BP should transform itself into a recognized industry leader in process safety management.

In making its recommendations, the panel singled out the company's chief executive at the time, Lord Browne, by saying, "In hindsight, the panel believes if Browne had demonstrated comparable leadership on and commitment to process safety [as he did for responding to climate change] that would have resulted in a higher level of safety at refineries."

Overall, the Baker panel found that BP's top management had not provided "effective leadership" on safety. It found that the failings went to the very top of the organization, to the company's chief executive, and to several of his top lieutenants. The Baker panel emphasized the importance of top management commitment, saying, for instance, that "it is imperative that BP leadership set the process safety tone at the top of the organization and establish appropriate expectations regarding process safety performance." It also said BP "has not provided effective leadership in making certain its management and U.S. refining workforce understand what is expected of them regarding process safety performance."

Lord Browne, the chief executive, stepped down about a year after the explosion. About the same time, some BP shareholders were calling for the company's executives and board directors to have their bonuses more closely tied to the company's safety and environmental performance in the wake of Texas City. In October 2009, OSHA announced it was filing the largest fine in its history for this accident, for $87 million, against BP. One year later, BP's Horizon oil rig in the Gulf of Mexico exploded, taking 11 lives. In September 2014, the U.S. District judge presiding over negligence claims in the ensuing case found BP guilty of gross negligence, basically reckless and extreme behavior; the company will appeal his ruling.

Questions

22. The text defines ethics as "the principles of conduct governing an individual or a group," and specifically as the standards one uses to decide what his or her conduct should be. To what extent do you believe that what happened at BP is as much a breakdown in the company's ethical systems as it is in its safety systems, and how would you defend your conclusion?
23. Are the Occupational Safety and Health Administration's standards, policies, and rules aimed at addressing problems like the ones that apparently existed at the Texas City plant? If so, how would you explain the fact that problems like these could have continued for so many years?
24. Since there were apparently at least three deaths in the year prior to the major explosion, and an average of about one employee death per 16 months for the previous 10 years, how would you account for the fact that mandatory OSHA inspections missed these glaring sources of potential catastrophic events?
25. The text lists numerous suggestions for "how to prevent accidents." Based on what you know about the Texas City explosion, what do you say Texas City tells you about the most important three steps an employer can take to prevent accidents?
26. Based on what you learned in Chapter 14, would you make any additional recommendations to BP over and above those recommendations made by the Baker panel and the CSB? If so, what would those recommendations be?

27. Explain specifically how strategic human resource management at BP seems to have supported the company's broader strategic aims. What does this say about the advisability of always linking human resource strategy to a company's strategic aims?

Source: Notes for BP Texas City: Sheila McNulty, "BP Knew of Safety Problems, Says Report," *Financial Times*, October 31, 2006, p. 1; "CBS: Documents Show BP Was Aware of Texas City Safety Problems," *World Refining & Fuels Today*, October 30, 2006; "BP Safety Report Finds Company's Process Safety Culture Ineffective," *Global Refining & Fuels Report*, January 17, 2007; "BP Safety Record Under Attack," *Europe Intelligence Wire*, January 17, 2007; Mark Hofmann, "BP Slammed for Poor Leadership on Safety, Oil Firm Agrees to Act on Review Panel's Recommendations," *Business Intelligence*, January 22, 2007, p. 3; "Call for Bonuses to Include Link with Safety Performance," *Guardian*, January 18, 2007, p. 24; www.bp.com/genericarticle.do?categoryId=9005029&contentId=7015905, accessed July 12, 2009; Steven Greenhouse, "BP Faces Record Fine for '05 Blast," *New York Times*, October 30, 2009, pp. 1, 6; Kyle W. Morrison, "Blame to Go Around," *Safety & Health*, 183, no. 3, March 2011, p. 40; Ed Crooks, "BP Had Tools to End Spill Sooner, Court Told," www.ft.com/cms/s/0/40d7b076-2ae8-11e3-8fb8-00144feab7de.html?ftcamp=published_links%2Frss%2Fhome_uk%2Ffeed%2F%2Fproduct#axzz2gZshHFOc, accessed October 2, 2013; Daniel Gilbert and Justin Scheck, "Judge Hammers BP for Gulf Disaster", *Wall Street Journal*, September 5, 2014, pp. B1, B2.

GLOSSARY

4/5ths rule Federal agency rule that a minority selection rate less than 80% (4/5ths) of that for the group with the highest rate is evidence of adverse impact.

401(k) plan A defined contribution plan based on section 401(k) of the Internal Revenue Code.

action learning A training technique by which management trainees are allowed to work full-time analyzing and solving problems in other departments.

adaptability screening A process that aims to assess the assignees' (and spouses') probable success in handling a foreign transfer.

adverse impact The overall impact of employer practices that result in significantly higher percentages of members of minorities and other protected groups being rejected for employment, placement, or promotion.

affirmative action Steps that are taken for the purpose of eliminating the present effects of past discrimination.

Age Discrimination in Employment Act of 1967 (ADEA) The act prohibiting arbitrary age discrimination and specifically protecting individuals over 40 years old.

agency shop A form of union security in which employees who do not belong to the union must still pay union dues on the assumption that union efforts benefit all workers.

alternation ranking method Ranking employees from best to worst on a particular trait, choosing highest, then lowest, until all are ranked.

alternative dispute resolution or ADR program Grievance procedure that provides for binding arbitration as the last step.

alternative staffing The use of nontraditional recruitment sources.

Americans with Disabilities Act (ADA) The act requiring employers to make reasonable accommodations for disabled employees; it prohibits discrimination against disabled persons.

annual bonus Plans that are designed to motivate short-term performance of managers and that are tied to company profitability.

applicant tracking systems Online systems that help employers attract, gather, screen, compile, and manage applicants.

application form The form that provides information on education, prior work record, and skills.

appraisal interview An interview in which the supervisor and subordinate review the appraisal and make plans to remedy deficiencies and reinforce strengths.

apprenticeship training A structured process by which people become skilled workers through a combination of classroom instruction and on-the-job training.

arbitration The most definitive type of third-party intervention, in which the arbitrator usually has the power to determine and dictate the settlement terms.

authority The right to make decisions, direct others' work, and give orders.

authorization cards In order to petition for a union election, the union must show that at least 30% of employees may be interested in being unionized. Employees indicate this interest by signing authorization cards.

bargaining unit The group of employees the union will be authorized to represent.

behavior modeling A training technique in which trainees are first shown good management techniques in a film, are asked to play roles in a simulated situation, and are then given feedback and praise by their supervisor.

behavior modification Using contingent rewards or punishment to change behavior.

behavior-based safety Identifying the worker behaviors that contribute to accidents and then training workers to avoid these behaviors.

behavioral interview A series of job-related questions that focus on how the candidate reacted to actual situations in the past.

behaviorally anchored rating scale (BARS) An appraisal method that aims at combining the benefits of narrative critical incidents and quantified ratings by anchoring a quantified scale with specific narrative examples of good and poor performance.

benchmark job A job that is used to anchor the employer's pay scale and around which other jobs are arranged in order of relative worth.

benefits Indirect financial and nonfinancial payments employees receive for continuing their employment with the company.

bias The tendency to allow individual differences such as age, race, and sex to affect the appraisal ratings employees receive.

bona fide occupational qualification (BFOQ) Requirement that an employee be of a certain religion, sex, or national origin where that is reasonably necessary to the organization's normal operation. Specified by the 1964 Civil Rights Act.

boycott The combined refusal by employees and other interested parties to buy or use the employer's products.

broadbanding Consolidating salary grades and ranges into just a few wide levels or "bands," each of which contains a relatively wide range of jobs and salary levels.

burnout The total depletion of physical and mental resources caused by excessive striving to reach an unrealistic work-related goal.

business process reengineering Redesigning business processes, usually by combining steps, so that small multifunction process teams using information technology do the jobs formerly done by a sequence of departments.

candidate-order (or contrast) error An error of judgment on the part of the interviewer due to interviewing one or more very good or very bad candidates just before the interview in question.

career The occupational positions a person has had over many years.

career development The lifelong series of activities that contribute to a person's career exploration, establishment, success, and fulfillment.

career management The process for enabling employees to better understand and develop their career skills and interests, and to use these skills and interests more effectively.

career planning The deliberate process through which someone becomes aware of personal skills, interests, knowledge, motivations, and other characteristics and establishes action plans to attain specific goals.

case study method A development method in which the manager is presented with a written description of an organizational problem to diagnose and solve.

cash balance plans Plans under which the employer contributes a percentage of employees' current pay to employees' pension plans every year, and employees earn interest on this amount.

central tendency A tendency to rate all employees the same way, such as rating them all average.

citation Summons informing employers and employees of the regulations and standards that have been violated in the workplace.

Civil Rights Act of 1991 (CRA 1991) The act that places the burden of proof back on employers and permits compensatory and punitive damages.

classes Grouping jobs based on a set of rules for each group or class, such as amount of independent judgment, skill, physical effort, and so forth, required. Classes usually contain similar jobs.

closed shop A form of union security in which the company can hire only union members. This was outlawed in 1947 but still exists in some industries (such as printing).

cloud (the) Refers to placing software programs and services on vendors' remote servers, from which they can then deliver these programs and services seamlessly to employees' digital devices.

coaching Educating, instructing, and training subordinates.

Co-determination An employee representation system in which workers elect their own representatives to the supervisory (management) board of the employer and have the legal right to a viice in setting company policies on matters such as company organizatio, hiring, and performance appraisal.

collective bargaining The process through which representatives of management and the union meet to negotiate a labor agreement.

college recruiting Sending an employer's representatives to college campuses to prescreen applicants and create an applicant pool from the graduating class.

compa ratio Equals an employee's pay rate divided by the pay range midpoint for his or her pay grade.

comparable worth The concept by which women who are usually paid less than men can claim that men in comparable rather than in strictly equal jobs are paid more.

compensable factor A fundamental, compensable element of a job, such as skills, effort, responsibility, and working conditions.

competency model A graphic model that consolidates, usually in one diagram, a precise overview of the competencies (the knowledge, skills, and behaviors) someone would need to do a job well.

Competency-based job analysis Describing the job in terms of measurable, observable, behavioral competencies (knowledge, skills, and/or behaviors) that an employee doing that job must exhibit to do the job well.

competency-based pay Where the company pays for the employee's range, depth, and types of skills and knowledge, rather than for the job title he or she holds.

competitive advantage Any factors that allow an organization to differentiate its product or service from those of its competitors to increase market share.

competitive strategy A strategy that identifies how to build and strengthen the business's long-term competitive position in the marketplace.

compressed workweek Schedule in which employee works fewer but longer days each week.

construct validity A test that is construct valid is one that demonstrates that a selection procedure measures a construct and that construct is important for successful job performance.

content validity A test that is content valid is one that contains a fair sample of the tasks and skills actually needed for the job in question.

controlled experimentation Formal methods for testing the effectiveness of a training program, preferably with before-and-after tests and a control group.

corporate campaign An organized effort by the union that exerts pressure on the corporation by pressuring the company's other unions, shareholders, directors, customers, creditors, and government agencies, often directly.

corporate-level strategy Type of strategy that identifies the portfolio of businesses that, in total, comprise the company and the ways in which these businesses relate to each other.

criterion validity A type of validity based on showing that scores on the test (predictors) are related to job performance (criterion).

critical incident method Keeping a record of uncommonly good or undesirable examples of an employee's work-related behavior and reviewing it with the employee at predetermined times.

cross training Training employees to do different tasks or jobs than their own; doing so facilitates flexibility and job rotation.

Davis-Bacon Act A 1931 law that sets wage rates for laborers employed by contractors working for the federal government.

decertification Legal process for employees to terminate a union's right to represent them.

deferred profit-sharing plan A plan in which a certain amount of profits is credited to each employee's account, payable at retirement, termination, or death.

diary/log Daily listings made by workers of every activity in which they engage along with the time each activity takes.

digital dashboard Presents the manager with desktop graphs and charts, and so a computerized picture of where the company stands on all those metrics from the HR scorecard process.

direct financial payments Pay in the form of wages, salaries, incentives, commissions, and bonuses.

discrimination Taking specific actions toward or against a person based on the person's group.

dismissal Involuntary termination of an employee's employment with the firm.

disparate rejection rates A test for adverse impact in which it can be demonstrated that there is a discrepancy between rates of rejection of members of a protected group and of others.

distributive justice Refers to a system of distributing rewards and discipline in which the actual results or outcomes of are evenhanded and fair.

diversity The variety or multiplicity of demographic features that characterize a company's workforce, particularly in terms of race, sex, culture, national origin, handicap, age, and religion.

downsizing The process of reducing, usually dramatically, the number of people employed by a firm.

early retirement window A type of offering by which employees are encouraged to retire early, the incentive being liberal pension benefits plus perhaps a cash payment.

earnings-at-risk pay plan Plan that puts some portion of employees' normal pay at risk if they don't meet their goals, in return for possibly obtaining a much larger bonus if they exceed their goals.

economic strike A strike that results from a failure to agree on the terms of a contract that involves wages, benefits, and other conditions of employment.

Electronic Communications Privacy Act (ECPA) The ECPA is a federal law intended to help restrict interception and monitoring of oral and wire communications.

electronic performance monitoring (EPM) Having supervisors electronically monitor the amount of computerized data an employee is processing per day, and thereby his or her performance.

electronic performance support systems (EPSS) Sets of computerized tools and displays that automate training, documentation, and phone support; integrate this automation into applications; and provide support that's faster, cheaper, and more effective than traditional methods.

employee assistance program (EAP) A formal employer program for providing employees with counseling and/or treatment programs for problems such as alcoholism, gambling, or stress.

employee compensation All forms of pay or rewards going to employees and arising from their employment.

employee engagement The extent to which an organization's employees are psychologically involved in, connected to, and committed to getting their jobs done.

employee orientation A procedure for providing new employees with basic background information about the firm.

employee recruiting Finding and/or attracting applicants for the employer's open positions.

employee relations The activity that involves establishing and maintaining the positive employee–employer relationships that contribute to satisfactory productivity, motivation, morale, and discipline, and to maintaining a positive, productive, and cohesive work environment.

Employee Retirement Income Security Act (ERISA) The 1974 law that provides government protection of pensions for all employees with company pension plans. It also regulates vesting rights (employees who leave before retirement may claim compensation from the pension plan).

employee stock ownership plan (ESOP) A corporation contributes shares of its own stock to a trust in which additional contributions are made annually. The trust distributes the stock to employees on retirement or separation from service.

Equal Employment Opportunity Commission (EEOC) The commission, created by Title VII, empowered to investigate job discrimination complaints and sue on behalf of complainants.

Equal Pay Act of 1963 The act requiring equal pay for equal work, regardless of sex.

ethics The study of standards of conduct and moral judgment; also the standards of right conduct.

ethnocentric The notion that home-country attitudes, management style, knowledge, evaluation criteria, and managers are superior to anything the host country has to offer.

ethnocentrism The tendency to view members of other social groups less favorably than members of one's own group.

executive coach An outside consultant who questions the executive's associates in order to identify the executive's strengths and weaknesses, and then counsels the executive so he or she can capitalize on those strengths and overcome the weaknesses.

exit interviews Interviews with employees who are leaving the firm, conducted for obtaining information about the job or related matters, to give the employer insight about the company.

expatriates (expats) Noncitizens of the countries in which employees are working.

expectancy chart A graph showing the relationship between test scores and job performance for a group of people.

expectancy A person's expectation that his or her effort will lead to performance.

fact finder A neutral party who studies the issues in a dispute and makes a public recommendation for a reasonable settlement.

fair day's work Output standards devised based on careful, scientific analysis.

Fair Labor Standards Act This 1938 act provides for minimum wages, maximum hours, overtime pay, and child labor protection. The law, amended many times, covers most employees.

fair treatment Reflects concrete actions, such as "employees are treated with respect," and "employees are treated fairly."

family-friendly (or work–life) benefits Benefits such as child care and fitness facilities that make it easier for employees to balance their work and family responsibilities.

Federal Violence Against Women Act of 1994 The act that provides that a person who commits a crime of violence motivated by gender shall be liable to the party injured.

financial incentives Financial rewards paid to workers whose production exceeds some predetermined standard.

flexible benefits plan/cafeteria benefits plan Individualized plans allowed by employers to accommodate employee preferences for benefits.

flextime A work schedule in which employees' workdays are built around a core of midday hours, and employees determine, within limits, what other hours they will work.

forced distribution method Similar to grading on a curve; predetermined percentages of ratees are placed in various performance categories.

foreign service premiums Financial payments over and above regular base pay, typically ranging between 10% and 30% of base pay.

functional strategy A strategy that identifies the broad activities that each department will pursue in order to help the business accomplish its competitive goals.

gainsharing plan An incentive plan that engages employees in a common effort to achieve productivity objectives and share the gains.

gender-role stereotypes The tendency to associate women with certain (frequently nonmanagerial) jobs.

geocentric The belief that the firm's whole management staff must be scoured on a global basis, on the assumption that the best manager of a specific position anywhere may be in any of the countries in which the firm operates.

golden parachute A payment companies make in connection with a change in ownership or control of a company.

good faith bargaining Both parties are making every reasonable effort to arrive at agreement; proposals are being matched with counterproposals.

good-faith effort strategy An affirmative action strategy that emphasizes identifying and eliminating the obstacles to hiring and promoting women and minorities, and increasing the minority or female applicant flow.

grade definition Written descriptions of the level of, say, responsibility and knowledge required by jobs in each grade. Similar jobs can then be combined into grades or classes.

grades A job classification system like the class system, although grades often contain dissimilar jobs, such as secretaries, mechanics, and firefighters. Grade descriptions are written based on compensable factors listed in classification systems.

graphic rating scale A scale that lists a number of traits and a range of performance for each. The employee is then rated by identifying the score that best describes his or her level of performance for each trait.

grievance procedure Formal process for addressing any factor involving wages, hours, or conditions of employment that is used as a complaint against the employer.

group life insurance Provides lower rates for the employer or employee and includes all employees, including new employees, regardless of health or physical condition.

halo effect In performance appraisal, the problem that occurs when a supervisor's rating of a subordinate on one trait biases the rating of that person on other traits.

hardship allowances Payments that compensate expatriates for exceptionally hard living and working conditions at certain locations.

health maintenance organization (HMO) A prepaid health-care system that generally provides routine round-the-clock medical services as well as preventive medicine in a clinic-type arrangement for employees, who pay a nominal fee in addition to the fixed annual fee the employer pays.

high-performance work system (HPWS) A set of human resource management policies and practices that promote organizational effectiveness.

home-country nationals Citizens of the country in which the multinational company has its headquarters.

HR audit An analysis by which an organization measures where it currently stands and determines what it has to accomplish to improve its HR functions.

HR scorecard A process for assigning financial and nonfinancial goals or metrics to the human resource management–related chain of activities required for achieving the company's strategic aims and for monitoring results.

human resource management (HRM) The process of acquiring, training, appraising, and compensating employees, and of attending to their labor relations, health and safety, and fairness concerns.

human resource metrics The quantitative gauge of a human resource management activity, such as employee turnover, hours of training per employee, or qualified applicants per position.

illegal bargaining items Items in collective bargaining that are forbidden by law; for example, a clause agreeing to hire "union members exclusively" would be illegal in a right-to-work state.

impasse Collective bargaining situation that occurs when the parties are not able to move further toward settlement, usually because one party is demanding more than the other will offer.

in-house development center A company-based method for exposing prospective managers to realistic exercises to develop improved management skills.

indirect financial payments Pay in the form of financial benefits such as insurance.

injunction A court order compelling a party or parties either to resume or to desist from a certain action.

inside games Union efforts to convince employees to impede or to disrupt production—for example, by slowing the work pace.

instrumentality The perceived relationship between successful performance and obtaining the reward.

insubordination Willful disregard or disobedience of the boss's authority or legitimate orders; criticizing the boss in public.

interest arbitration Arbitration enacted when labor agreements do not yet exist or when one or both parties are seeking to change the agreement.

interest inventory A personal development and selection device that compares the person's current interests with those of others now in various occupations so as to determine the preferred occupation for the individual.

international human resource management (IHRM) The human resource management concepts and techniques employers use to manage the human resource challenges of their international operations.

intrinsic motivation Motivation that derives from the pleasure someone gets from doing the job or task.

job aid A set of instructions, diagrams, or similar methods available at the job site to guide the worker.

job analysis The procedure for determining the duties and skill requirements of a job and the kind of person who should be hired for it.

job classification (or job grading) A method for categorizing jobs into groups.

job descriptions A list of a job's duties, responsibilities, reporting relationships, working conditions, and supervisory responsibilities—one product of a job analysis.

job enlargement Assigning workers additional same-level activities.

job enrichment Redesigning jobs in a way that increases the opportunities for the worker to experience feelings of responsibility, achievement, growth, and recognition.

job evaluation A systematic comparison done in order to determine the worth of one job relative to another.

job hazard analysis A systematic approach to identifying and eliminating workplace hazards before they occur.

job instruction training (JIT) Listing each job's basic tasks, along with key points, in order to provide step-by-step training for employees.

job posting Publicizing an open job to employees (often by literally posting it on bulletin boards) and listing its attributes, like qualifications, supervisor, working schedule, and pay rate.

job requirements matrix A more complete description of what the worker does and how and why he or she does it; it clarifies each task's purpose and each duty's required knowledge, skills, abilities, and other characteristics.

job rotation A management training technique that involves moving a trainee from department to department to broaden his or her experience and identify strong and weak points.

job sharing Allows two or more people to share a single full-time job.

job specifications A list of a job's "human requirements," that is, the requisite education, skills, personality, and so on—another product of a job analysis.

job-related interview A series of job-related questions that focus on relevant past job-related behaviors.

Landrum-Griffin Act of 1959 Also known as the *Labor Management Reporting and Disclosure Act*, this law aimed at protecting union members from possible wrongdoing on the part of their unions.

layoff An employer sending employees home due to a lack of work; this is typically a temporary situation.

lifelong learning Provides employees with continuing learning experiences over their tenure with the firm, with the aims of ensuring they have the opportunity to learn the skills they need to do their jobs and to expand their occupational horizons.

line authority The authority exerted by an HR manager by directing the activities of the people in his or her own department and in service areas (like the plant cafeteria).

line manager A manager who is authorized to direct the work of subordinates and is responsible for accomplishing the organization's tasks.

locals Citizens of the countries in which employees are working; also called *host-country nationals*.

lockout A refusal by the employer to provide opportunities to work.

management assessment center A simulation in which management candidates are asked to perform realistic tasks in hypothetical situations and are scored on their performance. It usually also involves testing and the use of management games.

management development Any attempt to improve current or future management performance by imparting knowledge, changing attitudes, or increasing skills.

management game A development technique in which teams of managers compete by making computerized decisions regarding realistic but simulated situations.

management process The five basic functions of planning, organizing, staffing, leading, and controlling.

manager The person responsible for accomplishing the organization's goals, and who does so by managing (planning, organizing, staffing, leading, and controlling) the efforts of the organization's people.

managing To perform five basic functions: planning, organizing, staffing, leading, and controlling.

managing diversity Maximizing diversity's potential benefits while minimizing its potential barriers.

mandatory bargaining items Items in collective bargaining that a party must bargain over if they are introduced by the other party—for example, pay.

market-competitive pay plan Pay plan where pay rates are equitable both internally (based on each job's relative value) and externally (in other words when compared with what other employers are paying).

mass interview A panel interviews several candidates simultaneously.

mediation Intervention in which a neutral third party tries to assist the principals in reaching agreement.

mentoring Advising, counseling, and guiding.

merit pay (merit raise) Any salary increase awarded to an employee based on his or her individual performance.

miniature job training and evaluation Training candidates to perform several of the job's tasks, and then evaluating the candidates' performance prior to hire.

mission statement Summarizes the answer to the question, "What business are we in?"

"mixed-motive" case A discrimination allegation case in which the employer argues that the employment action taken was motivated not by discrimination, but by some nondiscriminatory reason such as ineffective performance.

mobility premiums Typically, lump-sum payments to reward employees for moving from one assignment to another.

national emergency strikes Strikes that might "imperil the national health and safety."

National Labor Relations (or Wagner) Act This law banned certain types of unfair practices and provided for secret-ballot elections and majority rule for determining whether a firm's employees want to unionize.

National Labor Relations Board (NLRB) The agency created by the Wagner Act to investigate unfair labor practice charges and to provide for secret-ballot elections and majority rule in determining whether or not a firm's employees want a union.

negligent hiring Hiring workers with questionable backgrounds without proper safeguards.

negligent training A situation where an employer fails to train adequately, and the employee subsequently harms a third party.

Norris-LaGuardia Act of 1932 This law marked the beginning of the era of strong encouragement of unions and guaranteed to each employee the right to bargain collectively "free from interference, restraint, or coercion."

occupational illness Any abnormal condition or disorder caused by exposure to environmental factors associated with employment.

Occupational Safety and Health Act of 1970 The law passed by Congress in 1970 "to assure so far as possible every working man and woman in the nation safe and healthful working conditions and to preserve our human resources."

Occupational Safety and Health Administration (OSHA) The agency created within the Department of Labor to set safety and health standards for almost all workers in the United States.

Office of Federal Contract Compliance Programs (OFCCP) This office is responsible for implementing the executive orders and ensuring compliance of federal contractors.

on-demand recruiting services (ODRS) Services that provide short-term specialized recruiting to support specific projects without the expense of retaining traditional search firms.

on-the-job training Training a person to learn a job while working on it.

operational safety reviews Reviews conducted by agencies to ascertain whether units under their jurisdiction are complying with all the applicable safety laws, regulations, orders, and rules.

organization People with formally assigned roles who work together to achieve the organization's goals.

organization chart A chart that shows the organization-wide distribution of work, with titles of each position and interconnecting lines that show who reports to and communicates with whom.

organizational climate The perceptions a company's employees share about the firm's psychological environment, for instance, in terms of things like concern for employees' well-being, supervisory behavior, flexibility, appreciation, ethics, empowerment, political behaviors, and rewards.

organizational culture The characteristic values, traditions, and behaviors a company's employees share.

organizational development A special approach to organizational change in which employees themselves formulate and implement the change that's required.

organization-wide incentive plan Incentive plan in which all or most employees can participate.

outplacement counseling A formal process by which a terminated person is trained and counseled in the techniques of self-appraisal and securing a new position.

paired comparison method Ranking employees by making a chart of all possible pairs of the employees for each trait and indicating which is the better employee of the pair.

panel interview An interview in which a group of interviewers questions the applicant.

pay (or rate) ranges A series of steps or levels within a pay grade, usually based upon years of service.

pay (or wage) grade A pay grade is comprised of jobs of approximately equal difficulty.

Pension Benefits Guarantee Corporation (PBGC) Established under ERISA to ensure that pensions meet vesting obligations; also insures pensions should a plan terminate without sufficient funds to meet its vested obligations.

pension plans Plans that provide a fixed sum when employees reach a predetermined retirement age or when they can no longer work due to disability.

performance analysis Verifying that there is a performance deficiency and determining whether that deficiency should be corrected through training or through some other means (such as transferring the employee).

performance appraisal Evaluating an employee's current and/or past performance relative to his or her performance standards.

performance appraisal process A three-step appraisal process involving (1) setting work standards, (2) assessing the employee's actual performance relative to those standards, and (3) providing feedback to the employee with the aim of helping him or her to eliminate performance deficiencies or to continue to perform above par.

performance management The *continuous* process of identifying, measuring, and developing the performance of individuals and teams and *aligning* their performance with the organization's *goals*.

personnel replacement charts Company records showing present performance and promotability of inside candidates for the most important positions.

picketing Having employees carry signs announcing their concerns near the employer's place of business.

piecework A system of pay based on the number of items processed by each individual worker in a unit of time, such as items per hour or items per day.

point method The job evaluation method in which a number of compensable factors are identified and then the degree to which each of these factors is present on the job is determined.

polycentric A conscious belief that only the host-country managers can ever really understand the culture and behavior of the host-country market.

portability Instituting policies that enable employees to easily take their accumulated pension funds when they leave an employer.

position analysis questionnaire (PAQ) A questionnaire used to collect quantifiable data concerning the duties and responsibilities of various jobs.

position replacement card A card prepared for each position in a company to show possible replacement candidates and their qualifications.

preferential shop Union members get preference in hiring, but the employer can still hire nonunion members.

Pregnancy Discrimination Act An amendment to Title VII of the Civil Rights Act that prohibits sex discrimination based on "pregnancy, childbirth, or related medical conditions."

problem-solving teams Teams that identify and research work processes and develop solutions to work-related problems.

procedural justice Refers to just procedures in the allocation of rewards or discipline, in terms of the actual procedures being evenhanded and fair.

process chart A workflow chart that shows the flow of inputs to and outputs from a particular job.

productivity The ratio of outputs (goods and services) divided by the inputs (resources such as labor and capital).

profit-sharing plan A plan whereby employees share in the company's profits.

programmed learning A systematic method for teaching job skills, involving presenting questions or facts, allowing the person to respond, and giving the learner immediate feedback on the accuracy of his or her answers.

promotion Advancement to a position of increased responsibility.

protected class Persons such as minorities and women protected by equal opportunity laws, including Title VII.

qualified individuals Under ADA, those who can carry out the essential functions of the job.

quality circle A special type of formal problem-solving team, usually composed of 6 to 12 specially trained employees who meet once a week to solve problems affecting their work area.

ranking method The simplest method of job evaluation that involves ranking each job relative to all other jobs, usually based on overall difficulty.

ratio analysis A forecasting technique for determining future staff needs by using ratios between, for example, sales volume and number of employees needed.

reality shock Results of a period that may occur at the initial career entry when the new employee's high job expectations confront the reality of a boring or otherwise unattractive work situation.

recruiting yield pyramid The historical arithmetic relationships between recruitment leads and invitees, invitees and interviews, interviews and offers made, and offers made and offers accepted.

reliability The consistency of scores obtained by the same person when retested with the identical tests or with alternate forms of the same test.

restricted policy Another test for adverse impact, involving demonstration that an employer's hiring practices exclude a protected group, whether intentionally or not.

reverse discrimination Claim that due to affirmative action quota systems, white males are discriminated against.

right to work A term used to describe state statutory or constitutional provisions banning the requirement of union membership as a condition of employment.

rights arbitration Arbitration that interprets existing contract terms, for instance, when an employee questions the employer's right to have taken some disciplinary action.

role-playing A training technique in which trainees act out parts in a realistic management situation.

safety awareness program Program that enables trained supervisors to orient new workers arriving at a job site regarding common safety hazards and simple prevention methods.

salary survey A survey aimed at determining prevailing wage rates. A good salary survey provides specific wage rates for specific jobs. Formal written questionnaire surveys are the most comprehensive, but telephone surveys and newspaper ads are also sources of information.

savings and thrift plan Plan in which employees contribute a portion of their earnings to a fund; the employer usually matches this contribution in whole or in part.

Scanlon plan An incentive plan developed in 1937 by Joseph Scanlon and designed to encourage cooperation, involvement, and sharing of benefits.

scatter plot A graphical method used to help identify the relationship between two variables.

scientific management movement Management approach based on improving work methods through observation and analysis.

self-managing/self-directed work team A small (usually 8 to 10 members) group of carefully selected, trained, and empowered employees who basically run themselves with little or no outside supervision, usually for the purpose of accomplishing a specific task or mission.

severance pay A one-time payment some employers provide when terminating an employee.

sexual harassment Harassment on the basis of sex that has the purpose or effect of substantially interfering with a person's work performance or creating an intimidating, hostile, or offensive work environment.

sick leave Provides pay to an employee when he or she is out of work because of illness.

situational interview A series of job-related questions that focus on how the candidate would behave in a given situation.

situational test A test that requires examinees to respond to situations representative of the job.

social responsibility Refers to the extent to which companies should and do channel resources toward improving one or more segments of society other than the firm's owners or stockholders.

Social Security Federal program that provides three types of benefits: retirement income at the age of 62 and thereafter, survivor's or death benefits payable to the employee's dependents regardless of age at time of death, and disability benefits payable to disabled employees and their dependents. These benefits are payable only if the employee is insured under the Social Security Act.

staff authority Staff authority gives the manager the right (authority) to advise other managers or employees.

staff manager A manager who assists and advises line managers.

standard hour plan A plan by which a worker is paid a basic hourly rate but is paid an extra percentage of his or her rate for production exceeding the standard per hour or per day. Similar to piecework payment but based on a percent premium.

Standard Occupational Classification (SOC) Classifies all workers into one of 23 major groups of jobs that are subdivided into minor groups of jobs and detailed occupations.

stereotyping Ascribing specific behavioral traits to individuals based on their apparent membership in a group.

stock option The right to purchase a stated number of shares of a company stock at today's price at some time in the future.

straight piecework An incentive plan in which a person is paid a sum for each item he or she makes or sells, with a strict proportionality between results and rewards.

strategic human resource management Formulating and executing human resource policies and practices that produce the employee competencies and behaviors the company needs to achieve its strategic aims.

strategic management The process of identifying and executing the organization's strategic plan by matching the company's capabilities with the demands of its environment.

strategic plan The company's plan for how it will match its internal strengths and weaknesses with external opportunities and threats in order to maintain a competitive advantage.

strategy A course of action the company can pursue to achieve its strategic aims.

strategy map A strategic planning tool that shows the "big picture" of how each department's performance contributes to achieving the company's overall strategic goals.

strategy-based metrics Metrics that specifically focus on measuring the activities that contribute to achieving a company's strategic aims.

stress interview An interview in which the applicant is made uncomfortable by a series of often rude questions. This technique helps identify hypersensitive applicants and those with low or high stress tolerance.

strictness/leniency The problem that occurs when a supervisor has a tendency to rate all subordinates either high or low.

strike A withdrawal of labor.

structured (or directive) interview An interview following a set sequence of questions.

structured sequential interview An interview in which the applicant is interviewed sequentially by several persons; each rates the applicant on a standard form.

structured situational interview A series of job-relevant questions with predetermined answers that interviewers ask of all applicants for the job.

succession planning The ongoing process of systematically identifying, assessing, and developing organizational leadership to enhance performance.

suggestion teams Temporary teams whose members work on specific analytical assignments, such as how to cut costs or raise productivity.

supplemental pay benefits Benefits for time not worked such as unemployment insurance, vacation and holiday pay, and sick pay.

supplemental unemployment benefits Provide for a "guaranteed annual income" in certain industries where employers must shut down to change machinery or due to reduced work. These benefits are paid by the company and supplement unemployment benefits.

sympathy strike A strike that takes place when one union strikes in support of the strike of another.

Taft-Hartley Act of 1947 Also known as the *Labor Management Relations Act*, this law prohibited unfair union labor practices and enumerated the rights of employees as union members. It also enumerated the rights of employers.

talent management The goal-oriented and integrated process of planning, recruiting, developing, managing, and compensating employees.

task analysis A detailed study of a job to identify the specific skills required.

task statement Written item that shows *what* the worker does on one particular job task; *how* the worker does it; the *knowledge, skills, and aptitudes required* to do it; and the *purpose of the task*.

team (or group) incentive plan A plan in which a production standard is set for a specific work group, and its members are paid incentives if the group exceeds the production standard.

terminate at will In the absence of a contract, either the employer or the employee can terminate at will the employment relationship.

termination interview The interview in which an employee is informed of the fact that he or she has been dismissed.

test validity The accuracy with which a test, interview, and so on measures what it purports to measure or fulfills the function it was designed to fill.

third-country nationals Citizens of a country other than the parent or the host country.

Title VII of the 1964 Civil Rights Act The section of the act that says an employer cannot discriminate on the basis of race, color, religion, sex, or national origin with respect to employment.

tokenism When a company appoints a small group of women or minorities to high-profile positions, rather than more aggressively seeking full representation for that group.

training The process of teaching new or current employees the basic skills they need to perform their jobs.

transfer Reassignments to similar positions in other parts of the firm.

trend analysis Study of a firm's past employment needs over a period of years to predict future needs.

unclear standards An appraisal that is too open to interpretation.

unemployment insurance (or compensation) Provides benefits if a person is unable to work through some fault other than his or her own.

unfair labor practice strike A strike aimed at protesting illegal conduct by the employer.

Uniform Guidelines Guidelines issued by federal agencies charged with ensuring compliance with equal employment federal legislation explaining recommended employer procedures in detail.

union salting A union organizing tactic by which workers who are in fact employed full-time by a union as undercover organizers are hired by unwitting employers.

union shop A form of union security in which the company can hire nonunion people, but they must join the union after a prescribed period of time and pay dues. (If they do not, they can be fired.)

unsafe conditions The mechanical and physical conditions that cause accidents.

unstructured (or nondirective) interview An unstructured conversational-style interview in which the interviewer pursues points of interest as they come up in response to questions.

unstructured sequential interview An interview in which each interviewer forms an independent opinion after asking different questions.

valence The perceived value a person attaches to the reward.

variable pay Any plan that ties pay to productivity or profitability, usually as one-time lump payments.

video-based simulation A situational test in which examinees respond to video simulations of realistic job situations.

virtual classroom Teaching method that uses special collaboration software to enable multiple remote learners, using their PCs or laptops, to participate in live audio and visual discussions, communicate via written text, and learn via content such as PowerPoint slides.

virtual teams Groups of geographically dispersed coworkers who interact using a combination of telecommunications and information technologies to accomplish an organizational task.

vision statement A general statement of the firm's intended direction; it shows, in broad terms, "what we want to become."

Vocational Rehabilitation Act of 1973 The act requiring certain federal contractors to take affirmative action for disabled persons.

voluntary (or permissible) bargaining items Items in collective bargaining over which bargaining is neither illegal nor mandatory—neither party can be compelled against its wishes to negotiate over those items.

wage curve Shows the relationship between the value of the job and the average wage paid for this job.

Walsh-Healey Public Contract Act A 1936 law that requires minimum wage and working conditions for employees working on any government contract amounting to more than $10,000.

Web 2.0 learning Training that uses online technologies such as social networks, virtual worlds (such as Second Life), and systems that blend synchronous and asynchronous delivery with blogs, chat rooms, bookmark sharing, and tools such as 3-D simulations.

wildcat strike An unauthorized strike occurring during the term of a contract.

work samples Actual job tasks used in testing applicants' performance.

work sampling technique A testing method based on measuring performance on actual basic job tasks.

work sharing Refers to a temporary reduction in work hours by a group of employees during economic downturns as a way to prevent layoffs.

workers' compensation Provides income and medical benefits to work-related accident victims or their dependents regardless of fault.

workflow analysis A detailed study of the flow of work from job to job in a work process.

workforce (or employment or personnel) planning The process of deciding what positions the firm will have to fill, and how to fill them.

works councils Formal, employee-elected groups of worker representatives.

NAME/ORGANIZATION INDEX

Note: Page numbers with *f* indicate figures; those with *n* indicate endnotes; those with *t* indicate tables

A

ABB Inc., 516
Abbatiello, A., 28*n*42, 28*n*52, 162*n*83
Abbott, G., 586*n*98
ABC Virtual Communications Inc., 248–249
Abdow, D., 270*n*146
Abel, A. L., 270*n*149
Abelson, R., 510*n*2
Abosch, K., 412*n*5
Abrahamson, E., 271*n*161
Abudy, M., 414*n*100
Accenture, 12, 85, 141, 287*f*, 311
Achille, R. S., 383*n*96
Adams, E., 476*n*41
Adams, G., 163*n*151
Adams, Susan, 337*n*141
Adkins, J., 557*n*141
Adler, S., 198*n*93
ADP, 371
Aetna Insurance, 247
Agnello, P., 197*n*42
Agnew, J., 556*n*106
Agnvall, E., 162*n*62, 270*n*116
Aguinis, H., 197*n*24, 305*n*57, 305*n*104
Ahearne, M., 413*n*62
Ahmad, A., 226*n*58
Akhtar, S., 584*n*22
Alansky, K., 269*n*102
Albrecht, K., 539, 557*n*154
Alcoa, 505
Alder, S., 304*n*50
Aldrich, C., 269*n*85
Allen, D., 335*n*45
Allen, J., 92*n*10
Allen, R., 557*n*122
Allen, W. C., 268*n*29
Alliance of Motion Picture & Television Producers, 508
Alliant Techsystems, 318
Altman, Y., 586*n*81, 586*n*85
Ambos, Bjorn, 585*n*48
Ambrose, Maureen, 304*n*50, 304*n*51, 475*n*11
American Arbitration Association (AAA), 497
American Federation of Labor and Congress of Industrial Organizations (AFL-CIO), 483–484
American Management Association, 251, 255, 596
American Psychological Association (APA), 173
American Society for Training and Development (ASTD), 237–238
Anders, G., 163*n*115
Andersen, E., 556*n*96
Anderson, B., 586*n*90
Anderson, E., 93*nn*52–53
Andors, A., 446*n*48
Andrews, L., 477*n*79
Andrews, T., 556*n*71
Andrus, B., 557*n*147
Anfuso, D., 558*n*192
Antila, E., 92*n*12
Antonioni, D., 304*n*21, 304*n*23
Apex Door Company, 265–266
Apex Environmental, 222
Apple, 8, 10, 13, 20, 69, 72, 136, 147, 45
Applegate, J., 610*n*61
Aquino, K., 63*n*76
Arends, Brett, 336*n*126
Arkin, A., 556*n*105
Armour, S., 163*n*146
Armstrong, C., 65*n*130
Armstrong-Stassen, M., 62*n*9
Arneson, J., 268*n*32
Arnold, E., 511*n*47
Arnold, J., 162*nn*85–86, 162*n*88, 268*n*10, 268*n*11, 270*n*112
Arthur, W., 198*n*77
Aryee, Samuel, 93*n*57, 475*n*4
Asacker, T., 477*n*84
Ash, M., 510*n*6
Ashworth, S., 271*n*166
AT&T, 237, 505, 576
Athavaley, A., 225*n*27
Atkins, P., 304*n*20
Atkinson, W., 412*n*19, 558*n*158
Atlantic American Insurance Co., 99–100
Attaway, M., 477*n*90
Atwater, L., 304*n*25
Atwood, C., 161*n*28, 270*n*130
Austin, J., 271*n*160, 304*n*22, 305*n*79
Authoria ATS, 78
Aytemur, J. O., 335*n*26

B

Babcock, P., 335*n*73, 585*n*43
Bacharach, S., 557*n*136
Bachmann, D., 381*n*6
Baglieri, T., 446*nn*35–37
Bahlis, J., 268*n*39
Bain & Company, 205
Bain, T., 511*n*49
Baker, S., 93*n*47
Bakke, Allen, 57–60
Ball Corporation, 275
Ball, Deborah, 584*n*20
Ballentine, G., 268*n*41
Baltes, B., 448*n*178
Bamberger, P., 381*n*11
Barbazette, J., 269*n*53
Barnes, J., 63*n*78
Barrett, G., 305*n*82
Barrett, M., 610*n*78
Barrett, R., 27*n*8
Barrick, M., 164*n*164, 197*n*52, 198*n*83
Barron, T., 268*n*36
Barsness, Z., 584*n*6
Bartol, K., 414*n*105
Baruch, Y., 335*n*16
Barwick, K., 556*n*105
Bashline, D., 556*n*58
Bates, B., 27*n*4
Bates, S., 27*n*4, 304*n*32, 304*n*36
Bateson, J., 198*n*63
Batt, R., 335*n*50
Bauer, T., 268*n*3
Baum, M., 162*n*63
Baumann, E., 28*n*41
Bayer, R., 336*n*99, 336*n*102
Bayo-Moriones, A., 414*n*110
Beatty, R., 476*n*67
Beauchamp, T., 476*n*53
Bebchuk, L., 383*n*86, 414*n*95
Beck, R., 610*n*62, 610*n*64
Becker, B., 92*nn*32–33
Beehr, T., 63*n*75
Beer, M., 271*n*161, 271*n*163
Beeson, J., 270*n*125
Belcher, D. W., 383*n*78, 412*n*17
Belcourt, M., 269*n*52
Bell, C., 271*n*165
Bell, J., 198*n*100
Belogolovsky, E., 381*n*11
Belson, K., 445*n*12
Benelogic, 434
Bennington, E., 610*n*19
Berdahl, J., 63*n*64
Bergman, M., 63*n*73
Bergmann, T., 445*n*2
Berka, C., 199*n*141
Berliner, W., 269*n*60
Bernardin, H. J., 164*n*169, 305*n*82
Bernstein, E., 557*n*153
Berry, Paul, 585*n*58

Bersin, J., 28*n*44, 93*n*43, 197*n*16, 269*n*74
Berta, D., 269*n*78
Best Buy, 179
Betz, N., 196*n*11
Beus, J., 555*n*11
Bevilacqua, C., 414*n*101
Bielema, M., 556*n*88
Bindrum, K., 610*n*44
Bingham, J., 476*n*62
Birkner, G., 199*n*123
Biron, M., 558*n*163
Bittel, L., 477*n*110, 477*n*112, 477*n*115
Blakley, B. R., 197*n*44
Blanchard, P. N., 268*n*31, 268*n*38, 268*n*40, 269*n*75, 269*n*79, 269*nn*81–82, 269*nn*98–99
Bland, T., 65*n*120
Bledsoe, B., 270*n*125
Block, S., 163*n*146
Blood, M., 304*n*42
Blotzer, M., 556*n*60, 556*n*96
Bobko, P., 64*n*87, 198*n*73
Bock, Laszlo, 162*n*73, 172*n*74, 226*n*83, 226*n*90, 268*n*22, 303*n*12, 304*n*46, 334*n*11, 335*n*55, 336*n*74, 448*n*147, 476*n*29
Boeing Corp., 134
Bohlander, George, 477*n*116
Bohner, R., 162*n*103
Bolch, M., 225*n*22, 336*n*82
Bolino, M. C., 224*n*19
Bolles, R., 334*n*7, 334*n*8
Bompey, S., 65*nn*121–122
Bond, M., 447*n*80
Bon-Ton Stores Inc., 169
Born, M. P., 198*n*59
Borofsky, G., 556*n*88
Boswell, W., 163*n*129
Bottano, R., 413*n*75
Boudreau, G., 305*n*100
Bovis Lend Lease, 260
Bowie, Norman, 476*n*53
Bowles, R., 556*n*85
Bowling, N., 63*n*75
Bradley, D., 92*n*16
Brady, D., 270*nn*156–157
Branham, F. L., 336*n*106
Breaugh, J., 162*n*80, 162*n*82, 162*n*92, 163*n*120, 163*n*124, 163*n*129, 164*n*165, 198*n*84
Breslin, M., 198*n*65, 384*n*128
Brett, J. M., 584*n*6
Bretz, R., 161*n*115, 381*n*5
Brewster, C., 584*n*11
Bright, J., 335*n*18
British Petroleum (BP), 120–121, 251, 321
Brockbank, W., 17, 28*n*76
Bronfenbrenner, K., 511*n*39
Brotherton, P., 163*n*147
Brown, B., 227*n*72
Brown, D. W., 304*n*41
Brown, Duncan, 381*n*3, 384*n*125
Brown, R. D., 304*n*41
Bruce, R., 556*n*95
Brumback, G., 476*n*64
Brynjolfsson, E., 93*n*40, 93*n*46
Buchenroth, P., 382*n*45
Bucher, R., 65*n*144
Buckley, M. R., 224*n*19, 305*n*72, 477*n*85
Buddin, R., 448*n*144
Budworth, M., 305*n*103
Bull, R. A., 225*n*41, 225*n*53
Buller, P., 92*n*22
Burger, J., 225*n*48
Burke, M., 448*n*145, 556*n*94
Burlingame, H., 447*n*115
Burlington Industries, 40
Burns, J., 198*n*100
Burns, Sheila, 586*n*106
Bush, George H.W., 35
Buss, D., 476*n*70
Butts, M., 448*n*153
Byham, W., 477*n*78

C

Cable, D. M., 64*n*102, 271*n*164
Cable, J., 446*n*75, 556*n*100
Cabot, S., 512*n*74
Cadrain, D., 198*n*56, 199*n*140, 382*n*34, 412*n*15, 557*n*144
Caldwell, D., 225*n*48
Caldwell, Sandy, 409
Caligiuri, P., 197*n*54, 270*n*126, 585*n*68, 585*n*71, 585*n*74
Callender, J., 226*n*68
Caminiti, S., 161*n*36
Campbell, David, 477*n*111
Campbell, J. P., 412*n*13
Campion, M., 125*n*53, 125*n*55, 125*n*57, 224*n*8, 224*n*9, 225*n*41, 225*n*51, 225*n*53, 226*n*70, 226*n*72, 226*n*77, 226*n*79
Campoy, A., 63*n*78
Camps, J., 476*n*61
Camuso, M., 336*n*110
Canadian Auto Workers Union, 500
Canadian Red Cross, 546
Cannon-Bowers, J. A., 268*nn*47–49
Cantrell, Susan, 28*n*53, 587*n*137
Capelli, P., 197*n*38
Career FAQs, 207
Career Key, 310
Careerbuilder.com, 364
Carey, S., 512*n*92
Carlson, D, 475*n*10
Carlson, R. E., 225*nn*45–46, 226*n*80
Carnes, B., 269*n*102
Carpenter, M., 585*n*68
Carr, J. G., 476*n*27
Carr, L., 271*n*166
Carrell, M., 65*n*132, 382*n*58, 511*n*26, 511*n*43, 511*n*48, 511*n*53
Carter Cleaning Company, 25, 60, 89, 123, 159, 194, 223, 265, 302, 332, 379, 410, 443, 473, 509, 553, 582
Carter, Jennifer and Jack, 26, 60, 89, 194, 195, 223, 379, 410, 582
Carter, N., 335*n*27
Cascio, W., 124*n*12, 305*n*82
Casey, J., 163*nn*141–142
Casey, M., 268*n*31
Castagnera, J., 198*n*100
Castellano, S., 163*n*135
Castellano, W., 161*n*42
Caterpillar Inc., 500
Cauldron, S., 162*n*102
CEMEX, 574
Central Steel Door Corporation, 582
Cerner, 256
Chafkin, M., 610*n*66, 610*n*71
Chambers, A., 558*n*170
Chan, T. S., 65*n*138
Change to Win Coalition, 483, 504
Chapman, C., 557*n*112
Chapman, D., 224*n*1
Chappell, L., 125*n*56
Chaudhuri, A., 225*n*43
Cheesecake Factory, 179, 245, 248
Chelan County Public Utility District, 132
Chen, P. Y., 585*n*70
Chen, Peter Y., 585*n*70
Chen, S., 476*n*64
Childs Jr., J. T., 65*n*148
Chima, F., 558*n*167
China Post, 250
Ching-Hsing, 585*n*77
Christadore, R., 447*n*86
Christian, M., 28*n*69, 93*n*60, 476*n*56
Christiansen, N., 198*n*58
Chu, K., 412*n*8
Cingular Wireless, 504
Cioffi, Regina, 410
Cisco, 81, 247, 248, 567, 568
City Garage, 602–603
Clark, D., 414*n*93
Clark, L., 383*n*121
Clark, R., 270*n*110
Claus, L., 584*n*21, 586*n*122
Claussen, L., 557*n*137
Clemetson, L., 586*n*103
Clifford, J., 124*n*6

Clifford, S., 199*n*113
Cobb, A., 92*n*14
Coca-Cola, 69, 72, 235, 249
Cocchiara, F., 65*n*143
Coetzer, Alan, 335*n*67
Cohan, J., 478*n*149
Cohen, Alan, 447*n*92
Cohen, J., 383*n*121
Cohen, L., 199*n*122
Cohen, S., 585*n*48
Cohen, Susan, 585*n*48
Coil, J., 336*n*99, 336*n*102, 336*n*105
Colella, A., 65*n*140
Coleman, J., 382*n*21
Colvin, A., 335*n*50
Condeluci, C., 447*n*78
Conlin, B., 413*nn*67–68
Conlin, M., 611*n*83
Connolly, K., 65*n*145
Conseco, 402
Constans, J., 304*n*43
Constantin, S. W., 225*n*41
Conyon, M., 383*n*88
Cook, E., 336*n*77
Cooke, D., 199*n*127
Coombs, J., 448*n*168
Coomes, S., 415*n*123
Costco, 481
Cotter, M., 447*n*104
Cottereau, T., 162*n*61
Couchman, B., 92*n*15
Courtis, P., 448*n*133
Covey, S., 598, 610*n*42
Cox, T., 65*n*133, 65*n*135, 65*n*137, 65*n*144
Cox, W., 414*n*116
Coy, B., 92*n*37
Coy, P., 27*n*33
Coyle-Shapiro, J., 414*n*109
Craig, S.B., 303*n*16
Crawford, M. S., 197*n*44
Cropanzano, Russell, 477*n*80
Crowley, Mark, 477*n*124, 477*n*130, 478*n*139
Cruz, Lisa, 90, 123, 137, 160, 175, 195, 223, 266, 302, 333, 346, 380, 391, 411, 418, 444, 473, 474, 509, 553, 583, 608, 609
Csizmar, C., 586*n*88
Cuerton, G., 512*n*74
Cullen, L., 557*n*113
Cullen, S., 304*n*33
Cullison, J., 448*n*145
Culpan, T., 475*n*17
Culpepper, S., 197*n*24
Cummings, L. L., 584*n*6
Cummings, T., 271*n*161
Curcio, J., 446*n*66
Current, W., 557*n*142, 557*n*143
Custers, Michael, 448*n*151
CVS Caremark, 437

D

Dahl, D., 610*n*20, 610*n*22, 610*n*24, 610*n*26
Daimler, 95–96, 119–120
Dalessio, A., 225*n*40
Dallas-Fort Worth Airport, 435
Danaher, M., 335*n*70
Daniel, T., 475*n*19
Daniels, A., 412*n*14
Dartmouth University, 256
Dash, E., 415*n*126
Dash, J., 335*n*15
Davenport, T., 93*n*45
David, F., 92*n*6
David, J., 415*n*129
Davidshofer, C., 196*n*9, 197*n*12, 197*nn*22–23, 197*n*41, 224*n*17
Davis, R., 558*n*175
Davis-Howard, 269*n*59
Davison, Sue Canney, 585*n*47
Davlin, L., 610*n*63
Day, D., 161*n*27, 161*n*28
De Aenlle, Conrad, 382*n*42
De Avila, J., 162*n*59
De Fruyt, Filip, 336*n*128
De Kok, J., 610*n*33
De La Torre, P., 304*n*39
De Witt, L., 610*n*65
Deci, Edward, 412*n*11
DeConinck, J., 381*n*6
DeCotiis, T., 304*n*41
Dee, T. S., 412*n*22
DeGroot, T., 225*n*50
Del Carmen Triana, M., 65*n*140
Delaney, Jim, 265
Dell, 10, 247
Dell'omo, G., 336*n*90
Deloitte Touche Tohmatsu Limited, 139
Demby, E. R., 381*n*1, 382*nn*47–48
DeNisi, A., 304*n*40
Denison, D., 475*n*15
Dennis, D., 448*n*169
Deresky, Helen, 584*n*2, 586*n*94
DeRue, D. S., 512*n*62
Derven, M., 268*n*2
Deschenaux, J., 446*n*63, 558*n*177
DeShon, R. P., 476*n*27
Dessler, G., 226*n*87, 268*n*16, 335*n*29, 478m140
DeTuncq, T., 124*n*2
Deutsche Bank, 314
Development Dimensions International, 118, 178
DeVries, G., 446*n*76
Diamond, K., 558*n*198
Dickmeyer, W., 162*n*67
DiColo, J., 414*n*93
Diefendorff, J., 197*n*45
Dierdorff, E., 303*n*13
Dietz, G., 609*n*7, 609*n*9, 610*n*16, 610*n*36
Digh, P., 65*n*144
DiMarie, S., 585*n*48
Dipboye, R., 225*n*42
Discovery Benefits Inc., 434
Dixon, M., 224*n*18
Dizik, A., 164*n*162
Dodes, R., 268*n*1, 268*n*27
Doerpinghaus, H., 162*n*105
Doherty, L., 162*n*95–96
Doherty, M., 225*n*41
Dolan, M., 512*n*77
Dole Foods, 135
Dolezalek, H., 269*n*100, 270*n*150
Donham, C., 163*n*109
Donovan, M., 475*n*7
Doody, M., 335*n*24
Dormann, C., 335*n*68
Dougherty, C., 383*n*113
Dougherty, T., 226*n*68
Doverspike, D., 268*n*31
Dowling, D., 585*n*66, 586*n*87
Downes, M., 585*n*75
Doz, Y., 270*n*138
Dragoni, L., 270*n*137
Drake, J., 610*n*38
Dries, N., 124*n*3
Drucker, Peter, 27*n*24
Druskat, V., 303*n*13
Dube, L. E., 198*n*101
Ducharme, M. J., 303*n*4, 412*n*2
Dudley, J., 383*n*119
Dufresne, R., 477*n*78
Duke Power Co., 34, 58
Duncan, D., 609*n*5
Dunford, B., 414*n*92
Dunkelberger, K., 446*n*59
Dunnette, M. D., 412*n*12, 412*n*13
DuPont, 376, 515
Dvorak, P., 414*n*93
Dwyer, Timothy, 585*n*40
Dychtwald, K., 336*n*80, 336*n*85

E

Earhart, K., 448*n*141
Eckberg, S., 445*n*19
Eder, P., 335*n*61, 335*n*67
Eisenberger, R., 335*n*61
Eisenhardt, K., 92*n*4
Eisenstat, R., 271*n*161, 271*n*163
Electronic Arts (EA), 142
Elkeles, T., 271*n*172
Ell, R., 381*n*5

Ellig, B., 383*n*89, 414*n*79
Ellin, A., 163*n*154
Ellis, C., 268*n*25
Elswick, J., 586*n*97
Emerson, S., 383*n*110
Enron, 472
Environmental Tectonics Corporation, 248
Erdem, F., 335*n*26
Ericson, R., 413*n*77
Ernest, D., 335*n*45
Esen, E., 448*n*145
Esposito, J., 447*n*111
Etkind, S., 415*n*123
Evans, P., 270*n*138
Evered, J., 125*n*29
Express Auto, 409–410
Exxon, 191

F

Facebook, 9, 12, 42, 141, 142, 186, 248, 251, 276, 294, 341, 371, 376, 434, 435, 463, 500, 593, 594, 595
FaceTime, 207
Facteau, J., 303*n*16
Fair Labor Association (FLA), 450, 453
Falcon, P., 336*n*98, 477*n*112, 477*n*115
Falk, K., 610*nn*54–55
Famularo, J., 336*n*88
Fandray, D., 476*n*65
FBI, 155*f*, 255
Federal Mediation and Conciliation Service, 497
FedEx, 61*n*2, 138, 318, 467, 468, 469, 470
Feild, H., 63*n*86, 197*n*25
Feinberg, Mortimer, 293
Feintzeig, R., 28*n*54, 304*n*38, 308*n*88, 512*n*77
Feldacker, B., 61*n*4, 62*n*21
Feldman, D., 162*n*75, 162*n*105, 163*nn*152–153
Feliu, A., 558*n*172, 558*n*193, 558*nn*195–196
Fernandez Garcia, M., 65*n*140
Fernandez, Maria, 222–223
Ferrante, P., 558*n*174
Ferrell, L., 476*n*51, 476*n*52
Ferrell, O. C., 476*n*51, 476*n*52, 476*n*61
Ferris, D., 161*n*35
Fiester, M., 65*n*150
Figura, S., 556*n*50
Finch, R., 446*n*71
Finder, A., 199*n*102
Finkel, E., 477*n*86
First Advantage Corporation, 186
First Tennessee Bank, 397
Fischlmayr, I., 586*n*85
Fisher, J., 446*n*29
Fisher, Mel, 582
Fisher, S. L., 558*n*171
Fishman, C., 476*n*43
Fitzpatrick, L., 383*n*112
Fleischmann, S. T., 225*n*47
Fleites, L., 336*n*83
Flin, R., 556*n*106
Flynn, G., 446*n*31, 511*n*35
Fogli, L., 304*n*42
Folker, C., 609*n*8
Fong, S. C. L., 413*n*36
Fontenelle, G., 225*n*42
Foote, D., 335*n*14
Ford Motor Company, 137, 178, 246
Ford, J. K., 476*n*27
Fortunato, V. J., 304*n*22
Fossum, J., 511*n*55, 511*n*66, 512*n*65
Foulke, E., 555*n*22
Fox, A., 27*n*4, 28*n*47, 28*n*70, 93*n*61, 304*n*40, 305*n*60, 335*n*38, 584*n*16, 610*n*37
Fox, E. J., 446*n*44
Foxconn, 20, 450, 453
Fraedrich, J., 476*n*51, 476*n*52
France, A., 477*n*91
Francesco, A. M., 584*n*3, 584*nn*28–30
Frase-Blunt, M., 62*n*36, 163*n*122, 163*n*132, 224*n*16, 447*n*81, 585*n*39
Frauenheim, E., 93*n*46, 161*n*24, 163*n*111, 198*n*62, 198*n*67, 268*n*10, 335*n*54
Frazier, E., 383*n*115
French, W., 271*n*165
Freund, J. C., 511*n*59
Frey, C., 510*n*2
Freyvogel, T., 610*nn*47–49
Fried, J., 382*n*28, 383*n*86
Fried, Y., 92*n*12
Friedman, J., 382*n*28, 382*n*33
Friedman, L., 268*n*3
Friedman, S., 414*n*112
Fritz, N., 199*n*125
Fry, Erica, 27*n*21, 337*n*135, 337*n*138
Fuhrmanns, Vanessa, 446*n*67
Furst, S., 271*n*164
Fyfe-Mills, K., 334*n*1, 335*n*28

G

G. Neil Company, 170, 604
Galactica, S., 447*n*95
Galagan, P., 269*n*104, 270*n*119
Gale, S., 162*n*78, 197*n*28, 268*n*25
Garber, J., 557*n*118, 558*n*180, 558*n*183
Garcia, M., 65*n*140
Gardner, A. C., 414*n*115, 414*n*118
Garner, K., 225*n*42
Garvey, C., 414*n*105
Garvin, D., 93*n*48
Garza, A., 28*n*69, 93*n*60
Gatewood, R., 63*n*49, 63*n*86, 197*n*25
Gaugler, B., 198*n*77
Gaugler, E., 584*n*16
Gawker Media, 135
Gaylor, K., 335*n*34
GE Medical, 151, 367
GE, 10, 54, 136, 149, 151, 252, 257, 280, 287, 293, 367, 455
Gebler, D., 478*n*148
Geisel, J., 446*n*68, 447*n*115
Geisel, R., 448*n*138
Geller, E. S., 556*n*71, 556*n*86
Gellman, L., 304*n*24
General Dynamics Armament Systems (GDAS), 298–299
General Mills, 372
General Motors, 250, 505
Gentry, J., 585*n*69, 586*n*95
Gerbman, R., 200*n*160, 270*n*150
Gerhart, B., 381*n*14
Giancola, F., 383*n*102, 412*n*26, 445*n*5
Gibson, C., 585*n*48
Gilbert, S., 270*n*108
Gillette, 570
Gilliland, S., 226*n*86
Gilster, P., 162*n*68
Gino, F., 476*n*61
Giumetti, G., 304*n*34
Gladis, S., 270*n*151
Glairon, S., 163*n*145
Glassman, M., 413*n*42
Glendinning, P., 305*n*104, 413*n*65
Glomb, T., 475*n*20
Glover, W., 225*n*41
Gnyawali, D., 92*n*14
Goffin, R., 304*n*44
Gold, B., 584*n*5, 584*nn*28–30
Goldsmith, H., 383*n*38, 413*n*73, 413*n*75, 414*n*80, 414*n*86
Goldstein. H. W., 197*n*42
Goldwasser, D., 269*n*57
Gombar, R., 555*n*26
Goodfellow, M., 491, 511*n*35
Goodman, J. S., 268*nn*47–49
Goodman, M., 199*n*104
Goodroe, J., 415*n*119
Goodyear Tire & Rubber Company, 49
Google, 8, 9, 13, 21, 33, 62*n*10, 68, 69, 81, 82, 136, 140, 166, 178, 214, 218, 219, 234, 235, 250, 276, 285, 311, 318, 363, 371, 391, 401, 437, 467, 468, 469
Goomas, D. T., 304*n*51
Gooty, J., 225*n*50
Gopakumar, K., 335*n*22
Gordon, T., 557*n*110

Gorman, C., 225*n*41
Grady, T. O., 269*n*71
Graham-Moore, B., 414*n*115
Grant, D., 446*n*30
Grant, Tavia, 448*n*180
Graphic Media, 248
Graves, L., 224*n*3
Gray, C., 610*n*40
Green, J., 163*n*116
Green, P., 226*n*76
Greenberg, E., 336*nn*113–115
Greene, Robert, 415*n*121
Greengard, S., 198*n*95
Greenhaus, J. H., 65*n*138
Greenhouse, S., 510*n*2, 511*n*22, 511*n*28, 511*n*40, 512*n*102
Greenwald, J., 477*n*92
Gregersen, H., 586*n*104
Greguras, G., 305*n*70
Grensing-Pophal, L., 92*n*35, 92*n*37, 447*n*102
Griggs, K., 270*n*148
Griggs, Wilie, 34
Groce, D., 556*n*63
Grossman, R. J., 28*n*61, 65*n*136, 162*n*97, 162*n*103, 163*n*150, 198*n*82, 445*n*13, 445*n*16, 477*n*88, 477*n*114, 511*n*12, 512*n*99, 611*n*83
Grote, D., 477*n*118
Groysberg, B., 65*n*145
Gruman, J., 305*n*90
Grunberg, L., 336*nn*113–115
Guenole, N., 335*n*67
Gully, S., 63*n*36, 125*n*29, 125*n*48, 161*n*8, 161*n*25, 161*n*42, 196*n*3, 197*n*30, 198*n*85, 335*n*32, 335*n*41, 335*n*43
Gulotta, M., 447*n*115
Gundy, P., 413*n*59
Gurchiek, K., 164*n*163, 448*n*140
Guthrie, J., 27*n*24, 610*n*15

H

Haaland, D., 555*n*57
Hagerty, J., 512*n*84
Haggerty, James, 584*n*20
Hagmann, L., 414*n*105
Hahn, J. M., 199*n*114
Hahn, V., 335*n*68
Hakel, M., 125*n*17
Hall, M. J., 270*n*120, 511*n*33, 555*n*35
Hambrick, D., 414*n*94, 585*n*47
Hammer, W., 555*n*12
Han, K., 161*n*42
Hannah, R., 336*n*100, 475*n*6
Hannah, Sean, 475*n*6
Hannay, M., 448*n*138
Hansen, F., 161*n*10, 162*n*103, 196*n*8, 383*n*71, 383*n*93, 412*n*23, 414*n*86, 445*n*2, 586*n*123
Hao Zhao Oh, 163*n*130
Harbin, J., 163*n*110
Hargis, M., 92*n*16
Harmer, Mike, 610*n*78
Harpe, L., 162*n*65, 198*n*64
Harper, S., 447*n*124
Harris, D., 413*n*51
Harris, J., 93*n*45
Harris, M., 381*n*7, 412*n*21
Harris, P., 268*n*26, 269*n*87, 270*n*122, 448*n*159, 610*n*28
Harris, W. G., 199*n*126
Harrison, D., 65*nn*150–151, 161*n*6, 335*n*67, 476*n*54, 586*n*91
Hart, K., 197*n*39
Hartley, D., 124*n*10
Hartman, S., 477*n*114, 512*n*86
Hartshorn, D., 556*n*90
Hartwell, C., 224*n*8
Harvard Business Review, 82
Harvard, 256
Harvey, M., 335*n*19, 585*n*49, 585*n*65, 586*n*96
Harvey, T., 335*nn*19–20
Hasbro, 256
Hassink, W. H. J., 445*n*17
Hastings, Reed, 476*n*46, 607–608
Hatch, D. D., 511*n*3, 555*n*35
Hathaway Manufacturing, 409
Hauenstein, N., 304*n*41, 304*n*42
Haus, M., 199*n*136
Hausdorf, P., 609*n*5
Hauser, S., 63*n*48, 65*n*146
Hautelook, 298
Hayday, S., 305*n*95
Hayes, B., 335*n*23
Health maintenance organization (HMO), 426
Heath, C., 303*n*19
Heath, D., 224*n*3
Heavrin, C., 382*n*58, 511*n*26, 511*n*43, 511*n*48, 512*n*66, 512*n*88, 512*n*108
Hebl, M., 226*n*62
Heffes, E., 610*n*50
Heidemeier, H., 303*n*18
Heilman, M., 226*n*55, 305*n*67, 305*n*68, 336*n*75
Heineman Jr., B., 163*n*10
Heizer, J., 412*n*1
Heller, M., 198*n*91, 198*n*94
Henderson, N., 197*n*43
Henderson, R., 124*n*8, 124*n*11, 125*n*28, 197*n*43, 381*n*2, 381*n*14, 383*n*74, 412*n*16
Hendrickson, A., 585*n*48, 610*n*78
Heneman III, H., 304*n*41
Heneman, R., 383*n*102, 584*n*27
Henneman, T., 27*n*9, 162*n*46
Hernandez, L., 586*n*112
Herold, D., 271*n*161
Hershcovis, M. S., 558*n*190
Herskowitz, E., 335*n*71
Herzberg, Frederick, 100, 387, 388
Hibbing Taconite Steel Plant, 499
Hicks, S., 268*n*3, 268*n*4
Higgins, C., 225*n*53
Higgs, A. C., 271*n*166
Hijazi, S. T., 383*n*85
Hilbert, Dan, 130
Hill, C., 585*nn*61–65
Hill, J., 306*n*110
Hill, L., 37*n*36
Hillmer, B., 335*n*35
Hillmer, S., 335*n*35
Hills, F., 445*n*2
Hindman, H., 305*n*79
Hira, N., 269*n*65
Hirschman, C., 161*n*7, 162*n*106, 163*n*107, 336*n*88, 447*n*96, 447*n*131, 475*n*25, 448*n*160
Ho, A., 475*n*17
Hodson, S., 557*n*110
Hoffman, B., 198*n*76, 198*n*77, 198*n*86, 303*n*14
Hoffman, J., 556*n*88
Hofmann, D., 555*n*54
Hofmann, J., 270*n*109
Hofrichter, D., 383*nn*108–109
Hofstede, Geert, 562
Hogan, J., 197*n*46
Holland, J., 310, 336*n*127, 337
Hollande, Francois, 90
Home Depot, 152, 404
Hon Hai, 453
Honda, 181
Honoree, A., 381*n*8, 382*n*33
Hoobler, J., 558*n*187
Hopkins, C. D., 413*n*54, 413*n*59
Hopkins, W., 448*n*141
Hospital Management Corp., 188
Hostess Brands, 497
Hotel Paris, 21, 74, 90, 91, 108, 123, 137, 160, 175, 195, 206, 223, 243, 266, 267, 299, 302, 309, 333, 346, 380, 391, 411, 418, 444, 473, 474, 509, 510, 524, 553, 554, 565, 583, 604, 608
Hough, L. M., 412*n*12
Howe, N., 162*n*104
Howie, R., 199*n*121
HR Certification Institute (HRCI), 20
Hsi-An Shih, 586*n*104
Huff, C., 413*n*35
Huffcutt, A., 225*n*52, 226*n*57, 226*n*73
Hulin, C., 304*n*42
Hults, B., 92*n*15
Humphrey, S., 124*n*13, 125*n*17
Hunger, J. D., 92*n*5

Hung-Wen Lee, 585*n*77
Hunt, S., 125*n*46
Huntington Hospital, 539
Huselid, M., 92*n*33–34
Hutcheson, P., 335*n*13
Hymowitz, C., 163*n*116
Hyundai, 497

I

Ibarra, H., 335*n*27
IBM, 16, 55, 138, 144, 234, 249, 251, 420, 429, 459, 460, 565, 566, 567, 568, 572, 578, 579, 595, 608
Ilies, R., 197*n*51
Iliescu, D., 198*n*61
Imberman, W., 414*n*116, 414*n*119
Immelt, Jeffrey, 252
Inc. magazine, 595
In-Sook Kim, 586*n*104
Intel Corp., 134
International Association for Human Resource Information Management, 605
International Atomic Energy Agency (IAEA), 528
International Brotherhood of Teamsters, 483
International Coach Federation, 257
International Fitness Holdings, 376
Interstate, 52
InterviewStream Inc., 207
Intuit, 250, 311, 371, 392
Irlenbusch, B., 414*n*108
Isler, E., 336*n*104

J

J. P. Morgan, 251
Jackson, B., 555*n*27
Jackson, H., 163*n*109
Jackson, K. A., 224*n*19
Jaffee, C., 197*n*41
Jago, I. A., 197*n*44
Janov, J., 63*n*77
Janssens, M., 584*n*6
Jargon, Julie, 446*n*54
Jarventaus, J., 269*n*84
Jawahar, I. M., 305*n*64
Jean, S., 337*n*140
Jenkins, A., 197*n*37
Jenks, J., 92*n*2
Jensen, Jaclyn, 475*n*20
JetBlue Airways, 150
JLG, 372, 373
Johnson & Johnson, 257
Johnson Lane Corp., 52
Johnson, R., 28*n*51
Johnson, S., 268*n*51
Joie de Vivre Hospitality (JDV), 75, 402
Joinson, C., 335*n*17, 586*n*130
Jones, C., 198*n*71, 198*n*79
Jones, J., 199*n*124
Jorgensen, J., 446*n*40
Jossi, F., 586*n*124, 586*n*125
Judge, T., 64*n*102, 197*n*47, 197*n*51, 225*n*53, 334*n*3
Jun, S., 585*n*69, 586*n*95
Juniper Networks Inc., 287

K

Kabst, R., 162*n*63
Kahanar, E., 446*n*61
Kahn, R., 610*n*78
Kaiser Permanente, 149, 482
Kakkonen, A., 92*n*12
Kaleba, K., 269*n*62, 269*n*92
Kalkstein, H. M., 415*n*124
Kamm, N., 477*n*95
Kammeyer-Mueller, J., 268*n*5
Kane, D., 558*n*189, 558*n*197
Kanfer, R., 412*n*12, 412*n*13
Kaplan, R., 558*n*185
Kaplan, S. L, 381*n*2
Kapur, K., 448*n*144
Karau, S. J., 336*n*106
Karr, A., 558*n*175
Karren, R., 224*n*3
Katz, H., 511*n*38
Katzenbach, J., 476*n*40
Kauffman, J., 556*n*101
Kaul, P., 226*n*81
Kaupin, G., 477*n*106
Kearney, D., 125*n*39–40
Keaveny, T., 63*n*67
Keller, C., 447*n*78
Keller, E., 383*n*117
Kernan, M., 305*n*82
Kesselring, R., 199*n*148
Ketter, P., 93*n*73, 269*n*72, 269*n*91
Keys, B. J., 412*n*22
Kiger, P., 334*n*12, 447*n*120, 448*n*139
Kilgour, J., 382*n*55, 382*n*60, 383*n*63, 383*n*65, 383*n*73, 383*n*76, 383*n*77, 383*n*81, 447*n*100
Kim Soonhee, 335*n*36
Kim, A., 161*n*42
Kim, E., 475*n*20, 475*n*21
Kim, S., 27*n*2, 161*n*26, 161*n*30, 270*n*128, 270*n*132, 335*n*36, 414*n*109,
Kim, Y., 93*n*55
Kimberly-Clark, 528
King-Metters, K., 584*n*24
Kinicki, A., 305*n*104
Kirkman, B., 584*n*10, 585*n*57, 585*n*59
Kish-Gephart, J., 476*n*54
Klaas, B., 162*n*75, 336*n*90, 383*n*110
Klaff, L., 586*n*132
Klamm, D., 337*n*136
Klass, L., 584*n*31
Klein, H., 268*n*3
Kleps, K., 269*n*82
Klinefelter, J., 63*n*84
Kobata, M., 62*n*25
Koch, D., 270*n*117
Koelling, C. P., 415*n*120
Koen, C., 512*n*86
Koen, D., 337*n*133
Kohl, J., 62*n*13
Kohler, B., 65*n*133
Kolman, D., 557*n*113
Komaki, J., 556*n*105
Konrad, A., 93*n*71, 337*n*134
Korkke, P., 337*n*139
Korsgaard, M. A., 303*n*18
Kotey, B., 609*n*8
Kotter, J. P., 271*n*161, 271*n*162
Kraft, 574
Kraimer, M., 587*nn*133–135
Kranz, G., 269*n*88, 448*n*186
Krausert, A., 93*n*57
Krell, E., 92*n*1, 92*n*38, 162*n*47, 162*n*91, 268*n*50, 335*n*49
Kristof, A. L., 225*n*52
Kristof-Brown, A., 225*n*49
Krohe, J., 476*n*77, 557*n*154
Kroll, M., 414*n*106
Kronos, 371
Krueger, J., 383*n*122, 414*n*78
Krug, J. A., 414*n*106
Kruse, K., 93*n*62
Kujawa, P., 447*n*105, 447*n*106
Kulkarni, M., 268*n*8, 335*n*22
Kurbanoglu, N. I., 269*n*69
Kwoh, L., 162*n*52, 304*n*30, 306*n*109

L

Lachnit, C., 198*n*90
Lacy, D. A., 62*n*9
Ladd, S., 413*n*53
Ladika, S., 161*n*34, 162*n*97, 200*n*159, 269*n*89, 447*n*90
Laff, M., 161*n26,* 269*nn*79–80, 448*n*145
Lance, C., 305*n*61, 305*n*63
Landis, R., 335*n*45
Lane, I., 197*n*41, 198*n*74
Langdale, J., 225*n*45
Lanza, R., 336*n*94
Lapolice, C., 125*n*42
Lapowsky, I., 162*n*48
Larcker, D. F., 611*n*83
Larraza-Kintana, M., 414*n*110
Larsen, S., 556*n*70
Lasek, M., 196*n*6, 198*n*100

Latham, G., 226*n*72, 268*n*44, 269*n*56, 271*n*167, 271*n*169, 303*n*9, 304*n*41
Laudon, J., 610*n*78
Laudon, K., 610*n*78
Lauffs, A., 584*n*23
Laurent, A., 270*n*138
Lavelle, L., 414*n*98
Lawler, E., 28*n*50, 304*n*47, 305*n*99, 605*n*99
Lazarus, H., 415*n*124
Leaman, C., 270*n*143
Learning management systems (LMS), 250
LeBlanc, P., 383*n*102
Ledford, G., 383*n*103
Ledvinka, J., 62*n*20, 63*n*49, 64*n*98, 197*n*14
Lee, K., 268*n*49, 269*n*52
Leffler, F., 477*n*97
Lefkowitz, J., 476*n*78
Leiter, M., 558*n*160m 558*n*161
Lengnick-Hall, M., 63*n*45, 268*n*8
Lenius, P., 476*n*31
Lenox Hill Hospital, 158
Leonard, B., 65*n*152, 163*n*115, 197*n*26, 199*n*133, 447*n*98, 477*n*91, 610*n*52
Leonard, D., 477*n*91
Leung, Rebecca, 477*n*125
Levashina, J., 224*n*8
Levere, Jane, 586*n*129
Levi Strauss, 387, 403
Levine, D., 555*n*8
Levinson, E., 334*n*6
Levy, W., 511*n*41
Lewin, Kurt, 258–259
Li, J., 270*n*149
Liccione, William, 383*n*76
Licht, T., 62*n*38
Liddick, B., 447*n*86
Liden, R., 163*n*130
Liemandt, Joe, 159
Lievens, F., 163*n*127
Lincoln Electric Company, 405
LinkedIn, 12, 137, 186, 251, 341, 594–595
Lionel, T., 448*n*149
Liptak, A., 65*n*127, 65*n*129, 65*n*154
Lisko, R., 199*n*148
LivingSocial, 13, 298
Livingston, B., 270*n*117
Lloyd's of London, 135
Locke, E. A., 303*n*8
Lockheed Martin Corp., 81, 221, 456, 460
Lockwood, F., 557*n*146
Lohr, Steve, 477*n*107
London, M., 305*n*62, 305*n*81
Long, C., 475*n*3
Longnecker, B., 383*n*122, 414*n*78
Lopez, T. B., 413*n*54, 413*n*59
Los Angeles, city of, 541
Love, C., 92*n*4
Lowe, Linda, 122
Lowry, P., 226*n*74
Lowsky, Bram, 336*n*107
Lublin, J., 163*n*116, 336*n*117
Luchak, A., 336*n*84
Luecke, R., 305*n*84
Lundy, J., 162*n*90
Lunser, G. K., 414*n*108
Luo, S., 413*n*52, 413*n*54
Lurie, M., 512*n*90
Lutes, M., 446*n*57
Luthans, F., 412*n*14, 412*n*28, 413*n*38
Luxottica, 250
Luzzi, V. I., 199
Lyness, K., 305*n*67, 336*n*75
Lytle, A. L., 584*n*6
Lytle, T., 476*n*37

M

Mabey, C., 610*n*40
Macan, T., 224*n*4, 226*n*84
MacDonald, S., 199*n*137, 199*nn*142–144, 448*n*133
Macy's, 232, 236
Madera, J., 226
Madhani, P., 413*n*49, 413*n*56
Madison Square Garden, 60–61
Maher, C., 226*n*93, 511*n*11, 511*n*30, 512*n*93
Maher, K., 513*n*98
Mahmood, M., 226*n*66
Maier, A., 270*n*148
Maier, N., 270*n*148
Maiorca, J., 304*n*42
Makino, 144
Maltby, E., 224*n*20
Malveaux, Courtney, 555*n*48
Mamorsky, J. D., 415*n*124
Mangalindan, J. P., 445*n*1, 448*n*158
Manjoo, F., 27*n*18, 27*n*22, 29*n*86, 383*n*98, 478*n*133
Mann, E., 65*n*132
Mann, Phil, 122–123
Manolopoulos, D., 383*n*99
Marakas, G., 93*n*41
Marion, C., 269*n*73
Mark, B., 555*n*54
Markham, S., 414*nn*116–117
Markowich, M. M., 445*n*19
Marks, Mitchell Lee, 336*n*108
Marks, S., 383*n*82, 415*n*128
Marlowe, C., 226*n*55, 226*n*56
Maroney, K., 446*n*62
Marquardt, M., 270*n*139
Marquez, J., 382*n*46, 447*n*108, 512*n*63, 586*n*120
Marriott, 421
Marshall, J., 610*n*50
Martin, D., 305*n*77
Martin, S., 446*n*26
Martineau, J., 269*n*63
Martineau, Y., 337*n*132
Martinez, A., 124*n*14
Martinez, M., 163*n*113
Martocchio, J., 381*n*14, 382*nn*55–56, 382*n*62, 383*n*64, 383*n*72, 383*n*79, 383*n*88, 383*n*97, 383*n*104, 414*n*114, 445*n*6, 447*n*102, 448*n*163
Maslach, C., 558*n*160
Mason, J. F., 477*n*111
Masterson, S., 475*n*14
Mathews, Anna, 446*n*54
Mathis, T., 557*n*110
Matthews, M., 269*n*71
Mattioli, D., 336*n*92
Maurer, R., 558*n*200, 558*n*203, 558*n*205, 558*n*212
Maurer, T., 226*n*74, 226*n*77
Mavity, Howard, 556*n*65
Mayer, D., 65*n*142, 476*n*73, 477*n*113
Mayer, M., 198*n*90
Mayfield, J., 62*n*13
Mayfield, M., 62*n*13
Maylett, T., 304*n*25
Mayo Clinic, 233
Mayrhofer, W., 586*n*85
Mayson, S., 27*n*8
McAfee, A., 93*n*40
McCall, A., 611*n*83
McCarthy, J., 225*n*34, 226*n*71, 305*n*73
McCord, P., 305*n*87
McCormick, E. J., 125*n*45
McCreary, C., 163*n*118
McCunney, R. J., 199*n*143
McDaniel, M., 198*n*75, 199*n*149, 224*n*3, 224*n*6, 224*n*11, 225*n*37, 225*n*39
McDaniel, T., 557*n*111
McDonald, J., 62*n*31
McDonald's, 55
McDonnell-Douglas Corporation, 44–45
McElligott, J., 447*n*83
McEntire, L., 125*n*25
McEvoy, G., 92*n*22
McFarland, L., 198*n*73, 225*n*49
McGregor, J., 304*n*31
McGrory, K., 447*n*84
McIntyre, 413*n*70
McKay, P., 65*n*139
McKinsey & Co., 287
McLarney, W., 269*n*60
McMullen, Tom, 383*n*124, 384*n*126, 384*n*130, 384*n*136, 415*n*130
McQueen, M. P., 62*n*37

MCR Safety, 528
McRoberts, G., 335*n*35
Meade, J., 304*n*27
Mehta, K., 197*n*45
Meinert, D., 63*n*51, 163*n*106, 198*n*96, 199*n*118, 448*n*169, 448*n*173
Melchers, K. G., 226*n*72
Meltzer, M., 383*n*88, 413*n*73, 413*n*75
Melymuka, K., 336*n*78
Men's Wearhouse, 243
Merck, 54
Meredith, R., 163*n*110, 585*n*75
Meriac, J., 198*n*78
Meritor Savings Bank FSB, 40
Merrell Dow Pharmaceuticals, 567
Merriman, K., 414*n*105, 414*n*107
Messersmith, J., 93*n*59, 610*n*15
Messmer, M., 335*n*47, 335*n*48
Metters, R., 584*n*24
Meyer, D., 511*n*49
Miceli, S., 226*n*59
Michalak, D., 269*n*67
Michel, J. W., 198*n*86
Microsoft, 82, 147, 206, 242, 258, 280, 398, 406
Middendorf, C., 226*n*84
Middlemist, R. D., 448*n*141
Mihelich, M., 162*n*97, 163*n*131, 199*n*112, 336*n*95, 336*n*97, 512*n*104
Mikes, A., 558*n*185
Miller, B., 382*n*32
Miller, J. G., 162*n*99
Miller, M., 162*n*99
Miller, R., 124*n*9, 270*n*146
Miller, S., 162*n*104
Milliken & Co., 534
Milne, S., 336*n*106
Miner, 270*n*109
Minton-Eversole, T., 163*n*134
Mitchell, M., 475*n*11, 476*n*62
Mo Wang, 336*n*81
Moberg, D., 476*n*55
Moen, P., 334*n*2
Mohn, T., 586*n*130
Mone, E., 305*n*62, 305*n*81
Moore, S., 336*n*113
Moran, J., 63*n*82, 63*n*85
Moran, Patricia, 446*n*52
Morgan, R., 303*n*4
Morgeson, F., 124*n*13, 125*n*17, 198*n*57, 198*n*58, 225*n*41, 225*n*53
Morin, W. J., 336*n*106
Morrell, D., 413*n*35
Morris, B., 61*n*3
Morris, D., 335*n*72
Morris, G. J., 270*n*136
Morris, S., 476*n*55
Mosar, K., 303*n*18
Moser, P., 162*n*56
Mosley, E., 306*n*107
Moynihan, L. M., 224*n*21
Muczyk, J. P., 269*n*69
Muldowney, P., 446*n*59
Mullenweg, M., 225*n*29
Mullich, J., 163*n*126
Munniksma, L., 163*n*123, 163*n*128
Murdy, Al, 556*n*106
Murphy, K., 196*n*9, 197*n*12, 197*n*14, 197*n*19, 197*n*22, 197*n*41, 198*n*58, 224*n*17, 303*n*17, 304*n*43
Murray Supply Co., 454
Musinski, L., 585*n*75
Musselwhite, C., 270*n*146
Myers, B., 585*n*76
Myers, J., 555*n*27
Myers, R., 226*n*82

N

Nahrgang, J., 557*n*109
Nancherla, A., 224*n*14, 269*n*64
Napier, 586*n*85
Nash, G. N., 269*n*69
Nash, J., 556*n*103, 558*n*181
National Association of Manufacturers (NAM), 252, 596
National Football League, 495
National Institute for Occupational Safety and Health (NIOSH), 530, 546
National Labor Relations (Wagner) Act (1935), 352, 457, 484, 487–488, 490, 499
National Labor Relations Board (NLRB), 352, 484, 488, 499
Neary, D. B., 303*n*2, 305*n*58
Needleman, S., 197*n*40, 200*n*154
Nelson, B., 413*n*36
Nelson, C., 226*n*55
Nelson, Jack, 25
Nelson, M., 381*n*10
Netflix, 607–609
New United Motor Manufacturing Inc. (NUMMI), 505
New York Knicks, 60–61
Newport, M. G., 512*n*90
Ng, T., 163*n*147, 163*n*152
Nicas, J., 512*n*92
Nichols, G., 447*n*103
Nicholson, G., 609*n*1, 610*n*72
Niederkohr, T., 476*n*26
Nighswonger, T., 556*n*59, 557*n*154, 558*n*164
Nishii, L., 65*n*142
Noa, Jesse, 446*n*49
Nobile, R., 382*n*43
Nolan, Hamilton, 448*n*179, 448*n*187, 510*n*1, 511*n*7
Northam, M., 448*n*138
Northrop Grumman Corp., 437
Northrup, H., 512*n*76, 512*n*82
Nucor Corp., 406
Nutt, P., 92*n*8
NuView Inc., 595

O

O'Boyle, E., 305*n*57
O'Connell, B., 413*n*55
O'Connell, J., 447*n*132
O'Leary, B., 65*n*131
Occupational Safety and Health Administration (OSHA) citing supervisors, 517
inspections, citations, 518–520
responsibilities, rights, 520–523
standards, record keeping of, 517
Occupational Safety and Health Review Commission (OSHRC), 520
Office Depot, 603
Office of Federal Contract Compliance Programs (OFCCP), 32
Offstein, E., 92*n*14, 477*n*78
Okimoto, Y., 305*n*68
Olson, M. H., 414*n*118
Ones, D., 198*n*58
O*NET, 107–108, 112–117, 119, 134, 310, 331, 338, 593
Optima Air Filter Company, 122–123
Oracle, 370
Ordonez, L., 476*n*56
Orlitzky, M., 163*n*123
Orsburn, J., 476*n*42
Osawa, J., 162*n*56
Ostroff, S., 304*n*19
Ostrower, Jon, 512*n*85, 512*n*85
Otte, F., 335*n*13
Outback Steakhouse, 172
Overman, S., 163*n*114, 586*n*106
Overtime Calculator Advisor, 593
Overtime Security Advisor, 593
Ovide, S., 304*n*38
Owens, D., 446*n*40, 448*n*134

P

Pace, A., 269*n*88
Pacific Gas & Electric Company, 255
Pacific Timesheet, 348
Pajo, K., 335*n*67
Palais, L., 477*n*97
Palank, J., 512*n*64
Palmer, D., 226*n*77, 226*n*79
Panepento, P., 163*n*110
Pappas, M., 65*n*121–122
Paquette, Roger, 556*n*73
Paradise, A., 269*n*63
Parasuraman, S., 65*n*138
Park, H., 304*n*23
Park, S., 412*n*22

Park, T., 335*n*33, 335*n*37
Parker-Pope, T., 557*n*150
Parmenter, E., 447*n*117
Pascale, D. L., 304*n*50
Patagonia, 21, 173
Patel, A., 415*n*119
Pater, R., 555*n*56, 556*n*79, 556*n*85
Pati, G., 557*n*141
Patterson, M., 197*n*41, 198*n*100
Payless ShoeSource, 353
Payne, D., 512*n*86
Payne, R., 226*n*96, 337*n*144, 337*n*147
Peak, M., 270*n*149
Pearson Corporation, 4
Pearson Pennsylvania Hospital, 281
Pedigo, L., 197*n*41
Peiperl, Maury, 585*n*72
Pell, A., 226*n*67, 226*n*69, 226*n*71
Pelled, L. H., 335*n*63
Penney, L., 197
Pension Benefits Guarantee Corporation (PBGC), 433
PepsiCo, 17, 69, 71–72, 75, 400, 572
Performance Programs Inc. (PPI), 395
Perlez, J., 27*n*16
Perry, B., 268*n*37, 556*n*68
Perry, P., 610*n*56
Perryman, S., 305*n*95
Peters, L., 304*n*40
Peters, M., 270*n*140
Peters, T., 476*n*44
Petersen, D., 555*n*50
Peterson, C., 198*n*83
Peterson, S., 305*n*104, 412*n*14, 412*n*28, 413*n*38
Pettus, M., 414*n*106
Pflug, W., 511*n*13
Phillips, J., 63*n*86, 125*n*29, 125*n*48, 161*n*8, 161*n*25, 161*n*42, 196*n*3, 197*n*30, 198*n*85, 271*n*170
Phillips, P., 271*n*170, 270*n*172
Phillips, Z., 586*n*126
Pierce, C., 197*n*24
Pierce, F. D., 555*n*13
Pinellas County, 6
Pirie, C., 270*n*115
Pitt-Catsouphes, M., 163*n*141
Pittman, J., 199*n*148
Piturro, M., 336*n*109
Plachy, R., 125*n*29, 382*n*63
Ployhart, R., 93*n*55, 197*n*19
Poe, A., 226*n*81, 336*n*86, 477*n*105
Poerio, M., 383*n*117
Pohley, K., 198*n*77
Polaroid Corp., 20
Polimeni, R. S., 269*n*87
Pomeroy, A., 29*n*80, 270*n*137, 270*n*146, 305*n*72, 448*n*174, 477*n*85
Porter, M., 93*n*10
Porter, T., 161*n*38
Portman Hotel, 67, 74
Posthuma, R., 225*n*51, 226*n*70
Powell, C., 584*n*18
Powell, M., 557*n*119, 557*n*127
Predictive Index, 594
Preferred provider organizations (PPOs), 426
Prezant, F., 226*n*60
Prichard, R., 412*n*13
Pridgen, ., 447*n*109
Pringle, J. K., 585*n*76
Probst, T., 555*n*5
Procter & Gamble (P&G), 73, 579, 370, 578
Prussia, G., 305*n*104
PTC, 324
Pulakos, E., 182, 198*n*72, 279, 305*n*75, 305*n*82
Puncochar, P., 557*n*129
Pursell, E., 226*n*72, 226*n*75, 512*n*121, 512*n*122
Pyrillis, R., 64*n*107, 447*n*87, 447*n*116

Q

Quinones, M., 197*n*44, 199*n*77

R

Rafter, M. V., 412*n*30, 447*n*127, 585*n*36
Railton, W. S., 555*n*28
Rampell, C., 198*n*80
Rao, L., 306*n*107, 306*n*108
Rau, B., 163*n*151
Raymond, M. A., 413*n*54, 413*n*59
Ready, D., 27*n*36
Reagan, B., 447*n*129
Red Door Interactive, 455
Red Robin Gourmet Burgers, 49
Reda, J., 383*n*84, 414*n*79
Reeves, M., 93*n*4
Regini, Marino, 586*n*119
Reider, M. H., 225*n*41, 226*n*53
Reilly, Peter, 225*n*40, 225*n*42, 384*n*125
Reis, M., 269*n*94
Reiter-Palmon, R., 124*n*22
Reitz, D., 610*n*70
Rekus, J., 556*n*91
Render, B., 412*n*1
Rent A Center, 430
Reynolds, J., 414*n*116
Reynolds, M., 415*n*119
Reynolds, S., 476*n*55
Rice, C., 336*n*99, 336*n*102, 336*n*105
Rice, J., 65*n*147
Rich, B. L., 93*n*67, 93*n*70
Rich, M., 555*n*10
Richardson, R., 496, 511*n*61, 512*n*89
Risher, H., 93*n*48, 303*n*3, 304*n*29, 304*n*45, 305*n*74, 305*n*103, 306*n*115, 381*n*12, 412*n*21, 413*n*45
Ritz-Carlton Company, 74, 78
Robb, D., 269*n*86, 446*n*72, 447*n*125
Robbins, J., 475*n*9
Robbins, S., 334*n*3, 335*n*42, 476*n*27
Roberson, Q., 478*n*150
Roberts, B., 93*n*54, 161*n*11, 161*n*17, 161*n*31, 17*n*17, 198*n*92, 199*n*129, 270*n*114, 270*n*133, 447*n*94, 448*n*164, 477*n*96, 477*n*98, 584*n*15
Roberts, S., 557*n*145
Robinson, A., 413*n*43
Robinson, D., 305*n*95
Robinson, S., 336*n*111
Roble, D., 414*n*116
Rockwell International, 52
Rodgers, D., 225*n*23
Rodgers, J., 447*n*122
Rodriguez, A., 226*n*60
Roehling, P., 334*n*2
Rogers, E., 556*n*81
Rogers, K., 270*n*136, 304*n*50
Rosen, D., 62*n*27, 62*nn*29–30
Rosenblum, K., 556*n*89
Ross, A., 125*n*36
Ross, J. D., 305*n*101
Ross, T., 414*n*115
Rossler, P., 415*n*120
Roth, P., 64*n*87, 198*n*73, 226*n*57
Rotundo, M., 63*n*75
Rowe, M., 63*n*79
Rowe, P., 225*n*42
Rubenfeld, S., 415*n*129
Rubinger, J., 556*n*99
Ruiz, G., 162*n*60, 163*n*138, 610*n*43, 610*n*46
Ruiz, R., 125*n*27
Rusli, Evelyn, 610*n*13
Russell, R., 555*n*56
Ryan, A. M., 196*n*6, 587*n*139, 587*n*143
Ryan, M., 384*n*127
Ryan, R., 197*n*42
Rynes, S., 161*n*37, 163*n*123, 381*n*14
Ryu, S., 27*n*2

S

Sadri, G., 268*n*40
Saidler, J. M., 556*n*100
Sainfort, P. C., 304*n*50
Saks, A. M., 226*n*71, 269*n*52, 305*n*90
Salary.com, 347, 364
Salasko, E., 162*n*103
Salopek, J., 268*n*33, 269*n*92, 269*n*96, 271*n*173
Salz, L., 270*n*109

Sam's Club, 441, 481
Sammer, J., 305*n*71, 446*n*58, 447*n*83, 447*n*105
Sanchez, J., 304*n*39
Sandberg, J., 125*n*44
Sanders, W. G., 414*n*94
Sands, S. S., 413*n*58
Sankpill, J. P., 556*n*77
Sanofi SA, 493–494
Sapper, A., 555*n*26, 555*n*30, 555*n*47
Sarbanes-Oxley Act (2002), 375, 398, 461
Sarchione, C., 197*n*53
Saru, E., 610*n*41
Saruwatari, L., 226*n*55
SAS Institute Inc., 435
Saudi Petrol Chemical Co., 535
Sauer, Robert, 586*n*119
Scanlon, Joseph, 404–405
Scarpello, V., 445*n*2, 446*n*45
Schaffer, B., 412*nn*12–13
Schein, E., 337*n*131
Scherbaum, C., 197*n*42
Schleicher, D. J., 304*n*36
Schlemglmich, B., 585*n*48
Schmidt, A. M., 476*n*27
Schmidt, F., 225*n*36
Schmidt, J., 269*n*68
Schmidt, L., 124*n*2
Schminke, M., 476*n*77
Schneider, B., 271*n*166
Schneider, S., 226*n*55
Schoeff, M., 512*n*110, 586*n*113, 587*n*142
Schoenfelt, E., 197*n*41
Schramm, J., 27*n*26, 448*n*143, 512*n*95
Schroeder, A., 304*n*34
Schroeder, D., 413*n*43
Schultz, D., 224*n*5, 225*n*52, 269*n*69, 555*n*55
Schultz, S. E., 224*n*5, 225*n*52, 269*n*69, 555*n*55
Schumann, Paul, 476*n*51
Schuster, J., 383*n*97, 383*n*132, 413*n*43, 413*n*75
Schwab, D., 304*n*41
Scott, C., 511*n*47
Scott, D., 383*n*124, 383*n*130, 415*n*130, 512*n*101
Scott, D. R., 92*n*38
Scott, J. C., 305*n*62, 305*n*81
Scott, K. D., 414*n*116
Scott, L., 56*n*105
Scroggins, W. A., 197*n*53
Scullion, H., 586*n*85
Seabrook, K., 557*n*131
Seago, J., 510*n*6
Seaman, R., 414*n*106
Searcey, D., 414*n*85, 477*n*94, 477*n*97
Securities and Exchange Commission (SEC), 375
Segal, J., 161*n*39, 305*n*59, 336*n*101, 511*n*44
Selmer, J., 585*n*69, 585*n*76, 586*n*95
Sels, L., 610*n*14
Servais, S., 610*n*73
Service Employees International Union (SEIU), 483, 508
Sesil, J., 415*n*125
Shaffer, M., 335*n*67, 413*n*36, 585*n*74, 586*n*91
Shaller, E. H., 62*n*27, 62*n*29–30
Shanker, T., 303*n*10
Shannon, J., 161*n*6, 161*n*9
Shao, Alsoruodan, 584*n*6
Shapiro, C., 448*n*154
Shapiro, J., 93*n*45
Shapiro, L., 199*n*121
Shaw, J., 335*n*33, 335*n*37, 412*n*10
Shay, R., 336*n*79
Shell China, 287
Shellenbarger, S., 163*n*148, 163*n*150, 446*n*33
Shelton, T., 586*n*106, 586*n*109
Shepherd, B., 476*n*69
Shippmann, J., 125*n*52
Shonk, J. H., 476*n*38
Short, Kevin, 448*n*182
Short, L., 446*n*61
Shortland, S., 586*n*81, 586*n*85
Shoss, M., 475*n*5
Shuit, D., 269*n*101
Shultz, K. S., 199*n*129, 199*n*136
Shust, E., 414*n*100
Siegel, L., 197*n*41, 198*n*74
Siemens, 89
Silva, C., 335*n*27
Silver, D., 162*n*55
Silver-Greenberg, J., 199*n*113
Silverhart, T., 225*n*40
Silverman, D., 512*n*86
Silverman, R. E., 27*n*20, 164*n*161, 306*n*109, 334*n*10, 337*n*137, 381*n*12, 383*n*114, 412*n*24, 476*n*28
Silverstein, M., 556*n*80
Silverstone, Yaarit, 587*n*137
Simester, D., 93*n*52
Simmons, A., 305*n*65
Simon, M., 270*n*108
Simons, T., 478*n*150
Simpson, M., 382*n*41
Sims Jr., Bill, 556*n*82
Sims, E. N., 162*n*95
Sinclair, A., 304*n*41
Singer, N., 199*n*106
Singer, S., 557*n*107
Singh, P., 124*n*7, 414*n*101
Sipek, Sarah, 558*n*179
Sitzmann, T., 270*n*111
Skarlicki, Daniel, 584*n*6
Skelton, B., 412*n*27
Skinner, B. F., 388
Skrzypinski, C., 270*n*118
Skype, 106, 207, 567
Slaughter, J., 28*n*69, 93*n*60
Sloane, A., 511*n*16, 511*n*24, 511*n*27, 511*n*49, 511*n*55
Sloman, Colin, 587*n*137
Smailes, Andy, 585*n*79
Small Business Administration (SBA), 252, 596, 601
Small, B., 224*n*12, 225*n*34
Smerd, J., 269*n*90, 476*n*74
Smith, A. F. R., 304*n*22
Smith, D., 476*n*40
Smith, J., 125*n*17
Smith, M. J., 304*n*50
Smith, R., 268*n*24, 270*n*125
Smith, S. L., 557*n*131
Smith, S., 555*n*15–16, 555*n*46, 556*n*70, 556*n*75, 556*n*105, 556*n*107, 558*n*173, 558*n*210, 610*n*34
Smith, Tom, 389–390
Smith, W., 415*n*124
Smither, J., 270*n*153, 304*n*22, 304*n*26
Snell, S., 585*n*47
Snow, C., 585*n*47
Snyder, Deidre, 476*n*56
Society for Human Resource Management (SHRM), 5, 18, 79–80, 119, 133, 182–183, 185, 257, 291, 364
Solamon, J., 226*n*74, 226*n*77
Solander, A., 446*n*57
Solem, A., 270*n*148
Solomonson, A., 305*n*61, 305*n*63
Sonnentag, S., 557*n*155, 558*n*162
Sony Corp., 575
Sorensen, R., 336*n*111
Sosnin, B., 336*n*99, 336*n*102
South Florida Sun-Sentinel, 364
Southwest Airlines, 76–77
Sovereign, K., 65*n*126, 161*n*43, 164*n*160, 197*n*35, 305*n*78, 336*n*89
Sozbilir, M., 269*n*69
Spector, B., 271*n*161, 271*n*163
Spencer, M., 511*n*50
Spicer, C., 125*n*59
Spychalski, A., 198*n*77
Stahl, G., 305*n*56, 585*n*68
Stanley, J., 556*n*102
Starbucks, 89–90, 561
Starkman, J., 610*n*62, 610*n*64
Starkman, P., 125*n*39
Staw, B. M., 584*n*6
Steel, P., 584*n*10
Steen, M., 163*n*108

Steenburgh, T., 413*n*62
Steer, D., 270*n*118
Stern, I., 225*n*47
Stetz, T. A., 124*n*8
Stetzer, A., 555*n*54
Stevens, C. K., 225*n*52
Stevenson, C., 93*n*44, 93*n*50
Stewart, T., 163*n*137
Stivarius, T. B., 199*n*117
Stock, K., 199*n*135
Stone, Brad, 448*n*188
Stone, D., 125*n*20, 163*n*133
Stoneman, B., 224*n*15
Stout, Hilary, 412*n*33
Stradley, B., 414*n*81
Straub, C., 163*n*44
Strauss, K., 334*n*5
Strauss, S., 225*n*22
Stretch, L., 413*n*57
Stuller, J., 196*n*6, 225*n*52
Sturman, M., 412*n*22
Styers, B. A., 199*n*129, 199*n*136
Sudbury, D. A., 226*n*63, 226*n*65
Suddath, C., 477*n*108
Sull, D., 92*n*4
Sullivan, F., 511*n*41
Sullivan, J., 92*n*32
Sun Microsystems, 245
Sunoo, B. P., 447*n*99, 512*n*74
Surface, E., 303*n*13
Swanberg, J., 558*n*187
Sweetwater State University, 301
Swider, B., 226*n*54
Switzer III, F., 64*n*87, 304*n*34
Switzer, F., 64*n*87

T

Tae-Youn Park, 335*n*33
Taft, P., 584*n*18
Tammaro, P., 226*n*61
Tanguay, D. M., 412*n*22
Taras, S., 584*n*10
Taussig, R., 413*n*44
Tayan, B., 611*n*83
Taylor, B., 511*n*17
Taylor, P., 199*n*120, 224*n*12, 225*n*34, 226*n*73, 260*n*70
Taylor, Sully, 28*n*67, 586*n*85
Tebbetts, C., 557*n*122
Teladoc.Inc, 430
Tenneco Corporation, 532
Tepedino, L., 92*n*12
Tepper, B., 475*n*4, 475*n*8
Terpstra, D., 381*n*8
Terris, W., 199*n*124
Tett, R., 198*n*58
Thacker, J., 268*n*31, 268*n*38, 268*n*40, 269*n*75, 269*n*79, 269*n*81, 269*n*98
Tharenou, P., 271*n*171
Thau, Stefan, 476*n*57
Thelan, J., 558*n*194
Thibodeau, P., 27*n*28
Thomas International USA, 603
Thomas, B. W., 414*n*118
Thomas, D., 65*n*148
Thomas, Isaiah, 60–61
Thomas, R., 27*n*36
Thomas, S., 381*n*5
Thompkins, J., 63*n*84
Thomson Reuters Company, 78
Thornburg, L., 225*n*23
Thornton, G., 335*n*72
3M Co., 575
Tillmann, P., 92*n*4
Tinsley, C. H., 584n6
Tobenkin, D., 446*n*64, 447*n*88
Toker, S., 558*n*63
Tomlinson, G., 86, 93*n*77
Tormey, D., 383*n*89
Torpey, E. M., 448*n*166
Torres, K., 556*n*76, 557*n*120
Towers Watson, 73, 85, 128–129, 394
Townsend, A., 585n48
Toyota, 10, 36, 217–218, 505
Traxler, F., 511*n*38
Trevino, L. K., 305*n*73, 475*n*12, 477*n*54, 477*n*79, 477*n*82
Treviño, Linda, 475*n*12, 476*n*54, 477*n*79, 477*n*82
Triandis, H. C., 412*n*12
Trilogy Enterprises Inc., 159
Trottman, M., 63*n*53, 63*n*61
TRW, 273, 288
Tucker, D., 93*n*72, 196*n*7
Tucker, M., 225*n*42
Tungli, Z., 585*n*72
Turban, D., 226*n*68
Turnasella, T., 305*n*63, 412*n*9
Turnley, W., 162*n*105
Twitter
  for company news, information, training, 251
  for emergencies, 546
  for job seekers, 141, 154
  for small businesses, 593
Tye, M. G., 585*n*70
Tyler, Kathryn, 28*n*71, 93*n*66, 125*n*26, 162*n*105, 195*n*41, 197*n*41, 268*n*46, 269*n*58, 305*n*68, 335*n*44, 477*n*83, 511*n*57, 556*n*92, 558*n*157, 586*n*82, 586*n*131
Tziner, A., 304*n*43

U

U.K. Driver and Vehicle Licensing Agency, 421
U.S. Bureau of Labor Statistics, 134
U.S. Congressional Budget Office, 133
U.S. Department of Homeland Security, 192, 203
U.S. Department of Labor, 105–106, 106*t*, 112*f*, 244*f*, 519*f*, 522, 594*f*
  Office of Disability Employment Policy, 154
Office of Federal Contract Compliance Programs (OFCCP), 32, 48, 379
U.S. Department of Transportation, 191
U.S. Equal Employment Opportunity Commission, 592
U.S. Navy, 107, 108*f*, 437
Ulrich, Dave, 17
Ulrich, Dave, 17*f*
Umphress, E., 476*n*62, 476*n*64
Unicru, 178
Unilever, 287
UNITE HERE, 483
United Airlines, 46
United Auto Workers (UAW), 436, 497, 500, 505, 506
United Steelworkers of America, 499
University of California, 57, 530
UPS, 245, 247
Ursel, N., 62*n*9

V

Valentine, S., 476*n*50, 477*n*100
Valentino, L., 336*n*83
Valero Energy, 130, 134
Van Dyke, M., 384*n*127
Van Hasselt, C., 512*n*84
Van Hoot, E. A. J., 198*n*59
Van Iddekinge, C., 197*n*19, 224*n*9
VanDerhei, J., 447*n*112
Vanguard, 205, 432
Vanthournout, D., 270*n*117
Varicent, D., 413*n*48, 413*n*66
Varner, I. I., 585*n*75
Velasquez, M., 476*n*52
Vellios, G., 269*n*52
Velshi, Ali, 611*n*80, 611*n*82
Veranges, T., 306*n*112
Vesely, R., 447*n*89
Vettori, F. L., 269*n*69
Vijayan, J., 336*n*103
Viking Range Corp., 429
Villanova, P., 305*n*79
Viollis, P., 558*n*189, 558*n*197
Voelker, Keith, 586*n*119
Voss, Wendy, 446*n*49
Vroom, Victor, 388

W

Wade, 381*n*4
Wagner, David, 557*n*130
Wagner, J., 224*n*21
Wagner, W., 197*n*44
Wah, L., 125*n*28

Wahl, Asbjørn, 586*n*118
Walgreens, 37, 235, 429
Walker, A., 304*n*22
Walker, J., 197*n*16
Wallace, J., 335*n*34
Walley, E., 226*n*82
Walmart, 36, 54, 72–74, 76, 81, 146, 150–151, 181, 317, 353, 355, 441, 481, 575
Walsh, L., 198*n*87
Walsh, W. B., 196*n*11
Walt Disney Corporation, 370
Walter, B., 611*n*79
Walter, L., 556*n*62, 556*n*72, 556*n*78, 556*n*93
Wanberg, C., 268*n*5, 336*n*90
Wareham, J., 163*n*118, 337*n*134
Warford, Marissa, 445*n*20
Warren, M., 336*n*94
Wasserman, 609*n*10
Watkins, M., 92*n*12
Watson Wyatt Worldwide, 17, 84
Watson, T., 382*n*32
Waxer, C., 269*n*61
Wayne, T., 163*n*131
WD-40, 72, 85
Weaver, 268*n*3
Weaver, G. R., 305*n*73, 475*n*12, 477*n*79, 477*n*82
Weber, L., 27*n*20, 28*n*54, 63*n*58, 63*n*61, 162*n*52, 162*n*56, 162*n*66, 162*n*71, 163*n*117
Weber, Y., 92*n*12
Weekley, J., 198*n*71, 198*n*79
Wegmans Foods, 345, 352, 353
Weiner, 383*n*110
Weinstein, M., 224*n*13
Weintraub, R., 269*n*63
Weitz, J., 225*n*44
Welch, J., 293, 305*n*86
Wellins, R. S., 125*n*55
Wellner, A., 163*n*149
Wells Fargo, 255
Wells, D., 476*n*77
Wells, S., 28*n*66, 63*n*46, 161*n*28, 163*n*112, 199*n*137, 270*n*130, 446*nn*73–74, 446*n*77, 448*n*137, 476*n*45
Welsh, David, 476*n*56
West, D., 27*n*37
Westphal, J., 225*n*47
Wexley, K., 268*n*44, 269*n*56, 269*n*71, 271*n*167, 271*n*169
Whalen, J., 511*n*50
Wheelen, T., 92*n*5
Whetzel, D., 198*n*75
Whitaker, J., 445*n*23
Whitcomb, C., 270*n*141
White, B., 65*n*152
White, M., 448*n*72
White, R., 199*n*125, 586*n*115
Whitehouse, K., 414*n*111
Wiatrowski, W., 556*n*81
Wiegand, R., 269*n*67
Wiersma, U., 304*n*41
Wilk, S., 197*n*38
Wille, B., 336*n*128
Williams, C., 305*n*64
Williams, G., 334*n*2
Williams, J., 555*n*13
Williams, K. J., 198*n*86
Williamson, D., 556*n*101
Williamson, L. G., 224*n*9–10, 225*n*35, 226*n*77
Wilson Learning, 243
Wilson, D., 335*n*60, 335*n*62
Wilson, H. J. 304*n*52
Wilson, T., 412*n*18
Winchester, Rob, 301
Winerip, M., 61*n*1
Winfred, A., 198*n*77, 269*n*66
Wingrove, C., 304*n*37, 305*n*69
Winkler, C., 92*n*29
Wiscombe, J., 415*n*127
Witney, F., 511*nn*16–17, 511*n*24, 51*n*27, 511*n*49, 511*n*55
Witt, E., 610*n*65
Witt, L. A., 197*n*46, 197*n*50
Woehr, D., 303*n*14
Wojcik, J., 447*n*86
Wolf, A., 197*n*37
Wolf, S., 303*n*13
Wonderlic Inc., 170, 171
Wong, 584*n*4
Wood, M. S., 336*n*106
Wood, R., 304*n*20, 556*n*61
Woodward, H., 336*n*87, 336*n*90, 447*n*97
Woodward, N., 62*n*14, 226*n*81
Workforce Rypple, 298
Worley, C., 271*n*161
Wright, A.D., 162*n*84, 196*n*2, 198*n*69
Wright, G., 269*n*103
Wright, P., 414*n*106
Wright, Thomas, 477*n*80
Writers Guild of America (WGA), 508
Wuittner, J., 413*n*69
Wymer, J. F., 226*n*63, 226*n*65

X

Xerox Corp., 318
Xie Xiaogang, 453
Xin, K. R., 335*n*63

Y

Yager, E. G., 269*n*67
Yahoo! 69, 152, 440, 461
Yancey, G., 413*n*76
Yandrick, R., 448*n*142
Yang, Claira, 587*n*137
Yegge, Steve, 412*n*26 same
Yerkes, L., 412*n*34
York, K., 62*n*22
Young, E., 511*n*41
Young, J. P., 198*n*100
Yule, S., 556*n*106
Yun-Hwa Chiang, 586*n*104
Yusko, K., 197*n*42

Z

Zalewski, E., 556*n*74
Zall, M., 477*n*89
Zappe, J., 162*n*101
Zappos, 75
Zarandona, J., 336*n*110
Zatzick, C., 336*n*120
Zeidner, R., 27*n*15, 199*n*108, 199*n*139, 269*n*93, 445*n*22m 477*n*109
Zheng, Y., 65*n*152
Zielinski, D., 93*n*49, 162*n*72, 197*n*27, 198*n*68, 200*n*155, 382*n*24, 384*n*129, 556*n*97
Zimmerman, E., 199*n*103, 337*n*139
Zimmerman, R., 164*n*164, 196*n*7, 198*n*54, 198*n*83, 225*n*36
Zingheim, P., 383*n*97, 383*n*103, 384*n*132, 413*n*43, 413*n*75
Zipcar, 216
Zohar, D., 556*n*106
Zonneveld, J., 269*n*105
Zook, C., 92*nn*10
Zugelder, M., 63*n*70
Zweig, D., 224*n*1, 224*n*5

SUBJECT INDEX

Note: Page numbers with *f* indicate figures; those with *n* indicate endnotes; those with *t* indicate tables

A

Accountable care organizations, (ACO), 430
Action learning, 255
Adaptability screening, 569
ADDIE five-step process, 236, 251
Adverse impact, 42–45
Affirmative action, 32, 55–57
Age Discrimination in Employment Act (ADEA) (1967), 33, 39*t*, 45, 570, 592
Agency shop, 483
AIDA (attention, interest, desire, action), 142
Albemarle Paper Co. v. Moody, 34, 39*t*
Alternation ranking method, 278, 282*f*
Alternative dispute resolution (ADR) program, 52
Alternative staffing, 144–145
Americans with Disabilities Act (ADA) (1990), 35–36, 39*t*, 58, 112, 177, 190, 422
Americans with Disabilities (ADA) guidelines, 37*f*
Americans with Disabilities Amendments Act (ADAAA) (2008), 36, 39*t*
Analytics software, 78
Annual bonus, 398
Applicant tracking system (ATS), 78, 138–140
Application forms, 48, 154–156, 155*f*
Appraisal by subordinates, 277
Appraisal interview, 292–295, 294*f*, 295*f*
Apprenticeship training, 243–244, 244*f*
Aptitude tests, 175, 175*f*
Arbitration, 497
Audits, internal and external, 69
Authority, 5
Authorization cards, 488, 489*f*

B

Bakke v. Regents of the University of California (1978), 57
Bargaining unit, 490
Behavior modeling, 246
Behavior modification, 388
Behavioral interview, 204, 205
Behaviorally anchored rating scale (BARS), 283, 284*f*
Behavior-based safety, 532
Benchmark job, 356
Benefits, 418
Benefits and services
  current picture of
    about, 418, 418*f*, 419*t*
    policy issues, 418
  exercise, cases for, 443–444
  flexible, 438
    cafeteria plans, 438
    employee preference for, 438, 439*f*
    work schedules, 440
  insurance
    cost-control trends, 428–430
    hospitalization, health, disability, 425–426
    life insurance, 430
    for long-term care, 430
    for part-time, contingent workers, 431
    and striking workers, 443–444
    workers' compensation, 424–425, 443
  personal
    for domestic partners, 437
    executive perquisites, 438
    family-friendly (work-life), 436–437, 442
    personal service, 435–436
  retirement
    early, 433
    online systems for, 434
    pension plans, 431–433
    Social Security, 431, 443
  for time not worked
    online form for, 423*f*
    parental leave, 422
    severance pay, 423–424
    sick leave, 421
    and social media, 421
    supplemental unemployment benefits, 424
    unemployment insurance, 419
    vacations, holidays, 419–420
Benefits purchasing alliances, 429
Bias, 172, 290
Biodata, 156
Bona fide occupational qualification (BFQQ), 45
Boycott, 500
Boulwareism, 511*n*56
Broadbanding, 373–384, 374*f*
Burden of proof, 34
Burk v. California Association of Realtors (2003), 59
Burlington Industries v. Ellerth, 40
Burnout, 540
Business model, 69
Business necessity, 34, 46–47
Business process reengineering, 99–100

C

CAGE screening, 537
California Federal Savings and Loan Association v. Guerra, 62*n*12
Candidate-order (contrast) error, 210
Can't do/won't do problems, 239
Career, 309
Career coaches, 311
Career development, 309
Career management
  careers today, 309
  coaching, 314
  diversity issues, 313
  employee engagement guide for managers, 314–315
  employee's role, 310
  employer's role, 311
  improving performance through HRIS, 312
  mentoring, 313
  psychological contract, 309–310
Career planning, 309
Case interviews, 205
Case study method, 255
Cash balance plans, 432
Centers of expertise, 7
Central tendency, 289
Centralized call centers, 7
Cerner, 256
Change to Win Coalition, 483–484
Child labor provisions, 347
Child Labor Rules Advisor, 593
China, 564–565
Citation, 518
Civil Rights Act (1866), 32, 62*n*4
Civil Rights Act (1964), 32
Civil Rights Act (CRA 1991), 39*t*, 58
Classes, 357
Closed shop, 483
Coaching, 314
Codetermination, 563
Collective bargaining, 494
College recruiting, 149–150
Compa ratio, 368
Comparable worth, 374
Compensable factor, 355
Compensation managers, 7
Competency model, 237
Competency-based job analysis, 119, 121
Competency-based pay, 372
Competitive advantage, 69, 72

Compressed workweek, 440
Computerized, web-based appraisal, 286, 286*f*
Concentration statistics, 64*n*86
Consolidated Omnibus Budget Reconciliation Act (COBRA), 427
Construct validity, 169
Consumer-driven health plans (CDHPs), 429
Content validity, 169
Contingency-based recruiters, 147
Contract employees, 145
Controlled experimentation, 260
Controlling, 3
Coordinative function, 7
Coordinators, for EEO, 7
Corporate campaign, 499
Corporate HR teams, 7
Corporate-level strategy, 71–72
County of Washington v. Gunther (1981), 374
Coverage and Employment Status Advisor, 593
Co-working sites, 13
Criterion validity, 168
Critical incident method, 280
Cross training, 249
Crowd sourcing, 178
Customized talent management, 257, 287

D

Data analytics, 81, 82
Data mining, 81
Davis-Bacon Act (1931), 347
Decertification, 493
Defense of Marriage Act, 437
Deferred profit-sharing plans, 432
Defined benefit plan, 431
Defined contribution health insurance plans, 429
Defined contribution plan, 432
Deloitte Touche Tohmatsu Limited, 139
Demographics, and workforce, 7–8, 8*t*
Depression, employee, 539
Diary/log, 105
Digital and social media tools
  background-checking process, 186
  cloud-based training and systems, 242, 605
  digital unions, 500
  e-mail monitoring, 463–464
  emergency information, 546
  employee benefits, 434–435
  employee engagement/retention process, 318
  employee involvement, 455–456
  employer's benefit and reason for caution, 42
  HR democratization, 112
  job searching, 341–343
  mobile learning, 250–251
  mobile-based interviews, 207
  new human resource management, 14–15
  performance management, 297–298
  recognition/appreciation rewards, 376, 392
  safety compliance, 522–523, 533
  sales commissions, 397
  small business recruiters, 593–594
  talent analytics, 169
  transnational and virtual teams, 567
  Web-based recruiting, 141–142
Digital dashboard, 77, 77*f*
Direct financial payments, 346
Discriminatory practices, 47–49
Dismissal, 324, 466
Disparate impact, 42, 62*n*23
Disparate rejection rates, 43
Disparate treatment, 35
Distributive justice, 452
Diversity
  defined, 53
  and employee training, 248–249
  and equal opportunity, 53–57
  in workforce, 151–154
Diversity Counts, 21, 108, 153, 174, 211, 290, 321, 437, 465, 528, 570, 591
Dodd-Frank Law (2010), 375
Domestic partners, 437
Downsizing, 329
Drug Free Workplace Act (1988), 191
Dual-career ladders, 392

E

Early retirement window, 433
Earnings-at-risk plan, 405
Economic strike, 497
Educational subsidies, 436–437
Effective Psychology for Managers, 293
Elder care, 436
Electronic Communications Privacy Act (ECPA), 462
Electronic performance monitoring (EPM), 286
Electronic performance support systems (EPSS), 247
Embedded HR teams, 7
Employee assistance program (EAP), 435–436, 538, 540
Employee compensation, 346
Employee costs lever, 16
Employee discipline management
  appeals process, 465
  best companies, examples, 467–470
  discipline without punishment, 466
  fair discipline guidelines, 465–466
  gender bias, 465
  penalties, 464
  rules and regulations, 464
Employee engagement guide
  appraisal interview, 295–296
  around the globe, 577
  best companies to work for, 467
  career development, 314–315
  compensation plan at Costco's, 441
  desirable traits, 118
  incentive pay, 407
  onboarding, Toyota example, 234
  performance and productivity, 84
  promotion from within, 138
  selection program, 217
  total rewards programs, 376
  workplace safety, Milliken & Company, 534
Employee Free Choice Act, 504
Employee incentives, 387–389
  at-risk pay plan, 405
  designing, 402–403
  and employment law, 389
  ESOP plan, 406
  exercise, cases for, 265–267, 300–302, 409–411
  gainsharing plan, 405
  and the gender gap, 390
  inequities in, 404
  internationally, 401–402
  long-term, 400–402
  for managers, executives, 406
  maximizing sales results, 396–397
  merit pay, 390–392, 392*t*
  as performance booster, 393–394
  piecework, 389–390, 407
  plans, 395
  in practice, 406
  profit-sharing, 404
  recognition, 408–409
  recognition-based awards, 392
  salary, commission, combination for salespeople in action, 397
  Scanlon plan, 404–405
  short-term and annual, 398–400, 400*t*
  and social media, 392–393
  strategy for, 387, 397–398
  team incentive plans, 408
Employee leasing, 439
Employee life-cycle career management
  gender gap, 321–322
  promotion process, 320–321
  retirement, 322–324
  transfers, 322
Employee Polygraph Protection Act (1988), 188
Employee recruiting, 135
Employee relations, 451

Employee relations programs
bullying, 453–454
communication, 454
employee involvement programs, 455–456
ethics, 457–458
fair treatment, 451
protecting employee rights, 457–458
recognition/relations programs, 454–455
victimization, 453–454
Employee Reliability Index (ERI), 529
Employee retention, engagement
career management, 329–330
employee role in, 310–311
employer role in, 311
manager's role in, 311, 312*f*
and psychological contact, 309
talent management, 312
terminology for, 309
dismissals, 330
downsizing, 329
and employment law, 320
exit process, **termination interview**, 327–328
grounds for, 324–325
layoffs, plant closing law, 328–329
security measures for, 326–327
severance pay for, 325*f*
supervisor liability in, 327
wrongful discharge suits, 326
exercise, cases for, 332–333
life-cycle career managment, 319–320
managing transfers, retirements, 322
promotion decisions, 320
managing turnover
approach to retaining, 316
intangible costs of, 316
job withdrawal, 319
with social media, 319
talent management, 317
voluntary, 317
Employee Retirement Income Security Act (ERISA)(1974), 38, 351, 406, 427, 433, 442
Employee stock ownership plan (ESOP), 406, 432
Employee testing, selection
background investigations, reference checks, 183
and employment law, 184
form for, 185*f*
graphology, 189
human lie detectors, 190
immigration law, 191–192
physical exams, 189–190
polygraph, honesty testing, 188
from preemployment information services, 186–187
procedure for, 184
reasons for, 183
and social media, 186
substance abuse screening, 190–191
value of, 187–188
basics of, 192
bias, 172
to cut costs, boost profits, 172
and employment law, 173
evidence-based test validation, 170–172, 170*f*, 171*f*
gender issues in, 173
individual rights, security, 173
reliability, 167–168, 167*f*
use of, 174–175
utility analysis, 172
validity, 168–169
validity generalization, 173
exercise, cases for, 193–195
types of tests, 192
for achievement, 177
for cognitive ability, 175
computerization of, 178
for motor, physical abilities, 175–176
for personality, interests, 176–177
work samples, simulations, 178
choosing selection method, 181–182
management assessment center, 179–180
miniature job training, evaluation, 181
realistic previews, 181
situational, video-based testing, 180
situational judgment tests, 179
using, 178–179
Employee training, development
employee handbook for, 233–234
implementing program for
apprenticeship training, 243–244, 244*f*
audiovisual-based training, 246
behavior modeling, 246
computer-based training (CBT), 247
electronic performance support systems (EPSS), 247
informal learning, 245
internationally, 248–249
Internet-based training, 249–250
job instruction training (JIT), 245
on-the-job training, 243
lectures, 245–246
lifelong and literacy techniques, 248
mobile learning, 250
programmed learning, 246
simulated learning, 247–248
and social media, 250
team training, 249
vestibule training, 247
videoconferencing, 247
virtual classroom, 250
Web 2.0 learning, 251
importance of, 167
management development
candidate assessment, 9-Box Grid, 253–254
leadership development, 255
on, off the job, 254–257, 263
organizational change programs
evaluating training, 260–262
Lewin's change process, 258–259
organizational development, 259, 260*t*
orientation/onboarding, 233
process of, 252, 263
talent management, 257
training process, 235
ADDIE five-step process, 236
conducting needs analysis, 236–239
designing program for, 239–241
developing program for, 242
Employers Liability Act (1969), 196n8
Employment law
and application forms, 154–155
and discrimination, 47–49
and dismissals, 324
and drug testing, 191
and electronic monitoring, 462, 462*f*
and employee handbook, 233–234
and FMLA guidelines, 422
and gender, minority problems, 321–322
and hazard communication, 537
and health benefits, 426
and parental leave, 422
and pay incentives, 389
and pay rates, 347–353
and pension planning, 433
and performance management, 291–292
and personnel recruiting, 146
and promotions, 320
and references, giving, 184
state, local, 37
and termination, 325
and testing, selection, 173
and training process, 235
and union drive, election, 493
and vacations, 422
Entrepreneurs, 590
Environmental scan, 70*f*
Equal Employment Opportunity Act (1972), 32, 64*n*93
Equal employment opportunity (EEO), 7

Equal opportunity
1964-91 laws enacted, 32–34
1991-present laws enacted
Americans with Disabilities Act (ADA)(1990), 35–37
Civil Rights Act (CRA 1991), 35
discrimination allegation defense, 58
adverse impact, 42–45
bona fide occupational qualification (BFQQ), 45
business necessity, 46–47
knowing employment law, 47–49
treatment vs. impact, 42
diversity management, 58
affirmative action programs for, 55–57
benefits of, 54–55
reverse discrimination, 57
threats to, 53
enforcement process for, 58
filing file charge, 49
mandatory arbitration, 52
voluntary mediation, 51
exercises, cases for, 59–61
religious, other discrimination, 37–38
sexual harassment, 38–41
and social media, 42
state, local laws, 37
Equal Pay Act (1963), 33, 39*t*, 57, 351
Equity theory of motivation, 346
Ethics, 19, 456
Ethnocentric practices, 568
Ethnocentrism, 53
European Union (EU), 10, 563–564
E-Verify, 191–192
Evidence-based HR decisions, 17, 84, 170, 404, 492
Executive coach, 256–257
Executive Order 11246, 32, 39*t*, 55, 379
Executive Order 11375, 32, 39*t*
Exempt/nonexempt FLSA provisions, 348–349
Exit interviews, 317, 328, 454
Expatriates (expats), 566
Expectancy, 388
Expectancy chart, 171, 171*f*
Experimentation, scientific, 82
Extended workforce, 9, 146

F

Fact finder, 497
Fair Credit Reporting Act (1970), 184
Fair day's work, 387
Fair Labor Standards Act (FSLA) (1938), 347–348
Family and Medical Leave Act, 352, 422, 441
Family Education Rights and Privacy Act (1974), 184
Family-friendly (work-life) benefits, 436–437
Faragher v. City of Boca Raton, 40
Federal Privacy Act, 173
Federal Violence Against Women Act (1994), 39, 58
Fifth Amendment (1791), 32
Financial incentives, 387
FirstStep Employment Law Advisor, 592, 592*f*
Flexible benefits plan/cafeteria benefits plan, 438
Flextime, 440
Flow statistics, 64*n*86
Focus group, 454
Forced distribution method, 280
Ford Motor Company, 137, 178, 246
Foreign service premiums, 574
401(k) plan, 248, 432, 441
4/5*t*hs rule, 43
Freedom of Information Act (1966), 184
Functional strategy, 73

G

Gainsharing plan, 405
Gender, as BFQQ, 46
Gender-Motivated Violence Act, 544
Gender-role stereotypes, 53
Generation Y (Millenials), 8
Genetic Information Nondiscrimination Act (GINA)(2008), 37, 39*t*
Geocentric practices, 568
Geographic range, 72
Gilmer v. Interstate/Johnson Lane Corp., 52
Glass ceiling, 53, 322
Global human resources
exercise, cases for, 581–583
intercountry differences
in China, 564–565
cultural factors, 562–563
economic systems, 563
in the EU, 563–564
HR effects of, 561–562, 562*f*
managing
about, 561
in practice
developing effective system, 579
implementing program for, 579
making system acceptable, 579
study on, 578–579
staffing, 580
early returns, 570–571
ethics, codes of conduct, 568
expatriates vs. nationals, 566–568
female managers, 570
management values, staffing policy, 568
selecting managers for, 569–570
taxation issues, 582
training, maintaining employees abroad, 580–581
compensation abroad, 573–575, 580
orientation for, 571–572
performance appraisals, 572–573
repatriation, 576–577
terrorism, safety, 575, 580
See also **Human Resource Management (HRM)**
Globalization, 10
Golden parachute, 402
Good faith bargaining, 494
Good-faith effort strategy, 55
Grade definition, 358, 358*f*
Grades, 357
Graphic rating scale, 278
Graphology, 189
Grievance procedure, 501–502
Griggs v. Duke Power Co., 34, 39*t*, 58
Gross national product (GNP), 10, 10*f*
Group life insurance, 430
Guidelines, ADA, 37*f*
Guidelines, federal agency, 33–34

H

Halo effect, 289
Hardship allowance, 574
Health savings account (HSA), 429
Hierarchy of goals, 68*f*
High-performance work systems (HPWS), 17, 83
High-tech jobs, 14
Home-based salary plan, 354
Home-country nationals, 566
Host-based salary plan, 354
Hostile environments, 40
Hours Worked Advisor, 593
In-house development center, 256
HR audit, 80
HR data, safety of, 133*f*
HR department lever, 16
HR performance tools
for accident prevention, 516
and background, reference checks, 187–188
developing pay plan, 368–369
for EEO problems, 52
and employee incentives, 393
and employee leasing, 439
and employee testing, selection, 182

for the expatriate challenge, 571
firing high-risk employee, 544
free online safety, health services, 521
for handling grievances, 503
for intercountry differences, 565
for internal recruiting, 148
interviewing, 597
setting effective goals, 275
and small business ethics, 460
training employees, 251–252
using applications, 154
using O*NET, 113–114
HR scorecard, 77, 92*n*24
HR Value Proposition, 17
Human capital, 9, 81
Human lie detectors, 189
Human Resource Information System (HRIS)
analyzing incentives, 397
applicant tracking, 139
building, 607
career, succession planning, 312
defined, 605
for global companies, 577, 583
improving performance with analytics, 15–18
Internet-based training, 249
managing benefits, 434
online testing, data analytics, 177
payroll administration, 371
personnel forecasting, 132
for safety training, 530
succession systems, 253
talent management software, 96
tracking applicant metrics, 78
workforce planning, 128
Human resource management (HRM)
adding value, services, 17
aspects of, 5
basic functions of, 3
competencies for, 18
defined, 3
and **ethics**, 19
evidence-based decisions for, 17
exercises, cases for, 25–26
importance of, 3–5, 23
improving performance in, 15–18
measuring performance, results, 16
organizational chart for, 6*f*
philosophy of, 20
strategic, 15
talent management for, 13
trends in
demographics, workforce, 7–9, 8*t*
nature of work, 8
See also Global human resources; Small business human resources; Strategy and analysis, in HRM
Human resource metrics, 78

I

Identity theft, 192
Illegal bargaining items, 495
Impasse, 497
Improving Performance: Around the Globe, 176, 211, 248, 254, 298, 315, 354, 372, 401, 453, 493, 535, 565, 576
Improving Performance: HR as a Profit Center, 9, 54, 55, 75, 99, 134, 151, 172, 275, 316, 421, 430, 456, 515, 530, 567
Improving Performance: HR Practices Around the Globe, 176, 211, 248, 254, 298, 315, 354, 372, 401, 453, 493, 535, 265, 276
Improving Performance: HR Tools for Line Managers and Entrepreneurs, 21, 52, 113, 148, 182, 213, 251, 275, 368, 393, 439, 460, 503, 521, 571, 597
Improving Performance Through HRIS, 21, 78, 96, 139, 177, 253, 312, 371, 434, 530
Incentives. *See* Employee incentives
Independent contractors, 9, 350
Indirect financial payments, 346
Informal learning, 245
Injunction, 500
Inside games, 500
Instrumentality, 388
Insubordination, 324
Integrated case scenarios, 255
Intellectual disabilities, 36
Intelligence (IQ) tests, 175
Interest arbitration, 497
Interest inventory, 177
International human resource management (IHRM), 401, 561
Internet job recruiting, 139
Internet-based training, 249–250
Internships, 150
Interviewing
basics of, 220
about, 101–102
questions to ask, 204–206
designing, conducting, 206–207, 220
effective, 213–214, 214*f*
structured situational interview, 212
and talent management, 215*f*–216*f*
developing, extending job offer, 219
errors in, 220
applicant disability, 211
candidate-order, pressure to hire, 210
first impressions, 209
interviewer behavior, 212
job requirements, 209
nonverbal behavior, impression management, 210
personal characteristics, 210
exercise, cases for, 221–223
guide for interviewees, 230
internationally, 211
structured guide for, 227–229
structured vs. unstructured, 203, 204*f*–205*f*
usefulness of, 208
web-based, computerized, 207
Intrinsic motivation, 388

J

Job aid, 247
Job analysis
collecting information, 121
electronic methods, 106–107
interviewing, 102–103
observation, 105
participant diary/log, 105
quantitative techniques, 105–106
questionnaires, 103–105, 104*f*–105*f*
competency-based job analysis, 121
conducting
boosting productivity with, 99
enlargement, rotation, enrichment, 100
using information from, 98–99, 99*f*
and worker evaluation, 100
descriptions, specifications for, 97–98, 120–121
exercise, cases for, 122–124
talent management, 96–97
competency-based job analysis, 119–120, 120*f*
models, profiles used for, 118–120
using information from, 97
writing descriptions, 121
ADA compliance for, 112–113
benefits of, 108–109
job identification, summary, 109
relationship statement for, 109
responsibilities, duties in, 109–112, 110*f*–111*f*, 112*f*
standards, conditions of, 113–116, 114*f*–115*f*
writing specifications, 121
based on judgment, 117
based on statistical analysis, 117
job requirements matrix, 117
trained vs. untrained personnel, 116–117
Job analysts, 7
Job classification (grading), 357
Job Creation and Worker Assistance Act, 433
Job evaluation, 354
Job hazard analysis, 527
Job instruction training (JIT), 245
Job rotation, 254

Job search, 337–343
Job sharing, 440
Job-related interview, 205

K

Kehr v. Consolidated Freightways of Delaware, 198*n*99
Kidnapping and ransom (K&R) insurance, 575
KSACs (knowledge, skills, abilities, competencies), 167

L

Labor relations
about, 550
collective bargaining, 507
defined, 507
in good faith, 507–508
hints for, 496–497
impasses, mediation, strikes, 497–498, 499*f*
items for, 495, 496*t*
negotiating skills for, 495–496
negotiating team, contract for, 495
online, 499
disputes, grievances, 507
guidelines for handling, 502
procedure for, 501–502, 502*f*
and social media, 500
sources of, 501–502
exercise, cases for, 507–509
future of union movement, 506
about, 503
card check, other tactics, 504–505
cooperative clauses, 505–506
labor movement
about, 481
AFL-CIO, SEIU, 484
reasons for organizing, 481–482
union aims, 482
Labor relations (*continued*)
union drive, election, 506
decertification, 493
and employment law, 493
reasons for losing, 491–492
reasons for winning, 492
steps in forming, 487–494, 491*f*
supervisor's role in, 492–493
unions and the law, 505–506
acts passed for, 484–487
internationally, 494
rights of employees, employers, 486
unfair practices, 486
Labor relations specialists, 7
Landrum-Griffin Act (1959), 487, 506
Layoff, 328
Leading, 3
Learning management systems (LMS), 250
Learning portals, 250
Ledbetter v. Goodyear Tire & Rubber Company, 49, 64*nn*111–112
Leniency/strictness, 289
Lifelong learning, 248
Lilly Ledbetter Fair Pay Act, 49
Limited health-care plans, 429
Lincoln incentive system, 405
Line authority, 5
Line manager, 5, 23–24
Literacy training, 248
Locals, 566
Lockout, 500

M

Management by objectives (MBO), 285
Management game, 255
Management planning, 68, 87
Management process, 3
Manager, 4, 7–9
Mandatory arbitration, 52
Mandatory bargaining items, 495
Market-competitive pay system, 362
Markov analysis, 133
Mass interview, 206
McDonnell-Douglas test, 44, 58
Mediation, 497
Medical tourism, 429
Medicare Modernization Act (2003), 429
Mental Health Parity Act (1996), 426
Mental impairments, 36
Mentoring, 313–314
Mergers and acquisitions (M&A), 73
Merit pay (raise), 390–391, 392
Meritor Savings Bank FSB v. Vinson, 40
Michigan Alcoholism Screening Test (MAST), 537
Miniature job training and evaluation, 181
Minimum wage, 348
Minnesota Multiphasic Personality Inventory (MMPI), 177
Mission statement, 71
Mixed standard scales, 285
Mixed-motive case, 35
Mobile learning, 250
Mobility impairment, 36*f*
Mobility premiums, 574
Money damages, 35

N

Narrative form, for appraisals, 282–283, 282*f*
National emergency strikes, 487
National Labor Relations (Wagner) Act (1935), 352, 506
National origin, as BFQQ, 45
Negligent hiring, 167
Negligent training, 235
9-Box Grid, 253–254, 321
Nonpunitive discipline, 466
Nontraditional workers, 8
Norris-LaGuardia Act (1932), 484
North American Free Trade Agreement (NAFTA), 10

O

O*NET, 107, 108*f*, 112, 113–116, 115*f*
Observation, 105
Occupational illness, 517
Occupational Safety and Health Act (1970), 516, 547
Offshoring, 567–568
On-demand recruiting services (ODRS), 149
Online testing, 177
On-the-job training (OJT), 243
Operational safety reviews, 528
Organization, 3
Organization chart, 98
Organizational climate survey, 454
Organizational culture, 460, 472
Organizational development (OD), 259–260
Organization-wide incentive plan, 404
Organizing, 3
Outback Steakhouse, 1762
Outplacement counseling, 328
Outsourcing health care, 430
Overseas Assignment Inventory (OAI), 569
Overtime pay, 347
Overview, of book, 22–23

P

Paired comparison method, 278, 282*f*
Panel interview, 206
Patient Protection and Affordable Care Act (2010), 426
Pay (rate) ranges, 367–368, 367*t*
Pay (wage) grade, 366–367, 366*f*
Pay plans, strategic
compensable factors, weights for
broadbanding, 373–374, 374*f*
comparable worth, 374–375
executive pay oversight, 375
gender gaps, 375
competency-based pay, 371–375
determining rates, 35–36
by geography, 353
impact of equity, 346–347
internationally, 354
legal considerations in, 347–352
pay policies, 352–353
rewards and strategy, 346, 346*t*
union influences, 352
exercise, cases for, 379–380

job evaluation, 354
about, 354–359
compensable factors, 354
computerized, 358, 358*f*
job classification (grading), 357, 358*f*
point method, 358
preparing for, 355
ranking method, 356–357, 357*f*
market-competitive
about, 359
add remaining jobs, 368
choosing benchmark jobs, 359
comparing, adjusting wage rates, 366
compensable factors, weights for, 359–360, 360*f*
correct rates, 368–369
developing workable, 368
evaluating jobs, 362–363, 362*f*
factors for, 360, 361*t*
pay grades, 366–367, 366, 366*f*, 367*t*
pay ranges, 367
reviewing job descriptions, specifications, 360, 362
salary surveys, 363–364, 377
wage curves, 362*f*, 363*f*, 365*f*
pricing managerial, professional jobs, 377
determinants for, 369–370
executive, managerial pay, 370
payroll administration, 371
professional employees, 370–371
Peer appraisal, 276
Pension plans, 431
Performance achievement plan, 402
Performance analysis, 237–239
Performance appraisal, 274
Performance appraisal process, 274
Performance management, 261
Performance management, appraisal
appraisal interview, 292–295, 294*f*, 295*f*, 299
basics of, 296
appraisals, 276–278, 277*f*
defining employee goals, standards, 275–276
management of, 296
process of, 274–275, 274*f*
bias, 290
and employment law, 291–292
tools available, 291f, 291*t*
types of problems, 288–289, 289*t*
and talent management, 287*f*
techniques for
alternation ranking method, 278, 282*f*
behaviorally anchored rating scale (BARS), 283, 284*f*
computerized, web-based appraisal, 286
conversation days, 287
critical incident method, 282*t*
electronic performance monitoring (EPM), 286
forced distribution method, 280
forms for rating, 272*f*, 273*f*, 279*f*, 280*f*, 281*f*
graphic rating scale, 278
internationally, 288
management by objectives (MBO), 285
mixed standard scale, 285
narrative form, for appraisal, 282–283, 282*f*
paired comparison method, 278, 282*f*
Performance pay, incentives, 387
Performance-contingent restricted stock, 402
Personal appearance, 48
Personal protective equipment (PPE), 528
Personality Profile Analysis (PPA), 603
Personnel recruiting
application forms, 157
developing, using, 154–156, 155*f*
and employment law, 155–156
of diverse workforce, 157
the disabled, 153
minorities, 153–154
older workers, 152–153
women, single parents, 151
and employment law, 137
exercise, cases for, 158–160
importance of, 136–137
internal sources, 137–138, 157
outside sources
advertising, 141*f*, 142–143, 143*f*
applicant tracking systems (ATS), 139–140
college recruiting, internships, 149–150
cutting costs of, 151
on-demand recruiting services (ODRS), 149
employment agencies, 142–143
informal recruiting, 138
military personnel, 150
offshoring, outsourcing, 146–147
private agencies, 143–144
recruiters (headhunters), 147–148
referrals, walk-ins, 149–150
telecommuters, 150
temp workers, alternative staffing, 145–146
via the Internet, 138–142
workforce planning, forecasting, 157
about, 128–129, 128*f*
action plan for, 134
computerized, 131*f*, 132–133
and inside candidates, 132–133, 132*f*
labor demand, 134
and outside candidates, 133
succession planning, 134–135
Personnel replacement charts, 132, 132*f*
Person-organization fit, 167
Phone interview, 207
Picketing, 498
Piecework, 389–390
Planning, 3
Podslurping, 463
Point method, 358–359
Policies and procedures, 68
Polycentric practices, 568
Ponticas v. K.M.S. Investments, 167
Pooled paid leave plans (banks), 421
Population comparisons, for adverse impact, 44
Portability, 432
Position analysis questionnaire (PAQ), 105
Position replacement card, 132
Predictive validation, 171
Preferential shop, 483
Pregnancy Discrimination Act (1978), 33, 39*t*, 57
Prejudice, 53
Privacy Act (1974), 184
Problem-solving teams, 455
Procedural justice, 452
Process chart, 99
Product scope, 72
Productivity, 387
Professionals in Human Resources (PHR), 5
Profit-sharing plan, 404
Programmed learning, 246
Promotion, 320–322
Protected class, 34
Puzzle questions, 206

Q

Qualifications (skills) inventories, 132
Qualified individuals, 36
Quality circle, 455
Questionnaires, 102–105, 103*f*–104*f*
Quid pro quo, 40, 58

R

Ranking method, 356–357
Rating committee, 276
Ratio analysis, 130–131
Reactivity, 105
Reality shock, 311
Real-time translation captioning, 36*f*
Reasonable accommodation, 36, 37*f*
Recency effects, 290
Recruiters, 7
Recruitment law, 47
Reliability, 167–169, 168*f*
Reliability coefficient, 168
Religious discrimination, 38, 46

Restricted policy, 44
Retention management
comprehensive approach, 317–318
job withdrawal, 319
organizational performance, 316–317
at SAS, 318–319
turnover rate, 316
voluntary turnover, 317
Reverse discrimination, 57–58
Ricci v. DeStefano, 57
Right to work, 483
Rights arbitration, 497
Role-playing, 246

S

Safety, health, of employees
accident cause, 523–524
accident prevention
audits, inspections, 533–534
behavior-based safety, awareness, 532
culture of safety, 532–533
online safety training, 530
positive reinforcement, 530
poster, incentives, 530
reducing unsafe acts, 529, 547
reducing unsafe conditions, 524, 528
supervisor safety checklist, 525*f*–527*f*
for vulnerable workers, 528
workers' compensation costs, 535
exercise, cases for, 548–552
manager
importance of safety to, 515, 547
and occupational safety law, 516–523
role in safety, 515–516
occupational security, risk management
about, 542
company security, employee privacy, 545–546
emergency plans, 546
enterprise risk management, 542
setting up security program, 544–545
and social media, 546
terrorism, 546
violence at work, 542–544, 543*f*, 547
self-inspection safety and health checklist, 549*f*–552*f*
workplace health hazards
alcohol, substance abuse, 537–538, 538*t*
asbestos exposure, air quality, 537
chemical, industrial hygiene, 535–536
computer-related ergonomics, 540
infectious diseases, 541
repetitive motion disorders, 541
smoking, 541
stress, burnout, depression, 539
See also **Occupational Safety and Health Administration (OSHA)**
Safety awareness program, 532
Salary survey, 363–364, 363*f*, 364*t*
Savings and thrift plan, 432
Scanlon plan, 404–405
Scatter plot, 131, 157, 362*f*, 363f, 365*f*
Science in talent management, 82, 140, 218
Scientific management, 387
Screening, employee, 542
Section 14(c) Advisor, 593
Selection standards, 46
Self-Directed Search(SDS) test, 310
Self-managing/self-directed work team, 455
Self-rating, 277
Seminars, 255
Senior Professional in Human Resources (SPHR) designation, 5, 20
Severance pay, 423–424
Sexual harassment
EEOC definition, 39
employee feelings, options, 40
in hostile environment, 38
implications of, 40
proving, 40
Supreme Court decisions on, 40–41
under Title VII, 38
Sick child benefits, 436
Sick leave, 421–422
On-site health clinics, 429
Situational interview, 204
Situational test, 180
Small business human resources
building system for, 607
challenge of, 606
differences in, 590–591
importance of HRM, 591
women in, 591
exercise, cases for, 607–609
familiarity, flexibility, fairness, informality, 606
in benefits, rewards, 598–599
in a family business, 600
in interviewing, hiring, 597–598
in training, 598
and professional employer organizations (PEOs), 606
guidelines for, 602*f*
operation of, 601
systems, procedures, paperwork, 606
automating, 604
basics of, 603–604, 603*t*
using Internet, government tools, 602–603, 606
appraisal, compensation, 596
for employment planning, recruiting, 593
employment selection, 594–595
employment training, 596
for law compliance, 592–593
safety and health, 596
social media, 593–594
Social media
and background, reference checks, 184
and employee retention, 317
for employee training, 251
for expatriates, 576
during interview process, 212
and job recruitment, 139–140
and labor relations, 503
and performance management, 298
and sick leave, 421
for small businesses, 593–594
used in emergencies, 546
and workplace ethics, 462–463
See also Facebook; LinkedIn; Twitter
Social responsibility, 453
Social Security Act (1935), 352
Speed dating interview, 206
Spurlock v. United Airlines, 46
Staff authority, 5
Staff manager, 5
Staffing, 3
Standard deviation rule, 43–44
Standard hour plan, 390
Standard Occupational Classification, 110
Stereotyping, 53
Stock appreciation rights, 402
Stock options, 400–401
Straight piecework, 390–391
Strategic human resource management, 87
Strategic human resource management (SHRM) practices
City Garage, 602
Clif Bar, 437–438
Cognizant Corporation, 314
Costco's, 481
Daimler Alabama, 119
Deepwater Horizon, 516
Fast-Food Chain, 394
Four Seasons, 129
Google, 178
Hitachi, 578
L.L.Bean's, 15–16
May Department Stores Co., 236
Shanghai Ritz-Carlton Portman Hotel, 74
TRW's, 288
Urban Outfitters, 208
Wegmans Food Markets, 353
Strategic plan, 69
Strategic results lever, 16
Strategic training needs analysis, 236
Strategy, 69

Strategy and analysis, in HRM
exercises, cases for, 89–91
high-performance work systems (HPWS), 83–84, 84*f*
HR metrics, benchmarking, 67
evidence-based, scientific HR, 82–83
improving performance with analytics, 81
and needs analysis, 78–79
strategy-based, 79–80
tracking, 78
types of, 78
international practices, 74
management planning, 68, 83
mergers, acquisitions, 73
planning process for, 87
strategic human resource management, 74
strategic management
and diversity, 108
hierarchy of goals, 68*f*
planning process for, 68–73
process of, 69*f*
SWOT chart, 71*f*
types of
competitive, 68, 72
corporate, 68, 71
functional, 68, 71
Strategy map, 76–77, 76*f*, 78*f*
Strategy-based metrics, 79–80
Stress and the Manager, 539
Stress interview, 205
Strike, 496
Structured (directive) interview, 203
Structured sequential interview, 206
Structured situational interview, 212–213
Subsidized child care, 436
Succession planning, 134–135
Suggestion teams, 455
Supplemental pay benefits, 419
Supplemental unemployment benefits, 424
Survey Feedback Action (SFA) program, 468
Sustainability performance
PepesiCo's, 17, 71, 75
SWOT chart, 70*f*
Sympathy strike, 497

T

Taft-Hartley Act (1947), 485, 506
Talent management
defined, 96
and differential development assignments, 257
and employee retention, 318
features of, 96
manager's perspective on, 120
and pay plans, 374
and performance appraisal, 287*f*, 294
as top concern, 12
and training process, 236–237
Talent value model, 76
Task analysis, 237, 238*t*
Task statement, 117
Team (group) incentive plan, 402
Telecommuting, 440
Temporary workers, 144–148
Terminate at will, 325
Termination interview, 327
Terrorism, and workplace safety, 546
Test validity, 168
Third-country nationals, 566
Thirteenth Amendment (1865), 32
360-degree feedback, 277–278
Title VII (1964 Civil Rights Act)
about, 32
applicable for, 602
on discrimination, 235, 320
on dismissals, 326
on employment law, 48, 57
on pay rates, 347
purpose of, 39*t*
Tokenism, 53
Training, 235. *See also* employee training.
Training specialists, 7
Transactional HR teams, 7
Transfer, 322
Transnational teams, 567
Trend analysis, 130

U

Unclear standards, 288
Unemployment insurance (compensation), 399*t*, 419
Unfair labor practice strike, 497
Uniform guidelines, 58, 173
Uniformed Services Employment and Reemployment Rights Act (1994), 37
Union salting, 488
Union shop, 483
Unions. *See* Labor relations
Unsafe conditions, 523
Unstructured (nondirective) interview, 203
Unstructured sequential interview, 206

V

Valence, 388
Variable pay, 387
Vertical integration, 72
Vesting, for retirement, 433
Vibrating text pagers, 36
Video-based simulation, 180
Vietnam Era Veterans' Readjustment Assistance Act (1974), 39*t*
Virtual classroom, 250
Virtual reality, 247
Virtual teams, 567
Vision impairment, 36*f*
Vocational Rehabilitation Act (1973), 33, 39*t*, 57
Voice-recognition software, 36*f*
Voluntary (permissible) bargaining items, 495
Voluntary mediation, 51

W

Wage curve, 362–363, 362*f*, 365
Walsh-Healey Public Contract Act (1936), 347
Ward Cove v. Atonio, 39*t*
Web 2.0 learning, 251
Whistleblowers, 460
Wildcat strike, 497
Word-recognition software, 36*f*
Work Sampling Test, 597
Work sharing, 440
Workers' compensation, 425
Workflow analysis, 99
Workforce, U.S., 7–8, 82
Workplace violence training, 543–544
Works councils, 563

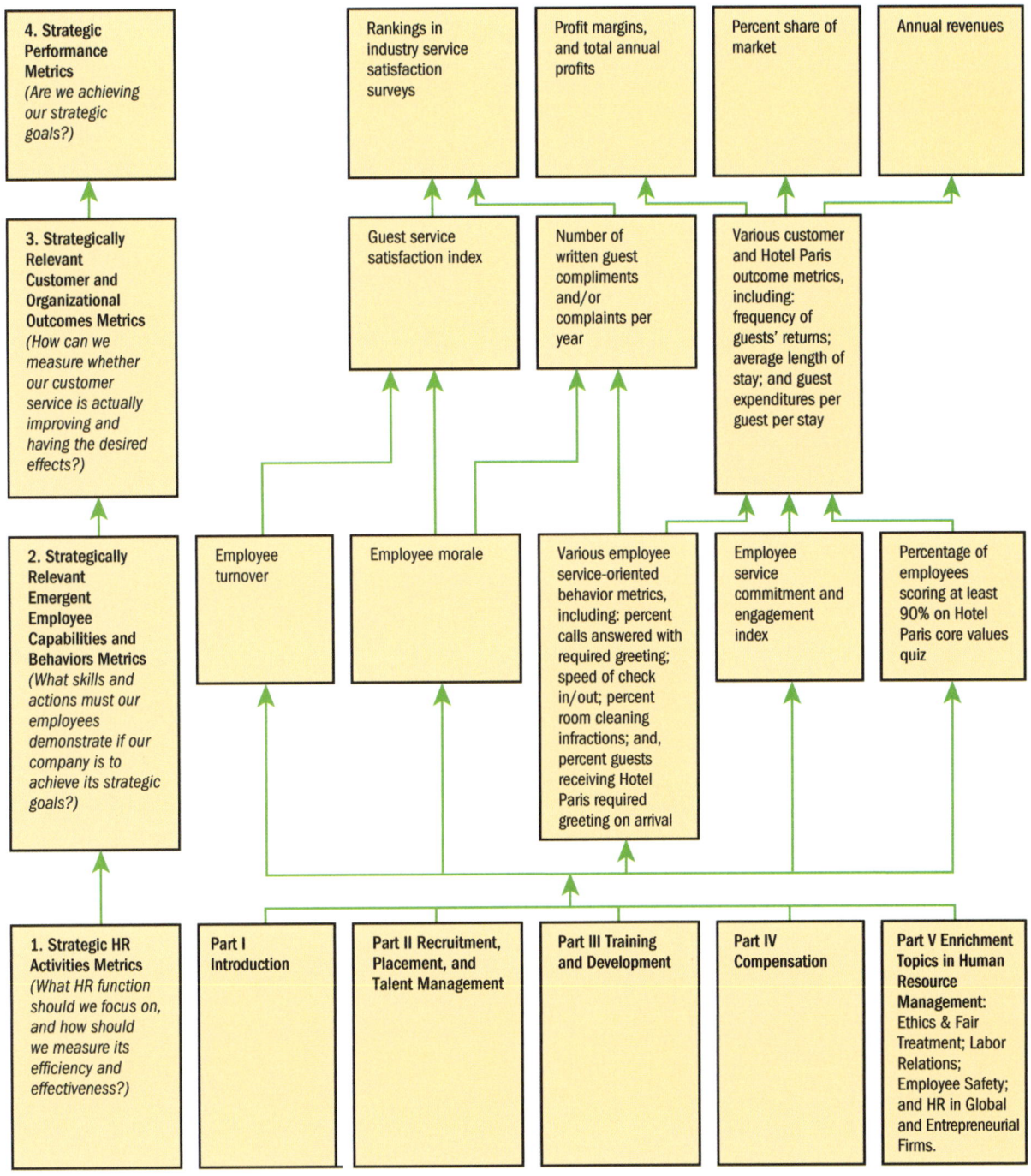

HR Scorecard for Hotel Paris International

Note: An abbreviated example showing selected HR practices and outcomes aimed at implementing the competitive strategy,"To use superior guest services to differentiate the Hotel Paris properties and thus increase the length of stays and the return rate of guests, and thus boost revenues and profitability and help the firm expand geographically.

The specialized strategy map for each chapter's Hotel Paris case is in the chapter's accompanying MyManagementLab.